FREE WITH NEW COPIES OF THIS TEXTBOOK*

Start using my BusinessCourse Today: www.mybusinesscourse.com

my BusinessCourse is a web-based learning and assessment program intended to complement your textbook and faculty instruction.

Student Benefits

- **eLectures**: These videos review the key concepts of each Learning Objective in each chapter.
- **Guided examples**: These videos provide step-by-step solutions for select problems in each chapter.
- **Auto-graded assignments**: Provide students with immediate feedback on select assignments. **(with Instructor-Led course ONLY)**.
- **Quiz and Exam preparation**: myBusinessCourse provides students with additional practice and exam preparation materials to help students achieve better grades and content mastery.

You can access my BusinessCourse 24/7 from any web-enabled device, including iPads, smartphones, laptops, and tablets.

Interactive content that runs on any device.

Built for PCs, iPads, Laptops, Tablets, Smartphones

Volume 2 Chapters 14–23

Intermediate Accounting

FOURTH EDITION

Michelle Hanlon
Massachusetts Institute of Technology

Leslie Hodder
Indiana University

Karen Nelson
Texas Christian University

Darren Roulstone
Ohio State University

Amie Dragoo
formerly Edgewood College

Cambridge
BUSINESS PUBLISHERS
A Sage Imprint

To my undergraduate accounting professors, Dr. Charles Wooton and Dr. Roann Kopel for answering my many questions about the details of intermediate accounting when I was an undergrad. And to my husband Chris and our children, Clark and Josie, for providing so much joy and laughter.
—MH

To my extended family, but especially Pat, Brian, Lisa, Maggie, and Will for your support and indulgence as I pursue my dreams. You are my reason.
—LH

To my students who indulge my passion for teaching accounting.
—KN

To Cindy, Kyle, Sariah, and Rachel for their much appreciated love and support.
—DR

To my husband Mike and our children, Jake, Justin, Julia, and Josie—for your love and steadfast support.
—AD

The FASB material used in this textbook is copyrighted by the Financial Accounting Foundation, 401 Merritt 7, Norwalk, CT 06856, USA, and is used with permission.

Cambridge Business Publishers

INTERMEDIATE ACCOUNTING, Fourth Edition, by Michelle Hanlon, Leslie Hodder, Karen Nelson, Darren Roulstone, and Amie Dragoo.

INSTRUCTOR EDITION ISBN: 978-1-61853-678-5

STUDENT EDITION
Volume 1 ISBN: 978-1-61853-676-1
Volume 2 ISBN: 978-1-61853-677-8

Bookstores & Faculty: To order this book, contact the company via email customerservice@cambridgepub.com or call 800-619-6473.

Students: To order this book, please visit the book's website and order directly online.

Printed in Canada.
10 9 8 7 6 5 4 3 2 1

About Our Team

 **Michelle L. Hanlon** is the Howard W. Johnson Professor at the MIT Sloan School of Management. She earned her doctorate degree at the University of Washington. Professor Hanlon has taught undergraduates, MBA students, Executive MBA students, and Masters of Finance students. She has won many awards for her teaching and research, including the 2021 Outstanding Teacher Award, 2020 Presidential Scholar, American Accounting Association, 2020 Distinguished Contribution to Accounting Literature Award, American Accounting Association, 2020 MIT Teaching with Digital Technology Award, and 2013 Jamieson Prize for Excellence in Teaching at MIT Sloan. Professor Hanlon's research focuses primarily on the intersection of financial accounting and taxation. She has published research studies in many journals including the leading accounting and finance journals. Professor Hanlon has served on several editorial boards and recently finished serving as one of the editors at the *Journal of Accounting and Economics*. Professor Hanlon is a co-author on two other textbooks—*Financial Accounting* and *Taxes and Business Strategy*. She has testified in front of the U.S. Senate Committee on Finance and the U.S. House of Representatives Committee on Ways and Means about the interaction of financial accounting and tax policy and international tax policy. She served as a U.S. delegate to the American-Swiss Young Leaders Conference in 2010 and worked as an Academic Fellow at the U.S. House Ways and Means Committee in 2015.

 **Leslie D. Hodder** is the David Thompson Chair of Accounting and at Indiana University's Kelley School of Business. She received her B.B.A and M.B.A./M. Acc from the University of New Mexico and her Ph.D. from the University of Texas at Austin. Prior to obtaining her Ph.D., Professor Hodder was Chief Financial Officer of a publicly traded commercial bank holding company in southern California. Professor Hodder was on faculty at Stanford University before joining the Indiana University faculty in 2003. Her research has appeared in top accounting journals, including *The Accounting Review*, *Review of Accounting Studies*, *Contemporary Accounting Research*, and *Accounting Organizations and Society*. She is the past winner of the American Accounting Association's Wildman Award for research relevant to practice, is a past Editor at *The Accounting Review*, and previously served as Finance Director on the Executive Board of the American Accounting Association. She currently serves on the International Financial Reporting Standards Advisory Council. Professor Hodder teaches financial-accounting-related topics in the undergraduate, master, and doctoral programs. Over her teaching career, she has developed or co-developed six courses in financial accounting, including Intermediate Financial Accounting I and II, Applied Audit and Accounting Research, Accounting Theory, and Detecting Earnings Management with a focus on data analytics. Currently, Professor Hodder is teaching a variety of financial accounting courses, including an online Intermediate Accounting course for working adults.

Karen K. Nelson is the M. J. Neeley Professor of Accounting in the M. J. Neeley School of Business at Texas Christian University. She earned her Ph.D. from the University of Michigan and a bachelor's degree (summa cum laude) from the University of Colorado. Prior to joining TCU, Professor Nelson served on the faculty at Stanford University and Rice University, and as a Visiting Professor at the University of Michigan. A Certified Public Accountant in Colorado, she is a past member of the Standing Advisory Group of the Public Company Accounting Oversight Board. Professor Nelson's research focuses on financial reporting and disclosure issues, including the role of regulators, auditors, and private securities litigation in monitoring financial reporting quality. She has held research seminars at numerous conferences and business schools in the U.S. and abroad. Her research is published in several leading academic journals including *The Accounting Review*, *Journal of Accounting and Economics*, *Journal of Accounting Research*, and the *Review of Accounting Studies*, and has been featured in the popular financial press. She is an Editor at *Accounting Horizons* and a past Associate Editor at the *Journal of Accounting and Economics* and was previously on the Editorial Board member at *The Accounting Review*. She is also an author of *Financial Accounting* and has taught financial and intermediate accounting and reporting at the undergraduate, MBA, and Ph.D. levels. Professor Nelson is the recipient of numerous awards for teaching excellence and was recently named a Top 50 Undergraduate Business Professor by Poets & Quants.

Darren T. Roulstone is the John W. Berry Sr., Fund for Faculty Excellence Professor of Accounting at the Ohio State University's Fisher College of Business. He earned his doctorate at the University of Michigan's Ross School of Business and BS and MAcc degrees from Brigham Young University's Marriott School of Business. During his time at Fisher, he spent 11 years directing the Accounting PhD program and three years as department chair. He teaches a PhD seminar on accounting research, the core course in Financial Reporting in Fisher's MAcc program, and a Financial Statement Analysis elective in the MAcc program. He has extensive experience teaching intermediate accounting at the undergraduate and graduate levels and was named MAcc Professor of the Year in 2024. Prior to joining Fisher, he was on the faculty at the University of Chicago's Booth School of Business where he taught financial accounting and financial statement analysis in the full-time, evening, and weekend MBA programs. Professor Roulstone's research focuses on information intermediaries, information acquisition by investors, and textual analysis of corporate disclosures. He has served on the editorial boards of several accounting journals and is currently an associate editor at *Management Science*. His research has been published in a variety of leading academic journals including *The Accounting Review, Journal of Accounting and Economics, Journal of Accounting Research, Review of Accounting Studies*, and *Management Science*. He is a past president of the American Accounting Association's Financial Accounting and Reporting Section.

Amie L. Dragoo is a Professor of Accounting and Independent Scholar. Former Accounting Department Chair and Associate Professor at Edgewood College, Dr. Dragoo earned her BA and MBA from Michigan State University, and her doctorate from Edgewood College. She holds a CPA license, and for nearly 15 years has been a Becker Professional Education faculty instructor. Prior to her experiences in higher education, she was a senior business assurance associate with PricewaterhouseCoopers LLP (PwC). Dr. Dragoo has extensive teaching experiences, including courses in Intermediate Accounting I and II, Cost Accounting, Advanced Cost Management, Strategic Financial Management, and other advanced courses in financial and managerial accounting. She has received a number of teaching awards including the School of Business Outstanding Faculty Award and the Estervig-Beaubien Excellence in Teaching and Mentoring Award. She has also worked as an independent scholar, emphasizing projects in higher education, and she has consulted with several corporate clients. Dr. Dragoo is a co-author of other leading textbooks including *Managerial Accounting* 9e by Kulp et al., 2022, and *Cost Accounting* 10e by Kinney et al., 2021. In addition, her research has been published in the *Journal of Education for Business,* and the *Journal of Continuing Higher Education* and she has contributed to numerous articles published by organizations affiliated with the AICPA. Dr. Dragoo is also involved in many community-oriented programs including having previously led her college's Volunteer Income Tax Assistance (VITA) program.

How Today's Accounting Students Learn

As we developed the concept for this Intermediate Accounting learning system, we conducted extensive research with accounting students and faculty to understand the changing learning and study behavior of accounting students. The findings of that research led to the development of the first three editions. We have continued to conduct research that focuses on how accounting students learn and how faculty teaching has evolved in the post-pandemic educational environment. In preparation for the 4th edition, we conducted 4 surveys of accounting students with over 5,000 student participants.

Findings of this research indicate that the vast majority of accounting students prefer:

- Attempting homework assignments before reading the textbook or using other course resources
- Watching videos that explain the accounting rather than reading the textbook
- Digestible chunks of information as opposed to lengthy, multi-topic explanations
- Online learning systems that they can access 24/7 from any type of device

Learning Style

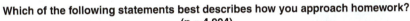

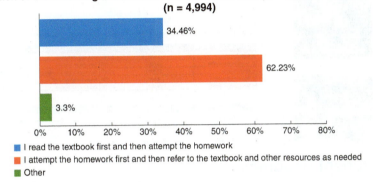

Which of the following statements best describes how you approach homework?
(n = 4,994)

- 34.46%
- 62.23%
- 3.3%

■ I read the textbook first and then attempt the homework
■ I attempt the homework first and then refer to the textbook and other resources as needed
■ Other

Takeaways:
Only 34.5% of accounting students read the textbook before attempting the homework

Preferred Learning Materials

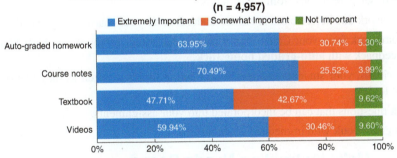

Which items are most important to you when learning accounting?
(n = 4,957)

■ Extremely Important   ■ Somewhat Important   ■ Not Important

	Extremely Important	Somewhat Important	Not Important
Auto-graded homework	63.95%	30.74%	5.30%
Course notes	70.49%	25.52%	3.99%
Textbook	47.71%	42.67%	9.62%
Videos	59.94%	30.46%	9.60%

Takeaways:
After course notes, auto-graded homework and videos are most valued by students.

Students Value myBusinessCourse

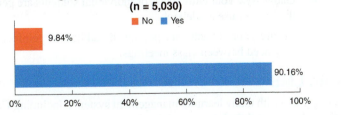

Would you encourage your professor to continue using myBusinessCourse?
(n = 5,030)

■ No   ■ Yes

- 9.84%
- 90.16%

Takeaways:
Over 90% of students recommend MBC use, which underscores how much they value it.

As is explained in the Preface, we used these findings and others to create an intermediate accounting product that complements and facilitates how today's students learn.

Technology that Improves Learning and Complements Instruction

myBusinessCourse is an online learning and assessment program intended to complement your textbook and faculty instruction. Access to **myBusinessCourse** is FREE ONLY with the purchase of a new textbook, but access can be purchased separately.

MBC is ideal for faculty seeking opportunities to augment their course with an online component. **MBC** is also a turnkey solution for online courses. The following are some of the features of **MBC**.

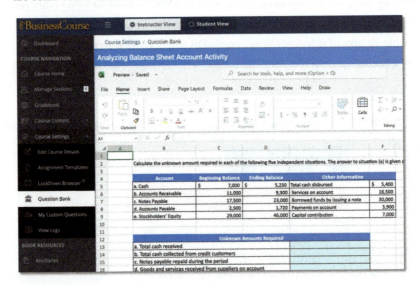

Increase Student Readiness

- **eLectures** cover each chapter's learning objectives and concepts. Consistent with the text and created by the authors, these videos are ideal for remediation and online instruction.

- **Guided Examples** are narrated video demonstrations created by the authors that show students how to solve select problems from the textbook.

- Make homework due before class to ensure students enter your classroom prepared.

- Assign homework from your Cambridge Business Publishers' textbook and have **MBC** provide mediate feedback with **auto-graded homework**.

- With our videos, your students can revisit accounting topics as often as they like or until they master the topic.

- **Test Bank** questions that can be incorporated into your assignments.

- Instructor **gradebook** with immediate grade results.

Make Instruction Needs-Based

- Identify where your students are struggling and customize your instruction to address their needs.

- Gauge how your entire class or individual students are performing by viewing the easy-to-use gradebook.

- Ensure your students are getting the additional reinforcement and direction they need between class meetings.

Integrate with LMS

myBusinessCourse integrates with many learning management systems, including **Canvas**, **Blackboard**, **Moodle**, **D2L**, **Schoology**, and **Sakai**. Your gradebooks sync automatically.

---

* These statistics are based on the results of five surveys in which 4,195 students participated.

Preface

Welcome to the Fourth Edition of *Intermediate Accounting*. This product is the result of extensive market research that included both faculty and students. We created this learning system because, as educators, we didn't feel that the existing textbooks in the intermediate market recognized how the **study habits of today's students have evolved**, nor did we feel that existing textbooks fully embraced the **power of technology** in the learning process. This product is not so much a textbook as it is an **integrated learning system**. Although the print textbook can be used on its own, we created extensive digital resources that integrate with and complement the print book.

The emphasis in our approach is to provide students with a demonstration and review problem for each key learning objective. In this way, students see the application of concepts through a **step-by-step illustration** and then have the opportunity to **immediately practice** similar review problems electronically in **myBusinessCourse** (MBC), our online homework platform. In addition, MBC contains hundreds of instructional videos that were created by the authors. There are four general categories of videos: **concept overviews**, **demonstration videos**, **worked-out review problems**, and **highlights & tips videos**. With nearly **1,000 author-created videos**, our text has broad appeal among the YouTube/TikTok generation as confirmed by our adopter feedback. The combination of textbook, videos, and online practice comprise an **active learning** system that recognizes and embraces how today's students prefer to learn and provides students with the tools to master intermediate accounting.

"**Intermediate Accounting, by Hanlon et al., is superior in comparison to the previous text that we used for decades. Students appreciate the tight narrative of each learning objective delivered in `chunks of information' which is how today's students learn.**"

Nate Sharp
Texas A&M University

Our approach steers away from dense text (which the average student is not reading) and moves to an active-learning approach where content is delivered in **short bursts followed by immediate practice**. Because each learning objective for every chapter is self-contained, faculty have the flexibility to pick and choose learning outcomes.

We note the need in the market for a direct incorporation of **authoritative guidance**. Although other intermediate accounting textbooks include some references to the FASB's standards in a footnote to a chapter, direct citations are rarely included. In our approach, we provide succinct yet thorough, to-the-point explanations along with direct citations of the most relevant references from the **Codification**. Direct citations best prepare the intermediate accounting student, who will often reference and cite the authoritative standards **in practice**. This novel approach of combining active-learning with real life authoritative guidance best prepares intermediate accounting students for life in practice.

Target Audience

As the title suggests, *Intermediate Accounting* is intended for use following the introductory financial accounting course at either the undergraduate or graduate level. This book supports an intermediate accounting series offered to accounting and finance majors, typically in a two-course sequence (three-course series in some cases). The topics in intermediate accounting are relevant to approximately 70% of the Financial Accounting Reporting (FAR) section of the current Uniform CPA Examination. In response to the recently updated CPA exam, we have provided the resources needed to prepare your students. We have mapped the learning objectives from each chapter to the learning objectives in the **CPA Exam Blueprints**. With this update, faculty and students will better understand how the topics in each chapter match up with the CPA exam learning objectives in the Financial Analysis and Reporting Section (FAR) and the Business Analysis and Reporting Section (BAR). This is useful for assessment purposes and will allow faculty and accounting departments the flexibility to separate FAR from BAR topics in the intermediate courses. Being current is important to our author team as we continually monitor updates to the CPA exam to provide the most up-to-date materials.

Action Plan

To establish our active-learning approach and highlight its user friendly organization, each chapter opens with an **Action Plan** that identifies each learning objective for the chapter, the related page numbers, the demonstrations, the review applications, the assignments, and the learning objectives tied to the CPA Exam Blueprints. This table allows students and faculty to quickly grasp the chapter contents and to efficiently navigate to the desired topic.

> **"The Action Plan with the Demos, Reviews, and Assignments is my HANDS DOWN favorite. I have specific topics that are important to me, so I use the Action Plan to convey to my students where to focus. The design of the plan allows them to spend more time focused specifically on the topics that I intend to cover in detail."**
>
> **Stephani Mason**
> *DePaul University*

Action Plan summarizes each chapter's resources and categorizes them by learning objective.

Demos are illustrative examples accompanied by videos (available in myBusinessCourse, MBC) that give 3-5 minute demonstrations of each learning objective.

Assignments reinforce learning and can be completed within MBC.

CPA cross-lists learning objectives from CPA Exam Blueprints.

Action Plan

LO	Topic/Subtopic	Page	Demos	Reviews	Assignments	CPA
LO 4-1	**Describe classification of asset, liability, and equity accounts on the balance sheet** Current Assets :: Noncurrent Assets :: Current Liabilities :: Noncurrent Liabilities :: Paid-in Capital :: Retained Earnings :: Accumulated Other Comprehensive Income :: Treasury Stock :: Noncontrolling Interests	4-3	D4-1A D4-1B D4-1C	R4-1	MC4-1, MC4-2, BE4-1, BE4-2, BE4-3, E4-1, E4-2, E4-3, E4-4, P4-1, P4-13, AD&J4-1, AD&J4-2, AD&J4-5, AD&J4-6, DA4-2	FAR I.A.1.a I.A.7.b
LO 4-2	**Prepare a classified balance sheet** Current and Noncurrent Classifications :: Working Capital :: Balance Sheet Classifications :: Management Judgment :: Report Format and Account Format	4-12	D4-2	R4-2	MC4-3, MC4-4, BE4-4, BE4-5, BE4-6, BE4-7, BE4-8, BE4-9, BE4-10, BE4-11, BE4-12, BE4-13, E4-5, E4-6, E4-7, E4-8, E4-9, E4-10, P4-2, P4-3, P4-4, P4-5, P4-6, P4-7, P4-8, P4-9, P4-10, P4-11, P4-12, P4-13, P4-14, AD&J4-3, AD&J4-4,	FAR I.A.1.a I.A.1.b I.A.1.c I.A.2.a I.A.7.a

Learning Objectives identify the key learning goals of the chapter. A video prepared by the authors is included with each LO, providing a brief topical overview.

Reviews are practice problems that follow Demos and that are accompanied by videos (available in MBC) that demonstrate how to solve each problem. Within MBC, Reviews can be assigned and graded.

Gray font denotes that Chapter LO ties indirectly to Evolution Model LO.

Black font denotes that a Chapter LO ties directly to Evolution Model LO.

Overview, Demo, and Review

We have adopted a straightforward, effective layout throughout every chapter of the book. We have included carefully crafted learning objectives that are not extraneous or all-encompassing. Each key learning objective is clearly identified with a distinct orange and blue banner and is followed by its own overview, demo, and review.

> **LO 7-3**   **Identify the performance obligations in the contract—Step 2**

In fact, each learning objective represents a **separate learning module**, allowing students and faculty to break down complex topics into manageable subtopics. Our text is comprised of approximately 200 learning objectives and unlike other textbooks in the market, each learning objective is structured in the same way with a **consistent layout and resources** (in type and quality) associated with each learning objective. Students appreciate this style of learning uniquely adopted in *Intermediate Accounting* because of the current trend in learning preferences. **Students prefer to learn by doing** with convenient access to explanations and authoritative references for help in the process. For additional support, students have access to short videos for each Overview, Demo, and Review. The videos can be accessed in MBC.

To help students, we employ a **3-step process** for each learning objective.

1. Overview → 2. Demo → 3. Review

Market research indicates that students benefit from this consistent pedagogical approach to learning.

1. Overview

Following each learning objective is a brief explanation of the topic with visual references (diagrams) when helpful. We also include an overview box for each learning objective to provide students with a quick overview of key topics. For topics where relevant authoritative guidance is important, we included an excerpt from the Codification. **This presentation of the accounting guidance minimizes authors' biases and places both students and faculty in a unique authoritative position.** Our approach incorporates ASC Glossary definitions whenever possible and terminology that is common in the Codification such as the terms recognition, measurement, derecognition, and disclosure. References to authoritative guidance are distinctly highlighted with black block text as shown below. While we take the text exactly as it is from the standard, we sometimes include only the main part of the standard and do not include more detailed portions in the interest of parsimony. Also, we include the most recently approved Codification references, even if the effective date is in the future.

"I'm really impressed with the book and like the integration of the codification. I encourage my colleagues to seriously consider adopting the book."
Maef Woods
Heidelberg University

Because a sale on account could be considered a short-term loan (depending on the specific terms), there is a financing component to a sale on account. Sellers initiating a revenue contract with transfer expected within one year do not have to recognize the financing component. This means short-term accounts receivable are typically recorded at the full amount that the seller expects to receive (not adjusted to present value). The authoritative support follows.

606-10-32-15 In determining the transaction price, an entity shall adjust the promised amount of consideration for the effects of the time value of money if the timing of payments agreed to by the parties to the contract (either explicitly or implicitly) provides the customer or the entity with a significant benefit of financing the transfer of goods or services to the customer. In those circumstances, the contract contains a significant financing component.

We cite the Codification including excerpts where appropriate.

The presentation of the Codification within the text makes our text unique within the marketplace. This aspect of the text is also relevant to students who are now expected to analyze sections of the Codification on the CPA exam so exposure to the Codification is critical to student success.

2. Demo

A presentation focused on demos inspires the contemporary college learner. Demos are included for each learning objective to illustrate the accounting concept discussed. We include color-coded solutions within the Demo (the **blue text**) because this is the student's first exposure to the relevant topic. In older intermediate textbooks, it is common for an accounting concept or a variation to an accounting method to be explained in a page or more of text instead of through an illustration. In our approach, **accounting concepts are predominantly demonstrated**. The active learner can reconstruct the steps independently. In addition, each demo is accompanied by a short video clip (typically 3 minutes or less) that walks students through the solution to the demo.

Videos, created by the authors that provide step-by-step guidance on solving the problem, are available in MBC.

Periodic Inventory System—Gross Method		LO9-2	DEMO 9-2A

CostKo Inc. uses a periodic inventory system and begins the month of June with $300 in inventory.
Part One: Record journal entries for the following seven transactions, listed in chronological order, using the *gross method* for recording purchase discounts.

1. **Purchase of Inventory** CostKo purchased inventory on June 2 for $800, with terms 2/10, n/30.

    June 2—To record inventory purchases using gross method

    | Purchases.. | 800 | |
    | Accounts Payable................................ | | 800 |

2. **Incur Transportation Costs** On June 2, CostKo paid shipping charges of $75 related to the purchase of inventory (f.o.b. shipping point).

    June 2—To record transportation costs on purchases

    | Freight-In.. | 75 | |
    | Cash.. | | 75 |

3. **Payment on Account within Discount Period** CostKo paid half its account payable

Demo
MBC

Gross Method

Assets = Liabilities + Equity
              +800   −800
              AP   Temp

Accounts Payable	Purchases
800	800

Assets = Liabilities + Equity
−75   −75
Cash   Temp

Cash	Freight-In
75	75

3. Review

At the conclusion of each learning objective, a review problem is provided with answers included at the end of the chapter. These review problems are presented to reinforce concepts presented in the section and to ensure student comprehension. By not pro-

viding the review solutions on the same page as the review, we are encouraging students to **'learn by doing.'** The demo, along with the overview material, provides the foundation for students to complete the review problems. **Students have the opportunity to practice the same problem online in myBusinessCourse.** We believe that many students will take

"Students tend not to read textbooks the way they did in the past. My students learn better by seeing an example and then doing a similar problem. The Overview/Demonstration/Review approach used in the book worked well for my students for that reason."
Lindsay Meermans
Wittenberg University

advantage of the opportunity to work through the problem online because they will gain instant feedback as to whether they completed the solution accurately—and frankly, a digital environment is more in line with how we all function every day. Further, each review is accompanied by a short video clip (typically 3 minutes or less) that walks students through the solution to the review. **All reviews are included in MBC with algorithmic options, which means they can be assigned and auto-graded.**

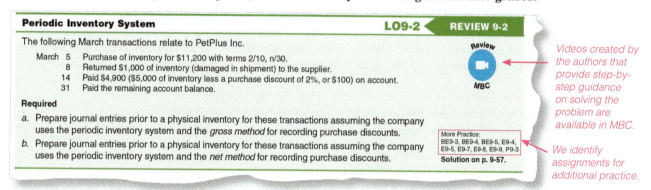

Periodic Inventory System　　**LO9-2**　**REVIEW 9-2**

The following March transactions relate to PetPlus Inc.

March	5	Purchase of inventory for $11,200 with terms 2/10, n/30.
	8	Returned $1,000 of inventory (damaged in shipment) to the supplier.
	14	Paid $4,900 ($5,000 of inventory less a purchase discount of 2%, or $100) on account.
	31	Paid the remaining account balance.

Required

a. Prepare journal entries prior to a physical inventory for these transactions assuming the company uses the periodic inventory system and the *gross method* for recording purchase discounts.

b. Prepare journal entries prior to a physical inventory for these transactions assuming the company uses the periodic inventory system and the *net method* for recording purchase discounts.

More Practice:
BE9-3, BE9-4, BE9-5, E9-4, E9-5, E9-7, E9-8, E9-9, P9-3
Solution on p. 9-57.

Videos created by the authors that provide step-by-step guidance on solving the problem are available in MBC.

We identify assignments for additional practice.

Integrated Videos in MBC Author-created videos are an integral part of our learning system. Time and again, our market research on student preferences and study habits indicates today's students

like and rely heavily on video instruction as they learn and apply accounting concepts to homework assignments and projects. Our videos are available through MBC and **can be accessed 24/7 by students**. To facilitate students' use of the instructional videos while doing their homework, we identify the appropriate video in the margin next to many assignments.

"The book does an excellent job of breaking the content into smaller chunks that are more digestible for students. The students also really like the video content that is available with the text."
Josh Filzen
Boise State University

Assume Ikeo Inc. sold $100,000 of gift cards during the last two weeks of December of Year 1. No gift cards were redeemed in calendar Year 1. A total of $90,250 of the gift cards were redeemed for store purchases during calendar Year 2. On December 31 of Year 2, Ikeo Inc. calculates the remaining balance of unredeemed gift cards as $9,750 ($100,000 less $90,250). Based on previous experiences, Ikeo estimates gift card breakage to be 5% of total gift card sales. Ikeo uses the proportional method to recognize income on gift card breakage.

Exercise 15-6
Accounting for Gift Cards **LO2**
Hint: See Review 15-2

We identify for student guidance an appropriate video aid in the margin next to assignments.

Required

a. Record the sale of gift cards in Year 1.

b. Record the redemption of gift cards in Year 2.

c. Record revenue in Year 2 due to gift card breakage using the proportional method.

Accounting Equation and T-Accounts

We have received overwhelmingly positive feedback on the inclusion of the accounting equation and use of T-accounts. Faculty recognize the value of these tools in explaining the impact transactions have on accounts and financial statements. **Students typically encounter the accounting equation and T-accounts in their introductory financial accounting course, and they appreciate the continuity between courses that these tools create.** An additional benefit of using the accounting equation is that **Finance majors**, who are more focused on the impact of transactions than the recording of them, leave the course with a better understanding of the affect transactions have on financial statements.

In the 4th edition, we expand our use of the accounting equation and T-accounts. In the margin adjacent to the journal entries, we show the impact of the accounting equation and T-accounts to aid in student comprehension.

To aid in student comprehension, we show the impact on the accounting equation and T-accounts in addition to the journal entries. New to this edition, abbreviated accounts names have been added to increase usefulness to students.

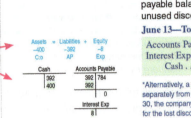
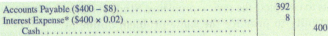

3. Payment on Account after the Discount Period CostKo paid the remaining accounts payable balance on June 13, after the discount period, recording interest expense for the unused discounts.

June 13—To record payment on account after discount period

Accounts Payable ($400 – $8).................................	392	
Interest Expense* ($400 × 0.02)..............................	8	
Cash...		400

*Alternatively, a company may use a separate expense account, Purchase Discount Lost, to track amounts separately from other interest expense. If CostKo had not paid the remaining account balance as of June 30, the company would record an entry to accrue interest (Dr. Interest Expense and Cr. Interest Payable) for the lost discount.

Assets = Liabilities + Equity
-400   -392   -8
C:o   AP   Exp

Cash   Accounts Payable
392 | 392 | 784
400 | 392 |
                      | 0
            Interest Exp
            8 |

Abbreviated Account Names and Cash Flow Identifier

New to this edition, abbreviated accounts names have been added to the accounting equation to increase usefulness to students. When a transaction affects cash, we also use notation to indicate if it is an operating cash flow (**C:o**), or an investing cash flow (**C:i**) or a financing cash flow (**C:f**).

*Notation indicates whether cash flow is operating (**C:o**), investing (**C:i**), or financing (**C:f**),.*

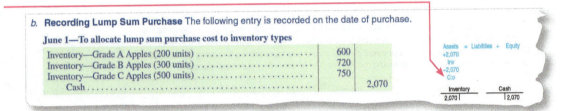

b. Recording Lump Sum Purchase The following entry is recorded on the date of purchase.

June 1—To allocate lump sum purchase cost to inventory types

Inventory—Grade A Apples (200 units)......................	600	
Inventory—Grade B Apples (300 units)......................	720	
Inventory—Grade C Apples (500 units)......................	750	
Cash...		2,070

Assets = Liabilities + Equity
+2,070
Inv
-2,070
C:o

Inventory   Cash
2,070 | | 2,070

New Assignments Requiring Use of the Accounting Equation

To complement the accounting equations shown in the text, a number of assignments are now offered in the accounting equation format in addition to the journal entry format. Faculty will have the flexibility to assign the traditional journal entry approach and/or the accounting equation approach for this set of problems. These questions will be well received by finance majors interested in the financial statement impact of transactions.

Exercise 9-7
Recording Purchase Entries Using the Gross Method (Periodic) **LO2**
Hint: See Demo 9-2A

Tanglewood Corp. began the month of February with $1,800 in inventory. Record the following transactions using the *gross* method for recording purchase discounts under a periodic inventory system.
1. Feb. 1   Purchased inventory for $22,000, with terms 1/10, n/30.
2. Feb. 2   Paid shipping charges of 5% of the February 1 invoice price (f.o.b. shipping point).
3. Feb. 8   Paid half of the accounts payable balance ($11,000 of the invoice less the cash discount).
4. Feb. 15   Paid remaining balance due on the February 1 invoice, after the discount period.
5. Feb. 20   Sold inventory with a retail price of $15,000.
6. Feb. 29   Physically counted month-end inventory valued at $14,400 and recorded cost of goods sold.

Exercise 9-8
Analyzing Purchase Transactions (Periodic System; Gross Method) Using the Accounting Equation **LO2**

a. Referring to E9-7, show the effect on the accounting equation for each transaction, including identifying the individual accounts affected, and the total impact on assets, liabilities, and stockholders' equity.
b. What is the net effect on the income statement? What does this number represent?

This icon identifies the assignments that require use of the accounting equation.

Excel Skills & Integrated Excel

Proficiency with Excel continues to be one of the most **sought-after skills among employers**. To facilitate Excel skill development, MBC now includes short videos that show students how to use various features and functions in **Excel**. The videos can be accessed within myBusinessCourse as part of your MBC course.

In addition, Cambridge Business Publishers has a new relationship with **Microsoft** that allows for a seamless integration of **Excel** within myBusinessCourse. Faculty can assign homework through MBC that requires students to use Excel. These assignments are **auto-graded** and scores are captured in the MBC gradebook.

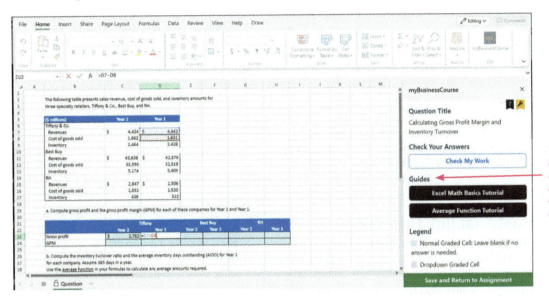

Videos are provided to show students the Excel functions required to complete each integrated Excel assignment.

Data Analytics and Data Visualizations

The world in which we live has changed dramatically in recent years. Technology is rapidly altering how accounting is performed and what can be done with the data once they are collected. In this edition, we have incorporated data analytic and data visualization assignments tailored to each chapter's content. An Excel solution is provided for instructors and all assignments have been added to MBC for an auto-grading option. Additional assignments are available in **Appendix A** which also provides an overview of the topic of data analytics.

"The only book on the market that seriously integrates the AACSB data analytics requirement."

Stephani Mason
DePaul University

Data analytic assignments require students to create and analyze charts in Excel or Tableau.

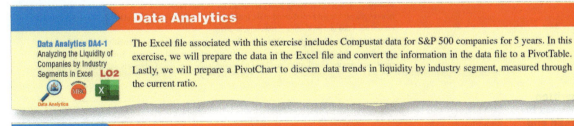

Data Analytics

Data Analytics DA4-1
Analyzing the Liquidity of Companies by Industry Segments in Excel **LO2**

The Excel file associated with this exercise includes Compustat data for S&P 500 companies for 5 years. In this exercise, we will prepare the data in the Excel file and convert the information in the data file to a PivotTable. Lastly, we will prepare a PivotChart to discern data trends in liquidity by industry segment, measured through the current ratio.

Data Visualization Activities

Data Visualization Activities are available in *myBusinessCourse*. These assignments use Tableau Dashboards to expose students to visual depictions of data and introduce students to data analytics through data visualizations. These exercises are assignable and auto graded by MBC.

Data visualization assignments require students to analyze charts in Tableauu dashboards accessible in MBC.

Learning in Context

Real World

Students appreciate and become more engaged when they see the real-world relevance of the content they are learning in class. We include current, real-world examples of financial reporting throughout each chapter in Real World boxes.

WELLS FARGO BANK   Real World—VALIDITY OF CONTRACTS

Wells Fargo Bank N.A. was the subject of an investigation by the Consumer Financial Protection Bureau (CFPB), which resulted in the largest penalty ever imposed by the CFPB. A press release issued by the CFPB (https://www.consumerfinance.gov/) indicated that Wells Fargo must pay a $100 million fine for the widespread practice of opening accounts without knowledge of its customers. To boost sales to reach targets, Wells Fargo secretly opened new accounts on behalf of its customers and transferred money from existing accounts. The estimate of the number of unauthorized new accounts was two million! Wells Fargo's violations included (1) opening deposit accounts and transferring funds without authorization, (2) applying for credit card accounts without authorization, (3) issuing and activating debit cards without authorization, and (4) creating phony email addresses for the purposes of online services. In reviewing the criteria included in this section for a valid contract, it is clear that Wells Fargo did not have a valid contract with its customers. Both parties did not approve the arrangements (a condition of a valid contract). Even though this occurred while the previous revenue standard (ASC 605) was in place, recognition of revenue is not supported under either standard.

Sustainability Reporting

Companies continue to expand disclosures on different aspects of sustainability. In the fourth edition, we have expanded our Real World coverage of recent 10-K disclosures with sustainability considerations and added other sustainability content where appropriate to describe current financial statement reporting requirements (primarily SEC guidance). Also new to this edition, we have added assignments requiring students to review and analyze recent sustainability disclosures. These new assignments are available in MBC.

SLEEP NUMBER, MACY'S, CONTAINER STORE, GAP
Real World—RISKS RELATED TO ENVIRONMENTAL, SOCIAL, AND GOVERNANCE MATTERS

Item 1A of a company's Form 10-K requires a discussion of risk factors. Companies often discuss how risks related to ESG matters could have a material impact on profitability in the future. Excerpts from certain companies' recent Form10-Ks follow, which describe potential *income statement* impacts.

- **Sleep Number Corp.:** New climate disclosure rules passed by California, as well as those proposed by the SEC, will increase the Company's compliance costs and may subject the Company to litigation or other risks, which would materially and adversely affect its future results of operations and financial condition. (Fiscal year 2023)
- **Macy's, Inc.:** Extreme weather conditions, including those that may be caused by climate change, in the areas in which our stores are located could negatively affect our business and results of operations. For example, frequent or unusually heavy snowfall, ice storms, rainstorms, or other extreme weather conditions over a prolonged period could make it difficult for our customers to travel to our stores and, thereby, reduce our sales and profitability. (Fiscal year 2023)
- **Container Store Group, Inc.:** Changes in the regulatory environment potentially increase the costs of compliance and subject us to possible government penalties and litigation. Specifically, significant or rapid increases to federal, state, and local minimum wage rates could adversely affect our earnings if we

AD&J3-7
Analyzing Climate Related Risks on Profitability **LO1**

Real World Analysis Review Item 1A. of **Mattel**'s 2023 Form 10-K, which can be found on the SEC Edgar website (https://www.sec.gov/edgar/searchedgar/companysearch.html) and answer the following questions.

a. What is the potential exposure risk for Mattel pertaining to a possible earthquake, tsunami, flood, fire, or power outage? What is the related potential income statement impact?
b. What is Mattel's goal for the reduction of Scope 1 and Scope 2 carbon emissions?
c. What are sources of increases to climate-related litigation? What is the related potential income statement impact?
d. How can customer preferences drive up Mattel's cost to source materials? What is the potential income statement impact of meeting expectations? Not meeting expectations?

Management Judgment

In each chapter, we emphasize how **management judgment** is required to apply the authoritative guidance. We feel it is important for students to understand that applying accounting rules is often subjective and requires professional judgment.

Management Judgment

Management judgment is sometimes needed to classify a stock dividend as a small stock dividend or a stock split effected in the form of a dividend. The accounting guidance provides a minimum range of 20% to 25% where a stock issuance becomes large enough to materially influence the unit market price of the stock. However, this is a range (not a bright line), and the guidance allows for some exceptions outside of this range.

Assume that WayMart Inc. issued a 24% common stock dividend on 100,000 shares of $1 par common stock issued and outstanding on May 1. The market price of the common stock is $5 per share. The impact on financial statements of these two options follows.

	Capital Stock	Paid-In Capital in Excess of Par	Retained Earnings	Total Stockholders' Equity
Small stock dividend.	$24,000	$96,000	$(120,000)	No change
Stock split effected through dividend . . .	24,000	—	(24,000)	No change

Retained earnings would have been $96,000 lower ($120,000 less $24,000) had the dividend been classified as a small stock dividend rather than a stock split effected in the form of a dividend. If the

Expanding Your Knowledge

Expanding Your Knowledge sections extend the coverage of a learning objective to novel situations that are illustrated with excerpts and examples from practice. These topics can enhance classroom discussions or simply allow the curious student to go beyond the usual coverage. A representative sample follows.

EXPANDING YOUR KNOWLEDGE — Effect of Foreign Exchange Rate Fluctuations

The Gap Inc. included the *effect of foreign exchange rate fluctuation* in determining the net increase (decrease) in cash and cash equivalents. ASC 830 requires that companies report the effect of exchange rate changes on cash, cash equivalents, and restricted cash held in foreign currencies as a separate part of the reconciliation in the statement of cash flows. The following table was constructed from information included in Gap's Consolidated Statements of Cash Flows in its recent report on Form 10-K.

$ millions	Fiscal Year 2023
Net cash provided by operating activities	$1,532
Net cash used for investing activities	(334)
Net cash provided by financing activities	(567)
Effect of foreign exchange rate fluctuations on cash and cash equivalents . . .	(3)
Net increase (decrease) in cash and cash equivalents	628
Cash, cash equivalents, and restricted cash at beginning of period	1,273
Cash, cash equivalents, and restricted cash at end of period	$1,901

Chapter Assessment

The challenge in intermediate accounting is applying the concepts to different scenarios. Our assignment material consists of a wide variety of formats, varying levels of complexity, a thorough coverage of learning objectives, and selections with real world data. The materials increase in complexity as you move through the different categories: **Questions**, **Multiple-Choice**, **Brief Exercises**, **Exercises**, and **Problems**. The questions in each end of chapter section are numbered sequentially from start to finish to avoid confusion for students. All learning objectives are represented in the end of chapter materials.

Each chapter contains Questions, Multiple-Choice, Brief Exercises, Exercises, and Problems. The Multiple-Choice section is new to this edition. At least one question is provided for each learning objective of the text. The computational questions are included in MBC with algorithmic options.

New to this edition: *at least one multiple choice question for each LO is offered in a new MC assignment section that can be assigned and auto-graded in MBC.*

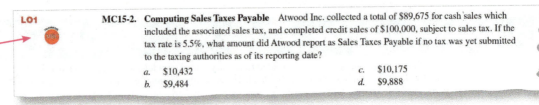

LO1

MC15-2. **Computing Sales Taxes Payable**   Atwood Inc. collected a total of $89,675 for cash sales which included the associated sales tax, and completed credit sales of $100,000, subject to sales tax. If the tax rate is 5.5%, what amount did Atwood report as Sales Taxes Payable if no tax was yet submitted to the taxing authorities as of its reporting date?

a. $10,432
b. $9,484
c. $10,175
d. $9,888

We prepared a grid plotting each chapter's content across the best competing texts in the marketplace, arranged by learning objective, to ensure that our coverage exceeds the competition. Importantly, our assignments correspond with the listed learning objective to ensure that students have the necessary foundational material to complete the corresponding problems.

The last section (**Accounting Decisions and Judgments**) includes more application-type problems, which are identified as follows.

Data Analytics   Problems that require skills including: data extraction, data cleaning, creation of data visualizations, analysis of data trends and visualizations

Real World Analysis   Includes real-world material from publicly available financial statements.

Communication Case   Allows students to apply chapter content through a written presentation.

Judgment Case   Pushes students to levels of evaluation, analysis, and decision-making involving relevant content.

Ethics Case   Shows students how decisions have ethical consequences.

Codification Skills   Includes research in the ASC glossary and in the Codification on specific topics and through an applied example.

Challenge Problem   Problems either integrate content from multiple chapters or require students to apply the chapter's content in a more complex environment that pushes students beyond the usual coverage.

Deloitte Trueblood Case   References are provided to cases in the Trueblood case series, prepared by Deloitte professionals, based on recent accounting technical issues that require research and judgment.

New to this edition, Integrated Excel questions have been added to MBC which allows for the auto-grading of student Excel formulas.

Chapter Organization—Updated this Edition

Chapters in this text are organized into two parts.

Part 1:   Chapters 1 through 6 offer a review of introductory financial reporting. We begin with the accounting environment and the underlying conceptual framework. We review the accounting double-entry system, including the preparation and presentation of the four financial statements: income statement (including comprehensive income), balance sheet, statement of equity, and statement of cash flows. We also introduce the DuPont framework, which is useful for analysis and interpretation of accounting reports. The first part of the book concludes with a review of time value of money.

Part 2:   The second part launches with the chapter on revenue recognition. This chapter is helpful to understanding the remaining chapters, including when revenue (and assets) are recognized, and when expenses (and liabilities) are recognized. Chapters 8 through 23 loosely follow the accounting equation. Specifically, we begin with the chapters covering assets—Chapters 8 through 14, followed by chapters generally covering liabilities or equity (with some asset implications)—Chapters 15 through 20. The last part of part 2 includes a new chapter to the fourth edition, **Chapter 21 on Accounting Changes and Error Analysis**. Previously offered as an Appendix, we now offer this content in a dedicated chapter with supporting resources. Next, Chapter 23 revisits the statement of cash flows (from Chapter 5), addressing the cash flows related to some special topics introduced in part 2. New to this edition, we moved the content on Pensions and Postretirement Benefits to the final chapter (Chapter 23) in recognition of its elimination from topical coverage on the CPA exam. Finally, **Appendix A** introduces Data Analytics and **Appendix B** (Online) describes key areas of differences between U.S. GAAP and IFRS.

Book-Wide Changes To This Edition

In addition to the chapter-specific changes listed below, we have made several enhancements that affect the entire book.

General Updates to the Text

- Chapter organization was revised to now include a new chapter (Chapter 21) on Accounting Changes and Error Analysis and the chapter on pensions and postretirement benefits was moved to the end of the book (Chapter 23) to recognize its elimination on the CPA exam. (See the new flow of chapters from Chapter 19 to Chapter 23).

- The CPA column of the Action Plan was updated to now reference sections of the CPA Exam Blueprints (2025) which can help instructors with curriculum assessment.

- The balance sheet equation (BSE) included in the text margin next to each journal entry now includes abbreviated account name. One key benefit of incorporating the BSE with account names is that students can readily see the impact of each transaction on the financial statements.

- New real world sustainability reporting examples were added throughout the text.

- We have updated disclosures for real companies on the chapter opening pages, Real World boxes, and Management Judgment sections.

General Udpates to End-of-Chapter Assignments and MBC

- A new multiple-choice section was added to every chapter of the text. At least one question is offered for each learning objective of the text.

- Many existing assignments are now offered in the balance sheet equation format in addition to the journal entry format.

- Overall, we assessed the coverage of assignments for each learning objective and added additional assignments as needed.

- A number of new assignments have been updated with current, real data.

- Additional questions in the problems and AD&J sections were added to MBC.

- New assignments asking students to analyze actual sustainability disclosures were added.

- Faculty will have the option to turn on relevant demo and review video resources that match numerous end-of-chapter assignments. This allows students convenient access to videos while solving similar problems in myBusinessCourse.

- Data Visualization assignments were added to the assignment offerings which allows students to analyze charts without creating them.

- New Integrated Excel assignments were also added which test students on the Excel formulas entered. This new auto-graded offering is completed by students within MBC, not requiring students to have Excel on their computers.

- Test Bank was updated to correspond with changes to the fourth edition and supplemented with additional questions.

- Additional videos were created for each chapter to align with new edition updates.

Chapter Specific Changes To This Edition

CHAPTER 14—Investments in Debt and Equity Securities

- The dual presentation on accounting for investments upon sale was changed from a side-by-side comparative approach to a separate LO presentation approach to improve the student learning experience. (The former accounting method one was moved to multiple appendices to the chapter.)

- HTM examples for the bondholder (company names and dollar amounts) were updated to mirror examples in Chapter 16 for the bond issuer. This update more easily allows faculty to show each side of a bond transaction.

- Dropped prior appendix 14B on special purpose funds and life insurance, with some discussion items moved to Chapter 4.

- Updated Demo 14-1A to include bond retirement.

- Added reclassification disclosure to Demo 14-3A and simplified reconciliation presentation.

- Added sustainability reporting topic of ESG classification of investment funds in the European Union.

- Added 31 new assignments including multiple-choice, accounting equation, and more plus additional appendix assignments to support alternative method to account for investments upon a sale.

CHAPTER 15—Current Liabilities and Contingencies

- Added Codification reference on commitment disclosures to LO15-6.

- Updated payroll rates in LO15-3.

- Added sustainability reporting content on environmental liabilities.

- Added 30 new assignments including multiple-choice, accounting equation, reporting of environmental liabilities, and more.

CHAPTER 16—Long-Term Liabilities

- Bond examples for the bond issuer (company names and dollar amounts) were updated to mirror examples in Chapter 14 for the bondholder. A new side-by-side comparison exhibit is also included in Chapter 16.

- Updated amortization schedules to include a column for the unamortized discount or premium

- Moved creditor section on troubled debt to Chapter 8.

- Added sustainability content on the issuance of green bonds.

- Added new Codification disclosure of unused commitments in LO16-10.

- Revised the content of LO16-8 to reflect ASU 2024-04 on induced conversions.

- Added 33 new assignments including multiple choice, accounting equation, questions asking for debtor and investor entries, green bond issuance, and more.

CHAPTER 17—Accounting for Leases

- Added new Demo 17-8C on unguaranteed residual value in sales-type lease.

- Added part 5 to Demo 17-1 to illustrate the fifth lease classification criterion.

- Added part *k* to Demo 17-6 to account for a lease where the lessor determines payments by the lessee are not probable.

- Added more clarity to the distinction between the terms net investment in lease and lease receivable for a sales-type lease (LO17-6, LO17-8, and LO17-10).

- Added 28 new assignments including multiple-choice, accounting equation, and more.

CHAPTER 18—Income Taxes

- The tax chapter was revamped to improve the student experience. We now start with a broad introduction and then build on the example with more complexity in later learning objectives.

- In this update, some content was reordered and revised in the chapter to improve the flow and presentation of topical content.

- A number of demos and reviews were revised throughout the chapter.
- Show that the term "permanent" difference is referenced as nontaxable, nondeductible, and other differences in the Codification.
- Expanded examples of tax rate reconciliation disclosures under ASU 2023-09 showing nontaxable amounts, nondeductible amounts, and tax rate changes. Also discussed the effect on rate reconciliation for tax credits.
- Moved LO18-10 to Chapter 21.

CHAPTER 19—Stockholders' Equity (Formerly Chapter 20)

- Illustrated noncontrolling interest through Coca-Cola in LO19-1.
- Expanded LO19-7 to include the statement of stockholders' equity.
- Added 27 new assignments including multiple-choice, accounting equation, diluted EPS, compensation expense, and more.

CHAPTER 20—Share-Based Compensation and Earnings per Share (Formerly Chapter 21)

- Added new Codification reference on EPS disclosures in LO20-9.
- Added new sustainability Real World box on executive compensation.
- Added 32 new assignments including multiple-choice, accounting equation, diluted EPS, compensation expense, and more.

CHAPTER 21—Accounting Changes and Error Analysis (Formerly Appendix A)

- Converted Appendix in prior edition to a new chapter complete with related chapter supplements.
- Includes a review of concepts covered in prior chapters along with expanded coverage.
- Significantly increased the number of end of chapter assignments.

CHAPTER 22—Statement of Cash Flows Revisited

- Added new Codification reference in LO22-5 related to disclosures.
- Moved pension references to Expanding Your Knowledge text box.
- Added 10 new assignments including multiple-choice.

CHAPTER 23—Pensions and Postretirement Benefits (Formerly Chapter 19)

- The pension chapter has been moved to later in the book in recognition of its elimination from topical coverage on the CPA exam.
- New teaching notes were added to suggest coverage and related assignments for faculty who wish to provide a brief topical overview of defined benefit plans.
- Included a new Expanding Your Knowledge box on pension fund financial statements (content included on BAR exam).
- Added 16 new assignments including multiple-choice and more.

APPENDIX A—Data Analytics

- Expanded background discussion to include the analytics mindset and best practices in data visualization
- Added additional assignments in Tableau and Excel

APPENDIX C (CHAPTER 6)—Time Value of Money

- Expanded PV and FV graphics to show discounting and accretion by year.
- Added 8 new multiple-choice questions.

APPENDIX D (CHAPTER 7)—Revenue Recognition

- Added Demo 7-5C on transaction price allocation with customer options.
- Added 42 new assignments including multiple-choice, accounting equation, real world problems on revenue recognition, regulatory credits, and more.

Additional Resources

Financial Accounting Bootcamp

This interactive tutorial is intended for use in programs that either require or would like to offer a tutorial that can be used as a refresher of topics introduced in the first financial accounting course. It is designed as an asynchronous, interactive, self-paced experience for students. Available Learning Modules (You Select) follow.

1. Introducing Financial Accounting (approximate completion time 2 hours)
2. Constructing Financial Statements (approximate completion time 4 hours)
3. Adjusting Entries and Completing the Accounting Cycle (approximate completion time 4 hours)
4. Reporting and Analyzing Cash Flows (approximate completion time 3.5 hours)
5. Analyzing and Interpreting Financial Statements (approximate completion time 3.5 hours)
6. Excel and Time-Value of Money Basics (approximate completion time 2 hours)

This is a separate, saleable item. Contact your sales representative to receive more information or email customerservice@cambridgepub.com.

Guide to Intermediate Accounting Research

The *Guide to Intermediate Accounting Research*, Third Edition, by Shelby Collins, is intended to serve as a supplement to the materials used in an intermediate accounting course. It includes many opportunities to apply Codification guidance to related accounting topics (including, for example, leases, investment accounting, revenue recognition, and consolidation). Students will learn to confidently address and communicate accounting research issues, from start to finish. Students will not only take away the ability to identify the accounting problem (the "researchable question"), but will gain experience locating and applying guidance within the FASB Codification. This is a separate, saleable text (ISBN: 978-1-61853-316-6). Contact your sales representative to receive a desk copy or email customerservice@cambridgepub.com

Acknowledgments

This product has benefited greatly from the valuable feedback of focus group attendees, survey respondents, reviewers, students, colleagues, and adopters. We are extremely grateful to them for their help in making this project a success for both instructors and students.

Mohamed Abualhaija	Kevin Baxter	Jason Call	Xiaoyan Cheng
Ronnie Abukhalaf	Laura Bearden	John Campbell	Yu-Ho Chi
Sara Adams	David Beck	Katherine Campbell	Wen-Wen Chien
Darlene Adkins	Sheila Bedford	Linda Campbell	Preeti Choudhary
Rohit Agarwal	Kentaya Beeler	Logan Carlisle	Bob Churchman
JK Aier	Rick Berschback	Greg Carlton	Cheryl Clark
Ahmad Alkosani	Carol Bishop	Rodney Carmack	Mary Catherine Cleaveland
Carl Allocca	Heidi Blakeway-Phillips	Thomas Carnes	Lynn Clements
Anthony Amoruso	Marie Blouin	Charles Carpenter	Kayla Cline
Alex Ampadu	Emily Blum	Matthew Carroll	Janice Cobb
Benjamin Anderson	Eveline Bogdanski	Mary Ellen Carter	Emily Cokeley
H. Kyle Anderson	Lisa Bostick	Al Case	Robert Collier
Angela Andrews	Brian Bratten	Nancy Cassidy	Norman Colter
Yunita Anwar	Daniel Brickner	Jack Cathey	Christie Comunale
Dennis Applegate	William Brink	Richard Cazier	Jenelle Conaway
Kalena Armstrong-Henry	Jake Brock	Diane Chabes	Rena Corbett
Balbir Arora	Marilyn Brooks-Lewis	Sumantra Chakravarty	Cheryl Corke
Muhammed Azim	Lisa Brown	Mary Chance	Claire Costin
Thomas Badley	Philip Brown	Nandini Chandar	Keaton Councell
David Baglia	Robert Brown	Amy Chang	John Crawford
Wendy Bailey	Lakeesha Browne	Jasmine Chen	Patricia Crenny
Marie Bakari	Esther Bunn	Jeff Chen	Cindy Cuccia
Patricia Ball	Megan Burke	Zeyun Chen	Marc Cussatt
Anandi Banerjee	Angela Busila	Zhenhua Chen	Abbie Daly
Dereck Barr-Pulliam	Regina Butts	Kang Cheng	Steve Davenport
Tami Barton	Holly Caldwell	Stephanie Cheng	William Davenport

Angela Davis	Kim Guerts	Jenny Kim	Katie Maxwell
Patricia Davis	Annie Guier	Jung Hoon Kim	Roger Mayer
Mady Day	Hongtao Guo	Oksana Kim	Brian McAllister
Mollie DeBrunner	Meng Guo	Taewoo Kim	Sarah Shonka McCoy
Scott Dell	Joohyung Ha	Wambui Kimani	Mindy McCready
Allison Dellapelle	Amy Haas	Beckett Kitaen	Terra McGhee
Travis Demsher	Kevin Hale	Gordon Klein	Michelle McNeil-Brown
Ming Deng	Richard Hale	Tyler Kleppe	McKelle Meek
John Dexter	Jade Hallum	Eric Knight	Lindsay Meermans
Charles Dick	Billie Hamilton	Robin Knowles	Tammy Metze
Cynthia Dittmer	Susan Hamlen	David Knutsen	Danya Mi
Mia Dizon	Glen Hansen	Polly Knutson	Jeanette Millius
Lei Dong	Pilar Hanson	Jared Koreff	Ashley Minnich
James Douthit	Izhar Haq	Elida Kraja	Don Minyard
Tom Downen	Michael Harding	Lakshmana Krishna Moorthy	Jose Miranda-Lopez
Hui Du	David Harr	Anita Jo Kroll	Marilyn Misch
Michael Dugan	Mary Healy	Gaurav Kumar	Robert Mocadlo
Devon Dunkle	Rebekah Heath	Anthony Kurek	Toni Molinari
Tim Eaton	Abby Helton	Melvin Lamboy-Ruiz	Joon Seok Moon
Pennie Eddy	Jacques Hendieh	Benjamin Lansford	Carmen Morgan
Gertrude Eguae-Obazee	Karen Hennes	Donna Larner	Arnica Mulder
Lisa Eiler	John Hepp	David B. Law	Martin Mulyadi
Dina El Mahdy	Young-won Her	Howard Lawrence	Volkan Muslu
David Emerson	Jessica Hildebrand	Judy Lawrence	Al Nagy
Cole Engel	Hannah Hoang	Ethan Layman	Tammy Naples
Sedat Erdogan	James Hodge	Yvette Lazdowski	Lisa Nash
Matthew Erikson	Benjamin Hoffman	Megan Leach	Sia Nassiripour
Jordan Evar	Robert Hogan	Anna Leftwich	Ashley Newton
Hayden Durant	Mike Hoppe	Deborah Leitsch	Joseph Nicassio
Joseph Faello	Jana Hosmer	Aaron Lewis	Daniel Nugent
Connie Fajardo	Md Enayet Hossain	Ji Li	Maria Nykyforovych
Farima Fakoor	Pei-Hui Hsu	Kristin Li	Daniel O'Connor
Yun Fan	Julie Huang	Lynn Li	Suzanne Ogilby
Tatiana Fedyk	Xiaochuan Huang	Yifan Li	Landri Ognowski
Kevin Feeney	Jason Hughes	Zining Li	Henrietta Okoro
Jennifer Feng	Susan Hughes	Lihong Liang	Christina Olear
Nathaniel Fields	Steven Hunt	Qunfeng Liao	Jen Oliver
Josh Filzen	David Hurtt	Sharon Lightner	Roshelle Overton
Mary Fischer	Helen Hurwitz	Lucy Lim	Randy Paape
Linda Flaming	Janet Huston	Betsy Lin	Sangshin Pae
Lisa Flynn	Paul D. Hutchison	Hui Lin	Shanshan Pan
Arno Forst	Mohammad Nazrul Islam	Jacky Lin	Ganesh Pandit
Thomas Francl	Derek Jackson	Zhilu Lin	Young Park
Mitchell Franklin	Mark Jackson	Qianhua Ling	Clay Partridge
Diana Franz	Harvey Jacobs	Ellen Lippman	Ronald Pearson
Laurel Franzen	Marianne James	Caixing Liu	Melanie Peddicord
Chad Frawley	Jackie Jamsheed	Carol Liu	Cindy Phipps
Donna Free	Adrian Jarrell	Cathy Liu	Marc Picconi
Fabio Gaertner	Shannon Jemiolo	Linxiao Liu	Hilari Pickett
Patricia Galletta	Amy Ji	Heather Lively	Chuck Pier
Nathan Garrett	John Jiang	Suzanne Long	James Pierson
Kelly Gebhart	Hengda Jin	Frank Longo	Byron Pike
Christina Gehrke	Vicki Jobst	Jackie Looser	Lincoln Pinto
Miriam Gerstein	Bret Johnson	Martha Loudder	Cynthia Planita
John Giles	Marilyn Johnson	Lucy Lu	Kendell Poch
Lisa Gillespie	Bill Jones	Yan Luo	Paul Polinski
Sunita Goel	Kevin Jones	William Lyle	Ronald Premuroso
Shawn Granitto	Megan Jones	Thomas Madison	Jean Price
Marina Grau	Erin Jordan	Daphne Main	Richard Price
Pamela Graybeal	Sarah Judge	Frank Manzi	Shay Blanchette Proulx
David Greenwell	Phyllis Kapetakis	Amanda Sue Marcy	Lauren Psomostithis
Tony Greig	Tanya Kausler	Jasna Marker	Linda Quick
Jennifer Grennan	Laura Kauzlarich	Blair Marquardt	Lance Radziej
Andrew Griffith	Mike Onder Kaymaz	DeAnna Martin	Tharindra Ranasinghe
Matt Griffith	Marsha Keune	Roger Martin	Robert Rankin
Teri Grimmer	Suzanne Kiess	Sharon Martin	Caleb Rawson
Thomas Guarino	Irene Kim	Stephani Mason	Andrew Reeder

Arnouk Rein
Robert Resutek
Will Riccardi
Jennifer Rivers
Cecile Roberti
Roslyn Roberts
Ethel Robinson
Karen Robinson
Shani Robinson
Steve Rock
Andrea Roerdink
Tina Rolling
Tom Rosengarth
Mark Ross
Sharon Ross
John Rossi
Brian Routh
Ivan Rubel
Pinky Rusli
Fangjun Sang
Sayan Sarkar
Jorge Eduardo Scarpin
Philipp Schaberl
Kathryn Schaefer
Paul Schloemer
Bryce Schonberger
Matthew Schultz

Michael Schultz
Andy Schut
Nadia Schwartz
Natalia Scott
Phillipp Shaberl
Emily Shafron
Joe Shangguan
Anish Sharma
Deanne Shimala
Haeyoung Shin
Alice Shiotsugu
Jacob Shortt
Evan Shough
Laura Simeoni
Debra Sinclair
Bhaskar Singh
Sonia Singh
Justyna Skomra
Philip Slater
Patricia Smith
Sheldon Smith
Nancy Snow
Greg Sommers
Mohsen Souissi
Lynn Stallworth
James Stanker
Vicki Stewart

Randall Stone
Brooke Stout
Sandra Streitenberger
Steve Stubben
Sarah Stuber
Ron Stunda
Rob Stussie
Amy Sun
Estelle Sun
Yan Sun
Nancy Swanson
Brian Sweeney
Lucas Swider
Brandon Szerwo
Kyle Tackett
Paul Tanyi
Ian Tarrant
Isaac Taylor
Mary Teal
Maya Thevenot
Paula Thomas
Robin Thomas
Geoffrey Tickell
Surjit Tinaikar
Pamela Trafford
Joseph Trainor
Madeline Trimble

Ben Trnka
Carmelita Troy
Peggy Tsirigotis
Eric Typpo
Kimberly Ulrich
Mark Ulrich
David Van Rijt
Jay Vega
Nathan Walck
Robin Overweg Walker
Huishan Wan
Lin Wang
Shane Warrick
Edie Wasyliszyn
Olena Watanabe
Pamela Watkins
Christine Wayne
James Webb
Jill Weber
Kyle Webster
Stephen Weiss
Mary Jeanne Welsh
Lei Wen
Winnie Wen
Ben Whipple
Donna Whitten
Tyler Wilkinson

Jeff Wilks
Gayle Williams
Tomeika Williams
Veronda Willis
Jennifer Winchel
Mindy Wolfe
Hannah Wong
JoAnn Wood
Maef Woods
Phil Woodward
Michelle Wray
Suzanne Wright
Di Wu
Wentao Wu
Hong Xie
Yan Xiong
Helen Xu
Li Xu
Rong Yang
Chunlai Ye
Xiaoli Yuan
Joseph Zhang
Qiuhong Zhao
Aleksandra Zimmerman

We received many helpful suggestions from adopters of the 3rd edition, and we are particularly thankful for the feedback from Jennifer Rivers who provided detailed chapter-by-chapter suggestions. We are also grateful for the feedback and contributions from Paul Hutchison who made meaningful contributions to the test bank. JoAnn Wood has been a tireless advocate for the book, and we appreciate all her efforts on our behalf. Accuracy is the hallmark of any best-selling accounting textbook, and we are thankful for the amazing job Gayle Williams did accuracy checking the 4th edition. Lastly, we thank George Werthman, Lorraine Gleeson, Jocelyn Mousel, Karen Amundson, Debbie McQuade, Terry McQuade, and the entire team at Cambridge Business Publishers for their encouragement, enthusiasm, and guidance.

Michelle Hanlon   *Leslie Hodder*   *Karen Nelson*   *Darren Roulstone*   *Amie Dragoo*

January 2025

Brief Contents

Contents

Chapter 17

Accounting for Leases 17-1

Chapter 20

Share-Based Compensation and Earnings per Share 20-1

Chapter 21

Accounting Changes and Error Analysis 21-1

Chapter 22

Statement of Cash Flows Revisited 22-1

Appendix D (Chapter 7)
Revenue Recognition 7-1

14 Investments in Debt and Equity Securities

Intel Corporation

Note 9: Investments

Short-term Investments

Short-term investments include marketable debt investments in corporate debt, government debt, and financial institution instruments, and are recorded within cash and cash equivalents and short-term investments on the Consolidated Balance Sheets. Government debt includes instruments such as non-US government bills and bonds and US agency securities. Financial institution instruments include instruments issued or managed by financial institutions in various forms, such as commercial paper, fixed- and floating-rate bonds, money market fund deposits, and time deposits. As of December 30, 2023 and December 31, 2022, substantially all time deposits were issued by institutions outside the US.

The fair value of our economically hedged marketable debt investments was $17.1 billion as of December 30, 2023 ($16.2 billion as of December 31, 2022). For hedged investments still held at the reporting date, we recorded net gains of $534 million in 2023 (net losses of $748 million in 2022 and net losses of $606 million in 2021). Net losses on the related derivatives were $472 million in 2023 (net gains of $752 million in 2022 and net gains of $609 million in 2021).

Our remaining unhedged marketable debt investments are reported at fair value, with unrealized gains or losses, net of tax, recorded in accumulated other comprehensive income (loss). The adjusted cost of our unhedged investments was $4.7 billion as of December 30, 2023 ($10.2 billion as of December 31, 2022), which approximated the fair value for these periods.

The fair value of marketable debt investments, by contractual maturity, as of December 30, 2023, was as follows:

(In Millions)	Fair Value
Due in 1 year or less	$ 9,575
Due in 1–2 years	2,375
Due in 2–5 years	7,134
Due after 5 years	442
Instruments not due at a single maturity date	2,274
Total	**$21,800**

Intel Corporation

Equity Investments

(In Millions)	Dec 30, 2023	Dec 31, 2022
Marketable equity securities	$1,194	$1,341
Non-marketable equity securities	4,630	4,561
Equity method investments	5	10
Total	**$5,829**	**$5,912**

[1] Over 90% of our marketable equity securities are subject to trading-volume or market-based restrictions, which limit the number of shares we may sell in a specified period of time, impacting our ability to liquidate these investments. The trading volume restrictions generally apply for as long as we own more than 1% of the outstanding shares. Market-based restrictions result from the rules of the respective exchange.

The components of gains (losses) on equity investments, net for each period were as follows:

Years Ended (In Millions)	Dec 30, 2023	Dec 31, 2022	Dec 25, 2021
Ongoing mark-to-market adjustments on marketable equity securities	$(36)	$787	$(130)
Observable price adjustments on non-marketable equity securities	17	299	750
Impairment charges	(214)	(190)	(154)
Sale of equity investments and other[1]	273	4,946	2,263
Total gains (losses) on equity investments, net	**$40**	**$4,268**	**$2,729**

[1] Sale of equity investments and other includes initial fair value adjustments recorded upon a security becoming marketable, realized gains (losses) on sales of non-marketable equity investments, and our share of equity method investee gains (losses) and distributions.

Intel Corporation
Consolidated Balance Sheets
(In Millions, Except Par Value)

	Dec. 30, 2023	Dec. 31, 2022
Assets		
Current assets:		
Cash and cash equivalents	$ 7,097	$ 11,144
Short-term investments	17,955	17,194
Accounts receivable, net	3,402	4,133
Inventories	11,127	13,224
Other current assets	3,706	4,712
Total current assets	43,269	50,407
Property, plant and equipment, net	96,647	80,860
Equity investments	5,829	5,912
Goodwill	27,591	27,591
Identified intangible assets, net	4,589	6,018
Other long-term assets	13,647	11,315
Total assets	**$191,572**	**$182,103**

Intel Corporation

Net unrealized gains and losses for our marketable and non-marketable equity securities still held at the reporting date were as follows:

(In Millions)	Dec 26, 2023	Dec 28, 2022	Dec 29, 2021
Net gains (losses) recognized during the period on equity securities	$19	$(314)	$1,210
Less: Net (gains) losses recognized during the period on equity securities sold during the period	(5)	1	(259)
Net unrealized gains (losses) recognized during the period on equity securities still held at the reporting date	**$14**	**$(313)**	**$ 951**

McAfee Corp.

During 2022, the sale of McAfee's consumer business was completed and we received $4.6 billion in cash for the sale of our remaining share of McAfee, recognizing a $4.6 billion gain in sale of equity investments and other. In 2021, we recognized McAfee dividends of $1.3 billion, which included a special dividend of $1.1 billion paid in connection with the sale of McAfee's enterprise business, and recognized $228 million related to the partial sale of our investment in McAfee.

Beijing Unisoc Technology Ltd.

We account for our interest in Beijing Unisoc Technology Ltd. (Unisoc) as a non-marketable equity security. During 2021, we recognized $471 million in observable price adjustments in our investment in Unisoc and as of December 30, 2023, the net book value of the investment was $1.1 billion ($1.1 billion as of December 31, 2022).

Chapter Preview

In this chapter, we describe the accounting for various classifications of debt and equity investments. The accounting treatment of a particular investment depends on its classification. We explain other topics related to investment accounting including the recognition of impairment losses and the use of fair value option. The appendices include a discussion on accounting for derivatives, which are financial instruments purchased to speculate on future prices or to hedge against risk.

Teaching note: (1) When an investment is recognized at fair value and it is later sold, a company can either (a) adjust the investment to fair value at the sale date and period-end or (b) delay adjusting the fair value adjustment account to period-end. For instructors who prefer (a), assign LO 14-2, LO 14-3, and LO 14-4. For instructors who prefer (b), assign LO 14-7, LO 14-8, and LO 14-9. (2) In the area of derivative accounting, the CPA Exam Blueprints indicate that the BAR section coverage of derivatives requires recall skills only, with the exception of the fair value hedge and the cash flow hedge, which require preparation of journal entries. See LO 14-11.

Action Plan

LO	Topic/Subtopic	Page	Demos	Reviews	Assignments	CPA*
LO 14–1	**Account for debt securities measured at amortized cost** HTM :: Amortized Cost :: Par :: Discount :: Premium :: Effective Interest Method :: Straight-Line Interest Method	14-4	D14-1A D14-1B D14-1C D14-1D D14-1E	R14-1	MC14-1, MC14-2, MC14-3, BE14-1, BE14-2, BE14-3, BE14-4, BE14-5, BE14-6, BE14-7, BE14-8, BE14-14, BE14-23, BE14-36, E14-1, E14-2, E14-3, E14-4, E14-5, E14-6, E14-32, P14-1, P14-2, P14-3, P14-4, P14-9, P14-16, AD&J14-5, AD&J14-7, AD&J14-9, AppP14-1, AppP14-7, AppP14-9	FAR II.E.2.a II.E.2.b
LO 14–2	**Account for debt securities measured at FV-NI with fair value adjustments at sale date and period-end** TS :: Fair Value Option Election :: Fair Value Adjustment :: Unrealized Gain or Loss—Income	14-13	D14-2A D14-2B	R14-2	MC14-4, MC14-5, BE14-9, BE14-10, BE14-11, BE14-12, BE14-13, BE14-14, BE14-23, BE14-36, E14-1, E14-7, E14-8, E14-9, E14-10, E14-11, E14-12, E14-32, P14-5, P14-6, P14-9, P14-14, P14-16, AD&J14-5, AD&J14-7, AD&J14-8, AppBE14-16, AppAD&J14-3, AppAD&J14-4, AppAD&J14-5	FAR II.E.1.a II.E.1.b II.E.1.c
LO 14–3	**Account for debt securities measured at FV-OCI with fair value adjustments at sale date and period-end** AFS :: Fair Value Adjustment :: Unrealized Gain or Loss—OCI :: Reclassification Adjustment	14-17	D14-3A D14-3B	R14-3	MC14-6, BE14-15, BE14-16, BE14-17, BE14-18, BE14-19, BE14-20, BE14-21, BE14-22, BE14-23, BE14-36, E14-1, E14-12, E14-13, E14-14, E14-15, E14-16, E14-17, E14-18, E14-32, P14-2, P14-3, P14-7, P14-8, P14-9, P14-14, P14-16, AD&J14-5, AD&J14-7, AD&J14-8, AppAD&J14-3, AppAD&J14-4, DA14-1	FAR II.E.1.a II.E.1.b II.E.1.c
LO 14–4	**Account for equity securities measured at FV-NI with fair value adjustments at sale date and period-end** Equity Securities :: Insignificant Influence :: Dividend :: Fair Value Adjustment :: Unrealized Gain or Loss—Income	14-24	D14-4	R14-4	MC14-7, MC14-9, BE14-24, BE14-24, BE14-26, BE14-27, BE14-31, BE14-36, E14-1, E14-19, E14-20, E14-21, E14-22, E14-23, E14-24, E14-32, P14-9, P14-10, P14-11, P14-16, AD&J14-6, AD&J14-7	FAR II.E.1.a II.E.1.b II.E.1.c
LO 14–5	**Account for equity securities following the equity method** Equity Securities :: Significant Influence :: Proportionate Share of Income :: Depreciation Adjustment :: Fair Value Option	14-27	D14-5	R14-5	MC14-8, MC14-9, BE14-28, BE14-29, BE14-30, BE14-31, BE14-32, BE14-36, E14-1, E14-23, E14-24, E14-25, E14-26, E14-27, E14-28, E14-29, E14-30, E14-31, E14-32, P14-11, P14-12, P14-13, P14-15, P14-16, AD&J14-1, AD&J14-2, AD&J14-3, AD&J14-4, AD&J14-7, AppP14-9	FAR II.E.3.a II.E.3.b
LO 14–6	**Adjust debt and equity securities for impairment** Impairment Loss :: HTM :: AFS :: Equity Method Investments	14-31	D14-6	R14-6	MC14-10, BE14-33, BE14-34, BE14-35, E14-33, E14-34, E14-35, P14-17, AD&J14-7	FAR II.E.1.d II.E.2.c
LO 14–7	**APPENDIX 14A—Account for debt securities measured at FV-NI with fair value adjustments only at period-end** TS :: Fair Value Option Election :: Fair Value Adjustment :: Unrealized Gain or Loss—Income	14-36	D14-7A D14-7B	R14-7	AppMC14-1, AppMC14-2, AppBE14-1, AppBE14-2, AppBE14-3, AppBE14-4, AppBE14-5, AppBE14-6, AppBE14-7, AppBE14-16, AppE14-1, AppE14-2, AppE14-3, AppE14-4, AppP14-1, AppP14-2, AppP14-7, AppP14-9	FAR II.E.1.a II.E.1.b II.E.1.c
LO 14–8	**APPENDIX 14B—Account for debt securities measured at FV-OCI with fair value adjustments only at period-end** AFS :: Fair Value Adjustment :: Unrealized Gain or Loss—OCI :: Reclassification Adjustment	14-39	D14-8A D14-8B	R14-8	AppMC14-3, AppBE14-8, AppBE14-9, AppBE14-10, AppBE14-11, AppBE14-12, AppBE14-13, AppBE14-14, AppBE14-15, AppBE14-16, AppBE14-17, AppBE14-18, AppE14-2, AppE14-5, AppE14-6, AppE14-7, AppE14-8, AppE14-9, AppP14-3, AppP14-4, AppP14-5, AppP14-7, AppP14-9	FAR II.E.1.a II.E.1.b II.E.1.c
LO 14–9	**APPENDIX 14C—Account for equity securities measured at FV-NI with fair value adjustments only at period-end** Equity Securities :: Insignificant Influence :: Dividend :: Fair Value Adjustment :: Unrealized Gain or Loss—Income	14-46	D14-9	R14-9	AppMC14-9, AppBE14-19, AppBE14-20, AppBE14-21, AppBE14-22, AppE14-10, AppE14-11, AppE14-12, AppE14-13, AppE14-14, AppP14-6, AppP14-7, AppP14-8, AppP14-9, AppAD&J14-5, AppAD&J14-6	FAR II.E.1.a II.E.1.b II.E.1.c
LO 14–10	**APPENDIX 14D—Explain the accounting for transfers of investments** Transfer Investment Category :: No Retrospective Treatment :: Disclosure	14-50	D14-10	R14-10	AppBE14-23, AppBE14-24, AppE14-15, AppE14-16, AppP14-10, AppAD&J14-1, AppAD&J14-2, AppAD&J14-3, AppAD&J14-4, AppAD&J14-5	FAR II.E.1.b II.E.2.b II.E.3.b
LO 14–11	**APPENDIX 14E—Describe and account for derivatives** Speculative Instrument :: Call Option :: Hedging Instrument :: Put Option :: Interest Rate Swap :: Futures Contract	14-51	D14-11A D14-11B D14-11C D14-11D	R14-11	AppBE14-25, AppBE14-26, AppBE14-27, AppBE14-28, AppE14-17, AppE14-18, AppE14-19, AppE14-20, AppP14-11, AppP14-12, AppP14-13	BAR II.H.1 II.H.2 II.H.3 II.H.4

*Black (Gray) font in CPA column indicates that the LO ties directly (indirectly) to the CPA Exam Blueprint LO.

Expanded Chapter Preview

Companies invest in the securities of other companies and government agencies for a variety of reasons. Companies often have cash available that is not needed at present but will be needed in the near future. Rather than allow idle cash to remain in a nonearning account, companies find temporary investments where they can earn a return. These investments are usually low risk and can be quickly and easily converted to cash. They often include securities of federal, state, and local government agencies but can also include securities of other companies. A second reason companies invest in securities of other companies, especially in securities representing ownership interests, is to develop a beneficial intercompany relationship that will increase the profitability of the investing company, both directly and indirectly.

This chapter explains how to account for investments in debt and equity securities from the perspective of the *investor*. In general, a **security** is a share, participation, or interest that is (1) represented by an instrument or is registered, (2) commonly recognized or dealt with on exchanges or markets, and (3) either one of a class or is divisible. Investments in debt and equity securities are known as **financial assets**.

> **ASC Glossary** Financial Assets: Cash, evidence of an ownership interest in an entity, or a contract that conveys to one entity a right to do either of the following:
> a. Receive cash or another financial instrument from a second entity.
> b. Exchange other financial instruments on potentially favorable terms with the second entity.

The first step in accounting for investments in securities is to determine whether an investment is a **debt security** or an **equity security**, the differences of which are outlined below. **For purposes of illustration in this chapter, we use bond investments to illustrate debt securities, and investments in common or preferred stock to illustrate equity securities.**

Investment	Definition	Examples	
Debt security	**ASC Glossary** Any security representing a creditor relationship with an entity.	• U.S. Treasury securities • Municipal securities • Corporate bonds	• Securitized debt instruments • Convertible debt • Commercial paper
Equity security[1]	**ASC Glossary** Any security representing an ownership interest in an entity (for example, common, preferred, or other capital stock) or the right to acquire (for example, warrants, rights, forward purchase contracts, and call options) or dispose of (for example, put options and forward sale contracts) an ownership interest in an entity at fixed or determinable prices.	• Common, preferred, and other capital stock • Stock options, warrants, and stock rights • Options to purchase (call options) or to sell (put options) equity securities at fixed or determinable prices	

[1] While ASC 321 describes the accounting for equity securities and other ownership interests in an entity such as investments in partnerships, the discussion in this chapter focuses on equity securities.

The next step is to determine the method to account for debt and equity securities, *which will have a direct impact on both recording of transactions and financial statement presentation*. Determining which method to use to account for *debt investments* requires an analysis of both the intent and the ability of the investor to trade or hold the securities until maturity.

Methods to Account for Debt Securities (BONDS)		
Amortized Cost	**FV-NI**	**FV-OCI**
Held-to-Maturity Securities: Investor has the intent and ability to hold to maturity	**Trading Securities:** Investor intends to sell in the near term.	**Available-for-Sale Securities:** Investor intends to hold the securities for an unspecified period.
LO 14-1	**LO 14-2 (or LO 14-7)**	**LO 14-3 (or LO 14-8)**
Recognize at amortized cost. Ignore adjustment to fair value.	Recognize at fair value (FV) with adjustment affecting NI.	Recognize at fair value (FV) with adjustment affecting OCI.

In the case of *equity securities*, extent of influence or control over the investee is important.

Methods to Account for Equity Securities (STOCK)		
FV-NI Investor Lacks Significant Influence (< 20% Ownership Interest)	**Equity Method** Investor Has Significant Influence (20% to 50% Ownership Interest)	**Consolidation** Investor Has Controlling Influence (> 50%* Ownership Interest)
LO 14-4 (or LO 14-9)	**LO 14-5**	**Advanced accounting courses**
Recognize at fair value (FV) with adjustment affecting net income.	Recognize at cost, adjusted for investor's share of net income and dividends.	Financial statements are consolidated for the investor and investee.

*In this chapter, we assume that a company with >50% ownership interest has obtained a controlling influence over the investee, even though there may be exceptions to this general guideline.

Account for debt securities measured at amortized cost

LO 14-1

Of the three methods to account for debt investments, we begin with debt investments measured at amortized cost. **Amortized cost** is the *acquisition cost* of an investment, adjusted for any premium or discount (as defined below but explained in greater detail in later sections). For this method, changes in fair value are considered irrelevant because it is assumed that the investor will hold the debt investment for its full term.

> **HTM at Amortized Cost**
> - Recognize at amortized cost (par, discount, or premium)
> - Ignore changes in fair value
> - Recognize interest revenue in net income using the effective interest method or straight-line interest method
> - Recognize gain or loss from a sale in net income

LO 14-1 Overview

Held-to-Maturity Securities

Debt investments measured at amortized cost are called **held-to-maturity securities** (**HTM**). The HTM classification is determined at acquisition, where a company has both **the positive intent and ability to hold an investment to its maturity date.** This implies that the investor (1) intends to hold the security until maturity, and (2) does not anticipate a need to sell the security before its maturity date to access cash quickly or to respond to interest rate changes. We illustrate HTM securities in this section using a common type of debt investment—bonds issued by another company. **Exhibit 14-1** defines terms commonly used in accounting for bond investments.

Amortized cost	Amount at which an investment is acquired, adjusted for amortization of any premium or a discount.
Discount	Amount equal to the excess of a bond investment's face value over its present value. A discount reduces the investment account to its amortized cost. A discount represents deferred interest revenue that will be recognized over the term of the bond investment.
Premium	Amount equal to the excess of the present value of a bond investment over its face value. A premium increases the investment account to its amortized cost. A premium represents a reduction of interest revenue that will be recognized over the term of the bond investment.
Fair value	ASC Glossary The price that would be received to sell an asset or paid to transfer a liability in an orderly transaction between market participants at the measurement date.
Face value (also called maturity value, principal amount, par or stated value)	Contractual cash flow receivable at a bond's maturity date.
Stated rate (also called coupon, nominal, or contractual rate)	Rate used to determine the cash interest receipts on a bond investment. Stated as an annual percentage of face value.
Market rate (also called effective rate or yield)	Rate on a similar bond investment in the market involving similar risk and where the issuer has a similar crediting rating. Stated as an annual percentage.

EXHIBIT 14-1
Bond Investment Terminology

The HTM classification is further described in the accounting guidance.

320-10-25-3   Amortized cost is relevant only if a security is actually held to maturity. Use of the held-to-maturity category is restrictive because the use of amortized cost must be justified for each investment in a debt security. At acquisition, an entity shall determine if it has the positive intent and ability to hold

Methods to Account for Debt Securities		
Amortized Cost	FV-NI	FV-OCI
LO 14-1	LO 14-2	LO 14-3

a security to maturity, which is distinct from the mere absence of an intent to sell. If management's intention to hold a debt security to maturity is uncertain, it is not appropriate to carry that investment at amortized cost. In establishing intent, an entity shall consider pertinent historical experience, such as sales and transfers of debt securities classified as held-to-maturity. A pattern of sales or transfers of those securities is inconsistent with an expressed current intent to hold similar debt securities to maturity.

Sale of HTM Securities Before Maturity Because an investor must have the intent and ability to hold an HTM security for its entire life, a sale before maturity is rare. However, due to unforeseen events an investor may decide to sell an HTM security before its maturity date. A sale of an HTM security due to *unforeseen circumstances* is not inconsistent with the original classification of HTM. For example, a company may sell an HTM debt security due to a downgrade of the investor's credit rating, or a tax law change. However, if a company sells an HTM security before maturity, without the justification of a major unforeseen event, the early sale may call into question the company's intention to hold to maturity. In such a case, the investor may be required to reclassify *all* of its debt securities as either trading or available-for-sale (debt categories discussed in later sections). The accounting guidance provides examples of unforeseen circumstances—three examples are provided below.

`320-10-25-6` The following changes in circumstances may cause the entity to change its intent to hold a certain security to maturity without calling into question its intent to hold other debt securities to maturity in the future. The sale or transfer of a held-to-maturity security due to one of the following changes in circumstances shall not be considered inconsistent with its original classification:

a. Evidence of a significant deterioration in the issuer's creditworthiness (for example, a downgrading of an issuer's published credit rating).
b. A change in tax law that eliminates or reduces the tax-exempt status of interest on the debt security . . .
c. A major business combination or major disposition . . . that necessitates the sale or transfer of held-to-maturity securities to maintain the entity's existing interest rate risk position or credit risk policy.
d. A change in statutory or regulatory requirements significantly modifying either what constitutes a permissible investment or the maximum level of investments in certain kinds of securities, thereby causing an entity to dispose of a held-to-maturity security.
e. A significant increase by the regulator in the industry's capital requirements that causes the entity to downsize by selling held-to-maturity securities.
f. A significant increase in the risk weights of debt securities used for regulatory risk-based capital purposes.

EXPANDING YOUR KNOWLEDGE   **Maturity of HTM Securities**

If a sale of the HTM debt security occurs near enough to its maturity date such that interest rate risk is substantially eliminated, or the sale occurs after substantial collection of the principal, the security is considered to be held the full-term for purposes of classification.

`320-10-25-14` Sales of debt securities that meet either of the following conditions may be considered as maturities for purposes of the classification of securities and the disclosure requirements under this Subtopic:

a. The sale of a security occurs near enough to its maturity date . . . that interest rate risk is substantially eliminated as a pricing factor. That is, the date of sale is so near the maturity or call date (for example, within three months) that changes in market interest rates would not have a significant effect on the security's fair value.
b. The sale of a security occurs after the entity has already collected a substantial portion (at least 85 percent) of the principal outstanding at acquisition due either to prepayments on the debt security or to scheduled payments on a debt security payable in equal installments (both principal and interest) over its term.

Measurement of HTM Securities

HTM investments are initially measured at acquisition cost, which is equal to the price paid for the security. In the absence of an observable price, the acquisition cost may be measured as the present value of the cash principal and interest expected to be collected based upon the stated rate, discounted at the market rate in effect at the time of acquisition. The market rate fluctuates with investors' expectations and is based upon many factors including changes in risks, market conditions, and more. However, the stated rate, which determines the periodic cash interest receipts, is fixed by the bond agreement and therefore does not fluctuate with market conditions. Any incidental costs related to the acquisition such as brokerage fees and transfer costs are added to the acquisition cost.

A **bond holder** initially recognizes a bond investment at face value, at a discount, or at a premium.

- If a bond investment's present value and face value do not differ materially, the bond investment is recognized at face value.

- If the face value of the bond investment is greater than its present value, a **discount** is recorded.
- If the face value of the bond investment is less than its present value, a **premium** is recorded.

A discount (premium) is amortized over the life of the bond investment as an increase (decrease) to a bond's amortized cost and as an increase (decrease) to interest revenue. **In practice, companies generally record a net bond investment rather than record separate accounts for discounts or premiums.** Because the process of amortization of discounts and premiums is used in accounting for debt instruments by the issuer, it is also addressed in Chapter 16. (In fact, Chapter 16 includes a side-by-side comparison of the bondholder's journal entries next to the bond issuer's journal entries for the same bonds in this section.) **Demo 14-1A** illustrates an HTM investment purchased at face value, **Demo 14-1B** and **Demo 14-1D** illustrate an HTM investment purchased at a discount (< face value), and **Demo 14-1C** and **Demo 14-1E** illustrate an HTM investment purchased at a premium (> face value).

If a security is sold between interest payment dates, the investor pays both the purchase price of the security and the interest accrued from the most recent prior interest payment date to the purchase date. Then, on the next interest payment date, the investor receives interest for the latest full interest period. We illustrate the accounting for a debt security sold between interest payment dates in LO 14-2, but the concept applies to all debt securities.

Subsequent measurement of HTM securities ignores changes in the fair value of the securities. **Therefore, no adjustment is made to the carrying amount of the security over the life of the investment for changes in fair value.** Although there is no financial statement impact for changes in fair value, the aggregate fair value of an HTM investment and any unrecognized holding gain (loss) are disclosed in the notes accompanying the financial statements. However, if the investment is considered impaired, a loss may need to be recognized as discussed in LO 14-6.

HTM Investment Purchased at Face Value

Demo 14-1A illustrates the case where the cost of a bond investment is equal to its face value.

Investment in HTM Purchased at Face Value	**LO14-1**	DEMO 14-1A

Demo

MBC

On January 1 of Year 1, Bold Corp. (Bold) purchased a 5% bond investment at an amount equal to its face value of $100,000 from Rush Inc. (Rush). The bond matures in 4 years and pays interest semiannually on June 30 and December 31. Bold has the intent and ability to hold the bond to its maturity date.

a. Record the entry for Bold's purchase of the bonds on January 1 of Year 1.
b. Record interest received on June 30 of Year 1.
c. Record the entry upon maturity of the bonds on December 31 of Year 4. Assume the final interest entry was already recorded.

Solution

a. The investment in bonds is classified as a held-to-maturity investment because Bold has both the intent and the ability to hold the bonds to maturity. HTM investments are accounted for at amortized cost. In exchange for the purchase price of the bonds, Bold will receive semiannual cash interest of $2,500 (2.5% x $100,000), and the face value of $100,000 at the end of the bond term. Because the bonds pay interest semiannually, interest rates and periods must be adjusted to reflect semiannual compounding periods. Because the bonds were sold at face value, we can assume that the market rate equals the stated rate of 5% at bond issuance.

- Semiannual market rate: 5% ÷ 2 = 2.5%
- Semiannual periods:
  - 4 years × 2 = 8 periods
- Semiannual cash interest payment:
  - 5% ÷ 2 × $100,000 = $2,500

	RATE	NPER	PMT	PV	FV	Excel Formula
Given	2.5%	8	2,500	?	100,000	=PV(0.025,8,2500,100000)
Solution				$(100,000)		

Purchase of Bond Investment at Face Value

January 1, Year 1—To record investment purchase

Investment in HTM Securities—Rush Bonds	100,000	
Cash		100,000

Assets = Liabilities + Equity
+100,000
HTM
−100,000
C:i

Invest—HTM		Cash	
100,000			100,000

continued

continued from previous page

b. Receipt of Interest

Bold records the following journal entry for the first semiannual interest cash receipt of $2,500.

June 30, Year 1—To record interest revenue

Cash	2,500	
Interest Revenue.		2,500

Assets = Liabilities + Equity
+2,500   +2,500
C:o   Rev

Cash	Interest Rev
2,500 | 100,000	| 2,500

c. Bond Maturity

Upon maturity, Bold records the cash receipt for the face value of the bond investment and derecognizes the bond investment.

December 31, Year 4—To derecognize bond investment

Cash	100,000	
Investment in HTM Securities—Rush Bonds		100,000

Assets = Liabilities + Equity
+100,000
C:i
−100,000
HTM

Cash	Invest-HTM
20,000 | 100,000	100,000 | 100,000
100,000 |	

Investment in HTM Purchased at a Discount—Effective Interest Method

EXHIBIT 14-2

Fluctuation in Bond Price

Bond Sells at a Premium (Market rate < Stated rate)

Bond Sells at a Face Value (Market rate = Stated rate)

Bond Sells at a Discount (Market rate > Stated rate)

Bond Selling Price

The present value of contractual bond payments (discounted at the market rate) does not equal the bond investment's face value when the stated rate is not equal to the market rate. More specifically, if the market rate is *greater* than the stated rate of the bond, the bond will sell at a discount as shown in **Exhibit 14-2**. This means the investor is expecting a *higher* rate of return than the stated rate, based upon expected returns on investments of similar risk. Thus, the investor who is not satisfied with the periodic cash interest receipts on the bond will counter by paying a lower price for the bond to *effectively* yield a higher rate of return. Regardless of the price paid up front for the bond, the investor will receive the face value of the bond upon maturity. The difference between the lower price paid for the bond and the face value of the bond is the **bond discount**.

The amount of interest revenue to be recognized periodically over the life of the bond is typically determined using the effective interest method. Under the **effective interest method**, interest revenue each period is measured by multiplying the market rate at the bond's inception by the amortized cost of the bond investment at the beginning of each interest period. For a bond investment purchased at a discount, interest revenue increases each period because the interest revenue increases with the increasing amortized cost of the bond investment. In other words, the base for calculating interest revenue each period is increasing as the bond investment moves toward the face value.

The cash interest received each period is calculated by multiplying the face value of the bonds by the stated rate. The difference between the market interest revenue and the cash interest received is discount amortization, which increases the carrying value of the investment each period until the investment reaches its face value.

DEMO 14-1B ▶ LO14-1   **Investment in HTM Purchased at a Discount (Effective Interest)**

Demo

MBC

Bold acquires $100,000 of Rush 5% bonds on January 1 of Year 1. Bold has the ability and intent to hold the bonds until they mature on December 31 of Year 4. The bonds pay cash interest semiannually on June 30 and December 31. Bold has acquired the bonds at the market price, which yields a market rate of 6%. Bold uses the effective interest method to amortize any discounts or premiums on HTM investments. Bold's accounting period ends on December 31.

Required

a. Determine the classification and purchase price of the bond investment.
b. Record Bold's entry to purchase the bond investment on January 1 of Year 1.
c. Prepare an amortization schedule and record the entry on June 30 of Year 1 to record interest revenue and discount amortization.
d. Record the entry at maturity of the bonds on December 31 of Year 4.
e. Assume that instead of holding the Rush bonds until maturity at December 31 of Year 4, Bold sells the Rush bonds on July 1 of Year 4 for $99,850 (due to a significant unforeseen event). Record the entry for the sale on July 1 of Year 4.

continued

continued from previous page

Solution

a. Classification of a Bond Investment and Computation of Purchase Price

The investment in bonds is classified as a held-to-maturity investment because Bold has both the intent and the ability to hold the bonds to maturity. HTM investments are accounted for at amortized cost. In exchange for the purchase price of the bonds, Bold will receive semiannual cash interest of $2,500 (2.5% × $100,000), and the face value of $100,000 at the end of the bond term. Because the bonds pay interest semiannually, interest rates and periods must be adjusted to reflect semiannual compounding periods.

- Semiannual market rate: 6% ÷ 2 = 3%
- Semiannual periods:
    4 years × 2 = 8 periods
- Semiannual cash interest payment: 5% ÷ 2 × $100,000 = $2,500

	RATE	NPER	PMT	PV	FV	Excel Formula
Given	3%	8	2,500	?	100,000	=PV(0.03,8,2500,100000)
Solution				$(96,490)		

The selling price of the bonds of $96,490 is measured by calculating the present value of the semiannual cash interest receipts and the present value of the bonds' maturity value using the semiannual market rate of 3%.

b. Purchase of Bond Investment at a Discount

The HTM debt investment purchased at a discount is recorded at a net value of $96,490. This means that the investment is recorded at an amount net of the discount of $3,510 ($100,000 − $96,490).

January 1, Year 1—To record investment purchase

Investment in HTM Securities—Rush Bonds	96,490	
Cash		96,490

Assets = Liabilities + Equity
+96,490
HTM
−96,490
C:i

Invest-HTM   Cash
96,490 | | 96,490

c. Amortization Schedule and Interest Revenue Recognition

The following amortization schedule illustrates how the amortization of the bond discount affects interest revenue recognition over the life of the bonds under the effective interest method. Interest revenue each period is measured by multiplying the market rate by the amortized cost of the bonds at the beginning of the period. For example, in the first semiannual period, interest revenue of $2,895 is equal to 3% multiplied by $96,490. The $395 difference between market interest of $2,895 and cash interest of $2,500 is the discount amortized in the first semiannual period. This amount increases the amortized cost of the bond to its new carrying amount of $96,885 on June 30 of Year 1. The components of the journal entries each period to record the receipt of cash interest and amortization of the discount can be found in this schedule.

	Effective Interest Method—Discount			
	A	**B**	**C**	**D**
	Cash*	Interest Revenue	Discount	Bond Investment, Net
	(Stated Interest)	(Market Interest)	Amortization	(Amortized Cost)
Date	2.5% × Face Value	3% × D Beg. Period Bal.	B − A	D Beg. Period Bal. + C
Jan. 1, Year 1 . . .				$ 96,490
June 30, Year 1 . . .	$ 2,500	$ 2,895	$ 395	96,885
Dec. 31, Year 1 . . .	2,500	2,907	407	97,292
June 30, Year 2 . . .	2,500	2,919	419	97,711
Dec. 31, Year 2 . . .	2,500	2,931	431	98,142
June 30, Year 3 . . .	2,500	2,944	444	98,586
Dec. 31, Year 3 . . .	2,500	2,958	458	99,044
June 30, Year 4 . . .	2,500	2,971	471	99,515
Dec. 31, Year 4 . . .	2,500	2,985	485	100,000
	$20,000	$23,510	$3,510	

*In some cases, a company may accrue interest receivable at period-end when interest earned will be received next period.

In the following entry, we do not use a separate account for the discount. Instead, the amortization of the discount results in a direct addition of $395 to the investment account.

Assets = Liabilities + Equity
+2,500   +2,895
C:o   Rev
+395
HTM

June 30, Year 1—To record interest revenue and discount amortization

Cash	2,500	
Investment in HTM Securities—Rush Bonds	395	
Interest Revenue		2,895

Cash   Interest Rev
2,500 | 96,490 | 2,895

Invest—HTM
96,490 |
395 |

continued

continued from previous page

d. Bond Maturity

The carrying amount of the bonds has increased $3,510 by the end of the four years; thus the carrying amount of the investment is equal to its face value of $100,000 at December 31 of Year 4. On this date, Bold receives the face value of the bonds and derecognizes the bond investment.

December 31, Year 4—To derecognize bond investment

Assets = Liabilities + Equity
+100,000
C:i
−100,000
HTM

Cash			Invest—HTM	
20,000	96,490	Bal.	100,000	100,000
100,000			0	

Cash	100,000	
Investment in HTM Securities—Rush Bonds		100,000

e. Sale of Bond Investment *Before* Maturity

On July 1 of Year 4, Bold records a gain on the sale of the investment of $335 when the bonds are sold before maturity at $99,850. The gain is the difference between the cash received of $99,850 and the carrying amount of the bonds of $99,515 (obtained from the amortization schedule). The realized gain on the sale of a security is included in other income in the income statement.

Assets = Liabilities + Equity
+99,850   +335
C:i   Gain
−99,515
HTM

Cash			Gain on Sale of Invest	
17,500	98,000			
99,850				335

	Invest—HTM	
Bal.	99,515	99,515
	0	

July 1, Year 4—To record sale of bond investment before maturity

Cash	99,850	
Investment in HTM Securities—Rush Bonds		99,515
Gain on Sale of Investment ($99,850 – $99,515)		335

HTM Investment Purchased at a Premium—Effective Interest Method

If the market rate is *less* than the stated rate of the bonds, the bonds will sell at a premium. In this case, the issuer of the bonds would be unwilling to sell the bonds for the face value because the market rate for debt securities of similar risk is less than the stated rate at which the bonds will pay interest to the investor. Pricing the bonds to yield a lower market rate results in a selling price that exceeds the face value.

Regardless of the price paid for the bonds, Bold will receive the face value of the bonds upon maturity. The excess of the price paid over the face value of the bonds is the **bond premium**. Over the term of the bonds, the premium is amortized, reducing interest revenue and the carrying amount of the bond by each period's amortization amount.

DEMO 14-1C ▶ **LO14-1**   **Investment in HTM Purchased at a Premium (Effective Interest)**

Demo

MBC

Refer to the information in **Demo 14-1B** but now assume that Bold paid *more* than the face value of the 5%, $100,000 bonds because the market rate is 4%

Required

a. Determine the purchase price of the bond investment.
b. Record Bold's entry to purchase the bond investment on January 1 of Year 1.
c. Prepare an amortization schedule and record the entry on June 30 of Year 1 for interest revenue and premium amortized.
d. Report the investment in bonds on the balance sheet on June 30 of Year 1 and the effects on the period-end income statement.
e. Record the entry at the maturity of the bonds on December 31 of Year 4.

Solution

a. Computation of Bond Purchase Price

Because the bonds pay interest semiannually, interest rates and periods must be adjusted to reflect semiannual compounding periods.

- Semiannual market rate: 4% ÷ 2 = 2%
- Semiannual periods: 4 years × 2 = 8 periods
- Semiannual cash interest payment:
  5% ÷ 2 × $100,000 = $2,500

	RATE	NPER	PMT	PV	FV	Excel Formula
Given	2%	8	2,500	?	100,000	=PV(0.02,8,2500,100000)
Solution				$(103,663)		

The selling price of the bonds of $103,663 is measured by calculating the present value of the semiannual cash interest receipts and the present value of the bonds' maturity value using the semiannual market rate of 2%.

continued

continued from previous page

b. **Purchase of Bond Investment at a Premium**

The entry to record the bond investment purchase is a debit to Investments in HTM Securities for the net proceeds of $103,663. This means that the investment is recorded at an amount including the premium of $3,663 ($103,663 – $100,000).

January 1, Year 1— To record investment purchase

Investment in HTM Securities—Rush Bonds	103,663	
Cash		103,663

Assets = Liabilities + Equity
+103,663
HTM
–103,663
C:i

Invest—HTM	Cash
103,663		103,663

c. **Amortization Schedule and Interest Revenue Recognition**

Utilizing the effective interest method, interest revenue each period is measured by multiplying the market rate by the amortized cost of the bonds at the beginning of the period. For example, in the first semiannual period, interest revenue of $2,073 is equal to 2% multiplied by $103,663. Interest revenue decreases each period because the interest revenue is a function of the decreasing bond amortized cost.

	Effective Interest Method—Discount			
	A	B	C	D
	Cash	**Interest Revenue**	**Premium**	**Bond Investment, Net**
	(Stated Interest)	**(Market Interest)**	**Amortization**	**(Amortized Cost)**
Date	**2.5% × Face Value**	**2% × D Beg. Period Bal.**	**A – B**	**D Beg. Period Bal. – C**
Jan. 1, Year 1 ...				$103,663
June 30, Year 1 ...	$ 2,500	$ 2,073	$ 427	103,236
Dec. 31, Year 1 ...	2,500	2,065	435	102,801
June 30, Year 2 ...	2,500	2,056	444	102,357
Dec. 31, Year 2 ...	2,500	2,047	453	101,904
June 30, Year 3 ...	2,500	2,038	462	101,442
Dec. 31, Year 3 ...	2,500	2,029	471	100,971
June 30, Year 4 ...	2,500	2,019	481	100,490
Dec. 31, Year 4 ...	2,500	2,010	490	100,000
	$20,000	$16,337	$3,663	

The entry to record interest revenue on June 30 follows.

June 30, Year 1—To record interest revenue and premium amortization

Cash	2,500	
Investment in HTM Securities—Rush Bonds		427
Interest Revenue		2,073

Assets = Liabilities + Equity
+2,500   +2,073
C:o   Rev
–427
HTM

Cash	Interest Rev
2,500	103,663		2,073

At June 30 of Year 1 the carrying amount of the bond investment is $103,236 or ($103,663 – $427).

Invest—HTM	
103,663	427

d. **Financial Statement Presentation of Bond Investment**

Balance Sheet Excerpt **June 30, Year 1**	**Income Statement Excerpt** **for Period Ended June 30, Year 1**
Assets	Other revenues (expenses)
Investment in HTM securities $103,236	Interest revenue 2,073

e. **Bond Maturity**

The amortized cost of the Rush bonds has decreased $3,663 by the end of the four years; thus, the carrying value of the investment at December 31 of Year 4 is its face value of $100,000. On this date, Bold receives the face value of the bonds and derecognizes the bond investment.

Assets = Liabilities + Equity
+100,000
C:i
–100,000
HTM

December 31, Year 4—To derecognize bond investment

Cash	100,000	
Investment in HTM Securities—Rush Bonds		100,000

Cash	Invest—HTM
20,000	103,663	103,663	3,663
100,000			100,000
		0	

HTM Investment—Straight-Line Interest Method

Although the effective interest method for amortizing discounts (and premiums) is the preferred method, there is an alternative method. The **straight-line interest method** can be used if the results are not materially different from the results using the effective interest method.

835-30-55-2   Generally accepted accounting principles (GAAP) require use of the interest method. There is no basis for using an alternative to the interest method except if the results of alternative methods do not differ materially from those obtained by using the interest method. Therefore, methods other than the interest method, such as the rule of 78s, sum of the years' digits, and straight-line interest methods shall not be used if their results materially differ from the interest method.

What would the amortization of the Rush bonds look like if the bonds were amortized using the straight-line interest method? Instead of computing the discount (premium) amortization as a function of the carrying value of the bonds, the discount (premium) is amortized evenly over the bond life. In other words, the total discount (premium) is divided and amortized equally over the term of the bonds. See **Demo 14-1D** for an illustration of straight-line amortization of a discount and **Demo 14-1E** for straight-line amortization of a premium.

| **DEMO 14-1D** | **LO14-1** | **Investment in HTM Purchased at a Discount (Straight-Line Interest)** |

Demo

MBC

Referring to **Demo 14-1B**, prepare an amortization schedule using the straight-line interest method and record Bold's June 30, Year 1 entry for interest revenue and discount amortized.

Solution

The following amortization schedule illustrates how the amortization of the bond discount impacts interest revenue recognition over the term of the bonds. For each period, cash interest ($100,000 × 2.5%) plus the discount amortization ($3,510 ÷ 8) equals interest revenue of $2,939.

	Effective Interest Method—Discount			
	A	**B**	**C**	**D**
	Cash	**Interest Revenue**	**Discount**	**Bond Investment, Net**
	(Stated Interest)	**(Market Interest)**	**Amortization***	**(Amortized Cost)**
Date	**2.5% × Face Value**	**A + C**	**$3,510 ÷ 8**	**D Beg. Period Bal. + C**
Jan. 1, Year 1 . . .				$ 96,490
June 30, Year 1 . . .	$ 2,500	$ 2,939	$ 439	96,929
Dec. 31, Year 1 . . .	2,500	2,939	439	97,368
June 30, Year 2 . . .	2,500	2,939	439	97,807
Dec. 31, Year 2 . . .	2,500	2,939	439	98,246
June 30, Year 3 . . .	2,500	2,939	439	98,685
Dec. 31, Year 3 . . .	2,500	2,939	439	99,124
June 30, Year 4 . . .	2,500	2,939	439	99,563
Dec. 31, Year 4 . . .	2,500	2,937	437	100,000
	$20,000	$23,510	$3,510	

*Discount amortization per period equals Total bond discount ÷ Total number of periods (with the exception of the last period where the amount reflects rounding differences).

Bold records the receipt of interest and discount amortization on June 30 of Year 1. Bold records this same entry each semiannual period for four years, at which time the discount is fully amortized.

Assets = Liabilities + Equity
+2,500   +2,939
C:o   Rev
+439
HTM

Cash		Interest Rev
2,500		2,939

Invest—HTM	
439	

June 30, Year 1—To record interest revenue and discount amortization

Cash	2,500	
Investment in HTM Securities—Rush Bonds	439	
Interest Revenue.		2,939

Investment in HTM Purchased at a Premium (Straight-Line Interest)   **LO14-1** **DEMO 14-1E**

Referring to **Demo 14-1C**, prepare an amortization schedule using the straight-line interest method and record Bold's June 30, Year 1 entry to recognize interest revenue and amortize the premium.

Solution

The amortization schedule under the straight-line interest method is prepared as follows. For each semiannual period, cash interest ($100,000 × 2.5%) minus the premium amortization ($3,663 ÷ 8) equals interest revenue of $2,042.

	A	B	C	D
	Straight-Line Interest Method—Premium			
	Cash	**Interest Revenue**	**Premium**	**Bond Investment, Net**
	(Stated Interest)	(Market Interest)	Amortization*	(Amortized Cost)
Date	2.5% × Face Value	A – C	$3,663 ÷ 8	D Beg. Period Bal. – C
Jan. 1, Year 1 ...				$103,663
June 30, Year 1 ...	$ 2,500	$ 2,042	$ 458	103,205
Dec. 31, Year 1 ...	2,500	2,042	458	102,747
June 30, Year 2 ...	2,500	2,042	458	102,289
Dec. 31, Year 2 ...	2,500	2,042	458	101,831
June 30, Year 3 ...	2,500	2,042	458	101,373
Dec. 31, Year 3 ...	2,500	2,042	458	100,915
June 30, Year 4 ...	2,500	2,042	458	100,457
Dec. 31, Year 4 ...	2,500	2,043	457	100,000
	$20,000	$16,337	$3,663	

*Premium amortization per period equals Total bond premium ÷ Total number of periods (with the exception of the last period in which the amount reflects rounding differences).

The following entry records interest and premium amortization on June 30 of Year 1. Bold would record the same entry each period for four years, at which time the premium is fully amortized.

June 30, Year 1—To record interest revenue and premium amortization

Cash	2,500	
Investment in HTM Securities—Rush Bonds		458
Interest Revenue		2,042

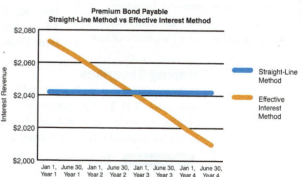

Assets = Liabilities + Equity
+2,500   +2,042
C:I   Rev
-458
HTM

Cash   Interest Rev
2,500 | | 2,042

Invest—HTM
| 458

Interest Revenue: Straight-line versus Effective Interest Method

As shown in the demos in this section, how interest revenue is recognized over a bond term varies depending on (1) whether a company accounts for the investment using the effective interest method or the straight-line interest method and (2) whether the bond was acquired at a premium or a discount. The graphs below illustrate how interest revenue is recognized at a constant rate under the straight-line interest method. Under the effective interest method, however, interest revenue increases each period for a bond acquired at a discount and decreases each period for a bond acquired at a premium because of the corresponding changes in the amortized cost of the bond investments (a factor in the calculation).

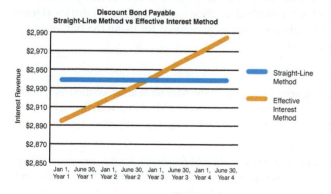

PEPSICO   **Real World—HELD-TO-MATURITY SECURITIES**

PepsiCo Inc. described its holdings in held-to-maturity securities in Note 9 of a recent Form 10-K.

Held-to-Maturity Debt Securities   Investments in debt securities that we have the positive intent and ability to hold until maturity are classified as held-to-maturity. Highly liquid debt securities with original maturities of three months or less are recorded as cash equivalents. Our held-to-maturity debt securities consist of commercial paper. As of December 30, 2023, we had $309 million of investments in commercial paper recorded in cash and cash equivalents. As of December 31, 2022, we had no investments in held-to-maturity debt securities. Held-to-maturity debt securities are recorded at amortized cost, which approximates fair value, and realized gains or losses are reported in earnings. As of December 30, 2023, gross unrecognized gains and losses and the allowance for expected credit losses were not material.

REVIEW 14-1	**LO14-1**			**Investment in HTM Securities**

Review
MBC

On January 2 of Year 1, New Apple Inc. purchased for cash six $10,000 bonds of Mack Corporation. The bonds pay 6% cash interest, payable on an annual basis each December 31, and mature in eight years on December 31. The bonds are classified as held-to-maturity securities. The annual reporting period ends December 31. Complete the following table for the five separate scenarios.

	(1) Bonds Yield 6%	(2) Bonds Yield 8% (Apply the effective interest method)	(3) Bonds Yield 8% (Apply the straight-line interest method)	(4) Bonds Yield 5% (Apply the effective interest method)	(5) Bonds Yield 5% (Apply the straight-line interest method)
Indicate whether bonds will sell at par, discount, or premium					
Purchase price of HTM investment					
Interest revenue for Year 1					
Interest revenue for Year 2					

More Practice:
BE14-1, BE14-2, BE14-3,
BE14-4, BE14-5, BE14-6,
E14-2, E14-3, E14-4, P14-4
Solution on p. 14-99.

Teaching note: To proceed to the presentation that assumes investments are adjusted to fair value only at period-end, proceed to LO 14-7, LO14-8, and LO14-9. Resume topical coverage at LO14-5.

LO 14-2 ▶ Account for debt securities measured at FV-NI with fair value adjustments at sale date and period-end

LO 14-2 Overview

TS Measured at FV-NI and Investments under Fair Value Option Election
- Recognize interest earned in net income
- Recognize adjustment to fair value (unrealized gain or loss) in net income
- Adjust and eliminate FVA at time of sale

Certain debt investments are measured at fair value with adjustments reflected in net income (**FV-NI**). This means that instead of recognizing investments at amortized cost, the amortized cost amount is adjusted to fair value. The resulting unrealized gain or loss is recognized in net income. The FV-NI method applies to (1) trading securities (**Demo 14-2A**) and (2) debt investments accounted for using the fair value option (**Demo 14-2B**).

Trading Securities

Debt securities that are bought and held primarily to be sold in the near term are classified as **trading securities (TS)**. Trading generally reflects active and frequent buying and selling with the objective of generating profits on short-term changes in price. Trading securities are typically classified as current assets on a classified balance sheet.

ASC Glossary   Trading Securities: Securities that are bought and held principally for the purpose of selling them in the near term and therefore held for only a short period of time. Trading generally reflects active and frequent buying and selling, and trading securities are generally used with the objective of generating profits on short-term differences in price.

Trading securities are adjusted to fair value through the income statement. The total **unrealized holding gain (or loss)** is the difference between the amortized cost and fair value of an investment—*unrealized* because the asset has not been sold. The change in the unrealized gain or loss for the period is included in the determination of earnings in the income statement and is classified as other income. Amortized cost is equal to the cost of the bond if the bond is purchased at par. If the bond is purchased at a discount (premium), the discount (premium) is amortized as an adjustment to interest revenue as illustrated in LO 14-1. As a result, the amortized cost of a bond changes over time.

Methods to Account for Debt Securities		
Amortized Cost	FV-NI	FV-OCI
LO 14-1	LO 14-2	LO 14-3

320-10-35-1   a. Trading securities. Investments in debt securities that are classified as trading shall be measured subsequently at fair value in the statement of financial position. Unrealized holding gains and losses for trading securities shall be included in earnings.

320-10-35-4 Dividend and interest income, including amortization of the premium and discount arising at acquisition, for all three categories of investments in debt securities shall be included in earnings.

In computing changes in the fair value of trading securities, more than one security may be analyzed as part of an **investment portfolio**. By adjusting trading securities to fair value on reporting dates instead of waiting until the assets are sold, financial statement users have more timely information to assess the performance of the company's investment strategies.

Instead of directly adjusting the investment account to fair value, an investor creates a valuation account, the **Fair Value Adjustment (FVA)** account. *This balance sheet account is debited for holding gains and credited for holding losses.* The carrying amount of TS is the net of its amortized cost and the Fair Value Adjustment account. A debit balance in the FVA account is added to the investment account whereas a credit in the FVA account is subtracted from the investment account. The Fair Value Adjustment account enables the accounting system to maintain a record of the amortized cost of the investment and the net amount of increase or decrease in carrying amount recognized over time. **We use the Fair Value Adjustment account in all examples and assignments.**

Sale of TS   If a TS is sold, the investment's carrying amount is first adjusted to fair value through the FVA account. Next, the sale is recorded and the associated FVA balance is eliminated.

320-10-40-1   . . . With respect to trading securities, because all changes in a trading security's fair value are reported in earnings as they occur, the sale of a trading security does not necessarily give rise to a gain or loss. Generally, a debit to cash (or trade date receivable) is recorded for the sales proceeds, and a credit is recorded to remove the security at its fair value (or sales price) . . . Some adjustment to this procedure will be necessary for entities that have not yet recorded the security's change in fair value up to the point of sale (perhaps because fair value changes are recorded at the end of each day).

EXPANDING YOUR KNOWLEDGE   **Noncash Consideration**

When noncash consideration (property or services) is given for an investment, the cost assigned to the securities should be measured by the fair value of the consideration given or the fair value of the securities received, whichever can be more reliably determined.

Investment in Trading Securities   **LO41-2**   ◀   **DEMO 14-2A**

Demo

MBC

On November 1 of Year 1, Bold purchased at par, $30,000 of Rush 8% bonds (dated July 1 of Year 1) that mature on June 30 of Year 6. Cash interest is paid semiannually on June 30 and December 31. Bold classifies the investment as trading securities (TS). Bold's accounting period ends on December 31.

Required
a. Record the entry to purchase TS on November 1 of Year 1,
b. Record the receipt of cash interest on December 31 of Year 1.
c. Record the entry to adjust the TS to fair value assuming that the fair value of the Rush bonds is $28,000 on December 31 of Year 1.
d. Report the investment in bonds on the balance sheet on December 31 of Year 1, and the effects on the Year 1 income statement.
e. Record the sale of the investment in TS on January 1 of Year 2 for $28,500, adjusting the investment to fair value at the date of sale using FV-NI; then, record the sale, eliminating the associated Fair Value Adjustment account balance.

continued

continued from previous page

Solution

a. Purchase of Bond Investment between Interest Payment Dates

Because the bonds were purchased outside of an interest payment date, Bold pays Rush accrued interest from the last interest payment date to the purchase date. Bold pays four months of interest up front because on December 31 of Year 1, Bold will automatically *receive the full six months of interest* totaling $1,200. Because Bold would have only *earned two months of interest* from November 1 of Year 1 to December 31 of Year 1, Bold must pay Rush four months of interest at the date of purchase. The journal entry for Bold at the date of purchase is as follows.

November 1, Year 1—To record investment purchase

Investment in TS—Rush Bonds..........................	30,000	
Interest Receivable ($30,000 × 0.08 × 4/12)...............	800	
Cash...		30,800

Assets = Liabilities + Equity
+30,000
TS
+800
Int Rec
−30,000
C:i
−800
C:o

Invest—TS	Interest Receiv
30,000		800	

Cash	
	30,800

b. Interest Revenue

On December 31 of Year 1, Bold records the full six months of interest received as cash, derecognizes interest receivable, and records two months of interest revenue. The journal entry is as follows.

December 31, Year 1—To record receipt of interest

Cash ($30,000 × 0.08 × 6/12)	1,200	
Interest Receivable..........................		800
Interest Revenue ($30,000 × 0.08 × 2/12)...............		400

Assets = Liabilities + Equity
+1,200
C:o
−800
Int Rec
+400
Rev

Cash		Interest Rev
1,200	30,800		400

Interest Receiv	
800	800

c. Adjustment of Bond Investment to Fair Value

At each balance sheet date, all securities classified as TS are reported at fair value. The unrealized holding loss on December 31 of Year 1, is measured and recorded as follows.

TS Investment	Amortized Cost	Fair Value Year-End	Unrealized Holding Gain (Loss)
Rush bonds	$30,000	$28,000	$(2,000)
Existing FVA account balance			0
Amount of increase (decrease) to FVA account needed			$(2,000)

December 31, Year 1—To adjust investment to fair value

Unrealized Gain or Loss—Income	2,000	
Fair Value Adjustment—TS...........................		2,000

Assets = Liabilities + Equity
−2,000
FVA
−2,000
Loss

FVA—TS	Unreal Gain or Loss—Inc
	2,000	2,000	

With this entry, the carrying value of TS is adjusted to fair value and the net change, an unrealized loss of $2,000, is recorded. For TS, the net unrealized holding gain or loss is treated as a component of other income on the income statement.

d. Financial Statement Presentation of Bond Investment

Balance Sheet Excerpt December 31, Year 1	Income Statement Excerpt for Year Ended December 31, Year 1
Current assets	Other revenues (expenses)
Investment in trading securities.....$28,000	Interest revenue ....$ 400
	Unrealized holding loss on trading securities ... (2,000)

e. Sale of Bond Investment

At the sale date, the company first adjusts the investment to fair value (FV-NI).

Required FVA account balance at date of sale*..............	$(1,500)
Less existing FVA account balance	(2,000)
Amount of increase (decrease) to FVA account needed	$ 500

*$28,500 fair value − $30,000 amortized cost.

January 1, Year 2—To adjust investment to fair value

Fair Value Adjustment—TS.................................	500	
Unrealized Gain or Loss—Income		500

Assets = Liabilities + Equity
+500
FVA
+500
Gain

FVA—TS	Unreal Gain or Loss—Inc
500	2,000	2,000	500

continued

continued from previous page

Next, the company records the sale, eliminating the related Fair Value Adjustment credit balance of $1,500. No gain or loss is recorded upon the sale because the investment was adjusted to fair value in the prior entry. This means net income already reflects any difference between fair value and the amortized cost of bonds.

January 1, Year 2—To record sale of bond investment

Cash	28,500	
Fair Value Adjustment—TS	1,500	
Investment in TS—Rush Bonds		30,000

Assets = Liabilities + Equity
+28,500
C:i
+1,500
FVA
-30,000
Invest

Cash		Invest—TS	
1,200	30,800	30,000	30,000
28,500			

FVA—TS	
500	2,000
1,500	
0	

Note: The total loss on sale of $1,500 is recognized in the financial statements over the ownership period of the TS.

Loss in Year 1 income statement	$(2,000)
Gain in Year 2 income statement	500
Loss recognized over ownership period	$(1,500)

Real World—TRADING SECURITIES

COCA-COLA

The Coca-Cola Company included its trading securities in the category of marketable securities in the current asset section of its balance sheet as indicated by the following excerpt from Note 4 in its Form 10-K.

The carrying values of our debt securities were included in the following line items in our consolidated balance sheets (in millions):

December 31, 2023	Trading Securities	Available-for-Sale Securities
Marketable securities	$41	$ 914
Other noncurrent assets	—	220
Total debt securities	$41	$1,134

Fair Value Option—Debt Securities

Under the fair value option, an investment is adjusted to fair value through net income each reporting period (**FV-NI**). The fair value option is an election that may be applied to debt securities that would otherwise be recognized at amortized cost (such as HTM securities) or where unrealized gains or losses are reflected in other comprehensive income (OCI). (FV-OCI is reviewed in the next section.) While the fair value option is not applicable for TS (as it's already recorded at FV-NI), the accounting treatment under the fair value option is *similar to that of TS*. This election must be selected on the purchase date of the asset, applied to each investment individually, and the decision is generally irrevocable. The company must include a disclosure on the fair value option election (825-10-50-28).

Investment Using the Fair Value Option	**LO14-2** ◀ **DEMO 14-2B**

Demo / MBC

On July 1, Bold purchased at par $30,000 of Rush 8% bonds that mature on June 30 in five years. Bold classifies the investment as HTM. However, on July 1, Bold chooses to account for the HTM investment using the fair value option. If the fair value of the Rush bonds is $31,500 on December 31, record the year-end adjusting entry for Bold. (Assume that interest revenue was recorded during the year.)

Solution

Assets = Liabilities + Equity
+1,500   +1,500
FVA   Gain

December 31—To adjust investment to fair value

Fair Value Adjustment—Fair Value Option ($31,500 – $30,000)	1,500	
Unrealized Gain or Loss—Income		1,500

Unreal Gain or Loss—Inc

FVA—Fair Val Opt		Loss—Inc	
1,500			1,500

REVIEW 14-2 ▸ LO14-2   Investment in Trading Securities

Review

MBC

On September 30 of Year 1, New Apple Inc. purchased $20,000 of Mack Corp. bonds. These bonds pay 5% cash interest annually on September 30 and mature September 30 in Year 11. The investment is classified as a TS investment and the company uses the effective interest method to amortize any bond discount or premium. The market rate on the bonds is 6%. New Apple's accounting period ends on December 31.

a. Do Mack Corp. bonds sell at a discount or premium? Determine the selling price of the bonds.

b. Record the entry for the purchase of the bonds by New Apple Inc.

c. Record the entry on December 31 of Year 1 to record interest revenue.

d. Record the entry on December 31 of Year 1 to adjust the investment to fair value, determined to be $21,000 on December 31 of Year 1.

e. Record the entry to sell the bonds on January 1 of Year 2 for $21,000, plus accrued interest, adjusting the investment to fair value at the date of sale using FV-NI; then record the sale, eliminating the associated Fair Value Adjustment account balance.

More Practice:
BE14-9, BE14-10, BE14-12, E14-7, E14-9, E14-10
Solution on p. 14-99.

f. How would your answers to parts *a* to *e* change if instead, the bond investment was classified as an HTM security and the company elected to account for the bonds using the fair value option on the acquisition date?

LO 14-3 ▸ Account for debt securities measured at FV-OCI with fair value adjustments at sale date and period-end

LO 14-3 Overview

AFS Securities Measured at FV-OCI
- Recognize interest earned in net income
- Recognize adjustment to fair value (unrealized gain or loss) in OCI
- Recognize realized gain or loss from a sale in net income
- Adjust and eliminate FVA at time of sale

Certain debt investments are measured at fair value with adjustments reflected in other comprehensive income (**FV-OCI**). Instead of recognizing investments at amortized cost, the amortized cost amount is adjusted to fair value with the resulting unrealized gain or loss recognized in other comprehensive income. The FV-OCI method applies to available-for-sale securities.

Available-for-Sale Securities

Debt investments that are *not* classified as trading securities or held-to-maturity securities are classified as **available-for-sale securities (AFS)**. The AFS category includes debt securities expected to be held for an unspecified period of time, such as those that *might be* sold to meet liquidity needs or to implement a company's risk management program. AFS investments are classified as short-term or long-term depending on the intent and ability of the investor to sell the investment within the next year (or operating cycle, if longer).

Methods to Account for Debt Securities		
Amortized Cost	FV-NI	FV-OCI
LO 14-1	LO 14-2	LO 14-3

ASC Glossary   Available-for-Sale Securities: Investments not classified as either trading securities or as held-to-maturity securities.

Unlike trading securities, subsequent adjustments to fair value affect OCI (other comprehensive income) rather than net income as shown in **Demo 14-3A** and **14-3B**. The Fair Value Adjustment (FVA) account is debited for holding gains and credited for holding losses. However, the offsetting unrealized gain or loss account is included in OCI. Recall from Chapter 3 that comprehensive income includes all changes in equity during a period from transactions and other events and circumstances from nonowner sources, including unrealized holding gains and losses on available-for-sale securities. Comprehensive income consists of net income and OCI. At the end of each reporting period, other comprehensive income is closed to accumulated other comprehensive income (AOCI) and is reported in the statement of stockholders' equity. Similarly, net income is closed to retained earnings and is reported in the statement of stockholders' equity.

320-10-35-1   b. Available-for-sale securities. Investments in debt securities that are classified as available for sale shall be measured subsequently at fair value in the statement of financial position. Unrealized holding gains and losses for available-for-sale securities (including those classified as current assets) shall be excluded from earnings and reported in other comprehensive income until realized except as indicated in the following sentences. All or a portion of the unrealized holding gain and loss of an available-for-sale security that is designated as being hedged in a fair value hedge that is not a portfolio layer method hedge shall be recognized in earnings during the period of the hedge . . .

Justification for Accounting of AFS Investments Justification for the different accounting treatment of unrealized holding gains or losses arising from trading securities and available-for-sale securities stems from the different purposes of the investments. Since the TS investments are actively managed and expected to be bought and sold continually, the inclusion of unrealized gains or losses in income reflects the economic consequences of TS investments in a timely manner. However, investments in AFS investments are often made for purposes other than profiting from increases in security prices, such as being part of a risk management strategy. The AFS investments and the liabilities of the investor interact to reduce the exposure of the investor to interest rate risk. Including in earnings only the unrealized gain or loss on the investment and not that on the related liabilities may result in misleading information in the financial statements about the impact of economic events on the overall financial condition of the company. Therefore, to avoid volatility to earnings, the gain or loss is instead included in AOCI, a separate component of stockholders' equity.

Sale of AFS Securities When an AFS investment is sold, first the investment is adjusted to fair value through OCI. Next, the sale is recorded, including the reclassification of the holding gain or loss in AOCI to net income, and the elimination of the associated Fair Value Adjustment account balance. Only at the time of sale is a gain or loss recognized in the income statement (other than for a possible impairment, which is discussed in a later section).

Disclosure of Reclassification Adjustment Disclosure of the amount reclassified out of AOCI and into net income is required for financial reporting. The amount of the reclassification adjustment from AOCI to net income is equal to the realized gain or loss on the sale.

`320-10-50-9` For each period for which the results of operations are presented, an entity shall disclose . . . d. The amount of the net unrealized holding gain or loss on available-for-sale securities for the period that has been included in accumulated other comprehensive income and the amount of gains and losses reclassified out of accumulated other comprehensive income into earnings for the period.

Investment in Available-for-Sale Securities	LO14-3	DEMO 14-3A

On July 1 of Year 1, Bold purchased for par $30,000 of Rush 8% bonds that mature on June 30 of Year 6. Cash interest is paid semiannually on June 30 and December 31. Bold classifies the investment as AFS. Bold's accounting period ends on December 31.

Demo

MBC

Required
a. Record the entry to purchase the investment on July 1 of Year 1.
b. Record the receipt of cash interest on December 31 of Year 1.
c. Record the entry to adjust AFS securities to fair value assuming that the fair value of the Rush bonds is $28,000 on December 31 of Year 1.
d. Report the investment in AFS securities in the Year 1 income statement and statement of comprehensive income, and the December 31 of Year 1 balance sheet for Bold. Assume a zero beginning balance in AOCI and no other current year adjustments to OCI other than any amounts related to this bond investment.
e. Assume that Bold made no changes to the current holdings of AFS securities in Year 2. Record the entry to adjust the AFS securities to fair value assuming that the fair value of the Rush bonds is $31,000 on December 31 of Year 2.
f. Record the sale of AFS securities on January 1 of Year 3 for $31,800, adjusting the investment to fair value at the date of sale using FV-OCI; then record the sale, including the reclassification of holding gains or losses in AOCI to net income and the elimination of the associated Fair Value Adjustment account balance.
g. Show the December 31 of Year 3 Accumulated OCI reclassification disclosure after the sale in part f, assuming no other changes to accumulated OCI during the year.

continued

continued from previous page

Solution

a. Purchase of Bond Investment at Face Value

July 1, Year 1—To record investment purchase

Assets = Liabilities + Equity
+30,000
AFS
−30,000
C:i

Invest—AFS	Cash
30,000	30,000

Investment in AFS Securities—Rush Bonds	30,000	
Cash		30,000

b. Recognition of Interest Revenue

December 31, Year 1—To record interest revenue

Assets = Liabilities + Equity
+1,200   +1,200
C:o   Rev

Cash	Interest Rev
1,200 | 30,000	1,200

Cash ($30,000 × 0.08 × 6/12)	1,200	
Interest Revenue......................................		1,200

c. Adjustment of Bond Investment to Fair Value—Year 1

At each balance sheet date, all securities classified as AFS are reported at fair value. The difference between fair value ($28,000) and amortized cost ($30,000) is recorded in a Fair Value Adjustment account and the unrealized holding loss is included in other comprehensive income through the following journal entry.

December 31, Year 1—To adjust investment to fair value

Assets = Liabilities + Equity
−2,000   −2,000
FVA   OCI

FVA—AFS	Unreal Gain or Loss—OCI
2,000	2,000

Unrealized Gain or Loss—OCI	2,000	
Fair Value Adjustment—AFS ($30,000 − $28,000).........		2,000

d. Financial Statement Presentation of Bond Investment

Balance Sheet Excerpt December 31, Year 1	
Assets	
Investment in available-for-sale securities	$28,000
Stockholders' equity	
Accumulated other comprehensive income (loss)	(2,000)

Income Statement Excerpt for Year Ended December 31, Year 1	
Other revenues (expenses)	
Interest revenue	$1,200

Statement of Comprehensive Income Excerpt for Year Ended December 31, Year 1	
Net income	$ ####
Other comprehensive income	
Unrealized holding loss on available-for-sale securities ...	(2,000)
Comprehensive income	$ ####

e. Adjustment of Bond Investment to Fair Value—Year 2

AFS Investment	Amortized Cost	Fair Value Year-End	Unrealized Holding Gain (Loss)
Rush bonds	$30,000	$31,000	$ 1,000
Existing FVA account balance			(2,000)
Amount of increase (decrease) to FVA account needed			$ 3,000

Based on this summary, Bold records the following entry to adjust its AFS investment to fair value.

December 31, Year 2—To adjust investment to fair value

Assets = Liabilities + Equity
+3,000   +3,000
FVA   OCI

FVA—AFS	Unreal Gain or Loss—OCI
3,000 | 2,000	2,000 | 3,000
1,000	

Fair Value Adjustment—AFS	3,000	
Unrealized Gain or Loss—OCI...........................		3,000

continued

continued from previous page

f. Sale of Bond Investment

At the sale date, the company first adjusts the investment to fair value (FV-OCI).

Required FVA account balance at the date of sale*	$1,800
Less existing FVA account balance	1,000
Amount of increase (decrease) to FVA account needed	$ 800

*$31,800 fair value – $30,000 amortized cost.

January 1, Year 3—To adjust investment to fair value

Fair Value Adjustment—AFS	800	
Unrealized Gain or Loss—OCI		800

Next, the company records the realized gain on sale of $1,800 ($31,800 cash proceeds – $30,000 amortized cost) by reclassifying it from AOCI to net income while converting the investment accounts to cash.

January 1, Year 3—To record sale of bond investment

Cash	31,800	
Unrealized Gain or Loss—OCI	1,800	
Investment in AFS—Rush Bonds		30,000
Gain on Sale of Investment		1,800
Fair Value Adjustment—AFS		1,800

g. Reclassification Disclosure

The Year 3 loss in OCI of $1,000 is made up of two components:
(1) the current year fair value adjustment gain of Rush bonds of $800 and
(2) the reclassification adjustment related to the gain on sale of Rush bonds of $1,800. The component amounts summarized in the table below are obtained from the Year 3 entries that affected Unrealized Gain or Loss—OCI.

Reconciliation of Accumulated Other Comprehensive Income		
Accumulated other comprehensive income, January 1, Year 3		$1,000
Current period unrealized gain on AFS securities	$ 800	
Reclassification adjustment for gain included in net income	(1,800)	(1,000)
Accumulated other comprehensive income, December 31, Year 3		$ 0

Note: The following AOCI summary highlights how the volatility in the fair value of the investment over the holding period is recognized in OCI and not net income.

Loss recognized in Year 1 OCI	$(2,000)
Gain recognized in Year 2 OCI	3,000
Gain recognized in Year 3 OCI	800
Reclassification adjustment to Year 3 NI.	(1,800)
Net effect in AOCI.	$ 0

Margin notes (T-accounts and accounting equation effects):

Assets = Liabilities + Equity
+800   +800
FVA   Unreal Gain or Loss—OCI

FVA—AFS			Unreal Gain or Loss—OCI	
3,000	2,000		2,000	3,000
800				800
1,800				

Assets = Liabilities + Equity
+31,800   –1,800
C:i   OCI
–30,000   +1,800
AFS   Gain
–1,800
FVA

Cash			Gain on Sale of Invest	
1,200	30,000			1,800
31,800				

Invest—AFS			Unreal Gain or Loss—OCI	
30,000	30,000		2,000	3,000
			1,800	800

FVA—AFS				
3,000	2,000			0
800	1,800			
0				

Real World—AVAILABLE-FOR-SALE SECURITIES

An excerpt from Note 1 of a recent Form 10-K for **PayPal Holdings, Inc.** described the accounting treatment of unrealized gains and losses on available-for-sale securities.

Our available-for-sale debt securities are reported at fair value using the specific identification method. Unrealized gains and losses are reported as a component of other comprehensive income (loss), net of related estimated tax provisions or benefits.

DEMO 14-3B   **LO14-3**   **Portfolio of Available-for-Sale Securities**

Demo

MBC

Assume that on December 31 of Year 2, Gold Inc. had the following AFS portfolio consisting of investments in two bonds: Blue bonds and Cait Corp. bonds.

AFS Investment	Amortized Cost	Fair Value Year-End	Unrealized Holding Gain (Loss)
Blue bonds	$ 30,000	$ 29,000	$ (1,000)
Cait bonds	100,500	120,000	19,500
	$130,500	$149,000	$18,500*

* Amount represents the December 31, Year 2, balance in AOCI and FVA.

Blue bonds are sold on January 1 of Year 3 for $31,000. The remaining AFS investment in Cait bonds (originally purchased at par value) had a fair value of $116,500 on December 31 of Year 3. Besides the sale of the Blue bonds on January 1 of Year 3, no other AFS transactions took place during the year. Gold's accounting period ends on December 31.

a. Adjust the investment in Blue bonds to fair value as of the date of sale using FV-OCI; then record the sale, including the reclassification of holding gains or losses in AOCI to net income and the elimination of the associated Fair Value Adjustment account balance.

b. Record the entry to adjust the Fair Value Adjustment account for Cait bonds on December 31 of Year 3.

c. Show the December 31 of Year 3 Accumulated OCI reclassification disclosure.

Solution

a. **Sale of Bond Investment**

At the sale date, the company first adjusts the investment in Blue bonds to fair value (FV-OCI).

Required FVA account balance at date of sale*	$1,000
Less existing FVA account balance	(1,000)
Amount of increase (decrease) to FVA account needed	$2,000

*$31,000 fair value − $30,000 amortized cost.

Assets = Liabilities + Equity
+2,000   +2,000
AFS   OCI

FVA—AFS		Unreal Gain or Loss—OCI	
18,500			2,000
2,000			

January 1, Year 3—To adjust investment in Blue bonds to fair value

Fair Value Adjustment—AFS	2,000	
Unrealized Gain or Loss—OCI		2,000

Next, the company records the realized gain on sale of $1,000 ($31,000 cash proceeds − $30,000 amortized cost) by reclassifying it from AOCI to net income while converting the investment accounts to cash.

Assets = Liabilities + Equity
+31,000   −1,000
Cash   OCI
−30,000   +1,000
Inv   Gain
−1,000
FVA

January 1, Year 3—To record sale of bond investment

Cash	31,000	
Unrealized Gain or Loss—OCI	1,000	
Investment in AFS—Blue Bonds........................		30,000
Gain on Sale of Investment		1,000
Fair Value Adjustment—AFS		1,000

Cash		Gain on Sale of Invest	
31,000			1,000

Invest—AFS		Unreal Gain or Loss—OCI	
130,500	30,000	1,000	2,000

FVA—AFS	
18,500	1,000
2,000	
19,500	

b. **Adjustment of the FVA Account**

The company adjusts the Cait bonds held at year-end to fair value (FV-OCI).

Required FVA ending account balance*	$16,000
Less existing FVA account balance	19,500
Amount of increase (decrease) to FVA account needed	$(3,500)

*$116,500 fair value − $100,500 amortized cost.

Assets = Liabilities + Equity
−3,500   −3,500
FVA   OCI

FVA—AFS		Unreal Gain or Loss—OCI	
Bal. 18,500	1,000	1,000	2,000
2,000	3,500	3,500	
16,000			

December 31, Year 3—To adjust investment to fair value

Unrealized Gain or Loss—OCI	3,500	
Fair Value Adjustment—AFS		3,500

continued

continued from previous page

c. **Reclassification Adjustment Disclosure**

The Year 3 loss in OCI of $2,500 is made up of two components:

(1) the current year fair value adjustment for the Blue and Cait bonds [$2,000 (Blue) – $3,500 (Cait) = $(1,500)] and

(2) the reclassification adjustment related to the Blue bonds sold during the year of $(1,000). The component amounts summarized in the table below are obtained from the Year 3 entries that impacted Unrealized Gain or Loss—OCI.

Reconciliation of Accumulated Other Comprehensive Income		
Accumulated other comprehensive income, January 1, Year 3		$18,500
Current period unrealized loss on AFS securities	$(1,500)	
Reclassification adjustment for gain included in net income	(1,000)	(2,500)
Accumulated other comprehensive income, December 31, Year 3		$16,000

APPLE   Real World—FAIR VALUE OF FINANCIAL INSTRUMENTS

Certain investment classifications require adjustments of investments to fair value on reporting dates. Financial statement disclosures provide information on how the fair value estimates are determined by categorizing the investments into the three levels of the fair value hierarchy introduced in Chapter 1. **Apple Inc.** in the following disclosure communicates how cash, cash equivalents, and marketable securities include both Level 1 and Level 2 investments. For example, a Level 1 investment may be publicly traded, while a Level 2 investment may be estimated based upon the quoted market price of a similar investment.

Cash, Cash Equivalents, and Marketable Securities The following table shows the Company's cash, cash equivalents and marketable securities by significant investment category as of September 30, 2023 (in millions):

	2023						
	Adjusted Cost	Unrealized Gains	Unrealized Losses	Fair Value	Cash and Cash Equivalents	Current Marketable Securities	Noncurrent Marketable Securities
Cash	$ 28,359	$—	$ —	$ 28,359	$28,359	$ —	$ —
Level 1:							
Money market funds	481	—	—	481	481	—	—
Mutual funds and equity securities	442	12	(26)	428	—	428	—
Subtotal	923	12	(26)	909	481	428	—
Level 2:							
U.S. Treasury securities	19,406	—	(1,292)	18,114	35	5,468	12,611
U.S. agency securities	5,736	—	(600)	5,136	36	271	4,829
Non-U.S. government securities	17,533	6	(1,048)	16,491	—	11,332	5,159
Certificates of deposit and time deposits	1,354	—	—	1,354	1,034	320	—
Commercial paper	608	—	—	608	—	608	—
Corporate debt securities	76,840	6	(5,956)	70,890	20	12,627	58,243
Municipal securities	628	—	(26)	602	—	192	410
Mortgage- and asset-backed securities	22,365	6	(2,735)	19,636	—	344	19,292
Subtotal	144,470	18	(11,657)	132,831	1,125	31,162	100,544
Total	$173,752	$30	$(11,683)	$162,099	$29,965	$31,590	$100,544

Investment in Available-for-Sale Securities	**LO14-3**	REVIEW 14-3

On January 1 of Year 1, Big Apple Inc. purchased for cash eight $10,000 bonds of Mack Corporation to yield 5%. The bonds pay 6% interest, payable on an annual basis each January 1, and mature on January 1 in five years. The bonds are classified as AFS. The annual reporting period for Big Apple Inc. ends December 31. Big Apple uses the effective interest method to amortize discounts and premiums. Provide the entries and reporting for the following transactions for Big Apple.

Review

MBC

a. Record the entry for the purchase of AFS securities on January 1 of Year 1.

b. Record adjusting entries on December 31 of Year 1 to accrue interest revenue and recognize change in value. The bonds were quoted on the market on this date at 95.

c. Indicate the effects of this investment on the current year income statement, statement of comprehensive income, and its year-end balance sheet. Assume a zero beginning balance in AOCI and no other current year adjustments to OCI other than any amounts related to this bond investment.

continued

continued from previous page

> *d.* Record the receipt of cash interest on January 1 of Year 2.
>
> *e.* After the interest payment on January 1 of Year 2, two of the bonds were sold for $19,000 cash. Record the sale, including the reclassification of holding gains or losses in AOCI to net income and the elimination of the associated Fair Value Adjustment account balance. *Hint:* No adjustment to fair value is required before the sale because the fair value has not changed since December 31 of Year 1.
>
> **More Practice:** *f.* Record adjusting entries on December 31 of Year 2, to accrue interest revenue and adjust the
> BE14-15, BE14-17, BE14-18, FVA account. The bonds were quoted on the market on this date at 95.
> E14-13, E14-15, E14-17
> **Solution on p. 14-100.**

Review of Accounting for Debt Securities

The following table compares journal entries for (1) held-to-maturity securities, (2) trading securities, and (3) available-for-sale securities.

Transaction	HTM LO 14-1	TS LO 14-7	AFS LO 14-8

Purchase of debt security	Dr. Investment in HTM
	    Cr. Cash
		Dr. Investment in TS
		    Cr. Cash
			Dr. Investment in AFS
			    Cr. Cash

Receipt of interest for debt security purchased at par	Dr. Cash
	    Cr. Interest Revenue
		Dr. Cash
		    Cr. Interest Revenue
			Dr. Cash
			    Cr. Interest Revenue

Receipt of interest for debt security purchased at a discount	Dr. Cash
	Dr. Investment in HTM
	    Cr. Interest Revenue
		Dr. Cash
		Dr. Investment in TS
		    Cr. Interest Revenue
			Dr. Cash
			Dr. Investment in AFS
			    Cr. Interest Revenue

Receipt of interest for debt security purchased at a premium	Dr. Cash
	    Cr. Investment in HTM
	    Cr. Interest Revenue
		Dr. Cash
		    Cr. Investment in TS
		    Cr. Interest Revenue
			Dr. Cash
			    Cr. Investment in AFS
			    Cr. Interest Revenue

Adjust debt security to fair value with a gain	No entry	Dr. Fair Value Adjustment
		    Cr. Unrealized Gain or Loss—Income
			Dr. Fair Value Adjustment
			    Cr. Unrealized Gain or Loss—OCI

Adjust debt security to fair value with a loss	No entry	Dr. Unrealized Gain or Loss—Income
		    Cr. Fair Value Adjustment
			Dr. Unrealized Gain or Loss—OCI
			    Cr. Fair Value Adjustment

The difference in accounting treatment across investment categories relates to adjusting to fair value. Securities classified as HTM are not adjusted to fair value; thus, no journal entry is required. Securities classified as TS are adjusted to fair value through the income statement (FV-NI) while securities classified as AFS are adjusted to fair value through OCI (FV-OCI).

Financial Presentation and Disclosure Requirements for Debt Securities

An investment is recognized on the balance sheet as *current* or *noncurrent* depending upon when the investment matures or is expected to be sold. The investment amounts in the categories of HTM, TS, and AFS may be presented separately on the face of the balance sheet or in a note accompanying the financial statements.

320-10-45-1   An entity shall report its investments in available-for-sale securities and trading securities separately from similar assets that are subsequently measured using another measurement attribute on the face of the statement of financial position. To accomplish that, an entity shall do either of the following:

a. Present the aggregate of those fair value and non-fair-value amounts in the same line item and parenthetically disclose the amount of fair value included in the aggregate amount

b. Present two separate line items to display the fair value and non-fair-value carrying amounts . . .

Investing and Operating Activities   In the statement of cash flows, cash inflows from investing activities include receipts from the sale of debt securities of other entities and cash outflows from investing activities include payments to acquire debt securities of other entities (other than certain trading securities).

Cash inflows and outflows resulting from trading securities specifically bought and sold for the purpose of generating profits on short-term differences in market prices are presented as operating activities in the statement of cash flows.

230-10-45-19   Cash receipts and cash payments resulting from purchases and sales of securities classified as trading debt securities accounted for in accordance with Topic 320 and equity securities accounted for in accordance with Topic 321 shall be classified pursuant to this Topic based on the nature and purpose for which the securities were acquired.

In the notes to the financial statements, the following items should be disclosed where applicable.

- Amortized cost and maturity dates
- Aggregate fair value
- Allowance for credit losses
- Gross realized and unrealized holding gains and losses
- Change in net unrealized holding gains and losses
- Information about contractual maturities of securities
- Impairment disclosures
- Inputs in determining fair value (Level 1, 2, or 3 in the fair value hierarchy) and other required fair value disclosures

Real World—ESG CLASSIFICATION OF INVESTMENT FUNDS IN THE EUROPEAN UNION

MORGAN STANLEY

The Sustainable Finance Disclosure Regulation (SFDR) is a European Union regulation that requires financial market participants (such as banks and insurance companies) to disclose sustainability information about their products and services. The SFDR can impact U.S. companies, such as those that sell to companies in the European Union. Among the requirements, companies classify investment funds into categories based on sustainability. The Morgan Stanley website for the United Kingdom* included the following explanation.

The Sustainable Finance Disclosure Regulation requires Morgan Stanley to classify all of its in scope products and accounts. SFDR product classifications fall under 3 categories: Article 8, Article 9 and 'Other.' Article 8 and Article 9 products consider sustainability in a binding way. In addition, Article 8 products promote social and or environmental characteristics and Article 9 products have a sustainable objective. Products which do not meet either the definition of Article 8 or Article 9 are classified as 'other.'

*Disclosure accessed on Nov. 3, 2024 at https://www.morganstanley.com/im/en-gb/intermediary-investor/about-us/newsroom/press-release/sustainable-finance-disclosure-regulation.html.

Sustainability

Account for equity securities measured at FV-NI with fair value adjustments at sale date and period-end

LO 14-4

In determining the appropriate accounting for equity investments, the extent of ownership interest is a critical factor. When the investor has *insignificant influence* over the investee and the fair value of the investment is *readily determinable*, the equity investment is measured at fair value with adjustments recognized in net income (**FV-NI**). It is generally presumed that an investor with an ownership interest of less than 20% of the voting stock of the investee *does not have* **significant influence** over the investee. However, the key issue is influence, which can occur at lower ownership levels. If the investor has significant influence (but not a controlling interest), the investment is accounted for under the equity method (**Demo 14-5**). If an investor has a controlling interest, the financial statements of the investor (parent) and investee (subsidiary) are consolidated and treated as one economic entity. Generally, controlling interest occurs when a company controls more than 50% of the investee's voting common stock. For example, the Coca-Cola consolidated financial statements are labeled "Coca-Cola Company and Subsidiaries." Accounting for consolidations is the subject of advanced accounting courses.

LO 14-4 Overview

Equity Securities Measured at FV-NI

- Adjust to fair value
- Recognize adjustment to fair value (unrealized gain or loss) in net income
- Recognize dividends declared in net income
- Record sale of investment
- Adjust and eliminate FVA at time of sale

Methods to Account for Equity Securities		
FV-NI LO 14-4	Equity Method LO 14-5	Consolidation

Equity investments measured at FV-NI

For an investment measured at FV-NI, the investment is initially recorded at its purchase price plus other incidental costs, such as brokerage fees, excise taxes, and other transfer costs incurred as part of the purchase. Subsequently, the investment is recognized at fair value on reporting dates and any unrealized holding gains and losses are recognized in net income (FV-NI) as illustrated in **Demo 14-4**.

321-10-35-1 Except as provided in paragraph 321-10-35-2, investments in equity securities shall be measured subsequently at fair value in the statement of financial position. Unrealized holding gains and losses for equity securities shall be included in earnings.

Because the investor does not have significant influence over the investee, the investor is unable to dictate whether net income will be retained in the company or distributed. Therefore, revenue is only recognized by the investor with a declaration of a dividend.

321-10-35-6 Dividend income from investments in equity securities shall be included in earnings.

Sale of Equity Securities Measured at FV-NI: When an equity security measured at FV-NI is sold, first the investment account is adjusted to fair value using FV-NI. Next, the sale is recorded including the elimination of the associated Fair Value Adjustment account balance. As a result, for any securities sold during the reporting period, the net effect on the income statement for the reporting period reflects any change in fair value from the last report date to the date of sale.

321-10-40-1 . . . With respect to equity securities, because all changes in an equity security's fair value are reported in earnings as they occur, the sale of an equity security does not necessarily give rise to a gain or loss. Generally, a debit to cash (or trade date receivable) is recorded for the sales proceeds, and a credit is recorded to remove the security at its fair value (or sales price) . . . An entity that has not yet recorded the security's change in fair value to the point of sale (perhaps because fair value changes are recorded at the end of each day) will need to adjust this procedure.

Balance Sheet Classification Equity investments are classified as short term or long term depending upon the intent and ability of the investor to sell the investment within the next year (or operating cycle, if longer).

DEMO 14-4 ▶ **LO14-4**   **Investment in Equity Securities Measured at FV-NI**

Demo

MBC

On July 1 of Year 1, Bold purchased 5,000 of Kale Inc.'s 50,000 outstanding shares of common stock for $20 per share. Commissions paid on the common stock purchase were $500. Bold's investment represents a 10% interest in Kale (5,000 shares/50,000 shares). Bold does *not* have significant influence over Kale. Provide the entries and reporting for the following transactions of Bold. Bold has an accounting period ending December 31.

a. Record the entry to purchase the investment in equity securities on July 1 of Year 1.
b. Record the entry for the declaration and payment of dividends of $5,000 by Kale on December 15 of Year 1.
c. Record the entry to adjust the investment of common stock to fair value assuming that the fair value of Kale's stock is $22 per share on December 31 of Year 1.
d. Report the investment in common stock on the December 31 of Year 1 balance sheet and the Year 1 income statement.
e. Record the sale of the investment in common stock on January 5 of Year 2 for $111,300. Adjust the investment to fair value at the date of sale using FV-NI; then record the sale, eliminating the associated Fair Value Adjustment account balance.

Solution

a. **Purchase of Equity Investment with Insignificant Influence**
The entry to record the purchase of common stock by Bold includes commissions as part of the purchase price.

Assets = Liabilities + Equity
+100,500
Inv
−100,500
C:i

Invest—CS		Cash
100,500		100,500

July 1, Year 1—To record investment purchase

Investment in Kale Stock.	100,500	
Cash ([5,000 × $20] + $500)		100,500

b. **Dividend Revenue**
Because Bold doesn't have significant influence over Kale, it is unable to direct whether net income will be retained in the company or distributed. Therefore, revenue is only recognized by Bold with a declaration of a dividend by Kale. Bold would record the following journal entry for its share of declared and paid dividends of $500 ($5,000 × 10%).

continued

continued from previous page

December 15, Year 1—To record dividend revenue

Cash	500	
Dividend Revenue ($5,000 × 0.10)		500

Assets = Liabilities + Equity
+500   +500
C:o   Rev

Cash	Dividend Rev
500 | 100,500	| 500

c. Adjustment of Investment to Fair Value

At each balance sheet date, equity securities held with insignificant influence are reported at fair value. The difference between fair value and the original cost is recorded in the Fair Value Adjustment account. The unrealized holding gain is measured as follows.

Investment	Cost	Fair Value Year-End	Unrealized Holding Gain (Loss)
Kale common stock	$100,500	$110,000*	$9,500
Existing balance in FVA account balance.....................			0
Amount of increase (decrease) to FVA account needed			$9,500

* $22 × 5,000 shares

The unrealized gain of $9,500 is reflected in the following entry.

December 31, Year 1—To adjust investment to fair value

Fair Value Adjustment—Equity Securities	9,500	
Unrealized Gain or Loss—Income		9,500

Assets = Liabilities + Equity
+9,500   +9,500
FVA   Gain

	Unreal Gain or
FVA—Eq Sec	Loss—Inc
9,500 |	| 9,500

This entry adjusts the carrying value to its current fair value and records an unrealized gain of $9,500. The net unrealized holding gain (or loss) is treated as a component of other income and is included in the determination of the earnings for the period in the income statement.

d. Financial Statement Presentation of Investment in Common Stock

Balance Sheet Excerpt December 31, Year 1	Income Statement Excerpt for Year Ended December 31, Year 1
Assets	Other revenues (expenses)
Investment in equity securities .. $110,000	Dividend revenue .... $ 500
	Unrealized holding gain on equity securities... 9,500

e. Sale of Investment in Common Stock

At the sale date, the company first adjusts the investment to fair value (FV-NI).

Required FVA account balance at sale date*.....................	$10,800
Less existing FVA account balance	9,500
Amount of increase (decrease) to FVA account..................	1,300

*$111,300 fair value – $100,500 original cost.

Assets = Liabilities + Equity
+1,300   +1,300
FVA   Gain

FVA—Eq Sec	Unreal Gain or Loss—Inc
9,500	| 9,500
1,300	| 1,300
10,800	

January 5, Year 2—To adjust investment to fair value

Fair Value Adjustment—Equity Securities	1,300	
Unrealized Gain or Loss—Income		1,300

Assets = Liabilities + Equity
+111,300
C:i
–100,500
Inv
–10,800
FVA

Next, the sale is recorded, including elimination of the associated Fair Value Adjustment balance. No gain is recorded because the gain was recorded in the prior entry.

January 5, Year 2—To record sale of equity securities

Cash..	111,300	
Investment in Kale Stock................................		100,500
Fair Value Adjustment—Equity Securities		10,800

Cash	FVA—Eq Sec
500 | 100,500	9,500 | 10,800
111,300 |	1,300 |
Invest—CS	0 |
100,500 | 100,500	
0 |	

Note: The gain on sale of $10,800 is recognized in the financial statements over the ownership period of the investment.

Gain in Year 1 income statement	$ 9,500
Gain in Year 2 income statement	1,300
Total gain recognized over ownership period ...	$10,800

and Dividend Revenue accounts. Assume that Shay Inc. (but not Clark Inc.) has significant influence over Nashville Inc.

Investor	Dividend Amount Declared and Received	Change in Investment Account	Increase in Dividend Revenue
Clark Inc.	$ _____	$ _____	$ _____
Shay Inc.	_____	_____	_____

On January 1, Evergreen Inc. purchased 3,750 of the 15,000 outstanding shares of common stock of Nature Net Inc., resulting in significant influence over Nature Net Inc. The shares were purchased for $5,000 cash and Evergreen elected to account for the investment under the fair value option. During the year, Nature Net reported net income of $26,000 and declared and paid dividends of $12,000. The 3,750 shares of Nature Net Inc. stock had a fair value of $5,500 at the company's year-end of December 31.

a. Prepare Evergreen's entry to record the purchase of the common stock of Nature Net Inc. on January 1.
b. Prepare Evergreen's entry to record the cash receipt of declared dividends on December 31.
c. Prepare Evergreen's entry to adjust the securities to fair value on December 31.
d. What is the carrying value of the investment on December 31?

Brief Exercise 14-32
Recording Entries
Using the Fair Value
Option **LO5**

Tracking Co. holds an HTM bond investment in Fields Corp. The carrying value of the investment is $4,500 at December 31. Tracking Co. estimates the present value of the amounts expected to be collected on the bond investment to be $2,000. The company does not intend to sell the asset, nor is it likely to be required to sell the investment before recovery of any unrealized loss. Prepare the journal entry, if any, to record an impairment loss on December 31.

Brief Exercise 14-33
Recording Entries for
Impairment—HTM **LO6**
Hint: See Demo 14-6

Determine the amount of impairment loss (if any) to record in income under the following three separate scenarios for an AFS debt investment. In all three cases, the company does not intend to sell and does not believe it is *more likely than not* that it will be required to sell the investment before recovery of any unrealized loss. Assume that the company has already adjusted the AFS debt investments to fair value through OCI.

Brief Exercise 14-34
Recording Entries for
Impairment—AFS **LO6**
Hint: See Demo 14-6

Scenario	1	2	3
Fair value	$90,000	$70,000	$60,000
Amortized cost	80,000	80,000	80,000
Expected credit loss	15,000	15,000	15,000

Refer to the information in BE14-34 except now assume that the company intends to sell the AFS debt securities. Determine the amount of impairment loss (if any) to record in income under the three separate scenarios.

Brief Exercise 14-35
Recording Entries for
Impairment—AFS **LO6**

For the following six items, indicate which financial statement category would be affected: (1) net income or (2) other comprehensive income.

a. Realized gain on sale of AFS debt investment.
b. Realized loss on sale of HTM debt investment.
c. Unrealized gain on an AFS debt investment.
d. Unrealized loss on a TS debt investment.
e. Unrealized gain on an AFS debt investment accounted for using the fair value option.
f. Unrealized loss on an equity investment measured at FV-NI.

Brief Exercise 14-36
Classifying
Financial Statement
Amounts **LO1, 2, 3, 4, 5**

Exercises

Match each security listed below with its usual classification: (1) trading securities, (2) available-for-sale securities, (3) equity method securities, (4) held-to-maturity securities, or (5) equity securities measured at FV-NI.

____ a. Abbit common stock, no-par; acquired to use temporarily idle cash with intent to sell next month.
____ b. 30% interest in Packherd Inc.; acquired to drive costs down through vertical integration.
____ c. Mack Inc. stock held in trading account.
____ d. Hasten Inc.'s 10-year bonds acquired with intent to hold to maturity, but may need to sell the bonds earlier for cash.
____ e. Staufer common stock, par $5; acquired to gain a significant influence, but not control.
____ f. Frazer bonds, 9%, maturing at the end of 10 years; acquired with the intent and ability to hold for 10 years.

Exercise 14-1
Classifying Investments
in Securities **LO1, 2, 3, 4, 5**

_____ g. FTC Corp. common stock; a 30% interest acquired, but difficulties encountered in an attempt to obtain representation on FTC's board of directors. Intent is to hold stock indefinitely.

_____ h. Astroid common stock, par $1; acquired as an investment (with insignificant influence) that management plans to hold indefinitely.

Exercise 14-2
Recording Entries for HTM Debt Securities—Par **LO1**
Hint: See Demo 14-1A

On January 1 of Year 1, Lazer Inc. purchased for cash, ten $1,000, 4% bonds of Star Corp. at par. The bond interest is paid annually on January 1 of each year, and the bonds' maturity date is January 1 of Year 10. Lazer has the intent and ability to hold the bonds over the full term. The fair value of the bonds on December 31 of Year 1 is $9,800.

a. Record the entry for the purchase of the bonds on January 1 of Year 1.
b. Record the year-end entry to accrue interest revenue on December 31 of Year 1.
c. Record the entry for the receipt of interest on January 1 of Year 2.

Exercise 14-3
Recording Entries for HTM Debt Securities—Effective Interest Method **LO1**
Hint: See Demo 14-1C

On January 1 of Year 1, Baker Corp. purchased $20,000 of Chocolate Inc. bonds. These bonds pay 5% interest annually on December 31 and mature in 10 years on December 31. The investment is classified as a held-to-maturity investment because Baker has the intent and the ability to hold the bonds for 10 years. The effective rate on the bonds is 4.5%. Baker's annual accounting period ends on December 31.

Required

a. Were the bonds purchased at a discount or premium?
b. Prepare an amortization schedule for Year 1 and Year 2, using the effective interest method.
c. Prepare the journal entry for the purchase of the investment on January 1 of Year 1.
d. Prepare journal entries to record interest revenue and to update the investment's amortized cost on December 31 of Year 1 and December 31 of Year 2.
e. Indicate the carrying value of the Chocolate bonds on Baker's December 31 of Year 2 balance sheet assuming that the fair value of the bonds on December 31 of Year 2 was $20,800.

Exercise 14-4
Recording Entries for HTM Debt Securities—Effective Interest Method **LO1**
Hint: See Demo 14-1B

On July 1 of Year 1, West Company purchased for cash, eight $10,000 bonds of North Corporation to yield 10%. The bonds pay 9% interest, payable on a semiannual basis each July 1 and January 1, and mature in three years on July 1. The bonds are classified as held-to-maturity securities. West Company's annual reporting period ends December 31. Assume the effective interest method of amortization of any discount or premium.

Required

a. Prepare an amortization schedule for Year 1 and Year 2 using the effective interest method.
b. Record the entry for the purchase of the bonds by West Company on July 1 of Year 1.
c. Record the adjusting entry by West Company on December 31 of Year 1. The fair value of the bonds at December 31 of Year 1 was $81,000.
d. Indicate the effects of this investment on the Year 1 income statement and the year-end balance sheet.
e. Record the receipt of interest on January 1 of Year 2.
f. After the interest was received on July 1 of Year 2, two of the bonds were sold for $19,300 cash. Provide the required entries on July 1 of Year 2 for the (1) receipt of interest and (2) sale of the two bonds.

Exercise 14-5
Reporting Transactions for HTM Securities (Effective Interest Method) Using the Accounting Equation **LO1**

 A L E

Referring to the information in E14-4, show the effect on the accounting equation for the following transactions, including identifying the individual accounts affected, and the total impact on assets, liabilities, and stockholders' equity.

a. Purchase of the bonds by West Company on July 1 of Year 1.
b. Adjusting entry on December 31 of Year 1.
c. Receipt of interest on January 1 of Year 2.
d. Receipt of interest on July 1 of Year 2.
e. Sale of two bonds for $19,300 cash on July 1 of Year 2, after the receipt of interest.

Exercise 14-6
Recording Entries for HTM Debt Securities—Straight-Line Method **LO1**
Hint: See Demo 14-1D

Refer to E14-4, but now assume discounts and premiums are amortized using the straight-line interest method.

Exercise 14-7
Recording Entries for TS—Effective Interest Method **LO2**

On July 1 of Year 1, West Company purchased for cash, eight $10,000 bonds of North Corporation at a market rate of 6%. The bonds pay 5% interest, payable on a semiannual basis each July 1 and January 1, and mature in three years on July 1. The bonds are classified as trading securities. West Company's annual reporting period ends December 31. Assume the effective interest method of amortization of any discounts or premiums.

Required

a. Prepare an amortization schedule for the life of the bonds using the effective interest method.
b. Record the entry for the purchase of the bonds by West Company on July 1 of Year 1.
c. Record the adjusting entries by West Company on December 31 of Year 1 to (1) accrue interest revenue and to update the investment's amortized cost and (2) record the unrealized gain or loss. The fair value of the bonds on December 31 of Year 1 was $83,000.
d. Record the receipt of interest on January 1 of Year 2.
e. Record the sale of all of the bonds on January 2 of Year 2 for $83,050, eliminating the related Fair Value Adjustment account balance. Prior to recording the sale, adjust the investment to fair value.

Refer to E14-7, but instead of journal entries, show the effect on the accounting equation for the transactions, including identifying the individual accounts affected, and the total impact on assets, liabilities, and stockholders' equity.

Exercise 14-8
Reporting Transactions for TS (Effective Interest Method) Using the Accounting Equation **LO2**

Refer to E14-7 except now assume that the market rate is 4% on July 1 of Year 1.

Exercise 14-9
Recording Entries for TS—Effective Interest Method **LO2**

At year-end on December 31 of Year 1 the investments in the portfolio of the trading securities of Kennedy Company consist of the following.

Exercise 14-10
Recording Entries for TS— Par Value **LO2**

Security	Purchase Date	Original Purchase Price
Atlanta Corp. bonds, 5%, $100,000	October 1, Year 1	$100,000
Dallas Inc. bonds, 4%, $50,000	July 1, Year 1	50,000

Required

a. Record the entry for the receipt of quarterly interest from the Atlanta Corp. bonds on December 31 of Year 1.
b. Record the entry for the receipt of semiannual interest from the Dallas Inc. bonds on December 31 of Year 1.
c. Record the entry to adjust the bonds to fair value on December 31 of Year 1. The fair value of the Atlanta Corp. bonds and the Dallas Inc. bonds on December 31 of Year 1 were $110,000 and $45,000, respectively.
d. Indicate the total amount to be included on the December 31 of Year 1 balance sheet of Kennedy Company as investments in trading securities.
e. Record the entry to sell the Atlanta Corp. bonds on January 2 of Year 2 for $112,500. First adjust the bonds to fair value and then eliminate the associated Fair Value Adjustment account upon the sale of the securities.
f. Record the entry to sell the Dallas Inc. bonds on January 3 of Year 2 for $44,500. First adjust the bonds to fair value and then eliminate the associated Fair Value Adjustment account upon the sale of the securities.
g. Determine the investment related impact on net income for Year 1 and for Year 2.

On January 1, Josie Inc. purchased for cash, ten $1,000, 4% bonds of Star Corp. at par. The bond interest is paid annually on January 1 of each year, and the bonds mature in 10 years on January 1. Josie has the intent and ability to hold the bonds over the full term and has elected to account for the bonds using the fair value option. The fair value of the bonds at year-end on December 31 is $9,500.

Exercise 14-11
Recording Entries under the Fair Value Option—HTM **LO2**
Hint: See Demo 14-2B

Required

Prepare the following entries for Josie Inc.

a. Record the entry for the purchase of the bonds on January 1.
b. Record adjusting entries at year-end December 31 to adjust (1) interest revenue and (2) investment to fair value.
c. Record the entry for the receipt of interest on January 1 of the following year.

On October 31, West Company purchased $10,000 of East Company bonds. West Company plans to hold the bonds for an indefinite period of time. West Company elects to account for the debt investment using the fair value option.

Required

a. If the fair value of the East Company bonds is $11,000 at the company's year-end of December 31, what year-end adjusting entry would West Company record?

b. If West Company had not elected the fair value option, what year-end adjusting entry would West Company record?

On January 1, Jules Company purchased for cash, $50,000 bonds (consisting of ten $5,000 bonds) of Android Corporation at a market rate of 6%. The bonds pay 6.5% interest, payable on a semiannual basis each June 30 and December 31, and mature on December 31 in five years. The bonds are classified as available-for-sale securities. The annual reporting period of Jules Company ends December 31. Assume the effective interest method of amortization of any discounts or premiums.

Required

a. Prepare an amortization schedule for the first year using the effective interest method.

b. Record the entry for the purchase of the bonds by Jules Company on January 1.

c. Record the entry for the receipt of interest and to update the investment's amortized cost on June 30.

d. Record the entry for the receipt of interest and to update the investment's amortized cost on December 31.

e. Record the adjusting entry on December 31 to adjust the debt investment to fair value. The fair value of the bonds on December 31 is $49,000.

f. Determine the impact on the following financial statement categories for the year, assuming no transactions other than those of the AFS securities.

1. Other comprehensive income
2. Net income
3. Comprehensive income
4. Other revenues (expenses)

g. Determine the balance in the Investment account on the balance sheet of December 31.

Refer to E14-13, but instead of journal entries, show the effect on the accounting equation for the transactions, including identifying the individual accounts affected, and the total impact on assets, liabilities, and stockholders' equity.

On July 1 of Year 1, West Company purchased for cash, eight $10,000 bonds of North Corporation to yield 10%. The bonds pay 9% interest, payable on a semiannual basis each July 1 and January 1, and mature in three years on July 1. The bonds are classified as AFS securities. West Company's annual reporting period ends December 31. Assume the effective interest method of amortization of any discount or premium.

Required

a. Prepare an amortization schedule for Year 1 and Year 2 using the effective interest method.

b. Record the entry for the purchase of the bonds by West Company on July 1 of Year 1.

c. Record the adjusting entries by West Company on December 31 of Year 1 to (1) accrue interest revenue and to update the investment's amortized cost and (2) adjust the investment to fair value. The fair value of the bonds at December 31 of Year 1 was $81,000.

d. Indicate the effects of this investment on the Year 1 income statement and the year-end balance sheet.

e. Record the receipt of interest on January 1 of Year 2.

f. After the interest receipt on July 1 of Year 2, two of the bonds were sold for $19,300 cash.

1. Record the receipt of interest and to update the investment's amortized cost on July 1 of Year 2.
2. Record the entry to adjust the two bonds to fair value (FV-OCI).
3. Record the sale, eliminating the related Fair Value Adjustment account balance in one entry. For simplicity, ignore any fair value adjustments in Year 2 related to the six remaining bonds.

Refer to E14-15, but instead of journal entries, show the effect on the accounting equation for the transactions, including identifying the individual accounts affected, and the total impact on assets, liabilities, and stockholders' equity.

A portfolio of investments of available-for-sale securities held by Dow Inc. follows.

Exercise 14-17
Adjusting AFS Debt
Securities to Fair
Value **LO3**

December 31, Year 1	Cost	Fair Value
Eastern Corp. bonds.	$120,000	$128,000
Western Corp. bonds	200,000	205,000
Total	$320,000	$333,000

December 31, Year 2	Cost	Fair Value
Eastern Corp. bonds.	$120,000	$140,000
Western Corp. bonds	200,000	190,000
Total	$320,000	$330,000

The Fair Value Adjustment account had a $0 balance on January 1 of Year 1. No sales or purchases took place in the available-for-sale investment portfolio in Year 1 and Year 2.

Required

a. Record the adjusting entry on December 31 of Year 1 to adjust the debt investments to fair value at year-end.
b. Record the adjusting entry on December 31 of Year 2 to adjust the debt investments to fair value at year-end.
c. Indicate how the adjustment to fair value in part (b) would be reported in Dow's income statement for the year ended December 31 of Year 2.

Exercise 14-18
Recording and Reporting
AFS Securities **LO3**

On December 31 of Year 1, Banff Company held an investment in Glacier Inc. bonds with an original cost of $23,000. The investment was classified as an available-for-sale security, had a fair value of $21,500 on December 31 of Year 1, and was the only investment in the available-for-sale security portfolio in Year 1. On June 1 of Year 2, Banff sold the investment in Glacier Inc. bonds for $20,000. On December 31 of Year 2, assume that Banff Company has an $8,000 net unrealized holding gain on other available-for-sale securities purchased during Year 2 and held on December 31 of Year 2. No other AFS securities were sold during the year. Banff's annual accounting period ends on December 31.

Required

Complete the following requirements for Banff Company.

a. Record the adjusting entry on December 31 of Year 1 to adjust the AFS debt investments to fair value.
b. Record the entry to adjust the Glacier bond investment to fair value at the date of sale using FV-OCI.
c. Record the sale of the Glacier bond investment, eliminating the associated Fair Value Adjustment account balance.
d. Record the adjusting entry on December 31 of Year 2 to adjust the AFS debt investments to fair value.
e. Indicate the effect on net income and other comprehensive income in Year 2 for these transactions.
f. Prepare the reclassification disclosure of accumulated other comprehensive income to include in the notes accompanying the financial statements of Banff Company for Year 2.

Exercise 14-19
Recording and Reporting
Equity Investment:
FV-NI **LO4**
Hint: See Demo 14-4

On November 1 of Year 1, Drucker Co. acquired the following investments in equity securities measured at FV-NI.

    Kelly Corporation—500 shares of common stock (no par) at $60 per share.
    Keefe Corporation—300 shares preferred stock ($10 par) at $20 per share.

On December 31 of Year 1, the company's year-end quoted market prices follow: Kelly Corporation common stock, $52, and Keefe Corporation preferred stock, $24.

    Following are the data for Year 2.

Mar. 2, Year 2   Dividends per share, declared and paid: Kelly Corp., $1, and Keefe Corp., $0.50.
Oct. 1, Year 2   Sold 100 shares of Keefe Corporation preferred stock at $25 per share.
Dec. 31, Year 2   Fair values: Kelly common, $46 per share, Keefe preferred, $26 per share.

Required

a. Prepare the entry for Drucker Company to record the purchase of securities at November 1 of Year 1.
b. Prepare any adjusting entry needed at December 31 of Year 1.
c. Indicate the items and amounts that should be reported on the Year 1 income statement of Drucker and its year-end balance sheet. Assume that the investments are classified as current.

d. Prepare the entries required in Year 2 to record (1) dividend revenue, (2) the sale of stock, and (3) the fair value adjustment. Update the Fair Value Adjustment account prior to recording any sale. Eliminate the associated Fair Value Adjustment account upon recording the sale of any investment.

e. Indicate items and amounts that should be reported on the Year 2 income statement and the year-end balance sheet.

Exercise 14-20
Reporting Transactions for
FV-NI Equity Investments
Using the Accounting
Equation **LO4**

Refer to E14-19, but instead of journal entries, show the effect on the accounting equation for the transactions, including identifying the individual accounts affected, and the total impact on assets, liabilities, and stockholders' equity.

Exercise 14-21
Recording Entries for
Equity Investment:
FV-NI **LO4**
Hint: See Demo 14-4

At December 31 of the prior year, the portfolio of investments in equity securities measured at FV-NI held by Athletes Inc. follows.

Investment Security	Cost	Fair Value	Unrealized Holding Gain (Loss)
Badger Common Stock (1,000 shares)	$ 40,000	$ 39,500	$ (500)
Spartan Common Stock (1,600 shares).	50,000	51,000	1,000
Wildcat Common Stock (500 shares).	25,000	23,500	(1,500)
	$115,000	$114,000	$(1,000)

In the current year on June 1, Athletes Inc. sold 400 shares of Spartan stock for $33 per share and 100 shares of Wildcat stock for $55 per share. Athletes Inc. purchased 400 shares of Gopher common stock for $35 per share on August 1. The fair value of the remaining stock held on December 31 follows: Badger common stock, $42,000; Spartan common stock, $36,000; Wildcat common stock, $20,800; and Gopher common stock, $14,400.

Required

a. Prepare the entry for (1) the sale of Spartan and (2) the sale of Wildcat common stock on June 1. Prior to recording the sale, update the investments to fair value. Eliminate the associated Fair Value Adjustment balances upon sale of the investments.

b. Record the purchase of Gopher common stock on August 1.

c. Prepare any adjusting entry needed at the current year-end of December 31.

Exercise 14-22
Adjusting Fair
Value Adjustment
Account—Equity
Investments **LO4**

Five separate scenarios of equity investment holdings, measured at FV-NI, follow.

Scenario	Original Cost of Investment	Fair Value at Dec. 31, Prior Year	Fair Value at Dec. 31, Current Year
1.	$10,000	$10,000	$10,500
2.	10,000	10,500	11,000
3.	10,000	8,500	9,200
4.	10,000	12,000	9,500
5.	10,000	8,200	7,900

Required
For each of the five separate scenarios, record the adjustment to fair value required on December 31 of the current year. Assume that each investment was purchased in the prior year and that there were no purchases or sales related to the investment in the current year.

Exercise 14-23
Recording Entries for
Equity Investment: FV-NI
and Equity Method
LO4, 5

On January 1, Allen Corporation purchased 30% of the 30,000 outstanding common shares of Towne Corporation at $17 per share as a long-term investment. On the date of purchase, the carrying amount and the fair value of the net assets of Towne Corporation were equal. During the year, Towne Corporation reported net income of $24,000 and declared and paid dividends of $8,000. As of December 31, common shares of Towne Corporation were trading at $20 per share. Both Towne and Allen's annual accounting periods end on December 31.

Required

a. Assume that Allen Corporation had significant influence over Towne Corporation. Prepare Allen's entries for the year to record (1) the purchase of the investment, (2) the receipt of declared dividends, and (3) the proportionate share of net income.

b. Assume that Allen Corporation did *not* have significant influence over Towne Corporation. Record Allen's entries during the year for (1) the purchase of the investment, (2) the receipt of declared dividends, and (3) the fair value adjustment.

c. Indicate the amount of income that would be reported on the income statement and the investment balance on the year-end balance sheet under (1) requirement (*a*) and (2) requirement (*b*).

Refer to E14-23, but instead of journal entries, show the effect on the accounting equation for the transactions, including identifying the individual accounts affected, and the total impact on assets, liabilities, and stockholders' equity.

Exercise 14-24
Reporting Investment Transactions as FV-NI and Under Equity Method Using the Accounting Equation **LO4, 5**

Assume that Fleetwood Inc. purchased 40% of the voting stock of Mac Corporation on January 1 for $100,000, an amount equal to 40% of Mac's carrying amount. Assume that the fair value and carrying amount of all net assets of Mac were the same at that time. During the year, Fleetwood Inc. debited the Investment account for $12,000 and credited the Investment account for $4,000. The ending balance of Fleetwood's Investment account is $108,000 at December 31. Assume that Fleetwood Inc. has significant influence over Mac Corporation. The accounting periods for both companies end on December 31.

Exercise 14-25
Analyzing Investment Account: Equity Method **LO5**
Hint: See Demo 14-5

Required

a. What did Mac Corporation report as net income for the year? What is Fleetwood's share of Mac Corporation's net income for the year?

b. What did Mac Corporation report as dividends for the year? What is Fleetwood's share of Mac Corporation's dividends for the year?

On January 1, Allen Corporation purchased 30% of the 30,000 outstanding common shares of Towne Corporation at $15 per share as a long-term investment. On the date of purchase, the carrying amount and the fair value of the net assets of Towne Corporation were equal. During the year, Towne Corporation reported net income of $24,000. Towne Corporation declared and paid cash dividends of $8,000 on December 30 to shareholders on record. As of December 31, common shares of Towne Corporation were trading at $20 per share. Both Towne and Allen's annual accounting periods end on December 31.

Exercise 14-26
Recording Entries for Equity Investment: Equity Method **LO5**
Hint: See Demo 14-5

Required

a. Record the entries for Allen Corporation on (1) January 1, (2) December 30, and (3) December 31, assuming that Allen Corporation had significant influence over Towne Corporation.

b. Indicate the effects of this investment on the income statement and year-end balance sheet.

On January 1, Mercedez Company purchased 400 of the 1,000 outstanding shares of Auto Supplies Inc. for $40,000. At that date, the balance sheet of Auto Supplies Inc. showed the following selected values.

Exercise 14-27
Recording Entries for Equity Investment: Equity Method **LO5**
Hint: See Demo 14-5

Assets not subject to depreciation	$40,000*
Assets subject to depreciation	26,000**
Liabilities	6,000*
Common stock (par $1)	50,000
Retained earnings	10,000

* Same as fair value.   ** Fair value $30,000; the assets have a 10-year remaining useful life (straight-line depreciation).

Note: The excess of the purchase price of the investment over the fair value of the net assets purchased was attributable to goodwill.

Required

a. Provide the entry by Mercedez Company to record the acquisition at a cost of $40,000.

b. Assume that on December 31 (end of the accounting period), Auto Supplies Inc. reported net income of $12,000. Provide all December 31 year-end entries for Mercedez Company.

c. In February of the following year, Auto Supplies Inc. declared and paid a $2 per share cash dividend. Provide the necessary entry for Mercedez Company.

Refer to E14-27, but instead of journal entries, show the effect on the accounting equation for the transactions, including identifying the individual accounts affected, and the total impact on assets, liabilities, and stockholders' equity.

Exercise 14-28
Reporting Investment Transactions Under Equity Method Using the Accounting Equation **LO5**

Exercise 14-29
Determining Value of
Investment Account:
Equity Method **LO5**

On January 1, Case Corporation purchased 3,000 of the 10,000 outstanding shares of common stock of Dow Corporation for $28,000 cash. At that date, Dow's balance sheet reflected the following selected carrying amounts. Dow reported net income of $18,000 during the year and declared and paid a $1 per share cash dividend.

Assets not subject to depreciation	$25,000*
Assets subject to depreciation	30,000**
Liabilities.	5,000*
Common stock (par $4)	40,000
Retained earnings	10,000

* Same as fair value.   ** Fair value $38,000; the assets have a 10-year remaining useful life (straight-line depreciation).

Note: The excess of the purchase price of the investment over the fair value of the net assets purchased was attributable to goodwill.

Required

Assuming that the equity method is used, determine the value of Case Corporation's Investment account at year-end on December 31 for its holding of common stock of Dow Corporation.

Exercise 14-30
Recording Entries for
Equity Investment:
Equity Method, Partial
Year **LO5**
Hint: See Demo 14-5

On July 1, Allen Corporation purchased 30% of the 30,000 outstanding common shares of Towne Corporation at $17 per share as a long-term investment. On the date of purchase, the carrying amount and the fair value of the net assets of Towne Corporation were equal. During the year, Towne Corporation reported net income of $24,000. Towne Corporation declared and paid cash dividends of $8,000 on December 30 to shareholders on record. As of December 31, common shares of Towne Corporation were trading at $20 per share. Both Towne and Allen's annual accounting periods end on December 31.

Required

a. Record Allen's entries on (1) July 1, (2) December 30, and (3) December 31, assuming that Allen Corporation had significant influence over Towne Corporation.

b. Indicate the effects of this investment on Allen's income statement and its year-end balance sheet.

Exercise 14-31
Recording Entries under
the Fair Value Option—
Equity Method **LO5**

Assume that Fireside Inc. purchased 30% of the common stock of Theater Supplies Corporation on January 1 for $100,000. Fireside Inc. elected to account for its investment using the fair value option. During the year, Theater Supplies reported net income of $80,000 and declared and paid dividends of $15,000. The fair value of Fireside's investment in Theater Supplies common stock is $105,000. Assume that Fireside Inc. has significant influence over Theater Supplies Corporation. The accounting periods for both companies end on December 31.

Required

a. What amount would Fireside Inc. report on its balance sheet on December 31 for its investment in Theater Supplies Corporation?

b. What amount would Fireside Inc. report in its income statement for the year ended December 31 for its investment in Theater Supplies Corporation?

Exercise 14-32
Reporting Various
Investment
Securities **LO1,
2, 3, 4, 5**

Complete the following table for four types of investment securities.

Security Type	Carrying Value	Fair Value	Current Asset	Non-current Asset	Unrealized Gain or Loss—Income	Unrealized Gain or Loss—Equity
Example: AFS Debt Investment[1]. . . .	*$ 9,000*	*$ 8,000*	*—*	*$8,000*	*—*	*$(1,000)*
1. AFS Debt Investment[1]	3,000	3,300				
2. TS Debt Investment[2]	8,000	7,500				
3. HTM Debt Investment[3]	18,000	17,000				
4. Equity Investment—at FV-NI[2]. . . .	21,000	23,000				

[1] Investor intends to hold investment for at least one year but less than full term of debt.
[2] Investor intends to hold for less than one year.
[3] Debt investment is purchased with a remaining term of 10 years.

Exercise 14-33
Recording Entries
for Impairment
of Investments—
HTM **LO6**
Hint: See Demo 14-6

Atlanta Inc. holds an HTM bond investment issued by Falcons Corporation. The carrying value of the investment is $140,500 on December 31. Atlanta Inc. determines the present value of the amounts expected to be collected under the debt contract under the CECL model to be $120,000. Atlanta's annual accounting period ends on December 31.

Required

a. For Atlanta Inc, record the impairment loss, if any, on December 31.

b. Assume that Atlanta Inc. holds the HTM bond investment from Falcons Corporation on December 31 of the following year. Record the adjusting entry, if any, if the present value of the amounts expected to be collected under the debt contract under the CECL model is now estimated to be $130,000.

Eagle Software has an equity investment in Finch Enterprises accounted for under the equity method. The carrying value and the fair value of the investment are $45,000, and $32,000, respectively at Eagle's year-end of December 31. Eagle management decides that the decline is other-than-temporary because Finch lost a patent protection suit during the year and can no longer profit from some of its products.

Required

a. Record Eagle's journal entry on December 31 to recognize the impairment.

b. What is the adjusted cost basis of the equity investment on December 31?

c. Assume that the fair value of the investment is $36,000 on December 31 of the following year. Record the applicable journal entry.

Exercise 14-34
Recording Entries
for Impairment of
Investments—Equity
Method **LO6**
Hint: See Demo 14-6

Atlanta Inc. holds an AFS bond investment issued by Falcons Corporation. The amortized cost of the investment is $140,500 on December 31. Atlanta Inc. estimates the fair value of the bonds to be $130,000. The unrealized loss of $10,500 is partially due to a credit loss of $8,000, with the remaining portion due to other factors. The company adjusted the AFS bonds to fair value through OCI on December 31, the company's year end.

Required

a. Record the impairment loss on December 31, assuming that the company does not intend to sell the investment and does not believe it is *more likely than not* that it will be required to sell the investment before recovery of any unrealized loss.

b. Record the impairment loss on December 31, now assuming that the company intends to sell the investment.

Exercise 14-35
Recording Entries
for Impairment of
Investments—AFS **LO6**

Problems

On July 1 of Year 1, Scarlet Company acquired the following bonds, which Scarlet intends to hold to maturity.

Security	Purchase Price	Face Value Purchased
Gold 10% bonds, maturity date July 1, Year 6	$101.5	$30,000
Green 8% bonds, maturity date December 31, Year 3	97.0	40,000

Both bonds pay interest annually on December 31. Premiums and discounts are amortized on a straight-line basis and the company's period ends on December 31.

Required

a. Provide the entries to record the purchase of the investments on July 1 of Year 1. Assume that cash payments for purchase prices include accrued interest.

b. Provide the entries on December 31 of Year 1 to record the receipt of interest and to update the investment's amortized cost.

c. Provide the items and amounts that would be reported in the Year 1 income statement and end of year balance sheet related to the investments.

d. Provide the entries on December 31 of Year 2 to record the receipt of interest and to update the investment's amortized cost.

e. Provide the items and amounts that would be reported in the Year 2 income statement and end of year balance sheet related to the investments.

Problem 14-1
Recording and Reporting
HTM Securities: Premium,
Discount, Straight-Line,
Accrued Interest **LO1**

On January 1 of Year 1, Pitt Company acquired the following bonds, which Pitt intends to hold to maturity.

Security	Purchase Price	Face Value Purchased
Hollywood 5% bonds, maturity date January 1, Year 11 . . .	$277,684	$300,000

Problem 14-2
Recording and Reporting
HTM and AFS Securities:
Discount, Semiannual,
Effective Interest
LO1, 3

The bonds pay interest semiannually on June 30 and December 31. Premiums and discounts are amortized using the effective interest method and a market rate of 6%. The fair value of the bonds was $275,000 on December 31 of Year 1. Pitt's annual accounting period ends on December 31.

Required

a. Provide the entry to record the purchase of the investment on January 1 of Year 1.

b. Provide the entry on June 30 of Year 1 to record the receipt of interest and to update the investment's amortized cost.

c. Provide the entry on December 31 of Year 1 to record the receipt of interest and to update the investment's amortized cost, plus any adjustment to fair value (if required).

d. Provide the items and amounts that would be reported in the Year 1 income statement, Year 1 statement of comprehensive income, and year-end balance sheet related to this investment.

e. Provide the entry on June 30 of Year 2 to record the receipt of interest and to update the investment's amortized cost.

f. Provide the entry on December 31 of Year 2 to record the receipt of interest and the adjustment to fair value (if required). The fair value of the bonds was $277,000 on December 31 of Year 2.

g. Provide the items and amounts that would be reported in the Year 2 income statement, Year 2 statement of comprehensive income, and year-end balance sheet related to this investment.

h. Repeat *a* through *g* assuming that Pitt was uncertain as to how long to hold the security.

Problem 14-3
Recording and Reporting HTM and AFS Securities: Premium, Semiannual, Effective Interest
LO1, 3

On January 1 of Year 1, Pitt Company acquired the following bonds, which Pitt intends to hold to maturity.

Security	Purchase Price	Face Value Purchased
Hollywood 5% bonds, maturity date January 1, Year 11...	$324,527	$300,000

The bonds pay interest semiannually on June 30 and December 31. Premiums are amortized using the effective interest method and a market rate of 4%. The fair value of the bonds was $325,000 on December 31 of Year 1. Pitt's annual accounting period ends on December 31.

Required

a. Provide the entry to record the purchase of the investment on January 1 of Year 1.

b. Provide the entry on June 30 of Year 1 to record the receipt of interest and to update the investment's amortized cost.

c. Provide the entry on December 31 of Year 1 to record the receipt of interest and to update the investment's amortized cost, plus any adjustment to fair value (if required).

d. Provide the items and amounts that would be reported in the Year 1 income statement, Year 1 comprehensive income statement, and year-end balance sheet related to this investment.

e. Provide the entry on June 30 of Year 2 to record the receipt of interest and to update the investment's amortized cost.

f. Provide the entry on December 31 of Year 2 to record the receipt of interest and to update the investment's amortized cost plus any adjustment to fair value (if required). The fair value of the bonds was $323,000 on December 31 of Year 2.

g. Provide the items and amounts that would be reported in the Year 2 income statement, Year 2 comprehensive income statement, and year-end balance sheet related to this investment.

h. Repeat *a* through *g* assuming that Pitt was uncertain as to how long to hold the security.

Problem 14-4
Computing Selling Price and Bond Interest Revenue— Effective Interest and Straight-Line **LO1**
Hint: See Review 14-1

On January 1 of Year 1, Olympians Inc. purchased for cash, ten $10,000 bonds of Ring Corporation. The bonds pay 4% interest, payable on an annual basis each December 31, and mature in 10 years on December 31. The bonds are classified as held-to-maturity securities. The annual reporting period of Olympians Inc. ends December 31. The following table includes five separate scenarios pertaining to these bonds.

	(1) Bonds Yield 4%	(2) Bonds Yield 5% (Use effective interest method)	(3) Bonds Yield 5% (Use straight-line interest method)	(4) Bonds Yield 3% (Use effective interest method)	(5) Bonds Yield 3% (Use straight-line interest method)
Were the bonds sold at par, discount, or premium?					
Compute the purchase price of bonds					
Compute interest revenue for Year 1					
Compute interest revenue for Year 2					

Required

a. Prepare an amortization schedule for Year 1 and Year 2 for each of the five bond scenarios.

b. Complete the table above.

Problem 14-5
Recording and Reporting
TS: Premium, Semiannual,
Straight-Line **LO2**

On July 1, JB Enterprises purchased for cash, eight $1,000, 9% bonds of Star Corporation at 102 plus accrued interest. The bond interest is paid semiannually each May 1 and November 1, and the maturity date of the bonds is November 1 of next year. JB's annual reporting period ends on December 31. JB classifies this investment as a trading security and uses the straight-line interest method to amortize discounts and premiums on bonds. At December 31, the Star Corporation bonds were quoted at 97.

Required

a. Prepare the entry for JB Enterprises to record the purchase of the bonds on July 1.

b. Prepare the November 1 entry for interest collected and to update the investment's amortized cost.

c. Prepare any adjusting entry(ies) required on December 31.

d. Indicate what items and amounts should be reported on the income statement for the year and on the December 31 balance sheet.

Problem 14-6
Recording and Reporting
TS: Discount, Annual,
Effective Interest **LO2**

On January 1 of Year 1, New Edition Co. purchased for cash, ten $1,000, 4% bonds of Brown Corporation at a market rate of 5.5%. The Brown Corp. bond interest is paid annually each January 1, and the bonds mature in eight years. New Edition's annual reporting period ends on December 31. New Edition classifies this investment as a trading security and uses the effective interest method to amortize discounts and premiums on bonds. At December 31, the Brown bonds were quoted at 97.

Required

a. Prepare the entry for New Edition to record the purchase of the bonds on January 1.

b. Prepare any adjusting entries required on December 31.

c. Indicate what items and amounts should be reported on the current year income statement and the December 31 balance sheet.

d. New Edition sold the bonds on January 2 of Year 2 at 95. First adjust the investment to fair value. Next, record the sale, eliminating the associated Fair Value Adjustment balance.

Problem 14-7
Recording and Reporting
AFS Debt Securities,
Reclassification **LO3**

Universe Inc. had the following portfolio of available-for-sale securities on December 31 of the prior year, which were previously purchased at par.

AFS Investment	Amortized Cost	Fair Value at Dec. 31, Prior Year	Unrealized Holding Gain (Loss)
Saturn Inc. bonds	$ 81,500	$ 85,000	$3,500
Venus bonds.	50,800	49,000	(1,800)
	$132,300	$134,000	$1,700

The Saturn bonds are sold on January 5 of the current year for $85,500. Universe's annual reporting period ends on December 31. At the end of the current year, the Venus bonds (originally purchased at par value) have a fair value of $50,000. Besides the sale of Saturn bonds on January 5, no other AFS transactions took place during the year.

Required

a.   Record the fair value adjustment of the Saturn bonds on January 5 prior to the sale.

b.   Record the sale of Saturn bonds on January 5, reversing the associated Fair Value Adjustment account balance.

c.   Adjust the Fair Value Adjustment account on December 31 of the current year.

d.   Prepare a reconciliation of other comprehensive income from January 1 to December 31 of the current year.

Problem 14-8
Recording Fair Value Adjustments of AFS Debt Investments   **LO3**

Given the following amortization schedule for available-for-sale bonds, answer the questions that follow.

Date	Stated Interest	Market Interest	Amortization	Bond Amortized Cost
Jan. 1, Year 1				$2,922.69
Dec. 31, Year 1	$210.00	$233.81	$23.81	2,946.50
Dec. 31, Year 2	210.00	235.72	25.72	2,972.22
Dec. 31, Year 3	210.00	237.78	27.78	3,000.00

Required

a.   Were the bonds purchased at a discount or premium?

b.   Assume that the estimated fair value for the bonds is $3,100 at year-end on December 31 of Year 1. Provide the adjusting entry to record the bonds at fair value on December 31 of Year 1. Assume that the Fair Value Adjustment account had a balance of $0 at January 1 of Year 1.

c.   Assume that the estimated fair value for the bonds is $2,800 at year-end on December 31 of Year 2. Provide the adjusting entry to record the bonds at fair value on December 31 of Year 2.

Problem 14-9
Recording and Reporting Investments in Securities—Fair Value, HTM   **LO1, 2, 3, 4**

During the year, Shale Company purchased equity shares of two corporations and debt securities of a third company. Related transactions follow.

1.   On February 1, Shale Company purchased 200 of the 10,000 shares outstanding of common stock of Tee Corporation at $31 per share plus a 4% brokerage fee and a transfer cost of $52. Shale Company intends to hold these shares for more than one year.

2.   On March 3, Shale Company purchased 300 of 4,000 outstanding shares of preferred stock (nonvoting) of Stone Corporation at $78 per share plus a 3% brokerage fee and a transfer cost of $198. Shale Company intends to hold the stock for an indefinite period.

3.   On August 15, Shale Company purchased an additional 20 shares of common stock of Tee Corporation at $35 per share plus a 4% brokerage fee and a transfer cost of $4. Shale Company intends to take advantage of short-term gains on these 20 shares.

4.   Shale Company purchased $10,000 of Container Corporation 9% bonds at par plus accrued interest and a transfer fee of $200. The purchase is made on November 1; interest is paid semiannually on January 31 and July 31. The Shale Company intends to hold these bonds through maturity.

5.   On December 31, Shale Company received $4 per share cash dividend on the Stone Corporation stock (declared December 15). Interest receivable on the Container bonds is accrued on December 31.

6.   At December 31, the fair value of the shares held at the end of the year were Tee stock, $34, and Stone stock, $75. The Container Corporation bonds were quoted at 100.

Required

a.   Provide the entries of Shale Company for each transaction 1 through 6, assuming the company's annual period ends on December 31.

b.   Indicate the financial items and amounts to recognize on the current year income statement and the December 31 year-end balance sheet.

Problem 14-10
Recording and Reporting Investments in Equity Securities—FV-NI   **LO4**

Raven Company's portfolio of securities measured at FV-NI at the end of the annual reporting period on December 31 of Year 1 follows. The equity securities were purchased on September 1 of Year 1.

Security	Shares	Unit Cost	Unit Market Price
Bic Corp., common stock, no par	50	$186	$187
Cross Corp., preferred stock, 6%, par $40	200	40	35

Transactions relating to this portfolio during Year 2 follow.

Jan. 25	Received a 6% declared dividend on the Cross shares.
Apr. 15	Sold 30 shares of Bic Corporation stock at $151 per share.
July 25	Received a $45 declared dividend on the Bic shares.
Oct. 1	Sold the remaining shares of Bic Corporation at $149.50 per share.
Dec. 1	Purchased 100 shares of Pilot Corporation common stock at $47 per share plus a $30 brokerage fee.
Dec. 5	Purchased 400 shares of Sanford Corporation common stock, par $1, at $15 per share.

On December 31 of Year 2, the following unit market prices were available: Bic stock, $140; Cross stock, $38; Pilot stock, $51; and Sanford stock, $14. Raven updates its Fair Value Adjustment account for its investment port-folio at year-end on December 31.

Required

a. Prepare entries that Raven Company should make on (1) September 1 of Year 1 and (2) December 31 of Year 1.

b. Provide the investment items and amounts that should be reported on the Year 1 income statement and year-end balance sheet.

c. Prepare the entries for the Year 2 transactions, plus any required year-end adjusting entries. Record an entry to adjust to market any securities sold during the year. As part of the entry to record the sale, eliminate any associated balances in the Fair Value Adjustment account.

d. Provide the investment items and amounts that should be reported on the Year 2 income statement and year-end balance sheet.

On January 3, American Company purchased 2,000 shares of the 10,000 outstanding shares of common stock of United Corporation for $14,600 cash with the intention of holding the securities indefinitely. At that date, the bal-ance sheet of United Corporation reflected the following: nondepreciable assets, $50,000 (same as fair value); de-preciable assets (net), $30,000 (fair value, $33,000); total liabilities, $20,000; and stockholders' equity, $60,000. Assume a 10-year remaining useful life (straight-line depreciation) on the depreciable assets. United Corporation recorded net income of $15,000 during the year. *Note:* The excess of the purchase price of the investment over the fair value of the net assets purchased was attributable to goodwill. The accounting periods for both American and United end on December 31.

Problem 14-11
Recording and Reporting Investments in Equity Securities—FV-NI, Equity Method **LO4, 5**

Required

a. Provide the entries, if any are required, on American's books for each item 1 through 5 below assuming that FV-NI method is appropriate.
  1. Entry at date of acquisition.
  2. Entry on December 31 to record net income reported by United.
  3. Entry on December 31 for additional depreciation expense.
  4. Entry on December 31 to recognize the decrease in fair value of United stock; quoted market price is $7 per share.
  5. Entry on December 31 for a cash dividend of $1 per share declared and paid by United.

b. Repeat part (a) assuming that the equity method is appropriate.

c. Indicate the ending balance in the Investment account under each method, a and b, as of December 31.

d. Indicate what items and amounts should be reported on the current year income statement and statement of cash flows (indirect method) under each method, a and b.

On January 1, Redmond Company purchases 3,000 of the 15,000 outstanding shares of common stock of Decca Computer (DC) Corporation for $80,000 cash as a long-term investment (the only long-term equity investment held). The assets and liabilities of DC Corporation at the date of purchase approximate fair value. During the year, DC re-ported net income of $25,000 and declared and paid cash dividends of $10,000. The fair value of DC Corporation at December 31 is $25 per share. The annual accounting periods for both Redmond and DC end on December 31.

Problem 14-12
Recording Investments in Securities—Equity Method, Fair Value Option **LO5**

Required

a. Prepare Redmond's journal entries to record (1) the purchase of the investment, (2) the receipt of dividends, and (3) the year-end adjusting entry, assuming that the investment is recorded under the equity method.

b. Record the journal entries described in part a assuming instead that Redmond Company opted on the pur-chase date to account for the investments using the fair value option.

On January 1 of Year 1, Rae Company purchased 8,000 of the 40,000 shares outstanding of common stock (par $1) of Sundem Corporation for $80,000 cash. Assume that the fair value and the carrying amount of all net assets of Sundem were the same at that time. This is the only long-term equity investment held, and the ownership of Sun-dem shares represents a significant interest. The accounting periods for both Rae and Sundem end on December 31.

Problem 14-13
Recording Investments in Securities—Equity Method **LO5**

Sundem Corporation	
Year 1	
Income reported	$40,000
Cash dividend per share declared and paid on December 15	1.50
Market price per share of stock, December 31	12.00
Year 2	
Income reported	$50,000
Cash dividend per share declared and paid on December 15	1.50
Market price per share of stock, December 31	11.00

Required

a. Provide all of the entries required for Rae Company for Year 1 and Year 2 including the investment purchase, receipt of declared dividends, and year-end adjusting entries.

b. Show how the long-term investments in equity securities and the related investment income would be reported on the balance sheet and income statement of Rae Company at the end of each year.

Problem 14-14
Recording and Reporting Investments in Debt Securities—AFS, Fair Value Option   **LO2, 3**

On January 1 of Year 1, Sage Company acquired $50,000 of the 4% bonds of Thyme Company, purchased to yield 6% interest. Interest is received semiannually on June 30 and December 31. The bonds mature in 10 years on December 31. Sage Company intends to hold the bonds longer than one year but doesn't anticipate holding the bonds until maturity. The fair value of the bonds on December 31 of Year 1 is $41,000. Sage Company's annual accounting period ends on December 31.

Required

a. Prepare an amortization schedule for Year 1 and Year 2 for the bonds purchased by Sage Company.

b. Provide the entry to record the purchase of the bonds on January 1 of Year 1.

c. Provide the entry to record interest received on June 30 of Year 1 and December 31 of Year 1.

d. Provide any necessary adjusting entries to reflect the fair value of the bonds at December 31 of Year 1.

e. On June 30 of Year 2, after interest was received, Sage Company sold the bonds for $44,000. Record (1) the interest entry, (2) the entry to adjust the bonds to fair value, (3) the sale entry, and (4) the entry to eliminate the Fair Value Adjustment account on June 30 of Year 2.

f. Repeat requirements b through e, assuming Sage Company elected to account for the bonds under the fair value option.

g. Summarize the income statement impact in Year 1 and Year 2 under each of the two methods from above.

Problem 14-15
Recording and Reporting Investments—Equity Method   **LO5**

Refer to the information in Problem 14-13, but now assume that on January 1 of Year 1, Rae Company elects to account for the investment using the fair value option.

Required

a. Provide all of the entries required for Rae Company for Year 1 and Year 2 including the investment purchase, receipt of declared dividends, and year-end adjusting entries. Assume that Rae Company accounts for the investment similarly to an asset measured at FV-NI except that the investment account is adjusted directly for market adjustments.

b. Show how the long-term investments in equity securities and the related investment income would be reported on the financial statements of Rae Company at the end of each year.

c. Instead, now assume that Rae Company records entries for this investment under the equity method during the year and adjusts the Investment account to fair value at year-end. Provide the entries required for Rae Company for Year 1 and Year 2 to record the investment purchase, share of net income, receipt of dividend, and year-end adjusting entries.

d. Show how the long-term investments in equity securities and the related investment income would be reported on the financial statements of Rae Company at the end of each year for requirement (c).

e. How do the net results on the balance sheet and income statement compare for requirement (b) and requirement (d)?

The following are descriptions of various debt and equity securities.

Problem 14-16
Classifying
Securities **LO1, 2,**
3, 4, 5

MBC

Investment Description	Debt or Equity Security	Investment Classification	Current or Noncurrent Asset
1. Starbucks Corporation's 50% ownership in President Starbucks Coffee (Shanghai).			
2. Starbucks Corporation's corporate debt securities, not held for short-term trading gains or expected to be retained for the full term. The company does not intend to sell the security sooner than one year.			
3. 3M's long-term investment in a municipal bond with NYC. The company does not intend to hold the bond to maturity.			
4. General Electric holds shares of corporate stock with intention of immediate resale.			
5. 3M's 3-month certificate of deposit, not held for short-term trading.			
6. U.S. Bancorp's mortgage-backed security investment that the company intends to hold for the full term.			
7. Kellogg's 50% interest in Multipro Singapore Pte. Ltd., a leading distributor of a variety of food products in Nigeria and Ghana.			
8. Alphabet has excess cash invested in money market funds.			
9. GM Corporation holds a significant influence on its equity investment in a joint venture in China.			
10. Lowe's holds shares of a mutual fund held for short-term gains.			

Required

Complete the table by identifying the type of security (debt or equity), the investment classification, and whether the investment is a current or noncurrent asset. For the investment classifications, use the following categories: (1) investment in trading securities, (2) investment in available-for-sale securities, (3) investment in equity method securities, (4) investment in held-to-maturity securities, and (5) investment in FV-NI securities. Choose the most likely classification based on the information provided.

Olympians Inc. holds a bond investment in LAX Corporation. The amortized cost of the investment is $280,000 at Olympians year-end on December 31. Olympians Inc. estimates the fair value of the bonds to be $250,000. The unrealized loss of $30,000 is partially due to a credit loss of $20,000 with the remaining portion due to other factors.

Problem 14-17
Accounting for Impairment
of Investments **LO6**

Required

Record any journal entries required for each of the following separate scenarios. Include the elimination of any fair value adjustment account with an entry if appropriate.

a. Record the impairment loss on December 31 assuming that (1) the company does not intend to sell the asset and does not believe it is *more likely than not* that it will be required to sell the investment before recovery of any unrealized loss, (2) the company classifies the investments as AFS, and (3) the AFS bonds were adjusted to fair value through OCI on December 31.

b. Record the impairment loss on December 31 assuming that (1) the company does not intend to sell the asset and does not believe it is *more likely than not* that it will be required to sell the investment before recovery of any unrealized loss, (2) the company classifies the investments as AFS, (3) the AFS bonds were adjusted to fair value through OCI on December 31, and (4) the estimated credit loss is $40,000.

c. Record the impairment loss on December 31 assuming that (1) the company intends to sell the asset, (2) the company classifies the investment as AFS, and (3) the AFS bonds were adjusted to fair value through OCI on December 31.

d. Record the impairment loss on December 31 assuming that (1) the company intends to sell the asset, (2) the company classifies the investment as HTM, and (3) an estimate of the allowance for credit losses is $20,000.

e. Record the impairment loss on December 31 assuming that (1) the company does not intend to sell the asset and does not believe it is *more likely than not* that it will be required to sell the investment before recovery of any unrealized loss, (2) the company classifies the investments as TS, and (3) the TS bonds were adjusted to fair value through net income on December 31.

Accounting Decisions and Judgments

AD&J14-1
Analyzing Equity
Method **LO5**

Real World Analysis In its Year 8 annual report, **Xerox Corporation** has several items in its financial statements that refer to investments measured using the equity method (which are labeled "affiliated companies" by Xerox).

$ millions	Year 8	Year 7
From the income statement:		
Equity in net income of unconsolidated affiliated companies and other income.	$ 74	$ 127
From the balance sheet:		
Investment in affiliates, at equity	1,456	1,332
From the statement of cash flows:		
Adjustments to reconcile income to cash flows		
Undistributed equity in net income of affiliates*.	(27)	(84)

*These are amounts added back (subtracted from) net income to obtain cash flow from operations.

Assume that there are no adjustments required for differences between carrying amount and fair value at the date of acquisition, associated with the affiliated companies.

Required

a. On the income statement, equity income is combined with "other income." From the information presented, what is the maximum amount that Xerox could have received in declared dividends from its affiliated companies in Year 8? In Year 7? Now suppose Xerox received no dividends from its affiliated companies in Year 8. In this case, how much of the $74 million is other income?

b. Did Xerox increase or decrease its investments in affiliated companies during Year 8 beyond the amount of Xerox's equity in earnings retained by the investee? If so, by how much?

c. What rate of return on average assets did Xerox earn on its investment in affiliated companies in Year 8? Assume that other income in Year 8 is zero.

d. Suppose there is only one affiliated company in Xerox's investment, and it is a 50% owned joint venture. What would you estimate the total stockholders' equity of that company to be at December 31 of Year 8?

AD&J14-2
Analyzing Equity
Method **LO5**

Real World Analysis **Kimberly-Clark** is a global consumer products company with total assets in excess of $11 billion. In Year 8, total revenues were over $12 billion from sales in over 150 countries. To conduct its global operations, Kimberly-Clark has an equity interest in over 60 companies. Some of these are wholly (100%) owned, while others have lesser percentages of ownership.

Data from the Year 8 annual report provide information referring to its investments measured using the equity method (which are labeled "equity companies" by Kimberly-Clark).

$ millions	Year 8	Year 7
From the balance sheet:		
Investments in equity companies	$ 813.1	$ 567.7
From the income statement:		
Share of net income of equity companies.	137.1	157.3
From the statement of cash flows:		
Increases (decreases) to adjust net income to cash flows from operations		
Equity companies' earnings in excess of dividends paid.	(15.1)	(62.1)
Notes disclosures:		
Net income of equity companies.	294.6	338.1
Total stockholders' equity of equity companies	1,522.3	1,063.2

Required

a. In the notes, Kimberly-Clark provides information on the percentage ownership of its various affiliated companies. How would you expect Kimberly-Clark to account for each of the following companies, based on the percentage of ownership reported?

1. Kimberly-Clark Southern Africa Holdings Limited, Johannesburg, South Africa (50% plus one share)
2. Kimberly-Clark Canada Inc. (100%)
3. Kimberly-Clark Pudumjee Limited, Pune, India (51%)
4. Hogla-Kimberly, Hadera, Israel (49.9%)
5. Tecnosura, Colombia (29%)

b.   Based on the information given in the statement of cash flows, it is apparent that in Year 8 Kimberly-Clark received cash dividends from its equity companies of $122.0 million (equal to $137.1 million minus the undistributed portion of $15.1 million). Provide the journal entries to record the recognition of Kimberly-Clark's share of net income of the equity companies and the receipt of dividends (assume declared and paid in current year) from these companies.

c.   Kimberly-Clark increased its interest in equity companies during Year 8. Determine the amount of investment Kimberly-Clark made in the equity companies during Year 8.

d.   For both Year 7 and Year 8, estimate the average percent ownership that Kimberly-Clark has in equity companies based on its share of net income. Is the direction of change in ownership consistent with increasing or decreasing investment in equity companies?

e.   Suppose there was no change in percent ownership. What effect would consolidating the equity companies have on Kimberly-Clark's Year 8 net income? In general terms, what effect would consolidating have on the reported total assets of Kimberly-Clark?

Real World Analysis   Refer to Note 6 from the Year 4 Coca-Cola annual report provided below and answer the questions that follow.

AD&J14-3
Analyzing Equity
Method **LO5**

NOTE 6: EQUITY METHOD INVESTMENTS

Our consolidated net income includes our Company's proportionate share of the net income or loss of our equity method investees. When we record our proportionate share of net income, it increases equity income (loss)—net in our consolidated statements of income and our carrying value in that investment. Conversely, when we record our proportionate share of a net loss, it decreases equity income (loss)—net in our consolidated statements of income and our carrying value in that investment. The Company's proportionate share of the net income or loss of our equity method investees includes significant operating and nonoperating items recorded by our equity method investees. These items can have a significant impact on the amount of equity income (loss)—net in our consolidated statements of income and our carrying value in those investments. Refer to Note 17 for additional information related to significant operating and nonoperating items recorded by our equity method investees. The carrying values of our equity method investments are also impacted by our proportionate share of items impacting the equity investee's AOCI.

We eliminate from our financial results all significant intercompany transactions, including the intercompany portion of transactions with equity method investees.

The Company's equity method investments include our ownership interests in Coca-Cola FEMSA, Coca-Cola Hellenic and Coca-Cola Amatil. As of December 31, Year 4, we owned 28 percent, 23 percent and 29 percent, respectively, of these companies' outstanding shares. As of December 31, Year 4, our investment in our equity method investees in the aggregate exceeded our proportionate share of the net assets of these equity method investees by $1,671 million. This difference is not amortized.

A summary of financial information for our equity method investees in the aggregate is as follows (in millions):

For Year Ended December 31	Year 4	Year 3	Year 2
Net operating revenues	$52,627	$53,038	$47,087
Cost of goods sold	31,810	32,377	28,821
Gross profit	$20,817	$20,661	$18,266
Operating income	$ 4,489	$ 4,380	$ 4,605
Consolidated net income	$ 2,440	$ 2,364	$ 2,993
Less: Net income attributable to noncontrolling interests	74	62	89
Net income attributable to common shareowners	$ 2,366	$ 2,302	$ 2,904
Equity income (loss) — net	$ 769	$ 602	$ 819

At December 31	Year 4	Year 3
Current assets	$16,184	$19,229
Noncurrent assets	40,080	40,427
Total assets	$56,264	$59,656
Current liabilities	$12,477	$14,386
Noncurrent liabilities	16,657	17,779
Total liabilities	$29,134	$32,165
Equity attributable to shareowners of investees	$26,363	$26,668
Equity attributable to noncontrolling interests	767	823
Total equity	$27,130	$27,491
Company equity investment	$ 9,947	$10,393

Net sales to equity method investees, the majority of which are located outside the United States, were $10,063 million, $9,178 million, and $7,082 million in Year 4, Year 3, and Year 2, respectively. Total payments, primarily marketing, made to equity method investees were $1,605 million, $1,807 million, and $1,587 million in Year 4, Year 3, and Year 2, respectively. In addition, purchases of finished products from equity method investees were $381 million, $415 million, and $392 million in Year 4, Year 3, and Year 2, respectively.

If valued at the December 31, Year 4, quoted closing prices of shares actively traded on stock markets, the value of our equity method investments in publicly traded bottlers would have exceeded our carrying value by $5,443 million.

Total net receivables due from equity method investees were $1,448 million and $1,308 million as of December 31, Year 4 and Year 3, respectively. The total amount of dividends received from equity method investees was $398 million, $401 million, and $393 million for the years ended December 31, Year 4, Year 3, and Year 2, respectively. Dividends received included a $35 million special dividend from Coca-Cola Hellenic during Year 2. We classified the receipt of the special dividend in cash flows from operating activities because our cumulative equity in earnings from Coca-Cola Hellenic exceeded the cumulative distributions received; therefore, the dividends were deemed to be a return on our investment and not a return of our investment.

Required

a. Does Coca-Cola have investments in affiliated companies for which it accounts using the equity method? What is the percentage ownership of each investee?

b. At December 31, Year 4 (the most current year), what is the total amount of assets over which Coca-Cola has "significant influence" as a result of its equity investments? What is the total amount of "investment" Coca-Cola reports in its financial statements for investees? What is the fair value for these investments?

c. What is the reported income from all of Coca-Cola's equity investments in Year 4? Considering only this income, does it appear that Coca-Cola is earning a large return on its equity investments?

d. In what additional ways does Coca-Cola benefit from its equity investments other than its equity in the earnings of these companies?

e. If all the equity method investments were consolidated into the Coca-Cola financial statements, what would be the effect on Coca-Cola's net income in Year 4? Assuming there are no intercompany receivables or payables to be eliminated, what would be the effect on Coca-Cola's total assets?

f. Comment on why Coca-Cola might use a strategy of acquiring a significant but less than 50% ownership in its various bottlers.

AD&J14-4
Identifying Significant
Influence **LO5**

Real World Analysis The Trueblood case series, prepared by Deloitte professionals, are based on recent accounting technical issues that require research and judgment. The cases are accessed through the Deloitte foundation at: https://www2.deloitte.com/us/en/pages/about-deloitte/articles/trueblood-case-studies-deloitte-foundation.html.

The following case is relevant to the content provided in this chapter: Case: 22-6 Zoovest Capital. This case requires an analysis of whether an investor has significant influence over an investee.

AD&J14-5
Classifying Investments in
Debt Securities **LO1,
2, 3**

Judgment Case GAAP requires investments in debt securities to be classified as held-to-maturity, as trading securities, or as available-for-sale securities.

Required

a. At what carrying value are investments in debt securities recorded for each of the three classifications? What treatment is given to differences between carrying value and original cost, if any, in terms of how they are reported in the financial statements?

b. Suppose a company makes an investment in a debt security at the beginning of its fiscal year. The debt security is acquired at face value (that is, there is no premium or discount), and the security matures in three years. At the purchase of the securities, management overlooks the issue of how to classify the investment security.

1. At year-end the market price of the security has declined significantly because of a substantial increase in interest rates for investment securities of similar risk. What are some reasons management might wish to classify this investment into each of the three categories to manage its reported earnings?

2. At year-end the market price of the security has increased significantly because of a substantial decline in interest rates for investment securities of similar risk. What are some reasons management might wish to classify this investment into each of the three categories to manage its reported earnings?

AD&J14-6
Recording Investments in
Equity Securities: Cash and
Stock Dividends, Stock
Split **LO4**

Challenge Problem Hewlett Company purchased common stock (par value $10 and 50,000 shares outstanding) of Packard Corporation as a long-term investment. Transactions (which occurred in the order given) related to this investment follow.

1. Purchased 600 shares of Packard common stock at $90 per share (designated lot 1).
2. Purchased 2,000 shares of Packard common stock at $96 per share (designated lot 2).

3. At the end of the first year, Packard Corporation declared and paid a cash dividend of $2.00 per share.
4. At the end of the first year, Packard Corporation reported net income of $52,000 and the stock was selling at $97 per share.
5. After reporting net income of $5,000 for the second year, Packard Corporation issued a stock dividend whereby each stockholder received one additional share for every two shares owned.
6. After the stock dividend at the end of the second year, the stock was selling at $85.
7. Packard Corporation revised its charter to provide for a stock split. The par value was reduced to $5. The old common stock was turned in, and the holders received in exchange two shares of the new stock for each old share turned in.

Required

Provide the entries for each transaction 1 through 6 for Hewlett Company. Hewlett has an insignificant influence over Packard. *Hint:* Review concepts in Chapter 19.

Codification Skills How are the terms (1) equity security, (2) fair value, (3) holding gain or loss, (4) readily determinable fair value, and (5) debt security defined in the Codification?

AD&J14-7
Defining Terms **LO1, 2, 3, 4, 5, 6**

Codification Skills Our audit client is trying to determine whether a debt security should be classified as a trading security or an available-for-sale security. Does the Codification provide guidance on a specific time period that an investor intends to hold a security? Is there a defined cut-off for an intended holding period?

Identify the relevant authoritative guidance.

FASB ASC ☐ - ☐ - ☐ - ☐

AD&J14-8
Performing Accounting Research **LO2, 3**

Codification Skills The Codification provides guidance on the criteria of holding a debt security as a held-to-maturity security. The holder must have a positive intent and ability to hold the security to maturity. If the security may be sold before its maturity date because of possible changes such as market rate changes or foreign currency risk changes, or due to liquidity needs, the holder should not classify the security as a held-to-maturity security.

Assume a company meets the requirements to classify a security as held-to-maturity in both intent and ability. What unanticipated circumstances may arise that could change the status of a particular held-to-maturity security, without calling into question other held-to-maturity classifications?

Identify the relevant authoritative guidance.

FASB ASC ☐ - ☐ - ☐ - ☐

AD&J14-9
Performing Accounting Research **LO1**

Appendices—Multiple Choice

Complete MC14-4.

AppMC 14-1
Determining FVA Balance for TS **LO7**

Complete MC14-5.

AppMC 14-2
Computing Bond Price Including Any Accrued Interest **LO7**

Complete MC14-6.

AppMC 14-3
Determining Financial Statement Effects of AFS Security **LO8**

Complete MC14-7.

AppMC 14-4
Determining Financial Statement Effects of Equity Securities **LO9**

Appendices—Brief Exercises

AppBE14-1
Recording Entries for
TS **LO7**

Complete BE14-9.

AppBE14-2
Recording Entries for
TS **LO7**

Complete BE14-10.

AppBE14-3
Reporting TS Transactions
Using the Accounting
Equation **LO7**

Complete BE14-11.

AppBE14-4
Reporting TS Transactions
Using the Accounting
Equation **LO7**

Complete BE14-13.

AppBE14-5
Recognizing Income
Under the Fair Value
Option **LO7**

Complete BE14-14.

AppBE14-6
Recording the Entry for
Sale of TS Debt Trading
Securities **LO7**

Referring to information in BE14-9, assume that Henry Inc. sold its holdings of Container Corporation bonds on July 2 for $4,800. Assume that the company adjusts the Fair Value Adjustment account only at year-end.

a.   Record the sale of the debt investment.

b.   Adjust the Fair Value Adjustment account on December 31, the company's year-end.

AppBE14-7
Reporting the Sale of TS
Debt Trading Securities
Using the Accounting
Equation **LO7**

Refer to AppBE14-6, but instead of journal entries, show the effect on the accounting equation for the transactions, including identifying the individual accounts affected, and the total impact on assets, liabilities, and stockholders' equity.

AppBE14-8
Recording Entries for AFS
Securities **LO8**

Complete BE14-15.

AppBE 14-9
Reporting Transactions
for AFS Securities
Using the Accounting
Equation **LO8**

Complete BE14-16.

AppBE14-10
Adjusting AFS Securities to
Fair Value **LO8**

Complete BE14-17.

AppBE14-11
Adjusting AFS Securities to
Fair Value **LO8**

Complete BE14-18.

Complete BE14-19.

AppBE14-12
Determining Impact on
Financial Reporting of
Unrealized Losses **LO8**

Complete BE14-20.

AppBE14-13
Reporting Comprehensive
Income with
Reclassification
Adjustments **LO8**

Complete BE14-21.

AppBE14-14
Recording Transactions for
AFS Security **LO8**

Complete BE14-22.

AppBE14-15
Reporting Transactions
for AFS Security
Using the Accounting
Equation **LO8**

Complete BE14-23.

AppBE14-16
Determining
Adjustments to Debt
Securities **LO1, 7, 8**

Clyde Inc. purchased a bond investment at its face value on March 1 of Year 1 for $100,000 and classified it as an available-for-sale security. At its year-end of December 31, the company adjusted the investment to its fair value of $98,000. On March 31 of Year 2, the company sold the security for $102,000. Record the following entries, ignoring any interest revenue entries for simplicity. Assume that the company adjusts the Fair Value Adjustment account only at year-end on December 31.

a. Purchase of investment on March 1 of Year 1.
b. Adjusting entry on December 31 of Year 1.
c. Sale on March 31 of Year 2.
d. Adjusting entry on December 31 of Year 2.

AppBE14-17
Recording the Entry for
Sale of AFS Debt Trading
Securities **LO8**

Refer to AppBE14-17, but instead of journal entries, show the effect on the accounting equation for the transactions, including identifying the individual accounts affected, and the total impact on assets, liabilities, and stockholders' equity.

AppBE14-18
Reporting the Sale of AFS
Debt Trading Securities
Using the Accounting
Equation **LO8**

Complete BE14-26.

AppBE14-19
Recording Entries
for Equity Securities:
FV-NI **LO9**

Complete BE14-27.

AppBE14-20
Analyzing Fair
Value Adjustment
Account **LO9**

AppBE14-21
Reporting Entries of Equity Securities: FV-NI **LO9**

An investor purchased 100 shares of Mallard common stock at $20 per share on March 15 of Year 1. On December 31 of Year 1, the stock was quoted at $19 per share and Mallard declared and paid a dividend of $1.50 per share. On June 5 of Year 2, the investor sold all 100 shares for $22 per share. At year-end on December 31 of each year, the Fair Value Adjustment account is adjusted. Assuming the investment is measured at FV-NI, provide the journal entries to be made at each of the following dates.

a.	March 15, Year 1.	*c.*	June 5, Year 2.
b.	December 31, Year 1.	*d.*	December 31, Year 2.

AppBE14-22
Reporting Entries of Equity Securities (FV-NI) Using the Accounting Equation **LO9**

Refer to AppBE14-21, but instead of journal entries, show the effect on the accounting equation for the transactions, including identifying the individual accounts affected, and the total impact on assets, liabilities, and stockholders' equity.

AppBE14-23
Recording the Transfer from FV-NI to Equity Method **LO10**

On January 1, Big Apple Inc.'s holding of 1,800 shares of the 10,000 shares outstanding of common stock of Mack Corporation was originally purchased for $15 per share and has been measured at FV-NI. However, due to recent changes, Big Apple Inc. determined that it now has significant influence over Mack Corporation and should account for the investment as an equity investment. The fair value of Mack Corporation stock on January 1 is $30 per share. If Big Apple had accounted for the investment since the purchase date under the equity method, the Investment account would have a balance of $45,000. Record the entry on January 1 to transfer the Investment account from the accounting treatment of FV-NI to the equity method. Assume that the investment was adjusted to fair value on December 31 of the prior year.

AppBE14-24
Recording the Transfer from AFS to TS **LO10**
Hint: See Demo 14-7

Franklin Inc. makes the decision to change the classification of its current holding of Washington bonds, with an amortized cost of $20,000, from AFS to TS on January 1. On January 1, the fair value of the Washington investment is $15,000. Record the entry to transfer the security from AFS to TS on January 1.

AppBE14-25
Determining Gain or Loss on Call Option Settlement **LO11**
Hint: See Demo 14-9A

On January 1 of the current year, a call option was purchased by Beats Co. for $40, which allows Beats Co. to purchase 50 shares of Bieber Inc. stock at a strike price of $25 per share through December 31 of the following year. On January 1, the fair value of the stock is $25 per share. On June 30, the fair value of each share of Bieber Inc. stock is $28 per share, and the fair value of the option is $190. Assuming that Beats Co. settles the call option on June 30, what is the gain or loss (if any) recorded on June 30? Assume that the call option was adjusted to fair value before settlement.

AppBE14-26
Recording Entries for a Fair Value Hedge: Put Option **LO11**
Hint: See Demo 14-9B

Anchor Inc. is holding a put option classified as a fair value hedge, with an estimated value of $300 effective December 31. Assume that one month later, the fair value of the put option is $375.

Record the month-end adjusting entry (if any) required on January 31 of the following year to adjust the put option to fair value.

AppBE14-27
Recording Entries for a Fair Value Hedge: Interest Rate Swap **LO11**
Hint: See Demo 14-9C

Arial Inc. entered into a 3-year interest swap agreement, which requires Arial Inc. to make interest payments based on a designated benchmark interest rate and receive fixed interest payments based on 4.2% of a notional amount of $100,000. The interest rate swap hedges against Arial's $100,000 note payable, which calls for fixed interest payments over 3 years at 4.2%. The fair value of the interest rate swap at the initiation of the agreement is zero. Assuming that the interest rate swap meets the GAAP effectiveness criteria, record any required adjusting entries related to the fair value of the swap and underlying liability at the first reporting date of December 31, if at that time, the interest rate swap is valued at $1,200. Assume a benchmark interest rate of 4% at the reporting date.

AppBE14-28
Recording the Entry to Adjust Futures Contract **LO11**
Hint: See Demo 14-9D

A-Plus Company is holding a futures contract classified as a cash flow hedge with a value of $500 effective December 31. Assume that one month later, the fair value of the futures contract is $300.

Record the month-end adjusting entry (if any) required on January 31 of the next year to adjust the futures contract to fair value.

Complete E14-11.

AppE14-1
Recording Entries
under the Fair Value
Option—HTM **LO7**

Complete E14-12.

AppE14-2
Recording Entries under
the Fair Value Option—
AFS **LO7, 8**

Referring to E14-7, answer the following questions.

a. Prepare an amortization schedule for the life of the bonds using the effective interest method.

b. Record the entry for the purchase of the bonds by West Company on July 1 of Year 1.

c. Record the adjusting entries by West Company on December 31 of Year 1 to (1) accrue interest revenue and to update the investment's amortized cost (2) record the unrealized gain or loss. The fair value of the bonds at year-end on December 31 of Year 1 was $83,000.

d. Record the receipt of interest on January 1 of Year 2.

e. Record the sale of all of the bonds on January 2 of Year 2, for $83,050.

f. Record the adjustment to the Fair Value Adjustment account at year-end on December 31 of Year 2 assuming no additional TS investments.

AppE14-3
Reporting Entries for
TS—Effective Interest
Method **LO7**

Referring to E14-10, answer the following questions.

a. Record the entry for the receipt of quarterly interest from the Atlanta Corp. bonds on December 31 of Year 1.

b. Record the entry for the receipt of semiannual interest from the Dallas Inc. bonds on December 31 of Year 1.

c. Record the entry to adjust the bonds to fair value on December 31 of Year 1. The fair value of the Atlanta Corp. bonds and the Dallas Inc. bonds on December 31 of Year 1 were $110,000 and $45,000, respectively.

d. Indicate the total amount to be included on the December 31 of Year 1 balance sheet of Kennedy Company as investments in trading securities.

e. Record the entry to sell the Atlanta Corp. bonds on January 2 of Year 2 for $112,500.

f. Record the entry to sell the Dallas Inc. bonds on January 3 of Year 2 for $44,500.

g. Adjust the Fair Value Adjustment account on December 31 of Year 2.

h. Determine the investment-related impact on net income for Year 1 and for Year 2.

AppE14-4
Reporting Entries for TS—
Par Value **LO7**

Complete E14-13.

AppE14-5
Recording Entries for AFS
Debt Securities—Effective
Interest Method **LO8**

Complete E14-14.

AppE14-6
Reporting Transactions
for AFS (Effective
Interest Method)
Using the Accounting
Equation **LO8**

Complete E14-17.

AppE14-7
Adjusting AFS Debt
Securities to Fair
Value **LO8**

Referring to E14-15, answer the following questions.

a. Prepare an amortization schedule for Year 1 and Year 2 using the effective interest method.

b. Record the entry for the purchase of the bonds by West Company on July 1 of Year 1.

AppE14-8
Reporting Entries for AFS
Debt Securities—Effective
Interest Method **LO8**

c.   Record the adjusting entries by West Company on December 31 of Year 1 to (1) accrue interest revenue and to update the investment's amortized cost and (2) adjust the investment to fair value. The fair value of the bonds at December 31 of Year 1 was $81,000.

d.   Indicate the effects of this investment on the Year 1 income statement and the year-end balance sheet.

e.   Record the receipt of interest on January 1 of Year 2.

f.   After the interest receipt on July 1 of Year 2, two of the bonds were sold for $19,300 cash. Record the entry for (1) the receipt of interest and (2) the sale of the bond investment.

g.   On December 31 of Year 2, the company's year-end, record the entry to eliminate the Fair Value Adjustment balance associated with the two bonds sold.

AppE14-9
Recording and Reporting
AFS Securities   **LO8**

Referring to E14-18, answer the following questions.

a.   Record the adjusting entry on December 31 of Year 1 to adjust the AFS debt investments to fair value.

b.   What is the balance in the Fair Value Adjustment—AFS account on January 1 of Year 2?

c.   Record the sale of the Glacier bond investment.

d.   Record the adjusting entry on December 31 of Year 2 to adjust the AFS debt investments to fair value. Assume that no adjustments to Fair Value Adjustment—AFS were made during the year.

e.   Indicate the effect on net income and other comprehensive income in Year 2 for these transactions.

f.   Prepare the reclassification disclosure of accumulated other comprehensive income to include in the notes accompanying the financial statements of Banff Company for Year 2.

AppE14-10
Recording and Reporting
Equity Investment:
FV-NI   **LO9**

Refer to E14-19, but for part *d*, now assume that the Fair Value Adjustment account is adjusted for the investment portfolio on December 31 of Year 2.

AppE14-11
Recording Entries for Equity
Investment: FV-NI   **LO9**

On September 1, Tech Company purchased 2,000 shares of common stock of Eagle Inc. for $200,000 while not obtaining significant influence over Eagle Inc. On November 1, Tech Company sold 1,000 shares of the Eagle Inc. stock for $105 per share and incurred brokerage fees of $480 on the sale. At December 31, Eagle Inc. declared and paid dividends of $5 per share. The fair value of the remaining investment in Eagle Inc. was $110,000 on December 31. The annual accounting periods for both Tech and Eagle end on December 31.

Required

a.   Purchase on September 1.   *c.*   Dividends declared and received on December 31.

b.   Sale of shares on November 1.   *d.*   Adjustment to fair value on December 31.

AppE14-12
Recording Entries for Equity
Investment: FV-NI   **LO9**

Referring to E14-21, answer the following questions.

a.   Prepare the entry for (1) the sale of Spartan and (2) the sale of Wildcat common stock on June 1.

b.   Record the purchase of Gopher common stock on August 1.

c.   Prepare any adjusting entry needed at the current year-end of December 31.

AppE14-13
Adjusting Fair
Value Adjustment
Account—Equity
Investments   **LO9**

Complete E14-22.

AppE14-14
Recording Entries for Equity
Investment: FV-NI   **LO9**

5M Corporation completed the following transactions, in the order given, for the portfolio of stocks held as equity investments measured at FV-NI. Assume the annual accounting periods for all companies end on December 31.

Year 1

1.   Purchased 150 shares of Starbux Corporation common stock (par value $1) at $50 per share plus a brokerage commission of 4% and transfer costs of $50 on August 1.

2.   Purchased 300 shares of Kolgate Corporation Class A common stock (par value $0.50) at $35 per share plus transfer costs of $75 on September 15.

Year 2

1.   Purchased 275 shares of Starbux Corporation common stock at $55 per share plus a brokerage commission of 4% and transfer costs of $60 on February 1.

2.   Received the declared cash dividends of $2.00 per share on the Kolgate Corporation Class A common stock on June 30.

3. Sold 75 shares of Starbux Corporation common stock at $58 per share on August 15.

4.

Year-End Stock Prices	Year 1	Year 2
Starbux, common stock	$48	$60
Kolgate, Class A common stock.	38	50

Required

a. Provide entries for 5M Corporation for the purchases of equity securities in Year 1.
b. Provide entries for 5M Corporation to adjust securities to fair value on December 31 of Year 1.
c. Record the purchase of Starbux Corporation common stock in Year 2.
d. Record the receipt of declared dividends on the Kolgate common stock in Year 2.
e. Record the sale of Starbux common stock in Year 2. Assume FIFO (first-in, first-out) order when shares are sold.
f. Provide the entry for 5M Corporation on December 31 of Year 2 to adjust the Fair Value Adjustment account.

Glacier Inc. held the following investments in an HTM security portfolio at December 31 of Year 1.

AppE14-15
Accounting for Transfer
from HTM to AFS **LO10**

Security	Cost	Fair Value at Dec. 31, Year 1	Unrealized Gain (Loss)
Rain Gear Company bonds	$ 57,000	$ 65,000	$ 8,000
Camping Unlimited Inc. bonds . . .	76,000	86,000	10,000
Total	$133,000	$151,000	$18,000

Both bonds were purchased at par value. At January 1 of Year 2 Glacier Inc. changed its intent from holding the bonds to maturity to holding these securities for an indefinite period of time due to a decrease in the credit standings of both investees. As a result, Glacier Inc. will begin to account for the securities as AFS beginning January 1 of Year 2.

Required
Record the entry on January 1 of Year 2, the date of transfer.

Refer to the information in App E14-15, but now assume that the bonds were originally recorded as AFS securities but are transferred to HTM bonds on January 1 of Year 2 due to a change in Glacier's ability and intent to now hold the securities to maturity. Both bonds have a remaining term of 10 years. Assume the company straight-line amortizes the unrealized gain to income.

AppE14-16
Accounting for
Transfer from AFS to
HTM **LO10**

Required

a. Record the entry on January 1 of Year 2, the date of transfer.
b. Record any required year-end adjusting entries on December 31 of Year 2 related to the HTM bonds.

On January 2, Starz Inc. established an agreement with Silver Co. allowing Starz Inc. to call 100 shares of Gold Inc. stock at a strike price of $45 per share through June 30 of the following year. On January 2, the current market price of Gold Inc. is $45 and the option premium is $200. On June 30, the fair value of the option is $900.

AppE14-17
Accounting for Call
Options **LO11**
Hint: See Demo 14-9A

Required

a. Prepare the journal entry on January 2 to record the purchase of the call option.
b. Prepare the entry to adjust the call option to fair value on June 30, assuming that the company is reporting mid-year financial statements.
c. At what price per share of Gold Inc. will the call option become valuable to Starz Inc.?

PierTwo purchased at par 100 $100 5% bonds of Supplier Inc. on January 1. To avoid exposure to fluctuations in the fair value of Supplier Inc. bonds, PierTwo acquires a 12-month put option on January 1 to sell 100 bonds of Supplier Inc. at a price of $100 per bond. The hedge is considered to be highly effective. On December 31, the market price per share of Supplier Inc. bonds fell to $90 per bond while the value of the put option is estimated to be $1,000. For simplicity, ignore interest on the bonds and assume the purchase price of the put option is zero.

AppE14-18
Accounting for Fair
Value Hedge: Put
Option **LO11**

Required

a. Prepare the year-end entry to adjust the investment to fair value on December 31.
b. Prepare the year-end entry to adjust the put option to fair value on December 31.

AppE14-19
Accounting for Fair Value
Hedge: Interest Rate
Swap **LO11**
Hint: See Demo 14-9C

On January 2, Badger Corp. enters into a 5-year interest rate swap contract to effectively hedge a 5-year, 5%, $10,000 note, issued on January 2. The swap calls for Badger Corp. to receive payments semiannually on June 30 and December 31 from the counterparty at a 5% interest rate based on a notional amount of $10,000 and to make payments to the counterparty based upon a designated benchmark interest rate. The benchmark interest rate is 4.2% as of January 2 and the rate will be adjusted every 6 months to the current benchmark interest rate. For simplicity, assume that the swap has zero value on January 2 and on June 30.

Required

a. Prepare the journal entry on January 2 to record the issuance of the note and initiation of the interest rate swap agreement.
b. Prepare the entries related to the note payable and the interest rate swap on June 30 assuming the benchmark interest rate is unchanged.

AppE14-20
Accounting for Cash
Flow Hedge: Futures
Contract **LO11**

In October, Rye Company, a producer of a grain-based product, determined that it would need 10,000 bushels of grain near the end of February of the following year. Rye Company expects the current price of $4 per bushel of grain to change and does not want to assume the risk of such market price changes. As a result, Rye Company enters into a futures contract with Chicago Clearing House Inc. (CCH) to hedge the risk of market price changes of grain. The cost of the cash flow hedge (futures contract) is zero. The futures contract provides that Rye Company purchases the grain at the date needed at market price, but CCH must pay Rye Company any differences above $4/bushel while Rye Company pays to CCH any differences below $4/bushel. Assume that the market price of grain is $4.20/bushel on December 31 and that Rye Company settles the futures contract with CCH and purchases the 10,000 bushels on February 20 of the following year in the market for $4.30/bushel.

Required
Prepare the following entries for Rye Company related to the futures contract.

a. Prepare the journal entry required on November 1 (if any) related to the purchase of the futures contract.
b. Prepare the journal entry required on December 31 (if any) for the futures contract.
c. Prepare the journal entry required on February 20 of the following year for the settlement of the futures contract and purchase of the grain.
d. Record the entry needed to reclassify any unrealized gain or loss when the inventory is sold.

Appendices—Problems

AppP14-1
Recording and Reporting
TS: Premium, Semiannual,
Straight-Line **LO7**

Complete P14-5.

AppP14-2
Recording Entries for
Equity Investment:
FV-NI **LO7**

Refer to P14-6 to answer the following questions.
a. Prepare the entry for New Edition to record the purchase of the bonds on January 1.
b. Prepare any adjusting entries required on December 31.
c. Indicate what items and amounts should be reported on the current year income statement and the December 31 balance sheet.
d. New Edition sold the bonds on January 2 of Year 2 at 95. Record the sale of the investment.
e. On December 31 of Year 2, the company's year-end, record the entry to eliminate the Fair Value Adjustment account associated with the bonds

---

AppP14-3
Recording and
Reporting HTM and AFS
Securities: Discount,
Semiannual, Effective
Interest **LO1,8**

Complete P14-2.

AppP14-4
Recording and Reporting
HTM and AFS Securities:
Premium, Semiannual,
Effective Interest **LO8**

Complete P14-3.

Refer to P14-7 to answer the following questions.

AppP14-5
Recording and Reporting
AFS Debt Securities;
Reclassification **LO8**

a. Record the sale of Saturn bonds on January 5 of the current year.

b. Adjust the Fair Value Adjustment account on December 31 of the current year.

c. Prepare a reconciliation of other comprehensive income from January 1 to December 31 of the current year.

Refer to P14-10 to answer the following questions.

AppP14-6
Recording and Reporting
Investments in Equity
Securities—FV-NI **LO9**

a. Prepare entries that Raven Company should make on (1) September 1 of Year 1 and (2) December 31 of Year 1.

b. Provide the investment items and amounts that should be reported on the Year 1 income statement and year-end balance sheet.

c. Prepare the entries for the Year 2 transactions, plus any required year-end adjusting entries.

d. Provide the investment items and amounts that should be reported on the Year 2 income statement and year-end balance sheet.

Complete P14-9.

AppP14-7
Recording and Reporting
Investments in
Securities—Fair Value,
HTM **LO1, 7, 8, 9**

On January 1 of Year 1, Laker Company acquired the following equity securities and classified them as having insignificant influence.

AppP14-8
Recording and Reporting
Investments in Equity
Securities—FV-NI **LO9**

Co.	Description	Quantity	Unit Cost
T	Common stock (no par)	1,000 shares	$20
U	Common stock (par $10)	1,000 shares	15
V	Preferred stock (par $20, nonconvertible)	400 shares	30
W	Common stock (no par)	1,000 shares	10

Per share data subsequent to the acquisition follow.

Dec. 31, Year 1   Fair values: T stock, $16; U stock, $15; V stock, $35; and W stock, $9.90.
Feb. 10, Year 2   Cash dividends declared and received: T stock, $1.50; U stock, $1; and V stock, $0.50.
Nov. 1, Year 2   Sold the shares of V stock at $38.
Dec. 31, Year 2   Fair values: T stock, $13; U stock, $17; and W stock, $10.15.

The company adjusts securities to fair value on its December 31 reporting dates.

Required

a. Provide the following entries for Laker Company for Year 1 and Year 2, assuming that the Fair Value Adjustment account for the investment portfolio is updated annually at its December 31 year-end.

   1. Purchase of equity securities on January 1 of Year 1.
   2. Adjustment to fair value on December 31 of Year 1.
   3. Receipt of declared dividends on February 10 of Year 2.
   4. Sale of V stock on November 1 of Year 2.
   5. Adjustment to fair value on December 31 of Year 2.

b. Provide the income statement and balance sheet presentation for Laker Company that would reflect these investments for Year 1 and for Year 2.

Spectrum Inc. is involved in a variety of investment transactions during the second quarter of the year ended June 30. To begin the quarter, Spectrum Inc. held shares of Atlanta Co. stock, the details follow.

AppP14-9
Recording Investments
in Debt and Equity
Securities—FV-NI, Equity
Method **LO1, 5, 7,
8, 9**

Investment holdings on April 1
Atlanta Co.: 2,000 shares of common stock purchased at $20,000; accounted for under FV-NI.

Second quarter transactions follow.

Apr.	1	Spectrum Inc. purchases $30,000 of face amount bonds issued by Madison Inc. at par plus accrued interest. The bonds have an interest rate of 5% and pay interest semiannually on April 30 and October 31. The investment is classified as AFS.
Apr.	2	Purchased 2,000 shares of the 8,000 shares outstanding of Detroit Inc. stock at $50 per share. Assume that Spectrum accounts for the investment using the equity method.
Apr.	15	Dividends of $1.00 per share are declared and received on the Atlanta Co. common shares.
Apr.	30	Received interest on the Madison bonds.
May	5	Sold 150 shares of Atlanta Co. stock for $15 a share.

June 30   Detroit Inc. reports net income of $20,000 for the second quarter of the year.
June 30   Detroit Inc. declares and pays dividends of $2.00 per share.
June 30   Market price per share of Atlanta Co. and Detroit Inc. is $18 and $54, respectively. The market
            price of the Madison Inc. bonds is 98.

Required

Record the entries for the second quarter of the year, assuming a $10,000 debit balance in the Fair Value Adjustment
account on March 30. Spectrum Inc. updates its Fair Value Adjustment account for its investment portfolio quarterly.

AppP14-10
Accounting for Transfer
from FV-NI to Equity
Method **LO10**

Duluth Travel Adventures reported the following regarding its investment in Superior Company common stock
at year-end on December 31 of Year 1.

Investments in Superior	$78,000
Less: Fair Value Adjustment	(6,000)
Investment in Superior, at fair value	$72,000

Duluth has only one security, Superior Company common stock, measured at FV-NI and purchased at the beginning
of Year 1. Duluth owns 1,000 of the 5,000 outstanding voting shares of Superior common but was not allowed to
influence the company. On January 2 of Year 2, Duluth is able to elect two of its senior management to Superior's
board of directors and determines that it can now exert significant influence over Superior.

Required

Provide the January 2 of Year 2 entry to record the reclassification of the investment in Superior from the FV-NI
measurement to the equity method.

AppP14-11
Accounting for Call
Options **LO11**

Champion Inc. purchased a call option as a speculative investment on January 1 of Year 1 for $125, allowing
Champion Inc. to purchase 200 of Rising Star Co. common shares at $100 per share through January 1 of Year 2.
Champion Inc. prepared the following table to track the activity of this investment during Year 1.

Date	Rising Star Co.: Market Price per Share	Call Option: Fair Value per Option
Jan. 1.	$100	$125
June 30.	90	50
Dec. 31.	102	400

Required

a. Prepare the following journal entries for Champion Inc.
    1. Purchase of the call option on January 1 of Year 1.
    2. Adjust the call option to fair value on June 30 of Year 1 assuming that the company is reporting mid-
        year financial statements.
    3. Adjust the call option to fair value on December 31 of Year 1 assuming that the company is reporting
        year-end financial statements.
b. What is the impact on the income statement of holding this speculative investment during the year?

AppP14-12
Accounting for Fair Value
Hedge: Interest Rate
Swap **LO11**

On January 1 of Year 1, Innovative Lab issued a 4-year $50,000 note to a local bank with fixed interest payments
based on 6%, payable annually on December 31. To hedge the risk of a fixed interest payment, Innovative Lab
entered into a 4-year interest rate swap agreement on January 1 of Year 1, calling for interest payments tied to a
designated benchmark interest rate to a counterparty and receipt of interest based on 6%, negotiated at a notional
amount of $50,000. The settlement date for the net cash payment is on December 31 of each year. The follow-
ing table provides additional information related to the interest rate swap as forecasted at year-ends for the the
next four years.

	Dec. 31, Year 1	Dec. 31, Year 2	Dec. 31, Year 3	Dec. 31, Year 4
Fair value: interest rate swap	$ 200	$ 400	$ 0	$ 0
Fair value: note payable	$50,200	$50,400	$50,000	$50,000
Benchmark interest rate	4.2%	4.0%	5.2%	5.8%

Required

a. Record the required journal entries for Year 1, Year 2, Year 3, and Year 4 related to the note payable and interest rate swap agreement.

b. Compute the effect on net income for each year, Year 1 through Year 4, ignoring income tax.

c. What change(s) in the forecast would make the interest rate swap more valuable than it is projected to be currently?

Mellogs is a small company that produces corn-based breakfast foods. On November 1 of Year 1, the company obtains a contract to supply 2 million pounds of its corn-based breakfast product to a large customer based in Germany, with delivery to be made in May of Year 2. As a result, Mellogs will need to acquire 100,000 bushels of corn in March of Year 2 to fulfill this contract. The price of corn, currently at $3.60 per bushel, could increase dramatically between November 1 of Year 1 and March of Year 2. As a result, Mellogs entered into a futures contract with Capitol Clearing House Inc. (CCH) to hedge the risk of market price changes of corn. The cost of the cash flow hedge (futures contract) is zero. The futures contract provides that Mellogs Company purchases the corn needed at the date needed at market price, but CCH must pay Mellogs Company any differences above $3.60/bushel while Mellogs Company pays to CCH any differences below $3.60/bushel. Assume that the market price of corn is $3.80/bushel on December 31 of Year 1, and that Mellogs Company purchases the 100,000 bushels on March 3 of Year 2 for $3.50/bushel.

AppP14-13
Accounting for Cash
Flow Hedge: Futures
Contract   **LO11**

Required

a. Prepare the journal entry required on November 1 of Year 1 (if any) related to the purchase of the futures contract.

b. Prepare the year-end journal entry required on December 31 of Year 1 (if any) for the futures contract.

c. Prepare the journal entry required on March 3 of Year 2 for the (1) purchase of the corn and (2) execution of the futures contract.

d. Assuming that the 100,000 bushels of corn were utilized to fulfill the order in May of Year 2, at what amount is the cost of the corn included in the reported COGS on the sale?

Appendices—Accounting Decisions and Judgments

Judgment Case   Petersen Company purchased debt securities at a cost of $500,000 on March 1 of Year 1 and classified them as AFS, as it intended to hold them for more than one year. At December 31 of Year 1, the fair value of the securities was $470,000, and the investment was carried at this value on that year-end balance sheet date. At the end of the third quarter of the next year (September 30 of Year 2), management is considering reclassifying the securities as trading securities. Alternatively, management is considering waiting until December 31, the end of the fiscal year, to record the reclassification.

AppAD&J14-1
Reclassifying
Investments in Debt
Securities   **LO10**

Required

Suppose the securities have a fair value of $525,000 at September 30 of Year 2, have a fair value $515,000 on December 31 of Year 2, and are sold on May 1 of Year 3 for $510,000.

a. What are the effects on Year 2 income if the securities are (a) reclassified on September 30, (b) reclassified on December 31, or (c) not reclassified during Year 2? What would be the effect of the May sale on Year 3 income if the securities (a) were reclassified on September 30, (b) were reclassified on December 31, or (c) were not reclassified prior to their sale? Does the reclassification affect the total gain recorded over the two-year period?

b. The authoritative guidance indicates the following. How should this guidance inform management's decision in considering a reclassification?

> **320-10-35-12**   In addition, given the nature of a trading security, transfers into or from the trading category also should be rare.

Judgment Case   Bell Company acquired a 20% ownership interest in the outstanding voting stock of Harris Inc. on January 1 three years prior, at a cost of $800,000. At the time, Bell did not have significant influence over Harris, and so Bell measured the investment at FV-NI. As time passed, Bell gained more influence over Harris, culminating in the election of two members of Bell's management to the board of directors of Harris on December 31 of the current year. The investment has a current carrying value of $840,000 on Bell's books. An analysis of Harris Inc. reveals that 20%

AppAD&J14-2
Reclassifying Investments
from FV-NI to Equity
Method   **LO10**

of its carrying amount equals $750,000 and that 20% of its net assets measured at fair value equals $820,000. The accounting periods for both Bell and Harris end on December 31.

Required

a. Should Bell continue to account for its investment in Harris using FV-NI, or should it use the equity method? What issues would influence the answer to this question?

b. Suppose Bell adopts the equity method effective December 31 of the current year. What effect would the decision have on its current year income statement and year-end balance sheet?

c. Suppose Bell adopts the equity method effective on January 1 of the next year. What effect would the decision have on its next year income statement and balance sheet, relative to adoption as described in part b?

d. By adopting the equity method, what are some of the changes that Bell will make in recording its investment income from its investment in Harris?

AppAD&J14-3
Reclassifying Investments from TS to AFS: Management Incentives
LO2, 3, 10

Ethics Case Ace Investors Company buys and sells various debt securities. These security investments represent approximately 90% of the company's total assets. Ace has a policy of classifying all its investments as trading securities, since it has traditionally sold any individual security when management felt it advantageous to do so. The company is reconsidering this classification policy because securities are often held for many accounting periods before they are sold. Many members of senior management feel that the entire investment portfolio should be classified as AFS debt securities. A number of managers, however, are opposed to the change in classification policy. They are concerned about the effects of the policy change on their retirement pay, which is based on a formula involving the three-year average earnings of the company in the year of retirement. We have been asked to advise Ace on its decision regarding changing its classification policy.

Required

a. What are the fundamental distinctions between the classifications as trading securities and as available-for-sale securities?

b. Give possible reasons why the Ace managers are concerned about their retirement pay.

c. Do you see any ethical issues involved in the task we have been asked to undertake?

AppAD&J14-4
Recording and Reporting Investments in Debt Securities: Accrued Interest on Purchase and Sale, Transfer
LO2, 3, 10

Challenge Problem On September 1 of Year 1, New Company purchased 20 bonds of Old Corporation ($1,000, 6%) as an investment in trading securities at par plus accrued interest. The bonds pay annual interest each July 1. New Company paid cash, including accrued interest. New Company's annual reporting period ends December 31. At December 31, Old Corporation's bonds were quoted at 99.

Required

a. Provide the journal entry for New Company to record the purchase of the bonds.

b. Provide any adjusting entries required at December 31 of Year 1.

c. Provide the items and amounts that should be reported on New Company's Year 1 income statement and its December 31 of Year 1 balance sheet.

d. Provide the required entry on July 1 of Year 2.

e. On August 1 of Year 2, New Company sold 8 of the bonds at 100.5 plus accrued interest. The remaining 12 bonds were transferred to an AFS securities portfolio. Provide the required entry(ies). First adjust investments to fair value and derecognize the associate Fair Value Adjustment balance upon sale or transfer.

f. At December 31 of Year 2, the Old Corporation bonds were quoted at 101.5. There were no additional transactions during Year 2. Provide the entry(ies) to be made at December 31 of Year 2.

g. List the investment items and amounts that would be reported on the Year 2 income statement and the December 31 of Year 2 balance sheet.

AppAD&J14-5
Recording and Reporting Investment in Trading Securities: Purchases, Sale, Accrued Interest, Reclassification
LO2, 10

Challenge Problem At December 31 of Year 1, the portfolio of investments in trading securities held by Dow Company follows. Dow's annual reporting period ends on December 31.

Security	Par Value	Interest Rate	Interest Payable	Cash Cost*	Date Purchased	Maturity Date
X Corp. Bonds	$30,000	6%	Nov. 1	$30,000	Sept. 1, Year 1	Nov. 1, Year 6
Y Corp. Bonds	20,000	9%	Dec. 31	20,000	Dec. 31, Year 1	Dec. 31, Year 3

*Excluding any accrued interest

At December 31 of Year 1, the X Corporation bonds were selling at 100.5.

Transactions relating to the portfolio of short-term investments in debt securities during Year 2 follow.

continued from previous page

b. Repeat part *a* assuming that the note is noninterest-bearing and the present value of the note payable is $48,285. The company amortizes the discount using the straight-line method.

Example Two—Balance Sheet Reporting of Notes Payable

Complete the following table by indicating the amount of debt (ignoring any interest payable amounts) that will be classified as current and noncurrent on Blues Company's December 31 of Year 10 balance sheet. Assume that Year 10 financial statements are issued on March 1 of Year 11.

More Practice: BE15-25, E15-16, E15-17, P15-6

Debt Scenario (at December 31, Year 1)	Dec. 31, Year 10 Current Liability	Dec. 31, Year 10 Noncurrent Liability
1. Blues Company borrowed $500,000 by issuing an 8% note payable on December 31 of Year 6. The principal is due on December 31 of Year 11.		
2. On December 31 of Year 10, Blues Company had a $100,000 outstanding note payable with First Bank due in five years. The loan agreement with First Bank requires Blues Company to maintain a minimum current ratio of 1.5 for each monthly reporting period. On December 31 of Year 10, Blues Company's current ratio slips to 1.25 (current assets of $250,000 divided by current liabilities of $200,000) with the note payable classified as long-term. Blues Company obtains a letter from First Bank, waiving the bank's right to call the $100,000 loan in Year 11.		
3. Blues Company borrowed $500,000 by issuing an 8% note payable on December 31 of Year 6. The principal is due on January 31 of Year 11. However, the company extinguished the debt through a common stock issuance in January of Year 11.		
4. Blues Company has a $500,000 note payable due June 15 of Year 11. At the financial statement date of December 31 of Year 10, Blues Company signed an agreement to borrow up to $500,000 to refinance the note payable on a long-term basis. The financing agreement called for borrowings not to exceed 80% of the value of the collateral Blues Company was providing. Upon issuance of the December 31 of Year 10 financial statements, the value of the collateral was $600,000 and was not expected to fall below this amount during Year 11.		

Solution on p. 15-65.

Describe accounting for subsequent events and contingencies including litigation, warranties, and other contingencies

LO 15-5

In this section, we explain the accounting for contingencies and subsequent events. A **contingency** is an existing condition that must be resolved in the future in order to determine whether the company will recognize a gain or a loss in the current period. The accounting guidance provides criteria to help companies determine whether a potential loss associated with a contingency is accrued, disclosed, or ignored in the current period. A **subsequent event** takes place after the balance sheet date but before the financial statements are issued. Depending on whether the subsequent event is tied to conditions that existed at the

Loss Contingencies
- Accrue: Probable and reasonably estimable
- Disclose: Reasonably possible or probable but not reasonably estimable

Subsequent Events
- Recognized subsequent events
- Nonrecognized subsequent events

LO 15-5 Overview

balance sheet date, a *material* subsequent event will either be accrued or disclosed. In some cases, a subsequent event is connected to conditions existing at the balance sheet date, such as the settlement of a current year-end loss contingency through a post year-end lawsuit settlement. In other cases, a subsequent event is a new event, such as a post year-end fire that took place before financial statements are issued and the fire is unrelated to conditions existing at year-end. We examine the accounting for (1) loss contingencies in general (**Demo 15-5A**), (2) subsequent events (**Demo 15-5B**), (3) specific loss contingencies (**Demo 15-5C**), and (4) gain contingencies (**Demo 15-5D**).

Loss Contingencies

The accounting guidance defines a contingency as follows.

> **ASC Glossary**   **Contingency:** An existing condition, situation, or set of circumstances involving uncertainty as to possible gain (gain contingency) or loss (loss contingency) to an entity that will ultimately be resolved when one or more future events occur or fail to occur.

A contingency related to litigation is the most commonly reported loss contingency as shown in **Exhibit 15-2**. Consider an example where a company is involved in a legal dispute over an action that took place prior to a company's accounting year-end of December 31 of Year 1. Because this legal matter will not be settled until after the calendar year-end financial statements are issued, the litigation is a contingency for purposes of financial reporting in Year 1. The definition of a contingency indicates that an uncertain outcome impacts the settlement of *an existing condition*. Therefore, for the legal dispute to be classified as a contingency, the event leading to the litigation needs to have taken place *on or before the balance sheet date.*

EXHIBIT 15-2

Common Types of Reported Loss Contingencies

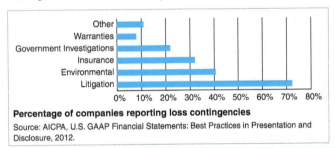

Percentage of companies reporting loss contingencies

Source: AICPA, U.S. GAAP Financial Statements: Best Practices in Presentation and Disclosure, 2012.

Loss contingencies can have an impact on periodic financial reporting through accruals of losses or through disclosures. Whether and how a loss contingency is reported in the financial statements first depends on the likelihood of an uncertain outcome relating to an existing condition occurring. The likelihood can be classified as remote, reasonably possible, or probable. These terms are defined as follows.

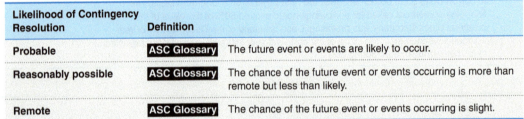

Likelihood of Contingency Resolution	Definition	
Probable	**ASC Glossary**	The future event or events are likely to occur.
Reasonably possible	**ASC Glossary**	The chance of the future event or events occurring is more than remote but less than likely.
Remote	**ASC Glossary**	The chance of the future event or events occurring is slight.

The proper accounting treatment for the loss contingency depends on the likelihood of contingency resolution and whether the amount of the loss is reasonably estimable, as outlined in **Exhibit 15-3**.

EXHIBIT 15-3

Accounting Treatment of a Contingent Liability

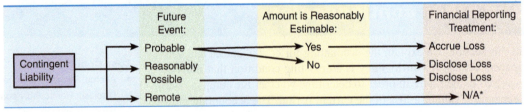

*Except in the case of certain guarantees where disclosure is required.

Accrual of a Loss Contingency   A loss contingency must be accrued (debit loss or expense and credit liability or contra-asset) if an estimated loss from a loss contingency is both probable and reasonably estimable.

> **450-20-25-2**   An estimated loss from a loss contingency shall be accrued by a charge to income if both of the following conditions are met:
>
> a. Information available before the financial statements are issued or are available to be issued . . . indicates that it is probable that an asset had been impaired or a liability had been incurred at the date of the financial statements. Date of the financial statements means the end of the most recent accounting period for which financial statements are being presented. It is implicit in this condition that it must be probable that one or more future events will occur confirming the fact of the loss.
>
> b. The amount of loss can be reasonably estimated . . .

The satisfaction of an obligation may ultimately require expenditures that differ from the amount of the original estimate of the obligation. When a subsequent estimate or actual settlement differs from the original estimated liability, the difference is accounted for as a change in estimate. If the loss can only be estimated within a range, with no better estimate within that range, the company accrues the *minimum* point in the range.

450-20-30-1   If some amount within a range of loss appears at the time to be a better estimate than any other amount within the range, that amount shall be accrued. When no amount within the range is a better estimate than any other amount, however, the minimum amount in the range shall be accrued. Even though the minimum amount in the range is not necessarily the amount of loss that will be ultimately determined, it is not likely that the ultimate loss will be less than the minimum amount . . .

Disclosure of a Loss Contingency

A loss contingency must be disclosed (and not accrued) if the loss is at least reasonably possible and *either* of the following conditions exists: (1) the loss is not both probable and estimable or (2) there is an exposure to a range of loss where only the minimum point in the range was accrued.

450-20-50-3   Disclosure of the contingency shall be made if there is at least a reasonable possibility that a loss or an additional loss may have been incurred and either of the following conditions exists:

a. An accrual is not made for a loss contingency because any of the conditions in paragraph 450-20-25-2 are not met.

b. An exposure to loss exists in excess of the amount accrued pursuant to the provisions of paragraph 450-20-30-1.

Disclosure includes the nature of the contingency and an estimate of the loss (or range of loss) or a statement that an estimate is not possible at this time. However, management is unlikely to disclose a belief that a contingent *legal loss* is probable and can be reliably estimated because generally the outcome of a lawsuit is hard to predict. In addition, doing so could imply that it may be advisable for the other party to settle out of court. To disclose a tacit expectation of loss in advance may prejudice the outcome of the trial. For this reason, information will appear, if at all, in the notes to the financial statements. Even then, it is unusual for a company to mention specific amounts unless court judgments have already been rendered.

Even if the loss contingency arises after the date of the company's financial statements, disclosure may be necessary. (Events arising after the balance sheet date are discussed further in the next section on subsequent events.)

450-20-50-9   Disclosure of a loss, or a loss contingency, arising after the date of an entity's financial statements but before those financial statements are issued . . . may be necessary to keep the financial statements from being misleading if an accrual is not required . . .

Accounting for a Remote Possibility of a Loss

The general rule is that a loss contingency is neither accrued nor disclosed if the possibility of a loss is remote. However, disclosure is required of certain guarantees when the possibility of a loss is remote.

460-10-50-2   An entity shall disclose certain loss contingencies even though the possibility of loss may be remote. The common characteristic of those contingencies is a guarantee that provides a right to proceed against an outside party in the event that the guarantor is called on to satisfy the guarantee. Examples include the following:

a. Guarantees of indebtedness of others, including indirect guarantees of indebtedness of others.

b. Obligations of commercial banks under standby letters of credit.

c. Guarantees to repurchase receivables (or, in some cases, to repurchase the related property) that have been sold or otherwise assigned

d. Other agreements that in substance have the same guarantee characteristic.

Accounting for Loss Contingencies   **LO15-5** ◀ **DEMO 15-5A**

Blues Brothers Inc. is subject to a lawsuit, initiated in the last quarter of Year 1, because of an accident that occurred during Year 1 involving a vehicle owned and operated by the company. Blues Brothers Inc.'s year-end is December 31 and the Year 1 financial statements were issued on March 1 of Year 2. The plaintiff is seeking $100,000 in damages. Provide the information indicated for each of the following *separate* scenarios.

Demo

MBC

continued

continued from previous page

a. Blues Brothers Inc. determines that a reasonable estimate of a probable loss on the settlement of the lawsuit is $50,000, although a settlement had not been reached prior to the issuance of the financial statements. On March 15 of Year 2, the lawsuit was settled in $40,000 cash. Record the required journal entries on December 31 of Year 1 and on March 15 of Year 2.

b. Blues Brothers Inc. estimates that a loss on the lawsuit is probable but the company is not able to reasonably estimate the settlement prior to the issuance of the financial statements. On March 15 of Year 2, the suit was settled in $40,000 cash. Record the required journal entries on December 31 of Year 1 and on March 15 of Year 2.

c. Blues Brothers Inc. estimates that a loss on the lawsuit is reasonably possible and the company is not able to reasonably estimate the settlement prior to the issuance of the financial statements. On June 30 of Year 2, the suit was settled in $25,000 cash. Record the required journal entries on December 3 of Year 1 and on June 30 of Year 2.

d. Blues Brothers Inc. determines that a loss on the lawsuit is remote. Indicate the proper financial statement impact on December 31 of Year 1.

Solution

a. **Loss Contingency—Probable and Reasonably Estimable**

Because the loss is probable and reasonably estimable, Blues Brothers Inc. records an accrual on December 31 of Year 1 for the amount of loss reasonably estimated.

December 31, Year 1—To accrue for a loss contingency

Loss on Litigation Settlement	50,000	
Estimated Litigation Liability		50,000

```
Assets  = Liabilities + Equity
         +50,000      −50,000
          LitLiab      Loss

Litig Liab          Litig Loss
    | 50,000    50,000 |
```

March 15, Year 2—To record settlement of loss contingency

Estimated Litigation Liability	50,000	
Gain on Litigation Settlement		10,000
Cash		40,000

```
Assets  = Liabilities + Equity
−40,000    −50,000     +10,000
  C:o       LitLiab      Gain

   Cash            Litig Liab
 | 40,000    50,000 | 50,000
                   Litig Gain
                       | 10,000
```

b. **Loss Contingency—Probable and Not Reasonably Estimable**

December 31, Year 1

No entry is recorded because the loss is not reasonably estimable but the company will disclose information relating to the lawsuit in the notes accompanying the financial statements.

March 15, Year 2—To record settlement of legal contingency

Loss on Litigation Settlement	40,000	
Cash		40,000

```
Assets  = Liabilities + Equity
−40,000                 −40,000
  C:o                    Loss

   Cash            Litig Loss
 | 40,000    40,000 |
```

c. **Loss Contingency—Reasonably Possible and Not Reasonably Estimable**

December 31, Year 1

No entry is recorded because the loss is reasonably possible and not reasonably estimable, but the company will disclose information relating to the lawsuit in the notes accompanying the financial statements.

June 30, Year 2—To record settlement of legal contingency

Loss on Litigation Settlement	25,000	
Cash		25,000

```
Assets  = Liabilities + Equity
−25,000                 −25,000
  C:o                    Loss

   Cash            Litig Loss
 | 25,000    25,000 |
```

d. **Loss Contingency—Remote**

Because the loss is considered remote, the company is not required to record an entry or disclose information relating to the lawsuit in the Year 1 financial statements.

Subsequent Events

Subsequent events are material financial events that take place between the balance sheet date and the issuance date (or the date available to be issued) of the financial statements. The accounting guidance indicates two types of subsequent events: recognized and nonrecognized.

ASC Glossary **Subsequent events**—Events or transactions that occur after the balance sheet date but before financial statements are issued or are available to be issued. There are two types of subsequent events:

a. The first type consists of events or transactions that provide additional evidence about conditions that existed at the date of the balance sheet, including the estimates inherent in the process of preparing financial statements (that is, recognized subsequent events).

b. The second type consists of events that provide evidence about conditions that did not exist at the date of the balance sheet but arose subsequent to that date (that is, nonrecognized subsequent events).

Determining when financial statements are issued or are available to be issued is explained in the accounting guidance.

> **ASC Glossary**   **Financial statements are issued**—Financial statements are considered issued when they are widely distributed to shareholders and other financial statement users for general use and reliance in a form and format that complies with GAAP.

> **ASC Glossary**   **Financial statements are available to be issued**—Financial statements are considered available to be issued when they are complete in a form and format that complies with GAAP and all approvals necessary for issuance have been obtained, for example, from management, the board of directors, and/or significant shareholders.

The subsequent event period is outlined in **Exhibit 15-4**. Events taking place in the subsequent event period may involve information that could influence a user's evaluation of the future prospects of a company. Some events may be completely new, or unconnected to conditions existing at the balance sheet date. These events are important to a financial statement user who is forecasting balance sheet amounts into a future period. Some events, however, can clarify or add information to conditions that existed at the balance sheet date.

EXHIBIT 15-4

Subsequent Event Period

Balance Sheet Date	Subsequent Event Period Jan. 1, Year 2 – Feb. 28, Year 2	Financial Statement Issuance* Mar. 1, Year 2
Dec. 31, Year 1	■ **Recognized subsequent event:** If the event reflects conditions existing during Year 1, *recognize* the effects in the Year 1 financial statements. ■ **Nonrecognized subsequent event:** If the event does not reflect conditions existing during Year 1 and is required to keep financial statements from being misleading, *disclose* the event in the Year 1 financial statements.	

*Or available to be issued

Recognized Subsequent Events

The effects of subsequent events must be recognized in the financial statements if they provide additional evidence about conditions that existed at the balance sheet date or affect assumptions made in preparing the financial statements. Subsequent events may affect the realization of assets existing on the balance sheet date, such as inventories, or receivables, or the settlement of estimated liabilities. Information from the subsequent event period is used to adjust the accounts recognized in the balance sheet at year-end.

Events that take place during the subsequent period may shed light on the nature of a contingency that existed at the balance sheet date. Judgment is necessary to determine whether the likelihood of a loss based on the resolution of a contingency is remote, reasonably possible, or probable. In making this judgment, management uses *all information available up to the date of the release of financial statements*. For example, if the events that gave rise to litigation take place before December 31 (balance sheet date) and that litigation is settled after December 31 but before the financial statements are issued on March 1 of the following year, then the settlement amount should be considered in estimating the amount of liability recognized on December 31.

> **855-10-25-1**   An entity shall recognize in the financial statements the effects of all subsequent events that provide additional evidence about conditions that existed at the date of the balance sheet, including the estimates inherent in the process of preparing financial statements . . .

> **855-10-55-1**   The following are examples of recognized subsequent events addressed in paragraph 855-10-25-1:
>
> *a.* If the events that gave rise to litigation had taken place before the balance sheet date and that litigation is settled after the balance sheet date but before the financial statements are issued or are available to be issued, for an amount different from the liability recorded in the accounts, then the settlement amount should be considered in estimating the amount of liability recognized in the financial statements at the balance sheet date.
>
> *b.* Subsequent events affecting the realization of assets, such as inventories, or the settlement of estimated liabilities, should be recognized in the financial statements when those events represent the culmination of conditions that existed over a relatively long period of time.

Nonrecognized Subsequent Events Subsequent events are disclosed in the notes and not recognized within the financial statements if they (1) result from conditions that did not exist at the balance sheet date and (2) are required to keep the financial statements from being misleading. The following examples would typically require financial statement disclosure:

- The sale of a bond or issuance of capital stock after the date of the balance sheet.
- Litigation related to an event that transpired after the date of the balance sheet.
- Inventory losses due to a casualty occurring after the date of the balance sheet.
- Losses caused by a condition that arose after the balance sheet date, such as a fire or flood.

855-10-25-3   An entity shall not recognize subsequent events that provide evidence about conditions that did not exist at the date of the balance sheet but arose after the balance sheet date but before financial statements are issued or are available to be issued . . .

855-10-50-2   Some nonrecognized subsequent events may be of such a nature that they must be disclosed to keep the financial statements from being misleading. For such events, an entity shall disclose the following:

a. The nature of the event
b. An estimate of its financial effect, or a statement that such an estimate cannot be made.

Examples of subsequent events that are neither disclosed nor reported through financial statements (but may be communicated through other means) are changes in the market price of a company's stock, employee strike, new product development, management changes, recognition or decertification of a union, and new sales or marketing agreements.

DEMO 15-5B ▶ **LO15-5**   **Accounting for Subsequent Events**

Demo
MBC

Example One—Recognized Subsequent Event
Blues Brothers Inc. is subject to a lawsuit initiated during the last quarter of calendar Year 1 because of an accident that occurred during the year involving a vehicle owned and operated by the company. The plaintiff is seeking $100,000 in damages. A settlement in the amount of $50,000 was reached on February 1 of Year 2, prior to the issuance of the financial statements on March 1 of Year 2. Record the required journal entries dated December 31 of Year 1 and February 1 of Year 2.

Solution
Because the lawsuit (considered a subsequent event) is settled before the financial statements are issued and the accident took place during Year 1, Blues Brothers Inc. records an accrual dated December 31 of Year 1 equal to the amount of the settlement.

December 31, Year 1—To accrue for legal loss contingency

Assets = Liabilities + Equity
        +50,000   −50,000
        LitLiab   Loss

Litig Liab   Litig Loss
    | 50,000   50,000 |

| Loss on Litigation Settlement . . . . | 50,000 | |
| Estimated Litigation Liability . . . . | | 50,000 |

The subsequent settlement of the lawsuit is recorded as follows.

February 1, Year 2— To record settlement of legal contingency

Assets = Liabilities + Equity
−50,000   −50,000
C:o   LitLiab

Cash   Litig Liab
    | 50,000   50,000 | 50,000

| Estimated Litigation Liability . . . . | 50,000 | |
| Cash . . . . | | 50,000 |

Example Two—Nonrecognized Subsequent Event
Repeat the requirements of Example One except now assume that the accident took place on January 1 of Year 2 instead of Year 1.

Solution

December 31, Year 1
No entry is recorded in Year 1 because the actual event (accident) took place after the Year 1 reporting period. However, the company would disclose information relating to this subsequent event in the notes accompanying the financial statements if required to keep the financial statements from being misleading.

The subsequent settlement of the lawsuit is recorded as follows.

February 1, Year 2—To record settlement of legal contingency

Assets = Liabilities + Equity
−50,000   −50,000
C:o   Loss

Cash   Litig Loss
    | 50,000   50,000 |

| Loss on Litigation Settlement . . . . | 50,000 | |
| Cash . . . . | | 50,000 |

Real World—SUBSEQUENT EVENT

Macy's Inc. recorded the following note related to a March event that occurred after the December 31 balance sheet date.

> **Financing Subsequent Event** On March 17, 2021, MRH completed an offering of $500 million in aggregate principal amount of 5.875% senior notes due 2029 (the "2029 Notes") in a private offering (the "Notes Offering"). The 2029 Notes mature on April 1, 2029. The 2029 Notes are senior unsecured obligations of MRH and are unconditionally guaranteed on a senior unsecured basis by Macy's, Inc. MRH used the net proceeds from the Notes Offering, together with cash on hand, to fund a separately announced tender offer in which $500 million of senior notes and debentures were tendered for early settlement and purchased by MRH on March 17, 2021.

Special Loss Contingencies

Further explanations are provided for the following special set of loss contingencies: (1) unasserted claims and assessments, (2) injury or damage caused by products sold, (3) risk of loss, (4) expropriation of assets, (5) coupons, and (6) warranties (**Demo 15-5C**).

Unasserted Claims and Assessments An unasserted claim exists when a specific party has an existing claim against a company but the company has no evidence of the claim. Disclosure or accrual of losses for unasserted claims is not required unless it is probable a claim will be asserted.

- If it is *probable* that an unasserted claim or assessment will be asserted, the company will assess the contingency following the steps outlined in **Exhibit 15-3**. This means that we assume that the unasserted claim is effectively asserted and analyze it accordingly.

- If it is *not probable* that an unasserted claim or assessment will be asserted, no accrual or disclosure is required. This means that no further analysis is required.

`450-20-50-6` Disclosure is not required of a loss contingency involving an unasserted claim or assessment if there has been no manifestation by a potential claimant of an awareness of a possible claim or assessment unless both of the following conditions are met: (a) It is considered probable that a claim will be asserted. (b) There is a reasonable possibility that the outcome will be unfavorable.

For example, Tyler Inc. owns a facility that sustained fire damage. There is a possibility that the company could be fined for noncompliance with certain laws. Assuming that a claim is only reasonably possible of materializing, no disclosure or accrual will be necessary at year-end related to the potential for a fine for noncompliance.

Injury or Damage Caused by Products Sold A company can become aware of potential litigation claims resulting from injury or damages caused by a product defect, as in the case of a product recall for safety reasons. If claims are probable, accrual for losses may be necessary. For example, Pharmaceutical Inc. sells a drug product for which a safety hazard related to the product is discovered. If it is considered probable that a loss will occur and Pharmaceutical Inc.'s experience enables the company to make a reasonable estimate of the loss, the estimated loss would be accrued.

`450-20-55-2` If it is probable that a claim resulting from injury or damage caused by a product defect will arise with respect to products or services that have been sold, accrual for losses may be appropriate . . .

Risk of Loss A mere risk of loss from a future event is distinguished from a loss contingency. A company can choose not to insure against risk of loss that may result from injury to others, casualty losses (such as fire or natural disaster), interruption of its business operations, or other business risks. A contingency requires the existence of a condition as of a balance sheet date. Therefore, simply the risk of a future loss, not based upon an actual event, does not qualify as a contingency.

`450-20-55-5` The absence of insurance does not mean that an asset has been impaired or a liability has been incurred at the date of an entity's financial statements . . .

For example, a company that operates manufacturing equipment should not accrue for injury to employees that might be caused by the use of the equipment in the future, even if the amount of those losses may be reasonably estimable. In accounting for a possible loss contingency, the company considers only actual events that have taken place prior to the date of the financial statements, including those that the company will not become aware of until after the financial statement release date.

Expropriation of Assets The threat of expropriation of assets (where a government takes private property for the benefit of public interest) can lead to recognition of a contingent loss. In evaluating the accounting for a loss contingency, the company must determine if the expropriation is imminent (occurring soon) and compensation from the government will be less than the carrying amount of the assets.

450-20-55-9 The threat of expropriation of assets is a contingency (as defined) because of the uncertainty about its outcome and effect. The condition in paragraph 450-20-25-2(a) is met if both of the following are true:

a. Expropriation is imminent.

b. Compensation will be less than the carrying amount of the assets . . .

Accrual will be required if the amount of loss can be reasonably estimated and both conditions are met.

EXPANDING YOUR KNOWLEDGE   Asset Retirement Obligations

A company records an *asset retirement obligation* for an existing long-term legal obligation associated with costs that will take place upon retirement of a noncurrent asset, such as costs for remediation, dismantling, disposal, restoration, etc. Because of the uncertain outcomes, an asset retirement obligation is a type of a loss contingency. See Chapter 11 for issues in evaluating this loss contingency.

Coupons—Separate from a Revenue Contract Sometimes coupons are offered outside of a revenue contract (such as in newspapers). In this case, a company records a liability for the estimated value of redeemed coupons at the time of coupon distribution if redemption is considered probable and the amount of redemption can be reasonably estimable. (Coupons offered as part of a revenue contract fall under the guidance of revenue recognition.)

Accounting for Warranties It is common for a company to offer a warranty in connection with the sale of a product or service. A **warranty** is a guarantee or a commitment by a company selling a product or providing a service, to provide repairs or substitutions in the event that the product or service does not function as planned or intended. Warranties can be included as part of a sales contract or warranties can be implied by legal requirements or as part of customary business practices. Warranties either (a) provide an assurance that the product or service will comply with agreed-upon specifications or (b) provide a service in addition to assurance that the product will comply with agreed-upon specifications.

Assurance-Type Warranties provide assurance that the related product will function as intended because it complies with agreed-upon specifications. This type of warranty is connected to the sale of the product or service and the warranty is typically included as part of the selling price of the product. Assurance-type warranties are accounted for on an accrual basis and are considered loss contingencies because they relate to existing but unidentified defects in products sold.

606-10-55-32 If a customer does not have the option to purchase a warranty separately, an entity should account for the warranty in accordance with the guidance on product warranties in Subtopic 460-10 on guarantees, unless the promised warranty, or a part of the promised warranty, provides the customer with a service in addition to the assurance that the product complies with agreed-upon specifications.

Warranty expense for an assurance-type warranty should be estimated and recognized fully in the year of the sale of the related product or service (when probable and reasonably estimable) even though repairs or exchanges may take place in later periods. In cases where the warranty extends over two or more years and the probabilities of estimated future cash flows can be estimated, the expected cash flow technique may be used to estimate the warranty liability. See **Demo 6-3C** in Chapter 6 for an example of estimating a warranty liability using the expected cash flow technique.

Service-Type Warranties provide customers with a service in addition to the assurance that the product complies with agreed-upon specifications. Typically, a service-type warranty is sold separately from the product. Because the additional service is a separate performance obligation, the cash collected for service-type warranties is recorded initially as deferred revenue and generally recognized as revenue on a straight-line basis over the service contract. Thus, **a service-type warranty is considered to be a separate performance obligation accounted for under revenue recognition and is not considered a loss contingency.**

`606-10-55-31`   If a customer has the option to purchase a warranty separately (for example, because the warranty is priced or negotiated separately), the warranty is a distinct service because the entity promises to provide the service to the customer in addition to the product that has the functionality described in the contract. In those circumstances, an entity should account for the promised warranty as a performance obligation . . .

How do you distinguish between an assurance-type warranty and a service-type warranty?

- If a customer has the option to purchase the warranty separately, the warranty is a service-type warranty.

- The longer the coverage period, the more likely it is that the warranty is a service-type warranty because it is more likely to be providing an *additional* service.

- If the entity is required by law to provide a warranty, the warranty is typically an assurance-type warranty because it is protecting customers from the risk of purchasing defective products.

Recognition of revenue and expense related to assurance-type and service-type warranties is summarized in **Exhibit 15-5**.

EXHIBIT 15-5
Assurance-Type and Service-Type Warranty Recognition

Assurance-Type Warranty (Loss Contingency)	Service-Type Warranty (Separate Performance Obligation)
At time of sale: ■ Recognize revenue on (combined) sale of product and warranty ■ Recognize estimated warranty expense and warranty liability	**At time of sale:** ■ Recognize revenue on sale of product ■ Recognize deferred revenue on warranty
Over warranty period: ■ Reduce liability for actual warranty costs incurred	**Over warranty period:** ■ Recognize warranty expense as costs are incurred ■ Recognize warranty revenue as performance obligation is satisfied, typically on a straight-line basis

3M

Real World—WARRANTY CONTINGENCY

3M Corporation provided the following disclosure in its recent Form 10-K regarding warranty accruals.

Note 18 Commitments and Contingencies
Warranties/Guarantees: 3M's accrued product warranty liabilities, recorded on the Consolidated Balance Sheet as part of current and long-term liabilities, are estimated at approximately $55 million at December 31, 2023, and $48 million at December 31, 2022. Further information on product warranties are not disclosed, as the Company considers the balance immaterial to its consolidated results of operations and financial condition. The fair value of 3M guarantees of loans with third parties and other guarantee arrangements are not material.

Accounting for Warranty Loss Contingencies   **LO15-5**   ◄ **DEMO 15-5C**

Example One—Assurance-Type Warranty
Rollex Company sells merchandise for $200,000 cash during the year. The merchandise includes a two-year warranty against manufacturing defects as part of the selling price of the product. The company's experience has indicated that warranty costs will approximate 0.5% of sales.

a. Record the sale of merchandise during the year, ignoring the cost entry.
b. Record the accrual of warranty costs on the company's annual reportng date of December 31. Assume no actual warranty costs were incurred during the year.
c. Record the expenditures for actual warranty costs of $1,100 in the following year.

Solution

a. **Sale of Merchandise**

Year 1—To record sale of merchandise

Cash...	200,000	
Sales.......................................		200,000

Assets = Liabilities + Equity
+200,000   +200,000
C:o   Rev

Cash	Sales
200,000		200,000

continued

continued from previous page

b. Accrual of Warranty Costs

December 31—To accrue warranty costs

Assets = Liabilities + Equity
+1,000   −1,000
WarrLiab   Exp

Warranty Liab	Warranty Exp
1,000	1,000

Warranty Expense	1,000	
Warranty Liability ($200,000 × 0.005)		1,000

c. Actual Warranty Costs

Year 2—To record warranty costs incurred

Assets = Liabilities + Equity
−1,100   −1,000   −100
C:o   WarrLiab   Exp

Cash	Warranty Liab
200,000 | 1,100	1,000 | 1,000

	Warranty Exp
	1,000
	100

Warranty Liability	1,000	
Warranty Expense ($1,100 − $100)	100	
Cash (and other resources used)		1,100

Example Two—Service-Type Warranty

Rollex sells merchandise for $10,000 cash on January 1 but also sells extended 2-year warranties for $50 per product, beginning on January 1. The stand-alone selling price of the merchandise is $10,000 and the stand-alone selling price of the extended warranties is $50 per warranty. Rollex sold 10 extended warranties on January 1 and incurred costs of $200 related to servicing the warranties during the year.

a. Record the sale of warranties and merchandise on January 1, ignoring the cost entry for the merchandise.

b. Record the expenditures for actual warranty costs of $200 during the year.

c. Record the recognition of warranty revenue on a straight-line basis on the company's year-end reporting date of December 31.

Solution

a. Sale of Merchandise and Warranties

Revenue on service-type warranties is initially deferred in Deferred Warranty Revenue, a current liability account.

January 1—To record sale of merchandise and extended warranties

Assets = Liabilities + Equity
+10,500   +500   +10,000
C:o   DWarrRev   Rev

Cash	Def Warr Rev
10,500	500

	Sales
	10,000

Cash [$10,000 + ($50 × 10)]	10,500	
Deferred Warranty Revenue ($50 × 10)		500
Sales		10,000

b. Actual Warranty Costs

To record warranty service costs incurred

Assets = Liabilities + Equity
−200   −200
C:o   Exp

Cash	Warranty Exp
10,500 | 200	200

Warranty Expense	200	
Cash (and other resources used)		200

c. Recognition of Warranty Revenue

Deferred warranty revenue is recognized as revenue on a straight-line basis over the two-year service period.

December 31—To recognize warranty revenue

Assets = Liabilities + Equity
−250   +250
DWarrRev   Rev

Def Warr Rev	Warranty Rev
250 | 500	250

Deferred Warranty Revenue ($500/2)	250	
Warranty Revenue		250

EXPANDING YOUR KNOWLEDGE   Guarantees

A guarantee that a company makes may result in the recognition or disclosure of an obligation. For example, a guarantor may agree to make payments to a guaranteed party in the event that another entity fails to perform under an obligating agreement (such as a loan). The authoritative guidance considers two aspects to a guarantee:

460-10-25-2   The issuance of a guarantee obligates the guarantor (the issuer) in two respects:

a. The guarantor undertakes an obligation to stand ready to perform over the term of the guarantee in the event that the specified triggering events or conditions occur (the noncontingent aspect).

b. The guarantor undertakes a contingent obligation to make future payments if those triggering events or conditions occur (the contingent aspect) . . .

The **stand ready aspect** of the guarantee, a noncontingent obligation, is recorded as a liability at fair value. The **potential credit loss aspect** of the agreement is treated as a loss contingency where the probability of default is assessed as outlined in **Exhibit 15-3**.

Gain Contingencies

For a gain contingency to be *disclosed*, the characteristics of a contingency must be present: there must be a probable increase in assets or a decrease in liabilities, and the gain must depend upon the occurrence of future events. An example of a gain contingency is a probable favorable outcome in a pending legal dispute. **Contingent gains are never accrued but may be disclosed provided that the disclosure does not mislead financial statement users as to the likelihood the gain will be realized.**

450-30-50-1   Adequate disclosure shall be made of a contingency that might result in a gain, but care shall be exercised to avoid misleading implications as to the likelihood of realization.

Accounting for a Gain Contingency   **LO15-5** ◀ **DEMO 15-5D**

Demo

MBC

Bower Inc. sold its hockey apparel division in December of Year 1. The sale agreement provides for $100 million to be paid to the company at closing plus an amount contingent on sales of apparel over a 12-month period beginning April 1 of Year 2. An estimate of the contingent amount based upon Bower's 20 years of experience is $500,000. Record the journal entry on December 31 of Year 1 related to the contingent amount.

Solution

A contingent gain is not recorded in financial statements as an asset or as income. This means that the company would record no revenue in Year 1 for the gain contingency.

Reporting of Contingencies and Subsequent Events   **LO15-5** ◀ **REVIEW 15-5**

Review

MBC

Complete the following table by indicating whether each item *a* through *f* will result in the reporting of any revenue or expense in the income statement of MJM Inc. for the year ended December 31 of Year 1. Assume that MJM Inc. issued its financial statements on February 15 of Year 2.

Contingency Scenario	Revenue and/ or Expense in Year 1
a. The company believes it is probable that it will incur $50,000 in additional charges in January of Year 2 related to its medical coverage for employees for medical conditions and related treatments occurring in Year 1.	
b. The company believes it is probable that it will incur $75,000 in additional charges in January of Year 2 related to its medical coverage for employees for medical conditions and related treatments occurring in early January of Year 2.	
c. The company sells merchandise of $1 million in Year 1 that includes a two-year limited warranty as part of the selling price. Warranty costs are estimated to be 1% of sales.	
d. The company sells merchandise at a stand-alone selling price of $2 million in Year 1. The company also sells 200 two-year warranties separately for $75 each. Total warranty costs are estimated to be $10,000 for the 200 products sold. The company incurred actual warranty costs of $8,000 in Year 1. Warranty revenue is recognized on a straight-line basis.	
e. The company issued $250,000 of bonds payable at par on January 31 of Year 2.	
f. The attorneys for the company believe that it is highly probable that the company will win a court settlement in the amount of $150,000, expected to be settled in the second quarter of Year 2.	

More Practice:
E15-24, E15-26, P15-10,
P15-11

Solution on p. 15-65.

EXPANDING YOUR KNOWLEDGE   **Revenue Contracts**

Revenue contracts can result in obligations to provide a good or service in the future to a customer such as a rebate, discount on future product sales, or a free product. As we discussed in Chapter 7, these items are accounted for as part of the revenue contract; thus, they are not treated distinctly as a contingent liability.

continued

continued from previous page

- **Customer options** grant rights to customers to acquire additional goods and services as part of a revenue contract. Options include loyalty rewards programs, coupons affixed to a product, and premiums (such as a promotion where a toy is received in exchange for cereal box tops). In these cases, the customer option is considered to be a separate performance obligation (if material to the context of the contract), and revenue is deferred for the amount allocated to the customer option until control of a promised good or service is transferred to the customer.
- **Consideration payable** results from a payment to a customer as a result of a revenue contract. Examples include rebates, credits, and volume discounts. Consideration payable is treated as a reduction to the transaction price unless the payment is exchanged for a distinct good or service. Consideration paid for a distinct good or service is accounted for in the same way as a typical purchase from a supplier.
- **Refund liability** is recorded if a company receives consideration from a customer and expects to refund some or all of the consideration in the future (such as is the case with a sale with a right of return). The estimated amount of returns is recorded as a liability (refund liability) at the time of sale.

LO 15-6 ▶ Explain liability, commitment and contingency disclosures and analyses using liquidity ratios

LO 15-6 Overview

Disclosures
- Current liabilities, contingencies

Liquidity ratios
- Current ratio

$$\frac{\text{Current assets}}{\text{Current liabilities}}$$

- Quick ratio

$$\frac{\text{Cash + Marketable securities + Receivables}}{\text{Current liabilities}}$$

In a classified balance sheet, current liabilities are included on the face of the balance sheet. The notes to the financial statements often include additional details on the composition of current liabilities.

The balance sheet may include a line titled *Commitments and Contingencies*, to direct financial statement users to information included in the notes. The notes will include additional information on contingencies accrued and on contingencies and commitments requiring disclosure but not accrual.

Disclosure of Current Liabilities, Commitments, and Contingencies

Current Liabilities The SEC requires its registrants to state separately any component of current liabilities in excess of 5% of total current liabilities on the balance sheet or in the notes.

> 210-10-S99-1   20. Other current liabilities. State separately, in the balance sheet or in a note thereto, any item in excess of 5 percent of total current liabilities. Such items may include, but are not limited to, accrued payrolls, accrued interest, taxes, indicating the current portion of deferred income taxes, and the current portion of long-term debt. Remaining items may be shown in one amount.

The following is an example of a disclosure of accrued and current liability amounts from a recent Form 10-K of **Target Corporation**.

Accrued and Other Current Liabilities (millions)	February 3, 2024
Wages and benefits	$1,535
Gift card liability, net of estimated breakage	1,162
Real estate, sales, and other taxes payable	827
Dividends payable	508
Current portion of operating lease liabilities	329
Workers' compensation and general liability[a]	192
Interest payable	122
Other	1,415
Accrued and other current liabilities	$6,090

[a] We retain a substantial portion of the risk related to general liability and workers' compensation claims. We estimate our ultimate cost based on analysis of historical data and actuarial estimates. General liability and workers' compensation liabilities are recorded at our estimate of their net present value. *Note 20* provides the noncurrent balance of these liabilities.

Further, companies must disclose the methodology used to recognize breakage of gift cards and significant judgments made in applying the methodology.

405-20-50-2   An entity that recognizes a breakage amount in accordance with paragraph 405-20-40-4 shall disclose the methodology used to recognize breakage and significant judgments made in applying the breakage methodology.

Commitments
When a company enters into an agreement for a future obligation, it creates a commitment that may require disclosure in its financial statements. Because a commitment for a future obligation is not a present obligation, it is not recorded on the balance sheet as a liability. The following accounting guidance outlines specific items requiring disclosure.

440-10-50-1   Notwithstanding more explicit disclosures required elsewhere in this Codification, all of the following situations shall be disclosed in financial statements:

a. Unused letters of credit
b. Leases (see Section 842-20-50)
c. Assets mortgaged, pledged, or otherwise subject to lien; the approximate amounts of those assets; and the related obligations collateralized
d. Pension plans (see Section 715-20-50)
e. The existence of cumulative preferred stock dividends in arrears
f. Commitments, including: 1. A commitment for plant acquisition; 2. An obligation to reduce debts; 3. An obligation to maintain working capital; 4. An obligation to restrict dividends.

Contingencies
Disclosures required for contingencies are also outlined in the accounting guidance.

450-20-50-4   The disclosure in the preceding paragraph shall include both of the following:

a. The nature of the contingency
b. An estimate of the possible loss or range of loss or a statement that such an estimate cannot be made.

As discussed earlier, certain remote contingencies, including guarantees, require disclosure. In addition, guarantors must disclose information for product warranties and other guarantee contracts including the nature of the guarantee and a schedule of changes in the guarantees.

460-10-50-8   A guarantor shall disclose all of the following information for product warranties and other guarantee contracts described in paragraph 460-10-15-9:

a. The information required to be disclosed by paragraph 460-10-50-4 . . .
b. The guarantor's accounting policy and methodology used in determining its liability for product warranties
c. A tabular reconciliation of the changes in the guarantor's aggregate product warranty liability for the reporting period . . .

An example of a litigation contingency disclosure for **Ford Motor Company** follows where the company disclosed an estimate of reasonably possible losses in a range of up to approximately $1.4 billion.

NOTE 25. Commitments and Contingencies

Various legal actions, proceedings, and claims (generally, "matters") are pending or may be instituted or asserted against us. These include, but are not limited to, matters arising out of alleged defects in our products; product warranties; governmental regulations relating to safety, emissions, and fuel economy or other matters; government incentives; tax matters, including trade and customs; alleged illegal acts resulting in fines or penalties; financial services; employment-related matters; dealer, supplier, and other contractual relationships; intellectual property rights; environmental matters; shareholder or investor matters; and financial reporting matters. Certain of the pending legal actions are, or purport to be, class actions. Some of the matters involve or may involve claims for compensatory, punitive, or antitrust or other treble damages in very large amounts, or demands for field service actions, environmental remediation programs, sanctions, loss of government incentives, assessments, or other relief, which, if granted, would require very large expenditures.

    The extent of our financial exposure to these matters is difficult to estimate. Many matters do not specify a dollar amount for damages, and many others specify only a jurisdictional minimum. To the extent an amount is asserted, our historical experience suggests that in most instances the amount asserted is not a reliable indicator of the ultimate outcome.

    We accrue for matters when losses are deemed probable and reasonably estimable. In evaluating matters for accrual and disclosure purposes, we take into consideration factors such as our historical experience with matters of a similar nature, the specific facts and circumstances asserted, the likelihood that we will prevail, and the severity of any potential loss. We reevaluate and update our accruals as matters progress over time.

continued

continued from previous page

For the majority of matters, which generally arise out of alleged defects in our products, we establish an accrual based on our extensive historical experience with similar matters. We do not believe there is a reasonably possible outcome materially in excess of our accrual for these matters.

For the remaining matters, where our historical experience with similar matters is of more limited value (i.e., "non-pattern matters"), we evaluate the matters primarily based on the individual facts and circumstances. For non-pattern matters, we evaluate whether there is a reasonable possibility of a material loss in excess of any accrual that can be estimated. Our estimate of reasonably possible loss in excess of our accruals for all material matters currently reflects indirect tax and customs matters, for which we estimate the aggregate risk to be a range of up to about $1.4 billion.

As noted, the litigation process is subject to many uncertainties, and the outcome of individual matters is not predictable with assurance. Our assessments are based on our knowledge and experience, but the ultimate outcome of any matter could require payment substantially in excess of the amount that we have accrued and/or disclosed.

In Note 15 of **General Motors'** recent Form 10-K the following table was reported, which summarizes information related to year-end liabilities recorded for commitments and contingencies.

Litigation-related liability and tax administrative matters	$1,155
Product liability	712
Ignition Switch Recall compensation program	66
Credit card programs	
Redemption liability—recorded in Accrued liabilities	115
Deferred revenue—recorded in other liabilities	258
Environmental liability	124
Guarantees	72

Each item is explained in more detail in the disclosure and where applicable, ranges of possible losses are disclosed. For the ignition switch recall, the company disclosed a rollforward of activity for the program, explained as follows.

NOTE 15. Commitments and Contingencies

Ignition Switch Recall Compensation Program

In the three months ended June 30 of Year 4 we created a compensation program (the Program) for accident victims who died or suffered physical injury (or for their families) as a result of a faulty ignition switch related to the 2.6 million vehicles recalled in the three months ended March 31 of Year 4. The Program is being administered by an independent program administrator, who established a protocol that defined the eligibility requirements to participate in the Program. The Program accepted claims from August 1 of Year 4 through January 31 of Year 5 and received a total of 4,343 claims. The Program completed its claims review process in the three months ended September 30 of Year 5, and the independent program administrator determined that 399 claims were eligible for payment under the Program. Payments to eligible claimants began in the three months ended December 31 of Year 4 and will continue through the first quarter of Year 6. At January 29 of Year 6 we had paid 345 eligible claimants $554 million out of the 362 claimants who accepted offers under the Program. The other 37 accident victims (or their families) chose not to participate in the Program and could pursue litigation against us. Accident victims (or their families) that accept a payment under the Program agree to settle all claims against GM related to the accident.

We recorded a charge of $400 million in the year ended December 31 of Year 4 and based on the Program's claims experience we recorded an additional $195 million in the year ended December 31 of Year 5. These charges were recorded in Automotive selling, general and administrative expense in Corporate and were treated as adjustments for EBIT-adjusted reporting purposes. Based on currently available information we believe our accrual at December 31 of Year 5 is adequate to cover the estimated costs under the Program. The following table summarizes the activity for the Program since its inception (dollars in millions):

Balance at April 1 of Year 4	$ —
Provisions	400
Payments	(85)
Balance at December 31 of Year 4	315
Provisions	195
Payments	(444)
Balance at December 31 of Year 5	$ 66

Liquidity Ratios and Analyses

The **current ratio** is a measure of short-term liquidity and is calculated by dividing current assets by current liabilities. It indicates a company's ability to meet short-term obligations from current resources. Investors and creditors use this ratio to assess whether a company has the ability to pay debts coming due within the year. A higher ratio indicates a stronger level of liquidity. However, a large ratio, such as a ratio of 3, may indicate that the company has idle assets that should be invested or returned to the shareholders.

$$\frac{\text{Current assets}}{\text{Current liabilities}}$$

    The current ratio considers all current assets while the **quick ratio** considers *only* the most liquid assets of cash, cash equivalents, marketable securities (i.e., short-term investment), and accounts receivable. The intent of the quick ratio is to estimate a company's ability to pay its current debts with only its most liquid assets. Thus, this ratio is a more rigorous measure of liquidity than the current ratio. The purpose of these two ratios is not to assess profitability or long-term debt paying ability, but instead to assess whether a company can remain solvent in the short-run. The current ratio and the quick ratio are illustrated in **Demo 15-6**.

$$\frac{\text{Cash + Marketable securities}}{\text{Current liabilities}}$$

Liquidity Ratios   **LO15-6** ◀ **DEMO 15-6**

The following financial information is provided for **Target Corporation**. Compute the current asset ratio and the quick ratio for the two years presented. Provide a brief analysis of your results.

($ millions)	Current Year-End	Prior Year-End
Current assets		
Cash and cash equivalents, including short-term investments of $1,110 and $3,008	$ 2,512	$ 4,046
Inventory	8,309	8,601
Assets of discontinued operations	69	322
Other current assets	1,100	1,161
Total current assets	$11,990	$14,130

($ millions)	Current Year-End	Prior Year-End
Current liabilities		
Accounts payable	$7,252	$7,418
Accrued and other current liabilities	3,737	4,236
Current portion of long-term debt and other borrowings	1,718	815
Liabilities of discontinued operations	1	153
Total current liabilities	$12,708	$12,622

Solution

Current Ratio

$ millions		Current Year-End	Prior Year-End
Current Ratio =	$\dfrac{\text{Current assets}}{\text{Current liabilities}}$	$\dfrac{\$11,990}{\$12,708} = 0.94$	$\dfrac{\$14,130}{\$12,622} = 1.12$

Quick Ratio

$ millions		Current Year-End	Prior Year-End
Quick Ratio =	$\dfrac{\text{Cash + Marketable securities + Receivables}}{\text{Current liabilities}}$	$\dfrac{\$2,512}{\$12,708} = 0.20$	$\dfrac{\$4,046}{\$12,622} = 0.32$

continued

continued from previous page

For the past two years, Target had a current ratio of approximately 1.0. This means that for every dollar of current liabilities, Target has approximately one dollar of current assets. We see that the large decrease in the denominator for the quick ratio (relative to the current ratio) is due to the exclusion of inventory. Inventory takes longer to convert to cash because it first must be sold, and if sold on account, the accounts receivable must be collected. The quick ratio decreased for Target from the prior year to the current year mainly because of the excess cash from the sale of its pharmacy and clinic businesses disclosed in its annual report in the prior year. Without this one-time bump due to a non-recurring item, the quick ratio for Target was roughly 0.20 for the prior year.

REVIEW 15-6	LO15-6		Calculating Liquidity Ratios

Compute the current asset ratio and the quick ratio for **Starbucks Corporation** at two year-ends.

Review

MBC

$ millions	Current Year-End	Prior Year-End
Current assets		
Cash and cash equivalents..........................	$2,462.3	$2,128.8
Short-term investments............................	228.6	134.4
Accounts receivable, net...........................	870.4	768.8
Inventories	1,364.0	1,378.5
Prepaid expenses and other current assets	358.1	347.4
Total current assets............................	$5,283.4	$4,757.9
Current liabilities		
Accounts payable	$ 782.5	$ 730.6
Accrued liabilities	1,934.5	1,999.1
Insurance reserves	215.2	246.0
Stored value card liability	1,288.5	1,171.2
Current portion of long-term debt	—	399.9
Total current liabilities	$4,220.7	$4,546.8

More Practice:
BE15-41, E15-31, E15-32
Solution on p. 15-65.

Management Judgment

Accounting for Contingencies

In applying the accounting guidance outlined in this chapter for contingencies, the judgment of management is important. Following are examples.

- Identifying contingencies is a subjective process—by their very nature, contingencies represent circumstances with uncertain outcomes.
- Determining whether a future outcome resulting in a loss is probable, reasonably possible, or remote is often a difficult process. It requires in-depth analysis and consultation with legal experts and a final decision based on management judgment.
- Determining a reasonably estimable amount of a loss contingency is not a straightforward process—for example, such an amount is not on a vendor invoice. Determining a warranty accrual or a legal accrual is a subjective process, resulting at times in a range of losses instead of a single estimate of a loss.

Ratio Analysis

Decisions made by management have a direct impact on ratio analysis. For example, management decisions result in the accrual, disclosure, or exclusion of contingencies in the financial statements. Financial statement users can assess whether contingencies not accrued (but disclosed) should be considered in ratio analysis.

Q15-1. Provide the definition of a liability.

Q15-2. Provide the definition of a current liability.

Q15-3. Explain how the measurement of a liability is related to its cause.

Q15-4. Why are most current liabilities recognized at maturity value at the beginning of their term?

Q15-5. In evaluating a balance sheet, some creditors say the liability section is one of the most important sections. What are some reasons justifying this position?

Q15-6. Some liabilities are reported at their maturity amount. In general, when should liabilities, prior to the maturity date, be reported at less than their maturity amount?

Q15-7. Explain why the amount of cash salaries paid to employees does not equal salaries expense for the employer.

Q15-8. Differentiate between secured and unsecured liabilities. Explain the reporting procedures for each.

Q15-9. What are examples of secured and unsecured liabilities?

Q15-10. Distinguish between the stated rate and the market rate on a debt.

Q15-11. Briefly define the following terms related to a note payable: present value of the note and maturity value of the note.

Q15-12. Distinguish between an interest-bearing note and a noninterest-bearing note.

Q15-13. How is gift card breakage recognized as revenue using the proportional method?

Q15-14. Why is deferred revenue classified as a liability?

Q15-15. What is a compensated absence? When should the expense related to compensated absences be recognized?

Q15-16. What is the accounting definition of a contingency? What are the three characteristics of a contingency? Why is this concept important?

Q15-17. How is the likelihood of the outcome of a contingency measured? In general, how does this affect the accounting for and reporting of contingencies?

Q15-18. Briefly explain the accounting and reporting for loss contingencies.

Q15-19. Under what conditions may a debt due within the next year (as measured at year-end) be reported as a noncurrent liability? Under what conditions may a long-term debt (as measured at year-end) be reported as a current liability?

Q15-20. What is the purpose of the current ratio and quick ratio?

For this exercise, download the Excel file "Table 3: State Tax Collections by State and Type of Tax 2021" obtained at the United States Census Bureau at https://www.census.gov/data/tables/2021/econ/qtax/historical.html. For this exercise, we extract data for *sales and gross receipts taxes by state* for the first quarter of 2021. We then convert the data to a U.S. map chart and analyze the results.

Data Analytics DA15-1
Preparing an Excel Map Visualization of Sales Tax Across States **LO1**

Refer to PA-27 in Appendix A. This problem uses Tableau to analyze liquidity of S&P 500 companies through the current ratio. The visualization is exported to PowerPoint for communication purposes.

Data Analytics DA15-2
Preparing Tableau Visualizations to Analyze Liquidity through the Current Ratio **LO4**

Data Visualization Activities are available in **myBusinessCourse**. These assignments use Tableau Dashboards to expose students to visual depictions of data and introduce students to data analytics through data visualizations. These exercises are assignable and auto graded by MBC.

Data Visualization

Multiple Choice

LO1

MC15-1. Determining Income Effect of a Payment on Inventory Purchase   On September 1, Elver Inc. purchases merchandise for resale. The merchandise has an invoice price of $8,000 and terms of 2/10, n/30. The company accounts for inventory using the gross method in a perpetual inventory system and pays the balance in full on September 8. How does the journal entry prepared on September 8 affect income?

   a. $160 decrease   *c.* $160 increase
   b. $7,840 decrease   *d.* $0

LO1

MC15-2. Computing Sales Taxes Payable   Atwood Inc. collected a total of $89,675 for cash sales which included the associated sales tax, and completed credit sales of $100,000, subject to sales tax. If the tax rate is 5.5%, what amount did Atwood report as Sales Taxes Payable if no tax was yet submitted to the taxing authorities as of its reporting date?

   a. $10,432   *c.* $10,175
   b. $9,484   *d.* $9,888

LO2

MC15-3. Computing Deferred Revenue Balance   On December 1, Electronic Repair Inc. collects an advance payment of $900 from a customer for three months of computer repair services. What is the company's balance in Deferred Revenue on December 31?

   a. $600   *c.* $900
   b. $300   *d.* $0

LO2

MC15-4. Computing Gift Card Breakage Revenue   Best Gifts Inc. gathered the following information related to its gift card sales for Year 1, its first year of selling gift cards.

Gift card redemptions, Year 1	$ 8,400
Sales of nonrefundable gift cards, Year 1	16,000

Best Gifts Inc. estimates that 75% of the value of gift cards sold in Year 1 will be redeemed while 25% will remain unclaimed. Under the proportional method, what would Best Gifts Inc. recognize for gift card breakage revenue in Year 1?

   a. $2,100   *c.* $4,000
   b. $2,800   *d.* $1,900

LO3

MC15-5. Computing Salaries Payable   Consider the following payroll information summarized for Cali Inc.

Weekly payroll, October 8 to 14	$565,000
Withholdings taxes payable (federal and state)	141,250
Federal unemployment taxes payable	3,390
State unemployment taxes payable	30,510
FICA taxes payable (employer share)	43,223
FICA taxes payable (employee share)	43,223
Health care savings account payable	45,000
Retirement contributions payable (employee share)	56,000

Employees are paid weekly, one week after the week worked. What amount would Cali recognize as salaries payable on October 14?

   a. $245,627   *c.* $279,527
   b. $236,304   *d.* $322,750

LO3

MC15-6. Computing Payroll Tax Expense   Referring to MC15-5, what amount would Cali recognize as payroll tax expense for the October weekly payroll?

   a. $33,900   *c.* $218,373
   b. $77,123   *d.* $184,473

LO4

MC15-7. Accounting for Noninterest-Bearing Note   Black Oak Corp. signs a $420,000, six-month, non-interest-bearing note when the market rate is 4%. The present value of the note is $411,765 and the company uses the straight-line method to amortize discounts. What is the impact on the income statement after an adjusting entry was recorded one month later?

    a. $8,235 increase to expense   *c.* $1,373 decrease to expense

    b. $1,373 increase to expense   *d.* $8,235 decrease to expense

MC15-8. Classifying a Note Payable as Current or Noncurrent   On December 31 of Year 10, Copper Company issued a nine-month, 5% interest-bearing note in the amount of $518,000. On February 1 of Year 11, Copper retires the notes with proceeds from a sale of 15,000 shares of its common stock at $30 per share plus additional cash. The common stock issuance took place before the Year 10 financial statements ended December 31 were issued. What amount of the short-term note payable should be *excluded* from current liabilities as of December 31 of Year 10?

LO4

    a. $0   *c.* $518,000

    b. $68,000   *d.* $450,000

MC15-9. Accounting for Loss Contingency   On December 31, of Year 1, the attorneys of Kendall Inc. believe it is probable that the company will be responsible for damages in a court settlement. A reasonable estimate of damages is between $500,000 and $1,500,000. On February 15 of Year 2, at the time of issuance of its financial statements, the attorneys revised the estimate to a range of $600,000 to $1,000,000. After the financial statements were issued, the dispute was settled for $850,000. What amount should be reported as a liability for this contingency on December 31 of Year 1?

LO5

    a. $600,000   *c.* $850,000 (as an error correction)

    b. $500,000   *d.* $1,000,000

MC15-10. Computing Current Ratio   Mallard Corp. reported the following amounts in its recent financial statements:

LO6

Noncurrent assets	$225,000	Total liabilities	$158,000
Noncurrent liabilities	$120,000	Total stockholders' equity . . .	$102,000

What is the company's current ratio?

    a.   1.88   *c.*   0.92

    b.   1.64   *d.*   1.09

Brief Exercises

On June 15, Red Buckle Inc. purchased merchandise for resale for $12,000 on credit terms 2/10, *n*/30. On June 20, Red Buckle paid for the merchandise. Record (1) the entry on June 15 and (2) the entry on June 20 using the perpetual inventory system and the gross method for recording discounts.

Brief Exercise 15-1
Recording Accounts
Payable Entries **LO1**
Hint: See Demo 15-1A

Refer to BE15-1, but instead of journal entries, show the effect on the accounting equation for the transactions, including identifying the individual accounts affected, and the total impact on assets, liabilities, and stockholders' equity.

Brief Exercise 15-2
Reporting Accounts
Payable Transactions
Using the Accounting
Equation **LO1**

Target Shoppers Inc. reported cash sales of $18,000 for the month of June. Sales taxes payable are recorded at the point of sale.

    a.   Assume that sales are subject to a 6% sales tax. Record the sales entry.

    b.   Assume that the cash collected on sales includes the 6% sales tax. Record the sales entry.

Brief Exercise 15-3
Recording Sales Tax
Payable Entries **LO1**
Hint: See Demo 15-1B

On June 1, Sunset Inc. sells merchandise with a sales price of $220 subject to a 5% sales tax to a customer on account (n/30). On June 25, the customer pays the full account balance. On June 30, Sunset remits the sales taxes to taxing authorities. The company uses a perpetual inventory system. Assume that the company records sales taxes payable with each sale and the cost of the item is 60% of its sales price. Record the company's entries on June 1, June 25, and June 30.

Brief Exercise 15-4
Recording Sales Tax
Payable Entries **LO1**
Hint: See Demo 15-1B

Brief Exercise 15-5
Reporting Sales Tax
Transactions Using
the Accounting
Equation **LO1**

Refer to BE15-4, but instead of journal entries, show the effect on the accounting equation for the transactions, including identifying the individual accounts affected, and the total impact on assets, liabilities, and stockholders' equity.

Brief Exercise 15-6
Recording Sales Tax
Payable Entries **LO1**
Hint: See Demo 15-1B

On June 25, Sunrise Inc. collects cash of $525 for the sale of merchandise plus the related 5% sales tax. On July 15, Sunset remits the sales taxes to taxing authorities. The company uses a perpetual inventory system. Assume that the company does not separately record sales taxes payable at the point of sale and the cost of the item is 60% of its sales price. Record the journal entries for (1) the sale and cost of sales on June 25 (2) the adjusting entry on June 30 to identify amounts owed to taxing authorities, and (3) the remittance of sales tax to the taxing authorities on July 15.

Brief Exercise 15-7
Reporting Sales Tax
Transactions Using
the Accounting
Equation **LO1**

Refer to BE15-6, but instead of journal entries, show the effect on the accounting equation for the transactions, including identifying the individual accounts affected, and the total impact on assets, liabilities, and stockholders' equity.

Brief Exercise 15-8
Recording Customer
Advances **LO2**
Hint: See Demo 15-2B

Jet Air Inc. collected $300 cash from a customer who purchased a one-way airline ticket on June 1 for a flight from Minneapolis to New York on August 15. Record (1) the entry on June 1, and (2) the entry on August 15 for Jet Air Inc.

Brief Exercise 15-9
Reporting Customer
Advance Using
the Accounting
Equation **LO2**

Refer to BE15-8, but instead of a journal entry, show the effect on the accounting equation for the transaction, including identifying the individual accounts affected, and the total impact on assets, liabilities, and stockholders' equity.

Brief Exercise 15-10
Recording Entries for
Returnable Deposits &
Deferred Revenue **LO2**
Hint: See Demo 15-2A

On August 10, Rental Inc. collected a $1,200 cash deposit plus the rental fee of $2,000 from a customer that rented banquet chairs and tables for a wedding. If the chairs and tables are returned in good condition, the deposit will be returned to the customer. The customer returns the chairs and tables in good condition on August 12 and the deposit is released to the customer. Prepare the entries on August 10 and August 12 by Rental Inc.

Brief Exercise 15-11
Reporting Returnable
Deposit & Deferred
Revenue Transactions
Using the Accounting
Equation **LO2**

Refer to BE15-10, but instead of journal entries, show the effect on the accounting equation for the transactions, including identifying the individual accounts affected, and the total impact on assets, liabilities, and stockholders' equity.

Brief Exercise 15-12
Recording Gift Card
Entries **LO2**
Hint: See Demo 15-2C

Chica's Inc. sold a $50 gift card on February 1. The gift card was redeemed on February 14. Record (1) the entry on February 1 and (2) the entry on February 14 for Chica's Inc.

Brief Exercise 15-13
Recording Entries for
Gift Cards that Do Not
Qualify for Proportional
Method **LO2**
Hint: See Demo 15-2C

Golf Pros Inc. sold $5,000 of nonrefundable gift cards during its first year of operations. Customers redeemed $3,510 of the gift cards for golf equipment purchases during the year. Assume that the company does not meet the requirements to use the proportional method to account for gift cards. On December 31, Golf Pros Inc. estimates a remote chance that 40% of the remaining unredeemed gift cards will be redeemed and a slight possibility that 60% will be redeemed. Record the adjusting year-end entry on December 31 (if any).

Brief Exercise 15-14
Recording Entries for
Gift Cards—Proportional
Method **LO2**
Hint: See Demo 15-2C

Golf Pros Inc. sold $5,000 of nonrefundable gift cards during its first year of operations. Customers redeemed $3,510 of the gift cards for golf equipment purchases during the year. Assume that the company meets the requirements to use the proportional method to account for gift cards. The company estimates gift card breakage to be 10% of total gift card sales. Record the adjusting year-end entry on December 31 (if any).

BNW Inc. had a weekly payroll of $5,000 for three employees with mandatory withholdings of social security tax (7.65%), federal withholdings of $1,000, and state withholdings of $200. Voluntary withholdings included retirement plan contributions of $100 and health care savings account contributions of $150.

Record the company's weekly payroll entry.

Brief Exercise 15-15
Recording Payroll Entries **LO3**
Hint: See Demo 15-3A

Total payroll for Fritz Corp. was $350,000. Income taxes withheld are $70,000 and retirement contributions payable are $8,000. The FICA tax rate is 7.65%, FUTA tax rate is 0.6% and SUTA tax rate is 5.4% on total payroll. Record the company's (1) payroll entry, (2) payroll tax entry, (3) payroll obligation remittance entry.

Brief Exercise 15-16
Recording Entries for Payroll **LO3**
Hint: See Demo 15-3B

The following information relating to compensated absences was available from Graf Company's accounting records at December 31.

■ Employees' rights to vacation pay vest and are attributable to services already rendered. Payment is probable, and Graf's obligation was reasonably estimated at $220,000.

■ Employees' rights to sick pay benefits do not vest but accumulate for possible future use. The rights are attributable to services already rendered, the total accumulated sick pay was reasonably estimated at $100,000, and payment is possible.

a. What amount is Graf required to report as the liability for compensated absences on its December 31 balance sheet?

b. Record the appropriate journal entry on December 31.

Brief Exercise 15-17
Recording Liability for Compensated Absences **LO3**
Hint: See Demo 15-3C

On December 15, the board of directors of Limited Inc. approved a bonus payout of $70,000 to executives, based upon services performed during the year. The bonus is payable on January 25 of the following year.

Record the entries required on (1) December 15, and (2) January 25 of the following year.

Brief Exercise 15-18
Recording Bonus Payable **LO3**
Hint: See Demo 15-3D

Aguilera Co. established a defined contribution plan in which the company matches the employees' contributions to a traditional 401(k) plan. The amount of the current year employer matching contribution is calculated as $150,000 based upon annual employee contributions in the period of service. Record the entry for Aguilera Co. at year-end assuming the company's payment to the pension fund will be made in January of the following year.

Brief Exercise 15-19
Recording Entry for Defined Contribution Retirement Plan **LO3**

On August 31 of Year 1, Pine Company issued a 9-month, 12% note payable to National Bank in the amount of $900,000. Interest is due at maturity. Record the entries for Pine Company on the following dates.

a. Issuance of the note on August 31 of Year 1.

b. Adjusting entry on December 31 of Year 1, the company's year-end.

c. Payment of the note payable on May 31 of Year 2.

Brief Exercise 15-20
Recording Interest-Bearing Note Payable Entries **LO4**
Hint: See Demo 15-4A

Refer to BE15-20, but instead of journal entries, show the effect on the accounting equation for the transactions, including identifying the individual accounts affected, and the total impact on assets, liabilities, and stockholders' equity.

Brief Exercise 15-21
Reporting Interest-Bearing Note Payable Transactions Using the Accounting Equation **LO4**

Choice Company buys equipment on October 1 of Year 1 providing as payment a noninterest-bearing note for $22,000 to be paid in one year. The equipment could be purchased for $20,000 in cash today. Record the entries for Choice Company on the following dates.

a. Issuance of the note for the equipment on October 1 of Year 1.

b. Adjusting entry on December 31 of Year 1, the company's year-end. Amortize any discount on the note using the straight-line method.

c. Payment of the note payable on October 1 of Year 2.

Brief Exercise 15-22
Recording Noninterest-Bearing Note Payable Entries **LO4**
Hint: See Demo 15-4B

Brief Exercise 15-23
Reporting NonInterest-Bearing Note Payable Transactions Using the Accounting Equation **LO4**

Refer to BE15-22, but instead of journal entries, show the effect on the accounting equation for the transactions, including identifying the individual accounts affected, and the total impact on assets, liabilities, and stockholders' equity.

Brief Exercise 15-24
Computing the Present Value of a Noninterest-bearing Note **LO4**

Compute the present value of a $10,000, one-year note payable that specifies no interest, although 10% would be a realistic rate. Is the present value less than, greater than, or equal to the maturity value?

Brief Exercise 15-25
Comparing an Interest-bearing and a Noninterest-bearing Note **LO4**

Assume that $4,000 cash is borrowed on a $4,000, 10%, one-year note payable that is interest-bearing and that another $4,000 cash is borrowed on a $4,400 one-year note that is noninterest-bearing. For each note, provide the following:

a. Present value of the note.   b. Maturity amount.   c. Total interest paid.

Brief Exercise 15-26
Recording Debt Issued at a Discount **LO4**
Hint: See Demo 15-4B

The face value of a company's commercial paper borrowings (loan) at December 31 was $6 million. This six-month loan originated on September 1.

a. Prepare the journal entry for issuance of the loan on September 1, assuming that the loan is discounted at 5.7%. *Hint:* Discount on Note Payable is equal to 6 months of interest.
b. Prepare the adjusting entry at December 31, the company's year-end. Amortize the discount on the note using the straight-line method.
c. Prepare the entry to repay the loan on February 28 of the following year.
d. Calculate the market rate of the loan.

Brief Exercise 15-27
Classifying Refinanced Debt **LO4**
Hint: See Demo 15-4C

Maple Co. has a $50,000, 5%, 10-year note issued July 31 of Year 1.

a. How will the $50,000 be classified on the balance sheet at December 31 of Year 10?
b. If the $50,000 is refinanced into a five-year note on January 31 of Year 11 (before the Year 10 financial statements are issued), how will the $50,000 note payable be classified on the balance sheet at December 31 of Year 10?

Brief Exercise 15-28
Callable Debt **LO4**
Hint: See Demo 15-4C

Leaf Co. has a $50,000, 5%, 10-year note issued July 31 of the current year. The debt agreement requires that Leaf maintain a total liabilities-to-equity ratio of 1.0 or less, or else the lender is able to call the debt immediately. At the end of the current year, Leaf's year-end financial statements as of December 31 indicate that it has a total liabilities-to-equity ratio of 1.05.

a. Show how the debt is classified on the balance sheet at the current year-end.
b. Assume that Leaf obtained a 6-month waiver of the debt covenant beginning this year-end from the lender. The waiver letter was dated on February 1 of the following year (before financial statements were issued). Describe how the debt is classified on the balance sheet at the current year-end.
c. How would the answer to part *b* change (if at all), if a 15-month waiver was obtained?

Brief Exercise 15-29
Recording Assurance-Type Warranty Liability **LO5**
Hint: See Demo 15-5C

Finisher Inc. sells merchandise for $250,000 during the year that includes a three-year limited warranty. Warranty costs are estimated to be 1% of sales. The company incurred actual costs of $800 during the year related to the warranties.

a. Record the warranty accrual at the time of sale.
b. Record the adjustment to the warranty accrual for actual warranty costs during the year. Assume actual warranty costs involve cash payments.

Brief Exercise 15-30
Reporting Assurance-Type Warranties Using the Accounting Equation **LO5**

Refer to BE15-29, but instead of journal entries, show the effect on the accounting equation for the transactions, including identifying the individual accounts affected, and the total impact on assets, liabilities, and stockholders' equity.

During Year 1, Madison Co. sold merchandise for $250,000 along with a two-year warranty (for Year 1 and Year 2) for $25 per product. Warranty costs are estimated to be 0.5% of sales. In Year 1, the company sold $2,500 of warranties and incurred actual costs of $800 related to the warranties. The company uses straight-line recognition of warranty revenue.

a.   Record the sale of the merchandise and warranties, ignoring the cost of goods sold entry. Assume cash sales.
b.   Record the warranty service costs for Year 1. Assume cash payments.
c.   Record the warranty revenue recognized in Year 1.

Brief Exercise 15-31
Recording Service-Type Warranty
Liability **LO5**
Hint: See Demo 15-5C

Refer to BE15-31, but instead of journal entries, show the effect on the accounting equation for the transactions, including identifying the individual accounts affected, and the total impact on assets, liabilities, and stockholders' equity.

Brief Exercise 15-32
Reporting Service-Type Warranties
Using the Accounting
Equation **LO5**

On November 5, Shipper Inc.'s vehicle was in an accident with another vehicle driven by R. Bell. Shipper received notice on January 12 of the following year of a lawsuit for $350,000 in damages for personal injuries suffered by Bell. The company's legal counsel believes it is probable that Bell will be awarded an estimated amount in the range between $100,000 and $225,000, and that $150,000 is a better estimate of potential liability than any other amount. The company's accounting year ends on December 31, and the current calendar year-end financial statements were issued on March 2 of the following year.

a.   What liability should the company accrue on December 31?
b.   How would your answer to *(a)* change if the company's legal counsel believes it is reasonably possible that Bell will be awarded a settlement?
c.   How would your answer to *(a)* change if the company's legal counsel believes there is only a remote possibility that Bell will be awarded a settlement?

Brief Exercise 15-33
Reporting a Legal
Contingency **LO5**
Hint: See Demo 15-5A

Pitt Company is the defendant in a lawsuit filed by Hoffman in Year 1 disputing the validity of a copyright held by Pitt. At December 31 of Year 1, Pitt determined that Hoffman would probably be successful against Pitt for an estimated amount of $800,000. Appropriately, an $800,000 loss was accrued by a charge to income of Pitt for the year ended December 31 of Year 1. On December 15 of Year 2, Pitt and Hoffman agreed to a settlement providing for cash payment of $500,000 by Pitt to Hoffman and transfer of Pitt's copyright to Hoffman. The carrying amount of the copyright on Pitt's accounting records was $120,000 at December 15 of Year 2.

a.   What would be the effect of the settlement of this liability on Pitt's pretax income in Year 2?
b.   Record the entry on December 15 of Year 2 for Pitt Company.

Brief Exercise 15-34
Recording and
Reporting a Legal
Contingency **LO5**

The following information pertains to a fire insurance policy in effect during the calendar year covering Vail Company's inventory:

Face amount of policy.	$400,000
Deductible.	25,000
Amount of premium	2,000

Vail's inventory averages $500,000 uniformly throughout the year. How much of a contingent liability should Vail accrue at December 31 to cover possible future fire losses?

Brief Exercise 15-35
Reporting a Loss
Contingency **LO5**

Marathon Inc. estimates that it will be required to spend approximately $40,000 to remove an underground storage tank in 10 years that was constructed during the current year for $300,000. The present value of this obligation based on the company's discount rate of 8% is $18,528. Record the entry (if any) during the current year related to the expected removal of the storage tank in 10 years.

Brief Exercise 15-36
Recording Asset
Retirement
Obligation **LO5**

A manufacturer of household appliances has potential losses due to the discovery of a possible defect in one of its products. The occurrence of the loss is reasonably possible, and the costs can be reasonably estimated at $50,000. How should this potential loss be treated for financial statement purposes?

Brief Exercise 15-37
Reporting a Loss
Contingency **LO5**

The Occupational Safety and Health Administration (OSHA) is in the process of conducting a workplace inspection at Kenny Corp. to determine whether the company is in compliance with standards on health and safety in the workplace. While the investigation is currently in process, Kenny Corp. estimates that it is probable that an assessment will be made. The range of a reasonably possible assessment is between $25,000 and $100,000. How should this potential loss be treated for financial statement purposes?

Brief Exercise 15-38
Reporting a Loss
Contingency **LO5**

Brief Exercise 15-39
Analyzing a Gain
Contingency **LO5**
Hint: See Demo 15-5D

During the year, a driver for Commuters Inc. was involved in an accident. Commuters Inc. brought a suit against the negligent party for $1 million. The suit is pending on December 31. Commuters Inc. believes it is virtually certain that it will receive a settlement of $1 million.

   How should this potential gain be treated for financial statement purposes on December 31?

Brief Exercise 15-40
Reporting Subsequent
Events **LO5**
Hint: See Demo 15-5B

In January, an explosion occurred at Nilo Company's plant, causing damage to area properties. In March, Nilo received notification of lawsuits filed against the company. Nilo's management and legal counsel concluded that it was reasonably possible that Nilo would be held responsible for negligence and that $1,500,000 was a reasonable estimate of the damages. Nilo's $2,500,000 comprehensive public liability policy contains a $150,000 deductible clause. In Nilo's December 31 financial statements for the year prior to the accident, how should this casualty be reported if the financial statements were released on March 31?

Brief Exercise 15-41
Calculating Liquidity
Ratios **LO6**
Hint: See Demo 15-6

Compute the (1) current ratio and the (2) quick ratio for **Nike Inc.** using the following excerpt from the balance sheet reported in a recent 10-K of Nike Inc.

At May 31 (in millions)			
Current assets		Current liabilities	
Cash and equivalents	$ 3,852	Current portion of long-term debt	$ 107
Short-term investments	2,072	Notes payable	74
Accounts receivable, net	3,358	Accounts payable	2,131
Inventories	4,337	Accrued liabilities	3,951
Deferred income taxes	389	Income taxes payable	71
Prepaid expenses and other current assets	1,968		
Total current assets	$15,976	Total current liabilities	$ 6,334

Exercises

Exercise 15-1
Recording Sales Taxes
Payable **LO1**
Hint: See Demo 15-1B

Cash sales for Zubra Inc. during the year were $9 million. The majority of sales were subject to a sales tax rate of 6%. The company records sales taxes payable at the point of sale.

Required
a. Record the sales and sales tax entry for the year assuming that $180,000 of sales were not subject to tax.
b. Now assume that cash collections for the year were $9 million, which included a 6% sales tax along with the sales amount. Of the amount collected, $180,000 of sales were *not* subject to tax. Record the sales and sales tax entry for the year.

Exercise 15-2
Recording Inventory
Purchase **LO1**

On September 1, Global Tech Inc. purchased merchandise for resale for $8,000 on credit terms 2/15, *n*/60 using the gross method and a perpetual inventory system. Global Tech incurred a shipping charge of $300 on the purchase, shipped f.o.b. shipping point, which was immediately paid. On September 10, Global Tech paid for half of the merchandise. On October 25, Global Tech paid the remaining balance.

Required
Record the following entries for Global Tech related to the merchandise purchase.

a. Record (1) the purchase of inventory on account and (2) the freight payment on September 1.
b. Record the payment on September 10.
c. Record the payment on October 25.
d. Assume that instead of making payments on September 10 and October 25, Global Tech issued a 12-month note in payment of the $8,000 account balance on October 31. Interest on the note is 10%, due in full upon maturity of the note. Record the issuance of the note payable.

Exercise 15-3
Recording Inventory
Purchases and Sales
on Account **LO1**
Hint: See Review 15-1

Record the entries for the following transactions for Shoppers Inc. Shoppers uses a perpetual inventory system and records sales taxes payable at the point of sale. *Hint:* For parts *b* and *d*, include the sales and cost of sales entries. *Hint:* Refer to Chapter 9 to review entries under a perpetual system.

a. On January 1, Shoppers Inc. purchased merchandise for resale for $35,000 on credit terms 1/15, *n*/30. Shoppers Inc. incurred a shipping charge of $180 on the purchase, which was immediately paid. Shoppers Inc. uses the gross method to record purchases.
b. Shoppers Inc. sells $14,000 of inventory during the first week of January to customers for $25,000, with a sales tax rate of 5%. Of the total sales for the week, 30% are cash sales, and 70% are credit sales (*n*/30).

c. On January 14, Shoppers Inc. pays the balance for purchases on account.

d. On January 15, Shoppers Inc. sells $15,000 of inventory to customers for $28,000, which includes a 5% sales tax. Of that total sales, 30% are cash sales, and 70% are credit sales. Record the sales entry.

Manchester Co. operates as a manufacturer of industrial equipment. On March 28, Manchester Co. received an advance payment of $100,000 from a customer on a special order of equipment. On May 1, Manchester Co. prepared an invoice and delivered the equipment to the customer. Total sales price is $400,000 and the remaining balance is due upon delivery of the equipment.

Exercise 15-4
Recording and Reporting Customer Advances **LO2**
Hint: See Demo 15-2B

Required

a. Record the entry on March 28 for Manchester Co.'s receipt of the advance payment.

b. Indicate how the payment would be reported on Manchester's March 31 financial statements.

c. Record the entry on May 1 for the sale of the equipment assuming that the advance payment was applied to the balance due. Ignore the cost of goods sold entry.

During the year, Neighbor Co-Op sells 500 beverages in glass bottles and receives a $1.00 deposit for each returnable bottle sold. As of December 31, a total of 400 glass bottles were returned, and deposits on 60 bottles were forfeited because it is the company's policy that a deposit must be claimed within 30 days. The remaining 40 bottles are still with customers within the 30-day claim period.

Exercise 15-5
Recording Customer Deposits **LO2**
Hint: See Demo 15-2A

Required

a. Record the collection of deposits during the year.

b. Record the return of glass bottles during the year.

c. Record the forfeiture of deposits during the year assuming that the cost of each bottle is $0.80. *Hint:* Include the sales and cost of sales entries.

Assume Ikeo Inc. sold $100,000 of gift cards during the last two weeks of December of Year 1. No gift cards were redeemed in calendar Year 1. A total of $90,250 of the gift cards were redeemed for store purchases during calendar Year 2. On December 31 of Year 2, Ikeo Inc. calculates the remaining balance of unredeemed gift cards as $9,750 ($100,000 less $90,250). Based on previous experiences, Ikeo estimates gift card breakage to be 5% of total gift card sales. Ikeo uses the proportional method to recognize income on gift card breakage.

Exercise 15-6
Accounting for Gift Cards **LO2**
Hint: See Review 15-2

Required

a. Record the sale of gift cards in Year 1.

b. Record the redemption of gift cards in Year 2.

c. Record revenue in Year 2 due to gift card breakage using the proportional method.

Refer to E15-6, but instead of journal entries, show the effect on the accounting equation for the transactions, including identifying the individual accounts affected, and the total impact on assets, liabilities, and stockholders' equity.

Exercise 15-7
Reporting Gift Card Transactions Using the Accounting Equation **LO2**

Aloha Company has a personnel policy that allows each employee with at least one year's employment to receive 20 days vacation time and two holidays with regular pay. Unused days are carried over to the next year. If not taken during the next year, the vacation and holiday times are lost. Aloha's accounting period ends December 31. At the end of Year 1, the personnel records showed the following:

Exercise 15-8
Recording and Reporting Compensated Absences **LO3**

Vacations Carried Over to Year 2		Holidays Carried Over to Year 2	
Total Days	Total Salaries	Total Days	Total Salaries
70	$16,800	10	$2,580

During Year 2, all of the Year 1 vacation time that was carried over and eight days of the holiday time that was carried over were taken. Salary increases in Year 2 for these employees relating to the days carried over amounted to $1,600. Total cash wages paid were: Year 1, $1,780,000; and Year 2, $1,860,000. There was no carryover of vacation time earned in Year 2.

Required

a. Provide the entries in Year 1 to record (1) salaries, and (2) accrued compensated absences. Disregard payroll taxes.

b. Provide the entry in Year 2 to record salaries. Disregard payroll taxes.

c. Show how the effects of the transactions should be reported in the Year 1 and Year 2 financial statements.

of the interest period. The difference between interest expense and the cash interest payment each period is the amount of discount amortized. As the discount is amortized over the term of the bonds, the carrying amount of the bonds increases toward the face value. Interest expense *increases* each period because of the increasing carrying amount of the bonds. See **Demo 16-4A**.

Effective Interest Method

Interest Expense			Cash Interest Payment			
Market Rate	×	Bond Payable, Net (Beg. of Year)	Stated Rate	×	Bond Face Value	= Discount Amortization

Straight-Line Interest Method   Although the effective interest method for amortizing discounts (and premiums) is the preferred method, there is an alternative method. The **straight-line interest method** can *only* be used, however, if the results are not materially different from the results using the preferred method.

835-30-55-2   Generally accepted accounting principles (GAAP) require use of the interest method. There is no basis for using an alternative to the interest method except if the results of alternative methods do not differ materially from those obtained by using the interest method. Therefore, methods other than the interest method, such as the rule of 78s, sum of the years' digits, and straight-line interest methods, shall not be used if their results materially differ from the interest method.

Under the straight-line interest method, the discount is recognized as interest expense *evenly* over the bond term. This method produces a stable dollar amount of interest expense each period equal to the cash interest paid *plus* the straight-line

Straight-Line Interest Method

Cash Interest Payment			Discount Amortization			
Stated Rate	×	Bond Face Value	Total Discount	÷	Bond Term	= Interest Expense

discount amortized each interest period. The carrying amount of the bonds increases by the discount amortization each period until the carrying amount of the bonds equals the face value upon maturity of the bonds (see **Demo 16-4B**). **Although interest expense per period varies depending upon the method followed, total interest expense over the life of the bonds is the same under both methods.**

Account for Bonds Issued at a Discount [Effective Interest Method]   **LO16-4**   **DEMO 16-4A**

Demo
MBC

Rush authorizes and issues $100,000 of 5% interest-bearing bonds on January 1 of Year 1. The bonds mature December 31 of Year 4 and pay cash interest on June 30 and December 31. The bonds were sold to yield a market rate of 6%. Rush amortizes the bond discount using the effective interest method.

a. Prepare an amortization schedule over the term of the bonds.
b. Prepare the entry for the issuance of the bonds on January 1 of Year 1.
c. Prepare the journal entry for the semiannual interest payment and amortization of the bond discount on June 30 of Year 1 and December 31 of Year 1.
d. Show the December 31 of Year 1 balance sheet and the Year 1 income statement effect of the bonds.
e. Assume the company prepares financial statements for the month of January of Year 2. Record the entry for the accrual of bond interest and amortization of the discount on January 31 of Year 2.
f. Record the entry upon maturity of the bonds, including the final interest payment, assuming no prior balance in Interest Payable.

Solution

a. **Amortization Schedule—Effective Interest Method [Stated Rate = 5% and Market Rate = 6%]**
Because the bonds pay interest semiannually, interest rates and periods must be adjusted to reflect semiannual compounding periods.

- Semiannual market rate: 6% ÷ 2 = 3%
- Semiannual periods: 4 years × 2 = 8 periods
- Semiannual cash interest payment: 5% ÷ 2 × $100,000 = $2,500

	RATE	NPER	PMT	PV	FV	Excel Formula
Given	3%	8	(2,500)	?	(100,000)	=PV(0.03,8,–2500,–100000)
Solution				$96,490		

The following amortization schedule illustrates how interest expense is recognized over the term of the bonds using the effective interest method. The components of the journal entry for each period include Cash, Interest Expense, and Discount on Bonds Payable. The carrying amount of the bonds indicated for each period is equal to the present value of the remaining cash flows discounted at the market rate in effect at the inception of the bonds.

continued

continued from previous page

Let's review the calculations for June 30 of Year 1. As shown above, the semiannual cash interest payment is equal to $2,500. Interest expense of $2,895 is equal to the market rate of 3% multiplied by the bond carrying amount at the beginning of the period of $96,490. The discount amortization of $395 is equal to interest expense of $2,895 less cash of $2,500. The discount amortized of $395 is subtracted from the beginning of period unamortized discount of $3,510 to arrive at the adjusted unamortized discount of $3,115. The carrying amount of bonds payable increases to $96,885, or $100,000 – $3,115. We see that over the bond term, stated interest (cash) is constant because it is contractual and is tied to the bond indenture. Interest expense each period increases with the increase in the bond carrying amount. At the end of the bond term, the carrying amount of the bonds equals the face value of $100,000, and the unamortized discount is zero. Total interest expense of $23,510 exceeds total cash interest of $20,000 because the bonds were sold at a discount.

	A	B	C	D	E
	Cash* (Stated Interest)	**Interest Expense** (Market Interest)	**Discount Amortization**	**Unamortized Discount**	**Bonds Payable, Net** (Carrying Amount)
Date	2.5% × Face Value	3% × E Beg. Period Bal.	B – A	D Beg. Period Bal. – C	Face Value – D
Jan. 1, Year 1 ...				$3,510	$ 96,490
June 30, Year 1 ...	$ 2,500	$ 2,895	$ 395	3,115	96,885
Dec. 31, Year 1 ...	2,500	2,907	407	2,708	97,292
June 30, Year 2 ...	2,500	2,919	419	2,289	97,711
Dec. 31, Year 2 ...	2,500	2,931	431	1,858	98,142
June 30, Year 3 ...	2,500	2,944	444	1,414	98,586
Dec. 31, Year 3 ...	2,500	2,958	458	956	99,044
June 30, Year 4 ...	2,500	2,971	471	485	99,515
Dec. 31, Year 4 ...	2,500	2,985	485	0	100,000
Totals	$20,000	$23,510	$3,510		

* In the case of an accrual, in this chapter, the company would record interest receivable at period-end.
Note: Amounts rounded to the dollar to simplify journal entries that follow.

b. Issuance of Bonds at a Discount

January 1, Year 1—To record bonds sold at a discount

Assets = Liabilities + Equity
+96,490   –3,510
C:f   Disc BP
        +100,000
          BP

Cash	Bonds Payable
96,490	100,000

Discount on BP
3,510

Cash	96,490	
Discount on Bonds Payable ($100,000 – $3,510)...............	3,510	
Bonds Payable		100,000

c. Interest Expense and Discount Amortized on Bonds [Effective interest method]

On June 30 of Year 1, the company records the following journal entry for the first semiannual cash interest payment and amortization of the discount on bonds payable.

June 30, Year 1—To record payment of interest and bond discount amortization

Assets = Liabilities + Equity
–2,500   +395   –2,895
C:o   Disc BP   Exp

Cash	Discount on BP
96,490	2,500	3,510	395

Interest Exp
2,895

Interest Expense......................................	2,895	
Discount on Bonds Payable...........................		395
Cash		2,500

At June 30 of Year 1, the carrying amount of the bonds is $96,885 ($96,490 + $395).

On December 31 of Year 1, the company records the following journal entry for the second semiannual cash interest payment and amortization of the discount.

December 31, Year 1—To record payment of interest and bond discount amortization

Assets = Liabilities + Equity
–2,500   +407   –2,907
C:o   Disc BP   Exp

Cash	Discount on BP
96,490	2,500	3,510	395
	2,500		407

Interest Exp
2,895
2,907

Interest Expense......................................	2,907	
Discount on Bonds Payable...........................		407
Cash		2,500

Using the effective interest method, Rush continues to amortize the discount through the four years of the bond term by crediting Discount on Bonds Payable each period. Interest expense is computed each period using the market rate in effect at the issuance of the bonds. Upon maturity, Discount on Bonds Payable will be fully amortized.

continued

continued from previous page

d. Financial Statement Presentation

In the balance sheet on December 31 of Year 1, the company recognizes bonds payable of $100,000 net of the unamortized discount of $2,708. In the income statement for the 12 months ended December 31 of Year 1, Rush recognizes 12 months of interest expense of $5,802 ($2,895 + $2,907).

Balance Sheet Excerpt December 31, Year 1		Income Statement Excerpt For Year Ended December 31, Year 1	
Liabilities		Other revenues (expenses)	
Bonds payable	$100,000	Interest expense	$(5,802)
Less: Discount on bonds payable	2,708		
Bonds payable, net	$ 97,292		

e. Accrual of Bond Interest

In the previous example, the interest payment dates were the same as the reporting dates of June 30 and December 31. On January 31 of Year 2, however, the financial reporting date does not match the cash interest payment date, so proration of interest is necessary. On January 31 of Year 2, Rush records one month of interest, prorated from the six months of interest of $2,919 (see June 30 of Year 2, interest expense from the amortization schedule).

January 31, Year 2—To record accrual of bond interest expense

Interest Expense ($2,919 × 1/6)	487	
Discount on Bonds Payable ($419 × 1/6)		70
Interest Payable ($2,500 × 1/6)		417

Assets = Liabilities + Equity
+70 −487
Disc BP Exp
+417
IntP

Interest Payable	Discount on BP
417	3,510	395
	407
	70

Interest Exp
2,895
2,907
487

f. Derecognition of Bonds Payable at Maturity

Upon maturity, the company records the final interest payment and the payment of the face value of the bonds to bondholders.

December 31, Year 4—To record final interest payment

Interest Expense	2,985	
Discount on Bonds Payable		485
Cash		2,500

Assets = Liabilities + Equity
−2,500 +485 −2,985
C:o Disc BP Exp

Interest Payable	Discount on BP
2,500 Bal.	485	485

Interest Exp
2,985

December 31, Year 4—To derecognize bonds payable at maturity

Bonds Payable	100,000	
Cash		100,000

Assets = Liabilities + Equity
100,000 −100,000
C:f BP

Cash	Bonds Payable
100,000	100,000	100,000 Bal.

Account for Bonds Issued at a Discount [Straight-Line Interest Method] LO16-4   DEMO 16-4B

Refer to the information in **Demo 16-4A** for Rush, but now assume that the company amortizes the bond discount using the straight-line interest method.

a. Prepare an amortization schedule over the term of the bonds.
b. Prepare the journal entry for the semiannual interest payment and amortization of the bond discount on June 30 of Year 1 and December 31 of Year 1.
c. Record the entry upon maturity of the bonds. Ignore the final interest payment entry.

Solution

a. **Amortization Schedule—Straight-Line Interest Method [Stated Rate = 5% and Market Rate = 6%]**

The following amortization schedule illustrates how interest expense is recognized over the term of the bonds under the straight-line interest method. The components of the journal entry for each period include Cash, Interest Expense, and Discount on Bonds Payable are included in this schedule.

Let's review the calculations for June 30 of Year 1. The semiannual cash interest payment is equal to $2,500. The discount amortization of $439 is equal to the total discount of $3,510 divided by 8 semiannual periods. Interest expense of $2,939 is equal to cash interest

continued

continued from previous page

of $2,500 plus the discount amortized of $439. The discount amortized of $439 is subtracted from the beginning of period uamortized discount of $3,510 to arrive at adjusted unamortized discount of $3,071. The carrying amount of bonds payable increases to $96,929, or $100,000 – $3,071. We see that over the bond term, stated interest is constant because it is contractual and is tied to the bond indenture. The amortized discount and interest expense are also the same each period over the term of the bonds (except for a minor rounding difference applied to the last period). At the end of the bond term, the carrying amount of the bonds equals the face value of $100,000, and the unamortized discount is zero. Total interest expense of $23,510 exceeds total cash interest of $20,000 because the bonds were sold at a discount.

	Straight-Line Interest Method—Discount				
	A	**B**	**C**	**D**	**E**
	Cash (Stated Interest)	**Interest Expense** (Market Interest)	**Discount** Amortization*	**Unamortized Discount**	**Bonds Payable, Net** (Carrying Amount)
Date	2.5% × Face Value	A + C	$3,510 ÷ 8	D Beg. Period Bal. – C	Face Value – D
Jan. 1, Year 1 ...				$3,510	$ 96,490
June 30, Year 1 ...	$ 2,500	$ 2,939	$ 439	3,071	96,929
Dec. 31, Year 1 ...	2,500	2,939	439	2,632	97,368
June 30, Year 2 ...	2,500	2,939	439	2,193	97,807
Dec. 31, Year 2 ...	2,500	2,939	439	1,754	98,246
June 30, Year 3 ...	2,500	2,939	439	1,315	98,685
Dec. 31, Year 3 ...	2,500	2,939	439	876	99,124
June 30, Year 4 ...	2,500	2,939	439	437	99,563
Dec. 31, Year 4 ...	2,500	2,937	437	0	100,000
	$20,000	$23,510	$3,510		

*Total bond discount ÷ Total number of periods (with the exception of the last period where the amount reflects rounding differences).

b. **Interest Expense and Discount Amortized on Bonds [Straight-line interest method]**
On June 30 of Year 1, the company records the following journal entry for the first semiannual cash interest payment and amortization of the discount.

Assets	=	Liabilities	+	Equity
–2,500		+439		–2,939
C:o		Disc BP		Exp

Cash		Discount on BP	
2,500	Bal.	3,510	439

Interest Exp	
2,939	

June 30, Year 1—To record payment of interest and bond discount amortization

Interest Expense..	2,939	
Discount on Bonds Payable.............................		439
Cash..		2,500

At June 30 of Year 1, carrying amount of the bonds is $96,929.
On December 31 of Year 1, the company records the following journal entry for the second semiannual cash interest payment and amortization of the discount.

Assets	=	Liabilities	+	Equity
–2,500		+439		–2,939
C:o		Disc BP		Exp

Cash		Discount on BP	
2,500	Bal.	3,510	439
2,500			439

Interest Exp	
2,939	
2,939	

December 31, Year 1—To record payment of interest and bond discount amortization

Interest Expense..	2,939	
Discount on Bonds Payable.............................		439
Cash..		2,500

c. **Derecognition of Bonds Payable at Maturity**
Under the straight-line interest method, the company continues to amortize the discount through the four years of the bond term. Upon maturity, Discount on Bonds Payable will be fully amortized.

Assets	=	Liabilities	+	Equity
–100,000		–100,000		
C:f		BP		

Cash		Bonds Payable	
100,000		100,000	100,000 Bal.

December 31, Year 5—To derecognize bonds payable at maturity

Bonds Payable	100,000	
Cash		100,000

Debt Issuance Costs

Debt issuance costs include legal, accounting, underwriting, commission, engraving, printing, registration, and promotion costs. These costs are paid by the issuer and reduce the net proceeds from the bond issue, thus raising the market rate for the issuer. By decreasing the cash received upon the sale of bonds, debt issuance costs increase the market rate on the transaction (meaning that borrowing costs go up).

Debt issuance costs are added to the bond discount (subtracted from the bond premium) and recorded in a valuation account, Discount and Debt Issuance Costs (Premium and Debt Issuance Costs). Amortization is recognized as interest expense over the term of the bonds. The effective rate that equates the net bonds payable amount to the future cash flows is calculated and applied to the beginning-of-period bond carrying amount to determine periodic interest expense.

835-30-45-1A   . . . Similarly, debt issuance costs related to a note shall be reported in the balance sheet as a direct deduction from the face amount of that note. The discount, premium, or debt issuance costs shall not be classified as a deferred charge or deferred credit.

835-30-45-3   Amortization of discount or premium shall be reported as interest expense in the case of liabilities or as interest income in the case of assets. Amortization of debt issuance costs also shall be reported as interest expense.

Account for Debt Issuance Costs   LO16-4 ◄ DEMO 16-4C

Demo

MBC

Refer to the information in **Demo 16-4A** for Rush. Assume that the bonds were sold to yield a market rate of 6% and that the company amortizes the bond discount using the effective interest method. Debt issuance costs are $5,000.

a. Record the entry upon issuance of the bonds, including the recording of debt issuance costs.
b. Prepare an amortization schedule over the term of the bonds.
c. Prepare the journal entry for the first semiannual interest payment and amortization of Discount and Debt Issuance Costs on June 30 of Year 1.

Solution

a. **Issuance of Bonds at a Discount with Debt Issuance Costs**
The $5,000 in issuance costs are subtracted from the bond proceeds and added to the bond discount of $3,510 calculated in **Demo 16-4A**, resulting in a debit to Discount and Debt Issue Costs of $8,510.

January 1, Year 1—To record bonds sold at a discount

Cash ($96,490 – $5,000)	91,490	
Discount and Debt Issuance Costs ($3,510 + $5,000)	8,510	
Bonds Payable		100,000

Assets = Liabilities + Equity
+91,490   –8,510
   C:f   Disc-Iss
             +100,000
                BP

Cash		Bonds Payable
91,490		100,000

Disc and Iss Cost
8,510 |

b. **Amortization Schedule—Effective Interest Method**
The carrying amount of the bonds on January 1 of Year 1 is now $91,490. The market rate increases to 3.751%, the rate that equates the present value of the bonds ($91,490) with the future value of the semiannual cash interest payments of $2,500 and the face value of $100,000.

	RATE	NPER	PMT	PV	FV	Excel Formula
Given	?	8	(2,500)	91,490	(100,000)	=RATE(8–2500,91490,–100000)
Solution	3.751%					

Effective Interest Method—Discount and Debt Issuance Costs				
A	B	C	D	E
Cash (Stated Interest)	Interest Expense (Market Interest)	Discount and Debt Issuance Costs Amortization	Unamortized Discount	Bonds Payable, Net (Carrying Amount)
Date	2.5% × Face Value	3.751% × E Beg. Period Bal.	B – A	D Beg. Period Bal. – C	Face Value – D
Jan. 1, Year 1 . . .				$8,510	$ 91,490
June 30, Year 1 . . .	$ 2,500	$ 3,432	$ 932	7,578	92,422
Dec. 31, Year 1 . . .	2,500	3,467	967	6,611	93,389
June 30, Year 2 . . .	2,500	3,503	1,003	5,608	94,392
Dec. 31, Year 2 . . .	2,500	3,541	1,041	4,567	95,433
June 30, Year 3 . . .	2,500	3,580	1,080	3,487	96,513
Dec. 31, Year 3 . . .	2,500	3,620	1,120	2,367	97,633
June 30, Year 4 . . .	2,500	3,662	1,162	1,205	98,795
Dec. 31, Year 4 . . .	2,500	3,705*	1,205	0	100,000
Totals	$20,000	$28,510	$8,510		

*Rounded.

continued

continued from previous page

C. Interest Expense and Discount and Debt Issuance Costs Amortized on Bonds

Assets	=	Liabilities	+	Equity
−2,500		+932		−3,432
C:o		Disc BP		Exp

Cash		Disc and Iss Cost	
91,490	2,500	8,510	932

Interest Exp	
3,432	

June 30, Year 1—To record payment of interest and amortization

Interest Expense.....................................	3,432	
Discount and Debt Issuance Costs...................		932
Cash...		2,500

REVIEW 16-4 > **LO16-4**   Account for Bonds Issued at a Discount

Review

MBC

More Practice:
BE16-9, BE16-10, BE16-13,
BE16-14, BE16-17, E16-10,
E16-11, E16-12, E16-13
Solution on p. 16-76.

5M Corp. authorized and issued $150,000, 5%, 10-year bonds on January 1. The bonds pay cash interest semiannually on July 1 and January 1 and are issued to yield 7%.

a. Record the entries on (1) January 1 for the issuance of the bonds, (2) July 1 for the payment of interest, and (3) December 31 for the accrual of interest, assuming that the company amortizes bond discounts using the effective interest method.

b. Record the entries on (1) January 1 for the issuance of the bonds, (2) July 1 for the payment of interest, and (3) December 31 for the accrual of interest, assuming that the company amortizes bond discounts using the straight-line interest method.

LO 16-5 > Account for bonds issued at a premium

LO 16-5 Overview

Bonds Issued at a Premium
- Stated rate > Market rate
- Proceeds > Face value
- Total cash interest payments > Total interest expense over bond term
- Premium reduces interest expense over the bond term
  - Effective interest method
  - Straight-line interest method

If the proceeds of a bond issuance are greater than the face value of the issued bonds, a premium on bonds payable is recorded. When bonds are sold at a premium, the amount of premium is initially recorded as an adjunct account to bonds payable. Over the term of the bonds, the premium reduces interest expense, resulting in total interest expense that is *less than* total cash interest payments. The premium is amortized using the effective interest method.

Effective Interest Method Under the **effective interest method**, interest expense is equal to the market rate in effect at the bonds issuance multiplied by the carrying amount of the bonds at the *beginning* of the interest period. The difference between the cash interest payment and interest expense for the period is the amount of premium amortized. As the premium is amortized over the term of the bonds, the carrying amount of the bonds decreases toward the face value. Interest expense *declines* each period as the carrying amount of the bonds declines to the face value. See **Demo 16-5A**.

Effective Interest Method

Cash Interest Payment				Bond Interest Expense			Premium Amortization
Stated Rate	×	Bond Face Value	−	Market Rate	×	Bond Payable, Net (Beg. of Year)	=

Straight-Line Interest Method The **straight-line interest method** can be used if the results are not materially different from using the effective interest method. Under the straight-line interest method, the premium is amortized evenly over the bond term. Thus, this method produces a stable dollar amount of interest expense each period equal to the cash interest paid *less* the premium amortized each interest period. The carrying amount of the bonds decreases by the premium amortization each period until the carrying amount of the bonds equals the face value upon maturity of the bonds (see **Demo 16-5B**).

Straight-Line Interest Method

Cash Interest Payment				Premium Amortization			Interest Expense
Stated Rate	×	Bond Face Value	−	Total Premium	÷	Bond Term	=

| Account for Bonds Issued at a Premium [Effective Interest Method] | **LO16-5** | DEMO 16-5A |

Demo

MBC

Rush authorizes and issues $100,000 of 5% interest-bearing bonds on January 1 of Year 1. The bonds mature in four years on December 31 and pay cash interest on June 30 and December 31. The bonds were sold to yield a market rate of 4%, and the company amortizes the bond premium using the effective interest method.

a. Prepare an amortization schedule over the term of the bonds.
b. Prepare the entry for the issuance of the bonds on January 1 of Year 1.
c. Prepare the journal entry for the semiannual interest payment and amortization of the premium on June 30 of Year 1 and December 31 of Year 1.
d. Show the December 31 of Year 1 balance sheet and the Year 1 income statement effect of the bonds.
e. Record the entry upon maturity of the bonds, including the final interest payment.

Solution

a. **Amortization Schedule—Effective Interest Method [Stated Rate = 5% and Market Rate = 4%]**
   Because the bonds pay interest semiannually, interest rates and periods must be adjusted to reflect semiannual compounding periods.
   - Semiannual market rate: 4% ÷ 2 = 2%
   - Semiannual periods: 4 years × 2 = 8 periods
   - Semiannual cash interest payment: 5% ÷ 2 × $100,000 = $2,500

	RATE	NPER	PMT	PV	FV	Excel Formula
Given	2%	8	(2,500)	?	(100,000)	=PV(0.02,8,–2500,–100000)
Solution				$103,663		

The following amortization schedule shows the components of the journal entry for each period for Cash, Interest Expense, and Premium on Bonds Payable. Over the bond term, stated interest is constant because it is contractual and is tied to the bond indenture. Interest expense each period decreases with the decrease in the bond carrying amount. The premium amortized is equal to the cash payment less interest expense. The premium amortized is subtracted from the beginning of period uamortized premium to arrive at adjusted unamortized premium. At the end of the bond term, the carrying amount of the bonds equals the face value of $100,000, and the unamortized premium equals zero. Total interest expense of $16,337 is less than total cash interest of $20,000 because the bonds were sold at a premium.

	Effective Interest Method—Premium				
	A	B	C	D	E
	Cash (Stated Interest)	Interest Expense (Market Interest)	Premium Amortization	Unamortized Premium	Bonds Payable, Net (Carrying Amount)
Date	2.5% × Face Value	2% × E Beg. Period Bal.	A – B	D Beg. Period Bal. – C	Face Value + D
Jan. 1, Year 1 . . .				$3,663	$103,663
June 30, Year 1 . . .	$ 2,500	$ 2,073	$ 427	3,236	103,236
Dec. 31, Year 1 . . .	2,500	2,065	435	2,801	102,801
June 30, Year 2 . . .	2,500	2,056	444	2,357	102,357
Dec. 31, Year 2 . . .	2,500	2,047	453	1,904	101,904
June 30, Year 3 . . .	2,500	2,038	462	1,442	101,442
Dec. 31, Year 3 . . .	2,500	2,029	471	971	100,971
June 30, Year 4 . . .	2,500	2,019	481	490	100,490
Dec. 31, Year 4 . . .	2,500	2,010	490	0	100,000
Totals	$20,000	$16,337	$3,663		

b. **Issuance of Bonds at a Premium**

January 1, Year 1—To record bonds sold at a premium

Cash.	103,663	
Premium on Bonds Payable ($103,663 – $100,000).		3,663
Bonds Payable		100,000

Assets = Liabilities + Equity
+103,663   +3,663
C:f   Prem BP
             +100,000
             BP

Cash		Bonds Payable
103,663		100,000

	Premium on BP
	3,663

continued

continued from previous page

c. **Interest Expense and Premium Amortized on Bonds [Effective interest method]**

On June 30 of Year 1, the company records the following journal entry for the first semiannual cash interest payment and amortization of the bond premium.

Assets	=	Liabilities	+	Equity
−2,500		−427		−2,073
C:o		Prem BP		Exp

Cash		Premium on BP
103,663	2,500	427	3,663

Interest Exp
2,073	

June 30, Year 1—To record payment of interest and bond premium amortization

Interest Expense......................................	2,073	
Premium on Bonds Payable.........................	427	
Cash..		2,500

At June 30 of Year 1, carrying amount of the bonds is $103,236 ($100,000 + $3,236).

On December 31 of Year 1, the company records the following journal entry for the second semiannual cash interest payment and amortization of the bond premium.

Assets	=	Liabilities	+	Equity
−2,500		−435		−2,065
C:o		Prem BP		Exp

Cash		Premium on BP
103,663	2,500	427	3,663
	2,500	435	

Interest Exp
2,073	
2,065	

December 31, Year 1—To record payment of interest and bond premium amortization

Interest Expense......................................	2,065	
Premium on Bonds Payable.........................	435	
Cash..		2,500

Under the effective interest method, the company continues to amortize the premium through the four years of the bond term by debiting Premium on Bonds Payable each period. Upon maturity, Premium on Bonds Payable will be fully amortized, with a carrying amount of zero.

d. **Financial Statement Presentation**

On the balance sheet on December 31 of Year 1, the company recognizes bonds payable of $100,000 plus the unamortized premium of $2,801. In the income statement for the 12 months ended December 31 of Year 1, the company recognizes 12 months of interest expense of $4,138 ($2,073 + $2,065).

Balance Sheet Excerpt December 31, Year 1		Income Statement Excerpt For Year Ended December 31, Year 1
Liabilities		Other revenues (expenses)
Bonds payable $100,000		Interest expense .... $(4,138)
Plus: Premium on bonds payable ... 2,801		
Bonds payable, net $102,801		

e. **Derecognition of Bonds Payable at Maturity**

Upon maturity, the company records the final interest payment and the payment of the face value of the bonds to the bond holders.

Assets	=	Liabilities	+	Equity
−2,500		−490		−2,010
C:o		Prem BP		Exp

Cash		Premium on BP
	2,500	490	490 Bal.

Interest Exp
2,010	

December 31, Year 4—To record final interest payment

Interest Expense......................................	2,010	
Premium on Bonds Payable.........................	490	
Cash..		2,500

Assets	=	Liabilities	+	Equity
−100,000		−100,000		
C:f		BP		

Cash		Bonds Payable
	100,000	100,000	100,000 Bal.

December 31, Year 4—To derecognize bonds payable at maturity

Bonds Payable	100,000	
Cash..		100,000

SKY HARBOUR

Real World—BONDS ISSUED AT A PREMIUM

Sky Harbour Group Corporation, an aviation infrastructure development company, described a debt issuance in a recent annual report. As disclosed, the Series 2021 Bond was issued at a premium.

The Series 2021 Bonds have principal amounts, interest rates, and maturity dates as follow: $21.1 million bearing interest at 4.00%, due July 1, 2036; $30.4 million bearing interest at 4.00%, due July 1, 2041; and $114.8 million bearing interest at 4.25%, due July 1, 2054. The Series 2021 Bond that has a maturity date of July 1, 2036 was issued at a premium, and the Company received bond proceeds that were $0.2 million above its face value. The bond premium is being amortized as a reduction of interest expense over the life of the bond. Interest is payable on each January 1 and July 1, commencing January 1, 2022. Principal repayments due under the Series 2021 Bonds are paid annually, commencing July 1, 2032.

Account for Bonds Issued at a Premium [Straight-Line Interest Method]   LO16-5   DEMO 16-5B

Refer to the information in **Demo 16-5A** for Rush. Now assume that the company amortizes the bond premium using the straight-line interest method.

a. Prepare an amortization schedule over the term of the bonds.
b. Prepare the journal entry for the first semiannual cash interest payment and amortization of the premium on June 30 of Year 1.

Solution

a. **Amortization Schedule—Straight-Line Interest Method [Stated Rate = 5% and Market Rate = 4%]**

The following amortization schedule shows the components of the journal entry for each period of Cash, Interest Expense, and Premium on Bonds Payable. Over the bond term, stated interest is constant because it is contractual and is tied to the bond indenture. The amortized premium and interest expense are also the same each period over the term of the bonds (except for a minor rounding difference applied to the last period). At the end of the bond term, the carrying amount of the bonds equals the face value of $100,000, and the unamortized premium equals zero. Total interest expense of $16,337 is less than total cash interest of $20,000 because the bonds were sold at a premium.

	Straight-Line Interest Method—Premium				
	A	**B**	**C**	**D**	**E**
	Cash (Stated Interest)	**Interest Expense** (Market Interest)	**Premium** Amortization*	**Unamortized Premium**	**Bonds Payable, Net** (Carrying Amount)
Date	2.5% × Face Value	A – C	$3,663 ÷ 8	D Beg. Period Bal. – C	Face Value + D
Jan. 1, Year 1 . . .				$3,663	$103,663
June 30, Year 1 . . .	$ 2,500	$ 2,042	$ 458	3,205	103,205
Dec. 31, Year 1 . . .	2,500	2,042	458	2,747	102,747
June 30, Year 2 . . .	2,500	2,042	458	2,289	102,289
Dec. 31, Year 2 . . .	2,500	2,042	458	1,831	101,831
June 30, Year 3 . . .	2,500	2,042	458	1,373	101,373
Dec. 31, Year 3 . . .	2,500	2,042	458	915	100,915
June 30, Year 4 . . .	2,500	2,042	458	457	100,457
Dec. 31, Year 4 . . .	2,500	2,043	457	0	100,000
Totals	$20,000	$16,337	$3,663		

*Total bond premium ÷ Total number of periods (with the exception of the last period where the amount reflects rounding differences).

b. **Interest Expense and Premium Amortized on Bonds [Straight-line interest method]**

June 30, Year 1—To record payment of interest and bond premium amortization

Interest Expense.	2,042	
Premium on Bonds Payable.	458	
Cash		2,500

Assets	=	Liabilities	+	Equity
–2,500		–458		–2,042
C:o		Prem BP		Exp

Cash		Premium on BP	
	2,500	458	3,663 Bal.

Interest Exp	
2,042	

At June 30 of Year 1, the carrying amount of the bonds is $103,205 ($100,000 + $3,205).

For both bonds issued at a discount and bonds issued at a premium, the carrying amount moves toward the face value over the term of the bond using either the effective interest or straight-line interest method.

Exhibit 16-2 shows the carrying amount of the Rush bonds issued at a discount (**Demo 16-4B**) and at a premium (**Demo 16-5B**) with the discount or premium amortized on a straight-line basis. Note that the carrying amount of the bond issued at a discount is originally recorded at an amount less than the face amount and gradually increases over the term of the bond. In contrast, the carrying amount of the bond issued at a premium is originally recorded at an amount greater than the face value and gradually decreases over the term of the bond. At maturity, the carrying amount equals the face value of the bonds regardless of whether the bonds were issued at par, a discount, or a premium.

EXHIBIT 16-2
Discount and
Premium
Amortization

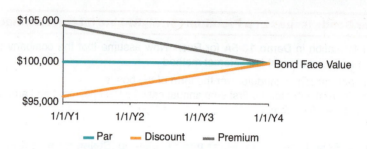

Comparing Debtor and Investor Transactions

Bonds issued from a debtor perspective are reviewed in Chapter 16 and from an investor perspective in Chapter 14. The journal entries are summarized here in chronological order, listed side-by-side.

For bonds issued at par, the journal entries recorded by the debtor and investor are a "mirror image." The debtor records Bonds Payable and Interest Expense while the investor records Investment in HTM Securities and Interest Revenue.

Bonds Issued at Par				
Bond Issuer/Debtor—Demo 16-3			**Bond Holder/Investor—Demo 14-1A**	
Jan. 1, Year 1	Cash	100,000	Investment in HTM Securities	100,000
	Bonds Payable	100,000	Cash	100,000
	To record bonds sold at face value		*To record investment purchased at face value*	
June 30, Year 1	Interest Expense	2,500	Cash	2,500
	Cash	2,500	Interest Revenue	2,500
	To record interest payment		*To record receipt of interest*	
Dec. 31, Year 4	Bonds Payable	100,000	Cash	100,000
	Cash	100,000	Investment in HTM Securities	100,000
	To derecognize bonds payable		*To derecognize bond investment*	

When bonds are issued at a discount, the debtor records a separate Discount on Bonds Payable account, which is amortized to Interest Expense over the term of the bonds. The investor records Investment in HTM Securities net of the bond discount and amortizes the discount to Interest Revenue through the investment account. Otherwise, the debtor and investor journal entries mirror each other.

Bonds Issued at a Discount—Effective Interest Method				
Bond Issuer/Debtor—Demo 16-4A			**Bond Holder/Investor—Demo 14-1B**	
Jan. 1, Year 1	Cash	96,490	Investment in HTM Securities	96,490
	Discount on Bonds Payable	3,510	Cash	96,490
	Bonds Payable	100,000	*To record investment purchased at a discount*	
	To record bonds sold at a discount			
June 30, Year 1	Interest Expense	2,895	Cash	2,500
	Discount on Bonds Payable	395	Investment in HTM Securities	395
	Cash	2,500	Interest Revenue	2,895
	To record interest payment		*To record receipt of interest and discount amortization*	
Dec. 31, Year 4	Bonds Payable	100,000	Cash	100,000
	Cash	100,000	Investment in HTM Securities	100,000
	To derecognize bonds payable		*To derecognize bond investment*	

Finally, when bonds are issued at a premium, the debtor records a separate Premium on Bonds Payable account while the investor records Investment in HTM Securities net of the bond premium.

Bonds Issued at a Premium—Effective Interest Method				
Bond Issuer/Debtor—Demo 16-5A			**Bond Holder/Investor—Demo 14-1C**	
Jan. 1, Year 1	Cash	103,663	Investment in HTM Securities	103,663
	Premium on Bonds Payable	3,663	Cash	103,663
	Bonds Payable	100,000	*To record investment purchased at a premium*	
	To record bonds sold at a premium			

continued

continued from previous page

June 30, Year 1	Interest Expense................	2,073			Cash............................	2,500	
	Premium on Bonds Payable.......	427			Investment in HTM Securities...		427
	Cash....................		2,500		Interest Revenue.............		2,073
	To record interest payment				*To record receipt of interest and premium amortization*		
Dec. 31, Year 4	Bonds Payable................	100,000			Cash............................	100,000	
	Cash....................		100,000		Investment in HTM Securities...		100,000
	To derecognize bonds payable				*To derecognize bond investment*		

Account for Bonds Issued at a Premium   LO16-5   REVIEW 16-5

Review

5M Corp., with a calendar year-end, authorized and issued $50,000, 6%, 10-year bonds on January 1. The bonds pay cash interest semiannually on July 1 and January 1 and were issued to yield 5%.

a. Record entries on (1) January 1 for issuance of the bonds, (2) July 1 for payment of interest, and (3) December 31 for accrual of interest, assuming that the company amortizes premiums using the effective interest method.

b. Record entries on (1) January 1 for issuance of the bonds, (2) July 1 for payment of interest, and (3) December 31 for accrual of interest, assuming that the company amortizes premiums using the straight-line interest method.

MBC

More Practice:
BE16-11, BE16-15, E16-15,
E16-16, E16-18, E16-20
Solution on p. 16-76.

Measure and record notes at issuance and after issuance   LO 16-6

A note is a formal document that specifies the terms of a debt. **Long-term notes** are often used for specific asset acquisitions, while bonds are more likely to be used to raise large amounts of capital for general purposes. Notes typically have shorter maturities than bonds and are not traded on organized exchanges. A note typically is a contract with one creditor, while bonds are contracts with multiple creditors.

Notes Payable
- Note issued for cash
  - Measure note at present value of cash flows
- Note issued for noncash consideration
  - Measure note at fair value of asset or debt, whichever is more clearly evident

LO 16-6 Overview

    The measurement basis for a note payable is the present value of the cash expected to be paid on the note. The market rate in effect at inception of the note is used in the present value calculation as the discount rate. If present value and face value do not differ materially, the note is recognized at face value. If the face value of the note is greater than the present value of the note, a discount on note payable is recognized. If the face value of the note is less than the present value of the note, a premium on note payable is recognized. A discount (premium) is amortized over the life of the note as an increase (decrease) to interest expense.

Notes Payable Issued for Cash

The three examples in **Demo 16-6A** illustrate the accounting for a note payable exchanged for cash. The first example is a typical exchange where a company issues a note for cash (a form of a loan) at the note's face value. In this case, the market rate is equal to the stated rate. Although issuers usually attempt to set the stated rate close to the expected market rate at issuance (minimizing the discount or premium), a zero-interest-bearing note is an exception. A zero-interest-bearing note (illustrated in example two) provides no separate interest payments. Instead, upon issuance of the note, the face value of the note exceeds the present value of the note—the difference representing a discount, or the interest on the note. The note described in example three illustrates a case where the stated rate is less than the market rate, causing the note to be issued at a discount. Although not illustrated, if the present value of the cash flows exceeds the stated value of the note, the note is recorded at a premium. The difference between the present value and face value of the note decreases interest expense over the term of the note.

DEMO 16-6A ▶ **LO16-6**   Note Payable Issued for Cash

Demo

MBC

Example One: Note Payable—Issued at Face Value [Stated Rate = 8% and Market Rate = 8%]
On January 1 of Year 1, Frazier Inc. borrowed $1,000 cash by issuing a 3-year, $1,000 note payable to Seattle Corp. at face value, with cash interest payable annually on December 31 at 8%. Record the following entries for Frazier Inc. related to the note payable. Frazier has an accounting period that ends on December 31.

a. Record the issuance of the note on January 1 of Year 1.
b. Record interest expense on the note payable on December 31 of Year 1, Year 2, and Year 3.
c. Record the entry upon maturity of the note payable on December 31 of Year 3.

Solution

a. **Issuance of Note Payable**

The issue price is equal to the present value of the principal ($1,000) and interest payments ($80), discounted at the market rate of 8%. The present value of the note on January 1 of Year 1 is equal to the face value of the note because the stated and market rates are equal.

	RATE	NPER	PMT	PV	FV	Excel Formula
Given	8%	3	(80)	?	(1,000)	=PV(0.08,3,-80,-1000)
Solution				$1,000		

The company records the following entry upon issuance of the note.

January 1, Year 1—To record note payable issued at face value

Cash	1,000	
Note Payable		1,000

Assets = Liabilities + Equity
+1,000   +1,000
C:f   NP

Cash		Note Payable
1,000		1,000

b. **Interest Expense on Note Payable**
The company recognizes interest expense each annual period as follows.

December 31, Year 1, Year 2, and Year 3—To record payment of interest

Interest Expense ($1,000 × 8%)	80	
Cash		80

Assets = Liabilities + Equity
−80   −80
C:o   Exp

Cash		Interest Exp
1,000	80	80
	80	80
	80	80

c. **Derecognition of Note Payable**
Upon maturity, Frazier Inc. records the full cash payment of the face value of the note to Seattle Corp.

December 31, Year 3—To record retirement of note

Note Payable	1,000	
Cash		1,000

Assets = Liabilities + Equity
−1,000   −1,000
C:f   NP

Cash		Note Payable
1,000	80	1,000	1,000
	80		
	80		
	1,000		

Example Two: Note Payable—Zero-Interest-Bearing [Stated Rate = 0% and Market Rate = 8%]
On January 1 of Year 1, Frazier Inc. issued a 3-year, $1,000 zero-interest-bearing note payable to Seattle Corp. for cash of $794. Record the following entries for Frazier Inc. related to the note payable, assuming that the market rate on the note is 8%.

a. Record the issuance of the note on January 1 of Year 1.
b. Prepare an amortization schedule over the term of the note payable that uses the effective interest method to amortize the discount on note payable.
c. Record interest expense on the note payable at year-end on December 31 of Year 1, Year 2, and Year 3.
d. Record the entry upon maturity of the note payable.

Solution

a. **Issuance of Note Payable**
Frazier Inc. borrows $794 in cash but will pay back the face value of the note of $1,000 at maturity. The difference of $206 is the discount that will be amortized to interest expense over the term of the note. Frazier Inc. recognizes the following entry upon issuance of the zero-interest-bearing note payable.

	RATE	NPER	PMT	PV	FV	Excel Formula
Given	8%	3	0	?	(1,000)	=PV(0.08,3,0,-1000)
Solution				$794		

continued

continued from previous page

January 1, Year 1—To record issuance of zero-interest-bearing note payable

Cash.....................................	794	
Discount on Note Payable ($1,000 – $794).....................	206	
Note Payable..		1,000

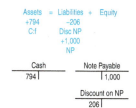

Assets = Liabilities + Equity
+794　　−206
C:f　　Disc NP
　　+1,000
　　NP

Cash		Note Payable	
794			1,000

	Discount on NP	
206		

b. **Amortization Schedule—Effective Interest Method [Stated Rate = 0% and Market Rate = 8%]**
The following amortization schedule shows the components of the journal entry for each period to record Interest Expense and adjust Discount on Note Payable.

	Effective Interest Method—Discount			
	Cash	Interest Expense	Discount on N.P.	Note Payable, Net
Date	(Stated Interest)	(Market Interest)	Amortization	(Carrying Amount)
Jan.　1, Year 1 ...				$ 794
Dec. 31, Year 1 ...	$0	$ 64	$ 64	858
Dec. 31, Year 2 ...	0	69	69	927
Dec. 31, Year 3 ...	0	73*	73	1,000
Totals	$0	$206	$206	

* rounded

c. **Interest Expense on Note Payable**
Even though no cash interest is paid during the note term, the debtor still records interest expense as the discount is amortized.

December 31, Year 1—To record interest expense

Interest Expense.......................	64	
Discount on Note Payable		64

Assets = Liabilities + Equity
　　+64　　−64
　　Disc NP　　Exp

Discount on NP		Interest Exp	
206	64	64	

December 31, Year 2—To record interest expense

Interest Expense.......................	69	
Discount on Note Payable		69

Assets = Liabilities + Equity
　　+69　　−69
　　Disc NP　　Exp

Discount on NP		Interest Exp	
206	64	64	
	69	69	

December 31, Year 3—To record interest expense

Interest Expense.......................	73	
Discount on Note Payable		73

Assets = Liabilities + Equity
　　+73　　−73
　　Disc NP　　Exp

Discount on NP		Interest Exp	
206	64	64	
	69	69	
	73	73	
0			

d. **Derecognition of Note Payable**
Upon maturity, Frazier Inc. records the payment of the face value of the note to Seattle Corp.

December 31, Year 3—To record retirement of note at maturity

Note Payable..	1,000	
Cash..		1,000

Assets = Liabilities + Equity
−1,000　　−1,000
C:f　　NP

Cash		Note Payable	
794	1,000	1,000	1,000

Example Three: Note Payable—Interest-Bearing [Stated Rate = 8% and Market Rate = 9%]

On January 1 of Year 1, Frazier Inc. issued a 3-year, $1,000 note payable to Seattle Corp. for $975 in cash, with cash interest payable annually on December 31 at 8%. The market rate of a note with similar risks is 9%. Record the following entries for Frazier Inc. related to the note payable.

a. Record the issuance of the note on January 1 of Year 1.
b. Prepare an amortization schedule over the term of the note payable that uses the effective interest method to amortize the discount on note payable.
c. Record interest expense on the note payable at year-end on December 31 of Year 1.
d. Record the entry upon maturity of the note payable (ignoring the interest entry) on December 31 of Year 3.

continued

continued from previous page

Solution

a. Issuance of Note Payable

The issue price of $975 is equal to the present value of the principal ($1,000) plus the present value of the interest payments ($80 or $1,000 × 0.08), discounted at the 9% market rate. The difference between the cash received and the face value of the note is recorded as a discount on note payable.

	RATE	NPER	PMT	PV	FV	Excel Formula
Given	9%	3	(80)	?	(1,000)	=PV(0.09,3,-80,-1000)
Solution				$975		

January 1, Year 1—To record issuance of interest-bearing note payable

Cash...	975	
Discount on Note Payable ($1,000 – $975)...............	25	
Note Payable.........................		1,000

Assets = Liabilities + Equity
+975   +1,000
C:f   NP
                  –25
              Disc NP

Cash		Note Payable
975		1,000

Discount on NP
25

b. Amortization Schedule—Effective Interest Method [Stated Rate = 8% and Market Rate = 9%]

The following amortization schedule shows the components of the journal entry for each period of Cash, Interest Expense, and Discount on Note Payable.

	Effective Interest Method—Discount			
	Cash	Interest Expense	Discount on N.P.	Note Payable, Net
Date	(Stated Interest)	(Market Interest)	Amortization	(Carrying Amount)
Jan. 1, Year 1...				$ 975
Dec. 31, Year 1...	$ 80	$ 88	$ 8	983
Dec. 31, Year 2...	80	88	8	991
Dec. 31, Year 3...	80	89	9	1,000
Totals.........	$240	$265	$25	

c. Interest Expense on Note Payable

December 31, Year 1—To record payment of interest and discount amortization

Assets = Liabilities + Equity
–80   +8   –88
C:o   Disc NP   Exp

Interest Expense........................	88	
Discount on Note Payable................		8
Cash......................................		80

Cash		Discount on NP	
	80	25	8

Interest Exp
88

The company records interest expense each period as indicated by the amortization schedule.

d. Derecognition of Note Payable

Upon maturity, Frazier Inc. records the payment of the face value of the note to Seattle Corp.

December 31, Year 3—To record retirement of note at maturity

Assets = Liabilities + Equity
–1,000   –1,000
C:f   NP

Note Payable............................	1,000	
Cash......................................		1,000

Cash		Note Payable	
	1,000	1,000	1,000

Notes Payable Issued for Noncash Consideration

Although most notes represent loans, notes payable can also arise from purchases of goods or services or through extension of payment periods of accounts payable. Measuring the value of such transactions is more difficult because cash is not exchanged. In this case, the transaction should be recorded at the fair value of the asset or debt, whichever is more clearly evident.

If the fair value of the consideration received is known, the market rate can be measured by equating the present value of the cash flows called for in the note to the fair value of the consideration. **What happens when the fair value of the consideration received is not readily determinable?** The fair value of the debt can be used to measure the transaction. However, the interest rate stated in a note *may not equal* the market rate prevailing on obligations involving a similar credit rating or risk, although the stated rate is always used to determine the cash interest payments. If the stated rate and market rate differ, the market rate (imputed interest rate) is used to discount the note and to measure interest expense. The market rate is the rate accepted by two parties with opposing interests engaged in an arm's-length transaction.

835-30-05-2   Business transactions often involve the exchange of cash or property, goods, or service for a note or similar instrument. When a note is exchanged for property, goods, or service in a bargained transaction entered into at arm's length, there should be a general presumption that the rate of interest stipulated by the parties to the transaction represents fair and adequate compensation to the supplier for the use of the related funds. That presumption, however, must not permit the form of the transaction to prevail over its economic substance and thus would not apply if interest is not stated, the stated interest rate is unreasonable, or the stated face amount of the note is materially different from the current cash sales price for the same or similar items or from the fair value of the note at the date of the transaction . . .

The following three examples in **Demo 16-6B** illustrate the exchange of a note payable for noncash consideration. In the first example, a note payable is exchanged for equipment with a determinable fair value. In the second example, the fair value of the equipment and the note are not determinable; therefore, the note is measured by discounting the note using the prevailing market rate of notes with similar risks (also called the **imputed interest rate**). In the third example, rather than arranging to pay off the entire principal balance at the end of the loan as in the previous examples, the contract requires the debtor to make periodic, equal payments that include both principal and interest. This is similar to a typical house or vehicle loan where payments are made up of principal and interest. This type of note is an **installment note,** which allows for the obligation to be satisfied at the end of the note term through equal periodic payments.

Note Payable Issued for Noncash Consideration	LO16-6	DEMO 16-6B

Example One: Note Payable Exchanged for Equipment [Fair Value of Asset Determinable]
Frazier Inc. purchased equipment on January 1 of Year 1 by issuing a 2-year, $1,000 note with a 5% stated rate. Interest is payable each December 31, and the entire principal is payable December 31 of Year 2. The equipment has a fair value of $947. A market rate of 8% is implicit in this agreement. Record the following entries for Frazier Inc. related to the note payable.

Demo

MBC

a. Record the issuance of the note on January 1 of Year 1.
b. Prepare an amortization schedule over the term of the note that uses the effective interest method to amortize the discount on note payable.
c. Record interest expense on the note payable at year-end on December 31 of Year 1 and Year 2.
d. Record the entry upon maturity of the note payable on December 31 of Year 2.

Solution
a. **Issuance of Note Payable**
    The issuance of the note payable is recorded as follows based upon the fair value of the equipment received.

January 1, Year 1—To record issuance of note payable

Equipment	947	
Discount on Note Payable ($1,000 – $947)	53	
Note Payable	.	1,000

Assets = Liabilities + Equity
+947   –53
Equip   Disc NP
            +1,000
              NP

Equipment	Note Payable
947		1,000

Discount on NP
53	

b. **Amortization Schedule—Effective Interest Method [Stated Rate = 5% and Market Rate = 8%]**
    The following amortization schedule illustrates how the Discount on Note Payable is amortized to interest expense using the market rate of 8% implicit in the agreement. The components of the journal entry for each period to record Cash, Interest Expense, and Discount on Note Payable are included in this schedule.

	Effective Interest Method—Discount			
Date	Cash (Stated Interest)	Interest Expense (Market Interest)	Discount on N.P. Amortization	Note Payable, Net (Carrying Amount)
Jan. 1, Year 1 . . .				$ 947
Dec. 31, Year 1 . . .	$ 50	$ 76	$26	973
Dec. 31, Year 2 . . .	50	77*	27	1,000
Totals	$100	$153	$53	

* rounded

continued

continued from previous page

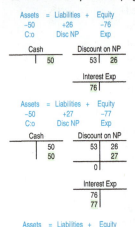

c. **Interest Expense on Note Payable**

December 31, Year 1—To record interest expense

Interest Expense..	76	
Discount on Note Payable		26
Cash		50

December 31, Year 2—To record interest expense

Interest Expense..	77	
Discount on Note Payable		27
Cash		50

d. **Derecognition of Note Payable at Maturity**
Upon maturity, Frazier Inc. records the payment of the face value of the note.

December 31, Year 2—To record retirement of note at maturity

Note Payable	1,000	
Cash		1,000

Example Two: Note Payable Exchanged for Equipment [Fair Value of Asset and Liability Not Determinable]

Frazier Inc. purchased used equipment on January 1 of Year 1 and issued a 2-year, $1,000 note with a 3% stated rate. Interest is payable each December 31, and the principal is payable December 31 of Year 2. The equipment does not have a readily determinable fair value and the 3% stated rate on the note is not equal to the market rate prevailing on obligations of similar risk. The prevailing market rate for similar notes is 8%. Record the following entries for Frazier Inc. related to the note payable.

a. Record the issuance of the note on January 1 of Year 1.
b. Prepare an amortization schedule over the term of the note payable that uses the effective interest method to amortize the discount on note payable.
c. Record interest expense on the note at year-end on December 31 of Year 1 and Year 2.
d. Record the entry upon maturity of the note payable on December 31 of Year 2.

Solution

a. **Issuance of Note Payable**
Because the fair value of the equipment (and the note) is not readily determinable, the present value of the note is measured by discounting the note using the prevailing market rate of notes with similar risks. The present value of the note is equal to the principal of $1,000 and annual interest of $30 or 3% × $1,000, discounted at the market rate for similar notes of 8%.

	RATE	NPER	PMT	PV	FV	Excel Formula
Given	8%	2	(30)	?	(1,000)	=PV(0.08,2,-30,-1000)
Solution				$911		

The entry for the issuance of the note payable is as follows.

January 1, Year 1—To record issuance of note payable

Equipment	911	
Discount on Note Payable ($1,000 – $911).................	89	
Note Payable		1,000

b. **Amortization Schedule—Effective Interest Method [Stated Rate = 3% and Market Rate = 8%]**
The following amortization schedule shows the components of the journal entry for each period of Cash, Interest Expense, and Discount on Note Payable.

	Effective Interest Method—Discount			
Date	**Cash** (Stated Interest)	**Interest Expense** (Market Interest)	**Discount on N.P.** Amortization	**Note Payable, Net** (Carrying Amount)
Jan. 1, Year 1...				$ 911
Dec. 31, Year 1....	$30	$ 73	$43	954
Dec. 31, Year 2...	30	76	46	1,000
Totals	$60	$149	$89	

continued

continued from previous page

c. Interest Expense on Note Payable

December 31, Year 1—To record interest expense

Interest Expense......................................	73	
Discount on Note Payable		43
Cash...		30

Assets = Liabilities + Equity
−30   +43   −73
C:o   Disc NP   Exp

Cash | Discount on NP
30 | 89 | 43

Interest Exp
73 |

December 31, Year 2—To record interest expense

Interest Expense......................................	76	
Discount on Note Payable		46
Cash...		30

Assets = Liabilities + Equity
−30   +46   −76
C:o   Disc NP   Exp

Cash | Discount on NP
30 | 89 | 43
30 | | 46
    0 |

Interest Exp
73 |
76 |

d. Derecognition of Note Payable

December 31, Year 2—To record retirement of note at maturity

Note Payable	1,000	
Cash...		1,000

Assets = Liabilities + Equity
−1,000   −1,000
C:f   NP

Cash | Note Payable
30 | 1,000 | 1,000
30 |
1,000 |

Example Three: Installment Note Payable Exchanged for Equipment [Fair Value of Asset Determinable]

On January 1 of Year 1, Frazier Inc. purchases equipment with a cash price of $10,000 (representing fair value) in exchange for a note with the following payment schedule: $6,000 due December 31 of Year 1 and Year 2. The note does not explicitly require interest payments. However, the interest rate implied by this transaction is 13.07%, computed as shown.

	RATE	NPER	PMT	PV	FV	Excel Formula
Given	?	2	(6,000)	10,000	0	=RATE(2,-6000,10000,0)
Solution	13.07%					

Record the following entries for Frazier Inc. related to the note payable.

a. Record the issuance of the note on January 1 of Year 1.
b. Prepare an amortization schedule over the term of the note payable that uses the effective interest method to amortize the discount on note payable.
c. Record installment payments on the note payable at year-end on December 31 of Year 1 and Year 2.

Solution

a. Issuance of Note Payable

This note is a form of an installment note because each payment of $6,000 includes interest and principal. The reduction in principal is sufficient to pay off the note upon maturity. The entry for the issuance of the note payable is as follows.

January 1, Year 1—To record issuance of installment note in exchange for equipment

Equipment	10,000	
Note Payable		10,000

Assets = Liabilities + Equity
+10,000   +10,000
Equip   NP

Equipment | Note Payable
10,000 | | 10,000

b. Amortization Schedule —Installment Note

For an installment note, the note carrying amount is reduced to zero at the end of the note term. Each installment payment is allocated to market interest and the reduction of principal of the note. The components of the journal entry for each period to record Cash, Interest Expense, and Note Payable are included in this schedule.

	A	B	C	D
	Cash	Interest Expense (Market Interest)	Note Payable (Reduction)	Note Payable, Net (Carrying Amount)
Date	Payment (Given)	D Beg. Period Bal. × 13.07%	A − B	D Beg. Period Bal. − C
Jan. 1, Year 1...				$10,000
Dec. 31, Year 1...	$ 6,000	$1,307	$ 4,693	5,307
Dec. 31, Year 2...	6,000	693*	5,307	0
Totals	$12,000	$2,000	$10,000	

continued

continued from previous page

Assets	=	Liabilities	+	Equity
−1,307		−4,693		−1,307
C:o		NP		Exp
−4,693				
C:f				

Cash		Note Payable	
	6,000	4,693	10,000

Interest Exp	
1,307	

Assets	=	Liabilities	+	Equity
−693		−5,307		−693
C:o		NP		Exp
−5,307				
C:f				

Cash		Note Payable	
	6,000	4,693	10,000
	6,000	5,307	
		0	

Interest Exp	
1,307	
693	

c. Installment Payments on Note Payable

December 31, Year 1—To record installment payment

Interest Expense..	1,307	
Note Payable	4,693	
Cash..		6,000

December 31, Year 2—To record installment payment

Interest Expense..	693	
Note Payable	5,307	
Cash..		6,000

After the recording of this entry, the note payable is reduced to a zero balance ($10,000 − $4,693 − $5,307).

EXPANDING YOUR KNOWLEDGE   Mortgage Note Payable

A debtor can obtain financing for a real estate asset through a mortgage where the real estate asset serves as collateral for the mortgage loan. Mortgage notes secured by real property have longer terms than the previous notes discussed in this section (such as 15 or 30 years), but are otherwise similar. A mortgage note can have a fixed rate over its term, or a variable rate that readjusts to market rates at specified dates. Payments on mortgage notes typically include both interest and principal, as illustrated with an installment note payable.

High and unstable interest rates gave rise to innovative mortgage notes, including point-system mortgages and adjustable-rate mortgages. The proceeds to the borrower are reduced in a point-system mortgage as a way of increasing the market rate. The monthly payment is based on the face amount of the note before the points are assessed. The interest rate on an adjustable-rate mortgage (ARM) fluctuates as market conditions change, periodically requiring a recalculation of the monthly payment based on the current loan balance, new interest rate, and remaining mortgage term.

REVIEW 16-6 ▶ LO16-6   Accounting for Notes Payable

Review

MBC

5M Corp. purchased merchandise for resale on January 1 of Year 1 for $100,000 cash plus a note payable. The fair value of the inventory on January 1 of Year 1 is $149,108. The market rate on obligations of similar risk is 8%. 5M Corp. uses the effective interest method to amortize discounts and premiums. Record the entries over the term of the note payable for the following three *separate* scenarios for the structuring of the note payable.

a. The principal of $50,000 is due on December 31 of Year 2, and the note specified 7% interest payable each December 31 over a 2-year period.

b. The face value of the note payable is instead $57,280 and is due on December 31 of Year 2. The note is structured as a zero-interest-bearing note payable over a 2-year period.

c. The loan is extended to three years with equal payments of $19,055.55 due on each December 31 over the term of the note. The note will be fully paid upon maturity.

More Practice:
BE16-20, BE16-21, BE16-22,
BE16-23, BE16-24, E16-24,
E16-25, E16-26, E16-27,
E16-28

Solution on p. 16-77.

LO 16-7 ▶ Account for extinguishment of debt

LO 16-7 Overview

Account for Early Debt Extinguishment
- Update interest expense to retirement date
- Derecognize liability including unamortized discounts/premiums
- Record transfer of cash or other assets
- Record gain or loss
- Record bond refunding if applicable

Companies typically use the proceeds from long-term debt issuances for the duration of the debt term. At maturity, any discounts or premiums are fully amortized so that the carrying amount of the debt is equal to the face value, as illustrated in the prior examples. The liability is then **derecognized** (removed) from the company's balance sheet at maturity.

Early Debt Extinguishment At times, however, a company may find it advantageous to extinguish debt early. This might be motivated by a desire to reduce interest costs, debt levels, or for other reasons. For example, early retirement of debt decreases the total liabilities-to-equity ratio and can facilitate future financing opportunities.

The incentives for retiring debt differ depending on whether interest rates have increased or decreased since the debt was issued. (When the call price is specified in the bond indenture, companies must decide whether it is more beneficial to extinguish the debt at the established price or issue new (additional) debt.) Let's consider an early retirement of bonds.

- If market rates have *increased* since the issuance of bonds, the market price (the amount paid to retire the bonds early) has fallen, sometimes below carrying amount. The result is a gain recognized by the issuer on retirement.

- If market rates have *decreased* since the issuance of bonds, the market price of the bonds has increased. In this case, the issuing company retires higher-interest-rate bonds, thus reducing future interest costs. However, a loss is recognized because the market price of the bonds exceeds carrying amount. Many companies take this opportunity to issue lower-rate debt in a refinancing of the higher-rate debt, just as homeowners do when they refinance their home mortgages when rates decline.

Accounting for Early Debt Extinguishment Accounting for debt extinguishment involves:

Adjusting the carrying amount of bond

- Recording interest expense and adjusting discount, premium, and related issue costs (as applicable) to the retirement date.

Recording the debt extinguishment

- Removing the liability accounts, including any unamortized discounts, premiums or related issue costs.

- Recording the transfer of cash, other resources, or debt securities.

- Recognizing a gain or loss in net income.

470-50-40-2 A difference between the reacquisition price of debt and the net carrying amount of the extinguished debt shall be recognized currently in income of the period of extinguishment as losses or gains and identified as a separate item . . .

In **Demo 16-7** we review an extinguishment of bonds at maturity in Example One and a partial early extinguishment of bonds in Example Two. In Example Three, an early bond retirement is immediately followed by a new bond issue. When such a **bond refunding** takes place, one bond issue is replaced with another bond issue. One way of refunding is to issue new bonds in exchange for the old bonds. Cash is involved if the bond issues have different market values. A second more common way is where the proceeds from a new bond issue are used to retire the old issue because the holders of the old issue do not necessarily wish to become the new creditors. In both cases, the accounting for refunding is similar to all other forms of debt extinguishment where gains and losses are recognized in net income in the period of refunding.

Extinguishment of Debt **LO16-7** **DEMO 16-7**

Example One: Extinguishment of Debt at Maturity
On January 1 of Year 1, Frazier Inc. issued $10,000 of 5%, 5-year bonds at a discount of $1,800. Assuming that Frazier holds the bonds to maturity, record the entry at maturity in five years on December 31.

Solution

December 31, Year 5—To record retirement of bonds at maturity

Bonds Payable	10,000	
Cash		10,000

Assets = Liabilities + Equity
−10,000   −10,000
   Cf   BP

Cash	Bonds Payable
10,000	10,000 | 10,000 Bal.

Example Two: Extinguishment of Debt Before Maturity
On January 1 of Year 1, Frazier Inc. issued a 3-year, $10,000 bond payable for $9,485, with cash interest payable annually on December 31 at 6%. The bonds were priced to yield 8%. Two years later, on December 31 of Year 2, after year-end adjusting entries were made and cash interest was paid, Frazier recalled 40% of the bonds at 101. At that time, the total unamortized discount was $184, as indicated in the following amortization schedule.

continued

continued from previous page

Effective Interest Method—Discount				
A	**B**	**C**	**D**	**E**
Cash (Stated Interest)	**Interest Expense** (Market Interest)	**Discount** Amortization	**Unamortized** Discount	**Bonds Payable, Net** (Carrying Amount)
Date / 6% × Face Value	8% × E Beg. Period Bal.	B – A	D Beg. Period Bal. – C	Face Value – D
Jan. 1, Year 1...			$515	$ 9,485
Dec. 31, Year 1... $ 600	$ 759	$159	356	9,644
Dec. 31, Year 2... 600	772	172	184	9,816
Dec. 31, Year 3... 600	784*	184	0	10,000
Totals $1,800	$2,315	$515		

* rounded

Required

a. Record Frazier Inc.'s entry upon recall of 40% of the bonds on December 31 of Year 2.

b. Record Frazier Inc.'s entry on December 31 of Year 3 to pay interest and to derecognize the remaining bonds.

Solution

a. **Early Redemption of Bonds Payable**

Frazier pays $4,040 upon redemption of the bonds or ($10,000 × 40% × 1.01). Frazier Inc. derecognizes 40% of the carrying amount of the bonds on December 31 of Year 2. The unamortized bond discount in total is $184. However, only 40% of this amount (as well as the bonds payable amount) is derecognized. Frazier Inc. records the following entry on redemption.

Assets = Liabilities + Equity
−4,040   −4,000   −114
C:f   BP   Loss
           +74
           Disc BP

Cash
| 4,040
Loss on Bond Red
114 |
Bonds Payable
4,000 | 10,000 Bal.
Discount on BP
Bal. 184 | 74

December 31, Year 2—To record bond redemption

Bonds Payable ($10,000 × 40%)	4,000	
Loss on Redemption of Bonds ($4,040 – [$4,000 – $74])	114	
Discount on Bonds Payable ($184 × 40%)		74
Cash ($10,000 × 40% × 1.01)		4,040

b. **Interest Payment and Retirement of Remaining Bonds Payable**

Debt extinguishment does not affect the accounting for the remaining 60% of the bond issue; 60% of the values in the amortization schedule are used to record entries over the remaining bond term.

Assets = Liabilities + Equity
−360   +110   −470
C:o   Disc BP   Exp

Cash
| 4,040
| 360
Discount on BP
184 | 74
    | 110
Interest Exp
470 |

December 31, Year 3—To record interest payment on bonds

Interest Expense ($784 × 60%)	470	
Discount on Bonds Payable ($184 × 60%)		110
Cash ($600 × 60%)		360

Assets = Liabilities + Equity
−6,000   −6,000
C:f   BP

Cash
| 4,040
| 360
| 6,000
Bonds Payable
4,000 | 10,000
6,000 |
      | 0

December 31, Year 3—To record retirement of remaining bonds at maturity

Bonds Payable	6,000	
Cash ($10,000 × 60%)		6,000

Example Three: Extinguishment of Debt Before Maturity with Refunding

On January 1 of Year 1, Frazier Inc. issues $10,000 of 10-year, 5% bonds at face value with cash interest payable each June 30 and December 31. On January 1 of Year 5, Frazier Inc. retires the 5% bond issue at 86 and immediately issues at face value, $8,600 of 20-year, 8% bonds with the same interest dates as the 5% bonds. Record Frazier's entry on January 1 of Year 5, to retire the 5% bonds and issue the new 8% bonds.

Assets = Liabilities + Equity
−8,600   −10,000   +1,400
C:f   BP   Gain

Cash
| 8,600
Bonds Payable
10,000 | 10,000 Bal.
Gn on Bond Ext
       | 1,400

Solution

January 1, Year 5—To record retirement of the 5% bonds payable

Bonds Payable	10,000	
Cash ($10,000 × 0.86)		8,600
Gain on Redemption of Bonds ($10,000 – $8,600).........		1,400

Assets = Liabilities + Equity
+8,600   +8,600
C:f   BP

Cash
8,600 | 8,600
Bonds Payable
10,000 | 10,000 Bal.
        | 8,600

January 1, Year 5—To record issuance of the 8% bonds payable

Cash	8,600	
Bonds Payable		8,600

On January 1, 5M Inc. issued $300,000 of bonds at 95. The bonds pay 5% cash interest semiannually on June 30 and December 31. The bonds are scheduled to mature in five years on December 31. The company retired $30,000 of the bonds on October 1, when the bonds were selling at 89 plus accrued interest. Assume the straight-line interest method is used to amortize the bond discount.

Required

a. Record the entry for the bond issuance on January 1.

b. Record the entry for the interest payment on June 30.

c. Provide the entry to recognize interest expense for the portion of the bond issue retired on October 1.

d. Provide the entry to record the bond retirement on October 1.

More Practice:
BE16-25, E16-33, E16-34,
E16-35, E16-36, E16-37
Solution on p. 16-78.

Account for conversion of debt into equity   LO 16-8

A **convertible bond** is exchangeable for capital stock, usually common stock, of the issuer at the option of the investor. A convertible bond is a **hybrid security** because it is a security that has characteristics of both debt and equity. Convertible bonds often are marketable at lower interest rates than conventional bonds because investors assign a value to the conversion privilege.

The primary attraction of convertible bonds to investors is the potential for increased value if the stock appreciates. If it does not, the investor continues to receive both interest and principal (although usually at a lower rate than nonconvertible bonds would provide).

Convertible bonds are advantageous to the issuer for several reasons.

Account for a Debt Conversion
- Record issuance as a straight-debt issue
- Record conversion
- Record no gain or loss upon conversion
- Expense conversion inducement costs

LO 16-8 Overview

- Prospect for raising debt capital often is improved.
- Typically pay a lower interest rate than do nonconvertible bonds.
- If such bonds are converted, the face value is never paid.
- Less shares may be issued on conversion than in a direct sale of stock; thus, less control is given up.

Convertible bonds are not without disadvantages. If the stock price rises, the issuing company forgoes the higher proceeds that would be possible from a direct sale of stock. If the stock price falls, the company must continue to service the debt.

BURLINGTON

Real World—CONVERTIBLE DEBT

The following example found in a recent Burlington Stores Inc. annual report illustrates an issuance of convertible debt. The notes are convertible into Burlington's common stock at the option of the debt holders.

Note 7—Long Term Debt: Excerpt from 2025 Convertible Notes Section

Prior to the close of business on the business day immediately preceding January 15, 2025, the 2025 Convertible Notes will be convertible at the option of the holders only upon the occurrence of certain events and during certain periods. Thereafter, the 2025 Convertible Notes will be convertible at the option of the holders at any time until the close of business on the second scheduled trading day immediately preceding the maturity date. The 2025 Convertible Notes have an initial conversion rate of 4.5418 shares per $1,000 principal amount of 2025 Convertible Notes (equivalent to an initial conversion price of approximately $220.18 per share of the Company's common stock), subject to adjustment if certain events occur. The initial conversion price represents a conversion premium of approximately 32.50% over $166.17 per share, the last reported sale price of the Company's common stock on April 13, 2020 (the pricing date of the offering) on the New York Stock Exchange.

Issuance of Convertible Debt Although convertible debt has an equity feature, it is typically recorded as a straight debt issuance. This means that there is no amount allocated to an equity account for the conversion feature of the debt. A separate market does not exist for either the bonds standing alone or the conversion privilege. There is no objective basis (such as a market or an exchange transaction) for allocating the bond price to the bonds and the conversion feature. The value of the conversion feature is contingent on a future stock price that cannot be predicted.

470-20-25-12   A debt with an embedded conversion feature shall be accounted for in its entirety as a liability, and no portion of the proceeds from the issuance of the convertible debt instrument shall be accounted for as attributable to the conversion feature unless the conversion feature is required to be accounted for separately as an embedded derivative under Subtopic 815-15 or the conversion feature results in a premium that is subject to the guidance in paragraph 470-20-25-13.

Conversion of Convertible Debt   When the bonds are converted under terms of the debt agreement, first the issuer updates interest expense and any amortization of premium or discount to the date of conversion. Then, bonds payable and any unamortized bond discount or premium are derecognized. If the debt is converted into common stock, the stockholders' equity accounts replace the bond accounts for the issuer, and *no gain or loss is recorded in net income*.

470-20-40-4   If a convertible debt instrument . . . is converted into shares, cash (or other assets) . . . in accordance with the conversion privileges provided in the terms of the instrument, upon conversion the carrying amount of the convertible debt instrument, including any unamortized premium, discount, or issuance costs, shall be reduced by, if any, the cash (or other assets) transferred and then shall be recognized in the capital accounts to reflect the shares issued and no gain or loss is recognized.

Induced Conversion   Convertible debt agreements can include provisions that allow the issuer to change the terms of the debt to induce prompt conversion. For example, declining interest rates can motivate an issuer to lower its debt levels which can be accomplished by debt holders converting debt to common stock. To induce a conversion, the issuer could offer cash (or other forms of consideration). In order to qualify for accounting as an induced conversion, the offer of consideration to the debt holder must be available for a limited time period, the form and amount of consideration in the offer must be provided in the terms of the existing debt agreement, and it must be reasonably possible that the offer would be exercised. If the criteria are not met, the transaction is instead accounted for as a debt extinguishment. For simplicity, we will consider all induced conversion examples in this chapter to qualify for induced conversion accounting. This means that the issuer recognizes an expense equal to the fair value of consideration offered in excess of the fair value of the consideration issuable under the original conversion terms as demonstrated in **Demo 16-8**.

470-20-40-16   If a convertible debt instrument is converted pursuant to an inducement offer . . . the issuer shall recognize an expense equal to the fair value of all securities and other consideration transferred in the transaction in excess of the fair value of securities and other consideration issuable pursuant to the conversion privileges provided in the terms of the existing instrument. The fair value of the securities or other consideration shall be measured as of the date the inducement offer is accepted by the convertible debt holder . . .

EXPANDING YOUR KNOWLEDGE   Value of a Conversion Feature

Accounting for the issuance of convertible bonds poses a conceptual problem. A popular view holds that the economic value of the conversion feature, reflected in the bond price, should be recorded as stockholders' equity. However, ASC 470 specifies that convertible bonds be generally recorded only as debt. The FASB reasoned that the debt and equity features of convertible bonds are inseparable and do not exist independently of each other. In addition, the FASB's aim was to reduce the complexity for preparers and improve decision usefulness and relevance of the information provided to financial statement users.

DEMO 16-8   **LO16-8**   **Accounting for Convertible Debt**

Demo
MBC

On January 1 of Year 1, Tollen Corporation sells $100,000 of 8% convertible bonds for $106,000. Each $1,000 bond is convertible into 10 shares of Tollen Corporation $10 par common stock. All of Tollen bonds are converted into common stock on December 31 of Year 2 when the unamortized premium is $3,000 and the common stock is trading at $110 per share.

Required
a. Record the issuance of convertible bonds on January 1 of Year 1.
b. Record the conversion of debt to common stock on December 31 of Year 2.
c. Record the conversion of debt to common stock on December 31 of Year 2, assuming Tollen makes a $5,000 payment to bondholders to induce conversion.

continued

continued from previous page

Solution

a. Issuance of Convertible Debt

January 1, Year 1—To record issuance of bonds

Cash	106,000	
Premium on Bonds Payable ($106,000 – $100,000)		6,000
Bonds Payable		100,000

Assets = Liabilities + Equity
+106,000   +6,000
C:f   Prem BP
           +100,000
           BP

Cash		Bonds Payable	
106,000			100,000

Premium on BP	
	6,000

b. Conversion of Convertible Debt to Equity

December 31, Year 2—To record conversion of bonds

Bonds Payable	100,000	
Premium on Bonds Payable.............................	3,000	
Common Stock ($100,000/$1,000 × 10 shares × $10 par) ...		10,000
Paid-In Capital in Excess of Par—Common Stock*		93,000

*($100,000 + $3,000 – $10,000)

Assets = Liabilities + Equity
         –100,000   +10,000
         BP   CS
         –3,000   +93,000
         Prem BP   PIC—CS

Bonds Payable		Premium on BP		
100,000	100,000	3,000	3,000	Bal.

Common Stock		Paid-In Cap—CS	
	10,000		93,000

c. Induced Conversion of Convertible Debt

December 31, Year 2—To record induced conversion of bonds

Bonds Payable	100,000	
Debt Conversion Expense	5,000	
Premium on Bonds Payable.............................	3,000	
Common Stock ($100,000/$1,000 × 10 shares × $10 par) ...		10,000
Paid-In Capital in Excess of Par—Common Stock*		93,000
Cash		5,000

*($100,000 + $3,000 – $10,000)

Assets = Liabilities + Equity
–5,000   –100,000   –5,000
C:f   BP   Exp
         –3,000   +10,000
         Prem BP   CS
                     +93,000
                     PIC—CS

Cash		Bonds Payable	
	5,000	100,000	100,000

Debt Convers Exp		Premium on BP		
5,000		3,000	3,000	Bal.

Common Stock		Paid-In Cap—CS	
	10,000		93,000

Accounting for Conversion of Debt   LO16-8 ◄ REVIEW 16-8

Review · MBC

5M Corp. issued $200,000 of 5%, 5-year convertible bonds. Each $1,000 bond is convertible into 5 shares of common stock ($1 par value per share) of 5M Corp. The bonds were sold at 98 on January 1 of Year 1.

Required

a. Provide the entry on January 1 of Year 1 for issuance of convertible bonds.

b. The conversion privilege for 50% of the bonds is exercised on December 31 of Year 2. Assume that any discount or premium has been amortized through the date of conversion using the straight-line interest method and that the common stock is selling at $125 per share at the conversion date. Provide the entry for conversion of the bonds to common stock.

More Practice:
BE16-26, BE16-27, E16-38, E16-39, P16-14

Solution on p. 16-79.

Apply the fair value option for liabilities   LO 16-9

The previous sections accounted for bonds and notes at amortized cost. Yet, debtors can opt to record most financial liabilities, including bonds and notes payable, under the **fair value option**. Under this method, a bond or note payable is adjusted to fair value each reporting date. The argument for reporting liabilities at fair value is that fair value enhances relevance and comparability and provides a better starting point for understanding and analyzing risks by reflecting changes in risks *in the period in which they occur*.

The decision to invoke the fair value option must be made on the election date of the debt or established through a company policy. The election date is the date that the company first recognizes the liability or meets another condition specified in the accounting guidance. The decision is applied to each debt instrument individually, and the decision is generally

Accounting for Fair Value Option
- Elect to value long-term liabilities at fair value
- Measure liability at fair value
  - General risk: Adjust NI
  - Instrument risk: Adjust OCI

LO 16-9 Overview

irrevocable (decision to report at fair value cannot be changed). A company should apply the method consistently to each financial liability from period to period. A company may choose to account for some debt instruments at fair value and others at amortized cost.

825-10-25-2   The decision about whether to elect the fair value option:

a. Shall be applied instrument by instrument, except as discussed in paragraph 825-10-25-7

b. Shall be irrevocable (unless a new election date occurs, as discussed in paragraph 825-10-25-4)

c. Shall be applied only to an entire instrument and not to only specified risks, specific cash flows, or portions of that instrument.

An entity may decide whether to elect the fair value option for each eligible item on its election date. Alternatively, an entity may elect the fair value option according to a preexisting policy for specified types of eligible items.

Fair value can be determined through market prices quoted on an exchange (readily observable). Otherwise, fair value can be measured by taking the present value of remaining cash flows, calculated by discounting cash flows at the market rate. Amortized cost of the debt is determined through the entries shown in previous sections. When adjusting liabilities to fair value from amortized cost, the adjustment is recorded in the **Fair Value Adjustment** account, which is a contra or adjunct account to the liability account. The offsetting debit or credit is an unrealized gain or loss recognized in either other comprehensive income or net income.

■ **General Risk** Recognize the portion of the total change in the fair value of the liability that results from a change in general risk (such as a change in the risk-free rate or a benchmark interest rate) in *net income*.

■ **Instrument-Specific Credit Risk** Recognize the portion of the total change in the fair value of the liability that results from a change in a company's own credit risk (called instrument-specific credit risk) in *other comprehensive income*. Instrument-specific credit risk is the risk that the bond issuer will not pay interest payments and the principal balance at the times and in the amounts specified in the bond indenture. The gain or loss recognized in accumulated other comprehensive income is reclassified to net income when the bond matures or is redeemed.

825-10-45-5   If an entity has designated a financial liability under the fair value option in accordance with this Subtopic, or Subtopic 815-15 on embedded derivatives, the entity shall measure the financial liability at fair value with qualifying changes in fair value recognized in net income. The entity shall present separately in other comprehensive income the portion of the total change in the fair value of the liability that results from a change in the instrument-specific credit risk. The entity may consider the portion of the total change in fair value that excludes the amount resulting from a change in a base market risk, such as a risk-free rate or a benchmark interest rate, to be the result of a change in instrument-specific credit risk. Alternatively, an entity may use another method that it considers to faithfully represent the portion of the total change in fair value resulting from a change in instrument-specific credit risk. The entity shall apply the method consistently to each financial liability from period to period.

In general, a company reports a gain from an increase in risk or, alternatively, a loss from a decrease in risk related to the underlying instrument. For example, a general increase in interest rates (due to an increase in risk) will cause the fair value of a bond issued at its face value to decrease. (Discounting the bond to present value using a higher rate of interest causes a lower fair value.) A decrease in bonds payable or a debit to Fair Value Adjustment causes a gain or a credit to Unrealized Gain—Income. The fair value option is illustrated in **Demo 16-9**.

EXPANDING YOUR KNOWLEDGE   **Instrument-Specific Credit Risk**

Bonds associated with an increase in instrument-specific risk result in a recognized gain under the fair value option. (Discounting of bonds at a higher interest rate causes the value of the bonds to decrease, resulting in an unrealized gain.) Many financial statement users consider recognizing a gain due to a decrease in credit standing to be *potentially misleading* because a company often lacks the ability to realize those gains by repurchasing the bonds at fair value. Thus, the inclusion of such gains in OCI (rather than net income) is supported by the FASB's observation that liabilities typically are not settled with a third party. This means that the fair value changes attributed to changes in a company's own credit risk usually are not realized. Plus, it is counterintuitive for a company to report an increase in its net income when its own credit risk increases and a decrease in net income if its own credit risk decreases.

Fair Value Option Accounting for Liabilities   LO16-9   DEMO 16-9

Demo

MBC

On January 1, Frazier Inc. issued 3-year bonds to Seattle Corp. at face value for $10,000, with cash interest payable annually on December 31 at 4%. On January 1, Frazier Inc. chooses to account for the bonds using the *fair value option*. The fair value of the bonds on December 31 is $9,200 because the stated rate is now less than the market rate due to an increase in the risk-free rate. (A market rate increase will cause comparable debt instruments to now offer a higher interest rate.)

a. Record the adjusting entry on December 31 to adjust the bonds to fair value. Assume that interest expense has been recorded during the year.
b. Now assume that the bonds were originally issued at a discount to yield a market rate of 5%. Record the adjusting entry on December 31 to adjust the bonds to fair value. Assume that interest expense has been recorded during the year. *Hint:* First compute the amortized cost of the bonds using the effective interest method.

Solution

a. **Fair Value Adjustment—Bond Issued at Face Value**

At December 31, the year-end adjusting entry adjusts the bonds to the fair value of $9,200. Because the change in fair value is attributed to an increase in the risk-free rate, net income will be adjusted.

December 31—To record fair value option adjustment and the net unrealized gain

Fair Value Adjustment—Bond Payable ($10,000 – $9,200)	800	
Unrealized Gain or Loss—Income		800

Assets	=	Liabilities	+	Equity
		−800		+800
		FVA		Gain

FVA—BP		Unreal Gain—Inc
800			800

b. **Fair Value Adjustment—Bond Issued at a Discount**

The bonds originally sold at a price of $9,728 (PV(0.05,3,–400,–10000)). On December 31, the amortized cost of the bonds is $9,814 ($9,728 + ($486 – $400)). Frazier records an entry to adjust the bonds to fair value from amortized cost.

December 31—To record fair value option adjustment and the net unrealized gain

Fair Value Adjustment—Bond Payable ($9,814 – $9,200)	614	
Unrealized Gain or Loss—Income		614

Assets	=	Liabilities	+	Equity
		−614		+614
		FVA		Gain

FVA—BP		Unreal Gain—Inc
614			614

Real World—FAIR VALUE OPTION

American International Group, Inc. (AIG), an insurance organization, reported the following related to its election of the fair value method in a recent Form 10-K.

Fair Value Measurements (excerpt)—Under the fair value option, we may elect to measure at fair value financial assets and financial liabilities that are not otherwise required to be carried at fair value. Subsequent changes in fair value for designated items are reported in earnings . . . The following table presents the gains or losses recorded related to the eligible instruments for which we elected the fair value option:

Years Ended December 31 (in millions)	Gain (Loss)	
	2023	2022
Liabilities:		
Long-term debt	$3	$225

Accounting for Debt Using the Fair Value Option   LO16-9   REVIEW 16-9

Review

MBC

On January 1, Frazier Inc. issued 3-year bonds to Seattle Corp. at face value for $10,000, with cash interest payable annually on December 31 at 4%. On January 1, Frazier Inc. chooses to account for the bonds using the *fair value option*. The fair value of the bonds on December 31 is $8,000 because Frazier Inc. was in violation of a debt covenant.

More Practice:
BE16-28, E16-41,
E16-42, E16-43

Required

Record the adjusting entry on December 31.

Solution on p. 16-79.

LO 16-10 Describe financing disclosures and analyses using leverage ratios

In general, notes accompanying financial statements provide information relevant to investors and creditors not conveniently disclosed within financial statements. Various aspects of debt agreements are disclosed in notes as they are relevant to investors and creditors.

Debt Disclosures with Financial Statements

The nature of debt, related interest rates, maturity dates, restrictions, call provisions, and conversion privileges are disclosed in notes to financial statements. Any assets pledged as collateral for debt, or other creditor restrictions, also are disclosed in the notes.

If it is practical to estimate the fair value of long-term debt, fair value should be disclosed.

825-10-50-10   A reporting entity shall disclose either in the body of the financial statements or in the accompanying notes, the fair value of financial instruments and the level of the fair value hierarchy within which the fair value measurements are categorized in their entirety (Level 1, 2, or 3). For financial instruments recognized at fair value in the statement of financial position, the disclosure requirements of Topic 820 also apply.

EXPANDING YOUR KNOWLEDGE   **Off-Balance-Sheet Financing**

Off-balance-sheet financing arises when commitments that expose the company to credit risk are not recorded on the balance sheet. For example, a company may be at risk for debt incurred by an unconsolidated subsidiary, or a company may agree to pay the debt of another party (in return for a fee) if that party defaults. A *direct guarantee of indebtedness* is an agreement in which a guarantor states that if the debtor fails to make payment to the creditor when due, the guarantor will pay the creditor. If the debtor defaults, the creditor has a direct claim on the guarantor. *An indirect guarantee of indebtedness* is an agreement that obligates the guarantor to transfer funds to a debtor upon the occurrence of specified events under certain conditions. For example, a guarantor may be obligated to advance funds if a debtor's net income, coverage of fixed charges, or working capital falls below a specified minimum.

The SEC requires its registrants to provide information on commitments and obligations within the Management Discussion and Analysis section of Form 10-K. This discussion is expected to include information about off-balance-sheet arrangements. **Coca Cola Company** disclosed the following off-balance-sheet arrangement in a recent Form 10-K.

We were contingently liable for guarantees of indebtedness owed by third parties of $431 million, of which $109 million was related to VIEs. These guarantees are primarily related to third-party customers, bottlers, vendors, and container manufacturing operations and have arisen through the normal course of business. These guarantees have various terms, and none of these guarantees is individually significant. These amounts represent the maximum potential future payments that we could be required to make under the guarantees. However, management has concluded that the likelihood of any significant amounts being paid by our Company under these guarantees is not probable . . . We were not directly liable for the debt of any unconsolidated entity, and we did not have any retained or contingent interest in assets as defined above.

Debt disclosures also include the aggregate amount of maturities and sinking-fund requirements for all long-term debt for each of the five years following the balance sheet date (illustrated in **Demo 16-10A**) as well as unused long-term financing arrangements.

470-10-50-1   The combined aggregate amount of maturities and sinking fund requirements for all long-term borrowings shall be disclosed for each of the five years following the date of the latest balance sheet presented . . .

470-10-50-6   An entity shall separately disclose the following in the notes to financial statements:
a. The amount and terms of unused commitments for long-term financing arrangements (including commitment fees and the conditions under which commitments may be withdrawn).
b. The amount and terms of unused lines of credit for short-term financing arrangements (including commitment fees and the conditions under which lines may be withdrawn) and the amount of those lines of credit that support commercial paper borrowing arrangements or similar arrangements.

Debt Disclosures for Cash Flows   Generally, proceeds from the issuance of long-term debt are reported as a cash inflow from *financing activities* while cash paid to retire long-term debt is reported as a cash outflow from financing activities. (If a debt is incurred to purchase inventory, repayment of that debt is classified as an operating outflow. This is true even for long-term debt.) Cash paid for interest is included in cash flows from *operating activities*. Interest expense is included in the computation of net income, the starting point of the operating activities section when using the indirect method. Noncash adjustments to net income include (1) changes in interest payable, (2) amortization of discounts and premiums, and (3) gains and losses on the retirement of debt. Chapter 22 discusses the statement of cash flows in more detail.

Disclosure of Five-Year Debt Maturities   **LO16-10** ◂ **DEMO 16-10A**

Demo

MBC

Frazier Inc. had three debt obligations as of December 31 of Year 1, summarized as follows.

1. Unsecured note payable of $838,000, with full payment due on December 31 of Year 5.
2. Secured note payable of $555,000, with installment payments of $55,500 due over the next 10 years.
3. Redeemable bond issuance of $200,000, with full payment due on December 31 of Year 11.

Prepare a table to present debt maturities and prepare the related disclosure.

Solution
The following table summarizes the projected principal debt payments.

Debt	Year 2	Year 3	Year 4	Year 5	Year 6	Beyond Year 6
1. Unsecured note payable				$838,000		
2. Secured note payable	$55,500	$55,500	$55,500	55,500	$55,500	$277,500
3. Redeemable bonds payable. . . .						200,000
Total	$55,500	$55,500	$55,500	$893,500	$55,500	$477,500

The following is included in the financial statement disclosure notes at December 31 of Year 1.

December 31, Year 1—Debt Disclosure
The requirements for principal payments on long-term debt are approximately $55,500, $55,500, $55,500, $893,500, and $55,500 for Year 2 through Year 6, respectively, and $477,500 thereafter.

PEPSICO

Real World—LONG-TERM DEBT

PepsiCo Inc. Form 10-K illustrates disclosure of maturities of long-term debt obligations.

Debt Obligations and Commitments—The following table summarizes the Company's debt obligations:

Short-Term Debt Obligations[b] ($ millions)	2023[a]
Current maturities of long-term debt.	$ 3,924
Commercial paper (5.5%).	2,286
Other borrowings (7.8% and 15.0%)	300
	$ 6,510

Long-Term Debt Obligations[b] ($ millions)	2023
Notes due 2023 (1.7%).	$ —
Notes due 2024 (3.0% and 2.2%)	3,919
Notes due 2025 (3.2% and 2.7%)	3,994
Notes due 2026 (3.7% and 3.1%)	3,961
Notes due 2027 (2.4% and 2.5%)	2,544
Notes due 2028 (2.1% and 1.5%)	3,323
Notes due 2029–2060 (3.0% and 2.9%)	23,725
Other due 2023–2033 (3.6% and 1.3%).	53
	41,519
Less: current maturities of long-term debt obligations	3,924
Total	$37,595

[a] Amounts are shown net of unamortized net discounts of $225 million and $227 million for 2023 and 2022, respectively.

[b] The interest rates presented reflect weighted-average effective interest rates at year-end. See Note 9 for further information regarding our interest rate derivative instruments.

Financial Leverage Ratios

The balance sheet provides information concerning liquidity and financial flexibility. For example, is a company in a position to finance new activities with relative ease without incurring excessive debt? Is a company in a position to pay interest on outstanding debt? Is a company able to respond to new competitive conditions? Is a company at risk of defaulting on its obligations? If a company carries a high debt load, it will be less flexible to cover unexpected expenses or take advantage of unexpected opportunities.

The balance sheet is the basis for calculating financial ratios measuring liquidity and financial flexibility. A number of ratios assist investors and creditors in analyzing the financial position of a company. The following three financial leverage ratios are illustrated in **Demo 16-10B**.

$$\frac{\text{Total liabilities}}{\text{Total stockholders' equity}}$$

Total liabilities-to-equity ratio (total liabilities/total stockholders' equity) provides a direct comparison between debt and stockholders' equity. It measures the balance between resources provided by creditors and resources provided by owners (including retained earnings). The higher the ratio, the more **leverage** the company is using and the more risk that is borne by owners. Because interest is a required expense and creditors have a priority claim on the assets of the company, investors are concerned if this ratio is high relative to the inherent risk of the operations of the company. On the other hand, a company may also have too low a ratio if management is not using debt financing at an appropriate level. A more detailed analysis of a computed ratio includes a comparison to the following: prior year ratios, current year's forecasted or budgeted ratios, competitor ratios, and average industry ratios.

$$\frac{\text{Total liabilities}}{\text{Total assets}}$$

Total liabilities-to-total assets ratio (total liabilities/total assets) measures the proportion of assets financed by creditors (an indicator of leverage). Again, a higher ratio indicates higher risk of default on debt.

$$\frac{\text{Income before taxes and interest expense}}{\text{Interest expense}}$$

Times interest earned ratio (income before taxes and interest expense/interest expense) measures the number of times a company could pay for interest from its current earnings. This ratio helps creditors and investors determine whether a company can make its required interest payments. Generally, the lower the ratio, the more risk of a company's default on interest payments.

DEMO 16-10B ▶ **LO16-10**   **Calculating Financial Leverage Ratios**

Demo

MBC

The following financial information is provided for **PepsiCo Inc.** from a recent annual report. Compute the company's (a) total liabilities-to-equity ratio, (b) total liabilities-to-total assets ratio, and (c) times interest earned ratio.

Balances at December 31 ($ millions)		Results for Year Ended December 31 ($ millions)	
Total assets.	$74,129	Operating profit before interest and taxes	$9,785
Total liabilities	62,930	Interest expense.	1,342
Total shareholders' equity	11,199		

Solution

$$\text{Total liabilities-to-equity} = \frac{\text{Total liabilities}}{\text{Total stockholders' equity}} = \frac{\$62,930}{\$11,199} = 5.62$$

$$\text{Total liabilities-to-total assets} = \frac{\text{Total liabilities}}{\text{Total assets}} = \frac{\$62,930}{\$74,129} = 0.85$$

$$\text{Times interest earned} = \frac{\text{Income before taxes and interest expense}}{\text{Interest expense}} = \frac{\$9,785}{\$1,342} = 7.29$$

This analysis illustrates that PepsiCo relies heavily on debt from creditors for financing yet demonstrates an ability to pay interest on its debt out of current earnings.

Calculating Financial Leverage Ratios   LO16-10   REVIEW 16-10

Coca-Cola Company reported the following amounts (in millions) in a recent Form 10-K.

Balance at December 31		Results for Year Ended December 31	
Total assets	$87,270	Total earnings	$6,550
Total liabilities	64,050	Interest expense	733
Total stockholders' equity	23,220	Net earnings before taxes and interest	8,626

Compute the following ratios.

a. Total liabilities-to-equity   b. Total liabilities-to-total assets   c. Times interest earned

Review

MBC

More Practice:
BE16-29, E16-45,
AD&J16-21

Solution on p. 16-79.

Account for bonds with stock warrants   LO 16-11

Companies can issue debt securities that grant the investor the right to acquire capital stock without having to relinquish the debt. In this case, the investor receives a right to become a shareholder (in the future) and then participate in stock price appreciation in addition to principal and cash interest payments.

One example of debt sold with rights is a bond sold with stock warrants attached. A **stock warrant** conveys the option to purchase from the issuer a specified number of shares of common stock at a designated price per share (the exercise price) within a stated time period (the exercise period). If the fair value of the common stock rises above the exercise price, the warrant becomes valuable to the holder because it enables the holder to buy stock at a discounted price. This means that warrants attached to a bond issue generally increase the bond price.

Accounting treatment for bonds with warrants depends on whether the warrants are detachable or nondetachable.

> **Account for Bonds with Stock Warrants**
> - Bonds with nondetachable warrants
>   - Record as a straight-debt issue
> - Bonds with detachable warrants
>   - Record warrants as equity (separate from debt) following either the incremental or the proportional method
>
> LO 16-11 Overview

- **Nondetachable stock warrants** cannot be sold separately from the bond. Because no separate market for the warrants exists, the entire bond price is allocated to the bonds.

- **Detachable stock warrants** have a readily determinable fair value and are traded as separate securities. This means a portion of the bond price is allocated to equity through the incremental method or the proportional method.

`470-20-25-2`   Proceeds from the sale of a debt instrument with stock purchase warrants (detachable call options) shall be allocated to the two elements based on the relative fair values of the debt instrument without the warrants and of the warrants themselves at time of issuance. The portion of the proceeds so allocated to the warrants shall be accounted for as paid-in capital. The remainder of the proceeds shall be allocated to the debt instrument portion of the transaction. This usually results in a discount (or, occasionally, a reduced premium) . . .

- If bonds are sold with *detachable warrants*, and the fair value of only one security is known, the **incremental method** is used. Fair value is applied to the security with a known fair value. The remaining or incremental portion of the proceeds is allocated to the other security with an unknown fair value.

- If bonds are sold with *detachable warrants*, and the fair value of both securities is known, the **proportional method** is used. Proceeds from the issuance are allocated based upon the relative fair value of the two securities.

In **Demo 16-11** we show how to account for bond issuances with nondetachable and detachable stock purchase warrants.

DEMO 16-11 ▶ **LO16-11**   **Accounting for Bonds with Stock Warrants**

Example One: Bonds with Nondetachable Warrants
Embassy Corporation issues $100,000 of 8%, 10-year nonconvertible bonds with *nondetachable* stock purchase warrants on January 1. Each $1,000 bond carries 10 warrants. Each warrant entitles the holder to purchase one share of $10 par common stock for $15. Assume the bond issue sells for 105. Record the entry on January 1 to issue the bonds with nondetachable warrants.

Solution

Assets = Liabilities + Equity
+105,000   +5,000
C:f   Prem BP
            +100,000
              BP

Cash		Bonds Payable	
105,000			100,000

	Premium on BP	
		5,000

January 1—To record issuance of bonds with nondetachable warrants

Cash ($100,000 × 1.05)	105,000	
Premium on Bonds Payable ($105,000 – $100,000)		5,000
Bonds Payable		100,000

Example Two: Bonds with Detachable Warrants–Incremental Method
Embassy Corporation issues $100,000 of 8%, 10-year nonconvertible bonds with *detachable* stock purchase warrants on January 1. Each $1,000 bond carries 10 warrants. Each warrant entitles the holder to purchase one share of $10 par common stock for $15. Assume the bonds with detachable stock warrants sell for 105. Shortly after issuance, the warrants trade for $4 each. Fair value is not determinable for the bonds selling without warrants. Record the entry on January 1 to issue the bonds with detachable warrants using the incremental method.

Solution
Because the warrants are detachable, we determine a separate measurement for the warrants from the bonds. Also, because we only know the fair value of the warrants (and not the fair value of the bonds without the warrants), we use the incremental method to measure and record a separate value for the bonds and the warrants.

Incremental Method: Allocation of Selling Price to Bonds and Warrants	
Selling price of bonds with warrants ($100,000 × 1.05)	$105,000
Fair value of warrants ($100,000/$1,000 × 10 warrants × $4)	4,000
Allocation of proceeds to bonds	$101,000

At January 1, the entry for issuance of the bonds follows.

Assets = Liabilities + Equity
+105,000   +100,000   +4,000
C:f   BP   PIC—SW
            +1,000
            Prem BP

Cash		Bonds Payable	
105,000			100,000

Premium on BP		Paid-In Cap—War	
	1,000		4,000

January 1—To record issuance of bonds with detachable warrants: Incremental method

Cash ($100,000 × 1.05)	105,000	
Paid-In Capital—Stock Warrants ($100,000/$1,000 × 10 × $4) ...		4,000
Premium on Bonds Payable ($101,000 – $100,000)		1,000
Bonds Payable (face value)		100,000

Example Three: Bonds with Detachable Warrants–Proportional Method
Embassy Corporation issues $100,000 of 8%, 10-year nonconvertible bonds with *detachable* stock purchase warrants on January 1. Each $1,000 bond carries 10 warrants. Each warrant entitles the holder to purchase one share of $10 par common stock for $15. Assume the bond issue sells for 105. Shortly after issuance, the warrants trade for $4 each and the bonds were quoted at 103 without warrants attached. Record the entry on January 1 to issue the bonds with detachable warrants using the proportional method.

Solution
Because the warrants are detachable, we determine a separate measurement for the warrants from the bonds. Also, because we know the fair value of the warrants and the fair value of the bonds without the warrants, we use the proportional method to measure and record a separate value for the bonds and the warrants.

continued

continued from previous page

Proportional Method: Allocation of Selling Price to Bonds and Warrants		
	Total	Proportion of Total
Fair value of bonds ($100,000 × 1.03)	$103,000	$103,000/$107,000
Fair value of warrants ($4 × 100 bonds × 10 warrants per bond)	4,000	$4,000/$107,000
	$107,000	
Allocation of proceeds to bonds ($105,000 × 103/107)	$101,075	
Allocation of proceeds to warrants ($105,000 × 4/107)	3,925	
	$105,000	

At January 1, the entry for issuance of the bonds follows.

January 1—To record issuance of bonds with detachable warrants: Proportional method

Cash	105,000	
Paid-In Capital—Stock Warrants		3,925
Premium on Bonds Payable ($101,075 – $100,000)		1,075
Bonds Payable (face value)		100,000

Assets = Liabilities + Equity
+105,000   +1,075   +3,925
C:f   Prem BP   PIC—SW
          +100,000
            BP

Cash   Bonds Payable
105,000 | | 100,000

Premium on BP   Paid-In Cap—War
| 1,075 | 3,925

Example Four: Bonds with Detachable Warrants–Conversion and Expiration

Assume that Embassy Corporation accounted for its warrants using the incremental method (see Example 2) and that the warrants issued on January 1 of Year 1 expire on January 31 of Year 2. On January 15 of Year 2, 900 warrants were exercised by warrant holders. Record the entry on January 15 of Year 2 for the exercise of the 900 warrants, and the expiration of the remaining 100 warrants on January 31 of Year 2.

Solution

On January 15 of Year 2, a prorated amount of stock warrants is derecognized ($3,600 or 900 warrants/1,000 warrants × $4,000). One share of common stock is issued for each of the 900 warrants, totaling 900 shares and $15 cash is collected for each warrant. Par value of the common stock is recorded for $9,000 (900 shares × $10 par), and the entry is balanced through a credit to Paid-In Capital in Excess of Par—Common Stock.

January 15, Year 2—To record conversion of warrants to common stock

Cash (900 × $15)	13,500	
Paid-In Capital—Stock Warrants ($4,000 × 900/1,000)	3,600	
Common Stock (900 × 1 share × $10 par)		9,000
Paid-In Capital in Excess of Par—Common Stock (to balance)		8,100

Assets = Liabilities + Equity
+13,500   –3,600
C:f   PIC—SW
           +9,000
            CS
           +8,100
            PIC—CS

Cash   Paid-In Cap—War
13,500 | 3,600 | 4,000 Bal.

Common Stock   Paid-In Cap—CS
| 9,000 | 8,100

An expiration entry is recorded at the end of the exercise period for any warrants that remain outstanding, whether through oversight or because of an unfavorable stock price. This entry simply reclassifies the equity amount in Paid-In Capital—Stock Warrants to Paid-In Capital in Excess of Par—Common Stock.

January 31, Year 2—To record expiration of 100 warrants

Paid-In Capital—Stock Warrants ($4,000 × 100/1,000)	400	
Paid-In Capital in Excess of Par—Common Stock		400

Assets = Liabilities + Equity
                 –400
                PIC—SW
                +400
                PIC—CS

Pd-In Cap—War   Pd-In Cap—CS
3,600 | 4,000 Bal. | 8,100
400 | | 400
        | 0

Accounting for Bonds with Stock Warrants   **LO16-11**   **REVIEW 16-11**

On January 1, CostKo Corporation issued $100,000 of 6%, 5-year nonconvertible bonds with *nondetachable* stock purchase warrants. Each $1,000 bond carried 10 warrants, each of which was for one share of CostKo common stock, par value $1, at a specified option price of $40 per share. The bonds (including the warrants) sold at 102. No bond price without warrants was available.

Review

MBC

continued

continued from previous page

Required

More Practice:
BE16-30, E16-46, E16-47, P16-18

Solution on p. 16-79.

a. Provide the entry at the date of issuance of the bonds.

b. Provide the entry at the date of issuance of the bonds assuming instead that the warrants are *detachable*. Immediately after the date of issuance, the detachable stock purchase warrants were selling at $5 each.

Management Judgment

There are many financing decisions that management must make related to debt issues. For example, management determines the type and features of new debt and the terms and timing of the issue. Management must also determine whether or not to extinguish debt early, refund debt with alternative debt, or entice debt holders to convert debt to equity in cases of convertible debt. Let's consider a sample of the judgments that management must make in accounting for long-term debt.

- Management determines the method to amortize discounts or premiums and whether a method other than the effective interest method produces results that are not materially different from the effective interest method (p. 16-12).

- In a case where a note is issued at a stated rate that does not equal the market rate, the market rate of a note with similar risks must be determined (p. 16-25).

- In a case where a note is issued for noncash consideration, management must determine whether the fair value of the debt or the fair value of the noncash consideration is more clearly evident. Further, in cases where the fair value of the debt is used to measure the transaction, a market rate must be determined (p. 16-25).

- Management must decide whether or not to elect the irrevocable fair value option on an individual debt security basis (p. 16-35).

- If the fair value option is selected, management must determine whether a gain or loss is attributable to general or instrument-specific credit risk (p. 16-35).

- For disclosure purposes, management must estimate the fair value of long-term debt through the categories of the fair value hierarchy when it is practical to do so (p. 16-37).

- SEC registrants must identify off-balance sheet disclosures for the MD&A analysis (p. 16-37).

- When bonds with detachable warrants are issued, management must determine the fair value of warrants and the fair value of the bonds without the warrants (p. 16-40).

APPENDIX 16A
LO 16-12   Account for debt settlement and restructuring

LO 16-12 Overview

Debt Settlement and Restructuring
- **Debtor perspective**
  - Settlement though transfer of assets or equity interest
  - Restructuring of debt terms

Rising interest rates, nonperforming loans, unsatisfactory return on investments, and lack of demand for a company's products and services contribute to troubled debt. Rather than write off nonperforming loans or pursue legal action, creditors can agree to a debt restructure, allowing the debtor to remain in operation in the hope that the debtor can resolve its financial difficulties. Creditors usually receive more on restructured debt than through bankruptcy by the debtor.

Debt restructuring includes:

- Settlement of debt through cash payment or transfer of other assets or equity securities.

- Modifications of a debt through a reduction in the interest rate, extension of the maturity date, reduction in the face amount of the debt, or reduction of accrued interest.

In a **troubled debt restructure**, the creditor grants a concession to the debtor that it would not otherwise consider. The concession is granted by the creditor in an attempt to protect its investment.

> **ASC Glossary**   Troubled debt restructuring: A restructuring of a debt constitutes a troubled debt restructuring if the creditor for economic or legal reasons related to the debtor's financial difficulties grants a concession to the debtor that it would not otherwise consider.

Troubled Debt Restructure—Debtor

We review and illustrate in **Demo 16-12** the following four scenarios from the debtor perspective.

Settlement of Debt through Transfer of Assets

Settlement of Debt through Transfer of Assets   In a full settlement of debt through the transfer of assets (such as land, receivables, building, or other assets), the debtor measures the assets given up at fair value, derecognizes the debt and the assets given up, and records a gain or loss on the income statement.

> **470-60-35-3**   A difference between the fair value and the carrying amount of assets transferred to a creditor to settle a payable is a gain or loss on transfer of assets. The carrying amount of a receivable encompasses not only unamortized premium, discount, acquisition costs, and the like but also an allowance for uncollectible amounts and other valuation accounts, if any. The debtor shall include that gain or loss in measuring net income for the period of transfer, reported as provided in Topic 220...

Settlement of Debt through Transfer of Equity Interest   In a full settlement of debt through the transfer of equity (such as common stock of the debtor), the debtor derecognizes the debt, records the equity issuance at fair value, and records a gain or loss on the income statement.

> **470-60-35-4**   A debtor that issues or otherwise grants an equity interest to a creditor to settle fully a payable shall account for the equity interest at its fair value. The difference between the fair value of the equity interest granted and the carrying amount of the payable settled shall be recognized as a gain on restructuring of payables.

Restructuring of Debt When Payments Are Less than Debt Carrying Amount   In a debt restructuring where the future revised cash flows are less than the debt carrying amount, the debtor reduces the carrying amount of the debt to the future modified cash payments (undiscounted), and a gain is recognized.

> **470-60-35-6**   If, however, the total future cash payments specified by the new terms of a payable, including both payments designated as interest and those designated as face amount, are less than the carrying amount of the payable, the debtor shall reduce the carrying amount to an amount equal to the total future cash payments specified by the new terms and shall recognize a gain on restructuring of payables equal to the amount of the reduction . . .

Restructuring of Debt When Payments Exceed Debt Carrying Amount   In a debt restructuring where the future revised cash flows exceed the debt carrying amount, the debtor does not adjust the carrying amount of the debt. Instead, the debtor computes a new effective interest rate to equate the present value of the future cash flows with the debt carrying amount. The new effective interest rate is used to prepare an amortization schedule, which becomes the basis for the recording of interest expense over the remaining term of the debt agreement.

> **470-60-35-5**   A debtor in a troubled debt restructuring involving only modification of terms of a payable—that is, not involving a transfer of assets or grant of an equity interest—shall account for the effects of the restructuring prospectively from the time of restructuring and shall not change the carrying amount of the payable at the time of the restructuring unless the carrying amount exceeds the total future cash payments specified by the new terms . . . Interest expense shall be computed in a way such that a constant effective interest rate is applied to the carrying amount of the payable at the beginning of each period between restructuring and maturity (in substance the interest method prescribed by paragraphs 835-30-35-2 and 835-30-35-4 through 35-5). The new effective interest rate shall be the discount rate that equates the present value of the future cash payments specified by the new terms (excluding amounts contingently payable) with the carrying amount of the payable.

Demo

MBC

On January 1 of Year 1, Debb Company issues a 10%, 2-year, $500,000 note paying annual interest each December 31 to Credex Company in exchange for $500,000 of merchandise. Debb is unable to make the December 31 of Year 1 interest payment. Debb is a calendar-year company and accrued the Year 1 interest.

We illustrate four possible debt restructuring arrangements at January 1 of Year 2 from the *debtor's perspective*.

- Example One: Settlement of debt through transfer of assets.
- Example Two: Settlement of debt through transfer of equity interest.
- Example Three: Restructuring of debt when payments exceed debt carrying amount.
- Example Four: Restructuring of debt when payments are less than debt carrying amount.

Example One: Settlement of Debt through Transfer of Assets

On January 1 of Year 2, Debb agrees to transfer land and a building to Credex in full settlement of the note. Information regarding the land and building follow.

	Land	Building
Fair value, January 1, Year 2.	$100,000	$250,000
Original cost to Debb	75,000	300,000
Accumulated depreciation through January 1, Year 2		100,000
Carrying amount, January 1, Year 2	75,000	200,000

Required
Record the entries for Debb (debtor) related to the debt settlement on January 1 of Year 2.

Solution

January 1, Year 2—To adjust assets to fair value for Debb (debtor)

Land ($100,000 – $75,000)	25,000	
Building ($250,000 – [$300,000 – $100,000])	50,000	
Gain on Disposal		75,000

January 1, Year 2—To record troubled debt restructure for Debb (debtor)

Note Payable	500,000	
Interest Payable ($500,000 × 10%)	50,000	
Accumulated Depreciation.	100,000	
Land.		100,000
Building		350,000
Gain on Restructuring of Debt (to balance).		200,000

Example Two: Settlement of Debt through Transfer of Equity Interest

Instead, let's assume that on January 1 of Year 2, Debb issues 2,500 shares of its $10 par common stock in full settlement of the note. The market price per share is $60 on January 1 of Year 2, and the increase in outstanding shares is not expected to affect the stock price appreciably.

Required
Record the entries for Debb (debtor) related to the debt settlement on January 1 of Year 2.

Solution

January 1, Year 2—To record troubled debt restructure for Debb (debtor)

Note Payable	500,000	
Interest Payable	50,000	
Common Stock (2,500 × $10)		25,000
Paid-In Capital in Excess of Par—Common Stock		
(2,500 × [$60 – $10]).		125,000
Gain on Restructuring of Debt (to balance).		400,000

Example Three: Restructuring of Debt at Less than Debt Carrying Amount

Now let's assume that on January 1 of Year 2, Debb and Credex agree to a debt restructure agreement with the following provisions:

continued

Margin T-accounts (left column):

Assets = Liabilities + Equity
+25,000   +75,000
Land   Gain
+50,000
Bldg

Land		Building	
Bal. 75,000		Bal. 300,000	
25,000		50,000	

Gain on Disposal	
	75,000

Assets = Liabilities + Equity
+100,000   –500,000   +200,000
AD   NP   Gain
–100,000   –50,000
Land   Int P
–350,000
Bldg

Land		Building	
Bal. 75,000	100,000	Bal. 300,000	350,000
25,000		50,000	
0		0	

Accum Deprec		Interest Payable	
100,000	100,000 Bal.	50,000	50,000 Bal.
	0		0

Note Payable		Gain—Debt Restr.	
500,000	500,000 Bal.		200,000
	0		

Assets = Liabilities + Equity
     –500,000   +25,000
     NP   CS
     –50,000   +125,000
     Int P   PIC—CS
            +400,000
            Gain

Interest Payable		Note Payable	
50,000	50,000 Bal.	500,000	500,000 Bal.
	0		0

Common Stock		Paid-In-Cap—CS	
	25,000		125,000

Gain—Debt Restr	
	400,000

- Face value of note is reduced to $400,000.
- Accrued interest for Year 1 is forgiven.
- Maturity is extended to January 1 of Year 4 (a 1-year extension).
- Interest rate is reduced to 5%; interest payments are due December 31 of Year 2 and Year 3.

Required

Record the entries for Debb (debtor) related to the debt restructuring on January 1 of Year 2.

Solution

The excess of the debt carrying amount over the restructured cash flows is calculated as follows.

Carrying amount of debt, January 1, Year 2 ($500,000 + $50,000)		$550,000
Sum of restructured cash flows:		
Face value payable, January 1, Year 4	$400,000	
December 31, Year 2, interest payment (5% × $400,000)	20,000	
December 31, Year 3, interest payment (5% × $400,000)	20,000	440,000
Excess of debt carrying amount over restructured cash flows		$110,000

Debb (debtor) will reduce the value of the interest payable and note payable by $110,000, net.

January 1, Year 2—To record troubled debt restructure for Debb (debtor)

Note Payable	500,000	
Interest Payable	50,000	
Note Payable		440,000
Gain on Restructuring of Debt (to balance)		110,000

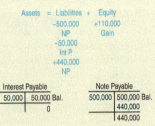

Assets	=	Liabilities	+	Equity
		−500,000		+110,000
		NP		Gain
		−50,000		
		Int P		
		+440,000		
		NP		

Interest Payable		
50,000	50,000	Bal.
	0	

Note Payable		
500,000	500,000	Bal.
	440,000	
	440,000	

Gain—Debt Restr	
	110,000

Example Four: Restructuring of Debt When Restructured Payments Exceed Debt Carrying Amount

Let's assume on January 1 of Year 2, Debb and Credex agree to a debt restructure agreement providing the following:

- Accrued interest for Year 1 is forgiven.
- Maturity is extended to January 1 of Year 4 (a 1-year extension), and regular interest payments are required December 31 of Year 2 and Year 3.

Required

Record the entries for Debb (debtor) related to the (1) debt restructuring on January 1 of Year 2, (2) the interest payments on December 31 of Year 2 and Year 3, and (3) the payment of the note on January 1 of Year 4.

Solution

The excess of the restructured cash flows over the debt carrying amount is calculated as follows.

Sum of restructured cash flows		
Face value payable, January 1, Year 4	$500,000	
December 31, Year 2, interest payment (10% × $500,000)	50,000	
December 31, Year 3, interest payment (10% × $500,000)	50,000	$600,000
Less carrying amount of debt, January 1, Year 2		550,000
Excess of restructured cash flows over debt carrying amount		$ 50,000

Debb computes a new effective interest rate using the revised debt payment schedule through the following calculation.

	RATE	NPER	PMT	PV	FV	Excel Formula
Given	?	2	(50,000)	550,000	(500,000)	=RATE(2,−50000,550000,−500000)
Solution	4.6487%					

Using the market rate of 4.6487%, Debb (debtor) prepares the following amortization schedule.

continued

continued from previous page

Debb (Debtor)				
		Effective Interest Method		
	Cash	Interest Expense	Note Payable	Note Payable, Net
Date	(Stated Interest)	(Market Interest)	Reduction	(Carrying Amount)
Jan. 1, Year 2 . . .				$550,000
Dec. 31, Year 2 . . .	$ 50,000	$25,568	$24,432	525,568
Dec. 31, Year 3 . . .	50,000	24,432	25,568	500,000
Totals	$100,000	$50,000	$50,000	

On January 1 of Year 2, outstanding interest is combined with the outstanding principal into the new note payable account.

Assets = Liabilities + Equity
−500,000
NP
− 50,000
Int P
+550,000
NP

January 1, Year 2—To record troubled debt restructure for Debb (debtor)

Note Payable	500,000	
Interest Payable . . . . :	50,000	
Note Payable		550,000

Interest Payable
50,000 | 50,000 Bal.

Note Payable
500,000 | 500,000 Bal.
| 550,000

Assets = Liabilities + Equity
−24,432   −24,432   −25,568
C:f   NP   Exp
−25,568
C:o

December 31, Year 2—To record interest payment for Debb (debtor)

Note Payable	24,432	
Interest Expense.	25,568	
Cash		50,000

Cash
| 50,000

Note Payable
500,000 | 500,000 Bal.
24,432 | 550,000

Interest Exp
25,568 |

Assets = Liabilities + Equity
−25,568   −25,568   −24,432
C:f   NP   Exp
−24,432
C:o

December 31, Year 3—To record interest payment for Debb (debtor)

Note Payable	25,568	
Interest Expense.	24,432	
Cash		50,000

Cash
| 50,000
| 50,000

Note Payable
500,000 | 500,000 Bal.
24,432 | 550,000
25,568 |

Interest Exp
25,568 |
24,432 |

Assets = Liabilities + Equity
−500,000   −500,000
C:f   NP

January 1, Year 4—To record principal payment for Debb (debtor)

| Note Payable . . . . | 500,000 | |
| Cash . . . . | | 500,000 |

Cash
| 50,000
| 50,000
| 500,000

Note Payable
500,000 | 500,000 Bal.
24,432 | 550,000
25,568 |
500,000 |
| 0

REVIEW 16-12 ▶ **LO16-12**   **Debtor's Accounting for Debt Settlement and Debt Restructuring**

Review

MBC

Example One: Settling Debt through a Transfer of Assets

Atlanta Corporation is experiencing financial struggles and is negotiating a settlement of its $40,000, 8% note payable to Johnson Company. On January 1 of Year 2, the note's carrying amount is $35,000 (with no interest due), and its present value at the current market rate is $28,000. Atlanta agreed to give Johnson Company equipment in full settlement of the note payable on January 1 of Year 2. The equipment's original cost was $50,000. On January 1 of Year 2, the equipment's carrying amount is $28,000, and its fair value is $32,000. Record the entries by Atlanta Corporation to record the gain or loss on disposal of equipment and the settlement of the note. Interest has been paid through December 31 of Year 1.

continued

continued from previous page

Example Two: Settling Debt through a Transfer of Equity

Now assume that instead of settling the note with equipment, Atlanta Corporation settles the note with an equity interest. On January 1 of Year 2, Atlanta Corporation issues 3,000 shares of its $1 par common stock in full settlement of the note. The market price per share is $10 on January 1 of Year 2, and the increase in outstanding shares is not expected to affect the stock price appreciably. Record the entry by Atlanta Corporation to settle the note.

Example Three: Restructuring Debt at Less than Debt Carrying Amount

Now assume that instead of settling the note, Johnson Company agrees to restructure the note. On January 1 of Year 2, Johnson Company agrees to reduce the note to $25,000 and decrease the interest rate to 5% (due annually). The note payable is now due December 31 of Year 3. Record the entry by Atlanta Corporation to restructure the note.

Example Four: Restructuring Debt in Excess of Debt Carrying Amount

Now assume that terms of the restructure are as follows. On January 1 of Year 2, Johnson Company agrees to reduce the note to $30,000 and decrease the interest rate to 9% (due annually). The note payable is now due December 31 of Year 4. Record the entry by Atlanta Corp. to restructure the note.

More Practice: AppBE16-1, AppBE16-2, AppBE16-3, AppBE16-4
Solution on p. 16-79.

Questions

Q16-1. List and briefly explain the primary characteristics of long-term debt securities. What are the primary distinctions between a debt security and an equity security?

Q16-2. Explain the difference between the stated rate and the market rate on a long-term debt security.

Q16-3. How is the issue price of a zero-interest-bearing note payable determined?

Q16-4. Briefly explain the effects on interest recognized when the stated and market rates of interest are different.

Q16-5. What are the primary characteristics of a bond? What distinguishes it from capital stock?

Q16-6. Contrast the following classes of bonds: (a) corporate versus municipal, (b) secured versus unsecured, (c) term versus serial, and (d) callable versus convertible.

Q16-7. What are the principal advantages and disadvantages of issuing bonds versus common stock for (a) the issuer and (b) the investor?

Q16-8. Distinguish between the face value and the issue price of a bond. When are they the same? When are they different? Explain.

Q16-9. Explain the impact on interest of a bond discount and bond premium to (a) the issuer and (b) the investor.

Q16-10. Assume that a $1,000, 8% (payable semiannually), 10-year bond is sold to yield a market rate of 6%. Explain how to compute the price of this bond.

Q16-11. Explain why and how bond discount and bond premium affect (a) the balance sheet and (b) the income statement of the investor.

Q16-12. What is the primary conceptual difference between the straight-line and effective interest methods of amortizing bond discount and premium?

Q16-13. Under GAAP, when is it appropriate to use the (a) straight-line interest method and (b) effective interest method of amortization for bond discount or premium?

Q16-14. When the end of the accounting period of the issuer is not on a bond interest date, adjusting entries must be made for (a) accrued interest and (b) discount or premium amortization. Explain in general terms what each adjustment amount represents.

Q16-15. When bonds are sold (or purchased) between interest dates, accrued interest must be recognized. Explain why.

Q16-16. What are convertible bonds? What are the primary reasons for their use?

Q16-17. Define extinguishment of debt.

Q16-18. When may extinguishment of debt occur? List the various ways in which extinguishment of debt occurs.

Q16-19. Explain how an accounting gain or loss to the debtor may occur when a call privilege is exercised.

Q16-20. When the issuer purchases its own debt securities in the open market to extinguish the debt, two entries must usually be made. Explain.

Q16-21. What is meant by refunding?

Q16-22. Interest rates have increased since a company issued its bonds. Why would the company want to refund the bonds with another issue of bonds paying a higher rate?

Q16-23. A company retired a bond issue early, at a loss. Is the company in an economically worse position after the retirement?

Q16-24. Why is the accounting different for nonconvertible bonds with detachable stock purchase warrants and nonconvertible bonds with nondetachable stock purchase warrants?

Data Analytics

Data Analytics DA16-1
Preparing Excel Schedules to Determine Compliance with Debt Agreements **LO1**

For this exercise, we calculate key financial amounts with data provided for Monroe Inc. to determine whether the company is in compliance with its debt covenants. The IF statement is used to show compliance or noncompliance. We also create new scenarios and check for debt compliance.

Data Visualization

Data Visualization

Data Visualization Activities are available in **myBusinessCourse**. These assignments use Tableau Dashboards to expose students to visual depictions of data and introduce students to data analytics through data visualizations. These exercises are assignable and auto graded by MBC.

Multiple Choice

LO1

MC16-1. Analyzing Bond Issuance   Iris Corp. authorized and issued 15-year, $225,000 bonds on January 1 of Year 10 at 96, bearing interest at 4%, payable semiannually on June 30 and December 31. For this bond issuance, what is the face value, selling price, and stated interest amount per payment period?

	Face Value	Selling Price	Stated Interest Amount per Payment Period
a.	$224,999	$225,000	$4,320
b.	$225,000	$216,000	$4,500
c.	$225,000	$216,000	$9,000
d.	$224,999	$225,000	$8,640

LO2

MC16-2. Computing Bond Selling Price   On January 1 of Year 1, Bryant Inc. authorizes and issues $400,000, 4% interest-bearing bonds. The bonds mature December 31 of Year 10, and pay interest semiannually on June 30 and December 31. Compute the selling price of the bonds under two different market rate assumptions.

	3% Market Rate	5% Market Rate
a.	$459,510	$350,151
b.	$367,297	$432,703
c.	$345,639	$454,361
d.	$434,337	$368,822

LO2

MC16-3. Computing Bond Selling Price Including Accrued Interest   Dixie Inc. authorized $60,000, 5%, 5-year bonds on January 1. The bonds pay interest semiannually on June 30 and December 31. If the bonds are sold on April 30 at 98, what amount of cash did Dixie receive, including any accrued interest?

a. $58,800   c. $60,800
b. $59,780   d. $59,800

LO3

MC16-4. Determining Financial Statement Effect for Bonds Issued at Par   On January 1 of Year 1, Timely Co. authorizes and issues $140,000, 6% interest-bearing bonds at par. The bonds mature December 31 of Year 10 and pay interest semiannually on June 30 and December 31. By what amount is Timely's stockholders' equity reduced on January 1 of Year 1 due to this transaction?

a. $0   c. $4,200
b. $700   d. $8,400

MC16-5. Determining Financial Statement Effect of Bond Interest—Effective Interest Method   On January 1 of Year 1, Eagle Inc. issued $250,000, 4%, 5-year debenture bonds for $239,176 to yield a market rate of 5%. Eagle also incurred costs of $12,000 to issue the bonds. The bonds pay interest annually on December 31 and the company applies the effective interest method to amortize any bond discount or premium. What amount of bond interest expense should Eagle report in its income statement for the year ended December 31 of Year 1?   **LO4**

    a. $11,358   c. $14,035

    b. $11,959   d. $13,631

MC16-6. Determining Carrying Amount of Bonds—Effective Interest Method   On July 1 of Year 10, Miller Company issued for $255,368, 4%, 10-year bonds with a face value of $300,000. Interest is paid semiannually on December 31 and June 30. The bonds were issued to yield 6%. Miller uses the effective interest method to amortize any bond discount or premium. What is the carrying amount of the bonds in Miller's December 31 of Year 10 balance sheet?   **LO4**

    a. $258,690   c. $253,707

    b. $257,029   d. $251,475

MC16-7. Determining Carrying Amount of Bonds—Effective Interest Method   On July 1 of Year 10, Spring Company issued for $349,054, 6%, 10-year bonds with a face value of $300,000. Interest is paid semiannually on December 31 and June 30. The bonds were issued to yield 4%. Spring uses the effective interest method to amortize any bond discount or premium. What is the carrying amount of the bonds in Spring's June 30 of Year 11 balance sheet?   **LO5**

    a. $344,976   c. $345,016

    b. $347,035   d. $357,998

MC16-8. Computing Interest Expense on Zero-Interest Bearing Note   Grafton Inc. issued a 5-year, $115,000, zero-interest bearing note to Lee Corp. on January 1 of Year 1 in exchange for equipment with a fair value of $85,935. The implicit interest rate is 6%. What is the amount of interest expense recognized for the first six months of Year 1?   **LO6**

    a. $5,156   c. $3,450

    b. $0   d. $2,578

MC16-9. Recording a Loss on Bond Redemption   Ten-year, 4% bonds of $200,000 with an unamortized discount of $10,000 are recalled at 103 on December 31 of Year 1 after interest was recognized and paid. The costs of the bond recall total $3,000. What is the loss recorded on the bond redemption?   **LO7**

    a. $6,000 loss   c. $16,000 loss

    b. $9,000 loss   d. $19,000 loss

MC16-10. Accounting for Convertible Bonds   On January 1 of Year 1, Joss Inc. sells $300,000 of 5% convertible bonds for $270,000. Each $1,000 bond is convertible into 5 shares of Joss $1 par value common stock. On December 31 of Year 2, Joss records the conversion of 70% of its bonds into common stock when the total unamortized discount is $24,000. What is the amount of Paid-in Capital in Excess of Par recognized upon the conversion, assuming that the common stock is trading at $210 per share?   **LO8**

    a. $62,850   c. $225,750

    b. $193,200   d. $192,150

MC16-11. Accounting for Bonds Under the Fair Value Option   Lee Inc. sold 5-year, 5%, $180,000 bonds at par. At the sales date, Lee chose to account for the bonds under the fair value option. One year later, the bonds had a fair value of $166,000. At that date, what is the unrealized gain or loss recorded?   **LO9**

    a.   Unrealized loss—income of $14,000   c.   Unrealized loss—income of $23,000

    b.   Unrealized gain—income of $14,000   d.   Unrealized gain—income of $23,000

MC16-12. Computing Times Interest Earned   Brook Inc. reported the following amounts at the end of Year 5.   **LO10**

Interest revenue	$ 800
Interest expense	$ 2,200
Income before taxes and interest expense . . .	$12,500
Net income	$ 7,210

Calculate the times interest earned ratio.

a.   3.28   c.   5.68
b.   8.93   d.   5.15

LO11

MC16-13. Issuing Bonds with Detachable Warrants   Lark Corp. issues $120,000 of 6%, 5-year bonds with detachable stock warrants on January 1. Each $1,200 bond carries 5 warrants. Each warrant entitles the holder to purchase one share of $1 par common stock for $12. Assume the bond issue sells for 102. Shortly after issuance, the warrants trade for $10 each and the bonds were quoted at 100 without warrants attached. Upon issuance of the bonds, the company would record a

a.   Credit to Paid-in Capital—Stock Warrants of $5,000
b.   Debit to Premium on Bonds Payable of $2,496
c.   Credit to Paid-in Capital —Stock Warrants of $4,896
d.   Debit to Cash of $120,000

Brief Exercises

Brief Exercise 16-1
Determining Bond
Type **LO1**
Hint: See Demo 16-1A

For each of the following debt scenarios *a* through *d*, identify the bond or note type that applies.

Debt Scenario	Choose from Bond or Note Type
a. Bonds issued by a public corporation	• Corporate bonds or Municipal bonds
b. Mortgage note issued for commercial property	• Secured note or Debenture note
c. Bonds issued at a discount, pay interest periodically and principal at bond maturity	• Term bonds or Serial bonds
d. Bonds that can be converted to equity securities at the option of the holder	• Redeemable bonds or Convertible bonds

Brief Exercise 16-2
Determining Bond
Features **LO1**
Hint: See Demo 16-1B

Rowe Corporation authorized $5,000 of 8% (cash interest payable semiannually) 10-year bonds. The bonds were dated January 1; interest dates are June 30 and December 31. Assume three different cases with respect to the sale of the bonds: **Case A**: Bonds sold on January 1 at par; **Case B**: Bonds sold on January 1 at 98; **Case C**: Bonds sold on February 1 at 102. Complete the following table.

	Case A	Case B	Case C
Face value of bonds			
Semiannual interest payment			
Bond selling price (excluding accrued interest)			
Bond issue date			

Brief Exercise 16-3
Computing Bond Selling
Price **LO2**
Hint: See Demo 16-2

An 8-year, 6%, $1,000 bond (cash interest payable annually) is sold to yield 6% interest. Compute the bond selling price.

Brief Exercise 16-4
Computing Bond Selling
Price **LO2**
Hint: See Demo 16-2

A 10-year, 7%, $1,000 bond (cash interest payable 3.5% semiannually) is sold to yield 6% interest. Compute the bond selling price.

Brief Exercise 16-5
Computing Bond Selling
Price **LO2**
Hint: See Demo 16-2

A 10-year, 6%, $1,000 bond (cash interest payable 3% semiannually) is sold to yield 8% interest. Compute the bond selling price.

Brief Exercise 16-6
Computing Bond Issue
Price—Sold Between
Interest Payment
Dates **LO2**
Hint: See Demo 16-2

Rowe Corporation authorized $600,000 of 8% (cash interest payable semiannually) 10-year bonds. The bonds are dated January 1. Interest dates are June 30 and December 31. Assuming that the bonds were sold on March 1 at face value, record the following journal entries.

a.   March 1: Issuance of bonds.   b.   June 30: First interest payment.

Yale Corporation issued $60,000, 8% (cash interest payable semiannually on July 1 and January 1) 10-year bonds dated and sold on January 1 of Year 1. If the bonds were sold at face value, provide the journal entries to be made at each of the following dates. Yale's fiscal year ends on December 31.

a.   Jan. 1, Year 1, for issuance of bonds.   *d.*   Jan. 1, Year 2, for interest payment.

b.   July 1, Year 1, for interest payment.   *e.*   Dec. 31, Year 10, bond retirement.

c.   Dec. 31, Year 1, for the adjusting entry.

Brief Exercise 16-7
Recording Bonds Issued at Face Value **LO3**
Hint: See Demo 16-3

Refer to BE16-7, but instead of journal entries, show the effect on the accounting equation for the transactions, including identifying the individual accounts affected, and the total impact on assets, liabilities, and stockholders' equity.

Brief Exercise 16-8
Reporting Transactions for Bonds Issued at Face Value Using the Accounting Equation **LO3**

Yale Corporation issued $60,000, 8% (cash interest payable semiannually on June 30 and December 31) 10-year bonds dated and sold on January 1. Yale amortizes any bond discount or premium using the straight-line amortization method. If the bonds were sold at 97, provide journal entries to be made at each of the following dates.

a.   January 1, for issuance of bonds.   *b.*   June 30, for the first interest payment.

Brief Exercise 16-9
Recording Bonds Issued at a Discount—Straight-Line **LO4**
Hint: See Demo 16-4B

Refer to BE16-9, but instead of journal entries, show the effect on the accounting equation for the transactions, including identifying the individual accounts affected, and the total impact on assets, liabilities, and stockholders' equity.

Brief Exercise 16-10
Reporting Transactions for Discount Bonds—Straight-Line Using the Accounting Equation **LO4**

Yale Corporation issued $60,000, 8% (cash interest payable semiannually on June 30 and December 31) 10-year bonds dated and sold on January 1. Yale amortizes any bond discount or premium using the straight-line amortization method. If the bonds were sold at 103, provide journal entries to be made at each of the following dates.

a.   January 1, for issuance of bonds.

b.   March 31, for accrual of interest for quarterly reporting.

c.   June 30, for the first interest payment. (No reversing entry was made on June 1.)

Brief Exercise 16-11
Recording Bonds Issued at a Premium—Straight-Line **LO5**

Refer to BE16-11, but instead of journal entries, show the effect on the accounting equation for the transactions, including identifying the individual accounts affected, and the total impact on assets, liabilities, and stockholders' equity.

Brief Exercise 16-12
Reporting Transactions for Premium Bonds—Straight-Line Using the Accounting Equation **LO5**

Yale Corporation issued $60,000, 8% (cash interest payable semiannually on June 30 and December 31) 10-year bonds dated and sold on January 1. Yale amortizes any bond discount or premium using the effective interest amortization method. If the bonds were sold to yield 9%, provide journal entries to be made at each of the following dates.

a.   January 1, for issuance of bonds.   *b.*   June 30, for the first interest payment.

Brief Exercise 16-13
Recording Bonds Issued at a Discount—Effective Interest **LO4**
Hint: See Demo 16-4A

Refer to BE16-13, but instead of journal entries, show the effect on the accounting equation for the transactions, including identifying the individual accounts affected, and the total impact on assets, liabilities, and stockholders' equity.

Brief Exercise 16-14
Reporting Transactions for Discount Bonds—Effective Interest Using the Accounting Equation **LO4**

Yale Corporation issued $60,000, 8% (cash interest payable semiannually on June 30 and December 31) 10-year bonds dated and sold on January 1. Yale amortizes any bond discount or premium using the effective interest amortization method. If the bonds were sold to yield 7%, provide journal entries to be made at each of the following dates.

a.   January 1, for issuance of bonds.   *b.*   June 30, for the first interest payment.

Brief Exercise 16-15
Recording Bonds Issued at a Premium—Effective Interest **LO5**
Hint: See Demo 16-5A

Brief Exercise 16-16
Reporting Transactions for Premium Bonds—Effective Interest Using the Accounting Equation **LO5**

Refer to BE16-15, but instead of journal entries, show the effect on the accounting equation for the transactions, including identifying the individual accounts affected, and the total impact on assets, liabilities, and stockholders' equity.

Brief Exercise 16-17
Reporting Bonds on the Balance Sheet **LO4**
Hint: See Demo 16-4A

For the Yale Corporation bonds in BE16-13, show how the bonds and any related bond discount or premium would be presented on the balance sheet as of June 30.

Brief Exercise 16-18
Recording Debt Issuance Costs **LO4**
Hint: See Demo 16-4C

Yale Corporation issued $60,000, 8% (cash interest payable semiannually on June 30 and December 31) 10-year bonds dated and sold on January 1. Yale amortizes any bond discount or premium using the effective interest amortization method and bond issuance costs are $1,500. If the bonds were sold to yield 9%, provide journal entries to be made at each of the following dates.

a. January 1, for issuance of bonds.
b. June 30, for the first interest payment.

Brief Exercise 16-19
Reporting Debt Issuance Costs Using the Accounting Equation **LO4**

Refer to BE16-18, but instead of journal entries, show the effect on the accounting equation for the transactions, including identifying the individual accounts affected, and the total impact on assets, liabilities, and stockholders' equity.

Brief Exercise 16-20
Recording Entries for Note Payable Exchanged for Cash **LO6**
Hint: See Demo 16-6A

Lacey Corp. issued a 3-year, $5,000 note with an 8% stated rate to Hayley Co. on January 1, and received cash of $5,000. The note requires semiannual interest payments on June 30 and December 31. Provide journal entries to be made by Lacey at each of the following dates.

a. January 1, for issuance of bonds.
b. June 30, for the first interest payment.

Brief Exercise 16-21
Recording Entries for Zero-Interest-Bearing Note Payable Exchanged for Cash **LO6**
Hint: See Demo 16-6A

On January 1, Landry Inc. issued a 3-year, $5,000, zero-interest-bearing note to Dillon LLP and received $4,198. The implied interest rate is 6% on this note transaction. Provide journal entries to be made by Landry at each of the following dates.

a. January 1, for issuance of the note.
b. December 31, for accrual of interest for the first year.

Brief Exercise 16-22
Recording Entries for Interest-Bearing Note Payable Exchanged for Noncash Consideration **LO6**
Hint: See Demo 16-6B

Fern Company purchased goods on January 1 and issued a 2-year, $2,500 note with a 5% stated rate. The fair value of the goods is $2,366. The note requires annual interest payments on December 31. The market rate for this note is 8%. The company uses the effective interest method to amortize any discount or premium. Provide journal entries to be made at each of the following dates.

a. January 1, for issuance of bonds.
b. June 30, for the first interest payment.

Brief Exercise 16-23
Recording Entries for Note Payable Exchanged for Cash and Noncash Consideration **LO6**

On January 1, Allen Corp. issued a 3-year, zero-interest-bearing note payable for $10,000 to Town Corp. for a cash receipt of $10,000. In lieu of interest payments, Allen Corp. agreed to sell merchandise to Town Corp. at a discount and provide free shipping during the 3-year period. The market rate for this note is 8%. Record the journal entry for Allen Corp. on January 1 for issuance of the note payable.

Brief Exercise 16-24
Computing Installment Payment on Note Payable **LO6**

On January 1, a borrower signed a long-term note, face amount $50,000, with time to maturity of 6 years. The interest rate is 7%, and equal annual installment payments will pay off the loan after six years.

a. How much is each annual installment payment?
b. Record the first installment payment on December 31.

Darien Inc. redeemed $5,000 of its bonds at 102 on January 1. At this date, the unamortized discount was $690. Prepare the journal entry on January 1 for the bond redemption. Assume Darien has a December 31 year-end and all necessary adjusting entries were made.

Brief Exercise 16-25
Recording Bond
Redemption **LO7**
Hint: See Demo 16-7

Stonewall Corporation issued $20,000 of 5%, 10-year convertible bonds. Each $1,000 bond is convertible to 10 shares of common stock (par $50) of Stonewall Corporation. The bonds were sold at 105 on January 1 of Year 1. Provide the entry for Stonewall Corporation on January 1 of Year 1 to record the issuance of the bonds.

Brief Exercise 16-26
Recording the Issuance of
Convertible Bonds **LO8**
Hint: See Demo 16-8

Refer to BE16-26 but now assume that five years later on December 31 of Year 5, the bonds were converted into common stock when the unamortized premium is $500. The company spent $1,500 cash to induce the conversion. Record the entry upon conversion.

Brief Exercise 16-27
Recording the Conversion of
Convertible Bonds **LO8**

Josie Corporation issued 10-year, 8% interest-bearing bonds payable at face value for $10,000 on January 1. At that time, Josie Corporation elected to account for the bonds payable using the fair value option method. At year-end on December 31, the fair value of the bonds payable was $9,900 due to an increase in Josie Corporation's borrowing rate because of general market risk changes.

a. Prepare the journal entry to adjust the bonds payable under the fair value option method on December 31.

b. How would your answer to part *a* change if the decrease in the fair value of bonds payable was instead due to an increase in Josie Corporation's borrowing rate due to a decline in corporate liquidity?

Brief Exercise 16-28
Adjusting Bonds Payable
Under the Fair Value
Option **LO9**

Target Corporation reported the following amounts (in millions) in a recent Form 10-K.

- Total assets: $44,553
- Total liabilities: $28,322
- Total noncurrent liabilities: $15,545
- Total stockholders' equity: $16,231

- Net earnings: $1,971
- Interest expense: $1,126
- Net earnings before taxes and interest: $4,229

Compute the following ratios.

a. Total liabilities-to-equity   *b.* Total liabilities-to-total assets   *c.* Times interest earned

Brief Exercise 16-29
Calculating Leverage
Ratios **LO10**
Hint: See Demo 16-10B

On December 1, Junction Company issued 4,000 of its 9%, 10-year, $1,000 par value, nonconvertible bonds with detachable stock purchase warrants at 104. Each bond carried two detachable warrants; each warrant was for one share of common stock at an option price of $15 per share. Shortly after issuance, the warrants were quoted on the market for $3 each. Fair value for the bonds without the warrants cannot be determined. Interest is payable on December 1 and June 1. Provide the entry to record issuance of the bonds by Junction Company on December 1.

Brief Exercise 16-30
Recording the Issuance
of Bonds with Detachable
Warrants **LO11**
Hint: See Demo 16-11

Exercises

For each account *a* through *m* listed below, indicate the account type (asset, liability, or equity) and the financial statement (balance sheet or statement of comprehensive income) where the account would be reported.

a. Discount on Bonds Payable (10-year bonds)
b. Premium on Bonds Payable (10-year bonds)
c. Bonds Payable (Due in 5 years)
d. Note Payable (Due in 2 years)
e. Interest Expense
f. Unrealized Gain or Loss—Income
g. Unrealized Gain or Loss—OCI

h. Gain on Redemption of Bonds
i. Debt Conversion Expense
j. Interest Payable
k. Gain on Extinguishment of Bonds
l. Mortgage Payable
m. Paid-In Capital—Stock Warrants

Exercise 16-1
Classifying
Financial Statement
Accounts **LO1, 2, 3,
4, 5, 6, 7, 8, 11**

For each of the following bond scenarios *a* through *e* described below, identify a bond type that applies from the following: callable, convertible, debenture, municipal, secured, serial, and term.

a. Harrison County Flood Control Improvement Bonds issued in the state of Texas.
b. Bonds backed by liens on equipment are issued.
c. Treasury bill where the registered owner receives the face value of the bill at maturity with no principal payments during the term.
d. Corporate bonds where the holder has the option to trade in the bonds for the company's common stock.
e. Corporate bond that can be retired early at the option of the issuer.

Exercise 16-2
Determining Bond
Type **LO1**
Hint: See Demo 16-1A

Exercise 16-3
Determining Bond Features
and Selling Price
LO1, 2
Hint: See Review 16-1

On January 1 of Year 1, the following debt was authorized and issued by Anderson Company.

1. $50,000, 5-year, 9% convertible bonds payable, cash interest payable semiannually on June 30 and December 31 to yield 10%.

2. $10,000, 8-year, 10% note payable, cash interest payable semiannually on June 30 and December 31 to yield 9.5%.

3. $30,000, 10-year, zero-interest-bearing bonds to yield 11% annually.

Required

For each debt, indicate the following:

a. Face value.

b. Stated rate per interest period.

c. Stated interest amount per interest period.

d. Market rate per interest period.

e. Number of interest periods over life of the debt.

f. Selling price.

g. Maturity date.

h. Authorization date.

Exercise 16-4
Determining Bond Selling
Price and Recording of
Bond Issuance   LO2
Hint: See Review 16-2

Calculate the bond selling price and the entry at bond issuance for the following four separate scenarios.

a. 33M Corp. authorized and issued $200,000, 6%, 5-year bonds payable on January 1. Calculate the selling price of the bonds if the bonds pay cash interest annually on December 31, and the market rate on similar bonds is 6%.

b. 33M Corp. authorized and issued $100,000, 6%, 20-year bonds payable on January 1. Calculate the selling price of the bonds if the bonds pay cash interest semiannually on July 1 and January 1, and the market rate on similar bonds is 8%.

c. 33M Corp. authorized and issued $250,000, 7%, 10-year bonds payable on January 1. Calculate the selling price of the bonds if the bonds pay cash interest semiannually on July 1 and January 1, and the market rate on similar bonds is 6%.

d. 33M Corp. issued $75,000, 5%, 10-year bonds payable on March 31 of Year 1. The bonds were authorized on January 1 of Year 1. Calculate the selling price of the bonds (including interest) if the bonds pay cash interest annually on January 1, and the market rate on similar bonds is 6%.

Exercise 16-5
Reporting Transactions
for Bonds Issuance
Using the Accounting
Equation   LO2

Refer to E16-4, but instead of journal entries, show the effect on the accounting equation for the transactions, including identifying the individual accounts affected, and the total impact on assets, liabilities, and stockholders' equity. **For the cash account, indicate the effect on the statement of cash flows by selecting from C:o (cash from operating activities), C:i (cash from investing activities), or C:f (cash from financing activities).**

Exercise 16-6
Recording Entries for
Bonds Sold Between
Interest Dates   LO2, 3

On May 1 of Year 1, Setup Inc. sold an issue of 5%, $1,000 bonds dated January 1 of Year 1 to yield 5%. The bonds pay interest every June 30 and December 31 and mature December 31 of Year 5.

Required

a. Provide journal entries to be made by Setup Inc. at each of the following dates.

    1. May 1 of Year 1, bond issuance.
    2. June 30 of Year 1, first interest payment.

b. Indicate the amount of interest expense to be recorded in the company's income statement for the six months ended June 30 of Year 1.

Exercise 16-7
Reporting Transactions
for Bonds Issued
Between Interest Dates
Using the Accounting
Equation   LO2, 3

Refer to E16-6, but instead of journal entries for part *a*, show the effect on the accounting equation for the transactions, including identifying the individual accounts affected, and the total impact on assets, liabilities, and stockholders' equity.

Exercise 16-8
Recording Journal Entries
for At-Par-Bonds
LO2, 3

On October 1 of Year 1, Nell Co. issued an 8-year, 6%, $1,000 bond at face value, with cash interest payable semiannually on April 1 and October 1.

Required

Provide journal entries at each of the following dates.

a. October 1 of Year 1—Issuance.

b. December 31 of Year 1—Interest expense adjusting entry.

c. April 1 of Year 2—First interest payment. (No reversing entries made in Year 2.)

On January 1 of Year 1, Williams Inc. issued 4-year, $50,000, 5% bonds, priced to yield 6%, with cash interest payable semiannually on June 30 and December 31. The company amortizes the bond discount using the effective interest method.

Required

Provide an amortization schedule of interest and discount amortization for the 4-year bond term.

Exercise 16-9
Preparing an Amortization Schedule—Effective Interest Method, Discount **LO4**

On January 1 of Year 1, Williams Inc. issued 4-year, $50,000, 5% bonds at 98, with cash interest payable semiannually on June 30 and December 31. The company amortizes the bond discount using the straight-line interest method.

Required

Provide an amortization schedule of interest and discount amortization for the 4-year bond term.

Exercise 16-10
Preparing an Amortization Schedule —Straight-Line Interest Method, Discount **LO4**
Hint: See Demo 16-4B

Mitchell Inc. issued 40 of its 6%, $1,000 bonds on January 1 of Year 1 for $38,950. The bonds pay cash interest annually each December 31 and were issued to yield 7%. The bonds mature in three years on December 31, and the company uses the effective interest method to amortize bond discounts or premiums.

Required

a. Prepare an amortization schedule for the full bond term.
b. Prepare journal entries on the following dates.
   1. January 1 of Year 1, bond issuance.   2. December 31 of Year 1, interest payment.
c. Explain why, in economic terms, the interest expense recognized each year exceeds the cash interest paid.

Exercise 16-11
Recording Bond Entries and Preparing an Amortization Schedule—Effective Interest Method, Discount **LO4**

Mitchell Inc. issued 40 of its 6%, $1,000 bonds on January 1 of Year 1. The bonds pay cash interest semiannually each July 1 and December 31 and were issued to yield 7%. The bonds mature in three years on December 31, and the company uses the effective interest method to amortize bond discounts or premiums.

Required

a. Determine the selling price of the bonds.
b. Prepare an amortization schedule for the first year of the bond term.
c. Prepare journal entries on the following dates.
   1. January 1 of Year 1, bond issuance.   3. December 31 of Year 1, interest payment.
   2. July 1 of Year 1, interest payment.

Exercise 16-12
Recording Bond Entries and Preparing an Amortization Schedule—Effective Interest Method, Discount **LO4**
Hint: See Demo 16-4A

Refer to the information in E16-12. However, now assume that the interest payments are made on July 1 and January 1.

Required

a. Determine the selling price of the bonds.
b. Prepare an amortization schedule for the first year of the bond term.
c. Prepare journal entries on the following dates.

   1. January 1 of Year 1, bond issuance.   3. December 31 of Year 1, interest accrual.
   2. July 1 of Year 1, interest payment.   4. January 1 of Year 2, interest payment.

Exercise 16-13
Recording Bond Entries and Preparing an Amortization Schedule—Effective Interest Method, Discount, Interest Accrual **LO4**
Hint: See Demo 16-4A

Mitchell Inc. issued 40 of its 6%, $1,000 bonds on January 1 of Year 1. The bonds pay cash interest semiannually each July 1 and December 31 and were issued to yield 7%. Debt issuance costs were $800. The bonds mature in three years on December 31, and the company uses the effective interest method to amortize bond discounts and debt issuance costs.

Required

a. Determine the selling price of the bonds, net of debt issuance costs.
b. Prepare an amortization schedule for the first year of the bond term.
c. Prepare journal entries on the following dates.
   1. January 1 of Year 1, bond issuance.   3. December 31 of Year 1, interest payment.
   2. July 1 of Year 1, interest payment.

Exercise 16-14
Recording Bond Entries and Preparing an Amortization Schedule—Debt Issuance Costs **LO4**
Hint: See Demo 16-4C

continued from previous page

Lease Scenario	Applicable Lease Criterion	Explanation	Lease Criterion Met
3. Lessee Inc. signs a lease contract for an office building for 10 years. The contract includes an option for a 10-year renewal, with rents determined by market prices at the time of renewal. Due to the amount invested in leasehold improvements, the lessee expects to renew the lease. The estimated useful life of the office building is 20 years.	Lease term length	There is an economic incentive to renew the lease, so the lease term is considered to be 20 years. Because the lease term is 100% of the building's estimated life, the lease term is a *"major part"* of the asset's economic life.	✔
4. Lessee Inc. leases equipment for 5 years. The annual payment is $3,000, with the first payment due immediately. *Other information* • Lessee's incremental borrowing rate: 6% • Implicit interest rate, known by lessee: 5%. • Fair value of equipment: $15,000.	Present value of lease payments	The present value of the lease payments ($13,638) is greater than 90% of the fair value ($13,500, or 0.90 × $15,000).	✔
5. Lessor Inc. entered into a lease agreement to rent specialized equipment to Lessee Inc. for five years. The equipment was tailored specifically to the Lessee's operations and would require significant adjustments to resell the equipment at lease end to another company, which the lessor would be reluctant to make.	No alternative use	The specialized equipment meets this criterion because of the restrictions on the use of the equipment at lease end.	✔

Scenario 4 detail:

	RATE	NPER	PMT	PV	TYPE	Excel Formula
Given	5%	5	(3,000)	?	1	=PV(0.05,5,−3000,0,1)
Solution				$13,638		

Effective control is considered transferred to the lessee because the present value of lease payments is *"substantially all"* of the fair value of the leased asset.

Determine Lease Classification   LO17-1   REVIEW 17-1

Jefferson Inc. is in the process of negotiating a lease of equipment with a fair value of $200,000 and must determine the proper lease classification. The following table describes four scenarios under negotiation.

	Option One	Option Two	Option Three	Option Four
Ownership transfer	No	No	No	No
Purchase option	No	No	$20,000 purchase option, considered a discounted price.	No
Length of lease term	8	10	8	8
Economic life of equipment	12	12	12	12
No alternative use of equipment at lease end	No	No	No	No
Annual lease payment	$25,000	$25,000	$28,000	$28,000
Implicit rate of lease	Unknown to lessee	Unknown to lessee	5.5232% Known by lessee	Unknown to lessee
Incremental borrowing rate of lessee	6%	6%	6%	6%
Payment type	Beginning of period	Beginning of period	Beginning of period	End of period

Determine the proper lease classification for each of the four separate scenarios assuming that Jefferson Inc. is the lessee.

More Practice: BE17-3, BE17-4, E17-1

Solution on p. 17-91.

LO 17-2 ⟩ Account for a basic finance lease for a lessee

LO 17-2 Overview

Lessee Accounting—Basic Finance Lease
- At least one of the lease classification criteria is met
- Establish a right-of-use asset and amortize the asset using the straight-line method
- Establish a lease liability and record interest expense using the effective interest method

It is essential that financial statement users understand a lessee's rights and obligations associated with leasing transactions. This means that these transactions must be faithfully represented in financial statements. The FASB determined that faithful representation requires that lessees recognize assets and liabilities for all leases with lease terms of more than 12 months. On the balance sheet, a lessee recognizes an asset for the right to use an underlying asset for the lease term and a liability for the obligation to make lease payments. This concept is similar to financing the purchase of a fixed asset with debt.

ASU 2016-02   The core principle of Topic 842 is that a lessee should recognize the assets and liabilities that arise from leases. All leases create an asset and a liability for the lessee in accordance with FASB Concepts Statement No. 6, Elements of Financial Statements.

842-20-25-1   At the commencement date, a lessee shall recognize a right-of-use asset and a lease liability.

Finance Lease This section explains the lessee's accounting for a *finance lease*, applicable when at least one of the five lease classification criteria is met. We illustrate the accounting for a basic finance lease with zero estimated residual value in **Demo 17-2**. An overview of a lessee's accounting for a finance lease follows.

Balance Sheet	Income Statement
Recognize a right-of-use asset and test for impairment.	Recognize amortization expense on the right-of-use asset typically using the straight-line method. Amortize over the (a) lease term or (b) useful life if there is an ownership transfer or the exercise of a purchase option is reasonably certain.
Recognize a lease liability.	Recognize interest expense on the lease liability using the effective interest method.

Lease Liability On the lease commencement date, the lessee records a **lease liability** equal to the present value of lease payments discounted using the rate implicit in the lease (or if that rate cannot be readily determined, the lessee's incremental borrowing rate). This section looks at examples where periodic lease payments are fixed and there are no adjustments to the lease liability.

Right-of-Use-Asset The right to use an asset through a lease results in the recognition of an asset called a "Right-of-Use-Asset." On the lease commencement date, a **right-of-use asset (ROU asset)** is recognized in the balance sheet at an amount equal to the liability (calculated above), adjusted for certain items such as lease incentives that are discussed in a later section. The right-of-use asset is amortized as expense over the period of economic benefit typically using the straight-line method. The period of economic benefit is normally the lease term.

EXPANDING YOUR KNOWLEDGE   Benefits and Disadvantages of Leasing

In considering the purchase of property, plant, and equipment, a lessee should consider the advantages and disadvantages of leasing.

Benefits of Leasing
- Financing for up to 100% of the lease asset's value. (Bank loans are typically limited to 80% of the asset's value.)
- Fixed interest rate option. (Some bank loans feature only variable rates.)
- Ready-to-use leased equipment can be attractive over a lengthy build-to-order asset.
- Solution for temporary, seasonal, or sporadic needs.
- Protection from equipment obsolescence where upgrades to newer equipment are possible.
- Income tax advantages derived from the deductibility of accelerated depreciation and interest expense.
- Tailored lease payment schedules to coordinate with expected cash inflows from operations.

continued

continued from previous page

Disadvantages of Leasing

- 100% financing of the lease assets also means a higher total dollar outlay for interest.
- Leasing ready-to-use (versus custom-built) equipment may result in a lower-quality product and lost sales.
- Equipment may be unavailable under lease when needed.
- Short-term leases may provide protection from product obsolescence, but short-term leasing rates are normally set at a premium over longer-term rates (to compensate the lessor for assuming the obsolescence risk).

Lessee—Basic Finance Lease   LO17-2 ◄ DEMO 17-2

Demo

MBC

On January 1 of Year 1, the lease commencement date, Lessor Inc. and Lessee Inc. sign a 3-year noncancellable lease for equipment that is routinely leased to other companies. Details follow.

1. The equipment has an estimated economic life of 3 years.
2. The three lease payments are $34,972.24, payable January 1 of Year 1, Year 2, and Year 3.
3. The fair value of the asset at the lease commencement is $100,000.
4. The lease does not contain a renewal or purchase option, and the asset reverts to the lessor at the end of the 3-year period.
5. The asset's residual value is estimated to be $0 and there is no guaranteed residual value.
6. The lessor's implicit interest rate, the rate that equates the present value of the payments to the asset's fair value, is 5% and is known by the lessee. The lessee's incremental borrowing rate is 5%.

Answer the following questions from the perspective of Lessee Inc. which has an accounting period that ends on December 31.

a. Determine the proper lease classification.
b. Calculate the lease liability and the right-of-use asset. For this basic example, assume that there are no adjustments to the lease liability to arrive at the right-of-use asset measurement.
c. Prepare a lease liability schedule.
d. Prepare the lessee's journal entries for Year 1.
e. Show the impact on the lessee's balance sheet and income statement for Year 1.
f. Prepare the lessee's journal entries for Year 2.
g. Show the impact on the lessee's balance sheet and income statement for Year 2.
h. Prepare the lessee's journal entries for Year 3.
i. How would your answers change if the lessee's incremental borrowing rate is 4.5% instead of 5%?

Solution

a. Lease Classification

At lease commencement, the lease is classified as a finance lease to the lessee because *at least one* of the lease classification criteria is met as shown in the following analysis.

Classification Criteria	Analysis	Met
1. Ownership transfer	Asset reverts to the lessor at the end of the 3-year period.	
2. Purchase option	Lease does not contain a purchase option.	
3. Lease term length	Three-year lease term is 100% of the asset's 3-year useful life.	✔
4. PV of lease payments	$100,000 (PV of lease payment) > $90,000 (90% of fair value of $100,000).	✔
5. No alternative use	There are alternative uses for the equipment as the lessor often leases this equipment to other companies.	

	RATE	NPER	PMT	PV	TYPE	Excel Formula
Given	5%	3	(34,972.24)	?	1	=PV(0.05,3,– 34972.24,0,1)
Solution				$100,000		

b. Lease Liability and Right-of-Use-Asset

The present value of the lease payments (consisting only of fixed periodic lease payments) is $100,000 using the rate implicit in the lease of 5% as calculated above in the lease classification test. There are no adjustments to the lease liability of $100,000 to arrive at the right-of-use asset of $100,000.

continued

continued from previous page

c. **Lease Liability Schedule**

The lessee prepares a lease liability schedule using the effective interest method.

- The Lease Payment column includes the lease payment (determined by the lessor). The lease payment reduces cash and the lease liability.
- The Interest on Liability column includes periodic interest which increases the lease liability and increases interest expense (however, no interest is calculated on the first payment because the payment was made on day one of the lease, before interest has time to accrue). Interest is calculated by taking the interest rate multiplied by beginning of period, lease liability.
- The Lease Liability Change column is the net of the lease payment and the interest on the liability. This amount reduces the lease liability for the period.
- The Lease Liability column shows the cumulative balance of the lease liability.

This schedule illustrates how each lease payment is allocated between interest and the reduction of the liability. Notice after the first payment (applied completely to principal because it took place on day one of the lease), the interest expense per period decreases due to the corresponding decrease in the lease liability.

Lease Liability Schedule

Date	Lease Payment[a] Dr. Lease Liability Cr. Cash	Interest on Liability[b] Dr. Interest Expense Cr. Lease Liability	Lease Liability Change[c]	Lease Liability[d]
Jan. 1, Year 1				$100,000
Jan. 1, Year 1	$ 34,972	$ —	$ 34,972	65,028
Jan. 1, Year 2	34,972	3,251	31,721	33,307
Jan. 1, Year 3	34,972	1,665	33,307	0
	$104,916	$4,916	$100,000	

[a] Lease payment (given).
[b] Interest rate (5%) × Beginning of period lease liability (with exception of first payment applied 100% to principal).
[c] Lease payment less interest on liability.
[d] Lease liability (beginning of period) less the change in lease liability.

Adjusting entries The lease liability schedule is based on the lease payment date which may not coincide with the reporting date. To calculate the lease liability at a date other than the lease payment date, add accrued interest up to the measurement date to the lease liability balance as of the most recent payment date. For example, the lease liability balance on December 31 of Year 1 is equal to $68,279 which is equal to $3,251 (12/12 months x $3,251) plus $65,028. For another example, the lease liability on October 31 of Year 1 is equal to $67,737, which is equal to $2,709 (10/12 months x $3,251) plus $65,028.

d. **Lessee's Journal Entries—Year 1**

Assets = Liabilities + Equity
+100,000   +100,000
ROU Asset Lease Liab

ROU Asset	Lease Liab
100,000	100,000

January 1, Year 1—To record right-of-use asset and lease liability

| Right-of-Use Asset.. | 100,000 | |
| Lease Liability .... | | 100,000 |

Assets = Liabilities + Equity
−34,972   −34,972
Cash   Lease Liab

Cash	Lease Liab
34,972	34,972 | 100,000

January 1, Year 1—To record lease payment

| Lease Liability .... | 34,972 | |
| Cash .... | | 34,972 |

Assets = Liabilities + Equity
+3,251   −3,251
Lease Liab Exp

Lease Liab	Interest Exp
34,972 | 100,000	3,251
3,251	
68,279	

December 31, Year 1—To record interest expense

| Interest Expense....................................... | 3,251 | |
| Lease Liability .... | | 3,251 |

Assets = Liabilities + Equity
−33,333   −33,333
ROU Asset Exp

ROU Asset	Amort Exp
100,000 | 33,333	33,333
66,667	

December 31, Year 1—To record amortization on right-of-use asset

| Amortization Expense .... | 33,333 | |
| Right-of-Use Asset ($100,000/3)*................... | | 33,333 |

*The company chooses to credit the right-of-use asset directly for the amortization expense instead of crediting an accumulated amortization account, as we see in all examples in this chapter.

continued

continued from previous page

e. Lessee's Financial Statements—Year 1

Balance Sheet	Dec. 31, Year 1
Assets	
Noncurrent assets	
Right-of-use asset* ($100,000 – $33,333) . . .	$66,667
Liabilities	
Current liabilities	
Lease liability ($3,251 + $31,721)	34,972
Noncurrent liabilities	
Lease liability† ($68,279 – $34,972)	33,307

Income Statement	Year 1
Expenses	
Interest expense—lease liability	$ 3,251
Amortization expense—right-of-use asset . . .	33,333

* The right-of-use asset is shown net of accumulated amortization in the asset section.

† The noncurrent portion is equal to the total lease liability of $68,279 (calculated as $65,028 + $3,251) less the current lease liability.

f. Lessee's Journal Entries—Year 2

Cash is credited for the payment of $34,972. Lease Liability is debited for the same amount of $34,972, reflecting cash payment of $31,721 of principal and $3,251 of accrued interest on the Year 1 lease liability balance.

January 1, Year 2—To record lease payment

Lease Liability	34,972	
Cash		34,972

Assets = Liabilities + Equity
–31,721   –34,972
C:f   Lease Liab
–3,251
C:o

Cash		Lease Liab	
	34,972	34,972	100,000
	34,972	34,972	3,251

December 31, Year 2—To record interest expense

Interest Expense	1,665	
Lease Liability		1,665

Assets = Liabilities + Equity
    +1,665   –1,665
    Lease Liab   Exp

Lease Liab		Interest Exp	
34,972	100,000	3,251	
34,972	3,251	1,665	
	1,665		
	34,972		

December 31, Year 2—To record amortization on right-of-use asset

Amortization Expense	33,333	
Right-of-Use Asset ($100,000/3)		33,333

Assets = Liabilities + Equity
–33,333   –33,333
ROU Asset   Exp

ROU Asset		Amort Exp	
100,000	33,333	33,333	
	33,333	33,333	
33,334			

g. Lessee's Financial Statements—Year 2

Balance Sheet	Dec. 31, Year 2
Assets	
Current assets	
Right-of-use asset ($66,667 – $33,333) . . .	$33,334
Liabilities	
Current liabilities	
Lease liability ($1,665 + $33,307)	34,972

Income Statement	Year 2
Expenses	
Interest expense—lease liability	$ 1,665
Amortization expense—right-of-use asset . . .	33,333

h. Lessee's Journal Entries—Year 3

January 1, Year 3—To record lease payment

Lease Liability	34,972	
Cash		34,972

Assets = Liabilities + Equity
–33,307   –34,972
C:f   Lease Liab
–1,665
C:o

Cash		Lease Liab	
	34,972	34,972	100,000
	34,972	34,972	3,251
	34,972	34,972	1,665
			0

December 31, Year 3—To record amortization on right-of-use asset

Amortization Expense	33,334	
Right-of-Use Asset ($100,000/3)*		33,334

*Amount adjusted due to rounding.

Assets = Liabilities + Equity
–33,334   –33,334
ROU Asset   Exp

ROU Asset		Amort Exp	
100,000	33,333	33,333	
	33,333	33,333	
	33,334	33,334	
0			

After the journal entries of Year 3 and the expiration of the lease, both the right-of-use asset and the lease liability have a balance of $0.

i. Change in Incremental Borrowing Rate

The solution remains unchanged as the lessee will use the lessor's implicit rate when known, even if it differs from its incremental borrowing rate.

Lessee Company enters into a 4-year finance lease of nonspecialized manufacturing equipment with Lessor Company on January 1. Lessee Company has agreed to pay $10,000 annually beginning immediately on January 1. The economic life of the asset is 4 years. The lessee's incremental borrowing rate is 5% and the lessor's implicit rate is not readily determinable by the lessee.

a. Determine the proper lease classification by the lessee.

b. Prepare a schedule of the lease liability.

c. Prepare the entries for Lessee Company for Year 1 and Year 2.

LO 17-3 ▶ Account for a basic operating lease for a lessee

Operating Leases—Lessee
- Meets *none* of the lease classification criteria
- Establish a right-of-use asset and a lease liability
- Recognize lease expense as a single amount using straight-line amortization in the income statement

From the perspective of the lessee, an *operating lease* is any lease other than a finance lease. In accounting for an operating lease, a lessee records a right-of-use asset and a lease liability on the balance sheet (calculated in the same way as presented earlier for a finance lease). However, unlike a finance lease, an equal amount of expense is recorded in subsequent periods on the income statement, using the straight-line method for expense recognition.

Balance Sheet	Income Statement
Recognize a right-of-use asset and test for impairment.	Recognize lease expense as a single amount on the income statement.
Recognize a lease liability.	■ Single amount is called lease expense.
	■ Lease expense is calculated through straight-line amortization.

Straight-Line Lease Expense A lessee in an operating lease is not receiving substantially all of the *remaining* benefits of the asset. The accounting reflects this. Recognizing an equal expense amount each period is consistent with a lessee receiving generally equal benefits each period. This means that the lessee in an operating lease is not normally exposed to changes in the value of the underlying asset. For example, the lease period is not the major part of the asset's remaining useful life, and legal title of the asset does not automatically transfer to the lessee at the end of the lease.

Straight-line lease expense is measured by taking the total cost of the lease at the commencement of the lease, divided by the total number of lease periods **Total cost of the lease** equals the undiscounted total of all lease payments. As in the last section, we consider only fixed periodic lease payments for now. In the absence of other lease payments or adjustments, *recognized straight-line lease expense each period is equal to the periodic cash lease payment paid to the lessor.* (Note that an unguaranteed residual value—estimated value of the underlying asset at the end of the lease term but not guaranteed by the lessee—is not considered a lease payment and will not impact the accounting for the lessee.)

`842-20-25-6` After the commencement date, a lessee shall recognize all of the following in profit or loss, unless the costs are included in the carrying amount of another asset in accordance with other Topics: *a.* A single lease cost, calculated so that the remaining cost of the lease . . . is allocated over the remaining lease term on a straight-line basis unless another systematic and rational basis is more representative of the pattern in which benefit is expected to be derived from the right to use the underlying asset . . . unless the right-of-use asset has been impaired . . .

In the same way as the finance lease, we prepare a lease liability schedule to determine the change in the lease liability over the lease term using the effective amortization method to determine 'interest' for the period. Next, the periodic reduction in the right-of-use asset is determined by subtracting the 'interest' for the period from the straight-line lease amortization expense as shown in the following graphic. Calculating the change in the right-of-use asset in this way ensures that the total periodic lease expense recognized equals the straight-line lease amortization expense.

Straight-Line Lease Amortization Expense	minus	Current Period 'Interest'	=	Change in Right-of-Use Asset
Recognized on Income Statement				Reduces ROU Asset to Carrying Value

Importantly, the goal of operating lease accounting is to achieve a straight-line lease expense pattern over the lease term. While 'interest' on the liability is computed to determine the change in the right-of-use asset, neither the 'interest' nor the change in the right-of-use asset ('amortization') is recognized separately on the income statement—only a single number, lease expense, is recognized. An example of a basic operating lease is illustrated in **Demo 17-3**.

Lessee—Basic Operating Lease	**LO17-3**	**DEMO 17-3**

Demo

MBC

On January 1 of Year 1, the lease commencement date, Lessor Inc. and Lessee Inc. sign a 3-year non-cancellable lease for equipment that is routinely leased to other companies. Details follow.

1. The equipment has an estimated economic life of six years.
2. The three lease payments are $34,972.24, payable January 1 of Year 1, Year 2, and Year 3.
3. Fair value of the asset at the commencement of the lease is $150,000.
4. The lease does not contain a renewal or purchase option, and the asset reverts to the lessor at the end of the 3-year period.
5. The lessee does not guarantee the residual value of the equipment.
6. The lessor's implicit interest rate is 5% and is known by the lessee. The lessee's borrowing rate is 5%.

Answer the following questions from the perspective of Lessee Inc. which has an accounting period that ends on December 31.

a. Determine the proper lease classification.
b. Calculate the lease liability and the right-of-use asset. For this basic example, assume that there are no adjustments to the lease liability to arrive at the right-of-use asset measurement.
c. Prepare a lease liability schedule and a right-of-use asset schedule.
d. Prepare the lessee's journal entries for Year 1.
e. Show the impact on the lessee's balance sheet and income statement for Year 1.
f. Prepare the lessee's journal entries for Year 2.
g. Show the impact on the lessee's balance sheet and income statement for Year 2.
h. Prepare the lessee's journal entries for Year 3.

Solution

a. **Lease Classification**

The lease is classified as an operating lease to the lessee because none of the lease classification criteria are met as shown in the following analysis.

Lease Classification Criteria	Analysis	Lease Criterion Met
1. Ownership transfer	Asset reverts to the lessor at the end of the 3-year period.	
2. Purchase option	Lease does not contain a purchase option.	
3. Lease term length	Three-year lease term < 75% of the 6-year useful life (4.5 years).	
4. PV of lease payments	PV of lease payments of $100,000 (rounded) < $135,000 (90% of fair value of $150,000).	
5. No alternative use	There are alternative uses for the equipment as the lessor often leases this equipment to other companies.	

Within criterion 4:

RATE	NPER	PMT	TYPE	PV	Excel Formula
5%	3	(34,972.24)	1	?	=PV(0.05,3,−34972.24,0,1)
				$99,999.99	

b. **Calculation of the Lease Liability and the Right-of-Use Asset**

With an operating lease, a lease liability and a right-of-use asset are initially recognized on the balance sheet in the same way as a finance lease. The lease liability is equal to the present value of the lease payments of $100,000 as calculated above in the lease classification test. The right-of-use asset is equal to the lease liability of $100,000.

c. **Lease Liability Schedule and Right-of-Use Asset Schedule**

The lease liability schedule is prepared first. 'Interest' on the liability determined in the lease liability schedule is an input to the right-of-use asset schedule below.

continued

continued from previous page

Lease Liability Schedule

Date	Lease Payment	Interest on Liability	Lease Liability Change	Lease Liability
Jan. 1, Year 1				$100,000
Jan. 1, Year 1	$ 34,972	$ 0	$ 34,972	65,028
Jan. 1, Year 2	34,972	3,251	31,721	33,307
Jan. 1, Year 3	34,972	1,665	33,307	0
	$104,916	$4,916	$100,000	

Note: Certain amounts adjusted for rounding differences.

Right-of-Use Asset Schedule

Date	Lease Expense[a]	Interest on Liability[b]	Right-of-Use Asset Change[c]	Right-of-Use Asset[d]
	Dr. Lease Expense	Cr. Lease Liability	Cr. Right-of-Use Asset	
Jan. 1, Year 1 ...				$100,000
Dec. 31, Year 1 ...	$ 34,972	$3,251	$ 31,721	68,279
Dec. 31, Year 2 ...	34,972	1,665	33,307	34,972
Dec. 31, Year 3 ...	34,972	—	34,972	0
	$104,916	$4,916	$100,000	

[a] Straight-line lease amortization expense equals total lease payments divided by total number of periods ($34,972 + $34,972 + $34,972)/3 = $34,972.

[b] 'Interest' on the liability is calculated in the lease liability schedule.

[c] Change in the right-of-use asset is the difference between *a* and *b* (Straight-line lease expense less interest on liability).

[d] Beginning right-of-use asset balance less change in right-of-use asset.

d. **Lessee's Journal Entries—Year 1**

Assets = Liabilities + Equity
+100,000   +100,000
ROU Asset   Lease Liab

ROU Asset	Lease Liab
100,000	100,000

January 1, Year 1—To record right-of-use asset and lease liability

Right-of-Use Asset...................................	100,000	
Lease Liability		100,000

Assets = Liabilities + Equity
−34,972   −34,972
C:o   Lease Liab

Cash	Lease Liab
34,972	34,972	100,000

January 1, Year 1—To record lease payment

Lease Liability	34,972	
Cash		34,972

Assets = Liabilities + Equity
−31,721   +3,251   −34,972
ROU Asset   Lease Liab   Exp

ROU Asset	Lease Liab
100,000	31,721	34,972	100,000
68,279			3,251
			68,279

Lease Exp	
34,972	

December 31, Year 1—To record lease expense

Lease Expense	34,972	
Lease Liability		3,251
Right-of-Use Asset............................		31,721

An option is to record Dec. 31 entry in two parts.

Right-of-Use Asset	3,251	
Lease Liability		3,251

Lease Expense........	34,972	
Right-of-Use Asset ...		34,972

e. **Lessee's Financial Statements—Year 1**

For an operating lease, the full cost of the lease results in periodic lease expense, which is classified as an operating expense on the income statement.

Balance Sheet	Dec. 31, Year 1
Assets	
Noncurrent assets	
Right-of-use asset ($100,000 − $31,721) ..	$68,279
Liabilities	
Current liabilities	
Lease liability.....................	34,972
Noncurrent liabilities	
Lease liability* ($68,279 − $34,972)	33,307

Income Statement	Year 1
Expenses	
Lease expense	$34,972

*The noncurrent portion equals the total lease liability of $68,279 (calculated as $65,028 + $3,251) less the current lease liability.

continued

continued from previous page

f. Lessee's Journal Entries—Year 2

January 1, Year 2—To record lease payment

Lease Liability	34,972	
Cash		34,972

Assets = Liabilities + Equity
−34,972   −34,972
C:o   Lease Liab

Cash		Lease Liab	
34,972		34,972	100,000
	34,972	34,972	3,251

December 31, Year 2—To record lease expense

Lease Expense	34,972	
Lease Liability		1,665
Right-of-Use Asset		33,307

Assets = Liabilities + Equity
−33,307   +1,665   −34,972
ROU Asset   Lease Liab   Exp

ROU Asset		Lease Liab	
100,000	31,721	34,972	100,000
	33,307	34,972	3,251
34,972			1,665
			34,972

Lease Exp	
34,972	
34,972	

g. Lessee's Financial Statements—Year 2

Balance Sheet	Dec. 31, Year 2		Income Statement	Year 2
Assets			**Expenses**	
Current assets			Lease expense . . .	$34,972
Right-of-use asset ($68,279 – $33,307) . . .	$34,972			
Liabilities				
Current liabilities				
Lease liability.	34,972			

h. Lessee's Journal Entries—Year 3

January 1, Year 3—To record lease payment

Lease Liability	34,972	
Cash		34,972

Assets = Liabilities + Equity
−34,972   −34,972
C:o   Lease Liab

Cash		Lease Liab	
	34,972	34,972	100,000
	34,972	34,972	3,251
	34,972	34,972	1,665
			0

December 31, Year 3—To record amortization on right-of-use asset

Lease Expense	34,972	
Right-of-Use Asset		34,972

Assets = Liabilities + Equity
−34,972   −34,972
ROU Asset   Exp

ROU Asset		Lease Exp	
100,000	31,721	34,972	
	33,307	34,972	
	34,972	34,972	
0			

After the journal entries of Year 3 and the expiration of the lease, both the right-of-use asset and the lease liability have a value of $0 at December 31 of Year 3.

Accounting for a Basic Operating Lease by a Lessee   LO17-3   REVIEW 17-3

Review

MBC

On January 1 of Year 1, Lessee Inc. leased equipment at an annual payment of $25,000, payable at the beginning of each year (including the current year) for 5 years. The equipment has a fair value of $250,000, an estimated useful life of 10 years, and is commonly purchased or leased by customers. Lessor's implicit rate is 6%, which is unknown to the lessee. The lessee's incremental borrowing rate is 5%. The lease does not contain a purchase option.

a. How would Lessee Inc. classify the lease? Explain.

b. Prepare a schedule of the lease liability.

c. Prepare a schedule of the right-of-use asset.

d. Prepare the entries for Lessee Inc. for Year 1 and Year 2, assuming Lessee Inc. has a calendar year end.

More Practice:
BE17-11, BE17-12, BE17-13,
E17-7, E17-8, E17-9

Solution on p. 17-93.

LO 17-4 ▶ Account for complex finance leases for a lessee

LO 17-4 Overview

Lessee Accounting—Complex Finance Lease

Lease liability
- Consider only probable amount owed on residual

Right-of-Use Asset
- Subtract lease incentives received
- Add initial direct costs incurred

This section builds on the basic finance lease presented in LO17-2. We illustrate the accounting for (1) a finance lease with initial direct cost and a lease incentive payment in **Demo 17-4A**, (2) a finance lease with a guaranteed residual value in **Demo 17-4B**, and (3) a finance lease with a purchase option expected to be exercised in **Demo 17-4C**.

Lease Classification Criterion No. 4 Revisited

Lease Classification Criteria
1. Ownership transfer
2. Purchase option
3. Lease term length
4. **PV of lease payments**
5. No alternative use

Before we review more complex examples, we first expand on our previous discussion of lease classification criteria. Recall that a lessee accounts for a lease as a finance lease when at least one of the five lease classification criteria is met. In our basic finance lease example, only fixed periodic lease payments were considered for purposes of criterion number four. However, there are up to four additional types of lease payments found in more complex lease scenarios as shown in **Exhibit 17-2**. All five types of lease payments need to be considered when determining whether a lease meets lease classification criterion number four.

EXHIBIT 17-2
Lease Payment Components

Lease Payments for Purposes of Lease Classification

1. Fixed periodic payments   2. Variable payments   3. Purchase option   4. Termination penalty   5. Guaranteed residual

Lease Payments
1. **Fixed payment**
2. Variable payment
3. Purchase option
4. Penalty
5. Guaranteed residual

Fixed Payment **Fixed payments** are required periodic payments that are stable or change over time based upon a predetermined rate. For example, a lease payment is considered fixed if it is specified in the contract as $2,000 per month for the first 2 years, increasing to $2,500 for the remaining 3 years of a 5-year lease.

For purposes of lease classification, fixed payments are calculated net of lease incentives. **Lease incentives** are incentives to encourage a lessee to sign a lease, such as an up-front cash payment to a lessee, reimbursement of lessee costs (such as moving expenses), or the payment by a lessor of a lessee's preexisting lease. Lease incentives are paid to the lessee before the commencement of the lease or during the lease term. While lease incentives received prior to commencement reduce the total cost of the lease, they do not reduce the amount of the initially recognized lease obligation.

Variable Payment **Variable payments** are payments that vary because of changes in factors or circumstances occurring *after* the lease commencement date.

Lease Payments
1. Fixed payment
2. **Variable payment**
3. Purchase option
4. Penalty
5. Guaranteed residual

842-10-30-5   b. Variable lease payments that depend on an index or a rate (such as the Consumer Price Index or a market interest rate), initially measured using the index or rate at the commencement date.

Variable payments are classified as *lease payments* only if the variability is based on an index or rate in effect at the time of the lease commencement. Otherwise, the variable payment is excluded from what the authoritative standards define as a *lease payment*. Why only include variable payments based upon an index or a rate? Such payments are unavoidable and thus are similar to fixed lease payments—only the measurement of the payment varies, not the existence of a payment.

One exception to the exclusion of variable payments that are not based on an index or rate, is the occurrence of an **in-substance fixed payment**. For example, a lease payment may be variable or contingent on a future event (such as sales volumes) but the lease indicates a required minimum payment level. Only the minimum payment level is considered a fixed lease payment.

While variable payments that do not depend on an index or rate are not included in total lease payments, they are recognized as expense in the period in which the achievement of the specified target that triggers the variable lease payments becomes probable. For example, if rent is based on a certain lessee sales target, expense is recorded when it is probable that the lessee will meet the sales target.

842-20-55-1   A lessee should recognize costs from variable lease payments (in annual periods as well as in interim periods) before the achievement of the specified target that triggers the variable lease payments, provided the achievement of that target is considered probable.

Purchase Option A **purchase option** (sometimes called a bargain purchase option in practice) is a provision of a lease contract giving the lessee an option to purchase the underlying asset for a specific price at a specific time. Only when it is *reasonably certain* that the lessee will exercise the option to purchase the underlying asset is the purchase option included as a lease payment. An option to purchase the asset for less than fair value is an indicator that the lessee would exercise the option. However, the amount of discount that makes an exercise reasonably certain is subject to judgment.

Lease Payments
1. Fixed payment
2. Variable payment
3. Purchase option
4. Penalty
5. Guaranteed residual

842-10-30-5 c. The exercise price of an option to purchase the underlying asset if the lessee is reasonably certain to exercise that option (assessed considering the factors in paragraph 842-10-55-26).

Lease Termination Penalty A payment for penalties for terminating a lease is included as a lease payment if the termination of the lease by the lessee is *reasonably certain.*

Lease Payments
1. Fixed payment
2. Variable payment
3. Purchase option
4. Penalty
5. Guaranteed residual

842-10-30-5 d. Payments for penalties for terminating the lease if the lease term (as determined in accordance with paragraph 842-10-30-1) reflects the lessee exercising an option to terminate the lease.

In the case where a purchase option or termination penalty is classified as a lease payment, the lease term ends at the time of the expected exercise of the purchase option or termination of the lease.

Residual Value Guarantee A **guaranteed residual value** is a guarantee by a lessee to a lessor that an underlying asset returned to the lessor at the end of a lease term will be valued at a minimum amount. **For the purposes of applying lease classification criterion number four, 100% of the guaranteed residual value is included when calculating the present value of the lease payments.**

Lease Payments
1. Fixed payment
2. Variable payment
3. Purchase option
4. Penalty
5. Guaranteed residual

An unguaranteed residual is treated differently. Because there is no obligation on the part of the lessee to return an asset at a particular value, an unguaranteed residual is *not* considered to be a lease payment for the lessee. While the lessor expects the underlying asset to be returned at a particular value, there is no guarantee by the lessee that it will happen. (For a discussion of lease contracts where the residual guarantee is guaranteed to the lessor by a third party, see Appendix 17A.)

The guidance treats a guaranteed residual value differently for purposes of measuring and recognizing the lease liability. In measuring a lease liability, the lease payment consists of the amount *probable of being owed*, which is equal to any excess of the *guaranteed* residual value over an estimate of the *expected* residual value. For example, a 3-year vehicle lease may require that a lessee return the vehicle at the end of 3 years with a fair value of $15,000 based upon its physical condition and mileage levels. If the lessee estimates that the fair value of the vehicle at lease end will be $12,000, the lease payment is only $3,000 ($15,000 – $12,000). If, however, it is assumed that it is reasonably certain that the lessee will exercise a purchase option, a guaranteed residual value is not considered a payment because the underlying asset would revert to the lessee at the end of the lease.

842-10-30-5 f. For a lessee only, amounts probable of being owed by the lessee under residual value guarantees (see paragraphs 842-10-55-34 through 55-36).

Nonlease Component It is important for a lessee to identify the lease components and nonlease components of a contract because consideration is allocated separately to each **lease component** and **nonlease component**, unless the lessee applies the practical expedient described in the *Expanding Your Knowledge* box that follows. For example, costs that contribute to obtaining control of a building (an underlying asset), including insurance and real estate taxes, should be included in lease payments. However, considerations allocated to a nonlease component, such as maintenance, cleaning, or snow removal costs, are not classified as a lease payment.

842-10-15-30 The consideration in the contract shall be allocated to each separate lease component and nonlease component of the contract . . . Components of a contract include only those items or activities that transfer a good or service to the lessee . . .

842-10-15-31 An entity shall account for each separate lease component separately from the nonlease components of the contract . . . Nonlease components are not within the scope of this Topic and shall be accounted for in accordance with other Topics.

For example, a lessor charges a lessee $10,000 to lease a building, $1,000 for real estate taxes, $500 for hazard insurance, and $800 for maintenance of the building. The maintenance fee is a nonlease cost, separate from obtaining control of the leased building, and thus is separately recognized as maintenance expense. However, charges for rent, real estate taxes, and insurance are fixed payments that relate to obtaining control of the leased building, and thus are included as part of the lease payment.

Accounting for a Complex Finance Lease

In more complex lease scenarios, the lease liability, calculated as the present value of the lease payments, can involve any of the additional types of lease payments outlined above. Also, as explained in detail below, the right-of-use asset, which has an initial basis equal to the lease liability, might require adjustment.

Calculate Lease Liability

Present value of lease payments
- Fixed payment
- Variable payment
- Purchase option
- Penalty
- Guaranteed residual: only probable amount owed

Lease Liability As illustrated in the basic finance lease example, on the lease commencement date, the lessee initially records a lease liability equal to the present value of the lease payments discounted using the rate implicit in the lease (or if that rate cannot be readily determined, the lessee's incremental borrowing rate). Any lease payments made on or prior to the commencement date will be applied to the lease liability on the commencement date (Dr. Lease Liability and Cr. Prepaid Lease Payment).

842-20-30-1 At the commencement date, a lessee shall measure both of the following:
  a. The lease liability at the present value of the lease payments not yet paid, discounted using the discount rate for the lease at lease commencement (as described in paragraphs 842-20-30-2 through 30-4)
  b. The right-of-use asset as described in paragraph 842-20-30-5.

Lease payments used to measure the lease liability are the same lease payments used to determine the appropriate lease classification (see lease classification criterion No. 4) with the following exceptions:

- To classify a lease, fixed lease payments will be reduced by lease incentives received prior to the commencement date. However, lease incentives received prior to the commencement date will not affect the measurement of the initial lease obligation.

- To classify a lease, 100% of the guaranteed residual value is included in lease payments. However, only *probable amounts* expected to be owed for a residual value guarantee are used to measure the lease liability as explained on the prior page.

Calculate Right-of-Use Asset

Initial measurement of lease liability
− Subtract lease incentive received
+ Add initial direct cost incurred

Right-of-use asset

Right-of-Use-Asset A **right-of-use asset** is recognized in the balance sheet as an asset at the measurement of the liability (calculated above) adjusted for the following items occurring *at or before the lease commencement date*: subtract lease incentives and add initial direct costs. Specifically:

- If the lessee had received a lease incentive prior to the commencement of the lease (debit Cash and credit Lease Incentive Liability), the lease incentive liability would offset the right-of-use asset at the lease commencement date. Lease incentives received by a lessee before the lease begins are initially recorded as a liability because they reflect a performance obligation. Upon commencement, the obligation is satisfied and the incentives reduce the cost of the lease recognized as a right-of-use asset.

Reclass Entry at
Lease Commencement
Right-of-Use Asset . . . . #
Lease Incentive Liab. . . #
  Initial Direct Cost. . . .   #
  Lease Liability . . . . . .   #

- If the lessee had paid an initial direct cost (debit Initial Direct Cost, an asset account, and credit Cash) the initial direct cost would be reclassified to the right-of-use asset at the lease commencement date.

`842-20-30-5`   At the commencement date, the cost of the right-of-use asset shall consist of all of the following:

a. The amount of the initial measurement of the lease liability b. Any lease payments made to the lessor at or before the commencement date, minus any lease incentives received c. Any initial direct costs incurred by the lessee . . .

`842-10-30-10`   Costs to negotiate or arrange a lease that would have been incurred regardless of whether the lease was obtained, such as fixed employee salaries, are not initial direct costs. The following items are examples of costs that are not initial direct costs:

a. General overheads . . . b. Costs related to activities performed by the lessor for advertising, soliciting potential lessees. . . c. Costs related to activities that occur before the lease is obtained, such as costs of obtaining tax or legal advice, negotiating lease terms and conditions, or evaluating a prospective lessee's financial condition.

Initial direct costs are incremental costs of a lease that would not have been incurred if the lease had not taken place. Initial direct costs are *not* considered "lease payments" as defined earlier in this section. Examples of what to include and exclude in initial direct costs are listed in the following table.

Items Included in Initial Direct Costs	Items Excluded from Initial Direct Costs
Commissions paid to secure a lease.	Fixed employee salaries.
Payments to an existing tenant as an incentive for the tenant to terminate its lease.	General overhead including depreciation, equipment costs, engineering costs, and unsuccessful origination efforts.
Legal fees incurred from the execution of the lease or after the execution of the lease.	Advertising, solicitation, and travel costs.
Consideration paid to an unrelated third party for a guarantee of a residual value.	Servicing of existing leases.
Lease document preparation fees.	Tax or legal fees for advice or assistance in negotiations before the lease is executed.

The right-of-use asset is amortized as expense over the period of economic benefit (the lease term) typically using the straight-line method. **However, if ownership transfers to the lessee at the end of the lease or the exercise of a purchase option is reasonable, the lessee amortizes the right-of-use asset over the underlying asset's useful life.** A lessee assesses a right-of-use asset for impairment and recognizes any impairment losses following the procedures applicable to long-lived assets described in Chapter 12.

`842-20-35-7`   A lessee shall amortize the right-of-use asset on a straight-line basis, unless another systematic basis is more representative of the pattern in which the lessee expects to consume the right-of-use asset's future economic benefits . . .

`842-20-35-8`   A lessee shall amortize the right-of-use asset from the commencement date to the earlier of the end of the useful life of the right-of-use asset or the end of the lease term. However, if the lease transfers ownership of the underlying asset to the lessee or the lessee is reasonably certain to exercise an option to purchase the underlying asset, the lessee shall amortize the right-of-use asset to the end of the useful life of the underlying asset.

In summary, the accounting for a lease by a lessee is outlined in the following timeline. These steps are illustrated in the demonstrations that follow.

Contract Inception			Lease Commencement	Subsequent Measurement
Identify a lease ▪ Identified asset ▪ Right to control use	Segregate nonlease components	Record any ▪ Prepaid lease payments ▪ Lease incentives* ▪ Initial direct costs*	Classify the lease. Measure and record: ▪ Lease liability ▪ Right-of-use asset	Record lease payments Record adjusting entries

*Amounts recorded through the lease commencement enter into measurement of the right-of-use asset.

Leasehold Improvements

Along with a right-of-use asset, companies recognize leasehold improvements. **Leasehold improvements** are improvements made to leased property by a lessee that revert to the lessor at the end of the lease, such as the construction of a new building, addition, or a modification to a leased space. As in the case with other fixed assets, the leasehold improvements are capitalized as noncurrent typically in property, plant, and equipment on the balance sheet and are depreciated over the shorter of their useful life or the lease term.

`842-20-35-12`   Leasehold improvements . . . shall be amortized over the shorter of the useful life of those leasehold improvements and the remaining lease term, unless the lease transfers ownership of the underlying asset to the lessee or the lessee is reasonably certain to exercise an option to purchase the underlying asset, in which case the lessee shall amortize the leasehold improvements to the end of their useful life.

DEMO 17-4A ▶ **LO17-4**   **Lessee—Finance Lease with Initial Direct Cost, Lease Incentive**

Demo

MBC

On January 1 of Year 1, the lease commencement date, Lessor Inc. and Lessee Inc. sign a 3-year non-cancellable lease for equipment that is routinely leased to other companies. Details follow.

1. The equipment has an estimated economic life of three years.
2. The three lease payments are $34,972.24, payable January 1 of Year 1, Year 2, and Year 3.
3. The fair value of the asset at the lease commencement is $100,000.
4. The lease does not contain a renewal or purchase option, and the asset reverts to the lessor at the end of the 3-year period.
5. The asset's residual value is estimated to be $0 and there is no guaranteed residual value.
6. The lessor's implicit interest rate is 5% and is known by the lessee. The lessee's incremental borrowing rate is 5%.
7. Initial direct costs of $800 (legal fees incurred related to the execution of the lease) were paid by the lessee prior to the lease commencement date.

Answer the following questions from the perspective of Lessee Inc. which has an accounting period that ends on December 31.

a. Prepare the journal entry to record the initial direct costs paid prior to lease commencement.
b. Determine the proper lease classification on January 1 of Year 1.
c. Calculate the lease liability.
d. Calculate the right-of-use asset.
e. Prepare a lease liability schedule.
f. Prepare the lessee's journal entries for Year 1.
g. Show the impact on the lessee's balance sheet and income statement for Year 1.
h. Prepare the lessee's journal entries for Year 2.
i. Show the impact on the lessee's balance sheet and income statement for Year 2.
j. Prepare the lessee's journal entries for Year 3.
k. Assume no other changes to the lease arrangement except that the lessor had paid the lessee $1,200 prior to the lease commencement as an incentive for the lessee to sign the lease. The lessee recorded the receipt of the lease incentive as a debit to Cash and a credit to Lease Incentive Liability for $1,200. Prepare the revised entry at the lease commencement on January 1 of Year 1.

Solution

a. **Lessee's Journal Entry—Prior to Lease Commencement**

To record initial direct cost paid prior to lease commencement

Initial Direct Cost.	800	
Cash		800

Assets = Liabilities + Equity
+800
In Dir Cost
−800
C:o

Init Dir Cost	Cash
800		800

b. **Lease Classification**

At lease commencement, the lease is classified as a finance lease to the lessee because *at least one* of the lease classification criteria is met as shown in the following analysis. *Note:* The initial direct cost does not impact the lease classification analysis.

Classification Criteria	Analysis	Met
1. Ownership transfer	Asset reverts to the lessor at the end of the three-year period.	
2. Purchase option	Lease does not contain a purchase option.	
3. Lease term length	Three-year lease term is 100% of the equipment's three-year useful life.	✔
4. PV of lease payments	$100,000 (PV of lease payments) > $90,000 (90% of fair value of $100,000).	✔
5. No alternative use	There are alternative uses for the equipment as the lessor often leases this equipment to other companies.	

	RATE	NPER	PMT	PV	TYPE	Excel Formula
Given	5%	3	(34,972.24)	?	1	=PV(0.05,3,−34972.24,0,1)
Solution				$100,000		

continued

continued from previous page

c. **Lease Liability**

The lease liability of $100,000 is measured at the present value of the lease payments (consisting only of fixed periodic lease payments) using the rate implicit in the lease of 5% as calculated above in the lease classification test.

d. **Right-of-Use-Asset**

The initial measurement of the lease liability of $100,000 is increased by the initial direct cost of $800 to arrive at the right-of-use asset balance of $100,800.

Calculate Right-of-Use Asset	
Initial measurement of lease liability....	$100,000
− Subtract lease incentive received......	0
+ Add initial direct cost incurred.........	800
Right-of-use asset	$100,800

e. **Lease Liability Schedule**

Date	Lease Payment Dr. Lease Liability Cr. Cash	Interest on Liability Dr. Interest Expense Cr. Lease Liability	Lease Liability Change	Lease Liability
Jan. 1, Year 1				$100,000
Jan. 1, Year 1	$ 34,972	$ —	$ 34,972	65,028
Jan. 1, Year 2	34,972	3,251	31,721	33,307
Jan. 1, Year 3	34,972	1,665	33,307	0
	$104,916	$4,916	$100,000	

f. **Lessee's Journal Entries—Year 1**

January 1, Year 1—To record right-of-use asset and lease liability

Right-of-Use Asset.....................................	100,800	
Lease Liability		100,000
Initial Direct Cost...............................		800

Assets = Liabilities + Equity
+100,800   +100,000
ROU Asset   Lease Liab
    −800
In Dir Cost

ROU Asset		Lease Liab	
100,800			100,000

Init Dir Cost	
800	800
0	

January 1, Year 1—To record lease payment

Lease Liability	34,972	
Cash		34,972

Assets = Liabilities + Equity
−34,972   −34,972
  Cⴕ   Lease Liab

Cash		Lease Liab	
	800	34,972	100,000
	34,972		

December 31, Year 1—To record interest expense

Interest Expense.......................................	3,251	
Lease Liability		3,251

Assets = Liabilities + Equity
    +3,251   −3,251
    Lease Liab   Exp

Lease Liab		Interest Exp	
34,972	100,000	3,251	
	3,251		
	68,279		

December 31, Year 1—To record amortization on right-of-use asset

Amortization Expense	33,600	
Right-of-Use Asset ($100,800/3).....................		33,600

Assets = Liabilities + Equity
−33,600   −33,600
ROU Asset   Exp

ROU Asset		Amort Exp	
100,800	33,600	33,600	
67,200			

g. **Lessee's Financial Statements—Year 1**

Balance Sheet	Dec. 31, Year 1
Assets	
Noncurrent assets	
Right-of-use asset* ($100,800 − $33,600)...	$67,200
Liabilities	
Current liabilities	
Lease liability ($3,251 + $31,721)	34,972
Noncurrent liabilities	
Lease liability† ($68,279 − $34,972)........	33,307

Income Statement	Year 1
Expenses	
Interest expense—lease liability	$ 3,251
Amortization expense—right-of-use asset ...	33,600

* The right-of-use asset is shown net of accumulated amortization in the asset section.

† The noncurrent portion is equal to the total lease liability of $68,279 (calculated as $65,028 + $3,251) less the current lease liability.

h. **Lessee's Journal Entries—Year 2**

Cash is credited for the payment of $34,972. Lease Liability is debited for the same amount of $34,972, which is equal to the principal portion of the lease payment of $31,721 plus the interest accrued of $3,251 on the Year 1 lease liability balance.

continued

continued from previous page

Assets = Liabilities + Equity
-31,721   -34,972
C:f   Lease Liab
-3,251
C:o

Cash		Lease Liab	
	800	34,972	100,000
	34,972	34,972	3,251
	34,972		

Assets = Liabilities + Equity
         +1,665   -1,665
         Lease Liab Exp

Lease Liab		Interest Exp	
34,972	100,000	3,251	
34,972	3,251	1,665	
	1,665		
	34,972		

Assets = Liabilities + Equity
-33,600   -33,600
ROU Asset   Exp

ROU Asset		Amort Exp	
100,800	33,600	33,600	
	33,600	33,600	
33,600			

January 1, Year 2— To record lease payment

Lease Liability	34,972	
Cash		34,972

December 31, Year 2—To record interest expense

Interest Expense.......................................	1,665	
Lease Liability		1,665

December 31, Year 2—To record amortization on right-of-use asset

Amortization Expense	33,600	
Right-of-Use Asset ($100,800/3).....................		33,600

i. **Lessee's Financial Statements—Year 2**

Balance Sheet	Dec. 31, Year 2	Income Statement	Year 2
Assets		**Expenses**	
Current assets		Interest expense—lease liability	$ 1,665
Right-of-use asset ($67,200 – $33,600) ...	$33,600	Amortization expense—right-of-use asset ...	33,600
Liabilities			
Current liabilities			
Lease liability ($1,665 + $33,307)	34,972		

j. **Lessee's Journal Entries—Year 3**

Assets = Liabilities + Equity
-33,307   -34,972
C:f   Lease Liab
-1,665
C:o

Cash		Lease Liab	
	800	34,972	100,000
	34,972	34,972	3,251
	34,972	34,972	1,665
	34,972		0

January 1, Year 3—To record lease payment

Lease Liability	34,972	
Cash		34,972

Assets = Liabilities + Equity
-33,600   -33,600
ROU Asset   Exp

ROU Asset		Amort Exp	
100,800	33,600	33,600	
	33,600	33,600	
	33,600	33,600	
0			

December 31, Year 3—To record amortization on right-of-use asset

Amortization Expense	33,600	
Right-of-Use Asset ($100,800/3).....................		33,600

After the journal entries of Year 3 and the expiration of the lease, both the right-of-use asset and the lease liability have a balance of $0.

k. **Lease Incentive**

The lease incentives could potentially affect lease classification through classification criterion #4. Subtracting the lease incentives from the first fixed lease payment made on January 1 results in a PV of lease payments of $98,800. For this problem, this amount is still greater than 90% of the fair value of the asset. At commencement the lease incentive reduces the right-of-use asset by $1,200 resulting in an adjusted balance of the right-of-use asset on January 1 of Year 1 of $99,600. At lease commencement, the Right-of-Use Asset is debited for $99,600, the Lease Incentive Liability and Initial Direct Cost balances are derecognized, and the Lease Liability is credited for $100,000 (unchanged from the prior calculation).

Calculate Right-of-Use Asset	
Initial measurement of lease liability....	$100,000
– Subtract lease incentive received......	(1,200)
+ Add initial direct cost incurred........	800
Right-of-use asset	$ 99,600

Assets = Liabilities + Equity
+99,600   +100,000
ROU Asset Lease Liab
-800   -1,200
In Dir Cost Incent Liab

ROU Asset		Lease Liab	
99,600			100,000

Int Dir Cost		Incent Liab	
Bal. 800	800	1,200	1,200 Bal.
0			0

January 1, Year 1—To record right-of-use asset and lease liability

Right-of-Use Asset..	99,600	
Lease Incentive Liability	1,200	
Initial Direct Cost.......................................		800
Lease Liability..		100,000

Real World—FINANCE LEASE DISCLOSURE

Microsoft Corporation disclosed information related to its finance leases in a recent Form 10-K (Note 14).

We have operating and finance leases for datacenters, corporate offices, research and development facilities, Microsoft Experience Centers, and certain equipment. Our leases have remaining lease terms of 1 year to 17 years, some of which include options to extend the leases for up to 5 years, and some of which include options to terminate the leases within 1 year. The components of lease expense were as follows.

Year Ended June 30 ($ millions)	2024
Finance lease cost	
Amortization of right-of-use assets	$1,800
Interest on lease liabilities	734
Total finance lease cost	$2,534

Supplemental balance sheet information related to leases follows ($ millions).

Finance Leases	2024
Property and equipment, at cost	$32,248
Accumulated depreciation	(6,386)
Property and equipment, net	$25,862
Other current liabilities	$ 2,349
Other long-term liabilities	24,796
Total finance lease cost	$27,145

Lessee—Finance Lease with Guaranteed Residual Value   LO17-4   DEMO 17-4B

On January 1 of Year 1, the lease commencement date, Lessor Inc. and Lessee Inc. sign a 3-year non-cancellable lease for equipment that is routinely leased to other companies. Details follow.

1. The equipment has an estimated economic life of three years.
2. The three lease payments are $33,461.73, payable January 1 of Year 1, Year 2, and Year 3.
3. The fair value of the asset at the commencement of the lease is $100,000.
4. The lease does not contain a renewal or purchase option, and the asset reverts to the lessor at the end of the 3-year period.
5. The contract requires the lessee to guarantee the residual value of the equipment at the end of the lease for $5,000. Lessee Inc. estimates that the residual value of the equipment at the end of the lease will be $3,000.
6. The lessor's implicit interest rate is 5% and is known by the lessee.

Answer the following questions from the perspective of Lessee Inc. which has an accounting period that ends on December 31.
a. Determine the proper lease classification.
b. Calculate the lease liability and the right-of-use asset.
c. Prepare a lease liability schedule.
d. Prepare the lessee's journal entries for Year 1.
e. Show the impact on the lessee's balance sheet and income statement for Year 1.
f. Prepare the lessee's journal entries for Year 2.
g. Show the impact on the lessee's balance sheet and income statement for Year 2.
h. Prepare the lessee's journal entries for Year 3.
i. Prepare the lessee's journal entry on January 1 of Year 4 to return the equipment to the lessor. The fair value of the equipment is determined to be $3,000 as expected.

Solution
a. **Lease Classification**

First, the lease is classified as a finance lease to the lessee because at least one of the lease classification criteria is met as shown in the following analysis.

continued

continued from previous page

Classification Criteria	Analysis	Met
1. Ownership transfer	The asset reverts to the lessor at the end of the three-year period.	
2. Purchase option	The lease does not contain a purchase option.	
3. Lease term length	Three-year lease term > 75% of the three-year useful life (2.25 years).	✔
4. PV of lease payments	$100,000 (PV of lease payments including 100% of the residual guarantee) > $90,000 (90% of fair value of $100,000).	✔
5. No alternative use	There are alternative uses for the equipment as the lessor often leases this equipment to other companies.	

	RATE	NPER	PMT	PV	FV	TYPE	Excel Formula
Given	5%	3	(33,461.73)	?	(5,000)	1	=PV(0.05,3,−33461.73,−5000,1)
Solution				$100,000			

b. Lease Liability and Right-of-Use Asset

On the lease commencement date, the lessee records a lease liability. The present value of the lease payments from the lease classification test computed above is $100,000, which includes 100% of the guaranteed residual value. To calculate the lease liability, however, only the *probable payment* on a residual guarantee is included, or $2,000 ($5,000 − $3,000). Thus, the lease liability measurement is $97,408. The right-of-use asset measurement is equal to the liability balance of $97,408, with no applicable adjustments for lease incentives or initial direct costs.

	RATE	NPER	PMT	PV	FV	Excel Formula
Given	5%	3	(33,461.73)	?	(2,000)	=PV(0.05,3,−33461.73,−2000,1)
Solution				$97,408		

c. Lease Liability Schedule

The lessee prepares a lease liability schedule with the final payment consisting of the $2,000 probable payment under the residual value guarantee.

Lease Liability Schedule

Date	Lease Payment Dr. Lease Liability Cr. Cash	Interest on Liability Dr. Interest Expense Cr. Lease Liability	Lease Liability Change	Lease Liability
Jan. 1, Year 1				$97,408
Jan. 1, Year 1	$ 33,462	$ 0	$33,462	63,946
Jan. 1, Year 2	33,462	3,197	30,265	33,681
Jan. 1, Year 3	33,462	1,684	31,778	1,903
Jan. 1, Year 4	2,000	97*	1,903	0
	$102,386	$4,978	$97,408	

*Amount rounded

Note: Amounts adjusted to whole numbers to simplify recording of journal entries that follow. If we prepare this schedule in Excel with unlimited decimals, the numbers slightly vary.

d. Lessee's Journal Entries—Year 1

January 1, Year 1—To record right-of-use asset and lease liability

Assets = Liabilities + Equity
+97,408   +97,408
ROU Asset   Lease Liab

ROU Asset		Lease Liab
97,408		97,408

| Right-of-Use Asset. . . . . | 97,408 | |
| Lease Liability . . . . | | 97,408 |

January 1, Year 1—To record first lease payment

Assets = Liabilities + Equity
−33,462   −33,462
C:f   Lease Liab

Cash		Lease Liab	
	33,462	33,462	97,408

| Lease Liability . . . . | 33,462 | |
| Cash . . . . | | 33,462 |

December 31, Year 1—To record interest expense

Assets = Liabilities + Equity
            +3,197   −3,197
            Lease Liab Exp

Interest Exp		Lease Liab	
3,197		33,462	97,408
			3,197
			67,143

| Interest Expense. . . . . | 3,197 | |
| Lease Liability . . . . | | 3,197 |

December 31, Year 1—To record amortization on right-of-use asset

Assets = Liabilities + Equity
−32,469   −32,469
ROU Asset   Exp

ROU Asset		Amort Exp	
97,408	32,469	32,469	
64,939			

| Amortization Expense . . . . | 32,469 | |
| Right-of-Use Asset ($97,408/3). . . . . | | 32,469 |

continued

continued from previous page

e. Lessee's Financial Statements—Year 1

Balance Sheet	Dec. 31, Year 1
Assets	
Noncurrent assets	
Right-of-use asset ($97,408 – $32,469) . . .	$64,939
Liabilities	
Current liabilities	
Lease liability ($3,197 + $30,265)	33,462
Noncurrent liabilities	
Lease liability* ($67,143 – $33,462)	33,681

Income Statement	Year 1
Expenses	
Interest expense—lease liability	$ 3,197
Amortization expense—right-of-use asset . .	32,469

*The noncurrent portion is equal to the total lease liability of $67,143 (calculated as $63,946 + $3,197) less the current lease liability.

f. Lessee's Journal Entries—Year 2

January 1, Year 2—To record lease payment

Lease Liability	33,462	
Cash		33,462

Assets	=	Liabilities	+	Equity
–30,265		–33,462		
C:f		Lease Liab		
–3,197				
C:o				

Cash		Lease Liab	
33,462		33,462	97,408
33,462		33,462	3,197

December 31, Year 2—To record interest expense

Interest Expense.	1,684	
Lease Liability		1,684

Assets	=	Liabilities	+	Equity
		+1,684		–1,684
		Lease Liab		Exp

Interest Exp		Lease Liab	
3,197		33,462	97,408
1,684		33,462	3,197
			1,684
			35,365

December 31, Year 2—To record amortization on right-of-use asset

Amortization Expense	32,469	
Right-of-Use Asset ($97,408/3).		32,469

Assets	=	Liabilities	+	Equity
–32,469				–32,469
ROU Asset				Exp

ROU Asset		Amort Exp	
97,408	32,469	32,469	
	32,469	32,469	
32,470			

g. Lessee's Financial Statements—Year 2

Balance Sheet	Dec. 31, Year 2
Assets	
Current assets	
Right-of-use asset ($64,939 – $32,469) . . .	$32,470
Liabilities	
Current liabilities	
Lease liability.	33,462
Noncurrent liabilities	
Lease liability* ($35,365 – $33,462)	1,903

Income Statement	Year 2
Expenses	
Interest expense—lease liability	$ 1,684
Amortization expense—right-of-use asset . .	32,469

*The noncurrent portion is equal to the total lease liability of $35,365 (calculated as $33,681 + $1,684) less the current lease liability.

h. Lessee's Journal Entries—Year 3

January 1, Year 3—To record lease payment

Lease Liability	33,462	
Cash		33,462

Assets	=	Liabilities	+	Equity
–31,778		–33,462		
C:f		Lease Liab		
–1,684				
C:o				

Cash		Lease Liab	
33,462		33,462	97,408
33,462		33,462	3,197
33,462		33,462	1,684

December 31, Year 3—To record interest expense

Interest Expense.	97	
Lease Liability		97

Assets	=	Liabilities	+	Equity
		+97		–97
		Lease Liab		Exp

Interest Exp		Lease Liab	
3,197		33,462	97,408
1,684		33,462	3,197
97		33,462	1,684
			97
			2,000

continued

continued from previous page

December 31, Year 3—To record amortization on right-of-use asset

Assets	=	Liabilities	+	Equity
−32,470				−32,470
ROU Asset				Exp

ROU Asset		Amort Exp	
97,408	32,469	32,469	
	32,469	32,469	
	32,470	32,470	
0			

Amortization Expense	32,470	
Right-of-Use Asset ($97,408/3)*		32,470

*Adjusted for rounding.

After the journal entries of Year 3 and the expiration of the lease, the right-of-use asset has a value of $0 and the lease liability has a value of $2,000, which equals the probable payment under the residual value guarantee.

Assets	=	Liabilities	+	Equity
−1,903		−2,000		
C:f		Lease Liab		
−97				
C:o				

Cash		Lease Liab	
	33,462	33,462	97,408
	33,462	33,462	3,197
	33,462	33,462	1,684
	2,000	2,000	97
			0

i. **Lessee's Journal Entry—End of Lease**

On December 31 of Year 3, upon the expiration of the lease, the lessee records the following entry because, as expected, the value of the equipment is $3,000, which is $2,000 short of the guaranteed residual value of $5,000.

December 31, Year 3—To record payment to satisfy guaranteed residual value

Lease Liability	2,000	
Cash		2,000

DEMO 17-4C   LO17-4   Lessee—Finance Lease with Purchase Option Expected to Exercise

Demo

MBC

A lease incorporates a purchase option when the lessee can purchase the underlying asset at the end of the lease for a specified amount. The purchase option, if it is reasonably certain that the lessee will exercise the option, will be included as a lease payment in evaluating the lease for its proper classification and in valuing the lease liability at the start of the lease. The following two examples include a purchase option.

Example One—Finance Lease with Purchase Option

Assume the same facts from **Demo 17-4B** above, except that the lease contract now (a) includes a purchase option for $2,000 expected to be exercised and (b) excludes a guaranteed residual value. Also assume that it is reasonably certain that Lessee Inc. will exercise the purchase option at lease end. Determine how the lessee's journal entries would change from the solution shown in **Demo 17-4B**.

Solution

In this case, the present value of the lease payments used to classify the lease is $97,408. The $2,000 purchase option is included as an additional payment on the lease (refer to **Exhibit 17-2**). The present value of the lease payments will be recorded as the lease liability because there are no adjustments to the lease liability. The lease liability of $97,408 matches the earlier example with a guaranteed residual value. There is no change to the initial recording of the right-of-use asset, which would be amortized over three years, which is the lease term and economic life of the asset. Therefore, the *journal entries and the financial statement presentation are identical to the solution for* **Demo 17-4B**. Although the lessee owns the asset at the end of the lease term, it has a carrying amount of zero because its cost basis has been fully amortized.

	RATE	NPER	PMT	PV	FV	TYPE	Excel Formula
Given	5%	3	(33,461.73)	?	(2,000)	1	=PV(0.05,3,−33461.73,−2000,1)
Solution				$97,408			

Example Two—Finance Lease with Purchase Option—Economic Life of Asset Differs from Lease Term

Assume the same information in Example One, except that the economic life of the equipment is estimated to be four years instead of three years **and that the lessee's accounting policy is to depreciate fixed assets using the straight-line method.** Determine how the accounting for the lessee would change from the solution shown in **Demo 17-4B**.

Solution

If a lease indicates that the underlying asset automatically reverts to the lessee at the end of the lease, or if the lease includes a purchase option that the lessee is reasonably certain to exercise, *the right-of-use asset is expensed over the asset's economic life.*

Dec. 31, Year 1	Amortization expense ($97,408/4)	$24,352
Dec. 31, Year 2	Amortization expense ($97,408/4)	24,352
Dec. 31, Year 3	Amortization expense ($97,408/4)	24,352
Dec. 31, Year 4	Depreciation expense ($24,352/1)	24,352

continued

continued from previous page

> Upon the expiration of the lease at the end of Year 3, the remaining balance in the right-of-use asset of $24,352 is transferred to an equipment account. The unamortized cost basis at the time the asset is purchased would be depreciated over its remaining life, which in this case is one year. While there were no initial direct costs in this example, any initial direct costs are amortized over the lease term, not the economic life of the asset. Thus, at the end of the lease term, the balance of initial direct costs should be zero.

Exhibit 17-3 summarizes the treatment of guaranteed and unguaranteed residual value, purchase options, and termination penalties for the lessee.

Accounting for the Lessee	Guaranteed Residual Value	Unguaranteed Residual Value	Purchase Option or Penalty*
PV of lease payment criterion of the lease classification test	Included	Not included	Included
Calculation of lease liability and right-of-use asset	Include only probable amount owed	Not included	Included

EXHIBIT 17-3

Lessee Accounting Treatment of Residual Value, Purchase Options, and Penalties

* Assume that it is reasonably certain that the lessee will exercise the purchase option or it is reasonably certain that the lessee will terminate the lease. If the exercise of a purchase option is reasonably certain, residual value is ignored in the lessee's calculations.

EXPANDING YOUR KNOWLEDGE   **Multiple Lease Components**

After determining that a contract contains a lease, a company must identify separate lease components (or individual right-of-use assets) in a contract. The right-of-use of an asset is considered a *separate lease component* if both of the following criteria are met.

> `842-10-15-28` *a.* The lessee can benefit from the right of use either on its own or together with other resources that are readily available to the lessee. Readily available resources are goods or services that are sold or leased separately (by the lessor or other suppliers) or resources that the lessee already has obtained (from the lessor or from other transactions or events).
>
> *b.* The right of use is neither highly dependent on nor highly interrelated with the other right(s) to use underlying assets in the contract. A lessee's right to use an underlying asset is highly dependent on or highly interrelated with another right to use an underlying asset if each right of use significantly affects the other.

After the separate lease components are identified, consideration in the contract is allocated to the separate lease components and nonlease components on a relative standalone selling price basis—see allocation methods in Chapter 7.

Finance Lease by Lessee with a Guaranteed Residual Value   **LO17-4** ◀   **REVIEW 17-4**

Review

MBC

Lessor Company and Lessee Company signed a four-year lease for equipment on January 1 of Year 1. The equipment has a fair value of $65,002 at commencement of the lease, an estimated life of six years, and reverts to Lessor Company at the end of the lease term. Lease payments of $16,000 are payable on January 1 of each year and were set to yield Lessor Company a return of 9%, which was known to Lessee Company. The estimated residual value at the end of the lease term is $12,000 and is guaranteed by Lessee Corporation. Lessee expects the residual value at the end of the lease term to be $12,000. The lease contains no purchase option. The Lessee has an accounting period that ends on December 31.

a. How would Lessee Company classify the lease?

b. Prepare a schedule of the lease liability.

c. Prepare entries for Lessee Company for Year 1 to (1) record the right-of-use asset and liability, (2) record the first lease payment, and (3) record adjusting entries at year end.

d. Repeat parts (*b*) and (*c*) but assume instead that Lessee Company expects the estimated residual value at the end of the lease term to be $3,500.

More Practice:
BE17-17, BE17-18, BE17-19, E17-12, E17-13, E17-14, E17-17

Solution on p. 17-94.

LO 17-5 ▶ **Account for Complex Operating Leases for a Lessee**

LO 17-5 Overview

> **Lessee Accounting—Complex Operating Lease**
> Lease liability
> - Consider only probable amount owed on residual
> - Reduce liability for any lease prepayments
>
> Right-of-use asset
> - Subtract lease incentives received
> - Add initial direct costs incurred
>
> Recognize straight-line lease expense as a single amount in the income statement

Recall from the basic operating lease example that the lessee records a right-of-use asset and a lease liability on the balance sheet at commencement of the lease, calculated the same way as in a finance lease. This means that adjustments to the right-of-use asset required in more complex finance leases described in LO17-4 (for lease incentives and initial direct costs) apply to operating leases as well. However, after the initial recognition of the lease liability and right-of-use asset, an equal amount of expense is recorded in the income statement using the straight-line method as discussed in LO 17-3 for a basic operating lease. Recall that the total cost of the lease equals the undiscounted total of all lease payments. Lease payments include not only fixed periodic lease payments, but other lease payments as detailed in the last section. The total cost of the lease at the commencement date is divided by the total number of lease periods to equal the straight-line lease expense for the period.

Straight-Line Lease Amortization Expense	minus	**Current Period 'Interest'**	=	**Change in Right-of-Use Asset**
Recognized on Income Statement				Reduces ROU Asset to Carrying Value

---

DEMO 17-5 | **LO17-5**   *Lessee—Operating Lease with Initial Direct Cost, Incentive, Prepayment*

Demo

MBC

On January 1 of Year 1, the lease commencement date, Lessor Inc. and Lessee Inc. sign a 3-year noncancellable lease for equipment that is routinely leased to other companies. Details follow.

1. The equipment has an estimated economic life of six years.
2. The three lease payments are $34,972.24, payable January 1 of Year 1, Year 2, and Year 3.
3. Fair value of the asset at the commencement of the lease is $150,000.
4. The asset reverts to the lessor at the end of the three-year period.
5. The asset's unguaranteed residual value is estimated to be $57,882.
6. The lessor's implicit interest rate is 5% and is known by the lessee.
7. Prior to the lease commencement, the lessee received $5,000 cash as a partial payment for the lessee's preexisting lease and incurred legal fees to execute the lease of $620.

Answer the following questions from the perspective of Lessee Inc. which has an accounting period that ends on December 31.

a. Record the entries for the lease incentive received and legal fees paid, prior to the lease commencement.
b. Determine the proper lease classification.
c. Calculate the lease liability and the right-of-use asset.
d. Prepare a lease liability schedule and a right-of-use asset schedule.
e. Prepare the lessee's journal entries for Year 1.
f. Show the impact on the lessee's balance sheet and income statement for Year 1.
g. Prepare the lessee's journal entries for Year 2.
h. Show the impact on the lessee's balance sheet and income statement for Year 2.
i. Prepare the lessee's journal entries for Year 3.
j. Now assume no other changes to the lease arrangement except that the lessee prepaid the first lease payment prior to the commencement of the lease. At that time, the lessee recorded the lease prepayment as a debit to Prepaid Lease Payment and a credit to Cash for $34,972. Prepare the revised entry at the lease commencement on January 1 of Year 1.

continued

continued from previous page

Solution

a. Lessee's Journal Entries—Prior to Lease Commencement

To record lease incentive received prior to lease commencement

Cash	5,000	
Lease Incentive Liability		5,000

Assets = Liabilities + Equity
+5,000   +5,000
C:o   Incent Liab

Cash	Incent Liab
5,000	5,000

To record initial direct cost paid prior to lease commencement

Initial Direct Cost.	620	
Cash		620

Assets = Liabilities + Equity
+620
In Dir Cost
–620
C:o

Cash	Init Dir Cost
5,000	620	620

b. Lease Classification

The lease is classified as an operating lease to the lessee because none of the lease classification criteria are met as shown in the following analysis.

Lease Classification Criteria	Analysis	Lease Criterion Met
1. Ownership transfer	Asset reverts to the lessor at the end of the three-year period.	
2. Purchase option	Lease does not contain a purchase option.	
3. Lease term length	Three-year lease term < 75% of the six-year useful life (4.5 years).	
4. PV of lease payments	$95,000 (PV of lease payments of $100,000 *less* lease incentive of $5,000) < $135,000 (90% of fair value of $150,000).	
5. No alternative use	There are alternative uses for the equipment as the lessor often leases this equipment to other companies.	

RATE	NPER	PMT	PV	Excel Formula
5%	3	(34,972.24)	?	=PV(0.05,3,–34972.24,0,1)
			$100,000	

Guaranteed Residual Scenario Assume instead that the residual value of $57,882 is guaranteed. Recall that a guaranteed residual value is considered an additional payment by the lessee. For lease classification criterion No. 4, the present value of lease payments is $150,000, instead of $100,000, calculated as =PV(0.05,3,-34972.24,-57882,1).

Present value of lease payments criterion:
$145,000 (PV of lease payments of $150,000 less lease incentive of $5,000) > **$135,000** (90% of $150,000 fair value)

Because the present value of the lease payments is greater than 90% of the fair value of the asset, the lease would be considered a finance lease, *not an operating lease,* for the lessee.

c. Calculation of the Lease Liability and the Right-of-Use Asset

The lease liability is equal to $100,000, the present value of the lease payments (see calculation above). The right-of-use asset is equal to the lease liability of $100,000 adjusted for items incurred at or before the lease commencement (lease incentive and initial direct costs).

Calculate Right-of-Use Asset	
Initial measurement of lease liability...	$100,000
− Subtract lease incentive received.....	(5,000)
+ Add initial direct costs incurred.......	620
Right-of-use asset	$ 95,620

d. Lease Liability Schedule and Right-of-Use Asset Schedule

The lease liability schedule is prepared first. 'Interest' determined in the lease liability schedule is an input to the right-of-use asset amortization schedule below.

continued

continued from previous page

Lease Liability Schedule

Date	Lease Payment	Interest on Liability	Lease Liability Change	Lease Liability
Jan. 1, Year 1				$100,000
Jan. 1, Year 1	$ 34,972	$ 0	$ 34,972	65,028
Jan. 1, Year 2	34,972	3,251	31,721	33,307
Jan. 1, Year 3	34,972	1,665	33,307	0
	$104,916	$4,916	$100,000	

Right-of-Use Asset Schedule

Date	Lease Expense[a] — Dr. Lease Expense	Interest on Liability — Cr. Lease Liability	Right-of-Use Asset Change — Cr. Right-of-Use Asset	Right-of-Use Asset
Jan. 1, Year 1				$ 95,620
Dec. 31, Year 1	$ 33,512	$3,251	$30,261	65,359
Dec. 31, Year 2	33,512	1,665	31,847	33,512
Dec. 31, Year 3	33,512	—	33,512	0
	$100,536	$4,916	$95,620	

[a] Straight-line amortization expense equals total lease payments divided by total number of periods ($34,972 + $34,972 + $34,972 + $620 − $5,000)/3 = $33,512).

Lease expense recognized in the income statement each period is $33,512 (straight-line amortization expense).

e. **Lessee's Journal Entries—Year 1**

Lease Incentive Liability and Initial Direct Cost are reclassified to the right-of-use asset account through this entry.

January 1, Year 1—To record right-of-use asset and lease liability

Right-of-Use Asset.	95,620	
Lease Incentive Liability	5,000	
Lease Liability		100,000
Initial Direct Cost.		620

January 1, Year 1—To record lease payment

Lease Liability	34,972	
Cash		34,972

December 31, Year 1—To record lease expense

Lease Expense	33,512	
Lease Liability		3,251
Right-of-Use Asset.		30,261

Assets = Liabilities + Equity
+95,620   −5,000
ROU Asset   Incent Liab
−620   +100,000
In Dir Cost Lease Liab

ROU Asset		Incent Liab	
95,620		5,000	5,000

Init Dir Cost		Lease Liab	
620	620		100,000

Assets = Liabilities + Equity
−34,972   −34,972
C:o   Lease Liab

Cash		Lease Liab	
5,000	620	34,972	100,000
	34,972		

Assets = Liabilities + Equity
−30,261   +3,251   −33,512
ROU Asset Lease Liab Exp

ROU Asset		Lease Liab	
95,620	30,261	34,972	100,000
65,359			3,251
			68,279

Lease Exp	
33,512	

f. **Lessee's Financial Statements—Year 1**

Balance Sheet	Dec. 31, Year 1		Income Statement	Year 1
Assets			**Expenses**	
Noncurrent assets			Lease expense	$33,512
Right-of-use asset ($95,620 − $30,261) . . .	$65,359			
Liabilities				
Current liabilities				
Lease liability.	34,972			
Noncurrent liabilities				
Lease liability*($68,279 − $34,972).	33,307			

*The noncurrent portion is equal to the total lease liability of $68,279 (calculated as $65,028 + $3,251) less the current lease liability.

continued

continued from previous page

g. **Lessee's Journal Entries—Year 2**

January 1, Year 2—To record lease payment

Lease Liability	34,972	
Cash		34,972

Assets = Liabilities + Equity
-34,972   -34,972
C:o   Lease Liab

Cash		Lease Liab	
5,000	620	34,972	100,000
	34,972	34,972	3,251
	34,972		

December 31, Year 2—To record lease expense

Lease Expense	33,512	
Lease Liability		1,665
Right-of-Use Asset		31,847

Assets = Liabilities + Equity
-31,847   +1,665   -33,512
ROU Asset   Lease Liab   Exp

ROU Asset		Lease Liab	
95,620	30,261	34,972	100,000
	31,847	34,972	3,251
33,512			1,665
			34,972

Lease Exp	
33,512	
33,512	

h. **Lessee's Financial Statements—Year 2**

Balance Sheet	Dec. 31, Year 2	Income Statement	Year 2
Assets		**Expenses**	
Current assets		Lease expense	$33,512
Right-of-use asset ($65,359 – $31,847) . . .	$33,512		
Liabilities			
Current liabilities			
Lease liability.	34,972		

i. **Lessee's Journal Entries—Year 3**

January 1, Year 3—To record lease payment

Lease Liability	34,972	
Cash		34,972

Assets = Liabilities + Equity
-34,972   -34,972
C:o   Lease Liab

Cash		Lease Liab	
5,000	620	34,972	100,000
	34,972	34,972	3,251
	34,972	34,972	1,665
	34,972		0

December 31, Year 3—To record amortization on right-of-use asset

Lease Expense	33,512	
Right-of-Use Asset		33,512

Assets = Liabilities + Equity
-33,512   -33,512
ROU Asset   Exp

ROU Asset		Lease Exp	
95,620	30,261	33,512	
	31,847	33,512	
	33,512	33,512	
0			

After the journal entries of Year 3 and the expiration of the lease, both the right-of-use asset and the lease liability have a balance of $0.

j. **Lessee's Journal Entries—Lease Prepayment**

Consistent with the prior example, we calculate the gross lease liability as the present value of lease payments, or $100,000 (=PV(0.05,3,-34,972.24)). Next we adjust the right-of-use asset for lease incentives and initial direct costs, resulting in net Right-of-Use Asset of $95,620 at the lease commencement date. We then adjust the lease liability for the prepaid lease payment, resulting in a net Lease Liability of $65,028 ($100,000 – $34,972).

Calculate Right-of-Use Asset	
Initial measurement of lease liability. . .	$100,000
– Subtract lease incentive received	(5,000)
+ Add initial direct cost incurred.	620
Right-of-use asset	$ 95,620

January 1, Year 1—To record right-of-use asset and lease liability

Right-of-Use Asset.	95,620	
Lease Incentive Liability	5,000	
Lease Liability		100,000
Initial Direct Cost.		620

Assets = Liabilities + Equity
+95,620   -5,000
ROU Asset   Incent Liab
-620   +100,000
Init Dir Cost   Lease Liab

ROU Asset		Incent Liab	
95,620		5,000	5,000

Init Dir Cost		Lease Liab	
620	620		100,000

January 1, Year 1—To adjust lease liability for advance lease payment

Lease Liability	34,972	
Prepaid Lease Payment		34,972

Assets = Liabilities + Equity
-34,972   -34,972
Prep Lease   Lease Liab

Prepaid Lease		Lease Liab	
34,972	34,972	34,972	100,000

MICROSOFT

Real World—OPERATING LEASE DISCLOSURE

Microsoft Corporation disclosed lease expense related to its operating leases in a recent Form 10-K.

The components of lease expense were as follows.

Year Ended June 30 ($ millions)	2024
Operating lease cost.	$3,555

Supplemental balance sheet information related to leases was as follows ($ millions).

June 30 Operating Leases	2024
Operating lease right-of-use assets	$18,961
Other current liabilities	3,580
Operating lease liabilities	15,497
Total operating lease liabilities	$19,077

Leases and Statement of Cash Flows

On the statement of cash flows for an operating lease of a lessee, the full lease payment is classified as an outflow from operating activities. However, for a finance lease, only the interest portion of the lease payment is included in expense, and thus only the cash outflows related to interest are incorporated into cash flows from operating activities. The reduction in principal is reported as an outflow for financing activities. For a lessor, lease cash receipts are treated as a cash inflow from operating activities.

Income Statement Presentation—Operating Lease versus Finance Lease

Whether a lease is classified as an operating or a finance lease, an asset and liability are recorded on the balance sheet. However, the timing and presentation on the income statement differs between an operating and finance lease.

842-20-45-4   In the statement of comprehensive income, a lessee shall present both of the following:

a. For finance leases, the interest expense on the lease liability and amortization of the right-of-use asset are not required to be presented as separate line items and shall be presented in a manner consistent with how the entity presents other interest expense and depreciation or amortization of similar assets, respectively.

b. For operating leases, lease expense shall be included in the lessee's income from continuing operations.

Let's consider two scenarios: one where the lease is classified as operating and one where the same lease is classified as a finance lease (for example, if the estimated economic life of the asset was 4 years, causing the lease term length criterion to be met). Using the lease example in **Demo 17-5**, lease expense is recorded on a straight-line basis, over the term of the lease, as one expense amount in income from operations. However, under the finance lease:

- Interest expense is reported separately from the amortization of the right-of-use asset. Interest expense is reported in other expense while amortization expense is reported as part of income from operations.

- Total expense is higher in earlier years (lower in later years) for a finance lease (under the effective interest method) as compared to an operating lease (straight-line method).

- Lessees likely prefer the operating lease classification over the finance lease classification as it produces stronger operating results in the earlier years. However, a finance lease permits lessees to classify a portion of the lease expense as financing instead of operating, resulting in higher operating income and higher cash flow from operating activities. We see, however, that while total expense recognized differs each year between the two methods, the total expense recognized over the term of the lease of $100,536 is the same under both methods.

	Operating Lease	Finance Lease		
	Lease Expense	Interest Expense	Amortization of Right-of-Use Asset	Total
Year 1..	$ 33,512	$3,251	$31,873	$ 35,124
Year 2..	33,512	1,665	31,873	33,538
Year 3..	33,512	—	31,874	31,874
	$100,536	$4,916	$95,620	$100,536

Because the amortization of the right-of-use asset differs, the net balance in the right-of-use asset for the first two years also differs as follows.

Balance, Net	Operating Lease Right-of-Use Asset	Finance Lease Right-of-Use Asset
Dec. 31, Year 1	$65,359	$63,747
Dec. 31, Year 2	33,512	31,874
Dec. 31, Year 3	0	0

Operating Lease by Lessee with Renewal Option and Initial Direct Costs   LO17-5   REVIEW 17-5

Review

MBC

On January 1 of Year 1, Lessee Inc. signed a 10-year lease for office space for $75,000 annually, with the first payment due immediately. Lessee Inc. has the option to renew the lease for an additional 4-year period on or before January 1 of Year 11 at market lease rates at the time of renewal. Lessee Inc. intends to evaluate rental options at the time of the option to renew. The economic life of the rental space is 30 years and the fair value of the rental space is $1 million. Lessee Inc. is not aware of the implicit rate of the lease but has an incremental borrowing rate of 6%. Lessee Inc. paid $1,000 on January 1 of Year 1 in initial direct costs. The lessee has an accounting period that ends on December 31.

a. How would Lessee Inc. classify the lease?

b. Prepare a schedule for the lease liability.

c. Prepare a schedule for the right-of-use asset.

d. Prepare the entries for Lessee Inc. for Year 1 and Year 2 to record the right-of-use asset and lease liability, to record the lease payments, and to record lease expense.

More Practice:
BE17-23, BE17-24, E17-18, E17-19, E17-20, E17-21
Solution on p. 17-95.

Determine lease type and account for a basic sales-type lease for a lessor

LO 17-6

LO 17-6 Overview

We now consider lease accounting for the *lessor*. Although the lessor and the lessee use nearly identical classification criteria, the lessee and lessor may have access to different information and may apply judgment differently. While many of our examples suggest the lessor and the lessee would classify a given lease in the same way, in the real world, this may not be the case.

Lessor Accounting—Basic Sales-Type Lease

- At least one of the lease classification criteria is met
- Record selling profit (if applicable) at lease commencement
- Derecognize underlying asset
- Record a lease receivable and recognize interest revenue on the receivable using the effective interest method

Lessor Lease Classification   If a lease meets at least one of the five lease classification criteria in **Exhibit 17-1** and payments from the lessee are probable, the lessor accounts for the lease as a sales-type lease. If, however, the lessor determines that payments are not **probable**, the lessor records lease payments received as a deposit liability (debit Cash and credit Deposit Liability) until either the payments become probable or the lease is terminated.

842-30-25-3   . . . If collectibility of the lease payments, plus any amount necessary to satisfy a residual value guarantee provided by the lessee, is not probable at the commencement date, the lessor shall not derecognize the underlying asset but shall recognize lease payments received—including variable lease payments—as a deposit liability . . .

If the lease does not meet any of the lease classification criteria outlined in **Exhibit 17-1**, the lease is classified as an operating lease (discussed in a later section) or as a direct financing lease (discussed in Appendix 17A to this chapter).

* Not classified as operating if it meets the criteria of direct financing lease—see Appendix 17A.

Accounting for a Basic Sales-Type Lease

In a sales-type lease, the lessor effectively transfers ownership of the underlying asset to the lessee. We illustrate the accounting for a basic sales-type lease with no residual value in **Demo 17-6**. A summary of the accounting for the lessee for a sales-type lease follows.

Balance Sheet	Income Statement
Recognize a net investment in lease and derecognize the underlying asset.	Recognize selling profit or loss at the commencement of the lease (if applicable).
Increase the net investment in lease by interest revenue and decrease net investment in lease for lease payments collected.	Recognize interest revenue on the net investment in lease using the effective interest method.

Net Investment in Lease   Upon commencement of a sales-type lease, the lessor recognizes a **net investment in lease** on the balance sheet and derecognizes Inventory (or Fixed Asset) from the balance sheet.

> **Glossary**   **Net investment in the lease** For a sales-type lease, the sum of the lease receivable and the unguaranteed residual asset.

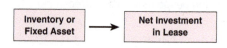

Assuming no residual values in this basic scenario, *net investment in lease* consists only of the **lease receivable** which is equal to the present value of the lease payments discounted at the rate implicit in the lease. (Residual value scenarios are explained in LO17-8.)

■   If the amount of the lease receivable exceeds (is less than) the carrying value of the inventory (or fixed asset), the lessor will immediately recognize profit (loss) on the transaction. Reporting on the income statement depends on whether the asset is held in inventory or fixed assets.

•   If the asset is held in inventory, the lessor will recognize Revenue and Cost of Goods Sold.

•   If the asset is held in fixed assets, the lessor will recognize a net Gain or Loss.

Asset Held as Inventory:

Sales revenue
– Cost of goods sold
= Gross profit

■   If the lease receivable is equal to the carrying value of the inventory (or fixed asset), the asset will be derecognized and Lease receivable will be recognized, but no Revenue or Cost of Goods sold will be recognized on the income statement.

Because the lease receivable is measured at present value, the lessor will prepare a lease receivable schedule to recognize interest revenue over the lease term using the effective interest method.

No gross profit:

Carrying value = Fair value

Calculation of Lease Payment A lessor determines the lease payment using the lessor's expected rate of return. The expected return varies across leases and lessees as the return depends upon factors specific to the contract and the lessee, such as the lessee's credit rating and the amount of expected residual value. The lease term includes reasonably certain renewals. For purposes of calculating lease payments in this section, only fixed periodic lease payments are considered. (See LO17-8 for more complex examples.)

DEMO 17-6 ▶	**LO17-6**	**Lessor—Basic Sales-Type Lease**

On January 1 of Year 1, the lease commencement date, Lessor Inc. and Lessee Inc. sign a 3-year non-cancellable lease for equipment that is routinely leased to other companies. This is the same lease contract as discussed in Demo 17-2 from the perspective of the lessee. Details follow.

1. The equipment has an estimated economic life of three years and the lessor manufactured the equipment at a cost of $80,000. The equipment is held in the lessor's Inventory account.

continued

continued from previous page

2. The three lease payments are $34,972.24, payable January 1 of Year 1, Year 2, and Year 3.
3. The fair value of the asset at the commencement of the lease is $100,000.
4. The asset reverts to the lessor at the end of the three-year period.
5. The asset's residual value is estimated to be $0 and there is no guaranteed residual value.
6. The lessor's implicit interest rate is 5%.

Answer the following questions from the perspective of Lessor Inc. which has an accounting period that ends on December 31.

a. Determine the proper lease classification assuming that the receipt of lease payments is probable.
b. Confirm the lease payment of $34,972 (rounded).
c. Calculate the lease receivable.
d. Prepare a lease receivable schedule.
e. Prepare the lessor's journal entries for Year 1.
f. Show the impact on the lessor's balance sheet and income statement for Year 1.
g. Prepare the lessor's journal entries for Year 2.
h. Show the impact on the lessor's balance sheet and income statement for Year 2.
i. Prepare the lessor's journal entry for Year 3.
j. Assume instead that the lessor is a merchant and that the carrying value of the equipment is $100,000 (recorded in the Inventory account). Record the entry at the commencement of the lease on January 1 of Year 1 to recognize the lease receivable.
k. Now assume that on January 1 of Year 1, the lessor determines that payments by the lessee are not probable. Record the lessor's entry on January 1 of Year 1.

Solution

a. **Lease Classification**

The lease is classified as a sales-type lease because at least one of the lease classification criteria is met. The lease term is 100% of the useful life of the asset. Also, the present value of the lease payments of $100,000 is equal to the fair value of the underlying asset of $100,000.

Classification Criteria	Criteria Met
1. Transfer of ownership	
2. Option to purchase	
3. Length of lease term.	✔
4. Present value of lease payments . . .	✔
5. No alternative use.	

b. **Calculation of Lease Payment**

To calculate the lease payment, enter an expected return on investment of 5% (RATE) from leasing an asset with a fair value of $100,000 (PV) over three years (NPER), with no expected residual value (FV) and with beginning-of-period payments (TYPE, 1), and solve for payment (PMT).

	RATE	NPER	PMT	PV	TYPE	Excel Formula
Given	5%	3	(34,972.24)	?	1	=PV(0.05,3,– 34,972.24,0,1)
Solution				$100,000		

	RATE	NPER	PMT	PV	TYPE	Excel Formula
Given	5%	3	?	(100,000)	1	=PMT(0.05,3,–100000,0,1)
Solution			$34,972			

c. **Calculation of Lease Receivable**

The lease receivable is $100,000, or the present value of the annual lease payments of $34,972.24 for three years, as calculated previously.

d. **Lease Receivable Schedule**

Date	Lease Payment[a] Dr. Cash Cr. Lease Receivable	Interest on Receivable[b] Dr. Lease Receivable Cr. Interest Revenue	Lease Receivable Change[c]	Lease Receivable[d]
Jan. 1, Year 1 . . .				$100,000
Jan. 1, Year 1 . . .	$ 34,972	$ 0	$ 34,972	65,028
Jan. 1, Year 2 . . .	34,972	3,251	31,721	33,307
Jan. 1, Year 3 . . .	34,972	1,665	33,307	0
	$104,916	$4,916	$100,000	

Note: Certain amounts adjusted for rounding differences.
[a] Lease payment.
[b] Interest rate (5%) × Beginning of period lease receivable (with exception of first payment applied 100% to principal).
[c] Lease payment less interest on receivable.
[d] Lease receivable (beginning of period) less the change in lease receivable.

continued

continued from previous page

e. Lessor's Journal Entries—Year 1

Lessor Inc. records gross profit of $20,000 ($100,000 less $80,000). The lessor also removes the asset to be leased (inventory) and records a net investment in the lease (lease receivable).

Sales revenue	$100,000
− Cost of goods sold	(80,000)
= Gross profit	$ 20,000

Assets	= Liabilities +	Equity
+100,000		−80,000
Lease Rec		Exp
−80,000		+100,000
Inv		Rev

Lease Receiv		COGS	
100,000		80,000	

Inventory		Sales Rev	
	80,000		100,000

January 1, Year 1—To derecognize asset and recognize lease receivable

Lease Receivable	100,000	
Cost of Goods Sold	80,000	
Sales Revenue		100,000
Inventory		80,000

Assets	= Liabilities +	Equity
+34,972		
C:o		
−34,972		
Lease Rec		

Cash		Lease Receiv	
34,972		100,000	34,972

January 1, Year 1—To record receipt of lease payment

| Cash | 34,972 | |
| Lease Receivable | | 34,972 |

Assets	= Liabilities +	Equity
+3,251		+3,251
Lease Rec		Rev

Lease Receiv		Interest Rev	
100,000	34,972		3,251
3,251			
68,279			

December 31, Year 1—To recognize interest revenue

| Lease Receivable | 3,251 | |
| Interest Revenue | | 3,251 |

f. Lessor's Financial Statements—Year 1

Balance Sheet	Dec. 31, Year 1
Assets	
Current assets	
Net investment in lease ($3,251 + $31,721)	$34,972
Noncurrent assets	
Net investment in lease* ($68,279 − $34,972)	33,307

Income Statement	Year 1
Sales revenue	$100,000
Less cost of goods sold	80,000
Gross margin	20,000
Other revenue (expense)	
Interest revenue	3,251

*The noncurrent portion is equal to the total lease receivable less the current lease receivable. Recall that in this scenario, the lease receivable is the only component of Net investment in lease.

g. Lessor's Journal Entries—Year 2

Assets	= Liabilities +	Equity
+34,972		
C:o		
−34,972		
Lease Rec		

Cash		Lease Receiv	
34,972		100,000	34,972
34,972		3,251	34,972

January 1, Year 2—To record receipt of lease payment

| Cash | 34,972 | |
| Lease Receivable | | 34,972 |

Assets	= Liabilities +	Equity
+1,665		+1,665
Lease Rec		Rev

Lease Receiv		Interest Rev	
100,000	34,972		3,251
3,251	34,972		1,665
1,665			
34,972			

December 31, Year 2—To recognize interest revenue

| Lease Receivable | 1,665 | |
| Interest Revenue | | 1,665 |

h. Lessor's Financial Statements—Year 2

Balance Sheet	Dec. 31, Year 2
Assets	
Current assets	
Net investment in lease ($1,665 + $33,307)	$34,972

Income Statement	Year 2
Other revenue (expense)	
Interest revenue	$1,665

i. Lessor's Journal Entry—Year 3

Assets	= Liabilities +	Equity
+34,972		
C:o		
−34,972		
Lease Rec		

Cash		Lease Receiv	
34,972		100,000	34,972
34,972		3,251	34,972
34,972		1,665	34,972
		0	

January 1, Year 3—To record receipt of lease payment

| Cash | 34,972 | |
| Lease Receivable | | 34,972 |

After the journal entry of Year 3 and the expiration of the lease, the lease receivable has a balance of $0.

continued

continued from previous page

j. Lessor's Initial Journal Entry—Carrying Value Equals Fair Value

The carrying value of the equipment of $100,000 is equal to its fair value. The lessor will not recognize a profit at the inception of the lease but will record interest revenue over the term of the lease.

No gross profit
Carrying value = Fair value

January 1, Year 1—To derecognize asset and recognize lease receivable

Lease Receivable	100,000	
Inventory		100,000

Assets	=	Liabilities	+	Equity
+100,000				
Lease Rec				
−100,000				
Inv				

Lease Receiv		Inventory	
100,000		Bal. 100,000	100,000

k. Lessor's Initial Journal Entry—Payment is not Probable

The lessor does not record a lease receivable or derecognize inventory. Instead, the lessor records the first lease payment as a deposit liability.

January 1, Year 1—To record receipt of lease payment

Cash	34,972	
Deposit Liability		34,972

Assets	=	Liabilities	+	Equity
+34,972		+34,972		
C:o		Dep		

Cash		Dep Liab	
34,972			34,972

Comparing Lessee and Lessor Transactions

A basic lease contract was reviewed in LO17-2 from the lessee perspective (finance lease) and in LO17-6 from the lessor perspective (sales-type lease). For simplicity, we assume that the facts and circumstances known to the lessor and the lessee are exactly the same and both have applied management judgment similarly. The journal entries are summarized here in chronological order, listed side-by-side.

	Lessee—Basic Finance Lease (LO17-2)			Lessor—Basic Sales-Type Lease (LO17-6)		
Jan. 1, Year 1	Right-of-Use Asset	100,000		Lease Receivable	100,000	
	Lease Liability		100,000	Cost of Goods Sold	80,000	
	To record right-of-use asset and lease liability			Sales Revenue		100,000
				Inventory		80,000
				To derecognize asset and record investment in lease		
Jan. 1, Year 1	Lease Liability	34,972		Cash	34,972	
	Cash		34,972	Lease Receivable		34,972
	To record lease payment			*To record receipt of lease payment*		
Dec. 31, Year 1	Interest Expense	3,251		Lease Receivable	3,251	
	Lease Liability		3,251	Interest Revenue		3,251
	To record interest expense			*To record interest revenue*		
Dec. 31, Year 1	Amortization Expense	33,333				
	Right-of-Use Asset		33,333			
	To record amortization of right-of-use asset					
Jan. 1, Year 2	Lease Liability	34,972		Cash	34,972	
	Cash		34,972	Lease Receivable		34,972
	To record lease payment			*To record receipt of lease payment*		
Dec. 31, Year 2	Interest Expense	1,665		Lease Receivable	1,665	
	Lease Liability		1,665	Interest Revenue		1,665
	To record interest expense			*To record interest revenue*		
Dec. 31, Year 2	Amortization Expense	33,333				
	Right-of-Use Asset		33,333			
	To record amortization of right-of-use asset					
Jan. 1, Year 3	Lease Liability	34,972		Cash	34,972	
	Cash		34,972	Lease Receivable		34,972
	To record lease payment			*To record receipt of lease payment*		
Dec. 31, Year 3	Amortization Expense	33,334				
	Right-of-Use Asset		33,334			
	To record amortization of right-of-use asset					

REVIEW 17-6 ▶ **LO17-6**   **Accounting for a Basic Sales-Type Lease for a Lessor**

Review

MBC

Lessor Company leased equipment with an estimated economic life of four years to Lessee Company over a four-year period. Lessor paid $78,000 for the equipment, its current carrying value. The lease started on January 1 of Year 1 with the first of four annual payments due of $21,236. Lessor Company uses a target rate of return of 6% in all lease contracts. Lessor Company's accounting periods end on December 31. The equipment reverts to Lessor Company at the end of the lease term, at which time Lessor Company estimates that the equipment will have no residual value.

Required

More Practice:
BE17-25, BE17-26, BE17-27,
BE17-29, E17-23, E17-24,
E17-25, E17-26

Solution on p. 17-96.

a. Prepare a schedule of the lease receivable for the lessor.
b. Provide journal entries for Year 1 and Year 2 for the lessor assuming that the equipment is held in the lessor's Inventory account prior to the start of the lease.

LO 17-7 ▶ Account for an operating lease for a lessor

Operating Lease—Lessor
- Meets *none* of the lease classification criteria
- Continue to recognize asset on the balance sheet
- Record depreciation expense over asset's useful life
- Record lease revenue each period

From the perspective of the lessor, an *operating lease* is any lease other than a sales-type lease or a direct financing lease.

Accounting for Operating Lease by Lessor In accounting for an operating lease, a lessor continues to maintain the leased asset on its balance sheet as shown in **Demo 17-7**. The asset is depreciated over its economic useful life (unless the lessor classifies the asset as inventory) and lease revenue is recognized over the term of the lease. Revenue is generally recognized on a straight-line basis. This means that if lease payments are $1,000 for the first two years and $1,600 for the third year of a three-year lease, lease revenue would be recognized as $1,200 per year ($3,600 ÷ 3). With an operating lease, the lessor will capitalize and amortize initial direct costs over the lease term rather than expense them at lease commencement as they do for sales-type leases.

842-30-25-11 After the commencement date, a lessor shall recognize all of the following:

a. The lease payments as income in profit or loss over the lease term on a straight-line basis unless another systematic and rational basis is more representative of the pattern in which benefit is expected to be derived from the use of the underlying asset, subject to paragraph 842-30-25-12

b. Variable lease payments as income in profit or loss in the period in which the changes in facts and circumstances on which the variable lease payments are based occur

c. Initial direct costs as an expense over the lease term on the same basis as lease income (as described in (a)).

A summary of the accounting for the lessor for an operating lease follows.

Balance Sheet	Income Statement
Underlying asset remains on the balance sheet.	Depreciate asset over its useful life. Recognize lease revenue, depreciation expense, and initial direct cost amortization expense in the income statement.

DEMO 17-7 ▶ **LO17-7**   **Lessor—Operating Lease with Initial Direct Cost**

Demo

MBC

On January 1 of Year 1 (lease commencement date), Lessor Inc. and Lessee Inc. sign a 3-year noncancellable lease for equipment that is routinely leased to other companies. This is the same lease contract as discussed in Demo 17-3 from the perspective of the lessee. Details follow.

1. The equipment has an estimated economic life of six years.
2. The three lease payments are $34,972.24, payable January 1, of Year 1 Year 2, and Year 3.
3. Fair value of the asset at the commencement of the lease is $150,000, which is also the carrying value (cost) on the lessor's books, carried in its Equipment account.
4. The asset reverts to the lessor at the end of the three-year period.
5. The asset's unguaranteed residual value is estimated to be $57,882 at the end of the lease term.
6. The lessor's implicit interest rate is 5%.

continued

continued from previous page

Answer the following questions from the perspective of Lessor Inc. which has an accounting period that ends on December 31.

a. Determine the proper lease classification.

b. Prepare the lessor's journal entries for Year 1, Year 2, and Year 3. Assume that the lessor depreciates fixed assets using the straight-line method.

c. Show the impact on the lessor's balance sheet and income statement for Year 1.

d. How would your answers change to parts *a*, *b*, and *c* if initial direct costs of the lessor were $900 (legal fees related to the execution of the lease), paid in cash on January 1 of Year 1?

Solution

a. **Lease Classification**

The lease is classified as an operating lease because none of the lease classification criteria are met.

Lease Classification Criteria	Analysis	Lease Criterion Met
1. Ownership transfer	Asset reverts to the lessor at the end of the three-year period.	
2. Purchase option	Lease does not contain a purchase option.	
3. Lease term length	Three-year lease term < 75% of the six-year useful life (4.5 years).	
4. PV of lease payments	$100,000 (PV of lease payments) < $135,000 (90% of fair value of $150,000).	
5. No alternative use	There are alternative uses for the equipment as the lessor often leases this equipment to other companies.	

RATE	NPER	PMT	PV	Excel Formula
5%	3	(34,972.24)	?	=PV(0.05,3,−34972.24,0,1)
			$100,000	

b. **Lessor's Journal Entries—Years 1 through 3**

Because the lease contract specifies payments on January 1 of each year, the lessor initially records the cash collected as Deferred Lease Revenue.

January 1, Year 1, Year 2, and Year 3—To record receipt of lease payment

Cash	34,972	
Deferred Lease Revenue		34,972

Assets = Liabilities + Equity
+34,972   +34,972
C:o   Def Lease Rev

Cash	Def Lease Rev
34,972	34,972

At the end of the year, the Deferred Lease Revenue is recognized as Lease Revenue.

December 31, Year 1, Year 2, and Year 3—To record lease revenue

Deferred Lease Revenue	34,972	
Lease Revenue		34,972

Assets = Liabilities + Equity
−34,972   +34,972
Def Lease   Rev

Def Lease Rev	Lease Rev
34,972	34,972	34,972

The equipment is depreciated over its useful life of six years, rather than the lease term because the lessor has control of the asset over its useful life.

December 31, Year 1, Year 2, and Year 3—To record depreciation expense

Depreciation Expense	25,000	
Accumulated Depreciation ($150,000/6)		25,000

Assets = Liabilities + Equity
−25,000   −25,000
AD   Exp

Accum Deprec	Deprec Exp
25,000	25,000

c. **Lessor's Financial Statements—Year 1**

Lessor Inc. recognizes the following amounts in its financial statements in Year 1.

Balance Sheet	Dec. 31, Year 1	
Noncurrent assets		
Equipment.	$150,000	
Accumulated depreciation.	(25,000)	$125,000

Income Statement	Year 1
Revenue	
Lease revenue	$34,972
Expenses	
Depreciation expense . . .	25,000

d. **Lessor's Journal Entries—Initial Direct Costs**

The initial direct costs would have no impact on the lease classification test; thus, the lease would still be classified as an operating lease. Lessor Inc. records the following entry at payment of the initial direct cost.

continued

continued from previous page

Assets = Liabilities + Equity
+900
In Dir Cost
−900
C:o

January 1, Year 1—To record initial direct cost

Initial Direct Cost..................................	900	
Cash		900

Init Dir Cost	Cash
900	| 900

The initial direct cost would be amortized on a straight-line basis over the lease term.

Assets = Liabilities + Equity
−300   −300
In Dir Cost   Exp

December 31, Year 1, Year 2, and Year 3—To amortize deferred cost (initial direct cost)

Amortization Expense	300	
Initial Direct Cost ($900/3)		300

Amort Exp	Init Dir Cost
300 |	900 | 300

The lessor would recognize on the year-end balance sheet of Year 1 a current asset of $300 and a noncurrent asset of $300 for the initial direct cost ($900 original balance − $300 Year 1 amortization = $600 ending balance). On the Year 1 income statement, the lessor would recognize amortization expense of $300.

Comparing Lessee and Lessor Transactions

The basic operating lease was described in LO17-3 from the lessee perspective and in LO17-7 from the lessor perspective. For simplicity, we assume that the facts and circumstances known to the lessor and the lessee are exactly the same and both have applied management judgment similarly. The journal entries in chronological order are listed side-by-side as follows.

	Lessee—Basic Operating Lease (LO17-3)			Lessor—Basic Operating Lease (LO17-7)		
Jan. 1, Year 1	Right-of-Use Asset........ Lease Liability .... *To record right-of-use asset and lease liability*	100,000	100,000			

Jan. 1, Year 1	Lease Liability ....
	     Cash ....
	 To record lease payment
		34,972	34,972	Cash ....
				     Deferred Lease Revenue ....
				 To record receipt of lease payment
					34,972	34,972

Dec. 31, Year 1	Lease Expense ....
	     Lease Liability ....
	     Right-of-Use Asset ...
	 To record lease expense
		34,972	3,251
			 31,721
				Deferred Lease Revenue ....
				     Lease Revenue ....
				 To record lease revenue
					34,972	34,972

Dec. 31, Year 1				Depreciation Expense .... Accumulated Depreciation... *To record depreciation expense*	25,000	25,000

Jan. 1, Year 2	Lease Liability ....
	     Cash ....
	 To record lease payment
		34,972	34,972	Cash ....
				     Deferred Lease Revenue ....
				 To record receipt of lease payment
					34,972	34,972

Dec. 31, Year 2	Lease Expense ....
	     Lease Liability ....
	     Right-of-Use Asset ...
	 To record lease expense
		34,972	1,665
			 33,307
				Deferred Lease Revenue ....
				     Lease Revenue ....
				 To record lease revenue
					34,972	34,972

Dec. 31, Year 2				Depreciation Expense .... Accumulated Depreciation... *To record depreciation expense*	25,000	25,000

Jan. 1, Year 3	Lease Liability ....
	     Cash ....
	 To record lease payment
		34,972	34,972	Cash ....
				     Deferred Lease Revenue ....
				 To record receipt of lease payment
					34,972	34,972

Dec. 31, Year 3	Lease Expense ....
	     Right-of-Use Asset....
	 To record lease expense
		34,972	34,972	Deferred Lease Revenue ....
				     Lease Revenue ....
				 To record lease revenue
					34,972	34,972

Dec. 31, Year 3				Depreciation Expense .... Accumulated Depreciation... *To record depreciation expense*	25,000	25,000

Operating Lease by Lessor with Initial Direct Costs   LO17-7 ◄ REVIEW 17-7

On January 1 of Year 1, Lessor Inc. purchased a building for $3 million to be leased. The building is expected to have a 50-year life with no salvage value. The building was leased immediately by Lessee Inc. for $180,000 a year, payable January 1 of each year starting January 1 of Year 1. The lease term is seven years with no renewal or purchase option reasonably expected to be exercised. There are no uncertainties surrounding collection. The implicit rate of the lease is 6% known by Lessee Inc.

a. How would Lessor Inc. classify the lease?
b. Prepare the entries for Lessor Inc. for Year 1 to record the lease payment received, lease revenue, and depreciation.
c. Assume that Lessor Inc. paid initial direct costs of $1,200 in cash on January 1 of Year 1 for the execution of the lease. Prepare the entries for Lessor Inc. to record the initial direct costs and the adjusting entry at year-end on December 31 of Year 1.

More Practice:
BE17-30, BE17-31, E17-27, E17-28, E17-29
Solution on p. 17-97.

Account for complex sales-type leases for a lessor   LO 17-8

In this section, we build on the basic sales-type lease concepts for the lessor as shown in LO17-6. Specifically, we consider leases where the lessor anticipates a residual value at the end of the lease term and where the lessor incurs initial direct costs. We illustrate the accounting for (1) a sales-type lease with initial direct costs in **Demo 17-8A**; (2) a sales-type lease with a guaranteed residual value in **Demo 17-8B**; and (3) a sales-type lease with an unguaranteed residual value in **Demo 17-8C**.

> **Lessor Accounting—Sales-Type Lease**
> - At least one of the lease classification criteria is met
> - Recognize net investment in lease and derecognize existing asset
> - Record any selling profit
> - Recognize interest revenue over lease term
>
> LO 17-8 Overview

Net Investment in Lease

As illustrated earlier for a basic sales-type lease, the lessor effectively transfers ownership of the underlying asset to the lessee. However, now we account for residual value in the calculation of *net investment in lease*.

842-30-30-1   At the commencement date, for a sales-type lease, a lessor shall measure the net investment in the lease to include both of the following:

a. The lease receivable, which is measured at the present value, discounted using the rate implicit in the lease, of:
  1. The lease payments . . . not yet received by the lessor
  2. The amount the lessor expects to derive from the underlying asset following the end of the lease term that is guaranteed by the lessee or any other third party unrelated to the lessor

b. The unguaranteed residual asset at the present value of the amount the lessor expects to derive from the underlying asset following the end of the lease term that is not guaranteed by the lessee or any other third party unrelated to the lessor, discounted using the rate implicit in the lease.

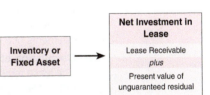

Lease Receivable   To calculate the lease receivable, lease payments are discounted at the rate implicit in the lease. Lease payments include fixed lease payments as well as any guaranteed residual value or any option fee that the lessor reasonably expects the lessee to exercise in the future. Any residual value is ignored when a purchase option is expected to be exercised because the lessee will not be returning the residual to the lessor.

Unguaranteed Residual Value   Any unguaranteed residual value is also discounted at the rate implicit in the lease. The amount discounted is equal to the residual value that the lessor *expects* to receive at lease end. The lease receivable and the unguaranteed residual value can be accounted for in two separate accounts However, **to simplify the accounting for a sales-type lease with an unguaranteed residual value, we combine the lease receivable and the unguaranteed residual value into one account—Net Investment in Lease.**

Initial Direct Costs

In a sales-type lease, the lessor will expense initial direct costs as selling expense in cases where the lessor records a gross profit. However, in cases where there is no gross profit (the lessor's carrying value of the underlying asset approximates its fair value), initial direct costs are deferred and amortized over the lease term.

DEMO 17-8A > **LO17-8**   **Lessor—Sales-Type Lease with Initial Direct Costs**

Demo
MBC

Using Demo 17-6 as a starting point, we consider initial direct costs in part 7. All problem facts are repeated here for convenience. On January 1 of Year 1, the lease commencement date, Lessor Inc. and Lessee Inc. sign a 3-year noncancellable lease for equipment that is routinely leased to other companies. Details follow.

1. The equipment has an estimated economic life of three years and the lessor manufactured the equipment at a cost of $80,000. The equipment is held in the lessor's Inventory account.
2. The three lease payments are $34,972.24, payable January 1 of Year 1, Year 2, and Year 3.
3. The fair value of the asset at the commencement of the lease is $100,000.
4. The asset reverts to the lessor at the end of the three-year period.
5. The asset's residual value is estimated to be $0 and there is no guaranteed residual value.
6. The lessor's implicit interest rate is 5%.
7. Initial direct costs of the lessor are $800 (legal fees related to the execution of the lease paid in cash on January 1 of Year 1).

Answer the following questions from the perspective of Lessor Inc.
a. Determine the proper lease classification assuming that the receipt of lease payments is probable.
b. Calculate the lease receivable.
c. Record initial direct costs of $800.

Solution

a. **Lease Classification**

The initial direct costs do not change the lease classification or the amount of the lease receivable as shown in **Demo 17-6**. The lease is still classified as a sales-type lease because at least one of the lease classification criteria is met. The lease term is 100% of the useful life of the asset. Also, the present value of the lease payments of $100,000 is equal to the fair value of the underlying asset of $100,000.

Classification Criteria	Criterion Met
1. Transfer of ownership	
2. Option to purchase	
3. Length of lease term.	✔
4. Present value of lease payments . . .	✔
5. No alternative use.	

b. **Calculation of Lease Receivable**

The lease receivable is $100,000, or the present value of the annual lease payments of $34,972.24 for three years. This is the same calculation as in part a.

	RATE	NPER	PMT	PV	TYPE	Excel Formula
Given	5%	3	(34,972.24)	?	1	=PV(0.05,3,–34972.24,0,1)
Solution				$100,000		

c. **Initial Direct Costs**

Because this lease has a selling profit ($100,000, fair value, less $80,000, carrying value), the initial direct costs are expensed as incurred.

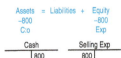

January 1, Year 1—To record initial direct costs

Selling Expense	800	
Cash		800

Assets = Liabilities + Equity
–800   –800
C:o   Exp

Cash	Selling Exp
800	800

DEMO 17-8B > **LO17-8**   **Lessor—Sales-Type Lease with a Guaranteed Residual Value**

Demo
MBC

Let's review another sales-type lease. In this case we include a guaranteed residual value. On January 1 of Year 1, the lease commencement date, Lessor Inc. and Lessee Inc. sign a 3-year noncancellable lease for equipment that is routinely leased to other companies. Details follow.

1. The equipment has an estimated economic life of three years and the lessor manufactured the equipment at a cost of $80,000. The cost of equipment is held in the lessor's Inventory account.
2. The three lease payments are $33,461.73 each, payable January 1 of Year 1, Year 2, Year 3.

continued

continued from previous page

3. The fair value of the asset at the commencement of the lease is $100,000.
4. The asset reverts to the lessor at the end of the three-year period.
5. The contract requires the lessee to guarantee the residual value of the equipment at the end of the lease for $5,000.
6. The lessor's implicit interest rate is 5%.

Answer the following questions from the perspective of Lessor Inc. which has an accounting period that ends on December 31.

a. Determine the proper lease classification assuming that lease payments are probable.
b. Confirm the lease payment of $33,462 (rounded).
c. Calculate the lease receivable.
d. Prepare a lease receivable schedule.
e. Prepare the lessor's journal entries for Year 1.
f. Show the impact on the lessor's balance sheet and income statement for Year 1.
g. Prepare the lessor's journal entries for Year 2.
h. Show the impact on the lessor's balance sheet and income statement for Year 2.
i. Prepare the lessor's journal entries for Year 3.
j. Show the impact on the lessor's balance sheet and income statement for Year 3.
k. Prepare the lessor's journal entry on January 1 of Year 4. Assume that the inventory was returned with a fair value of $3,000.

Solution

a. Lease Classification

The lease is classified as a *sales-type lease* because at least one of the lease classification criteria is met. The lease term is 100% of the useful life of the asset. Also, the present value of the lease payments is equal to the fair value of the underlying asset of $100,000 indicating that control of the underlying asset has transferred from the lessor to the lessee.

Classification Criteria	Criterion Met
1. Ownership transfer	
2. Purchase option	
3. Lease term length.	✔
4. Present value of lease payments . . .	✔
5. No alternative use.	

	RATE	NPER	PMT	PV	FV	TYPE	Excel Formula
Given	5%	3	(33,461.73)	?	(5,000)	1	=PV(0.05,3,−33461.73,−5000,1)
Solution				$100,000			

b. Calculation of Lease Payment

To calculate the lease payment, enter an expected return on investment of 5% (RATE) from leasing an asset with a fair value of $100,000 (PV) over three years (NPER), with a guaranteed residual value of $5,000 (FV), and with beginning of period payments (TYPE 1), and solve for the payment (PMT). Because there is a guaranteed residual value, the lease payments to achieve a 5% return to the lessor ($33,462) are lower than in **Demo 17-8A** ($34,972). The more value the lessor recovers through the residual, the lower the fixed lease payments.

	RATE	NPER	PMT	PV	FV	TYPE	Excel Formula
Given	5%	3	?	(100,000)	5,000	1	=PMT(0.05,3,−100000,5000,1)
Solution			$33,462				

c. Calculation of Lease Receivable

The lease receivable is equal to $100,000 calculated as the present value of the annual lease payments of $33,462 (PMT) and the guaranteed residual value of $5,000 (FV) as calculated in part a.

d. Lease Receivable Schedule

Date	Lease Payment Dr. Cash Cr. Lease Receivable	Interest on Receivable Dr. Lease Receivable Cr. Interest Revenue	Lease Receivable Change	Lease Receivable
Jan. 1, Year 1 . . .				$100,000
Jan. 1, Year 1 . . .	$ 33,462	$ 0	$ 33,462	66,538
Jan. 1, Year 2 . . .	33,462	3,327	30,135	36,403
Jan. 1, Year 3 . . .	33,462	1,820	31,642	4,761
Jan. 1, Year 4 . . .	5,000*	239**	4,761	0
	$105,386	$5,386	$100,000	

*Amount reclassified to inventory at lease end

** Amounts adjusted to whole numbers to simplify recording of journal entries that follow. If we prepare this schedule in Excel with unlimited decimals, the numbers slightly vary.

continued

continued from previous page

Sales revenue	$100,000
− Cost of goods sold	(80,000)
= Gross profit	$ 20,000

e. Lessor's Journal Entries—Year 1

Gross profit of $20,000 is equal to sales revenue of $100,000 less cost of goods sold of $80,000.

January 1, Year 1—To record lease receivable and derecognize inventory

Assets	=	Liabilities	+	Equity
+100,000				−80,000
Lease Rec				Exp
−80,000				+100,000
Inv				Rev

Lease Receiv		COGS	
100,000		80,000	

Inventory		Sales Rev	
	80,000		100,000

Lease Receivable	100,000	
Cost of Goods Sold	80,000	
Sales Revenue		100,000
Inventory		80,000

January 1, Year 1—To record receipt of lease payment

Assets	=	Liabilities	+	Equity
+33,462				
C:o				
−33,462				
Lease Rec				

Cash		Lease Receiv	
33,462		100,000	33,462

Cash	33,462	
Lease Receivable		33,462

December 31, Year 1—To recognize interest revenue

Assets	=	Liabilities	+	Equity
+3,327				+3,327
Lease Rec				Rev

Lease Receiv		Interest Rev	
100,000	33,462		3,327
3,327			
69,865			

Lease Receivable	3,327	
Interest Revenue...		3,327

f. Lessor's Financial Statements—Year 1

Balance Sheet	Dec. 31, Year 1	Income Statement	Year 1
Assets		Sales revenue...........	$100,000
Current assets		Less cost of goods sold ...	80,000
Net Investment in Lease ($3,327 + $30,135)	$33,462	Gross margin	$ 20,000
Noncurrent assets		Other revenue (expense)	
Net Investment in Lease* ($69,865 − $33,462) ...	36,403	Interest revenue	3,327

*The noncurrent portion is equal to the total lease receivable of $69,865 (calculated as $66,538 + $3,327) less the current lease receivable. In this scenario, the lease receivable (which incorporates the guaranteed residual value) is the only component of Net investment in lease.

g. Lessor's Journal Entries—Year 2

January 1, Year 2—To record lease receipt of payment

Assets	=	Liabilities	+	Equity
+33,462				
C:o				
−33,462				
Lease Rec				

Cash		Lease Receiv	
33,462		100,000	33,462
33,462		3,327	33,462

Cash	33,462	
Lease Receivable		33,462

December 31, Year 2—To recognize interest revenue

Assets	=	Liabilities	+	Equity
+1,820				+1,820
Lease Rec				Rev

Lease Receiv		Interest Rev	
100,000	33,462		3,327
3,327	33,462		1,820
1,820			
38,223			

Lease Receivable	1,820	
Interest Revenue...		1,820

h. Lessor's Financial Statements—Year 2

Balance Sheet	Dec. 31, Year 2	Income Statement	Year 2
Assets		Other revenue (expense)	
Current assets		Interest revenue	$1,820
Net Investment in Lease ($1,820 + $31,642).....	$33,462		
Noncurrent assets			
Net Investment in Lease* ($38,223 − $33,462) ...	4,761		

*The noncurrent portion is equal to the total lease receivable of $38,223 (calculated as $36,403 + $1,820) less the current lease receivable.

i. Lessor's Journal Entries—Year 3

Assets	=	Liabilities	+	Equity
−33,462				
C:o				
−33,462				
Lease Rec				

Cash		Lease Receiv	
33,462		100,000	33,462
33,462		3,327	33,462
33,462		1,820	33,462

January 1, Year 3—To record receipt of lease payment

Cash	33,462	
Lease Receivable		33,462

continued

continued from previous page

December 31, Year 3—To recognize interest revenue

Lease Receivable	239	
Interest Revenue		239

Assets = Liabilities + Equity
+239   +239
Lease Rec   Rev

Lease Receiv		Interest Rev
100,000	33,462	3,327
3,327	33,462	1,820
1,820	33,462	239
239		
5,000		

j. Lessor's Financial Statements—Year 3

Balance Sheet	Dec. 31, Year 3	Income Statement	Year 3
Assets		Other revenue (expense)	
Current assets		Interest revenue	$239
Net Investment in Lease	$5,000		

k. Lessor's Journal Entry at Lease Termination

After the journal entries of Year 3 and the expiration of the lease, the lease receivable has a value of $5,000. When the inventory is returned to the lessor, the lease receivable is derecognized, inventory is recognized for $3,000, and the $2,000 cash payment in satisfaction of the guaranteed residual value ($5,000 – $3,000) is recognized.

January 1, Year 4—To record return of underlying asset to lessor

Inventory	3,000	
Cash	2,000	
Lease Receivable		5,000

Assets = Liabilities + Equity
+3,000
Inv
+2,000
C:o
–5,000
Lease Rec

Cash		Lease Receiv	
33,462		100,000	33,462
33,462		3,327	33,462
33,462		1,820	33,462
2,000		239	5,000
		0	

Inventory
3,000

Unguaranteed Residual Value

The accounting becomes more complex for a sales-type lease when the lease includes an unguaranteed residual value. In this case, the lease standard requires that the lessor deduct the present value of the unguaranteed residual value from both sales revenue and cost of goods sold to avoid overstatement. However, this treatment does not affect the total gross profit that is reported. This treatment is necessary because of the lessor's uncertainty in receiving the unguaranteed residual value at the end of the lease term.

Lessor—Sales-Type Lease with an Unguaranteed Residual Value   **LO17-8**   **DEMO 17-8C**

Now assume the same information for Lessor Inc. in **Demo 17-8B**, except that the lessor reasonably expects an unguaranteed residual value of $5,000 at the end of the lease.
a. Determine the proper lease classification assuming that lease payments are probable.
b. Calculate the net investment in lease, which is equal to the lease receivable plus the present value of the unguaranteed residual value.
c. Prepare the lessor's journal entry at the commencement of the lease to recognize sales revenue.
d. Prepare the lessor's entries for the lease payment on January 1of Year 1, and for the recognition of interest revenue on December 31 of Year 1.
e. Show the impact on the lessor's balance sheet and income statement for Year 1.
f. Assume instead that residual value is only partially guaranteed. The lessor expects the asset to be returned with a fair value of $5,000, but the lessee only guarantees a residual of $3,500. The inventory is returned with a fair value of $3,000. Prepare the lessor's journal entry on January 1 of Year 4.

Solution

a. The lease is classified as a sales-type lease because at least one of the lease classification criteria is met. The lease term is 100% of the useful life of the asset. Also, the present value of the lease payments ($95,681) is greater than 90% of the fair value of the asset of $100,000, indicating control has passed to the lessee.

	RATE	NPER	PMT	PV	FV	TYPE	Excel Formula
Given	5%	3	(33,461.73)	?	0	1	=PV(0.05,3,–33461.73,0,1)
Solution				$95,681			

b. Net investment in lease is equal to $100,000, or the present value of the lease payments calculated above of $95,681 plus the present value of the unguaranteed residual value of $4,319.

	RATE	NPER	PV	FV	TYPE	Excel Formula
Given	5%	3	?	(5,000)	1	=PV(0.05,3,0 –5000,1)
Solution			$4,319			

continued

continued from previous page

c. On January 1 of Year 1, the lessor records Net Investment in Lease and derecognizes Inventory. Both Sales and Cost of Goods sold are reduced by the present value of the unguaranteed residual value.

Assets	=	Liabilities	+	Equity
100,000				–75,681
Inv in Lease				Exp
–80,000				95,681
Inv				Sales Rev

Inv in Lease		Sales	
100,000			95,681

Inventory		COGS	
	80,000	75,681	

January 1, Year 1—To record net investment in lease and derecognize inventory

Net Investment in Lease............................	100,000	
Cost of Goods Sold ($80,000 – $4,319)	75,681	
Sales ($100,000 – $4,319)...........................		95,681
Inventory		80,000

d. The Lease Receivable Schedule in part d of **Demo 17-8B** is adjusted to a Net Investment in Lease Schedule and the amounts are used in the entries that follow.

Date	Lease Payment Dr. Cash Cr. Net Investment in Lease	Interest on Net Investment in Lease Dr. Net Investment in Lease Cr. Interest Revenue	Net Investment in Lease Change	Net Investment in Lease
Jan. 1, Year 1 ...				$100,000
Jan. 1, Year 1 ...	$ 33,462	$ 0	$ 33,462	66,538
Jan. 1, Year 2 ...	33,462	3,327	30,135	36,403
Jan. 1, Year 3 ...	33,462	1,820	31,642	4,761
Jan. 1, Year 4 ...	5,000	239	4,761	0
	$105,386	$5,386	$100,000	

Assets	=	Liabilities	+	Equity
+33,462				
C:o				
–33,462				
Inv in Lease				

Cash		Inv in Lease	
33,462		100,000	33,462

January 1, Year 1—To record receipt of lease payment

Cash	33,462	
Net Investment in Lease............................		33,462

Assets	=	Liabilities	+	Equity
+3,327				+3,327
Inv in Lease				Int Rev

Lease Receiv		Interest Rev	
100,000	33,462		3,327
3,327			

December 31, Year 1—To recognize interest revenue

Net Investment in Lease............................	3,327	
Interest Revenue..................................		3,327

e. **Lessor's Financial Statements—Year 1**

Balance Sheet	Dec. 31, Year 1		Income Statement	Year 1
Assets			Sales revenue...........	$95,681
Current assets			Less cost of goods sold ...	75,681
Net Investment in Lease ($3,327 + $30,135)	$33,462		Gross margin	$ 20,000
Noncurrent assets			Other revenue (expense)	
Net Investment in Lease* ($69,865 – $33,462) ...	36,403		Interest revenue	3,327

*The noncurrent portion is equal to the total net investment in lease of $69,865 (calculated as $66,538 + $3,327) less the current net investment in lease.

f. **Lessor's Journal Entry at Lease Termination with a Partial Residual Guarantee**

Because the lessor based its lease payment on the expected residual value of $5,000, the Net Investment in Lease would still have a value of $5,000. When the inventory is returned, the Net Investment in Lease is derecognized, inventory is recognized for $3,000, cash of $500 is recognized for the lessor payment ($3,500 – $3,000), and the difference of $1,500 is recognized as a loss.

Assets	=	Liabilities	+	Equity
+3,000				–1,500
Inv				Loss
+500				
C:o				
–5,000				
Inv in Lease				

Cash		Inv in Lease	
500		Bal. 5,000	5,000

Inventory		Loss on Lease	
3,000		1,500	

Inventory	3,000	
Cash	500	
Loss on Lease.....................................	1,500	
Net Investment in Lease............................		5,000

Exhibit 17-4 summarizes the treatment of guaranteed and unguaranteed residual value, purchase options, and termination penalties for the lessor.

Accounting for the Lessor	Guaranteed Residual Value	Unguaranteed Residual Value	Purchase Option or Penalty*
PV of lease payment criterion of the lease classification test	Included	Not included	Included
Net investment in lease calculation	Included	Included	Included
Lease payment calculation (fixed payment)	Included	Included	Included

EXHIBIT 17-4

Lessor Accounting for Residual Value, Purchase Options, and Penalties

* Assumes that exercise of the purchase option or termination option is reasonably certain. If the exercise of a purchase option is reasonably certain, residual value is ignored in the lessor's calculations.

LXP

Real World—SALES-TYPE LEASE DISCLOSURE

LXP Industrial Trust, a real estate investment trust, invests in single-tenant warehouse/distribution real estate investments. LXP reported on its balance sheet on December 31, 2023, Investment in sales-type lease, net of approximately $63.5 million (shown net of an allowance for credit losses of $61,000). LXP disclosed the following accounting policy related to sales-type leases.

Investment in Sales-Type Leases Investments in sales-type leases are accounted for under ASC 842 "Leases" ("ASC 842")...If the lease is determined to be a direct financing or sales-type lease, the Company records a net investment in the lease, which is equal to the sum of the lease receivable and the unguaranteed residual asset, discounted at the rate implicit in the lease. Any difference between the fair value of the asset and the net investment in the lease is considered selling profit or loss and is either recognized upon execution of the lease or deferred and recognized over the life of the lease, depending on the lease classification and the collectibility of the minimum lease payments.

Sales-Type Lease by Lessor with a Guaranteed Residual Value LO17-8 REVIEW 17-8

Review

MBC

Lessor Company leased equipment (recorded as inventory) to Lessee Company for a three-year period. Lessor paid $300,000 for the equipment (its fair value) and immediately leased it on January 1. The equipment has an estimated useful life of four years, and the estimated residual value at the end of the lease term is $60,000. Lessor's expected rate of return is 8%. The lessee agreed to guarantee the estimated residual value of $60,000. The first lease payment is due on January 1 and the accounting periods for both entities end on December 31. At the lease termination date, an independent appraiser provided an estimate of the residual value of $25,000. The lessee immediately paid the difference of $35,000 ($60,000 guaranteed residual value minus $25,000, the actual residual value). The lessor's accounting period ends on December 31.

Required

a. Compute the lease payment for the lessor. Compute the lease receivable to be capitalized by the lessor.

b. Provide the entry for the lessor on January 1 to derecognize inventory and record the lease receivable.

c. Provide a schedule of the lease receivable.

d. Provide the entries for the lessor through the lease term to record the lease payments, the year-end adjusting entries, and the lease termination.

More Practice:
BE17-32, BE17-33, E17-31

Solution on p. 17-98.

LO 17-9 Explain the accounting policy election for short-term leases and other lease disclosures

LO 17-9 Overview

Short-term Lease Policy Election
- Lease with a duration of one year or less
- Lessee records lease expense on a straight-line basis over the lease term.
- Lessee does not record a right-of-use asset or a lease liability.

Disclosures
- Qualitative disclosures
- Quantitative disclosures

This section explains the policy election available for short-term leases (leases with a duration of one year or less). We also highlight the general requirements for reporting leases in the financial statements and notes to the financial statements.

Short-Term Leases

A **short-term lease** is defined by the lease standard as a lease with a duration of 12 months or less with no purchase option that the lessee is reasonably expected to exercise. Recall that the lease criterion on the length of a lease requires lessees to consider renewal periods where the lessee is reasonably certain of renewal. Thus, a one-year lease where there is a reasonable certainty that the lessee will renew the lease for another year is *not* considered a one-year lease under this short-term lease exception.

JAN FEB MAR APR
MAY JUN JUL AUG
SEP OCT NOV DEC

ASC Glossary   Short-term lease: A lease that, at the commencement date, has a lease term of 12 months or less and does not include an option to purchase the underlying asset that the lessee is reasonably certain to exercise.

If a lessee identifies a short-term lease, the lessee may *elect* to expense the lease payments on a straight-line basis and not record a right-of-use asset and lease liability as illustrated in **Demo 17-9**. Once a lessee establishes a **short-term lease election** for a class of underlying assets, all future short-term leases for that class should consistently follow the lessee's policy. Otherwise, the company would need to account for a future change in policy as a change in accounting principle. A company would provide a short-term lease disclosure along with a number of qualitative and quantitative disclosures in the notes accompanying the financial statements. The short-term lease exception applies only to the lessee, not the lessor.

842-20-25-2   As an accounting policy, a lessee may elect not to apply the recognition requirements in this Subtopic to short-term leases. Instead, a lessee may recognize the lease payments in profit or loss on a straight-line basis over the lease term and variable lease payments in the period in which the obligation for those payments is incurred . . .

DEMO 17-9   **LO17-9**   **Short-Term Leases**

Demo
MBC

Lessee Inc. enters into a lease with Lessor Inc. for a 6-month rental of a storage unit for use during a construction project. The lease contract includes a 6-month renewal that the lessee is reasonably certain that it will exercise based upon the estimated completion date of the construction project. Because the lease plus the renewal is one year or less, the lease qualifies for the short-term lease exception. The lessee elects to account for the lease as a *short-term lease*. Record the entry for Lessee Inc. in Year 1 if the monthly rent is $10,000. Assume each payment is made at the end of each month.

Solution
The lessee records the following entry for each of the 12 months of the lease period.

Assets	=	Liabilities	+	Equity
−10,000				−10,000
C:o				Exp

Cash		Lease Exp
10,000		10,000

To record monthly lease expense

Lease Expense (Short-Term)	10,000	
Cash		10,000

Financial Statement Reporting of Leases

Lessee Reporting A lessee presents (or discloses) right-of-use lease assets and lease liabilities on its balance sheet separately from each other and from other assets or liabilities. It is common to see material *operating lease* right-of-use assets and liabilities reported separately on the balance sheet. However, *finance lease* right-of-use assets and liabilities are typically embedded in other balance sheet accounts such as fixed assets (for finance lease asset) and long-term debt (for finance lease liability).

842-20-45-1 A lessee shall either present in the statement of financial position or disclose in the notes all of the following:

a. Finance lease right-of-use assets and operating lease right-of-use assets separately from each other and from other assets

b. Finance lease liabilities and operating lease liabilities separately from each other and from other liabilities.

Right-of-use assets and lease liabilities shall be subject to the same considerations as other nonfinancial assets and financial liabilities in classifying them as current and noncurrent in classified statements of financial position.

In income, a lessee reports interest expense and amortization expense for a finance lease as it would report other such expenses. Lease expense for an operating lease would be reported in income from continuing operations.

The objective of lease disclosure is described in the authoritative guidance.

842-20-50-1 The objective of the disclosure requirements is to enable users of financial statements to assess the amount, timing, and uncertainty of cash flows arising from leases. To achieve that objective, a lessee shall disclose qualitative and quantitative information about all of the following:

a. Its leases . . .

b. The significant judgments made in applying the requirements in this Topic to those leases . . .

c. The amounts recognized in the financial statements relating to those leases . . .

Lessor Reporting A lessor of a sales-type (and direct financing) lease presents lease assets separately from other items on its balance sheet and identifies income arising from leases. Conversely, a lessor of an operating lease continues to report assets according to other standards (such as continuing to report assets as property, plant, and equipment).

842-30-45-1 A lessor shall present lease assets (that is, the aggregate of the lessor's net investment in sales-type leases and direct financing leases) separately from other assets in the statement of financial position.

842-30-45-3 A lessor shall either present in the statement of comprehensive income or disclose in the notes income arising from leases. If a lessor does not separately present lease income in the statement of comprehensive income, the lessor shall disclose which line items include lease income in the statement of comprehensive income.

842-30-45-6 A lessor shall present the underlying asset subject to an operating lease in accordance with other Topics.

Qualitative Items—Lessee and Lessor The following **qualitative items** should be disclosed in the notes accompanying the financial statements of both lessees and lessors.

1. Information about the nature of leases, including:

   • Lease description.

   • Basis on which variable lease payments are determined.

   • Terms and conditions of options to extend or terminate a lease.

   • Terms and conditions of residual value guarantees provided by a lessee.

   • The restrictions or covenants imposed by leases.

2. Information about leases creating significant rights and obligations that have not commenced.

3. Information about significant assumptions including determining whether a lease exists, allocation between lease and nonlease components, and the determination of a discount rate.

Quantitative Items—Lessee The following **quantitative items** should be disclosed in the notes accompanying the financial statements of lessees.

■ Total lease costs including the following:

   • Finance lease cost.   • Short-term lease cost.

   • Operating lease cost.   • Variable lease cost.

■ Cash paid for amounts included in the measurement of lease liabilities, segregated between operating and financing cash flows.

■ Supplemental noncash information on lease liabilities due to obtaining right-of-use assets.

■ Weighted-average remaining lease term and weighted-average discount rate.

- Maturity analysis showing the undiscounted cash flows on an annual basis for a minimum of each of the first five years and the total for the remaining years (separately for finance and operating leases).

Quantitative Items—Lessor The following **quantitative items** should be disclosed in the notes accompanying the financial statements of lessors.

- Profit or loss recognized at the commencement date.

- Interest revenue either in aggregate or separated by components of the net investment in the lease.

- For operating leases, lease income relating to lease payments.

- Lease income relating to variable lease payments not included in measurement of a lease receivable.

- Information about the management of risk associated with the residual value of leased assets.

- Significant changes in the balance of its unguaranteed residual assets and deferred selling profit on direct financing leases.

- Maturity analysis of its lease receivables, showing the undiscounted cash flows to be received on an annual basis for a minimum of each of the first five years and a total of the amounts for the remaining years.

MICROSOFT

Real World—DISCLOSURE OF FUTURE MINIMUM LEASE PAYMENTS

Microsoft Corporation disclosed the following future minimum lease payments in a recent Form 10-K.

Maturities of lease liabilities were as follows.

Year Ending June 30 (In millions)	Operating Leases	Finance Leases
2025	$ 4,124	$ 3,311
2026	3,549	3,021
2027	2,981	3,037
2028	2,405	3,026
2029	1,924	2,638
Thereafter	6,587	19,116
Total lease payments	21,570	34,149
Less imputed interest	(2,493)	(7,004)
Total	$19,077	$27,145

REVIEW 17-9	▶ LO17-9	Accounting for a Short-Term Lease

Review

MBC

More Practice:
BE17-38, E17-44

Solution on p. 17-99.

Lessee Inc. entered into a contract on January 1 to lease a vehicle for one year, with monthly payments of $500 due at the end of each month. The vehicle has a fair value of $35,000. The lease agreement does not contain an option for purchase or renewal. The lessor's implicit rate of return is 6%. Lessee Inc. recognizes the lease under the short-term lease accounting election. Prepare the entries for Lessee Inc. for the year related to the lease.

Management Judgment

Identifying a Lease

Leases are sometimes embedded in arrangements such as supply contracts, data center agreements, or outsourcing agreements. At the inception of a contract, judgment is involved in determining whether an arrangement includes an embedded lease. Recall that a lease gives the right to control the use of an identified asset to a lessee in exchange for consideration for a period of time. Any *nonlease* components not meeting the criteria must be identified and separately accounted for (unless management elects the practical expedient explained on p. 17-18).

Classifying a Lease

In applying the lease classification test, management must determine whether the lease term is a *major part* of the remaining economic life of the underlying asset. Management must also determine whether the present value of the lease payments is *substantially all* of the fair value of the underlying asset. Although a bright-line threshold of 75% for the economic life test is described in the accounting guidance as a "reasonable approach" (along with the 90% threshold for the fair value test), the accounting standards do *not* require the bright-line tests, leaving room for management judgment. In addition, if the contract includes a renewal option or a purchase option, management must determine whether it is reasonably certain that the company will renew the lease or take advantage of a purchase option. These decisions are often not clear-cut in practice.

Accounting for a Lease

Management must value the following items, and each requires judgment.

- Estimated economic life of equipment and its estimated residual value
- Fair value of the underlying asset at inception of the lease.
- Lessee's incremental borrowing rate.
- Lease term.

Amounts associated with these items require management to make assumptions and provide estimations. For example, the lease term includes any renewal or termination options that a lessee is *reasonably certain* to exercise. The estimated economic life of equipment depends on how a company plans to use and maintain the equipment. The fair value of an underlying asset would be more difficult to determine if the asset were self-constructed or purchased years earlier. The residual value is subjective and influenced by the lease term and the expected usage of the asset. The lessee's incremental borrowing rate varies by each underlying asset because it depends on a hypothetical borrowing under similar terms to the lease. The authoritative guidance requires disclosing qualitative and quantitative information about the judgments made in applying the lease standard.

Account for direct financing leases by the lessor

APPENDIX 17A
LO 17-10

Typically, a lease that does not meet any of the lease classification criteria would be classified as an operating lease by the lessor. However, there is an exception for lessors when a third-party guarantee of the residual value is involved. A lease is classified as a *direct financing lease* if the lessor determines that control of the underlying asset is transferred to the lessee when taking into account a guarantee of the residual value by a third party (typically an insurance company).

For a lease to be classified as a **direct financing lease**, it must first *not* qualify for a sales-type lease. Second, the lease must meet the present value of lease payments criterion **but** only by considering both the present value of the lease payments (as previously defined) *plus the present value of a residual guaranteed by a third party, arranged by the lessor.* In addition, the collection of the lease payments and any amounts necessary to satisfy a guaranteed residual value is considered probable.

Lessor Accounting—Direct Financing Lease
- Control passes to the lessee with an involvement by a third party
- Defer selling profit at lease commencement
- Recognize selling loss at lease commencement
- Derecognize underlying asset and recognize lease receivable
- Recognize interest revenue over lease term using the effective interest method

LO 17-10 Overview

Direct Financing Lease

| Does not qualify for sales-type lease | Meets lease criterion #4 when considering third-party residual guarantee | Collection of lease payments and guaranteed residual value is probable |

Lease Classification Criteria
1. Ownership transfer
2. Purchase option
3. Lease term length
4. PV of lease payments
5. No alternative use

842-10-25-3   *b.* A lessor shall classify the lease as either a direct financing lease or an operating lease. A lessor shall classify the lease as an operating lease unless both of the following criteria are met, in which case the lessor shall classify the lease as a direct financing lease:

1. The present value of the sum of the lease payments and any residual value guaranteed by the lessee that is not already reflected in the lease payments . . . and/or any other third party unrelated to the lessor equals or exceeds substantially all of the fair value of the underlying asset.

2. It is probable that the lessor will collect the lease payments plus any amount necessary to satisfy a residual value guarantee.

A summary of the accounting for the lessor for a direct financing lease follows. Note that the accounting guidance defines a net investment in the lease for a direct financing lease differently than for a sales-type lease.

Balance Sheet	Income Statement
Recognize a net investment in lease as defined below for a direct financing lease and derecognize the underlying asset.	Defer selling profit but recognize selling loss at the commencement of the lease.
Increase the net investment in lease by interest revenue and decrease the net investment in lease for lease payments collected.	Recognize interest revenue on the net investment in lease using the effective interest method.

Glossary   **Net Investment in the Lease**   For a direct financing lease, the sum of the lease receivable and the unguaranteed residual asset, net of any deferred selling profit.

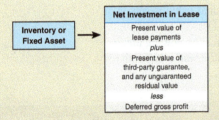

The lessor records a net investment in lease and derecognizes the leased asset. The net investment in lease is equal to the lease receivable (including the present value of the third-party guarantee) net of deferred gross profit. A selling loss would be recognized at the lease commencement. The decrease in the net investment in lease causes the implicit rate of the lease to increase. The lessor computes the new discount rate that equates the balance in the net investment in lease to the lease payments and residual value. The new rate is used to produce a net investment in lease schedule to determine interest revenue recognized over the lease term.

DEMO 17-10   ▶   **LO17-10**   **Lessor—Direct Financing Lease**

Demo

MBC

Lessor Inc. enters into a 5-year lease of equipment with Lessee Inc. on January 1 of Year 1. The equipment is not specialized in nature and has a 10-year economic life, and ownership is not transferred to the lessee at lease end. In addition, the following information applies to this lease.

- Lease payments of $12,800 are due at the end of each year.
- The expected residual value of the equipment at lease end is $12,000. The lessor contracts with a third party (an insurance company) to ensure the guaranteed residual value of $12,000.
- The rate implicit in the lease is 4.909%.
- The lessor concludes that the collection of lease payments (including the amount insured by a third party on the residual value) is probable.
- The fair value of the equipment is $65,000 and the carrying value of the equipment (recorded as inventory) to the lessor is $60,000.

Answer the following questions from the perspective of Lessor Inc. which has an accounting period that ends on December 31.

a. Determine the proper lease classification.
b. Record the net investment in lease on January 1 of Year 1.
c. Prepare the lessor's journal entry on December 31 of Year 1.
d. Prepare the lessor's journal entry at lease end.

continued

continued from previous page

Solution

a. Lease Classification

Without considering the guaranteed residual value by a third party, the lease does not meet the criteria to qualify as a sales-type lease.

	Lease Classification Criteria	Analysis	Lease Criterion Met
1.	Ownership transfer	Asset reverts to the lessor at the end of the five-year period.	
2.	Purchase option	Lease does not contain a purchase option,	
3.	Lease term length	Five-year length of the lease is < 75% of the equipment's useful life.	
4.	PV of lease payments	$55,557 (PV of lease payments) < $58,500 (90% of fair value of $65,000).	
5.	No alternative use	There are alternative uses for the equipment as the lessor often leases this equipment to other companies.	

	RATE	NPER	PMT	PV	Excel Formula
Given	4.909%	5	(12,800)	?	=PV(0.04909,5,–12800)
Solution				$55,557	

The lease does not meet any of the lease classification criteria, thus, it is not classified as a sales-type lease. However, in considering the guarantee by a third party for the residual value, the lease does meet the present value of lease payments test.

4.	PV of lease payments	$65,000 (PV of lease payments) > $58,500 (90% of fair value of $65,000)	✔

Therefore, the lease meets the criteria of a direct financing lease, given that the payments are considered probable.

	RATE	NPER	PMT	PV	FV	Excel Formula
Given	4.909%	5	(12,800)	?	(12,000)	=PV(0.04909,5,–12800,–12000)
Solution				$65,000		

b. Initial Recording of the Net Investment in Lease

In the case of a direct financing lease, a net investment in lease is recorded of $60,000. The net investment in lease is equal to the lease receivable of $65,000, net of the deferred gross profit of $5,000 ($65,000 – $60,000).

January 1, Year 1—To record net investment in lease

Net Investment in Lease..............................	60,000	
Inventory		60,000

Assets = Liabilities + Equity
+60,000
Inv in Lease
–60,000
Inv

Lease Receiv, Net	Inventory
60,000		60,000

Calculation of Net Investment in Lease

Lease receivable*.........................	$65,000
Deferred gross profit.......................	(5,000)
Net Investment in Lease....................	$60,000

*Including present value of third party guarantee on residual

c. Lessor's Journal Entry—Year 1

The net investment in lease is amortized over the lease term using the effective interest method, where the discount rate is a rate that equates the balance in the net investment in lease to the lease payments and residual value.

Discount Rate....................	7.583%

We see that this rate is higher than the rate implicit in the lease of 4.909% because we are using the net investment in lease balance as the present value instead of the fair value of the equipment and recognizing the interest revenue of the deferred gross profit over the lease term. Using this discount rate of 7.583%, we can construct the amortization schedule of the net investment in lease using the effective interest method. In this example, the lease payment date falls on the company's year-end reporting date.

	RATE	NPER	PMT	PV	FV	Excel Formula
Given	?	5	12,800	(60,000)	12,000	=RATE(5, 12800, –60000, 12000)
Solution	7.583%					

continued

continued from previous page

Net Investment in Lease Schedule

Date	Lease Payment — Dr. Cash Cr. Net Investment in Lease	Interest on Net Investment in Lease — Dr. Net Investment in Lease Cr. Interest Revenue[a]	Net Investment in Lease Change	Net Investment in Lease
Jan. 1, Year 1 . . .				$60,000
Dec. 31, Year 1 . . .	$ 12,800	$4,550	$ 8,250	51,750
Dec. 31, Year 2 . . .	12,800	3,924	8,876	42,874
Dec. 31, Year 3 . . .	12,800	3,251	9,549	33,325
Dec. 31, Year 4 . . .	12,800	2,527	10,273	23,052
Dec. 31, Year 5 . . .	24,800[b]	1,748	23,052	0

[a] Interest revenue is equal to 7.583% multiplied by the beginning-of-period net investment in lease balance.
[b] Final payment includes the lease payment of $12,800 and the residual value of $12,000 to be reclassified to inventory.

The entry to record the first lease payment uses amounts from the schedule above.

Assets = Liabilities + Equity
+12,800   +4,550
C:o   Rev
−8,250
Inv in Lease

Cash		Inv in Lease	
12,800		60,000	8,250
		51,750	

Interest Rev	
	4,550

December 31, Year 1—To record receipt of lease payment

Cash	12,800	
Net Investment in Lease ($12,800 − $4,550)		8,250
Interest Revenue.		4,550

The net investment in lease is recorded in the balance sheet as $51,750* ($60,000 − $8,250) on December 31 of Year 1. The lessor will continue to amortize the net investment in lease over the term of the lease.

*The net investment in lease of $51,750 is equal to the gross lease receivable of $55,391 less the deferred gross profit of $3,641. *Gross lease receivable* is equal to the original lease receivable of $65,000 less the amortization of $9,609 [($65,000 × 0.04909) − $12,800]. *Deferred gross profit* is equal to $5,000 (original gross profit) less the amortization of $1,359 [($60,000 × 0.07583) − ($65,000 × 0.04909)]. The components of net investment in lease will be disclosed in the notes accompanying the financial statements.

d. **Lessor's Journal Entry—Lease End**

At the end of the lease, assuming that the residual value was equal to $12,000, the lessor records the following entry.

Assets = Liabilities + Equity
+12,000
Inv
−12,000
Inv in Lease

Inventory		Inv in Lease	
12,000		Bal. 12,000	12,000
		0	

December 31, Year 5—To record inventory at lease end

Inventory	12,000	
Net Investment in Lease.		12,000

REVIEW 17-10 ▶ LO17-10   **Accounting for Direct Financing Leases**

Review

MBC

On January 1, Lessor Inc. entered into a 4-year lease agreement with Lessee Inc. to lease equipment with a useful life of six years. The equipment will be returned to the lessor at the end of the lease term and is expected to have alternative uses. The lessor obtained a guarantee from a third party (insurance company) for the expected residual of $5,000 at the end of the lease term. Lease payments are $10,000 due annually at the end of each year. The implicit rate of the lease is 6.65682%. The fair value of the equipment is $38,000 and the carrying value is $35,000.

a. Determine the proper classification of the lease for the lessor.

b. Record the lessor's entry on January 1.

More Practice:
AppBE17-1, AppBE17-2,
AppE17-1

Solution on p. 17-99.

c. Compute the discount rate used to amortize the net investment in lease.

d. Prepare the schedule to amortize the net investment in lease.

e. Prepare the lessor's entry at year-end on December 31.

Explain lease modifications and lease remeasurements

Lease modifications are changes to the terms and conditions of a contract that take place after a lease is in effect. For example, a lease term may be extended or terminated, or the timing of lease payments may be adjusted. A lease modification is treated as (1) a separate lease or (2) a modification to an existing lease depending on whether the modification grants additional rights at a **standalone price** (price at which a lessee would purchase the right separately). The treatment of lease modifications, along with cases for lease classification reassessment and remeasurement, are described as follows and illustrated in **Demo 17-11.**

> **Lease Modifications**
> - Does *not* grant the lessee additional rights at standalone price: Results in a reassessment of lease classification and remeasurement
> - Does grant the lessee additional rights at standalone price: Results in a new lease

LO 17-11 Overview

Lease Modifications

If a modification grants the lessee an additional right at a standalone price, a **separate lease** is recorded at the lease modification date. This means that a separate lease (apart from the original lease) is created with additional rights at standalone prices. If these conditions are not met, the lease is considered to be a **single, modified lease**. In the case of a single, modified lease, the lease classification is reassessed and the lease liability is remeasured accordingly.

Modification with additional rights at standalone prices? → **Yes** → Treat Modification as a Separate Lease

→ **No** → Treat as a Single, Modified Lease
- Reassess lease classification
- Remeasure accordingly

842-10-25-8   An entity shall account for a modification to a contract as a separate contract (that is, separate from the original contract) when both of the following conditions are present:

a. The modification grants the lessee an additional right of use not included in the original lease (for example, the right to use an additional asset).

b. The lease payments increase commensurate with the standalone price for the additional right of use, adjusted for the circumstances of the particular contract . . .

842-10-25-9   If a lease is modified and that modification is not accounted for as a separate contract in accordance with paragraph 842-10-25-8, the entity shall reassess the classification of the lease in accordance with paragraph 842-10-25-1 as of the effective date of the modification.

Additional Cases of Lease Classification Reassessment and Lease Remeasurement

For the lessee, a lease classification reassessment and/or a remeasurement of a lease liability may take place for reasons *other than a lease modification.* A lessor, on the other hand, is not required to reassess a lease unless the lease contract is modified.

A lessee reassesses its lease classification and remeasures its lease payments in the following cases: change in lease term, and a change in whether the lessee is reasonably certain to exercise an option to purchase the underlying asset.

A lessee remeasures the lease payments (without a lease classification reassessment) in the following cases: resolution of a contingency affecting variable lease payments such that those payments become fixed, and a change in the probable amounts owed for a guaranteed residual value.

842-10-25-1   . . . In addition, a lessee also shall reassess the lease classification after the commencement date if there is a change in the lease term or the assessment of whether the lessee is reasonably certain to exercise an option to purchase the underlying asset . . .

> **Remeasure a Lease Liability**
> - Modification not treated as a separate lease
> - Change in assessment of lease term or exercise of purchase option
> - Change in probable amount owed for guaranteed residual value
> - Contingency resolution making variable payments fixed

842-10-35-4   A lessee shall remeasure the lease payments if any of the following occur:

a. The lease is modified, and that modification is not accounted for as a separate contract . . .

b. A contingency upon which some or all of the variable lease payments that will be paid over the remainder of the lease term are based is resolved such that those payments now meet the definition of lease payments. For example, an event occurs that results in variable lease payments that were linked to the performance or use of the underlying asset becoming fixed payments for the remainder of the lease term. However, a change in a reference index or a rate upon which some or all of the variable lease payments in the contract are based does not constitute the resolution of a contingency subject to (b). (See paragraph 842-10-35-5 for guidance on the remeasurement of variable lease payments that depend on an index or a rate.)

c. There is a change in any of the following:

1. The lease term . . . A lessee shall determine the revised lease payments on the basis of the revised lease term.
2. The assessment of whether the lessee is reasonably certain to exercise or not to exercise an option to purchase the underlying asset . . . A lessee shall determine the revised lease payments to reflect the change in the assessment of the purchase option.
3. Amounts probable of being owed by the lessee under residual value guarantees. A lessee shall determine the revised lease payments to reflect the change in amounts probable of being owed by the lessee under residual value guarantees.

In the case of remeasurement, the lease liability is remeasured and the adjustment to the lease liability is applied to the right-of-use asset. Generally, the lease liability is remeasured using the new information and any required changes are treated prospectively, similar to a change in estimate.

842-20-35-4   After the commencement date, a lessee shall remeasure the lease liability to reflect changes to the lease payments as described in paragraphs 842-10-35-4 through 35-5. A lessee shall recognize the amount of the remeasurement of the lease liability as an adjustment to the right-of-use asset . . .

The discount rate used for the remeasurement is updated at the time of remeasurement with the following exceptions. In the three cases outlined below in the authoritative guidance, the discount rate at the time of the lease commencement is used.

842-20-35-5   If there is a remeasurement of the lease liability in accordance with paragraph 842-20-35-4, the lessee shall update the discount rate for the lease at the date of remeasurement on the basis of the remaining lease term and the remaining lease payments unless the remeasurement of the lease liability is the result of one of the following:

a. A change in the lease term or the assessment of whether the lessee will exercise an option to purchase the underlying asset and the discount rate for the lease already reflects that the lessee has an option to extend or terminate the lease or to purchase the underlying asset.
b. A change in amounts probable of being owed by the lessee under a residual value guarantee (see paragraph 842-10-35-4(c)(3)).
c. A change in the lease payments resulting from the resolution of a contingency upon which some or all of the variable lease payments that will be paid over the remainder of the lease term are based (see paragraph 842-10-35-4(b)).

DEMO 17-11 ▶   **LO17-11**   **Lease Modifications and Lease Remeasurements**

Demo

MBC

Lease modifications resulting in a separate lease or modification to an existing lease for a lessee and a lessor are illustrated in the following three examples.

Example One—Lease Modification Resulting in a Separate (New) Lease
Lessee Corp. signs a 3-year lease contract to rent 500 square feet of office space from Lessor Corp. for $1,000 per month. At the end of the first year, Lessee Corp. and Lessor Corp. agree to amend the contract to include an additional 200 square feet of office space in the same building for the remaining two years of the lease. Lessee Corp pays an additional $400 per month for the additional space. The additional rent is the going rate for rental of office space ($2 per square foot). Lessee Corp. will make one monthly payment of $1,400 per month after the modification. Determine whether the lease modification results in a separate lease or a lease remeasurement.

Solution
Lessee Corp. receives an additional right-of-use at a standalone price. Thus, the modification results in a new and separate lease. Lessee Corp. would account for the following items separately:

- Original lease for 3 years of 500 square feet.
- New lease for 2 years of 200 square feet.

The accounting for the original lease is not impacted. The new lease would be analyzed as any other new lease, starting with the lease classification analysis.

Example Two—Modification of an Existing Lease Leading to Lease Remeasurement
Lessee Corp. signs a 3-year lease contract to rent 500 square feet of office space with Lessor Corp. for $1,000 per month. At the end of the first year, Lessee Corp. and Lessor Corp. agree to amend the contract to include an additional 200 square feet of office space in the same building for the remaining two years of the lease. Lessee Corp. pays an additional $200 per month for the additional space.

continued

continued from previous page

The additional rent at $1 per square foot is offered at a significant discount under the going rate of $2 per square foot. Lessee Corp. will make one monthly payment of $1,200 per month after the modification. Determine whether the lease modification results in a separate lease or a lease remeasurement.

Solution
In this case, the modification is considered an extension of the current lease because the additional rent is not at a standalone price. As a result, the current lease classification would be reassessed. After the lease classification is determined, the lease would be accounted for accordingly.

Example Three—Event Leading to Lease Remeasurement
On January 1 of Year 1, Lessee Corp. signs a lease contract with Lessor Corp. to lease equipment with an estimated useful life of six years. The lease has a 5-year term with no renewal option. Annual lease payments are $100,000 beginning on January 1 of Year 1. The lessee's discount rate is 5%. The lease contains a purchase option at the end of the lease for $30,000, but Lessee Corp. is not reasonably certain that it will exercise the purchase option. Lessee Corp. appropriately records the lease as a finance lease. The discount rate does not reflect the purchase option.

On January 1 of Year 3, Lessee Corp. now reasonably expects to purchase the equipment at the end of the lease term because of a significant increase in the sales forecasts of products produced by the equipment. After evaluating the classification criteria, Lessee Corp. determines that the lease remains a finance lease.

On the date of remeasurement of January 1 of Year 3 (before the lease payment is made), Lessee Corp.'s incremental borrowing rate is 4% and the carrying value of the right-of-use asset and lease liability are $272,757 and $185,941, respectively.

Record the entry required on January 1 of Year 3.

Solution
The lease liability is remeasured using the updated discount rate because the lessee changed the assessment of whether to exercise a purchase option.

	RATE	NPER	PMT	PV	FV	TYPE	Excel Formula
Given	4%	3	(100,000)	?	(30,000)	1	=PV(0.04,3,−100000,−30000,1)
Solution				$315,279			

The revised lease liability is $315,279, which is an increase of $129,338 ($315,279 − $185,941). The increase to the liability is recorded as an adjustment to the right-of-use asset.

Assets = Liabilities + Equity
+129,338   +129,338
ROU Asset   Lease Liab

January 1, Year 3—To remeasure lease liability

Right-of-Use Asset.	129,338	
Lease Liability		129,338

ROU Asset		Lease Liab	
Bal. 272,757			185,941 Bal.
129,338			129,338
402,095			315,279

Lease Modifications and Lease Remeasurements   LO17-11   REVIEW 17-11

Review

MBC

Determine whether the following changes would result in a (1) new lease (2) remeasurement, or (3) lease classification reassessment and remeasurement.

Lease Scenario	(1) New Lease, (2) Remeasurement, or (3) Lease Classification Reassessment and Remeasurement
a. Lessee Inc. guarantees the residual value of a vehicle (underlying) at the end of the lease term. The lessee now anticipates exceeding the allotted miles of the vehicle, causing the lessee's estimate of the residual value to drop by $5,000.	
b. A lessee of a manufacturing facility expands its current lease to include additional warehouse space at a standalone lease price.	
c. An existing lease was modified to extend the lease for an additional two years.	
d. Lessee Inc. unexpectedly disposed of a purchased vehicle during the year. This event caused Lessee Inc. to now reasonably expect to exercise a purchase option on a leased vehicle at the end of its lease term in two years, while before, a purchase was not expected by the lessee.	

More Practice:
AppBE17-3, AppE17-2, AppE17-3

Solution on p. 17-99.

Describe the difference in accounting for a sale-leaseback versus a failed sale

Sale-Leaseback or Failed Sale

- Sale-leaseback
  - Control of asset is transferred to the buyer
  - Lessee records a sale and accounts for an operating lease
- Failed sale
  - Control of asset is not transferred to the buyer
  - Lessee records a finance liability

Sale-leaseback transactions are essentially financing transactions. In a sale-leaseback, one party (seller/lessee) sells an asset to another party (buyer/lessor) and then simultaneously leases the same asset back from the buyer.

Companies engage in sale-leaseback transactions for a variety of reasons. For a lessee, a sale-leaseback reduces exposure to the risk of owning assets and provides an immediate cash inflow. If a company owns fully depreciated assets that afford no tax savings beyond maintenance and insurance expenses, selling the equipment and leasing it back may increase tax benefits through deductible lease payments.

In the majority of sale-leaseback transactions, the sale of assets generates immediate cash. If liquidity is a problem, or if expansion capital is needed, the sale-leaseback of assets (without giving up operating possession) provides an immediate inflow of cash of up to 100% of the asset's current fair value. In contrast, asset-secured bank loans are typically limited to 75% or 80% of the asset's fair value. The lessor, on the other hand, is at an advantage in that the earnings on the leaseback arrangement may be higher than under conventional loans.

In accounting for a sale-leaseback, it is important to determine whether the buyer has obtained control of the asset to record a sale of the asset. In determining whether a sale has taken place, a review of the indicators in the revenue recognition standard may be helpful: buyer has a right to payment, legal title, physical possession, significant risks and rewards of ownership, and has accepted the asset. See Chapter 7 for further discussion on these indicators. Not all indicators must be met for a sale to have taken place. Another factor in determining whether control has transferred is through a review of the lease classification. If a seller classifies a leaseback as a finance lease, no sale has occurred and this would be considered a **failed sale**. Classifying a lease as a finance lease indicates an effective purchase of an asset and not a lease. On the other hand, if a seller classifies a leaseback as an operating lease, a sale has occurred and would be appropriately recorded as a lease. We illustrate the accounting for a sale-leaseback and a failed sale in **Demo 17-12**.

If a transfer of an asset is *considered a sale*, the seller/lessee accounts for the transaction as follows.

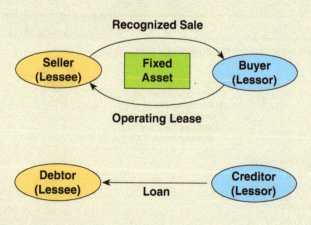

- Recognize the sales price when buyer/lessor takes control of asset.
- Derecognize the carrying amount of asset and record a gain or loss.
- Account for the operating lease as discussed previously in this chapter.

If a transfer of the asset is *not considered a sale* (also called a failed sale), the debtor/lessee accounts for the transaction as follows.

- Do not adjust the carrying value of asset at the transaction date but continue to depreciate the asset over its useful life.
- Recognize "sales" proceeds as a loan.
- Allocate payments to interest expense and to principal reduction of the loan over the lease term.

Sale-Leaseback and Failed Sale   LO17-12 ◀ DEMO 17-12

Demo

MBC

Example One—To Record Sale-Leaseback

To obtain an immediate cash flow, Merill Co. negotiated a sale-leaseback agreement with Leasing Solutions Inc. On January 1, Merill Co. sells a warehouse to Leasing Solutions Inc. for $95,000, the fair value of the warehouse. The warehouse is carried on Merill's books at $80,000 (cost of $200,000 less accumulated depreciation of $120,000) and has an estimated remaining useful economic life of 10 years (total life, 25 years).

In conjunction with the sale of the warehouse, Merill Co. and Leasing Solutions Inc. enter into a 5-year lease. The lease contains no transfer of title or purchase option, and the warehouse could have alternative uses as the warehouse is used primarily for storage. The implicit rate of the lease is 8%, known by the lessee. Annual lease payments, starting January 1 are $16,890, due at the end of each year. The lessor estimates that the warehouse will have a $40,500 residual value that is *not* guaranteed by the lessee. Answer the following questions from the perspective of Merill Co.

a. Determine the appropriate lease classification.
b. Prepare Merill's journal entries on January 1.
c. Prepare Merill's journal entries at year-end on December 31.

Solution

a. **Lease Classification**

To determine whether control of the warehouse has transferred from Leasing Solutions Inc. (Lessor) to Merill Co. (Lessee) it is necessary to determine the classification of the lease.

	Lease Classification Criteria	Analysis	Lease Criterion Met
1.	Ownership transfer	Asset reverts to the lessor at the end of the five-year period.	
2.	Purchase option	Lease does not contain a purchase option.	
3.	Lease term length	Length of the lease is only 50% of the economic life of warehouse.	
4.	PV of lease payments	$67,437 (PV of lease payments) < $85,500 (90% of fair value of $95,000).	
5.	No alternative use	There are alternative uses for the warehouse.	

	RATE	NPER	PMT	PV	Excel Formula
Given	8%	5	(16,890)	?	=PV(0.08,5,–16890)
Solution				$67,437	

None of the lease classification criteria are met, which indicates that the lease is classified as an operating lease. Because the lease does not transfer control to the lessee, the transaction is treated as a sale-leaseback for reporting purposes.

b. **Lessee's Journal Entries—January 1**

Merill Inc. records a gain on the sale of the warehouse to Leasing Solutions Inc. as follows.

January 1—To record gain on sale of warehouse

Cash	95,000	
Accumulated Depreciation.	120,000	
Warehouse		200,000
Gain on Sale-Leaseback.		15,000

Assets = Liabilities + Equity
+95,000   +15,000
Cash   Gain
+120,000
AD
–200,000
Whouse

Cash		Accum Deprec	
95,000		120,000	120,000 Bal.

Warehouse		Gain—Leaseback	
Bal. 200,000	200,000		15,000

Also, on the same day, Merill Inc. records a right-of-use asset and lease liability related to the operating lease.

January 1—To record right-of-use asset and lease liability

Right-of-Use Asset.	67,437	
Lease Liability		67,437

Assets = Liabilities + Equity
+67,437   +67,437
ROU Asset   Lease Liab

ROU Asset		Lease Liab	
67,437			67,437

c. **Lessee's Journal Entries—December 31**

On December 31, Merill Inc. records the following entries related to the first lease payment obtained from the partial schedules included below.

continued

continued from previous page

Assets	=	Liabilities	+	Equity
−11,495		+5,395		−16,890
ROU Asset		Lease Liab		Exp

ROU Asset		Lease Liab	
67,437	11,495		67,437
55,942			5,395

	Lease Exp	
	16,890	

Assets	=	Liabilities	+	Equity
−16,890		−16,890		
C:o		Lease Liab		

Cash		Lease Liab	
95,000	16,890	16,890	67,437
			5,395
			55,942

December 31—To record lease expense

Lease Expense	16,890	
Lease Liability		5,395
Right-of-Use Asset.		11,495

December 31—To record lease payment

Lease Liability	16,890	
Cash		16,890

Lease Liability Schedule (Partial)

Date	Lease Payment	Interest on Liability	Lease Liability Change	Lease Liability
Jan. 1 . . .				$67,437
Dec. 31 . . .	$16,890	$5,395	$11,495	55,942

Right-of-Use Asset Schedule (Partial)

Date	Lease Expense	Interest on Liability	Right-of-Use Asset Change	Right-of-Use Asset
Jan. 1 . . .				$67,437
Dec. 31 . . .	$16,890	$5,395	$11,495	55,942

Example Two—To Record a Failed Sale

Assume the same circumstances as Example One, except that the lease term is 8 years and the payments are now $16,531.40. Answer the following questions from the perspective of Merill Co.

a. Determine the appropriate lease classification.
b. Prepare Merill's journal entry at January 1.
c. Prepare Merill's journal entries at December 31.

Solution
a. **Lease Classification**

	Lease Classification Criteria	Analysis	Lease Criterion Met
1.	Ownership transfer	Asset reverts to the lessor at the end of the five-year period.	
2.	Purchase option	Lease does not contain a purchase option.	
3.	Lease term length	Length of the lease is 80% of the economic life of warehouse.	✔
4.	PV of lease payments	$95,000 (PV of lease payments) > $85,500 (90% of fair value of $95,000).	✔
5.	No alternative use	There are alternative uses for the warehouse.	

Criterion 4 table:

	RATE	NPER	PMT	PV	Excel Formula
Given	8%	8	(16,531.40)	?	=PV(0.08,8,−16531.40)
Solution				$95,000	

The lease qualifies as a finance lease because two lease criteria are met. This qualification as a finance lease precludes the recording of a sale of the warehouse to Leasing Solutions Inc. Thus, this transaction will be recorded similarly to a loan.

b. **Lessee's Journal Entry—January 1**

For a failed sale, the transaction results in the recording of a note payable by Merill.

Assets	=	Liabilities	+	Equity
+95,000		+95,000		
C:f		NP		

Cash		Note Payable	
95,000			95,000

January 1—To record note payable on failed sale

Cash	95,000	
Note Payable		95,000

c. **Lessee's Journal Entries—December 31**

On December 31, the lease payment and depreciation expense are recorded as follows.

continued

continued from previous page

December 31—To record lease payment

Interest Expense (0.08 × $95,000)...................	7,600	
Note Payable ($16,531 − $7,600)	8,931	
Cash................................		16,531

Assets = Liabilities + Equity
−8,931   −8,931   −7,600
C:f   NP   Exp
−7,600
C:o

Cash		Note Payable	
95,000	16,531	8,931	95,000

Interest Exp	
7,600	

December 31—To record depreciation expense

Depreciation Expense ($80,000/10)...................	8,000	
Accumulated Depreciation..........................		8,000

Assets = Liabilities + Equity
−8,000   −8,000
AD   Exp

Accum Deprec		Deprec Exp	
	8,000	8,000	

Accounting for Sale-Leaseback   LO17-12   REVIEW 17-12

Wal-Market Inc. sells a building currently used to Diversified Investors for $9 million, its current fair value. Prior to the sale, the carrying value of the building was $7 million (original cost of $15 million). The estimated remaining useful life of the building is 20 years, with no estimated residual value; straight-line depreciation is used. On January 1, Wal-Market Inc. signed a 15-year noncancellable leaseback agreement. The lessee's incremental borrowing rate is 8% and the lessor's implicit rate is unknown to the lessee. Annual payments of $1,051,466 start on December 31. The lease agreement does not contain a purchase option, the lessee does not guarantee a residual value, and the building does not revert to the lessee at lease end. The building would have alternative uses at lease end.

a. Determine the lease classification for Wal-Market Inc.
b. Record the journal entries for Wal-Market Inc. for the year.

Review

MBC

More Practice:
AppBE17-4, AppBE17-5,
AppE17-4, AppE17-5
Solution on p. 17-100.

Questions

Q17-1. What are the advantages of leasing from the lessee's perspective?

Q17-2. How does a lessee determine whether or not a contract includes a lease?

Q17-3. What is meant by capitalization of a lease from the viewpoint of the lessee?

Q17-4. What types of leases are capitalized by a lessee? Under what condition would a lessee not capitalize a lease?

Q17-5. From a lessee's standpoint, leases are classified as finance or operating leases. What criteria are used to identify a finance lease?

Q17-6. What lease payments are used in determining whether the present value of lease payments is greater than or equal to substantially all of the fair value of the underlying asset?

Q17-7. How is a lease liability calculated?

Q17-8. How is a right-of-use asset calculated?

Q17-9. How does a lessee determine what interest rate is appropriate to discount the lease liability?

Q17-10. How does an unguaranteed residual value in a sales-type lease affect the lessor's accounting in recording the entries at the date of inception of the lease?

Q17-11. How is a guaranteed residual value treated differently by the lessee when determining the classification of leases as compared to the recording of a lease liability?

Q17-12. Define initial direct costs.

Q17-13. How does a lessee derecognize a right-of-use asset and lease liability over the term of an operating lease?

Q17-14. How does a lessee derecognize a right-of-use asset and lease liability over the term of a finance lease?

Q17-15. If a lessee records a right-of-use asset related to a finance lease, over what period would the lessee recognize amortization expense? What conditions impact your answer?

Q17-16. How does a lessor account for an operating lease?

Q17-17. How does a lessor account for a sales-type lease?

Q17-18. If a lessor determines that payments from a lessee pertaining to a sales-type lease are not probable, how would the lessor account for the lease?

Q17-19. What qualifies as a short-term lease and how would a lessee account for a short-term lease?

Q17-20. What types of qualitative information should be disclosed about a company's leases?

Data Analytics

Data Analytics DA17-1
Using Excel Visualizations to Analyze the Impact of an Accounting Change **LO3**

Information included in the Excel file associated with this exercise was extracted or inferred from disclosures made by **Walgreens Boots** and **Verizon** in the year of adoption of the lease standard. Using this data, we will calculate ratios before and immediately after the adoption of the lease standard to better understand the impact of the accounting standard on financial statement results.

Data Analytics DA17-2
Explaining the Role of Artificial Intelligence in Accounting **LO3**

For this exercise, we match a specific example to the six uses of artificial intelligence summarized by the authors Nigel Duffy and Karsten Fuser in a post called "Six Ways the CFO Can Use Artificial Intelligence, Today" (found at https://www.ey.com/en_us/ai/six-ways-the-cfo-can-use-artificial-intelligence-today).

Data Visualization

Data Visualization

Data Visualization Activities are available in **myBusinessCourse**. These assignments use Tableau Dashboards to expose students to visual depictions of data and introduce students to data analytics through data visualizations. These exercises are assignable and auto graded by MBC.

Multiple Choice

LO1

MC17-1. Determining Lease Classification On January 1 of Year 1, a lessee entered into a 10-year noncancellable lease for equipment with a fair value of $78,000. The lease requires annual payments beginning January 1 of Year 1. The lessee's incremental borrowing rate is 7%, and the lessor's implicit interest rate, known to the lessee, is 8%. Ownership of the property remains with the lessor at expiration of the lease. The leased property has an estimated economic life of 18 years. What is the lowest annual lease payment that indicates classification of the lease by the lessee as a finance lease?

a. $9,341   c. $10,462
b. $9,687   d. $9,995

LO2

MC17-2. Determining Lease Liability for a Lessee On January 2 of Year 1, Laurel Company entered into a 12-year noncancellable lease requiring year-end payments of $40,000. Laurel's incremental borrowing rate is 6%, and the lessor's implicit interest rate, known to Laurel, is 8%. Ownership of the property remains with the lessor at expiration of the lease. The leased property has an estimated economic life of 15 years. What amount should Laurel record as Lease Liability on January 2 of Year 1?

a. $301,443   c. $342,379
b. $335,354   d. $388,490

LO3

MC17-3. Determining Current and Noncurrent Lease Liability of an Operating Lease Sauk Inc. purchased equipment for leasing purposes on January 1 of Year 1 for $440,000 and immediately leased the equipment to Ski Company for $58,000 a year for a five-year period. The first payment was made by Ski Company on January 1 of Year 1. At the end of the lease, the equipment will be returned to Sauk. Ski Company estimates the equipment's useful life to be 10 years. Ski is not aware of the implicit rate of the lease, but Ski's incremental borrowing rate is 4%. If Ski Company properly classifies the lease as an operating lease, what are the current and noncurrent lease liability amounts at the end of the accounting period on December 31 of Year 2?

	Current Lease Liability	Noncurrent Lease Liability
a.	$58,000	$160,955
b.	$49,579	$160,955
c.	$58,000	$109,393
d.	$49,579	$109,393

MC17-4. Computing Amortization of ROU Asset for Finance Lease A lessor and lessee sign a 5-year non-cancellable lease for equipment with a useful life of 5 years and a fair value of $70,713. The contract calls for annual lease payments of $15,000 payable starting on the lease commencement date. The contract requires the lessee to guarantee the residual value at the end of the lease term of $5,000. The lessee, however, estimates that the residual value at the end of the lease term will only be $2,000. The lessor's implicit rate known by the lessee is 6%. If the lessee properly classifies the lease as a finance lease, what is the amount of amortization on the right-of-use asset that the lessee will recognize in Year 2?

LO4

a.	$13,844	*c.*	$14,143
b.	$13,694	*d.*	$22,571

MC17-5. Computing ROU Asset for an Operating Lease Considering Legal Fees Refer to the information in MC17-3, but now assume that the lessee incurred $2,000 in legal fees to execute the lease. What is the amount of the ROU asset recognized on December 31 of Year 2?

LO5

a.	$166,593	*c.*	$161,120
b.	$167,393	*d.*	$168,593

MC17-6. Calculating Carrying Value of Inventory for Lessor of Sales-Type Lease A lessor enters into a 3-year lease properly classified as a sale-type lease and calculates the following amounts at the lease commencement date: lease receivable of $250,000, a residual value of $0, annual lease payments of $80,000, and gross profit of $50,000. What is the carrying value of the inventory to be leased?

LO6

a.	$250,000	*c.*	$200,000
b.	$190,000	*d.*	$130,000

MC17-7. Calculating Lease Revenue for Lessor's Operating Lease A lessor enters into a 4-year lease with a lessee with a lease payment of $8,000 per year. As an incentive for the lessee to sign the lease, the lessor reduces the first-year lease payment to 50% of the normal charge. If the lessor properly classifies the lease as an operating lease, what amount of lease revenue would the lessor recognize in Year 1?

LO7

a.	$4,000	*c.*	$8,000
b.	$6,000	*d.*	$7,000

MC17-8. Calculating Gross Profit for Lessor in Sales-Type Lease On January 1 of Year 1, a lessor leases equipment to a lessee for a four-year period. The equipment has a carrying value of $47,000, an economic life of four years, and was held in the lessor's inventory account prior to the lease. The lessor's implicit rate is 6% and there is a guaranteed residual value at the end of the lease of $5,000. The annual lease payment is $19,340.95, with the first payment due immediately on January 1 of Year 1. What is the gross profit (if any) recognized on January 1 of Year 1 by the lessor?

LO8

a.	$0	*c.*	$24,040
b.	$28,000	*d.*	$25,300

MC17-9. Analyzing Short-Term Lease Election On January 1 of Year 1, a lessee enters into an agreement to lease equipment for a 6-month period ending June 30 of Year 1. The present value of the 6 lease payments is $28,000. If the lessee elects to account for the lease under the short-term lease election, what amount would the lessee recognize as lease liability on March 31 of Year 1, the end of its annual reporting period?

LO9

a.	$28,000	*c.*	$0
b.	$14,000	*d.*	More information is required.

Brief Exercises

A customer enters into a contract with Auto Inc. where Auto Inc. provides a vehicle for the customer to use at any time over a three-year period for a monthly fee. The vehicle is maintained by and stored with Auto Inc. but is dropped off at the customer's residence at the customer's request when needed. Auto Inc. can substitute any vehicle without the customer's consent as long as it has the seating capacity per the contract. Does this contract include a lease that would be accounted for under the lease standard?

Brief Exercise 17-1
Identifying a
Lease **LO1**

Required

a. Calculate the annual lease payment calculated by the lessor.

b. Is this an operating lease or a finance lease to the lessee?

c. Prepare a lease liability schedule and right-of-use asset schedule for the lessee for the first two years of the lease term.

d. Provide journal entries for the lessee on January 1 and at year-end on December 31 of Year 1 and Year 2.

On July 1 of Year 1, Stanley Company leased a small building and its site to East Company on a five-year contract. The lease provides for an annual fixed lease payment of $40,000 payable each July 1 starting in Year 1. There is no renewal agreement. Stanley's accounts showed the following data on January 1 of Year 1: initial cost of the building, $250,000 (accumulated depreciation, $60,000); estimated remaining life, 15 years; and estimated residual value, $10,000. The accounting period for each company ends December 31. Stanley Company appropriately classifies the lease as operating.

Problem 17-8
Recording Entries for Operating Lease—Lessor **LO7**

Required

a. Provide journal entries for the lessor on July 1 and December 31 of Year 1 and Year 2. Assume adjusting entries are recorded annually at December 31.

b. Instead, assume that the initial payment is still $40,000, but the payment increases by $1,000 each year of the lease. Provide journal entries for the lessor on July 1 and December 31 of Year 1 and Year 2.

Lessor Sales Company and Lessee Manufacturing agreed to a noncancellable lease. The following information is available to both entities regarding the lease terms and the underlying asset.

Problem 17-9
Analyzing and Recording Entries for Operating Lease—Lessee and Lessor **LO5, 7**

1. Lessor's cost of the underlying asset was $30,000. The asset was new at the inception of the lease term.
2. Lease term is three years starting January 1 of Year 1.
3. Estimated useful life of the underlying asset is six years. Estimated residual value at end of six years is zero.
4. On January 1 of Year 4, the estimated unguaranteed residual value of the underlying asset one day after the end of the lease term is $10,000.
5. Lessor's implicit rate is 7%.
6. Lessee's incremental borrowing rate on January 1 of Year 1 is 8% and the lessee is unaware of the lessor's implicit rate.
7. Title to the underlying asset is retained by the lessor at the end of the lease term.
8. The fair value of the underlying asset on January 1 of Year 1 is $45,000.
9. Annual lease payments are due each January 1 with the first payment due at the inception of the lease.
10. The accounting period for the lessor and the lessee ends on December 31.

Required

a. Compute the annual lease payment calculated by the lessor.

b. Determine the lease classification for the (1) lessee and the (2) lessor.

c. Provide journal entries for the lessee on January 1 and December 31 of Year 1 and Year 2.

d. Provide journal entries for the lessor on January 1 and December 31 of Year 1 and Year 2.

Box Inc. leases a building from Lessor Corp. The following is a summary of information about the lease and the leased building.

Problem 17-10
Recording Operating Lease Entries—Lessee
LO1, 5

Lease term: 5 years with no options for renewal	Box Inc.'s incremental borrowing rate: 4.5%
Annual lease payments: $1,100,000	Remaining economic life of the building: 35 years
Payment date: Annually in advance on January 1	Purchase option: None
Fair value of the underlying asset: $40,000,000	

Additional information

- Rate implicit in the lease that Lessor Corp. charges Box Inc. is not readily determinable by Box Inc.
- Title to the building remains with Lessor Corp. throughout the period of the lease and upon lease expiration.
- Box Inc. does not guarantee the residual value of the building.
- Box Inc. pays for all property taxes, insurance, and maintenance of the building separately from the lease payments.
- Lessor Corp. pays Box Inc. $125,000 prior to the lease commencement date for packing and moving expenses as a lease incentive, recorded initially as a liability by Box.

Required

a. Is this an operating lease or a finance lease to the lessee?

b. Prepare a lease liability schedule and right-of-use asset schedule for the lessee for the first two years of the lease term.

c. Provide journal entries for the lessee on January 1 and December 31 of Year 1 and Year 2. The accounting period for the lessee ends on December 31.

Problem 17-11
Reporting a Sales-Type Lease with an Unguaranteed Residual Value—Lessor **LO8**

On December 31 of Year 1, a lessor acquired a machine at a cost of $35,000 to be held for lease and classified as inventory. The machine was leased on January 1 of Year 2, for five years in a sales-type lease that requires annual payments of $14,099 at the end of each year. At inception of the lease, the sales value of the underlying asset was $55,000. The machine will revert to the lessor at the end of the lease term, at which time the estimated residual value will be $2,500 (none of which is guaranteed by the lessee). The lessor's implicit rate of interest is 10% on the investment. The estimated fair value of the residual at lease end is $2,500. The accounting period for the lessor ends December 31

Required

a. Show how the lessor computed the annual payment of $14,099.
b. What type of lease is this to the lessor?
c. Calculate the value of the net investment in lease at the lease commencement.
d. Prepare a net investment in lease schedule for the lessor for the first two years of the lease term.
e. Provide journal entries for the lessor on January 1 of Year 2 and December 31 of Year 2 and Year 3.
f. Provide the journal entry at termination of the lease on December 31 of Year 6 for receipt of the final payment and the lease asset, assuming the estimate of residual value is confirmed.

Problem 17-12
Reporting a Sales-Type Lease with a Guaranteed Residual Value—Lessor **LO8**
Hint: See Demo 17-8B

On January 1 of Year 1, Lansing Leasing leased equipment to a lessee for an eight-year term during which $59,139 is payable each January 1, starting on January 1 of Year 1. The guaranteed residual value of the equipment at the end of the lease term is $41,000. The interest rate implicit in the lease is 6%. The accounting period for the lessor ends on December 31. The lessor manufactured the equipment at a cost of $380,000 and the fair value at commencement of the lease was $415,000.

Required

a. Show how the lessor computed the annual payment of $59,139.
b. What type of lease is this to the lessor?
c. Prepare a lease receivable schedule for the lessor for the first two years of the lease term.
d. Provide journal entries for the lessor on January 1 and December 31 of Year 1 and Year 2.
e. What balances (account titles and amounts) appear on the lessor's balance sheet on December 31 of Year 1 related to the lease?
f. What balances (account titles and amounts) appear on the lessor's income statement for Year 1 related to the lease?

Problem 17-13
Determining Lease Type and Recording Journal Entries—Lessee and Lessor; Unguaranteed Residual Value **LO1, 4, 8**

Rentals Inc. leases a vehicle to United Inc. for four years on January 1 of Year 1, requiring equal annual payments on each January 1, with the first payment due at the lease commencement. The underlying asset, recently purchased new, cost the lessor $45,000. The estimated unguaranteed value of the asset at the end of the lease term is $5,000. The annual lease payments were computed to yield Rentals Inc. 6%, a rate known to United Inc. The underlying asset has a six-year life with zero residual value at the end of Year 6. There is no purchase option, and the asset is retained by Rentals Inc. at the end of the lease term. The accounting period for both lessor and lessee ends December 31.

Required

a. Compute the annual lease payment calculated by the lessor.
b. What type of lease is this to the lessor and lessee?
c. Prepare a lease liability schedule and right-of-use asset schedule for the lessee for the first two years of the lease term.
d. Provide journal entries for the lessee on January 1 and December 31 of Year 1 and Year 2.
e. Calculate the value of the net investment in lease at the lease commencement. Prepare a schedule of net investment in lease for the first two years of the lease term.
f. Provide journal entries for the lessor on January 1 and December 31 of Year 1 and Year 2.
g. What balances (account titles and amounts) appear on the lessee's balance sheet on December 31 of Year 1 related to the lease?
h. What balances (account titles and amounts) appear on the lessee's income statement for Year 1 related to the lease?

i.   What balances (account titles and amounts) appear on the lessor's balance sheet on December 31 of Year 1 related to the lease?

j.   What balances (account titles and amounts) appear on the lessor's income statement for Year 1 related to the lease?

Key Company uses leasing as a secondary means of selling its products. On January 1 of Year 1, it contracted with Lock Corporation to lease machinery for six years that had a sales price of $90,000 and that cost Key $60,000 (its carrying value in inventory). Equal annual lease payments of $18,786 are to be made each January 1, starting on January 1 of Year 1. Key's implicit interest rate, based on the sales price, is 10% (known to Lock). There is no residual value expected at the end of the lease term. The accounting period for both companies ends on December 31. The economic life of the machinery is six years. Both parties paid $500 in legal fees to execute the lease on the lease commencement date.

Problem 17-14
Determining Lease Type and Recording Journal Entries—Lessee and Lessor; Initial Direct Cost: No Residual Value **LO1, 4, 8**

Required

a.   What type of lease is this for the lessee and the lessor?

b.   Provide journal entries for the lessee on January 1 and December 31 of Year 1 and Year 2.

c.   Provide journal entries for the lessor on January 1 and December 31 of Year 1 and Year 2.

On January 1 of Year 1, lessor Alpha and lessee Beta sign a four-year lease. The equipment, recorded as inventory, cost Alpha $900,000 and the sales price is $1,400,000. The equipment has a six-year estimated useful life. Estimated residual values follow: end of Year 4, $200,000, and end of Year 6, $80,000. The lease provides Beta an option to buy the equipment at the end of Year 4 for $150,000 cash, and Beta is reasonably expected to exercise the option. The lease requires four equal annual payments starting on January 1 of Year 1. Alpha's expected rate of return on the lease is 6%, and the incremental borrowing rate for Beta is 5%. Beta is aware of Alpha's rate. The accounting period for both companies ends on December 31.

    On December 31 of Year 4, the lessee exercises the purchase option, at which time a new estimate of residual value is $175,000.

Problem 17-15
Determining Lease Type and Recording Journal Entries—Lessee and Lessor; purchase option **LO1, 4, 8**

Required

a.   Compute the annual lease payment calculated by the lessor.

b.   What type of lease is this to the lessor and to the lessee?

c.   Prepare a lease liability schedule and right-of-use asset schedule for the lessee for the first two years of the lease term.

d.   Prepare a schedule of the lease receivable for the first two years of the lease term.

e.   Provide journal entries for the lessee on January 1 and December 31 of Year 1 and Year 2.

f.   Provide journal entries for the lessor on January 1 and December 31 of Year 1 and Year 2.

g.   Record the entries for the (1) lessee and (2) lessor on December 31 of Year 4 for the exercise of the purchase option.

On January 1, Star Leasing (the lessor) leased equipment to lessee Convers Inc. The equipment cost the lessor $400,000, and the lessor's expected rate of return was 8%. Lease payments of $12,500 are due at the end of each quarter over the lease term of one year.

Problem 17-16
Recording Entries for a Short-Term Lease **LO9**

Required

a.   What options does Convers Inc. have in accounting for the lease?

b.   Prepare the quarterly entries for the lease assuming that Convers elects the short-term lease election.

c.   If the lease had an option for annual renewals at market prices, and the lessee was reasonably certain to exercise such an option, how would your answer to part *a* change, if at all?

Accounting Decisions and Judgments

Real World Analysis   **Norfolk & Southern** is a major transportation company. This is an excerpt (adapted by the authors) from Note 6 to Norfolk & Southern's Year 8 annual report.

AD&J17-1
Estimating Lease Liability **LO4**

Long-Term Debt   The Company's noncancellable long-term leases generally include options to purchase at fair value and to extend the terms. Finance leases have been discounted at rates ranging from 3.09% to 14.26% and are collateralized by assets with a carrying amount of $332 million at December 31 of Year 8. Minimum commitments, exclusive of nonlease costs borne by the Company are:

$ millions	Finance Leases
Year 9	$ 92
Year 10	76
Year 11	60
Year 12	57
Year 13	52
Year 14 through Year 28	194
Total	$531
Imputed interest on finance lease at an average rate of 8.4%	(140)
Lease liability included in debt	$391

Required

Provided that lease payments occur evenly throughout the year, estimate the decline in the finance lease liability in Year 8.

AD&J17-2
Performing Lease
Calculations **LO4**

Real World Analysis **Turner Broadcasting Company**'s Note 6 to its Year 5 annual statements, dealing with long-term debt, includes the following information.

December 31 ($ thousands)	Year 5	Year 4
Bank credit facilities	$1,435,044	$1,490,000
8 3/8% Senior Notes due July 1, Year 23, net of unamortized discount of $2,558 and $2,619	297,442	297,381
7.4% Senior Notes due Year 14, net of unamortized discount of $334 and $363.	249,666	249,637
8.4% Senior Debentures due Year 34, net of unamortized discount of $154 and $155	199,846	199,845
Zero coupon subordinated convertible notes, 7.25% yield, due February 13, Year 17, net of unamortized discount of $318,362 and $336,487	263,694	245,569
Convertible subordinated debentures of a wholly owned subsidiary	29,075	29,075
Obligations under finance leases due in varying amounts through Year 9, net of imputed interest of $684 and $931	5,254	6,200
Other debt, net of imputed interest of $1,175 and $29, due in varying amounts through Year 9, interest at fixed rates ranging from 6.00% to 9.49%	1,336	1,386
	$2,481,313	$2,519,093
Less current portion	1,543	1,345
	$2,479,770	$2,517,748

Other information obtained from Note 6 to Turner Broadcasting Company's financial statements.

> Included in the maturities of long-term debt amounts are obligations under finance lease of $1,492,000; $1,798,000; $1,534,000; $1,097,000; and $17,000 for each of the five years following December 31 of Year 5.

Required

Estimate the company's average implicit interest rate on its lease liability. Assume there are no further long-term lease obligations after December 31, Year 13. All payments are made at the end of the year.

AD&J17-3
Analyzing Lease Reporting
Entries **LO4**

Real World Analysis **United Airlines** leases aircraft, airport passenger terminal space, aircraft hangars and related maintenance facilities, cargo terminals, other airport facilities, real estate, office and computer equipment, and vehicles. Portions of the United Airlines (UAL) liability section of its Year 8 annual report and portions of Note 10 (adapted) are provided below.

Balance Sheet Liabilities at Dec. 31, $ millions	Year 8	Year 7
Current obligations under finance leases	$ 176	$ 171
Long-term obligations under finance leases.	2,113	1,679

Note 10: Lease Obligations Payable during, $ millions	Finance Leases
Year 9	$ 317
Year 10	308
Year 11	399
Year 12	341
Year 13	242
After Year 13	1,759
Total lease payments	3,366
Imputed interest (at rates of 5.3% to 12.2%)	(1,077)
Lease liability	2,289
Current portion	(176)
Long-term obligations under finance leases.	$2,113

The statement of cash flows reports principal payments under finance lease obligations of $322 million.

Required

a. What was the value of the equipment acquired under finance lease obligations in Year 8?

b. What principal was paid on these new leases in Year 8?

Communication Case Prior to the recent lease standard (ASC 824), operating leases were not required to be shown on the balance sheet. For example, prior to the updated lease standard, if United Airlines' operating leases on December 31 of Year 8 were added to its liabilities reported in AD&J17-3, its current ratio would decline from 0.69 to 0.57, while its total debt would increase from $239 million to $1,105 million. There would also be significant changes in the measured return on assets because assets would be increased and the related increase in amortization and interest expense exceeds the lease expense included in its Year 8 income statement.

AD&J17-4
Assessing the Capitalization of Operating Leases **LO5**

Comment on this situation with regard to economic reality and the provision of useful information to decision makers. Do you support the capitalization of operating leases? Why or why not? Put your answer in the form of a memo to the FASB.

Judgment Case If the rate implicit in the lease is not readily determinable, the lessee will use its incremental borrowing rate when determining the present value of lease payments. A lessor assesses a lease's classification using the rate implicit in the lease.

AD&J17-5
Analyzing Interest Rates Implicit in Leases **LO4, 8**

ASC Glossary **Rate Implicit in the Lease**—The rate of interest that, at a provided date, causes the aggregate present value of (a) the lease payments and (b) the amount that a lessor expects to derive from the underlying asset following the end of the lease term to equal the sum of (1) the fair value of the underlying asset minus any related investment tax credit retained and expected to be realized by the lessor and (2) any deferred initial direct costs of the lessor.

ASC Glossary **Incremental Borrowing Rate**—The rate of interest that a lessee would have to pay to borrow on a collateralized basis over a similar term an amount equal to the lease payments in a similar economic environment.

Required

Evaluate the foregoing criteria in light of each of the following assertions.

a. Asking a lessor what interest rate is inherent in a lease transaction would be similar to asking a farmer what rate is implicit in the price the farmer can expect now for next fall's corn crop. There are varying degrees of risk in any operation having a distant future; the higher the farmer's future risks are thought to be, the higher the farmer will set his or her rate, and the lessor will do likewise.

b. The assumption that a lease has an implicit interest rate, in many cases, represents circular reasoning in that the fair value of the underlying asset itself (that is, the benchmark value used in determining the implicit rate) is determined by market forces. The value of the property stems from the payments it will command rather than the payments stemming from the value of the property.

c. One determinant of the implicit interest rate in a lease is the residual value of the property to be leased. This is a subjective judgment that, depending on the property, can be substantially in error. Lessors will not disclose what their guess is.

Judgment Case Speedware Corporation has entered into a debt agreement that restricts its debt-to-equity ratio to less than 2 to 1. The corporation is planning to expand its facilities, creating a need for additional financing. The board of directors is considering leasing the additional facilities but is concerned that leasing may violate its existing debt agreement; a violation would place the corporation in default. Speedware's board has asked you to analyze the following alternatives.

AD&J17-6
Analyzing Debt Ratios **LO4, 5**

Alternative A—Speedware would enter into a lease that qualifies as a finance lease (to Speedware). If this alternative is selected, Speedware's reported debt-to-equity ratio would be 1.9, and its ability to issue debt in the future would be seriously constrained.

Alternative B—Speedware would enter into a lease that would be structured in such a way as to qualify as an operating lease to Speedware and as a finance lease to the lessor.

Required

Analyze and explain the consequences of each scenario.

AD&J17-7
Reporting Interest
Expense **LO4**

`Judgment Case` Spectrum Inc. reported the following information.

Liability account balances at December 31 of Year 1 included:	
Note payable to bank	$800,000
Liability under finance lease	354,595

Additional information

1. The note payable, dated October 1 of Year 1, bears interest at an annual rate of 10% payable semiannually on April 1 and October 1. Principal payments are due annually on October 1 (beginning October 1 of Year 2) in four equal installments.
2. The finance lease is for a 10-year period beginning December 31 of five years earlier, with payment due in advance. Equal annual payments of $100,000 are due on December 31 of each year. The 5% interest rate implicit in the lease is known by Spectrum.
3. On July 1 of Year 2, Spectrum issued $1,000,000 face amount of 10-year, 4% bonds for $922,000, to yield 5%. Interest is payable annually on July 1. Bond discount is amortized by the effective interest method.
4. All required principal and interest payments were made on schedule in Year 3.

Required

a. What is the theoretical basis for requiring lessees to capitalize certain long-term leases? Do not discuss the specific criteria for classifying a lease as a finance lease.
b. Prepare the long-term liabilities section of Spectrum's balance sheet at December 31 of Year 2.
c. Prepare a schedule showing interest expense that should appear in Spectrum's income statement for the year ended December 31 of Year 2.

AD&J17-8
Analyzing Lease
Disclosures **LO9**

`Judgment Case` The following excerpts are from disclosures of a *telecommunications company* for the year ended December 31 of Year 2.

Long-Term Debt Note The following table sets forth interest rates and other information on long-term debt outstanding at December 31 (in thousands).

Interest Rates	Maturities	Year 2	Year 1
4.5%–6.5%	2–8 years	$1,800	$ 650
6.6%–8.0%	3–18 years	2,500	2,400
8.1%–9.0%	2–6 years	45	180
9.1%–9.5%	6–17 years	90	90
		4,435	3,320
Finance lease obligations		400	450
Other		2	1
Unamortized discount, net . . .		(36)	(40)
Total		$4,801	$3,731

Commitments—Finance Lease	
Years	
Year 3	$150
Year 4	100
Year 5	150
Year 6	50
Year 7	50
Thereafter	50
Total rental commitments	550
Less interest costs	40
Present value of lease payments	$510

Required

a. Is the company a lessee or lessor?

b. Where would the lease liabilities appear on the Year 2 balance sheet, and in what amounts?

c. What entries would the company make to account for its finance leases during Year 3 based on those leases currently on the company's balance sheet?

Trueblood Case The Trueblood case series, prepared by Deloitte professionals, is based on recent accounting technical issues that require research and judgment. The cases are accessed through the Deloitte Foundation: https://www2.deloitte.com/us/en/pages/about-deloitte/articles/trueblood-case-studies-deloitte-foundation.html The following case is relevant to the content provided in this chapter: **Case: 19-1 The Terminator**. In this case, lease renewal options are examined from a lessee perspective.

AD&J17-9
Analyzing Lease Renewal Options **LO1**

Trueblood Case The Trueblood case series, prepared by Deloitte professionals, is based on recent accounting technical issues that require research and judgment. The cases are accessed through the Deloitte Foundation: https://www2.deloitte.com/us/en/pages/about-deloitte/articles/trueblood-case-studies-deloitte-foundation.html The following case is relevant to the content provided in this chapter: **Case: 18-6 Logistical Logistics Inc.** In this case, a lessee needs to identify vendor contracts to determine whether or not they contain a lease.

AD&J17-10
Identifying a Lease **LO1**

Codification Skills How are the terms (1) lease, (2) lessee, (3) lessor, (4) underlying asset, and (5) unguaranteed residual asset defined in the Codification?

AD&J17-11
Defining Terms **LO1**

Codification Skills Through research in the Codification, identify the specific citation for each of the following items included as guidance in this chapter.

a. Specific topics not covered by ASC 842 (lease standard)   FASB ASC ☐ - ☐ - ☐ - ☐

b. Explicit or implicit specification of an identified asset in a contract   FASB ASC ☐ - ☐ - ☐ - ☐

c. Consideration in a contract for a lessee that depends on variable rates depending on an index or rate   FASB ASC ☐ - ☐ - ☐ - ☐

d. Lease classification criteria   FASB ASC ☐ - ☐ - ☐ - ☐

AD&J17-12
Performing Accounting Research **LO1, 4**

Codification Skills A company is preparing annual financial statements, including the valuation of a finance lease. The lease was modified during the current year from the original term of five years to a modified term of 10 years. The extension was not part of a renewal option. The company believes that it needs to remeasure the lease liability but is uncertain as to what interest rate to use to discount the lease liability. What guidance is available in the Codification?

FASB ASC ☐ - ☐ - ☐ - ☐

AD&J17-13
Performing Accounting Research **LO11**

Appendices—Multiple Choice

Computing Net Investment in Direct Financing Lease Through a 4-year lease, a lessor leased equipment to a lessee with a fair value of $63,000 and a carrying value of $57,000 with the following terms.

AppMC17-1 LO10

Lease Terms	
Rate implicit in the lease.	6.49648%
Annual lease payment, first payment due at the end of the year . . .	$ 4,000
Guaranteed residual value by an insurance company	$20,000

What is the net investment in the direct financing lease at lease commencement?

a. $57,514   c. $63,514

b. $41,965   d. $57,000

Classifying a Lease Modification A contract for a lessee to lease equipment provided by a lessor is modified to include additional equipment rentals at standalone lease prices. The change to the lease contract is classified by the lessee as a

a. New lease

b. Lease remeasurement

c. Lease classification reassessment and remeasurement

d. Lease disqualification

AppMC17-2 LO11

AppMC17-3
LO12

Analyzing a Sale-Leaseback On December 31 of Year 1, Spruce Inc. sold equipment to Maple and simultaneously leased it back for 8 years. Pertinent information at this date is as follows.

Sales price	$70,000
Cost of equipment	50,000
Accumulated depreciation on equipment	5,000

At December 31 of Year 1, how much should Spruce report as a gain from the sale of the equipment if the lease is properly accounted for as an operating lease?

a. $20,000   c. $25,000
b. $3,215   d. $0

Appendices—Brief Exercises

AppBE17-1
Classifying a
Lease **LO10**
Hint: See Demo 17-10

Lessor Inc. entered into a five-year lease agreement with Lessee Inc. to lease equipment with a useful life of seven years. The equipment will be returned to the lessor at the end of the lease term and is expected to have alternative uses. The lessor obtained a guarantee from a third party (insurance company) for the expected residual of $5,000 at the end of the lease term. Lease payments are $3,500 due annually at the end of each annual period. The implicit rate of the lease is 5.117%. The fair value of the equipment is $19,000 and the carrying value is $17,000. Determine the proper classification of the lease for the lessor.

AppBE17-2
Recording a Direct
Financing Lease **LO10**
Hint: See Demo 17-10

Using the information from AppBE17-1, record the lessor's entry at commencement of the lease.

AppBE17-3
Remeasuring a Lease
Liability **LO11**
Hint: See Demo 17-11

Universal Inc. signed a contract to lease equipment for a four-year term on January 1 of Year 1 for $20,000 annually beginning immediately. The lease included a purchase option at the end of the lease for $8,000; at the commencement of the lease, Universal did not believe it would exercise the option. On December 31 of Year 2, two years later, circumstances had changed causing Universal to now reasonably expect to exercise the option. Universal's incremental borrowing rate changed from 5% at the lease commencement date to 7% at the end of Year 2. The incremental borrowing rate at lease commencement did not reflect the purchase option. On December 31 of Year 2, the lease liability and right-of-use asset had balances of $37,188 and $37,233, respectively. What is the adjusted lease liability on December 31 of Year 2?

AppBE17-4
Recording a
Sale-Leaseback **LO12**
Hint: See Demo 17-12

Olympia Co. owns a building with a current carrying value on January 1 of $450,000, an original cost of $700,000, a 10-year remaining useful life, and no residual value. The building is sold on January 1 to Beta Investor Inc. for $500,000 cash. Simultaneously, the two parties executed a five-year lease with a 7% implicit rate of interest, known by both parties. Each annual payment of $78,000 is due on December 31. Assuming that the lease is classified as an operating lease, record Olympia's journal entry(s) on January 1.

AppBE17-5
Recording a Failed
Sale-Leaseback **LO12**
Hint: See Demo 17-12

Olympia Co. owns a building with a current carrying value on January 1 of $450,000, an original cost of $700,000, a 10-year remaining useful life, and no residual value. The building is sold on January 1 to Beta Investor Inc. for $500,000 cash. Simultaneously, the two parties executed a 10-year lease with a 7% implicit rate of interest, known by both parties. Each annual payment of $75,000 is due on December 31. Assuming that the lease is classified as a finance lease, record Olympia's journal entry(s) on January 1.

Appendices—Exercises

AppE17-1
Recording a Direct
Financing Lease **LO10**
Hint: See Demo 17-10

On January 1 of Year 1, Lessor Inc. entered into a five-year lease agreement with Lessee Inc. to lease equipment with a useful life of seven years. The equipment will be returned to the lessor at the end of the lease term and is expected to have alternative uses. The lessor obtained a guarantee from a third party (insurance company) for the expected residual of $100,000 at the end of the lease term. Lease payments are $95,000 due annually at the end of each annual period. The implicit rate of the lease is 4.3265%. The fair value of the equipment is $500,000 and the carrying value is $475,000.

Required

a. Determine the proper classification of the lease for the lessor.
b. Record the lessor's entry on January 1 of Year 1.
c. Compute the discount rate used to amortize the lease receivable.
d. Prepare the lease receivable schedule.
e. Prepare the lessor's entry on December 31 of Year 1.

On January 1 of Year 1, Lessee Corp. commences a finance lease contract for equipment with the following terms.

AppE17-2
Remeasuring
Leases   **LO11**

- Lease term: 5 years
- Economic life: 6 years
- Annual lease payments: $100,000 (due at the beginning of each period)
- Guaranteed residual value: $15,000
- Lessee's incremental borrowing rate: 6% (lessor's implicit rate unknown to the lessee)

At the commencement of the lease, Lessee Corp. did not anticipate having to make a payment for the guaranteed residual value requirement.

On January 1 of Year 3, the company determined that a payment would be due to the lessor as a result of a change in technology, which lowered the estimated fair value of the residual, causing an expected $10,000 payment.

Required

a. Will the change in expected payment on the guaranteed residual value result in a lease reclassification assessment or a lease remeasurement?
b. What is the value of the right-of-use asset and lease liability of the existing lease on January 1 of Year 3, prior to the change in the estimated residual value?
c. If applicable, calculate the remeasured value of the lease liability on January 1 of Year 3. Use the discount rate of 6% at the time of the lease commencement to compute remeasurement differences, if applicable.
d. Record the entry required on January 1 of Year 3.
e. What are the adjusted balances for the lease liability and right-of-use asset after the entry recorded in part d?
f. What is the income statement impact for Year 3 related to the lease?

Determine whether the following changes would result in a new lease, or a lease classification reassessment and/ or a lease remeasurement.

AppE17-3
Identifying
Remeasurement   **LO11**
Hint: See Demo 17-11

a. Lessee and Lessor enter into a 10-year lease for 10,000 square feet of office space in a building with a remaining economic life of 50 years. Annual payments are $100,000, paid at the end of the period. Lessee's incremental borrowing rate at the commencement date is 6%. The lease is classified as an operating lease. At the beginning of Year 6, Lessee and Lessor agree to modify the lease such that the total lease term increases from 10 years to 15 years. The annual lease payments increase to $110,000 per year for the remaining 10 years after the modification. Lessee's incremental borrowing rate is 7% at the date the modification is agreed to by the parties.
b. Lessee enters into a 10-year lease for 10,000 square feet of office space. At the beginning of Year 6, Lessee and Lessor agree to modify the lease for the remaining five years to include an additional 10,000 square feet of office space in the same building. The increase in the lease payments is commensurate with the market rate of office space at the date the modification became effective.

On January 1 of Year 1, Metalwork Manufacturing Inc. enters into a sales agreement with 4M Inc. to sell a building for $950,000 with a simultaneous agreement to lease the building back for five years. Other information about the transaction follows.

AppE17-4
Recording a
Sale-Leaseback   **LO12**
Hint: See Demo 17-12

- Net carrying amount of the building at the date of sale is $800,000 (original cost $1.2 million).
- Lease payment is $100,000 (end of year payments).
- Annual depreciation on the building is $75,000.
- Metalwork does not guarantee the residual value at the end of the lease term, but the agreement allows for Metalwork to repurchase the building at market price for equivalent property.
- Metalwork's incremental borrowing rate is 8% and the implicit rate on the lease is unknown to Metalwork.
- There are no alternative assets readily available.

Required

a. Determine the lease classification for Metalwork Manufacturing.
b. Record the journal entries for Metalwork Manufacturing for the first year.
c. Record the journal entry on December 31 of Year 5, at the conclusion of the lease.

AppE17-5
Recording a
Sale-Leaseback **LO12**
Hint: See Demo 17-12

On January 1, Wal-Market Inc. sells a building to Diversified Investors for $9,000,000, its current fair value. Prior to the sale, the carrying value of the building was $7,000,000 (original cost of $15 million). The estimated remaining useful life of the building is 20 years, with no residual value; straight-line depreciation is used. On January 1, Wal-Market Inc. signed a 10-year noncancellable leaseback agreement that has an 8% implicit rate of return for the lessor, unknown to the lessee. The lessee's incremental borrowing rate is 7%. The annual payments of $992,000 start on December 31. The lease agreement does not contain a purchase option, the lessee does not guarantee a residual value, and the building does not revert to the lessee at lease end. The building would have alternative uses at lease end.

Required
a. Determine the lease classification for Wal-Market Inc.
b. Record the journal entries for Wal-Market Inc. for the first year.

Appendices—Problem

AppP17-1
Remeasuring a Lease
Liability **LO11**

Omega Co. (lessor) enters into a lease agreement with Nino Co. (lessee) to lease retail space in an outlet mall. The five-year lease commenced on January 1 of Year 1 with no renewal options. The lease payments of $105,000 are due at the beginning of each period and the lessee incurred initial direct costs of $10,000. The lessee's incremental borrowing rate is 5% and the lease is properly classified as an operating lease.

On January 1 of Year 2, the lease is amended to decrease the lease term to three years and increase the annual rent to $110,000. The lease continues to qualify as an operating lease.

Required
a. Determine the balance of the lease liability and right-of-use asset on January 1 of Year 2.
b. Determine the proper treatment of the modification of the lease for the lessee.
c. Record the entry to adjust the lease liability and right-of-use asset, if applicable, using the lessee's current discount rate of 6%.
d. Determine the adjusted balances of the lease liability and right-of-use asset on January 1 of Year 2.

Answers to Review Exercises

Review 17-1

Option One

Lease Classification Criteria	Analysis	Criterion Met?
1. Ownership transfer	Title does not transfer	No
2. Purchase option	No purchase option	No
3. Lease term length	8 < 9 (75% of life of 12)	No
4. Present value of lease payments	PV of lease payments of $164,560 (rounded)[1] < 90% of fair value of $200,000	No
5. No alternative use	No indication of limited use	No
Lease Classification: Operating lease as no criteria met		

[1] PV(0.06,8,–25000,0,1)

Option Two

Lease Classification Criteria	Analysis	Criterion Met?
1. Ownership transfer	Title does not transfer	No
2. Purchase option	No purchase option	No
3. Lease term length	10 > 9 (75% of life of 12)	Yes
4. Present value of lease payments	PV of lease payments of $195,042[2] > 90% of fair value of $200,000	Yes
5. No alternative use	No indication of limited use	No
Lease Classification: Finance lease as two criteria are met		

[2] PV(0.06,10,–25000,0,1)

Option Three

Lease Classification Criteria	Analysis	Criterion Met?
1. Ownership transfer	Title does not transfer	No
2. Purchase option	Yes, discounted purchase option	Yes
3. Lease term length	8 < 9 (75% of life of 12)	No
4. Present value of lease payments	PV of lease payments of $200,000[3] > 90% of fair value of $200,000	Yes
5. No alternative use	No indication of limited use	No
Lease Classification: Finance lease as two criteria are met		

[3] PV(.055232,8,−28000,−20000,1)

Option Four

Lease Classification Criteria	Analysis	Criterion Met?
1. Ownership transfer	Title does not transfer	No
2. Purchase option	No purchase option	No
3. Lease term length	8 < 9 (75% of life of 12)	No
4. Present value of lease payments	PV of lease payments of $173,874[4] < 90% of fair value of $200,000	No
5. No alternative use	No indication of limited use	No
Lease Classification: Operating lease as no criteria met		

[4] PV(0.06,8,−28000,0,0)

Review 17-2

a. The contract is classified as a finance lease because it meets at least one lease criterion—lease criterion No. 4.—because the estimated useful life of the equipment of four years equals the lease term.

b.

Date	Lease Payment	Interest on Liability	Lease Liability Change	Lease Liability
Jan. 1, Year 1				$37,232
Jan. 1, Year 1	$10,000	$ 0	$10,000	27,232
Jan. 1, Year 2	10,000	1,362	8,638	18,594
Jan. 1, Year 3	10,000	930	9,070	9,524
Jan. 1, Year 4	10,000	476	9,524	0
	$40,000	$2,768	$37,232	

Note: Amounts rounded to the dollar.   Initial lease liability: PV(0.05,4,−10000,0,1)

c.   **January 1, Year 1**

Right-of-Use Asset.	37,232	
Lease Liability		37,232

Assets = Liabilities + Equity
+37,232   +37,232

ROU Asset	Lease Liab
37,232			37,232

January 1, Year 1

Lease Liability	10,000	
Cash		10,000

Assets = Liabilities + Equity
−10,000   −10,000

Cash	Lease Liab
	10,000	10,000	37,232

December 31, Year 1

Interest Expense.	1,362	
Lease Liability		1,362

Assets = Liabilities + Equity
    +1,362   −1,362

Lease Liab	Interest Exp
10,000	37,232	1,362	
	1,362	

December 31, Year 1

Amortization Expense	9,308	
Right-of-Use Asset ($37,232/4).		9,308

Assets = Liabilities + Equity
−9,308   −9,308

ROU Asset	Amort Exp
37,232	9,308	9,308	

Assets = Liabilities + Equity
−10,000   −10,000

Cash		Lease Liab	
10,000	10,000	10,000	37,232
	10,000	10,000	1,362

January 1, Year 2

| Lease Liability . . . . | 10,000 | |
| Cash . . . . | | 10,000 |

Assets = Liabilities + Equity
          +930   −930

Lease Liab		Interest Exp	
10,000	37,232	1,362	
10,000	1,362	930	
	930		

December 31, Year 2

| Interest Expense . . . . | 930 | |
| Lease Liability . . . . | | 930 |

Assets = Liabilities + Equity
−9,308   −9,308

ROU Asset		Amort Exp	
37,232	9,308	9,308	
	9,308	9,308	

December 31, Year 2

| Amortization Expense . . . . | 9,308 | |
| Right-of-Use Asset ($37,232/4) . . . . | | 9,308 |

Review 17-3

a.

Lease Classification Criteria	Analysis	Criterion Met?
1. Ownership transfer	Title does not transfer	No
2. Purchase option	No purchase option	No
3. Lease term length	5-year term is only 50% of the asset's useful life.*	No
4. PV of lease payments	PV of lease payments of $113,649 is less than 90% of fair value, which is $250,000	No
5. No alternative use	Asset commonly leased	No
Lease Classification: Operating as no criterion met.		

* PV(0.05,5,−25000,0,1)

b. Lease Liability Schedule

Date	Lease Payment	Interest on Liability	Lease Liability Change	Lease Liability
Jan. 1, Year 1				$113,649*
Jan. 1, Year 1	$ 25,000	$ 0	$ 25,000	88,649
Jan. 1, Year 2	25,000	4,432	20,568	68,081
Jan. 1, Year 3	25,000	3,404	21,596	46,485
Jan. 1, Year 4	25,000	2,324	22,676	23,809
Jan. 1, Year 5	25,000	1,191	23,809	0
	$125,000	$11,351	$113,649	

Note: Amounts in schedule are rounded.   * PV(0.05,5,−25000,0,1)

c. Right-of-Use Asset Schedule

Date	Lease Expense	Interest on Liability	Right-of-Use Asset Change	Right-of-Use Asset
Jan. 1, Year 1				$113,649
Dec. 31, Year 1	$ 25,000	$ 4,432	$ 20,568	93,081
Dec. 31, Year 2	25,000	3,404	21,596	71,485
Dec. 31, Year 3	25,000	2,324	22,676	48,809
Dec. 31, Year 4	25,000	1,191	23,809	25,000
Dec. 31, Year 5	25,000	0	25,000	0
	$125,000	$11,351	$113,649	

d.

Assets = Liabilities + Equity
+113,649   +113,649

ROU Asset		Lease Liab	
113,649			113,649

January 1, Year 1

| Right-of-Use Asset . . . . | 113,649 | |
| Lease Liability . . . . | | 113,649 |

January 1, Year 1

Lease Liability	25,000	
Cash		25,000

Assets = Liabilities + Equity
−25,000   −25,000

Cash	Lease Liab
25,000	25,000 | 113,649

December 31, Year 1

Lease Expense	25,000	
Lease Liability		4,432
Right-of-Use Asset.....................................		20,568

Assets = Liabilities + Equity
−20,568   +4,432   −25,000

ROU Asset	Lease Liab
113,649 | 20,568	25,000 | 113,649
	4,432

	Lease Exp
	25,000 |

January 1, Year 2

Lease Liability	25,000	
Cash		25,000

Assets = Liabilities + Equity
−25,000   −25,000

Cash	Lease Liab
25,000	25,000 | 113,649
25,000	25,000 | 4,432

December 31, Year 2

Lease Expense	25,000	
Lease Liability		3,404
Right-of-Use Asset.....................................		21,596

Assets = Liabilities + Equity
−21,596   +3,404   −25,000

ROU Asset	Lease Liab
113,649 | 20,568	25,000 | 113,649
| 21,596	25,000 | 4,432
	3,404

	Lease Exp
25,000 |	
25,000 |	

Review 17-4

a.

Lease Classification Criteria	Analysis	Criterion Met?
1. Ownership transfer	Title does not transfer	No
2. Purchase option	No purchase option	No
3. Lease term length	4 < 4.5 (75% of life of 6)	No
4. Present value of lease payments	PV of lease payments of $65,002* = 100% of fair value of $65,002	Yes
5. No alternative use	No information indicating customization	No
Lease Classification: Finance lease as one criterion is met		

*PV(0.09,4,−16000,−12000,1)

b.

Date	Lease Payment	Interest on Liability	Lease Liability Change	Lease Liability
Jan. 1, Year 1				$56,501[1]
Jan. 1, Year 1	$16,000	$ 0	$16,000	40,501
Jan. 1, Year 2	16,000	3,645	12,355	28,146
Jan. 1, Year 3	16,000	2,533	13,467	14,679
Jan. 1, Year 4	16,000	1,321	14,679	0
	$64,000	$7,499	$56,501	

[1] PV(0.09,4,−16000,0,1)

c. **January 1, Year 1—To record right-of-use asset and lease liability**

Right-of-Use Asset.......................................	56,501	
Lease Liability		56,501

Assets = Liabilities + Equity
+56,501   +56,501

ROU Asset	Lease Liab
56,501 |	| 56,501

January 1, Year 1—To record lease payment

Lease Liability	16,000	
Cash		16,000

Assets = Liabilities + Equity
−16,000   −16,000

Cash	Lease Liab
| 16,000	16,000 | 56,501

December 31, Year 1—To record interest expense

Interest Expense..	3,645	
Lease Liability		3,645

Assets = Liabilities + Equity
+3,645   −3,645

Interest Exp	Lease Liab
3,645 |	16,000 | 56,501
	| 3,645
	| 44,146

December 31, Year 1—To record amortization of right-of-use asset

Amortization Expense	14,125	
Right-of-Use Asset ($56,501/4).......................		14,125

Assets = Liabilities + Equity
−14,125   −14,125

ROU Asset	Amort Exp
56,501 | 14,125	14,125 |
42,376 |	

d. The result of the lease classification test does not change because the total guaranteed residual value is used in the present value of lease payment test. Therefore, the lease is still classified as a finance lease.

Date	Lease Payment	Interest on Liability	Lease Liability Change	Lease Liability
Jan. 1, Year 1				$62,522[1]
Jan. 1, Year 1	$16,000	$ 0	$16,000	46,522
Jan. 1, Year 2	16,000	4,187	11,813	34,709
Jan. 1, Year 3	16,000	3,124	12,876	21,833
Jan. 1, Year 4	16,000	1,965	14,035	7,798
Jan. 1, Year 5	8,500	702	7,798	0
	$72,500	$9,978	$62,522	

[1] =PV(0.09,4,–16000,–8500,1)

January 1, Year 1— To record right-of-use asset and lease liability

Right-of-Use Asset..	62,522	
Lease Liability		62,522

Assets = Liabilities + Equity
+62,522   +62,522

ROU Asset | Lease Liab
62,522 | | 62,522

January 1, Year 1—To record lease payment

Lease Liability	16,000	
Cash		16,000

Assets = Liabilities + Equity
−16,000   −16,000

Cash | Lease Liab
| 16,000 | 16,000 | 62,522

December 31, Year 1—To record interest expense

Interest Expense.......................................	4,187	
Lease Liability		4,187

Assets = Liabilities + Equity
+4,187   −4,187

Interest Exp | Lease Liab
4,187 | | 16,000 | 62,522
| | 4,187
| | 50,709

December 31, Year 1—To record amortization of right-of-use asset

Amortization Expense	15,631	
Right-of-Use Asset ($62,522/4).........................		15,631

Assets = Liabilities + Equity
−15,631   −15,631

ROU Asset | Amort Exp
62,522 | 15,631 | 15,631 |
46,891 |

Review 17-5

a.

Lease Classification Criteria	Analysis	Criterion Met?
1. Ownership transfer	Title does not transfer	No
2. Purchase option	No purchase option	No
3. Lease term length	10-year term is only 1/3 of the asset's useful life.	No
4. PV of lease payments	PV of lease payments of $585,127* is less than 90% of fair value or $1 million.	No
5. No alternative use	Asset commonly leased	No
Lease Classification: Operating as no criterion met.		

*PV(.06,10,75000,0,1)

b. **Lease Liability Schedule**

Date	Lease Payment	Interest on Liability	Lease Liability Change	Lease Liability
Jan. 1, Year 1				$585,127*
Jan. 1, Year 1	$ 75,000	$ —	$ 75,000	510,127
Jan. 1, Year 2	75,000	30,608	44,392	465,735
Jan. 1, Year 3	75,000	27,944	47,056	418,679
Jan. 1, Year 4	75,000	25,121	49,879	368,800
Jan. 1, Year 5	75,000	22,128	52,872	315,928
Jan. 1, Year 6	75,000	18,956	56,044	259,884
Jan. 1, Year 7	75,000	15,593	59,407	200,477
Jan. 1, Year 8	75,000	12,029	62,971	137,506
Jan. 1, Year 9	75,000	8,250	66,750	70,756
Jan. 1, Year 10	75,000	4,244	70,756	0
	$750,000	$164,873	$585,127	

* =PV(0.06,10,–75000,0,1)

c. **Right-of-Use Asset Schedule**

Date	Lease Expense*	Interest on Liability	Right-of-Use Asset Change	Right-of-Use Asset
Jan. 1, Year 1				$586,127**
Dec. 31, Year 1	$ 75,100	$ 30,608	$ 44,492	541,635
Dec. 31, Year 2	75,100	27,944	47,156	494,479
Dec. 31, Year 3	75,100	25,121	49,979	444,500
Dec. 31, Year 4	75,100	22,128	52,972	391,528
Dec. 31, Year 5	75,100	18,956	56,144	335,384
Dec. 31, Year 6	75,100	15,593	59,507	275,877
Dec. 31, Year 7	75,100	12,029	63,071	212,806
Dec. 31, Year 8	75,100	8,250	66,850	145,956
Dec. 31, Year 9	75,100	4,244	70,856	75,100
Dec. 31, Year 10	75,100	—	75,100	0
	$751,000	$164,873	$586,127	

* (($75,000 × 10) + $1,000)/10

** $585,127 + $1,000

d. **January 1, Year 1—To record right-of-use asset and lease liability**

Right-of-Use Asset.	586,127	
Lease Liability		585,127
Cash		1,000

Assets = Liabilities + Equity
+586,127   +585,127
−1,000

ROU Asset	Lease Liab
586,127		585,127

Cash	
	1,000

January 1, Year 1—To record lease payment

Lease Liability	75,000	
Cash		75,000

Assets = Liabilities + Equity
−75,000   −75,000

Cash	Lease Liab
	1,000	75,000	585,127
	75,000	

December 31, Year 1—To record lease expense

Lease Expense	75,100	
Lease Liability		30,608
Right-of-Use Asset.		44,492

Assets = Liabilities + Equity
−44,492   +30,608   −75,100

Lease Liab	Lease Exp
75,000	585,127	75,100	
	30,608	

ROU Asset	
586,127	44,492

January 1, Year 2—To record lease payment

Lease Liability	75,000	
Cash		75,000

Assets = Liabilities + Equity
−75,000   −75,000

Cash	Lease Liab
	1,000	75,000	585,127
	75,000	75,000	30,608
	75,000	

December 31, Year 2—To record lease expense

Lease Expense	75,100	
Lease Liability		27,944
Right-of-Use Asset.		47,156

Assets = Liabilities + Equity
−47,156   +27,944   −75,100

ROU Asset	Lease Liab
586,127	44,492	75,000	585,127
	47,156	75,000	30,608
		27,944

Lease Exp	
75,100	
75,100	

Review 17-6

a.

Date	Lease Payment	Interest on Receivable	Lease Receivable Change	Lease Receivable
Jan. 1, Year 1				$78,000[1]
Jan. 1, Year 1	$21,236	$ 0	$21,236	56,764
Jan. 1, Year 2	21,236	3,406	17,830	38,934
Jan. 1, Year 3	21,236	2,336	18,900	20,034
Jan. 1, Year 4	21,236	1,202	20,034	0
	$84,944	$6,944	$78,000	

[1] PV(0.06,4,−21236,0,1)

Permanent differences never reverse so they do not result in recognition of deferred tax assets and liabilities. As a result, when the company only has permanent differences, income tax expense for financial reporting is equal to the amount computed as total income taxes on the tax return for the period.

In **Demo 18-4A**, we combine a taxable temporary difference, a deductible temporary difference, and a nontaxable item into one example. This Demo incorporates concepts from this section and prior sections.

Multiple Book-Tax Differences	LO18-4 DEMO 18-4A

Demo

MBC

We continue with the Vail example in **Demo 18-1A**, but now, we extend the example through Year 3. Thus, we present the problem a bit differently in the interest of parsimony. Assume pretax GAAP income after all items of revenue and expense are considered is $100,000 in Year 1, $125,000 in Year 2, and $90,000 in Year 3. The enacted tax rate for all years is 25%. The two temporary differences originating in Year 1 are repeated here for convenience. The municipal bond interest revenue of $500 is assumed now for all three years. The accounting and tax periods both end December 31.

- Prepaid insurance in the amount of $20,000 was recorded on December 31 of Year 1 for Year 2 insurance coverage. The cost of insurance is deductible for tax purposes in the year paid.
- A warranty accrual of $30,000 recorded on December 31 of Year 1 is not deductible for tax purposes until the warranty costs are settled. The amount is paid evenly over Year 2 through Year 4.
- The company recorded interest revenue of $500 each year (Year 1, Year 2, and Year 3) on municipal bonds. Interest revenue on municipal bonds is not taxable.

GAAP asset > Tax asset

GAAP liability > Tax liability

Nontaxable item

Required
a. Compute the increase in income tax payable on December 31 of Year 1, Year 2, and Year 3.
b. Prepare a schedule to compute the deferred tax liability balance and a schedule to compute the deferred tax asset balance on December 31 of Year 1, Year 2, and Year 3.
c. Record the income tax journal entries in Year 1, Year 2, and Year 3.

Solution
a. **Computation of the Increase in Income Tax Payable**

Calculation of Income Tax Payable Increase (Dec. 31)	Year 1	Year 2	Year 3
Pretax GAAP income	$100,000	$125,000	$90,000
Insurance expense adjustment	(20,000)	20,000	
Warranty expense adjustment	30,000	(10,000)	(10,000)
Interest revenue—municipal bond	(500)	(500)	(500)
Taxable income	109,500	134,500	79,500
Tax rate	× 25%	× 25%	× 25%
Income tax payable increase	$ 27,375	$ 33,625	$19,875

b. **Deferred Tax Schedules**

Schedule to Compute Deferred Tax Liability Balance (Dec. 31)	Year 1	Year 2	Year 3
GAAP basis of prepaid insurance	$20,000	$ 0	$ 0
Tax basis of prepaid insurance	0	0	0
Difference between GAAP and tax bases	20,000	0	0
Tax rate	× 25%	× 25%	× 25%
Deferred tax liability, ending balance	$ 5,000	$ 0	$ 0

Schedule to Compute Deferred Tax Asset Balance (Dec. 31)	Year 1	Year 2	Year 3
GAAP basis of accrued warranty liability	$30,000	$20,000	$10,000
Tax basis of accrued warranty liability	0	0	0
Difference between GAAP and tax bases	30,000	20,000	10,000
Tax rate	× 25%	× 25%	× 25%
Deferred tax asset, ending balance	$ 7,500	$ 5,000	$ 2,500

continued

continued from previous page

Assets	=	Liabilities	+	Equity
+7,500		+5,000		−24,875
DTA		DTL		Exp
		+27,375		
		Tax Pay		

Def Tax Asset		Inc Tax Pay	
7,500			27,375

Inc Tax Exp		Def Tax Liab	
24,875			5,000

c. Income Tax Journal Entries

Vail Inc. records the following entries in Year 1, Year 2, and Year 3.

December 31, Year 1

Income Tax Expense ($27,375 + $5,000 − $7,500)................	24,875	
Deferred Tax Asset..	7,500	
Deferred Tax Liability		5,000
Income Tax Payable................................		27,375

Assets	=	Liabilities	+	Equity
−2,500		−5,000		−31,125
DTA		DTL		Exp
		+33,625		
		Tax Pay		

Def Tax Asset		Inc Tax Pay	
7,500	2,500		27,375
			33,625

Inc Tax Exp			
24,875			
31,125		Def Tax Liab	
		5,000	5,000
			0

December 31, Year 2

Income Tax Expense ($33,625 + $2,500 − $5,000)............	31,125	
Deferred Tax Liability* ($0 − $5,000)	5,000	
Deferred Tax Asset* ($5,000 − $7,500).................		2,500
Income Tax Payable...................................		33,625

*Adjustment calculated by taking Year 2 account ending balance minus Year 1 account ending balance.

Assets	=	Liabilities	+	Equity
−2,500		+19,875		−22,375
DTA		Tax Pay		Exp

Def Tax Asset		Inc Tax Pay	
7,500	2,500		27,375
	2,500		33,625
2,500			19,875

Inc Tax Exp			
24,875			
31,125			
22,375			

December 31, Year 3

Income Tax Expense ($19,875 + $2,500)	22,375	
Deferred Tax Asset ($2,500 − $5,000).................		2,500
Income Tax Payable.................................		19,875

At the end of Year 3, the deferred tax liability has a zero balance because the entire liability reverses in Year 2. The deferred tax asset has a balance of $2,500 ($7,500 − $2,500 − $2,500), which represents one-third of the warranty liability balance expected to reverse in Year 4. Municipal bond interest income produces neither a deferred tax asset nor a deferred tax liability because the difference it creates between GAAP and taxable incomes never reverses.

Rate Reconciliation Disclosure

Companies must disclose a rate reconciliation, which is a reconciliation (in dollars and in percentages) between the U.S. statutory tax rate and the effective tax rate.

- The statutory tax rate, or simply **statutory rate**, is the legally imposed tax rate of a jurisdiction. For statutory tax in dollars, multiply pretax GAAP income by the statutory tax rate.
- The **effective tax rate** is calculated by dividing income tax expense by pretax GAAP income. For the effective tax in dollars, enter the amount of income tax expense.

The effective tax rate will often differ from the statutory rate, and one reason for the difference is the existence of permanent differences. When a company has permanent differences such as nontaxable revenue or deductions for tax purposes not reportable in the financial statements, the effective tax rate is reduced. On the other hand, when a company has nondeductible items, the effective tax rate is increased. A rate reconciliation schedule is illustrated in **Demo 18-4B**. We note that effective in 2025 for calendar year-end companies, FASB has issued new disclosure requirements (ASU 2023-09). The new rules require more disclosure and, at times, more details by jurisdiction. We describe the relevant new rules below, but we cannot show "Real World" disclosures using the new guidance because companies have not reported using the new rule as of the time of the writing of this text.

EXPANDING YOUR KNOWLEDGE   **Other Items that Impact Effective Tax Rate**

There are several items that impact the rate reconciliation disclosure beyond nontaxable and nondeductible items. In fact, GAAP requires disclosure of specific items in a rate reconciliation highlighted in the categories below. In general, a company is required to separately disclose any reconciling item with a tax effect greater than 1.05 percent (21% × 5%) of income from continuing operations. If a reconciling item does not fit into one of the categories and does not meet the conditions for disaggregation on the threshold basis, it would be aggregated with other such reconciling items in an "Other Adjustments" category.

State income taxes In addition to federal income taxes, most companies have to pay state income taxes. This increases the company's effective tax rate beyond the U.S. federal income tax rate. Thus, a reconciling item for the effect of state income taxes is often necessary in the rate reconciliation. ASC 740-10-50-12B states, in part, that entities must "provide a qualitative description of the states and local jurisdictions that make up the majority (greater than 50 percent) of the effect of the state and local income tax category."

continued

continued from previous page

Tax credits The tax credit reduces the tax the company owes to the taxing authority, now and forever, but is not technically a difference between income measures. A company computes its income tax payable and reduces the amount by the tax credit which reduces the amount paid to the taxing authority. The net effect is a reduction in the effective tax rate below the statutory rate via a tax credit. Thus, a reconciling item is required for tax credits that directly reduces income tax payable. In this case, the rate adjustment is simply equal to the tax credit divided by pretax GAAP income.

Change in valuation allowance Management's estimate for the valuation allowance (see LO 18-5) in a reporting period after the deferred tax asset is recorded also impacts the effective tax rate. Management is just changing the accounting accrual in this case, so there is no change in the actual taxes paid during the period.

Effect of changes in tax laws or rates enacted in the current period Temporary differences scheduled to reverse in periods with enacted tax rates that differ from the current period's enacted tax rate will cause the effective tax rate to differ from the current period statutory rate.

Foreign tax effects Reconciling items attributable to the impact of income taxes imposed by foreign jurisdictions.

Effect of cross-border tax laws The effect of incremental income taxes imposed by the domestic jurisdiction (e.g., the US for a US company) on income earned in foreign jurisdictions. For US companies, this includes the impacts of the global intangible low-taxed income (GILTI) provision, the base erosion and anti-abuse tax (BEAT), and the foreign-derived intangible income (FDII) rules.

Changes in unrecognized tax benefits Reconciling items resulting from changes in judgment related to tax positions taken in prior annual reporting periods. For unrecognized tax benefits recorded in the current annual reporting period related to a tax position taken in the current reporting period, such benefit and its related tax position may be presented on a net basis in the category in which the tax position is presented.

Along with these items, the guidance requires disclosure for other items beyond the scope of this text but included in the rate reconciliation disclosures that meet a quantitative threshold as mentioned above (ASC 740-10-50-12A).

Rate Reconciliation   **LO18-4**   DEMO 18-4B

Referring to **Demo 18-4A**, prepare a reconciliation disclosure of the statutory tax rate to the effective tax rate in dollars and percentages.

Demo

MBC

Solution
The following reconciliation begins with the statutory (U.S. federal) rate of 25%. The nontaxable item of interest on the municipal bonds is never taxed, which decreases the effective tax rate. In Year 1 for example, the statutory rate of 25% is reduced to an effective rate of 24.875% due to the permanent difference.

Reconciliation from Statutory Tax Rate to Effective Tax Rate						
	Year 1		Year 2		Year 3	
	Dollar	Percentage	Dollar	Percentage	Dollar	Percentage
Statutory tax rate[1]	$25,000	25.000%	$31,250	25.000%	$22,500	25.000%
Tax exempt income[2]	–125	–0.125%	–125	–0.100%	–125	–0.139%
Effective tax rate[3]	$24,875	24.875%	$31,125	24.900%	$22,375	24.861%

[1] Statutory tax in dollars
Year 1 $100,000 × 25% = . . . $25,000
Year 2 $125,000 × 25% = . . . $31,250
Year 3 $90,000 × 25% = . . . $22,500

[2] Tax-exempt income calculations
Year 1 ($500 × 25%) = $125/$100,000 = . . . 0.125%
Year 2 ($500 × 25%) = $125/$125,000 = . . . 0.100%
Year 3 ($500 × 25%) = $125/$90,000 = . . . 0.139%

[3] Effective tax rate calculations
Year 1 $24,875/$100,000 = ... 24.875%
Year 2 $31,125/$125,000 = ... 24.900%
Year 3 $22,375/$90,000 = ... 24.861%

COCA-COLA

Real World—APPLYING THE CONSERVATISM RATIO TO COCA-COLA

While companies try to maximize profits, they also try to minimize or at least defer tax payments. One way to potentially assess (a) the extent to which managers have used discretion in reporting financial accounting earnings and/or (b) the extent to which managers have employed aggressive tax strategies is by computing the *conservatism ratio* (GAAP income before taxes divided by taxable income). The higher the ratio, the less conservative the accounting earnings and/or the more aggressive the tax strategies employed that defer (or eliminate in the case of permanent differences) tax payments to future periods. This ratio is computed for the Coca-Cola Company using amounts reported in recent financial statements.

continued

continued from previous page

Coca-Cola ($ millions)	2023	2022	2021
GAAP income before taxes	$12,952	$11,686	$12,425
Taxable income*	$10,719	$10,652	$ 8,223
Conservatism ratio	1.21	1.10	1.51

* A rough estimate of taxable income (which can vary greatly from actual) is to divide current tax expense by the statutory tax rate).

For Coca-Cola, the most aggressive tax policy year was 2021, where GAAP income before taxes was 151% of taxable income. This ratio could also inform us about the quality of financial accounting in some cases. It is important to realize that many differences between GAAP and tax are simply due to rule differences. Thus, while this metric provides a signal of possible aggressive behavior, we cannot infer that type of behavior with certainty.

HARTFORD

Real World—INCOME TAX RATE RECONCILIATION

The **Hartford Financial Services Group Inc.** provided the following income tax rate reconciliation in a recent Form 10-K. The pretax GAAP income from continuing operations on its income statement is $3,088 million. The tax rate reconciliation below starts with this income multiplied by the U.S. statutory tax rate of 21%, for a provision at the U.S. statutory rate of $648 million ($3,088 × 21%). We then see the tax effect of nontaxable net investment income and others. The effective tax rate for Hartford is 18.9% (= $584/$3,088).

Income Tax Rate Reconciliation	
For year ended December 31 (in millions)	**2023**
Tax provision at U.S. federal statutory rate	$648
Nontaxable net investment income	(41)
Other	(23)
Provision for income taxes	**$584**

REVIEW 18-4 ▶ **LO18-4**	**Multiple Temporary and Permanent Differences**

Review
MBC

For the year, Raleigh Corporation had pretax GAAP income of $250,000 and an income tax rate of 25%. Raleigh had a $5,000 credit balance in its Deferred Tax Liability account on January 1, which reversed during the year, and a zero balance in its Deferred Tax Asset account on January 1. The accounting and tax periods both end December 31. The company summarized the following items for the year.

- Depreciation for accounting purposes, $80,000, and for income tax purposes, $110,000. The related fixed asset was acquired for $400,000 at the beginning of the year and had an estimated 5-year useful life at that time.

- Installment sales revenue for accounting purposes was $80,000, and for income tax purposes, $40,000. The $40,000 receivable is expected to be collected evenly over the next four years.

- Payment of life insurance premiums on executive officers totaled $4,000 for the year.

More Practice:
BE18-23, BE18-24, BE18-25,
E18-16, E18-22, E18-24,
E18-26, E18-27

Solution on p. 18-67.

Required

a. Compute the increase in income tax payable on December 31.

b. Record the income tax journal entry required on December 31.

Explain how to record a valuation allowance and report deferred taxes

LO 18-5

To realize the benefit of a deferred tax asset, there must be future taxable income against which the future deductible amounts can be applied. Possible sources of future taxable income are reversals of taxable temporary differences, forecasted future taxable income, and the application of tax-planning strategies. If sufficient future taxable income is not likely, a company must reduce the carrying value of the deferred tax asset through a **valuation allowance**.

> **Valuation Allowance for Deferred Tax Assets**
> - Record as a contra asset to deferred tax asset
> - Record when it is *more likely than not* that the deferred tax asset will not be realized
> - Consider both negative and positive evidence
>
> **Recording deferred taxes, net**
> - Noncurrent tax asset or
> - Noncurrent tax liabliity
>
> *LO 18-5 Overview*

Valuation Allowance

The following guidance provides a definition of a valuation allowance and identifies possible sources of taxable income to realize a deferred tax asset.

ASC Glossary Valuation Allowance—The portion of a deferred tax asset for which it is more likely than not that a tax benefit will not be realized.

740-10-30-18 Future realization of the tax benefit of an existing deductible temporary difference or carryforward ultimately depends on the existence of sufficient taxable income of the appropriate character (for example, ordinary income or capital gain) within the carryback, carryforward period available under the tax law. The following four possible sources of taxable income may be available under the tax law to realize a tax benefit for deductible temporary differences and carryforwards:

a. Future reversals of existing taxable temporary differences
b. Future taxable income exclusive of reversing temporary differences and carryforwards
c. Taxable income in prior carryback year(s) if carryback is permitted under the tax law
d. Tax-planning strategies. . .

If, based on the weight of available evidence, it is *more likely than not* (>50%) that some portion of the deferred tax asset will not be realized, the deferred tax asset is reduced by a valuation allowance. The **Valuation Allowance for Deferred Tax Assets** is a contra asset account sufficient to reduce the deferred tax asset to the amount *likely* to be realized. **Demo 18-5** illustrates the establishment and adjustment of the valuation allowance.

740-10-30-5 e. Reduce deferred tax assets by a valuation allowance if, based on the weight of available evidence, it is more likely than not (a likelihood of more than 50 percent) that some portion or all of the deferred tax assets will not be realized. The valuation allowance shall be sufficient to reduce the deferred tax asset to the amount that is more likely than not to be realized.

To realize a deferred tax asset, a company must have positive taxable income in the future against which it can offset its deferred deductions. That is, a deferred tax asset related to future tax deductions of $10,000 can only be realized if the company has at least $10,000 of future taxable income before considering the deferred deductions. A company must consider all available evidence, both positive and negative, to make a determination of whether a deferred tax asset will be realized. For example, a strong history of positive taxable income is **positive evidence** that a company would realize the deferred tax asset. A taxable loss expected in the following year would be **negative evidence** indicating that the company may not realize the deferred tax asset. The valuation allowance is evaluated and adjusted at the end of each reporting period.

740-10-30-23 An entity shall use judgment in considering the relative impact of negative and positive evidence. The weight given to the potential effect of negative and positive evidence shall be commensurate with the extent to which it can be objectively verified. The more negative evidence that exists, the more positive evidence is necessary and the more difficult it is to support a conclusion that a valuation allowance is not needed for some portion or all of the deferred tax asset. A cumulative loss in recent years is a significant piece of negative evidence that is difficult to overcome.

Assessing the realizability of deferred tax assets is arguably more difficult when tax net operating losses can be carried forward indefinitely into the future. Generally speaking, estimates requiring projections farther into the future are more uncertain and less verifiable.

EXPANDING YOUR KNOWLEDGE   **Negative and Positive Evidence—Valuation Allowance**

The authoritative guidance includes a list of items that could be considered negative and positive evidence when considering whether or how much to reserve as a deferred tax valuation allowance.

Negative Evidence

740-10-30-21 Forming a conclusion that a valuation allowance is not needed is difficult when there is negative evidence such as cumulative losses in recent years. Other examples of negative evidence include, but are not limited to, the following:

a. A history of operating loss or tax credit carryforwards expiring unused
b. Losses expected in early future years (by a presently profitable entity)
c. Unsettled circumstances that, if unfavorably resolved, would adversely affect future operations and profit levels on a continuing basis in future years
d. A carryback, carryforward period that is so brief it would limit realization of tax benefits if a significant deductible temporary difference is expected to reverse in a single year or the entity operates in a traditionally cyclical business.

Positive Evidence

740-10-30-22 Examples (not prerequisites) of positive evidence that might support a conclusion that a valuation allowance is not needed when there is negative evidence include, but are not limited to, the following:

a. Existing contracts or firm sales backlog that will produce more than enough taxable income to realize the deferred tax asset based on existing sales prices and cost structures.
b. An excess of appreciated asset value over the tax basis of the entity's net assets in an amount sufficient to realize the deferred tax asset.
c. A strong earnings history exclusive of the loss that created the future deductible amount (tax loss carryforward or deductible temporary difference) coupled with evidence indicating that the loss (for example, an unusual or infrequent item) is an aberration rather than a continuing condition.

DEMO 18-5A   **LO18-5**   **Account for Deferred Tax Asset Valuation Allowance**

Demo

MBC

Referring to **Demo 18-4A**, Vail Inc. recorded a deferred tax asset on December 31 of Year 1, for $7,500. The company has a beginning balance of zero in its Valuation Allowance for Deferred Tax Asset account. The accounting and tax periods both end on December 31.

Required

a. On December 31 of Year 1, Vail determined that it was *more likely than not* that $2,000 of the deferred tax asset would not be realized. Record the entry required to establish a valuation allowance.
b. On December 31 of Year 2, the balance of the deferred tax asset account is reduced to $5,000 due to the deferred tax asset reversal during the year. The company determines that it is *more likely than not* that half of the balance will not be realized. The company considered all relevant available evidence to make this determination. Record the entry required to adjust the valuation allowance.

Solution

a. **Valuation Allowance for Deferred Tax Asset**

Assets	=	Liabilities	+	Equity
−2,000				−2,000
DTA Allow				Exp

DTA Val Allow		Inc Tax Exp
	2,000	2,000	

December 31, Year 1—To establish deferred tax asset valuation allowance

Income Tax Expense	2,000	
Valuation Allowance for Deferred Tax Asset		2,000

The Valuation Allowance for Deferred Tax Asset is a contra asset account. On the December 31 of Year 1 balance sheet, the net deferred tax asset recognized is $5,500 ($7,500 − $2,000).

b. **Valuation Allowance for Deferred Tax Asset Adjustment**

Because Vail has a beginning balance in the valuation allowance account of $2,000, a credit of $500 to the valuation account is required to arrive at an ending balance of $2,500 ($5,000 × 50%).

Valuation Allowance for Deferred Tax Asset	
2,000	Jan. 1, Year 2
500	**Adjustment**
2,500	Dec. 31, Year 2

continued

continued from previous page

Vail records the following entry to adjust the valuation allowance.

December 31, Year 2—To adjust deferred tax asset valuation allowance

Income Tax Expense	500	
Valuation Allowance for Deferred Tax Asset.		500

The net deferred tax asset on the balance sheet on December 31 of Year 2 is $2,500 ($5,000 – $2,500).

Assets = Liabilities + Equity
–500   –500
DTA Allow   Exp

DTA Val Allow	Inc Tax Exp
2,000	2,000
500	500

COCA COLA

Real World—DEFERRED TAX ASSET VALUATION ALLOWANCE

Coca Cola Company provided the following reconciliation of its deferred tax asset valuation allowance in a recent Form 10-K. The allowance balance as a percentage of total gross deferred tax assets was 8.2%.

Note 15: Income Taxes An analysis of our deferred tax asset valuation allowance is as follows:

Year Ended December 31 ($ millions)	2023
Balance at beginning of Year	$424
Additions.	28
Deductions	(56)
Balance at end of Year	$396

The Company's deferred tax asset valuation allowances are primarily the result of uncertainties regarding the future realization of recorded tax benefits on tax loss carryforwards and foreign tax credit carryforwards from operations in various jurisdictions and basis differences in certain equity investments. Current evidence does not suggest that we will realize sufficient taxable income of the appropriate character within the carryforward period to allow us to realize these deferred tax benefits. If we were to identify and implement tax planning strategies to recover these deferred tax assets or generate sufficient income of the appropriate character in these jurisdictions in the future, it could lead to the reversal of these valuation allowances and a reduction of income tax expense. The Company believes that it will generate sufficient future taxable income to realize the tax benefits related to the remaining net deferred tax assets in our consolidated balance sheet.

In 2023, the Company recognized a net decrease of $28 million in its valuation allowances, primarily due to net decreases in the deferred tax assets and related valuation allowances on a certain equity method investment, certain excess foreign tax credit carryforwards and the changes in net operating losses in the normal course of business.

Balance Sheet Presentation of Deferred Tax Accounts

Deferred tax assets, valuation allowances, and deferred tax liabilities are merged into either a *net noncurrent tax asset* or a *net noncurrent tax liability* on a classified balance sheet. As specified below and illustrated in **Demo 18-5B**, the larger value (of net assets or liabilities) determines the proper classification.

Criteria	Balance Sheet Classification
(Deferred tax asset – Valuation allowance) > Deferred tax liability	Noncurrent deferred tax asset, net
Deferred tax liability > (Deferred tax asset – Valuation allowance)	Noncurrent deferred tax liability, net

740-10-45-6 For a particular tax-paying component of an entity and within a particular tax jurisdiction, all deferred tax liabilities and assets, as well as any related valuation allowance, shall be offset and presented as a single noncurrent amount. However, an entity shall not offset deferred tax liabilities and assets attributable to different tax-paying components of the entity or to different tax jurisdictions.

Account for Deferred Tax Asset Valuation Allowance   **LO18-5**   **DEMO 18-5B**

Aspen Co. reports temporary differences resulting in a deferred tax asset of $100,000, a valuation allowance of $50,000, and a total deferred tax liability of $120,000. How would the company report deferred taxes on its balance sheet?

Solution

The company reports a net noncurrent deferred tax liability of $70,000, computed as $120,000 – [$100,000 – $50,000].

Demo

MBC

REVIEW 18-5 **LO18-5   Tax Asset Valuation Allowance and Reporting of Deferred Tax Accounts**

Review

MBC

Part One: Tax Asset Valuation Allowance

Dallas Corp. has a deferred tax asset balance of $300,000 on December 31 of the current year, due to a temporary difference related to a warranty expense accrual that is not deductible for tax purposes. The deferred tax asset balance has increased $20,000 over the prior year's ending balance of $280,000, and the Valuation Allowance for Deferred Tax Asset account has a zero balance. Taxable income for the current year is $880,000, and the tax rate is 25%.

a. Record the income tax journal entry on December 31, assuming that it is *more likely than not* that the deferred tax asset ending balance of $300,000 will be realized.

b. Record the income tax journal entries on December 31, assuming that it is *more likely than not* that 30% of the deferred tax asset ending balance of $300,000 will not be realized.

Part Two: Reporting of Deferred Tax Accounts

The following items create deferred tax assets and deferred tax liabilities at December 31 for Lee Inc. Assume no beginning balances in deferred tax accounts.

1. Prepaid operating expenses of $40,000 are tax deductible when paid.
2. Excess tax depreciation (MACRS) over GAAP depreciation (straight-line) is $30,000.
3. Bad debt expense amount of $10,000 is tax deductible when individual accounts are written off.
4. Installment sales of $35,000 are recorded on an accrual basis for reporting purposes and taxed when collected.
5. Valuation allowance for deferred tax asset is estimated to be 50% of the deferred tax asset balance.

Show how deferred taxes would be recognized on the company's December 31 balance sheet, assuming a tax rate of 25%.

More Practice:
BE18-30, BE18-31,
BE18-32, BE18-33,
E18-28, E18-30
Solution on p. 18-67.

LO 18-6 > # Explain how a change in tax rates impacts deferred taxes

LO 18-6 Overview

Tax Rate Changes
- Use new tax rate only if enacted into law
- Recognize income statement effect of a change in tax rate in period the new tax rate was enacted
- Apply new tax rate(s) to temporary taxable amounts in the year(s) of reversal

The legislature can change enacted tax rates for the current or future periods at any time, which impacts the accounting for income taxes. For example, in a prior administration, a new federal tax rate was enacted into law that significantly reduced the federal corporate statutory tax rate from 35% to 21%. Because deferred tax assets and liabilities are valued at the enacted tax rate that will be in effect when temporary differences reverse, any deferred tax assets or liabilities existing at the time of the change were reduced to reflect the change in the enacted tax rate. Rate adjustments are reflected in net income in the period that the enacted tax rate changed. Even if a company anticipates a tax law change, no adjusting entries are made until the law has been passed.

Adjusting Deferred Tax Accounts for a Change in Tax Rate A tax law change can result in a tax rate change effective immediately or at some point in the future. In some instances, a tax law can phase in different rates over several years causing a temporary difference that reverses over a multi-year period to be impacted by multiple tax rates. **To determine a deferred tax balance, future enacted tax rates must be matched to temporary differences in the year(s) of reversal.** This process is illustrated in **Demo 18-6**.

`740-10-25-47` The effect of a change in tax laws or rates shall be recognized at the date of enactment.

`740-10-35-4` Deferred tax liabilities and assets shall be adjusted for the effect of a change in tax laws or rates. A change in tax laws or rates may also require a reevaluation of a valuation allowance for deferred tax assets.

Change in Enacted Tax Rate   LO18-6   DEMO 18-6

Demo

MBC

GAAP asset > Tax asset

Consider each of the following three examples separately.

Example One: Enacted Tax Rate Change, Multiple Tax Rates, No Existing Deferred Tax

Springs Inc. has taxable income of $40,000 for the year ended December 31 of Year 1. In addition, Springs calculates a taxable temporary difference of $5,000 due to the excess of the carrying value of depreciable assets over the tax basis. The $5,000 temporary difference will result in future taxable amounts of $2,000 in Year 2, $2,000 in Year 3, and $1,000 in Year 4. The current year tax rate is 25%. Newly enacted future tax rates are as follows: Year 2: 25%, Year 3: 30%, and Year 4: 35%.

a. Prepare a schedule to compute the deferred tax liability balance on December 31 of Year 1. Assume a beginning balance of zero for the tax liability. Assume the accounting and tax periods both end on December 31.

b. Record the income tax journal entry on December 31 of Year 1.

Solution

a. **Schedule to Compute Deferred Tax Liability**

The future enacted tax rates are matched to the temporary taxable amounts in the relevant *years of reversal* as follows.

Schedule to Compute Deferred Tax Liability Balance (Dec. 31)	Year 2	Year 3	Year 4	Total
Reversal of differences between GAAP and tax bases	$2,000	$2,000	$1,000	$5,000
Tax rate in effect in the year of reversal	× 25%	× 30%	× 35%	
Year 1 Deferred tax liability, ending balance.............	$ 500	$ 600	$ 350	**$1,450**

b. **Income Tax Journal Entry**

The current tax rate is used to calculate the increase in income tax payable (the current tax expense) of $10,000 ($40,000 × 25%). The deferred tax liability account of $1,450 is calculated above. The journal entry to record income tax expense follows.

December 31, Year 1—To record income tax expense

Income Tax Expense ($1,450 + $10,000)	11,450	
Deferred Tax Liability		1,450
Income Tax Payable ($40,000 × 25%)		10,000

Assets = Liabilities + Equity
+1,450 −11,450
DTL   Exp
+10,000
Inc Tax Pay

Def Tax Liab	Inc Tax Exp
	1,450	11,450	

Inc Tax Exp	
	10,000	

Example Two: Enacted Tax Rate Change—Impact on Existing Deferred Tax Asset Account

Boulder Inc. has one deductible temporary difference of $50,000 due to a GAAP accrual for a pending lawsuit with a tax basis of zero. Originating in the current year through the entry that follows, the deferred tax asset has a balance of $20,000 ($50,000 × 40% current tax rate) on December 31 of Year 1 before considering a tax law change due.

Year 1—To record deferred tax asset

Deferred Tax Asset......................................	11,450	
Income Tax Expense		10,000

GAAP liability > Tax liability

On December 31 of Year 1, a new tax rate of 25% was enacted into law, effective in Year 2.

a. Prepare a schedule to compute the deferred tax asset balance on December 31 of Year 1.

b. Record the income tax journal entry on December 31 of Year 1, assuming taxable income of $110,000 (Pretax GAAP income of $60,000 + $50,000 deductible temporary difference).

Solution

a. **Schedule of Deferred Tax Asset Balance**

The enacted tax rate is used to determine the deferred tax asset value in the following calculation.

continued

continued from previous page

Schedule to Compute Deferred Tax Asset Balance (Dec. 31)	Year 1
GAAP basis of estimated litigation liability	$50,000
Tax basis of estimated litigation liability	0
Difference between GAAP and tax bases	$50,000
Tax rate in effect in the year of reversal	× 25%
Deferred tax asset, ending balance	$12,500

The Deferred Tax Asset account will require an adjustment of $7,500 (credit).

Deferred Tax Asset		
Dec. 31, Year 1 20,000		
	7,500	Adjustment
Dec. 31, Year 1 12,500		

b. **Income Tax Journal Entry**

Boulder Inc. records the following entry to recognize income tax expense for Year 1. The adjustment to the deferred tax asset due to the *decrease* in the tax rate causes an *increase* in income tax expense. Specifically, an asset is now valued at a lower amount and this devaluation of an asset reduces income.

December 31, Year 1—To record income tax expense

Income Tax Expense ($44,000 + $7,500)	51,500	
Deferred Tax Asset		7,500
Income Tax Payable ($110,000 × 40%)		44,000

Assets	=	Liabilities	+	Equity
–7,500		+44,000		–51,500
DTA		Tax Pay		Exp

Def Tax Liab		Inc Tax Exp	
Bal. 20,000	7,500		44,000
12,500			

	Inc Tax Exp	
	51,500	20,000 Bal.

GAAP asset > Tax asset

Example Three: Enacted Tax Rate Change—Impact on Existing Deferred Tax Liability Account

Boulder Inc. has one taxable temporary difference of $50,000 related to fixed assets with a GAAP basis of $50,000 and a tax basis of zero. Originating in the current year through the entry that follows, the Deferred Tax Liability account has a balance of $20,000 ($50,000 × 40% current tax rate) on December 31 of Year 1 before considering a tax law change.

Year 1—To record deferred tax liability

Income Tax Expense	20,000	
Deferred Tax Liability		20,000

On December 31 of Year 1, a new tax rate of 25% was enacted into law, effective in Year 2.

a. Prepare a schedule to compute the deferred tax liability balance on December 31 of Year 1.
b. Record the income tax journal entry on December 31 of Year 1, assuming taxable income of $10,000 (Pretax GAAP income of $60,000 - $50,000 taxable temporary difference).

Solution

a. **Schedule of Deferred Tax Liability Balance**

The enacted tax rate is used to determine the deferred tax liability value.

Schedule to Compute Deferred Tax Liability Balance (Dec. 31)	Year 1
GAAP basis of fixed assets	$50,000
Tax basis of fixed assets	0
Difference between GAAP and tax bases	$50,000
Tax rate in effect in the year of reversal	× 25%
Deferred tax liability, ending balance	$12,500

The Deferred Tax Liability account will require an adjustment of $7,500 (debit).

Deferred Tax Asset		
	20,000	Dec. 31, Year 1
Adjustment 7,500		
	12,500	Dec. 31, Year 1

continued

continued from previous page

b. **Income Tax Journal Entry**

Boulder Inc. records the following entry to recognize income tax expense for Year 1. The adjustment to the deferred tax liability due to the *decrease* in the tax rate causes a *decrease* in income tax expense.

Assets	=	Liabilities	+	Equity
		−7,500		−3,500
		DTL		Exp
		+4,000		
		Tax Pay		

December 31, Year 1—To record income tax expense

Deferred Tax Liability	7,500	
Income Tax Expense ($4,000 – $7,500)		3,500
Income Tax Payable ($10,000 × 40%).		4,000

Def Tax Liab		Inc Tax Exp	
7,500	20,000 Bal.	Bal. 20,000	3,500
	12,500		

Inc Tax Exp	
4,000	

EXPANDING YOUR KNOWLEDGE   **Computing Ratios Considering Deferred Tax Liabilities**

Recall that the **total liabilities-to-equity** ratio measures the proportion of liabilities to equity in a company's capital structure. It indicates how much a company relies on debt financing compared to equity financing. *As the liabilities-to-equity ratio increases, risk increases, and solvency decreases.* A ratio greater than 1.0 indicates that total liabilities exceed total stockholders' equity. Deferred tax liabilities are classified as liabilities and would seemingly be included as part of total liabilities in computing the debt-to-equity ratio. However, some analysts exclude deferred tax liabilities from total liabilities for ratio analyses. More specifically, if it is uncertain that the deferred tax liability will reverse over time, some financial analysts exclude the deferred tax liability from the numerator of the ratio. For example, continually replenishing fixed assets can cause tax depreciation to be indefinitely higher than GAAP depreciation, delaying the realization of the tax liability.

EXPANDING YOUR KNOWLEDGE   **Rate Reconciliation with Change in Enacted Tax Rate**

As described in the last section, temporary differences scheduled to reverse in periods with enacted tax rates that differ from the current period's enacted tax rate will cause the effective tax rate to differ from the current period statutory rate.

a. Referring to **Demo 18-6** Example Two, prepare a reconciliation of the statutory tax rate to the effective tax rate for Year 1.

b. Referring to **Demo 18-6** Example Three, prepare a reconciliation of the statutory tax rate to the effective tax rate for Year 1.

SOLUTION

a. **Deferred Tax Asset Affected by a Decrease in Statutory Rate** The effect of the litigation liability temporary difference increases the effective tax rate in Year 1 because the company will deduct $50,000 next year when the statutory tax rate is *lower* than it is in the current year. The reconciling amount is based on the difference between the current statutory rate and the rate in the year of reversal.

Example One: Reconciliation from Statutory Tax Rate to Effective Tax Rate		
	Dollars	**Percentages**
Statutory tax rate	$24,000[a]	40.00%[b]
Litigation liability difference reversing at lower tax rate in Year 2	7,500[c]	12.50%[d]
Effective tax rate.	$31,500[e]	52.50%[f]

[a]$60,000 × 40%   [b]$24,000/$60,000   [c]$50,000 × (40% – 25%)   [d]$7,500/$60,000   [e]$51,500 – $20,000   [f]$31,500/$60,000

b. **Deferred Tax Liability Affected by a Decrease in Statutory Rate** The effect of the fixed asset temporary difference decreases the effective tax rate in Year 1 because the company will pay tax on $50,000 next year when the statutory tax rate is lower than it is in the current year. The reconciling amount is based on the difference between the current statutory rate and the rate in the year of reversal.

Example Two: Reconciliation from Statutory Tax Rate to Effective Tax Rate		
	Dollars	**Percentages**
Statutory tax rate	$24,000[a]	40.00%[b]
Litigation liability difference reversing at lower tax rate in Year 2	(7,500)[c]	−12.50%[d]
Effective tax rate.	$16,500[e]	27.50%[f]

[a]$60,000 × 40%   [b]$24,000/$60,000   [c]–$50,000 × (40% – 25%)   [d]–$7,500/$60,000   [e]$20,000 – $3,500   [f]$16,500/$60,000

HARTFORD
HARTFORD
Real World—CHANGES IN TAX RATES FOR A COMPANY WITH DEFERRED TAX ASSETS

Hartford Financial Services Group Inc. reported an income tax item in a recent 10-K rate reconciliation for "Tax Reform" of $877 million. This amount is an *increase* to its income tax expense. This might seem puzzling because the U.S. tax rate *decreased*! However, Hartford had large deferred tax assets recorded on its balance sheet. When the U.S. tax rate is reduced, the value of those deferred tax assets is also reduced. Thus, the company must record a journal entry to reduce deferred tax assets (a credit) and increase deferred tax expense (a debit). There were no changes to the underlying non-tax assets and non-tax liabilities. The only change was the tax rate, affecting the valuation of the deferred tax assets and liabilities. Hartford reports the following in its Form 10-K tax note.

> The Company recognized an $877 increase in income tax expense in 2017 due to the effects of Tax Reform, primarily due to the reduction in net deferred tax assets as a result of the reduction in the Federal corporate income tax rate from 35% to 21%.

BOEING
Real World—CHANGES IN TAX RATES FOR A COMPANY WITH DEFERRED TAX LIABILITIES

Boeing had net deferred tax liabilities recorded when the TCJA was passed, and Boeing was required to revalue these liabilities at the new lower rate. (TCJA is the Tax Cuts and Jobs Act that reduced the corporate statutory tax rate from 35% to 21%.) As a result, the company showed a reduction in their effective tax rate.

> In the fourth quarter of 2017, we recorded provisional tax benefits of $1,210 related to the remeasurement of our net U.S. deferred tax liabilities to reflect the reduction in the corporate tax rate. We also recorded a provisional tax expense of $159 related to tax on non-U.S. activities resulting from the TCJA.

REVIEW 18-6	LO18-6	Change in Enacted Tax Rate

Review

MBC

More Practice:
BE18-35, BE18-36, E18-32,
E18-33, E18-37, E18-38

Solution on p. 18-68.

Billboard Company has a deferred tax liability in the amount of $6,900 at December 31 of Year 1, relating to a $23,000 installment sale receivable, $10,000 of which is collected in Year 2. The tax rate in Year 2 is 30%. However, the rate for Year 3 and thereafter is changed during Year 2 to 25%. Warranty expense in Year 2 included in the determination of pretax GAAP income is $22,000, with these amounts expected to be incurred and deductible for tax purposes in Year 3. Pretax GAAP income is $112,000 in Year 2.

Prepare the journal entry to record income taxes in Year 2.

LO 18-7 ▷ Describe accounting for net operating loss carryforwards and loss carryback|carryforwards

LO 18-7 Overview

NOL Carryforward
- Losses offset taxable income (maximum of 80%) in future years

NOL Carryback|Carryforward
- Allowed under certain circumstances
- Losses first offset prior years' taxable income
- Carryforward any excess loss not offset by prior years' taxable income

When a company has negative taxable income in a period, it has a **net operating loss** (NOL), which means it has no income tax obligation in the current period. Under current tax law, a company can carry such tax losses forward to offset future taxable income and, thus, reduce taxes in future years. While in most cases, companies will carryforward losses, some exceptions allow for losses to be first carried back for a specified number of years before any excess losses are carried forward.

ASC Glossary **Carryforwards**: Deductions or credits that cannot be utilized on the tax return during a year that may be carried forward to reduce taxable income or taxes payable in a future year.

ASC Glossary **Carrybacks**: Deductions or credits that cannot be utilized on the tax return during a year that may be carried back to reduce taxable income or taxes payable in a prior year. An operating loss carryback is an excess of tax deductions over gross income in a year; a tax credit carryback is the amount by which tax credits available for utilization exceed statutory limitations. Different tax jurisdictions have different rules about whether excess deductions or credits may be carried back and the length of the carryback period.

Net Operating Loss Carryforwards

Under current federal tax laws, a company can carry federal income tax losses forward indefinitely (but generally cannot carry losses back to prior periods). In future years, the company can use the losses to offset taxable income (earned in those future years). With few exceptions, net operating loss carryforwards can only offset a maximum of 80% of taxable income in each of the future years. **All assignments assume the 80% limitation applies to all carryforwards unless stated otherwise.** The

loss carryforward requires the recording of a deferred tax asset and a decrease to income tax expense as illustrated in **Demo 18-7A.** For presentation purposes, when income tax expense has a credit balance, it is called **Income Tax Benefit** on the income statement. (Recall that the ASC Glossary definition of a deferred tax asset included earlier directly references "carryforwards.") The realization of a future tax savings from loss carryforwards depends on a company's ability to earn profits in the future. As a result, the company must assess whether a valuation allowance is necessary.

Net Operating Loss Carryback|Carryforward

When loss carrybacks are allowed, losses are first carried back a specified number of years, in order of years, *starting with the earliest year* first, to secure a refund of prior years' taxes on income of an equivalent amount. For example, under current tax law, certain farming losses and NOLs of insurance companies (other than a life insurance company) can be carried back two years before carrying any excess losses forward (without the 80% limit). In addition, during times of crises such as the coronavirus pandemic or the financial crisis (2007 - 2008) the government may allow carrybacks in attempt to increase liquidity for taxpayers. With different rules applying to losses arising in different years, companies must track their losses by year. Also, some states and foreign jurisdictions have their own carryback|carryforward rules. The loss carryback|carryforward approach is illustrated in **Demo 18-7B.** The shift of the loss to prior and future periods has the effect of averaging income over time.

Net Operating Loss Carryforward	**LO18-7**	**DEMO 18-7A**

Whitewater Inc. experiences an operating loss for tax purposes of $65,000 in Year 1. Management estimates future taxable income will be $10,000, $5,000, $50,000, and $60,000, in Year 2, Year 3, Year 4, and Year 5, respectively. The tax rate is 25%. The accounting and tax periods both end on December 31.

a. Calculate Whitewater's deferred tax asset balance on December 31 of Year 1 related to its NOL carryforward.
b. Record the effect of the NOL carryforward. Assume that evidence indicates that it is *more likely than not* that the deferred tax asset will be realized.
c. Show the income statement presentation of the NOL carryforward in Year 1.
d. Whitewater becomes profitable in Year 2 (actual taxable income of $15,000). Record the income tax expense entry for Year 2. Assume that evidence indicates that it is *more likely than not* that only 70% of the deferred tax asset will be realized.

Solution
a. **Measurement of Deferred Tax Asset**
    The full $65,000 loss is carried forward to future years to create a deferred tax asset of $16,250, calculated as $65,000 × 25%. Carryforward amounts utilized are subject to a limit of 80% of the estimated future earnings. The cumulative amount utilized cannot exceed the carryforward of $65,000.
b. **Recording Effect of Net Operating Loss Carryforward**
    Whitewater records a deferred tax asset of $16,250, the estimated future tax benefit from the carryforward. No valuation allowance is recorded because evidence indicates that it is *more likely than not* that the deferred tax asset will be realized. Income tax expense is credited for the net benefit due to the recognition of the deferred tax asset related to the net operating loss carryforward.

    December 31, Year 1—To record income tax benefit

		Assets = Liabilities + Equity
		+16,250 +16,250
		DTA Exp

Deferred Tax Asset..................................	16,250	
Income Tax Expense		16,250

Def Tax Liab	Inc Tax Exp
16,250 │	│ 16,250

continued

continued from previous page

c. **Income Statement Presentation**

Schedule to Compute Deferred Tax Liability Balance (Dec. 31)	Year 1
Operating loss before income taxes..	$(65,000)
Income tax benefit...	16,250
Net loss...	$(48,750)

d. **Recording Effect of Net Operating Loss Carryforward—Year Two**

In Year 2, the company utilizes a carryforward loss of $12,000 or 80% of actual taxable income of $15,000. The $65,000 loss carryforward is reduced to $53,000. Thus, the deferred tax asset would be reduced to $13,250 ($53,000 × 25%).

Deferred Tax Asset			
Jan. 1, Year 2	16,250		
		3,000	Adjustment
Dec. 31, Year 2	13,250		

The company pays income tax on 20% of taxable income for Year 2.

$15,000 Taxable income × 20% (outside 80% limitation) × 25% Tax rate = $750 Income Tax Payable

Assets	=	Liabilities	+	Equity
−3,000		+750		−3,750
DTA		Tax Pay		Exp

Def Tax Liab		Inc Tax Exp	
16,250	3,000		750
13,250			

Inc Tax Exp	
3,750	16,250

December 31, Year 2—To record income tax expense

Income Tax Expense ($3,000 + $750)........................	3,750	
Deferred Tax Asset (see adjustment above)................		3,000
Income Tax Payable ($15,000 × 20% × 25%).............		750

The following entry is made to establish an allowance for the 30% amount of the deferred tax asset that is not expected to be realized.

Assets	=	Liabilities	+	Equity
−3,975				−3,975
DTA Allow				Exp

DTA Val Allow		Inc Tax Exp	
	3,975	3,750	16,250
		3,975	

December 31, Year 2—To adjust deferred tax asset valuation allowance

Income Tax Expense ($13,250 × 30%)........................	3,975	
Valuation Allowance for Deferred Tax Asset..............		3,975

DEMO 18-7B ▶ LO18-7   **NOL Carryback|Carryforward**

Wick Inc. began operations in Year 1 and has taxable income of $20,000, $30,000, and $5,000 in Year 1, Year 2, and Year 3 of its operations, respectively. In Year 4, Wick experiences an operating loss of $65,000. Wick qualifies for loss carryback for two years (starting with the earlier year) and carryforward for an unlimited number of Years with an 80% income limit. The accounting and tax periods both end December 31.

Prior and current taxable income, and management's estimates of future taxable income (Year 5 through Year 7) follow. Assume a tax rate for all years of 25%.

Year	Taxable Income	Tax Rate
1	$20,000	25%
2	30,000	25%
3	5,000	25%
4 (current year)	(65,000)	25%
5	12,500 Estimated	25%
6	6,250 Estimated	25%
7	18,750 Estimated	25%

Required

a. Calculate Wick's tax refund receivable for Year 4 (the current year).
b. Calculate Wick's deferred tax asset related to the tax loss carryforward on December 31 of Year 4.
c. Record the effect of the net operating loss assuming that it is *more likely than not* that the deferred tax asset will be realized.
d. Show the income statement presentation of the loss carryback and carryforward in Year 4.

continued

continued from previous page

e. Assume instead that on December 31 of Year 4 there is evidence that it is *more likely than not* that the deferred tax asset would not be realized, record the required adjusting entry and show the income statement presentation. Also assume a beginning balance of zero in the Deferred Tax Asset valuation account.

Solution

a. **Measurement of Tax Refund Receivable**

Wick can request a tax refund by first carrying back $30,000 of the loss to Year 2 (the earlier year) and then $5,000 of the loss to Year 3. The total tax refund is equal to $8,750 calculated as ($30,000 × 25%) + ($5,000 × 25%). Wick cannot carry back to Year 1, as this year is outside the two-year carryback window. The tax refund will be recorded as a tax receivable.

b. **Measurement of Deferred Tax Asset**

Wick will have $30,000 of NOL ($65,000 total NOL, less $35,000 carried back to Year 2 and Year 3) to carry forward to future years (subject to the 80% limit), starting with Year 5. Wick records a deferred tax asset for the estimated future tax benefit from the carryforward because the NOL creates future deductible amounts, calculated as follows.

$$\$30,000 \text{ NOL} \times 25\% \text{ Tax rate} = \$7,500$$

c. **Effect of Net Operating Loss Carryback and Carryforward**

Wick records a receivable for the tax refund requested of $8,750 and Wick records a deferred tax asset for the $7,500 of estimated future tax savings from the carryforward. No deferred tax asset valuation allowance is required because the company determines that it is more likely than not that the deferred tax asset will be realized.

December 31, Year 4—To record income tax benefit

Income Tax Refund Receivable..........................	8,750	
Deferred Tax Asset..	7,500	
Income Tax Expense		16,250

Assets	= Liabilities +	Equity
+8,750		+16,250
Tax Rec		Exp
+7,500		
DTA		

Inc Tax Rec		Inc Tax Exp
8,750 |		| 16,250
Def Tax Asset		
7,500 | 16,250		

d. **Income Statement Presentation**

Partial Income Statement	Year 4
Operating loss before income taxes..	$(65,000)
Income tax benefit	16,250
Net loss..	$(48,750)

e. **Deferred Tax Asset Valuation Allowance**

If there is evidence that it is *more likely than not* that all or part of the deferred tax asset will not be realized, the company must record a valuation allowance. The company records the following entry to establish the deferred tax asset valuation allowance.

December 31, Year 4—To adjust deferred tax valuation allowance

Income Tax Expense	7,500	
Valuation Allowance for Deferred Tax Asset..............		7,500

Assets	= Liabilities +	Equity
−7,500		−7,500
DTA Allow		Exp

DTA Val Allow		Inc Tax Exp
| 7,500		7,500 | 16,250

Partial Income Statement	Year 4
Operating loss before income taxes...	$(65,000)
come tax benefit ($16,250 − $7,500)	8,750
Net loss..	$(56,250)

Tyson Corporation has no differences between financial accounting and taxable incomes. During the year ended December 31, the corporation experienced an $18,000 pretax loss from operations. Assume an income tax rate of 25% in all years.

Review

MBC

continued

continued from previous page

Required

More Practice:
BE18-37, BE18-38, E18-41,
E18-43, E18-44
Solution on p. 18-68.

Provide the income tax entry assuming the laws only allow loss carryforwards. Assume that on December 31, there is evidence that it is *more likely than not* that 60% of the deferred tax asset would not be realized.

LO 18-8   Explain and demonstrate accounting for uncertainty in income tax decisions

LO 18-8 Overview

Uncertain Tax Benefits
- **Recognition threshold**: Recognize uncertain tax benefits if it is *more likely than not* the company will sustain it
- **Measurement of tax benefit**: Measure tax benefit as the largest amount greater than 50% likely of being realized

At times, companies can take a tax position on the tax return that may later be subject to a different interpretation by taxing authorities. For example, a company and a taxing authority can arrive at different conclusions about how the taxpayer should treat a particular transaction, a valuation computation that affects taxable income, or the timing of when an expense is taken (among other positions). The dispute can be solved through negotiation between the taxing authority and the taxpayer or through litigation if a settlement cannot be reached. The accounting for income taxes must consider tax positions where the outcome is not certain, known as **uncertain tax positions**.

740-10-55-4 Relatively few disputes are resolved through litigation, and very few are taken to the court of last resort. Generally, the taxpayer and the taxing authority negotiate a settlement to avoid the costs and hazards of litigation. As a result, the measurement of the tax position is based on management's best judgment of the amount the taxpayer would ultimately accept in a settlement with taxing authorities.

The intuition behind an unrecognized tax benefit is that if a company takes a tax position that results in lower current taxes due, that position might not be accepted upon a dispute with the taxing authorities. Therefore, the taxpayer should accrue a liability now for the tax that would be due if the tax authority disagrees with the position or amount of position and requires more tax payments. An unrecognized tax benefit is essentially a contingent liability of the company; the company may be liable for additional taxes in the future for positions taken in the current or prior periods. Determining the amount to record for the unrecognized tax benefit requires management judgment in assessing the likelihood a position is maintained and also in measuring the amount that is likely to be sustained. The decision process for the accounting treatment of uncertain tax positions is a two-step process that separates recognition from measurement (**Demo 18-8** illustrates this).

Step One: Recognition The first step is to determine whether a tax position has met the recognition threshold. If it is *more likely than not* (> 50% likelihood) the taxpayer will maintain the tax position in a dispute with taxing authorities, based on the technical merits of the company's position, the company

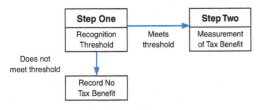

may recognize a financial statement benefit for a position taken on the tax return. If this condition is not met, the company cannot recognize the tax benefit on the financial statements for the position taken on the tax return. When making this determination the company is to assume that the taxing authority will audit the position and has full knowledge of all relevant information. In other words, the company cannot take the probability of an audit into account. If the recognition threshold is met, the company measures the tax benefit as described in step two.

Step Two: Measurement The second step is to measure the tax benefit that meets the *more likely than not* recognition threshold. The benefit is measured as the largest amount of tax benefit that is greater than 50% likely of being realized.

740-10-55-3 The application of the requirements of this Subtopic related to tax positions requires a two-step process that separates recognition from measurement. The first step is determining whether a tax position has met the recognition threshold; the second step is measuring a tax position that meets the recognition threshold. The recognition threshold is met when the taxpayer (the reporting entity) concludes that, consistent with paragraphs 740-10-25-6 through 25-7 and 740-10-25-13, it is more likely than not that the taxpayer will sustain the benefit taken or expected to be taken in the tax return in a dispute with taxing authorities if the taxpayer takes the dispute to the court of last resort.

740-10-25-6 An entity shall initially recognize the financial statement effects of a tax position when it is more likely than not, based on the technical merits, that the position will be sustained upon examination. The term *more likely than not* means a likelihood of more than 50 percent; the terms *examined* and *upon examination* also include resolution of the related appeals or litigation processes, if any. For example, if an entity determines that it is certain that the entire cost of an acquired asset is fully deductible, the more-likely-than-not recognition threshold has been met. The more-likely-than-not recognition threshold is a positive assertion that an entity believes it is entitled to the economic benefits associated with a tax position. The determination of whether or not a tax position has met the more-likely-than-not recognition threshold shall consider the facts, circumstances, and information available at the reporting date. The level of evidence that is necessary and appropriate to support an entity's assessment of the technical merits of a tax position is a matter of judgment that depends on all available information.

740-10-55-5 The recognition and measurement requirements of this Subtopic related to tax positions require that the entity recognize the largest amount of benefit that is greater than 50 percent likely of being realized upon settlement.

Uncertain Tax Positions   **LO18-8**   **DEMO 18-8**

Example One—Uncertain Tax Position—Does Not Meet Recognition Threshold

Boulder Inc. took a deduction of $100 on its Year 1 tax return with a tax rate of 25%, reducing current taxes payable by $25. Without taking the deduction, Boulder's tax payable would have been $5,025. Boulder believes the probability the deduction would be allowed if challenged by taxing authorities is less than 50%. Provide the entry to record income tax expense at year-end on December 31 of Year 1.

Demo
MBC

Solution

Although Boulder Inc. files a tax return showing taxes due of $5,000 ($5,025 – $25) based upon the tax position that it had taken, the income tax expense in the financial statements is reported as if the tax position will not be sustained.

December 31, Year 1—To record income tax expense

Income Tax Expense	5,025	
Income Tax Payable.		5,000
Liability for Unrecognized Tax Benefits ($100 × 25%)		25

Assets = Liabilities + Equity
           +5,000   Unrecog
           Tax Pay   Tax
           +25   –5,025

Inc Tax Rec   Inc Tax Exp
  | 5,000   5,025 |
Liab—Tax
Benefit
    | 25

Example Two—Uncertain Tax Position—Meets Recognition Threshold

Now assume Boulder Inc. does meet the recognition threshold (>50% probability that the tax position will be sustained). There is limited information about how a taxing authority will view the position. However, based upon judgment, management of Boulder Inc. believes it is likely Boulder would settle for less than the full amount of the entire position when examined by the taxing authority. Management estimates the probabilities of possible outcomes as follows.

Possible Estimated Outcome (Allowable Tax Deduction)	Individual Probability of Occurring	Cumulative Probability of Occurring
$100	25%	25%
68	40%	65%
42	30%	95%
0	5%	100%

Boulder Inc. takes the $100 deduction on the tax return, and income tax payable is $5,000 on December 31 of Year 1. Record the income tax expense entry on December 31 of Year 1, assuming a tax rate of 25%.

Solution

Because the deduction meets the recognition threshold, Boulder measures the benefit related to the largest deduction with a cumulative probability in excess of 50%. From the third column of the table, management estimates there is a 25% probability a deduction of $100 would be allowed, a 65% probability a deduction of **at least** $68 would be allowed, and a 95% probability a deduction

continued

continued from previous page

of *at least* $42 would be allowed. Because $68 is the largest deduction for which the cumulative probability exceeds 50%, Boulder will recognize the benefit of a $68 deduction and record a liability for the unrecognized benefit of $32 ($100 – $68) multiplied by the tax rate of 25%.

December 31, Year 1—To record income tax expense

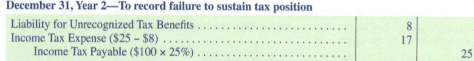

Income Tax Expense ($5,000 + $8)	5,008	
Income Tax Payable (given)		5,000
Liability for Unrecognized Tax Benefits ($32 × 25%)		8

Determining the possible estimated outcomes and the associated probabilities requires *management judgment*. For example, in the probability table above, management estimated that there is a 25% probability of an outcome where the full $100 would be allowed as a tax deduction. If we instead assume that management estimates there is a 55% probability the full $100 deduction is allowed, no liability would be recognized for uncertain tax benefits and income tax expense would be $5,000. Estimates prepared by management have a direct impact on net income reported in the financial statements.

Example Three—Uncertain Tax Position—Resolution

The uncertain tax position can be resolved in different ways including the following: (a) full benefit is lost, (b) full benefit is realized, or (c) some portion of the benefit is realized. In all three cases, assume that the company previously accrued $8 ($32 × 25%) as the liability for the unrecognized tax benefits on December 31 of Year 1.

a. **Full Tax Benefit Is Lost**

Assume that in December of Year 2, after negotiations with taxing authorities, Boulder Inc. does not sustain any portion of its tax position regarding the $100 tax deduction. Record Boulder's entry resolving the uncertain tax position on December 31 of Year 2.

Solution

December 31, Year 2—To record failure to sustain tax position

Liability for Unrecognized Tax Benefits	8	
Income Tax Expense ($25 – $8)	17	
Income Tax Payable ($100 × 25%)		25

In this case the effect on tax expense in Year 2 is only $17 because the company expensed $8 in a prior period when it accrued a liability for the uncertain tax position.

b. **Full Tax Benefit Is Realized**

Assume that in December of Year 2, after negotiations with taxing authorities, Boulder Inc. sustains its full tax position regarding the $100 tax deduction. Record Boulder's entry resolving the uncertain tax position on December 31 of Year 2.

Solution

December 31, Year 2—To record favorable resolution of tax position

Liability for Unrecognized Tax Benefits	8	
Income Tax Expense		8

In this case, we decrease income tax expense in Year 2 to account prospectively for the new information. The expense accrued in Year 1 is not considered an error and is not restated. Entries reflecting resolution of uncertainty are consistent with other changes in accounting estimates.

c. **Portion of Tax Benefit Is Realized**

Assume that in December of Year 2, after negotiations with taxing authorities, Boulder Inc. realizes $68 of the tax deduction. Record Boulder's entry resolving the uncertain tax position on December 31 of Year 2.

Solution

December 31, Year 2—To record negotiated resolution of tax position

Liability for Unrecognized Tax Benefits	8	
Income Tax Payable ($32 × 25%)		8

Assets = Liabilities + Equity
+5,000   –5,008
Tax Pay   Exp
+8
Unrecog Tax

Inc Tax Pay	Inc Tax Exp
5,000	5,008

Liab—Tax Benefit
8

Assets = Liabilities + Equity
–8   –17
Unrecog Tax   Exp
+25
Tax Pay

Inc Tax Pay	Inc Tax Exp
25	17

Liab—Tax Benefit
8 | 8 Bal.
0

Assets = Liabilities + Equity
–8   +8
Unrecog Tax   Exp

Liab—Tax Benefit   Inc Tax Exp
8 | 8 Bal. | 8
0

Assets = Liabilities + Equity
–8
Unrecog Tax
+8
Tax Pay

Liab—Tax Benefit   Inc Tax Pay
8 | 8 Bal. | 8
0

continued

continued from previous page

> In this case there is no effect on the income statement because the amount owed is equal to the amount as estimated. The amount is reclassified to Income Taxes Payable because the resolution of uncertainty results in a current obligation to pay $8.

TARGET

Real World—UNRECOGNIZED TAX BENEFITS

In a recent Form 10-K, **Target Corporation** recorded $352 million of unrecognized tax benefits based on the uncertainty of some tax positions. The following required disclosure reconciles the beginning of Year balance to the end of Year balance of the Liability for Unrecognized Tax Benefits. The company also reserved for potential interest and penalties that could result if the company does not sustain their position with taxing authorities.

Reconciliation of Liability for Unrecognized Tax Benefits (millions)	2023	2022	2021
Balance at beginning of period	$233	$125	$181
Additions based on tax positions related to the current year	128	115	32
Additions for tax positions of prior years	8	21	11
Reductions for tax positions of prior years	(13)	(23)	(95)
Settlements	(4)	(5)	(4)
Balance at end of period	$352	$233	$125

If we were to prevail on all unrecognized tax benefits recorded, the amount that would benefit the effective tax rate was $161 million, $107 million, and $67 million as of February 3, 2024, January 28, 2023, and January 29, 2022, respectively. In addition, the reversal of accrued interest and penalties would also benefit the effective tax rate. Interest and penalties associated with unrecognized tax benefits are recorded within income tax expense. During 2023, 2022, and 2021, we recorded an expense / (benefit) from accrued interest and penalties of $6 million, $(4) million, and $1 million, respectively. As of February 3, 2024, January 28, 2023, and January 29, 2022, total accrued interest and penalties were $14 million, $7 million, and $13 million, respectively.

   It is reasonably possible that the amount of the unrecognized tax benefits with respect to our other unrecognized tax positions will increase or decrease during the next twelve months; however, an estimate of the amount or range of the change cannot be made at this time.

Uncertain Tax Positions   **LO18-8** ◄ **REVIEW 18-8**

Review

MBC

Leah Inc. considered the possible outcomes of a recent tax position taken related to the deduction of $30,000 from taxable revenue. Leah determined that this position is *more likely than not* to be sustained in future discussions with taxing authorities. Using available information, Leah created the following summary of the probabilities of possible outcomes.

Individual probability of occurring	15%	20%	25%	20%	20%
Estimated allowable tax deduction	$30,000	$22,000	$20,000	$10,000	$5,000

Assuming taxable income of $450,000 (reflecting the inclusion of the uncertain tax expense in deductible expenses) and a tax rate of 25%, record the income tax journal entry for the year.

More Practice:
BE18-43, BE18-44, E18-48, E18-49

Solution on p. 18-68.

Disclosure Requirements for Income Tax

Notes to the financial statements should provide the following supplemental disclosures regarding income taxes (ASC 740-10-50).

- Total of all deferred tax liabilities and assets.

- Total adjustments to and net change in the valuation allowance.

- Approximate tax effect of each major source of temporary difference and carryforward that gives rise to significant portions of deferred tax assets and liabilities.

- Reconciliation between the effective tax rate and the U.S. statutory rate in percentages and dollars with the inclusion of specified categories of reconciling items.

- Current portion of income tax expense or benefit.

- Deferred portion of income tax expense or benefit.
- Tax credits.
- Government grants to the extent they are used as reductions of income tax expense.
- Benefits of and expiration dates of operating loss carryforwards.
- Adjustments of deferred tax assets or liabilities as a result of enacted tax law or rate changes or changes in the tax status of the company.
- Income or loss from continuing operations before income tax expense (or benefit) disaggregated between domestic and foreign.
- Income tax expense (benefit) from continuing operations disaggregated by federal, state, and foreign.
- Amount of income tax paid disaggregated by federal, state, and foreign taxes (with additional disclosures required for payments to individual jurisdictions meeting a specified threshold).

FASTENAL   **Real World—DISCLOSURE**

Fastenal Company included the following summary of current and deferred taxes in its disclosure of income taxes in a recent Form 10-K.

Components of income tax expense (benefit) were as follows:

2023 ($ millions)	Current	Deferred	Total
Federal	$273.3	$ (9.2)	$264.1
State	59.6	(1.3)	58.3
Foreign	44.9	(0.3)	44.6
Income tax expense	$377.8	$(10.8)	$367.0

Total income tax expense is also shown on the income statement.

Components of income tax expense (benefit) were as follows ($ millions):

Consolidated Statement of Earnings (excerpt)	2023
Earnings before income taxes	$1,522.0
Income tax expense	367.0
Net earnings	$1,155.0

While numerous detailed journal entries go into producing the disclosures a financial statement user sees, we can infer that the net of all these entries would be the following entry at an aggregated level ($ millions).

Income Tax Expense	367.0	
Net Deferred Tax Liability	10.8	
Income Tax Payable		377.8

Assets = Liabilities + Equity
−10.8   −367.0
Net DTL   Exp
+377.8
Tax Pay

Management Judgment

Deferred Tax Asset Valuation Allowance

Determining whether it is *more likely than not* that some or all of the balance of deferred tax assets will not be realized requires management judgment. Recall that deferred tax assets are realized only if a company has positive taxable income in the future to offset the deferred deductions (p. 18-18). Management must evaluate both positive and negative evidence to determine the portion (if not all of) the deferred tax asset for which an allowance is required. For example, a significant increase in expected compliance costs with newly enacted environmental regulations should have a significant impact on estimates of future taxable income.

740-10-30-24 Future realization of a tax benefit sometimes will be expected for a portion but not all of a deferred tax asset, and the dividing line between the two portions may be unclear. In those circumstances, application of judgment based on a careful assessment of all available evidence is required to determine the portion of a deferred tax asset for which it is more likely than not a tax benefit will not be realized.

The decisions made by management regarding the amount of the allowance impacts financial reporting. An adjustment to the allowance in a period results in lower or higher tax expense and, thus, higher or lower reported financial accounting income.

Uncertain Tax Position

The measurement of an unrecognized tax benefit is based on management's judgment of the amount that the company will settle with the taxing authority. Management must determine whether the company meets the recognition threshold, and if so, management must measure the tax benefit (p. 18-29). Both steps require management judgment depending on what factors management determines are relevant and the weight assigned to the factors based on all information available at the time. The uncertain tax position is revaluated as new information becomes available.

740-10-25-14 Subsequent recognition shall be based on management's best judgment given the facts, circumstances, and information available at the reporting date. A tax position need not be legally extinguised and its resolution need not be certain to subsequently recognize the position. Subsequent changes in judgment that lead to changes in recognition shall result from the evaluation of new information and not from a new evaluation or new interpretation by management of information that was available in a previous financial reporting period . . .

Apply intraperiod tax allocation

Intraperiod tax allocation is the allocation of tax expense (benefit) to different financial statement components. Intraperiod tax allocation is required for income (loss) from continuing operations and discontinued operations. In addition, income tax expense (benefit) related to items charged or credited directly to other comprehensive income are shown in other comprehensive income. This is done by showing the item net of the tax effect as illustrated in **Demo 18-9**.

Allocate Tax Expense (Benefit)
- To income (loss) from continuing operations
- To income (loss) from discontinued operations
- To other comprehensive income

LO 18-9 Overview

Intraperiod Tax Allocation   **LO18-9** ◀ **DEMO 18-9**

Demo

MBC

During the year, Hikers Corp. reports pretax GAAP income of $6,000, resulting from income of $8,000 from continuing operations and a loss from discontinued operations of $2,000. Unrealized loss on available-for-sale debt securities totaled $500 before tax. The tax rate is 25%. Assume taxable income equals pretax GAAP income. Present the income statement and the statement of comprehensive income for the year.

Solution
The income statement includes the following.

Income Statement	
Income before income taxes.	$ 8,000
Income tax expense ($8,000 × 25%)	2,000
Income from continuing operations	6,000
Discontinued operations	
Loss from discontinued operations, net of tax ($2,000 × 75%).	(1,500)
Net income.	$ 4,500

The statement of comprehensive income includes the following.

Statement of Comprehensive Income	
Net income.	$ 4,500
Other comprehensive income (loss)	
Unrealized loss on securities ($500 × 75%)	(375)
Comprehensive income	$ 4,125

J&J
Real World—INTRAPERIOD TAX ALLOCATION

Johnson & Johnson recognized (a) income from operations of discontinued segments net of tax and (b) other comprehensive income items net of tax in a recent Form 10-K, applying intraperiod tax allocation.

Consolidated Statements of Operations (millions)	2023	2022
Earnings before provision for income taxes	$15,062	$19,359
Provision for taxes on income taxes (Note 8)	1,736	2,989
Net earnings from continuing operations	13,326	16,370
Net earnings from discontinued operations, net of tax (Note 21)	21,827	1,571
Net earnings	**$35,153**	**$17,941**

Consolidated Statements of Comprehensive Income (millions)	2023	2022
Net earnings	$35,153	$17,941
Other comprehensive income/(loss), net of tax	(4,741)	91
Comprehensive income	$30,412	$18,032

REVIEW 18-9   **LO18-9**   **Intraperiod Tax Allocation**

Review

MBC

Athletics Inc. had the following pretax balances in its accounts on December 31.

Revenues	$180,000
Cost of goods sold	99,000
Operating expenses	15,000
Loss from discontinued operations	(14,000)
Unrealized gain on available-for-sale debt securities	3,000

More Practice:
AppBE18-1, AppBE18-2,
AppE18-1
Solution on p. 18-69.

Assuming an income tax rate of 25% and a simple company structure (with no differences between financial accounting and taxable incomes, no state taxes, no foreign earnings or taxes, and no tax credits), prepare a combined statement of comprehensive income using intraperiod tax allocation.

Questions

Q18-1.   Briefly explain intraperiod tax allocation.

Q18-2.   Briefly describe the balance sheet approach in accounting for income taxes.

Q18-3.   Explain why deferred income tax can be either an asset or a liability.

Q18-4.   Explain the main overriding reasons why pretax GAAP income and taxable income are often quite different.

Q18-5.   Differentiate between a temporary difference and permanent difference such as a nondeductible or a nontaxable item.

Q18-6.   Landend Corporation (a) uses straight-line depreciation for its financial accounting and uses accelerated depreciation on its income tax return and (b) holds a $50,000 investment in tax-free municipal bonds. What kind of tax difference is caused by each of these items? Explain.

Q18-7.   How are deferred tax accounts presented on the balance sheet?

Q18-8.   Explain the difference between a taxable temporary difference and a deductible temporary difference.

Q18-9.   Explain the difference between a deferred tax liability and a deferred tax asset.

Q18-10. Define net operating loss (NOL) carryforwards. Briefly explain the process of a tax loss carryforward.

Q18-11. With respect to NOL carryforwards, how does uncertainty affect the accounting treatment?

Q18-12. Is deferred tax arising from an NOL carryforward classified as current or noncurrent?

Q18-13. Explain the limitation on the carrying value of deferred income tax assets.

Q18-14. How does a company account for a change in tax rates?

Q18-15. Describe the two-step process required when uncertain tax positions are taken.

Data Analytics

Analyzing Excel Visualizations of Deferred Tax Accounts The Excel file associated with this exercise includes balance sheet tax account data for two years for fourteen large companies in the Consumer Discretionary segment. This exercise requires the preparation of visualizations used to analyze the deferred tax allowance in relation to the deferred tax asset balance and net deferred tax assets in relation to deferred tax liabilities.

Data Analytics DA18-1
Using Excel Visualizations to Analyze the Impact of an Accounting Change **LO1, 2, 3**

Data Visualization

Data Visualization Activities are available in **myBusinessCourse**. These assignments use Tableau Dashboards to expose students to visual depictions of data and introduce students to data analytics through data visualizations. These exercises are assignable and auto graded by MBC.

Data Visualization

Multiple Choice

MC18-1. Identifying Temporary Differences Which of the following typically results in temporary differences classified as expenses or losses for financial reporting but are deductible for taxes in a later period?   **LO1**

   a.   Regulatory fine   *c.*   Prepaid maintenance
   b.   Cash advances from customers   *d.*   Warranty liability

MC18-2. Identifying Temporary Differences Which of the following typically results in temporary differences classified as revenues or gains for financial reporting but are taxable in a later period?   **LO1**

   a.   Interest received on municipal bonds
   b.   Cash advances from customers
   c.   Unrealized gain recognized for investments accounted for under FV-NI
   d.   Website maintenance subscription fee received in advance

MC18-3. Determining Income Tax Expense Fox Inc. had current tax expense of $18,000 for the year ended December 31. The ending deferred tax liability balance was $22,000, which was a $3,000 increase from January 1. The tax rate is 25%. What was total income tax expense for the current year?   **LO2**

   a. $21,000   *c.* $20,250
   b. $15,750   *d.* $15,000

MC18-4. Calculating Deferred Tax Liability The following schedule reconciles Whitney Inc.'s pretax GAAP income to its taxable income for the current year: **LO2, 3**

Pretax GAAP income	$84,000
Nondeductible expense for fines.	1,000
Tax deductible insurance cost in excess of GAAP insurance expense.	(8,000)
Taxable subscription receipts in excess of GAAP subscription revenue.	4,000
Taxable income.	$81,000

Assuming a tax rate of 25%, what would the company calculate as a deferred tax liability (ignoring any deferred tax assets or permanent differences)?

   a. $2,000   *c.* $3,000
   b. $1,000   *d.* $0

MC18-5. Determining Income Tax Expense Regent Corp. recorded the following journal entry on December 31 of Year 1.   **LO3**

Cost of Goods Sold	3,500	
Allowance to Reduce Inventory to Net Realizable Value.		3,500

If Regent Corp. has a tax rate of 25% and taxable income of $38,000 for the year, what is income tax expense for the year?

   a. $10,375   *c.* $6,000
   b. $8,625   *d.* $9,500

LO4

MC18-6. **Computing Amounts for a Rate Reconciliation** Schultz Inc. reported pretax GAAP income of $50,000. The company calculated taxable income of $46,000 by subtracting a permanent difference of $500 and a taxable temporary difference of $3,500 from pretax GAAP income. What reconciling percentage(s) will the company show on its rate reconciliation from its statutory rate of 25% to its effective tax rate?

	Permanent Difference	Temporary Difference
a.	−0.25%	−1.75%
b.	−1.00%	−7.00%
c.	+0.25%	0%
d.	−0.25%	0%

LO5

MC18-7. **Adjusting Valuation Allowance** Raymond Inc. summarized the following balances on December 31.

	Dec. 31
Deferred tax asset, Dec. 31	$60,000 Dr.
Valuation allowance for deferred tax asset, unadjusted	5,000 Cr.

Management reviewed all available positive and negative evidence to estimate that it was more likely than not that 75% of the deferred tax asset would not be realized. The entry to adjust the valuation allowance to the desired ending balance would include:

a.   a debit to income tax expense for $40,000.

b.   a debit to Valuation Allowance for Deferred Tax Asset for $40,000.

c.   a credit to xDeferred Tax Asset for $45,000.

d.   a debit to income tax expense for $45,000.

LO5

MC18-8. **Determining Balance in Valuation Allowance** Sheridan Inc. reported a net deferred tax asset on its year-end balance sheet of $12,000. If the company's year-end records show a deferred tax asset of $24,000 and a deferred tax liability of $10,000, what was the balance in its deferred tax asset valuation allowance?

a. $2,000 debit   c. $22,000 debit

b. $2,000 credit   d. $22,000 credit

LO6

MC18-9. **Adjusting Deferred Taxes for Change in Enacted Tax Rate** Reid Inc. recognized a deferred tax asset of $15,000 on December 31 of Year 1 that is expected to reverse evenly over the next three years. On December 31 of Year 1, a new tax law is enacted which increases the tax rate of 25% to 35% beginning on January 1 of Year 3. What change should Reid make to the deferred asset balance on December 31 of Year 1?

a.   Increase by $1,000   c.   Increase by $4,000

b.   Decrease by $1,000   d.   Increase by $5,000

LO7

MC18-10. **Identifying Effects of NOL Carryforward** Sayle Inc. incurred a net operating loss for tax purposes of $38,000 in Year 1, the company's first year of operations. On December 31 of Year 1, evidence indicates that it is more likely than not that the deferred tax asset will be realized. In Year 2, the company calculates taxable income of $15,000. On December 31 of Year 2, the company determines that it is more likely than not that the deferred tax asset will be realized. What will the company recognize as income tax payable in Year 2 assuming a statutory rate of 25%?

a. $0   c. $3,000

b. $750   d. $3,750

LO8

MC18-11. **Accounting for Uncertain Tax Position** Lasso Inc. considered the probability of its recent tax position taken related to the deductibility of certain expenses of $20,000. Lasso Inc. is only 70% certain that its tax position supporting the deductibility of the full $20,000 will hold if the company is audited by the taxing authorities.

Lasso Inc. paid taxes based upon its tax position taken. Lasso's taxable income is $320,000 after considering the $20,000 deductible amount. Lasso's tax rate is 25%.

What will the company record as income tax expense for the year?

a. $81,500   c. $85,000

b. $83,500   d. $80,000

Consider the following three differences between financial and tax reporting due to current period activity.
1. Allowance for doubtful accounts has a $30,000 GAAP basis but a $0 tax basis.
2. Installment sale receivable has a $200,000 GAAP basis but a $0 tax basis.
3. Environmental fine expense recognized for GAAP purposes is never deductible for income tax purposes.

For each of the three items above, answer the following questions. Consider each item separately.
a. In the current period, will taxable income be greater than or less than pretax GAAP income?
b. In a future period(s), will taxable income be greater than or less than pretax GAAP income, or is there no impact on future financial and tax reporting?
c. Is the difference a taxable temporary difference, a deductible temporary difference, a nontaxable item, or a nondeductible item?

Brief Exercise 18-1
Identifying Temporary and Permanent Differences **LO1**
Hint: See Demo 18-1B

Consider the following three differences between financial and tax reporting due to current period activity.
1. The carrying amount of equipment for GAAP purposes is $300,000, but the tax basis of equipment is $200,000.
2. Estimated litigation accrual is $20,000 for GAAP purposes but is $0 for tax purposes.
3. Prepaid maintenance contract has a $25,000 GAAP basis but a $0 tax basis.

For each of the three items above, answer the following questions. Consider each item separately.
a. In the current period, will taxable income be greater than or less than pretax GAAP income?
b. In a future period(s), will taxable income be greater than or less than pretax GAAP income, or is there no impact on future financial and tax reporting?
c. Is the difference a taxable temporary difference, a deductible temporary difference, a nontaxable item, or a nondeductible item?

Brief Exercise 18-2
Identifying Temporary and Permanent Differences **LO1**
Hint: See Demo 18-1B

Consider the following three differences between financial and tax reporting due to current period activity.
1. Warranty liability has a $45,000 GAAP basis, but a $0 tax basis.
2. The investment account basis is lower than the tax basis of the investment account by $10,000 due to an unrealized holding loss recognized under GAAP.
3. Premiums paid on executive life insurance policies are recognized as insurance expense for GAAP purposes, but are never deductible for tax purposes.

For each of the three items above, answer the following questions. Consider each item separately.
a. In the current period, will taxable income be greater than or less than pretax GAAP income?
b. In a future period(s), will taxable income be greater than or less than pretax GAAP income, or is there no impact on future financial and tax reporting?
c. Is the difference a taxable temporary difference, a deductible temporary difference, a nontaxable item, or a nondeductible item?

Brief Exercise 18-3
Identifying Temporary and Permanent Differences **LO1**
Hint: See Demo 18-1B

Determine whether each of the following differences originating in the current year would result in a taxable temporary difference or a deductible temporary difference.

		GAAP Basis	Tax Basis
a.	Prepaid insurance..................	$ 20,000	$ 0
b.	Fixed asset, net	100,000	65,000
c.	Deferred revenue	33,000	0
d.	Installment receivable............	18,000	0
e.	Allowance for doubtful accounts...	2,500	0
f.	Investment*......................	20,000	25,000

*Investment accounted for at FV-NI for GAAP purposes and at cost for tax purposes.

Brief Exercise 18-4
Identifying Taxable and Deductible Temporary Differences **LO1**

For each of the following items, identify whether the difference between GAAP and tax reporting will result in a taxable temporary difference, a deductible temporary difference, or neither.
a. For Accounts Payable, the GAAP basis is identical to the tax basis.
b. For Equipment, net, the GAAP basis is greater than the tax basis.
c. For Accrued Litigation Liability, the GAAP basis is greater than the tax basis (which is $0).
d. For Organization Costs (asset), the tax basis is greater than the GAAP basis (which is $0).

Brief Exercise 18-5
Identifying Taxable and Deductible Temporary Differences **LO1**

Brief Exercise 18-6
Computing Net Income **LO2**

4M Inc. showed income tax on its tax return of $4,800 on December 31 and had a tax rate of 25%. If taxable income was equal to pretax GAAP income for the year, determine the amount of net income that 4M Inc. recognized during the year on its financial statements.

Brief Exercise 18-7
Recording Income Tax Expense **LO2, 3**

Aquafena Inc. recognized taxable income of $100,000 for the year ended December 31. Aquafena calculated a deferred tax asset and a deferred tax liability of $12,000 and $8,000, respectively, on December 31. The tax rate is 25%. Assume zero beginning balances in deferred tax accounts.

a. Determine the increase in income tax payable on December 31.
b. Prepare the income tax expense journal entry on December 31.

Brief Exercise 18-8
Reporting Income Tax Expense Using the Accounting Equation **LO2, 3**

Refer to BE18-7, but instead of a journal entry for part *b*, show the effect on the accounting equation for the transaction, including identifying the individual accounts affected, and the total impact on assets, liabilities, and stockholders' equity.

Brief Exercise 18-9
Recording Income Tax Expense **LO2, 3**

Alexa Inc. recorded the following deferred tax amounts.

	December 31, Year 1	December 31, Year 2
Deferred tax liability	$ 5,000	$8,500
Deferred tax asset	13,000	6,000

If the company had current tax expense of $26,000 in Year 2, determine total income tax expense for Year 2.

Brief Exercise 18-10
Reporting a Deferred Tax Liability **LO2**

On December 31, Lexxus Inc. recorded an unrealized gain in income of $5,000 related to its trading debt securities originally purchased on December 15 for $20,000. Lexxus recognized pretax GAAP income of $80,000 during the year and had a tax rate of 25%.

a. Determine the reported amount of trading securities in the financial statements on December 31.
b. Determine the tax basis of the trading securities on December 31.
c. Calculate the deferred tax balance and show how it would be reported in the December 31 balance sheet.

Brief Exercise 18-11
Recording Income Tax Expense **LO2**

Assuming the same information from BE18-10, record the income tax journal entry on December 31. Assume zero beginning balances in deferred tax accounts.

Brief Exercise 18-12
Reporting Income Tax Expense Using the Accounting Equation **LO2**

Refer to BE18-11, but instead of a journal entry, show the effect on the accounting equation for the transaction, including identifying the individual accounts affected, and the total impact on assets, liabilities, and stockholders' equity.

Brief Exercise 18-13
Recording Income Tax Expense **LO2**

Alexa Inc. purchased equipment two years ago for $50,000 with no residual value. At year-end on December 31, accumulated depreciation on the equipment using the straight-line method for financial reporting was $12,500. For tax purposes, Alexa uses MACRS depreciation resulting in $35,600 in accumulated depreciation for tax purposes on December 31. Taxable income was $100,000 and the company's tax rate is 25%.

a. Determine the GAAP basis of equipment (net) on December 31.
b. Determine the tax basis of equipment on December 31.
c. Assuming a deferred tax liability balance of $4,900 on January 1, record income tax expense for the year.

Brief Exercise 18-14
Calculating Income Tax Expense **LO3**

Underwood Co. had current tax expense of $20,000 for the year ended December 31. The ending deferred tax asset balance was $6,000, which was a $4,000 increase from January 1. The tax rate is 25%. Calculate income tax expense for the year.

Brief Exercise 18-15
Calculating Deferred Tax Asset Balance **LO3**

On December 31, Delta Inc. recorded $28,000 of deferred revenue (a liability) on customer deposits received in advance of the satisfaction of performance obligations. However, this amount is taxable during the year when cash was received. Assume a tax rate of 25% and pretax GAAP income of $160,000 for the year.

a. Determine the GAAP basis of deferred revenue on December 31.

b. Determine the tax basis of deferred revenue on December 31.

c. Determine the deferred tax asset balance on December 31.

Assuming the same information in BE18-15, record the income tax journal entry on December 31. Assume zero beginning balances in deferred tax accounts and there are no other differences between accounting and tax incomes.

Brief Exercise 18-16
Recording Income Tax
Expense **LO3**

Refer to BE18-16, but instead of a journal entry, show the effect on the accounting equation for the transaction, including identifying the individual accounts affected, and the total impact on assets, liabilities, and stockholders' equity.

Brief Exercise 18-17
Reporting Income
Tax Expense Using
the Accounting
Equation **LO3**

Rangee Rover Inc. had taxable income of $95,000 for the year. The GAAP basis of accounts receivable (net) is $6,000 less than the tax basis of accounts receivable. Assuming a tax rate of 25%, record the income tax journal entry on December 31. Assume zero beginning balances in deferred tax accounts.

Brief Exercise 18-18
Recording Income Tax
Expense **LO3**

Assume the same information as in BE18-18 except that the Deferred Tax Asset account had a January 1 debit balance of $1,800. Record the income tax journal entry on December 31.

Brief Exercise 18-19
Recording Income Tax
Expense **LO3**

ATW Corporation has completed an analysis of its pretax GAAP income, its taxable income, and temporary differences. Taxable income is $100,000, and there are several temporary differences that result in (a) a deferred tax asset of $15,000 and (b) a deferred tax liability of $20,000. The income tax rate for the current period and all future periods is 25%. There were no deferred tax assets or deferred tax liabilities as of the beginning of the current year. Provide the entry to record income taxes on December 31.

Brief Exercise 18-20
Recording Income Tax
Expense **LO2, 3**

Refer to BE18-20, but instead of a journal entry, show the effect on the accounting equation for the transaction, including identifying the individual accounts affected, and the total impact on assets, liabilities, and stockholders' equity.

Brief Exercise 18-21
Reporting Income
Tax Expense Using
the Accounting
Equation **LO2, 3**

Bell Corp. recognized $38,000 in current income tax expense during the year. Pretax GAAP income was $89,000 and deferred income tax expense is $6,000 for the year. Prepare (a) the income tax section of the income statement for the year and (b) the disclosure of current and deferred income tax expense.

Brief Exercise 18-22
Preparing Income Tax
Section of Income
Statement **LO2, 3**

Baltimore Inc. reported pretax GAAP income of $45,000 during the year. In analyzing differences between pretax GAAP income and taxable income, the company determined that it had properly deducted $5,000 in nondeductible fines and added $2,800 in tax-exempt municipal interest revenue to pretax GAAP income. Given a statutory tax rate of 25%, determine the following.

Brief Exercise 18-23
Analyzing Permanent
Differences **LO4**

a. Taxable income

b. Income tax payable

c. Income tax expense

d. Net income

e. Effective tax rate

Refer to information in BE18-23. Prepare a reconciliation between Baltimore Inc.'s statutory tax rate and its effective tax rate in dollars and percentages.

Brief Exercise 18-24
Reconciling between
Effective and Statutory Tax
Rates **LO4**

Lake Company has pretax GAAP income of $100,000 during its first year of operations. Lake Company has depreciation expense during the year for GAAP purposes that is $60,000 less than the amount of depreciation expense for tax purposes. In addition, $5,000 of regulatory fines included in the determination of pretax GAAP income are not tax deductible. Lake Company's tax rate is 25%. Prepare Lake Company's income tax entry on December 31.

Brief Exercise 18-25
Recording Income Tax
Expense **LO2, 4**

Brief Exercise 18-26
Reporting Income
Tax Expense Using
the Accounting
Equation **LO2, 4**

Refer to BE18-25, but instead of a journal entry, show the effect on the accounting equation for the transaction, including identifying the individual accounts affected, and the total impact on assets, liabilities, and stockholders' equity.

Brief Exercise 18-27
Recording Income Tax
Expense **LO3, 4**

Lake Company has pretax GAAP income of $100,000 during its first year of operations. Lake Company has warranty expense during the year for GAAP purposes that is $60,000 greater than the amount of warranty expense for tax purposes. In addition, $5,000 of regulatory fines included in the determination of pretax GAAP income are not tax deductible. Lake Company's tax rate is 25%. Prepare Lake Company's income tax entry on December 31.

Brief Exercise 18-28
Reporting Income
Tax Expense Using
the Accounting
Equation **LO3, 4**

Refer to BE18-27, but instead of a journal entry, show the effect on the accounting equation for the transaction, including identifying the individual accounts affected, and the total impact on assets, liabilities, and stockholders' equity.

Brief Exercise 18-29
Calculating Deferred Tax
Balance **LO2, 4**

Evergreen Company's reconciliation between pretax GAAP income and taxable income follows for the year.

Pretax GAAP income	$ 200,000
Depreciation adjustment.	(40,000)
Nondeductible item.	1,250
Taxable income.	$161,250

The company had one temporary difference due to the GAAP basis of equipment exceeding the tax basis of equipment. Record the income tax journal entry for the calendar year, assuming a tax rate of 25%. Assume that the January 1 deferred tax liability balance was $5,000.

Brief Exercise 18-30
Recording Tax Valuation
Allowance **LO5**
Hint: See Demo 18-5A

Maui Resort Inc. determined that the balance in its deferred tax asset account on December 31 was $50,000. Management reviewed all available positive and negative evidence to estimate that 30% of the deferred tax asset was *more likely than not* to be realized. The valuation allowance for deferred tax assets has a December 31 unadjusted balance of $4,000 (credit). Record the entry to adjust the allowance on December 31.

Brief Exercise 18-31
Analyzing Deferred
Taxes **LO5**

Assume Company A and Company B each had a balance in deferred tax assets of $250,000. However, Company A has a valuation allowance related to the deferred tax asset of $200,000 while Company B has a valuation allowance of $5,000. What can you infer about Company A and B based upon this information?

Brief Exercise 18-32
Analyzing Valuation
Allowance **LO5**

Starbucks Corporation recognized the following amounts in a recent Form 10-K.

$ millions	Current Fiscal Year-End	Prior Fiscal Year-End
Deferred tax asset	$1,651.1	$1,660.0
Valuation allowance	70.3	143.7
Net income attributable to Starbucks	2,817.7	2,757.4

a. Calculate the deferred tax asset valuation allowance as a percentage of deferred tax assets for both fiscal years presented.

b. Based on your results in part *a*, does it appear that the company considers deferred tax benefits to be realized at a higher or lower rate than the prior year?

Brief Exercise 18-33
Reporting Deferred Taxes
in Balance Sheet **LO5**
Hint: See Demo 18-5B

Kate Club Inc. has determined that there are four temporary differences between the tax basis and the GAAP basis of assets and liabilities that resulted in the following deferred taxes: (a) deferred tax liability related to accelerated tax depreciation over straight-line depreciation, $20,000; (b) deferred tax asset related to deferred contract revenue collected in advance, $24,000; (c) deferred tax asset related to bad debt expense recognized on an allowance basis, $10,000; and (d) deferred tax liability related to prepaid automobile insurance, $8,000. Prepare the balance sheet presentation of deferred taxes.

Taylor Co. reports temporary differences resulting in a deferred tax asset of $450,000, a valuation allowance of $150,000 and a total deferred tax liability of $220,000. How would the company report deferred taxes on its balance sheet?

Brief Exercise 18-34
Reporting Deferred Tax
Accounts **LO5**
Hint: See Demo 18-5B

In Year 1, Explorers Inc. completed installment sales of $80,000, recorded in full as accounts receivable and as revenue. For tax purposes, it recognizes income when cash is received. Cash related to the installment sales is expected to be received in the following years: Year 2 of $10,000; Year 3 of $40,000; Year 4 of $30,000. The enacted tax rate for Year 1, Year 2, and Year 3 is 25%. The newly enacted tax rate for Year 4 is 40%. Compute the value of the deferred tax liability at year-end on December 31 of Year 1.

Brief Exercise 18-35
Calculating a Deferred Tax
Liability Balance
LO2, 6

The Jets Company recorded a deferred tax liability of $18,750 at year-end on December 31 of Year 1, due to the book value of equipment exceeding the tax basis of equipment by $75,000. The difference will reverse equally over the next three years. In late Year 1, the enacted tax rate increased to 42.5% beginning in Year 3.
a. Determine the income tax rate that is the enacted rate for Year 1.
b. What journal entry should the Jets record to adjust the deferred tax liability, if any, on December 31 of Year 1?

Brief Exercise 18-36
Recording Income
Tax with Changing Tax
Rates **LO2, 6**
Hint: See Demo 18-6

During the current year, Lambeau Inc. suffered a loss of $100,000. The enacted tax rate is 25%. Prepare Lambeau's entry for the loss carryforward on December 31, assuming that management determined that it was *more likely than not* that the deferred tax asset would be realized.

Brief Exercise 18-37
Recording Net
Operating Loss
Carryforward **LO7**
Hint: See Demo 18-7A

In Year 1, Cardinals Company operated at a tax loss, totaling $(88,000) during its first year of business.
a. Assuming a tax rate of 25%, and that income is expected in Year 2, record the entry to reflect the tax benefit of the net operating loss on December 31 of Year 1.
b. Cardinals Company determined that it was *more likely than not* that 75% of the deferred tax asset would not be realized. Prepare the entry to record a deferred tax asset valuation allowance, assuming a zero beginning balance in that account.

Brief Exercise 18-38
Recording Net
Operating Loss
Carryforward **LO7**

Refer to BE18-38, but instead of journal entries, show the effect on the accounting equation for the transactions, including identifying the individual accounts affected, and the total impact on assets, liabilities, and stockholders' equity.

Brief Exercise 18-39
Reporting Net Operating
Loss Carryforward
Using the Accounting
Equation **LO7**

During Year 4, Lamb Inc. suffered a tax loss of $(100,000). Lamb qualifies for a two-year loss carryback option for tax purposes, using the earliest year first and with no income restrictions. Taxable income for the last three years (listed in chronological order) follows: Year 1: $90,000; Year 2: $80,000; and Year 3: $30,000. The tax rate is 40% for Year 3 and Year 4, and 25% for Year 1 and Year 2. Prepare Lamb's entry for the loss carryback at year-end on December 31 of Year 4.

Brief Exercise 18-40
Recording Net Operating
Loss Carryback **LO7**
Hint: See Demo 18-7B

Refer to BE18-40, but instead of journal entries, show the effect on the accounting equation for the transactions, including identifying the individual accounts affected, and the total impact on assets, liabilities, and stockholders' equity.

Brief Exercise 18-41
Reporting Net Operating
Loss Carryback
Using the Accounting
Equation **LO7**

Latt Inc. experienced a tax loss in Year 3. The company reported the following taxable income (loss) and tax rate for Year 1 through Year 3. There were no temporary differences from Year 1 to Year 3.

Brief Exercise 18-42
Recording Net Operating
Loss Carryback **LO7**

	Year 1	Year 2	Year 3
Taxable income (loss)............	$40,000	$15,000	$(50,000)
Income tax rate.................	25%	35%	40%

a. Record the Year 3 entry for a loss carryback assuming that the company qualifies for a two-year loss carryback option for tax purposes, using the earliest year first and with no income restrictions.

b. List the accounts and amounts that should be reported on the income statement and on the year-end balance sheet of Year 3.

Brief Exercise 18-43
Recording Income
Tax Expense with Tax
Uncertainty **LO8**

Springs Inc. has taken a tax position during the year that it believes is based on fairly clear tax law for the payment of $80,000 in salaries and benefits to employees. There are no limits on deductibility and all amounts were fully paid within the statutory time limit, although there is some question on the company's policies for capitalization of a portion of the salaries. Management has a fairly high confidence level in the technical merits of this position. It is clear that it is greater than 50% likely that the full amount of the tax position will be ultimately realized, but it is less than 100%. Springs estimates the probability of sustaining the entire tax position with taxing authorities at 60%. Springs Inc. taxable income is $100,000, which includes the salary deduction of $80,000 referenced previously. If Springs Inc. tax rate is 25% (with no other deferred items), record the income tax journal entry required on December 31.

Brief Exercise 18-44
Recording Income
Tax Expense with Tax
Uncertainty **LO8**

Sentinel Inc. took a deduction of $16,000 on its Year 1 tax return with a tax rate of 25%, reducing current taxes payable by $4,000. Without taking the deduction, the company's tax payable would have been $68,000. The company believes the probability the deduction would be allowed if challenged by taxing authorities is less than 50%. Provide the entry to record income tax expense at year-end on December 31 of Year 1.

Brief Exercise 18-45
Reporting Income Tax
Expense with Uncertainty
Using the Accounting
Equation **LO8**

Refer to BE18-44, but instead of a journal entry, show the effect on the accounting equation for the transaction, including identifying the individual accounts affected, and the total impact on assets, liabilities, and stockholders' equity.

Brief Exercise 18-46
Computing Ratios **LO8**

The following information was obtained from recent annual reports of **American Eagle Outfitters Inc.** For both the current and prior fiscal years, compute the debt-to-equity ratio (a) including deferred tax liabilities as part of total liabilities, and (b) excluding deferred tax liabilities as part of total liabilities.

$ thousands	Current Fiscal Year-End	Prior Fiscal Year-End
Deferred tax liabilities	$ 71,468	$ 67,332
Total liabilities	578,091	560,870
Total stockholders' equity	1,204,569	1,051,376

Exercises

Exercise 18-1
Differentiating Pretax
GAAP Income from
Taxable Income; Identifying
Temporary and Other
Differences **LO1**
Hint: See Review 18-1

For its first year of operation, Randall Inc.'s pretax GAAP income exceeds its taxable income. The difference is due to three items that are treated differently under the rules of GAAP versus tax: regulatory fines, customer advances, and depreciation expense. While $200,000 of revenues and $125,000 of expenses are identical in the pretax GAAP income and taxable income results, the three differences are described as follows.

- **Regulatory fines** Under GAAP, the company recognizes fine expense of $3,800 for the year. However, fines are not deductible for tax purposes.

- **Customer advances** Under GAAP, because cash collected from a customer of $1,800 relates to a promise to satisfy a performance obligation in a future period, Deferred Revenue is recognized. However, cash is taxable when collected by the company; thus, the tax basis of Deferred Revenue is $0.

- **Depreciable assets** Under GAAP, the company reported equipment purchased on December 31 of the current year at $55,000 (the company did not record any depreciation for GAAP purposes). Under tax rules however, the company opts for immediate expensing of the equipment resulting in a tax basis of Equipment of $0.

Required

a. Prepare a schedule showing the components of pretax GAAP income and taxable income for Year 1.
b. Answer the following questions for each of the three differences described above. Consider each difference separately.
   1. In the current period, will taxable income be greater than or less than pretax GAAP income?
   2. In a future period(s), will taxable income be greater than, less than, or have no impact on pretax GAAP income?
   3. Is the difference a taxable temporary difference, a deductible temporary difference, a nontaxable item, or a nondeductible item?

On January 1 of Year 1, Levery Inc. purchased equipment at a cost of $100,000 with a useful life of 5 years and no salvage value. For GAAP purposes, Levery depreciates fixed assets using the straight-line depreciation. Assume the following four alternate tax depreciation methods resulted in the following depreciation in the year of equipment purchase.

1. Tax depreciation method 1: $25,000
2. Tax depreciation method 2: $33,333
3. Tax depreciation method 3: $40,000
4. Tax depreciation method 4: $100,000

Exercise 18-2
Identifying GAAP Basis, Tax Basis, Temporary Difference **LO1**

Required

a. For each tax method, calculate the GAAP basis and tax basis of net equipment on December 31.

b. Calculate and classify the temporary difference in the current year ended December 31 under each tax method.

For Year 1, Reetz Corp. summarized the following differences between GAAP and tax reporting.

1. On December 31, a contingent liability was accrued for a probable loss on a litigation settlement of $50,000. The loss is not deductible for tax purposes until the lawsuit is settled.
2. Amortization on certain intangible assets held totaling $50,000 was $15,000 under GAAP and $20,000 under tax in Year 1.
3. Prepaid insurance premiums of $4,000 for a life insurance policy on the company's CEO.

Exercise 18-3
Identifying Differences and GAAP Basis, Tax Basis **LO1**

Required

a. Compute and classify each difference as a taxable temporary difference, a deductible temporary difference, a nontaxable item or a nondeductible item.

b. For any temporary differences, identify the GAAP basis and tax basis of the relevant asset or liability at year-end on December 31 of Year 1.

Staples Corporation would have had identical pretax income on both its income tax returns and its income statements for Year 1 through Year 4 except for a depreciable asset that cost $120,000. The asset was depreciated for income tax purposes at the following amounts: Year 1, $48,000; Year 2, $36,000; Year 3, $24,000; and Year 4, $12,000. However, for accounting purposes the straight-line method was used, resulting in $30,000 per year. The accounting and tax periods both end December 31. There were no deferred taxes at the beginning of Year 1. The depreciable asset has a four-year estimated life and no residual value. The tax rate for each year was 25%. Pretax GAAP income for each of the four years follows.

Exercise 18-4
Recording and Reporting Temporary Difference **LO2**
Hint: See Review 18-2

Year 1 .... $230,000	Year 2 .... $250,000	Year 3 .... $240,000	Year 4 .... $240,000

Required

a. Compute the increase to income tax payable on December 31 of Year 1, Year 2, Year 3, and Year 4.

b. Prepare a schedule to compute the deferred tax balance on December 31 of Year 1, Year 2, Year 3, and Year 4.

c. Record the income tax journal entry on December 31 of Year 1, Year 2, Year 3, and Year 4.

d. For each year, show the deferred tax amount that would be reported on the balance sheet.

e. Prepare the income tax section of the income statement for Year 1 and provide the disclosure of current and deferred tax expense.

Refer to E18-4, but instead of journal entries for part *c*, show the effect on the accounting equation for the transactions, including identifying the individual accounts affected, and the total impact on assets, liabilities, and stockholders' equity.

Exercise 18-5
Reporting Temporary Differences Using the Accounting Equation **LO2**

Repeat the requirements of E18-4, but assume instead that the asset was 100% expensed for tax purposes in Year 1.

Exercise 18-6
Recording and Reporting Temporary Difference **LO2**
Hint: See Review 18-2

Refer to E18-6, but instead of journal entries for part *c*, show the effect on the accounting equation for the transactions, including identifying the individual accounts affected, and the total impact on assets, liabilities, and stockholders' equity.

Exercise 18-7
Reporting Temporary Differences Using the Accounting Equation **LO2**

Exercise 18-8
Reporting a Temporary
Difference **LO2**

For the current year, Trendy Inc. calculated taxable income of $30,000 after taking into account one temporary difference: prepaid insurance expense on a GAAP basis exceeds its tax basis by $5,000. The tax rate is 25%, and there were no balances in deferred tax accounts at the beginning of the year.

Required

a. Indicate the deferred income tax amount that would be recognized on the balance sheet on December 31.
b. Prepare the income tax section of the income statement for the year and provide the disclosure of current and deferred tax expense.

Exercise 18-9
Recording and
Reporting Temporary
Difference **LO2**

On December 31, for GAAP purposes, Clubs Inc. reported a balance of $70,000 in Prepaid Maintenance Expense for services to be received over the following year. For tax purposes, however, prepaid costs are deducted when paid. Taxable income is $230,000, and the tax rate is 25%. Assume no other temporary differences or any beginning balances in deferred tax accounts.

Required

a. Record the income tax journal entry on December 31.
b. Prepare the income tax section of the income statement for the year and provide the disclosure of current and deferred tax expense.

Exercise 18-10
Recording a Temporary
Difference **LO3**
Hint: See Demo 18-3

On December 31, for GAAP purposes, Clubs Inc. reported a balance of $40,000 in a warranty liability for anticipated costs to satisfy future warranty claims. The tax basis for the warranty liability is zero. No claims were paid during the year. The increase to income tax payable on December 31 is $85,000, and the tax rate is 25%. Assume no other differences between the tax basis and GAAP basis of assets and liabilities, or any beginning balances in deferred tax accounts.

Required

a. Record the income tax journal entry on December 31.
b. Assume that there was a January 1 beginning balance of $4,000 in the deferred tax asset account related to the warranty liability. How would your answer to part a change?

Exercise 18-11
Recording Income Tax
Expense over Four
Year **LO3**
Hint: See Review 18-3

On December 31 of Year 1, Napper Corporation collected $90,000 cash in advance of satisfying performance obligations of a revenue contract and recognized $90,000 in deferred revenue. Napper recognized GAAP revenue of $30,000 in Year 2, Year 3, and Year 4. For tax purposes, the full $90,000 was recognized as taxable income in Year 1. The accounting and tax periods both end December 31. There were no deferred tax account balances at the beginning of Year 1. The tax rate for each year was 25%.

Pretax GAAP income amounts for each of the four years follow.

| Year 1.... $88,000 | Year 2.... $95,000 | Year 3.... $110,000 | Year 4.... $120,000 |

Required

a. Compute the increase to income tax payable on December 31 of Year 1, Year 2, Year 3, and Year 4.
b. Prepare a schedule to compute the deferred tax balance on December 31 of Year 1, Year 2, Year 3, and Year 4.
c. Record the income tax journal entry on December 31 of Year 1, Year 2, Year 3, and Year 4.

Exercise 18-12
Recording and Reporting
Income Tax Expense
and Deferred Tax
Account **LO3**
Hint: See Demo 18-3

Aspen Inc. estimates assurance-type warranty costs of $30,000 related to Year 1 sales. During the year, $10,000 warranty costs are incurred. On December 31 of Year 1, Aspen Inc. recorded a warranty accrual (debit Warranty Expense and credit Warranty Liability) for future estimated claims of $20,000 ($30,000 – $10,000). For tax purposes, however, only the $10,000 of actual warranty costs is deductible. Assume that the $20,000 of claims results in actual costs in Year 2.

The records of Aspen Inc. show the following.

Pretax GAAP Income	Year 1	Year 2	Total	Taxable Income	Year 1	Year 2	Total
Revenues	$100,000	$100,000		Revenues	$100,000	$100,000	
Other expense	(60,000)	(60,000)		Other expense	(60,000)	(60,000)	
Warranty expenses	(30,000)	0		Warranty expense	(10,000)	(20,000)	
Pretax GAAP income	$ 10,000	$ 40,000	$50,000	Taxable income	$ 30,000	$ 20,000	$50,000

Required

a. Compute the increase in income tax payable for Year 1 and Year 2. Assume a tax rate of 25%.
b. Prepare a schedule to compute the Deferred Tax Asset balance on December 31 of Year 1 and Year 2. Assume a zero-beginning balance in the Deferred Tax Asset account on January 1 of Year 1.

c.   Record the income tax journal entry on December 31 of Year 1.

d.   Indicate the amounts included on the balance sheet on December 31 of Year 1 and on the Year 1 income statement. Indicate the disclosure of current and deferred tax expense. Classify all deferred accounts as non-current on the balance sheet.

e.   Record the income tax journal entry on December 31 of Year 2.

The records of Anderson Inc. provide the following information for the current tax year ended December 31.

- There was no beginning balance in deferred tax account(s).
- Taxable income was $60,000.
- Tax rate is 25%.
- Three temporary differences were identified:
  1. Estimated litigation accrual of $20,000, not deductible for tax purposes until paid. Settlement is expected to take place two years from now.
  2. Excess of accelerated tax depreciation over GAAP depreciation of $12,000 caused a difference in the $50,000 GAAP basis and the $38,000 tax basis of equipment. One-third of the difference will reverse next year.
  3. Unrealized holding gain on equity securities of $3,500 not recognized for tax purposes. Anderson Inc. intends to sell those securities early next year. The investment (accounted for under FV-NI) is reported at its fair value of $10,000 at year-end in the financial statements.

Required

a.   Record the income tax journal entry on December 31.

b.   Record the income tax journal entry on December 31 of next year, assuming taxable income of $125,000.

Exercise 18-13
Recording Multiple
Temporary
Differences **LO2, 3**
Hint: See Demo 18-2,
Demo 18-3

Refer to E18-13, but instead of journal entries, show the effect on the accounting equation for the transactions, including identifying the individual accounts affected, and the total impact on assets, liabilities, and stockholders' equity.

Exercise 18-14
Reporting Multiple
Temporary Differences
Using the Accounting
Equation **LO2, 3**

Lake Company shows the following results of operations on December 31, its first year of operations.

1. Pretax GAAP income for the current year totals $100,000. Taxable income is $90,000.
2. Recorded an installment sale receivable totaling $60,000, with a tax basis of $0. This amount will be included in taxable income in future years.
3. Accrued $50,000 in its financial statements as a provision for future warranty costs. This amount was not deductible for tax purposes during the year but will be deductible in future years.
4. Enacted tax rate for the current year and all future years is 25%.

Required

a.   Provide the journal entry to record income tax expense for the year.

b.   Prepare the income tax section of the income statement for the year and provide the disclosure of current and deferred tax expense.

c.   Compute the effective tax rate for the year.

Exercise 18-15
Recording and Reporting
Multiple Temporary
Differences **LO2, 3**

Cross Corporation provided the following reconciliation between taxable income and pretax GAAP income.

Exercise 18-16
Recording and Reporting
Multiple Temporary
Differences
LO2, 3, 4, 5

	Year 1	Year 2	Year 3	Year 4
Taxable income............................	$59,500	$79,500	$84,400	$74,600
Interest revenue on tax-exempt municipal bonds ...	500	500	600	400
Depreciation expense.........................	15,000	(5,000)	(5,000)	(5,000)
Bad debt expense............................	(20,000)	(10,000)	(18,000)	25,000
Pretax GAAP income	$55,000	$65,000	$62,000	$95,000

- Depreciation adjustment results from a difference between the GAAP basis and tax basis of depreciable equipment.
- Bad debt expense adjustment results from a difference between the GAAP basis and tax basis of net accounts receivable.
- Deferred tax accounts have a zero balance at the start of Year 1. Tax rate is 25%.

Required

a. Record the income tax journal entry on December 31 of Year 1.
b. Record the income tax journal entry on December 31 of Year 2.
c. Record the income tax journal entry on December 31 of Year 3.
d. Record the income tax journal entry on December 31 of Year 4.
e. Prepare the income tax section of the income statement for Year 1 and provide the disclosure of current and deferred tax expense.
f. Indicate the deferred income tax that would be recognized on the balance sheet at December 31 of Year 1. *Hint*: See LO 18-5 for guidance.

Exercise 18-17
Recording and Reporting Multiple Temporary Differences
LO2, 3, 5

TNA Corporation reported the following year-end data related to income taxes.

■ Unrealized gain on the company's investment portfolio, $50,000; recognized in net income for GAAP purposes at the end of the year. Amount will be considered for tax purposes when sold, estimated to be in two years. Fair value of the investment portfolio on December 31 is $400,000.

■ Estimated litigation expense, $30,000; accrued for GAAP purposes at the end of the year. Amount will be considered for income tax purposes when paid, estimated to be at the end of next year.

■ Taxable income (from the tax return) at the end of the year, $100,000; the enacted income tax rate is 25%. There were no deferred tax amounts at the beginning of the year.

Required

a. Prepare schedules to compute the deferred tax balances on December 31.
b. Prepare the journal entry to record income tax expense for the year.
c. Determine pretax GAAP income for the year.
d. Prepare the income tax section of the income statement for the year and provide the disclosure of current and deferred tax expense.
e. Determine the deferred income tax that would be recognized on the balance sheet on December 31. *Hint*: See LO 18-5 for guidance.

Exercise 18-18
Recording Multiple Temporary Differences **LO2, 3**

The following annual information is available for Rapper Inc.

■ Taxable income: $115,000
■ Accounts receivable on installment sales
  • GAAP basis: $150,000
  • Tax basis: $0

■ Tax rate: 25%
■ Deferred revenue on services
  • GAAP basis: $35,000
  • Tax basis: $0
■ No deferred tax balances at beginning of the year

Required

a. Prepare schedules to compute the deferred tax balances on December 31.
b. Record the income tax journal entry on December 31.
c. Compute pretax GAAP income.

Exercise 18-19
Reporting Multiple Temporary Differences **LO2, 5**

For the current year, Raleigh Corporation had taxable income of $100,000 and an income tax rate of 25%. Raleigh had a $75,000 credit balance in its Deferred Tax Liability account. This credit balance was due to the following two temporary differences.

■ Carrying value of equipment for GAAP purposes, $300,000, tax basis of equipment, $200,000. The equipment has a five-year remaining life.

■ Installment sale receivable for GAAP purposes, $200,000, and for income tax purposes, $0. The collection period for the $200,000 receivable is the following four years with equal amounts each year.

Required

Indicate how the deferred tax amounts would be reported on the current year-end balance sheet.

Exercise 18-20
Recording Multiple Temporary Differences **LO2, 3**

Cruse Corporation started operations on January 1 of Year 1. Taxable income from the tax return is $2,850,000. Income tax rate is 25%. There were no beginning balances in deferred tax accounts.

Additional information

■ On December 31 of Year 1, GAAP basis of installment sale receivables, $330,000; tax basis, $0. Receivables will be collected equally over Year 2, Year 3, and Year 4.

■ On December 31 of Year 1, GAAP basis of litigation accrual, $270,000; tax basis, $0. Management expects the litigation loss to be recorded in the tax return in Year 4

Required

a. Prepare schedules to compute the deferred tax balances on December 31 of Year 1.

b. Record the income tax journal entry on December 31 of Year 1.

c. Record the income tax journal entry on December 31 of Year 1 for each of the following *separate* situations.

1. Taxable income is $1,650,000 for Year 1.

2. Deferred tax liability had a January 1 of Year 1 balance of $50,000 instead of $0.

3. Deferred tax asset had a January 1 of Year 1 balance of $28,000 instead of $0.

4. Litigation loss was estimated at $170,000 instead of $270,000.

5. GAAP basis of installment sales receivables was $440,000 instead of $330,000.

ACE Company had pretax GAAP income of $50,000 for the current tax year ended December 31.

Exercise 18-21
Computing Taxable
Income **LO2, 3**

Required

a. Determine taxable income for each of the following *separate* situations.

1. Excess accelerated depreciation for tax purposes, $5,000

2. Unrealized holding gain on securities accounted for under FV-NI, $2,000

3. Unrealized holding loss on securities accounted for under FV-NI, $2,000

4. Rental receipts received in advance, $30,000

5. Litigation contingency accrual, $10,000

6. Six-month prepaid rent deposit, $12,000

b. Classify each of the items in part *a* as one of the following:

1. GAAP revenue before taxable revenue

2. Taxable revenue before GAAP revenue

3. GAAP expense before taxable expense

4. Taxable expense before GAAP expense

Condensed income statements for Prince Inc. for Year 1 and Year 2 ended December 31 follow.

Exercise 18-22
Recording and Reporting
Multiple Differences
LO3, 4, 5

	GAAP		Tax	
	Year 1	Year 2	Year 1	Year 2
Service revenue	$ 0	$ 10,000	$ 10,000	$ 0
Sales revenue.	180,000	190,000	180,000	190,000
Environmental fines	(10,000)	(10,000)	0	0
Warranty expense.	(8,000)	0	0	(8,000)
Other expenses	(134,000)	(171,000)	(134,000)	(171,000)
Pretax GAAP income	$ 28,000	$ 19,000		
Taxable income.			$ 56,000	$ 11,000

Additional information

▪ Environmental fines are not deductible for income tax purposes.

▪ Amount collected in Year 1 related to deferred service revenue ($10,000) was taxable in Year 1.

▪ Accrued warranty costs of $8,000 are not deductible for income tax purposes until Year 2 when the expenditures are made.

▪ Income tax rate is 25% for both years.

▪ At the beginning of Year 1, deferred tax asset and liability balances were zero.

Required

a. Prepare schedules to compute the deferred tax balances on December 31 of Year 1.

b. Compute the increase to income tax payable on December 31 of Year 1 and Year 2.

c. Record the income tax journal entry on December 31 of Year 1.

d. Record the income tax journal entry on December 31 of Year 2.

e. Show how the tax accounts would be reported on the income statement and balance sheet (excluding income taxes payable) for Year 1 and Year 2. Include the disclosure of current and deferred tax expense.

f. Compute the effective tax rate for Year 1.

Exercise 18-23
Identifying Tax Differences
LO2, 3, 4

Listed below are ten separate situations. For each item indicate whether the difference is (1) temporary, creating a deferred tax asset or a deferred tax liability or (2) permanent.

		Deferred Income Tax		
	Item	Asset	Liability	Permanent
1.	Bad debt expense recognized under GAAP but not deductible for tax purposes until the account is written off.	____	____	____
2.	Dividend revenue recognized for accounting while a portion is deductible for taxes (dividends received deduction).	____	____	____
3.	Estimated warranty costs: accrual basis for accounting and cash basis for income tax.	____	____	____
4.	Fines expensed for accounting but not deductible for tax purposes.	____	____	____
5.	Straight-line depreciation for accounting and accelerated depreciation for income tax.	____	____	____
6.	Unrealized gain on investments: FV-NI recognized for accounting, but gain recognized only on disposal of the asset for income tax.	____	____	____
7.	Subscription revenue collected in advance: accrual basis for accounting, cash basis for income tax.	____	____	____
8.	Unrealized loss on investments: FV-NI recognized for accounting, but loss recognized only on disposal of the asset for income tax.	____	____	____
9.	Probable and estimable litigation contingency: accrual basis for accounting and cash basis for income tax.	____	____	____
10.	Interest received on investments in municipal bonds is not taxable.	____	____	____

Exercise 18-24
Preparing a Rate
Reconciliation Disclosure
with a Nontaxable
Item **LO4**
Hint: See Demo 18-4B

Springs Inc. has taxable revenues of $105,000 and tax-deductible expenses of $60,000 for the year ended December 31. In addition, Springs Inc. received interest from municipal bonds in the amount of $10,000, not subject to income taxation. All of these revenues and expenses are included in pretax GAAP income for the period. Assume that the tax rate is 25% for all periods.

Required
a. Record the income tax journal entry on December 31.
b. Prepare a reconciliation disclosure of the statutory tax rate in dollars and percentages.

Exercise 18-25
Recording Income Tax
Journal Entry: Temporary
and Nondeductible
Item; Multiple Tax
Rates **LO2, 3, 4, 6**

Fox Corporation purchased a machine on January 1 of Year 1 that cost $40,000. The machine had an estimated service life of five years and no residual value. Fox uses straight-line depreciation for accounting purposes and accelerated depreciation for the income tax return as follows: Year 1, 30%; Year 2, 25%; Year 3, 20%; Year 4, 15%; and Year 5, 10%. Taxable income on the tax return for Year 1 was $150,000. The Year 1 income statement showed a $15,000 expense for premiums paid for life insurance policies on company executive officers. The income tax rate is 25% in Year 1 and 35% in all subsequent years. The accounting and tax periods both end on December 31.

Required
a. Prepare a schedule to compute the deferred tax balance on December 31 of Year 1 through Year 5.
b. Record the income tax journal entry on December 31 of Year 1.
c. Repeat requirements a and b assuming instead that the machine is 100% expensed in Year 1 for tax purposes.

Exercise 18-26
Calculating Income Tax
Payable, Deferred Tax
Balances, Income Tax
Expense; Preparing a Rate
Reconciliation Disclosure
with a Nondeductible
Item **LO2, 4**
Hint: See Demo 18-4B

Sedona Corporation purchased equipment on January 1 of Year 1 that cost $24,000. The equipment has an estimated service life of four years and no residual value. The company uses straight-line depreciation for accounting purposes, but the equipment is 100% expensed in Year 1 for tax purposes. Pretax GAAP income is $120,000, $90,000, $100,000, and $110,000 for Year 1, 2, 3, and 4, respectively. An annual $5,000 expense for premiums paid for life insurance policies on company executive officers is included in GAAP income for all four years; this amount is not deductible for tax purposes. The income tax rate is 25% in all years. The accounting and tax periods both end December 31.

Required
a. Compute the increase to income tax payable on December 31 of Year 1, Year 2, Year 3, and Year 4.
b. Prepare a schedule to compute the deferred tax balance on December 31 of Year 1, Year 2, Year 3, and Year 4.
c. Determine income tax expense recognized in Year 1, Year 2, Year 3, and Year 4.

d. Prepare a reconciliation disclosure of the statutory tax rate to the effective tax rate in percentages only for Year 1, Year 2, Year 3, and Year 4.

e. Check the effective tax rates in the schedule in part *d* by calculating the effective tax rate as income tax expense divided by GAAP income.

Rafting Inc. had pretax GAAP income of $100,000 and the statutory tax rate is 25%. Rafting Inc. has no temporary differences, and so there is no deferred tax component to income tax expense. Rafting Inc. has the following permanent differences.

- Interest revenue of $20,000 resulting from an investment in tax-exempt municipal bonds.
- Fines paid of $30,000 for violation of environmental laws. The fines are not tax-deductible.

Required

a. Record the income tax expense journal entry.

b. Prepare a reconciliation of the statutory tax rate in dollars and percentages.

Exercise 18-27
Reconciling Effective and
Statutory Tax Rate **LO4**

Allied Corp. has a deferred tax asset balance of $50,000 at year-end on December 31 due to a temporary difference related to a warranty expense accrual that is not deductible for tax purposes. The deferred tax asset balance has increased $10,000 over the prior year ending balance of $40,000. Taxable income for the year is $210,000 and the tax rate is 25%. There was no deferred tax asset valuation allowance recorded on January 1.

Required

a. Record the income tax journal entries on December 31 to (1) adjust the deferred tax asset account and (2) adjust the deferred tax asset valuation allowance, assuming that it is *more likely than not* that the deferred tax asset ending balance of $50,000 will be realized.

b. Record the income tax journal entries on December 31 to (1) adjust the deferred tax asset account and (2) adjust the deferred tax asset valuation allowance, assuming that it is *more likely than not* that only 60% of the deferred tax asset ending balance of $50,000 will be realized.

Exercise 18-28
Recording a Deferred Tax
Asset Allowance **LO5**
Hint: See Demo 18-5A

Refer to E18-28, but instead of journal entries, show the effect on the accounting equation for the transactions, including identifying the individual accounts affected, and the total impact on assets, liabilities, and stockholders' equity.

Exercise 18-29
Reporting a Deferred
Tax Asset Allowance
Using the Accounting
Equation **LO5**

Assume the same information in E18-28, except that there is a $12,000 unadjusted December 31 credit balance in the deferred tax asset valuation allowance.

Required

a. Record the income tax journal entries on December 31 to (1) adjust the deferred tax asset account and (2) adjust the deferred tax asset valuation allowance, assuming that it is *more likely than not* that the deferred tax asset ending balance of $50,000 will be realized.

b. Record the income tax journal entries on December 31 to (1) adjust the deferred tax asset account and (2) adjust the deferred tax asset valuation allowance, assuming that it is *more likely than not* that only 60% of the deferred tax asset ending balance of $50,000 will be realized.

Exercise 18-30
Recording a Deferred Tax
Asset Allowance **LO5**

The following items create deferred tax assets and deferred tax liabilities for a company at year-end on December 31.

1. Prepaid operating expenses of $25,000 are tax deductible when paid.
2. Excess tax depreciation (MACRS) over GAAP depreciation (straight-line) is $22,000.
3. Warranty liability of $8,000 is tax deductible when incurred.
4. Installment sales of $80,000 are recorded on an accrual basis for GAAP purposes but taxed when collected.
5. Taxable income is $320,000 and the tax rate is 25%.

Required

Show how all tax-related items would be reported on the December 31 balance sheet.

Exercise 18-31
Reporting Tax Amounts on
the Balance Sheet **LO5**
Hint: See Review 18-5

Wittco Company reports pretax GAAP income in Year 1, its first year of operations, of $100,000. Temporary differences in the GAAP basis and tax basis of assets arose during the year from the following two sources.

- Prepayment of Year 2 website costs in the amount of $24,000 in Year 1.
- Installment sale totaling $36,000, with cash collections expected in two equal amounts in Year 3 and Year 4.

Exercise 18-32
Recording Multiple
Temporary Differences,
Multiple Tax Rates,
Change in Enacted Tax
Rate **LO2, 6**

The enacted tax rates are 25% in Year 1, 30% in Year 2, and 40% in Year 3 and thereafter. The accounting and tax periods both end December 31.

Required

a. Record the income tax journal entry on December 31 of Year 1.

b. Record the income tax journal entry on December 31 of Year 1, assuming that a new tax law is passed in Year 1 decreasing the tax rate to 20% for Year 1 and all years thereafter.

Exercise 18-33
Recording Multiple
Temporary Differences,
Change in Enacted Tax
Rate **LO2, 3, 6**

The Billboard Company has a deferred tax liability in the amount of $14,000 at year-end on December 31 of Year 1, relating to a $40,000 installment sale receivable, $20,000 of which is collected in Year 2. The tax rate in Year 2 is 35%. During Year 2, the rate for Year 3 and thereafter is changed to 25%. Warranty expense included in the determination of Year 2 pretax GAAP income is $100,000, with this amount expected to be incurred and deductible for tax purposes in Year 3. Pretax GAAP income is $280,000 in Year 2.

Required

Prepare the journal entry to record income taxes in Year 2.

Exercise 18-34
Preparing a Rate
Reconciliation Disclosure
with a Change in Enacted
Tax Rate; Challenging
LO2, 3, 4, 6

Referring to E18-33, prepare a reconciliation disclosure of the statutory tax rate to the effective tax rate for Year 2 in dollars and percentages. Combine the effects of the change in enacted tax rate into one line in the reconciliation disclosure. *Hint*: Refer to the Expanding Your Knowledge box on Page 18-24 for guidance.

Exercise 18-35
Preparing a Rate
Reconciliation Disclosure
with a Tax Credit;
Challenging **LO4**

Brite Inc. reported pretax GAAP income of $125,000 for the year. There are no differences between pretax GAAP income and taxable income. However, the company qualifies for a $2,000 tax credit that directly reduces its income tax payable amount. The company's tax rate is 25%. *Hint*: Refer to the Expanding Your Knowledge box on Page 18-16 for guidance.

Required

a. Record the income tax journal entry on December 31.

b. Prepare a reconciliation disclosure of the statutory tax rate to the effective tax rate for the year in dollars and percentages.

Exercise 18-36
Recording Temporary
Difference, Multiple Tax
Rates **LO3, 6**

In Year 1, Adele Company accrued a legal liability of $500,000 for payments expected to be paid (that will be deducted when paid) as follows: Year 2: $250,000; Year 3: $150,000; and Year 4: $100,000. The company's Year 1 pretax GAAP income is $5 million. Enacted tax rates follow: Year 1: 25%; Year 2: 25%; Year 3: 30%; Year 4 and beyond: 30%. The company had no other differences between GAAP and tax income, and its deferred tax accounts had zero balances at the beginning of Year 1.

Required

Prepare the journal entry to record income taxes in Year 1.

Exercise 18-37
Recording Temporary
Difference, Multiple Tax
Rates **LO2, 6**

A plant asset purchased by Krest Inc. for $100,000 late in Year 1 is to be depreciated as follows.

Year	Tax Depreciation	GAAP Depreciation
Year 2	$ 40,000	$ 20,000
Year 3	30,000	20,000
Year 4	20,000	20,000
Year 5	10,000	20,000
Year 6	0	20,000
	$100,000	$100,000

In Year 3, taxable income is $450,000, and the tax rate is 25%. Recently enacted tax rates follow: Year 4: 25%; Year 5: 30%; and Year 6: 30%. The deferred tax liability balance on January 1 of Year 3 is $5,000. The accounting and tax periods both end December 31.

Required

a. Prepare a schedule to compute the deferred tax balance on December 31 of Year 3.

b. Calculate the tax basis of the plant asset on December 31 of Year 3 and its reported amount in the financial statements.

c. Prepare the journal entry to record income tax expense in Year 3.

At year-end on December 31, Colgait Inc. had an installment sale receivable balance of $90,000 recognized on its financial statements, while the amount was not recognized for tax purposes. Colgait Inc. also had a warranty accrual of $20,000 on December 31 that is not deductible for tax purposes. The installment receivable will be settled equally over the next three years. The warranty will be settled equally over the next two years. Taxable income for the current year was $500,000. Enacted tax rates are 25% for the current and next year, and 30% for years thereafter.

Exercise 18-38
Recording Multiple Temporary Differences, Multiple Tax Rates
LO2, 3, 6

Required

a. Prepare schedules to compute the deferred tax balances on December 31.

b. Prepare the current year journal entry to record income tax expense, assuming zero beginning balances in deferred tax accounts.

Aim Inc. reported the following for Year 1 through Year 3.

- Prepaid maintenance contract: $30,000 on January 1 of Year 1, for a three-year period beginning January 1 of Year 1.

- Deferred revenue: $45,000 on January 1 of Year 1, for a three-year period beginning January 1 of Year 1.

- Pretax GAAP income is $500,000, $388,000, and 425,000 for Year 1, Year 2, and Year 3, respectively.

- Enacted tax rates are 25% for Year 1 and Year 2, and 30% for Year 3.

- There were no balances in the deferred tax accounts on January 1 of Year 1.

- The accounting and tax periods both end on December 31.

Exercise 18-39
Recording Multiple Temporary Differences, Multiple Tax Rates
LO2, 3, 6

Required

a. Compute the increase to income tax payable on December 31 of Year 1, Year 2, and Year 3.

b. Prepare schedules to compute the deferred tax balances on December 31.

c. Prepare the journal entry to record income taxes in Year 1, Year 2, and Year 3.

Refer to E18-39, but instead of journal entries for part c, show the effect on the accounting equation for the transactions, including identifying the individual accounts affected, and the total impact on assets, liabilities, and stockholders' equity.

Exercise 18-40
Reporting Multiple Temporary Differences with Multiple Tax Rates Using the Accounting
LO2, 3, 6

Tyson Corporation reported pretax income from operations in Year 1 of $80,000 (the first year of operations). In Year 2, the corporation experienced a $40,000 NOL (pretax loss from operations). Management is confident the company will have taxable income in excess of $50,000 in Year 3. Assume an income tax rate of 25% in Year 1 and thereafter. Tyson has no other temporary differences.

Exercise 18-41
Recording NOL Carryforward   **LO7**

Required

a. Provide the Year 1 and Year 2 income tax entries the company should make.

b. Show (1) income tax expense (benefit) on the Year 1 and Year 2 income statements and (2) net deferred tax asset (liability) and income tax payable on the Year 1 and Year 2 year-end balance sheets.

Refer to E18-41, but instead of journal entries, show the effect on the accounting equation for the transactions, including identifying the individual accounts affected, and the total impact on assets, liabilities, and stockholders' equity.

Exercise 18-42
Reporting NOL Carryforward Using the Accounting Equation
LO2, 3, 6

Decker Corporation reported the following for Year 1. There were no temporary differences in Year 1 other than potential differences arising from a net operating loss carryforward.

Exercise 18-43
Recording and Reporting NOL Carryforward   **LO7**

	Year 1
Taxable income (loss)...	$(65,000)
Income tax rate...	25%

Required

a. Record income taxes for Year 1 and Year 2 assuming the following.

- For Year 2, the company computed taxable income of $45,000 and recognized a deferred tax liability balance of $2,250 related to acquisition of depreciable assets in its year-end financial statements. These amounts were consistent with management's expectations.
- Income tax rate enacted in Year 1 and effective for Year 2 and thereafter is 30%.
- Management estimates the valuation allowance on the deferred tax asset related to its Year 1 NOL to be zero.

b. List the amounts that should be reported on the income statements and balance sheets for Year 1 and Year 2.

Exercise 18-44
Recording NOL Carryforward, Valuation Allowance **LO7**
Hint: See Demo 18-7A

DNSE Inc. began operations in Year 1. In its first year the company had a net operating loss of $(10,000), which was carried forward and used to reduce income tax payable in Year 2. In Year 2, DNSE had taxable income of $40,000 before the use of the NOL carryforward. At December 31 of Year 2, DNSE Inc. determines that it should have a deferred tax asset ending balance of $25,000 related to Year 2 deferred revenue. The income tax rate is 25%. No valuation allowance has been established.

Required

a. Provide the journal entry to record income taxes in Year 2, assuming that no valuation allowance is required.

b. Now assume DNSE has encountered stiff competition and is uncertain whether it will have any taxable income in the foreseeable future. DNSE determined that it was *more likely than not* that none of the deferred tax asset would be realized. Assume also that the temporary differences that give rise to the deferred tax asset are expected to reverse in Year 3 and Year 4. (1) Determine what amount, if any, should be recorded as a deferred tax asset valuation allowance at December 31 of Year 2, and (2) make the appropriate entry. Assume DNSE has already recorded the entry in part *a*.

c. Show how the December 31 of Year 2 balance sheet and income statement would present the information provided, assuming that a deferred tax asset valuation allowance is recorded.

Exercise 18-45
Recording and Reporting NOL Carryforward, Valuation Allowance **LO7**
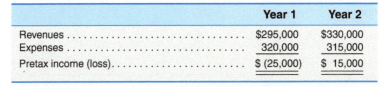

The financial statements of Gibson Corporation for the first two years of operations show the following.

	Year 1	Year 2
Revenues	$295,000	$330,000
Expenses	320,000	315,000
Pretax income (loss)	$ (25,000)	$ 15,000

Assume a tax rate of 25% for Year 1 and Year 2. Estimates of future earnings after Year 2 are zero. There are no temporary differences. *Note:* At the end of Year 1 and at the end of Year 2, management believes that any tax loss carryforward benefit will not be realized.

Required

a. Provide entries to record the NOL income tax effects for Year 1 and Year 2.

b. Show (1) income tax expense (benefit) on the Year 1 and Year 2 income statements and (2) net deferred tax asset (liability) and income tax payable on the Year 1 and Year 2, year-end balance sheets.

Exercise 18-46
Reporting NOL Carryforward and Valuation Allowance Using the Accounting Equation **LO7**

Refer to E18-45, but instead of journal entries, show the effect on the accounting equation for the transactions, including identifying the individual accounts affected, and the total impact on assets, liabilities, and stockholders' equity.

Exercise 18-47
Recording NOL Carryback|Carryforward **LO7**

ABC Inc. reported taxable income for Year 1 through Year 6 as follows.

Year 1	$175,000	Year 3	$(100,000)	Year 5	$ 80,000
Year 2	65,000	Year 4	(250,000)	Year 6	100,000

The enacted tax rate is 25% for Year 1 and 2, and 40% for years thereafter. There are no differences between taxable income/loss and pretax GAAP income/loss. Management believes that the full amount of any tax loss carryforward benefit is *more likely than not* to be realized.

Required

Prepare the journal entries to record income tax expense and/or the net operating loss carryback|carryforward for Year 2 through Year 6, assuming that the company qualifies for the NOL carryback method for two years (using the earlier year first) and carryforward indefinitely without an income limitation.

Randolph Inc. took a recent tax position related to the exclusion of $10,000 from taxable revenue. Randolph determined that this position is *more likely than not* to be sustained in future discussions with taxing authorities. Using available information, Randolph Inc. created the following summary of probabilities of sustaining its tax position.

Exercise 18-48
Recording Income Tax
Expense with an Uncertain
Tax Position   **LO8**
Hint: See Review 18-8

Possible Estimated Outcome (Allowable Revenue Exclusion)	Probability of Occurring
$10,000	10%
8,000	20
6,000	25
5,000	30
1,000	15

Required

Assuming taxable income of $50,000 (reflecting the exclusion of the $10,000 uncertain tax revenue) and a tax rate of 25%, record the income tax journal entry.

Lawrence Inc. took a $85,000 tax deduction on its tax return in Year 1. The company determined that $25,000 of the deduction would not be realized and therefore recognized a Liability for the Unrecognized Tax Benefits of $6,250 ($25,000 × 25%) at year-end on December 31 of Year 1. Consider each of the following cases separately.

Exercise 18-49
Recording Income Tax
Expense with an Uncertain
Tax Position   **LO8**
Hint: See Demo 18-8

a. In December of Year 2, after negotiations with taxing authorities, Lawrence did not sustain any portion of its tax position regarding the $85,000 tax deduction. Record Lawrence's entry resolving the uncertain tax position on December 31 of Year 2.

b. Now assume that in December of Year 2, after negotiations with taxing authorities, Lawrence sustained its full tax position regarding the $85,000 tax deduction. Record Lawrence's entry resolving the uncertain tax position on December 31 of Year 2.

c. Now assume that in December of Year 2, after negotiations with taxing authorities, Lawrence realized $60,000 of the tax deduction. Record Lawrence's entry resolving the uncertain tax position on December 31 of Year 2.

Terms frequently used in accounting for income taxes along with their descriptions follow.

Exercise 18-50
Defining Tax
Terminology   **LO2, 3, 4, 5, 6, 7, 8**

Terms

____ 1. Deferred tax asset
____ 2. Taxable temporary difference
____ 3. Permanent difference
____ 4. Valuation allowance
____ 5. Temporary difference

____ 6. Taxable income
____ 7. Noncurrent deferred tax asset, net
____ 8. Income tax expense
____ 9. NOL carryforward
____ 10. Intraperiod income tax allocation

Descriptions

a. Current tax expense plus net changes in the deferred tax liability, deferred tax asset, valuation allowance, and the unrecognized tax benefit balance sheet accounts.

b. Amount used to compute the cash taxes owed to the taxing authority.

c. Net of deferred tax assets, liabilities, and valuation allowance (relating to the same tax jurisdiction) presented on the balance sheet as a noncurrent asset.

d. Can reduce income tax paid to taxing authorities in future periods.

e. Difference between accounting income and taxable income that will reverse in the future.

f. Deferred tax balance sheet amount that has a debit balance.

g. Difference between accounting and taxable incomes that does not reverse.

h. Allocation of tax among components in the income statement and the statement of comprehensive income.

i. Contra asset account used to reduce deferred tax assets to the portion *more likely than not* to be realized.

j. Amount that represents a difference between GAAP and tax basis of an asset (liability) that will increase taxable income in future periods relative to financial accounting income.

Required

Match each of the terms 1 through 10 with the most closely aligned description a through j.

Problems

Problem 18-1
Recording Temporary
Differences **LO2**

On January 1 of Year 1, Keefe Corporation purchased equipment at a cost of $100,000. The equipment has a five-year life and no salvage value. The depreciation schedule for GAAP and tax purposes follows.

Year	GAAP Depreciation	Tax Depreciation
Year 1	$20,000	$25,000
Year 2	20,000	38,000
Year 3	20,000	37,000
Year 4	20,000	0
Year 5	20,000	0

Pretax GAAP income for each year ended December 31, Year 1 through Year 4, is $120,000, and the tax rate is 25%. There are no other differences between pretax GAAP income and tax income.

a.   Prepare a schedule to compute the deferred tax balance on December 31 of Year 1, Year 2, Year 3, and Year 4.
b.   Record the income tax journal entry on December 31 of Year 1.
c.   Record the income tax journal entry on December 31 of Year 2.
d.   Record the income tax journal entry on December 31 of Year 3.
e.   Record the income tax journal entry on December 31 of Year 4.
f.   Repeat (a) through (e) instead assuming that the company expensed 100% of the equipment in Year 1 for tax purposes.

Problem 18-2
Reporting Changes in
Enacted Tax Rates
LO2, 6

Refer to the data and information in P18-1 for Keefe Corporation. Assume that the tax rate for Year 1 through Year 3 is 25%, but that a new law is passed in Year 1 that will raise the tax rate in Year 4 and thereafter to 30%. Pretax GAAP income equals $120,000 in Year 1 and Year 2.

Required

a.   Record the income tax journal entry on December 31 of Year 1 (assuming the original tax depreciation schedule provided).
b.   Record the income tax journal entry on December 31 of Year 2 (assuming the original tax depreciation schedule provided).

Problem 18-3
Recording and
Reporting Temporary
Differences   **LO3, 5**

Whirlpools Corporation reported the following for the current year ended December 31: taxable income based on its tax return, $47,600; income tax rate, 25%. There were two temporary differences.

■   December 31, collected customer advances resulting in deferred revenue of $5,000. The $5,000 is included on its tax return.

■   December 31, the company recorded a $10,000 estimated expense, accrued as a liability to be paid next year. The $10,000 is not deductible for tax purposes.

Required

a.   Prepare schedules to compute the deferred tax balances on December 31.
b.   Record the income tax journal entry on December 31. Assume a zero-beginning balance in the deferred tax asset account on January 1.
c.   Show (1) income tax expense (benefit) on the current year income statement and (2) net deferred tax asset (liability) and income tax payable on the current year-end balance sheet. Include the disclosure of current and deferred tax expense.

Problem 18-4
Recording and
Reporting Temporary
Differences   **LO2, 5**

Financial statements of Drake Corporation for the recent four-year period show the following.

	Year 1	Year 2	Year 3	Year 4
Income statement (summarized)				
Revenues	$120,000	$134,000	$154,000	$174,000
Expenses other than depreciation	(80,000)	(92,000)	(95,000)	(128,000)
Depreciation expense (straight-line)	(20,000)	(20,000)	(20,000)	(20,000)
Pretax GAAP income	$ 20,000	$ 22,000	$ 39,000	$ 26,000
Balance sheet (partial)				
Equipment (four-year life, no residual value), at cost	$ 80,000	$ 80,000	$ 80,000	$ 80,000
Less accumulated depreciation	(20,000)	(40,000)	(60,000)	(80,000)
Carrying amount....................................	$ 60,000	$ 40,000	$ 20,000	$ 0

Drake has a tax rate of 25% each year and deducts accelerated depreciation for income tax purposes as follows: Year 1, $32,000; Year 2, $24,000; Year 3, $16,000; and Year 4, $8,000. There are no deferred tax assets or deferred tax liabilities at January 1 of Year 1.

Required

a.   Prepare a schedule to compute the deferred tax balance at year-end on December 31 of Year 1, Year 2, Year 3, and Year 4.

b.   Prepare the journal entries to record income tax expense for Year 1, Year 2, Year 3, and Year 4.

c.   For each year show the deferred income tax amount that should be reported on the balance sheet.

The records of Lane Corporation show the following pretax GAAP income for the past 4 years.

Problem 18-5
Recording and Reporting Temporary and Permanent Differences **LO2, 3, 4, 5**

	Year 1	Year 2	Year 3	Year 4
Pretax GAAP income	$90,000	$92,000	$95,000	$98,000

The income tax rate is 25%. The company had the following differences between GAAP basis and tax basis income.

■   For GAAP purposes, installment sales receivable is $30,000 at year-end on December 31 of Year 1. On the tax return, $10,000 will be recognized each year, Year 2 through Year 4, as cash is collected.

■   For GAAP purposes, warranty expenses of $4,000 are accrued in Year 1. On the tax return, $1,000 will be deducted each year, Year 1 through Year 4, as expenditures are made related to warranties.

The company also recorded interest revenue of $1,250 each year on municipal bonds, which is not taxable.

Required

a.   Prepare schedules to compute the deferred tax balances on December 31 of Year 1, Year 2, Year 3, and Year 4.

b.   Compute the increase to income tax payable on December 31 of Year 1, Year 2, Year 3, and Year 4.

c.   Prepare the journal entries to record income tax expense for Year 1, Year 2, Year 3, and Year 4.

d.   Show (1) income tax expense (benefit) on the Year 1, Year 2, Year 3, and Year 4 income statements and (2) net deferred tax asset (liability) and income tax payable on the Year 1, Year 2, Year 3, and Year 4, year-end balance sheets. Include the disclosure of current and deferred tax expense.

The first year of operations for Blair Corporation is Year 1. The accounting and income tax periods end on December 31. The company provided the following income tax-related data at the end of Year 1.

Problem 18-6
Recording and Reporting Temporary and Permanent Differences
LO1, 2, 4, 5

■   Tax rate is 25% for Year 1 through Year 3, but rises to 30% in Year 4. All of these rates are enacted as of January 1 of Year 1.

■   Year 1 taxable income: $150,000.

■   Temporary differences:

   • $300,000 estimated expense was accrued at the end of Year 1 for GAAP purposes and recorded as a liability; the expected settlement date is Year 5 for income tax purposes.

   • $200,000 of revenue on installment sales was recognized for GAAP purposes at the end of Year 1; the amount will be included in the income tax return as collected in equal amounts for Year 2 through Year 5.

   • $200,000 depreciable asset (estimated useful life five years and no residual value) is depreciated as follows.

	Year 1	Year 2	Year 3	Year 4	Year 5
GAAP purposes	$ 40,000	$ 40,000	$40,000	$40,000	$40,000
Income tax purposes	66,000	54,000	40,000	26,000	14,000
Difference	$(26,000)	$(14,000)	$ 0	$14,000	$26,000

   • $40,000 of revenue is collected in advance at the end of Year 1; revenue is recognized for GAAP purposes evenly in Year 2 and Year 3. The full amount must be included in the Year 1 income tax return.

■   Nondeductible item:

   •   Fines paid in Year 1 and Year 4 were $5,000 and $4,000, respectively.

Required

a.   Prepare schedules to compute the deferred tax balances on December 31 of Year 1.

b.   Prepare the journal entries to record income tax expense for Year 1.

c.   Show (1) income tax expense (benefit) on the Year 1 income statement and (2) net deferred tax asset (liability) and income tax payable on the year-end balance sheet for Year 1. Include the disclosure of current and deferred tax expense.

Problem 18-7
Recording Temporary
Differences: Change in
Enacted Rate   **LO2, 6**

The records of Morgan Corporation show the following income data for Year 1 through Year 4. At the end of Year 1, the enacted tax rate was 35%. During Year 2, the enacted tax rate was changed to 25%, retroactive to the beginning of Year 2, and remains in effect through Year 4.

	Year 1	Year 2	Year 3	Year 4
Pretax GAAP income	$58,000	$70,000	$80,000	$88,000
Taxable income.	28,000	80,000	90,000	98,000

There is only one temporary difference: At the end of Year 1, the company prepaid an expense of $30,000, which will be amortized for GAAP purposes over the next three years (straight line); the full amount is included in Year 1 for income tax purposes.

Required
Provide the entry to record income taxes for Year 1 through Year 4.

Problem 18-8
Recording Temporary
Differences: Change in
Enacted Tax Rates
LO3, 6

The records of Castle Corporation show the following income data. The income tax rate is 25%.

	Year 1	Year 2	Year 3	Year 4
Pretax GAAP income	$40,000	$70,000	$90,000	$100,000

The deferred tax account has a zero balance at the start of Year 1. There was only one temporary difference: estimated warranty expenses were recorded (accrued) for GAAP purposes in Year 1 for $20,000. The balance in the warranty liability for GAAP purposes follows.

	Year 1	Year 2	Year 3	Year 4
Warranty liability	$20,000	$30,000	$25,000	$0

Required
a. Provide the entry to record income taxes at the end of Year 1.
b. During Year 2, tax legislation was passed that changed the enacted tax rate to 40% for Year 3 and Year 4. Provide the entry to record income taxes at the end of Year 2.
c. Assume instead that during Year 2, tax legislation was passed that changed the enacted tax rate to 20% for Year 3 and Year 4. Provide the entry to record income taxes at the end of Year 2.

Problem 18-9
Recording Temporary
Differences: Change in
Enacted Tax Rates
LO3, 6

Beetle Corporation reported pretax GAAP income as follows: Year 1, $150,000; and Year 2, $176,000. Taxable income for each year would have been the same as pretax GAAP income except for a transaction in Year 1 in which $1,800 of revenue was collected in advance, to be applied to Year 2. Revenue is taxable in the year collected. The tax rate for Year 1 and Year 2 is 25%, and the year-end for both accounting and tax purposes is December 31. The revenue collected in advance is the only difference, and it is not repeated in October of Year 2.

Required
a. Prepare the income tax journal entry for Year 1.
b. Now assume that during Year 1, the tax rate changes to 35% for Year 2 and future years. Prepare the journal entry for income taxes in Year 1.

Problem 18-10
Recording Income Tax
Expense with Temporary
and Permanent
Differences; Preparing
Rate Reconciliation
Disclosure with Change in
Tax Rates; Challenging
LO2, 3, 4, 6

For its first year of operations, Altitude Inc. reports pretax GAAP income of $100,000 in Year 1. Assume pretax GAAP income in Year 2 and Year 3 of $125,000 and $90,000, respectively. The enacted tax rate is 25% for Years 1 and 2 and 40% for Year 3 and thereafter. The accounting and tax periods both end on December 31. The following additional information is available for the first three years of operations.

- Prepaid insurance in the amount of $20,000 was recorded on December 31 of Year 1 for Year 2 insurance coverage. The cost of insurance is deductible for tax purposes in the year paid.
- A warranty accrual of $30,000 recorded on December 31 of Year 1 is not deductible for tax purposes until the warranty costs are settled. The amount is paid evenly over Year 2 through Year 4.
- The company recorded interest revenue of $500 each year (Year 1, Year 2, and Year 3) on municipal bonds. Interest revenue on municipal bonds is not taxable.

Required
a. Compute the increase in income tax payable on December 31 of Year 1, Year 2, and Year 3.
b. Prepare a schedule to compute the deferred tax liability balance and a schedule to compute the deferred tax asset balance on December 31 of Year 1, Year 2, and Year 3.

c. Record the income tax journal entries in Year 1, Year 2, and Year 3.

d. Compute the effective tax rate for each year and prepare a schedule reconciling the statutory tax rate to the effective tax rate in percentages only. *Hint*: Refer to the "Expanding Your Knowledge" box on Page 18-24 for guidance.

Condensed pretax income statements of Bixler Corporation for the first four years of operations follow.

Problem 18-11
Recording NOL
Carryforward   **LO7**

Income Statements (summarized)	Year 1	Year 2	Year 3	Year 4
Revenue	$125,000	$155,000	$180,000	$250,000
Expenses	120,000	195,000	160,000	200,000
Pretax income (loss)	$ 5,000	$ (40,000)	$ 20,000	$ 50,000

There are no temporary differences other than those created by tax loss carryforwards. The income tax rate is 25%. Assume that future income is highly uncertain at the end of each year, so a valuation allowance is needed for any recognized deferred tax asset. Assume that no loss carrybacks are allowed.

Required

a. Provide entries to record the NOL income tax effects for each year.

b. Prepare summarized income statements for Year 1 through Year 4 (including income tax expense).

Toner Corporation computed the following: Year 1 taxable income, $10,000; Year 2 taxable loss, $(40,000). At the end of Year 2, Toner made the following estimates: Year 3 taxable income, $4,000; Year 4 taxable income, $11,000; and Year 5 taxable income, $50,000. On the basis of these estimates, Toner believes the full amount of the tax loss carryforward benefit is *more likely than not* to be realized. There are no other temporary differences. The tax rate is 25% in all years. Net operating loss carryforwards can only offset a maximum of 80% of taxable income in each of the future years.

Problem 18-12
Recording NOL
Carryforward and
Carryback|Carryforward
LO7

Required

a. Provide the income tax entry for Year 2.

b. Provide the income tax entry for Year 3, assuming that the actual taxable income was $6,000.

c. Provide the income tax entry for Year 4, assuming that Year 3 results were as described in part *b*, and that the actual Year 4 taxable income was $13,000.

d. Provide the entry for Year 5, assuming results for Year 3 and Year 4 were as described in parts *b* and *c*, and assuming that the actual Year 5 taxable income was $45,000.

e. Assume instead that the company qualifies for a two-year loss carryback for tax purposes, using the earlier year first and with no income restrictions. Assume also that any excess loss can then be carried forward indefinitely, with **no income restrictions**. Prepare the income tax journal entry for Year 2.

Randolph Inc. took a recent tax position related to a tax deduction of $250,000 on a research and development project. The company had uncertainty about the classification of some costs associated with the project. Randolph determined that this position is *more likely than not* to be sustained in any future investigation by taxing authorities. Using available information, Randolph Inc. created the following summary of probabilities of sustaining the tax position.

Problem 18-13
Recording Income Tax
Expense: Uncertain Tax
Position **LO8**

Possible Estimated Outcome (Allowable Deductible Expense)	Probability of Occurring
$250,000	15%
200,000	25
180,000	40
100,000	10
80,000	10

Required

a. Assuming taxable income of $1,000,000 (with the research and development tax deduction taken) and a tax rate of 25%, record the income tax journal entry for the year. Assume Randolph has no temporary differences between GAAP and taxable income.

b. Next year, assume the full benefit is realized, record the journal entry required.

c. Assume instead that next year the full benefit is lost, record the journal entry required.

Accounting Decisions and Judgments

AD&J18-1
Analyzing Texaco—Income
Tax Disclosure
LO2, 3, 5

Real World Analysis In the notes to its Year 8 financial statements, **Texaco Inc.**, a major U.S. oil producer, provides the following disclosure regarding the deferred tax asset and liability accounts at December 31 of Year 8.

$ millions	Asset (Liability)
Depreciation	$(1,079)
Depletion	(429)
Intangible drilling costs	(726)
Other deferred tax liabilities	(686)
Total	(2,920)
Employee benefit plans	532
Tax loss carryforwards	641
Tax credit carryforwards	368
Environmental liabilities	116
Other deferred tax assets	639
Total	2,296
Total before valuation allowance.	(624)
Valuation allowance	(815)
Total, net.	$(1,439)

Required

a. What is the total of deferred tax liability at December 31 of Year 8? What is the total of deferred tax asset? What is the net amount of deferred tax asset or liability reported on Texaco's December 31 of Year 8 balance sheet?

b. Assuming a federal tax rate of 35%, estimate the amount of temporary difference arising from GAAP versus tax differences for depreciable assets that exists for Texaco at December 31 of Year 8.

AD&J18-2
Analyzing Applied
Technology
Laboratories—Income Tax
Disclosure   **LO4, 7**

Real World Analysis **Applied Technology Laboratories (ATL)**, a medical equipment manufacturer, reported a loss before income taxes of $20.9 million in Year 4, yet the income tax effect was a tax benefit of $0.7 million. The effective income tax rate was only 3.3% ($0.7 million/$20.9 million). ATL reported a loss before income taxes of $1.7 million in Year 3 yet had income tax expense of $1.6 million. Assume a statutory income tax rate of 35%.

Notes to the Year 4 ATL annual report explains its deferred tax assets and deferred tax liabilities as follows.

$ thousands	Year 4	Year 3
Deferred tax assets		
Receivables	$ 3,230	$ 2,936
Inventories	11,564	8,800
Net operating loss carryforwards	3,969	3,157
State taxes	3,106	2,087
Compensation	2,623	2,171
Provision for litigation claim	1,700	—
Research and experimentation credit carryforwards	6,602	6,425
Other.	3,032	3,107
Gross deferred tax assets	$35,826	$28,683
Less valuation allowance	(27,249)	(19,709)
Net deferred tax assets	$ 8,577	$ 8,974
Deferred tax liabilities, primarily depreciation and intangible assets	(4,472)	(4,628)
Net deferred income taxes	$ 4,105	$ 4,346

Required

a. What are some reasons why ATL's effective tax rate might be so low in Year 4?

b. Why might ATL show an income tax expense in a year when it has a loss before income taxes for financial reporting?

c. In general terms, explain why ATL has such a large amount reported as a valuation allowance.

d. What effect did the increase in the valuation allowance from Year 3 to Year 4 have on ATL's income tax expense computation in fiscal Year 4?

e. Using a tax rate of 35%, estimate the amount of net operating loss carryforwards that ATL has as of December 31 of Year 4.

f. Using a tax rate of 35%, estimate the amount of "research and experimentation credit carryforwards" that ATL has as of December 31 of Year 4.

g. Using a tax rate of 35%, estimate the amount of accrued liability for litigation claim that ATL has as of December 31 of Year 4.

Real World Analysis Following are three **Coca-Cola Company** financial statement excerpts, with Year 5 being the most current year.

AD&J18-3
Analyzing Coca
Cola—Income Tax
Disclosure **LO2, 3, 5**

Note 14: Income Taxes   Income before income taxes consisted of the following (in millions).

Year Ended December 31	Year 5	Year 4	Year 3
United States	$1,801	$1,567	$ 2,451
International	7,804	7,758	9,026
Total	$9,605	$9,325	$11,477

A reconciliation of the statutory U.S. federal tax rate and our effective tax rate is as follows in percentages only for simplicity.

Year Ended December 31	Year 5	Year 4	Year 3
Statutory U.S. federal tax rate	35.0%	35.0%	35.0%
State and local income taxes—net of federal benefit	1.2	1.0	1.0
Earnings in jurisdictions taxed at rates different from the statutory U.S. federal rate	(12.7)	(11.5)	(10.3)
Equity income or loss	(1.7)	(2.2)	(1.4)
Other operating charges	1.2	2.9	1.2
Other—net	0.3	(1.6)	(0.7)
Effective tax rate	23.3%	23.6%	24.8%

December 31	Year 5	Year 4
Deferred tax assets:		
Property, plant and equipment	$ 192	$ 96
Trademarks and other intangible assets	68	68
Equity method investments (including foreign currency translation adjustment)	694	462
Derivative financial instruments	161	134
Other liabilities	1,056	1,082
Benefit plans	1,541	1,673
Net operating/capital loss carryforwards	413	729
Other	175	196
Gross deferred tax assets	$4,300	$4,440
Valuation allowances	(477)	(649)
Total deferred tax assets	$3,823	$3,791

Required

a. If Coca-Cola had no book-tax differences, and all earnings were subject to the federal statutory income tax rate, for what amount would Coca-Cola record income tax expense in Year 5?

b. Identify three sources and their percentage effects on income taxes that caused Coca-Cola's effective tax rate in Year 5 to differ from the federal statutory rate of 35%.

c. By how much did Coca-Cola increase or decrease its valuation allowance in Year 5? How did the valuation allowance as a percentage of deferred tax assets (gross) change from Year 4 to Year 5?

Communication Case Assume the statutory federal tax rate has been 35% for a number of Years. Assume that late in the third quarter of this year, a new rate, 40%, is approved as the new enacted rate, effective as of January 1. You are an assistant controller with Zenics Inc. The CEO of the company is concerned about what effect, if any, the new tax rate will have on earnings.

AD&J18-4
Analyzing a Change in
Enacted Tax Rate **LO6**

At the beginning of the year, Zenics had a deferred tax asset of $10 million and a deferred tax liability of $6 million. There was no need for a valuation allowance, nor is it expected that any will be needed this year. You estimate that pretax GAAP income will be approximately $5 million and that taxable income will be about $7 million. The company is publicly traded, with 500,000 shares outstanding all year.

Required

Write a memo to the CEO, Rihanna Star, explaining what effect the tax rate increase will have on the balance sheet and income statement for the company. Be specific, especially with regard to the effect the change will have on the balance sheet accounts, income statement accounts, net income, and earnings per share. If there is likely to be a negative impact on earnings, Rhianna would like your advice on what actions the company might consider taking in the last few days of the year to minimize the impact. Also comment on what effect, if any, you think the tax rate change will have on the company's stock price.

AD&J18-5
Explaining Tax Accounting and Financial Reporting
LO2, 3, 5, 7

Ethics Case A company had a tax refund of $2,000 but it reported income tax expense of $5,000 on its income statement.

Required

a. Is it appropriate and legal for a company to keep two sets of books: one for tax purposes and one for financial reporting purposes?

b. Explain how a company might have an income tax refund at the time it is reporting income tax expense.

AD&J18-6
Analyzing Deferred Income Taxes   **LO2, 3, 4**

Judgment Case Rimes Inc. has each of the following items on its balance sheet at December 31. The prepaid expenses have already been deducted for tax purposes; none of the other items have yet been deducted. The current and future income tax rate is 35%.

Current assets: Prepaid expenses	$ 50,000
Current liabilities: Warranty liability	100,000
Current liabilities: Insurance liability*	10,000

*Not tax deductible.

Required

a. Explain which of the items requires a deferred tax amount to be recorded, in what amount, and whether it is a deferred tax asset or deferred tax liability.

b. Determine how the amounts of deferred tax asset and deferred tax liability would be reported on the balance sheet.

AD&J18-7
Analyzing Valuation Allowance for Deferred Tax Assets   **LO5**

Judgment Case Soderstrom Company has a deferred tax asset of $1,000,000 at December 31, arising from the recording of its liability for postretirement benefits other than pensions. Soderstrom's CPA asks management whether a valuation allowance to reduce the deferred tax asset to zero should be recorded.

Required

a. Why would Soderstrom not want to report a valuation allowance? Outline what evidence, assuming it existed, that Soderstrom might use to argue against recording a valuation allowance.

b. Suppose in the final analysis it is determined that a valuation allowance of $400,000 is needed. How would the company have arrived at this determination, and what effect will it have on net income?

AD&J18-8
Reporting Comprehensive Long-Term Debt
LO2, 5

Challenge Problem The following are descriptions of long-term obligations for SuperK.

Income Tax—SuperK Corporation had identical income before taxes on both its income tax return and its income statement for Year 1 except for a temporary difference related to the difference between tax and GAAP depreciation. A depreciable asset that cost $250,000 was depreciated for income tax purposes using the following amounts: Year 1, $128,000; Year 2, $64,000; Year 3, $34,000; Year 4, $16,000; and Year 5, $8,000. However, for accounting purposes the straight-line method was used (5 years, no salvage value). The accounting and tax periods both end December 31. There were no deferred taxes at the beginning of Year 1. Taxable income was $298,000, and the income tax rate is 40% for Year 1.

Lease—On December 31 of Year 1, SuperK Corporation completed the first year of a 3-year lease. The lease is considered a finance lease. Annual payments of $36,556 are due on January 1, with the first payment due on January 1 of Year 1. The incremental borrowing rate of SuperK is 10%, and the fair value of the equipment at the origination of the lease was $100,000.

Long-term Debt—On January 1 of Year 1, SuperK issued $250,000 of bonds with a stated rate of 6%, accounted for using the effective interest method. The 10-year bonds pay interest annually on December 31 to yield 8%.

Pension—SuperK sponsors a defined benefit plan. December 31 of Year 1, ending balances for the projected benefit obligation, and fair value of plan assets totaled $800,000 and $725,000, respectively. The accumulated benefit obligation on December 31 of Year 1 was $700,000.

Required

a. Provide the entry to record income taxes at the end of Year 1.

b. Compute the amounts to be included in long-term liabilities on the balance sheet on December 31 of Year 1.

AD&J18-9
Reporting Income Tax
Expense: Comprehensive
Example   LO1, 2, 3,
4, 5, 6, 7, 8

Challenge Problem The Duesing Company began operations five years ago, engaging in a number of business activities ranging from manufacturing and marketing durable goods to editing technical business publications on which the company collects royalty income. The accounting for these many activities resulted in a number of differences between reporting for book and tax purposes. For financial reporting purposes, the company accrued estimated warranty costs when it sold products under warranty, deferred advance royalty payments it received, and prepaid many operating expenses. For tax purposes, it recognized warranty costs when paid, royalty income when cash was received, and operating expenses when cash was paid. The opening and closing balances in these accounts for Year 5 follow. Assume that each of these has a tax basis of zero and each is expected to reverse in the following year.

Debit (Credit)	January 1	December 31	Change During Year
Accrued warranty costs	$(50,000)	$(40,000)	$10,000
Deferred royalty income	(10,000)	(40,000)	(30,000)
Prepaid expenses.	33,000	25,000	(8,000)

The company depreciates its manufacturing equipment using an accelerated method for tax purposes and a straight-line method for financial reporting. The schedule of GAAP and tax depreciation for Year 5 and all remaining years for the company's existing equipment is as follows.

Year	GAAP Depreciation	Tax Depreciation
Year 5	$ 9,000	$14,000
Year 6	9,000	9,000
Year 7	9,000	6,000
Year 8	9,000	3,000
Total	$36,000	$32,000

The company's Year 5 pretax GAAP income was $8,000. This includes $2,000 of interest revenue on municipal bonds that is not taxable.

- The tax rate the company expected to be effective in Year 5 and Year 6 (and for all prior years) is 34%. However, during Year 5 a tax law was enacted that will change the tax rate to 40% for Year 7 and subsequent years.
- There are no prior taxes currently payable or any prior tax refunds currently receivable.
- At January 1 of Year 5, there are opening balances in the deferred tax asset account of $29,240, in the valuation allowance of $5,100, and in the deferred tax liability account of $15,980.
- The company determines that it is *more likely than not* that any deferred tax asset on December 31 of Year 5, will not be realized.

Required

a. Prepare the journal entry to record the company's income tax expense for Year 5.
b. Determine the deferred tax amount to be reported on the company's balance sheet.

AD&J18-10
Recording Multiple
Temporary Differences,
Change in Enacted Tax
Rate   LO2, 6

Challenge Problem On January 1 of each of the first four years of its existence, Allway Company purchases a new unit of equipment. Each unit has a four-year life and zero salvage value, costs $100,000, and is depreciated for GAAP and tax purposes as shown below. The income tax rate is 25%. Allway has a deferred tax liability of $12,500 at the end of Year 3. The current year is Year 4, and pretax GAAP income is $30,000. Amounts are in thousands.

	Prior Years			Current Year	Future Years		
	1	2	3	4	5	6	7
Equipment							
Beginning balance	$ 0	$100	$200	$300			
Purchases at January 1	100	100	100	100			
Retirements at December 31	0	0	0	(100)			
Ending balance	$100	$200	$300	$300			
GAAP depreciation							
Equipment 1	$ 25	$ 25	$ 25	$ 25			
Equipment 2		25	25	25	$25		
Equipment 3			25	25	25	$25	
Equipment 4				25	25	25	$25
Annual total	$ 25	$ 50	$ 75	$100	$75	$50	$25

continued

continued from previous page

	Prior Years			Current Year	Future Years		
	1	2	3	4	5	6	7
Tax depreciation							
Equipment 1	$ 40	$ 30	$ 20	$ 10			
Equipment 2		40	30	20	$10		
Equipment 3			40	30	20	$10	
Equipment 4				40	30	20	$10
Annual total	$ 40	$ 70	$ 90	$100	$60	$30	$10

Required

a. Record the income tax entry at the end of Year 4.

b. Assume that during Year 4, the tax rate is increased to 30% effective as of the beginning of Year 4. Repeat part *a* under this assumption.

c. Assume that during Year 4, the tax rate is increased to 30% effective in Year 5 and to 35% thereafter. Repeat part *a* under this assumption.

AD&J18-11
Defining Terms **LO2, 3, 4, 5, 6, 7, 8**

Codification Skills How are the terms (1) deferred tax asset, (2) deferred tax liability, (3) tax position, (4) valuation allowance, (5) income tax expense (or benefit), (6) carryforwards defined in the Codification?

AD&J18-12
Performing Accounting Research **LO2, 4, 5, 7, 8**

Codification Skills Through research in the Codification, identify the specific citation for each of the following items included as guidance in this chapter for income tax accounting.

a. *More likely than not* threshold in recording a valuation allowance   FASB ASC ☐ - ☐ - ☐ - ☐

b. Change in tax laws recognized at the date of enactment   FASB ASC ☐ - ☐ - ☐ - ☐

c. *More likely than not* threshold in evaluating tax positions   FASB ASC ☐ - ☐ - ☐ - ☐

d. Loss carryforwards resulting in deferred tax assets   FASB ASC ☐ - ☐ - ☐

e. Intraperiod tax allocation   FASB ASC ☐ - ☐ - ☐

AD&J18-13
Performing Accounting Research **LO8**

Codification Skills When a company is uncertain as to the disposition of a tax position, it becomes a question as to the amount of tax benefit to recognize in the financial statements. Resolution of tax positions may take years. A company is trying to determine how to estimate the benefit to recognize related to an anticipated tax settlement with a taxing authority.

What guidance is available in the Codification in reporting this information?

FASB ASC ☐ - ☐ - ☐ - ☐

Appendices—Brief Exercises

AppBE18-1
Reporting Intraperiod Tax Allocation **LO9**
Hint: See Demo 18-9

During the year, Roberts Inc. reports pretax GAAP income of $60,000, resulting from income from continuing operations of $65,000 and $5,000 from a loss from discontinued operations. If the company's tax rate is 25%, what amount will the company report for the loss from discontinued operations and net income in its income statement?

AppBE18-2
Reporting Intraperiod Tax Allocation **LO9**
Hint: See Demo 18-9

Bye Corporation is preparing its financial statements. Its pretax amounts are income before discontinued operations, $300,000, and gain from discontinued operations, $20,000. How much income tax should be allocated to each of the intraperiod amounts assuming a tax rate of 25%?

Appendices—Exercises

AppE18-1
Reporting Intraperiod Tax Allocation **LO9**
Hint: See Demo 18-9

Apple Inc. had the following balances in its accounts on December 31.

Revenues	$500,000
Cost of goods sold	210,000
Operating expenses	75,000
Loss from discontinued operations	(40,000)
Unrealized gain on available-for-sale debt securities	4,000

Required

Assuming an income tax rate of 25%, prepare a combined statement of comprehensive income using intraperiod tax allocation.

Appendices—Problems

Information for Lake Inc. for the year ended December 31 follows.

- Revenues, costs of goods sold, and operating expenses are $800,000, $350,000, and $100,000, respectively.
- One timing difference originating during the year results in a future taxable amount of $40,000.
- Fines paid of $2,500 included in operating expenses are not deductible.
- Loss from discontinued operations that is tax deductible in the current year of $10,000 is not included in the amounts above.
- Tax rate is 25% for all years.

AppP18-1
Reporting Intraperiod Tax
Allocation **LO9**

Required

a. Prepare the journal entry to record income tax expense.
b. Prepare an income statement using intraperiod tax allocation.

Answers to Review Exercises

Review 18-1

a.

	Pretax GAAP Income Year 1	Taxable Income Year 2
Other revenues.	$350,000	$350,000
Maintenance expense	0	(20,000)
Bad debt expense.	(30,000)	0
Regulatory fines	(500)	0
Other expense	(216,700)	(216,700)
Total	$ 102,800	$ 113,300

b.   **Maintenance contract**
Current period: Taxable income < Pretax GAAP income
Future period: Taxable income > Pretax GAAP income
Type of difference: Taxable temporary difference

Bad Debt expense
Current period: Taxable income > Pretax GAAP income
Future period: Taxable income < Pretax GAAP income
Type of difference: Deductible temporary difference

Regulatory fine
Current period: Taxable income > Pretax GAAP income
Future period: No impact
Type of difference: Nondeductible item

Review 18-2

Example One

a.

Calculation of Income Tax Payable Increase at Dec. 31	Year 1	Year 2	Year 3	Year 4
Pretax GAAP income	$145,000	$160,000	$160,000	$155,000
Accelerated depreciation adjustment	(5,000)	(12,000)	6,000	11,000
Taxable income.	140,000	148,000	166,000	166,000
Tax rate.	× 25%	× 25%	× 25%	× 25%
Income tax payable increase	$ 35,000	$ 37,000	$ 41,500	$ 41,500

b.

Schedule to Compute Deferred Tax Liability Balance (Dec. 31)	Year 1	Year 2	Year 3	Year 4
GAAP basis of depreciable asset................	$45,000	$30,000	$15,000	$ 0
Tax basis of depreciable asset	40,000	13,000	4,000	0
Difference between GAAP and tax bases	5,000	17,000	11,000	0
Tax rate...................................	× 25%	× 25%	× 25%	× 25%
Deferred tax liability, ending balance	$ 1,250	$ 4,250	$ 2,750	$ 0

Assets = Liabilities + Equity
       +1,250   −36,250
       +35,000

Inc Tax Pay	Inc Tax Exp
│ 35,000	36,250 │

Def Tax Liab
│ 1,250

c. **December 31, Year 1—To record income tax expense**

Income Tax Expense ($35,000 + $1,250)	36,250	
Deferred Tax Liability		1,250
Income Tax Payable.................................		35,000

Assets = Liabilities + Equity
       +3,000   −40,000
       +37,000

Inc Tax Pay	Inc Tax Exp
│ 35,000	36,250 │
│ 37,000	40,000 │

Def Tax Liab
│ 1,250
│ 3,000

December 31, Year 2—To record income tax

Income Tax Expense ($37,000 + $3,000)	40,000	
Deferred Tax Liability ($4,250 – $1,250)		3,000
Income Tax Payable.................................		37,000

Assets = Liabilities + Equity
       −1,500   −40,000
       +41,500

Inc Tax Pay	Inc Tax Exp
│ 35,000	36,250 │
│ 37,000	40,000 │
│ 41,500	40,000 │

Def Tax Liab	
1,500 │	1,250
	3,000

December 31, Year 3—To record income tax expense

Income Tax Expense ($41,500 – $1,500)	40,000	
Deferred Tax Liability ($4,250 – $2,750)	1,500	
Income Tax Payable.................................		41,500

Assets = Liabilities + Equity
       −2,750   −38,750
       +41,500

Inc Tax Pay	Inc Tax Exp
│ 35,000	36,250 │
│ 37,000	40,000 │
│ 41,500	40,000 │
│ 41,500	38,750 │

Def Tax Liab	
1,500 │	1,250
2,750 │	3,000
	0

December 31, Year 4—To record income tax expense

Income Tax Expense ($41,500 – $2,750)	38,750	
Deferred Tax Liability ($0 – $2,750)...................	2,750	
Income Tax Payable.................................		41,500

Example Two

a.

Calculation of Income Tax Payable Increase at Dec. 31	Year 1	Year 2	Year 3	Year 4
Pretax GAAP income	$145,000	$160,000	$160,000	$155,000
Expense adjustment..........................	(45,000)	15,000	15,000	15,000
Taxable income..............................	100,000	175,000	175,000	170,000
Tax rate....................................	× 25%	× 25%	× 25%	× 25%
Income tax payable increase	$ 25,000	$ 43,750	$ 43,750	$ 42,500

b.

Schedule to Compute Deferred Tax Liability Balance (Dec. 31)	Year 1	Year 2	Year 3	Year 4
GAAP basis of depreciable asset......................	$45,000	$30,000	$15,000	$ 0
Tax basis of depreciable asset	0	0	0	0
Difference between GAAP and tax bases	45,000	30,000	15,000	0
Tax rate....................................	× 25%	× 25%	× 25%	× 25%
Deferred tax liability, ending balance	$11,250	$ 7,500	$ 3,750	$ 0

c. **December 31, Year 1—To record income tax expense**

Income Tax Expense ($25,000 + $11,250)	36,250	
Deferred Tax Liability		11,250
Income Tax Payable		25,000

Assets = Liabilities + Equity
+11,250 −36,250
+25,000

Def Tax Liab | 11,250   Inc Tax Exp 36,250 |
Inc Tax Pay | 25,000

December 31, Year 2—To record income tax expense

Income Tax Expense ($43,750 − $3,750)	40,000	
Deferred Tax Liability ($11,250 − $7,500)	3,750	
Income Tax Payable		43,750

Assets = Liabilities + Equity
−3,750 −40,000
+43,750

Def Tax Liab 3,750 | 11,250   Inc Tax Exp 36,250 | 40,000 |
Inc Tax Pay | 25,000 | 43,750

December 31, Year 3—To record income tax expense

Income Tax Expense ($43,750 − $3,750)	40,000	
Deferred Tax Liability ($7,500 − $3,750)	3,750	
Income Tax Payable		43,750

Assets = Liabilities + Equity
−3,750 −40,000
+43,750

Def Tax Liab 3,750 | 11,250   3,750   Inc Tax Exp 36,250 40,000 40,000 |
Inc Tax Pay | 25,000 43,750 43,750

December 31, Year 4—To record income tax expense

Income Tax Expense ($42,500 − $3,750)	38,750	
Deferred Tax Liability ($3,750 − $0)	3,750	
Income Tax Payable		42,500

Assets = Liabilities + Equity
−3,750 −38,750
+42,500

Def Tax Liab 3,750 | 11,250; 3,750; 3,750 | 0   Inc Tax Exp 36,250 40,000 40,000 38,750 |
Inc Tax Pay | 25,000 43,750 43,750 42,500

Review 18-3

a.

Calculation of Income Tax Payable Increase at Dec. 31	Year 1	Year 2	Year 3	Year 4
Pretax GAAP income	$145,000	$155,000	$150,000	$148,000
Revenue adjustment	150,000	(50,000)	(50,000)	(50,000)
Taxable income	295,000	105,000	100,000	98,000
Tax rate	× 25%	× 25%	× 25%	× 25%
Income tax payable increase	$ 73,750	$ 26,250	$ 25,000	$ 24,500

b.

Schedule to Compute Deferred Tax Asset Balance (Dec. 31)	Year 1	Year 2	Year 3	Year 4
GAAP basis of deferred revenue	$150,000	$100,000	$50,000	$ 0
Tax basis of deferred revenue	0	0	0	0
Difference between GAAP and tax bases	150,000	100,000	50,000	0
Tax rate	× 25%	× 25%	× 25%	× 25%
Deferred tax asset, ending balance	$ 37,500	$ 25,000	$12,500	$ 0

c. **December 31, Year 1—To record income tax expense**

Income Tax Expense ($73,750 − $37,500)	36,250	
Deferred Tax Asset	37,500	
Income Tax Payable		73,750

Assets = Liabilities + Equity
+37,500 +73,750 −36,250

Def Tax Asset 37,500 | Inc Tax Exp 36,250 |
Inc Tax Pay | 73,750

December 31, Year 2—To record income tax expense

Income Tax Expense ($26,250 + $12,500)	38,750	
Deferred Tax Asset ($25,000 − $37,500)		12,500
Income Tax Payable		26,250

Assets = Liabilities + Equity
−12,500 +26,250 −38,750

Def Tax Asset 37,500 | 12,500   Inc Tax Exp 36,250 | 38,750 |
Inc Tax Pay | 73,750 | 26,250

Assets = Liabilities + Equity
−12,500   +25,000   −37,500

Def Tax Asset		Inc Tax Exp	
37,500	12,500	36,250	
	12,500	38,750	
		37,500	

Inc Tax Pay	
	73,750
	26,250
	25,000

December 31, Year 3—To record income tax expense

Income Tax Expense ($25,000 + $12,500)	37,500	
Deferred Tax Asset ($25,000 − $12,500)...............		12,500
Income Tax Payable...........................		25,000

Assets = Liabilities + Equity
−12,500   +24,500   −37,000

Def Tax Asset		Inc Tax Exp	
37,500	12,500	36,250	
	12,500	38,750	
	12,500	37,500	
		37,000	

Inc Tax Pay	
	73,750
	26,250
	25,000
	24,500

December 31, Year 4—To record income tax expense

Income Tax Expense ($24,500 + $12,500)	37,000	
Deferred Tax Asset ($12,500 − $0)		12,500
Income Tax Payable...........................		24,500

Review 18-4

a.

Calculation of Income Tax Payable Increase at Dec. 31	
Pretax GAAP income	$250,000
Depreciation adjustment.....................	(30,000)
Installment sales adjustment	(40,000)
Insurance premiums.....................	4,000
Taxable income.....................	184,000
Tax rate.....................	× 25%
Income tax payable increase	$ 46,000

b. **December 31—To record income tax expense**

Assets = Liabilities + Equity
+12,500   −58,500
+46,000

Def Tax Liab		Inc Tax Exp	
	5,000 Bal	58,500	
	12,500		
	17,500		

Inc Tax Pay	
	46,000

Income Tax Expense ($46,000 + $12,500)	58,500	
Deferred Tax Liability ($17,500* − $5,000)		12,500
Income Tax Payable...........................		46,000

*	Fixed Asset	Installment Receivable	Total
GAAP	$320,000	$40,000	
Tax	290,000	0	
	30,000	40,000	
	× 25%	× 25%	
Deferred tax liability bal........	$ 7,500	$10,000	$17,500

Review 18-5

Part One

Assets = Liabilities + Equity
+20,000   +220,000   −200,000

Def Tax Asset		Inc Tax Exp	
Bal. 280,000		200,000	
20,000			
300,000			

Inc Tax Pay	
	220,000

a. **December 31—To record income tax expense**

Income Tax Expense ($220,000 − $20,000)	200,000	
Deferred Tax Asset....................	20,000	
Income Tax Payable ($880,000 × 0.25).............		220,000

Assets = Liabilities + Equity
+20,000   +220,000   −200,000

Def Tax Asset		Inc Tax Exp	
Bal. 280,000		200,000	
20,000			
300,000			

Inc Tax Pay	
	220,000

b. **December 31—To record income tax expense**

Income Tax Expense ($220,000 − $20,000)	200,000	
Deferred Tax Asset....................	20,000	
Income Tax Payable ($880,000 × 0.25).............		220,000

Assets = Liabilities + Equity
−90,000   −90,000

DTA Val Allow		Inc Tax Exp	
	90,000	200,000	
		90,000	

December 31—To record valuation allowance

Income Tax Expense	90,000	
Valuation Allowance for Deferred Tax Asset*		90,000

*(30% × $300,000)

Part Two

	Deferred Tax Asset (Liability)
Prepaid operating expense................	$(10,000)
Excess accelerated depreciation	(7,500)
Installment sales......................	(8,750)
Deferred tax liabilities	26,250
Bad debt expense......................	2,500
Valuation allowance (50% × $2,500)	(1,250)
Deferred tax assets...................	1,250
Net deferred tax liability ($26,250 - $1,250) ...	$ 25,000

Balance Sheet (excerpt)	
Liabilities	
Noncurrent	
Deferred tax liability, net	25,000

Review 18-6

Calculation of Income Tax Payable Increase at Dec. 31	Year 2
Pretax GAAP income..................	$112,000
Installment sales adjustment	10,000
Warranty expense adjustment	22,000
Taxable income......................	144,000
Tax rate............................	× 30%
Income tax payable increase	$ 43,200

Deferred Tax Liability Adjustment, at Dec. 31	Year 2
Installment receivable ($13,000 × 0.25)..	$ 3,250
Beginning balance	6,900
Deferred tax liability adjustment	$(3,650)

December 31, Year 2—To record income tax expense

Income Tax Expense ($43,200 – $9,150)	34,050	
Deferred Tax Asset ($22,000 × 25%).......................	5,500	
Deferred Tax Liability	3,650	
Income Tax Payable.....................................		43,200

Assets = Liabilities + Equity
+5,500   –3,650   –34,050
        +43,200

Def Tax Asset	Inc Tax Exp
5,500		34,050	

Inc Tax Pay	Def Tax Liab
	43,200	3,650	6,900 Bal.
			3,250

Review 18-7

December 31—To record income tax benefit

Deferred Tax Asset ($18,000 × 25%).......................	4,500	
Income Tax Expense		4,500

Assets = Liabilities + Equity
+4,500   +4,500

Def Tax Asset	Inc Tax Exp
4,500			4,500

December 31—To record valuation allowance

Income Tax Expense ($4,500 × 60%)	2,700	
Valuation Allowance for Deferred Tax Asset..............		2,700

Assets = Liabilities + Equity
–2,700   –2,700

DTA Val Allow	Inc Tax Exp
	2,700	2,700	4,500

Review 18-8

December 31—To record income tax expense

Income Tax Expense	115,000	
Liability for Unrecognized Tax Benefits*		2,500
Income Tax Payable ($450,000 × 25%).................		112,500

Assets = Liabilities + Equity
        +2,500   –115,000
        +112,500

Liab—Tax Benefits	Inc Tax Exp
	2,500	115,000	

Inc Tax Pay	
	112,500	

* There is a 60% (15% + 20% + 25%) cumulative probability that a deduction of at least $20,000 will be allowed. Benefits related to the remaining $10,000 of deduction cannot be recognized. Liability for unrecognized tax benefits is $2,500, computed as 25% × $10,000 (= $30,000 – $20,000).

Review 18-9

Athletics Inc. Statement of Comprehensive Income For Year Ended December 31	
Revenues	$180,000
Cost of goods sold	99,000
Gross margin	81,000
Operating expenses	15,000
Income from continuing operations before income tax	66,000
Income tax expense ($66,000 × 25%)	16,500
Income from continuing operations	49,500
Discontinued operations	
Loss from discontinued operations, net of tax ($14,000 × 75%)	(10,500)
Net income	39,000
Other comprehensive income	
Unrealized gain on debt securities ($3,000 × 75%)	2,250
Comprehensive income	$ 41,250

19

Stockholders' Equity

Consolidated Statement of Equity
PepsiCo Inc. and Subsidiaries
Fiscal years ended December 30, 2023, December 31, 2022, and December 25, 2021 (in millions except per share amounts)

	2023 Shares	2023 Amount	2022 Shares	2022 Amount	2021 Shares	2021 Amount
Common Stock						
Balance, beginning of year	1,377	23	1,383	23	1,380	23
Change in repurchased common stock	(3)	—	(6)	—	3	—
Balance, end of year	1,374	23	1,377	23	1,383	23
Capital in Excess of Par Value						
Balance, beginning of year		4,134		4,001		3,910
Share-based compensation expense		379		346		302
Stock option exercises, RSUs and PSUs converted		(107)		(102)		(118)
Withholding tax on RSUs and PSUs converted		(140)		(107)		(92)
Other		(5)		(4)		(1)
Balance, end of year		4,261		4,134		4,001
Retained Earnings						
Balance, beginning of year		67,800		65,165		63,443
Net income attributable to PepsiCo		9,074		8,910		7,618
Cash dividends declared - common[a]		(6,839)		(6,275)		(5,896)
Balance, end of year		70,035		67,800		65,165
Accumulated Other Comprehensive Loss						
Balance, beginning of year		(15,302)		(14,898)		(15,476)
Other comprehensive (loss)/income		(232)		(404)		578
Balance, end of year		(15,534)		(15,302)		(14,898)
Repurchased Common Stock						
Balance, beginning of year	(490)	(39,506)	(484)	(38,248)	(487)	(38,446)
Share repurchases	(6)	(1,000)	(9)	(1,500)	(1)	(106)
Stock option exercises, RSUs and PSUs converted	3	223	3	240	4	303
Other	—	1	—	2	—	1
Balance, end of year	(493)	(40,282)	(490)	(39,506)	(484)	(38,248)
Total PepsiCo Common Shareholders' Equity		18,503		17,149		16,043
Noncontrolling interests						
Balance, beginning of year		124		108		98
Net income attributable to noncontrolling interests		81		68		61
Distributions to noncontrolling interests		(68)		(69)		(49)
Acquisitions		—		21		—
Other, net		(3)		(4)		(2)
Balance, end of year		134		124		108
Total Equity		$18,637		$17,273		$16,151

[a] Cash dividends declared per common share were $4.9450, $4.5250, and $4.2475 for 2023, 2022, and 2021, respectively.
See accompanying notes to the consolidated financial statements.

PepsiCo Inc. and Subsidiaries
PepsiCo Common Shareholders' Equity

	2023	2022
Common stock, par value 1⅔¢ per share (authorized 3,600 shares, issued, net of repurchased common stock at par value: 1,374 and 1,377 shares, respectively)	23	23
Capital in excess of par value	4,261	4,134
Retained earnings	70,035	67,800
Accumulated other comprehensive loss	(15,534)	(15,302)
Repurchased common stock, in excess of par value (493 and 490 shares, respectively)	(40,282)	(39,506)
Total PepsiCo Common Shareholders' Equity	18,503	17,149
Noncontrolling interests	134	124
Total Equity	18,637	17,273
Total Liabilities and Equity	$100,495	$92,187

Chapter Preview

In this chapter, we identify five main components of stockholders' equity and illustrate how these components are reported in the statement of stockholders' equity. We then examine in more detail common stock, preferred stock, and the related additional paid-in capital accounts, as well as treasury stock, which is a contra equity account. We examine the effect on retained earnings from different kinds of dividends: cash, property, liquidating, and stock. We also examine stock splits. Accumulated comprehensive income, a segment of stockholders' equity, is discussed, as well as the required reporting of the statement of comprehensive income. We wrap up the topic of equity with a discussion of required financial statement disclosures and the use of equity-based ratio analyses.

Action Plan

LO	Topic/Subtopic	Page	Demos	Reviews	Assignments	CPA*
LO 19–1	**Describe and report key components of stockholders' equity** Paid-In Capital :: Retained Earnings :: Accumulated OCI :: Treasury Stock :: Noncontrolling Interest	19-3	D19-1	R19-1	MC19-1, MC19-10, BE19-1, BE19-2, BE19-3, E19-1, E19-2, E19-30, E19-32, P19-1, P19-2, P19-3, P19-5, P19-6, P19-7, P19-9, P19-10, P19-11, AD&J19-1, AD&J19-5, AD&J19-6	FAR I.A.4.a II.I.1
LO 19–2	**Account for common stock issuance, including par and no-par, cash and noncash, and issue costs** Par Value :: No-Par :: Stated Value :: Noncash Consideration :: Multiple Securities Issuance :: Stock Issue Costs	19-8	D19-2A D19-2B D19-2C D19-2D D19-2E	R19-2	MC19-2, BE19-4, BE19-5, BE19-6, BE19-7, BE19-8, BE19-9, BE19-10, BE19-11, E19-3, E19-4, E19-5, E19-6, E19-7, E19-8, E19-18, E19-20, E19-30, P19-1, P19-4, P19-5, P19-7, P19-11, AD&J19-4, AD&J19-5, AD&J19-6, AD&J19-11, AD&J19-19, AD&J19-23	FAR I.A.4.b I.A.4.c II.I.1
LO 19–3	**Account for reacquisition of common stock** Treasury Stock :: Cost Method :: Direct Retirement	19-12	D19-3A D19-3B	R19-3	MC19-3, MC19-10, BE19-12, BE19-13, BE19-14, BE19-15, BE19-16, BE19-17, BE19-18, E19-9, E19-10, E19-11, E19-12, E19-13, E19-14, E19-15, E19-16, E19-17, E19-18, E19-30, P19-1, P19-4, P19-5, P19-6, P19-7, P19-11, AD&J19-4, AD&J19-5, AD&J19-10, AD&J19-13, AD&J19-14, AD&J19-23	FAR II.I.1
LO 19–4	**Describe and account for preferred stock** Callable :: Redeemable :: Convertible :: Cumulative Dividend Preference	19-15	D19-4	R19-4	MC19-4, BE19-19, BE19-20, BE19-21, BE19-22, BE19-23, E19-19, E19-20, E19-21, E19-30, P19-1, P19-2, P19-4, AD&J19-2, AD&J19-3, AD&J19-7, AD&J19-8, AD&J19-9, AD&J19-12, AD&J19-17, AD&J19-18, AD&J19-23	FAR II.I.1
LO 19–5	**Record dividend distributions, including cash, property, and liquidating** Cash Dividends :: Property Dividends :: Liquidating Dividends :: Declaration Date	19-18	D19-5A D19-5B D19-5C	R19-5	MC19-5, MC19-10, BE19-24, BE19-25, BE19-26, BE19-27, BE19-28, BE19-29, E19-19, E19-22, E19-23, E19-24, E19-25, E19-26, E19-30, P19-1, P19-2, P19-4, P19-5, P19-8, P19-12, AD&J19-2, AD&J19-8, AD&J19-9, AD&J19-15, AD&J19-16, AD&J19-17, AD&J19-18, AD&J19-20, DA19-3	FAR II.I.1
LO 19–6	**Account for stock dividends and stock splits** Small Stock Dividend :: Fractional Shares :: Stock Split Effected in the Form of Stock Dividend :: Stock Split :: Reverse Stock Split	19-23	D19-6A D19-6B D19-6C	R19-6	MC19-6, MC19-10, BE19-30, BE19-31, BE19-32, BE19-33, BE19-34, E19-27, E19-28, E19-29, E19-30, E19-31, E19-32, P19-1, P19-2, P19-9, AD&J19-4, AD&J19-16, AD&J19-21, AD&J19-22, AD&J19-24	FAR II.I
LO 19–7	**Describe the components of comprehensive income and prepare a statement of comprehensive income and a statement of stockholders' equity.** Net Income :: Retained Earnings :: Other Comprehensive Income :: Accumulated Other Comprehensive Income	19-28	D19-7	R19-7	MC19-7, MC19-8, BE19-35, BE19-36, E19-30, E19-32, E19-33, E19-34, E19-35, E19-36, P19-3, P19-11, AD&J19-22, AD&J19-23	FAR I.A.3.a I.A.3.b
LO 19–8	**Explain stockholders' equity disclosures and key ratios** Disclosures :: Book Value per Share :: Payout Ratio :: Return on Equity :: Price-to-Earnings Ratio	19-30	D19-8	R19-8	MC19-9, BE19-37, BE19-38, E19-37, E19-38, P19-3, P19-7, P19-10, P19-12, AD&J19-1, AD&J19-5, AD&J19-6, AD&J19-7, DA19-1, DA19-2	FAR II.I.1 I.F.2

*Black (Gray) font in CPA column indicates that the LO ties directly (indirectly) to the CPA Exam Blueprint LO.

LO 19-1 ▸ Describe and report key components of stockholders' equity

Key Components of Stockholders' Equity
- Paid-in capital
  - Capital stock and additional paid-in capital
- Retained earnings
- Accumulated other comprehensive income
- Treasury stock
- Noncontrolling interest

The corporate form of business has both advantages and disadvantages. An advantage of a public corporation is its ability to obtain funds from investors in the market. Another advantage is that the corporation is a separate entity from its owners, which means that the owners have limited personal liability for the debt of the corporation. The corporation's creditors cannot settle debt by collecting investors' personal assets. The disadvantages of a corporation include increased taxation and regulation and extensive reporting requirements. Owners or shareholders of the corporation are able to easily transfer ownership interests but are not able to exercise active control over management actions unless they own a controlling interest in the company.

The advantages of the corporate form of business often outweigh the disadvantages, making it a popular choice for businesses. The corporate form of business is the dominant form of U.S. business organization in terms of total capital invested. Generally accepted accounting principles apply to all forms of business organizations, whether a sole proprietorship, partnership, or corporation. Corporations, however, have legal and contractual implications that result in different accounting and reporting requirements for stockholders' equity. This chapter focuses on the corporate form of business and the accounting for its equity.

Stockholders' equity (also called **net assets** or **shareholders' equity**) is the difference between recorded assets and recorded liabilities for a corporation. Stockholders' equity is a residual interest and has no existence without the presence of assets. Stockholders' equity is not a claim on specific assets but rather a claim on total assets after liabilities are recognized.

Key Components of Stockholders' Equity

Stockholders' equity consists of five key components.

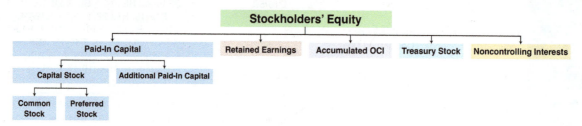

The end of period balances of components of stockholders' equity are recognized in the stockholders' equity section of the balance sheet. Changes in separate equity accounts for the periods reported are typically presented in a separate **statement of stockholders' equity**, although disclosure is an option, as indicated in authoritative guidance. A separate statement of stockholders' equity shows the beginning balance, additions, deductions, and ending balance for each major stockholders' equity component. See the statement of stockholders' equity for the Coca-Cola Company at the end of this section as one example.

505-10-50-2 If both financial position and results of operations are presented, disclosure of changes in the separate accounts comprising shareholders' equity (in addition to retained earnings) and of the changes in the number of shares of equity securities during at least the most recent annual fiscal period and any subsequent interim period presented is required to make the financial statements sufficiently informative. Disclosure of such changes may take the form of separate statements or may be made in the basic financial statements or notes thereto.

Paid-In Capital

Paid-in capital or **contributed capital** consists of capital stock (common stock and preferred stock) and additional paid-in capital.

Capital Stock The following table defines the terms used to describe capital stock.

Term	Explanation
Par value	Value per share of stock designated in the articles of incorporation.
Authorized shares	Number of shares of stock that can be issued legally, as specified in the charter of the corporation.
Issued shares	Number of shares of authorized capital stock that has been issued to stockholders.
Unissued shares	Number of shares of authorized capital stock that has not been issued—that is, the difference between authorized shares and issued shares.
Outstanding shares	Number of shares issued, less the number of shares repurchased and currently held by the company as treasury stock. Outstanding shares are used for earnings per share calculations.
Treasury shares	Shares previously issued and later repurchased by the corporation that are still held (equal to the difference between issued shares and outstanding shares).

Common stock is the primary issue of shares. When there is only one class of stock, all the shares are common stock (whether so designated or not). Although common stock is usually voting stock, some corporations issue two (or more) classes of common stock: at least one class has voting rights (often identified as Class A), and other classes such as Class B are nonvoting or hold different voting rights than Class A. When two or more classes of common stock are issued, one class of stock usually is traded publicly, while the other class of stock is often held by a smaller ownership group and traded privately. This arrangement permits greater control by that smaller group (perhaps as protection against takeovers) and still allows access to capital markets.

Common stockholders are the residual owners of the corporation. Their position is less secure than that of creditors and preferred stockholders because they are not guaranteed dividends or assets if the business fails. However, common stockholders often benefit most from a company's success.

Ownership of common stock normally entitles the holder the right to:

- Vote in stockholder meetings.
- Receive dividends declared by the board of directors.
- Share in the distribution of assets upon liquidation.
- Purchase new shares of common stock on a pro rata basis when new issues are offered for sale. This **preemptive right** gives each stockholder the opportunity to maintain a proportional ownership in the corporation.

The first three rights generally hold in all states. The fourth right is less consistently required across states, and in many instances may not exist. These rights are shared proportionately by all stockholders unless the charter or bylaws say otherwise. When there are two or more classes of stock, ownership rights vary depending on the class of stock.

For SEC registrants, the number of authorized shares is reported either on the face of the balance sheet or in the notes, while the number of shares issued or outstanding is reported on the face of the balance sheet.

`210-10-S99-1`   29. Common stocks. For each class of common shares state, on the face of the balance sheet, the number of shares issued or outstanding, as appropriate . . . and the dollar amount thereof. If convertible, this fact should be indicated on the face of the balance sheet. For each class of common shares state, on the face of the balance sheet or in a note, the title of the issue, the number of shares authorized, and, if convertible, the basis of conversion . . . Show in a note or statement the changes in each class of common shares for each period for which an income statement is required to be filed.

Preferred stock has preferences, or specific rights, that distinguish it from common stock. The most common preference is a priority claim on dividends, usually at a stated rate or amount. This means that if the board declares a dividend, preferred shareholders will receive the stated dividend before common stockholders receive dividends. In return, preferred stock may not have certain rights held by common shareholders, such as voting rights. For SEC registrants, the number of authorized and issued or outstanding shares are recognized on the face of the balance sheet or in a note.

210-10-S99-1   28. Non-Redeemable Preferred Stocks. Preferred stocks that are not redeemable or are redeemable solely at the option of the issuer. State on the face of the balance sheet, or if more than one issue is outstanding state in a note, the title of each issue and the dollar amount thereof . . . State on the face of the balance sheet or in a note, for each issue, the number of shares authorized and the number of shares issued or outstanding, as appropriate . . . Show in a note or separate statement the changes in each class of preferred shares reported under this caption for each period for which an income statement is required to be filed. . . .

Additional Paid-In Capital   **Additional paid-in capital**, or **paid-in capital in excess of par**, reports the value of assets received by the corporation above par or stated value. For financial reporting, the various types of additional paid-in capital accounts are aggregated and reported as one item in the equity section of the balance sheet. Examples of additional paid-in capital accounts include Paid-In Capital in Excess of Par—Common Stock, Paid-In Capital in Excess of Par—Preferred Stock, Paid-In Capital—Treasury Stock, and Paid-In Capital—Retired Stock. Other paid-in capital accounts are introduced throughout the text as needed.

Retained Earnings

Retained earnings, beginning balance
+/– Prior period adjustment (net of tax)
+/– Net income (loss)
– Dividends (cash, property, stock)
Retained earnings, ending balance

Retained earnings, or reinvested earnings, is the company's accumulated net income or net loss from its inception (including prior period adjustments net of tax) less accumulated dividends and other amounts transferred to contributed capital (paid-in capital) accounts. If the accumulated losses and distributions of retained earnings exceed accumulated earnings, a deficit exists (represented by a debit balance) in retained earnings.

Accumulated Other Comprehensive Income

Accumulated Other Comprehensive Income (Accumulated OCI or AOCI) represents changes in equity defined as other comprehensive income (OCI) that have accumulated over the years. Items affecting other comprehensive income are changes in equity during a period resulting from nonowner sources that are *not* included as part of net income. *Other comprehensive income amounts are reported net of tax.* The accumulated amount of OCI, net of tax, is reported as a separate section of stockholders' equity after retained earnings. Accumulated OCI is either added or subtracted in the stockholders' equity section of the balance sheet depending on whether it represents accumulated income or losses.

Accumulated OCI, beginning balance
+/– Other comprehensive income (loss)
Accumulated OCI, ending balance

Treasury Stock

Treasury stock is preferred or common stock that has been issued and reacquired by the issuing corporation but has not been resold or retired. The purchase of treasury stock does not reduce the number of issued shares but does reduce the number of outstanding shares. Treasury shares subsequently may be resold or, in some cases, retired. Treasury stock, a contra equity account, is deducted to arrive at total stockholders' equity.

Noncontrolling Interest

Noncontrolling interest represents the amount of a company's *net assets* (assets less liabilities) owned by outside investors in one of a company's subsidiaries that are not part of the controlling stockholders' interest. A controlling interest is typically achieved when a company owns more than 50% of the outstanding shares of another company. In this case, a parent company has a controlling interest in the other company (subsidiary). Generally, the full financial results of subsidiaries are consolidated into the results of the parent company. The noncontrolling interest is the amount of net assets of any subsidiaries *owned by investors other than the parent company*. The equity attributable to noncontrolling interests is shown separately from the equity attributable to the controlling interest. For example, the Coca-Cola Company financial statements on page 19-7 indicate that Cola-Cola Company's shareholders' equity is $25,941 million for the most recent year presented. The noncontrolling interest is $1,539 million, which is the share of the Coca-Cola Company's net assets owned by noncontrolling shareholders. Total equity is equal to the total of the controlling interest plus the noncontrolling interest ($ millions).

$25,941 Controlling interest by Coca-Cola Company + $1,539 Noncontrolling interest = $27,480 Total equity

In the stockholders' equity section of the balance sheet, the relevant components of stockholders' equity are typically presented in the order presented here and in **Demo 19-1**.

On December 31, Polar Inc. had the following account balances.

Preferred stock, $15 par, 20,000 shares authorized.	$ 30,000 Cr.
Paid-in capital in excess of par—preferred stock	25,000 Cr.
Common stock, $1 par, 100,000 shares authorized.	8,000 Cr.
Paid-in capital in excess of par—common stock	192,000 Cr.
Retained earnings	140,000 Cr.
Accumulated other comprehensive income (loss)	25,000 Dr.
Treasury stock, 500 shares.	15,000 Dr.

Prepare the stockholders' equity section of the balance sheet for Polar Inc. on December 31. State the par value per share, and the number of shares authorized, issued, and outstanding of common stock and preferred stock on the face of the balance sheet.

Solution

While 8,000 common shares were issued ($8,000 par value/$1 par value per share), only 7,500 are outstanding because 500 shares are held as treasury shares. For preferred stock, 2,000 shares were issued ($30,000 par value/$15 par value per share). Additional paid-in capital accounts for common stock ($192,000) and preferred stock ($25,000) are combined into a single amount of $217,000. The accumulated other comprehensive loss and treasury stock both have debit balances and are deducted within the stockholders' equity section.

Balance Sheet (excerpt) December 31	
Common stock, $1 par value, 100,000 shares authorized, 8,000 shares issued, 7,500 shares outstanding	$ 8,000
Preferred stock, $15 par value, 20,000 shares authorized, 2,000 shares issued and outstanding	30,000
Paid-in capital in excess of par.	217,000
Retained earnings	140,000
Accumulated other comprehensive loss.	(25,000)
Less: Treasury stock, 500 shares	(15,000)
Total stockholders' equity	**$355,000**

Components of Stockholders' Equity — LO19-1 — REVIEW 19-1

Match each of the financial statement items *a* through *k* with its proper stockholders' equity component 1 through 5.

Financial Statement Items

_____ a. Net income

_____ b. Foreign currency translation loss adjustment

_____ c. Paid-in capital in excess of par—preferred stock

_____ d. Cash dividends declared and paid

_____ e. Reacquired common shares

_____ f. Unrealized holding loss on securities classified as available-for-sale

_____ g. Prior period adjustment—error correction

_____ h. Common stock at par value

_____ i. Preferred stock at par value

_____ j. Paid-in capital in excess of par—common stock

_____ k. Net assets owned by non-parent investors

Stockholders' Equity Components

1. Paid-in capital
2. Retained earnings
3. Accumulated other comprehensive income
4. Treasury stock
5. Noncontrolling interest

More Practice: BE19-1, BE19-2, BE19-3, E19-1, E19-2

Solution on p. 19-64.

COCA-COLA

Real World—STOCKHOLDERS' EQUITY

The following financial statement excerpts of Coca-Cola Company illustrate various components of stockholders' equity. We see differences in terminology: *shareowners' equity* is used for stockholders' equity, *capital surplus* is used for paid-in capital in excess of par, and *reinvested earnings* is used for retained earnings.

Coca-Cola Company—Balance Sheets (excerpt) December 31 (in millions except par value)	2023	2022
Common stock, $0.25 par value; authorized—11,200 shares; issued—7,040 shares . . .	$ 1,760	$ 1,760
Capital surplus	19,209	18,822
Reinvested earnings.	73,782	71,019
Accumulated other comprehensive income (loss)	(14,275)	(14,895)
Treasury stock, at cost—2,732 and 2,712 shares, respectively	(54,535)	(52,601)
Equity attributable to shareowners of the Coca-Cola company	25,941	24,105
Equity attributable to noncontrolling interests.	1,539	1,721
Total equity	$27,480	$25,826

We see how each of the ending balances provided above, and the activity for the year, is presented on the consolidated statement of shareowners' equity shown below.

The COCA-COLA Company and Subsidiaries Consolidated Statements of Shareowners' Equity Year Ended December 31 (in millions except per share data)	2023	2022
Equity attributable to shareowners of the Coca-Cola company		
Number of common shares outstanding		
Balance at beginning of year	4,328	4,325
Treasury stock issued to employees related to stock compensation plans	17	24
Purchases of stock for treasury.	(37)	(21)
Balance at end of year	4,308	4,328
Common stock	$ 1,760	$1,760
Capital surplus		
Balance at beginning of year	$18,822	$18,116
Stock issued to employees related to stock-based compensation plans	177	373
Stock-based compensation expense	233	332
Acquisition of interests held by noncontrolling owners	(20)	—
Other activities	(3)	1
Balance at end of year	19,209	18,822
Reinvested earnings		
Balance at beginning of year	71,019	69,094
Net income attributable to shareowners of the Coca-Cola company	10,714	9,542
Dividends (per share—$1.64 and $1.60 in 2020 and 2019, respectively)	(7,951)	(7,617)
Balance at end of year	73,782	71,019
Accumulated other comprehensive income (loss)		
Balance at beginning of year	(14,895)	(14,330)
Net other comprehensive income (loss)	620	(565)
Balance at end of year	(14,275)	(14,895)
Treasury stock		
Balance at beginning of year	(52,601)	(51,641)
Treasury stock issued to employees related to stock compensation plans	255	376
Purchases of stock for treasury.	(2,189)	(1,336)
Balance at end of year	(54,535)	(52,601)
Total equity attributable to shareowners of the Coca-Cola company	$25,941	$24,105
Equity attributable to noncontrolling interests		
Balance at beginning of year	$ 1,721	$ 1,861
Net income attributable to noncontrolling interests.	(11)	29
Net foreign currency translation adjustment	(147)	(118)
Dividends paid to noncontrolling interests	(25)	(51)
Acquisition of interests held by noncontrolling owners	(2)	—
Other activities	3	—
Total equity attributable to noncontrolling interests.	$ 1,539	$ 1,721

Account for common stock issuance, including par and no-par, cash and noncash, and issue costs

LO 19-2

Articles of incorporation are prepared by a corporation's organizers to meet the legal requirements of the state that issues a **corporate charter**. The articles of incorporation describe the nature and purpose of the corporation and specify the number of shares of capital stock authorized. An initial **board of directors** is selected to approve corporate bylaws, to supplement the provisions of the charter, and to select corporate officers. While state laws vary regarding corporate procedures, many states have adopted the **Model Business Corporation Act,** which is a model corporate law established by the American Bar Association. Having a model act for guidance allows for some consistency and clarity across state statutes in the United States.

Accounting for Stock Issuance

- Par value common stock issuance
- No-par common stock issuance
- Stated value common stock issuance
- Noncash consideration
- Multiple securities issuance
- Stock issue costs

LO 19-2 Overview

Par Value Common Stock

No journal entry is made when stock is authorized with a company's state of incorporation. From the authorized shares, a company can issue shares to shareholders for cash or noncash consideration. The articles of incorporation can designate a **par value** per share of stock. Par value has *no particular relation to the fair value* of the company's stock. For example, **Facebook Inc.** has a par value per common share of $0.000006, which does not (and was not intended to) correlate with its stock price per share.

In the case of par value common stock, legal capital is specified in most states as the par value of the issued or outstanding shares. **Legal capital** is the minimum amount (defined by state law) that must be maintained in the company for the protection of its creditors. Generally, corporate laws prohibit a distribution of assets to shareholders if the distribution would reduce the remaining total capital below legal capital. For example, a corporation must refrain from paying dividends when the effect would be to impair legal capital. Further, any shareholders who purchased stock at an amount below par value would be liable for any shortages under par in the case of a company's liquidation. However, over time, par value has become less relevant (and in many cases irrelevant) because the assigned par value is typically very low, affording little, if any, protection for creditors.

When par value stock is issued, Common Stock is credited for the par value of stock issued equal to the number of shares issued multiplied by the par value per share. Any excess amount of cash over the par value is credited to Paid-In Capital in Excess of Par—Common Stock, as illustrated in **Demo 19-2A**.

Par Value Stock Issuance		**LO19-2**	**DEMO 19-2A**

Lopez Inc. issued 10,000 shares of common stock, $1 par value per share, for cash at $10.20 per share on January 2. Record the issuance of stock on January 2.

Demo

MBC

Solution

January 2—To record par value common stock issuance

Cash (10,000 × $10.20)	102,000	
Common Stock (10,000 × $1)		10,000
Paid-In Capital in Excess of Par—Common Stock (10,000 × [$10.20 – $1])...		92,000

Assets = Liabilities + Equity
+102,000   +10,000
C:f   CS
                              +92,000
                              PIC—CS

Cash		Common Stock	
102,000			10,000

Paid-In Cap—CS	
	92,000

No-Par and Stated Value Common Stock

Many state statutes permit two types of no-par stock: true no-par stock and stated value no-par stock. When true no-par stock is sold, the capital stock account is credited for the full amount received, with no impact on additional paid-in capital accounts. In some states, the full proceeds from the sale of no-par stock is considered legal capital, thus restricting a company's ability to distribute earnings in the future. Some states instead require no-par stock to be associated with a minimum amount or stated value. If shares of no-par stock are assigned a minimum **stated value** per share, the stated amount (number of shares issued × stated value per share) is credited to the capital stock account, with any remainder credited to the additional paid-in capital account. No-par stock with a stated value is accounted for in the same manner as par value stock, as illustrated in **Demo 19-2B**.

DEMO 19-2B	LO19-2	No-Par Common Stock Issuance

Demo

MBC

Example One—No-Par Stock
Lopez Inc. issued 10,000 shares of common stock, no-par, for cash at $10.20 per share on January 2. Record the issuance of stock on January 2.

Solution

Assets	=	Liabilities	+	Equity
+102,000				+102,000
C:f				CS

Cash		Common Stock	
102,000			102,000

January 2—To record no-par common stock issuance

Cash (10,000 × $10.20)	102,000	
Common Stock		102,000

Example Two—Stock with a Stated Value
Instead assume that Lopez Inc. issued 10,000 shares of common stock, no-par, stated value of $1 per share, for cash at $10.20 per share on January 2. Record the issuance of stock on January 2.

Solution

Assets	=	Liabilities	+	Equity
+102,000				+10,000
C:f				CS
				+92,000
				PIC—CS

Cash		Common Stock	
102,000			10,000

	Paid-In Cap—CS	
		92,000

January 2—To record no-par, stated-value common stock issuance

Cash (10,000 × $10.20)	102,000	
Common Stock (10,000 × $1)		10,000
Paid-In Capital in Excess of Stated Value—Common Stock (10,000 × [$10.20 – $1])		92,000

Common Stock Issued for Noncash Consideration

Corporations sometimes issue capital stock for noncash assets, as illustrated in **Demo 19-2C**. The fair value of the stock issued or the noncash consideration received, whichever is more clearly evident, is used to measure the transaction. If the current market value of neither the capital stock issued nor the noncash consideration received is clearly evident, appraised values are used. If neither market values nor appraisals are clearly evident, values are established by the corporation's board of directors using available data such as comparable asset sales or discounted expected future cash flows.

Common Stock Issuance for Noncash Consideration	**LO19-2** ◄ **DEMO 19-2C**

On January 1, Fields Corp. privately issued 100,000, $1 par, common shares in exchange for land. The fair value of the common shares is not clearly evident. However, a recent appraisal indicates that the land is valued at $240,000. Record the issuance of stock on January 1.

Solution

January 1—To record common stock issuance for noncash consideration

Land..	240,000	
Common Stock (100,000 × $1)...............................		100,000
Paid-In Capital in Excess of Par—Common Stock ($240,000 – $100,000) ...		140,000

Assets	=	Liabilities	+	Equity
+240,000				+100,000
Land				CS
				+140,000
				PIC—CS

Land		Common Stock	
240,000			100,000

		Paid-In Cap—CS	
			140,000

Multiple Securities Issuance

Although most corporations sell one class of stock when obtaining financing, they may sell two or more classes of capital stock for one lump-sum amount, as illustrated in **Demo 19-2D**. In the case of a sale of multiple securities, the total proceeds must be allocated logically among the securities. Two approaches are used. (1) When the fair value of each security is known, the lump sum received is allocated proportionately among the classes of stock on the basis of the *relative fair value* of each security. We illustrated the proportional method in LO11-2 with the lump-sum purchase of property, plant, and equipment, (2) When the fair value of one security is known, the known value is used as a basis for that security, with the remainder of the lump sum allocated to the other class. The company should use the approach that produces the most faithful depiction considering the data available.

Multiple Securities Issuance	**LO19-2** ◄ **DEMO 19-2D**

Example One—Proportional Allocation
On January 2, Vale Inc. issued a combined offering of 1,000 shares of common stock, $10 par, and 500 shares of preferred stock, $8 par. The common stock is selling at $40 per share, and the preferred stock at $20 per share. Total cash received is $48,000. Record the issuance of stock.

Solution
Because the fair value of each issue is known, proportional allocation is preferable as a basis for allocating the lump-sum amount.

Fair value of stock		
Fair value of common stock (1,000 shares × $40)	$40,000	($40,000/$50,000) or 80%
Fair value of preferred stock (500 shares × $20)	10,000	($10,000/$50,000) or 20%
	$50,000	

Proportional allocation of lump-sum sale price of $48,000	
Common stock allocation ($48,000 × 80%)	$38,400
Preferred stock allocation ($48,000 × 20%)	9,600
	$48,000

Assets	=	Liabilities	+	Equity
+48,000				+10,000
C:f				CS
				+28,400
				PIC—CS
				+4,000
				PS
				+5,600
				PIC—PS

January 2—To record multiple securities stock issuance—proportional allocation

Cash..	48,000	
Common Stock (1,000 × $10)...............................		10,000
Paid-In Capital in Excess of Par—Common Stock ($38,400 – $10,000) ...		28,400
Preferred Stock (500 × $8).................................		4,000
Paid-In Capital in Excess of Par—Preferred Stock ($9,600 – $4,000)		5,600

Cash		Common Stock	
48,000			10,000

Preferred Stock		Paid-In Cap—CS	
	4,000		28,400

Paid-In Cap—PS	
	5,600

Example Two—Incremental Allocation
On January 2, Vale Inc. issued 1,000 shares of common stock, $10 par, and 500 shares of preferred stock, $6 par. Total cash received is $48,000. The common stock of Vale Inc. is selling at $40 per share, but the market for the preferred stock is not known. Record the issuance of stock.

continued

continued from previous page

Solution

Because the fair value of only the common stock is known, incremental allocation is appropriate for allocating the lump-sum amount.

Assets	=	Liabilities	+	Equity
+48,000				+10,000
C:f				CS
				+30,000
				PIC—CS
				+3,000
				PS
				+5,000
				PIC—PS

Incremental allocation of lump-sum sale price of $48,000	
Common stock allocation ($40 × 1,000 shares).........	$40,000
Preferred stock allocation ($48,000 – $40,000)	8,000
	$48,000

Cash		Common Stock	
48,000			10,000

Preferred Stock		Paid-In Cap—CS	
	3,000		30,000

Paid-In Cap—PS	
	5,000

January 2—To record multiple securities stock issuance—incremental allocation

Cash..	48,000	
Common Stock (1,000 × $10)		10,000
Paid-In Capital in Excess of Par—Common Stock ($40,000 – $10,000) ...		30,000
Preferred Stock (500 × $6)...........................		3,000
Paid-In Capital in Excess of Par—Preferred Stock ($8,000 – $3,000)		5,000

Stock Issue Costs

Issuing capital stock can entail substantial expenditures, including registration fees, underwriter commissions, attorney and accountant fees, printing costs, administrative costs, and promotional costs. These expenditures are called **stock issue costs**.

Stock issue costs are treated as a reduction to paid-in capital in excess of par, as shown in **Demo 19-2E**. The cash received from the stock issuance is the net cash received (selling price less stock issue costs). Because the stock issue costs relate to the issuance of stock, not the operations of the company, they do not affect net income.

505-10-25-2 All of the following shall be excluded from the determination of net income or the results of operations under all circumstances:

a. Adjustments or charges or credits resulting from transactions in the entity's own capital stock.

b. Transfers to and from accounts properly designated as appropriated retained earnings . . .

c. Adjustments made pursuant to a quasi-reorganization. . .

DEMO 19-2E ▶ **LO19-2**

Common Stock Issue Costs

Demo

MBC

Vale Inc. issued 10,000 shares of common stock, $1 par, for cash of $10.20 per share on January 2. Vale also incurred $5,000 in stock issue costs. Record the issuance of stock on January 2, including the stock issue costs.

Solution

Assets	=	Liabilities	+	Equity
+97,000				+10,000
C:f				CS
				+87,000
				PIC—CS

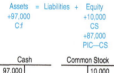

January 2—To record par value common stock issuance and stock issue costs

Cash		
97,000		

Common Stock	
	10,000

Paid-In Cap—CS	
	87,000

Cash ((10,000 × $10.20) – $5,000)	97,000	
Common Stock (10,000 × $1)...		10,000
Paid-In Capital in Excess of Par—Common Stock ([10,000 × {$10.20 – $1}] – $5,000)...		87,000

Accounting for Common Stock Issuance   LO19-2   REVIEW 19-2

Seven unrelated stock issue scenarios follow.

Review
MBC

a. Issue 20,000 shares of common stock at $20 per share ($1 par).

b. Issue 20,000 shares of common stock at $20 per share (no-par value).

c. Issue 20,000 shares of common stock at $20 per share (no-par value), with a stated value of $1 per share.

d. Issue 10,000 shares of common stock ($1 par) in exchange for equipment with a fair value of $180,000.

e. Issue 5,000 shares of common stock ($1 par) and 2,000 shares of preferred stock ($5 par) at a price of $160,000. At the time of issuance, the market price of the common stock is $20 per share, and the market price of the preferred stock is $35 per share.

f. Issue 5,000 shares of common stock ($1 par) and 2,000 shares of preferred stock ($5 par) at a price of $175,000. At the time of issuance, the market price of the common stock is $18 per share, and the market price of the preferred stock is unknown.

g. Issue 20,000 shares of common stock at $20 per share ($1 par). Related to this transaction, the company incurred legal and administrative costs totaling $4,000.

More Practice:
BE19-6, BE19-7, BE19-9,
BE19-11, E19-3, E19-4,
E19-6, E19-7, E19-8

Record journal entries for each of the seven *separate* scenarios described and dated as of January 1. Solution on p. 19-65.

Account for reacquisition of common stock   LO 19-3

It is common practice for a company to buy back its own shares of outstanding stock for a variety of reasons that include the following.

> **Reacquisition of Common Stock**
> - Treasury stock—Cost Method
>   - Deduct treasury stock from equity
>   - Shares remain issued
> - Direct retirement of stock
>   - Derecognize capital accounts
>   - Shares reclassified to unissued
>
> *LO 19-3 Overview*

- Shares may be repurchased and later reissued to satisfy stock compensation awards to employees or for business acquisitions, avoiding the dilution caused by issuing new shares for these purposes.

- Management may choose to buy back stock as a way to increase the market price of the stock. When stock is acquired, the number of outstanding shares decreases. This reduction in supply of stock results in an increase in fair value per share (and earnings per share) of the remaining shares outstanding.

- Repurchasing shares distributes excess cash to shareholders.

- Repurchasing shares may be used to thwart takeover attempts because it increases the ownership interest of the remaining shareholders and their ability to influence company decisions.

A company accounts for the purchase of its own outstanding stock either by holding the shares as **treasury stock**—see **Demo 19-3A**, or through **direct retirement**—see **Demo 19-3B**. The cost of shares held as treasury stock is deducted from stockholders' equity, and the shares remain as *issued* shares. However, treasury stock generally does not carry voting, dividend, preemptive, or liquidation rights and is not an asset of the company. On the other hand, in a direct retirement, the capital accounts are derecognized, and the shares are reclassified as *unissued*. These shares revert to the pool of authorized but unissued shares.

```
                    Purchase Own
                    Common Stock
                         |
        +----------------+----------------+
        |                                 |
Account for as Treasury Stock      Directly Retire
```

Treasury Stock

Under the **cost method**, the acquisition cost of treasury stock is reported as a deduction from total paid-in capital and retained earnings in the stockholders' equity section of the balance sheet. The entry to record the repurchase of shares for treasury stock is a debit to Treasury Stock, a contra stockholders' equity account, and a credit to Cash. The purchase of treasury stock decreases both assets and stockholders' equity.

(Alternatively, a company can account for treasury stock using the **par value method**, in which treasury stock is recognized as a deduction in the capital section of the statement of stockholders' equity. Because this method is used rarely in practice, only the cost method is demonstrated.)

505-30-45-1 If a corporation's stock is acquired for purposes other than retirement (formal or constructive), or if ultimate disposition has not yet been decided, the cost of acquired stock may be shown separately as a deduction from the total of capital stock, additional paid-in capital, and retained earnings, or may be accorded the accounting treatment appropriate for retired stock specified in paragraphs 505-30-30-7 through 30-10.

A company may later sell the treasury stock. If a company decides to sell the treasury stock, Cash is debited for the selling price, and Treasury Stock is credited for the original cost of acquiring the treasury stock. If a company has multiple purchases of treasury stock, purchased at different times and at different prices, the acquisition cost of the shares must be determined. A company may use any of the cost flow assumptions used in inventory (FIFO, LIFO, or weighted average) to measure the cost of treasury shares. If the selling price is not equal to the original acquisition cost of the treasury stock, the company will balance the journal entry as follows:

- When treasury stock is sold for *more* than its acquisition cost, the difference is credited to Paid-In Capital—Treasury Stock.

- When treasury stock is sold for *less* than its acquisition cost, the difference is debited to Paid-In Capital—Treasury Stock if the prior credit balance in that account is sufficient to absorb the debit. Any excess is debited to Retained Earnings.

505-30-30-10 Gains on sales of treasury stock not previously accounted for as constructively retired shall be credited to additional paid-in capital; losses may be charged to additional paid-in capital to the extent that previous net gains from sales or retirements of the same class of stock are included therein, otherwise to retained earnings.

Subsequent Retirement of Treasury Stock If treasury stock is formally retired, the company debits Common Stock and Paid-In Capital in Excess of Par—Common Stock at the amount of the original issuance of the shares, and credits Treasury Stock at cost. Any amounts needed to balance the entry are determined through the same procedures described above.

DEMO 19-3A ▶	**LO19-3**	**Reacquisition of Common Stock—Treasury Stock**

Demo

MBC

On January 1, Star Corp. sold 10,000 of its 50,000 authorized shares of common stock, par $1, at $26 per share. On June 30, Star Corp. reacquires 2,000 common shares for the treasury at $28 per share.

a. Record reacquisition of 2,000 shares of common stock on June 30.
b. Record sale of 500 shares of treasury stock on September 30 at $30 per share.
c. Record sale of 500 shares of treasury stock on December 31 at $19 per share.
d. Present the stockholders' section of the balance sheet on December 31. Assume a balance in retained earnings of $40,000 before any adjustments due to treasury stock.
e. The remaining 1,000 treasury shares (2,000 – 500 – 500) are retired and returned to unissued status on March 1 of the next year. Record the necessary entry.

Solution

a. **Acquisition of Common Shares**

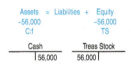

Assets = Liabilities + Equity
−56,000   −56,000
C:f   TS

Cash	Treas Stock
56,000	56,000

June 30—To record acquisition of common stock

Treasury Stock (2,000 × $28)	56,000	
Cash		56,000

b. **Sale of Treasury Stock**

Assets = Liabilities + Equity
+15,000   +14,000
C:f   TS
                   +1,000
                   PIC—TS

Cash	Treas Stock
15,000	56,000	56,000	14,000

Paid-In Cap—TS
1,000

September 30—To record sale of treasury stock (sales price > acquisition cost)

Cash (500 × $30)	15,000	
Treasury Stock (500 × $28)		14,000
Paid-In Capital—Treasury Stock (to balance)............		1,000

continued

continued from previous page

c. Sale of Treasury Stock

December 31—To record sale of treasury stock (sales price < acquisition cost)

Cash (500 × $19)	9,500	
Paid-In Capital—Treasury Stock[†]	1,000	
Retained Earnings (to balance)	3,500	
Treasury Stock (500 × $28)		14,000

[†]The credit balance of $1,000 in Paid-In Capital—Treasury Stock is derecognized. The debit to Paid-In Capital—Treasury Stock is limited to its previous $1,000 credit balance. The remaining difference of $3,500 to balance the journal entry is debited to Retained Earnings.

Assets	=	Liabilities	+	Equity
+9,500				−1,000
C:f				PIC—TS
				−3,500
				RE
				+14,000
				TS

Cash		Pd-In Cap—TS	
15,000	56,000	1,000	1,000
9,500			

Ret Earnings		Treas Stock	
3,500	40,000 Bal.	56,000	14,000
			14,000

d. Financial Statement Presentation of Treasury Stock

Stockholders' Equity	
Common stock, $1 par value, 50,000 shares authorized, 10,000 shares issued, 9,000 shares outstanding	$ 10,000
Paid-In capital in excess of par	250,000
Retained earnings	36,500*
Less: Treasury stock, 1,000 shares	(28,000)[†]
Total stockholders' equity	**$268,500**

*$40,000 − $3,500.   [†] $56,000 − $14,000 − $14,000.

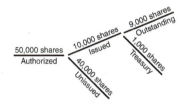

e. Subsequent Retirement of Treasury Stock

Treasury stock is credited for $28,000 (its ending balance), and common stock and paid-in capital are derecognized for the original issue amounts. Because there is no remaining balance in Paid-In Capital—Treasury Stock, the amount required to balance the entry is debited to Retained Earnings. The retirement of the stock does not affect the net balance in stockholders' equity. However, it does reduce the number of shares issued by the number of shares retired. After the retirement, Star Corp. has 50,000 shares authorized, 9,000 shares issued, and 9,000 shares outstanding.

March 1—To record subsequent retirement of treasury stock

Common Stock (1,000 × $1)	1,000	
Paid-In Capital in Excess of Par—Common Stock (1,000 × [$26 − $1])	25,000	
Retained Earnings (to balance)	2,000	
Treasury Stock (1,000 × $28)		28,000

Assets	=	Liabilities	+	Equity
				−1,000
				CS
				−25,000
				PIC—CS
				−2,000
				RE
				+28,000
				TS

Common Stock		Paid-In Cap—CS	
1,000	10,000 Bal.	25,000	250,000 Bal.

Ret Earnings		Treas Stock	
3,500	40,000	56,000	14,000
2,000			14,000
			28,000
		0	

Direct Retirement of Stock

Instead of holding repurchased shares in the treasury, a company can directly retire the shares. In this case, the company debits Common Stock and Paid-In Capital in Excess of Par—Common Stock at the amount of its original issuance and credits Cash. If the acquisition cost of the stock is not equal to the original issuance amount, the company will balance the journal entry as follows:

- When the cash paid to retire stock is *less* than its original issuance price, the difference is credited to Paid-In Capital—Retired Stock.

- When the cash paid to retire stock is *more* than its original issuance price, the difference is debited to Paid-In Capital—Retired Stock as long as the credit balance in that account is sufficient to absorb the debit. Any excess is debited to Retained Earnings.

Reacquisition of Common Stock—Direct Retirement   **LO19-3** ◀   DEMO 19-3B

Demo

MBC

On January 1, Star Corp. sold 10,000 shares of common stock, par $1, at $26 per share. On June 30, Star Corp. acquires 1,000 shares of its common stock at $28 per share and immediately retires the shares.

a. Record the entry for immediate retirement on June 30.
b. Instead, assume that Star Corp. acquires 1,000 shares at $24 per share for retirement. Record the entry for immediate retirement on June 30.

continued

continued from previous page

Solution

a. **Acquisition of Common Shares and Immediate Retirement**

Because there is no credit balance in Paid-In Capital—Retired Stock, the excess of the cash paid over the amount of the original issuance of the stock is debited to Retained Earnings.

Assets	=	Liabilities	+	Equity
−28,000				−1,000
C:f				CS
				−25,000
				PIC—CS
				−2,000
				RE

Cash		Common Stock	
28,000		1,000	10,000 Bal.

Paid-In Cap—CS		Ret Earnings	
25,000	250,000 Bal.	2,000	

June 30—To record direct retirement of common stock

Common Stock (1,000 × $1)	1,000	
Paid-In Capital in Excess of Par—Common Stock (1,000 × [$26 − $1]) . . .	25,000	
Retained Earnings (to balance)	2,000	
Cash (1,000 × $28)		28,000

b. **Acquisition of Common Shares and Immediate Retirement**

The excess of the original issuance price of the stock over the cash paid is credited to Paid-In Capital—Retired Stock.

Assets	=	Liabilities	+	Equity
−24,000				−1,000
C:f				CS
				−25,000
				PIC—CS
				+2,000
				PIC—RS

Cash		Common Stock	
24,000		1,000	10,000 Bal.

Paid-In Cap—CS		Pd-In Cap—RS	
25,000	250,000 Bal.		2,000

June 30—To record direct retirement of common stock

Common Stock (1,000 × $1)	1,000	
Paid-In Capital in Excess of Par—Common Stock (1,000 × [$26 − $1]) . . .	25,000	
Paid-In Capital—Retired Stock (to balance)		2,000
Cash (1,000 × $24)		24,000

REVIEW 19-3 ▶ **LO19-3**   **Reacquisition of Common Stock**

Review

MBC

On January 1, Baker Corporation issued 5,000 shares of $1 par value common stock at $25 per share. On June 15, Baker reacquired 1,000 shares of its common stock at $30 per share for the treasury. On November 15, the company sold 250 treasury shares for $33 per share.

a. Record the entry on January 1 for the issuance of common stock.

b. Record the entry on June 15 for the purchase of common shares for the treasury.

c. Record the entry on November 15 for the sale of treasury shares at $33 per share.

d. Assume that on December 31, all remaining treasury shares are retired. Provide the entry for subsequent retirement of treasury shares.

More Practice:
BE19-15, BE19-17, E19-9,
E19-11, E19-12, E19-15

Solution on p. 19-65.

e. Alternatively, assume that Baker Corporation purchased 1,000 shares on June 15 for $30 and immediately retired the shares rather than holding the shares as treasury shares. Provide the entry for immediate retirement of common shares.

LO 19-4 ▶ **Describe and account for preferred stock**

Features of Preferred Stock
- Callable
- Redeemable
- Mandatorily redeemable
- Convertible
- Cumulative dividend preference

LO 19-4 Overview

Preferred stock has preferences, or specific rights, that distinguish it from common stock. Preferred stock typically is par value stock with a dividend preference expressed as a percentage of par. For example, 6% preferred stock would pay a dividend of 6% of the par value of each share in any year that the board of directors declares dividends. In exchange for this preference, the preferred stockholders often sacrifice voting rights and the right to dividends beyond the stated rate or amount. Preferred stockholders also typically have preference over common stockholders in the case of a company liquidation.

The following terms are used to describe preferred stock.

Preferred Stock Feature	Description
Callable	Allows the issuer the option to recall (buy back) shares at a specified price.
Redeemable	Allows the stockholder the option to redeem stock (return stock to issuer for payment) at a specified price.
Mandatorily redeemable	**ASC Glossary** Mandatorily Redeemable Financial Instrument—Any of various financial instruments issued in the form of shares that embody an unconditional obligation requiring the issuer to redeem the instrument by transferring its assets at a specified or determinable date (or dates) or upon an event that is certain to occur.
Convertible	**ASC Glossary** Convertible security—A security that is convertible into another security based on a conversion rate. For example, convertible preferred stock that is convertible into common stock on a two-for-one basis (two shares of common for each share of preferred).
Cumulative dividend preference	Requires dividends not declared in a given year to accumulate at the preference rate for the stock. The issuer must pay cumulative dividends in full before dividends can be paid on common stock. If preferred dividends are not declared in a given year, they are said to have been passed and are called **dividends in arrears** on the cumulative preferred stock; see LO 19-5.

Initial Recognition of Preferred Stock

Other than mandatorily redeemable preferred stock, preferred stock is recognized initially as *equity,* as illustrated in **Demo 19-4**. As with common stock, Cash is debited and Preferred Stock is credited for the par value of the shares issued, and the excess cash received over the par value is credited to Paid-In Capital in Excess of Par—Preferred Stock.

Mandatorily redeemable preferred shares have financial characteristics of both debt and equity. They resemble equity securities in that dividend payments are not mandatory, and redeemable preferred shareholders are paid after debt holders in the event of liquidation. However, **they are similar to a debt instrument in that they must be either retired or refunded by the issuer at a specified or determinable date or upon an event that is certain to occur.** Therefore, the accounting standards require that mandatorily redeemable preferred stock be classified as a *liability* (measured at present value of payments) on the balance sheet.

`480-10-25-4` A mandatorily redeemable financial instrument shall be classified as a liability unless the redemption is required to occur only upon the liquidation or termination of the reporting entity.

`480-10-35-3` . . . [M]andatorily redeemable financial instruments shall be measured subsequently in either of the following ways:

a. If both the amount to be paid and the settlement date are fixed, those instruments shall be measured subsequently at the present value of the amount to be paid at settlement, accruing interest cost using the rate implicit at inception.

b. If either the amount to be paid or the settlement date varies based on specified conditions, those instruments shall be measured subsequently at the amount of cash that would be paid under the conditions specified in the contract if settlement occurred at the reporting date, recognizing the resulting change in that amount from the previous reporting date as interest cost.

Subsequent Recognition of Preferred Stock

Subsequent recognition for specific types of preferred stock follows.

- **Callable and Redeemable**—In the event that preferred stock is called in or redeemed, the preferred stockholder exchanges shares of preferred stock for cash. The issuer derecognizes preferred stock and its related paid-in capital account and reduces the cash balance (with any debit difference recorded in retained earnings and any credit difference in additional paid-in capital). *The net impact is a decrease to equity and to assets.*

- **Convertible**—In the event that preferred stock is converted into common stock, the issuer derecognizes preferred stock and its related paid-in capital account and increases common stock and its related paid-in capital account (with any debit difference recorded in retained earnings and any credit difference in additional paid-in capital). This means that if the carrying value of preferred stock exceeds the par value of common stock, credit Paid-In Capital in Excess of Par—Common Stock for the remainder. If the carrying value of preferred stock is less than the par value of the common stock, debit Retained Earnings for the remainder. *There is no net change to equity.*

EXPANDING YOUR KNOWLEDGE

Temporary Equity

SEC registrants have additional guidance to consider in determining whether to classify preferred stock as equity or as a liability. If preferred stock is not mandatorily redeemable (when it is required to be classified as a *liability*) but redemption is outside of the issuer's control (or triggered by the occurrence of an event that is not solely within the control of the issuer), the preferred stock is classified as **temporary equity** on the balance sheet. In this case, the preferred stock is shown between the liability and equity sections of the balance sheet. The balance sheet presentation of temporary equity is illustrated as follows.

Balance Sheet		
Total assets..	$200	
Total liabilities...	75	
Redeemable preferred stock	25	[Temporary equity]
Total stockholders' equity	100	
Total liabilities, redeemable preferred stock, and stockholders' equity	$200	

480-10-S99-3A 4   ASR 268 requires equity instruments with redemption features that are not solely within the control of the issuer to be classified outside of permanent equity (often referred to as classification in "temporary equity."

DEMO 19-4   **LO19-4**   **Accounting for Preferred Stock**

Demo

MBC

Example One—Callable Preferred Stock

On January 1 of Year 1, Ace Corp. issues 2,500 shares of callable preferred stock ($10 par value) at $104 per share. Ace Corp. has the option to repurchase the preferred stock from the shareholders at any point in the next five years at $104 per share. On March 15 of Year 2, the 2,500 shares of preferred stock were recalled at $104 per share. Record the entry for issuance of the preferred stock on January 1 of Year 1 and for the recall of preferred stock on March 15 of Year 2.

Solution

January 1, Year 1—To record issuance of preferred stock

Cash (2,500 × $104).......................................	260,000	
Preferred Stock (2,500 × $10).................................		25,000
Paid-In Capital in Excess of Par—Preferred Stock (2,500 × [$104 − $10]) ...		235,000

Assets = Liabilities + Equity
+260,000   +25,000
C:f   PS
                        +235,000
                        PIC—PS

Cash
260,000 |

Preferred Stock
| 25,000

Paid-In Cap—PS
| 235,000

March 15, Year 2—To record recall of preferred stock

Preferred Stock..	25,000	
Paid-In Capital in Excess of Par—Preferred Stock	235,000	
Cash (2,500 × $104)..		260,000

Assets = Liabilities + Equity
−260,000   −25,000
C:f   PS
                        −235,000
                        PIC—PS

Cash
260,000 | 260,000

Preferred Stock
25,000 | 25,000

Paid-In Cap—PS
235,000 | 235,000

Example Two—Mandatorily Redeemable and Redeemable Preferred Stock

Eagle Inc. issues for cash 5,000 shares of 5%, $20 par value, preferred stock that is mandatorily redeemable in five years on January 1 at a fixed price.

a. Indicate in which section of the balance sheet the preferred stock would be presented on a reporting date.
b. How would the answer to part *a* change if preferred stock can instead be redeemed at a fixed price at the option of the stockholder?

Solution

a. The preferred stock would be reported in the noncurrent liability section of the company's balance sheet.
b. The preferred stock would be reported in the stockholders' equity section of the company's balance sheet.

Example Three—Convertible Preferred Stock

On January 1 of Year 1, Ace Corp. issued 2,500 shares of preferred stock ($10 par value) at $104 per share. Each share of preferred stock is convertible into 5 shares of common stock ($1 par value) at the option of the holder. Record the entry for issuance of preferred stock on January 1 of Year 1, and for the conversion of all preferred stock into common stock on March 15 of Year 2.

continued

continued from previous page

Solution

January 1, Year 1—To record issuance of convertible preferred stock

Cash (2,500 × $104)...	260,000	
Preferred Stock (2,500 × $10)		25,000
Paid-In Capital in Excess of Par—Preferred Stock (2,500 × [$104 – $10]) ...		235,000

Assets = Liabilities + Equity
+260,000   +25,000
  C:f   PS
                 +235,000
                 PIC—PS

Cash	Preferred Stock
260,000	25,000

	Paid-In Cap—PS
	235,000

In the following entry, Preferred Stock and Paid-In Capital in Excess of Par—Preferred Stock are derecognized. Common Stock is credited for the par value of 12,500 shares (or 2,500 shares × conversion ratio of 5 × $1 par value per share), and the remainder is credited to Paid-In Capital in Excess of Par—Common Stock.

March 15, Year 2—To record conversion of preferred stock to common stock

Preferred Stock...	25,000	
Paid-In Capital in Excess of Par—Preferred Stock	235,000	
Common Stock (2,500 × 5 × $1)................................		12,500
Paid-In Capital in Excess of Par—Common Stock (to balance)		247,500

Assets = Liabilities + Equity
                 −25,000
                    PS
                −235,000
                 PIC—PS
                +12,500
                   CS
                +247,500
                   PIC—CS

Preferred Stock	Paid-In Cap—PS
25,000 | 25,000	235,000 | 235,000

Common Stock	Paid-In Cap—CS
| 12,500	| 247,500

EXPANDING YOUR KNOWLEDGE   Why Issue Preferred Stock Over Debt?

If redeemable preferred stock is really debt, why don't corporations just issue debt in the first place? After all, preferred dividends are not tax-deductible, and interest payments normally are. One answer lies in the requirements affecting debt capacity in debt agreements and covenants. The issuance of redeemable preferred stock instead of debt may avoid a debt covenant violation. A second answer is that the issuer might obtain capital at rates below the market rate of interest. Corporate buyers are willing to accept a dividend rate on redeemable preferred stock that is less than the market rate of interest because corporations can exclude a significant portion of their dividend income from taxable income. No such exclusion is available for interest income.

Accounting for Preferred Stock   LO19-4   REVIEW 19-4

Two separate scenarios follow for the issuance of preferred stock.

a. Bell Inc. issues 1,000 shares of 6% convertible preferred stock ($10 par value) on December 31 for $100,000.

b. Bell Inc. issues 1,000 shares of 6% redeemable preferred stock ($10 par value) on December 31 for $100,000.

Required
For each separate scenario, (1) record the issuance of preferred stock, and (2) indicate the financial statement presentation of preferred stock at December 31.

Review
MBC

More Practice:
BE19-19, E19-19, E19-21
Solution on p. 19-65.

Record dividend distributions, including cash, property, and liquidating   LO 19-5

A corporation has two alternative uses for the company's earnings.

1. Reinvest in the operations of the company.
2. Distribute to shareholders in the form of a dividend.

A **dividend** is a distribution of retained earnings to shareholders in the form of assets or shares of the issuing company's stock. A consistent dividend payment over time can create demand in a company's stock, especially for investors seeking a steady flow of income. Corporations are not *required* to pay dividends. It is rare that 100% of a company's current period earnings are distributed as dividends. Some state laws and contracts restrict the amount of retained earnings that can be distributed as dividends.

Accounting for Dividend Distributions
- Cash (reduce retained earnings)
  - Common stock dividends
  - Preferred stock dividends
- Property (reduce retained earnings)
- Liquidating (reduce additional paid-in capital)

LO 19-5 Overview

If a company has investment opportunities in which it expects to earn excess profits, management may advise that the earnings be retained and used as capital for financing the investment. Retaining earnings is a common way for a company to provide capital for growth. Many start-up companies pay little or no dividends. Generally, investors are not disappointed when a company retains earnings and reinvests

them, so long as the investment earns a high return or the company is building a buffer against possible cash shortages in the future. In this section, we review the accounting for cash dividends (**Demo 19-5A**), property dividends (**Demo 19-5B**), and liquidating dividends (**Demo 19-5C**).

Cash Dividend

When the decision is to pay out retained earnings through a cash dividend, cash is distributed to shareholders. Cash dividends are the most common form of distributions to stockholders. Cash dividends depend on the corporation having sufficient cash available for distribution. Before a cash dividend can be paid to common shareholders, any preference in dividends (including those in arrears) must first be paid to preferred stockholders.

A corporation's board of directors approves and announces a dividend payment on the **date of declaration**, for shareholders of record at a specified date, to be paid on a specified date. This timeline is illustrated in **Exhibit 19-1**.

- Declaration of a cash dividend is recorded as a debit to Retained Earnings and a credit to Dividends Payable. A liability is recorded because declaration of a cash dividend constitutes an enforceable contract between the corporation and the stockholders.

- **Ex-dividend date** is the first day shares are traded without the right to receive declared dividends. Thus, holders of the stock on the day prior to the stipulated ex-dividend date receive the dividend. The ex-dividend is often set one day before the date of record (discussed next), allowing time for the determination of the owners as of the date of record. Investors who buy shares on and after the ex-dividend date do not receive the dividend. *No entry is made on the ex-dividend date.*

- Eligible owners of stock on the **date of record** receive the dividend. No entry is made on the date of record. The record date selected by the board of directors is stated in the declaration. Usually the record date follows the declaration date by two to three weeks.

- **Date of payment** is determined by the board of directors and typically follows the declaration date by four to six weeks. Payment is recorded as a debit to Dividends Payable and a credit to Cash.

EXHIBIT 19-1
Cash Dividend
Timeline

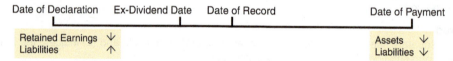

If a company declares a dividend, the dividend is allocated in a predetermined way to preferred and common shareholders. In the previous section, we identified a certain feature of preferred stock that would influence this allocation: *cumulative dividend preference*. The current year dividend on preferred stock and any cumulative dividends in arrears must be paid out to preferred shareholders before common shareholders are paid. After these obligations are satisfied, and unless the preferred shares are participating, the common shareholders receive the remainder of declared dividends. **Participating preference**, however, allows the preferred stockholder to share in additional dividends on a pro rata basis with common shareholders in the way defined by the company's charter.

DEMO 19-5A   **LO19-5**   **Cash Dividend Distributions**

Demo

MBC

Example One—Common Stock Dividends
The board of directors of Bass Company, at its meeting on January 20, declares a cash dividend of 50 cents per share, payable March 20 to stockholders of record on March 1. There are 10,000 shares of no-par common stock outstanding. The cash dividends are paid on March 20.
a. Record Bass Company's entry at the date of dividend declaration, January 20.
b. Record Bass Company's entry at the date of record, March 1.
c. Record Bass Company's entry at the date of payment, March 20.

continued

continued from previous page

Solution

a. **Date of Dividend Declaration**

January 20—To record cash dividends declared

Retained Earnings (10,000 × $0.50)	5,000	
Dividends Payable		5,000

Assets = Liabilities + Equity
+5,000   −5,000
Div Pay   RE

Div Payable	Ret Earnings
5,000	5,000

b. **Date of Record**

No entry is made on the date of record.

c. **Date of Dividend Payment**

March 20—To record cash dividend payment

Dividends Payable	5,000	
Cash		5,000

Assets = Liabilities + Equity
−5,000   −5,000
C:f   Div Pay

Cash	Div Payable
5,000	5,000	5,000

Example Two—Cumulative Preferred Stock Dividends

Sprite Inc. has the following capital structure.

Preferred stock, 5%, $10 par, 10,000 shares issued and outstanding	$100,000
Common stock, $5 par, 40,000 shares issued and outstanding	200,000
Total	$300,000

The preferred stock is cumulative, and dividends are in arrears for two preceding years. Cash dividends of $28,000 are declared on December 31. Determine the allocation of dividends between common and preferred shareholders, and record the declaration entry.

Solution

The annual preferred stock dividend is $5,000 ($100,000 × 5%). The declared dividend of $28,000 is allocated as follows.

	Preferred Dividends	Common Dividends
Preferred dividends in arrears (2 × $5,000) . . .	$10,000	
Preferred current dividend	5,000	
Balance to common		$13,000
Total	$15,000	$13,000

December 31—To record cash dividends declared

Retained Earnings ($15,000 + $13,000)	28,000	
Dividends Payable—Preferred Stock.		15,000
Dividends Payable—Common Stock.		13,000

Assets = Liabilities + Equity
+28,000   −28,000
Div Pay   RE

Ret Earnings	Div Payable
28,000	15,000
	13,000

EXPANDING YOUR KNOWLEDGE   Participating Dividends

Depending on the charter, a participating preference allows the preferred stockholder to share in additional dividends on a pro rata basis with common shareholders after receiving the stated amount. Let's assume the same capital structure for Sprite Inc. in Example Two of **Demo 19-5A** *except* that the preferred stock is fully participating and noncumulative. Cash dividends of $28,000 are declared. Allocation between the common and preferred shareholders is determined as follows.

	Preferred Dividends	Common Dividends
Preferred current dividend	$5,000	
Common to match (5% × $200,000)		$10,000
Allocation of remaining dividend of $13,000 ($28,000 − $15,000) based upon relative proportion to total par value:		
Preferred ($100,000/$300,000 × $13,000)	4,333	
Common ($200,000/$300,000 × $13,000)		8,667
Total	$9,333	$18,667

Property Dividend

Corporations occasionally pay **property dividends** with noncash assets. The property can be securities of *other* companies held by the corporation, real estate, or any other noncash asset designated by the board of directors. Most property dividends are the securities of other companies held as an investment because this kind of property dividend reduces the problem of indivisibility of units that would occur with most other noncash assets. For example, a mining company issues common shares of its fully owned subsidiary to shareholders as a property dividend equivalent to one share of its investment in subsidiary to every 200 shares held of the mining company.

A property dividend is recorded at the fair value of the assets transferred. When the corporation's carrying value of the property to be distributed as a dividend is different from its fair value on the declaration date, the corporation first recognizes a holding gain or loss to adjust the asset to fair value before recording the dividend declaration. Any changes in asset value after the dividend declaration date are ignored.

DEMO 19-5B ► **LO19-5** **Property Dividend Distributions**

Demo
MBC

On June 2, the board of directors of Sun Co. declares a property dividend of 1,000 shares of its investment in Nic Inc., originally purchased on January 1 for $10,000 (which is also the current carrying value). The property dividends are payable on June 30 to stockholders of record on June 15. The fair value of Sun Co.'s investment in Nic Inc. is $12,000 on June 2.

a. Record the declaration of property dividend on June 2.
b. Record the transfer of property on June 30.

Solution

a. **Declaration of Property Dividend**

Sun Co. must first recognize the gain in fair value over carrying value ($12,000 less $10,000, or $2,000) before recording the property dividend.

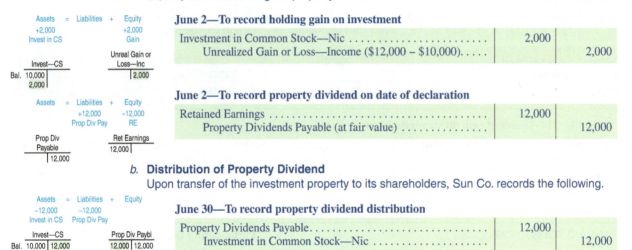

June 2—To record holding gain on investment

Investment in Common Stock—Nic	2,000	
Unrealized Gain or Loss—Income ($12,000 – $10,000)		2,000

June 2—To record property dividend on date of declaration

Retained Earnings	12,000	
Property Dividends Payable (at fair value)		12,000

b. **Distribution of Property Dividend**

Upon transfer of the investment property to its shareholders, Sun Co. records the following.

June 30—To record property dividend distribution

Property Dividends Payable	12,000	
Investment in Common Stock—Nic		12,000

Liquidating Dividend

Liquidating dividends are a return of stockholders' investment rather than a distribution of a company's profits. Stockholders must be informed of the portion of any dividend that represents a return of capital. For example, a liquidating dividend might be issued when a company is dissolving and is using the dividend as a way to distribute assets.

Liquidating Dividend Distributions   **LO19-5**   **DEMO 19-5C**

Demo

MBC

On May 31, Miners Inc. declares a cash dividend of $40,000 and informs the stockholders that 75% of it is a liquidating dividend. The dividends are payable June 25 to stockholders of record on June 10.

a. Record the declaration of the dividend on May 31.
b. Record the dividend payment on June 25.

Solution

a. **Declaration of Dividend**

The dividend declaration includes a debit to Retained Earnings for $10,000 (25% × $40,000) and a debit to Paid-In Capital in Excess of Par—Common Stock for $30,000 (75% × $40,000).

May 31—To record dividend on date of declaration

Retained Earnings ($40,000 × 25%)	10,000	
Paid-In Capital in Excess of Par—Common Stock ($40,000 × 75%)...	30,000	
Dividends Payable		40,000

Assets = Liabilities + Equity
+40,000   −10,000
Div Pay   RE
                −30,000
                PIC—CS

Ret Earnings	Paid-In Cap—CS
10,000		30,000	

Div Payable
	40,000

b. **Dividend Payment**

June 25—To record dividend payment

Dividends Payable	40,000	
Cash		40,000

Assets = Liabilities + Equity
−40,000   −40,000
C:f   Div Pay

Cash	Div Payable
	40,000	40,000	40,000

PROCTER & GAMBLE

Real World—DIVIDENDS

In the letter to shareholders included in a recent annual report, **Procter & Gamble Company** stated:

> In April, we announced a 7% dividend increase, again reinforcing our commitment to return cash to shareowners— the 68th consecutive annual dividend increase, and the 134th consecutive year P&G has paid a dividend. Only seven U.S. publicly traded companies have paid a dividend more consecutive years than P&G, and only three U.S. companies have raised their dividend more consecutive years.

Although not legally required to pay a dividend to shareholders each year, the long history of dividend payments by Procter & Gamble sets up an expectation for investors for stable dividend payments projecting into future years.

Recording Dividend Distributions   **LO19-5**   **REVIEW 19-5**

Review

MBC

Following are four separate dividend scenarios.

a. On June 1, Sox Inc. declared a cash dividend of $2.50 per share on its 50,000 outstanding shares of common stock ($0.10 par). The dividend is payable on June 15 to stockholders of record on June 1.

b. FX Inc. holds 1,000 shares of Den Co. common stock, purchased in May for $19 a share. On June 1, FX Inc. declared a property dividend of 1,000 shares of Den Co. common stock when the shares were selling at $22 per share. The carrying value of the shares on June 1 is $19 a share.

c. Lox Inc. declared a common stock cash dividend of $80,000 on August 15. Lox Inc. announced to shareholders that $20,000 of the dividend amount was a return of capital.

d. Vox Inc. has outstanding 2,000 shares of $10 par, cumulative, 5% preferred stock and 10,000 shares of $1 par common stock. Dividends are in arrears for one year. On June 1, the board of directors of Vox Inc. declared dividends of $25,000 to be paid to shareholders at the end of the fiscal year.

Record the entry for declaration of dividends for each of the four separate scenarios.

More Practice:
BE19-25, BE19-27, BE19-29,
E19-22, E19-24, E19-25

Solution on p. 19-65.

LO 19-6 ▶ Account for stock dividends and stock splits

Another form of dividend is a **stock dividend**. A stock dividend is a proportional distribution of additional shares of a company's stock to shareholders. The accounting treatment of stock dividends differs depending on the size of the stock dividend. A small stock dividend is illustrated in **Demo 19-6A**, and a large stock dividend called a *stock split effected in the form of a dividend* is illustrated in **Demo 19-6B**. A **stock split** is a change in the number of shares outstanding accompanied by an offsetting change in the par or stated value per share. A stock split is illustrated in **Demo 19-6C**.

Stock Dividends

400 Shares of Stock Outstanding
↓
Stock Dividend of 10%
↓
440 Shares of Stock Outstanding

A stock dividend proportionally grants new shares of stock to current shareholders without requiring consideration from the shareholders. For example, if a company has 400 shares of stock outstanding, after a 10% stock dividend, it would have an additional 40 shares outstanding (or 400 shares × 10%), resulting in a total of 440 shares of stock outstanding.

With the exception of cash payouts for fractional shares described below, a stock dividend does not result in a net change in total assets, liabilities, or stockholders' equity. The components of stockholders' equity change, but the net value does not change. The ownership percentage of each investor remains exactly the same before and after a stock dividend, as illustrated below.

Investor	Shares Before 10% Stock Dividend	Ownership %	Shares After 10% Stock Dividend	Ownership %
Investor A	120	30%	132	30%
Investor B	40	10%	44	10%
Investor C	100	25%	110	25%
Investor D	140	35%	154	35%
Totals	400	100%	440	100%

Companies issue stock dividends for several reasons, including the following.

- To continue dividend distributions without disbursing cash needed for operations. Shareholders may be willing to accept a stock dividend representing accumulated earnings because they can sell these additional shares.

- To increase the number of shares outstanding, reducing the market price per share and possibly leading to increased trading of shares in the market.

- To convey that the company plans to retain a portion of earnings permanently in the business because a stock dividend results in a shift from retained earnings to paid-in capital. (State law often restricts the extent of retained earnings that may be distributed in dividends.)

There is debate about whether the stock issued for the dividend should be recorded at fair value, at par or stated value, or at some other value. In support of the par value method, it is generally recognized that if a company doubles the number of shares outstanding by issuing a stock dividend, the competitive market price will roughly fall to one-half its previous level, absent any other market factors. At the time of the issuance of the accounting guidance on stock dividends, it was believed that the market price of the company's stock did *not* automatically adjust for the issuance of small stock dividends. There was concern that investors would view the small stock dividend as having an immediate value, when in fact, the investor's share of the company did not change after the small stock dividend distribution. Thus, the accounting guidance (still in effect today) requires the measurement of small stock dividends at fair value, perhaps even as a way to discourage its use.

505-20-05-2 Many recipients of stock dividends look upon them as distributions of corporate earnings, and usually in an amount equivalent to the fair value of the additional shares received. If the issuances of stock dividends are so small in comparison with the shares previously outstanding, such issuances generally do not have any apparent effect on the share market price and, consequently, the fair value of the shares previously held remains substantially unchanged.

This authoritative standard is not without controversy mainly because of evidence of market adjustments for small stock dividends. Nonetheless, this is the basis of the accounting treatment of stock dividends, which treats a small stock dividend differently from a large stock dividend: **accounting standards require *small* stock dividends to be measured at fair value and *large* stock dividends to be measured at par or stated value to the extent necessitated by legal requirements.**

Small Stock Dividends

If the proportion of the additional shares issued is small in relation to the shares previously outstanding (**small stock dividend**), the *fair value* of the additional shares is capitalized. Small in the accounting standards is generally described as less than 20 or 25 percent of the total previously outstanding shares.

505-20-25-3   The point at which the relative size of the additional shares issued becomes large enough to materially influence the unit market price of the stock will vary with individual entities and under differing market conditions and, therefore, no single percentage can be established as a standard for determining when capitalization of retained earnings in excess of legal requirements is called for and when it is not. Except for a few instances, the issuance of additional shares of less than 20 or 25 percent of the number of previously outstanding shares would call for treatment as a stock dividend as described in paragraph 505-20-30-3.

A small common stock dividend is recorded with a debit to Retained Earnings (at fair value) and a credit to Common Stock Dividends Distributable (at par value) and Paid-In Capital in Excess of Par—Common Stock (for the remainder). When the shares are officially issued, the company debits Common Stock Dividends Distributable and credits Common Stock. **With offsetting increases and decreases to stockholders' equity accounts, the net balance in stockholders' equity remains unchanged.**

505-20-30-3   In accounting for a stock dividend, the corporation shall transfer from retained earnings to the category of capital stock and additional paid-in capital an amount equal to the fair value of the additional shares issued. Unless this is done, the amount of earnings that the shareholder may believe to have been distributed to him or her will be left, except to the extent otherwise dictated by legal requirements, in retained earnings subject to possible further similar stock issuances or cash distributions.

Fractional Shares   When a stock dividend is issued, not all shareholders may own exactly the number of shares needed to receive whole shares. For example, if a company issues a 10% stock dividend and a shareholder owns 15 shares, the stockholder is entitled to 1.5 shares (15 shares × 10%). The shareholder has a right to 1 full share plus a fractional share of ½ share. A company can pay cash to shareholders for the fair value of the fractional shares to which they are entitled.

Accounting for Small Stock Dividends	**LO19-6** ◀ DEMO 19-6A

Example One— Small Stock Dividend
WayMart Inc. declared a 10% common stock dividend on 100,000 shares of $1 par common stock issued and outstanding on May 1. The market price of the common stock is $5 per share. The small stock dividend will be distributed on May 25 to stockholders of record on May 10. Record the entry on (1) the date of declaration and (2) the date of distribution.

Demo

MBC

Solution
The small stock dividend is recorded at fair value, with the excess of the fair value of $50,000 over the par value of $10,000 recorded as an increase to additional paid-in capital for $40,000.

May 1—To record small stock dividend on date of declaration

Retained Earnings (100,000 × 10% × $5)	50,000	
Common Stock Dividends Distributable (100,000 × 10% × $1)		10,000
Paid-In Capital in Excess of Par—Common Stock (to balance)		40,000

Assets = Liabilities + Equity
−50,000 RE
+10,000 CS DIST
+40,000 PIC—CS

Ret Earnings	CS Div Distrib
50,000	10,000

Paid-In Cap—CS
40,000

continued

continued from previous page

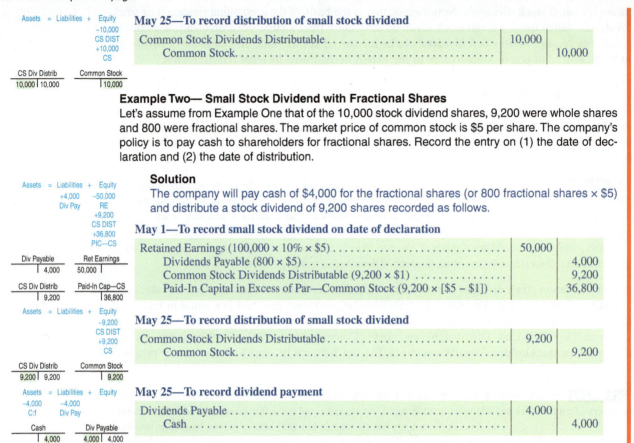

May 25—To record distribution of small stock dividend

Common Stock Dividends Distributable............................	10,000	
Common Stock..		10,000

Assets = Liabilities + Equity
−10,000
CS DIST
+10,000
CS

CS Div Distrib	Common Stock
10,000 | 10,000	| 10,000

Example Two— Small Stock Dividend with Fractional Shares

Let's assume from Example One that of the 10,000 stock dividend shares, 9,200 were whole shares and 800 were fractional shares. The market price of common stock is $5 per share. The company's policy is to pay cash to shareholders for fractional shares. Record the entry on (1) the date of declaration and (2) the date of distribution.

Solution

The company will pay cash of $4,000 for the fractional shares (or 800 fractional shares × $5) and distribute a stock dividend of 9,200 shares recorded as follows.

May 1—To record small stock dividend on date of declaration

Retained Earnings (100,000 × 10% × $5)............................	50,000	
Dividends Payable (800 × $5)...................................		4,000
Common Stock Dividends Distributable (9,200 × $1)................		9,200
Paid-In Capital in Excess of Par—Common Stock (9,200 × [$5 − $1])...		36,800

Assets = Liabilities + Equity
     +4,000 −50,000
     Div Pay   RE
            +9,200
            CS DIST
            +36,800
            PIC—CS

Div Payable	Ret Earnings
| 4,000	50,000 |

CS Div Distrib	Paid-In Cap—CS
| 9,200	| 36,800

May 25—To record distribution of small stock dividend

Common Stock Dividends Distributable............................	9,200	
Common Stock..		9,200

Assets = Liabilities + Equity
              −9,200
             CS DIST
             +9,200
             CS

CS Div Distrib	Common Stock
9,200 | 9,200	| 9,200

May 25—To record dividend payment

Dividends Payable..	4,000	
Cash..		4,000

Assets = Liabilities + Equity
−4,000 −4,000
 C:f   Div Pay

Cash	Div Payable
| 4,000	4,000 | 4,000

Stock Split Effected in the Form of a Dividend (Large Stock Dividend)

By default, a large stock dividend occurs when the proportion of the additional shares issued is 20 or 25 percent or more of the total previously outstanding shares. Because this is more in line with a stock split, a large stock dividend is often referred to as a **stock split effected in the form of a dividend**. As discussed in the next section, a stock split results in an increase in shares of stock with an offsetting decrease in par value per share. However, in the case of a large stock dividend, the par value per share remains unchanged, while the number of shares increases. Thus, the legal minimum (usually par, or stated value, or average paid-in capital for no-par stock) is capitalized into equity.

505-20-25-2   The number of additional shares issued as a stock dividend may be so great that it has, or may reasonably be expected to have, the effect of materially reducing the share market value. In such a situation… the substance of the transaction is clearly that of a stock split.

505-20-50-1   Paragraph 505-20-25-2 identifies a situation in which a stock dividend in form is a stock split in substance. In such instances every effort shall be made to avoid the use of the word dividend in related corporate resolutions, notices, and announcements and that, in those cases in which because of legal requirements this cannot be done, the transaction be described, for example, as a stock split effected in the form of a dividend.

A *stock split effected in the form of a dividend* is recorded through a debit to Retained Earnings and a credit to Common Stock Dividends Distributable (typically at par or stated value). When the shares are officially issued, the company debits Common Stock Dividends Distributable and credits Common Stock. **With offsetting increases and decreases to stockholders' equity accounts, the net balance in stockholders' equity remains unchanged.** The fair value of the stock is not relevant to the recording of the entry. In practice, companies can debit a paid-in capital account instead of retained earnings (if legally acceptable) because the codification does not provide direct guidance on the accounting entries for a large stock dividend.

505-20-30-6   In the case of a stock split, there is no need to capitalize retained earnings, other than to the extent occasioned by legal requirements.

Accounting for a Stock Split Effected in the Form of a Dividend **LO19-6** **DEMO 19-6B**

WayMart Inc. declares a 50% common stock dividend on 100,000 common shares ($1 par value) on May 1. The market price of the common stock is $5 per share. The new shares will be distributed to shareholders on May 25 to stockholders of record on May 10. Record the entry on (1) the date of declaration and (2) the date of distribution.

Solution

The stock split effected in the form of a stock dividend is recorded at par value.

May 1—To record stock split effected in the form of a dividend on date of declaration

Retained Earnings (100,000 × 50% × $1)	50,000	
Common Stock Dividends Distributable		50,000

May 25—To record stock split effected in the form of a dividend on date of distribution

Common Stock Dividends Distributable	50,000	
Common Stock.		50,000

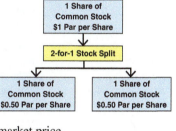

Stock Splits

A large distribution of stock might also be achieved through a **stock split**. A stock split is a change in the number of shares outstanding accompanied by an offsetting change in the par or stated value per share. For example, in a 2-for-1 stock split, the number of outstanding and unissued shares doubles (1 share becomes 2 shares), and the par value per share is reduced by one-half (such as $1.00 par becomes $0.50 par). The effect of a stock split is to increase the number of shares outstanding and *decrease* the market price per share. The lower market price after a stock split might increase potential investor participation. Increasing the number of shares outstanding also reduces earnings per share.

A company might also initiate a **reverse stock split** that will result in an *increase* in market price per share. For example, in a reverse 2-for-1 split, the number of shares is reduced by one-half (2 shares become 1 share) and the par value per share doubles (such as $0.50 par becomes $1.00 par). A company might initiate a reverse stock split to increase market price to a minimum price level to remain on a major stock exchange.

In a stock split or a reverse stock split, no accounting entry is needed because there is no change in the total dollar amounts in capital stock, additional paid-in capital, or retained earnings. The increase (decrease) in the number of shares is exactly counterbalanced by a proportional reduction (increase) in the par or stated value per share. The only items changed are par (or stated) value per share, and shares issued, outstanding, and in the treasury. The ownership percentage of each investor remains exactly the same, as illustrated below.

Investor	Shares Before 2-for-1 Stock Split	Ownership %	Shares After 2-for-1 Stock Split	Ownership %
Investor A	120	30%	240	30%
Investor B	40	10%	80	10%
Investor C	100	25%	200	25%
Investor D	140	35%	280	35%
Totals	400	100%	800	100%

Impact of Dividends and Stock Splits

We have reviewed the accounting for different types of dividends and stock splits. Dividends can be distributed through cash, property, or a company's own stock. A split either increases outstanding shares or, in the case of a reverse split, decreases the number of outstanding shares. The impact on a corporation's capital structure is summarized in **Exhibit 19-2**. These changes are reflected in the financial statements (including disclosures) of a company. These events will also have an impact on the market price of shares, which is not reflected in financial statements.

EXHIBIT 19-2
Impact of a
Dividend or Split

	Number of Shares Outstanding	Par Value per Share	Capital Stock	Paid-In Capital in Excess of Par	Retained Earnings	Total Stockholders' Equity
Declaration of cash dividend ...	No change	No change	No change	No change	Decrease	Decrease
Payment of cash dividend......	No change	No change	No change	No change	No change	No change
Declaration and distribution:						
Property dividend[1]...........	No change	No change	No change	No change	Decrease	Decrease
Liquidating dividend	No change	No change	No change	Decrease	No change	Decrease
Small stock dividend........	Increase	No change	Increase[2]	Increase[3]	Decrease[4]	No change
Large stock dividend........	Increase	No change	Increase[2]	No change	Decrease[2]	No change
Stock split	Increase	Decrease	No change	No change	No change	No change
Reverse stock split	Decrease	Increase	No change	No change	No change	No change

[1] Assets distributed are first adjusted to fair value.   [3] Excess of fair value over par value (or stated value).
[2] Par value (or stated value).   [4] Fair value.

DEMO 19-6C **LO19-6**   **Accounting for Stock Splits**

Demo

MBC

Cruz Co is authorized to issue 200,000 shares of common stock, $1 par, of which 40,000 shares were issued initially at $11 per share. Retained earnings has a balance of $450,000. Show the effect of a 2-for-1 stock split on the stockholders' equity section of the balance sheet.

Solution

Stockholders' Equity	Before 2-for-1 Stock Split	After 2-for-1 Stock Split
Common stock, $1 par value; 200,000 shares authorized; 40,000 shares issued and outstanding..................	$ 40,000	
Common stock, $0.50 par value; 400,000 shares authorized; 80,000 shares issued and outstanding..................		$ 40,000
Paid-In capital in excess of par..........................	400,000	400,000
Retained earnings	450,000	450,000
Total stockholders' equity	$890,000	$890,000

SHOE CARNIVAL

Real World—STOCK SPLIT

Shoe Carnival Inc. announced the following stock split effected in the form of a stock dividend through a business wire included on its website (ShoeCarnival.com).

Shoe Carnival, Inc. (Nasdaq: SCVL) (the "Company"), a leading retailer of footwear and accessories for the family, announced today that its Board of Directors has authorized a two-for-one stock split of the Company's common stock. The stock split will be effected by the payment of a stock dividend of one share on each share of common stock to shareholders of record at the close of business on Tuesday, July 6, 2021. The dividend shares are scheduled to be distributed on Monday, July 19, 2021. The Company expects the adjusted number of shares outstanding and adjusted per share stock price reported by the Nasdaq Stock Market to be effective Tuesday, July 20, 2021. The recently announced cash dividend of $0.14 per share, which is also payable on July 19, 2021, will be paid on a pre-split basis.

REVIEW 19-6 **LO19-6**   **Account for Stock Dividends and Stock Splits**

Review

MBC

The records of Round Corporation showed the following account balances on March 1.

Common stock, $1 par, 50,000 shares outstanding	$ 50,000
Paid-in capital in excess of par..........................	200,000
Retained earnings	175,000

The fair value of its common stock is $24 per share on March 1. Prepare journal entries for four separate scenarios.

a. The company declares (March 1) and issues (March 15) a 5% stock dividend.

b. The company declares (March 1) and issues (March 15) a 5% stock dividend. Of the stock dividend shares distributed, 200 shares are fractional shares. It is Round Corporation's policy to pay out fractional shares in cash.

More Practice:
BE19-30, BE19-32, BE19-34,
E19-27, E19-28

Solution on p. 19-66.

c. The company declares (March 1) and issues (March 15) a stock split in the form of a 100% stock dividend.

d. The company declares (March 1) and issues (March 15) a 3-for-1 stock split.

Describe the components of comprehensive income and prepare a statement of comprehensive income and a statement of stockholders' equity.

LO 19-7

Total **comprehensive income (or loss)** represents the change in equity (net assets) of a business entity during a period from transactions and other events and circumstances from nonowner sources. A statement of comprehensive income (illustrated in **Demo 19-7**) is required as part of a full set of financial statements.

Total comprehensive income is divided into two categories:

- Net income
- Other comprehensive income

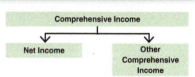

Comprehensive Income Components
- Net income (loss)
  - Accumulate in retained earnings
- Other comprehensive income (loss)
  - Accumulate in accumulated other comprehensive income (loss)

LO 19-7 Overview

Other comprehensive income includes gains and losses (net of tax) that are excluded from net income, but which are recognized separately in **other comprehensive income (or loss)**—often abbreviated OCI. The components of other comprehensive income are displayed as reconciling items between net income and comprehensive income. Gains and losses commonly reported in other comprehensive income include:

1. Gains or losses from foreign currency translation adjustments (Chapter 3).
2. Unrealized holding gains or losses on available-for-sale debt securities (Chapter 14).
3. Gains or losses from adjustments to a cash flow hedge (Chapter 14).

GAAP requires the reporting of comprehensive income in the financial statements either as a **single continuous statement of comprehensive income** *or* as **two separate statements of income and comprehensive income**. The expectation is that financial statement users are able to understand the relation between net income and comprehensive income and that this understanding leads to increased comparability of financial statements across companies.

Single Statement	Two Statements
Revenues	Revenues
(Expenses)	(Expenses)
Net income	Net income
OCI (net of tax)	
Comp Inc	Net income
	OCI (net of tax)
	Comp Inc

At the end of an accounting period, the process of closing out other comprehensive income differs from the process of closing out net income. While net income is closed to a permanent account, retained earnings, at the end of an accounting period, other comprehensive income is closed to a permanent account called **accumulated other comprehensive income (or loss)**—often abbreviated AOCI—at the end of an accounting period. Accumulated other comprehensive income is a separate component of stockholders' equity.

Reporting of Comprehensive Income and Accumulated OCI   **LO19-7**   **DEMO 19-7**

Demo

MBC

Whitefish Inc. recognizes net income of $50,000 for the current year ended December 31. The company's tax rate is 25%. Whitefish Inc. also reports a pretax net unrealized gain on available-for-sale debt securities of $4,000 ($3,000 after-tax) and a pretax loss on derivatives (cash flow hedges) of $6,400 ($4,800 after-tax) during the current year. Its prior year December 31 balances (all credit balances) are: common stock of $1,000, paid-in capital in excess of par of $300,000, retained earnings of $200,000, and accumulated other comprehensive income of $3,000. The company paid no dividends and had no transactions affecting common stock during the current year. Shares of common stock issued and outstanding for the current year were 10,000.

a. Prepare a separate statement of comprehensive income for the current year.
b. Prepare a statement of stockholders' equity for the current year. Use a columnar format with the account types as the column titles.
c. Prepare the stockholders' equity section of the balance sheet at December 31 of the current year.

Solution
a. Separate Statement of Comprehensive Income
A separate statement of comprehensive income begins with net income and adds/subtracts other comprehensive income to arrive at total comprehensive income. Other comprehensive income items are shown net of tax.

continued

continued from previous page

Statement of Comprehensive Income For Current Year Ended December 31		
Net income		$50,000
Other comprehensive income, net of tax		
Net unrealized holding gain on available-for-sale securities . . .	$3,000	
Loss on cash flow hedges.	(4,800)	
Other comprehensive loss.		(1,800)
Comprehensive income		$48,200

b. Statement of Stockholders' Equity

Statement of Stockholders' Equity					
	Common Stock		Paid-In Capital in Excess of Par	Retained Earnings	Accumulated Other Comprehensive Income	Total
	Shares	Amount				
Balance, Dec. 31, Prior Year	10,000	$1,000	$300,000	$200,000	$3,000	$504,000
Net income				50,000		50,000
Other comprehensive loss					(1,800)	(1,800)
Balance, Dec. 31, Current Year . . .	10,000	$1,000	$300,000	$250,000	$1,200	$552,200

c. Stockholders' Equity Presentation

Balance Sheet (excerpt) December 31, Current Year	
Stockholders' Equity	
Common stock	$ 1,000
Paid-in capital in excess of par	300,000
Retained earnings	250,000
Accumulated other comprehensive income	1,200
Total stockholders' equity	$552,200

PEPSICO

Real World—STATEMENT OF COMPREHENSIVE INCOME

PepsiCo Inc. reported the following statement of comprehensive income in a recent annual report. PepsiCo Inc. chose to report comprehensive income in a statement separate from the income statement.

Consolidated Statement of Comprehensive Income
PepsiCo, Inc. and Subsidiaries

Fiscal Years Ended Dec. 30, 2023 (in millions)	
Net income	$9,155
Other comprehensive (loss) income, net of taxes:	
Net currency translation adjustment	(307)
Net change on cash flow hedges	(32)
Net pension and retiree medical adjustments.	(358)
Net change on available-for-sale debt securities and other	465
	(232)
Comprehensive income	8,923
Less: Comprehensive income attributable to noncontrolling interests	81
Comprehensive income attributable to PepsiCo.	**$8,842**

Explain stockholders' equity disclosures and key ratios

LO 19-8

Stockholders' equity is an important component of financial statement presentation, disclosures, and analyses. Financial statement users find useful information in financial statements and in notes to financial statements that explain elements of equity. Using this information, ratios are computed to assess financial strength and long-term solvency.

Equity Analysis
- Disclosure
  - Number of shares
  - Changes in equity categories
  - Rights and privileges of outstanding securities
- Ratios
  - Book value per share
  - Payout ratio
  - Return on equity
  - Price-to-earnings ratio

LO 19-8 Overview

Equity Disclosures

For each issuance of equity, companies report the number of shares authorized, the number of shares issued, the number of shares outstanding, and any par value. A company must also disclose changes in the stockholders' equity categories and changes in the number of shares of equity securities.

Disclosure also includes the rights and privileges associated with a company's outstanding securities. Dividend and liquidation preferences, participation rights, call prices and dates, sinking fund requirements, and conversion rates are examples of information disclosed. For example, in notes to financial statements in a recent Form 10-K of **Bank of America**, the company described a liquidation preference for a preferred stock issuance of $1,000 per share. This means that preferred shareholders have a right to $1,000 per share in the event of a liquidation before common shareholders would be paid, but after creditors would be paid.

Accounting standards also require companies to provide the following additional specific disclosures for equity, several of which pertain to preferred stock.

1. Relevant rights and privileges of the various securities.*
2. Number of shares issued from the conversion, exercise of securities, or satisfaction of required conditions during the period.
3. Liquidation preference of preferred or of other senior stock must be disclosed in the equity section of the balance sheet when that preference is significantly greater than par or stated value.
4. Aggregate or per-share amounts at which preferred stock may be called or is subject to redemption.
5. Aggregate and per-share amounts of cumulative preferred stock dividends in arrears.
6. Significant terms (quantitative and qualitative) of the conversion features of contingently convertible securities.
7. Redemption requirement for all capital stock redeemable at fixed or determinable prices on fixed or determinable dates in each of the five years following the date of the balance sheet.

*505-10-50-3   An entity shall explain, in summary form within its financial statements, the pertinent rights and privileges of the various securities outstanding. Examples of information that shall be disclosed are dividend and liquidation preferences, participation rights, call prices and dates, conversion or exercise prices or rates and pertinent dates, sinking-fund requirements, unusual voting rights, and significant terms of contracts to issue additional shares or terms that may change conversion or exercise prices (excluding standard antidilution provisions) . . .

A portion of retained earnings may be **restricted** for a certain purpose. Retained earnings are restricted primarily to protect the cash position of the corporation by reducing the amount of cash dividends that otherwise might be paid. The restriction may be the result of a legal contract or a state law. For example, a company may have signed a debt agreement that protects the creditors by restricting the amount of retained earnings that can be paid out in dividends while the debt is outstanding. Restrictions of retained earnings are typically indicated in notes to financial statements.

Management of a company may restrict retained earnings more formally through an appropriation of retained earnings. In this case, the restricted amount of retained earnings is transferred to an account, **appropriated retained earnings**, which is clearly identified separately in financial statements. This means that the company would report retained earnings in two components: appropriated retained earnings and unappropriated retained earnings. Disclosure in the notes accompanying the financial statements includes the nature of the appropriation and the amount restricted.

`505-10-45-3` Appropriation of retained earnings is permitted, provided that it is shown within the shareholders' equity section of the balance sheet and is clearly identified as an appropriation of retained earnings.

Equity Ratios

We examine the following ratios in this section and in **Demo 19-8**: book value per share, payout ratio, return on equity, and price-to-earnings ratio.

Book Value per Share

$$\frac{\text{Common stock equity}}{\text{Number of common shares outstanding}}$$

This ratio measures the common shareholder investment per common share. Common stockholders' equity is total stockholders' equity less preferred stockholder claims, such as liquidation value and dividends in arrears on cumulative preferred stock. Book value per common share represents the liquidation value per share of common stock based on historical cost and other accounting principles affecting measurement and recognition in the financial statements. The ratio is less relevant as an estimation of liquidation value, however, if the amounts on the balance sheet do not reflect fair value.

Payout Ratio

$$\frac{\text{Cash common dividends}}{\text{Net income available to common stockholders}}$$

The payout ratio computes the proportion of income paid as dividends to common shareholders. If preferred shareholders receive a portion of profits through dividends (or preferred dividends are cumulative), this amount is subtracted from net income to arrive at the net income that is available to common shareholders. A higher ratio indicates that a larger percentage of income was paid out in common dividends.

Return on Equity

$$\frac{\text{Net income available to common stockholders}}{\text{Average common stockholders' equity}}$$

This ratio computes the return on investment by the company's owners or the dollars of income earned for each investment dollar of the owners. Average common stockholders' equity is a simple average of beginning and ending total common stockholders' equity. If preferred shareholders receive a portion of profits through dividends (or preferred dividends are cumulative), this amount is subtracted from net income to arrive at the net income that is available to common shareholders. A higher ratio indicates a higher return on investment of the shareholders.

Price-to-Earnings Ratio

$$\frac{\text{Market price per share}}{\text{Earnings per share}}$$

The price-to-earnings ratio measures the amount an investor is willing to pay (market price of stock) per each dollar of earnings per share. As this ratio increases, an investor would assume to have a higher expectation for the profitability of the company in the future.

DEMO 19-8 | **LO19-8**   **Equity Ratios**

Demo MBC

The following information is from **Target Corporation**, with Year 3 being the most recent year.

$ millions	Year 3	Year 2	Year 1
Total assets.	$51,248	$42,779	$41,290
Total liabilities	36,808	30,946	29,993
Shareholders' investment (common)	14,440	11,833	11,297

$ millions, except per share data	Year 3	Year 2
Common dividends paid.	$1,343	$1,330
Net income.	4,368	3,281
Basic earnings per share	8.72	6.42

continued

continued from previous page

Compute the book value per share, the payout ratio, the return on equity, and the price earnings ratio for Year 3 and Year 2. Market price per share of its stock was $181.17 at the end of Year 3, and $110.74 at the end of Year 2. Common shares outstanding were 500,877,129 at the end of Year 3 and 504,198,962 at the end of Year 2.

Solution

		Year 3	Year 2
Book value per share	$= \dfrac{\text{Common stock equity}}{\text{Number of common shares outstanding}}$	$\dfrac{\$14{,}440}{500.877} = \$28.83$	$\dfrac{\$11{,}833}{504.199} = \$23.47$
Payout ratio	$= \dfrac{\text{Cash common dividends}}{\text{Net income available to common}}$	$\dfrac{\$1{,}343}{\$4{,}368} = 0.31$	$\dfrac{\$1{,}330}{\$3{,}281} = 0.41$
Return on equity	$= \dfrac{\text{Net income available to common}}{\text{Average common stockholders' equity}^\dagger}$	$\dfrac{\$4{,}368}{\$13{,}137} = 0.33$	$\dfrac{\$3{,}281}{\$11{,}565} = 0.28$
Price-to-earnings ratio	$= \dfrac{\text{Market price per share}}{\text{Earnings per share}}$	$\dfrac{\$181.17}{\$8.72} = \$20.78$	$\dfrac{\$110.74}{\$6.42} = \$17.25$

† Average common stockholders' equity: Year 3 = ($14,440 + $11,833) / 2.   Year 2 = ($11,833 + $11,297) / 2.

Target increased book value per share by approximately 23% over the prior year. Although the dollar amount of dividends was relatively flat over the two-year period, as a percentage of profits, it decreased from 41% to 31%. Target investors had a higher rate of return on their investment, receiving 33 cents on each dollar invested compared to 28 cents per dollar in the prior year. Price to earnings also increased over the prior year, by approximately 20%.

GOLDMAN SACHS

Real World—FINANCIAL STATEMENT RATIOS

The Goldman Sachs Group Inc. provided the following ratios in its Management's Discussion and Analysis in a recent Form 10-K. Two ratios discussed above (return on equity and the payout ratio) are included in the three-year, comparative ratio analysis.

Year Ended December	2023	2022	2021
Net earnings to average total assets	0.5%	0.7%	1.6%
Return on shareholders' equity	7.3%	9.7%	21.3%
Average equity to average assets	7.5%	7.5%	7.4%
Dividend payout ratio	45.9%	29.9%	10.9%

Computing Equity Ratios

LO19-8   **REVIEW 19-8**

The following information is provided for **Starbucks Corporation**, where Year 3 is the most recent year.

In millions	Year 3	Year 2	Year 1
Common stock	$ 1.4	$ 1.5	$ 1.5
Additional paid-in capital	41.1	41.1	41.1
Retained earnings	5,563.2	5,949.8	5,974.8
Accumulated other comprehensive loss	(155.6)	(108.4)	(199.4)
Total shareholders' equity	$5,450.1	$5,884.0	$5,818.0
Common shares outstanding	1,431.6	1,460.5	1,485.1
Cash common dividends	$1,450.4	$1,178.0	$ 928.6
Net income	$2,884.7	$2,817.7	$2,757.4

Review

MBC

Required

Compute the following ratios for its fiscal Year 3 and Year 2.

a. Book value per share   *b.* Payout ratio   *c.* Return on equity

More Practice:
BE19-37, BE19-38, E19-37, E19-38

Solution on p. 19-67.

Management Judgment

Management judgment is sometimes needed to classify a stock dividend as a small stock dividend or a stock split effected in the form of a dividend. The accounting guidance provides a minimum range of 20% to 25% where a stock issuance becomes large enough to materially influence the unit market price of the stock. However, this is a range (not a bright line), and the guidance allows for some exceptions outside of this range.

Assume that WayMart Inc. issued a 24% common stock dividend on 100,000 shares of $1 par common stock issued and outstanding on May 1. The market price of the common stock is $5 per share. The impact on financial statements of these two options follows.

	Capital Stock	Paid-In Capital in Excess of Par	Retained Earnings	Total Stockholders' Equity
Small stock dividend................	$24,000	$96,000	$(120,000)	No change
Stock split effected through dividend ...	24,000	—	(24,000)	No change

Retained earnings would have been $96,000 lower ($120,000 less $24,000) had the dividend been classified as a small stock dividend rather than a stock split effected in the form of a dividend. If the balance in Retained Earnings before the stock dividend were $500,000, adjusted retained earnings would be $380,000 with a small stock dividend versus $476,000 with a stock split effected in the form of a dividend. Reporting a 20% lower retained earnings balance with a small stock dividend can have broad implications, such as lowering the availability of future cash dividend distributions or affecting debt covenant compliance requiring a minimum retained earnings balance.

Questions

Q19-1. Identify four basic rights of stockholders. How may one or more of these rights be withheld from the stockholders?

Q19-2. Explain the meaning of authorized capital stock, issued capital stock, unissued capital stock, outstanding capital stock, and treasury stock.

Q19-3. Describe the main categories of stockholders' equity in accounting for corporate capital.

Q19-4. What is a noncontrolling interest, and how is it presented in a company's statement of stockholders' equity?

Q19-5. Define legal capital.

Q19-6. Distinguish between par and no-par stock. Distinguish between common and preferred stock.

Q19-7. Identify and explain a transaction that causes paid-in capital to increase but does not result in any increase in the assets or decrease in the liabilities of the corporation.

Q19-8. Explain the difference between cumulative and noncumulative preferred stock.

Q19-9. Under what conditions is preferred stock reported as a liability?

Q19-10. Distinguish between callable and redeemable preferred stock.

Q19-11. How are assets valued when shares of stock are given in payment to acquire these assets?

Q19-12. Briefly describe the accounting for stock issue costs.

Q19-13. Define treasury stock.

Q19-14. What is the effect on the amounts of assets, liabilities, and stockholders' equity of (a) the purchase of treasury stock and (b) the sale of treasury stock?

Q19-15. Total stockholders' equity is not affected by the use of the cost method of accounting for treasury stock, yet some components of stockholders' equity are affected. Is this statement correct? Explain.

Q19-16. Why may states limit purchases of treasury stock to the amount reported as retained earnings?

Q19-17. In recording treasury stock transactions, explain why "gains" are recorded in additional paid-in capital account, whereas "losses" may involve a debit to retained earnings.

Q19-18. How is treasury stock reported on the balance sheet under the cost method?

Q19-19. When treasury stock is formally retired, retained earnings may be affected. Explain how this situation may occur.

Q19-20. What are the principal sources and uses of retained earnings?

Q19-21. Explain the significance of the declaration date, record date, and payment date related to dividends.

Q19-22. Distinguish between cash dividends and property dividends.

Q19-23. What is a liquidating dividend? What is the proper accounting treatment for such dividends?

Q19-24. What is the difference between a cash or property dividend and a stock dividend?

Q19-25. Explain this statement: When property dividends are declared and paid, a loss or gain often must be reported.

Q19-26. Contrast the effects of a stock dividend (declared and issued) versus a cash dividend (declared and paid) on assets, liabilities, and total stockholders' equity.

Q19-27. Contrast the effects of a typical small stock dividend (declared and issued and ignoring fractional shares) versus a typical cash dividend (declared and paid) on the components of stockholders' equity.

Q19-28. Explain why the amount of retained earnings reported on the balance sheet is often not the net amount of all accumulated earnings (and losses) less all accumulated cash and property dividends.

Q19-29. Distinguish between a stock split effected in the form of a dividend and a stock split.

Q19-30. What are the primary reasons for appropriating and for restricting retained earnings?

Data Analytics

The financial information in the Excel file associated with this exercise was obtained from 10-K reports for **Costco Wholesale Corporation**. In this exercise, we examine how changing the starting point (baseline) of the y-axis from 0.0 impacts the chart that is created. The chart that is created for Costco examines return on equity over a five-year period.

Data Analytics DA19-1
Critically Analyzing a Visualization in Excel **LO1, 2**

The Excel file associated with this exercise includes market price and ratio information for companies in the S&P 500. For this exercise, we examine trends in the price-to-earnings ratio of S&P 500 companies by industry segment.

Data Analytics DA19-2
Analyzing Trends in the Price-to-Earnings Ratio Using Excel **LO8**

Refer to PA28 in Appendix A. This problem uses Tableau to analyze dividend payout policies of S&P 500 companies through the dividend yield and dividend payout ratio.

Data Analytics DA19-3
Preparing Tableau Visualizations to Analyze Dividend Payout Policies through Ratios **LO5**

Data Visualization

Data Visualization Activities are available in **myBusinessCourse**. These assignments use Tableau Dashboards to expose students to visual depictions of data and introduce students to data analytics through data visualizations. These exercises are assignable and auto graded by MBC.

Data Visualization

Multiple Choice

MC19-1. Computing Total Stockholders' Equity Smithfield Corp. summarized the following account balances as of December 31.

LO1

Accumulated other comprehensive income (loss)	$ 14,000
Common stock, $1 par, 250,000 shares authorized, 40,000 shares issued	35,000
Investment in equity securities	55,000
Paid-in capital in excess of par—common stock	200,000
Retained earnings, ending balance	42,000
Treasury stock, 5,000 shares	8,000

Based on the information provided, what is total stockholders' equity on December 31?

a. $299,000   c. $255,000

b. $338,000   d. $283,000

LO2

MC19-2. Analyzing Common Stock Issuance Sylvan Inc. reported the following balances on December 31 of Year 5.

Common stock, $2 par, 400,0000 shares authorized, 125,000 shares issued and outstanding . . .	$125,000
Paid-in capital in excess of par—common stock	520,000

On January 1 of Year 6, Sylvan Inc. issued 10,000 common shares in exchange for equipment. Sylvan's shares of common stock are widely traded on a public stock exchange. On January 1, the common shares were trading for $7 per share. However, a recent appraisal indicates that the equipment is valued at $80,000.

After issuance of the common stock described above, what is the balance in the account Paid-in Capital in Excess of Par—Common Stock?

a. $570,000   c. $580,000
b. $590,000   d. $600,000

LO3

MC19-3. Analyzing Treasury Stock Transactions In its first year of business, Torrey Corp. issued 1,000 shares of stock at $25 per share. The company also acquired 100 shares at $26 per share for the treasury, reissued 20 treasury shares at $28 per share, and reissued 30 treasury shares at $24 per share. What is the net effect of all treasury share transactions during the year on Additional Paid-in Capital—Treasury Stock and the Retained Earnings accounts?

	Additional Paid-in Capital—TS	Retained Earnings
a.	$0	$20 credit
b.	$20 credit	$40 debit
c.	$0	$20 debit
d.	$20 credit	$0

LO4

MC19-4. Analyzing Conversion of Preferred Stock On January 1 of Year 1, Park Corp. issued 2,500 shares of preferred stock ($5 par value) at $25 per share. Each share of preferred stock is convertible into 10 shares of common stock ($1 par value) at the option of the holder. On March 15 of Year 2, half of the preferred stock was converted into common stock. The entry for the conversion on March 15 of Year 2 would include a credit to Additional Paid-in Capital—CS for

a. $37,500   c. $18,750
b. $30,000   d. $6,250

LO5

MC19-5. Computing Preferred Dividends Norwood Company has the following capital structure.
- Preferred stock, 5%, $35 par, 5,000 shares issued and outstanding
- Common stock, $1 par, 80,000 shares issued and outstanding

If the preferred stock is cumulative and 3 years of dividends are in arrears, how much would the common shareholders receive if the company declares dividends of $80,000?

a. $31,373   c. $53,750
b. $45,000   d. $71,250

LO6

MC19-6. Analyzing Effect of Stock Dividend on Retained Earnings Prior to issuing a stock dividend, Randall Inc. had a total stockholders' equity balance of $350,000 with 10,000 shares of $1 par common stock issued and outstanding. Randall is considering two options. The first is a 10% stock dividend, and the second is a 30% stock dividend. The current market price of the stock is $5 per share. If Randall has a current balance in Retained Earnings of $55,000, what is the balance in Retained Earnings after a 10% stock dividend and after a 30% stock dividend? Consider each option separately.

	10% Stock Dividend	30% Stock Dividend
a.	$50,000	$52,000
b.	$54,000	$52,000
c.	$50,000	$40,000
d.	$54,000	$40,000

LO7

MC19-7. Determining Balance of Accumulated OCI Lakewood Inc. reports net income of $70,000 for the year ended December 31 of Year 5. The company recorded an unrealized loss on available-for-sale debt securities of $15,000 (pre-tax) and a gain on cash flow hedges of $5,000 (pre-tax) for the year. The company declared dividends of $40,000 for the year and its tax rate is 25%. The December 31 of Year 4 balance in accumulated other comprehensive income is $18,000 (debit balance).

What is the ending balance in accumulated other comprehensive income on December 31 of Year 5?

a.	$10,500 debit	c.	$28,000 debit
b.	$25,500 debit	d.	$44,500 credit

MC19-8. Computing Comprehensive Income Referring to MC19-7, what will Lakewood Inc. report as comprehensive income for Year 5?   **LO7**

a.	$22,500	c.	$60,000
b.	$45,000	d.	$62,500

MC19-9. Analyzing Payout Ratio If a company's payout ratio is 0.25 and its net income available to common stockholders for the period is $180,000, what were cash common dividends for the period? Assume a tax rate of 25%.   **LO8**

a.	$33,750	c.	$45,000
b.	$18,000	d.	Requires additional information

MC19-10. Determining Effect of Various Transactions on Retained Earnings Lainey Inc. summarized the following information for Year 5.   **LO1, 3, 5, 6**

1. Cash dividends declared of $10,000.
2. Dividends declared of property with a carrying amount of $30,000 and a fair value of $28,000.
3. Excess of cash proceeds of treasury stock sold of $12,000 over the cost of treasury stock.
4. 10% stock dividend declared; just before the dividend declaration, the market price of Lainey's $1 par, 10,000 shares of common stock was $8 per share.
5. Net income of $137,000.

If the company reported a balance of $130,000 in retained earnings as of January 1 of Year 5, what is the December 31 of Year 5 balance in retained earnings?

a.	$228,000	c.	$209,000
b.	$219,000	d.	$221,000

Brief Exercises

On December 31, Polar Inc. had the following account balances. Prepare the stockholders' equity section of the balance sheet at December 31. Ignore the disclosure of number of shares.

Preferred stock, $10 par value	$150,000
Paid in capital in excess of par—Preferred stock	12,000
Common stock, $1 par value	8,000
Paid in capital in excess of par—Common stock	40,000
Retained earnings	220,000
Accumulated other comprehensive loss.	(6,000)

Brief Exercise 19-1
Preparing a
Stockholders' Equity
Section **LO1**
Hint: See Demo 19-1

Match each of the items *a* through *n* with its proper stockholders' equity component 1 through 7.

Brief Exercise 19-2
Classifying
Stockholders' Equity
Accounts **LO1**
Hint: See Review 19-1

Financial Statement Item
- _____ *a.* Net loss
- _____ *b.* Restriction on retained earnings
- _____ *c.* Goodwill
- _____ *d.* Gain from foreign currency translation adjustment
- _____ *e.* Cash dividends declared, not paid
- _____ *f.* Bond sinking fund
- _____ *g.* Treasury stock, cost method
- _____ *h.* Unrealized gain on available-for-sale debt securities
- _____ *i.* Net income
- _____ *j.* Correction of accounting error affecting prior years' net income
- _____ *k.* Legal capital
- _____ *l.* Net assets owned by investors other than the parent
- _____ *m.* Preferred stock
- _____ *n.* Paid-in capital in excess of par

Stockholders' Equity Component
1. Capital stock
2. Additional paid-in capital
3. Retained earnings
4. Accumulated other comprehensive income
5. Treasury stock
6. Noncontrolling interests
7. None of the above

Brief Exercise 19-3
Determining Issued
and Outstanding
Shares **LO1**

From the following information, determine (1) the number of common shares issued, (2) the number of common shares outstanding, and (3) the number of common shares unissued.

Common stock, $2 par value, 10,000 shares authorized	$8,000
Treasury stock, 250 shares.	2,500

Brief Exercise 19-4
Preparing Entry
to Issue Common
Stock **LO2**
Hint: See Demo 19-2A

On June 30, Ebae Inc. issued 120 shares of $1 par value common stock for $12 per share. Prepare Ebae's June 30 journal entry for stock issuance.

Brief Exercise 19-5
Reporting Common
Stock Issuance Using
the Accounting Equation
LO2

Refer to BE19-4, but instead of journal entries, show the effect on the accounting equation for the transactions, including identifying the individual accounts affected, and the total impact on assets, liabilities, and stockholders' equity.

Brief Exercise 19-6
Preparing Entry
to Issue Common
Stock **LO2**
Hint: See Demo 19-2B

On June 30, Ebae Inc. issued 120 shares of no-par common stock for $15 per share.

a.   Prepare Ebae's June 30 journal entry for stock issuance.
b.   Prepare Ebae's June 30 journal entry assuming instead that the company designated a stated value of $2 per share for common stock.

Brief Exercise 19-7
Preparing Entry for
Multiple Securities
Issuance **LO2**
Hint: See Demo 19-2D

Amazing Inc. issued 1,000 shares of common stock ($1 par) and 1,000 shares of preferred stock ($10 par) at a price of $100,000 on April 1. At the time of issuance, the market price of the common stock is $30 per share, and the market price of the preferred stock is $90 per share. Prepare the journal entry on April 1.

Brief Exercise 19-8
Reporting Multiple
Securities Issuance Using
the Accounting Equation
LO2

Refer to BE19-7, but instead of journal entries, show the effect on the accounting equation for the transactions, including identifying the individual accounts affected, and the total impact on assets, liabilities, and stockholders' equity.

Brief Exercise 19-9
Preparing Entry to Issue
Stock for Noncash
Consideration **LO2**
Hint: See Demo 19-2C

Ranier Corp. authorized the issuance of 400,000 shares of no-par common stock. The state of incorporation requires a minimum stated value of $4 per share of common stock issued. On February 1, Ranier issued 50 shares of common stock to a local law firm for legal services related to the start-up of the company with an estimated value of $1,500. Prepare the journal entry on February 1. *Hint:* Start-up costs are expensed as incurred.

Brief Exercise 19-10
Reporting Stock Issuance
for Noncash Consideration
Using the Accounting
Equation **LO2**

Refer to BE19-9, but instead of journal entries, show the effect on the accounting equation for the transactions, including identifying the individual accounts affected, and the total impact on assets, liabilities, and stockholders' equity.

Brief Exercise 19-11
Preparing Entry to
Issue Common Stock
with Stock Issue
Costs **LO2**
Hint: See Demo 19-2E

On January 1, Vera Clothing Inc. issued 5,000 shares of common stock, $5 par for $100,000. Related to this issuance, the company incurred legal and accounting fees of $2,500 and administrative fees of $2,500.

    Prepare the journal entry on January 1.

Brief Exercise 19-12
Preparing Entry for
Direct Retirement
of Reacquired
Shares **LO3**
Hint: See Demo 19-3B

Refer to the information in BE19-11. On June 30, Vera Clothing Inc. reacquired 500 shares of common stock at $21 per share and immediately retired the shares.

    Prepare the journal entry on June 30.

Refer to BE19-12, but instead of journal entries, show the effect on the accounting equation for the transactions, including identifying the individual accounts affected, and the total impact on assets, liabilities, and stockholders' equity.

Brief Exercise 19-13
Reporting Stock Direct Retirement Using the Accounting Equation
LO4

On January 30, Pier5 Inc. issued 500 shares of $1 par common stock for $15 per share. On June 30, Pier5 Inc. reacquired 50 shares of common stock at $12 per share and immediately retired the shares. On December 15, Pier5 Inc. reacquired 100 shares of common stock at $17 per share and immediately retired the shares. By what amount did retained earnings decrease as a result of the reacquisition of common stock on December 15?

Brief Exercise 19-14
Preparing Entry for Direct Retirement of Reacquired Shares   **LO3**
Hint: See Demo 19-3B

Harlee Inc. has 60,000 shares of $5 par common stock outstanding at the beginning of the year. Prepare entries for the following transactions affecting stockholders' equity. Assume Paid-In Capital—Treasury Stock has a zero beginning balance.

a.   Jan. 15:   Purchased common stock as treasury shares, 2,000 shares at $20 per share.
b.   June 15:   Sold common treasury stock, 800 shares at $14 per share.

Brief Exercise 19-15
Preparing Entries for Treasury Stock Transactions   **LO3**
Hint: See Demo 19-3A

Refer to BE19-15, but instead of journal entries, show the effect on the accounting equation for the transactions, including identifying the individual accounts affected, and the total impact on assets, liabilities, and stockholders' equity.

Brief Exercise 19-16
Reporting Treasury Stock Transactions Using the Accounting Equation
LO3

Charter Inc. has 600,000 shares of $1 par common stock outstanding at the beginning of the year. Prepare entries for the following transactions affecting stockholders' equity. Assume Paid-In Capital—Treasury Stock has a zero beginning balance.

a.   Jan. 31:   Purchased common stock as treasury shares, 1,200 shares at $15 per share.
b.   Sep. 15:   Sold common treasury stock, 200 shares at $17 per share.
c.   Dec. 20:   Sold common treasury stock, 250 shares at $13 per share.

Brief Exercise 19-17
Preparing Entries for Treasury Stock Transactions   **LO3**
Hint: See Demo 19-3A

Refer to BE19-17, but instead of journal entries, show the effect on the accounting equation for the transactions, including identifying the individual accounts affected, and the total impact on assets, liabilities, and stockholders' equity.

Brief Exercise 19-18
Reporting Treasury Stock Transactions Using the Accounting Equation
LO3

Regency Inc. issued 800 shares of $20 par value, 8%, cumulative preferred stock for $48,000 on June 30. Prepare the journal entry on June 30.

Brief Exercise 19-19
Preparing Entry to Issue Preferred Stock   **LO4**
Hint: See Demo 19-4

Refer to BE19-19, but instead of journal entries, show the effect on the accounting equation for the transactions, including identifying the individual accounts affected, and the total impact on assets, liabilities, and stockholders' equity.

Brief Exercise 19-20
Reporting Preferred Stock Issuance Using the Accounting Equation
LO4

On January 1 of Year 1, Leo Corp. issues 1,500 shares of callable preferred stock ($8 par value) at $50 per share. Leo Corp. has the option to repurchase the preferred stock from the shareholders at any point in the next three years at $50 per share. On June 30 of Year 3, the 1,500 shares of preferred stock were recalled at $50 per share. Record the entry for issuance of the preferred stock on January 1 of Year 1 and for the recall of preferred stock on June 30 of Year 3.

Brief Exercise 19-21
Preparing Entries for Issuance and Recall of Callable Preferred Stock   **LO4**
Hint: See Demo 19-4

Brief Exercise 19-22
Preparing Entries
for the Issuance
and Conversion of
Convertible Preferred
Stock **LO4**
Hint: See Demo 19-4

On January 1 of Year 1, Leo Corp. issues 1,500 shares of preferred stock ($8 par value) at $50 per share. Each share of preferred stock is convertible into 10 shares of common stock ($1 par value) at the option of the holder. Record the entry for issuance of preferred stock on January 1 of Year 1 and for the conversion of 500 shares of preferred stock into common stock on June 30 of Year 2.

Brief Exercise 19-23
Reporting Issuance and
Conversion of Convertible
Preferred Stock Using
the Accounting Equation
LO4

Refer to BE19-22, but instead of journal entries, show the effect on the accounting equation for the transactions, including identifying the individual accounts affected, and the total impact on assets, liabilities, and stockholders' equity.

Brief Exercise 19-24
Determining Dividend
Distributions **LO5**

During the year, Urban Inc. distributes $80,000 in cash dividends to shareholders. Urban Inc. has the following capital stock outstanding.

Common, $1 par, 30,000 shares issued and outstanding	$ 30,000
8% Preferred, $10 par, 20,000 shares issued and outstanding . . .	200,000

a. If the preferred stock is cumulative and dividends are in arrears for the past three years, what is the cash distribution to common shareholders and preferred shareholders?

b. What is the cash distribution to common shareholders and preferred shareholders if the preferred stock is noncumulative and dividends are in arrears for the past three years?

Brief Exercise 19-25
Preparing Dividend
Entries **LO5**
Hint: See Demo 19-5A

On September 1, Fox Corporation declared a cash dividend of $1 per share on its 800,000 outstanding shares of common stock ($1 par). The dividend is payable on October 15 to stockholders of record on October 1.
    Provide all journal entries directly related to this dividend.

Brief Exercise 19-26
Reporting Dividend
Transactions Using the
Accounting Equation
LO5

Refer to BE19-25, but instead of journal entries, show the effect on the accounting equation for the transactions, including identifying the individual accounts affected, and the total impact on assets, liabilities, and stockholders' equity. **For the cash account, indicate the effect on the statement of cash flows by selecting from C:o (cash from operating activities), C:i (cash from investing activities), or C:f (cash from financing activities).**

Brief Exercise 19-27
Preparing Entry
for Property
Dividends **LO5**
Hint: See Demo 19-5B

Zerizon Inc. holds 6,000 shares of Cable Co. common stock, which it acquired for $25 per share in May. On June 1, Zerizon Inc. declares a property dividend of 500 shares of Cable Co. common stock that it owns when the shares are selling at $28 per share. Provide the journal entries on June 1 for (1) adjustment of the investment to fair value and (2) the declaration of the property dividend. For part 1, ignore any adjustments required on shares not declared as a property dividend.

Brief Exercise 19-28
Reporting Property
Dividend Transactions
Using the Accounting
Equation **LO5**

Refer to BE19-27, but instead of journal entries, show the effect on the accounting equation for the transactions, including identifying the individual accounts affected, and the total impact on assets, liabilities, and stockholders' equity.

Brief Exercise 19-29
Preparing Entry for
Liquidating Dividend
Declaration **LO5**
Hint: See Demo 19-5C

Wellington Corp. declared a dividend on common stock of $250,000 on May 18. Wellington announced to shareholders that $175,000 of the dividend amount was a return of capital.
    Provide the journal entry on May 18 for the dividend declaration.

Brief Exercise 19-30
Preparing Entries
for Small Stock
Dividends **LO6**
Hint: See Demo 19-6A

Landry Inc. has 10,000 shares of $1 par common stock outstanding. On September 30, Landry declares a 10% stock dividend when the fair value of its common stock is $30 per share. Distribution of the dividend will be on October 15.

a. Prepare the journal entry for the declaration of the stock dividend on September 30.

b. Prepare the journal entry for the distribution of the stock dividend on October 15.

Refer to BE19-30, but instead of journal entries, show the effect on the accounting equation for the transactions, including identifying the individual accounts affected, and the total impact on assets, liabilities, and stockholders' equity.

Brief Exercise 19-31
Reporting Small Stock Dividends Using the Accounting Equation
LO6

Landry Inc. has 10,000 shares of $1 par common stock outstanding. On September 30, Landry declares a stock split effected in the form of a 100% stock dividend when the fair value of its common stock is $30 per share. Distribution of the dividend will be on October 15.

a. Prepare the journal entry for the declaration of the stock dividend on September 30.
b. Prepare the journal entry for the distribution of the stock dividend on October 15.

Brief Exercise 19-32
Preparing Entries for Stock Split Effected in the Form of a Dividend **LO6**
Hint: See Demo 19-6B

Refer to BE19-32, but instead of journal entries, show the effect on the accounting equation for the transactions, including identifying the individual accounts affected, and the total impact on assets, liabilities, and stockholders' equity.

Brief Exercise 19-33
Reporting Stock Split Effected in the Form of a Dividend Using the Accounting Equation
LO6

Refer to the information in BE19-32. Assume instead that Landry announces a 2-for-1 stock split *not* effected through a stock dividend.

a. Prepare the journal entry for the declaration of the stock split on September 30.
b. Prepare the journal entry for the distribution of the stock split on October 15.
c. What is the total par value of common stock before and after the stock split?
d. What is the par value per share before and after the stock split?
e. What are the total number of shares before and after the stock split?

Brief Exercise 19-34
Analyzing a Stock Split **LO6**

Fastco Corp. reports net income of $20,000, and other comprehensive income of $5,000 (net of tax) for the current year ended December 31. The prior year December 31 balance in accumulated other comprehensive income is $18,000 (credit balance) and the balance in retained earnings is $100,000 (credit balance). What is the ending balance in accumulated other comprehensive income on December 31 of the current year?

Brief Exercise 19-35
Determining the Balance in Accumulated OCI **LO7**
Hint: See Review 19-7

Identify whether the following items *a* through *j* are part of (1) net income or (2) other comprehensive income.
_____ a. Sales revenue
_____ b. Bad debt expense
_____ c. Loss from foreign currency translation adjustment
_____ d. Gain on sale of an available-for-sale debt investment
_____ e. Unrealized gain on an available-for-sale debt investment
_____ f. Unrealized gain on an equity investment where investor lacks significant influence
_____ g. Prior service cost amortization expense for a defined benefit plan
_____ h. Unrealized loss on cash flow hedge
_____ i. Loss on impairment of investment
_____ j. Loss on sale of land

Brief Exercise 19-36
Identifying Net Income and Other Comprehensive Income Amounts **LO7**

Bucky's Apparel Inc. is considering paying a dividend on December 31. A loan covenant stipulates that the payout ratio must be less than or equal to 10%. If the company has no preferred stock outstanding, and net income is expected to be $80,000, what is the maximum value that Bucky can pay out in dividends to the common shareholders?

Brief Exercise 19-37
Analyzing Payout Ratio **LO8**

The following information is provided for the **Coca-Cola Company** ($ millions).

Total common stockholders' equity on Dec. 31, Current Year....	$17,072
Total common stockholders' equity on Dec. 31, Prior Year......	23,062
Net income, Current Year............................	1,248

Brief Exercise 19-38
Computing Equity Ratios **LO8**
Hint: See Demo 19-8

Compute the following ratios for the current year. Total number of common shares outstanding is 4,259 million.
a. Book value per share
b. Return on equity

Exercises

Exercise 19-1
Reporting Stockholders'
Equity **LO1**

The following data are from the accounts of Mitar Corporation at December 31.

Retained earnings, beginning balance..	$ 900,000
Common stock, $__ par, 100,000 shares authorized, 50,000 shares issued.............	1,000,000
Treasury stock, 1,000 shares	20,000
Paid-in capital in excess of par...	400,000
Bonds payable	200,000
Net income (not included in retained earnings above)............................	190,000
Dividends declared and paid (not included in retained earnings above)	80,000

Required

a.   Determine the value of the following items.

1. Total retained earnings at year-end
2. Par value per share
3. Number of shares outstanding
4. Total stockholders' equity
5. Average original selling price per share
6. Cost per share of treasury stock

b.   Prepare the stockholders' equity section of the balance sheet at December 31.

Exercise 19-2
Reporting Stockholders'
Equity **LO1**
Hint: See Demo 19-1

On December 31, Nakoma Inc. summarized the following information.

Preferred stock, $100 par, 5,000 shares authorized............	$ 20,000
Paid-in capital in excess of par—Preferred stock.............	80,000
Common stock, $1 par, 250,000 shares authorized............	35,000
Paid-in capital in excess of par—Common stock	480,000
Retained earnings	360,000
Accumulated other comprehensive income (loss)	48,000
Treasury stock, 1,200 shares	55,000
Noncontrolling interests	5,000

Prepare the stockholders' equity section of the balance sheet for Nakoma Inc. on December 31. State the par value per share, and the number of shares authorized, issued, and outstanding for common stock and for preferred stock on the face of the statement.

Exercise 19-3
Recording Entries
for Common Stock
Issuance **LO2**
Hint: See Review 19-2

Record journal entries for the following separate transactions.

a.   Max Inc. issued 5,000 shares of $1 par value common stock for $20 per share.

b.   Max Inc. issued 1,000 shares of no-par common stock for $25 per share. The state of incorporation requires a minimum value per share of $2.

c.   Max Inc. issued 500 shares of no-par common stock for $18 per share.

d.   Max Inc. issued 5,000 shares of $1 par value common stock for $18 per share and incurred $1,000 in legal fees related to the stock issuance.

e.   Max Inc. issued 10,000 shares of common stock ($1 par) in exchange for equipment with a fair value of $178,000.

f.   Max Inc. issued 3,000 shares of Class A common stock ($1 par) and 4,000 shares of Class B common stock ($2 par) for $80,000 cash. At the time of issuance, the market price of the Class A common stock is $15 per share, and the market price of the Class B common stock is $10 per share.

g.   Max Inc. issued 3,000 shares of Class A common stock ($1 par) and 4,000 shares of Class B common stock ($2 par) for $85,000 cash. At the time of issuance, the market price of the Class A common stock is $16 per share, and the market price of the Class B common stock is unknown.

Exercise 19-4
Recording Entries
for Common Stock
Issuance **LO2**

Tridint Corporation is authorized to issue 100,000 shares of $5 par value common stock. The shares of stock are not publicly traded. During the year, the company completed the following transactions.

Jan. 8   Issued 40,000 shares of common stock at $12 per share.
Jan. 30   Issued 10,500 shares of common stock in exchange for equipment with an appraised value of $136,500.

Required

a.   Prepare the journal entry on January 8.

b.   Prepare the journal entry on January 30.

c.   Prepare the entry for part *b* assuming instead that the stock was traded on a registered stock exchange at $14 per share on January 30.

Refer to E19-4, but instead of journal entries, show the effect on the accounting equation for the transactions, including identifying the individual accounts affected, and the total impact on assets, liabilities, and stockholders' equity.

Exercise 19-5
Reporting Common
Stock Issuances Using
the Accounting Equation
LO2

Facebook raised over $16 billion in its initial public offering. Specifically, 421.2 million shares of Class A common stock, $0.000006 par value, were sold for $38 a share.

Required

Ignoring stock issue costs, record the journal entry for this stock issuance.

Exercise 19-6
Recording Entry for
Stock Issuance **LO2**
Hint: See Demo 19-2A

Gilmore Company has 20,000 authorized shares of common stock, $2 par, and 20,000 authorized shares of preferred stock, $10 par. On April 10, Gilmore sold 600 shares of common stock and 400 shares of preferred stock in one transaction for a total of $20,000 cash. The common stock was selling at $26 per share, while the preferred stock was selling at $16 per share.

Required

a. Prepare the entry on April 10 for the issuance of common and preferred stock.
b. Assume instead that only the market price of the common stock is known ($26 per share). Prepare the entry on April 10 for the issuance of common and preferred stock.

Exercise 19-7
Recording Entries for
Multiple Securities
Issuance **LO2**
Hint: See Demo 19-2D

Stellar Inc. issued 20,000 shares of common stock, $0.01 par value, for $28 per share on March 28. As part of this transaction, Stellar incurred legal and administrative costs totaling $4,000, paid in cash.

Required

Prepare the journal entry on March 28 for the issuance of common shares.

Exercise 19-8
Recording Stock Issue
Costs **LO2**
Hint: See Demo 19-2E

Laser Inc. has the following beginning account balances on January 1.

Common stock, $1 par, 10,000 shares issued	$ 10,000
Paid-in capital in excess of par.	140,000

Exercise 19-9
Recording Common
Stock Direct
Retirement **LO3**
Hint: See Demo 19-3B

Required

Prepare journal entries for the following three separate scenarios.

a. On January 15, Laser Inc. acquires and immediately retires 1,000 shares of stock at $15 per share.
b. On January 15, Laser Inc. acquires and immediately retires 1,000 shares of stock at $17 per share.
c. On January 15, Laser Inc. acquires and immediately retires 1,000 shares of stock at $14 per share.

Refer to E19-9, but instead of journal entries, show the effect on the accounting equation for the transactions, including identifying the individual accounts affected, and the total impact on assets, liabilities, and stockholders' equity.

Exercise 19-10
Reporting Common Stock
Direct Retirement Using
the Accounting Equation
LO3

Acer Inc. issued 50,000 shares of $0.01 par value common stock for $15 per share on January 1, the day of its initial stock offering.

Required

a. Record entries for the following subsequent transactions assuming that the company's policy is to directly retire any reacquired shares.
   1. On March 30, the company reacquires and retires 1,000 shares of common stock at $13.50 per share.
   2. On August 20, the company reacquires and retires 1,000 shares of common stock at $17.25 per share.
   3. On December 1, the company issues 5,000 shares of common stock at $17.00 per share.
b. Determine the number of shares issued and the number of shares outstanding on the following dates (after transactions have been recorded).
   1. March 30   2. August 20   3. December 1

Exercise 19-11
Recording Common
Stock Direct
Retirement **LO3**

Exercise 19-12
Recording
Treasury Stock
Transactions **LO3**

On January 2, Liberty Corporation was authorized to issue 100,000 shares of $5 par value common stock. Liberty issued 20,000 shares of common stock on January 15 at $15 per share.

Required

a. Record the entry on June 30 for purchase of 2,200 common shares for the treasury at $18 per share.

b. Record the entry on September 20 for sale of 800 treasury shares at $21 per share.

c. Record the entry on November 3 for sale of 500 treasury shares at $17 per share.

d. Record the entry on December 15 for sale of 400 treasury shares at $13 per share.

e. Determine the number of shares issued and the number of shares outstanding on the following dates (after transactions have been recorded): June 30; September 20; November 3; and December 15.

Exercise 19-13
Recording
Treasury Stock
Transactions **LO3**
Hint: See Demo 19-3A

On January 2, Pharro Corporation was authorized to issue 200,000 shares of $1 par value common stock. Pharro issued 50,000 shares of common stock on January 8 at $10 per share. In addition, the company completed the following transactions during the year.

Mar. 30   Purchased 5,000 shares of common stock for the treasury at $12 per share.
Apr. 20   Purchased 5,000 shares of common stock for the treasury at $9 per share.
Oct. 31   Sold 8,000 shares of treasury stock at $11 per share.

Required

a. Record the entry on March 30 for the purchase of common shares for the treasury.

b. Record the entry on April 20 for the purchase of common shares for the treasury.

c. Record the entry on October 31 for the sale of treasury shares at $11 per share. Assume a FIFO cost flow in accounting for the sale of treasury shares.

d. Repeat part c but instead assume a weighted average cost flow in accounting for the sale of treasury shares.

Exercise 19-14
Recording
and Reporting
Treasury Stock
Transactions **LO3**
Hint: See Review 19-3

On January 1, Jordan Corporation issued 20,000 shares of $1 par value common stock at $50 per share. On January 15, Jordan purchased 50 shares of its own common stock at $55 per share. On March 1, twenty shares of treasury stock were resold at $58. The balance in retained earnings was $25,000 prior to these transactions.

Required

a. Record the entry on January 1 for issuance of common stock. What is the impact on stockholders' equity of this transaction?

b. Record the entry on January 15 for purchase of common shares for the treasury. What is the impact on stockholders' equity of this transaction?

c. Record the entry on March 1 for sale of treasury shares at $58 per share. What is the impact on stockholders' equity of this transaction?

d. Provide the ending balances for each of the stockholders' equity accounts affected by these entries.

e. Assume that on March 30 all remaining treasury shares are retired. Provide the entry for retirement of the remaining treasury shares.

Exercise 19-15
Recording: Treasury
Stock vs. Direct Stock
Retirement **LO3**

On December 31, the records for Lakers Inc. provided the following data on stockholders' equity.

Common stock, $10 par, 30,000 shares issued	$300,000
Additional paid-in capital on common stock, $0.30 per share	9,000
Treasury stock, 3,000 shares (cost $9.80 per share)	29,400

On that date, the stockholders vote to retire all of the treasury stock immediately and to purchase for direct retirement another 4,000 shares of common stock currently trading at $12.50 per share.

Required

a. Provide the journal entry to retire the 3,000 shares of treasury stock.

b. Provide the journal entry for the purchase and immediate retirement of the 4,000 shares of outstanding common stock.

c. Assume instead for part b that the company holds the 4,000 shares in the treasury rather than retiring immediately. Record the journal entry.

d. Determine the change in stockholders' equity after part b and then again after part c.

Refer to E19-15, but instead of journal entries, show the effect on the accounting equation for the transactions, including identifying the individual accounts affected, and the total impact on assets, liabilities, and stockholders' equity.

Exercise 19-16
Reporting Treasury Stock vs. Direct Stock Retirement Transactions Using the Accounting Equation **LO3**

Lakers Inc. reacquired a number of its own shares in one transaction in December. (Assume no previous reacquisitions of stock.) Lakers Inc. could account for the reacquisition transaction using two different methods, illustrated as Option One and Option Two.

Exercise 19-17
Analyzing Common Stock Reacquisition Methods **LO3**

Stockholders' Equity Section at December 31	Option One	Option Two
Common stock, $1 par, 100,000 shares authorized...........	$ 8,000	$ 10,000
Paid-in capital in excess of par...........................	120,000	150,000
Retained earnings	31,000	35,000
Treasury stock, 2,000 shares	0	(36,000)
Total stockholders' equity	$159,000	$159,000

Required

a. Identify which accounting method the company used in Option One to account for the reacquisition of common stock—the direct retirement method or the treasury stock method. Re-create the accounting entry to record the reacquisition of common stock.

b. Identify which accounting method the company used in Option Two to account for the reacquisition of common stock—the direct retirement method or the treasury stock method. Re-create the accounting entry to record the reacquisition of common stock.

c. Determine the shares issued and shares outstanding on December 31 under Option One.

d. Determine the shares issued and shares outstanding on December 31 under Option Two.

In our review of the accounting records of Crew Corp., we discover that during the year, all stockholders' equity transactions were recorded in the common stock account. Our first step is to re-create the journal entries for the year that affected equity.

Exercise 19-18
Correcting Stockholders' Equity Account **LO2, 3**

Common Stock	
	0 Beginning balance
	7,500 June 1: Sold 500 shares of common stock ($1 par) at $15 per share
	5,400 July 31: Sold 300 shares of common stock ($1 par) at $18 per share
Oct. 15: Purchased 200 shares for treasury at $20 per share 4,000	
	2,100 Dec. 1: Sold 100 shares treasury stock at $21 per share
	11,000 Ending balance

Required

a. Provide the correct journal entries for the stockholders' equity transactions on (1) June 1, (2) July 31, (3) October 15, and (4) December 1.

b. What is the correct ending balance of common stock?

Cedar Corporation is authorized to issue 10,000 shares of 6%, $10 par, cumulative preferred stock. Early in Year 1, it sold 2,000 shares of preferred stock for $25 per share.

Exercise 19-19
Recording and Reporting Preferred Stock **LO4, 5**

Required

a. Record the entry for the issuance of preferred stock during Year 1.

b. Assume the company is preparing financial statements for Year 4. If the company had not declared or paid dividends in any year to preferred shareholders, what would the company report as dividends in arrears on December 31 of Year 4?

Gilmore Company has 20,000 authorized shares of common stock, $2 par, and 20,000 authorized shares of preferred stock, $10 par.

Exercise 19-20
Recording Common and Preferred Stock Transactions **LO2, 4**

Required

Record journal entries for the following *separate* transactions. Analyze and record each transaction separately.

a. On January 1, Gilmore sold 496 shares of common stock and 80 shares of preferred stock for a lump sum of $12,300. The common stock was selling at $20 per share, and the preferred at $31 per share. Round amounts to the nearest dollar.

b. On January 1, Gilmore issued 180 shares of preferred stock for used equipment. The equipment is appraised at $2,400, and the carrying amount recorded by the seller is $1,200. A fair value measurement on the preferred stock has not been established.

c. Assume that the 20,000 shares of preferred stock are callable for $12 per share at the option of the issuer, Gilmore. After issuing 500 shares of callable preferred stock on January 1 for $12, Gilmore called 100 shares of preferred stock on June 30 for $12. Record the entries for Gilmore on January 1 and on June 30.

d. Assume that each of the 20,000 shares of preferred stock is convertible into 2 shares of common stock at the option of the stockholder. After issuing 500 shares of convertible preferred stock on January 1 for $12, 100 shares of preferred stock were converted into common stock on June 30. Record the entries for Gilmore on January 1 and on June 30, assuming that the fair value of the preferred stock is $16 per share on June 30.

Exercise 19-21
Determining
Preferred Stock
Financial Statement
Presentation **LO4**

On December 31 of Year 1, Costko Corporation had 50,000 shares of 6%, $10 par, cumulative preferred stock.

Required

Indicate where the preferred stock is reported in the balance sheet for each separate scenario.

a. Preferred shares are nonredeemable.

b. Preferred shares will be called in by the company on December 31 of Year 5, for a fixed price. Although not obligated to pay dividends each year, the company intends to pay the 6% dividend to the preferred shareholders over the next 5 years.

c. Preferred shares may be redeemed by shareholders at a predetermined price at any point in time.

d. Preferred shares may be called in by the company at any point in time.

Exercise 19-22
Recording Dividend
Declarations **LO5**
Hint: See Review 19-5

Following are four separate dividend scenarios.

a. On April 1, Meriter Corporation declared a cash dividend of $5 per share on its 32,000 outstanding shares of common stock ($1 par). The dividend is payable on April 21 to stockholders of record on April 14.

b. Axe Co. has issued and outstanding 1,000 shares of $100 par, cumulative, 5% preferred stock, and also 20,000 shares of $5 par common stock. Dividends are in arrears for the past year (not including the current year). On December 15, the board of directors of Axe Co. declared dividends of $25,000 to be paid to shareholders at the end of its fiscal year.

c. Siri Corp. holds 1,000 shares of Mobile Co. common stock, purchased at the beginning of the year for $30 a share (which is the carrying value on February 1). On February 1, Siri Corp. declared a property dividend of 450 shares of Mobile Co. common stock when the Mobile Co. shares were selling at $28 per share.

d. Treck Corporation declared a common stock dividend of $45,000 on April 1. Treck Corporation announced to shareholders that 70% of the dividend amount was a return of capital.

Required

Record the entry(ies) for the declaration of dividends for each of the four separate scenarios.

Exercise 19-23
Reporting Dividend
Declarations Using the
Accounting Equation
LO5

Refer to E19-22, but instead of journal entries, show the effect on the accounting equation for the transactions, including identifying the individual accounts affected, and the total impact on assets, liabilities, and stockholders' equity.

Exercise 19-24
Determining
Preferred Dividend
Distributions **LO5**

Olivia Inc. had 30,000 outstanding shares of common stock, $0.01 par, and also 8,000 outstanding shares of 7%, cumulative preferred stock, $50 par, throughout its initial four years of operations. The company declared dividends of $0, $40,000, $40,000, $40,000, in Years 1, 2, 3, and 4, respectively.

Required

a. Determine how the dividends were shared between the preferred and common shareholders in Year 2 in total and on a per share basis.

b. Determine how the dividends were shared between the preferred and common shareholders in Year 3 in total and on a per share basis.

c. Determine how the dividends were shared between the preferred and common shareholders in Year 4 in total and on a per share basis.

On November 1 of Year 2, Toni Corp. declared a cash dividend of $3 per share on its 20,000 outstanding shares of common stock ($1 par, originally sold at $10 per share). The dividend is payable on January 5 of Year 3, to its stockholders of record on December 30 of Year 2. On its declaration date, the balance in the retained earnings account was $40,000.

Exercise 19-25
Recording Liquidating
Dividends **LO5**
Hint: See Demo 19-5C

Required
a. Provide the entry for declaration of the dividend on November 1 of Year 2.
b. Provide the entry for distribution of the dividend on January 5 of Year 3.
c. Are there any issues in recording the cash dividend?

Refer to E19-25, but instead of journal entries, show the effect on the accounting equation for the transactions, including identifying the individual accounts affected, and the total impact on assets, liabilities, and stockholders' equity.

Exercise 19-26
Reporting Liquidating
Dividends Using the
Accounting Equation
LO5

The records of Dixie Corporation showed the following beginning balances on November 1. The fair value of its stock is $18 per share.

Exercise 19-27
Recording Stock
Dividends and Stock
Splits **LO6**
Hint: See Review 19-6

Common stock, $10 par, 30,000 shares outstanding	$300,000
Paid-in capital in excess of par	102,000
Retained earnings	200,000

Required
Prepare journal entries for the following six separate scenarios.

a. The company declares (November 1) and issues (November 20) a 10% stock dividend.
b. The company declares (November 1) and issues (November 20) a 10% stock dividend. Of the 3,000 stock dividend shares, 2,800 shares are whole shares and the remaining were fractional shares making up 200 equivalent whole shares. It is the company's policy to pay out fractional shares in cash.
c. The company declares (November 1) and issues (November 20) a stock split effected in the form of a 100% stock dividend.
d. The company declares (November 1) and issues (November 20) a 2-for-1 stock split. Determine the total number of shares and the par value per share after the stock split.
e. The company declares (November 1) and issues (November 20) a 5-for-1 stock split. Determine the total number of shares and the par value per share after the stock split.
f. The company declares (November 1) and issues (November 20) a 3-for-1 reverse stock split. Determine the total number of shares and the par value per share after the stock split.

Tech Inc. issues a 5% common stock dividend on 50,000 shares of $1 par common stock issued and outstanding on August 1. The market price of its common stock is $20 per share. The small stock dividend will be distributed on August 15 to stockholders of record on August 7.

Exercise 19-28
Recording Stock
Dividends, Fractional
Shares **LO6**
Hint: See Demo 19-6A

Required
a. Record the entry on (1) the date of declaration and (2) the date of distribution.
b. Assume that of the 2,500 stock dividend shares, 2,200 were whole shares and the remaining were fractional shares making up 300 equivalent whole shares. The company's policy is to pay cash to shareholders for fractional shares. Record the entry on (1) the date of declaration and (2) the date of distribution.

Refer to E19-28, but instead of journal entries, show the effect on the accounting equation for the transactions, including identifying the individual accounts affected, and the total impact on assets, liabilities, and stockholders' equity.

Exercise 19-29
Reporting Stock Dividends
with Fractional Shares
Using the Accounting
Equation **LO6**

Exercise 19-30
Reporting Impact of
Equity Transactions
**LO1, 2, 3, 4, 5,
6, 7**

Fourteen equity transactions are included in the following table.

Transaction	Paid-In Capital	Retained Earnings	Accumulated OCI	Treasury Stock	Total Stockholders' Equity	Total Assets	Total Liabilities
1. Issue common stock for cash							
2. Issue common stock for land							
3. Retire common stock from the treasury							
4. Issue preferred stock for cash							
5. Incur stock issue costs							
6. Purchase shares for the treasury							
7. Resale of treasury stock above cost . . .							
8. Declare a cash dividend							
9. Pay a previously declared cash dividend							
10. Declare a liquidating dividend.							
11. Declare a 5% stock dividend							
12. Declare stock split effected in the form of a dividend.							
13. Declare a 2-for-1 stock split							
14. Record an unrealized gain on available-for-sale debt securities							

Required

Indicate how each transaction affects each financial statement category: increase, decrease, remain unchanged, or change not determinable.

Exercise 19-31
Reporting a Stock
Split **LO6**

Starbucks Corporation disclosed the following on a recent stock split in its annual Form 10-K for the year ended September 27 of Year 5.

> **Stock Split (excerpt from Note 1)**—On April 9 of Year 5, we effected a 2-for-1 stock split of our $0.001 par value common stock for shareholders of record as of March 30 of Year 5. All share and per-share data in our consolidated financial statements and notes has been retroactively adjusted to reflect this stock split. We adjusted shareholders' equity to reflect the stock split by reclassifying an amount equal to the par value of the additional shares arising from the split from retained earnings to common stock during the second quarter of fiscal Year 5, resulting in no net impact to shareholders' equity on our consolidated balance sheets.
>
> In addition, the statement of equity for Starbucks on September 27 of Year 5 reported the following: the company increased common shares by 749.4 million shares, increased the common stock account by $0.8 million, and decreased retained earnings by $0.8 million related to this effected stock split.

Required

a. What journal entry did the company record for this effected stock split on the date of declaration?

b. What was the impact of the effected stock split on (1) the number of common shares, (2) par value per common share, (3) retained earnings, (4) paid-in capital, (5) net income, (6) stockholders' equity, and (7) market price? Indicate whether the amount increased, decreased, or did not change.

c. Answer part *b* assuming instead that the company distributed a 2-for-1 stock split.

Exercise 19-32
Calculating the
Balance in Retained
Earnings **LO1, 6, 7**

The following information is provided for Fey Corp. for the year ended December 31.

Sales.	$110,000
Cost of goods sold	45,000
General and administrative expenses	25,000
Unrealized gain on available-for-sale securities	2,000
Dividends declared and paid	12,000
Prior period adjustment, net of tax (expense understatement). . . .	2,200
Stock dividends distributed.	6,000
Treasury stock at cost.	4,000
Retained earnings, beginning balance	130,000

Required

Assuming a 25% tax rate, calculate the ending balance in retained earnings for the year ended December 31.

The following excerpts are from the annual financial statements of KPNG Inc.

Exercise 19-33
Reporting
Comprehensive
Income, Retained
Earnings, Accumulated
OCI **LO7**

Statement of Comprehensive Income For Year Ended December 31, Current Year	
Net Income...	$100,000
Other comprehensive income, net of tax	
Net unrealized holding loss on available-for-sale securities	(12,000)
Gain on pension benefit plan*........................	1,200
Other comprehensive loss	(10,800)
Comprehensive income	$ 89,200

*Note: Certain gains/losses related to pension plans are recognized as other comprehensive income.

Stockholders' Equity Section		
As of December 31	Current Year	Prior Year
Common stock	$ 1,000	$ 1,000
Paid-in capital in excess of par......................	300,000	300,000
Retained earnings	250,000	150,000
Accumulated other comprehensive income (loss)	(7,800)	3,000
Total stockholders' equity	$543,200	$454,000

Required

a. Calculate comprehensive income (loss) for the current year ended December 31. Calculate the accumulated other comprehensive income (loss) as of December 31 of the current year.

b. Prepare a reconciliation of retained earnings from December 31 of the prior year to December 31 of the current year assuming that no dividends were declared in the current year.

c. Prepare a reconciliation of accumulated other comprehensive income (loss) from December 31 of the prior year to December 31 of the current year.

Eastridge Corp. recognizes net income of $38,000 for Year 12 ending on December 31. The company's tax rate is 25%. Eastridge also reports a pretax net unrealized loss on available-for-sale debt securities of $10,000 and a pretax gain on cash flow hedges of $20,000 during Year 12. Its December 31 of Year 11 balances (all credit balances) are common stock of $10,000, paid-in capital in excess of par of $4100,000, retained earnings $112,000, and accumulated other comprehensive income of $14,500. The company paid dividends of $15,000 and had issued 1,000 shares of $1 par common stock during the current year for $45,000. Shares of common stock issued and outstanding were 10,000 on January 1 of Year 12 and 11,000 on December 31 of Year 12.

Exercise 19-34
Preparing a Statement
of Comprehensive
Income, Statement of
Stockholders' Equity,
and the Stockholders'
Equity Section of the
Balance Sheet **LO7**
Hint: See Demo 19-7

Required

a. Prepare a separate statement of comprehensive income for the current year.

b. Prepare a statement of stockholders' equity for the current year. Use a columnar format with the account types as the column titles.

c. Prepare the stockholders' equity section of the balance sheet at December 31 of the current year.

Douglas Corporation recognizes net income of $115,000 along with an other comprehensive loss of $9,000 (net of tax) for Year 3. The December 31 of Year 2 balance in accumulated other comprehensive income is $4,000 (debit balance), and the balance in retained earnings is $45,000 (credit balance).

Exercise 19-35
Preparing a Statement
of Comprehensive
Income and
Determining Ending
Balance of Accumulated
OCI **LO7**
Hint: See Review 19-7

Required

a. Prepare a statement of comprehensive income for the current year.

b. Determine the ending balance in accumulated other comprehensive income on December 31 of Year 3.

The following items are included in the statement of comprehensive income of Raft Inc.

Exercise 19-36
Analyzing Amounts
Affecting Net
Income and Other
Comprehensive
Income **LO7**

_____ a. Dividend revenue

_____ b. Unrealized loss on available-for-sale securities

_____ c. Realized loss on available-for-sale securities

_____ d. Gain on sale of short-term investments

_____ e. Gain from foreign currency translation adjustment

_____ f. Loss on disposal of equipment

_____ g. Gain on sale of discontinued operations

_____ h. Interest revenue

_____ i. Unrealized gain on available-for-sale securities

_____ j. Gain on cash flow hedge derivative instrument

_____ k. Insurance gain on casualty (fire)

Required

For each item *a* through *k*, indicate whether the amount is included in comprehensive income as (1) net income or (2) other comprehensive income. Also indicate whether the item is accumulated in (3) retained earnings or in (4) accumulated other comprehensive income.

Exercise 19-37
Computing and
Analyzing Stockholders'
Equity Ratios **LO8**
Hint: See Demo 19-8

The balance sheets for Crosby Inc. and Gretzky Inc. reflect the following.

	Crosby Inc.	Gretzky Inc.
Current liabilities.	$ 30,000	$ 30,000
Long-term liabilities	30,000	230,000
Stockholders' equity		
Common stock, $5 par	170,000	46,000
6% Preferred stock, $10 par, cumulative	50,000	20,000
Retained earnings.	60,000	30,000
Total liabilities and stockholders' equity	$340,000	$356,000
Net income, included in above retained earnings amount	$ 40,000	$ 20,000
Common stockholders' equity, prior year	225,000	90,000

Required

a. Compute the total liabilities-to-equity ratio. *HInt:* Refer to Chapter 16.
b. Compute the return on equity ratio.
c. Compute book value per share of common stock.
d. Interpret the results from parts *a*, *b*, and *c*.

Exercise 19-38
Computing
Stockholders' Equity
Ratios **LO8**
Hint: See Demo 19-8

The following information is provided for ABC Retail Inc.

Shareholders' Equity	**Dec. 31**
Preferred stock, $50 par, 4,000,000 shares authorized, 61,000 shares outstanding . . .	$ 3,050,000
Common stock, $1 par, 1,000,000 shares authorized, 800,000 shares outstanding . . .	800,000
Paid-in capital in excess of par.	200,000
Retained earnings	35,730,000
Total shareholders' equity	$39,780,000

Additional information	
Preferred dividends paid during the year	$ 240,000
Common dividends paid during the year	1,840,000
Net income for year ended December 31.	2,250,000
Average common shareholders' equity.	35,000,000
Market price per share	$ 12.50
Earnings per share.	$ 2.51

Required

a. Compute book value per share of common stock.
b. Compute the payout ratio.
c. Compute the return on equity ratio.
d. Compute price-to-earnings ratio.

Problems

Problem 19-1
Recording Equity
Journal Entries and
Reporting Stockholders'
Equity **LO1, 2, 3,
4, 5, 6**

Haywood Co. is a publicly owned company whose shares are traded on a national stock exchange. At January 1 Haywood had 50 million shares of $10 par value common stock authorized, of which 30 million shares were issued and 28 million shares were outstanding.

The stockholders' equity accounts at January 1 had the following beginning balances ($ millions).

Common stock	$300
Paid-in capital in excess of par.	160
Retained earnings	100
Treasury stock	(36)

During the year, Haywood had the following transactions.

1. On February 1, a secondary distribution of 4 million shares of $10 par value common stock was completed. The stock was issued to the public at $18 per share, net of issue costs.
2. On February 15, issued at $110 per share, 200,000 shares of $100 par value, 8% cumulative preferred stock.
3. On March 1, reacquired 40,000 shares of its common stock for $18.50 per share for the treasury.
4. On March 31, declared a semi-annual cash dividend on common stock of 10 cents per share, payable on April 30 to stockholders of record on April 10.
5. On May 31, when the market price of the common stock was $20 per share, declared a 5% stock dividend distributable on July 1 to stockholders of record on June 1.
6. On June 30, sold the 40,000 treasury shares reacquired on March 1 and an additional 560,000 treasury shares costing $11.2 million that were held at the beginning of the year. The selling price was $25 per share.
7. On September 30, declared a semi-annual cash dividend on common stock of 10 cents per share and the yearly dividend on preferred stock, both payable on October 30 to stockholders of record on October 10.
8. Net income for the year was $50.0 million.

Required

a. Provide entries for each of the transactions.
b. Provide a summary of the year-end balances of the company's stockholders' equity accounts, including preferred stock, common stock, paid-in capital in excess of par, retained earnings, and treasury stock.

The Gilmore Company had the following stockholders' equity section as of January 1.

Problem 19-2
Recording Equity
Journal Entries and
Reporting Stockholders'
Equity   **LO1, 4,
5, 6**

Stockholders' Equity

Preferred stock, $100 par, 8% cumulative, 10,000 shares issued and outstanding	$1,000,000
Common stock, $20 par, 70,000 shares issued and outstanding.	1,400,000
Paid-in capital in excess of par.	800,000
Retained earnings	3,000,000
Total stockholders' equity	$6,200,000

There are no dividends in arrears on preferred shares. During the year, the following transactions occurred.

1. Earnings during the year total $600,000.
2. The board of directors declares and distributes a cash dividend totaling $280,000 to be paid as appropriate to preferred and common shareholders.
3. To familiarize stockholders with one of the company's new products, the board declares and distributes a property dividend of one ounce of a new perfume the company produces for every share of outstanding common stock. The cost of the perfume is 60 cents per ounce, and the product has a market value of $1 per ounce. Any gain or loss on this transaction has already been recorded and is included in the earnings reported above.
4. A stock dividend of 10% is declared and distributed on common stock. The fair value of common stock is $68 per share on the date the stock dividend is declared.
5. At the end of the year, the board declares and distributes a 3-for-2 stock split of its common stock, effected in the form of a dividend. At the date of the stock split, the fair value of common stock is $75 per share.

Required

a. Prepare entries to record the transactions.
b. Prepare the stockholders' equity section as of December 31.

The following information is available for Croton Corporation at December 31.

Problem 19-3
Reporting Stockholders'
Equity   **LO1, 7, 8**

Retained earnings appropriated for bond sinking fund.	$ 40,000
Preferred stock, 6%, $100 par, 1,000 shares authorized, cumulative	90,000
Bonds payable, 7%.	200,000
Common stock, no-par, 5,000 shares authorized and outstanding	250,000
Paid-in capital in excess of par—Preferred stock	15,000
Discount on bonds payable	1,000
Retained earnings	250,000
Accumulated other comprehensive income	5,000

Required

Prepare the stockholders' equity section of the balance sheet for Croton Corporation at December 31.

Problem 19-4
Recording Stock
Issuances, Dividends,
and Retirement **LO2,**
3, 4, 5

On June 2, Aerial Corporation issued 100,000 shares of $0.01 par value common stock for $1,000,000. One share of Aerial 5% preferred stock ($5 par) was issued with every 10 shares of common stock. The market price per share for the common stock was $6, and the market price per share for the preferred stock was $50 per share.

Required

a. Record the journal entry for issuance of common and preferred stock.

b. Assume that the market price for the common stock was $8 but the market price for the preferred stock was not easily determinable because the shares are not traded publicly. Aerial also incurred stock issue costs of $7,000. Record the journal entry for the issuance of common and preferred stock. Allocate stock issue costs proportionately to the common and preferred stock accounts.

c. On June 30, Aerial declares a cash dividend of $15,000. What is the allocation between common and preferred shareholders? Record the journal entry for the dividend declaration.

d. On December 31, Aerial purchases and immediately retires 5,000 shares of common stock at $8 per share. Record the journal entry for the purchase and retirement of the 5,000 shares. Assume the stock issuance was recorded as in part a.

Problem 19-5
Correcting Entries on
Stock issuance **LO1,**
2, 3, 5

Woods Corporation was organized on January 1 of Year 1 and began operations immediately.

- For Year 1 through Year 3, the company incorrectly presented an annual balance sheet that reported only one amount for stockholders' equity: Year 1, $137,700; Year 2, $156,600; and Year 3, $185,000.

- Its condensed income statement reported: Year 1, net loss of $17,500; Year 2, net income of $12,000; and Year 3, net income of $40,930 (cumulative earnings of $35,430).

- Given cumulative earnings of $35,430, the president recommended to the board of directors that a cash dividend of $35,000 be declared and paid in January of Year 4.

- An outside director on the board objects to the dividend on the basis that the company's financial statements contain significant errors (and there has never been an audit).

Assume we are engaged to clarify the situation. The single stockholders' equity account of the company follows.

Stockholders' Equity			
Year 1 Stock issue cost	1,300	160,000	Year 1 Common stock, $5 par, 20,000 shares issued
Year 1 Net loss	17,500		
Year 2 Bought 100 shares of company stock from stockholder Adams	700	22,000	Year 2 Net income (including $10,000 land write-up to appraisal value)
Depreciation expense* Year 1, $1,500; Year 2, $1,700; Year 3, $2,300	5,500	1,800	Year 2 Common stock, 200 shares issued
Cash Over and Short* Year 1, $2,000; Year 2; $2,500; Year 3, $500	5,000	270	Year 3 Sold 30 of the shares bought from Adams
Year 3 Cash loan to the company president	10,000	40,930	Year 3 Net income
	40,000	225,000	

* Recorded as expense but not shown on income statement.

Required

a. Determine the December 31 balance in Retained Earnings for Year 1, Year 2, and Year 3. Assume that the amounts are found to be arithmetically accurate and that there is no change in income tax. What amount of retained earnings is available to support a cash dividend at the end of Year 3?

b. Based on calculations in part a, prepare journal entries for declaration and later payment of the cash dividend.

c. What entry, prior to the dividend entries in part b, is necessary to reclassify amounts from the single stockholders' equity account to separate equity accounts? *Note:* Reclassify amounts through a single entry.

Problem 19-6
Recording
Treasury Stock
Transactions **LO1, 3**

Han Tire Corporation has outstanding 10,000 shares of preferred stock, $10 par, and also 10,000 shares of no-par common stock sold initially for $20 per share. Paid-in capital in excess of par on the preferred stock is $40,000. The retained earnings balance is $81,600.

The company then enters into the following transactions during the year.

Jan. 15   Purchased 500 shares of its common stock at $30 per share for the treasury.
Mar. 1   Sold 100 shares of the common treasury stock for $26 per share.
Oct. 15   Sold 50 shares of the common treasury stock for $32 per share.
Dec. 31   Sold 50 shares of the common treasury stock for $29 per share.

Required

a. Provide entries to record the treasury stock transactions.

b. Prepare the stockholders' equity section of the balance sheet after these transactions are recorded.

At January 1, the records of Frazer Corporation showed the following.

Problem 19-7
Recording, Reporting
Treasury Stock
Transactions **LO1,
2, 3, 8**

Common stock, $10 par, 60,000 shares outstanding..........	$600,000
Paid-in capital in excess of par..........................	240,000
Retained earnings	160,000

During the year, the following transactions affecting shareholders' equity occurred.

- On January 15, purchased 1,000 shares of common stock for the treasury at $20 per share.
- On March 1, purchased 1,000 shares of common stock for the treasury at $22 per share.
- On June 30, sold 1,200 shares of treasury stock at $25.

State law places a restriction on retained earnings where it must be equal to or greater than the cost of treasury stock held. Net income for the year was $45,000.

Required
a. Provide entries for each of the three transactions. Assume a FIFO flow for treasury stock.
b. Provide the entry to close net income to retained earnings.
c. Determine the ending balance for each capital account, including common stock, paid-in capital in excess of par, retained earnings, and treasury stock.
d. Prepare the required disclosure note, if any, related to the treasury stock.
e. Provide the journal entry on January 15 assuming instead that the company purchased and immediately retired the 1,000 shares of common stock at $20 per share.
f. Repeat part a but instead assume a weighted average flow for treasury stock.

The records of Palmer Corporation showed the following at the beginning of the year.

Problem 19-8
Determining Dividend
Preferences **LO5**

Preferred stock, 6% cumulative, nonparticipating, $20 par	$200,000
Common stock, no-par value, 50,000 shares issued and outstanding....	240,000
Paid-in capital in excess of par—Preferred stock	30,000
Retained earnings	125,000
Investment in stock of Ace Corporation (500 shares)................	30,000
Preferred stock has dividends in arrears for two prior years	

On January 15, the board of directors approved the following resolution:

> The dividend, to stockholders of record on February 1, shall be 6% on the preferred stock and $1.00 per share on the common stock; the dividends in arrears are to be paid on March 1 by issuing a property dividend using the requisite amount of Ace Corporation stock. All current dividends are to be paid in cash on March 1.

On January 15, the stock of Ace Corporation was selling at $60 per share; on February 1 at $61 per share; and on March 1 at $62 per share.

Required
a. Compute the dividends to be distributed to each class of stockholders, including the number of shares of Ace Corporation stock and the cash required by the declaration. Assume that divisibility of the shares of Ace Corporation poses no problem.
b. Provide journal entries to record the dividend declaration on January 15, and its subsequent payment on March 1.

Bailey Corporation has the following stockholders' equity account balances.

Problem 19-9
Recording and
Reporting Stock
Dividends and Stock
Splits **LO1, 6**

Common stock, $12 par, 20,000 shares outstanding...........	$240,000
Paid-in capital in excess of par..........................	70,000
Retained earnings	500,000
Total stockholders' equity	$810,000

The corporation will triple the number of shares currently outstanding (to 60,000 shares) by taking one of the following separate actions.

1. Issue a 200% stock dividend (40,000 additional shares) and capitalize retained earnings on the basis of par value.
2. Issue a stock split (3-for-1 stock split; where three new shares are issued for each old share) by changing par value per share proportionately.

Required

a. Provide the journal entry that should be made for each alternative action.

b. Complete the following schedule that compares the effects of the two alternative actions.

Item	Before Change	Option One	Option Two
Number of shares outstanding			
Par value per share			
Common stock			
Paid-in capital in excess of par			
Total paid-in capital			
Retained earnings			
Total stockholders' equity			

Problem 19-10
Preparing Income
Statement, Retained
Earnings **LO1, 8**

The following annual data were taken from the records of Baker Corporation at December 31.

Sales revenue.	$450,000
Cost of goods sold	230,000
General and administrative expenses	85,000
Gain on sale of equipment	30,000
Stock dividend issued.	80,000
Cash dividend declared and paid	25,000
Correction of accounting error involving understatement of	
depreciation expense from prior period (net of tax)	8,000
Current restriction for bond sinking fund.	10,000
Current appropriation for plant expansion	40,000

Assume an income tax rate of 25% on all items except the prior period adjustment. The following beginning of year balances are also reported.

	Jan. 1
Retained earnings, unappropriated	$120,000 Cr.
Retained earnings, restricted for bond sinking fund	20,000 Cr.
Retained earnings, appropriated for plant expansion	60,000 Cr.

Required

a. Prepare a single-step income statement for the year ended December 31. Disregard EPS.

b. Prepare a statement of retained earnings, reconciling the January 1 Total retained earnings balance to the December 31 Total retained earnings balance.

c. Prepare a disclosure that reconciles each of the three retained earnings amounts (Unappropriated, Restricted for bond sinking fund, and Appropriate for plant expansion) from the January 1 balance to the December 31 balance.

Problem 19-11
Analyzing an
Equity
Financial
Statement
**LO1, 2,
3, 7**

Following is an excerpt from the Fastenal Company's Form 10-K.

	Common Stock		Additional Paid-In Capital	Retained Earnings	Accumulated Other Comprehensive Income (Loss)	Total Stockholders' Equity
Consolidated Statements of Stockholders' Equity (in thousands)	**Shares**	**Amount**				
Balance as of December 31, Year 4	295,868	$2,959	$33,744	$1,886,350	$ (7,836)	$1,915,217
Dividends paid in cash	—	—	—	(327,101)	—	(327,101)
Purchases of common stock.	(7,100)	(71)	(60,042)	(232,838)	—	(292,951)
Stock options exercised	814	8	19,091	—	—	19,099
Stock-based compensation.	—	—	5,841	—	—	5,841
Excess tax benefits from stock-based compensation. . .	—	—	3,390	—	—	3,390
Net earnings	—	—	—	516,361	—	516,361
Other comprehensive income (loss)	—	—	—	—	(38,567)	(38,567)
Balance as of December 31, Year 5	289,582	$2,896	$ 2,024	$1,842,772	$(46,403)	$1,801,289

Required

a. What types of capital stock have been issued? What is the par value per share?

b. What is (1) net income, (2) other comprehensive income, and (3) total comprehensive income, for the year ended December 31 of Year 5?

c. What three activities in Year 5 are indicated by the change in the retained earnings account?

On November 1, the board of directors of Jax Mining Company declared the maximum cash dividend permitted by state law. The company had never declared a dividend before. There were 100 stockholders, each holding 400 shares of stock with a par value of $5 per share. The laws of the state provide that:

Problem 19-12
Reporting Stockholders'
Equity Including
Disclosures   **LO5, 8**

> Dividends may be paid equal to all accumulated profits prior to the recorded depletion expense.

Retained earnings showed a correct balance of $120,000; and depletion for the year was $24,000 (accumulated depletion was $40,000). The dividend was paid 60 days after the declaration date on January 31.

Required
a. Provide entries for the dividend declaration on November 1, and the dividend payment on January 31.
b. What note disclosure regarding the nature of the dividend, if any, should be reported to stockholders?
c. What items related to the dividend declaration are reported on the balance sheet dated December 31, assuming net income for the year of $15,000 (included in the $60,000 balance of retained earnings)? Prepare any note that may be needed to fully disclose the dividend.

Accounting Decisions and Judgments

Real World Analysis In its Year 5 annual report, **General Dynamics Corporation** showed the following regarding stockholders' equity.

AD&J19-1
Analyzing a Statement
of Stockholders'
Equity **LO1, 8**

| | Consolidated Statements of Shareholders' Equity | | | | | |
| | Common Stock | | | | Accumulated Other | Total |
$ millions	Par	Surplus	Retained Earnings	Treasury Stock	Comprehensive Loss	Shareholders' Equity
December 31, Year 4	$482	$2,548	$21,127	$ (9,396)	$(2,932)	$11,829
Net earnings	—	—	2,965	—	—	2,965
Cash dividends declared	—	—	(888)	—	—	(888)
Equity-based awards	—	182	—	237	—	419
Shares purchased	—	—	—	(3,233)	—	(3,233)
Other comprehensive loss . . .	—	—	—	—	(354)	(354)
December 31, Year 5	$482	$2,730	$23,204	$(12,392)	$(3,286)	$10,738

On December 31 of Year 5, we had 481,880,634 shares of common stock issued and 312,987,277 shares of common stock outstanding, including unvested restricted stock of 1,391,275 shares. On December 31 of Year 4, we had 481,880,634 shares of common stock issued and 332,164,097 shares of common stock outstanding. We repurchased 22.8 million of our outstanding shares for $3.2 billion in Year 5.

Required
a. What appears to be the par value, if any, of General Dynamics Corporation common stock? What amount was paid for purchases of stock for the treasury? What was the average price paid per share for these treasury shares?
b. What is the book value per common share of General Dynamics at December 31 of Year 4? At December 31 of Year 5?
c. At December 31 of Year 5, General Dynamics common stock had a market price of $136.36 per share. Briefly discuss why investors might pay so much, relative to the company's book value per share, for General Dynamics Corporation common stock.
d. How does the amount paid for treasury shares calculated in part a differ from the market price at December 31 of Year 5, included in part c?

Real World Analysis **Unocal** is the parent company of Union Oil, a fully integrated energy resources company. In its Year 5 annual report, Unocal showed the following regarding stockholders' equity.

AD&J19-2
Analyzing
Preferred Stock
Dividends **LO4, 5**

December 31 ($ millions)	Year 5	Year 4
Stockholders' equity		
Preferred stock, $0.10 par value; stated at liquidation value of $50 per share		
Shares authorized: 100,000,000		
Shares outstanding: 10,250,000 in Year 5 and Year 4	$513	$513
Common stock, $1 par value		
Shares authorized: 750,000,000		
Shares outstanding: 247,310,376 in Year 5; 244,198,701 in Year 4	247	244
Capital in excess of par value	319	237

In notes to financial statements, the following is provided regarding preferred stock.

Preferred Stock—The company has authorized 100,000,000 shares of preferred stock with a par value of $0.10 per share. In July of Year 2, the company issued 10,250,000 shares of $3.50 convertible preferred stock. The convertible preferred stock is redeemable on and after July 15, Year 6, in whole or in part, at the option of the company, at a redemption price of $52.10 per share declining to $50 per share on and after July 15, Year 12, together with accumulated but unpaid dividends. The convertible preferred stock has a liquidation value of $50 per share and is convertible at the option of the holder into common stock of the company at a conversion price of $30.75 per share, subject to adjustment in certain events. Dividends on the preferred stock at an annual rate of $3.50 per share are cumulative and are payable quarterly in arrears, when and as declared by Unocal's Board of Directors (the Board). Holders of the preferred stock have no voting rights. However, there are certain exceptions, including the right to elect two additional directors if the equivalent of six quarterly dividends payable on the preferred stock are in default.

Required

a. Suppose Unocal decides to redeem the outstanding preferred stock on July 15 of Year 6. Show the entry to record the transaction. Assume that dividends for the quarter ending June 30 of Year 6 have not been paid and that the shares were originally issued at their liquidation value.

b. Assume all preferred stock is converted to common stock on January 1 of Year 6. Show the entry to record this transaction. Assume that the shares were originally issued at their liquidation value.

c. Suppose that Unocal does *not* declare and pay the preferred dividends for Year 11 and the first half of Year 12. On July 15 of Year 12, Unocal calls and redeems the preferred stock. Show the entry to record this redemption.

AD&J19-3
Analyzing Preferred
Stock **LO4**

Real World Analysis **Con Ed** is a large public utility company. Similar to many other public utilities, Con Ed uses preferred stock for a portion of its financing. In its Year 5 annual report, Con Ed provided the following schedule regarding its capitalization.

Consolidated Statement of Capitalization Consolidated Edison Company of New York, Inc.				
	Shares Outstanding			
At December 31 ($ in thousands)	Year 5	Year 4	Year 5	Year 4
Common shareholders' equity (Note B)				
Common stock, $2.50 par value, authorized 340,000,000 shares	234,956,299	234,905,235	$1,464,305	$1,463,913
Retained earnings			4,097,305	3,888,010
Capital stock expense.			(38,606)	(38,926)
Total common shareholders' equity			$5,522,734	$5,312,997
Preferred stock (Note B)				
Subject to mandatory redemption				
Cumulative Preferred, $100 par value,				
7.20% Series I.	500,000	500,000	$ 50,000	$ 50,000
6 1/8 % Series J	500,000	500,000	50,000	50,000
Total subject to mandatory redemption			100,000	100,000
Other preferred stock				
$5 Cumulative Preferred, without par value, authorized 1,915,319 shares . . .	1,915,319	1,915,319	175,000	175,000
Cumulative Preferred, $100 par value authorized 6,000,000 shares*				
5 3/4% Series A	600,000	600,000	$ 60,000	$ 60,000
5 1/4 % Series B	750,000	750,000	75,000	75,000
4.65% Series C.	600,000	600,000	60,000	60,000
4.65% Series D.	750,000	750,000	75,000	75,000
5 3/4% Series E	500,000	500,000	50,000	50,000
6.20% Series F.	400,000	400,000	40,000	40,000
Cumulative Preference, $100 par value, authorized 2,250,000 shares 6%				
Convertible Series B.	49,174	53,102	4,917	5,310
Total other preferred stock			539,917	540,310
Total preferred stock.			$639,917	$640,310

* Represents total authorized shares of cumulative preferred stock, $100 par value, including preferred stock subject to mandatory redemption.

In notes to the financial statements, Con Ed provides the following information regarding its preferred stock.

Note B Capitalization—Common Stock and Preferred Stock Not Subject to Mandatory Redemption   Each share of Series B preference stock is convertible into 13 shares of common stock at a conversion price of $7.69 per share. During Year 5, Year 4, and Year 3, 1,993, 3,928 shares, 4,176 shares, and 5,208 shares of Series B preference stock were converted into 51,064 shares, 54,288 shares, and 67,704 shares of common stock, respectively.

     At December 31 of Year 5, 639,262 shares of unissued common stock were reserved for conversion of preference stock. The preference stock is subordinate to the $5 Cumulative Preferred Stock and Cumulative Preferred Stock with respect to dividends and liquidation rights.

     Redemption prices of preferred stock other than Series I and Series J (in each case, plus accrued dividends) are as follows:

$5 Cumulative Preferred Stock.	$105.00
Cumulative Preferred Stock	
Series A	$102.00
Series B	102.00
Series C	101.00
Series D	101.00
Series E	101.00
Series F.	102.50
Cumulative Preference Stock	
6% Convertible Series B.	$100.00

Preferred Stock Subject to Mandatory Redemption   The Company is required to redeem 25,000 of the Series I shares on May 1 of each year in the five-year period commencing with Year 12 and to redeem the remaining Series I shares on May 1 of Year 17. The Company is required to redeem the Series J shares on August of Year 12. In each case, the redemption price is $100 per share plus accrued and unpaid dividends to the redemption date. In addition, the Company may redeem Series I shares at a redemption price of $105.04 per share, plus accrued dividends, if redeemed prior to May 1 of Year 6 (and thereafter at prices declining annually to $100 per share, plus accrued dividends, after April 30 of Year 12); provided, however, that prior to May 1 of Year 7, the Company may not redeem any Series I shares with borrowed funds or proceeds from certain securities issuances having a cost to the Company of less than 7.20% per annum.

Required

a.   Outline the preference differences between the various types of preferred stock issued by Con Ed. Which of these issues is most like a debt issue? Which is most like a common equity issue? Explain.

b.   What were the proceeds per share for the preferred stock identified as $5 Cumulative Preferred, without par value? What were the proceeds per share for each of the Cumulative Preferred, $100 par value series (A through F)?

c.   Show the entry Con Ed would make if it elects to redeem the entire Series I preferred stock on April 30 of Year 6. Assume all preferred dividends are paid as of April 30.

d.   If Con Ed had not redeemed the preferred stock as stated in part c, show the entry Con Ed would make on May 1 of Year 12, for mandatory redemption of its Series I Cumulative Preferred Stock.

e.   Suppose that during Year 6, a total of 5,000 shares of the 6% Convertible Series B preference stock is tendered to the company for conversion into common stock. Provide the entry to record this transaction.

Real World Analysis   **T. Rowe Price's (TRP)** primary business is providing investment information services to Price Funds and individual private accounts. The Year 5 annual report for the company included the following Consolidated Statement of Stockholders' Equity.

AD&J19-4
Analyzing Common
Stock and Repurchased
Stock   **LO2, 3, 6**

$ thousands	Common Stock Shares	Common Stock Par Value	Capital in Excess of Par Value	Retained Earnings	Accumulated Other Comprehensive Income	Total Stockholders' Equity
Balance at December 31, Year 2	14,429,315	$2,886	$1,171	$150,141		$154,198
Common stock issued under						
stock-based compensation plans	254,629	51	2,963			3,014
2-for-1 stock split	14,491,095	2,898	(1,997)	(901)		
Purchases of common stock	(80,000)	(16)	(940)	(1,295)		(2,251)
Net income				48,539		48,539
Dividends declared.				(12,892)		(12,892)
Unrealized security holding gains.					$ 5,345	5,345
Balance at December 31, Year 3	29,095,039	5,819	1,197	183,592	5,345	195,953

continued

continued from previous page

$ thousands	Common Stock		Capital in Excess of Par Value	Retained Earnings	Accumulated Other Comprehensive Income	Total Stockholders' Equity
	Shares	Par Value				
Common stock issued under						
stock-based compensation plans	366,880	74	4,277			4,351
Purchases of common stock	(892,500)	(179)	(3,539)	(22,831)		(26,549)
Net income				61,151		61,151
Dividends declared.				(15,876)		(15,876)
Decrease in unrealized security holding gains . . .					(2,791)	(2,791)
Balance at December 31, Year 4	**28,569,419**	**5,714**	**1,935**	**206,036**	**2,554**	**216,239**
Common stock issued under						
stock-based compensation plans	465,553	93	5,555	(2)		5,646
Purchases of common stock	(369,500)	(74)	(4,578)	(8,789)		(13,441)
Net income				75,409		75,409
Dividends declared.				(19,720)		(19,720)
Increase in unrealized security holding gains. . . .					10,099	10,099
Balance at December 31, Year 5	**28,665,472**	**$5,733**	**$2,912**	**$252,934**	**$12,653**	**$274,232**

Required

a. From the information provided at December 31 of Year 2, estimate the par value of a share of common stock on that date. From the information provided at December 31 of Year 3, estimate the par value of a share of common stock on that date. Did TRP really split the par value of its shares two for one?

b. When TRP purchases common stock, is it held as treasury stock or as retired stock? If as treasury stock, is TRP using the cost method or the par value method or some variation of one of these methods for accounting for treasury stock? *Hint:* The par value method treats treasury stock as if it had been retired.

c. Determine the average price per share TRP paid for common stock repurchased during Year 5. Determine the average price per share TRP received for common stock issued under the stock-based compensation plans.

d. On December 31 of Year 5, TRP common stock had a market price of $48 per share. What is the company's total fair value on this date? What is the company's net book value on this date? Why do these two amounts differ?

AD&J19-5
Analyzing Stockholders'
Equity **LO1, 2, 3, 8**

Real World Analysis **Gtech Holdings Corporation** is a technology and communications services company. Its consolidated statement of shareholders' equity provides the following information.

$ thousands	Common Stock		Additional Paid-In Capital	Other	Retained Earnings	Treasury Stock	Total
	Shares	Par Value					
Balance at February 29, Year 2	36,293,642	$363	$31,570	$(6,783)	$ 5,595	$(30)	$ 30,715
Purchase of 73,463 shares of common stock				(113)		(113)	(113)
Common stock issued	5,900,000	59	90,294				90,353
Common stock issued under stock award plans . . .	765,867	8	8,747				8,755
Tax benefit from stock compensation			17,467				17,467
Net income					21,694		21,694
Foreign currency translation				(816)			(816)
Balance at February 27, Year 3	42,959,509	$430	$148,078	$(7,599)	$27,289	$(143)	$168,055

Required

a. What is the par value of Gtech common stock?

b. Record the entry for the issuance of 5,900,000 shares of stock in Year 3.

c. What is the book value per share of Gtech at February 29 of Year 2, assuming shares in the treasury total 40,090 shares? At February 27 of Year 3? Explain why book value per share changed so much from February 29 of Year 2, to February 27 of Year 3.

d. What was the average price per share paid for common shares acquired during the year ending February 27 of Year 3? What were the average proceeds per share for shares issued, other than those issued under stock award plans, during the year ending February 27 of Year 3? List any possible reasons why these amounts might significantly differ.

Real World Analysis The following information is included in the consolidated statement of equity for **Starbucks Corporation** in a recent Form 10-K.

AD&J19-6
Analyzing Stockholders'
Equity **LO1, 2, 8**

STARBUCKS CORPORATION
CONSOLIDATED STATEMENTS OF EQUITY

in millions, except per share data	Common Stock Shares	Amount	Additional Paid-In Capital	Retained Earnings	Accumulated Other Comprehensive Income/(Loss)	Shareholders' Equity
Balance, September 28, Year 4	749.5	$0.7	$ 39.4	$5,206.6	$ 25.3	$5,272.0
Net earnings......................	—	—	—	2,757.4	—	2,757.4
Other comprehensive income/(loss).............					(193.6)	(193.6)
Stock-based compensation expense	—	—	211.7	—	—	211.7
Exercise of stock options/vesting of RSUs, including tax benefit of $131.3	14.6	—	224.4	—	—	224.4
Sale of common stock, including tax benefit of $0.2 ...	0.6	—	23.5	—	—	23.5
Repurchase of common stock	(29.0)	—	(459.6)	(972.2)	—	(1,431.8)
Cash dividends declared, $0.680 per share........	—	—	—	(1,016.2)	—	(1,016.2)
Two-for-one stock split	749.4	0.8	—	(0.8)	—	—
Purchase of noncontrolling interest	—	—	1.7		(31.1)	(29.4)
Balance, September 27, Year 5	1,485.1	$1.5	$ 41.1	$5,974.8	$(199.4)	$5,818.0

Required

a. Does Starbucks have a par value for its common stock that can be determined from the information provided? If so, what is it?

b. Ignoring the tax benefit, record the entry for the sale of common stock during fiscal Year 5. Assume that the par value per common share is $0.001. What was the average price per share for which this stock was sold?

c. Compute Starbucks's book value per share at September 27 of Year 5, assuming that the number of outstanding shares is 1,499.1 million. What is the relation between the stock trading price at September 27 of Year 5, of $57.99 per share and its book value? What factors might explain this difference?

Real World Analysis Consider the following excerpt from a Year 10 Form 10-K of **Bank of America Corporation**.

AD&J19-7
Analyzing
Stockholders' Equity
Disclosure **LO4, 8**

Note 13—Shareholders' Equity (excerpt)

Series: Series L
Description: 7.25% Non-Cumulative Perpetual Convertible
Initial Issuance date: January of Year 3

Total Shares Outstanding: 3,080,182
Liquidation preference per share: $1,000
Carrying value: $3,080,000,000

The 7.25% Non-Cumulative Perpetual Convertible Preferred Stock, Series L (Series L Preferred Stock) listed in the Preferred Stock Summary table does not have early redemption/call rights. Each share of the Series L Preferred Stock may be converted at any time, at the option of the holder, into 20 shares of the Corporation's common stock plus cash in lieu of fractional shares. The Corporation may cause some or all of the Series L Preferred Stock, at its option, at any time or from time to time, to be converted into shares of common stock at the then-applicable conversion rate if, for 20 trading days during any period of 30 consecutive trading days, the closing price of common stock exceeds 130 percent of the then-applicable conversion price of the Series L Preferred Stock. If a conversion of Series L Preferred Stock occurs at the option of the holder, subsequent to a dividend record date but prior to the dividend payment date, the Corporation will still pay any accrued dividends payable. All series of preferred stock in the Preferred Stock Summary table have a par value of $0.01 per share, are not subject to the operation of a sinking fund, have no participation rights ... All outstanding series of preferred stock of the Corporation have preference over the Corporation's common stock with respect to the payment of dividends and distribution of the Corporation's assets in the event of a liquidation or dissolution.

Required
Complete the following table by identifying the relevant disclosure from the financial statement excerpt of Bank of America, related to the disclosure requirement listed.

Disclosure Requirements	Relevant Disclosure for Bank of America
a. Par value	
b. Number of shares outstanding	
c. Liquidation preference	
d. Dividend preferences	
e. Dividends in arrears	
f. Call prices and dates	
g. Sinking fund requirements	
h. Conversion rates	
i. Contingent conversion terms	

AD&J19-8
Determining
Participating
Preferred Dividend
Distributions **LO4, 5**

Challenge Problem Alexa Inc. has the following capital structure.

Common stock, $10 par, 6,000 shares issued and outstanding.	$60,000
6% Preferred stock, $100 par, 200 shares issued and outstanding . . .	20,000

Required

Alexa declared a cash dividend distribution of $20,000. Calculate the allocation of dividends between preferred and common shareholders under the following separate scenarios.

a. Preferred stock is cumulative and nonparticipating. Dividends are in arrears for the preceding year.
b. Preferred stock is noncumulative and fully participating.
c. Preferred stock is cumulative and fully participating. Dividends for the preferred stock are in arrears for the preceding two years.

AD&J19-9
Analyzing
Preferred Dividend
Disclosure **LO4, 5**

Real World Analysis Following is an excerpt from a recent Form 10-K of **Pandora Media Inc.** on its redeemable preferred stock.

In June of Year 7, we entered into an agreement with Sirius XM Radio, Inc. ("Sirius XM") to sell 480,000 shares of Series A for $1,000 per share, with gross proceeds of $480.0 million. The Series A shares were issued in two rounds: an initial closing of 172,500 shares for $172.5 million that occurred on June 9 of Year 7 upon signing the agreement with Sirius XM, and an additional closing of 307,500 shares for $307.5 million that occurred on September 22 of Year 7. In the year ended December 31 of Year 7, total proceeds from the initial and additional closing, net of preferred stock issuance costs of $29.3 million, was $450.7 million.

Conversion Feature. Holders of the Series A shares have the option to convert their shares plus any accrued dividends into common stock. We have the right to settle the conversion in cash, common stock, or a combination thereof. The conversion rate for the Series A is initially 95.2381 shares of common stock per each share of Series A, which is equivalent to an initial conversion price of approximately $10.50 per share of our common stock, and is subject to adjustment in certain circumstances. Dividends on the Series A will accrue on a daily basis, whether or not declared, and will be payable on a quarterly basis at a rate of 6% per year. We have the option to pay dividends in cash when authorized by the Board and declared by the Company or accumulate dividends in lieu of paying cash. Dividends accumulated in lieu of paying cash will continue to accrue and accumulate at rate of 6% per year.

Redemption Feature. As of December 31 of Year 7, there is no ability to redeem or require redemption of the Series A. Under certain circumstances, we will have the right to redeem the Series A on or after September 22 of Year 10. The Series A holders will have the right to require us to redeem the Series A on or after September 22 of Year 12. Any optional redemption of the Series A will be at a redemption price equal to 100% of the liquidation preference, or $1,000 per share, plus accrued and unpaid dividends to, but excluding, the redemption date. In the event of a future redemption, whether initiated by us or by the holders, we will have the option to redeem the Series A in cash, common stock or a combination thereof.

Required

a. Would we expect the redeemable preferred stock to be presented on the balance sheet as a liability or as equity?
b. Provide the summary entry for the issuance of the Series A redeemable stock in Year 7, assuming that the preferred stock has a par value of $0.0001 per share. Indicate how the stock issue costs affect the journal entry.
c. Provide the entry if 100,000 shares of Series A preferred stock were converted to common stock, assuming that the common stock has a par value of $0.001 per share.
d. Determine the amount of dividends that would be in arrears for a full year, assuming no dividend declaration, no change in the number of preferred shares outstanding, and that the dividend rate applies to the net preferred stock proceeds (not the par value).

Communication Case Arguments are made that treasury stock is an asset because it is purchased, owned, and paid for in cash like any other asset. Also, as with other assets, it can be sold for cash at any time in an established market. One possible conclusion is that because treasury stock has the overriding attributes of an asset, it should be reported and classified on the balance sheet as an asset.

AD&J19-10
Classifying Treasury
Stock **LO3**

Required

a. Assuming that we have no GAAP constraints to consider, explain in a memo how we believe treasury stock should be classified and why.

b. Assume that the issuing company has a bond sinking fund being accumulated to retire outstanding bonds payable at maturity date. It is administered by an independent outside trustee in accordance with the bond agreement. Assume that the sinking fund investments include stock of the issuing company. How should that particular stock be classified? Explain the basis for that conclusion.

Communication Case C. Banfield, an engineer, developed a special safety device to be installed in backyard swimming pools; when turned on, it would set off an alarm if anything fell into the water. Over a two-year period, Banfield's spare time was spent developing and testing the device. After receiving a patent, three of Banfield's friends, including an attorney, considered plans to produce and market the device. Accordingly, a charter was obtained, which authorized 200,000 shares of $10 par value stock. Each of the four organizers contributed $20,000, and each received in return 2,000 shares of stock. They also agree that for other consideration, each would receive 5,000 additional shares. The remaining shares were to be held as unissued stock. Each organizer made a proposal concerning how the additional 5,000 shares would be paid for. These individual proposals were made independently; then the group considered them as a package. The four proposals were:

AD&J19-11
Issuing Capital
Stock **LO2**

Banfield: Patent would be turned over to the corporation as payment for the 5,000 shares. An independent appraisal of the patent could not be obtained.

Attorney: 1,000 shares would be received for legal services already rendered during organization, 1,000 shares would be received as advance payment for legal retainer fees for the next three years, and the balance would be paid for in cash at par.

Friend #2: A small building, suitable for operations, would be given to the corporation for the 5,000 shares of stock. It was estimated that $20,000 would be needed for renovation prior to use. The owner estimates that the fair value of the building is $750,000, and there is a $580,000 loan on it to be assumed by the corporation.

Friend #3: To pay $10,000 cash on the stock and to give a 12% (the going rate) interest-bearing note for the total price of $40,000 (subscriptions receivable) to be paid out of dividends over the next five years.

Required

a. How would each of the above proposals be recorded? Assess the valuation basis for each, including alternatives.

b. What are your recommendations for an agreement that would be equitable to each organizer? Explain the basis for such recommendations.

Communication Case Onray Corporation reported the following items on its balance sheet dated December 31 of Year 1.

AD&J19-12
Analyzing Preferred
Stock: Equity versus
Debt **LO4**

Liabilities	
Long-term note payable, 12% interest payable each June 30 and December 31	
(maturity date December 31 of Year 6)	$ 500,000
Stockholders' equity	
Common stock, no-par	6,000,000
Preferred stock, $100 par, nonvoting, 9% cumulative, nonparticipating,	
and mandatory redemption at par no later than December 31 of Year 6;	
4,000 shares authorized and outstanding	400,000
Retained earnings.	800,000

Required

Evaluate the reporting classifications applied by Onray. Did Onray violate current GAAP? Explain.

Communication Case Ellis Corporation purchased equipment (cash price of $144,000) for $107,000 cash and a promise to deliver an indeterminate number of shares of its $5 par common stock, with a fair value of $15,000, on January 1 of each year for the next four years. Hence, $60,000 in fair value of shares will be required to discharge the $37,000 balance due on the equipment.

AD&J19-13
Analyzing
Treasury Stock
Transactions **LO3**

The corporation then acquired 5,000 shares of its own stock (which became treasury shares) in the expectation that the fair value of the stock would increase substantially before the delivery date.

Required

a. Discuss the propriety of recording the equipment at the following values.
  1. $107,000 (the cash payment).
  2. $144,000 (the cash price of the equipment).
  3. $167,000 (the $107,000 cash payment plus the $60,000 fair value of treasury stock that must be transferred to the vendor to settle the obligation per the agreement). Assume an ordinary annuity.

b. Discuss the arguments for treating the balance due as:
  1. A liability.
  2. Treasury stock subscribed. *Hint:* To subscribe treasury stock, we debit Subscriptions Receivable (contra equity account) and credit paid-in capital accounts.

c. Assuming that legal requirements do not affect the decisions, discuss the arguments for treating the corporation's treasury shares as follows:
  1. An asset awaiting ultimate disposition.
  2. A capital element awaiting ultimate disposition.

AICPA Adapted

AD&J19-14
Analyzing Use of Debt and Equity Securities to Purchase an Asset **LO3**

Judgment Case On January 1, Crefax Corporation purchased a tract of land, for long-term use as a possible future plant site, in exchange for $50,000 cash plus a five-year note with no interest, even though the current interest for similar debt is 15%. The note is to be paid in $20,000 annual amounts; the first $20,000 is due one year from the date of the land purchase, and the last $20,000 is due at the end of five years. The note also specifies (quite unusually) that instead of being payable in cash, each $20,000 annual amount is to be settled by issuance of 20,000 shares of Crefax common stock, $1 par, to the holder of the note. On the date land was purchased, the fair value of the stock set aside to be issued on the five dates by Crefax Corporation was $180,000.

Required

a. Prepare and explain the basis for the journal entry that Crefax should make on January 1.
b. Prepare and explain the basis for the entry(ies) that Crefax should make on December 31.
c. Explain how the following items should be reported on the financial statements of Crefax Corporation: (1) interest expense, (2) land, (3) debt, and (4) paid-in capital.

AD&J19-15
Determining Whether to Declare a Dividend **LO5**

Judgment Case Drake Company was started in Year 1 to manufacture a wide range of plastic products from three basic components. The company was originally owned by 23 stockholders; however, late in Year 11, the capital structure was expanded considerably, at which time preferred stock was issued. The preferred is nonvoting, cumulative, nonparticipating, 6% stock. The company has experienced a substantial growth in business over the years. This growth was due to two principal factors: (a) the dynamic management and (b) the geographical location. The company served a rapidly expanding area with relatively few regionally situated competitors.

The December 31 of Year 16 audited balance sheet showed the following (summarized):

Cash..........................	$ 11,000	Current liabilities........................	$ 38,000
Other current assets............	76,000	Long-term notes payable	60,000
Investment in Kile Co. stock	30,000	Preferred stock, $100 par, 500 shares*	50,000
Plant and equipment (net)	310,000	Common stock, $15 par, 10,000 shares*	150,000
Intangible assets...............	15,000	Premium on preferred stock	2,000
Other assets..................	8,000	Retained earnings	25,000
		Profits invested in plant.................	125,000
Total assets..................	$450,000	Total liabilities and equity	$450,000

*Authorized shares—preferred, 2,000; common, 20,000.

The board of directors has not declared any dividends since organization. Instead, profits were used to expand the company. This decision was based on the fact that the original capital was small and the number of stockholders was limited. At present, the common stock is held by slightly fewer than 50 individuals. Each of these individuals also owns preferred shares; their total holdings approximate 46% of the outstanding preferred. The preferred was issued at the time of the capital expansion.

The board of directors had been planning to declare a dividend during the early part of Year 17, payable June 30. However, the cash position as shown by the balance sheet has raised serious doubts about the advisability of a dividend in Year 17. The president has explained that most of the cash will be needed shortly to pay for inventory already purchased. The company has a chief accountant but no controller. The board relies on an outside CPA for advice concerning financial management. The CPA was asked to advise about the contemplated dividend declaration. Four of the seven members of the board felt very strongly that some kind of dividend must be declared and paid and that all stockholders "should get something."

Required

We have been asked to analyze the situation and make whatever dividend proposals appear worthy of consideration by the board. Show amounts to support our recommendations in a written form suitable for consideration by the board in reaching a decision. Provide the basis for all proposals and indicate any preferences that we may have in a memo to the board.

Challenge Problem To date, 3,000 shares of preferred stock (6%, $100 par value, cumulative, nonparticipating) and 100,000 shares of common stock (no-par) of Gomez Inc. have been issued. Authorized shares were as follows: common, 200,000; preferred, 3,000. No dividends were in arrears as of January 1. During the year, the following transactions affected stockholders' equity:

AD&J19-16
Recording Stock and Property Dividends **LO5, 6**

- **February 1:** Declared and immediately issued one share of the company's investment in AC Corporation stock for each share of preferred stock as a property dividend. The fair value of the AC stock was $3.50 per share. Original cost of the AC stock was $3.50 per share. In addition, a cash dividend was paid to complete payment of the dividends.
- **December 1:** Declared and issued a stock dividend, payable in common stock to holders of both preferred and common stock. The preferred holders are to receive value equivalent to 6%, and the common holders are to receive one share for each five shares held. The value and the amount to be capitalized per share as a debit to Retained Earnings is the fair value. The price per share of the common stock immediately after the stock dividend was $1.50.

Required

a. Provide the entry for declaration and distribution of the property and cash dividend on February 1.
b. Provide the entry for declaration and distribution of the stock dividend on December 1.

Challenge Problem Able Corporation has the following stock outstanding:

AD&J19-17
Computing Participating Preferred Dividend Distributions **LO4, 5**

> Common, $50 par, 6,000 shares
> Preferred, 6%, $100 par, 1,000 shares

Required

Compute dividends payable in total and per share on the common stock and the preferred stock for each separate case.

a. Preferred is cumulative and nonparticipating; two years in arrears; dividends declared, $34,000.
b. Preferred is noncumulative and fully participating; dividends declared, $40,000.
c. Preferred is cumulative and partially participating up to an additional 3%; three years in arrears; dividends declared, $60,000.
d. Preferred is cumulative and fully participating; three years in arrears; dividends declared, $50,000.

Challenge Problem The charter of Crew Corporation authorized: (1) 5,000 shares of 6% preferred stock, $20 par, and (2) 8,000 shares of common stock, $50 par. All of the authorized shares have been issued. In a five-year period, annual dividends paid in chronological order were (from oldest to most current) $4,000, $40,000, $32,000, $5,000, and $36,000, respectively.

AD&J19-18
Computing Participating Preferred Dividend Distributions **LO4, 5**

Required

Compute the amount of dividends that would be paid to each class of stock for each year under the following separate cases.

a. Preferred stock is noncumulative and nonparticipating.
b. Preferred stock is cumulative and nonparticipating.
c. Preferred stock is noncumulative and fully participating.
d. Preferred stock is cumulative and fully participating.
e. Preferred stock is cumulative and partially participating up to an additional 2%; *also* assume that the dividend for year 5 was $42,000 instead of $36,000.

AD&J19-19
Recording Exchanges
of Stock   **LO2**

Challenge Problem Rather Corporation had authorized an outstanding 100,000 shares of common stock, $2 par value. The stockholders approved the exchange of two new shares for each share of the old stock. *Hint:* Do not decrease paid-in capital accounts below zero; instead, debit retained earnings.

Required

Provide the journal entries to record the change under each of the following separate cases. (Assume a sufficient balance in retained earnings.)

a. Old stock was sold at par, and the new stock was no-par stock with no stated or assigned value.

b. Old stock was sold at a premium of $3 per share, and the new stock was no-par stock with a stated value of $2 per share.

c. Old stock was sold at a premium of $1.50 per share, and the new stock was no-par stock with a stated value of $2 per share.

d. Old stock was sold at par, and the new stock was no-par stock with a stated value of $1.50 per share.

e. Old stock originally was sold at a premium of $1.50 per share, and the new stock was $1 par value.

f. Old stock was sold at a premium of $3 per share, and the new stock was no-par stock with no stated or assigned value.

g. Old stock was sold at a premium of $1 per share, and the new stock was no-par stock with no stated or assigned value.

AD&J19-20
Recording and
Reporting Scrip
Dividends   **LO5**

Challenge Problem On June 1, Ward Corporation had outstanding 10,000 shares of capital stock, $10 par. The shares were held by 10 stockholders, each having an equal number of shares. The retained earnings account showed a credit balance of $60,000, although the company was short of cash.

The company owned 20,000 shares (2%) of the common stock of Carson Corporation that had been purchased as an investment. The fair value of this stock is $1.25 per share, an increase of $0.25 per share over its value at the beginning of the year.

On June 1, the board of directors of Ward Corporation declared a dividend of $4 per share "to be paid with the Carson stock 30 days after declaration date and scrip to be issued for the difference. The scrip will be payable at the end of 12 months from payment date of the property dividend and will earn 12% interest per annum." The accounting period ends December 31.

Required

a. Provide all entries related to the dividends through date of payment of the scrip, including accounts relating to the investment in Carson. *Hint:* Use the account, Scrip Dividends Payable.

b. Illustrate how all items related to the dividend declaration should be reported by Ward on (1) the balance sheet and (2) the income statement at the end of the year, including any notes needed for full disclosure.

AD&J19-21
Recording Adjustments
to Investments   **LO6**

Challenge Problem On January 1, Lambo Inc. purchased 200 shares of Farve Industries' common stock at $100 per share. The investment is measured as FV-NI. On June 30, Lambo received a 15% stock dividend on the Farve investment.

Required

Record the entry to adjust the investment to fair value on December 31, assuming that the Lambo stock is trading at $101 per share on December 31.

AD&J19-22
Defining
Terms   **LO6, 7**

Codification Skills How are the terms (1) comprehensive income, (2) other comprehensive income, (3) dividend, (4) stock dividend, and (5) stock split defined in the Codification?

AD&J19-23
Performing Accounting
Research   **LO2, 3, 4, 7**

Codification Skills Through research in the Codification, identify the specific citation for each of the following items included as guidance in this chapter for the accounting for equity.

a. Specific amounts included in other comprehensive income.   FASB ASC ☐ - ☐ - ☐ - ☐

b. Determination of value recorded for noncash consideration in a stock issuance.   FASB ASC ☐ - ☐ - ☐

c. Treatment of common stock issue costs.   FASB ASC ☐ - ☐ - ☐

d. Financial reporting of treasury stock.   FASB ASC ☐ - ☐

e. Preferred stock reported as a liability.   FASB ASC ☐ - ☐ - ☐

Codification Skills Ellis Company has experienced a sustained growth in its market price of common stock such that the company is considering offering either a stock dividend or a stock split. The company understands that adding new shares to the market place will result in a decrease in price per share of common stock, which would make the stock more attractive to an average investor. Every indication points to a continued growth in stock price over the next three years. The company has no experience with stock dividends but had heard that options include stock splits, small stock dividends, and large stock dividends. What research supports these options in the Codification?

AD&J19-24
Performing Accounting
Research **LO6**

FASB ASC [   ] - [   ]

Answers to Review Exercises

Review 19-1

a. 2	e. 4	i. 1
b. 3	f. 3	j. 1
c. 1	g. 2	k. 5
d. 2	h. 1	

Review 19-2

a. January 1—To record issuance of par value stock

Cash (20,000 × $20)..	400,000	
Common Stock (20,000 × $1)...............................		20,000
Paid-In Capital in Excess of Par—Common Stock ($400,000 – $20,000)		380,000

Assets = Liabilities + Equity
+400,000   +20,000
           +380,000

Cash	Common Stock
400,000	20,000

Paid-In Cap—CS
380,000

b. January 1—To record issuance of no-par stock

Cash (20,000 × $20)..	400,000	
Common Stock...		400,000

Assets = Liabilities + Equity
+400,000   +400,000

Cash	Common Stock
400,000	400,000

c. January 1—To record issuance of no-par stock with a stated value

Cash (20,000 × $20)..	400,000	
Common Stock (20,000 × $1)...............................		20,000
Paid-In Capital in Excess of Stated Value—Common Stock ($400,000 – $20,000) ...		380,000

Assets = Liabilities + Equity
+400,000   +20,000
           +380,000

Cash	Common Stock
400,000	20,000

Paid-In Cap—CS
380,000

d. January 1—To record issuance of stock for noncash consideration

Equipment	180,000	
Common Stock (10,000 × $1)...............................		10,000
Paid-In Capital in Excess of Par—Common Stock ($180,000 – $10,000)		170,000

Assets = Liabilities + Equity
+180,000   +10,000
           +170,000

Equipment	Common Stock
180,000	10,000

Paid-In Cap—CS
170,000

e. January 1—To record issuance of multiple securities—proportional allocation

Cash	160,000	
Common Stock (5,000 × $1)..................................		5,000
Paid-In Capital in Excess of Par—Common Stock ($94,400 – $5,000)		89,400
Preferred Stock (2,000 × $5)................................		10,000
Paid-In Capital in Excess of Par—Preferred Stock ($65,600 – $10,000)		55,600

Assets = Liabilities + Equity
+160,000   +160,000

Cash	Common Stock
160,000	5,000

Preferred Stock	Paid-In Cap—CS
10,000	89,400

Paid-In Cap—PS
55,600

f. January 1—To record issuance of multiple securities—incremental allocation

Cash	175,000	
Common Stock (5,000 × $1)..................................		5,000
Paid-In Capital in Excess of Par—Common Stock ([$18 × 5,000] – $5,000).......		85,000
Preferred Stock (2,000 × $5)................................		10,000
Paid-In Capital in Excess of Par—Preferred Stock (to balance)		75,000

Assets = Liabilities + Equity
+175,000   +175,000

Cash	Common Stock
160,000	5,000

Preferred Stock	Paid-In Cap—CS
10,000	85,000

Paid-In Cap—PS
75,000

g. **January 1—To record stock issue costs**

Assets = Liabilities + Equity
+396,000   +396,000

Cash	Common Stock
396,000		20,000

Paid-In Cap—CS
	376,000

Cash ([20,000 × $20] – $4,000)...	396,000	
Common Stock (20,000 × $1)..		20,000
Paid-In Capital in Excess of Par—Common Stock ($396,000 – $20,000).........		376,000

Review 19-3

a. **January 1—To record issuance of common stock**

Assets = Liabilities + Equity
+125,000   +5,000
+120,000

Cash	Common Stock
125,000		5,000

Paid-In Cap—CS
	120,000

Cash (5,000 shares × $25).................................	125,000	
Common Stock (5,000 shares × $1)........................		5,000
Paid-In Capital in Excess of Par—Common Stock ($125,000 – $5,000)		120,000

b. **June 15—To record acquisition of treasury stock**

Assets = Liabilities + Equity
–30,000   –30,000

Cash	Treasury Stock
125,000 | 30,000	30,000 |

Treasury Stock (1,000 shares × $30)...........................	30,000	
Cash...		30,000

c. **November 15—To record sale of treasury stock**

Assets = Liabilities + Equity
+8,250   +750
+7,500

Cash	Treasury Stock
125,000 | 30,000	30,000 | 7,500
8,250 |	

Paid-In Cap—TS
	750

Cash (250 shares × $33).................................	8,250	
Paid-In Capital—Treasury Stock (to balance)......................		750
Treasury Stock (250 shares × $30)...........................		7,500

d. **December 31—To record retirement of remaining treasury stock**

Assets = Liabilities + Equity
–22,500
+22,500

Paid-In Cap—CS	Common Stock
18,000 | 120,000	750 | 5,000

Paid-In Cap—TS	Ret Earnings
750 | 750	3,000 |
0	

Treasury Stock
30,000 | 7,500
| 22,500
0 |

Common Stock (750 shares × $1)................................	750	
Paid-In Capital in Excess of Par—Common Stock (750 shares × $24).........	18,000	
Paid-In Capital—Treasury Stock...................................	750	
Retained Earnings	3,000	
Treasury Stock (750 shares × $30)...........................		22,500

e. **June 15—To record direct retirement of stock**

Assets = Liabilities + Equity
–30,000   –30,000

Cash	Common Stock
	30,000	1,000 | 5,000 Bal.

Paid-In Cap—CS	Ret Earnings
24,000 | 120,000 Bal.	5,000 |

Common Stock (1,000 shares × $1).............................	1,000	
Paid-In Capital in Excess of Par—Common Stock (1,000 shares × $24).......	24,000	
Retained Earnings	5,000	
Cash (1,000 shares × $30).................................		30,000

Review 19-4

a. **December 31—To record issuance of convertible preferred stock**

Assets = Liabilities + Equity
+100,000   +10,000
+90,000

Cash	Preferred Stock
100,000		10,000

Paid-In Cap—PS
	90,000

Cash	100,000	
Preferred Stock (1,000 × $10)		10,000
Paid-In Capital in Excess of Par—Preferred Stock (to balance)		90,000

Financial statement presentation: $100,000 reported in paid-in capital in the stockholders' equity section.

b. **December 31—To record issuance of redeemable preferred stock**

Assets = Liabilities + Equity
+100,000   +10,000
+90,000

Cash	Preferred Stock
100,000		10,000

Paid-In Cap—PS
	90,000

Cash	100,000	
Preferred Stock (1,000 × $10)		10,000
Paid-In Capital in Excess of Par—Preferred Stock (to balance)		90,000

Financial statement presentation: $100,000 reported in paid-in capital in the stockholders' equity section.

Review 19-5

a. **June 1—To record declaration of cash dividends**

Assets = Liabilities + Equity
+125,000   –125,000

Ret Earnings	Div Payable
125,000		125,000

Retained Earnings (50,000 shares × $2.50).......................	125,000	
Dividends Payable		125,000

b. **June 1—To adjust investment to fair value**

Investment in Den Co. Stock	3,000	
Unrealized Gain or Loss—Income (1,000 × [$22 – $19]).		3,000

Assets = Liabilities + Equity
+3,000   +3,000

Invest—CS	Unreal Gain or Loss—Inc
3,000			3,000

June 1—To record declaration of property dividends

Retained Earnings	22,000	
Property Dividends Payable.		22,000

Assets = Liabilities + Equity
       +22,000   –22,000

Ret Earnings	Prop Div Payable
22,000			22,000

c. **August 15—To record a partial liquidating dividend**

Retained Earnings ($80,000 – $20,000)	60,000	
Paid-In Capital in Excess of Par—Common Stock	20,000	
Dividends Payable		80,000

Assets = Liabilities + Equity
       +80,000   –60,000
                –20,000

Ret Earnings	Paid-In Cap—CS
60,000			20,000

Div Payable
	80,000

d. **June 1—To record preferred and common stock dividend declaration**

Retained Earnings	25,000	
Dividends Payable—Preferred Stock (20,000 × 0.05 × 2 years). . . .		2,000
Dividends Payable—Common Stock ($25,000 – $2,000).		23,000

Assets = Liabilities + Equity
       +2,000   –25,000
       +23,000

Ret Earnings	Div Payable
25,000			25,000

Review 19-6

a. **March 1—To record declaration of stock dividend**

Retained Earnings (50,000 × 5% × $24)	60,000	
Common Stock Dividends Distributable (50,000 × 5% × $1).		2,500
Paid-In Capital in Excess of Par—Common Stock (to balance)		57,500

Assets = Liabilities + Equity
               –60,000
               +2,500
              +57,500

Ret Earnings	CS Div Distrib
60,000			2,500

Paid-In Cap—CS
	57,500

March 15—To record issuance of stock dividend

Common Stock Dividends Distributable	2,500	
Common Stock.		2,500

Assets = Liabilities + Equity
               –2,500
               +2,500

Common Stock	CS Div Distrib
	2,500	2,500	2,500

b. **March 1—To record declaration of stock dividend**

Retained Earnings (50,000 × 5% × $24)	60,000	
Dividends Payable (200 shares × $24).		4,800
Common Stock Dividends Distributable (2,300 × $1)		2,300
Paid-In Capital in Excess of Par—Common Stock (2,300 × $23).		52,900

Assets = Liabilities + Equity
       +4,800   –60,000
               +2,300
              +52,900

Div Payable	Ret Earnings
	4,800	60,000	

CS Div Distrib	Paid-In Cap—CS
	2,300		52,900

March 15—To record issuance of stock dividend

Common Stock Dividends Distributable	2,300	
Common Stock.		2,300

Assets = Liabilities + Equity
               –2,300
               +2,300

CS Div Distrib	Common Stock
2,300	2,300		2,300

March 15—To record issuance of cash dividend

Dividends Payable	4,800	
Cash		4,800

Assets = Liabilities + Equity
–4,800   –4,800

Cash	Div Payable
	4,800	4,800	4,800

c. **March 1—To record declaration of stock dividend**

Retained Earnings (50,000 × 100% × $1)	50,000	
Common Stock Dividends Distributable		50,000

Assets = Liabilities + Equity
               –50,000
               +50,000

Ret Earnings	CS Div Distrib
50,000			50,000

March 15—To record issuance of stock dividend

Common Stock Dividends Distributable	50,000	
Common Stock.		50,000

Assets = Liabilities + Equity
               –50,000
               +50,000

CS Div Distrib	Common Stock
50,000	50,000		50,000

d. There are no journal entries required on the declaration date or the date of the distribution. Total par value is the same before and after the stock split. Round Company would disclose that they have 50,000 × 3 = 150,000 common shares outstanding with a par value per share of $1/3 = $0.3333.

Review 19-7

a.

Net Income	$250,000
Other comprehensive gain, net of tax.	55,000
Comprehensive income	$305,000

b.

Accumulated OCI, beginning balance	$114,000
Other comprehensive gain, net of tax.	55,000
Accumulated OCI, ending balance.	$169,000

Review 19-8

Year 3			Year 2	
Book value per share . . .	$3.81	($5,450.1 ÷ 1,431.6)	$4.03	($5,884.0 ÷ 1,460.5)
Payout ratio.	0.50	(1,450.4 ÷ $2,884.7)	0.42	($1,178.0 ÷ $2,817.7)
Return on equity	0.51	$2,884.7 ÷ (($5,450.1 + $5,884.0)/2)	0.48	$2,817.7 ÷ (($5,884.0 + $5,818.0)/2)

20

Share-Based Compensation and Earnings per Share

THE HOME DEPOT INC.
CONSOLIDATED STATEMENTS OF EARNINGS

in millions, except per share data	Fiscal 2023	Fiscal 2022	Fiscal 2021
Net sales	$152,669	$157,403	$151,157
Cost of sales	101,709	104,625	100,325
Gross profit	50,960	52,778	50,832
Operating expenses:			
Selling, general and administrative	26,598	26,284	25,406
Depreciation and amortization	2,673	2,455	2,3862
Total operating expenses	29,271	28,739	27,792
Operating income	21,689	24,039	23,040
Interest and other (income) expense:			
Interest income and other, net	(178)	(55)	(44)
Interest expense	1,943	1,617	1,347
Interest and other, net	1,765	1,562	1,303
Earnings before provision for income taxes	19,924	22,477	21,737
Provision for income taxes	4,781	5,372	5,304
Net earnings	$ 15,143	$ 17,105	$ 16,433
Basic weighted-average common shares	999	1,022	1,054
Basic earnings per share	$ 15.16	$ 16.74	$ 15.59
Diluted weighted-average common shares	1,002	1,025	1,058
Diluted earnings per share	$ 15.11	$ 16.69	$ 15.53

THE HOME DEPOT INC.
8. Stock-Based Compensation

Stock Options. Under the terms of the Plans, incentive stock options and nonqualified stock options must have an exercise price at or above the fair market value of our stock on the date of the grant. Typically, nonqualified stock options vest at the rate of 25% per year commencing on the second anniversary date of the grant and expire on the tenth anniversary date of the grant. Additionally, a majority of our stock options may become non-forfeitable upon the associate reaching age 60, provided the associate has had five years of continuous service. No incentive stock options have been issued under the Omnibus Plan.

We estimate the fair value of stock option awards on the date of grant using the Black-Scholes option-pricing model. Our determination of fair value of stock option awards on the date of grant using the Black-Scholes option-pricing model is affected by our stock price as well as assumptions regarding a number of variables.

Restricted Stock and Performance Share Awards. Restrictions on the restricted stock issued under the Plans generally lapse over various periods up to five years. At the grant date of the award, recipients of restricted stock are granted voting rights and generally receive dividends on unvested shares, paid in the form of cash on each dividend payment date. Dividends paid on unvested shares were immaterial for fiscal 2023, fiscal 2022, and fiscal 2021. Additionally, the majority of our restricted stock awards may become non-forfeitable upon the associate's attainment of age 60, provided the associate has had five years of continuous service.

We have also granted performance share awards under the Plans. These awards provide for the issuance of shares of our common stock at the end of the three-year performance cycle based upon our performance against target average ROIC and operating profit over that performance cycle. Additionally, the awards become non-forfeitable upon the associate's attainment of age 60, provided the associate has had five years of continuous service and minimum performance targets are achieved. Recipients of performance share awards have no voting rights until the shares are issued following completion of the performance period. Dividend equivalents accrue on the performance shares (as reinvested shares) and are paid upon the payout of the award based upon the actual number of shares earned. The fair value of the restricted stock and performance shares is based on the closing stock price on the date of grant and is expensed over the period during which the restrictions lapse.

THE HOME DEPOT INC.
10. WEIGHTED-AVERAGE COMMON SHARES

The following table presents the reconciliation of our basic to diluted weighted-average common shares as well as the number of anti-dilutive securities excluded from diluted weighted average common shares:

in millions	Fiscal 2023	Fiscal 2022	Fiscal 2021
Basic weighted-average common shares	999	1,022	1,054
Effect of potentially dilutive securities [1]	3	3	4
Diluted weighted-average common shares	1,002	1,025	1,058
Anti-dilutive securities excluded from diluted weighted-average common shares	1	1	—

[1] Represents the dilutive impact of stock-based awards.

Chapter Preview

In this chapter we explain the accounting for share-based compensation plans where compensation is paid in a form other than cash. We examine the accounting for restricted stock plans, restricted stock unit plans, stock option plans, and employee stock purchase plans. We then describe the calculation of basic earnings per share, including the effects of dividends, share issuances, share buybacks, stock dividends, and stock splits. We also describe the diluted earnings per share calculation, which considers any financial instrument with a potential to increase common shares outstanding.

Action Plan

LO	Topic/Subtopic	Page	Demos	Reviews	Assignments	CPA*
LO 20–1	**Account for restricted stock plans** Restricted Stock Awards :: Restricted Stock Units :: Compensation Expense :: Requisite Service Period :: Forfeitures	20-3	D20-1A D20-1B	R20-1	MC20-1, BE20-1, BE20-2, BE20-3, BE20-4, E20-1, E20-2, E20-3, E20-4, E20-5, E20-6, E20-7, E20-8, E20-9, P20-1, P20-11, AD&J20-6, AD&J20-10, AD&J20-18, DA20-1	BAR II.D.1 II.D.2
LO 20–2	**Account for stock options** Stock Options :: Fair Value :: Option-Pricing Model :: Compensation Expense :: Forfeitures	20-8	D20-2	R20-2	MC20-2, BE20-5, BE20-6, BE20-7, BE20-8, BE20-9, BE20-10, BE20-11, BE20-12, E20-10, E20-11, E20-12, E20-13, E20-14, P20-2, P20-3, AD&J20-6, AD&J20-8, AD&J20-10, AD&J20-13, DA20-1	BAR II.D.1 II.D.2
LO 20–3	**Account for employee stock purchase plans** Employee Stock Purchase Plan :: Noncompensatory :: Compensatory	20-12	D20-3	R20-3	MC20-3, BE20-13, BE20-14, BE20-15, BE20-16, E20-15, P20-3	BAR II.D.1 II.D.2
LO 20–4	**Compute earnings per share (EPS) with a simple capital structure** Net Income Available to Common Shareholders :: Weighted-Average Common Shares	20-14	D20-4	R20-4	MC20-4, BE20-17, E20-16, P20-4, AD&J20-1, AD&J20-2, AD&J20-3, AD&J20-4, AD&J20-5, AD&J20-7, AD&J20-15, AD&J20-16, AD&J20-17	FAR I.D.3
LO 20–5	**Compute EPS given share issuances, buybacks, dividends, and splits** Weighted-Average Number of Common Shares :: Stock Issuance :: Treasury Stock :: Stock Dividends :: Stock Split	20-15	D20-5	R20-5	MC20-5, MC20-6, BE20-17, BE20-18, BE20-19, BE20-20, BE20-21, E20-17, E20-18, E20-19, E20-20, E20-21, E20-22, E20-29, E20-35, E20-38, P20-4, P20-5, P20-6, P20-7, P20-8, P20-9, AD&J20-1, AD&J20-2, AD&J20-3, AD&J20-4, AD&J20-5, AD&J20-7, AD&J20-11, AD&J20-12, AD&J20-15, AD&J20-16, AD&J20-17	FAR I.D.3
LO 20–6	**Compute EPS using *if-converted* method for convertible securities** Diluted EPS :: Convertible Preferred Stock :: Convertible Debt :: *If-Converted* Method	20-19	D20-6A D20-6B	R20-6	MC20-7, BE20-22, BE20-23, E20-17, E20-23, E20-24, E20-25, E20-26, E20-27, E20-28, E20-29, E20-38, P20-4, P20-5, P20-7, P20-8, P20-9, AD&J20-1, AD&J20-2, AD&J20-3, AD&J20-4, AD&J20-5, AD&J20-7, AD&J20-9, AD&J20-11, AD&J20-12, AD&J20-15, AD&J20-16, AD&J20-17	FAR I.D.3
LO 20–7	**Compute EPS using treasury stock method for options, warrants, and restricted stock** Diluted EPS :: Stock Options :: Stock Warrants :: Restricted Stock :: Treasury Stock Method	20-24	D20-7A D20-7B	R20-7	MC20-8, BE20-24, BE20-25, E20-30, E20-31, E20-38, P20-5, P20-5, P20-6, P20-7, P20-9, P20-11, AD&J20-1, AD&J20-2, AD&J20-3, AD&J20-4, AD&J20-5, AD&J20-7, AD&J20-12, AD&J20-14, AD&J20-15, AD&J20-16, AD&J20-17	FAR I.D.3
LO 20–8	**Compute EPS given contingently issuable shares** Diluted EPS :: Contingently Issuable Shares :: Satisfaction of Conditions	20-29	D20-8	R20-8	MC20-9, BE20-26, E20-32, E20-38, P20-10, AD&J20-1, AD&J20-2, AD&J20-3, AD&J20-4, AD&J20-5, AD&J20-7, AD&J20-15, AD&J20-16, AD&J20-17	FAR I.D.3
LO 20–9	**Compute EPS given multiple securities and describe EPS financial statement presentation** Multiple Securities :: Rank Securities :: Dilutive Effect :: EPS Presentation	20-30	D20-9	R20-9	MC20-10, BE20-27, BE20-28, E20-33, E20-34, E20-35, E20-36, E20-37, P20-4, P20-5, P20-7, P20-8, P20-12, AD&J20-1, AD&J20-2, AD&J20-3, AD&J20-4, AD&J20-5, AD&J20-7, AD&J20-12, AD&J20-15, AD&J20-16, AD&J20-17	FAR I.D.3
LO 20–10	**APPENDIX 20A—Describe accounting for stock appreciation rights** Stock Appreciation Rights (SARs) :: Equity :: Liability	20-34	D20-10	R20-10	AppBE20-1, AppBE20-2, AppBE20-3, AppE20-1, AppE20-2, AppP20-1	BAR II.D.1 II.D.2 II.D.3

*Black (Gray) font in CPA column indicates that the LO ties directly (indirectly) to the CPA Exam Blueprints LO.

LO 20-1 ▷ Account for restricted stock plans

Many companies have established plans under which employees receive compensation in a form other than cash such as shares of restricted stock or options to acquire shares of stock. We refer to the entire set of such plans as share-based compensation plans. **Share-based compensation plans**, also called stock-based compensation plans, are often awarded to select employees to encourage superior performance, and to help recruit and retain outstanding employees. Two types of share-based compensation plans are restricted stock awards and restricted stock unit awards. These are *restricted* awards because stock (or a right to stock) is awarded only after certain conditions are met. We illustrate the accounting for (1) **restricted stock awards** (awards of restricted stock) in **Demo 20-1A** and (2) **restricted stock unit** (awards for the right to receive a specified number of shares of stock) in **Demo 20-1B**.

Key terms related to restricted stock plans are defined as follows.

Grant date*	**ASC Glossary** The date at which a grantor and a grantee reach a mutual understanding of the key terms and conditions of a share-based payment award.
Vest*	**ASC Glossary** To earn the rights to. A share-based payment award becomes vested at the date that the grantee's right to receive or retain shares, other instruments, or cash under the award is no longer contingent on satisfaction of either a service condition or a performance condition. Market conditions are not vesting conditions.
Requisite service period	**ASC Glossary** The period or periods during which an employee is required to provide service in exchange for an award under a share-based payment arrangement. The service that an employee is required to render during that period is referred to as the requisite service. The requisite service period for an award that has only a service condition is presumed to be the vesting period, unless there is clear evidence to the contrary.
Vesting date	Date that a share-based compensation plan is exercisable by an employee.
Vesting period	Period from the grant date to the vesting date. Typically, the vesting period would align with the requisite service period.

*While the discussion in this chapter focuses on employer sponsored compensation plans, ASC 718 broadly applies to share-based payment transactions for acquiring goods and services from *nonemployees*. Accordingly, we see the terms "**grantee**" and "**grantor**" in the accounting guidance.

A restricted stock plan gives an employee shares (or rights to own shares) that cannot be awarded to the employee until the employee has satisfied vesting requirements. Such restrictions provide an incentive to the employee to stay with the company through the vesting date and to act in the best interest of shareholders. Thus, if an employee were to leave the company before the vesting period, the restricted shares (units) would be forfeited. Typically, the employee would be restricted from selling these shares during the vesting period.

Restricted Stock Awards

When a company compensates an employee through shares of restricted stock, the company issues stock to the employee at the grant date but holds the stock in a trust through the vesting period. **Unearned Compensation—Equity** (also called Deferred Compensation), a contra-equity account, is debited for the *fair value* of the stock at the **grant date**. Changes in the fair value of the stock after the grant date are irrelevant for purposes of valuation of the stock award. Unearned Compensation—Equity is amortized to Compensation Expense over the employee's **requisite service period** (typically the vesting period), using the straight-line amortization method.

718-10-30-6   The measurement objective for equity instruments awarded to grantees is to estimate the fair value at the grant date of the equity instruments that the entity is obligated to issue when grantees have delivered the good or rendered the service and satisfied any other conditions necessary to earn the right to benefit from the instruments (for example, to exercise share options). That estimate is based on the share price and other pertinent factors, such as expected volatility, at the grant date.

718-10-35-2 The compensation cost for an award of share-based employee compensation classified as equity shall be recognized over the requisite service period, with a corresponding credit to equity (generally, paid-in capital). The requisite service period is the period during which an employee is required to provide service in exchange for an award, which often is the vesting period. The requisite service period is estimated based on an analysis of the terms of the share-based payment award.

Restricted Stock Units

When a company chooses to compensate employees through restricted stock units, the employee is granted the *right* to receive stock at a future date under certain conditions. After the employee meets the conditions, the company distributes the common shares. Unlike restricted stock awards, the issuance of shares is delayed until after the vesting period. However, the fair value of the compensation is still determined at the grant date, as is the case with restricted stock award plans. Compensation expense (along with an increase in **Paid-in Capital—Restricted Stock**) is recognized over the employee's requisite service period using the straight-line amortization method. Paid-in Capital—Restricted Stock is credited instead of Common Stock and Paid-in Capital—Common Stock because the employee receives a right to receive stock in the future. This means the stock is not yet issued. When the stock is issued, Common Stock and Paid in Capital—Common Stock are credited, and Paid-in Capital—Restricted Stock is debited.

Forfeitures of Stock Awards or Stock Units

What if an employee does not meet the specified conditions and the restricted stock or units are forfeited? The accounting standards allow two different options in accounting for forfeitures.

- **Recording an estimate of forfeitures** Under this option, the fair value of the restricted stock award at the grant date is reduced by the percentage of shares estimated to be forfeited. Thus, compensation expense recorded each period is based on the net expected stock award. If the estimate changes in a later period, the *cumulative effect* of the change in estimate is recorded in the current period.

- **Recording forfeitures as they are incurred** As a practical expedient, companies can record forfeitures (due to employee turnover) in the period incurred.

718-10-35-3 . . . To determine the amount of compensation cost to be recognized in each period, an entity shall make an entity-wide accounting policy election for all employee share-based payment awards to do either of the following:

a. Estimate the number of awards for which the requisite service will not be rendered (that is, estimate the number of forfeitures expected to occur). The entity shall base initial accruals of compensation cost on the estimated number of instruments for which the requisite service is expected to be rendered. The entity shall revise that estimate if subsequent information indicates that the actual number of instruments is likely to differ from previous estimates. The cumulative effect on current and prior periods of a change in the estimated number of instruments for which the requisite service is expected to be or has been rendered shall be recognized in compensation cost in the period of the change.

b. Recognize the effect of awards for which the requisite service is not rendered when the award is forfeited (that is, recognize the effect of forfeitures in compensation cost when they occur). Previously recognized compensation cost for an award shall be reversed in the period that the award is forfeited.

Accounting for Restricted Stock Awards	**LO20-1**	**DEMO 20-1A**

Demo

MBC

On January 1 of Year 1, Jax Inc. grants 1,000, $1 par, restricted shares of its common stock to one senior corporate officer. The shares vest if the officer stays with the company for three years, which is the requisite service period. The fair value of the shares on January 1 of Year 1 is $15 per share.

a. Record the journal entry on January 1 of Year 1, the date of grant, for this compensatory plan.
b. Record the journal entry on December 31 of Year 1 to recognize compensation expense.
c. Show the December 31 of Year 1 financial statement presentation resulting from the restricted stock award.
d. Assume that the senior corporate officer resigned on January 1 of Year 2. Record the entry on January 1 of Year 2 to reflect the financial statement impact of the resignation. Assume that the company elects to record forfeitures as incurred.

continued

continued from previous page

Solution

a. Issuance of Restricted Stock

The journal entry at the date of grant follows.

January 1, Year 1—To record issuance of restricted stock

Unearned Compensation—Equity (1,000 × $15)	15,000	
Common Stock (1,000 × $1)		1,000
Paid-in Capital in Excess of Par—Common Stock ($15,000 – $1,000) ...		14,000

Assets = Liabilities + Equity
-15,000
Contra Eq
+1,000
CS
+14,000
PIC—CS

Unearned Comp—Eq		Common Stock
15,000		1,000

Paid-in Cap—CS
14,000

b. Recognition of Compensation Expense

Jax Inc. recognizes compensation expense at the end of the first year as follows.

December 31, Year 1—To record compensation expense

Compensation Expense	5,000	
Unearned Compensation—Equity ($15,000/3 years)		5,000

Assets = Liabilities + Equity
-5,000
Exp
+5,000
Contra Eq

Comp Exp		Unearned Comp—Eq	
5,000		15,000	5,000

Jax Inc. also records compensation expense of $5,000 in both of the next two years.

c. Financial Statement Presentation

In the financial statements for December 31, Jax Inc. presents the following for its restricted stock transactions.

Balance Sheet	Dec. 31, Year 1
Stockholders' equity	
Common stock	$ 1,000
Paid-in capital in excess of par	14,000
Unearned compensation—equity	
($15,000 – $5,000)	(10,000)

Income Statement	Year 1
Expense	
Compensation expense	$5,000

Assets = Liabilities + Equity
-1,000
CS
-14,000
PIC—CS
+10,000
Contra Eq
+5,000
Exp

d. Restricted Stock Forfeiture

The related equity accounts are derecognized and compensation expense previously recorded is now credited.

January 1, Year 2—To record restricted stock forfeiture

Common Stock...	1,000	
Paid-in Capital in Excess of Par—Common Stock	14,000	
Unearned Compensation—Equity ($15,000 – $5,000)...............		10,000
Compensation Expense		5,000

Unearned Comp—Eq		Common Stock	
15,000	5,000	1,000	1,000
	10,000		

Paid-in Cap—CS		Comp Exp	
14,000	14,000	5,000	5,000

DEMO 20-1B   **LO20-1**   **Accounting for Restricted Stock Units**

Demo

MBC

On January 1 of Year 1, Jax Inc. grants a total of 5,000 restricted stock units to five senior corporate officers. Each stock unit may be exchanged for 1 share of $1 par common stock. Each corporate officer will receive 1,000 shares if the officer stays with the company for three years, which is the requisite service period. The fair value of the shares on January 1 of Year 1, is $15 per share.

a. Record compensation expense in Year 1, Year 2, and Year 3 related to the award of the restricted stock units granted on January 1 of Year 1.

b. Record the issuance of the shares of restricted stock on January 1 of Year 4, assuming all five officers received the designated stock unit awards.

c. Assume the same information in the original scenario except that Jax Inc. now expects forfeitures due to employee turnover and Jax's policy is to recognize estimated forfeitures. On January 1 of Year 1, Jax Inc. estimates 1,000 units will be forfeited due to employee turnover during the three-year requisite service period.

   1. Record the entry on December 31 of Year 1 to recognize compensation expense.

   2. Record the entry on December 31 of Year 2 to recognize compensation expense, assuming that one officer left the company on that date and no further forfeitures are expected.

continued

continued from previous page

 d. Assume the same information in the original scenario except that Jax Inc. now expects forfeitures due to employee turnover and Jax elected to record forfeitures as incurred.

  1. Record the required entry on December 31 of Year 1 to recognize compensation expense.

  2. Record the entry on December 31 of Year 2 to recognize compensation expense, assuming one officer left the company on that date.

 e. Assume the same information as in part *c*. Record the entry on December 31 of Year 2 assuming the estimate of forfeitures increases to 2,000 restricted stock units and no forfeitures have occurred.

Solution

a. Recognition of Compensation Expense

No journal entry is required on January 1 of Year 1 (the date of grant). However, the total cost of compensation is calculated at that time as 5,000 units multiplied by $15 per share or $75,000. Compensation expense will be recognized at the end of each of the next three years or the requisite service period as follows.

December 31, Year 1, Year 2, and Year 3—To record compensation expense

Compensation Expense	25,000	
Paid-in Capital—Restricted Stock ($75,000/3 years)		25,000

Assets = Liabilities + Equity
−25,000 Exp
+25,000 PIC—RS

Comp Exp	Paid-in Cap—RS
25,000	25,000
25,000	25,000
25,000	25,000

b. Issuance of Vested Restricted Stock Units

On January 1 of Year 4, the restricted stock units are fully vested and the shares awarded to the corporate officer.

January 1, Year 4—To record issuance of restricted stock

Paid-in Capital—Restricted Stock ($25,000 × 3 years).................	75,000	
Common Stock (5,000 × $1)...................................		5,000
Paid in Capital in Excess of Par—Common Stock ($75,000 – $5,000) ...		70,000

Assets = Liabilities + Equity
−75,000 PIC—RS
+5,000 CS
+70,000 PIC—CS

Paid-in Cap—RS		Paid-in Cap—CS
75,000	25,000	70,000
	25,000	
	25,000	

Common Stock
5,000

c. Restricted Stock Unit Forfeitures—Estimated

 1. The fair value of the compensation related to the restricted stock units is reduced by the estimate of forfeiture of 1,000 units or 20% (1,000 units/5,000 units). Thus, the cost of compensation is estimated to be $60,000 ($75,000 × 80%). Jax Inc. recognizes compensation expense at the end of the first year of the requisite service period as follows.

December 31, Year 1—To record compensation expense

Compensation Expense	20,000	
Paid-in Capital—Restricted Stock ($60,000/3 years)		20,000

Assets = Liabilities + Equity
−20,000 Exp
+20,000 PIC—RS

Comp Exp	Paid-in Cap—RS
20,000	20,000

 2. Considering the forfeiture in Year 2, total compensation is $60,000 or $75,000 less $15,000 for the estimated forfeiture. Paid-in Capital—Restricted Stock should be $40,000 (or $60,000 × 2/3). Because $20,000 was expensed in Year 1, an additional $20,000 is expensed in Year 2. No adjustment is necessary for the actual units forfeited.

December 31, Year 2—To record compensation expense

Compensation Expense	20,000	
Paid-in Capital—Restricted Stock ($40,000 – $20,000)		20,000

Assets = Liabilities + Equity
−20,000 Exp
+20,000 PIC—RS

Comp Exp	Paid-in Cap—RS
20,000	20,000
20,000	20,000

d. Restricted Stock Unit Forfeitures—Recognized as Incurred

 1. Total compensation expense at the grant date is calculated as 5,000 shares multiplied by $15 shares or $75,000. One-third of the total amount is expensed in Year 1 as follows.

December 31, Year 1—To record compensation expense

Compensation Expense	25,000	
Paid-in Capital—Restricted Stock ($75,000/3 years)		25,000

Assets = Liabilities + Equity
−25,000 Exp
+25,000 PIC—RS

Comp Exp	Paid-in Cap—RS
25,000	25,000

 2. The company records the forfeiture as incurred in Year 2. Considering the forfeiture, total compensation is $60,000 or $75,000 less $15,000 for the forfeiture. Paid-in Capital—Restricted Stock should be $40,000 (or $60,000 × 2/3). Because $25,000 was expensed in Year 1, an additional $15,000 is expensed in Year 2.

continued

continued from previous page

December 31, Year 2—To record compensation expense

Compensation Expense	15,000	
Paid-in Capital—Restricted Stock ($40,000 – $25,000)		15,000

Assets = Liabilities + Equity
−15,000
Exp
+15,000
PIC—RS

Comp Exp		Paid-in Cap—RS	
25,000			25,000
15,000			15,000
			40,000

We see from parts *c* and *d* that total compensation expense is $40,000 over the two-year period of Year 1 to Year 2. Only the timing of expense recognition differs.

e. **Change in Estimate in Accounting for Forfeitures**

On December 31 of Year 2, the estimate of forfeitures increases to 2,000 units or 40% of the total compensation (2,000 units/5,000 units). Revised total compensation is $45,000 ($75,000 × 60%). Thus, on December 31 of Year 2, after two years, total Paid-in Capital—Restricted Stock should be $30,000 ($45,000 × 2/3). Because $20,000 was expensed in the prior year, an additional $10,000 is expensed in Year 2.

December 31, Year 2—To record compensation expense

Compensation Expense	10,000	
Paid-in Capital—Restricted Stock		10,000

Assets = Liabilities + Equity
−10,000
Exp
+10,000
PIC—RS

Comp Exp		Paid-in Cap—RS	
20,000			20,000
10,000			10,000
			30,000

FORD

Real World—RESTRICTED STOCK UNITS

Ford Motor Company described its share-based compensation plans, including its restricted stock unit plan for key employees in Note 6 to the financial statements in a recent Form 10-K. Some units are time-based and some are performance-based.

> Under our Long-Term Incentive Plans, we may issue restricted stock units ("RSUs"), restricted stock shares ("RSSs"), and stock options. RSUs and RSSs consist of time-based and performance-based awards. The number of shares that may be granted in any year is limited to 2% of our issued and outstanding Common Stock as of December 31 of the prior calendar year. The limit may be increased up to 3% in any year, with a corresponding reduction in shares available for grants in future years. Granted RSUs generally cliff vest or ratably vest over a three-year service period. Performance-based RSUs can be based on internal financial performance metrics or total shareholder return relative to a peer group or a combination of the two metrics. At the time of vest, RSU awards are net settled (i.e., shares are withheld to cover the employee tax obligation). Stock options ratably vest over a three-year service period and expire ten years from the grant date.

REVIEW 20-1	LO20-1	Accounting for Restricted Stock Plans

Review

MBC

On January 1, the board of directors of Instagraham Inc. granted awards to each of five key employees for 5,000 shares of restricted stock under the following terms.

- Restricted stock awards vest on December 31 of next year. Grantees must remain employed with the company to receive the common shares of stock without restriction. The requisite service period is considered to be 2 years.
- Each stock award represents one share of $1 par, common stock of Instagraham Inc.
- No forfeitures are anticipated.

On the date of grant, the common shares were trading at $75 per share. During this year and next year, the average price of common stock was $70 and $80 per share, respectively.

a. Prepare the journal entry on the date of grant, January 1.

b. Prepare the adjusting journal entry on December 31.

More Practice:
E20-1, E20-3, E20-5, E20-6, E20-8

Solution on p. 20-61.

c. Assume instead that the board of directors granted 5,000 restricted stock units instead of 5,000 shares of restricted stock. Each restricted stock unit may be exchanged for one share of common stock of Instagraham Inc. Prepare the related journal entries on January 1 and on December 31.

Account for stock options   LO 20-2

A stock option plan is another form of share-based compensation. **Stock options** give employees the right to buy a specified number of shares of stock of the employer at an established price (**exercise price**) over a specified time period. The accounting for stock option plans is illustrated in **Demo 20-2**.

Stock Option
- Determine total compensation at the date of grant using option-pricing model
- Recognize compensation expense in net income over the requisite service period
- Account for forfeitures

LO 20-2 Overview

Stock option plans are designed to incentivize employees to increase productivity and the share price of the company's stock. For example, options awarded to employees to purchase stock at the current market price exercisable in five years provide incentive to increase the market price of the stock over the next five years. Employees reap a reward equal to the increase in the share price times the number of shares under option. In this way, stock options are designed to align the interests of employees with the interests of shareholders. However, stock options are short-term focused as the holders benefit from an increase in stock price in a certain time period. Decisions made by management that lead to an increase in stock price in the short-term may be detrimental to the company in the long-term.

Key terms related to stock option plans are defined as follows.

Option	**ASC Glossary** Unless otherwise stated, a call option that gives the holder the right to purchase shares of common stock from the reporting entity in accordance with an agreement upon payment of a specified amount. Options include, but are not limited to, options granted and stock purchase agreements entered into with grantees. Options are considered securities.
Exercise price (Strike price)	**ASC Glossary** The amount that must be paid for a share of common stock upon exercise of an option or warrant.
Expiration date	Date that marks the point where the employee may no longer exercise the award under a share-based payment arrangement.
Performance condition	**ASC Glossary** A condition affecting the vesting, exercisability, exercise price, or other pertinent factors used in determining the fair value of an award that relates to both of the following: a. Rendering service or delivering goods for a specified (either explicitly or implicitly) period of time. b. Achieving a specified performance target that is defined solely by reference to the grantor's own operations (or activities) or by reference to the grantee's performance related to the grantor's own operations (or activities).

The cost of compensation is determined at the grant date based on the fair value of the options as determined by applying an option-pricing model such as the **Black-Scholes option-pricing model**. Changes in assumptions or selected valuation techniques are applied *prospectively* as explained in the authoritative guidance.

718-10-55-27   Assumptions used to estimate the fair value of equity and liability instruments granted in share-based payment transactions shall be determined in a consistent manner from period to period . . . The valuation technique an entity selects to estimate fair value for a particular type of instrument also shall be used consistently and shall not be changed unless a different valuation technique is expected to produce a better estimate of fair value. A change in either the valuation technique or the method of determining appropriate assumptions used in a valuation technique is a change in accounting estimate . . . and shall be applied prospectively to new awards.

Option-pricing models may require valuation inputs, such as the current market price of the stock, risk-free rate of interest, expected term of the options, expected volatility of the stock price, and expected dividend yield of the stock. Thus, an option-pricing model considers prospective information in deriving a fair value. For example, assume that a stock option with an exercise price of $20 per share was granted when the related stock was trading at $20 per share. The intrinsic value (or the amount by which the fair value of the underlying stock exceeds the exercise price of the option) is $0. However, the option-pricing model estimates the fair value of each option to be $5, based upon the variables considered in the option-pricing model. Options have option value even when their intrinsic value is zero because there is a non-zero chance the options will have a positive intrinsic value in the future. While the fair value of stock options is determined on the grant date, no journal entry is recorded at this time because compensation expense is recognized over the employees' service period.

The service period begins on the grant date and ends when the employee has no further service obligations or constraints imposed by the stock option plan. The entry to recognize expense each period includes a debit to **Compensation Expense** and a credit to **Paid-in Capital—Stock Options**. The compensation plan may specify the requisite service period; otherwise, the company must use a best estimate. A company may estimate forfeitures or elect to record forfeitures as incurred as described in LO 20-1.

Stock option plans may be structured to award the option to purchase shares based upon certain performance conditions or market conditions.

Performance conditions   In cases where a stock option award is based upon performance conditions, the company recognizes compensation expense when the company determines that it is *probable* that the performance condition will be met. Revisions of estimates of probability that affect amounts previously recorded are reflected *fully* in the year of the estimate revision.

Market conditions   In cases where a stock option award is based upon a market condition such as a target stock price, the share price models such as Black Scholes, have already taken market factors into account so no adjustments to fair values determined by the models are required. This means that the company recognizes compensation expense as if there is no target.

718-10-25-20   Accruals of compensation cost for an award with a performance condition shall be based on the probable outcome of that performance condition—compensation cost shall be accrued if it is probable that the performance condition will be achieved and shall not be accrued if it is not probable that the performance condition will be achieved. . . .

718-10-30-14   Some awards contain a market condition. The effect of a market condition is reflected in the grant-date fair value of an award. . . .

Upon exercise of the stock options, the employer debits Cash for the contractual amount paid by the employee, debits Paid-in Capital—Stock Options and credits the capital stock accounts. If instead, the stock options expire, the company transfers the balance of Paid-in Capital—Stock Options to Paid-in Capital—Expired Stock Options.

A stock option agreement may be structured to allow a performance obligation to be met *after* the employee retires. In this case, compensation is recognized when the company determines that it is probable that the condition is met, even if the condition is met after the employee retires.

718-10-30-28   In some cases, the terms of an award may provide that a performance target that affects vesting could be achieved after an employee completes the requisite service period or a nonemployee satisfies a vesting period. That is, the grantee would be eligible to vest in the award regardless of whether the grantee is rendering service or delivering goods on the date the performance target is achieved. A performance target that affects vesting and that could be achieved after an employee's requisite service period or a nonemployee's vesting period shall be accounted for as a performance condition. As such, the performance target shall not be reflected in estimating the fair value of the award at the grant date. . . .

As shown in this bar graph, restricted stock/unit awards are used more often (92%) than stock option awards (54%). The restricted stock/unit award is more popular because first, fewer shares are typically granted with restricted stock awards than with stock option plans. This results in less dilution to current shareholder ownership. For example, an executive officer may be just as satisfied with 200 shares of restricted stock as with stock options to purchase 500 shares of stock at a predetermined price; however, 200 shares represents less dilution to current shareholders. Second, restricted shares will generally retain some value despite market downturns, whereas stock options may become worthless.

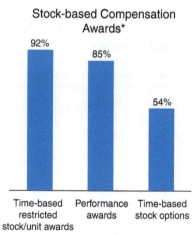

Stock-based Compensation Awards*

- Time-based restricted stock/unit awards: 92%
- Performance awards: 85%
- Time-based stock options: 54%

*Chart shows percentage usage by participants in the *Domestic Stock Plan Design Survey* by the National Association of Stock Plan Professionals and Deloitte Consulting LLP. For details see https://www2.deloitte.com/content/dam/Deloitte/us/Documents/human-capital/us-naspp-2019-full-report-v2.pdf.

Sustainability

APPLE INC.
THE CLOROX COMPANY
JOHNSON CONTROLS

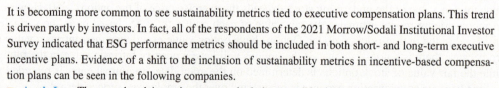

Real World—SUSTAINABILITY METRICS IN EXECUTIVE COMPENSATION PLANS

It is becoming more common to see sustainability metrics tied to executive compensation plans. This trend is driven partly by investors. In fact, all of the respondents of the 2021 Morrow/Sodali Institutional Investor Survey indicated that ESG performance metrics should be included in both short- and long-term executive incentive plans. Evidence of a shift to the inclusion of sustainability metrics in incentive-based compensation plans can be seen in the following companies.

- **Apple Inc.** The annual cash incentive program includes a modifier based on an executive's efforts to further values and key community initiatives (Proxy statement).

continued

continued from previous page

- **The Clorox Company** The annual incentive payouts for certain executives are affected by an individual performance multiplier that takes into account ESG factors (Proxy statement).
- **Johnson Controls** Executive compensation is linked to sustainability and diversity goals through an individual contribution multiplier that is applied to annual incentive award calculations (Proxy statement).

Accounting for Stock Options	**LO20-2**	**DEMO 20-2**

Demo

MBC

On January 1 of Year 1, Ram Co. awards a total of 100,000 stock options to acquire 100,000 shares of common stock ($1 par value) to 1,000 employees at an exercise price of $5 per share. The market price of Ram Co. common stock on the grant date is $5 per share. The options are exercisable after January 1 of Year 4 and expire when an employee leaves the company or on December 31 of Year 10, whichever is first. The requisite service period is three years. Using a fair value option-pricing model, management estimates that total compensation cost is $540,000 related to the stock options.

a. Record an entry (if applicable) on the date of grant.
b. Recognize compensation expense in Year 1 related to the stock options.
c. Employees exercised 90,000 options (90% of the options) that vested on January 1 of Year 4. On that date, the market price of Ram Co. stock was $7 per share. The amount collected from the employees totaled $450,000 or $5 × 90,000 options. Record the required journal entry on January 1 of Year 4.
d. The remaining 10,000 options (10% of the options) were *not* exercised before the expiration date of December 31 of Year 10. Record the required journal entry on December 31 of Year 10.
e. Assume the original scenario except that 20,000 options were associated with employees who left the company in Year 2. Record the required journal entry on December 31 of Year 2, assuming that the company recognizes forfeitures as incurred.
f. Assume the original scenario except that the company estimates forfeitures to be 10%. Record compensation expense related to the stock options in Year 1 assuming that it is the company's policy to recognize estimated forfeitures.
g. Assume the original scenario except that awards will only be granted to employees if sales of the company increase by 5% in each of the following three years: Year 1, Year 2, and Year 3. Management believes that it is probable that the company will achieve this performance target. Recognize compensation expense, if any, in Year 1.
h. Assume the original scenario except that the awards will only be granted to employees if sales of the company increase by 5% in each of the following three years: Year 1, Year 2, and Year 3. Management believes that it is *not* probable that the company will achieve this performance target. Recognize compensation expense, if any, in Year 1.

Solution

a. **Issuance of Stock Options**
   While the total cost of compensation of $540,000 is determined at the grant date, no journal entry is recorded at this time.

b. **Recognition of Compensation Expense**
   The cost of compensation of $540,000 determined at the grant date is recognized over the three-year requisite service period. This is the period that the employees earn the compensation.

December 31, Year 1—To record compensation expense

Compensation Expense	180,000	
Paid-in Capital—Stock Options ($540,000/3 years)		180,000

Assets = Liabilities + Equity
−180,000 Exp
+180,000 PIC—SO

Comp Exp	Pd-in Cap—SO
180,000	180,000

Ram Co. also records compensation expense of $180,000 in Year 2 and Year 3.

c. **Exercise of Stock Options**
   Ram Co. records the following entry upon the exercise of stock options by employees.

January 1, Year 4—To record exercise of stock options

Cash (90,000 × $5).	450,000	
Paid-in Capital—Stock Options ($540,000 × 90%)	486,000	
Common Stock (90,000 × $1)		90,000
Paid-in Capital in Excess of Par—Common Stock (to balance) . . .		846,000

Assets = Liabilities + Equity
+450,000   −486,000
C:f   PIC—SO
         +90,000
         CS
         +846,000
         PIC—CS

Cash	Pd-in Cap—SO
450,000	486,000	540,000 Bal.

Common Stock	Pd-in Cap—CS
90,000	846,000

continued

continued from previous page

d. **Expiration of Stock Options—Time Lapse**

On December 31 of Year 10, the company transfers the balance of Paid-in Capital—Stock Options to Paid-in Capital—Expired Stock Options.

December 31, Year 10—To record expiration of stock options

Paid-in Capital—Stock Options ($540,000 × 10%)	54,000	
Paid-in Capital—Expired Stock Options		54,000

Assets = Liabilities + Equity
-54,000
PIC—SO
+54,000
PIC—ExpSO

Pd-in Cap—SO		Pd-in Cap—ESO
486,000	540,000	54,000
54,000		
	0	

e. **Stock Option Forfeitures—Recognized as Incurred**

The company will recognize the forfeiture in Year 2 when incurred. The forfeiture of 20,000 options is a 20% (20,000 options/100,000 options) reduction of compensation cost. Total compensation cost reflecting the forfeiture is $432,000 or $540,000 × 80%. Total Paid-in Capital—Stock Options should be $288,000 or $432,000 × 2/3. Because $180,000 was expensed in Year 1, an additional $108,000 is expensed in Year 2.

December 31, Year 2—To record compensation expense adjusted for expiration of stock options

Compensation Expense	108,000	
Paid-in Capital—Stock Options ($288,000 – $180,000)		108,000

Assets = Liabilities + Equity
-108,000
Exp
+108,000
PIC—SO

Comp Exp		Pd-in Cap—SO	
108,000		180,000	Bal.
		108,000	
		288,000	

f. **Stock Option Forfeitures—Estimated**

Forfeitures are estimated to be 10%, which reduces total compensation cost to $486,000 ($540,000 × 90%). Thus, compensation expense is now $162,000 per year (or $486,000/3 years), recorded in Year 1 as follows.

December 31, Year 1—To record compensation expense

Compensation Expense	162,000	
Paid-in Capital—Stock Options ($486,000/3 years)		162,000

Assets = Liabilities + Equity
-162,000
Exp
+162,000
PIC—SO

Comp Exp		Pd-in Cap—SO	
162,000		162,000	

g. **Performance Based Measure**

Because the company believes that it is probable that it will achieve the performance target, allocated compensation expense is recognized in Year 1.

December 31, Year 1—To record compensation expense

Compensation Expense	180,000	
Paid-in Capital—Stock Options ($540,000/3 years)		180,000

Assets = Liabilities + Equity
-180,000
Exp
+180,000
PIC—SO

Comp Exp		Pd-in Cap—SO	
180,000		180,000	

h. **Performance Based Measure**

Because the company believes that it is *not* probable that it will achieve the performance target, compensation expense is not recorded in Year 1.

EXPANDING YOUR KNOWLEDGE   Graded Vesting of Stock Option Plans

Stock option plans may vest over several dates instead of on one particular date, which is called **graded vesting**. (**Cliff vesting**, as illustrated in **Demo 20-2**, is when *all* awards vest at the end of the vesting period.) In the case of graded vesting, a company may value each vesting group (or tranche) *separately* or in the *aggregate* using an average expected term. Compensation may be recognized using an accelerated approach or straight-line method, as long as the cumulative amount recognized each year is at least equal to the value of the awards vested to that date. For example, AAA Co. awards stock options that vest over a three-year period. The fair value of each group of options that vest is estimated to be $5,000, $12,000, and $21,000, for years 1, 2, and 3, respectively. The amounts are separately recognized as expense on a straight-line basis as follows.

Compensation Costs to be Recognized	Year 1	Year 2	Year 3	Total
Shares vesting in Year 1	$ 5,000	$ —	$ —	$ 5,000
Shares vesting in Year 2	6,000	6,000	—	12,000
Shares vesting in Year 3	7,000	7,000	7,000	21,000
	$18,000	$13,000	$7,000	$38,000

Under this approach, each year of expense exceeds the actual value of the awards vested to date.

Year 1: Compensation expense of $18,000 exceeds vested expense of $5,000.

Year 2: Compensation expense of $31,000 ($18,000 + $13,000) exceeds vested expense of $17,000 ($5,000 + $12,000).

Alternatively, the company may calculate amortization expense in the aggregate as $12,667 each year or $38,000/3.

PEPSICO

Real World—EMPLOYEE STOCK OPTIONS

PepsiCo Inc. described the assumptions used to value its stock options in a recent annual report.

Note 6—A stock option permits the holder to purchase shares of PepsiCo common stock at a specified price. We account for our employee stock options under the fair value method of accounting using a Black-Scholes valuation model to measure stock option expense at the date of grant.... weighted-average Black-Scholes fair value assumptions are as follows:

Expected life................	7 years	Expected volatility.............	16%
Risk-free interest rate..........	4.2%	Expected dividend yield........	2.7%

The expected life is the period over which our employee groups are expected to hold their options. It is based on our historical experience with similar grants. The risk-free interest rate is based on the expected U.S. Treasury rate over the expected life. Volatility reflects movements in our stock price over the most recent historical period equivalent to the expected life. Dividend yield is estimated over the expected life based on our stated dividend policy and forecasts of net income, share repurchases and stock price.

Accounting for Stock Options   **LO20-2**   **REVIEW 20-2**

Review   MBC

On April 1 of Year 1, Badger Corp. announced a stock option incentive plan for its top executives. The plan provides certain executives stock options for the company's common stock. Each option allows for the purchase of one share of common stock, par $1, at an exercise price of $25 per share. The rights are nontransferable and are exercisable three years after the grant date and prior to five years from the grant date. Continuing employment is required through the exercise date, and the requisite service period ends on the first possible exercise date.

On April 1 of Year 1, 2,000 options were granted to employees when the market price was $30 per share. Using an option-pricing model, the fair value of the options granted was $18,000. Employees exercised 1,200 options on June 30 of Year 4 when the market price of the stock was $45 per share.

a. Compute the total amount of compensation cost for the grant made on April 1 of Year 1.

b. Record the entry for compensation expense on December 31 of Year 1, Badger's year-end.

c. Record the entry for the exercise of options on June 30 of Year 4.

More Practice:
BE20-5, E20-10, E20-12

Solution on p. 20-61.

Account for employee stock purchase plans   LO 20-3

Employee stock purchase plans allow employees the opportunity to purchase shares of stock of their employer at a discounted price. The company records no compensation expense in this situation if all of the following conditions are met as outlined in the authoritative guidance.

`718-50-25-1` An employee share purchase plan that satisfies all of the following criteria does not give rise to recognizable compensation cost (that is, the plan is noncompensatory):

a. The plan satisfies either of the following conditions:

  1. The terms of the plan are no more favorable than those available to all holders of the same class of shares. . . .

  2. Any purchase discount from the market price does not exceed the per-share amount of share issuance costs that would have been incurred to raise a significant amount of capital by a public offering. A purchase discount of 5 percent or less from the market price shall be considered to comply with this condition without further justification. . . .

b. Substantially all employees that meet limited employment qualifications may participate on an equitable basis.

c. The plan incorporates no option features, other than the following:

  1. Employees are permitted a short period of time—not exceeding 31 days—after the purchase price has been fixed to enroll in the plan.

  2. The purchase price is based solely on the market price of the shares at the date of purchase, and employees are permitted to cancel participation before the purchase date and obtain a refund of amounts previously paid (such as those paid by payroll withholdings).

Employee Stock Purchase Plan

- Noncompensatory plan
  - Meets criteria
  - Recognize no compensation expense
- Compensatory plan
  - Does not meet criteria
  - Recognize compensation expense for employee discount on stock purchase

LO 20-3 Overview

If all of the conditions outlined above are met, no compensation is recorded related to the plan as illustrated in **Demo 20-3** (Example One). If all of the conditions outlined above are *not* met, the company must recognize compensation expense for the amount of the stock discount extended to employees—see **Demo 20-3** (Example Two).

EXPANDING YOUR KNOWLEDGE   Disclosure of Compensation Plans

Companies with a share-based payment arrangement(s) must disclose the following information described in the authoritative guidance.

718-10-50-1   An entity with one or more share-based payment arrangements shall disclose information that enables users of the financial statements to understand all of the following:

  a. The nature and terms of such arrangements that existed during the period and the potential effects of those arrangements on shareholders.
  b. The effect of compensation cost arising from share-based payment arrangements on the income statement.
  c. The method of estimating the fair value of the equity instruments granted (or offered to grant), during the period.
  d. The cash flow effects resulting from share-based payment arrangements.

HOME DEPOT

Real World—EMPLOYEE STOCK PURCHASE PLANS

Home Depot Inc. described employee stock purchase plans (ESPPs) in a recent annual report. The discount extended to employees for stock purchases is 15%.

> We maintain two ESPPs: a U.S. and a non-U.S. plan. The plan for U.S. associates is a tax-qualified plan under Section 423 of the Internal Revenue Code. The non-U.S. plan is not a Section 423 plan. At January 28, 2024, there were approximately 15 million shares available under the U.S. plan and approximately 18 million shares available under the non-U.S. plan. The purchase price of shares under the ESPPs is equal to 85% of the stock's fair market value on the last day of the purchase period, which is a six-month period ending on December 31 and June 30 of each year. During fiscal 2023, there were approximately 1 million shares purchased under the ESPPs at an average price of $277.19. Under the outstanding ESPPs at January 28, 2024, associates have contributed $22 million to purchase shares at 85% of the stock's fair market value on the last day of the current purchase period, June 30, 2024.

DEMO 20-3   **LO20-3**   **Accounting for Employee Stock Purchase Plans**

Demo
MBC

Example One—Share Issuance Under a Noncompensatory Employee Stock Purchase Plan
Evergreen Inc. has an employee stock purchase plan for all eligible employees. Under the plan, shares of the company's $1 par value common stock may be purchased at 95% of the fair value on the last day of each six-month period. On January 31, employees purchased 5,000 shares at a price of $18 per share, less the 5% discount. The plan is determined to be noncompensatory because it meets the criteria of a noncompensatory plan. Record the journal entry for the issuance of stock on January 31.

Solution
On January 31, Evergreen Inc. records the following journal entry for issuance of stock through the employee stock purchase plan.

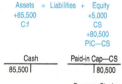

Assets	=	Liabilities	+	Equity
+85,500				+5,000
C:f				CS
				+80,500
				PIC—CS

Cash		Paid-in Cap—CS
85,500		80,500

Common Stock
5,000

January 31—To record issuance of stock for employee stock purchase plan

Cash (5,000 × $18 × 95%)............................	85,500	
Common Stock (5,000 × $1)		5,000
Paid-in Capital in Excess of Par—Common Stock (to balance) ...		80,500

Example Two—Share Issuance Under a Compensatory Employee Stock Purchase Plan
Let's assume the same facts described in Example One, except now the plan allows for the shares to be purchased at 90% of the fair value on the last day of each six-month period. In this case, the discount exceeds 5% of the stock price and the plan is considered compensatory. Record the journal entry for the issuance of stock on January 31.

Solution
On January 31, Evergreen Inc. records the following journal entry for the issuance of stock through the employee stock purchase plan.

Assets	=	Liabilities	+	Equity
+81,000				−9,000
C:f				Exp
				+5,000
				CS
				+85,000
				PIC—CS

Cash		Comp Exp
81,000		9,000

Common Stock		Paid-in Cap—CS
5,000		85,000

January 31—To record issuance of stock for employee stock purchase plan

Cash (5,000 × $18 × 90%).............................	81,000	
Compensation Expense (5,000 × $18 × 10%).....................	9,000	
Common Stock (5,000 × $1)		5,000
Paid-in Capital in Excess of Par—Common Stock (to balance) ...		85,000

Accounting for Employee Stock Purchase Plans   LO20-3   REVIEW 20-3

Review
MBC

Safe Inc. employees are all eligible to participate in a stock purchase plan. The plan allows employees to purchase $1 par value common stock at a 5% discount. On January 1, employees purchased 500 shares of common stock when the market price of the stock was $10 per share.

a. Record the journal entry for Safe Inc. on January 1, assuming the plan is determined to be noncompensatory.

b. Assume instead that only certain employees are eligible for the plan and that the discount is 15% on the market price of the stock. Record the entry on January 1 for the employee purchase of 500 shares of common stock when the market price of the stock was $10 per share.

More Practice:
BE20-13, BE20-15, E20-15
Solution on p. 20-62.

Compute earnings per share (EPS) with a simple capital structure   LO 20-4

Earnings per share (EPS) is the amount of earnings attributable to each share of common stock. This measure is important to investors because it is a factor in determining the market price of stock. Given the emphasis of this measure, the FASB, the SEC, and other investment regulatory agencies are concerned with how this financial statistic is measured. We begin with a discussion of basic earnings per share.

EPS—Simple Capital Structure
- Earnings attributable to each share of common stock
- Divide net income available to common stockholders by weighted-average common shares outstanding

LO 20-4 Overview

ASC Glossary   Basic earnings per share: The amount of earnings for the period available to each share of common stock outstanding during the reporting period.

In its most elementary form, **basic earnings per share** (EPS) for a period of time is calculated as follows and illustrated in **Demo 20-4**.

$$\text{Basic earnings per share} = \frac{\text{Net income available to common stockholders}}{\text{Weighted-average common shares outstanding}}$$

One implication of this expression is that preferred dividends declared in the period must be deducted from net income because these dividends are a part of net income that does not belong to common stockholders. The impact of preferred dividends on this calculation is explained in the next section. If a company incurs a net loss (instead of net income), the net loss is divided by weighted-average common shares to arrive at a net loss per share. Net income excludes the income attributable to any noncontrolling interest in subsidiaries.

A company has a **simple capital structure** if stockholders' equity consists only of common stock and no financial instruments exist that could be converted to common stock and dilute (decrease) earnings per existing common share. We will explore in a later section how to reflect the impact on EPS of issuing financial instruments or employee share-based awards that could result in an increase in common stock. If a company has several classes of common stock, the total of the weighted-average shares of the classes of common stock are used to compute basic EPS. **For a simple capital structure, a single EPS presentation showing basic earnings per share is appropriate on the face of the income statement.**

Earnings per Share Calculation—Simple Capital Structure   LO20-4   DEMO 20-4

Demo
MBC

Atlanta Co. has 300,000 common shares outstanding for the entire year and net income of $2 million.
a. Compute basic earnings per share for the year.
b. Show how basic earnings per share is presented in the financial statements.

Solution
a. **Computation of Basic EPS**

	Net Income Available to Common Stockholders		Weighted-Average Common Shares Outstanding		Per Share
Basic EPS . . .	$2,000,000	÷	300,000	=	$6.67

continued

continued from previous page

b. Financial Statement Presentation of Basic EPS
In the income statement for the year ended December 31, the company reports the following.

Income Statement	
Net income	$2,000,000
Basic earnings per share	$ 6.67

REVIEW 20-4   LO20-4   **Calculation of Basic EPS**

Review
MBC

More Practice:
BE20-17, E20-16
Solution on p. 20-62.

Compute basic earnings per share considering the following information for Badger Corp.

Common stock, $1 par, outstanding throughout the year	100,000 shares
Net income	$245,000

LO 20-5   Compute EPS given share issuances, buybacks, dividends, and splits

Factors Affecting EPS Calculation
- Numerator
  - Reduce net income for preferred dividends
- Denominator
  - Weight shares by the fraction of the period outstanding for issuances and buybacks
  - Weight shares from the beginning of the periods presented for stock dividends and stock splits

A number of factors cause adjustments to the numerator and the denominator in the computation of basic EPS. In the numerator, net income is adjusted for the impact of preferred dividends. In the denominator, weighted average common shares are adjusted for share issuances and share buybacks, stock splits, and stock dividends. The impact on EPS for these factors is illustrated in **Demo 20-5**.

Preferred Stock Dividends
The adjustment to the numerator for preferred dividends depends on whether the preferred stock is cumulative and whether a dividend was declared. If the preferred stock is *noncumulative*, only the dividends declared for the current period are subtracted. If the preferred stock is *cumulative*, one year's dividend claim is subtracted from earnings whether or not declared. Undeclared cumulative preferred dividends must be paid before current common dividends, which is why they are subtracted even if not declared. However, only the current-year claim is subtracted. Prior years' cumulative preferred stock dividends were subtracted in computing EPS in prior years and should not be subtracted again.

`260-10-45-11` Income available to common stockholders shall be computed by deducting both the dividends declared in the period on preferred stock (whether or not paid) and the dividends accumulated for the period on cumulative preferred stock (whether or not earned) from income from continuing operations (if that amount appears in the income statement) and also from net income. If there is a loss from continuing operations or a net loss, the amount of the loss shall be increased by those preferred dividends. An adjustment to net income or loss for preferred stock dividends is required for all preferred stock dividends, regardless of the form of payment. Preferred dividends that are cumulative only if earned shall be deducted only to the extent that they are earned.

If the company declared *common* stock dividends, there will be no impact on the EPS calculation. EPS calculates the income per common share available to common shareholders. The company may choose to distribute a portion of earnings as dividends, or to retain the earnings for internal growth. In either case, there is no adjustment to the EPS calculation.

Share Issuances and Buybacks

To properly reflect weighted-average number of common shares in the denominator, shares issued and reacquired must be weighted for the portion of the period that they were outstanding. The resources made available by the issuance (or buyback) of common shares during the period were available only for the part of the year for which the shares were outstanding.

260-10-45-10   Basic EPS shall be computed by dividing income available to common stockholders (the numerator) by the weighted-average number of common shares outstanding (the denominator) during the period. Shares issued during the period and shares reacquired during the period shall be weighted for the portion of the period that they were outstanding. See Example 1 (paragraph 260-10-55-38) for an illustration of this guidance.

Stock Dividends and Stock Splits

Stock dividends and stock splits are treated as if they occurred at the beginning of the earliest period presented. This differs from the treatment of share issuances because stock dividends and stock splits do not generate additional capital for the company,

Sometimes stock dividends and stock splits occur after the balance sheet date but before the issuance of financial statements. In this situation, all EPS amounts shown for the period just ended and for any previous periods shown comparatively must reflect the stock dividend or split. Restatement provides the most current and relevant information for the user. A description of the effects of such dividends and splits is disclosed in the notes to financial statements.

260-10-55-12   If the number of common shares outstanding increases as a result of a stock dividend or stock split (see Subtopic 505-20) or decreases as a result of a reverse stock split, the computations of basic and diluted EPS shall be adjusted retroactively for all periods presented to reflect that change in capital structure. If changes in common stock resulting from stock dividends, stock splits, or reverse stock splits occur after the close of the period but before the financial statements are issued or are available to be issued (as discussed in Section 855-10-25) the per-share computations for those and any prior-period financial statements presented shall be based on the new number of shares. If per-share computations reflect such changes in the number of shares, that fact shall be disclosed.

EPS Calculations—Simple Capital Structure	LO20-5	DEMO 20-5

Demo

MBC

Example One—Basic EPS Calculation with Share Issuance
Atlanta Co. has 100,000 common shares outstanding as of January 1 and net income of $300,000 for the year. On October 1, the company issues an additional 50,000 shares of common stock. Calculate basic EPS for the year.

Solution
The company first calculates weighted-average common shares for the year.

Inclusive Dates	A Actual Shares Outstanding	Months Outstanding	B Percentage of Full Year*	(A × B) Weighted-Average Shares Outstanding
Jan.–Sept.	100,000	9	75%	75,000
Oct.–Dec.	150,000	3	25%	37,500
		12	100%	112,500

* Divide months outstanding by total months of 12.

The weighted-average number of shares outstanding is 112,500 shares and reflects the number of months shares were outstanding. This means more weight (75%) is given to 100,000 shares (than 150,000 shares) because 100,000 shares were outstanding for a greater proportion of the year. The weighted-average common shares of 112,500 is used to calculate basic EPS.

	Net Income Available to Common Stockholders	Weighted-Average Common Shares Outstanding	Per Share
Basic EPS	$300,000	112,500	$2.67

continued

continued from previous page

Example Two—Basic EPS Calculation with Share Buyback

To extend Example One, now assume the same facts except that Atlanta Co. also purchased 5,000 common shares for the treasury on March 31. The company started the year with 100,000 shares, reduced the number of shares to 95,000 on March 31 (100,000 – 5,000), and increased the number of shares to 145,000 (95,000 + 50,000) on October 1. Calculate basic EPS for the year.

Solution

We first calculate weighted-average common shares for the year. Again, any changes in the number of common shares outstanding must be reflected in the calculation of EPS and weighted according to the period outstanding.

Inclusive Dates	A Actual Shares Outstanding	Months Outstanding	B Percentage of Full Year*	(A × B) Weighted-Average Shares Outstanding
Jan.–Mar.	100,000	3	25%	25,000
Apr.–Sept.	95,000	6	50%	47,500
Oct.–Dec.	145,000	3	25%	36,250
		12	100%	108,750

* Divide months outstanding by total months of 12.

The weighted-average common shares of 108,750 is used to calculate basic EPS.

	Net Income Available to Common Stockholders	Weighted-Average Common Shares Outstanding	Per Share
Basic EPS	$300,000	108,750	$2.76

Example Three—Basic EPS Calculation with Stock Dividends and Stock Splits

a. To extend Example Two, now assume that Atlanta Co. also distributed a stock dividend of 40% on October 31. On October 31, the shares outstanding increase by 40% to 203,000 shares (145,000 × 1.4). Calculate basic EPS for the year.

b. Instead of a stock dividend on October 31, now assume that Atlanta Co. declared a 2-for-1 stock split. Calculate basic EPS for the year.

Solution

a. **Stock Dividend**

The company calculates weighted-average common shares for the year as follows, applying the retroactive restatement adjustment of 140% (1.4) to all periods prior to the stock dividend.

Inclusive Dates	Actual Shares Outstanding	Retroactive Restatement for Stock Dividend	A Equivalent Shares Outstanding*	Months Outstanding	B Fraction of Year	(A × B) Weighted- Average Shares Outstanding
Jan.–Mar.	100,000	1.4	140,000	3	3/12	35,000
Apr.–Sept.	95,000	1.4	133,000	6	6/12	66,500
Oct.	145,000	1.4	203,000	1	1/12	16,917
Nov.–Dec.	203,000		203,000	2	2/12	33,833
				12	100.0%	152,250

* Shares outstanding × Retroactive restatement.

The weighted-average common shares of 152,250 is used to calculate basic EPS.

	Net Income Available to Common Stockholders	Weighted-Average Common Shares Outstanding	Per Share
Basic EPS	$300,000	152,250	$1.97

continued

continued from previous page

b. **Stock Split**

If the stock dividend were instead a 2-for-1 stock split on October 31, the retroactive restatement factor would be 2.0. (Had the stock dividend been instead a reverse, 1-for-2 stock split on October 31, the retroactive restatement factor would be 0.5.)

Inclusive Dates	Actual Shares Outstanding	Retroactive Restatement for Stock Split	A Equivalent Shares Outstanding*	Months Outstanding	B Fraction of Year	(A × B) Weighted-Average Shares Outstanding
Jan.–Mar.	100,000	2.0	200,000	3	3/12	50,000
Apr.–Sept.	95,000	2.0	190,000	6	6/12	95,000
Oct.	145,000	2.0	290,000	1	1/12	24,167
Nov.–Dec.	290,000		290,000	2	2/12	48,333
				12	100.0%	217,500

* Shares outstanding × Retroactive restatement.

The weighted-average common shares of 217,500 is used to calculate basic EPS.

	Net Income Available to Common Stockholders	Weighted-Average Common Shares Outstanding	Per Share
Basic EPS	$300,000	217,500	$1.38

Example Four—Basic EPS Calculation with Cash Dividends (Noncumulative Preferred)

Madison Co. has 100,000 common shares outstanding during the year, and net income of $300,000 for the year. During the year, the company also has 20,000 shares of 4%, $10 par value preferred stock outstanding. The preferred stock is *noncumulative* and preferred dividends of $6,000 were declared and paid during the year. Calculate basic EPS for the year.

Solution

The preferred dividends of $6,000 are subtracted from net income in calculating basic earnings per share. With noncumulative preferred stock, dividends are subtracted in the current year when dividends are declared in the current year. (Had the company declared no dividends on noncumulative preferred stock, no adjustment for dividends would have been required.)

December 31—To calculate basic EPS with noncumulative preferred stock

	Net Income Available to Common Stockholders	Weighted-Average Common Shares Outstanding	Per Share
Basic EPS	$294,000[1]	100,000	$2.94

[1] $300,000 (net income) – $6,000 (preferred dividends).

Example Five—Basic EPS Calculation with Cash Dividends (Cumulative Preferred)

Now assume Madison Co. has 100,000 common shares outstanding during the year, and net income of $300,000 for the year. During the year, the company also had 20,000 shares of 4%, $10 par value preferred stock outstanding. The preferred stock is *cumulative* and no preferred stock dividends were declared during the year. Calculate basic EPS for the year.

Solution

Even though no dividends were declared, because the preferred stock is cumulative, one year of dividends is subtracted in the numerator of the EPS calculation. The annual preferred stock dividend is $8,000 (4% × 20,000 × $10).

	Net Income Available to Common Stockholders	Weighted-Average Common Shares Outstanding	Per Share
Basic EPS	$292,000[1]	100,000	$2.92

[1] $300,000 (net income) – $8,000 (preferred dividends).

© Cambridge Business Publishers

REVIEW 20-5 ▶ LO20-5   Calculation of Basic EPS

Review

MBC

Seco Corporation was incorporated on January 2. The following information pertains to Seco's common stock transactions for the year.

Jan.	2	Number of shares issued	150,000
Mar.	31	Number of shares issued	60,000
Jul.	1	Number of shares reacquired but not canceled	5,000
Nov.	1	150% common stock dividend	

More Practice:
BE20-18, BE20-19, E20-19,
E20-20

Solution on p. 20-62.

Net income for the year was $825,000. The company also had 5,000 shares of noncumulative, preferred stock outstanding and declared and paid $3,500 in preferred dividends to shareholders during the year. Compute basic EPS for the year.

LO 20-6 ▶ Compute EPS using *if-converted* method for convertible securities

LO 20-6 Overview

Convertible Bonds: Effect on Diluted EPS
- Numerator: Add back interest expense, net of tax
- Denominator: Add new common shares

Convertible Preferred Stock: Effect on Diluted EPS
- Numerator: Add back preferred dividends
- Denominator: Add new common shares

To this point, we assumed that the company had a simple capital structure. *What if the company owns financial instruments that upon exercise or conversion could result in an increase to common shares?* A **complex capital structure** exists when a company owns financial instruments that have the *potential* to increase common shares. The exercise or conversion of such instruments could result in a decrease to EPS in the future. We consider the potential dilution of stockholders' interest in the company's earnings when we calculate **diluted EPS**.

ASC Glossary   Diluted earnings per share: The amount of earnings for the period available to each share of common stock outstanding during the reporting period and to each share that would have been outstanding assuming the issuance of common shares for all dilutive potential common shares outstanding during the reporting period.

260-10-10-2   The objective of diluted EPS is consistent with that of basic EPS—to measure the performance of an entity over the reporting period—while giving effect to all dilutive potential common shares that were outstanding during the period.

260-10-45-16   The computation of diluted EPS is similar to the computation of basic EPS except that the denominator is increased to include the number of additional common shares that would have been outstanding if the dilutive potential common shares had been issued. In computing the dilutive effect of convertible securities, the numerator is adjusted in accordance with the guidance in paragraph 260-10-45-40. . . .

A security is **dilutive** if EPS is reduced as a result of incorporating the effects of an *assumed* conversion or exercise of common stock into the EPS calculation. A security is **antidilutive** if EPS is *not* reduced as a result of incorporating the effects of an assumed conversion or exercise of common stock into the EPS calculation. If a security is determined to be antidilutive, the effects of the security are not considered in the diluted EPS calculation. This means we only want to consider securities that have the potential to *decrease* earnings per share without offsetting this impact by a security with a potential to increase earnings per share. First, we consider only one potentially dilutive security at a time. In a later section, we explore the impact of multiple potentially dilutive securities on a company's diluted earnings per share calculation.

Convertible Debt and Convertible Preferred Stock

Convertible debt and convertible preferred stock are instruments that have the potential to convert into common stock. Therefore, the effect of conversion must be considered in computing diluted earnings per share. This is accomplished by using the *if-converted* method to determine whether the convertible securities are dilutive and, if so, the amount needed to adjust diluted EPS.

The *if-converted* method assumes that conversion occurs as of the beginning of the period or at the date of issue, if later. This is a hypothetical calculation—no conversion to common stock has taken place during the year, but a conversion could have taken place during the year. The impact of such hypothetical conversions on EPS is shown in the **diluted EPS** calculation.

ASC Glossary   If-Converted Method: A method of computing EPS data that assumes conversion of convertible securities at the beginning of the reporting period (or at time of issuance, if later).

Convertible Debt

Convertible debt is assumed to have been converted into common stock as of the beginning of the period (or the issue date if later) under the *if-converted* method. If we assume that the debt is converted, the company would not incur interest expense. As a result, interest expense, adjusted for tax savings, is added back to the numerator of the basic EPS calculation and the new common shares are added to the denominator of the basic EPS calculation as we show in **Demo 20-6A**.

Effect on Diluted EPS Calculation of Convertible Debt
Numerator: Add back interest expense, net of tax
Denominator: Add new common shares

260-10-45-40b   If an entity has convertible debt outstanding:

1. Interest charges applicable to the convertible debt shall be added back to the numerator. For convertible debt for which the principal is required to be paid in cash, the interest charges shall not be added back to the numerator.
2. To the extent nondiscretionary adjustments based on income made during the period would have been computed differently had the interest on convertible debt never been recognized, the numerator shall be appropriately adjusted. Nondiscretionary adjustments include any expenses or charges that are determined based on the income (loss) for the period, such as profit-sharing and royalty agreements.
3. The numerator shall be adjusted for the income tax effect of (b)(1) and (b)(2).

260-10-45-40c   The convertible preferred stock or convertible debt shall be assumed to have been converted at the beginning of the period (or at time of issuance, if later), and the resulting common shares shall be included in the denominator. . . .

Impact of Net Losses on Calculation of Diluted EPS

If a company reports a *net loss* from continuing operations, the basic earnings per share amount will be negative. The dilutive earnings per share calculations will always result in a lower net loss, thus will have an antidilutive effect. Therefore, in the case of a loss from continuing operations, no potentially dilutive securities are considered; thus, **basic EPS and diluted EPS will be reported as the same amount.**

260-10-45-19   Including potential common shares in the denominator of a diluted per-share computation for continuing operations always will result in an antidilutive per-share amount when an entity has a loss from continuing operations or a loss from continuing operations available to common stockholders (that is, after any preferred dividend deductions). Although including those potential common shares in the other diluted per-share computations may be dilutive to their comparable basic per-share amounts, no potential common shares shall be included in the computation of any diluted per-share amount when a loss from continuing operations exists, even if the entity reports net income.

260-10-50-1   For each period for which an income statement is presented, including interim periods, an entity shall disclose all of the following: . . . c. Securities (including those issuable pursuant to contingent stock agreements) that could potentially dilute basic EPS in the future that were not included in the computation of diluted EPS because to do so would have been antidilutive for the period(s) presented. Full disclosure of the terms and conditions of these securities is required even if a security is not included in diluted EPS in the current period. . . .

EXPANDING YOUR KNOWLEDGE   **Convertible Debt Sold at a Discount or Premium**

If a convertible debt is sold at a discount or premium, interest expense on the income statement factors into the amortization of the discount or premium for the reporting period. This means the adjustment to the numerator described above should reflect *effective interest*. For example, assume that a $50,000, 10-year, 5% bond, is sold at $48,000 on January 1, and that the company's tax rate is 25%. What is the adjustment to the numerator in the diluted EPS calculation assuming that the discount is amortized using the straight-line method? *Answer:* The after-tax interest expense adjustment including the amortization of the discount of $200 [($50,000 − $48,000)/10 years] is: $2,025, computed as ([$50,000 × 5%] + $200) × 0.75.

DEMO 20-6A **LO20-6**   **EPS Calculations—Convertible Bonds**

Demo

MBC

Net income for the year for Gridley Inc. is $600,000. During the entire year, 1,000, 6%, $1,000 bonds, issued at par, were outstanding, each convertible into 20 common shares. The weighted-average shares outstanding before considering potentially dilutive securities is 200,000, and the tax rate is 25%.

a. Compute basic EPS for Gridley Inc. for the year.
b. Compute diluted EPS for the year using the *if-converted* method. Indicate the EPS amount(s) that the company would report in its income statement.
c. Assume instead that the convertible bonds were issued on October 1 resulting in interest expense for three months instead of twelve months. As a result, net income for the year is $633,750 (calculated as $600,000 + prorated after-tax interest of $33,750 (9/12 × $45,000). Compute diluted EPS for the year using the *if-converted* method.
d. Repeat the requirements of parts *a* and *b*, but now assume that the company reported a net loss of $600,000. Even though the company has an accounting loss, assume the company has sufficient taxable income to be able to deduct the interest on their tax return and there are no other complications.

Solution

a. **Basic EPS Calculation**

	Net Income Available to Common Stockholders	Weighted-Average Common Shares Outstanding	Per Share
Basic EPS	$600,000	200,000	$3.00

b. **Diluted EPS Calculation with Convertible Bond**

The impact on EPS assuming that all of the bonds were converted into common stock as of January 1 follows.

- **Adjustment to numerator:** After-tax interest of $45,000 is added, computed as (1,000 bonds × $1,000 par × 6%) × (1 − 25%). Had the bonds been converted at the beginning of the year, no interest would have been paid, causing earnings after tax to increase $45,000.
- **Adjustment to denominator:** 20,000 new common shares are added based on the assumed conversion (1,000 bonds × 20 shares per bond).

The impact on diluted EPS follows.

	Net Income Available to Common Stockholders	Weighted-Average Common Shares Outstanding	Per Share
Basic EPS	$600,000	200,000	$3.00
Effect of convertible bonds:			
Add back interest, net of tax . . .	45,000		
Add new common shares		20,000	
Diluted EPS	$645,000	220,000	$2.93

The convertible bonds are considered dilutive because EPS drops from $3.00 (basic EPS) to $2.93 (diluted EPS). The company reports both basic EPS of $3.00 and diluted EPS of $2.93 in its annual income statement.

c. **Diluted EPS Calculation with Convertible Bonds (Partial Year)**

Because the bonds were issued on October 1, the number of shares assumed converted is weighted by the period over which the new shares are assumed outstanding.

- **Adjustment to numerator:** After-tax interest of $45,000 is prorated based on the length of time the bonds were outstanding: $45,000 × 3/12, or $11,250.
- **Adjustment to denominator:** 20,000 new common shares are prorated: 20,000 shares × 3/12, or 5,000.

continued

continued from previous page

	Net Income Available to Common Stockholders	Weighted-Average Common Shares Outstanding	Per Share
Basic EPS	$633,750	200,000	$3.17
Effect of convertible bonds:			
Add back prorated interest, net of tax . . .	11,250		
Add new prorated common shares		5,000	
Diluted EPS	$645,000	205,000	$3.15

The convertible bonds issued on October 1 are considered dilutive because EPS drops from $3.17 (basic EPS) to $3.15 (diluted EPS). The company reports both basic EPS of $3.17 and diluted EPS of $3.15 in its income statement.

d. **Basic and Diluted EPS Calculations with a Net Loss**

	Net Income Available to Common Stockholders	Weighted-Average Common Shares Outstanding	Per Share	
Basic EPS	$(600,000)	200,000	$(3.00)	
Effect of convertible bonds:				
Add back interest, net of tax . . .	45,000			
Add new common shares		20,000		
Diluted EPS	$(555,000)	220,000	$(2.52)	antidilutive

Given a net loss, the convertible bonds are considered antidilutive because EPS increases from $(3.00) for basic EPS to $(2.93) for diluted EPS. The company reports both basic and diluted EPS as $(3.00) and discloses the information related to the convertible bonds with an *antidilutive* effect.

EXPANDING YOUR KNOWLEDGE   **Conversion of a Convertible Bond before Year-End**

How is the diluted EPS calculation impacted if a convertible bond converts to common shares before year-end? Because a conversion is assumed to have happened on January 1, the diluted EPS amount will reflect a full 12-months of dilution. For example, let's assume Gridley Inc. has 1,000, 6%, $1,000 bonds, each convertible into 20 common shares. Assume that all of these bonds were converted to common stock on May 1. The diluted EPS calculation includes the following adjustments for the period from January 1 to May 1, assuming a tax rate of 25%.

Adjustment to numerator: $1,000,000 \times 6\% \times 0.75 \times 4/12 = \$15,000$.

Adjustment to denominator: 1,000 bonds $\times$ 20 common shares $\times$ 4/12 = 6,667 shares.

With these adjustments, diluted EPS will now reflect *a full-year of dilution*. This means diluted EPS will be the same regardless if an actual conversion took place on a different day of the year or not at all.

Convertible Preferred Stock

Convertible preferred stock is assumed to have been converted into common stock as of the beginning of the period (or the issue date if later) under the *if-converted* method. If we assume that preferred stock is converted, the company would no longer pay preferred dividends. As a result, preferred dividends are added back to the numerator of the basic EPS calculation, if they were deducted when computing basic EPS, and the new common shares are added to the denominator of the basic EPS calculation as we show in **Demo 20-6B**.

Effect on Diluted EPS Calculation of Convertible Preferred Stock
Numerator: Add back preferred dividends
Denominator: Add new common shares

260-10-45-40   The dilutive effect of convertible securities shall be reflected in diluted EPS by application of the if-converted method. Under that method: a. If an entity has convertible preferred stock outstanding, the preferred dividends applicable to convertible preferred stock shall be added back to the numerator. The amount of preferred dividends added back will be the amount of preferred dividends for convertible preferred stock deducted from income from continuing operations (and from net income) in computing income available to common stockholders pursuant to paragraph 260-10-45-11. . .

DEMO 20-6B ▶ **LO20-6**   *EPS Calculations—Convertible Preferred Stock*

Now assume that instead of convertible debt, Gridley Inc. owns convertible preferred stock. Because convertible preferred stock has the potential to increase common shares upon conversion, the company has a complex capital structure. Current-year net income for the company is $600,000. During the entirety of this year, 10,000 shares of 4%, $100 par, cumulative convertible preferred stock were outstanding, each share convertible into five common shares. Dividends are declared and paid at the end of each quarter. The weighted-average shares outstanding before considering potentially dilutive securities is 200,000, and the tax rate is 25%.

a. Compute basic EPS.

b. Compute diluted EPS for the year using the *if-converted* method, assuming that the preferred stock is converted into common stock as of January 1. Indicate the EPS amount(s) that the company would report in its annual income statement.

Solution

a. **Basic EPS Calculation**

Preferred dividends of $40,000 (or 10,000 shares × $100 par × 4%) are subtracted from the numerator.

	Net Income Available to Common Stockholders	Weighted-Average Common Shares Outstanding	Per Share
Basic EPS	$560,000[1]	200,000	$2.80

[1] $600,000 (net income) − $40,000 (preferred dividends).

b. **Diluted EPS Calculation with Convertible Preferred Stock**

The impact on basic EPS assuming that the preferred stock is converted into common stock as of January 1 follows.

Adjustment to numerator: Dividends saved equal $40,000 (10,000 preferred shares × $100 par × 4%).

Adjustment to denominator: 50,000 common shares are added (10,000 preferred shares × 5 common shares).

	Net Income Available to Common Stockholders	Weighted-Average Common Shares Outstanding	Per Share
Basic EPS	$560,000	200,000	$2.80
Effect of convertible preferred stock:			
Add back preferred dividends	40,000		
Add new common shares		50,000	
Diluted EPS	$600,000	250,000	$2.40

The convertible preferred stock is considered dilutive because EPS drops from $2.80 (basic EPS) to $2.40 (diluted EPS). The company reports both basic EPS of $2.80 and diluted EPS of $2.40 in its annual income statement.

Real World—DILUTED EARNINGS PER SHARE

PepsiCo Inc.'s basic and diluted earnings per share amounts included on the face of its income statement for a recent fiscal year were $6.59 and $6.56, respectively. Note 10 accompanying the financial statements included the detail necessary to recalculate EPS.

$ millions, except per share amounts	2023	
	Income	Shares[a]
Basic net income attributable to PepsiCo per common share	$ 6.59	
Net income available for PepsiCo common shareholders	$9,074	1,376
Dilutive securities:		
Stock options, RSUs, PSUs and other[b]	—	7
Diluted	$9,074	1,383
Diluted net income attributable to PepsiCo per common share	$ 6.56	

(a) Weighted-average common shares outstanding (in millions).
(b) The dilutive effect of these securities is calculated using the treasury stock method.

Calculation of EPS—Convertible Bonds and Convertible Preferred Stock

LO20-6   **REVIEW 20-6**

Example One—Calculation of EPS with Convertible Bonds

A company has outstanding $100,000 of 5% convertible bonds due in five years. Each $1,000 convertible bond is convertible into 60 shares of common stock. Net income for the year was $365,000. Common shares outstanding for the year were 205,000. The relevant tax rate is 25%.

a. Compute basic earnings per share.
b. Compute diluted earnings per share. Indicate the EPS amount(s) that the company would report in its annual income statement.

Review

MBC

Example Two—Calculation of EPS with Convertible Preferred Stock

Charter Company earned net income of $248,000 for the year. The company had 85,000 shares of common stock outstanding during the year and 1,000 shares of noncumulative preferred stock, each preferred share convertible into 4 shares of common stock, $5 par value per share. The relevant tax rate is 25%. During the year, Charter Company declared and paid $15,000 in preferred dividends and no common stock dividends.

a. Compute basic earnings per share.
b. Compute diluted earnings per share. Indicate the EPS amount(s) that the company would report in its annual income statement.

More Practice:
BE20-22, BE20-23, E20-23,
E20-26, E20-27, E20-28

Solution on p. 20-62.

Compute EPS using treasury stock method for options, warrants, and restricted stock

LO 20-7

Equity contracts, including stock options and warrants (security giving the holder the right to purchase shares of common stock) are typically exercisable at the option of the holder. Restricted stock shares are granted to employees but are restricted until the employee completes a vesting period. These potentially dilutive securities enter into the calculation of diluted earnings per share if they result in a dilution of EPS.

Stock Options, Warrants, Restricted Stock: Effect on Diluted EPS
- Numerator: No effect
- Denominator: Add incremental common shares

LO 20-7 Overview

Stock Options and Warrants

For diluted EPS calculations, stock options and warrants are assumed to have been exercised as of the beginning of the period (or at time of issuance, if later). In most situations, there are no adjustments to the numerator of diluted EPS on the assumed exercise of options and warrants. Assumed exercise of

Effect on Diluted EPS Calculation of Stock Options and Warrants	
Numerator: No effect	
Denominator: Add incremental common shares	

options and warrants increases the number of common shares outstanding following the treasury stock method as we show in **Demo 20-7A**.

Recall that if an employee chooses to exercise stock options, the employee pays a designated amount of cash for those shares (presumably less than the fair value if the employee is electing to exercise the options). To ensure companies account consistently for assumed cash receipts in computing diluted EPS, the treasury stock method presumes hypothetical cash receipts are used to repurchase outstanding shares.

Under the required **treasury stock method**, *incremental* common shares are added to the denominator of the diluted EPS calculation. Incremental common shares are calculated as new assumed common shares issued, less shares assumed purchased for the treasury. Companies are *assumed* to repurchase their own common shares at an average market price for the treasury. In this chapter, assume that stock options are fully vested unless otherwise stated. Fully vested means that an employee's right to receive shares is not contingent on a service or performance condition.

ASC Glossary   Treasury stock method: A method of recognizing the use of proceeds that could be obtained upon exercise of options and warrants in computing diluted EPS. It assumes that any proceeds would be used to purchase common stock at the average market price during the period.

260-10-45-23   Under the treasury stock method:
a. Exercise of options and warrants shall be assumed at the beginning of the period (or at time of issuance, if later) and common shares shall be assumed to be issued.
b. The proceeds from exercise shall be assumed to be used to purchase common stock at the average market price during the period. . . .
c. The incremental shares (the difference between the number of shares assumed issued and the number of shares assumed purchased) shall be included in the denominator of the diluted EPS computation. . . .

Increases in the average market price above the strike price enhance the dilutive effect of options because the number of treasury shares that could be repurchased declines. If the market price is below the strike price, the assumed exercise of the stock options using the treasury stock method is always antidilutive. Therefore, calculations are unnecessary. This should make sense intuitively because holders have little incentive to exercise out-of-the-money options.

DEMO 20-7A ▶	**LO20-7**	**EPS Calculations—Stock Options**

Demo

MBC

Options to purchase 1,000 shares of common stock are outstanding at the beginning of the year at Lax Inc. The exercise price of the options is $30 per share. The average market price of Lax Inc.'s common stock is $50 for the year. Net income for the year is $4,000 and 2,000 common shares were outstanding the entire year.

a. Compute basic EPS for the year.
b. Compute diluted EPS for the year using the treasury stock method. Indicate the EPS amount(s) that the company would report in its annual income statement.
c. Compute diluted EPS for the year using the treasury stock method but now assume that the average market price of Lax Inc.'s common stock is $10 for the year. Indicate the EPS amount(s) that the company would report in its annual income statement.

Solution

a. **Basic EPS Calculation**

	Net Income Available to Common Stockholders	Weighted-Average Common Shares Outstanding	Per Share
Basic EPS	$4,000	2,000	$2.00

b. **Diluted EPS Calculation with Stock Options**
Rather than use the entire 1,000 option shares as the new shares, the assumed proceeds are used to purchase treasury shares, which reduces the 1,000 option shares to 400 incremental shares. Cash of $30,000 is calculated by taking the 1,000 options multiplied by the exercise price of $30. Then, the $30,000 is divided by $50 (average market price) to arrive at 600 shares assumed purchased for the treasury. Incremental shares are 400 or the option shares of 1,000 less the treasury shares of 600.

continued

continued from previous page

New shares upon exercise of stock options	1,000
Less treasury shares (1,000 shares × $30)/$50	(600)
Incremental shares	400

The impact on diluted EPS is as follows.
- **Adjustment to numerator:** No effect.
- **Adjustment to denominator:** 400 incremental common shares are added based on the treasury stock method.

	Net Income Available to Common Stockholders	Weighted-Average Common Shares Outstanding	Per Share
Basic EPS	$4,000	2,000	$2.00
Effect of stock options:			
Add incremental common shares . . .		400	
Diluted EPS	$4,000	2,400	$1.67

The stock options are considered dilutive because EPS drops from $2.00 (basic EPS) to $1.67 (diluted EPS). The company reports both basic EPS of $2.00 and diluted EPS of $1.67 in its annual income statement.

c. **Stock Options—Market Price is Less than the Exercise Price**
If the market price were $10, the number of treasury shares purchased would be 3,000 [(1,000 × $30)/10], resulting in a negative 2,000 incremental shares (or 1,000 − 3,000) thereby causing EPS to increase. Therefore, in this case, the options do *not* have a dilutive effect on EPS and no diluted EPS would be reported. The company reports only basic EPS of $2.00 in its annual income statement.

EXPANDING YOUR KNOWLEDGE   **Stock Options Exercised Before Year-End**

How is the diluted EPS calculation impacted if stock options are exercised before year-end? Because a conversion is assumed to have happened on January 1, the diluted EPS amount must reflect a full 12-months of dilution. This means diluted EPS will require an adjustment for the portion of the year *before* the conversion. (Basic EPS will reflect the new shares issued after the conversion date.)

Let's assume that 5,000 stock options are granted to executives prior to the current year, allowing the acquisition of common stock at an exercise price of $15 per share. On March 31 of the current year, executives exercised all of the options. The average market price for the period of January 1 to March 31 was $22 per share. *When calculating diluted EPS, what adjustment is required to basic EPS to account for the stock options?* Answer: To reflect dilution for the full-year, an adjustment to diluted EPS is required for the months *before* conversion consisting of an addition of 398 incremental shares to the denominator, calculated as follows:

New shares upon exercise of stock options	5,000 shares
Less treasury shares (5,000 shares × $15)/$22	(3,409)
Net shares	1,591
Prorated shares for partial year (3/12 × 1,591 shares)	398 shares

---

Unvested Restricted Stock

While vested restricted stock is issued to employees (via outstanding shares) and included in basic EPS, unvested restricted stock is considered only in the diluted EPS calculation. Unvested restricted stock is assumed to have been issued as of the beginning of the period (or at time of issuance, if later). In most situations, there are no adjustments to the numerator of diluted EPS on the assumed issuance of unvested restricted stock. Assumed issuance of restricted stock increases the number of common shares outstanding following the treasury stock method as we show in **Demo 20-7B**. (Refer to LO 20-1 to review the reporting for restricted stock and unit awards that affect the diluted EPS calculation.)

Effect on Diluted EPS Calculation of Unvested Restricted Stock
Numerator: No effect
Denominator: Add incremental common shares

Under the **treasury stock method**, *incremental* common shares are added to the denominator of the diluted EPS calculation. Incremental common shares are calculated as new assumed shares of restricted stock issued, less shares assumed purchased for the treasury. **The amount of unearned compensation at a reporting date is used to calculate an assumed purchase of shares for the treasury at an average market price.** The unearned compensation is equal to the amount of compensation expense yet to be recognized on the unvested restricted stock.

260-10-45-32   Fixed grantee stock options (fixed awards) and nonvested stock (including restricted stock) shall be included in the computation of diluted EPS based on the provisions for options and warrants in paragraphs 260-10-45-22 through 45-27. Even though their issuance may be contingent upon vesting, they shall not be considered to be contingently issuable shares. (see Section 815-15-55 and paragraph 260-10-45-48). However, because issuance of performance-based stock options (and performance-based nonvested stock) is contingent upon satisfying conditions in addition to the mere passage of time, those options and nonvested stock shall be considered to be contingently issuable shares in the computation of diluted EPS. A distinction shall be made only between time-related contingencies and contingencies requiring specific achievement.

DEMO 20-7B ▶ **LO20-7**   **EPS Calculations—Restricted Stock**

Demo

MBC

100 restricted common stock shares are outstanding at the beginning of the year and will vest after 4 years of service. Net income for the year is $4,000, and 2,000 common shares were outstanding the entire year. The fair value of the shares on January 1 is $10 per share. For simplicity, assume that the average market price of common shares is also $10 per share.

a. Compute basic EPS for the year.
b. Compute diluted EPS for the year. Indicate the EPS amount(s) that the company would report in its annual income statement.

Solution

a. **Basic EPS Calculation**

	Net Income Available to Common Stockholders	Weighted-Average Common Shares Outstanding	Per Share
Basic EPS	$4,000	2,000	$2.00

b. **Diluted EPS Calculation with Restricted Stock**
Rather than use the entire 100 shares as new shares in the diluted EPS calculation, the 100 unvested restricted shares are reduced by an assumed purchase of treasury shares. The treasury shares are purchased with the amount of *compensation that has not yet been expensed*. Total compensation of $1,000 is calculated by multiplying 100 shares by the market price at grant date of $10. One year of compensation has been expensed during the year for $250 ($1,000/4 years) leaving $750 of remaining compensation expense. Next, the $750 is divided by $10 (average market price) to arrive at 75 shares assumed purchased for the treasury. Incremental shares are 25 or the restricted shares of 100 less the treasury shares of 75.

New shares upon vesting of the restricted shares	100
Less treasury shares ($1,000 − $250)/$10	(75)
Incremental shares	25

The impact on diluted EPS follows.
• **Numerator:** No effect.
• **Denominator:** 25 common shares are added based on the treasury stock method.

	Net Income Available to Common Stockholders	Weighted-Average Common Shares Outstanding	Per Share
Basic EPS	$4,000	2,000	$2.00
Effect of restricted stock:			
Add incremental common shares . . .		25	
Diluted EPS	$4,000	2,025	$1.98

continued

continued from previous page

> The restricted stock is considered dilutive because EPS drops from $2.00 (basic EPS) to $1.98 (diluted EPS). The company reports both basic EPS of $2.00 and diluted EPS of $1.98 in its annual income statement.

EXPANDING YOUR KNOWLEDGE   Stock Options Not Fully Vested

How is the diluted EPS calculation impacted if stock options are not fully vested? The treasury shares are considered purchased with the amount of compensation that has not yet been expensed along with the cash expected to be collected by the employees holding the stock options. (Refer to LO 20-2 for the computation of compensation expense and its recognition over time.) Let's assume options to purchase 1,000 shares of common stock are outstanding at the beginning of the year at Lax Inc. The exercise price of the options is $30 per share. The average market price of Lax Inc.'s common stock is $50 for the year. In addition, compensation not yet expensed related to the stock options totals $5,000. *When calculating diluted EPS, what adjustment is required to basic EPS to account for the stock options?* Answer: Incremental shares of 300 to adjust the numerator of the diluted EPS using the treasury stock method are calculated as follows.

New shares upon exercise of stock options	1,000
Less treasury shares [(1,000 shares × $30) + $5,000]/$50	(700)
Incremental shares	300

HOME DEPOT

Real World—BASIC AND DILUTED EPS

Home Depot Inc. included both basic and diluted earnings per share on the face of its consolidated statements of earnings in its recent Form 10-K (in millions, except per share amounts).

Basic weighted average common shares	999
Basic earnings per share	$15.16
Diluted weighted average common shares	1,002
Diluted earnings per share	$15.11

EPS Calculations—Options and Restricted Stock   LO20-7 ◀ REVIEW 20-7

Review

MBC

Example One—EPS Calculation with Options

Lazer Inc. reported net income of $450,000 for the year. During the year, 300,000 shares were outstanding on average and Lazer's common stock sold at an average market price of $40 per share. In addition, Lazer had 2,000 stock options outstanding as part of executive compensation. The options allow certain executives the right to purchase a total of 8,000 common shares at $25 for each share of stock under option.

a. Compute basic EPS for the year.
b. Compute diluted EPS for the year. Indicate the EPS amount(s) that the company would report in its annual income statement.

Example Two—EPS Calculation with Restricted Stock

Lazer Inc. granted 2,000 shares of restricted stock (common shares, $1 par) to its president on January 1, when the stock was trading at $25 per share. Net income for the year was $480,000 and 220,000 shares were outstanding throughout the year. On average, the fair value of common shares during the year was $25 per share. The restricted shares vest after 3 years if the president remains with the company.

a. Compute basic EPS for the year.
b. Compute diluted EPS for the year. Indicate the EPS amount(s) that the company would report in its annual income statement.

More Practice:
BE20-24, BE20-25, E20-30, E20-31

Solution on p. 20-63.

LO 20-8 ▶ Compute EPS given contingently issuable shares

Contingently Issuable Shares: Effect on Diluted EPS
- Denominator
  - Add shares if conditions were satisfied by period end
  - Add shares assuming the reporting period-end is the contingency period-end and conditions were satisfied at that point

Effect on Diluted EPS Calculation of Contingently Issuable Shares	
Numerator: No effect	
Denominator: Add new common shares meeting criteria	

Contingently issuable shares are common shares of stock that will be issued only if certain conditions are satisfied such as a target income level or a target stock price. If all necessary conditions have been satisfied by the end of the period, the contingently issuable shares are considered outstanding for purposes of computing diluted EPS.

If all necessary conditions have *not* been satisfied by the end of the period, the number of contingently issuable shares included in diluted EPS shall be based on the number of shares, if any, that would be issuable if the end of the reporting period were the end of the contingency period. See **Demo 20-8**.

260-10-45-48   Shares whose issuance is contingent upon the satisfaction of certain conditions shall be considered outstanding and included in the computation of diluted EPS as follows:

a. If all necessary conditions have been satisfied by the end of the period (the events have occurred), those shares shall be included as of the beginning of the period in which the conditions were satisfied (or as of the date of the contingent stock agreement, if later).

b. If all necessary conditions have not been satisfied by the end of the period, the number of contingently issuable shares included in diluted EPS shall be based on the number of shares, if any, that would be issuable if the end of the reporting period were the end of the contingency period (for example, the number of shares that would be issuable based on current period earnings or period-end market price) and if the result would be dilutive. Those contingently issuable shares shall be included in the denominator of diluted EPS as of the beginning of the period (or as of the date of the contingent stock agreement, if later).

In these cases, the contingently issuable shares shall be included as of the beginning of the period or as of the date of the contingent stock agreement, if later.

DEMO 20-8 ▶ LO20-8   **Compute EPS Given Contingently Issuable Shares**

Demo / MBC

Assume Gridley Inc. reported net income for the current year of $100,000, and 10,000 common shares were outstanding the entire year. The company had a contingent stock agreement that granted 1,000 common shares to the company's chief executive officer if net income in the next year reached $95,000. Compute diluted EPS in the current year and indicate the EPS amount(s) that the company would report in its current year income statement.

Solution

Because the company surpassed the $95,000 net income target for the year, it is presumed that the company will reach this target level in the next year. This means that we assume that the end of the current year is the end of the contingency period and we determine that the contingency is met at that point. Therefore, the denominator will be increased by 1,000 shares in calculating diluted EPS.

	Net Income Available to Common Stockholders	Weighted-Average Common Shares Outstanding	Per Share
Basic EPS	$100,000	10,000	$10.00
Effect of contingently issuable stock:			
Add new common shares		1,000	
Diluted EPS	$100,000	11,000	$ 9.09

The company reports both basic EPS of $10.00 and diluted EPS of $9.09 in its current year income statement.

Calculation of EPS Given Contingently Issuable Shares   **LO20-8** ◄   **REVIEW 20-8**

In Year 1, Case Inc. initiated an agreement with its shareholders that if net income for Year 2 exceeded $600,000, an additional 42,000 shares of Case Inc. stock would be issued to shareholders in Year 3 as a stock dividend.

Review

MBC

Required

Compute basic and diluted EPS in Year 1 assuming net income of $500,000 and weighted-average common shares of 385,000 in Year 1. Indicate the EPS amount(s) that the company would report in its Year 1 income statement.

More Practice:
BE20-26, E20-32

Solution on p. 20-64.

Compute EPS given multiple securities and describe EPS financial statement presentation

LO 20-9

To this point, we have considered only one potentially dilutive security at a time. Diluted EPS is reported only if it results in a decline relative to basic EPS. If not, the security is **antidilutive** and no further disclosure is required.

In practice, companies can have several potentially dilutive securities outstanding at any one time. The order by which multiple securities are included in the diluted EPS calculation can affect the final amount reported. In response to this issue, the FASB requires that potentially dilutive securities be considered for inclusion in diluted EPS in sequence *from the most dilutive to the least dilutive.* It can be shown that this approach achieves maximum dilution (the lowest diluted EPS) as we show in **Demo 20-9**.

Diluted EPS with Multiple Securities
- Rank securities from most dilutive to least dilutive
- Determine the cumulative dilutive effect on EPS for each additional security

Financial Statement Presentation of EPS
- Face of the income statement
  - Income (loss) from continuing operations
  - Net income (loss)
- Face of the income statement or note
  - Income (loss) from discontinued operations

LO 20-9 Overview

`260-10-45-18` Convertible securities may be dilutive on their own but antidilutive when included with other potential common shares in computing diluted EPS. To reflect maximum potential dilution, each issue or series of issues of potential common shares shall be considered in sequence from the most dilutive to the least dilutive. That is, dilutive potential common shares with the lowest earnings per incremental share shall be included in diluted EPS before those with a higher earnings per incremental share… Options and warrants generally will be included first because use of the treasury stock method does not affect the numerator of the computation….

Compute EPS Given Multiple Securities   **LO20-9** ◄   **DEMO 20-9**

For the Palmento Company, net income for the year was $124,000, and 94,000 common shares were outstanding the entire year. Palmento Company holds four potentially dilutive securities. The numerator and denominator effects on the basic EPS calculation for the potentially dilutive securities are summarized and ranked as follows. The potentially dilutive securities are ranked from the most dilutive (lowest ratio of the numerator to the denominator) to the least dilutive.

Demo

MBC

Ranking of Potentially Dilutive Securities

Potentially Dilutive Security	Increase in Income	Increase in Number of Common Shares	Earnings per Incremental Share
Stock options	$ 0	400	$0.00
Convertible preferred stock. . . . ,. .	7,000	8,000	0.88
Series B convertible bonds.	30,000	25,000	1.20
Series A convertible bonds.	9,600	6,000	1.60

Required

a. Compute basic EPS for the year.
b. Compute diluted EPS for the year.
c. Show the financial statement presentation of earnings per share.

continued

continued from previous page

Solution

a. **Basic EPS Calculation—Multiple Securities**

	Net Income Available to Common Stockholders	Weighted-Average Common Shares Outstanding	Per Share
Basic EPS	$124,000	94,000	$1.32

b. **Diluted EPS—Multiple Securities**

Now consider the effect of potentially dilutive securities on the diluted EPS calculation, in the order previously established in the ranking from most dilutive to least dilutive.

	Net Income Available to Common Stockholders	Weighted Average Common Shares Outstanding	Per Share	
Basic EPS	$124,000	94,000	$1.32	
Effect of stock options:				
Additional common shares		400		
Tentative diluted EPS.............	$124,000	94,400	$1.31	dilutive
Effect of convertible preferred stock:				
Add back preferred dividends	7,000			
Additional common shares		8,000		
Tentative diluted EPS.............	$131,000	102,400	$1.28	dilutive
Effect of convertible bonds—series B:				
Add back interest	30,000			
Additional common shares		25,000		
Tentative diluted EPS.............	$161,000	127,400	$1.26	dilutive
Effect of convertible bonds—series A:				
Add back interest	9,600			
Additional common shares		6,000		
Tentative diluted EPS.............	$170,600	133,400	$1.28	antidilutive
Diluted EPS.....................	$161,000	127,400	$1.26	

After considering stock options, the tentative diluted EPS is $1.31 (which is less than basic EPS of $1.32) before considering the remaining securities. Next, we consider convertible preferred stock, which results in a tentative EPS of $1.28, which is less than $1.31. This means the convertible preferred stock is dilutive and is included in the diluted EPS calculation. Next, we consider series B convertible bonds, which results in an EPS of $1.26, which is less than $1.28. This means the convertible securities are dilutive and are included in the diluted EPS calculation. This is the final value for diluted EPS because adding the remaining Series A convertible bonds (ranked fourth) creates a larger EPS amount of $1.28, which exceeds $1.26. Including the Series A bonds would be antidilutive.

c. **Financial Statement Presentation**

Income Statement

Basic earnings per share	$1.32
Diluted earnings per share	1.26

Presentation and Disclosure of EPS

Companies with simple and complex capital structures must disclose basic EPS on the face of the income statement for the following line items, net of tax.

1. **Income (loss) from continuing operations**

2. **Net income (loss)**

EPS data must be presented for all periods for which an income statement or summary of earnings is presented. The EPS amounts for an annual period must equal the weighted-average of the EPS amounts reported on interim (quarterly) financial statements. In comparative disclosures, if any period reports diluted EPS, then all periods must report diluted EPS even if it is the same as basic EPS. If basic and diluted EPS are the same for all years presented, dual presentation can be accomplished in one line on the income statement.

260-10-45-2   Entities with simple capital structures, that is, those with only common stock outstanding, shall present basic per-share amounts for income from continuing operations and for net income on the face of the income statement. All other entities shall present basic and diluted per-share amounts for income from continuing operations and for net income on the face of the income statement with equal prominence.

Earnings per share in prior periods should be restated as a result of a declaration of stock dividends and stock splits, or a prior period adjustment due to an error or change in accounting principle. Income from continuing operations and net income exclude the income attributable to the noncontrolling interest in subsidiaries.

Income (loss) from discontinued operations must also be disclosed on a per-share basis (net of tax), either on the face of the income statement or in the notes accompanying the financial statements for simple and complex capital structures.

260-10-45-3   An entity that reports a discontinued operation in a period shall present basic and diluted per-share amounts for that line item either on the face of the income statement or in the notes to the financial statements.

For example, Johnson & Johnson reported the following earnings per share information related to continuing and discontinued operations on the face of its Consolidated Statement of Earnings in its recent report on Form 10-K.

Basic earnings per share	2023	2022
Continuing operations	$5.26	$6.23
Discontinued operations	8.62	0.60
Net earnings per share	$13.88	$6.83

Diluted earnings per share	2023	2022
Continuing operations	$5.20	$6.14
Discontinued operations	8.52	0.59
Net earnings per share	$13.72	$6.73

In a case where a company has discontinued operations, the company makes the determination of whether to report diluted EPS by considering the impact of potentially dilutive securities on income from continuing operations as indicated in the accounting guidance.

260-10-45-20   The control number for determining whether including potential common shares in the diluted EPS computation would be antidilutive should be income from continuing operations (or a similar line item above net income if it appears on the income statement). As a result, if there is a loss from continuing operations, diluted EPS would be computed in the same manner as basic EPS is computed, even if an entity has net income after adjusting for a discontinued operation. Similarly, if an entity has income from continuing operations but its preferred dividend adjustment made in computing income available to common stockholders in accordance with paragraph 260-10-45-11 results in a loss from continuing operations available to common stockholders, diluted EPS would be computed in the same manner as basic EPS.

Other disclosures required include the following:

260-10-50-1a   A reconciliation of the numerators and the denominators of the basic and diluted per-share computations for income from continuing operations. . . .

260-10-50-1b   The effect that has been given to preferred dividends in arriving at income available to common stockholders in computing basic EPS.

260-10-50-1c   Securities (including those issuable pursuant to contingent stock agreements) that could potentially dilute basic EPS in the future that were not included in the computation of diluted EPS because to do so would have been antidilutive for the period(s) presented. Full disclosure of the terms and conditions of these securities is required even if a security is not included in diluted EPS in the current period.

260-10-50-1d   The methods used in the diluted EPS computation for each type of dilutive instrument (for example, treasury stock method, if-converted method, two-class method, or reverse treasury stock method).

260-10-50-2   For the latest period for which an income statement is presented, an entity shall provide a description of any transaction that occurs after the end of the most recent period but before the financial statements are issued or are available to be issued (as discussed in Section 855-10-25) that would have changed materially the number of common shares or potential common shares outstanding at the end of the period if the transaction had occurred before the end of the period.

FORD   Real World—ANTIDILUTIVE SECURITIES

Ford Motor Company disclosed the income and shares used to calculate basic and diluted income per share in Note 8 in a recent Form 10-K report. On the income statement in 2023, basic EPS of $4.49 can be calculated as $17,937 ÷ 3,991. In cases where a company reports a loss, the diluted EPS will equal basic EPS as explained in an earlier section. The company discloses the number of shares excluded from the calculation due to their anti-dilutive effect.

Earnings/(Loss) Per Share Attributable to Ford Motor Company Common and Class B Stock Basic and diluted income/(loss) per share were calculated using the following (in millions).

	2021	2022	2023
Net Income/(Loss) Attributable to Ford Motor Company	$17,937	$(1,981)	$4,347
Basic and diluted shares			
Basic shares (average shares outstanding)	3,991	4,014	3,998
Net dilutive options, unvested restricted stock units, unvested restricted stock shares, and convertible debt[a]	43	—	43
Diluted shares...	4,034	4,014	4,041

(a) In 2022, there were 42 million shares excluded from the calculation of diluted earnings/(loss) per share, due to their antidilutive effect.

REVIEW 20-9 ▶ **LO20-9**   **Calculation of EPS—Multiple Securities**

Review

MBC

The following information relates to Jones Corporation on December 31.

Common stock, outstanding shares	140,000 shares
Convertible preferred stock, outstanding shares	25,000 shares
5% Convertible bonds	$300,000

During the year, Jones declared and paid dividends of $2.50 per share on its preferred stock. The preferred shares are convertible into 75,000 shares of common stock. The 5% bonds are convertible into 25,000 shares of common stock. Net income for the year is $820,000. Assume that the income tax rate is 25% and that the common stock, preferred stock, and the bonds were outstanding all year.

More Practice:
BE20-27, E20-33, E20-34,
E20-35, E20-36

Solution on p. 20-64.

a. Compute basic EPS for the year.

b. Compute diluted EPS for the year.

c. Show the financial statement presentation of earnings per share for the year.

Management Judgment

Share-Based Compensation

Management must make decisions on how to compensate employees (for example, through salaries, bonuses, restricted stock share awards, restricted stock unit awards, or stock options). In accounting for employee compensation, management judgment is required as shown in the following examples.

- For restricted stock awards, management must determine the fair value of the shares at the date of grant. If shares are publicly traded, estimating the fair value is not complicated. However, in cases when a company is not public or has been delisted from the market, estimating fair value requires judgment.

- Management must determine how to account for forfeitures of share-based awards: Record an estimate of forfeitures or record forfeitures as incurred. If management decides to record an estimate of forfeitures, management will need to apply judgment to determine the estimate (p. 20-4).

- For stock options, compensation expense is based on the fair value of the awards determined through an option-pricing model. The model is chosen by management and should be used consistently from period to period. The variables that are entered into the model are subjective, often including prospective information (p. 20-8). The significant assumptions are disclosed in the notes to the financial statements.

- If a stock option plan is based upon employees meeting certain performance conditions, management must determine when it is probable that the conditions will be met requiring an accrual of compensation expense (p. 20-9).

EPS Calculations

Management judgment is crucial in EPS calculations.

- The EPS calculation starts with net income. Therefore, all estimates that we have discussed in this text that impact net income through the recognition of revenues and expenses impact the calculation of EPS.

- In the use of the treasury stock method in computing EPS, companies must determine the fair value of common shares by determining the average market price (p. 20-26). As explained, when shares are not traded publicly, determining fair value is more difficult.

Describe accounting for stock appreciation rights

APPENDIX 20A
LO 20-10

Stock appreciation rights (SARs) were developed primarily to provide cash incentives to employees and to take advantage of favorable income tax provisions. SARs plans allow executives the right to compensation equal to the appreciation in market price of stock above a specified price level.

From the point of view of the employee, stock appreciation rights have two potential advantages over stock options.

- First, the employee does not have to purchase shares of stock as is required with stock options. If a large number of shares are involved, amassing the cash necessary to exercise a stock option may be difficult for the employee.

- Second, the difference between the market price and the exercise price for the acquired shares is usually taxable income for the employee when the shares are acquired. The employee must have the resources to pay this income tax, which presents another cash-flow problem, especially if the employee plans to hold the newly acquired shares. SARs minimize these cash flow problems. While this receipt of cash is taxable, the employee has the cash with which to pay the tax.

> **Stock Appreciation Rights (SARs)**
> - Record as equity (Employer may settle with stock)
>   - Estimate fair value at grant date
>   - Accrue as compensation expense over requisite service period
> - Record as liability (Settled with cash or employee chooses stock or cash)
>   - Continually adjust liability (and corresponding expense) to align with expected cash payment
>
> *LO 20-10 Overview*

Recording SARs as Equity

When the *employer* (not the employee) has the right to settle the SARs agreement in stock (rather than cash), the SARs are recorded as equity—see **Demo 20-10 Example One**. Similar to the accounting for restricted stock unit plans discussed in a previous section, total fair value is estimated at grant date, and compensation expense is recognized over the requisite service period on a straight-line basis. Because a transfer of assets is *not required,* no liability is recorded. In addition, no adjustment is made for changes in fair value of the underlying stock over the requisite service period.

Recording SARs as Liabilities

When the *employee* has the right to settle the SARs agreement in *cash*, the SARs are recorded as liabilities during the requisite service period as compensation is expensed—see **Demo 20-10 Example Two**. When SARs are recognized as liabilities, the company must continually adjust the liability account to align with the expected cash payment.

718-10-25-11 Options or similar instruments on shares shall be classified as liabilities if either of the following conditions is met:
a. The underlying shares are classified as liabilities.
b. The entity can be required under any circumstances to settle the option or similar instrument by transferring cash or other assets. A cash settlement feature that can be exercised only upon the occurrence of a contingent event that is outside the grantee's control (such as an initial public offering) would not meet this condition until it becomes probable that event will occur.

DEMO 20-10 ▶ **LO20-10**   **Stock Appreciation Rights**

Demo

MBC

Example One—Stock Appreciation Rights: Recorded as Equity

On January 1 of Year 1, Serenity Corporation began a stock appreciation rights plan. For each stock appreciation right, the grantee receives cash for the difference between the fair value per share of the company's common stock on the date the SARs are exercised and the market price per share on the grant date. The rights require continuing employment and may be exercised at any time between the end of the fourth year after the grant date and the expiration date. The rights expire at the end of the sixth year after the grant date or when employment is terminated, whichever is earlier. The requisite service period is from the grant date to the earliest exercise date (the vesting date), or in this case, four years.

On January 1 of Year 1, the company's common stock has a market price of $10 per share, and Ann Killian, CEO of Serenity, is granted 5,000 SARs under the incentive plan. The fair value of the SARs is estimated to be $25,000 as of January 1 of Year 1. The fair value of the SARs is estimated to be $1.00, $3.50, $2.00, and $4.00 per unit on December 31 of Year 1, Year 2, Year 3, and Year 4, respectively. The SARs may be settled by the employer, Serenity, through the issuance of stock.

Record the journal entry required for the SARs on December 31 of Year 1, Year 2, Year 3, and Year 4. Assume that Killian exercises the SARs on December 31 of Year 4, when the market price of the stock is $24 per share and Serenity settles the SARs in cash for $70,000 ([$24 – $10] × 5,000), (the difference between the fair value of common stock on the exercise date and date of grant).

Solution

Total compensation cost is expensed over a requisite service period that is from the date of grant to the vesting date.

Assets = Liabilities + Equity
-6,250
 Exp
+6,250
 PIC—SAR

Comp Exp		Pd-in Cap—SARs
6,250		6,250

December 31, Year 1—To record compensation expense

Compensation Expense	6,250	
Paid-in Capital—SARs Plan ($25,000/4 years).		6,250

Serenity records compensation expense of $6,250 for Year 2, Year 3, and Year 4.

Assets = Liabilities + Equity
-70,000   -25,000
 C:o   PIC—SAR
                   -45,000
                    Exp

Cash		Comp Exp
70,000		6,250
		6,250
		6,250
		6,250
		45,000

Pd-in Cap—SARs
25,000 6,250
6,250
6,250
6,250
0

December 31, Year 4—To record the exercise of SARs

Paid-in Capital—SARs Plan	25,000	
Compensation Expense	45,000	
Cash ([$24 – $10] × 5,000)		70,000

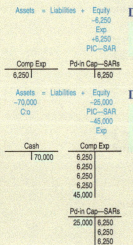

Example Two—Stock Appreciation Rights: Recorded as Liability

Refer to the information in Example One *except* now assume that the *employee* has the right to settle the SARs agreement in cash and that the fair value of the stock is $14 at the end of Year 4 and that the fair value of the SARs on December 31 of Year 4 is $4.

Record the journal entry required for the SARs on December 31 of Year 1, Year 2, Year 3, and Year 4. Assume that the employee settled the SARs contract in cash on December 31 of Year 4 for $20,000 ([$14 – $10] × 5,000), the difference between the fair value of common stock on the exercise date and date of grant.

continued

continued from previous page

Solution

This method for determining annual compensation expense for SARs is illustrated in this table.

Date	A Year-End Fair Value	B (A × 5,000 SARs) Aggregate Compensation	C % of Service Period Accrued	D (B × C) Total SARs Liability Accrued	E (D – Previous Liability) Annual Expense
Dec. 31, Year 1 . . .	$1.00	$ 5,000	25%	$ 1,250	$ 1,250
Dec. 31, Year 2 . . .	3.50	17,500	50%	8,750	7,500
Dec. 31, Year 3 . . .	2.00	10,000	75%	7,500	(1,250)
Dec. 31, Year 4 . . .	4.00	20,000	100%	20,000	12,500

December 31, Year 1—To record compensation expense

Compensation Expense	1,250	
SARs Liability		1,250

Assets = Liabilities + Equity
    +1,250   −1,250
    SAR   Exp

SARs Liab		Comp Exp	
	1,250	1,250	

December 31, Year 2—To record compensation expense

Compensation Expense	7,500	
SARs Liability		7,500

Assets = Liabilities + Equity
    +7,500   −7,500
    SAR   Exp

SARs Liab		Comp Exp	
	1,250	1,250	
	7,500	7,500	

December 31, Year 3—To record compensation expense

SARs Liability	1,250	
Compensation Expense		1,250

Assets = Liabilities + Equity
    −1,250   +1,250
    SAR   Exp

SARs Liab		Comp Exp	
1,250	1,250	1,250	1,250
	7,500	7,500	

December 31, Year 4—To record compensation expense

Compensation Expense	12,500	
SARs Liability		12,500

Assets = Liabilities + Equity
    +12,500   −12,500
    SAR   Exp

SARs Liab		Comp Exp	
1,250	1,250	1,250	1,250
	7,500	7,500	
	12,500	12,500	

December 31, Year 4—To record exercise of SARs plan

SARs Liability	20,000	
Cash		20,000

Assets = Liabilities + Equity
−20,000   −20,000
   Cio   SAR

Cash		SARs Liab	
	20,000	1,250	1,250
		20,000	7,500
			12,500
			0

Accounting for Stock Appreciation Rights   **LO20-10** ◄ **REVIEW 20-10**

Review

MBC

Brum Inc. established a SARs plan on January 1 of Year 1, that extends rights to certain company executives that can be redeemed for cash by the employee, equal to the difference between the market price of the company's common stock ($1 par) at a pre-determined price of $15 and market price at the first exercise date. The 400 SARs can be exercised two years from the grant date and expire one year from the first eligible exercise date or when employment is terminated, if earlier. The requisite service period is considered to be two years because exercise is expected (highly probable) to occur on December 31 of Year 2. The fair value of the SARs is estimated to be $5.50, $3.00, and $5.00 per unit on January 1 of Year 1, December 31 of Year 1, and December 31 of Year 2, respectively.

a. Record Brum Inc.'s entries for Year 1 and Year 2, assuming that the SARs are settled for $2,000 in cash on December 31 of Year 2.

b. Assume the same information *except* now Brum may settle the SARs contract with common stock. Record Brum's entries for Year 1 and Year 2, assuming that the SARs are settled for common stock on December 31 of Year 2. The market price of common stock per share on December 31 of Year 2, is $20 per share.

More Practice:
AppBE20-2, AppBE20-3,
AppE20-1, AppE20-2

Solution on p. 20-65.

Cash T-Account Approach   LO22-8   DEMO 22-8

Demo

MBC

Comparative balance sheets, an income statement, along with additional information follows for Eagle Heights Company.

Comparative Balance Sheets December 31	Prior Year	Current Year	Difference
Cash and cash equivalents	$ 100	$ 65	$ 35 decrease
Restricted cash	20	30	10 increase
Accounts receivable, net	280	170	110 decrease
Inventory	100	300	200 increase
Equipment	2,000	2,700	700 increase
Accumulated depreciation	(200)	(500)	300 increase
Total assets	$2,300	$2,765	$465
Accounts payable	$ 275	$ 240	$ 35 decrease
Salaries payable	50	25	25 decrease
Bonds payable	600	700	100 increase
Common stock, no-par	1,100	1,200	100 increase
Retained earnings	275	600	325 increase
Total liabilities and stockholders' equity	$2,300	$2,765	$465

Income Statement For Year Ended Dec. 31	Current Year
Sales revenue	$3,000
Cost of goods sold	(1,700)
Salary expense	(125)
Interest expense	(60)
Depreciation expense	(400)
Loss on equipment sale	(200)
Net income	$ 515

Additional information for the current year

- Equipment with an original cost of $400 and accumulated depreciation of $100 was sold for $100.
- Equipment purchases were made with cash.
- All dividends declared were paid in cash.

Required

Prepare and complete the cash T-account and then report the statement of cash flows for the current year following the direct method for the operating activities section.

Solution

The following *reconstructed* journal entries are recreated from the financial information above.

a.	Cash	3,110	
	Accounts Receivable		110
	Sales Revenue		3,000
b.	Cost of Goods Sold	1,700	
	Inventory	200	
	Accounts Payable	35	
	Cash		1,935
c.	Salary Expense	125	
	Salaries Payable	25	
	Cash		150
d.	Interest Expense	60	
	Cash		60
e.	Cash	100	
	Accumulated Depreciation	100	
	Loss on Sale of Equipment	200	
	Equipment		400
f.	Equipment	1,100	
	Cash		1,100
g.	Cash	100	
	Bonds Payable		100
h.	Cash	100	
	Common Stock		100
i.	Retained Earnings	190	
	Cash		190
j.	Depreciation Expense	400	
	Accumulated Depreciation		400

continued

continued from previous page

The recreated entries from above are entered into T-accounts as follows.

Cash and cash equivalents and restricted cash			
		25	(Net change in cash)
Operating Activities			
(a) From customers	3,110	1,935	(b) To suppliers
		150	(c) To employees
		60	(d) For interest
Investing Activities			
(e) Sale of equipment	100		
		1,100	(f) Purchase of equipment
Financing Activities			
(g) Issuance of bonds	100	190	(h) Payment of dividends
(i) Issuance of common stock	100		

Accounts Receivable, Net			Inventory			Equipment		
	110			200			700	
	110	(a)	(b)	200		(f)	1,100	400	(e)

Accumulated Depreciation			Accounts Payable			Salaries Payable		
		300			35			25
(e)	100	400	(j)	(b)	35		(c)	25

Bonds Payable			Common Stock			Retained Earnings		
		100			100			325
		100	(g)			100	(i)	(h)	190	515	(NI)

Sales Revenue			Loss on Sale of Equipment			Depreciation Expense		
		3,000		200			400	
		3,000	(a)	(e)	200		(j)	400	

Cost of Goods Sold			Salaries Expense			Interest Expense		
	1,700			125			60	
(b)	1,700		(c)	125		(d)	60	

The statement of cash flows is constructed from the cash flow T-account following the direct method.

Cash Flows from Operating Activities	
Collections from customers	$3,110
Payments to suppliers	(1,935)
Payments to employees	(150)
Interest payments.	(60)
Net cash provided by operating activities.	965
Cash Flows from Investing Activities	
Proceeds from sale of equipment.	100
Purchase of equipment.	(1,100)
Net cash used by investing activities	(1,000)
Cash Flows from Financing Activities	
Issuance of bonds	100
Dividends paid	(190)
Issuance of stock	100
Net cash provided by financing activities	10
Net decrease in cash and cash equivalents and restricted cash . . .	(25)
Cash and cash equivalents and restricted cash, Jan. 1	120
Cash and cash equivalents and restricted cash, Dec. 31.	$ 95

Cash T-Account Approach   LO22-8 ◄ REVIEW 22-8

Review

MBC

The following income statement and comparative balance sheets are from Redd Inc.

Balance Sheets, December 31	Prior Year	Current Year
Cash.	$ 3,500	$ 4,600
Accounts receivable	2,800	2,750
Inventory.	3,000	3,300
Investments	1,000	1,600
Total assets.	$10,300	$12,250
Accounts payable	$ 1,750	$ 1,400
Accrued expense	1,450	1,900
Retained earnings	2,575	4,325
Common stock	4,525	4,625
Total liabilities and stockholders' equity . . .	$10,300	$12,250

Income Statement For Year Ended Dec. 31	Current Year
Sales revenue.	$9,800
Cost of goods sold	3,900
Operating expense	4,150
Net income	$1,750

Construct the cash T-account only and prepare the current year statement of cash flows using the direct method for the operating activities section.

More Practice:
AppE22-1, AppP22-1
Solution on p. 22-72.

Questions

Q22-1. Explain the purpose of the statement of cash flows.

Q22-2. Explain the basic differences between the three activities reported in the statement of cash flows: operating, investing, and financing.

Q22-3. List three major cash inflows and three major cash outflows under (a) operating activities, (b) investing activities, and (c) financing activities.

Q22-4. Define a noncash investing activity. Give examples of two possible cases.

Q22-5. Define a noncash financing activity. Give examples of two possible cases.

Q22-6. Define a cash equivalent.

Q22-7. Explain the basic difference between the direct and indirect methods of reporting operating activities on the statement of cash flows. Use net income, $5,000, sales revenue, $100,000, and an increase in net accounts receivable, $10,000, to illustrate the basic difference. Which method provides the most relevant information to investors and creditors?

Q22-8. Explain why cash paid during the period for purchases and for salaries is not specifically reported on the statement of cash flows as cash outflows when presenting cash flows from operating activities under the indirect method.

Q22-9. Explain why a $50,000 increase in inventory during the year must be considered when developing disclosures for operating activities under both the direct method and the indirect method.

Q22-10. What three reconciling amounts must be reported at the bottom of the statement of cash flows? Which one(s) must agree with a key amount in another financial statement? Use assumed amounts for illustrative purposes.

Q22-11. One of the criticisms of the statement of cash flows indirect method is that it does not report each of the three activities consistently. Explain the basis for this argument.

Q22-12. Explain why an adjustment must be made to compute cash flows from operating activities for depreciation expense, bad debt expense, amortization of intangibles (such as patents, copyrights, franchises), and bond discount.

Q22-13. Explain why gains and losses reported on the income statement usually must be omitted (or removed) from operating activities to compute cash flows from operating activities.

Q22-14. Why are cash, cash equivalents, and restricted cash grouped together for purposes of the statement of cash flows?

Q22-15. Why is a two-year Treasury note purchased three months before maturity a cash equivalent for cash flow purposes, although the same security purchased one year before maturity is not?

Q22-16. If the intent is to hold an investment in common stock less than three months, why is the investment not a cash equivalent?

Q22-17. What general disclosure requirements are required related to the statement of cash flows?

Q22-18. How is a lease payment (after inception) on a finance lease classified in the statement of cash flows of a lessee?

Q22-19. Certain equity securities and trading debt securities are treated differently in the statement of cash flows. What are the major differences in treatment?

Data Analytics

Data Analytics 22-1
Analyzing Cash Flow
Ratio Trends by Industry
Segment **LO6**

For this exercise, we analyze trends in cash flow ratios by industry segment of S&P 500 companies through the use of PivotTables.

Data Visualization

Data Visualization

Data Visualization Activities are available in **myBusinessCourse**. These assignments use Tableau Dashboards to expose students to visual depictions of data and introduce students to data analytics through data visualizations. These exercises are assignable and auto graded by MBC.

Multiple Choice

LO1

MC22-1. Analyzing the Structure of the Statement of Cash Flows For the current year, Alpine Inc. determined its net cash flows from investing to be an outflow of $29,000 and its net cash flows from financing activities to be an inflow of $3,500, respectively. The company disclosed that it had received dividends of $5,000 and paid dividends of $8,000 for the year. If the company had a beginning cash balance of $8,500 and an ending cash balance of $34,000, what were cash flows from operating activities?

a. $56,000   c. $51,000
b. $59,000   d. $68,000

LO2

MC22-2. Calculating Net Cash Flows from Operating Activities Bramble Corp. summarized the following information for the year.

Net decrease in cash	$ 5,000	Net income	$48,000
Depreciation expense	21,000	Dividend revenue	2,500
Bond premium amortization	5,000	Decrease in prepaid insurance	1,400
Decrease in accounts receivable, net	11,200	Increase in accounts payable	6,200
Increase in inventory	15,500	Decrease in salaries payable	2,100
Decrease in income taxes payable	8,800	Gain on sale of equipment	2,400

Based on the information provided, what is net cash flows from operating activities for the year?

a. $54,000   c. $64,000
b. $56,500   d. $49,000

LO3

MC22-3. Analyzing a Sale of Equipment Brewster Inc. compiled the following information for its equipment.

	Jan. 1	Dec. 31
Equipment	$425,000	$450,000
Accumulated depreciation	122,000	178,000

In addition, the company purchased equipment for $48,000 cash and recorded depreciation of $62,000 for the year. If equipment was sold during the period for $20,000, what was the gain or loss recognized on the sale?

a. $14,000 gain   c. $3,000 loss
b. $3,000 gain   d. $6,000 loss

LO3

MC22-4. Calculating Net Cash Flows from Investing Activities A hurricane destroyed a building costing $800,000 with a carrying amount of $250,000. The insurance paid the company $200,000 cash and the company constructed a new building for $1,200,000 cash. What is the net cash outflow for investing activities for the period?

a.	$1,200,000		*c.*	$450,000
b.	$750,000		*d.*	$1,000,000

MC22-5. **Calculating Net Cash Flows from Financing Activities** Cambridge Inc. reported the following transactions in the current year.

Borrowed cash for inventory purchase by signing a six-month trade note payable	$ 35,000
Received cash dividends	5,000
Paid cash for dividends.	45,000
Issued preferred stock for cash	128,000
Retired a 15-year bond payable with cash	125,000
Sold investment in equity securities for cash	23,000
Paid interest on bonds payable.	1,000

Based on the information provided, what is net cash flows from financing activities for the year?

a.	$54,000 cash outflow		*c.*	$42,000 cash outflow
b.	$77,000 cash outflow		*d.*	$37,000 cash outflow

MC22-6. **Analyzing a Partial Noncash Transaction** Calico Inc. purchase land for $325,000. For payment, the seller accepted $210,000 in cash and the remainder in common stock with a fair value of $115,000. How would Calico report the transaction in its statement of cash flows?

	Investing Activities	**Financing Activities**
a.	$(325,000)	$(115,000)
b.	$(210,000)	$(115,000)
c.	$(325,000)	$ 0
d.	$(210,000)	$ 0

MC22-7. **Analyzing an Accounting Worksheet** The following is an excerpt from an accounting worksheet of Capri Corp. used to prepare a statement of cash flows using the indirect method to present net cash flows from operating activities.

	Dr.	**Cr.**
Net income	$4,500	
Depreciation expense.	4,800	
Decrease in accounts receivable	1,200	
Increase in inventory		$2,400
Decrease in accounts payable		4,200
Decrease in salaries payable		3,000
Purchase of equipment for cash.		2,900
Cash proceeds from sale of plant assets	1,000	
Dividends paid		3,400
Issuance of bonds for cash.	1,500	
Issuance of stock for cash	2,400	

Based on the partial worksheet, what is net change in cash for the period?

a.	Increase in cash of $500		*c.*	Increase in cash of $1,000
b.	Decrease in cash of $500		*d.*	Decrease in cash of $1,000

MC22-8. **Calculating Cash Collections under the Direct Method** Brewster Inc. compiled the following information.

	Jan. 1	**Dec. 31**
Accounts receivable	$45,500	$52,000
Allowance for doubtful accounts	1,800	2,000

If the company recognized revenue of $310,000, what is amount of cash collections from customers reported in the operating activities section of the statement of cash flows under the direct method?

a.	$303,700		*c.*	$303,500
b.	$316,300		*d.*	$316,500

LO7

MC22-9. Calculating Cash Paid to Suppliers under the Direct Method Comet Corp. summarized the following information for the current year.

Sales.	$600,000
Cost of goods sold	440,000
Increase in inventory balance.	50,000
Increase in accounts payable.	38,000

What is the amount of cash paid to suppliers that the company would report in the operating activities section of the statement of cash flows under the direct method?

a.	$172,000	c.	$452,000
b.	$428,000	d.	$352,000

Brief Exercises

Brief Exercise 22-1
Identifying Cash
Flows **LO1, 2**
Hint: See Demo 22-1

For each of the items listed below, indicate whether it would be included as an adjustment in the (1) operating, (2) investing, or (3) financing section of the statement of cash flows. Assume the indirect method is used to present cash flows from operating activities.

_____ a. Decrease in accounts receivable   _____ d. Depreciation expense

_____ b. Proceeds from the sale of equipment   _____ e. Principal payments on a note payable

_____ c. Cash dividend payment   _____ f. Increase in accounts payable

Brief Exercise 22-2
Solving for Statement
of Cash Flows
Amounts **LO1**
Hint: See Demo 22-1

Complete the following table for each of the four *separate* scenarios a through d.

	Net cash flows from operating activities	Net cash flows from investing activities	Net cash flows from financing activities	Cash at the beginning of the period	Cash at the end of the period
a.	$ 50,000	$ (40,000)	$ (4,500)	$5,000	$?
b.	250,000	(200,000)	(55,000)	?	45,000
c.	45,000	(50,000)	?	8,000	11,000
d.	?	5,000	(1,000)	6,000	6,500

Brief Exercise 22-3
Preparing Operating
Activities
Section **LO2**
Hint: See Demo 22-2

Quest Company reported net income of $45,000, which included depreciation expense of $2,000 and a loss on sale of equipment of $600. On the balance sheet, the company reported the following: increases in accounts receivable of $2,200 and accounts payable of $4,400 and decreases in inventory of $1,200 and in salaries payable of $800. Prepare the operating activities section of the statement of cash flows using the indirect method.

Brief Exercises 22-4
Preparing Operating
Activities
Section **LO2**
Hint: See Demo 22-2

Konverse Company reported net income of $200,000 for the year. Depreciation expense was $15,000 and amortization expense on patents was $2,500 for the year. In addition, the balance sheet reported the following account changes during the year.

Decrease in accounts receivable	$5,000
Increase in debt investments classified as available-for-sale securities.	4,500
Decrease in prepaid expenses.	2,000
Decrease in accounts payable	8,000
Increase in accrued expenses	4,500
Decrease in short-term nontrade notes payable	8,000

Prepare the operating activities section of the statement of cash flows using the indirect method.

Brief Exercise 22-5
Preparing Operating
Activities
Section **LO2**

Quest Company reported a net loss of $15,000, which included depreciation expense of $2,000 and a gain on sale of equipment of $800. On the balance sheet, the company reported the following: increases in accounts receivable of $650 and accounts payable of $2,300, and a decrease in inventory of $1,200. Prepare the operating activities section of the statement of cash flows using the indirect method.

Brief Exercise 22-6
Identifying Investing
Cash Flows **LO3**

Indicate items from the following list that would be included in the investing activities section of the statement of cash flows. Indicate whether an item would be added or subtracted in the investing section.

_____ a. Patent amortization recognized amounted to $30,000.

_____ b. Plant assets costing $4,000 were purchased with cash.

_____ c. Sold a long-term investment in another company's common stock for $5,000.

_____ d. Paid $40,000 cash for capital projects.

_____ e. Paid a cash dividend of $5,000.

_____ f. Depreciation recognized amounted to $80,000.

_____ g. Purchased land for $85,000 cash.

_____ h. Issued common stock, $1 par, for $200,000.

_____ i. Purchased a 3-month U.S. Treasury bill, $5,000. The company's accounting policy treats such securities as cash equivalents.

_____ j. Purchased a patent for $5,000.

_____ k. Purchased treasury stock, $3,500.

Frontier Company sold equipment on June 30 for $30,000. The equipment had been depreciated $1,500 for the first six months of the year, which is included in the accumulated depreciation balance of $10,000 on June 30. The original cost of the equipment was $50,000. Indicate the impact of this transaction on the operating, investing, and financing sections of the current year statement of cash flows. The indirect method is used to report cash flows from operating activities.

Brief Exercise 22-7
Analyzing Cash Flow
Effects of Equipment
Sale **LO2, 3**
Hint: See Demo 22-3

Considering the information in BE22-6, indicate items that would be included in the financing section of a statement of cash flows. Indicate whether an item would be added or subtracted in the financing section.

Brief Exercise 22-8
Identifying Financing
Cash Flows **LO4**

Cambell Inc. issued $100,000, 6%, 10-year bonds on January 1 for $86,580, with interest payments due annually at the end of each year. The amount of the discount amortization in year one is $926 using the effective interest method. Indicate the impact on the (a) operating activities section and the (b) financing activities section, of the current year statement of cash flows. The indirect method is used to report cash flows from operating activities.

Brief Exercise 22-9
Classifying Bond
Transactions on
Statement of Cash
Flows **LO2, 4**

Tiffany Inc. issued a 9% note payable to First Choice Bank for $100,000 with 10 equal payments of $15,582 (principal plus interest) due at the end of each year. Indicate the impact on the financing activities section of the statement of cash flows of Tiffany from the first installment payment.

Brief Exercise 22-10
Presenting Installment
Payment on Statement
of Cash Flows **LO4**

Marshall Inc. had beginning balances (January 1) of $200,000 and $5,000 for accounts receivable and the allowance for doubtful accounts, respectively. During the year, the company had the following transactions.

Sales.	$900,000
Write-off of accounts.	1,000
Cash collections on account receivable	850,000
Bad debt expense recorded	2,800

Brief Exercise 22-11
Adjusting Cash
Flows for Changes
in Accounts
Receivable **LO2**

a. Determine the ending balance (December 31) for accounts receivable and for the allowance for doubtful accounts.

b. Determine the adjustment to net income in the operating activities section in the statement of cash flows assuming the indirect method is used.

Pier2 Company purchased equipment with a useful life of 10 years for $36,000. Pier2 paid one-third down and signed a two-year, interest-bearing note for the balance. Indicate how the transaction would be reported in the statement of cash flows and/or any note disclosure.

Brief Exercise 22-12
Analyzing Noncash
Transactions **LO3, 5**

The investing and financing activities section of the statement of cash flows for Landry Inc. follow.

Brief Exercise 22-13
Analyzing Noncash
Transactions **LO5**
Hint: See Demo 22-5

Cash Flows from Investing Activities	
Proceeds from sale of equipment.	$ 80,000
Purchase of equipment.	(375,000)
Net cash used by investing activities . . .	$(295,000)

Cash Flows from Financing Activities	
Dividend payment.	$ (35,000)
Issuance of common stock.	200,000
Principal payment on note	(40,000)
Net cash provided by financing activities . . .	$125,000

While the company did purchase $375,000 of equipment and issue $200,000 of stock (amounts in the above statement), the company later determined that the $375,000 equipment purchase was made with cash of $240,000 and with common stock of $135,000.

    a.   Update the investing and financing sections based on this new information.

    b.   Prepare the disclosure of noncash items.

Brief Exercise 22-14
Preparing Entries for an Accounting Worksheet **LO6**
Hint: See Demo 22-6

Indicate the reconstructed entries that would be included on an accounting worksheet for each of the following items.

    a.   Depreciation expense of $10,000.   *c.*   Purchase of equipment of $100,000.

    b.   Increase in prepaid expenses of $2,500.   *d.*   Dividend payment of $12,000.

Brief Exercise 22-15
Determining Cash Receipts—Direct Method **LO7**
Hint: See Demo 22-7

Universal Company reported revenue in its income statement for the year of $350,000. The beginning and ending balances of accounts receivable, gross were $35,000 and $42,000, respectively. What amount would be reported as cash receipts from customers in the operating activities section of the statement of cash flows using the direct method?

Brief Exercise 22-16
Determining Cash Receipts—Direct Method **LO7**
Hint: See Demo 22-7

Using the information from BE22-11, determine the cash receipts from customers reported in the operating activities section in the statement of cash flows using the direct method.

Brief Exercise 22-17
Computing Cash Paid to Supplier—Direct Method **LO7**
Hint: See Demo 22-7

Park Place Company reported cost of goods sold of $280,000 for the year. Park Place also reported the following amounts on its balance sheets.

	Jan. 1	Dec. 31
Inventory.	$50,000	$55,000
Accounts payable	30,000	29,000

What amount would be reported as cash paid to suppliers in the operating activities section of the statement of cash flows using the direct method?

Brief Exercise 22-18
Computing Cash Paid to Employees—Direct Method **LO7**
Hint: See Demo 22-7

Park Place Company reported salaries expense of $100,000 for the year. Park Place also reported salaries payable of $18,000 and $12,000 on January 1 and December 31, respectively. What amount would be reported as cash paid to employees in the operating activities section of the statement of cash flows using the direct method?

Brief Exercise 22-19
Classifying Bond Transactions—Direct Method **LO7**

Using the information in BE22-9, indicate the impact on the (a) operating activities section and the (b) financing activities section of the statement of cash flows, using the direct method in presenting cash flows from operating activities.

Brief Exercise 22-20
Classifying a Sale of Equipment—Direct Method **LO7**

Frontier Company sold equipment on June 30 for $30,000. The equipment had been depreciated $1,500 for the first six months of the year, which is included in the accumulated depreciation balance of $10,000 on June 30. The original cost of the equipment was $50,000. Indicate the impact of this transaction on the operating, investing, and financing sections of the current year statement of cash flows. The direct method is used to report cash flows from operating activities.

Brief Exercise 22-21
Computing Cash from Customers—Direct Method **LO7**

A corporation's records showed the following: sales, $80,000, and gross accounts receivable decrease, $10,000, after the write-off of a $3,000 bad debt. Assuming the direct method, compute the cash inflow from customers.

Exercises

Exercise 22-1
Classifying Cash Flow Activities **LO1, 2, 5**

Sonic Company had the following activities during the current year ended December 31.

____   1.   Purchased treasury stock.

____   2.   Issuance of finance lease liability for equipment.

____ 3. Depreciation expense on equipment.

____ 4. Loss on sale of land.

____ 5. Increase in accounts receivable.

____ 6. Increase in accounts payable.

____ 7. Proceeds from issuance of preferred stock.

____ 8. Exchange of common stock for a building.

____ 9. Unrealized gain—income on equity securities.

____ 10. Increase in a current deferred tax asset.

____ 11. Decrease in deferred tax liability.

____ 12. Issued a short-term nontrade note payable for cash.

____ 13. Amortization expense on discount for a bond payable.

____ 14. Excess of the company's share of its investee's net income over the company's share of dividend payments (accounted for under the equity method).

____ 15. Decrease in interest payable.

____ 16. Decrease in prepaid expenses.

____ 17. Decrease in income taxes payable.

____ 18. Exchange of currently held equipment with replacement equipment.

____ 19. Proceeds from sale of a business segment.

____ 20. Purchase of land for cash.

Required

Assuming that the company uses the indirect method in presenting cash flows from operating activities, classify each activity as follows:

a.	Operating activity—add to net income	*e.*	Financing activity—cash inflow
b.	Operating activity—subtract from net income	*f.*	Financing activity—cash outflow
c.	Investing activity—cash inflow	*g.*	Noncash transaction
d.	Investing activity—cash outflow		

Savers Inc. had the following cash receipts and cash payments during the current year ended December 31.

Exercise 22-2
Classifying Cash Flow
Activities **LO1**
Hint: See Demo 22-1

____ 1. Cash receipt for issuance of preferred stock.

____ 2. Cash payment for dividends to shareholders.

____ 3. Cash outflow for a nontrade loan advanced to another entity.

____ 4. Cash payment for the redemption of bonds.

____ 5. Cash receipt from customers for services performed.

____ 6. Cash paid to the federal government for federal income taxes.

____ 7. Cash receipt for sale of a patent.

____ 8. Cash receipt for issuance of bonds at a premium.

____ 9. Cash receipt from dividends from investments.

____ 10. Cash payment on nontrade note payable (principal balance).

____ 11. Cash payment for interest on debt.

____ 12. Cash receipt from sale of equity securities (not held in trading account).

____ 13. Cash receipt for sale of equipment.

____ 14. Cash payment for employee salaries

Required

Indicate in which of the following three sections, each of the items would be reported on a statement of cash flows.

a.	Operating activity	*b.*	Investing activity	*c.*	Financing activity

The data below were provided by the accounting records of Franklin Company.

Exercise 22-3
Preparing the
Operating Activities
Section **LO2**
Hint: See Demo 22-2

Net income (accrual basis).............	$40,000	Increase in long-term liabilities.............	$10,000
Depreciation expense.................	8,000	Sale of capital stock for cash	25,000
Decrease in salaries payable	1,200	Amortization of premium on bonds payable ...	200
Decrease in trade accounts receivable....	1,800	Accounts payable increase................	4,000
Increase in merchandise inventory.......	2,500	Stock dividend issued...................	10,000
Amortization of patent	100		

Required

Prepare the reconciliation of net income to cash flow from operations for inclusion in the statement of cash flows (indirect method).

Exercise 22-4
Preparing the
Operating Activities
Section **LO2**
Hint: See Demo 22-2

The data below were provided by the accounting records of Marshall Company.

Net income (accrual basis).	$25,000	Amortization of patent	$	100
Depreciation expense.	3,000	Decrease in long-term liabilities		5,000
Increase in salaries payable.	500	Sale of capital stock for cash		12,500
Increase in trade accounts receivable . . .	900	Amortization of discount on bonds payable . . .		150
Decrease in merchandise inventory	1,150			

Required

Prepare the reconciliation of net income to cash flow from operations for inclusion in the statement of cash flows (indirect method).

Exercise 22-5
Preparing the
Operating Activities
Section **LO2**
Hint: See Demo 22-2

The following items are relevant to the preparation of a statement of cash flows for Maxwell Inc.

1. Net loss for the year was $20,000. Depreciation expense was $50,000.
2. Wrote off a $4,000 customer account. During the year, gross accounts receivable increased $100,000, and the allowance for doubtful accounts increased $10,000. Total sales of $600,000 are all on account.
3. Amortization expense on patents is $20,000 for the year.
4. Deferred tax liability increased $80,000, income taxes payable decreased $20,000, and income tax expense was $220,000.
5. $20,000 of interest was capitalized. Interest expense recognized is $100,000. There is no change in interest payable.
6. Sold short-term investments (not held in a trading account) at a $4,000 gain, proceeds $16,000.
7. Merchandise inventory decreased by $10,000, trade accounts payable decreased by $5,000, and salaries payable increased by $14,000.

Required

Prepare the reconciliation of net income to cash flow from operations for inclusion in the statement of cash flows (indirect method).

Exercise 22-6
Presenting Investment
Revenue on Statement
of Cash Flows
LO2, 3

On January 1, Allen Corporation purchased 30% of the 30,000 outstanding common shares of Towne Corporation at $17 per share as a long-term investment. On the date of purchase, the book value and the fair value of the net assets of Towne Corporation were equal. During the year, Towne Corporation reported net income of $24,000 and declared and paid dividends of $8,000. As of December 31, common shares of Towne Corporation were trading at $20 per share.

Required

a. Assume that Allen Corporation had significant influence over Towne Corporation. Record the entries for the year for Allen Corporation.
b. Indicate the impact of the transactions on the operating, investing, and financing sections of the current year statement of cash flows. The indirect method is used to report cash flows from operating activities.

Exercise 22-7
Presenting Installment
Note on Statement of
Cash Flows **LO2, 4**

United Company signed an 8% installment note with Bank One on January 1 for $100,000. The installment note calls for 5 equal annual payments beginning on December 31.

Required

a. Calculate the amount of each installment payment.
b. Indicate the impact of this transaction on the operating, investing, and financing sections of the current year statement of cash flows. The indirect method is used to report cash flows from operating activities.

Exercise 22-8
Presenting Bond
Payable on Statement
of Cash Flows **LO4**

Yale Corporation issued a 6%, $60,000 5-year bond dated January 1, with interest payable annually on December 31. The bond was sold to yield 8% interest. Assume that the company uses the effective interest method to amortize bond discounts or premiums.

Required

a. Provide journal entries to be made on January 1 and December 31 of this first year.
b. Indicate the impact of this transaction on the operating, investing, and financing sections of the current year statement of cash flows. The indirect method is used to report cash flows from operating activities.

On January 1, Lessee Inc. signs a three-year non-cancelable agreement to lease equipment (no residual value) from Lessor Inc. The lessee accounts for the lease as a finance lease, which requires three lease payments of $34,972 each, payable January 1 and December 31 of this year, and December 31 of next year. The lessor's implicit rate is 5%, which is known to the lessee, resulting in the recording of a right-of-use asset and lease liability of $100,000 (PV(0.05,3,34972,0,1)) at the inception of the lease. As a result, the lessee recorded the following entries in the current year (amounts rounded).

Exercise 22-9
Classifying Lessee
Transactions in
Statement of Cash
Flows **LO2, 4, 5**

January 1—To record right-of-use asset and lease liability

| Right-of-Use Asset.................................... | 100,000 | |
| Lease Liability.................................... | | 100,000 |

January 1—To record lease payment

| Lease Liability.................................... | 34,972 | |
| Cash.................................... | | 34,972 |

December 31—To record lease payment

Interest Expense....................................	3,251	
Lease Liability....................................	31,721	
Cash....................................		34,972

December 31—To record amortization on right-of-use asset

| Amortization Expense.................................... | 33,333 | |
| Right-of-Use Asset ($100,000/3).................................... | | 33,333 |

Required
Indicate the impact of the transactions on the operating, investing, and financing sections of the current year statement of cash flows. The indirect method is used to report cash flows from operating activities.

The following items are relevant to the preparation of a statement of cash flows for Pier Imports Inc.

Exercise 22-10
Determining Investing
and Financing
Activities **LO3, 4**

1. Comparative balance sheets show a decrease of $6,000 in accrued utilities payable for the current year.
2. Nontrade short-term notes payable to banks increased $80,000 during the current year due to new borrowings.
3. The following end-of-year adjusting entry was recorded. No other interest-related transactions or entries occurred during the year.

Interest Expense....................................	12,000	
Premium on Bonds Payable....................................	800	
Interest Payable....................................		12,800

4. A $500 cash payment was made to reduce the principal balance of a nontrade loan from a bank.
5. Gross equipment account increased $20,000 during the year, accumulated depreciation increased $8,000, and depreciation expense for the period is $10,000. One item of equipment (cost $10,000, accumulated depreciation $2,000) was sold during the year; a gain of $1,000 on the sale was recognized.
6. Purchase of treasury stock, $30,000 cash.
7. Distribution of cash dividends, $5,000.
8. Sale of available-for-sale debt securities for $16,000 cash, at a loss of $3,000.

Required
a. Determine the net cash flows that would be reported in the investing section of the statement of cash flows.
b. Determine the net cash flows that would be reported in the financing section of the statement of cash flows.

The following items are relevant to the preparation of a statement of cash flows for Tropical Inc.

Exercise 22-11
Determining Investing
and Financing
Activities **LO3, 4**

1. Sale of common stock, $500,000 cash.
2. Retirement of bonds payable, $355,000 cash.
3. Purchase of land, $10,000 cash.
4. Sale of equipment for $24,000 cash, at a loss of $5,000.
5. Purchase of equity securities (not held in a trading account), $10,000 cash.
6. Declaration of cash dividends, $40,000.
7. Loan of $30,000 cash resulting in a note receivable, nontrade.
8. Purchase of a patent, $20,000 cash.
9. Proceeds from the issuance of a short-term nontrade note, $10,000 cash.

Required

a. Determine the net cash flows that would be reported in the investing section of a statement of cash flows.

b. Determine the net cash flows that would be reported in the financing section of a statement of cash flows.

Exercise 22-12
Determining Cash
Flow Impact of
Retained Earnings
Changes **LO3, 4, 5**

The following items affected the retained earnings account for the year for Walker Inc.

1. Net loss, $15,000.
2. Cash dividend distributed, $3,000.
3. Stock dividend, $5,000 (1,000 shares, $1 par value common stock).
4. Property dividend, $4,000 (100 shares of common stock in another company held as an investment).
5. Sale of treasury shares for $5,000 cash, previously purchased in the prior year for $6,000.

Required

Indicate how each of the retained earnings transactions would affect the statement of cash flows for the year. The company uses the indirect method in presenting cash flows from operating activities.

Exercise 22-13
Preparing Statement of
Cash Flows—Indirect
Method **LO2, 3, 4**
Hint: See Demo 22-2,
22-3, 22-4

The accounting records of Zale Inc. provided the following data for the current year.

Balance Sheet, Dec. 31	Prior Year	Current Year
Cash.	$ 100	$ 265
Accounts receivable	300	200
Merchandise inventory	100	300
Equipment, net	1,800	2,100
Total assets.	$2,300	$2,865
Accounts payable	$ 275	$ 240
Salaries payable	50	25
Bonds payable	600	800
Common stock (no-par)	1,100	1,200
Retained earnings	275	600
Total liabilities and stockholders' equity . . .	$2,300	$2,865

Income Statement For Year Ended Dec. 31	Current Year
Revenues	$3,000
Cost of goods sold	(1,700)
Depreciation	(400)
Other expenses	(385)
Net income	$ 515

Additional information for the current year

1. Equipment was sold for its carrying amount of $500.

2. Equipment was purchased during the year for $1,200.

3. Cash dividends declared and paid were $190.

Required

Prepare the current year statement of cash flows following the indirect method in presenting cash flows from operating activities.

Exercise 22-14
Preparing Statement of
Cash Flows—Indirect
Method **LO2, 3, 4**
Hint: See Demo 22-2,
22-3, 22-4

Pier2 Inc. reported the following comparative balance sheets for the current year.

Balance Sheets	January 1	December 31
Cash.	$ 4,000	$ 9,750
Restricted cash.	1,000	1,000
Accounts receivable	3,000	2,000
Equipment	9,000	15,000
Accumulated depreciation	(1,000)	(2,000)
Total assets.	$16,000	$25,750
Salaries payable	$ 1,000	$ 2,000
Long-term notes payable	5,000	5,000
Capital stock	8,000	8,000
Retained earnings	2,000	10,750
Total liabilities and stockholders' equity	$16,000	$25,750

Additional information

1. Net income for the current year was $10,000.
2. No disposals of equipment took place during the year.

Required

Prepare the statement of cash flows following the indirect method in presenting cash flows from operating activities.

Denton Corporation's balance sheet accounts as of December 31 of the current and prior year, and information relating to current year activities, are presented below.

Exercise 22-15
Preparing a Statement of Cash Flows—Indirect Method **LO2, 3, 4**
Hint: See Demo 22-2, 22-3, 22-4

Balance Sheets, December 31	Current Year	Prior Year
Assets		
Cash.....................................	$ 230,000	$ 100,000
Short-term investments	300,000	—
Accounts receivable (net)...................	510,000	510,000
Inventory................................	680,000	600,000
Long-term investments.....................	200,000	300,000
Plant assets	1,700,000	1,000,000
Accumulated depreciation	(450,000)	(450,000)
Patent..................................	90,000	100,000
Total assets..........................	$3,260,000	$2,160,000
Liabilities and Stockholders' Equity		
Accounts payable and accrued liabilities	$ 825,000	$ 720,000
Short-term debt to financial institutions	325,000	—
Common stock, $10 par.....................	800,000	700,000
Additional paid-in capital...................	370,000	250,000
Retained earnings	940,000	490,000
Total liabilities and stockholders' equity	$3,260,000	$2,160,000

Information relating to current year activities

1. Net income for the current year was $690,000.
2. Cash dividends of $240,000 were declared and paid during the year.
3. Plant assets costing $400,000 and having a carrying amount of $150,000 was sold this year for $150,000.
4. A long-term investment was sold for $135,000 cash. There were no other transactions affecting long-term investments during the year.
5. 10,000 shares of common stock were issued for $22 per share.
6. Short-term investments consist of Treasury bills maturing on June 30 of the next year and are reported at fair value. Assume no change in fair value from the date of purchase has occurred.

Required

Prepare the statement of cash flows for the current year ended December 31, assuming the indirect method is used in presenting cash flows from operating activities.

Exon Corporation's recent comparative balance sheets and income statement follow.

Exercise 22-16
Preparing a Statement of Cash Flows—Indirect Method
LO2, 3, 4, 5

Balance Sheets, Dec. 31	Current Year	Prior Year
Assets		
Cash...........................	$ 49,000	$ 53,000
Cash equivalents	10,000	7,000
Accounts receivable (net)..........	34,000	24,000
Equipment	277,000	247,000
Accumulated depreciation	(178,000)	(167,000)
Total assets....................	$192,000	$164,000
Liabilities and Stockholders' Equity		
Bonds payable	$ 49,000	$ 46,000
Dividends payable	8,000	5,000
Common stock, $1 par............	22,000	19,000
Additional paid-in capital...........	9,000	3,000
Retained earnings	104,000	91,000
Total liabilities and stockholders' equity............	$192,000	$164,000

Income Statement For Year Ended Dec. 31	Current Year
Sales revenue.............	$155,000
Cost of goods sold	(107,000)
Gross margin	48,000
Depreciation expense.......	(33,000)
Gain on sale of equipment ...	13,000
Net income	$ 28,000

Additional information

1. During the current year, equipment costing $40,000 was sold for cash.
2. During the current year, $20,000 of bonds payable was issued in exchange for equipment. There was no amortization of bond discount or premium.

Required

Prepare the statement of cash flows for the current year ended December 31, assuming the indirect method is used in reporting cash flows from operating activities.

Sketchers Corporation's recent comparative balance sheets and income statement follow.

Balance Sheets, December 31	Prior Year	Current Year
Assets		
Cash and cash equivalents	$ 16,000	$ 68,000
Accounts receivable (net)	20,000	36,000
Inventory.	40,000	48,000
Investment, long-term.	8,000	—
Plant assets	120,000	188,000
Accumulated depreciation	(20,000)	(28,000)
Total assets.	$184,000	$312,000
Liabilities and Stockholders' Equity		
Accounts payable	$ 12,000	$ 20,000
Notes payable, short-term (nontrade). . . .	16,000	12,000
Notes payable, long-term	40,000	72,000
Common stock, no-par	100,000	160,000
Retained earnings	16,000	48,000
Total liabilities and stockholders' equity.	$184,000	$312,000

Income Statement For Year Ended Dec. 31	Current Year
Sales revenue.	$600,000
Cost of goods sold	(360,000)
Gross margin	240,000
Depreciation expense.	(8,000)
Other operating expenses . . .	(128,000)
Net income	$104,000

Additional Information

1. Sold the long-term investment at cost, for cash.
2. Declared and paid a cash dividend of $28,000.
3. Purchased plant assets that cost $68,000; gave a $48,000 long-term note payable and paid $20,000 cash.
4. Paid a $16,000 long-term note payable by issuing common stock; fair value, $16,000.
5. Issued a stock dividend, $44,000.

Required

Prepare the statement of cash flows for the current year ended December 31, assuming the indirect method is used in presenting cash flows from operating activities.

Sterling Corporation's recent comparative balance sheets and income statement follow.

Balance Sheets, December 31	Prior Year	Current Year
Assets		
Cash and cash equivalents	$ 34,000	$ 33,500
Accounts receivable (net)	12,000	17,000
Inventory.	16,000	14,000
Investment, long-term.	6,000	—
Fixed assets	80,000	98,000
Accumulated depreciation	(48,000)	(39,000)
Total assets.	$100,000	$123,500
Liabilities and Stockholders' Equity		
Accounts payable	$ 19,000	$ 12,000
Bonds payable	10,000	30,000
Common stock, no-par	50,000	65,000
Retained earnings	21,000	28,000
Treasury stock	—	(11,500)
Total liabilities and stockholders' equity . . .	$100,000	$123,500

Income Statement, For Year Ended December 31	Current Year
Sales revenue.	$70,000
Cost of goods sold	(42,000)
Gross margin	28,000
Depreciation expense.	(5,000)
Other operating expenses	(18,000)
Gain on sale of investments	3,000
Loss on sale of fixed assets	(1,000)
Net income	$ 7,000

Analysis of selected accounts and transactions

1. Sold fixed assets for cash; cost, $21,000, and two-thirds depreciated.
2. Purchased fixed assets for cash, $9,000.
3. Purchased fixed assets; exchanged bonds of $30,000 (face value equals fair value) in payment.
4. Sold the long-term investments for cash. Assume carrying value of the investment is equal to its original purchase price.
5. Purchased treasury stock for cash, $11,500.
6. Retired bonds payable at maturity date by issuing common stock, $10,000.
7. Issued common stock for cash, $5,000.

Required

Prepare the statement of cash flows for the current year ended December 31, assuming the indirect method is used in presenting cash flows from operating activities.

5M Corporation's recent comparative balance sheets and income statement follow.

Exercise 22-19
Preparing a Statement of Cash Flows—Indirect Method **LO2, 3, 4**

Balance Sheets, December 31	Prior Year	Current Year
Assets		
Cash and cash equivalents	$ 42,000	$ 76,000
Accounts receivable (net)..........	31,000	39,000
Plant assets	82,000	81,000
Accumulated depreciation	(20,000)	(14,000)
Total assets....................	$135,000	$182,000
Liabilities and Stockholders' Equity		
Salaries payable.................	$ 3,000	$ 5,000
Notes payable, long-term	46,000	40,000
Common stock, par $10	61,000	101,000
Additional paid-in capital..........	9,000	17,000
Retained earnings	16,000	27,000
Treasury stock	—	(8,000)
Total liabilities and stockholders' equity.............	$135,000	$182,000

Income Statement For Year Ended Dec. 31	Current Year
Sales revenue..............	$66,000
Salaries expense	(28,000)
Depreciation expense........	(4,000)
Administrative and selling expenses...............	(12,000)
Net income	$22,000

Additional information

1. Plant assets were sold for $21,000 with an original cost of $31,000 and accumulated depreciation of $10,000.
2. Borrowed cash for $40,000; and made principal payments of $46,000 on long-term notes during the year.

Required

Prepare the statement of cash flows for the current year ended December 31, assuming the indirect method is used in presenting cash flows from operating activities.

Crew Company recorded the following amounts in the selected accounts below.

Exercise 22-20
Analyzing the Statement of Cash Flows **LO2, 3, 4, 5**

Equipment				
Jan. 1	100,000			
Purchase of equipment	80,000	25,000	Cost of equipment sold	
Dec. 31	155,000			

Retained Earnings				
		88,000	Jan. 1	
Dividends	2,000	14,000	Net income	
		100,000	Dec. 31	

Accumulated Depreciation—Equipment				
		35,000	Jan. 1	
		12,000	Depreciation expense	
Accumulated depreciation on equipment sold	15,000			
		32,000	Dec. 31	

Common Stock			
	100,000	Jan. 1	
	40,000	Stock issuance	
	140,000	Dec. 31	

Additional Information

1. Equipment was sold for $12,500 cash during the year.
2. Dividends payable increased by $500 from the beginning of the year.
3. $10,000 of the equipment purchases were made by issuing common stock.

Required

a. Indicate items that would be included in the operating, investing, and financing sections of the statement of cash flows, assuming the indirect method is used in presenting cash flows from operating activities.

b. Indicate any noncash disclosures that would be required based upon the information provided.

Taser Corporation's recent comparative balance sheets and income statement follow.

Balance Sheets, December 31	Prior Year	Current Year
Assets		
Cash and cash equivalents	$ 39,000	$ 63,800
Accounts receivable (net)..........	68,000	68,000
Merchandise inventory	156,000	170,000
Investments, long-term............	—	20,000
Plant assets	337,000	361,000
Accumulated depreciation	(88,000)	(68,000)
Total assets......................	$512,000	$614,800
Liabilities and Stockholders' Equity		
Accounts payable	$ 42,000	$ 38,000
Salaries payable	3,000	1,000
Income taxes payable.............	4,000	7,000
Bonds payable	200,000	200,000
Premium on bonds payable	8,000	7,400
Common stock, no-par............	240,000	311,000
Retained earnings	15,000	50,400
Total liabilities and stockholders' equity.............	$512,000	$614,800

Income Statement For Year Ended Dec. 31	Current Year
Sales revenue...............	$240,000
Cost of goods sold	(96,000)
Depreciation expense........	(12,000)
Salaries expense	(44,000)
Income tax expense	(20,000)
Interest expense............	(14,000)
Other expenses	(4,600)
Gain on sale of plant assets...	6,000
Net income	$ 55,400

Additional information

1. Purchased a plant asset, $60,000; issued common stock in full payment.
2. Purchased a long-term investment in equity securities for cash, $20,000.
3. Declared and paid cash dividend, $20,000.
4. Sold a plant asset for $10,000 cash (cost, $36,000; accumulated depreciation, $32,000).
5. Issued common stock, 1,000 shares at $11 per share cash.

Required

a. Prepare a cash flow worksheet.

b. Prepare a reconciliation of the total of the three sections of net cash flows from operating, investing, and financing activities to the change in cash, and prepare the noncash disclosure note.

Guccii Corporation's recent comparative balance sheets and income statement follow.

Balance Sheets, December 31	Prior Year	Current Year
Assets		
Cash and cash equivalents	$ 30,000	$ 43,000
Investments, short-term	—	6,000
Accounts receivable (net)..........	34,000	42,000
Merchandise inventory	20,000	30,000
Investments, long-term............	—	20,000
Plant assets, net..................	120,000	118,000
Patents	6,000	5,400
Other assets.....................	14,000	14,000
Total assets.....................	$224,000	$278,400
Liabilities and Stockholders' Equity		
Accounts payable	$ 24,000	$ 44,000
Accrued expenses payable.........	—	17,400
Bonds payable	80,000	40,000
Common stock, par $10	70,000	80,000
Additional paid-in capital..........	—	9,000
Retained earnings	50,000	88,000
Total liabilities and stockholders' equity	$224,000	$278,400

Income Statement, For Year Ended December 31	Current Year
Sales revenue.............	$208,000
Cost of goods sold	(110,000)
Depreciation expense.......	(16,000)
Patent amortization.........	(600)
Other operating expenses ...	(35,400)
Net income	$ 46,000

Additional information

1. Retired bonds paying $40,000 cash.
2. Bought long-term investment in debt securities, $20,000 cash.
3. Purchased a plant asset, $14,000 cash.
4. Purchased short-term investment in securities (not held in a trading account), $6,000 cash.
5. Declared and paid cash dividends, $8,000.
6. Issued common stock, 1,000 shares at $19 cash per share.

Required

a. Prepare a cash flow worksheet.

b. Prepare a reconciliation of the total of the three sections of net cash flows from operating, investing, and financing activities to the change in cash.

ISPN Corporation's recent comparative balance sheets and income statement follow.

Exercise 22-23
Preparing a Cash Flow
Worksheet **LO6**

Balance Sheets, December 31	Prior Year	Current Year
Assets		
Cash.	$ 16,000	$ 32,000
Accounts receivable	56,000	52,000
Allowance for doubtful accounts.	(6,000)	(5,000)
Other receivables (nontrade)	3,000	2,000
Inventory.	30,000	32,000
Equipment	80,000	77,000
Accumulated depreciation	(6,000)	(5,000)
Intangibles, net	55,000	53,000
Total assets.	$228,000	$238,000
Liabilities and Stockholders' Equity		
Accounts payable	$ 50,000	$ 60,000
Income taxes payable.	70,000	50,000
Interest payable	2,000	1,000
Bonds payable	32,000	
Discount on bonds payable	(2,000)	
Common stock, no-par	70,000	80,000
Retained earnings	6,000	47,000
Total liabilities and stockholders' equity	$228,000	$238,000

Income Statement For Year Ended Dec. 31	Current Year
Sales revenue.	$300,000
Cost of goods sold	(80,000)
Depreciation expense.	(45,000)
Patent amortization.	(2,000)
Other expenses	(44,000)
Interest expense.	(3,000)
Income tax expense	(65,000)
Net income	$ 61,000

Additional information

1. $20,000 of cash dividends were declared and paid in the current year.
2. Equipment costing $66,000, with a carrying value of $20,000, was sold for cash at its carrying value. New equipment also was purchased; common stock was issued in partial payment, $10,000.
3. Bonds were retired at carrying value; $500 of bond discount was amortized in the current year.

Required

a. Prepare a cash flow worksheet.
b. Prepare a reconciliation of the total of the three sections of net cash flows from operating, investing, and financing activities to the change in cash, and prepare the noncash disclosure note.

Adjusted trial balances for Garboz Company, an industrial recycler, at December 31 of the current and prior year follow.

Exercise 22-24
Determining Operating
Cash Flows—Direct
Method **LO7**
Hint: See Demo 22-7

Debits, December 31	Current Year	Prior Year
Cash.	$ 35,000	$ 32,000
Accounts receivable	33,000	30,000
Inventory.	31,000	47,000
Property, plant, and equipment. . .	100,000	95,000
Discount on bonds payable	4,500	5,000
Cost of goods sold	250,000	380,000
Selling expenses	141,500	172,000
General and administrative expenses.	137,000	151,300
Interest expense.	4,300	2,600
Income tax expense	20,400	61,200
Total debits	$756,700	$976,100

Credits, December 31	Current Year	Prior Year
Allowance for doubtful accounts. . .	$ 1,300	$ 1,100
Accumulated depreciation	16,500	15,000
Trade accounts payable	25,000	17,500
Income taxes payable.	21,000	27,100
Deferred income tax liability	5,300	4,600
Callable bonds payable, 8%	45,000	20,000
Common stock	50,000	40,000
Additional paid-in capital.	9,100	7,500
Retained earnings	44,700	64,600
Sales.	538,800	778,700
Total credits	$756,700	$976,100

Additional information

1. Purchased $5,000 of equipment for cash in the current year.
2. Allocated one-third of its depreciation expense to selling expenses and the remainder to general and administrative expenses.
3. Assume no accounts receivable were written off or recovered during the year.

Required

What amounts are reported in the operating activities section of the statement of cash flows using the direct method for the current year ended December 31 for the following line items?

a. Cash collected from customers
b. Cash paid to suppliers
c. Cash paid for interest
d. Cash paid for income taxes
e. Cash paid for selling expenses

Exercise 22-25
Analyzing Cash Flows:
Sales **LO7**

The records of Morgan Company reported sales revenue of $100,000 (on the income statement) and a change in the balance of accounts receivable. To demonstrate the effect of changes in accounts receivable on cash inflows from customers, five separate cases are used.

Case	Sales Revenue (on Income Statement)	Accounts Receivable Increase (Decrease)	Cash Inflow
A.....	$100,000	$ 0	$_____
B.....	100,000	10,000	_____
C.....	100,000	(10,000)	_____
D.....	100,000	9,000*	_____
E.....	100,000	(9,000)*	_____

*Includes the effect of a $1,000 write-off of an uncollectible account.

Required
Complete the table above for each separate case.

Exercise 22-26
Analyzing Cash
Flows: Cost of Goods
Sold **LO7**

The records of Atlas Company showed cost of goods sold (on the income statement) of $60,000 and a change in the inventory and accounts payable balances. To demonstrate the effect of these changes on cash outflow for cost of goods sold (such as payments to suppliers), eight separate cases are used.

Case	Cost of Goods Sold (on Income Statement)	Inventory Increase (Decrease)	Accounts Payable Increase (Decrease)	Cash Outflow
A.....	$60,000	$ 0	$ 0	$_____
B.....	60,000	6,000	0	_____
C.....	60,000	(6,000)	0	_____
D.....	60,000	0	4,000	_____
E.....	60,000	0	(4,000)	_____
F.....	60,000	6,000	4,000	_____
G.....	60,000	(6,000)	(4,000)	_____
H.....	60,000	(6,000)	(6,000)	_____

Required
Complete the table above for each separate case.

Exercise 22-27
Determining Operating
Cash Flows—Direct
Method **LO7**
Hint: See Demo 22-7

Using the information provided in E22-18, prepare the operating activities section of the statement of cash flows, using the direct method. Assume there is no bad debt expense.

Exercise 22-28
Determining Operating
Cash Flows—Direct
Method **LO7**
Hint: See Demo 22-7

Using the information provided in E22-21, prepare the operating activities section of the statement of cash flows, using the direct method.

Exercise 22-29
Determining Operating
Cash Flows—Direct
Method **LO7**
Hint: See Demo 22-7

Using the information provided in E22-22, prepare the operating activities section of the statement of cash flows, using the direct method. Assume there is no bad debt expense

Exercise 22-30
Analyzing Changes in
Accounts Receivable
LO2, 7

The following information pertains to Medicoil Inc., producers of medical hardware, for the current year.

Balance Sheet Excerpts	January 1	December 31
Accounts receivable	$20,000	$35,000
Allowance for doubtful accounts...	(1,000)	(2,000)
Net accounts receivable	$19,000	$33,000

Income Statement Excerpts	
Net sales.	$80,000
Bad debt expense..........	5,500

Additional information

1. $6,000 of accounts receivable were written off during the year.
2. $1,500 was collected on accounts receivable written off in previous years.

Required

a. Determine the adjustment(s) to net income appearing in the operating activities section of the statement of cash flows for the current year under the *indirect* method.

b. Determine the cash collections appearing in the operating activities section of the statement of cash flows for the current year under the *direct* method.

The records of Atlas Company showed bond interest expense (on the income statement) of $20,000 and a change in the bond interest payable, premium, and discount balances. To demonstrate the effect of these changes on cash outflow for bond interest (such as payments to creditors) reported under the direct cash flow method, six separate cases are used.

Exercise 22-31
Analyzing Cash Flows:
Bond Interest   **LO7**

Case	Interest Expense	Change in Interest Payable	Change in Unamortized Discount	Change in Unamortized Premium	Cash Outflow
A.........	$20,000	$ 0	$ 0	n/a	$_____
B.........	20,000	500	(1,000)	n/a	_____
C.........	20,000	(500)	(1,800)	n/a	_____
D.........	20,000	0	n/a	$(2,000)	_____
E.........	20,000	800	(1,000)	n/a	_____
F.........	20,000	(500)	n/a	(2,000)	_____

Required

Complete the table above for each separate case. Assume the only change affecting the unamortized premium and discount accounts is amortization for the period.

The records of Atlas Company showed income tax expense (on the income statement) of $20,000 and a change in the income taxes payable and deferred tax accounts. To demonstrate the effect of these changes on cash outflow for income taxes, six separate cases are used.

Exercise 22-32
Analyzing Cash Flows:
Income Taxes   **LO7**

Case	Income Tax Expense	Change in Income Taxes Payable	Change in Deferred Tax Asset	Change in Deferred Tax Liability	Cash Outflow
A..........	$20,000	$ 0	$ 0	$ 0	$_____
B..........	20,000	1,000	0	0	_____
C..........	20,000	1,000	800	0	_____
D..........	20,000	1,000	0	800	_____
E..........	20,000	(1,000)	500	(800)	_____
F..........	20,000	1,000	(600)	700	_____

Required

Complete the table above for each separate case.

Using the information from E22-22 and E22-29, prepare a statement of cash flows assuming the direct method in presenting cash flows from operating activities. Assume there is no bad debt expense.

Exercise 22-33
Preparing a Statement
of Cash Flows—Direct
Method   **LO3, 4, 7**

The following three statements relate to Aude Company.

Exercise 22-34
Analyzing Interrelations
of Financial Statements
LO2, 3, 4, 7

Net Cash Flows from Operating Activities—Direct Method
For Year Ended December 31

Collections from customers	$240,000
Payments to suppliers	(114,000)
Payments for salaries......................................	(46,000)
Payments for income taxes................................	(17,000)
Payments for interest	(14,600)
Other operating expenses	(4,600)
Net cash provided by operating activities..............	$ 43,800

Income Statement
For Year Ended December 31

Sales revenue.	$ *a*
Cost of goods sold	*b*
Depreciation expense.	*c*
Salaries expense	*d*
Income tax expense	*e*
Interest expense.	*f*
Other expenses	*g*
Gain on sale of fixed assets	*h*
Net income	$ *i*

Net Cash Flows from Operating Activities—Indirect Method
For Year Ended December 31

Net income	$ *j*
Depreciation expense	12,000
Amortization of bond premium	(600)
Gain on sale of fixed assets	(6,000)
Increase in inventory.	(14,000)
Decrease in accounts payable	(4,000)
Decrease in salaries payable	(2,000)
Increase in income taxes payable.	3,000
Net cash provided by operating activities	$43,800

Required

Determine the missing amounts *a* through *j* in the statements above.

Problems

Problem 22-1
Identifying
Operating, Investing,
and Financing
Activities **LO1, 2, 5**
Hint: See Demo 22-1

Harlee Company had the following activities during the current year ended December 31.

_____ 1. Payment of a cash dividend.

_____ 2. Amortization expense on patent.

_____ 3. Compensation expense recognized for stock options.

_____ 4. Decrease in accounts payable.

_____ 5. Decrease in deferred revenue.

_____ 6. Purchase of land through the issuance of common stock.

_____ 7. Unrealized loss—income on equity securities.

_____ 8. Increase in deferred tax liability.

_____ 9. Increase in deferred tax asset.

_____ 10. Conversion of bonds payable to common stock.

_____ 11. Decrease in supplies.

_____ 12. Issued a short-term, nontrade note for cash.

_____ 13. Increase in salaries payable.

_____ 14. Acquisition of equipment through an increase in bonds payable.

_____ 15. Proceeds from cash sale of a patent.

_____ 16. Purchase of equipment for cash.

_____ 17. Excess of the company's share of its investee's net income over the company's share of dividend payments (accounted for under the equity method).

_____ 18. Cash proceeds from an insurance settlement on a property loss.

_____ 19. Increase in inventory.

_____ 20. Principal payment in cash on a mortgage payable.

_____ 21. Collection in cash of a nontrade note receivable.

_____ 22. Cash proceeds from long-term nontrade note payable.

_____ 23. Amortization expense on premium for a bond payable.

_____ 24. Cash sale of available-for-sale debt securities.

_____ 25. Retirement of preferred stock for cash.

_____ 26. Collection in cash on a trade note receivable (note received for inventory purchase).

Required

Assuming that the company uses the indirect method to present cash flows from operating activities, classify each activity listed into one of the seven following categories, *a* through *g*.

a. Operating activity—addition
b. Operating activity—subtraction
c. Investing activity—cash inflow
d. Investing activity—cash outflow
e. Financing activity—cash inflow
f. Financing activity—cash outflow
g. Noncash transaction

Label Corporation's recent comparative balance sheets and income statement, along with additional information follow.

Problem 22-2
Preparing a Statement of Cash Flows—Indirect Method
LO2, 3, 4, 5

Balance Sheets, December 31	Prior Year	Current Year		Income Statement, For Year ended December 31	Current Year
Assets				Sales revenue.	$80,000
Cash and cash equivalents	$ 15,000	$ 31,000		Cost of goods sold	(35,000)
Accounts receivable	30,000	28,500		Depreciation expense.	(5,000)
Allowance for doubtful accounts. . . .	(1,500)	(2,000)		Bad debt expense.	(1,000)
Inventory.	10,000	15,000		Insurance expense	(1,000)
Prepaid insurance.	2,400	1,400		Interest expense	(2,000)
Fixed assets	80,000	81,000		Salaries expense	(12,000)
Accumulated depreciation	(20,000)	(16,000)		Income tax expense	(3,000)
Land	40,100	81,100		Other expenses, including loss	
Total assets.	$156,000	$220,000		on sale of fixed assets	(15,000)
				Net income	$ 6,000
Liabilities and Stockholders' Equity					
Accounts payable	$ 10,000	$ 11,000			
Salaries payable.	2,000	1,000			
Interest payable	—	1,000			
Notes payable, long-term	20,000	46,000			
Common stock, no-par.	100,000	136,000			
Retained earnings	24,000	25,000			
Total liabilities and stockholders' equity	$156,000	$220,000			

Additional information

1. Wrote off $500 accounts receivable as uncollectible.
2. Sold a fixed asset for $4,000 cash (cost, $15,000; accumulated depreciation, $9,000).
3. Issued common stock for $5,000 cash.
4. Declared and paid a cash dividend, $5,000.
5. Purchased land, $20,000 cash.
6. Acquired land for $21,000 and issued common stock as payment in full.
7. Acquired fixed assets, cost $16,000; issued a $16,000, three-year, interest-bearing note payable.
8. Paid a $10,000 long-term note installment by issuing common stock to the creditor.
9. Borrowed cash on long-term note, $20,000.

Required

Prepare a current year statement of cash flows using the indirect method to report cash flows from operating activities.

Problem 22-3
Preparing a Statement
of Cash Flows—Indirect
Method
LO2, 3, 4, 5

The income statement and balance sheets of Kenwood Company and related analysis are provided below.

Balance Sheets, December 31	Current Year	Prior Year
Assets		
Cash and cash equivalents	$ 100,000	$ 90,000
Accounts receivable (net of allowance for doubtful accounts of $10,000 and $8,000, respectively)	210,000	140,000
Inventory	260,000	220,000
Land	325,000	200,000
Plant and equipment	580,000	633,000
Accumulated depreciation	(90,000)	(100,000)
Patents	30,000	33,000
Total assets	$1,415,000	$1,216,000
Liabilities and Stockholders' Equity		
Accounts payable	$ 260,000	$ 200,000
Salaries payable	200,000	210,000
Income tax payable	140,000	100,000
Bonds payable (due in nine year on December 15)	130,000	180,000
Common stock, par value $5, authorized 100,000 shares, issued and outstanding 50,000 and 42,000 shares, respectively	250,000	210,000
Additional paid-in capital	233,000	170,000
Retained earnings	202,000	146,000
Total liabilities and stockholders' equity	$1,415,000	$1,216,000

Income Statement, For Year Ended December 31	Current Year
Sales revenue	$1,000,000
Expenses and losses	
Cost of goods sold	(560,000)
Salaries	(190,000)
Depreciation	(20,000)
Patent amortization	(3,000)
Loss on sale of equipment	(4,000)
Interest expense	(16,000)
Miscellaneous expenses	(8,000)
Gain on early extinguishment of debt	12,000
Income tax expense	(90,000)
Net income	$ 121,000

Analysis of selected accounts and transactions

1. On February 2, issued a 10% stock dividend to stockholders of record on January 15. The market price per share of the common stock on February 2 was $15.
2. On March 1, issued 3,800 shares of common stock for land. The common stock had a fair value of approximately $40,000 on March 1.
3. On April 15, repurchased its long-term bonds payable with a face value of $50,000 for cash.
4. On June 30, sold equipment that cost $53,000, with a carrying amount of $23,000, for $19,000 cash.
5. On September 30, declared and paid a 4 cents per share cash dividend to stockholders of record on August 1.
6. On October 10, purchased land for $85,000 cash.

Required

Prepare a current year statement of cash flows using the indirect method to report cash flows from operating activities.

The following is Orem Corporation's comparative balance sheets for the current year and prior year.

Problem 22-4
Preparing a Statement
of Cash Flows—Indirect
Method
LO2, 3, 4, 5

Balance Sheets, December 31	Current Year	Prior Year
Assets		
Cash and cash equivalents	$ 400,000	$ 350,000
Accounts receivable (net).............................	564,000	584,000
Inventory.......................................	925,000	857,500
Right-of-use asset	200,000	—
Property, plant, & equipment	1,453,500	1,483,500
Accumulated depreciation	(582,500)	(520,000)
Investment in Belle Co....	152,500	137,500
Loan receivable	135,000	—
Total assets.....	$3,247,500	$2,892,500
Liabilities and Stockholders' Equity		
Accounts payable	$ 507,500	$ 477,500
Income taxes payable....	15,000	25,000
Dividends payable	40,000	45,000
Lease liability	200,000	—
Capital stock, common, $1 par....	250,000	250,000
Additional paid-in capital....	750,000	750,000
Retained earnings	1,485,000	1,345,000
Total liabilities and stockholders' equity	$3,247,500	$2,892,500

Additional information

1. On December 31 of the prior year, acquired 25% of Belle Company's common stock for $137,500. On that date, the carrying value of Belle's net assets and liabilities, which approximated fair value, was $550,000. Belle reported income of $60,000 for the current year ended December 31. No dividend was paid on Belle's common stock during the year.
2. During the year, loaned $150,000 cash to Chase Company, an unrelated company. Chase made the first semi-annual principal repayment of $15,000 cash, plus interest at 10% on October 1.
3. On January 2, sold equipment costing $30,000, with a carrying value of $17,500, for $20,000 cash.
4. On December 31, entered into a finance lease for an office building. Orem recorded a right-of-use asset and a lease liability for $200,000 at the lease commencement. Orem made the first rental payment of $30,000 cash when due on January 2 of the next year.
5. Net income for the year was $180,000. Taxes paid during the year were $70,000.

Required

Prepare a current year statement of cash flows using the indirect method to report cash flows from operating activities.

Differences between the Boole Inc. balance sheet accounts on December 31 of the current and prior year follow.

Problem 22-5
Preparing a Statement
of Cash Flows—Indirect
Method
LO2, 3, 4, 5

Balance Sheet Changes	Difference	Balance Sheet Changes	Difference
Assets		**Liabilities and Stockholders' Equity**	
Cash and cash equivalents	$ 60,000	Accounts payable and accrued liabilities ...	$ (2,500)
Short-term investments	150,000	Dividends payable	80,000
Accounts receivable, net.......	0	Short-term debt (nontrade).............	162,500
Inventory..................	40,000	Long-term debt......................	55,000
Investment, long-term.........	(50,000)	Common stock, $5 par.................	50,000
Plant assets	350,000	Additional paid-in capital.............	60,000
Accumulated depreciation	0	Retained earnings	145,000
Total assets..............	$550,000	Total liabilities and stockholders' equity	$550,000

Additional information for the current year

1. Both short- and long-term investments are reported at fair value. The fair value of the short-term investments and long-term investments did not change during the year. Investments were not held in a trading account.
2. A building costing $300,000 and having a carrying amount of $175,000 was sold for $175,000 cash.

3. Equipment costing $55,000 was acquired through the issuance of long-term debt.
4. A long-term investment was sold for $67,500 cash. There were no other transactions affecting long-term investments.
5. 10,000 shares of common stock were issued for $11 a share.
6. Net income was $395,000.
7. Interest and taxes paid during the year were $30,000 and $160,000, respectively.

Required

Prepare the current year statement of cash flows assuming that cash on January 1 of the current year was $30,000 and that the company presents cash flows from operating activities using the indirect method.

Problem 22-6
Preparing a Statement of Cash Flows—Indirect Method
LO2, 3, 4, 5, 6

At December 31 of the current year the following data for Lincoln Company were available.

Balance Sheets, December 31	Prior Year	Current Year
Assets		
Cash.	$ 7,000	$ 19,000
Cash equivalents	1,000	3,000
Accounts receivable (net).	18,000	24,000
Inventory.	16,000	10,000
Investment, long-term.	4,000	0
Plant	60,000	60,000
Equipment	40,000	44,000
Land	20,000	80,000
Patents	16,000	14,000
Accumulated depreciation—plant.	(14,000)	(20,000)
Accumulated depreciation—equipment	(20,000)	(16,000)
Total assets.	$148,000	$218,000
Liabilities and Stockholders' Equity		
Accounts payable	$ 16,000	$ 4,000
Salaries payable	2,000	0
Notes payable, long-term	20,000	38,000
Common stock, no-par	100,000	150,000
Retained earnings	10,000	26,000
Total liabilities and stockholders' equity	$148,000	$218,000

Income Statement, For Year Ended December 31	Current Year
Sales revenue.	$180,000
Cost of goods sold	(110,000)
Depreciation expense, plant.	(6,000)
Depreciation expense, equipment	(4,000)
Patent amortization.	(2,000)
Other operating expenses	(40,000)
Loss on sale of equipment	(2,000)
Gain on sale of long-term investment.	16,000
Income tax expense	(8,000)
Net income	$ 24,000

Analysis of selected accounts and entries

1. At the end of the year, sold equipment that cost $16,000 (50% depreciated) for $6,000 cash.
2. Purchased land that cost $20,000; paid $4,000 cash, issued a long-term note for the balance.
3. Paid $8,000 cash to retire a long-term note payable at maturity.
4. Issued $20,000 of common stock for cash.
5. Purchased equipment costing $20,000; paid half in cash, balance due in three years (interest-bearing note).
6. Issued 3,000 shares of common stock, fair value $30,000, for land that cost $40,000; the balance was paid in cash.
7. Sold the long-term investment for $20,000 cash. The investments were debt securities classified as available-for-sale. The securities were purchased December 31 of the prior year; therefore, no valuation allowance was established.
8. Declared and paid cash dividends, $8,000.
9. Income taxes paid and interest paid were $8,000 and $2,000, respectively.

Required

a. Prepare a cash flow worksheet for the current year.

b. Prepare the statement of cash flows using the indirect method to report cash flows from operating activities.

The records of Lopez Co. provided the following data.

Problem 22-7
Preparing a Statement
of Cash Flows—Indirect
Method
LO2, 3, 4, 5, 6

Balance Sheets, December 31	Prior Year	Current Year
Assets		
Cash and cash equivalents	$ 30,000	$ 69,000
Investments, short term	10,000	8,000
Accounts receivable	56,000	86,000
Allowance for doubtful accounts	(6,000)	(7,000)
Inventory	20,000	30,000
Prepaid rent	0	2,000
Land	60,000	25,000
Equipment	80,000	90,000
Accumulated depreciation	(20,000)	(26,900)
Other assets	29,000	39,000
Total assets	$259,000	$315,100
Liabilities and Stockholders' Equity		
Accounts payable	$ 33,000	$ 45,000
Salaries payable	5,000	2,000
Income taxes payable	2,000	8,000
Bonds payable	70,000	55,000
Discount on bonds payable	(1,000)	(900)
Common stock, no-par	100,000	131,000
Preferred stock, no-par	20,000	30,000
Retained earnings	30,000	45,000
Total liabilities and stockholders' equity	$259,000	$315,100

Income Statement, For Year Ended December 31	Current Year
Sales revenue	$180,000
Cost of goods sold	(90,000)
Depreciation expense	(6,900)
Bad debt expense	(1,000)
Salaries	(32,900)
Other operating expenses	(4,000)
Interest expense	(6,100)
Gain on sale of land	18,000
Loss on bond retirement	(1,000)
Income tax expense	(12,100)
Net income	$ 44,000

Analysis of selected accounts and transactions

1. Issued bonds payable for cash, $5,000. The bonds payable account represents more than one bond issue.

2. Sold land for $53,000 cash; carrying amount, $35,000.

3. Purchased equipment for cash, $10,000.

4. Purchased short-term investments (not held in a trading account) for cash, $2,000.

5. Declared a property dividend on the preferred stock and paid it with a short-term investment; fair value and carrying value are the same, $4,000.

6. Prior to maturity date, retired $20,000 (face) of bonds payable by issuing common stock; the common stock had a fair value of $21,000. The bonds retired had been issued at face value.

7. Acquired other assets by issuing preferred stock with a fair value of $10,000.

8. Cash dividends declared and paid were $15,000. A stock dividend with a fair value of $10,000 was issued on the common stock.

Required

a. Prepare a cash flow worksheet for the current year.

b. Prepare the statement of cash flows using the indirect method in presenting cash flows from operating activities.

Problem 22-8
Preparing a Statement
of Cash Flows—Indirect
Method
LO2, 3, 4, 5

The income statement, balance sheets and analysis of selected accounts of Cruz Co. are provided below.

Balance Sheets, December 31	Prior Year	Current Year
Assets		
Cash and cash equivalents	$ 80,000	$ 89,800
Accounts receivable (net)	120,000	105,000
Inventory	360,000	283,200
Prepaid insurance	4,800	2,400
Investment, long-term	60,000	—
Land	20,000	76,800
Plant assets	500,000	518,000
Accumulated depreciation	(130,000)	(158,000)
Patent (net)	3,200	2,800
Total assets	$1,018,000	$920,000
Liabilities and Stockholders' Equity		
Accounts payable	$ 100,000	$106,000
Salaries payable	4,000	3,000
Income taxes payable	18,000	26,800
Bonds payable	200,000	100,000
Premium on bonds payable	10,000	3,400
Common stock, par $10	600,000	612,000
Additional paid-in capital	30,000	36,000
Retained earnings	56,000	32,800
Total liabilities and stockholders' equity	$1,018,000	$920,000

Income Statement, For Year Ended December 31	Current Year
Sales revenue	$800,000
Cost of goods sold	(448,800)
Depreciation expense	(28,000)
Patent amortization	(400)
Gain on sale of long-term investment	20,000
Other expenses, including interest of $3,400 and taxes of $23,800 . . .	(306,000)
Net income	$ 36,800

Analysis of selected accounts and entries

1. Purchased plant assets; cost, $18,000; payment by issuing 1,200 shares of stock.
2. Cash payment at maturity date to retire bonds payable, $100,000.
3. Sold long-term investments for $80,000 cash. The fair value of these securities reported at fair value had not changed until the current year.
4. Purchased land, $56,800; paid cash.
5. Analysis of the retained earnings account follows.

Retained earnings, beginning balance	$56,000
Net income	36,800
Cash dividend paid	(60,000)
Retained earnings, ending balance	$32,800

Required

Prepare the current year statement of cash flows using the indirect method in presenting cash flows from operating activities.

Problem 22-9
Recording the
Effects of Bonds and
Leases **LO2, 4, 7**

Central Corporation issued $100,000, 6%, 10-year bonds (interest payable semiannually on June 30 and December 31) dated on January 1 of this year, when the market rate was 7%. Assume that the company uses the effective interest method to amortize bond discounts and premiums.

Central Corporation also leased equipment on January 1 of this year, recording a right-of-use asset and lease liability for $50,000. The lease calls for beginning of the year payments beginning on January 1, for five years. The implicit rate of interest (known by Central Corporation) is 10%. The estimated useful life of the equipment is five years and no salvage value is estimated.

Required

Part One

a. Indicate how the bond transactions would affect the statement of cash flows for the year, assuming that the company uses the indirect method.

b. Indicate how the lease transactions would affect the statement of cash flows for the year, assuming that the company uses the indirect method.

Part Two

a. Indicate how the bond transactions would affect the statement of cash flows for the year, assuming that the company uses the direct method to report cash flows from operating activities.

b. Indicate how the lease transactions would affect the statement of cash flows for the year, assuming that the company uses the direct method to report cash flows from operating activities.

The following items affected the retained earnings account for the year.

Problem 22-10
Analyzing Financing
Activities **LO4**

1. Net income, $35,000.
2. Cash dividend declared and distributed, $10,000.
3. Stock dividend distributed, $5,000 (1,000 shares, $1 par value common stock).
4. Retirement of common shares for $45,000 cash, resulting in a settlement of $4,500 in excess of the stock carrying value.

Required

Indicate how the retained earnings transactions would affect the statement of cash flows for the year, assuming that the company uses the indirect method to report cash flows from operating activities.

The following information is provided for Vale Inc.

Problem 22-11
Determining
Operating Activities—
Direct and Indirect
Approaches **LO2, 7**

Balance Sheets, December 31	Prior Year	Current Year
Assets		
Cash and cash equivalents	$ 45,000	$105,000
Accounts receivable, net.	75,000	65,000
Inventory.	100,000	78,000
Equipment	200,000	180,000
Accumulated depreciation	(40,000)	(20,000)
Land	30,000	35,000
Total assets.	$410,000	$443,000
Liabilities and Stockholders' Equity		
Accounts payable	$ 70,000	$ 87,000
Other current liabilities	10,000	8,000
Bonds payable	100,000	100,000
Premium on bonds payable	10,000	8,000
Common stock, no-par	120,000	90,000
Retained earnings	100,000	150,000
Total liabilities and stockholders' equity	$410,000	$443,000

Income Statement, For Year Ended December 31	Current Year
Sales revenue.	$255,000
Cost of goods sold	(125,000)
Depreciation expense.	(20,000)
Other operating expenses	(40,000)
Interest expense.	(10,000)
Gain on sale of equipment	25,000
Net income	$ 85,000

Other information

Equipment with an original cost of $60,000 and accumulated depreciation of $40,000 was sold for $45,000 cash. Assume there is no bad debt expense.

Required

a. Prepare the operating activities section of the statement of cash flows using the direct method.

b. Prepare the operating activities section of the statement of cash flows using the indirect method.

Problem 22-12
Preparing a Statement of Cash Flows—Direct Method **LO7**

Using the information provided in P22-2, prepare the operating activities section of the statement of cash flows using the direct method. Do not include a disclosure reconciling net income to cash flows from operating activities.

Problem 22-13
Preparing a Statement of Cash Flows—Direct Method **LO7**

Using the information provided in P22-3, prepare the statement of cash flows using the direct method for the operating activities section. Assume no accounts receivable were written off or recovered during the year. Do not include a disclosure reconciling net income to cash flows from operating activities.

Problem 22-14
Preparing a Statement of Cash Flows—Direct Method **LO7**

Using the information provided in P22-6, prepare the statement of cash flows using the direct method for the operating activities section. Do not include a disclosure reconciling net income to cash flows from operating activities.

Problem 22-15
Preparing a Statement of Cash Flows—Direct Method **LO7**

Using the information provided in P22-7, prepare the statement of cash flows using the direct method for the operating activities section. Assume no accounts receivable were written off or recovered during the year. Do not include a disclosure reconciling net income to cash flows from operating activities.

Problem 22-16
Preparing a Statement of Cash Flows—Direct Method **LO7**

The following information is provided for DHS Inc.

Balance Sheets, December 31	Prior Year	Current Year
Assets		
Cash.	$ 35,000	$ 49,582
Cash equivalents	20,000	10,000
Investment, short-term	8,000	5,000
Accounts receivable	50,000	75,000
Allowance for doubtful accounts.	(2,000)	(3,000)
Inventory.	120,000	40,000
Prepaid insurance.	20,000	30,000
Long-term investment.	40,000	45,000
Land	250,000	350,000
Equipment	100,000	130,000
Right-of-use asset	—	60,653
Accumulated depreciation, equipment.	(50,000)	(64,837)
Intangible assets, net	45,000	35,000
Total assets.	$636,000	$762,398
Liabilities and Stockholders' Equity		
Accounts payable	$ 40,000	$ 70,000
Income taxes payable.	5,000	8,000
Dividends payable	6,000	12,000
Lease liability, long-term.	—	63,398
Deferred tax liability	20,000	25,000
Mortgage payable.	—	80,000
Note payable.	—	100,000
Bonds payable	180,000	—
Unamortized bond discount	(12,000)	—
Common stock	300,000	300,000
Retained earnings	97,000	104,000
Total liabilities and stockholders' equity	$636,000	$762,398

Income Statement, For Year Ended December 31	Current Year
Sales revenue.	$620,000
Cost of goods sold	(400,000)
Depreciation expense.	(26,837)
Bad debt expense.	(18,000)
Interest expense.	(23,000)
Amortization of right-of-use asset	(15,163)
Amortization of intangibles . . .	(10,000)
Other operating expenses . . .	(85,000)
Gain on sale of short-term investments.	3,000
Gain on equipment sale	7,000
Gain on bond retirement.	20,000
Investment income	30,000
Income tax expense	(25,000)
Net income	$ 77,000

Additional information about events in the current year

1. On January 1, the fair value of the portfolio of short-term investments in debt securities, classified as available-for-sale, equaled cost. During the year, investments carried at $3,000 were sold for $6,000. No securities were purchased during the year. At December 31, the fair value of the portfolio is $5,000.
2. Cash equivalents were continually purchased and sold at cost. No gains or losses were incurred.
3. $20,000 of accounts receivable was written off during the year and $3,000 was collected on an account written off in the prior year. All sales are on account.

4. The long-term investment represents a 25% equity interest in Wickens Company and is accounted for under the equity method, purchased at book value. During the year, Wickens paid $100,000 in cash dividends and earned $120,000.

5. At the end of the year, DHS Inc. acquired land for $100,000 by assuming an $80,000 mortgage and paying the balance in cash.

6. Equipment (cost, $20,000; carrying value, $8,000) was sold for $15,000 cash.

7. Started and completed construction of equipment for its own use during the year. The cost of the finished equipment, $50,000, includes $5,000 of capitalized interest.

8. Entered into a finance lease on January 1, recording a right-of-use asset and a lease liability for $75,816. The interest rate used to capitalize the lease is 10%. Equal annual payments of $20,000 are due each December 31 for five years. Interest expense in the current year income statement includes interest on the lease liability of $7,582.

9. The bonds were retired for cash before maturity at a $20,000 gain, before taxes. Discount amortized during the year, $4,000.

10. Declared $70,000 of cash dividends during the year.

Required

Prepare the current year statement of cash flows using the direct method for the operating section. Include a note disclosure reconciling net income to cash flows from operating activities.

The following three statements relate to Sterling Co.

Problem 22-17
Analyzing Interrelations of Financial Statements—Direct and Indirect Method
LO2, 3, 4, 7

Income Statement
For Year Ended December 31

Sales revenue.	$ a
Cost of goods sold	b
Depreciation expense.	c
Salaries	d
Other operating expenses	e
Interest expense.	f
Gain on sale of equipment	g
Loss on bond retirement.	h
Income tax expense	i
Net income.	$ j

Net Cash Flows from Operating Activities, Direct Method
For Year Ended December 31

Collections from customers	$165,000
Payments to suppliers	(88,000)
Payments for salaries.	(35,900)
Payments for other operating expenses.	(4,900)
Payments for interest	(6,000)
Payments for income tax	(6,100)
Net cash provided by operating activities.	$ 24,100

Net Cash Flows from Operating Activities, Indirect Method
For Year Ended December 31

Net income.	$ k
Adjustments:	
Depreciation expense.	8,000
Gain on sale of equipment	(18,000)
Loss on bond retirement.	1,000
Amortization of bond discount	100
Increase in accounts receivable, net.	(29,000)
Increase in inventory.	(10,000)
Increase in prepaid rent	(2,000)
Increase in accounts payable	12,000
Decrease in salaries payable	(3,000)
Increase in income taxes payable.	6,000
Net cash provided by operating activities.	$ l

Required

Determine the missing amounts *a* through *l* in the statements above.

Accounting Decisions and Judgments

AD&J22-1
Interpreting the
Statement of Cash
Flows **LO2**

Real World Analysis A portion of the operating activities section of a telecommunication firm's Year 8 statement of cash flows is reproduced below ($ millions).

Cash flows from operating activities	
Net income	$3,606
Adjustments to net income	
Depreciation and amortization	2,717
Deferred income taxes, net (#1)	305
Investment tax credits, net (#2)	(25)
Change in accounts receivable, net	26
Change in material and supplies.	(95)
Change in other current assets	(213)
Change in accounts payable	(50)
Change in certain other current liabilities (#3).	1,322
Change in certain noncurrent assets and liabilities (#4) . . .	(959)
Gain on sale of TCNZ shares (#5).	(1,543)
(Combined other items—deleted by authors)	(281)
Net cash provided by operating activities	$4,810

The firm uses the deferral method to account for investment tax credits: the company amortizes part of the deferred investment tax credit account as a reduction in income tax expense over the lives of related plant assets.

Required

Using only the information provided, explain why each of the five numbered reconciling items appears in the operating section, and why it is added or subtracted.

AD&J22-2
Interpreting the
Statement of Cash
Flows **LO7**

Real World Analysis **Dole Food Company** is one of the largest international food processing and distribution companies. Partial information from the Year 8 annual report appears below ($ thousands).

Consolidated Statement of Income For Year Ended December 31, Year 8 ($ thousands)	
Revenue	$4,424,160
Cost of products sold	3,785,745
Gross margin	638,415
Selling, marketing and administrative expenses.	433,509
Hurricane loss.	100,000
Citrus charge	20,000
Operating income	84,906
Interest income	9,312
Other income (expense)—net	(7,996)
Earnings before interest and taxes	86,222
Interest expense	68,943
Income from operations before income taxes	17,279
Income taxes	5,200
Net income	$ 12,079

From the December 31 balance sheets ($ thousands)	Year 8	Year 7
Current assets		
Cash and short-term investments.	$ 35,352	$ 31,202
Receivables—net	616,579	534,844
Inventories	475,524	468,692
Prepaid expenses	43,200	48,438
Total current assets.	$1,170,655	$1,083,176
Current liabilities		
Notes payable	$ 29,637	$ 11,290
Current portion of long-term debt	6,451	2,326
Accounts payable	264,732	230,143
Accrued liabilities	504,058	432,680
Total current liabilities	$ 804,878	$ 676,439

Additional information

1. Payments for selling, marketing, and administrative expenses and other income expense—net can be determined by analyzing the change in prepaid expenses and accrued expenses.
2. Notes payable are due to financial institutions.
3. Net deferred tax liability increased $2,000 during Year 8.

Required
Use the information in this case to prepare the operating activities section of the Year 8 statement of cash flows, using the direct method. List any assumptions necessary to prepare this report.

`Real World Analysis` **Johnson & Johnson** is a leading personal care products manufacturer. The company's Year 2 statement of cash flow disclosed the following two reconciling adjustments in the operating activity section prepared under the indirect method ($ thousands).

AD&J22-3
Interpreting the Statement of Cash Flows **LO2**

Imputed interest on note..........................	$134
Increase in cash surrender value of life insurance	(251)

Required
Explain why the reconciliation includes these two adjustments and why they are added to or subtracted from net income.

`Real World Analysis` **Collins Industries Inc.** is a manufacturer of specialty vehicles, such as ambulances and school and shuttle buses. The company uses the direct method to prepare its statement of cash flows. Reproduced below from the Year 5 statement of cash flows are (1) the operating activities section and (2) the reconciliation schedule.

AD&J22-4
Reconstructing an Income Statement from a Statement of Cash Flows **LO2, 3, 7**

Operating Activities	
Cash received from customers.........................	$141,425,892
Cash paid to suppliers and employees..................	(132,956,101)
Interest paid, net......................................	(3,209,818)
Cash provided by operations	$ 5,259,973

Reconciliation of Net Loss to Net Cash Provided by Operations	
Net loss...	$ (340,759)
Depreciation and amortization	2,513,541
Common stock issued for benefit of employees.............	106,365
Decrease in receivables, net	700,827
Decrease in inventories	1,614,442
Decrease in prepaid expenses.........................	329,517
Increase (decrease) in accounts payable.................	276,782
Increase (decrease) in accrued expenses	(261,519)
Gain on sale of vacant land	(99,667)
Loss on early extinguishment of debt....................	420,444
Cash provided by operations	$5,259,973

Required
Reconstruct the Year 5 income statement for Collins Industries. Assume that accrued and prepaid expenses do not relate to interest or to income taxes, and that Collins had no interest income in Year 5. *Hint:* Aggregate cost of goods sold and operating expenses in one category.

`Real World Analysis` Obtain an electronic copy of the Form 10-K for the **Coca-Cola Company** for the year ended December 31, 2023, which can be found on the SEC Edgar website (https://www.sec.gov/edgar/searchedgar/companysearch.html). Answer the following questions.

AD&J22-5
Analyzing a Statement of Cash Flows **LO2, 3, 4, 5, 7**

a. Is Coca Cola's operating activities section on its statement of cash flows prepared under the direct method or the indirect method?
b. For 2023, provide the amount of dividends paid and the amount of dividends accrued.
c. Provide an estimate of cash receipts from sales for 2023, assuming that all net operating revenues are credit sales and that there were no write-offs of receivables in 2023.

d. What is the company's policy with respect to classification of investments fulfilling the definition of cash equivalents?

e. Did the company fulfill the requirement to disclose certain operating cash flows for 2023?

f. Can we estimate the amount of dividends received from investments accounted for under the equity method in 2023? Why is this amount not shown in the statement of cash flows?

AD&J22-6
Comparing Direct and Indirect Methods **LO1, 2, 7**

Communication Case The principal advantage of the direct method is that it shows operating cash receipts and payments relating to the major classes of revenues and expenses in the income statement. The principal advantage of the indirect method is that it focuses on reconciling items between net income and net cash flow from operating activities. There has been discussion over the years of requiring companies to use the direct method to be more consistent with the objective of a statement of cash flows—to provide information about cash receipts and cash payments—than the indirect method, which does not directly report operating cash receipts and payments. Assume the following are items separately reported in a company's financial statements.

Cash Inflows and Outflows (and related changes)	Direct Method	Indirect Method	Comparative Balance Sheet
1. Cash inflow from sales			
2. Cash inflow from services			
3. Cash inflow from interest			
4. Cash inflow from dividend received			
5. Accounts receivable increase or decrease			
6. Interest receivable increase or decrease			
7. Payments to suppliers (cash purchases)			
8. Inventory increase or decrease			
9. Accounts payable increase or decrease			
10. Payments for salaries			
11. Salaries payable increase or decrease			
12. Payments for income taxes			
13. Income taxes payable increase or decrease			
14. Net income			
15. Net cash flow from operating activities			
16. Cash flows from investing activities			
17. Cash flows from financing activities			
18. Net increase or decrease in cash during the period			
19. Cash, beginning balance			
20. Cash, ending balance			

Required

a. Complete the table indicating whether each item 1 through 20 is included in a statement of cash flows where the operating activities section is prepared using the direct method or the indirect method, and/or on a comparative balance sheet.

b. Prepare a one-page memorandum on the advantages of each method (direct and indirect).

AD&J22-7
Interpreting the Statement of Cash Flows **LO1, 2**

Ethics Case Honore Company has competed for many years in product lines that have recently experienced a great increase in global competition. Their products have long been dominated by U.S. firms. Honore has no foreign operations and few personnel with experience in international trade. Honore has made few product changes in recent years and is not actively engaged in product innovation or research and development. The following information is taken from the company's financial statements and notes for Year 1 through Year 4, where Year 4 is the most current year ($ thousands).

	Year 1	Year 2	Year 3
Net income.	$50,000	$30,000	$10,000
Net accounts receivable (ending).	40,000	12,000	6,000
Inventory (ending).	19,000	14,000	7,000
Net cash provided by operating activities.	15,000	7,000	4,500
Capital expenditures.	9,000	7,000	6,000
Proceeds from sale of plant assets	15,000	10,000	18,000
Net gain on sales of plant assets	16,000	12,000	15,000

The company executed the following activities during Year 4.

1. Recently negotiated with banks to extend payment terms on short-term loans.
2. Maintained very low levels of accounts payable during this period.
3. Significant investments in corporate bonds (interest revenue on bonds in Year 4 was $3,000).
4. Paid no dividends during this period.
5. Issued no stock or bonds during this period.

Statement of Cash Flows		
For Year Ended December 31, Year 4 (in thousands)		
Cash flows from operating activities:		
Net income	$ 7,000	
Items reconciling net income and net cash inflow from operating activities		
Accounts receivable decrease	1,000	
Inventory decrease	1,500	
Loss from building fire.	8,000	
Dividends received (equity investment)	6,000	
Investment revenue (equity investment)	(10,000)	
Gains on sales of plant assets	(14,000)	
Depreciation, amortization	4,000	
Net cash provided by operating activities		$ 3,500
Cash flows from investing activities:		
Purchase of plant assets.	(4,000)	
Insurance proceeds on building fire	20,000	
Sale of plant assets.	25,000	
Purchase of corporate bonds	(5,000)	
Purchase of corporate stocks	(10,000)	
Net cash provided by investing activities.		26,000
Cash flows from financing activities:		
Principal payments on short-term notes to financial institutions.	(15,000)	
Purchase of treasury stock	(6,000)	
Net cash used by financing activities		(21,000)
Net cash increase.		8,500
Beginning cash balance		12,000
Ending cash balance		$20,500

Required

Provide an interpretation of the statement of cash flows in light of Honore's situation. Weigh ethical considerations in terms of company strategy and financial disclosure.

Judgment Case The following transactions and end-of-year fair values refer to investments of BankOne Inc.

a. BankOne purchased securities of Smith Company for $10,000 in late December. The investment is held in a trading account.
b. The December 31 fair value of the investment in Smith Company is $12,000.
c. During January of the following year, BankOne sold the trading investment for $12,000.

AD&J22-8
Reporting Cash Flow for Investments in Securities
LO1, 2, 3

Required

For each of the above transactions and end-of-year adjusting entries, describe how the transaction will be reported assuming the indirect method in presenting cash flows from operating activities.

Judgment Case The reconciliation of a company's earnings to its net cash flow from operating activities is a required disclosure regardless of the method chosen to prepare the statement of cash flows. If the direct method is used, the reconciliation appears as a supporting schedule. If the indirect method is used, the reconciliation appears either as the operating activity section of the statement of cash flow or as a supporting schedule. This case asks us to look more closely at the reconciliation.

AD&J22-9
Reconciling Net Income and Net Operating Cash Flow **LO2, 7**

Required

Answer the following questions about the reconciliation.

a. What is the purpose of the reconciliation?
b. Why does the reconciliation result in the same amount for net operating cash flow as does the list of operating cash flows found in the operating activities section under the direct method?

c.   One of the most common adjustments found in the reconciliation is the change in operating working capital accounts, such as accounts receivable and prepaid expenses. Why are changes in dividends payable and short-term non-trade notes to financial institutions not found in the reconciliation?

d.   Are the reconciliation adjustments referred to in part *c* limited to changes in current assets and liabilities? Explain.

e.   Why is a cash flow not a common adjustment to be found in the reconciliation? Can we think of any cash flows that would appear in the reconciliation?

AD&J22-10
Improving the
Statement of Cash
Flows
LO1, 2, 3, 4, 5

Judgment Case Do you feel that the principles governing the statement of cash flows have produced the most useful statement possible? If you were a member of the FASB, would you suggest any changes to the statement of cash flows? Provide your thoughts to the Board on how the statement of cash flows might be improved.

AD&J22-11
Interpreting Interest
Disclosures in the
Statement of Cash
Flows   **LO2, 5**

Rubbermaid Inc., a manufacturer of home products, begins its Year 8 statement of consolidated cash flows with the following line:

| Net earnings..................................... | $142,536,000 |

In a supplement to its statement of cash flows, Rubbermaid reports:

| Interest paid during the year..................... | $33,407,000 |

Required

a.   Interest expense of $37,944,000 was reported in the income statement and no interest was capitalized during the period. Where is the $4,537,000 difference between interest expense and interest paid reported on the statement of cash flows?

b.   Now assume that interest expense of $28,870,000 is reported in the income statement, interest was capitalized during the period, and there was no change in interest payable from the beginning to the end of the year. Where is the $4,537,000 difference between interest expense and interest paid reported on the statement of cash flows?

AD&J22-12
Presenting Payments to
Employees in
Statement of Cash
Flows   **LO3, 5**

Trueblood Case The Trueblood case series, prepared by **Deloitte** professionals, are based on recent accounting technical issues that require research and judgment. The cases are accessed through the Deloitte foundation at:
https://www2.deloitte.com/us/en/pages/about-deloitte/articles/trueblood-case-studies-deloitte-foundation.html
The following case is relevant to the content provided in this chapter: **Case 23-1 Greener Houses Corp.** This case requires an analysis of the cash flow presentation of amounts related to emission allowances recognized as intangible assets.

AD&J22-13
Defining Terms   **LO1**

Codification Skills How are the terms (1) operating activities, (2) investing activities, (3) financing activities, and (4) cash equivalents defined in the Codification?

AD&J22-14
Performing Accounting
Research
LO3, 4, 5

Codification Skills Through research in the Codification, identify the specific citation for each of the following items.

a.   Cash flow classification of available-for-sale debt securities.   FASB ASC ☐ - ☐ - ☐ - ☐

b.   Examples of items classified as outflows from financing activities.

FASB ASC ☐ - ☐ - ☐ - ☐

c.   Describing the change in cash to include cash,   FASB ASC ☐ - ☐ - ☐
cash equivalents, and restricted cash.

d.   Requirement to disclose interest and taxes paid if   FASB ASC ☐ - ☐ - ☐ - ☐
specifically using the indirect method.

AD&J22-15
Performing Accounting
Research   **LO5**

Codification Skills A company is preparing annual financial statements including the statement of cash flows. The controller would like to report trends of cash flow on a per share basis over the last five years. What guidance is available in the Codification regarding such a presentation?

FASB ASC ☐ - ☐ - ☐ - ☐

continued from previous page

b. **Funded Status—Underfunded**

If instead, Taser calculated ending plan assets at fair value of $115,000, Taser would report a *net liability* of $3,550 ($118,550 – $115,000) on its balance sheet.

Underfunded plan: PBO > Plan assets

Determination of Funded Status	
Projected benefit obligation	$118,550
Plan assets at fair value	115,000
Funded status, Dec. 31.	$ (3,550)

c. **Funded Status—Fully-Funded**

If Taser calculated the ending balance of plan assets at fair value of $118,550, no balance would be reported on the balance sheet on December 31 because the difference between the plan assets ($118,550) and the PBO ($118,550) is zero. Similar to unrecognized contingencies, a line item for funded status would appear in the liability section with a reference to the notes to financial statements for more information.

PBO ≈ Plan assets

Determination of Funded Status	
Projected benefit obligation	$118,550
Plan assets at fair value	118,550
Funded status, Dec. 31.	$ 0

FORD

Real World—FUNDED STATUS

Ford Motor Company reported the following information in a recent Form 10-K summarizing its funded status for its defined benefit plans. The U.S. Plans, the Non-U.S. Plans, and the Worldwide OPEB (other postretirement benefit) plans are all in underfunded status for 2023.

Note 17: Retirement Benefits   The year-end status of these plans was as follows (in millions):

	Pension Benefits				Worldwide OPEB	
	U.S. Plans		Non-U.S. Plans			
Change in Benefit Obligation	2022	2023	2022	2023	2022	2023
Benefit obligation at January 1	$44,888	$32,867	$34,432	$21,605	$ 6,040	$ 4,459
Service cost	500	292	416	245	42	21
Interest cost	1,054	1,641	504	965	146	231
Amendments (a)	—	581	—	46	—	32
Separation programs/other	4	(18)	56	255	—	—
Curtailments	—	—	(2)	6	—	—
Settlements (b)	(1,172)	(1,479)	(674)	(21)	—	—
Plan participant contributions	18	16	12	11	1	—
Benefits paid	(2,466)	(2,417)	(1,302)	(1,257)	(363)	(359)
Foreign exchange translation	—	—	(2,877)	960	(92)	26
Actuarial (gain)/loss	(9,959)	1,193	(8,960)	1,189	(1,315)	286
Benefit obligation at December 31	32,867	32,676	21,605	24,004	4,459	4,696
Change in Plan Assets						
Fair value of plan assets at January 1	45,909	32,922	33,085	21,344	—	—
Actual return on plan assets	(9,548)	2,180	(7,516)	1,145	—	—
Company contributions	223	238	722	756	—	—
Plan participant contributions	18	16	12	11	—	—
Benefits paid	(2,466)	(2,417)	(1,302)	(1,257)	—	—
Settlements (b)	(1,172)	(1,479)	(674)	(21)	—	—
Foreign exchange translation	—	—	(2,973)	990	—	—
Other	(42)	(37)	(10)	(10)	—	—
Fair value of plan assets at December 31 . . .	32,922	31,423	21,344	22,958	—	—
Funded status at December 31	$ 55	$ (1,253)	$ (261)	$ (1,046)	$(4,459)	$(4,696)

Review

MBC

REVIEW 23-3 ▶ **LO23-3** **Reconciliation of Plan Assets and Determination of Funded Status**

Example One—Plan Asset Reconciliation

Raspberry Inc. implemented a defined benefit pension plan for its employees. The following data are provided for the year. Calculate the fair value of plan assets on December 31.

Balance	Jan. 1	Activity for the Year	
Projected Benefit Obligation...	$280,000 Cr.	Actual return on plan assets...	$12,000
Plan Assets...	300,000 Dr.	Benefits paid to employees....	30,000
		Employer contributions.......	22,000

Example Two—Funded Status

As of December 31, the projected benefit obligation and plan assets of a noncontributory defined benefit plan sponsored by Randall Inc. follow. Determine the funded status of the pension plan.

More Practice:
BE23-6, BE23-7, BE23-8,
E23-5
Solution on p. 23-62.

Projected Benefit Obligation..........................	$480,000 Cr.
Plan Assets.....................................	466,000 Dr.

LO 23-4 ▶ ## Determine the five components of pension expense

Components of Pension Expense
+ Service cost
+ Interest cost
− Expected return on plan assets
+ Amortization of prior service cost
−/+ Amortization of pension gain/loss

Pension expense (also referred to as **net periodic pension cost** for reporting purposes) is the amount of total pension cost allocated to each reporting period. Periodic pension expense is the sum of the five elements shown in the graphic below (as applicable).

Defined Benefit Pension Fund Information		
$ millions	Pension Exp. (Inc)	Pension Exp. (Inc) Divided by Revenue
Ford Motor.............	$2,510	1.8%
Boeing................	(527)	−0.7%
United Parcel Service....	1,212	1.3%

Service Cost

Service cost is the actuarial present value of additional pension benefits earned by employees as a result of completing additional service in the current year. Service cost increases pension expense and the PBO balance.

Interest Cost

Interest cost is the interest on the PBO for a given period. Interest cost is equal to the PBO balance at the beginning of the year (adjusted for any prior service cost amendment and pension gain or loss dated as of the beginning of the year), multiplied by the discount rate. Interest cost increases pension expense and the PBO balance. The interest rate or discount rate used to determine interest cost should reflect the rate at which the pension benefits could be effectively settled (this is why the discount rate is often referred to as the *settlement rate*). In estimating the discount rate, companies should look to available information about rates implicit in current prices of annuity contracts that could be used to settle the pension obligation.

715-30-35-8 The interest cost component of net periodic pension cost is interest on the projected benefit obligation, which is a discounted amount. Measuring the projected benefit obligation as a present value requires accrual of an interest cost at rates equal to the assumed discount rates.

715-30-35-43 Assumed discount rates shall reflect the rates at which the pension benefits could be effectively settled . . .

Expected Return on Plan Assets

Expected return on plan assets is calculated by multiplying the **expected rate of return** on plan assets by the **market-related value of plan assets** at the beginning of the reporting period, defined as follows.

> **ASC Glossary**   Market-Related Value of Plan Assets—A balance used to calculate the expected return on plan assets. The market-related value of plan assets is either fair value or a calculated value that recognizes changes in fair value in a systematic and rational manner over not more than five years.

The market-related value of plan assets reflects a smoothed average of fair values over a number of years; however, **for simplicity, we use fair value of plan assets as the market-related value of plan assets for pension calculations in this chapter.**

    The expected rate of return on plan assets should reflect long-term expected yields of asset classes in which plan assets are invested. A company investing in more risky assets has the potential for a higher rate of return than a company investing in less risky assets. A positive *expected* return on plan assets reduces the computation of pension expense. When expected and actual returns on plan assets differ, a **gain/loss on plan assets** results. Pension expense is adjusted for expected return on plan assets and the gain/loss on plan assets is deferred as an adjustment to accumulated other comprehensive income as discussed in LO 23-5. However, in certain cases, amortization of pension gains/losses accumulated in OCI can affect pension expense as described later.

Amortization of Prior Service Cost

Recall that prior service cost increases the PBO (and decreases OCI) and results from the granting of additional pension benefits for services provided by employees in *prior years*. Although the entire adjustment is added to projected benefit obligation immediately (assuming increased benefits), the adjustment is amortized to pension expense over time. (This does impact interest cost for the year because interest is based on the PBO balance.)

    Employers who increase pension benefits attributable to prior service are assumed to benefit in future periods from improved employee productivity and morale, reduced turnover, and reduced demand for pay raises. Therefore, the cost of retroactive benefits is subject to delayed recognition and is expensed or matched against the periods of benefit to the company (the average remaining service life of the employees affected by the prior service adjustment). While the accounting guidance suggests companies use the service method to allocate pension expense (illustrated in Appendix 23C), the guidance also indicates the **straight-line method** is acceptable, as long as more rapid amortization results.

> **715-30-35-11**   A plan amendment that retroactively increases benefits (including benefits that are granted to retirees) increases the projected benefit obligation. The cost of the benefit improvement shall be recognized as a charge to other comprehensive income at the date of the amendment. Except as specified in paragraphs 715-30-35-13 through 35-16, that prior service cost shall be amortized as a component of net periodic pension cost by assigning an equal amount to each future period of service of each employee active at the date of the amendment who is expected to receive benefits under the plan . . .

> **715-30-35-13**   To reduce the complexity and detail of the computations required, consistent use of an alternative approach that more rapidly amortizes the cost of retroactive amendments is acceptable. For example, a straight-line amortization of the cost over the average remaining service period of employees expected to receive benefits under the plan is acceptable.

Amortization of Pension Gain/Loss

We introduced two sources of pension gain/loss: actuarial gain/loss on the PBO (LO 23-2) and gain/loss on plan assets (earlier in this section). Unlike typical gains and losses that are recognized in income when they occur, pension gains and losses are recognized in other comprehensive income. The rationale is that recognizing pension gains and losses as part of periodic pension expense in the period in which they occur would add too much volatility to pension expense. Deferring income statement recognition of gains and losses achieves **income smoothing**. Over time, incurred gains may offset incurred losses resulting in a relatively small net unrecognized gain or loss in accumulated other comprehensive income. However, if the balance grows too large, the company must begin amortizing it.

    How does the FASB define whether an accumulated pension gain/loss is too large? If the unrecognized amount exceeds either 10% of the greater of the PBO at the beginning of the year (adjusted for any prior service cost amendment and pension gain or loss dated as of the beginning of the year) or the fair value of plan assets at the beginning of the year, then the gain or loss is considered to be too large. Because balances that are less than 10% of the greater of plan assets or the PBO are not considered large, the 10% limit is called the acceptable **corridor**. Larger balances that fall outside the corridor limit are subject to amortization. Amortization of a net loss increases pension expense and increases other comprehensive income. Amortization of a net gain decreases pension expense and decreases other comprehensive income.

The minimum required amortization to be recognized (see **Exhibit 23-4**) is computed as follows.

$$\frac{\text{Accumulated OCI—Pension Gain/Loss, beginning of year in excess of corridor limit}}{\text{Average remaining service period of employees expected to receive benefits}}$$

EXHIBIT 23-4

Corridor Approach

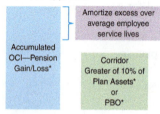

* Beginning of year balance

715-30-35-24 As a minimum, amortization of a net gain or loss included in accumulated other comprehensive income (excluding asset gains and losses not yet reflected in market-related value) shall be included as a component of net pension cost for a year if, as of the beginning of the year, that net gain or loss exceeds 10 percent of the greater of the projected benefit obligation or the market-related value of plan assets. If amortization is required, the minimum amortization shall be that excess divided by the average remaining service period of active employees expected to receive benefits under the plan. The amortization must always reduce the beginning-of-the-year balance. Amortization of a net gain results in a decrease in net periodic pension cost; amortization of a net loss results in an increase in net periodic pension cost. If all or almost all of a plan's participants are inactive, the average remaining life expectancy of the inactive participants shall be used instead of average remaining service.

The FASB allows a company to adopt any systematic method under certain conditions that results in faster recognition than the corridor approach as indicated in the accounting guidance. Based upon this guidance, companies can even elect to recognize the entire gain or loss directly on the income statement—see the excerpt from Ford Motor Company in the Real World segment below.

715-30-35-25 Any systematic method of amortizing gains or losses may be used in lieu of the minimum specified in the preceding paragraph provided that all of the following conditions are met:

a.   The minimum is used in any period in which the minimum amortization is greater (reduces the net balance included in accumulated other comprehensive income by more).

b.   The method is applied consistently.

c.   The method is applied similarly to both gains and losses.

In summary, pension expense is calculated as follows as illustrated below in **Demo 23-4**.

Measurement of Pension Expense

+ Service cost
+ Interest cost
– Expected return on plan assets
+ Amortization of prior service cost
–/+ Amortization of pension gain/loss

Total pension expense*

*Net amount of net periodic pension cost recognized could be income rather than expense. For example, Boeing reported a net periodic benefit for its pension plans of $527 million in 2023. This was a result of expected return on plan assets exceeding other components of pension expense.

FORD **Real World—IMMEDIATE RECOGNITION OF REMEASUREMENT GAINS/LOSSES**

The following excerpt from Ford Motor Company describes the company's move from the corridor approach to immediate income statement recognition of remeasurement gains and losses on plan assets.

Note 1—Presentation On December 31, 2015, we adopted a change in accounting method for certain components of expense related to our defined benefit pension and OPEB plans. Under the new method, we recognize remeasurement gains and losses immediately in net income and use fair value to calculate the expected return on plan assets. Historically, we recognized remeasurement gains and losses as a component of accumulated other comprehensive income/(loss) and amortized them as a component of net periodic benefit cost, subject to a corridor, over the remaining service period of our active employees.

Components of Pension Expense	LO23-4	DEMO 23-4

Demo

MBC

Taser Inc. reports the following related to its defined benefit pension plan.

Account Balances	Jan. 1
Projected Benefit Obligation............	$ 95,000 Cr.
Plan Assets (at fair value)..............	100,000 Dr.
Accumulated OCI—Prior Service Cost....	12,500 Dr.
Accumulated OCI—Pension Gain/Loss ...	25,000 Dr.

Activity for the Year	
Service cost	$12,000
Actual return on plan assets.....	6,000
Actuarial loss on PBO (determined Dec. 31)	4,000
Contribution amount...........	15,000
Benefits paid................	1,000
Prior service cost amortization...	1,250

Other	
Expected rate of return on plan assets.......	7%
Discount (Settlement) rate	9%
Average remaining service period	10 years

Determine the following components of pension expense for the year.
a. Service cost
b. Interest cost
c. Expected return on plan assets
d. Amortization of prior service cost—straight-line method
e. Amortization of pension gain/loss—corridor approach
f. Calculation of total pension expense

Solution

a. **Service Cost**

Component of Pension Expense	
Service cost	$12,000

b. **Interest Cost**
Interest cost is calculated by multiplying the discount rate by the PBO balance at the beginning of the reporting period.

Component of Pension Expense	
Interest cost ($95,000 × 0.09)	$8,550

c. **Expected Return on Plan Assets**
Expected return on plan assets is calculated by multiplying the expected rate of return on plan assets by the fair value of plan assets at the beginning of the reporting period.

Component of Pension Expense	
Expected return on plan assets ($100,000 × 0.07)	$(7,000)

Taser incurred an unexpected loss of $1,000 (expected return on plan assets of $7,000 less actual return on plan assets of $6,000). This is not recognized as part of current period pension expense. Refer to **Demo 23-5** to see how this is recorded.

d. **Amortization of Prior Service Cost**
The prior service cost is amortized over the average remaining service period.

Component of Pension Expense	
Prior service cost amortization ($12,500/10 service years)...	$1,250

e. **Amortization of Pension Gain/Loss—Corridor Approach**
The corridor is calculated as follows.

10% × $100,000* = $10,000	

*Greater of the beginning of year PBO ($95,000) or plan assets ($100,000).

The excess of the beginning balance of Accumulated OCI—Pension Gain/Loss over the corridor of $10,000 is amortized over the average remaining service years of 10.

continued

continued from previous page

$$\frac{\text{(Accumulated OCI—Pension Gain/Loss, January 1 − Corridor)}}{\text{Average remaining service period}} = \frac{(\$25,000 - \$10,000)}{10 \text{ years}} = \frac{\$15,000}{10} = \$1,500$$

Component of Pension Expense	
Amortization of Accumulated OCI—Pension Gain/Loss......	$1,500*

* Amount represents a loss.

f. **Calculation of Total Pension Expense**
The five components of pension expense are totaled below.

Components of Pension Expense	
Service cost	$12,000
Interest cost	8,550
Expected return on plan assets	(7,000)
Amortization of prior service cost..................	1,250
Amortization of net pension loss	1,500
Total pension expense	$16,300

UPS

Real World—PENSION EXPENSE

United Parcel Service (UPS) reported the following information regarding its benefit plans in a recent Form 10-K. Included in its pension expense total of $1,212 are the five components of pension expense described in LO 23-4.

Note 5 Company-Sponsored Employee Benefit Plans Information about net periodic benefit cost for the company-sponsored pension and postretirement defined benefit plans is as follows (in millions).

U.S. Pension Benefits	2023
Net Periodic Benefit Cost:	
Service cost	$1,172
Interest cost	2,508
Expected return on plan assets	(2,967)
Amortization of prior service cost...............................	106
Actuarial (gain) loss	393
Net periodic benefit cost......................................	$1,212

REVIEW 23-4	LO23-4	Components of Pension Expense

Review
MBC

Alexa Company started a noncontributory, defined benefit pension plan on January 1 of last year. The records of Alexa Company indicate the following for the current year.

Account Balances	Jan. 1	Activity for the Year	
Projected Benefit Obligation............	$75,000 Cr.	Service cost	$18,000
Plan Assets.........................	81,000 Dr.	Amortization of prior service cost...	1,000
Accumulated OCI—Pension Gain/Loss ...	12,900 Dr.	Pension benefits paid	(500)
Accumulated OCI—Prior Service Cost....	10,000 Dr.	Actual earnings on plan assets	
		(same as expected return)	4,000
		Employer contribution...........	15,000

More Practice:
BE23-9, BE23-10, BE23-11,
BE23-12, E23-7

Solution on p. 23-63.

Compute net pension expense for the year using the corridor approach to amortize any applicable pension gain/loss over a 10-year average remaining service period. Assume a discount rate of 6%.

Record prior service cost amendment, pension expense, gains and losses, funding, and benefits paid

LO 23-5

In this section, we explain the journal entries to record items for a defined benefit plan including a prior service cost amendment, pension expense, and a deferral of a pension gain or loss. We also present journal entries related to funding the plan and paying benefits. See **Demo 23-5** for entries related to these activities.

> **Pension Plan Recording (as applicable)**
> - Record prior service cost amendment
> - Record pension expense
> - Record deferral of pension gain/loss
> - Record employer contributions
> - Record benefits paid
>
> LO 23-5 Overview

Recording Prior Service Cost Amendment

When a company retroactively grants credit for prior service, the company debits OCI—Prior Service Cost and credits Projected Benefit Obligation to recognize the cost (assuming an increase in benefits). The adjusted beginning of year PBO balance (after the effect of the prior service cost amendment) is then used for any calculations requiring the beginning of year PBO, such as the interest cost calculation. The adjustment for a new prior service cost amendment is illustrated in **Review 23-5**.

```
OCI—Prior Service Cost . . . . .   #
    PBO . . . . . . . . . . . . . . . . . .       #
```

Recording Pension Expense

We summarize the effect on pension expense in a single entry in **Demo 23-5**. We explain each component of that entry as follows.

- Service cost: Debit Pension Expense and credit PBO.
- Interest cost: Debit Pension Expense and credit PBO.
- Expected return on plan assets: For an expected positive return, debit Plan Assets and credit Pension Expense. (In the next section, Plan Assets is adjusted to reflect *actual* return instead of *expected* return on plan assets.)
- Amortization of prior service cost: debit Pension Expense and credit OCI—Prior Service Cost.
- Amortization of pension gain/loss: credit(debit) Pension Expense and debit(credit) OCI—Pension Gain/Loss.

```
Pension Expense  . . . . . . . . . . #
Plan Assets . . . . . . . . . . . . . . . #
    PBO . . . . . . . . . . . . . . . . . .       #
    OCI—PSC . . . . . . . . . . . . . .       #
    OCI—Pension Gain/Loss. . .# or #
```

Recording Deferral of Pension Gains and Losses

We discussed how gain/loss on the PBO and gain/loss on plan assets do *not* affect net income unless they fall outside the acceptable corridor and must be amortized. Instead these gains or losses are deferred in other comprehensive income when incurred. To record an unexpected gain(loss) on plan assets, other comprehensive income and plan assets are both increased(decreased). As a result, the account Plan Assets, is now adjusted to reflect actual return on plan assets. To defer an actuarial gain(loss) on the PBO determined by the actuaries, other comprehensive income is increased(decreased), and the projected benefit obligation is decreased(increased).

```
To defer gain:
Plan Assets . . . . . . . . . . . . . . . #
    OCI—Pension Gain/Loss. . .       #

To defer loss:
OCI—Pension Gain/Loss. . . . . #
    Plan Assets . . . . . . . . . . . . . .       #

To defer gain:
PBO . . . . . . . . . . . . . . . . . . . . #
    OCI—Pension Gain/Loss. . .       #

To defer loss:
OCI—Pension Gain/Loss. . . . . #
    PBO . . . . . . . . . . . . . . . . . .       #
```

Recording Employer Contributions

When a company funds its pension plan, an amount is paid to the trustee who manages the fund investments. The company records a debit to Plan Assets and a credit to Cash. The amount of funding is based upon factors including legal minimum funding requirements, tax consequences, and cash flow capabilities.

```
Plan Assets . . . . . . . . . . . . . . . #
    Cash . . . . . . . . . . . . . . . . . .       #
```

Recording Benefits Paid

A trustee will make payments from the plan assets to eligible retirees based upon the pension benefit formula. The payment of benefits reduces the company's pension obligation and plan assets resulting in a debit to Projected Benefit Obligation and a credit to Plan Assets.

```
PBO . . . . . . . . . . . . . . . . . . . . #
    Plan Assets . . . . . . . . . . . . . .       #
```

DEMO 23-5 ▶ **LO23-5**   **Recording the Impact of Defined Benefit Plan**

Demo

MBC

Using the information from **Demo 23-4** for Taser Inc., provide the following journal entries for the year to record the activity related to its defined benefit plan. Taser Inc. did not incur a *new* amendment for prior service cost during the current year.

a. Record pension expense.
b. Record the deferral of current year pension losses.
c. Record the funding of plan assets.
d. Record the payment of retiree benefits.

Solution

a. **Recording Pension Expense**

Recall Demo 23-4 where we determined the components of pension expense.

Components of Pension Expense	
Service cost	$12,000
Interest cost	8,550
Expected return on plan assets	(7,000)
Amortization of prior service cost	1,250
Amortization of net pension loss	1,500
Total pension expense	$16,300

The journal entry to record pension expense follows.

December 31—To record pension expense

Assets = Liabilities + Equity
+7,000   +20,550   −16,300
PI Asset   PBO   Exp
                    +1,250
                    OCI
                    +1,500
                    OCI

Pension Expense	16,300	
Plan Assets	7,000	
Projected Benefit Obligation ($12,000 + $8,550)		20,550
OCI—Prior Service Cost		1,250
OCI—Pension Gain/Loss		1,500

b. **Recording Deferral of Pension Gains and Losses**

The following entries are required to defer (1) the unexpected loss on plan assets of $1,000 and (2) the actuarial loss on the PBO of $4,000. To defer the unexpected loss on plan assets of $1,000, other comprehensive income (rather than net income) and plan assets are both reduced. As a result, the account Plan Assets, is now adjusted for actual return on plan assets. The $7,000 expected return on plan assets from the pension expense entry (above) less the $1,000 unexpected loss (below), results in a net increase to plan assets of $6,000 which is equal to the actual return on plan assets.

December 31—To defer unexpected loss on plan assets to OCI

Assets = Liabilities + Equity
−1,000   −1,000
PI Asset   OCI

OCI—Pension Gain/Loss	1,000	
Plan Assets ($7,000 − $6,000)		1,000

To defer the actuarial loss on the PBO (determined by the actuaries as of December 31) other comprehensive income is decreased (rather than net income), and the projected benefit obligation is increased.

December 31—To defer actuarial loss on PBO to OCI

Assets = Liabilities + Equity
         +4,000   −4,000
         PBO   OCI

OCI—Pension Gain/Loss	4,000	
Projected Benefit Obligation		4,000

While these current year losses are recorded in OCI, remember that a portion of the *beginning* balance of Accumulated OCI—Pension Gain/Loss was amortized in the pension expense entry above because it exceeded the corridor. Amortization is always based on the beginning balance of Accumulated OCI—Pension Gain/Loss; therefore, adjustments made during the year will not affect amortization.

continued

continued from previous page

c. **Recording Employer Contributions**

Taser Inc. records the following entry for the funding of its pension plan.

December 31—To record funding of pension plan

Plan Assets..	15,000	
Cash..		15,000

Assets = Liabilities + Equity
+15,000
Pl Asset
−15,000
C:o

d. **Recording Benefits Paid**

Taser Inc. records the following entry for the payment of benefits to retirees.

December 31—To record benefits paid to retirees

Projected Benefit Obligation.........................	1,000	
Plan Assets..		1,000

Assets = Liabilities + Equity
−1,000   −1,000
Pl Asset   PBO

The following T-accounts illustrate how pension expense is affected by changes in the PBO, plan assets, and accumulated OCI accounts.

- Service cost and interest cost directly affect pension expense.
- While *expected* return on plan assets of $7,000 impacts pension expense, plan assets is adjusted for *actual* return on plan assets of $6,000 (equal to $7,000 minus $1,000), and the unexpected loss of $1,000 is deferred in accumulated OCI.
- Adjustments to prior service cost are deferred in accumulated OCI and only amortization of PSC affects pension expense.
- While current year losses (on the PBO and on plan assets) are deferred in accumulated OCI, the only impact on pension expense is for amortization of the beginning balance of Accumulated OCI—Pension Gain/Loss using the corridor approach.

Plan Assets

Beg. bal.	100,000		
(a) Expected return	7,000	1,000	(b) Unexpected loss
(c) Plan contrib.	15,000	1,000	(d) Benefits pd.
End. bal.	120,000		

See Demo 23-3A

Pension Expense

(a) Service cost	12,000	7,000	(a) Expected return
(a) Interest cost	8,550		
(a) PSC amortiz.	1,250		
(a) Pension loss amortiz.	1,500		
End. bal.	16,300		

See Demo 23-4

Just as revenue and expense accounts are closed to retained earnings at the end of a reporting period, OCI accounts are closed to accumulated OCI accounts:

Cash

		15,000	(c) Plan contrib.
		15,000	End. bal.

OCI—Prior Service Cost

Close to AOCI	1,250	1,250	(a) Amortiz.
		0	End. bal.

Accum. OCI—PSC

		Beg. bal.	12,500	1,250 Close OCI—PSC
		End. bal.	11,250	

PBO

(b) Benefits paid	1,000	95,000	Beg. bal.
		12,000	(a) Serv. cost
		8,550	(a) Int. cost
		4,000	(b) Act. loss on PBO
		118,550	End. bal.

See Demo 23-2

OCI—Pension Gain/Loss

(b) Act. loss on PBO	4,000	1,500	(a) Amortiz.
(b) Unexpected loss	1,000	3,500	Close to AOCI
End. bal.	0		

Accum. OCI—Pension Gain/Loss

Beg. bal.	25,000	
Close OCI—Pens G/L	3,500	
End. bal.	28,500	

EXPANDING YOUR KNOWLEDGE   **Recording as Pension Asset (Liability)**

Instead of separately recording in journal entries the pension asset and projected benefit obligation as we have demonstrated, some companies record amounts in a net account: Pension Asset (Liability). In either case, the *net amount* of pension asset and projected benefit obligation (PBO) is always recognized on the balance sheet.

REVIEW 23-5 ▶ **LO23-5**   **Recording the Impact of a Defined Benefit Plan**

Review

MBC

The following data relate to a pension plan for BMXX Inc.

Account Balances	Jan. 1	Activity for the Year	
Projected Benefit Obligation............	$300,000 Cr.	Service cost	$33,000
Plan Assets........................	350,000 Dr.	Contributions to pension fund....	40,000
Accumulated OCI—Pension Gain/Loss ...	5,000 Dr.	Benefits paid to retirees	22,000
		Expected return on plan assets...	15,000
		Actual return on plan assets.....	16,000

Other	
Prior service cost amendment on January 1	$30,000
(relates to an employee group with an average remaining service period of 10 years; use straight-line method for amortization)	

More Practice:
BE23-13, BE23-15, E23-15
Solution on p. 23-63.

Provide the entries to record pension activity for the year assuming a discount rate of 5%. Instead of using the corridor approach to amortize Accumulated OCI—Pension Gain/Loss, we amortize the account using the straight-line method over 10 years (an alternative, systematic approach resulting in a higher amortization amount).

LO 23-6 ▶ # Describe the reporting of pensions in financial statements

LO 23-6 Overview

Pension Reporting
- Income statement
- Statement of comprehensive income
- Stockholders' equity statement
- Balance sheet
- Disclosure requirements

The entries in the prior section result in account balances that are reported in a company's financial reports and note disclosures. We summarize how pensions are reported in the income statement, statement of comprehensive income, statement of stockholders' equity, and the balance sheet. We then continue with the Taser Inc. example to illustrate how accounts are shown in its financial statements in **Demo 23-6**.

Income Statement

Components of pension expense are recognized in the income statement as follows: service cost is included with other employee compensation costs within operations (if the subtotal is presented) while the remaining components of pension expense are included outside of operating income.

Sales
Operating expenses (includes service costs)
Operating income
Other revenue (expenses), net
Other components of net periodic pension cost
Net income

715-20-45-3A   An employer shall report in the income statement:

a. The service cost component of net periodic pension cost and net periodic postretirement benefit cost in the same line item or items as other compensation costs arising from services rendered by the pertinent employees during the period (except for the amount being capitalized, if appropriate, in connection with the production or construction of an asset such as inventory or property, plant, and equipment).

b. The other components. . . separately from the service cost component and outside a subtotal of income from operations, if one is presented. If a separate line item or items are used to present the other components, that line item or items shall be described appropriately.

Statement of Comprehensive Income and Statement of Stockholders' Equity

Other comprehensive income is affected by the following pension related items (net of tax) within a statement of comprehensive income.

Net income
Other comprehensive income
(Deferral of pension loss)
Amortization of pension loss
Deferral of pension gain
(Amortization of pension gain)
(Prior service cost adjustment for additional benefits)
Amortization of prior service cost
Comprehensive income

The other comprehensive income (OCI) accounts are collected in accumulated OCI accounts. Both the activity during the period and the balances in the accumulated OCI accounts are shown on the statement of stockholders' equity. The ending balances of the accumulated OCI accounts are carried over to the balance sheet.

Balance Sheet

The net pension asset or net pension liability is recognized on the balance sheet. A net pension asset is presented as a noncurrent asset labeled **Prepaid pension cost, net**. A net pension liability is presented as current or noncurrent depending on whether the benefit obligation is due within the next 12 months (or a combination of both). A net pension liability is labeled **Accrued pension cost, net**. If a company has more than one pension plan, plans with a net asset balance may be combined together while plans with a net liability balance may be combined together. Companies may *not* combine a plan with a net asset balance with a plan with a net liability balance on the balance sheet.

Net pension asset:
  Plan assets > PBO

Net pension liability:
  PBO > Plan assets

Note disclosure:
  PBO ≈ Plan assets

715-30-25-2   The employer shall aggregate the statuses of all overfunded plans and recognize that amount as an asset in its statement of financial position. It also shall aggregate the statuses of all underfunded plans and recognize that amount as a liability in its statement of financial position.

715-20-45-3   An employer that presents a classified statement of financial position shall classify the liability for an underfunded plan as a current liability, a noncurrent liability, or a combination of both. The current portion (determined on a plan-by-plan basis) is the amount by which the actuarial present value of benefits included in the benefit obligation payable in the next 12 months, or operating cycle if longer, exceeds the fair value of plan assets. The asset for an overfunded plan shall be classified as a noncurrent asset in a classified statement of financial position. The amount classified as a current liability is limited to the amount of the plan's unfunded status recognized in the employer's statement of financial position.

The ending balance in accumulated OCI accounts would be included on the balance sheet. Chapter 22 described the effects of a defined benefit plan on the statement of cash flows.

Pension Plan Reporting   **LO23-6**   **DEMO 23-6**

Demo

MBC

Considering the entries for Taser Inc. from **Demo 23-5**, present the effect on the following financial statements.

a. Income statement   b. Statement of comprehensive income   c. Balance sheet at year-end

Solution

a. **Income Statement**   The following income statement excerpt illustrates the inclusion of pension expense ($16,300 shown in two parts as $12,000 and $4,300) related to Taser's defined benefit plan.

Income Statement		
Revenue	$	#
Operating expenses (includes $12,000 of service costs). . .		#
Operating income.		#
Other components of net periodic pension cost.	4,300	
Net income	$	#

continued

continued from previous page

b. **Statement of Comprehensive Income**   The following abbreviated statement of comprehensive income illustrates the presentation of other comprehensive income account. This example ignores income taxes; but other comprehensive income must be shown net of tax.

Statement of Comprehensive Income	
Net income	$ #
Other comprehensive income (loss)	
Loss due to actuarial change in PBO	(4,000)
Unexpected loss on plan assets	(1,000)
Amortization of prior service cost	1,250
Amortization of pension loss.......................	1,500
Comprehensive income	$ #

c. **Balance Sheet**   The following balance sheet excerpt illustrates the inclusion of pension related accounts in the noncurrent asset section and the stockholders' equity section.

Balance Sheet	Year-End
Assets	
Noncurrent assets	
Prepaid pension cost, net ($120,000 – $118,550)	$ 1,450
Liabilities	
Stockholders' equity	
Retained earnings*	
Accumulated other comprehensive income	
Net pension loss	(28,500)
Prior service cost................................	(11,250)

*Retained earnings would include net income for the period which reflects pension expense.

Disclosure Requirements

Disclosure requirements for defined benefit pension plans are extensive so as to provide useful information to investors and creditors who are trying to assess the company's obligation to fulfill pension requirements. Due to the volatility of the liability and the nature of the assumptions needed to estimate the liability, a number of items are reported in note disclosures. Disclosure requirements (outlined in ASC 715-20-50-1) include the following.

- Reconciliation of beginning and ending balances of the PBO.
- Reconciliation of beginning and ending balances of the fair value of plan assets.
- Funded status of the plans and the amounts recognized on the balance sheet.
- Information on how investment allocation decisions are made.
- Fair value of each class of plan assets.
- Description of rate assumptions used.
- Accumulated benefit obligation.
- Benefits expected to be paid in each of the next five years, and in the aggregate for the next five years.
- Estimate of contributions expected to be paid to the plan during the next year.
- Amount (and components) of net benefit cost recognized.
- Pension gain/loss and net prior service cost or credit recognized in OCI.
- Amounts in accumulated OCI.
- On a weighted-average basis, assumptions used in accounting for the plans.
- Explanation of significant gains and losses related to changes in defined benefit obligation for the period; and any other significant changes not otherwise apparent.

Nonpublic companies are not required to provide a reconciliation of the beginning and ending balance of the PBO and fair value of plan assets.

Reporting a Defined Benefit Pension Plan

The following data relate to a pension plan for Vilas Inc.

Review

MBC

Account Balances	Year-End	Activity for the Year	
Projected Benefit Obligation............	$310,000 Cr.	Pension expense, including service cost of $50,000................	$75,000
Plan Assets.........................	350,000 Dr.	Unexpected gain on plan assets	8,500
Accumulated OCI—Prior Service Cost. ...	40,000 Dr.	Amortization of prior service costs ...	2,500
Accumulated OCI—Pension Gain/Loss ...	12,000 Dr.		

Use the information to present the effect on the following financial statements.

a. Income statement *b.* Statement of comprehensive income *c.* Balance sheet at year-end

More Practice:
BE23-18, BE23-19
Solution on p. 23-63.

Use a pension worksheet to record pension journal entries

LO 23-7

A pension worksheet is a tool used to organize the effects on pension accounts and for calculating ending balances in pension accounts—see **Demo 23-7**. The worksheet illustrates the changes in plan assets, projected benefit obligation, pension expense, and accumulated other comprehensive income accounts examined in this chapter. The worksheet also provides the funded status both at the beginning and end of the period. The information provided in the worksheet can be used to record end of period pension entries.

In completing the worksheet, first enter beginning balances. Next, enter both sides of the journal entries for the prior service cost amendment, service cost, interest cost, expected return on plan assets, unexpected gain or loss on plan assets, gain or loss on the PBO (provided by actuaries), prior service cost amortization, net pension gain or loss amortization, fund contributions, and benefit payments. Fill in the *Net Pension Asset/Liability* column by subtracting the projected benefit obligation from plan assets. Total all columns (except for the cash column) to arrive at ending balances.

> **Pension Worksheet**
> - Organizational tool
> - Presentation of funded status
> - Source for recording end of period pension journal entries
>
> LO 23-7 Overview

Preparation of a Pension Worksheet

LO23-7 ◄ DEMO 23-7

Assume the following information for Taser Inc. used in previous demonstrations.

Demo

MBC

Account Balance Jan. 1		Activity for the Year	
Projected Benefit Obligation............	$ 95,000 Cr.	Service cost	$12,000
Plan Assets.........................	100,000 Dr.	Actual return on plan assets........	6,000
Accumulated OCI—Prior Service Cost. ...	12,500 Dr.	Actuarial loss on PBO (determined December 31).............	4,000
Accumulated OCI—Pension Gain/Loss ...	25,000 Dr.	Contribution to pension fund.......	15,000
		Benefit payments	1,000
		Prior service cost amortization......	1,250

Other	
Expected rate of return on plan assets. ..	7%
Discount rate	9%
Average remaining service period	10 years

Required
Record the pension activity directly into a pension worksheet.

continued

continued from previous page

Solution

	Reported Net in Financial Statements		Reported on Balance Sheet				Reported in Comprehensive Income		
			Net Pension Asset/	Accumulated OCI			OCI		
	Plan Assets	PBO	Liability	Prior Service Cost	Pension Gain/Loss	Cash Outflow	Pension Expense	Prior Service Cost	Pension Gain/Loss
1. Balance, Jan. 1	$100,000	$ (95,000)	$ 5,000	$12,500	$25,000				
2. Service cost		(12,000)	(12,000)				$12,000		
Interest cost		(8,550)	(8,550)				8,550		
3. Expected return on plan assets . .	7,000		7,000				(7,000)		
4. Unexpected loss on plan assets . .	(1,000)		(1,000)		1,000				$1,000
5. Actuarial loss on PBO		(4,000)	(4,000)		4,000				4,000
6. Prior service cost amortization . . .				(1,250)			1,250	$(1,250)	
7. Net pension loss amortization . . .					(1,500)		1,500		(1,500)
8. Contributions to fund	15,000		15,000			$(15,000)			
9. Retiree benefits paid	(1,000)	1,000							
10. Balance, Dec. 31	$120,000	$(118,550)	$1,450	$11,250	$28,500		$16,300	$(1,250)	$3,500

Steps to Complete Pension Worksheet

1. Enter beginning balances for Plan Assets, PBO, Net Pension Asset/Liability, AOCI—Prior Service Cost, and AOCI—Pension Gain/Loss.

2. Enter service cost, $12,000 (given) and interest cost, $8,550 (0.09 × $95,000) as a credit to Projected Benefit Obligation and a debit to Pension Expense.

3. Enter expected return on plan assets, $7,000 (0.07 × $100,000) as debit to Plan Assets and a credit to Pension Expense.

4. Enter unexpected loss on return, $1,000 ($6,000 – $7,000) as a debit to Pension Gain/Loss in both the OCI column and the Accumulated OCI column and a credit to Plan Assets. This loss would be shown in OCI in the statement of comprehensive income. The OCI for the year would be closed out to AOCI, and the ending balance of AOCI would be shown on the balance sheet. While not illustrated in this worksheet, the amount of pension expense would be included in the end of year retained earnings balance on the balance sheet through the process of closing net income to retained earnings at year-end.

5. Enter actuarial loss on the PBO, $4,000 as a debit to Pension Gain/Loss in both the OCI column and the Accumulated OCI column and a credit to Projected Benefit Obligation.

6. Enter prior service cost amortization, $1,250 as a debit to Pension Expense and a credit to Prior Service Cost in both the OCI column and the Accumulated OCI column.

7. Enter amortization of pension loss, $1,500, as a debit to Pension Expense and a credit to Pension Gain/Loss in both the OCI column and the Accumulated OCI column. (Amortization equals beginning of year AOCI—Pension Gain/Loss of $25,000 less the corridor of $10,000, divided by service years of 10. Corridor is 10% of the greater of beginning of year PBO or Plan Assets [$100,000 × 10%].)

8. Enter contributions of $15,000 as a debit to Plan Assets and a credit to Cash.

9. Enter benefits of $1,000 as a debit to Projected Benefit Obligation and a credit to Plan Assets.

10. Total all columns (except the cash column) to arrive at ending balances. Funded status (net pension asset) is $1,450, which is pension assets of $120,000 less the PBO of $118,550.

REVIEW 23-7   **LO23-7**   **Record Pension Entries Using a Pension Worksheet**

Review

MBC

Fox Company has a noncontributory, defined benefit pension plan. The following information pertains to the pension plan.

Account Balances	Jan. 1	Activity for the Year	
Projected Benefit Obligation (before amendment)	$223,000 Cr.	Service cost	$80,000
Plan Assets	200,000 Dr.	Pension benefits paid	30,000
Accumulated OCI—Prior Service Cost		Contributions to pension fund	70,000
(before amendment)	0 Dr.	Actual return on plan assets	10,000
Accumulated OCI—Pension Gain/Loss . . .	30,000 Dr.	Loss on PBO due to changes in	
		actuarial assumptions*	8,000

*Determined December 31

continued

continued from previous page

Other

Prior service benefits granted through plan amendment on Jan. 1 (present value)	$15,000
Average remaining service period	10 years
Discount rate	8%
Expected rate of return on plan assets.	7%

Required

a. Record amounts above directly into a pension worksheet. Assume that the company follows the corridor approach for amortization.
b. Record journal entries using the pension worksheet.

More Practice:
BE23-20, E23-18, E23-20, E23-22
Solution on p. 23-64.

EXPANDING YOUR KNOWLEDGE   **Financial Statements Required for the Pension Plan Entity**

The pension plan fund is a separate legal entity, requiring the reporting of a separate set of financial statements. Financial statements required under GAAP for *defined benefit plans* are as follows:

- **Statement of net assets available for benefits:** Shows the net assets available for pension benefits at period end.
- **Statement of changes in net assets available for benefits:** Shows the changes in net assets for the period (for example, changes due to investment income, employer contributions, benefits paid, or administrative expenses).
- **Statement of accumulated plan benefits:** Reports the actuarial present value of the accumulated plan benefits at period beginning or end.
- **Statement of changes in accumulated plan benefits:** Reports the changes in accumulated plan benefits for the period (for example, changes due to plan amendments, actuarial assumptions, benefits accumulated, or benefits paid.)

ASC Glossary   **Accumulated plan benefits:** Future benefit payments that are attributable under the provisions of a pension plan to employees' service rendered to the benefit information date.

Because *defined contribution plans* do not owe a specified benefit, only the first two statements listed above are required under GAAP. The content of the statements for defined benefit and defined contribution plans are included in the CPA exam blueprints in the BAR section.

Management Judgment

Nearly every aspect of accounting for defined benefit plans requires judgment. The assumptions used directly impact the derived pension amounts. In the Taser Inc. example, let's consider how just three changes in assumptions would change the accounting results.

1. A change in the service cost estimate from $12,000 to $18,000 would increase pension expense and the PBO. Service cost is not an objective value as it is based on many assumptions such as the assumption of the final salary of an employee (before retirement).

2. The discount rate could change from 9% to 10%. This may increase or decrease pension expense and the PBO. For example, a higher rate is applied to the PBO which will be lower because the present value of the pension obligations will be discounted at a lower rate.

3. The expected rate of return could change from 7% to 6.5%. This would increase pension expense without affecting the PBO.

Changes in assumptions not only impact the amounts recognized on financial statements (pension expense and net pension asset/liability), but changes in assumptions impact the amount of funding contributions to the pension fund required by the company.

<table>
<tr><td>APPENDIX 23A
LO 23-8</td><td># Explain postretirement benefit plans and differences from pensions plans</td></tr>
</table>

LO 23-8 Overview

> **Employer Accounting for Postretirement Benefit Plans**
> - Determine expected postretirement benefit obligation
>   - Assign equally over attribution period
> - Recognize accumulated postretirement benefit obligation

Postretirement benefit plans other than pensions provide benefits to retirees in exchange for service at a company. These benefits may include health-care coverage (medical and dental), life insurance, tuition assistance, legal services, and housing subsidies. Benefits are often extended to the employee and the employee's spouse and dependents. For employers, health-care benefits are generally the most significant benefit.

An employee is fully eligible for postretirement benefits when the employee renders the service necessary to receive expected benefits. Full eligibility is attained by fulfilling age and service requirements, depending on the plan. For example, an employee may earn certain postretirement healthcare coverage if the employee provides at least 15 years of service with the company and reaches the age of 60 years old.

The company determines the EPBO (**expected postretirement benefit obligation**) or the present value of the expected postretirement benefits to be paid to retirees. An APBO (**accumulated postretirement benefit obligation**) is recognized as the present value of the expected benefits attributed to the employee's services rendered to date and expense is recognized through an attribution process. **Attribution** is the process of assigning the postretirement benefit costs to employee service periods. The attribution period typically extends from the employee's hire date to the full eligibility date (when the employee has met the requirements to receive the postretirement benefit). The employee may continue to provide service after the point of full eligibility, which does not impact (increase) postretirement benefits. The obligation is generally assigned equally to each year of service during the attribution period as illustrated in **Demo 23-8**.

ASC Glossary   Expected Postretirement Benefit Obligation—The actuarial present value as of a particular date of the postretirement benefits expected to be paid by the employer's plan to or for each employee, the employee's beneficiaries, and any covered dependents pursuant to the terms of the plan.

ASC Glossary   Accumulated Postretirement Benefit Obligation—The actuarial present value as of a particular date of all future benefits attributed to an employee's service rendered to that date assuming the plan continues in effect and that all assumptions about future events are fulfilled. The accumulated postretirement benefit obligation generally reflects a ratable allocation of expected future benefits to employee service already rendered in the attribution period.

ASC Glossary   Attribution period—The period of an employee's service to which the expected postretirement benefit obligation for that employee is assigned. The beginning of the attribution period is the employee's date of hire unless the plan's benefit formula grants credit only for service from a later date, in which case the beginning of the attribution period is generally the beginning of that credited service period. The end of the attribution period is the full eligibility date. Within the attribution period, an equal amount of the expected postretirement benefit obligation is attributed to each year of service unless the plan's benefit formula attributes a disproportionate share of the expected postretirement benefit obligation to employees' early years of service. In that case, benefits are attributed in accordance with the plan's benefit formula.

Key differences between pension plans and postretirement benefit plans that affect financial statement reporting are described as follows.

Comparison of Pension Plans and Postretirement Benefit Plans

	Pension Plans (LO 23-1 through LO 23-7)	Postretirement Benefit Plans (LO 23-8 and LO 23-9)
Determination of retiree benefit amount and employer's obligation	Benefit is calculated based upon a pension benefit formula.	The benefit is undefined, hard to estimate, based upon many factors, and varies by individual. As a result, prediction of expense is more difficult than under pension plans.
Typical vesting period	Total pension obligation typically changes (increases) for each year of service driven by the pension benefit formula. Gradually earn benefits ⊢⊢⊢⊢⊢⊢⊢⊢⊢⊢⊢⊢→ Years of service	Benefits are typically 100% earned when the employee meets the criteria. Therefore, the EPBO is generally assigned through attribution where the employee earns an equal amount of benefit for each year of service from the date of hire to the full eligibility date. Point of 100% eligibility ⊢⊢⊢⊢⊢⊢⊢⊢↓⊢⊢⊢⊢⊢⊢⊢⊢ Years of service
Measurement of Service Cost	Actuarial present value of additional pension benefits earned by employees based upon employee service in the current year.	EPBO equally assigned (through the attribution process) to each year of service from date of hire until date of 100% eligibility.

Disclosure

In addition to the disclosures required for pension plans, disclosures for postretirement benefit plans include the assumed cost trend rate(s) and assumed pattern of changes used to measure the expected cost of benefits covered by the plan (gross eligible charges). For health plans, accounting guidance requires the following:

715-20-50-1   *l.* The assumed health care cost trend rate(s) for the next year used to measure the expected cost of benefits covered by the plan (gross eligible charges), and a general description of the direction and pattern of change in the assumed trend rates thereafter, together with the ultimate trend rate(s) and when that rate is expected to be achieved.

EXPANDING YOUR KNOWLEDGE   Drivers of Postretirement Health-Care Plan Payments

Net incurred claims cost by age are the employer's share of the cost of providing postretirement health care for one year at each age plan participants are expected to receive benefits. The cost equals future gross eligible charges reduced by expected Medicare reimbursement, expected employee contributions (cost sharing), and deductibles. The net incurred claims cost amounts by age are the cash flow inputs into the actuarial present-value models. These cash estimates are affected by the following:

- Past and present claims data for the plan, or the experience of other employers.
- Health care trend rates or assumptions about annual rate of change of health-care costs for the benefits provided. These assumptions include health-care inflation, changes in utilization, technological advances, and health-care status of participants.
- Plan demographics or characteristics of a plan population, including geographical distribution, age, gender, and marital status.

Determining Obligations for Postretirement Benefit Plan   **LO23-8** ◄   **DEMO 23-8**

Demo

MBC

Rayovak Corp. sponsors a postretirement plan that provides postretirement health care coverage to employees who serve 15 years and reach the age of 60. On January 1 of Year 6, a 45-year-old employee, Michael has worked for the company for 5 years and is expected to retire at age 67 in Year 28. The postretirement plan provides benefits for 5 years and the benefit is estimated to be $5,000 per year.

Required
a. Determine the attribution period.
b. Calculate the expected postretirement benefit obligation (EPBO) on January 1 of Year 6 assuming the discount rate is 10%.
c. Calculate the accumulated postretirement benefit obligation (APBO) on January 1 of Year 6.
d. Compute service cost for one year.

continued

continued from previous page

Solution

a. Attribution Period

The attribution period of 20 years begins at date of hire (January 1 of Year 1) and ends at the full eligibility date of January 1 of Year 21 (the date Michael reaches the age of 60). On January 1 of Year 21, Michael has met both requirements of service years and age.

b. Expected Postretirement Benefit Obligation (EPBO)

To calculate the EPBO, we first compute the present value (at retirement date) of a 5-year, postretirement benefit cash flow stream (annuity), assuming a discount rate of 10%.

Present Value of Postretirement Benefit Cash Flow Stream at Retirement Date

	RATE	NPER	PMT	PV	Excel Formula
Given	10%	5	5,000	?	=PV(0.1,5,5000)
Solution				$18,954	

We then discount the cash flow stream to January 1 of Year 6 (the current date).

Present Value of Postretirement Benefit Cash Flow Stream on January 1 of Year 6

	RATE	NPER	PV	FV	Excel Formula
Given	10%	22	?	18,954	=PV(0.1,22,0,18954)
Solution			$2,328		

The expected postretirement benefit obligation for Michael is $2,328 on January 1 of Year 6, discounted back from Michael's expected retirement date of Year 28.

c. Accumulated Postretirement Benefit Obligation (APBO)

The APBO on January 1 of Year 6, is calculated as follows.

EPBO × (Years of service/Years in full attribution period)
$2,328 × 5/20 = $582

The APBO is the portion of the EPBO attributed to service rendered. On the full eligibility date of January 1 of Year 21, the APBO and the EPBO will be equal.

d. Service Cost

EPBO ÷ Years in Attribution Period
$2,328 ÷ 20 = $116

The service cost for the year is equal to the EPBO attributed to one year of service during the attribution period of 20 years.

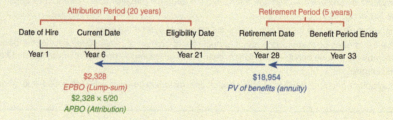

REVIEW 23-8 ▶ **LO23-8**   **Determining Obligations for Postretirement Benefit Plan**

Review

MBC

A postretirement plan promises 100% health care coverage for all employees who retire after age 62. Leah, employed on January 1 of Year 1, is expected to render a total of 14 years of service before reaching age 62. Expected benefits are $7,500 per year for an estimated 10 years commencing at an estimated retirement age of 67 years.

a. Calculate the attribution period.

b. Calculate the expected postretirement benefit obligation (EPBO) on January 1 of Year 5, using an interest rate of 6%.

More Practice:
AppBE23-1, AppBE23-2,
AppBE23-7, AppE23-4

Solution on p. 23-65.

c. Calculate the accumulated postretirement benefit obligation (APBO) on January 1 of Year 5, using an interest rate of 6%.

Record postretirement benefit expense, gains and losses, funding, and benefits paid

APPENDIX 23B
LO 23-9

The accounting for postretirement benefit plans is similar to the accounting for pension plans. The APBO is treated in a similar way for accounting purposes as the PBO. **Postretirement benefit expense**, or **net periodic postretirement benefit cost**, includes the same components as pension expense. For example, service cost is still recognized as expense for the period as under a pension plan even though the underlying calculations to derive service cost differ as illustrated in Appendix 23A. The amortization period, however, differs under a postretirement plan. Instead of amortizing over the remaining service years, amounts will be amortized over the remaining service years up to the point of full eligibility. (Recall from Appendix 23A that an employee may continue employment after the date of full eligibility.) **Demo 23-9** illustrates the similarities in the accounting treatment of postretirement benefits and pension plans.

> **Postretirement Benefit Plan Recording (as applicable)**
> - Record prior service cost amendment
> - Record postretirement benefit expense
> - Record deferral of benefit gain/loss
> - Record employer contributions
> - Record benefit payments
>
> *LO 23-9 Overview*

Recording Entries for Postretirement Benefit Plan   **LO23-9**   **DEMO 23-9**

Assume that MTV Inc. has a health-care benefit plan for retirees and the following information is available regarding the plan.

- Plan Assets, January 1: $200,000 Dr.
- Accumulated OCI—Prior Service Cost, January 1: $60,000 Dr.
- Accumulated OCI—Benefit Gain/Loss, January 1: $0
- APBO, January 1: $288,000 Cr.
- Expected 5% return on plan assets: $10,000
- Actual return on plan assets: $9,500
- Service cost: $40,000
- Contribution to fund: $75,000
- Benefit payments: $45,000
- Increase in estimated health care costs results in a $50,000 increase in the APBO on December 31
- Average remaining service years to full eligibility for active plan participants: 10 years
- Discount rate: 9%

Required

a. Compute postretirement benefit expense for the year.
b. Compute accumulated postretirement benefit obligation as of December 31.
c. Record postretirement benefit expense.
d. Record deferral of gain or loss on plan assets and on the APBO.
e. Record the funding of plan assets.
f. Record the benefits paid.
g. Prepare a postretirement benefit worksheet for the year.

Solution

a. **Measuring Postretirement Benefit Expense**

Postretirement benefit expense is measured as follows, using the same guidance as determined under pension plans. No amortization is recorded on the Accumulated OCI—Benefit Gain/Loss because there is a zero balance on January 1.

Measurement of Postretirement Benefit Expense	
Service cost	$40,000
Interest cost ($288,000 × 9%)	25,920
Expected return on plan assets	(10,000)
Amortization of prior service cost	6,000
Total postretirement benefit expense	$61,920

continued

continued from previous page

b. **Reconciliation of Accumulated Postretirement Benefit Obligation**

Accumulated postretirement benefit obligation for MTV Inc. is computed as follows, using the same guidance in determining the PBO under pension plans.

Measurement of APBO	
APBO, Jan. 1	$288,000
Service cost	40,000
Interest cost	25,920
Prior service cost adjustment	0
Loss on APBO	50,000
Payment of benefits	(45,000)
APBO, Dec. 31	$358,920

c. **Recording Postretirement Benefit Expense**

The journal entry to record postretirement benefit expense will include the following.

- A debit to Postretirement Benefit Expense for total postretirement benefit expense.
- A debit to Plan Assets for the expected return on plan assets.
- A credit to APBO for service cost plus interest cost.
- A credit to OCI—Prior Service Cost for amortization of prior service cost.
- A credit to OCI—Benefit Gain/Loss for amortization of gain/loss (not applicable in this example).

December 31—To record postretirement benefit expense

Postretirement Benefit Expense.	61,920	
Plan Assets.	10,000	
Accumulated Postretirement Benefit Obligation . . . . . . :.		65,920
OCI—Prior Service Cost		6,000

Assets = Liabilities + Equity
+10,000   +65,920   −61,920*
PI Asset   APBO   Exp
                    +6,000
                    OCI

Plan Assets		Postret Benefit Exp
Bal. 200,000		61,920
10,000		

APBO		OCI—PSC
	288,000 Bal.	6,000
	65,920	

d. **Recording Deferral of Benefit Gain/Loss**

The following entries are required to defer (1) the unexpected loss on plan assets of $500 and (2) the actuarial loss on the APBO of $50,000.

December 31—To defer unexpected loss on plan assets

OCI—Benefit Gain/Loss	500	
Plan Assets ($10,000 − $9,500)		500

Assets = Liabilities + Equity
−500   −500
PI Asset   OCI

Plan Assets		OCI—Benefit G/L
Bal. 200,000	500	500
10,000		

December 31—To defer actuarial loss on APBO

OCI—Benefit Gain/Loss	50,000	
Accumulated Postretirement Benefit Obligation		50,000

Assets = Liabilities + Equity
        +50,000   −50,000
        APBO   OCI

APBO		OCI—Benefit G/L
	288,000 Bal.	500
	65,920	50,000
	50,000	

e. **Recording Funding of Plan Assets**

At the time that MTV Inc. funds its postretirement benefit plan by making a payment to increase plan assets, MTV Inc. records the following entry.

December 31—To record funding of postretirement benefit plan

Plan Assets.	75,000	
Cash		75,000

Assets = Liabilities + Equity
+75,000
PI Asset
−75,000
C:o

Cash		Plan Assets	
	75,000	Bal. 200,000	500
		10,000	
		75,000	

The amount of funding is based upon factors including legal minimum funding requirements, tax consequences, and cash flow capabilities. Amounts are paid to the trustee who manages the fund investments.

f. **Recording Benefits Paid**

The trustee, on behalf of MTV Inc., will make payments to eligible retirees based upon the benefit payout ratio. As payments are made, both plan assets and the APBO decrease.

December 31—To record benefits paid to retirees

Accumulated Postretirement Benefit Obligation	45,000	
Plan Assets.		45,000

Assets = Liabilities + Equity
−45,000   −45,000
PI Asset   APBO

Plan Assets		APBO	
Bal. 200,000	500	45,000	288,000 Bal.
10,000	45,000		65,920
75,000			50,000
239,500			358,920

continued

continued from previous page

g. Postretirement Benefit Worksheet

| | Reported Net in Financial Statements | | Reported on the Balance Sheet | | | | Reported in Comprehensive Income | | |
	Plan Assets	APBO	Net Postretirement Asset/Liability	Accumulated OCI Prior Service Cost	Accumulated OCI Benefit Gain/Loss	Cash Outflow	Postretirement Benefit Expense	OCI Prior Service Cost	OCI Benefit Gain/Loss
Balance, Jan. 1	$200,000	$(288,000)	$ (88,000)	$60,000					
Service cost		(40,000)	(40,000)				$40,000		
Interest cost		(25,920)	(25,920)				25,920		
Expected return on plan assets	10,000		10,000				(10,000)		
Unexpected loss on assets	(500)		(500)		$ 500				$ 500
Loss on APBO		(50,000)	(50,000)		50,000				50,000
Prior service cost amortization				(6,000)			6,000	$(6,000)	
Contributions to fund	75,000		75,000			$(75,000)			
Retiree benefits paid	(45,000)	45,000							
Balance, Dec. 31	$239,500	$(358,920)	$(119,420)	$54,000	$50,500		$61,920	$(6,000)	$50,500

BOEING
Real World—POSTRETIREMENT BENEFIT EXPENSE

The Boeing Company, one of the world's major aerospace firms, sponsors defined benefit pension plans. However, nonunion and the majority of union employees that had participated in defined benefit pension plans transitioned to a company-funded defined contribution retirement savings plan within the past 5 years. Components of net periodic benefit cost for defined benefit and other postretirement benefits are summarized below. Other postretirement benefits consist primarily of health care coverage for eligible retirees and qualifying dependents, and to a lesser extent, life insurance to certain groups of retirees.

Note 16—Postretirement Plans—The components of net periodic benefit (income)/cost were as follows:

Years ended December 31, 2023 (in millions)	Pension	Other Postretirement Benefits
Service cost	$ 2	$ 49
Interest cost	2,820	148
Expected return on plan assets	(3,441)	(9)
Amortization of prior service credits	(81)	(22)
Recognized net actuarial loss/(gain)	173	(175)
Settlement/curtailment (gain)/loss	—	—
Net periodic benefit (income)/cost	$ (527)	$ (9)

Recording Entries for Postretirement Benefit Plan   LO23-9   REVIEW 23-9

Levii Corp. sponsors a postretirement benefit plan for health care. The following information relates to this plan.

Review MBC

Activity for the Year		Account Balances	January 1
Service cost	$320,000	Plan Assets	$125,000 Dr.
Contributions to the plan	150,000	APBO	250,000 Cr.
Benefits paid to retirees	50,000	Accumulated OCI—Prior Service Cost	60,000 Dr.
Amortization of prior service cost	10,000		
Interest cost	15,000		

Other

Expected (and actual) rate of return on plan assets . . . 6%

Record entries for postretirement benefit expense, benefit payments, and funding for the year.

More Practice:
AppBE23-4, AppBE23-5, AppBE23-6, AppE23-1, AppE23-2

Solution on p. 23-65.

APPENDIX 23C
LO 23-10 › Allocate prior service cost using the service method

LO 23-10 Overview

Allocation of Prior Service Cost
- Service method
  - Allocation over employee service years
- Straight-line method
  - Allocation over average service period

Prior service cost is deferred and recognized over time through either the service method, or through an alternative approach such as the straight-line method.

- **Service method**—allocates an equal amount of prior service cost to each service year and results in declining amortization as employees retire.
- **Straight-line method**—allocates an equal amount of prior service cost over the employees' average service period.

The service method is preferable because it logically relates prior service cost to years of service as rendered, with more expense allocated to the early years. The benefits the employer realizes are also greatest during those years. More employees are working, and the effect of the grant on performance is at its peak soon after the award. Both methods are illustrated in **Demo 23-10**.

DEMO 23-10 › LO23-10   **Allocation of Prior Service Cost**

Demo

MBC

A plan amendment for BWW Company results in a $48,000 prior service cost adjustment on January 1 of Year 1. The amendment affects 5 employees with service years estimated as follows: 5, 4, 2, and 1, for Year 1, Year 2, Year 3, and Year 4, respectively. This means that five employees are expected to work in Year 1, four employees in Year 2, two employees in Year 3, and one employee in Year 4. Total service years is equal to 12 years (5 + 4 + 2 + 1). Average service years is equal to 2.4 years (12 service years / 5 employees).

Required

a. Compute prior service cost amortization in Year 1 through Year 4 using the service method.
b. Compute prior service cost amortization in Year 1 through Year 4 using the straight-line method.

Solution

a. **Service Method**

Under the service method, $20,000 of prior service cost (5/12 × $48,000) is amortized in Year 1, when 5 of the total 12 service years are rendered. Pension expense is increased by $20,000 in Year 1. Similarly, in each of the remaining years, the amount of prior service cost is allocated based upon the number of employee service years.

Year	Service Years	Annual Amortization	
Year 1	5	$48,000 × 5/12 =	$20,000
Year 2	4	$48,000 × 4/12 =	16,000
Year 3	2	$48,000 × 2/12 =	8,000
Year 4	1	$48,000 × 1/12 =	4,000
	12		$48,000

b. **Straight-Line Method**

Under the straight-line method, prior service cost is amortized over the 2.4 average service years.

Year	Annual Amortization	
Year 1	$48,000/2.4 years	$20,000
Year 2	$48,000/2.4 years	20,000
Year 3	$8,000 (remaining)	8,000
Year 4		0
		$48,000

Allocation of Prior Service Costs   **LO23-10**   **REVIEW 23-10**

On January 1 of Year 1, Oracle Company amended its defined benefit pension plan by granting retroactive pension benefits for work performed before that date. The present value of those benefits was determined to be $80,000 at that date. The following employees expect to receive benefits under the plan, and they have the indicated expected number of years remaining in their careers at January 1 of Year 1: Jake: two years, Julia: five years.

Determine the amortization of prior service cost to be recognized in Year 3 under the:

a. Service method that associates an equivalent amount of prior service cost to each service year.

b. Straight-line method based on the average remaining service period of employees.

More Practice:
AppBE23-8, AppE23-5
Solution on p. 23-66.

Questions

Q23-1. Describe the key aspects of a defined benefit pension plan.

Q23-2. Describe the role and responsibilities of the employer, the trustee, and the employees in their involvement in a defined benefit pension plan.

Q23-3. What are actuarial assumptions used to develop estimates of future retirement benefit payments of a pension plan?

Q23-4. Distinguish between a contributory pension plan and a noncontributory pension plan.

Q23-5. Employer Mac sponsors a defined benefit pension plan. The estimated pension expense is $100,000 in the first year of the plan. Provide the balance sheet presentation for each of the following separate scenarios.

    a.   Mac contributes 100% of the pension expense

    b.   Mac contributes 80% of the expense

    c.   Mac contributes 120% of the expense

Q23-6. Employee Justin will receive an annual pension benefit of $12,000 for five years, starting on December 31. Assuming an interest rate of 8%, how much must be in the pension fund on January 1? Explain why the answer is not $60,000.

Q23-7. Employer Beeber must build a pension fund of $50,000 by December 31, four years from now. Five equal annual payments are made into the fund starting on December 31 of the current year. The fund will earn 8%. What is the amount of each payment? Explain why it is not $10,000.

Q23-8. Explain why accounting for defined benefit plans must be based on assumptions and estimates.

Q23-9. What is the pension benefit formula?

Q23-10. Explain why pension expense is not simply recognized when benefits are paid to employees.

Q23-11. What does attribution mean in pension accounting?

Q23-12. Two special features of pension accounting are (a) income smoothing in the income statement, and (b) offsetting in the balance sheet. Explain each feature.

Q23-13. What is the vested benefit obligation?

Q23-14. List and define the five components of pension expense.

Q23-15. Define and explain the projected benefit obligation (PBO).

Q23-16. What information is typically found in the report from the trustee on plan assets?

Q23-17. Explain what is meant by underfunded pension plan.

Q23-18. Explain the difference between the projected benefit obligation and the accumulated benefit obligation.

Q23-19. Explain the primary approaches for amortizing unrecognized pension costs.

Q23-20. In the case of unrecognized prior service cost, amortization may or may not be appropriate at the end of the year that the unrecognized prior service cost is first incurred. Explain why.

Data Analytics

In this exercise, we analyze the trend of (and the relations between) balances of the PBO and Plan assets over time. We also analyze the trends in service cost over time and determine possible causes of the trends.

Data Analytics DA23-1
Analyzing the Trends
of Plan Asset and PBO
Balances and Service
Cost Over Time in
Excel **LO2,3**

Data Visualization

Data Visualization

Data Visualization Activities are available in **myBusinessCourse**. These assignments use Tableau Dashboards to expose students to visual depictions of data and introduce students to data analytics through data visualizations. These exercises are assignable and auto graded by MBC.

Multiple Choice

LO1

MC23-1. **Computing ABO Liability Measurement** Consider the following employee of Rush Inc. who started work on January 1 of Year 1.

     Current salary: $60,000
     Projected salary at retirement, 10 years from now: $110,000
     Annual benefit formula: 4% × Number of years of service × Final salary
     Vesting percentage after 1 year: 10%

What is the present value at the employee's retirement date assuming a retirement period of 15 years and a discount rate of 8% under an ABO liability measurement? Assume the calculation is performed on December 31 of Year 1 after the employee completed one year of service.

   a. $16,104   c. $2,054
   b. $20,543   d. $22,186

LO1

MC23-2. **Computing PBO Liability Measurement** Referring to MC23-1, what is the present value at the employee's retirement date assuming a retirement period of 15 years and a discount rate of 8% under a PBO liability measurement? Assume the calculation is performed on December 31 of Year 1 after the employee completed one year of service.

   a. $29,524   c. $37,662
   b. $3,766   d. $40,675

LO2

MC23-3. **Calculating PBO Balance** Carson Corp.'s January 1 trial balance included a projected benefit obligation balance of $225,000. Assuming service cost of $48,000, interest cost of $14,000, actual return on plan assets of $8,000, and benefit payments of $28,000, what was the December 31 balance in the projected benefit obligation account?

   a. $259,000   c. $251,000
   b. $315,000   d. $287,000

LO3

MC23-4. **Calculating Actual Return on Plan Assets** Bristol Inc. compiled the following information for the current year.

Plan assets, December 31	$330,000
Plan assets, January 1	410,000
Benefits paid	99,000
Employer contributions	40,000

If the company's discount rate is 5%, what is the company's actual return on plan assets for the year?

   a. $139,000   c. $16,500
   b. $59,000   d. $21,000

LO4

MC23-5. **Computing Net Pension Expense** Chatham Inc. summarized the following information for the current year.

Account Balance	Jan. 1	Activity for the Year	
PBO	$40,000	Service cost	$8,000
Plan assets	42,000	Benefits paid	300
		Actual/Expected return on plan assets	1,900
		Employer contribution	8,000

Assuming a discount rate of 5%, compute net pension expense for the year.

   a. $10,000   c. $7,800
   b. $11,900   d. $8,100

MC23-6. Determining Effect of Pensions on Accounting Equation Referring to MC23-5, what is the net effect on the accounting equation for the reporting of pension expense, plan funding, and benefits paid?

LO5

	Assets	Liabilities	Stockholders' Equity
a.	+1,600	+9,700	–8,100
b.	+1,900	+10,000	–8,100
c.	+1,600	+10,000	–8,400
d.	+1,600	+8,000	–6,400

MC23-7. Computing Net Pension Expense Refer to MC23-5, but now assume a January 1 balance of $5,000 in Accumulated OCI—Prior Service Cost and amortization of prior service cost for the year of $500. If the company's discount rate is 5%, What is the net pension expense for the year?

LO4

a.	$12,400	c.	$8,300
b.	$8,600	d.	$7,600

MC23-8. Recording Pension Expense Referring to MC23-7, the entry to record pension expense would include which of the following?

LO5

a. Credit to Plan Assets for $1,900
b. Debit to OCI—Prior Service Cost for $500
c. Credit to PBO for $10,000
d. Debit to Plan Assets for $300

MC23-9. Reporting Net Pension Balance Referring to MC23-7, on January 1, the net pension balance would be reported on the balance sheet as a

LO6

a. Noncurrent accrued pension cost, net of $3,000
b. Noncurrent prepaid pension cost, net of $3,000
c. Noncurrent accrued pension cost, net of $2,000
d. Noncurrent prepaid pension cost, net of $2,000

MC23-10. Creating a Pension Worksheet Use the information MC23-7 to create a pension worksheet. How much did Net Pension Asset/Liability decrease for the year on the completed pension worksheet?

LO7

a.	$1,900	c.	$100
b.	$0	d.	$400

Brief Exercises

Aguilaera Co. maintains a defined benefit plan for its employees where vested employees earn an annual retirement payout of 2.5% of their projected final annual salary for each year worked. Benefits vest each year by 10% until the employee is 100% vested. Assume that new employee Smith earns a starting annual salary of $60,000, but is projected to earn $75,000 annually at her projected retirement date of fifteen years from now. After Smith's first year of service, determine the present value of the PBO retirement cash flow stream, measured at Smith's retirement date, assuming a 20-year retirement period and a 6% discount rate.

Brief Exercise 23-1
Computing PBO **LO1**
Hint: See Demo 23-1

Michael (age 35) commenced employment at Larkin Inc. on January 1 of Year 1. Larkin sponsors a defined benefit plan where employees vest 5% after year one, an additional 10% after year two, and an additional 15% each year after until 100%. Michael's current salary is $90,000 per year, and he is expected to retire in 20 years, at which time his salary is estimated to be $175,000 per year. The annual benefit formula is equal to 2.5% × number of years of service × final salary. Determine the gross annual benefit payment earned as of December 31 of Year 2, under a (1) VBO, (2) ABO, and (3) PBO pension liability measurement.

Brief Exercise 23-2
Computing Annual Benefit
Payment **LO1**
Hint: See Demo 23-1

Sharks Company implemented a defined benefit pension plan for its employees. The following data are provided for the current and prior year. Determine the benefit payments to retirees in the current year, assuming no PSC adjustment or gain or loss on the PBO in the current year and a discount rate of 7%.

Brief Exercise 23-3
Analyzing Change in PBO
Balance **LO2**
Hint: See Demo 23-2

	Current Year	Prior Year
Projected Benefit Obligation, December 31	$187,500	$175,000
Plan Assets, December 31	168,750	150,000
Service cost	22,500	

Brief Exercise 23-4
Analyzing Change in PBO
Balance **LO2**

Gaap Company sponsors a defined benefit plan covering all employees. Benefits are based on years of service and compensation levels at the time of retirement. Gaap determined that as of December 31, its accumulated benefit obligation was $270,000 and its plan assets had a $290,000 fair value. Gaap's December 31 trial balance included a projected benefit obligation balance of $297,075. Assuming service cost of $50,000, interest cost of $1,875, and benefit payments of $4,800, what was the January 1 balance of the PBO?

Brief Exercise 23-5
Analyzing Change in PBO
Balance **LO2**

Alpha Company sponsors a defined benefit plan covering all employees. Benefits are based on years of service and compensation levels at the time of retirement. Alpha's December 31 trial balance included a projected benefit obligation balance of $983,000, adjusted for an actuarially determined pension loss due to projected changes in interest rates. Assuming service cost of $155,000, discount rate of 5% applicable during the year (prior to the change in rates), benefit payments of $118,000, and a January 1 balance of $840,000 for the PBO, what was the loss recorded on the PBO during the year?

Brief Exercise 23-6
Analyzing Change in Plan
Asset Balance **LO3**
Hint: See Demo 23-3A

Blues Company implemented a defined benefit pension plan for its employees. The following data are provided for the current and prior year. Determine the employer's contribution in the current year.

	Current Year	Prior Year
Projected Benefit Obligation, December 31 . . .	$187,500	$175,000
Plan Assets, December 31	168,750	150,000
Actual return on plan assets	9,000	
Benefits paid to employees	3,000	

Brief Exercise 23-7
Analyzing Change in Plan
Asset Balance **LO3**
Hint: See Demo 23-3A

Blackhawk Company implemented a defined benefit pension plan for its employees. The following data are provided for the year.

Account Balances, Dec. 31		Activity for the Year	
Projected Benefit Obligation . . .	$280,000	Actual return on plan assets	$ 8,120
Plan Assets	280,020	Benefits paid to employees	12,000
		Employer contributions	15,000

  a.   Determine the balance in Plan Assets on January 1.
  b.   Determine the actual rate of return on plan assets for the year.

Brief Exercise 23-8
Determining Funded
Status **LO3**
Hint: See Review 23-3

As of December 31, the projected benefit obligation and plan assets of a noncontributory defined benefit plan sponsored by Durasell Inc. were as follows. Determine the funded status of this pension plan.

Projected benefit obligation	$312,000
Plan assets at fair value	300,000

Brief Exercise 23-9
Calculating Pension
Expense **LO4**
Hint: See Review 23-4

Lauren Inc. summarized the following information for the year.

Account Balances, Jan. 1		Activity for the Year	
Projected Benefit Obligation . . .	$229,000	Service cost	$55,000
Plan Assets	200,000	Actual and expected gain on plan assets . . .	16,000
		Annual interest on pension obligation	18,320
		Benefits paid	3,500

What amount should the company report as pension expense in its income statement?

Brief Exercise 23-10
Determining Pension
Expense **LO4**
Hint: See Demo 23-4

The following information pertains to Qdobe Corporation's defined benefit pension plan for the year. Assume no beginning balance in Accumulated OCI—Pension Gain/Loss. What amount should the company report as pension expense in its income statement?

Service cost	$160,000
Actual and expected gain on plan assets	35,000
Actuarial loss on PBO incurred during the year	40,000
Amortization of unrecognized prior service cost	5,000
Annual interest on pension obligation	50,000

Kent Co. approved a prior service obligation of $120,000 on January 1, which granted retroactive benefit to employees. Assuming an average remaining service period of 10 years for all active plan participants, what is the effect on pension expense in the current year?

Brief Exercise 23-11
Analyzing Prior Service
Cost **LO4**
Hint: See Demo 23-4

On June 1 of two years ago, West Corporation established a defined benefit pension plan for its employees. The following information is available for the current year.

Brief Exercise 23-12
Amortizing Pension Gain/
Loss **LO4**
Hint: See Demo 23-4

Balance	Jan. 1
Projected Benefit Obligation...............	$3,625,000 Cr.
Plan Assets...........................	3,750,000 Dr.
Accumulated OCI—Pension Gain/Loss	637,500 Cr.

For the current year, compute the amortization of the account, Accumulated OCI—Pension Gain/Loss, assuming that the company uses the corridor approach in determining the minimum amortization to recognize. Assume that the average remaining service life of employees is 10 years.

Kidman Inc. sponsors a defined benefit plan and determined that for the current year, service cost was $10,000, interest cost was $2,100, and the expected (and actual) return on plan assets was $2,000. Kidman contributes $1,800 to the plan on December 31. Record the journal entries (1) for pension expense and (2) to fund the plan for the year, assuming no benefits are paid during the year.

Brief Exercise 23-13
Recording Pension
Expense and Plan
Funding **LO5**
Hint: See Demo 23-5

Referring to BE23-13, show the effect on the accounting equation for each transaction, including identifying the individual accounts affected, and the total change in assets, liabilities, and stockholders' equity.

Brief Exercise 23-14
Reporting Pension
Expense and Plan Funding
Using the Accounting
Equation **LO5**

LetsGo Inc. sponsors a defined benefit plan and determined that for the current year, service cost was $250,000, amortization of prior service cost was $1,800, interest cost was $21,100, and the expected (and actual) return on plan assets was $18,000. LetsGo Inc. contributes $45,000 to the plan, and payments to retirees total $15,000. Record the journal entries (1) for pension expense, (2) to fund the plan, and (3) to pay benefits for the year.

Brief Exercise 23-15
Recording Pension
Expense, Plan
Funding, Benefit
Payments **LO5**
Hint: See Demo 23-5

Referring to BE23-15, show the effect on the accounting equation for each transaction, including identifying the individual accounts affected, and the total change in assets, liabilities, and stockholders' equity.

Brief Exercise 23-16
Reporting Pension
Expense, Plan Funding,
Benefit Payments Using
the Accounting Equation
LO5

The following pension-related values are determined on December 31 for BNW Inc. Compute the net pension asset (liability) to be recorded on the balance sheet on December 31.

Brief Exercise 23-17
Computing Net Pension
Asset (Liability) **LO6**
Hint: See Review 23-6

Projected benefit obligation	$100,000
Accumulated benefit obligation.................	80,000
Plan assets at fair value	90,000
Accumulated OCI—Prior Service Cost (Dr.).......	12,000

At the end of Year 1, after recording pension expense, Talent Co. has the following balances: Accumulated OCI—Pension Gain/Loss $6,000 (debit) and Projected Benefit Obligation $100,000 (credit). During Year 2, Talent Co. experienced a $500 actuarial gain on its PBO and an unexpected loss on plan assets of $80. Net income for Year 2 totaled $3,800. Talent Co. did not record amortization expense on the pension gain/loss because the beginning balance in Accumulated OCI—Pension Gain/Loss did not exceed the corridor. The company has no other items affecting OCI besides pension related items.

Brief Exercise 23-18
Reporting the Impact of
Pension Fund **LO6**

a.   What is other comprehensive income (loss) for Year 2, as reported in the financial statements?

b.   What is comprehensive income (loss) for Year 2, as reported in the financial statements?

c. What is the balance of accumulated other comprehensive income (loss) as of December 31 of Year 2 as reported in the financial statements?

Brief Exercise 23-19
Reporting the Impact of
Pension Fund **LO6**
Hint: See Demo 23-6

Pharrell Inc. sponsored a defined pension plan for its employees. For the year ended December 31, Pharrell recorded pension expense of $2,500 (including service cost of $1,500) and a $200 unexpected loss on plan assets. Pharrell calculated the December 31 balance in Accumulated OCI—Gain/Loss account to be $400 (debit) and calculated a net pension asset/liability of $250 (credit). Assuming no amortization of pension gain/loss, compute the impact of this plan on the (a) balance sheet, (b) income statement, and (c) statement of comprehensive income.

Brief Exercise 23-20
Preparing a Pension
Worksheet **LO7**
Hint: See Demo 23-7

Levine Co. sponsored a defined benefit plan, which included January 1 balances of $5,000 and $4,800 in Plan Assets and Projected Benefit Obligation, respectively. During the year, the company incurred $1,000 in service cost, made plan contributions of $210, and paid benefits to retirees for $150. The discount rate is 9% and the expected and actual rate of return on plan assets is 10%. Prepare a pension worksheet for the year.

Exercises

Exercise 23-1
Computing PBO;
Comparison to
Defined Contribution
Plan **LO1**

Hewlatt Inc. is considering the implications of establishing a defined benefit plan for its employees with the following three annual benefit payment options.

1. Annual retirement benefit = 2% × Final annual salary × Years of service; benefits would vest each year by 10% until the employee is 100% vested.
2. Annual retirement benefit = 1% × Final annual salary × Years of service; benefits would vest each year by 10% until the employee is 100% vested.
3. Lump sum payment at retirement date equal to the present value of the annual retirement benefit described in option 1, and assuming a 15-year retirement period.

The company determines that the average employee has a current annual salary of $50,000, is projected to earn $65,000 annually at the projected retirement date of 20 years from now, and will have an average retirement period of 15 years.

Required
a. After the first year of service, determine the present value of the PBO retirement cash flow stream for each option, 1 through 3, measured at the retirement date, and assuming a 6% discount rate and 300 employees.
b. As an alternative, the company is considering a defined contribution plan where the company matches each employee's retirement contribution, up to a maximum amount that varies by salary level. The company has no further obligations after making the defined contribution payment to the employees' plan. The estimated payment for the first year is $2,500 per employee. Determine the total liability at the end of the initial year of the plan, assuming that the first annual contribution will be made in January of the following year.

Exercise 23-2
Computing ABO, PBO
LO1
Hint: See Review 23-1

Mallard Company sponsors a pension plan with the following pension benefit:

$$\text{Benefit paid at each year-end during retirement} = \frac{\text{Number of years worked} \times \text{Annual salary at retirement}}{25}$$

Employee Josie began work with the company and received credit for service as of January 1 of Year 1. Josie is expected to work a total of 30 years with an annual salary at retirement of $100,000. She is expected to draw 10 years of retirement benefits. The discount rate is 10%.

Required
a. Compute the PBO on December 31 of Year 10, if Josie's current salary is $30,000.
b. Compute the ABO on December 31 of Year 10, if Josie's current salary is $30,000.

Exercise 23-3
Analyzing Changes in
PBO **LO2**
Hint: See Demo 23-2

Garcia Co. has a PBO balance on January 1 of $146,000. The actuaries provided the following information for the year: PBO December 31 balance, $140,000; interest cost, $13,000; actuarial gain on the PBO, $24,000; prior service cost amendment (causing additional obligations), $8,000; benefits paid to retirees, $19,000.

Required
Compute service cost for the year.

The following items are related to a defined pension plan.

Items relate to the current year

_____ *a.* December 31 projected benefit obligation balance

_____ *b.* December 31 plan asset balance

_____ *c.* Loss (gain) related to changes in actuarial assumptions

_____ *d.* Cash funding by the employer

_____ *e.* Prior service cost amendment

_____ *f.* Net periodic pension expense

_____ *g.* Actual return on plan assets

_____ *h.* Interest cost on PBO

_____ *i.* Amortization of prior service cost

_____ *j.* January 1 pension plan asset balance

_____ *k.* Pension benefits paid to retirees

_____ *l.* January 1 projected benefit obligation balance

_____ *m.* Expected return on plan assets

_____ *n.* Amortization of pension gain/loss

_____ *o.* Service cost

Exercise 23-4
Determining Amounts Affecting Pension Expense, PBO, and Plan Assets **LO2, 3, 4**

Required

Indicate whether each item *a* through *o* would be included in (1) a plan asset reconciliation, (2) a PBO reconciliation, and/or (3) a schedule of pension expense. An item may appear in more than one of these reports.

Kulver's Inc. sponsored a defined benefit plan during the year. Plan assets showed a January 1 balance at fair value of $130,000 and a December 31 balance at fair value of $134,800. The actual return on plan assets is 6%. The trustee paid $18,000 of benefits to retirees.

Exercise 23-5
Analyzing Changes in Plan Assets **LO3**
Hint: See Demo 23-3A

Required

Compute Kulver's current year contribution to the defined benefit plan.

The following information pertains to a company's defined benefit plan for the year.

Exercise 23-6
Analyzing Changes in Plan Assets and PBO **LO2, 3**

Balance		Activity for the Year	
Fair value of plan assets, Jan. 1	$5,000 Dr.	Actual return on plan assets	$300
Fair value of plan assets, Dec. 31	5,625 Dr.	Contributions to plan assets	450
Projected benefit obligation, Jan. 1	5,000 Cr.	Service cost	500
Net pension asset (liability), Dec. 31	200 Cr.		

Other	
Discount rate	8%
Expected rate of return on plan assets	7%

Required

a. Calculate benefits paid to retirees during the year.

b. Calculate any actuarial gain or loss on the PBO for the year.

Stars Inc. has a noncontributory defined pension plan for its employees. During the year, the company had service cost of $60,000, an expected return on plan assets of $9,280, amortization of prior service cost of $2,000, amortization of net pension loss of $2,222, and benefits paid to employees of $40,000. The January 1 balance in its projected benefit obligation was $194,000. The discount rate is 10%.

Exercise 23-7
Calculating Pension Expense **LO4**
Hint: See Demo 23-4

Required

Calculate pension expense for the year.

Determine how the following three defined benefit plans would be reported on Brittany Inc.'s balance sheet given the following information on December 31 (assuming all amounts are noncurrent).

Exercise 23-8
Determining and Reporting Funded Status **LO3**
Hint: See Review 23-3

Plan #1		Plan #2		Plan #3	
PBO	$100,000	PBO	$540,000	PBO	$85,000
ABO	60,000	ABO	450,000	ABO	50,000
Plan assets at fair value	80,000	Plan assets at fair value	600,000	Plan assets at fair value	95,000

Exercise 23-9
Analyzing Pension
Gain/Loss **LO4**

Spears Company presents the following information related to its pension plan for the year, before recording pension expense.

Account Balances	
Projected Benefit Obligation, Jan. 1	$300,000 Cr.
Projected Benefit Obligation, Dec. 31	325,000 Cr.
Accumulated OCI—Pension Gain/Loss, Jan. 1	12,000 Cr.
Plan Assets, Jan. 1	280,000 Dr.
Plan Assets, Dec. 31	295,000 Dr.

Activity for the Year	
Actuarial loss on PBO, determined at Dec. 31	$ 4,200
Contributions to pension fund	10,000
Benefits paid	15,000

Other	
Average remaining service period of employees, current and next year	20 years
Expected rate of return	10%

Required

a. Determine the amortization of Accumulated OCI—Pension Gain/Loss for the current year, using (1) corridor (minimum amortization) and (2) straight-line amortization based on average remaining service period.
b. Determine the Accumulated OCI—Pension Gain/Loss balance at January 1 of next year assuming straight-line amortization.
c. (1) Determine the impact on pension expense in the current year using the information provided and assuming straight-line amortization of Accumulated Pension Gain/Loss. (2) What information is missing to calculate total pension expense?
d. Determine the amortization of Accumulated OCI—Pension Gain/Loss for next year assuming straight-line amortization.

Exercise 23-10
Determining
Funded Status,
Recording Pension
Expense **LO3, 4, 5**

Rico Corporation initiated a defined benefit pension plan on January 1 of Year 1. The plan does not provide any retroactive benefits for existing employees. The pension funding payment is made to the trustee on December 31 of each year. The following information is available for Year 1 and Year 2.

	Year 1	Year 2
Service cost	$75,000	$82,500
Funding payment (contribution)	85,000	92,500
Interest on projected benefit obligation		7,500
Actual and expected return on plan assets		9,000

Required

a. In its December 31 of Year 1 balance sheet, Rico should report what amount of net pension asset/liability?
b. In its December 31 of Year 2 balance sheet, Rico should report what amount of net pension asset/liability?
c. Prepare the journal entries to record (1) pension expense and (2) plan funding for Year 2.

AICPA adapted

Exercise 23-11
Reporting Pension
Expense, Plan Funding
Using the Accounting
Equation **LO5**

Referring to E23-10 part c, show the effect on the accounting equation for each transaction, including identifying the individual accounts affected, and the total change in assets, liabilities, and stockholders' equity.

Exercise 23-12
Preparing a Pension
Worksheet **LO7**

Referring to Exercise 23-10, create a pension worksheet to summarize the pension data at the end of Year 2.

Exercise 23-13
Computing Amortization
of Pension Gain/
Loss **LO4**

On January 1, Crew Inc. reported a $6,000 credit balance in its Accumulated OCI—Pension Gain/Loss account related to its pension plan. During the year, the following events occurred.

■ Actual return on plan assets was $8,000, and expected return on plan assets was $10,000.
■ A gain on the PBO of $4,000 was determined by the actuary at December 31, based on changes in actuarial assumptions.

Crew amortizes unrecognized gains and losses using the corridor approach over the average remaining service life of active employees (20 years for this year and next year). Further information on this plan follows for the current year.

	Jan. 1	Dec. 31
PBO	$50,000	$56,000
Fair value of plan assets.	30,000	34,000

Required

a. Compute amortization of Accumulated OCI—Pension Gain/Loss for the current year using the corridor approach.

b. Compute the balance in Accumulated OCI—Pension Gain/Loss on December 31 of the current year.

c. Compute amortization of Accumulated OCI—Pension Gain/Loss for next year using the corridor approach.

d. Instead, now assume that the company elects to amortize Accumulated OCI—Pension Gain/Loss using the straight-line method. Compute amortization of Accumulated OCI—Pension Gain/Loss for (1) this year and (2) next year.

The following data relate to a defined benefit pension plan for Hollistir Co. for the year.

Exercise 23-14
Computing Pension Expense, Gain/Loss Amortization, PBO, and Plan Asset Balances
LO4, 5

Fair value of plan assets, Jan. 1	$16,000
PBO Jan. 1, not including any items below.	20,000
PSC from amendment dated Jan. 1, (10 years is the amortization period)	10,000
Gain from change in actuarial assumptions, computed as of Jan. 1	3,000
Actual return on plan assets.	2,000
Contributions to plan assets	4,000
Benefits paid to retirees	5,000
Service cost	9,000
Discount rate	8%
Expected rate of return on plan assets.	10%

Required

a. Compute pension expense for the year. The company amortizes the full pension gain/loss over average service life of 15 years, using the straight-line method.

b. Compute the PBO at December 31.

c. Compute fair value of plan assets at December 31.

Everglade Co. reported the following balances related to its noncontributory defined pension plan.

Exercise 23-15
Computing Amortization of Pension Gain/Loss
LO4

Account Balance	PBO	Plan Assets
Jan. 1, Year 1	$120,000	$ 95,000
Jan. 1, Year 2	194,000	116,000
Jan. 1, Year 3	221,400	219,200
Jan. 1, Year 4	248,000	233,000

Additional information related to the plan follows. The January 1 of Year 1 balance in OCI—Pension Gain/Loss is zero.

Account Balance	Current Year OCI—Pension Gain/Loss	Average Service Life
Dec. 31, Year 1	$50,000 Dr.	10
Dec. 31, Year 2	20,000 Dr.	10
Dec. 31, Year 3	12,000 Cr.	9
Dec. 31, Year 4	8,000 Dr.	9

Required

Using the corridor approach, compute the following.

a. Amortization of OCI—Pension Gain/Loss for Year 1 through Year 4.

b. Balance of Accumulated OCI—Pension Gain/Loss on December 31 of Year 1 through Year 4.

Exercise 23-16
Recording Pension
Expense, Gains/
Losses, Funding,
Benefit Payments and
Preparing Worksheet
LO5, 7

Amex Company started a noncontributory defined benefit pension plan on January 1 of last year. Company records show the following for the current year.

Account Balances	Jan. 1	Activity for the Year	
Projected Benefit Obligation...	$30,000 Cr.	Service cost	$10,000
Plan Assets..............	27,500 Dr.	Interest cost (interest rate, 10%)	3,000
Accumulated OCI—Pension		Gain in PBO due to change in actuarial	
Gain/Loss	1,500 Cr.	assumption	2,000
		Pension benefits paid	500
		Actual earnings on plan assets	
		(same as expected return)	2,500
		Plan funding payment (contributions)..........	15,000

Required

a. Compute net pension expense for the current year assuming that the January 1 Accumulated OCI—Pension Gain/Loss is amortized over a 15-year average remaining service period.

b. Prepare journal entries for (1) pension expense, (2) deferral of the gain, (3) funding, and (4) benefits paid.

c. Compute the underfunded (overfunded) pension balance as of December 31.

d. Create a worksheet to summarize the pension data at the end of the current year.

Exercise 23-17
Recording and
Reporting Pension
Accounts; Preparing
Worksheet **LO5, 6, 7**
Hint: See Review 23-7

Current year records of Lexxus Company provide the following data related to its noncontributory defined benefit pension plan.

Account Balances	Jan. 1	Activity for the Year	
Projected Benefit Obligation............	$3,000	Service cost	$1,200
Plan Assets........................	2,400	Interest cost	240
Accumulated OCI—Prior Service Cost....	0	Pension benefits paid........	400
Accumulated OCI—Pension Gain/Loss ...	0	Actual return on plan assets...	168
		Contributions	1,024

Other	
Expected rate of return of plan assets	7%
Discount rate	8%

Required

a. Compute net periodic pension expense reported for the year.

b. Prepare a reconciliation for (1) plan assets and (2) projected benefit obligation.

c. Provide the entries to record (1) pension expense, (2) funding, and (3) payment of benefits.

d. Determine the plan's funded status at the beginning and end of the year.

e. Indicate the amounts that would appear on the income statement and year-end balance sheet.

f. Create a worksheet to summarize the pension data at the end of the year.

Exercise 23-18
Preparing Pension
Journal Entries and
Pension Worksheet
LO5, 7
Hint: See Demo 23-7

Mac Company has a noncontributory defined benefit pension plan, with the following data for the year.

Account Balances	Jan. 1	Activity for the Year	
PBO balance, before PSC		Prior service cost (due to plan amendment	
adjustment	$45,000 Cr.	on Jan. 1)	$ 5,000
Plan Asset balance............	52,500 Dr.	Service cost	32,500
		Actual and expected return on plan assets .	2,500
		Cash funding (contributions).............	25,000
		Pension benefits paid to retirees	0

Required

a. Calculate interest cost assuming a discount rate of 8%.

b. Compute net pension expense. Assume that prior service cost will be amortized over a 10-year average remaining service period.

c. Prepare entries, as needed, to record (1) prior service cost deferral, (2) pension expense, (3) gain or loss deferral, (4) contributions, and (5) benefits for the year.

d. Provide the same entries in part *c* assuming cash funding from the employer of $35,500 and no other changes.

e. Determine the plan's funded status assuming all entries in part *c* are made.

f. Determine the plan's funded status assuming all entries in part *d* are made.

g. Create a worksheet to summarize the pension data at the end of the year based on part *c* entries.

The following data relate to a pension plan for ISPN Inc. for the year.

Exercise 23-19
Preparing and
Recording Pension
Entries and Preparing
Pension Worksheet
LO5, 6, 7

Account Balances	Jan. 1	Activity for the Year	
Projected Benefit Obligation............	$30,000 Cr.	Service cost	$7,000
Plan Assets.........................	30,000 Dr.	Contributions	9,000
Accumulated OCI—Pension Gain/Loss ...	5,000 Cr.	Prior service cost amortization...	1,000
Accumulated OCI—Prior Service Cost. ...	8,000 Dr.	Expected return on plan assets ..	2,000
		Actual return on plan assets.....	3,000

Required

a. Prepare entries to record (1) pension expense, (2) gain or loss deferral (if any), and (3) contributions for the year. Assume a discount rate of 8% and that no benefits were paid to retirees during the year. Include in pension expense, amortization of Accumulated OCI—Pension Gain/Loss using the straight-line method over 15 years.

b. Assuming pension expenses are not capitalized as part of inventory or other assets, indicate the effect on the income statement for the year ended December 31.

c. Indicate the changes in the following balance sheet accounts between January 1 and December 31: Net pension asset/liability, Cash, Retained earnings, and Accumulated other comprehensive income.

d. Create a worksheet to summarize the pension data at the end of the year.

Rollo Company has a defined benefit pension plan. At the end of the current reporting period, December 31, the following information was available.

Exercise 23-20
Preparing Pension
Entries and Pension
Worksheet **LO5, 7**
Hint: See Demo 23-7

Projected benefit obligation		Plan assets	
Balance, Jan. 1..........................	$150,000	Balance, Jan. 1.....................	$160,000
Service cost	40,000	Actual return on plan assets	
Interest cost ($150,000 × 10% discount rate)...	15,000	(same as expected)................	16,000
Change in actuarial assumptions on Dec. 31 ...	(400)	Funding of plan by Rollo..............	30,000
Pension benefits paid	(42,000)	Pension benefits paid to retirees........	(42,000)
Balance, Dec. 31........................	$162,600	Balance, Dec. 31....................	$164,000

Accumulated benefit obligation	$120,000	**Accumulated other comprehensive income**	**Jan. 1**
		Accumulated OCI—Prior Service Cost....	$20,000 Dr.
Vested benefit obligation..................	$ 40,000	Accumulated OCI—Pension Gain/Loss ...	2,000 Cr.

Required

a. Create a worksheet to summarize the pension data at the end of the year. The company uses the corridor approach in amortizing the pension gain/loss. Assume an average remaining service period of 10 years.

b. Prepare entries to record (1) pension expense, (2) gain or loss deferral (if any), (3) contributions, and (4) benefits for the year.

Information for the Jenkins Company defined benefit pension plan follows. The company uses the straight-line method to amortize prior service cost, and uses the corridor approach in amortizing pension gains and losses.

Exercise 23-21
Preparing Pension
Entries and Pension
Worksheet **LO5, 7**

Account Balances	Jan. 1	Activity for the Current Year	
Projected Benefit Obligation......	$700,000 Cr.	Service cost	$ 60,000
Plan Assets..................	500,000 Dr.	Actuarial loss determined Dec. 31	40,000
Accumulated OCI—		Actual return on plan assets............	55,000
Pension Gain/Loss	160,000 Cr.	Funding...........................	88,000
Accumulated OCI—PSC	120,000 Dr.	Benefits paid......................	0

Other	
Discount rate	8%
Expected rate of return on plan assets..................	10%
Average remaining service period of active plan participants ...	10 years

Required

a. Prepare the presentation of funded status as of December 31 of the prior year.
b. Prepare entries to record (1) pension expense, (2) gain or loss deferrals, (3) contributions, and (4) benefits for the current year.
c. Prepare the presentation of funded status as of December 31 of the current year.
d. Determine the amount of amortization of net unrecognized gain or loss required for next year, if any.
e. Prepare a pension worksheet for the current year.

Exercise 23-22
Preparing Pension
Entries and Pension
Worksheet   **LO5, 7**
Hint: See Demo 23-7

Laker Company has a noncontributory defined benefit pension plan. The company must record its pension expense for the year ended December 31. The following data are available for the year ($ thousands).

Activity for the Year	
Service cost	$ 60
Interest cost (at 8%)	48
Loss on PBO due to actuarial changes determined Dec. 31	20
Pension benefit paid to retirees	200
Actual return on plan assets	36
Employer contributions	120
Pension benefits paid	200

Account Balances	Jan 1
Accumulated OCI—Prior Service Cost. . . .	$ 72 Dr.
Accumulated OCI—Pension Gain/Loss . . .	8 Dr.
Projected Benefit Obligation	600 Cr.
Plan Assets.	400 Dr.

Other	
Average remaining service period	10 years
Expected return on plan assets	10%

Required

a. Create a pension worksheet to summarize the pension data at the end of the year. The company uses the corridor approach in amortizing any pension gain/loss.
b. Prepare entries to record (1) pension expense, (2) gain or loss deferrals, (3) contributions, and (4) benefits for the current year.

Exercise 23-23
Determining Reporting
Amounts and Preparing
Disclosures   **LO5, 6**

The following information relates to the contributory defined pension plan of Klarbrun Inc. for the year.

Account Balances	Jan. 1
Projected Benefit Obligation	$75,000 Cr.
Plan Assets.	78,750 Dr.
Accumulated OCI—Prior Service Cost. . .	49,500 Dr.

Activity for the Year	
Service cost	$ 49,000
Interest cost	6,000
Prior service cost amortization	500
Actual return on plan assets (same as expected return)	4,725
Cash funding by company	37,500
Cash funding by plan participants . . .	10,000
Pension benefits paid to retirees	5,000
Net income	500,000

Required

a. Prepare the portion of the pension disclosure showing the components of pension expense.
b. Prepare the portion of the pension disclosure showing the (1) reconciliation of the projected benefit obligation, (2) reconciliation of plan assets, and (3) funded status.
c. Prepare the statement of comprehensive income beginning with net income, assuming there are no other OCI items except those related to pensions.
d. Determine the ending balance in accumulated other comprehensive loss.

Terms relating to concepts discussed in this chapter along with descriptions of the terms follow.

Exercise 23-24
Defining Pension
Terminology   **LO1,
2, 3, 4, 5, 6**
MBC

____ 1. Projected benefit
obligation
____ 2. Expected return on
plan assets
____ 3. Amortization of
gains and losses
____ 4. Pension plan assets
____ 5. Pension expense
____ 6. Fair value (of plan
assets)
____ 7. Amortization of
prior service costs
____ 8. Net pension asset
____ 9. Accumulated
benefit obligation
____ 10. Interest cost
____ 11. Discount rate
____ 12. Service cost
____ 13. Vested benefit
obligation
____ 14. Actual return on
plan assets

a. Amount reported as pension expense for the period; has five components.
b. Allocation of the cost of retroactive pension benefits to periodic expense.
c. Actuarial present value of future pension benefits earned as of the
    measurement date excluding the effects of expected future compensation
    levels.
d. Cost of future pension benefits earned during the current accounting period.
e. The interest rate used to compute the present value of future pension
    benefits earned by employees.
f. Present value of the employee's benefits at the measurement date not
    contingent on future employee service.
g. Allocation of the difference between expected return and actual return on
    plan assets and changes in actuarial assumptions to periodic expense.
h. Cumulative fund assets in excess of the PBO.
i. Difference between plan assets at fair value at the beginning and end
    of the period minus contributions and plus distributions during the
    accounting period.
j. The value of plan assets between a willing buyer and a willing seller (not
    a forced sale).
k. Actuarial present value of future pension benefits earned as of
    the measurement date, including the effects of current and future
    compensation levels.
l. Projected benefit obligation at the beginning of the current accounting
    period multiplied by the discount rate.
m. Resources set aside to provide future pension benefits to retirees.
n. Beginning market-related value of pension plan assets multiplied by the
    expected rate of return.

Required

Match each term, 1 through 14, with the most appropriate description *a* through *n*.

Exercise 23-25
Determining How
Pension Items Affect
Accounts   **LO1, 2,
3, 4, 5, 6**
MBC

Pension items discussed in this chapter along with account effects follow.

Pension Items

a. Service cost
b. Expected return on plan assets
c. Excess of expected return over actual return on plan assets
d. Excess of actual return over expected return on plan assets
e. Amortization of prior service cost
f. Actuarial loss on the PBO (deferral)
g. Amendment to prior service cost (increase benefits)
h. Payment of retirement benefits
i. Actuarial gain on the PBO (deferral)
j. Employer contributions
k. Interest cost on the PBO
l. Amortization of actuarial pension loss

Account Effects

____ 1. Increase pension expense
____ 2. Decrease pension expense
____ 3. Increase projected benefit
        obligation
____ 4. Decrease projected benefit
        obligation
____ 5. Increase plan assets
____ 6. Decrease plan assets
____ 7. Increase other
        comprehensive income
____ 8. Decrease other
        comprehensive income
____ 9. Decrease cash

Required

Match each pension item, *a* through *l* with the account effect 1 through 9. More than one account effect may apply to a pension item.

Exercise 23-26
Presenting Pension
Funding on Statement
of Cash Flows **LO6**

Appleton Corporation initiated a defined benefit pension plan on January 1 of the prior year. The plan does not provide any retroactive benefits for existing employees. The pension funding payment is made to the trustee on December 31 of each year. The following information is available for the prior and current year.

	Prior Year	Current Year
Service cost	$75,000	$82,500
Funding payment (contribution)	85,000	92,500
Interest on projected benefit obligation.		7,500
Actual (and expected) return on plan assets		9,000

Required

a. Prepare the journal entries for the current year to record (1) pension expense and (2) the funding of plan assets.

b. Assuming that the company uses the indirect method in reporting operating cash flows, what noncash expense adjustment (if any) to net income would the company make in the operating activities section of the statement of cash flows? *Hint*: Refer to Chapter 22.

Problems

Problem 23-1
Calculating ABO and
PBO Balances   **LO1**
Hint: See Demo 23-1B

Bryan is a participant in a pension plan. Information on the plan and Bryan's involvement follows.

Plan inception: Jan. 1 of Year 1
Bryan's first day with the company: Jan. 1 of Year 1
Bryan's expected service period: 20 years
Bryan's expected final salary: $100,000
Retirement period: 10 years
Brian's salary for Year 1 and Year 2: $30,000
Discount rate: 10%
Pension benefit formula: Yearly benefit during retirement = [(Number of years worked) × (Final salary)]/25

Required

a. Compute projected benefit obligation at December 31 of Year 1.
b. Compute accumulated benefit obligation at December 31 of Year 1.
c. Compute projected benefit obligation at December 31 of Year 2.
d. Compute accumulated benefit obligation at December 31 of Year 2.

Problem 23-2
Calculating ABO and
PBO Balances   **LO1**
Hint: See Demo 23-1B

The Jets Company sponsors a pension plan with the following pension benefit formula.

$$\text{Benefit paid at each year-end during retirement} = 2\% \times (\text{Number of service years}) \times (\text{Annual salary at retirement})$$

Credit for service began January 1 of Year 1 for an employee (Shuler), which is Shuler's first day with the company with a starting salary of $45,000. Shuler is expected to work a total of 25 years with an annual salary at retirement of $150,000. Shuler is expected to draw 10 years of retirement benefits. The discount rate is 10%. Starting January 1 of Year 3, Shuler's new salary is $47,250 after a 5% raise.

Required

a. Compute the following amounts.
   1. PBO on January 1 of Year 2.
   2. ABO on January 1 of Year 2.
   3. PBO on January 1 of Year 3.
   4. ABO on January 1 of Year 3.

b. Consider the following three additional, separate scenarios, and compute the following amounts.
   1. PBO on January 1 of Year 2, assuming that the discount rate is 8%.
   2. PBO on January 1 of Year 2, assuming that the starting salary is $100,000 and final salary is $325,000.
   3. PBO on January 1 of Year 2, assuming that the retirement period is 20 years instead of 10.

Problem 23-3
Computing Pension
Expense, Two Years
LO4, 5

The following information pertains to a pension plan for Guccii Company that recognizes only the minimum amortization of unrecognized gains and losses using the corridor approach.

Account Balances	Jan. 1, Year 1
Accumulated OCI—Pension Gain/Loss ...	$ 0
Projected Benefit Obligation, not	
considering Year 1 actuarial loss.......	60,000
Plan Assets........................	24,000
Accumulated OCI—Prior Service Cost	
(average remaining service life of	
employees covered under prior service	
cost grant: 2 years)	8,000

Activity	
Actuarial loss, Year 1	
(determined Jan. 1, Year 1).....	$12,000
Service cost, Year 1	12,000
Service cost, Year 2	14,000
Funding amount, Year 1	16,000
Funding amount, Year 2	20,000
Actual return on fund in Year 1	1,800
Actual return on fund in Year 2	2,400

Other	
Discount rate	10%
Expected rate of return on fund assets..............................	12%
No benefits were paid in either year	
Average remaining service period in years for amortization of any pension gain/loss...	12

Required

a.   Compute pension expense for Year 1.

b.   For Year 2, compute the following amounts.

1.   Plan asset balance, January 1 of Year 2.
2.   PBO balance, January 1 of Year 2.
3.   Accumulated Pension Gain/Loss balance, January 1 of Year 2.
4.   Pension expense for Year 2.

Netflicks Inc. has a noncontributory defined benefit pension plan. The following data are for the current year.

Problem 23-4
Calculating PBO, Plan Assets, and Underfunding or Overfunding   **LO2, 3, 4**

Projected Benefit Obligation	
Balance, Jan. 1.....................	$164,000
Balance, Dec. 31	214,000

Plan Assets (at Fair Value)	
Balance, Jan. 1.....................	$ 80,000
Balance, Dec. 31	140,000

Required

a.   How much did the PBO increase during the year? Name five items that could have caused the PBO to change.

b.   How much did pension plan assets change during the year? Name three items that could have caused the change in plan assets.

c.   Compute the plan's funded status at (1) January 1 and (2) December 31. Explain what the amounts mean.

Current year information for a pension plan for Morgan Inc. follows.

Problem 23-5
Computing Pension Gain/Loss   **LO4**

Account Balances	
Accumulated OCI—Pension	
Gain/Loss, Jan. 1	$ 7,000 Cr.
Plan Assets, Jan. 1..............	200,000 Dr.
Plan Assets, Dec. 31	220,000 Dr.

Activity for the Year	
Contributions	$40,000
Benefits paid......................	32,000
Actuarial loss on PBO	
(computed on Dec. 31)	8,000

The company elects to amortize pension gain/loss into income for the period using the straight-line method (10-year average remaining service period) without applying the corridor approach. The expected rate of return on plan assets is 7%.

Required

Compute Accumulated OCI—Pension Gain/Loss at January 1 of the following year.

Mason Company has a noncontributory defined benefit pension plan. The following data are for the current year of the pension plan.

Problem 23-6
Preparing Entries and Reconciliations for Pension Plan   **LO3, 4, 5**

Projected Benefit Obligation, Jan. 1	$ 40,000
Service cost	60,000
Interest cost	3,600
Pension benefits paid	0
Projected Benefit Obligation, Dec. 31	103,600
Plan Assets, Jan. 1	50,000
Funding of plan.	37,000
Actual return and expected return on plan assets	10,000
Discount rate	9%

Required

a. Prepare a reconciliation of plan assets for the year.

b. Compute the plan's funded status at the beginning of the year and the end of the year.

c. Prepare entries to record (1) pension expense and (2) contributions for the year.

d. Provide the same entries in (c), assuming cash funding of $55,000 (instead of $37,000).

e. Provide the computation for the $3,600 of interest cost.

Problem 23-7
Reporting Pension
Expense, Plan Funding
Using the Accounting
Equation **LO3, 4, 5**

Referring to P23-6, show the effect on the accounting equation for each transaction, including identifying the individual accounts affected, and the total change in assets, liabilities, and stockholders' equity.

Problem 23-8
Preparing Entries and
Worksheet for Pension
Plan   **LO5, 7**

Luloo Inc. has a defined benefit pension plan. At the end of the current reporting period, December 31, the following information was available.

Account Balances	Jan. 1	Activity for the Year	
PBO	$2,400 Cr.	Service cost	$ 312
Plan Assets.	2,000 Dr.	Interest cost ($2,400 × 7% discount rate).	168
Accumulated OCI—		Loss on PBO due to a change in actuarial assumptions	
Prior Service Cost.	180 Dr.	determined Dec. 31	72
Accumulated OCI—		Pension benefits paid	(160)
Pension Gain/Loss	144 Dr.	Actual return on plan assets (same as expected)	120
		Pension funding payment	280

Required

a. Create a worksheet to summarize the pension data at the end of the year. Assume that the company amortizes accumulated prior service costs over a nine-year service period. The company amortizes its accumulated pension gain/loss using the corridor approach and amortizes over a nine-year average remaining service period.

b. Prepare entries to record (1) pension expense, (2) gain or loss deferral (if any), (3) contributions, and (4) benefits for the year.

Problem 23-9
Preparing Worksheet
for Pension Plan and
Analyze Changes
LO7

Cruise Company has a noncontributory defined benefit pension plan. The annual accounting period ends on December 31. The following plan information relates to the current year.

Projected Benefit Obligation		Plan Assets	
Balance, Jan. 1	$16,000	Balance, Jan. 1	$12,600
Service cost	1,920	Actual return on plan assets.	1,000
Interest cost ($16,000 × 8% discount rate). . . .	1,280	Funding to plan by Cruise.	3,000
Loss (gain) change in actuarial assumptions		Pension benefits paid to retirees . . .	(1,600)
determined Dec. 31.	660	Balance, Dec. 31	$15,000
Pension benefit paid to retirees	(1,600)		
Balance, Dec. 31	$18,260		

Other Information	
Accumulated OCI—Prior Service Cost, Jan. 1	$1,980 Dr.
Accumulated OCI—Pension Gain/Loss, Jan. 1	440 Cr.
Expected return on plan assets	1,000
Average remaining service period	11 years

Required

a. Create a worksheet to summarize the pension data at the end of the year. The company uses the corridor approach in amortizing any pension gain/loss.

b. Prepare entries to record (1) pension expense, (2) gain or loss deferral (if any), (3) contributions, and (4) benefits for the year.

c. The company president asked the following question: We paid $3,000 cash to the pension fund, but the projected benefit obligation increased over $2,000. Why? Prepare a written response with data and explanation.

The following schedule provides two years of information for Rhino Inc. related to its defined benefit plan.

Problem 23-10
Analyzing Pension
Information for Two
Years   **LO3, 4**

December 31	Prior Year	Current Year
Projected Benefit Obligation............	$120,000 Cr.	$194,000 Cr.
Plan Assets........................	95,000 Dr.	116,000 Dr.
Accumulated OCI—Prior Service Cost....	0 Dr.	18,000 Dr.
Accumulated OCI—Pension Gain/Loss ...	1,000 Cr.	3,450 Cr.

In the current year, the company made a contribution to pension plan assets. Payout to retirees in the current year totaled $40,000. The discount rate is 8%. Expected return on plan assets is 9%. Assume no amortization of prior service cost or pension gain/loss, and no new actuarial changes to the PBO in the current year.

Required

Determine the following amounts.

a. Funded status as of December 31 of the prior year.   d. Employer contributions.

b. Funded status as of December 31 of the current year.   e. Service cost.

c. Actual return on plan assets.   f. Total pension expense.

Voss Company has a noncontributory defined benefit pension plan for its employees. Year-end data follow.

Problem 23-11
Preparing Pension
Worksheets for Two
Years   **LO7**

Balance, Jan. 1	Prior Year	Current Year
Projected Benefit Obligation......................	$1,520 Cr.	$1,752 Cr.
Plan Assets......................	940 Dr.	1,084 Dr.
Accumulated OCI—Prior Service Cost...............	100 Dr.	108 Dr.
Accumulated OCI—Pension Gain/Loss	182 Dr.	199 Dr.

Activity	Prior Year	Current Year
Service cost	$200	$238
Interest cost	152	140
Prior service cost amendment, Jan. 1 (increase to PBO)...	20	13
Loss on PBO due to actuarial changes, Dec. 31	10	6
Pension benefits paid............................	150	170
Actual return on plan assets.......................	84	92
Plan funding	210	320

Other	Prior Year	Current Year
Expected return on plan assets	10%	10%
Average remaining service period	10 years	9 years

Required

Prepare worksheets to summarize the pension data at the end of the prior year and the current year. The company uses the corridor approach in amortizing any pension gain/loss.

Problem 23-12
Preparing Pension
Worksheets for Two
Years   **LO5, 7**

Andros Company has a noncontributory defined benefit pension plan. Data for the two recent years follow.

Balance, Jan. 1	Prior Year	Current Year
Projected Benefit Obligation.............................	$1,700 Cr.	$2,215 Cr.
Plan Assets..	1,000 Dr.	1,210 Dr.
Accumulated OCI—Prior Service Cost..................	0 Dr.	216 Dr.
Accumulated OCI—Pension Gain/Loss	150 Dr.	180 Dr.

Activity	Prior Year	Current Year
Service cost	$180	$210
Prior service cost (plan amended, Jan. 1)	240	0
Increase in PBO due to actuarial change, Dec. 31........	20	5
Pension benefits paid	80	125
Actual return on plan assets..........................	90	110
Contributions (funding)...............................	200	440

Other	Prior Year	Current Year
Expected return on plan assets	10%	10%
Discount rate	8%	9%
Average remaining service period	10 years	9 years

Required

a. Prepare worksheets to summarize the pension data at the end of the prior year and the current year. The company uses the corridor approach in amortizing any pension gain/loss.

b. Prepare entries (as applicable) to record (1) prior service cost deferral, (2) pension expense, (3) gain or loss deferrals, (4) contributions, and (5) benefits for each year.

Problem 23-13
Preparing Pension
Worksheet   **LO5, 7**

Jack Company has a noncontributory defined benefit pension plan. The following data are for the current year of the pension plan.

Balance	Jan. 1	Activity for the Year	
Projected Benefit Obligation.......	$300 Cr.	Service cost	$ 50
Plan Assets....................	170 Dr.	Gain on PBO due to change in actuarial	
Accumulated OCI—Prior		assumption (determined Dec. 31)........	10
Service Cost	40 Dr.	Pension benefit paid to retirees	124
Accumulated OCI—Pension		Actual return on plan assets..............	8
Gain/Loss	80 Dr.	Contributions	110
		Pension benefits paid..................	124

Other	
Expected return on plan assets	6%
Discount rate	8%
Average remaining service period	10 years

Required

a. Prepare a worksheet to summarize the pension data at the end of the year. The company uses the corridor approach in amortizing any pension gain/loss.

b. Prepare entries to record (1) pension expense, (2) gain or loss deferral (if any), (3) contributions, and (4) benefits for the year.

Problem 23-14
Preparing Pension
Entries for Three Years
LO3, 5

The defined benefit pension plan of Americo Inc. has been in existence for several years before January 1 of Year 1. The following data relates to the plan for Year 1 and is followed by comparative data from Years 1, 2, and 3.

Discount rate and expected rate of return	10%
PBO, Jan. 1 of Year 1 (before amendments)	$1,965
Plan assets at fair value, Jan. 1 of Year 1................	$2,094
Average remaining service period—Prior service cost.......	4 years
Average remaining service period—Pension gain/loss	10 years

	Year 1	Year 2	Year 3
Service cost	$ 800	$1,400	$1,700
Contributions	1,100	1,600	1,700
Actual return on plan assets. . .	209	300	600
Benefits paid.	0	0	0

Additional information

- On January 1 of Year 1, the company retroactively granted three employees an increase in benefits based on work performed before that date. The immediate present value of those benefits is $3,000.

- On January 1 of Year 1, the actuaries inform the company that on the basis of new estimates, the actuarial gain on the PBO is $1,200. The company elects minimum amortization of the net unrecognized gain or loss using the corridor approach.

- On January 1 of Year 3, the actuaries inform the company that on the basis of new estimates, average life expectancy of retirees and current employees is expected to be higher than previously anticipated. The immediate effect on the actuarial present value of benefits based on the budget formula is a $1,400 loss on the PBO.

Required

For Year 1, Year 2, and Year 3, complete the following requirements.

a. Prepare entries (as necessary) to record the (1) January 1 deferral(s), (2) pension expense, (3) December 31 gain or loss deferral(s), and (4) contributions.

b. Prepare the end of year presentation of funded status.

c. Determine the year-end balance in the accumulated other comprehensive income accounts.

Accounting Decisions and Judgments

Real World Analysis   **Ford Motor Company** (Ford) is a global automotive and mobility company. Below is an excerpt from a recent Form 10-K.

AD&J23-1
Analyzing Retirement
Benefits **LO3, 4**

NOTE 12. RETIREMENT BENEFITS   The year-end status of these plans was as follows (in millions):

Pension Benefits U.S. Plans	Current Year	Prior Year
Change in Benefit Obligation		
Benefit obligation at January 1	$47,103	$43,182
Service cost.	586	507
Interest cost.	1,817	1,992
Amendments.	99	—
Separation programs and other.	(27)	(50)
Plan participant contributions	26	26
Benefits paid	(2,949)	(3,028)
Actuarial (gain)/loss.	(1,719)	4,474
Benefit obligation at December 31	44,936	47,103
Change in Plan Assets		
Fair value of plan assets at January 1	44,844	41,217
Actual return on plan assets	(755)	6,542
Company contributions	130	130
Plan participant contributions	26	26
Benefits paid	(2,949)	(3,028)
Other.	(44)	(43)
Fair value of plan assets at December 31.	41,252	44,844
Funded status at December 31	$ (3,684)	$ (2,259)
Amounts Recognized on the Balance Sheet		
Prepaid assets	$ —	$ 76
Other liabilities	(3,684)	(2,335)
Total.	$ (3,684)	$ (2,259)
Amounts Recognized in Accumulated Other Comprehensive Loss (pre-tax)		
Unamortized prior service costs/(credits)	$ 553	$ 609

Required

a. What is the funded status of the plan in the current year?

b. Estimate the discount rate.

c. Determine as many components of current year pension expense as possible from the information.

AD&J23-2
Analyzing Defined
Pension Plan   **LO3, 4**

Real World Analysis   **United Parcel Service Inc.** (UPS), a package delivery company, reported the following in its annual report regarding its pension plans (company-sponsored employee benefit plans).

The UPS Retirement Plan is noncontributory and includes substantially all eligible employees of participating domestic subsidiaries who are not members of a collective bargaining unit, as well as certain employees covered by a collective bargaining agreement. This plan generally provides for retirement benefits based on average compensation levels earned by employees prior to retirement. Benefits payable under this plan are subject to maximum compensation limits and the annual benefit limits for a tax-qualified defined benefit plan as prescribed by the Internal Revenue Service ("IRS").

	Current Year
Discount rate	4.40%
Rate of compensation increase	4.29%
Expected return on assets	8.75%

U.S. Pension Benefits, $ millions	Current Year	Prior Year
Funded status		
Fair value of plan assets.	$28,887	$28,828
Benefit obligation	(36,846)	(37,521)
Funded status recognized at December 31	$ (7,959)	$ (8,693)
Funded Status Recognized in Balance Sheet		
Other non-current assets	$ 0	$ 0
Other current liabilities	(16)	(17)
Pension and postretirement benefit obligations	(7,943)	(8,676)
Net liability at December 31	$ (7,959)	$ (8,693)
Amounts Recognized in AOCI		
Unrecognized net prior service cost.	$ (954)	$ (1,122)
Unrecognized net actuarial gain (loss)	(3,263)	(3,752)
Gross unrecognized cost at December 31	(4,217)	(4,874)
Deferred tax assets (liabilities) at December 31.	1,585	1,833
Net unrecognized cost at December 31	$ (2,632)	$ (3,041)

The company also reported accumulated benefit obligation for U.S. pension plans as of the measurement dates in the current year and prior year of $34.210 and $34.725 billion, respectively.

Required

a. Estimate current year interest cost from the information provided.

b. Estimate the current year expected return on plan assets from the information provided.

c. What is the funded status of the plan in the current year?

d. What is the funded status in the current year comparing ABO to plan assets? Why is this different from your answer to part c?

AD&J23-3
Analyzing Pension
Plans   **LO3, 4, 6**

Real World Analysis   **3M Company** is a diversified technology company with a global presence in the following businesses: Industrial; Safety and Graphics; Electronics and Energy; Health Care; and Consumer. In its Year 8 to Year 10 annual reports, 3M Company shows the following regarding its defined benefit plans.

3M has company-sponsored retirement plans covering substantially all U.S. employees and many employees outside the United States. In total, 3M has over 80 defined benefit plans in 28 countries. Pension benefits associated with these plans generally are based on each participant's years of service, compensation, and age at retirement or termination. The primary U.S. defined benefit pension plan was closed to new participants effective January 1 of Year 4.

U.S. Defined Pension Plans ($ millions)	Year 10	Year 9	Year 8	Year 7
Projected benefit obligation	$15,856	$16,435	$13,967	$14,830
Accumulated benefit obligation	14,834	15,319	13,357	14,127
Fair value of plan assets	13,966	14,623	13,889	13,781
Pension Costs				
Service cost	$ 293	$ 241	$ 258	$ 254
Interest cost	655	676	598	587
Expected return on plan assets	(1,069)	(1,043)	(1,046)	(992)
Amortization of prior service cost (benefit)	(24)	4	5	5
Amortization of net actuarial (gain) loss	409	243	399	470
Other	2	—	—	26
Pension Expense	$ 266	$ 121	$ 214	$ 350
Changes to Other Comprehensive Income				
Prior service cost (benefit)	$ —	$ (266)	$ —	$ —
Amortization of prior service cost (benefit)	24	(4)	(5)	(5)
Net actuarial (gain) loss	312	2,167	(743)	(470)
Amortization of net actuarial (gain) loss	(409)	(243)	(399)	(470)
	$ (73)	$ 1,654	$(1,147)	$ (945)
Assumptions[1] ($ millions)	**Year 10**	**Year 9**	**Year 8**	**Year 7**
Discount rate	4.10%	4.98%	4.14%	4.15%
Return on plan assets	7.75%	7.75%	8.00%	8.25%
Cash Flow Information				
Pension and postretirement contributions	$(267)	$(215)	$(482)	$(1,146)
Financial Statement Information				
Total assets	$32,718	$31,209	$33,550	$33,876
Total liabilities	20,971	18,067	15,602	15,836
Total equity	11,747	13,142	17,948	18,040
Net income	4,841	4,998	4,721	4,511
Total other comprehensive income	(72)	(2,395)	755	231
Net cash provided by operating activities	6,420	6,626	5,817	5,300

[1] Weighted-average assumption used to determine net cost

Required

a. What is the funded status of the plan using the PBO over the four years presented? Comment on your results.

b. What is recorded in 3M's liabilities on the balance sheet related to the pension plans over the four years presented? Calculate the percentage of these amounts over the company's total liabilities. Calculate the percentage of the PBO over the company's total liabilities. Comment on your results.

c. Compute the funded status of the plan using the ABO for Year 7 to Year 10. How does this differ from your results in part a? Why?

d. Calculate the interest cost and expected return on plan assets for Year 8, Year 9, and Year 10.

e. When did 3M record prior period cost amendment(s) in the four years presented and for what amount? What was the impact on prior service cost amortization (if any)? Estimate the average service life related to the plan amendment.

f. Calculate the cash impact of pension plan contributions as a percentage of net cash provided by operating activities over the past four years. Comment on your results.

g. Calculate comprehensive income for the four years presented and compare to net income for the four years presented. Comment on the deferral of any significant amounts in other comprehensive income based upon your analysis. How do you think the company treats the allocation of pension gains/losses?

h. 3M reported the following in its Year 10 Form 10-K note on pension plans. How does 3M's shift from offering new employees defined pension plans to now offering 401(k) plans affect its pension plan accounting?

The Company also sponsors employee savings plans under Section 401(k) of the Internal Revenue Code. These plans are offered to substantially all regular U.S. employees. For eligible employees hired prior to January 1 of Year 4, employee 401(k) contributions of up to 6% of eligible compensation were matched in cash at rates of 60% or 75%, depending on the plan in which the employee participates. Employees hired on or after January 1 of Year 4, received a cash match of 100% for employee 401(k) contributions of up to 6% of eligible compensation and also received an employer retirement income account cash contribution of 3% of the participant's total eligible compensation.

AD&J23-4
Analyzing
Postretirement Benefit
Plans **LO3, 6, 8, 9**

Real World Analysis In its recent annual reports, **3M Company** shows the following regarding its postretirement benefit plans.

The Company also provides certain postretirement health care and life insurance benefits for substantially all of its U.S. employees who reach retirement age while employed by the Company. Most international employees and retirees are covered by government health care programs.

Postretirement Benefits ($ millions)	Year 10	Year 9	Year 8	Year 7
Change in benefit obligation				
Benefit obligation at beginning of year	$2,462	$2,017	$2,205	$2,108
Service cost	75	65	80	78
Interest cost	98	97	88	86
Participant contributions	14	18	30	52
Foreign exchange rate changes	(22)	(11)	(13)	(2)
Plan amendments.	(211)	—	(20)	—
Actuarial (gain)loss	(80)	415	(225)	31
Medicare Part D Reimbursement	1	1	2	8
Benefit payments	(122)	(140)	(130)	(156)
Other.	1	—	—	—
Benefit obligation at end of year	$2,216	$2,462	$2,017	$2,205
Change in plan assets				
Fair value of plan assets at beginning of year	$1,436	$1,405	$1,321	$1,209
Actual return on plan assets.	36	148	178	149
Company contributions.	3	5	6	67
Participant contributions	14	18	30	52
Benefit payments	(122)	(140)	(130)	(156)
Fair value of plan assets at end of year	$1,367	$1,436	$1,405	$1,321

Required

a. What is the funded status of the plan using the APBO over the four years presented? Comment on your results.

b. What is recorded in 3M's assets and/or liabilities on the balance sheet related to the postretirement plans over the four years presented?

c. In Note 11 of the 3M Company's Year 10 Form 10-K, the company reported the following. Comment on this change as it relates to the estimation of postretirement pension obligations.

The Company is in the process of transitioning all current and future retirees in the U.S. postretirement health care benefit plans to a savings account benefits-based plan. The contributions provided by the Company to the health savings accounts increase 3% per year for employees who retired prior to January 1 of Year 11 and increase 1.5% for employees who retire on or after January 1 of Year 11. Therefore, the Company no longer has material exposure to health care cost inflation.

AD&J23-5
Analyzing Components
of Pension
Loss **LO4, 6**

Communication Case At December 31, as a result of its defined benefit pension plan, Creste Company had a balance in Accumulated OCI—Pension Loss and an underfunded pension balance. Creste's pension plan and its actuarial assumptions have not changed since it began operations ten years ago. Creste has made annual contributions to the plan.

Required

Write a one-page report addressing the following questions.

a. Identify the components of net pension expense that should be recognized in Creste's current year financial statements.

b. What circumstances caused Creste's (1) net pension loss and (2) underfunded pension balance?

AD&J23-6
Assessing the Delayed
Recognition in Pension
Accounting **LO5**

Ethics Case GAAP accounting for pension plans has been criticized by those who maintain that it provides opportunity for sponsors to manipulate and smooth earnings. Would you propose changes to these standards?

Required

Briefly discuss the provisions of the accounting standards that contribute to opportunities for income smoothing or manipulation. For each point, give your opinion as to whether the provision is appropriate in terms of optimal measurement and reporting (as opposed to the economic consequences of such reporting).

Judgment Case An alternative conceptualization of pension expense that had been proposed at various times before the current standards, would have based annual pension expense on the required annual contribution needed to fully fund the estimated total pension benefit at retirement. It is called the cost approach because pension expense for a period is considered to be the contribution (annuity amount) required in that year to fund the plan. This approach is not allowed under GAAP.

AD&J23-7
Recording Pension
Expense Based on
Funding   **LO1**

Required

a. Using the following example from Demo 23-1, determine Year 1 pension expense using the cost approach, where funding is assumed to take place equally over Nicole's service period.

> Nicole (age 40) started working at Axe Company on January 1 of Year 1, at a starting annual salary of $45,000. Nicole's expected retirement date is December 31 of Year 25, with an annual salary of $150,000. Benefits vest as follows: 10% after the first year, 15% after the second year, and 20% each year after until 100%. Nicole's expected retirement period is 10 years. The relevant discount rate is 10%. The applicable pension benefit formula for the defined benefit plan is

> **Annual benefit payment during retirement = 2% × Number of service years × Final salary**

b. Assume the company funds its obligation to Nicole at the date she retires. How much funding is required?

c. Based on your findings above and your knowledge of GAAP, provide your opinion as to whether the cost approach would be a better approach to measuring pension expense than the current standards.

Ethics Case We are the auditors for Frito Inc., which is in considerable financial difficulty. In particular, debt covenants may be violated if liabilities are increased. In addition, the client's balance in retained earnings is minimal as a result of excessively high dividends and diminished earnings in the past several years.

AD&J23-8
Considering
Opportunities for
Managing Pension
Expense and Liabilities
LO2, 3, 4, 5

Frito Inc. is dominated by its CEO, a person who has served the company for 30 years. The CEO makes most of the major decisions in the company. This person is the company's primary representative working with the audit staff. There has been considerable turnover of audit committee members in the last two years. The CEO is very aggressive with respect to earnings.

From the minutes, we have discovered that extreme emphasis has been placed on meeting earnings projections. Department officers have been fired for not meeting earnings goals for two successive years. We know that, through PCAOB Audit Standard No. 8, part of our responsibility as an auditor is to develop an audit plan that is sensitive to audit risk. Audit risk is the probability that we may unknowingly fail to modify our audit report on financial statements that are materially misstated. Our audit plan should be designed to provide reasonable assurance that material errors and fraud are detected.

Required

We understand that the pressures faced by Frito Inc. may create incentives for unethical and fraudulent financial reporting. In a report of not more than two pages, discuss the aspects of pension accounting that should be considered with special care. What pension-related variables might be changed, and in what direction, to achieve reduced pension expense and liabilities? Include in your discussion reasons why you chose these variables.

Communication Case Rogers Inc., has a defined benefit pension plan for its 2,000 employees. It provides covered employees with a pension equal to 1.5% of their average salary during the two calendar years of highest pay times the number of years of service, with a maximum of 30 years. Benefits are based on an assumed retirement age of 65 and are reduced or increased to their actuarial equivalents for those employees who retire before or after age 65. The projected benefit obligation of Rogers' plan on December 31 of the prior year was $180 million, and the fair value of assets in the fund was $207 million.

AD&J23-9
Analyzing Pension
Expense; Assumed
Rate of Salary Increase
LO2

Early in the current year, Joleen Stave, CFO of Rogers Inc., received a report from the actuaries of Rogers' pension plan that recommended an increase in the assumed rate of increase in future salaries among other things. An annual rate of 3% per year had been used for several years; according to the actuaries' experience during the last five years, a period of relatively low inflation, average salaries increased considerably more than that. Actuaries recommended a 6% rate that would increase Rogers' year-end projected benefit obligation by 40%. The actuaries also sent a copy of the report to Aaron Rogers, CEO of Rogers Inc.

Several days after receiving the report, Joleen and Aaron were having lunch when the subject of the report came up. Rogers began by saying that initially he feared that a 40% increase in the pension obligation would wipe out prior year profits, but after discussing the prior year astronomical rise in the stock market with his broker, he began to think that since Rogers Inc.'s pension fund is heavily invested in equities, the effect of the increase in the salary increase rate might be offset to some extent by the large increase in return on plan assets last year. His broker had mentioned to him that the bull market last year caused his company's plan to go from underfunded to overfunded.

Rogers then asked Joleen what she thought a revision of the salary increase rate would do to prior year profits, but before she had a chance to respond, they were interrupted and did not have a chance to get back to the subject.

Later that day Joleen received an email from Rogers asking for a memo explaining what the proposed revision in the salary increase rate would do to profits. Joleen will be out of town for several days so she has asked you, her assistant, to draft an email to Rogers.

Required

Prepare a draft of the requested email.

AD&J23-10
Calculating Funding
Payment, Multiple
Employees   **LO1**

Challenge Problem Plans are being made to fund the prospective pension benefits of a group of employees of Forever 31 Inc. due to retire in nine years and to be paid in these amounts from one to five years after retirement.

End of Year 1	$ 90,000
End of Year 2	50,000
End of Year 3	30,000
End of Year 4	15,000
End of Year 5	5,000
Thereafter...	0
Total of pension payments	$190,000

Funds deposited with the pension fund trustee will earn 6% per year. The pension plan contract calls for the deposit of an amount sufficient to fund all of the expected payments from the fund by the date the employees retire.

Required

a.   Compute the amount required by the trustee on the employees' retirement date, assuming that the first pension payment is one year after retirement. Prepare an amortization schedule showing principal and interest payments on the pension liability over the 5 years.

b.   Assuming that eight equal payments are made to the trustee, with the last payment coinciding with the retirement date, compute the amount of the equal payment.

AD&J23-11
Preparing Pension
Worksheet for Two
Years with Corridor
(Minimum) Amortization
LO5, 6, 7

Challenge Problem Voss Company has a noncontributory defined benefit pension plan for its employees. Comparative data available at year-end December 31 follow.

$ thousands	Prior Year	Current Year
Projected benefit obligation, beginning.	$1,520	?
Service cost	200	$238
Interest cost	152	140
Loss (gain), actuarial changes, Dec. 31	10	6
Average remaining service period*.............	10 years	9 years
Plan assets, balance at beginning	1,450	?
Actual return on plan assets...................	135	155
Funding of plan.............................	210	320
Pension benefits paid to retirees	(150)	(170)
Expected return on plan assets	10%	10%
Accumulated OCI—Prior Service Cost, Jan. 1....	100 Dr.	?
Accumulated OCI—Pension Gain/Loss, Jan. 1 ...	182 Dr.	?

*Assume this for all unrecognized pension costs.

Required

a.   Prepare a worksheet to summarize the pension data at the end of the prior year and current year. The company uses the corridor approach in amortizing any pension gain/loss.

b.   Provide the following disclosures for both years: (1) the amount of pension expense for each period with separate disclosure of service cost, interest cost, actual return on plan assets, and net total of other components and (2) the presentation of funded status.

AD&J23-12
Determining Change in
Principle, Estimation,
or Error Correction
LO6

Challenge Problem Pension plan disclosures provide useful information for investors and creditors that is not available in the financial statements.

Required

For each of the following separate scenarios, briefly explain how the event would be treated (as a change in principle, correction of an error, or a change in estimate).

a. Recognition of pension gains/losses in net income rather than including in accumulated other comprehensive income and amortizing according to the corridor approach.

b. The expected rate of return of plan assets drops from 6.75% to 6.70%.

c. Employee contributions to a contributory plan were not included in the PBO reconciliation in the prior year.

d. The discount rate used by the actuary changed by a full percentage point from one year to the next.

e. The company disclosed estimated gross benefit payments for the next five years and the aggregate amount for the next five years after that. The amount disclosed for the next year does not match exactly to the actual payment.

Challenge Problem   Mac Company has a noncontributory defined benefit pension plan. On December 31, the following data (all presented before tax) are available.

> **AD&J23-13**
> Assessing the Tax
> Effect of Pension
> Entries   **LO5**

PBO balance, Jan. 1	$45,000
Plan Asset balance, Jan. 1	52,500
Actuarial loss on PBO determined Dec. 31	5,000
Prior service cost (10-year average service life)	5,000
Service cost	32,500
Interest cost	4,000
Pension benefits paid	3,500
Actual return on plan assets (same as expected return)	2,500
Cash funding	35,500
Tax rate	25%

Required

Prepare entries to record (1) pension expense, (2) amortization of prior service cost, (3) gain or loss deferral (if any), (4) contributions, and (5) benefits for the year. Include the income tax effect in your entries. Assume that the pension is considered overfunded for tax purposes. Tax assets and/or liabilities will need to be established for the timing differences between book and tax. *Hint*: Record items in other comprehensive income net of tax.

Codification Skills   How are the terms (1) attribution, (2) projected benefit obligation, (3) accumulated benefit obligation, (4) net periodic pension cost, (5) defined contribution plan, and (6) defined benefit plan defined in the Codification?

> **AD&J23-14**
> Defining Terms   **LO1**

Codification Skills   Through research in the Codification, identify the specific citation for each of the following items included as guidance in this chapter for pension accounting.

> **AD&J23-15**
> Performing Accounting
> Research   **LO4, 5,**
> **6, 8**
>

a. Amortizing of gains/losses using the corridor approach   FASB ASC ☐ - ☐ - ☐ - ☐

b. Whether or not to combine the funded status of separate   FASB ASC ☐ - ☐ - ☐ - ☐
defined benefit plans

c. Components of net periodic pension cost   FASB ASC ☐ - ☐ - ☐ - ☐

d. Disclosure of the accumulated benefit obligation for   FASB ASC ☐ - ☐ - ☐ - ☐
public companies

e. Attribution in postretirement benefit plan accounting   FASB ASC ☐ - ☐ - ☐

Codification Skills   A settlement is a transaction that is an irrevocable action, relieves the employer (or the plan) of primary responsibility for a pension or postretirement benefit obligation, and eliminates significant risks related to the obligation and the assets used to effect the settlement. How is a settlement recognized in the financial statements? Through research in the Codification, identify the specific citation where guidance is included.

> **AD&J23-16**
> Performing Accounting
> Research   **LO1**
>

FASB ASC ☐ - ☐ - ☐ - ☐

Appendices—Brief Exercises

Explain the difference between expected postretirement benefit obligation (EPBO) and accumulated postretirement benefit obligation (APBO) in accounting for postretirement benefits other than pensions.

> **AppBE23-1**
> Explaining Terms   **LO8**
> *Hint: See Demo 23-8*

AppBE23-2
Determining Attribution
Period **LO8**
Hint: See Demo 23-8

A postretirement plan promises 100% health care coverage for all employees who retire after age 62. It is expected that participants will have rendered an average of 15 years of service at age 62.

a. What is the full eligibility date for a participant?
b. What is the attribution period (the period the expected postretirement benefit obligation is assigned)?

AppBE23-3
Calculating
APBO **LO8**
Hint: See Demo 23-8

At December 31, Atlanta Inc. estimated the present value of postretirement health benefits of $75,000 for an employee. The employee is 50 years old and has been working for Atlanta Inc. for 8 years and is expected to retire at age 65. To be fully eligible, the employee must work for Atlanta Inc. for 15 years and remain at the company until age 55. Calculate the accumulated postretirement benefit obligation at December 31 for this employee.

AppBE23-4
Reporting of
Postretirement Benefit
Plans **LO9**

The following information is for a postretirement benefit plan where the average remaining service period for active plan participants is 15 years. What amount is recognized on the balance sheet and how it is classified?

Accumulated Postretirement Benefit Obligation	Plan Assets at Fair Value	Net Postretirement Asset/Liability
$100,000	$200,000	$100,000

AppBE23-5
Computing
Postretirement Benefit
Expense **LO9**
Hint: See Demo 23-9

Targets Corp. sponsored a postretirement benefit plan for health care. The following information relates to this plan. Compute postretirement benefit expense for the year assuming an expected (and actual) return on plan assets of 10%.

Activity for the Year		Account Balances	January 1
Service cost	$30,000	Plan Assets	$ 15,000
Contributions to the plan	75,000	APBO	228,000
Benefits paid to retirees	45,000		
Amortization of prior service cost	6,000		
Interest cost	25,920		

AppBE23-6
Recording Entries for
Postretirement Benefit
Plans **LO9**
Hint: See Demo 23-9

Refer to information in Brief Exercise 23-93. Record the entry for (1) postretirement benefit expense, (2) funding, and (3) benefit payments during the year.

AppBE23-7
Determining APBO
Balance **LO9**
Hint: See Demo 23-9

Refer to information in Brief Exercise 23-93. Calculate the APBO balance as of December 31.

AppBE23-8
Amortizing Prior
Service Costs **LO10**
Hint: See Demo 23-10

On January 1 of Year 1, Allied Co. amended its postretirement benefit plan to grant retroactive benefits for services already performed in prior years. The present value of the benefits on January 1 of Year 1 is $50,000 and it relates to two employees with the following expected years of service: Jeff, 2 years, and Erica, 4 years. Determine the amortization to be recognized in Year 1 by allocating an equivalent amount of prior service cost to each service year.

Appendices—Exercises

AppE23-1
Calculating EPBO and
APBO **LO8**
Hint: See Demo 23-8

A plan provides life insurance benefits to employees who serve 20 years, at which time the employees become fully eligible. The benefit equals $50,000. On December 31, a 45-year-old employee has worked 15 years for the company. He is expected to retire at age 65. The discount rate is 7%.

Required

a. What is the expected postretirement benefit obligation on December 31?
b. What is the accumulated postretirement benefit obligation on December 31?

The following information pertains to YNCA Inc. for the current year.

APBO: Jan. 1	$100,000
Plan Assets: Jan. 1	$75,000
Actual (and expected) return on plan assets	$7,500
Discount rate	12%
Service cost	$25,000
Contribution to asset fund, Dec. 31	$35,000
Benefit payments, Dec. 31	$10,000

AppE23-2
Recording
Postretirement
Benefit Expense and
Determining Funded
Status **LO9**
Hint: See Demo 23-9

Required

a. Provide the entry to record postretirement benefit expense.

b. Prepare a presentation of funded status on December 31.

The December 31, Year 1, presentation of funded status and accrued postretirement benefit cost for Audee Inc. with a postretirement benefit plan, along with activity for Year 2, follow.

AppE23-3
Recording
Postretirement
Benefit Expense and
Determining Funded
Status **LO9**
Hint: See Demo 23-9

Balance	Dec. 31, Year 1	Activity	Year 2
APBO	$(224,000)	Service cost	$50,000
Plan Assets	203,000	Actual return on plan assets	20,000
Underfunded APBO (funded status)	$ (21,000)	Contributions (end of year)	75,000
		Benefit payments (end of year)	85,000

At the beginning of Year 2, the plan was amended to increase future health-care benefits for retirees. The increase is attributable to service performed before Year 2. As a result, the APBO increased $56,000. The discount rate is 12%, and the expected rate of return on plan assets is 10%. The average remaining years of service to full eligibility for active plan participants is 15 years.

Required

a. Provide the entry to record Year 2 postretirement benefit expense.

b. Provide a presentation of funded status at December 31 of Year 2.

Information for the Krysler Company postretirement healthcare plan follows for the current year.

AppE23-4
Calculating
Postretirement
Benefit—Gain/Loss and
Postretirement Benefit
Expense **LO9**

APBO, Jan. 1	$300,000	Discount rate	8%
Plan Assets, Jan, 1	100,000	Expected rate of return on plan assets	7%
Accumulated OCI—Postretirement		Average service period	10 years
Benefit Gain/Loss, Jan. 1	80,000*		
Actual return on plan assets	6,000		
Service cost	60,000		

* Amount represents an accumulated loss.

Required

a. Calculate the amount of amortization related to Accumulated OCI—Postretirement Benefit Gain/Loss (if any) for the year. Krysler uses the corridor approach for amortization of postretirement gains and losses.

b. Compute postretirement benefit expense for the year.

On January 1 of Year 1, Oracle Company amended its postretirement benefit plan by granting retroactive pension benefits for work performed before that date. The present value of those benefits was determined to be $100,000 at that date. The following employees expect to receive benefits under the plan, and they have the indicated expected number of years remaining in their careers at January 1 of Year 1: Jake: three years, and Julia: five years.

AppE23-5
Allocating Prior Service
Cost **LO10**
Hint: See Demo 23-10

Required

Determine the amortization of prior service cost to be recognized in Year 5 under the following methods.

a. The method that associates an equivalent amount of prior service cost to each service year.

b. Straight-line method based on the average remaining service period of employees.

Appendices—Problems

AppP23-1
Calculating EPBO and
APBO   **LO8**

At December 31 of Year 1, Gyro Inc. estimated the following net incurred claims costs for one of its employees for each year of the employee's postretirement period to which the plan applies.

At Age	Estimated Net Incurred Claims Cost by Age
64	$4,194
65	4,640
66	1,284
67	1,421
68	1,577

The postretirement plan provides no benefits after age 68. For full eligibility, an employee must serve 20 years. The employee in question is 51 years old at December 31 of Year 1, and has served 15 years at that date. The employee is expected to retire at age 63. The discount rate for postretirement benefit accounting purposes is 8%.

Required

a. Determine the expected postretirement benefit obligation and accumulated postretirement benefit obligation at December 31 of Year 1, for this employee.

b. Assuming that the employee works another five years after December 31 of Year 1, and that there are no changes in expected net incurred claims costs, determine the expected postretirement benefit obligation and accumulated postretirement benefit obligation at December 31 of Year 6, for this employee.

AppP23-2
Differences in
Accounting for Pensions
vs. Nonpension
Postretirement
Benefits   **LO8**

Accounting for pensions is similar to accounting for nonpension postretirement benefits in many ways. However, there are some significant differences.

Required

Prepare a list of the differences and discuss some of these differences and their financial statement effects.

AppP23-3
Recording
Postretirement Benefit
Expense, Funded
Status, Preparing
Worksheet   **LO9**

The January 1 unadjusted balances for CTS Inc. with a postretirement benefit plan follow.

Account Balances	January 1
APBO	$450,000 Cr.
Plan Assets.	425,000 Dr.
Accumulated OCI—Prior Service Cost.	48,000 Dr.
Accumulated OCI—Benefit Gain/Loss	62,000 Dr.

Additional information

- Expected return on plan assets: 10%
- Discount rate: 8%
- Remaining years to amortize prior service cost: 8
- Average remaining service period: 10
- CTS Inc. recognizes the minimum amortization of gains and losses using the corridor approach.
- Service cost: $80,000
- Actual return on plan assets: $40,000
- APBO increased $100,000 on Dec. 31, due to an increase in health-care cost trend rates.
- Contributions to fund, Dec. 31: $100,000
- Benefit payments, Dec. 31: $80,000

Required

a. Prepare a worksheet to summarize the postretirement benefit data at the end of the year. The company uses the corridor approach in amortizing any benefit gain/loss.

b. Record the entry for (1) postretirement benefit expense, (2) deferral(s) of any gain or loss, (3) funding, and (4) benefit payments during the year.

AppP23-4
Allocating Prior Service
Cost   **LO10**

Pepsee Inc. amended its postretirement plan on January 1 of Year 1, by increasing health-care benefits attributable to services rendered by employees before the amendment date. The accumulated postretirement benefit obligation increased $90,000 (prior service cost). The three employees affected and their remaining years to full eligibility follow. The average remaining service period for all active plan participants is 10 years.

Remaining Years to Full Eligibility at Date of Amendment (January 1 of Year 1)					
Employee	Year 1	Year 2	Year 3	Year 4	Year 5
Miley..........................	1	1	1	1	1
Justin	1	1	—	—	—
Will	1	1	—	—	—
Total	3	3	1	1	1

Required

a. Determine amortization of prior service cost for each remaining year to full eligibility, using the service method.

b. Determine the amortization of prior service cost for each remaining year to full eligibility, using the straight-line method.

Answers to Review Exercises

Review 23-1

Annual pension benefit: (10 years worked × $200,000 final salary)/25	$ 80,000
PV of Ordinary Annuity: PV(0.06,15,−80000,0)	776,980
PBO: PV(0.06,15,0,−776980)	$324,207

Annual pension benefit: (10 years worked × $80,000 current salary)/25	$ 32,000
PV of Ordinary Annuity: PV(0.06,15,−32000,0)	310,792
ABO: PV(0.06,15,0,−310792)...	$129,683

Review 23-2

Measurement of PBO	
PBO, Jan. 1..	$375,000
Service cost	85,000
Interest cost	22,000
Actuarial loss on PBO...	2,800
Benefit payments	(46,000)
PBO, Dec. 31	$438,800

Review 23-3

Example One

Measurement of Plan Assets	
Plan assets, Jan. 1...	$300,000
Actual return on plan assets...	12,000
Employer contributions..	22,000
Benefit payments	(30,000)
Plan assets, Dec. 31...	$304,000

Example Two

Determination of Funded Status	
Projected benefit obligation	$480,000
Plan assets at fair value	466,000
Funded status, Dec. 31...	$ (14,000)

Review 23-4

Measurement of Net Pension Expense	
Service cost	$18,000
Interest cost ($75,000 × 0.06)	4,500
Expected return on plan assets	(4,000)
Amortization of prior service costs	1,000
Amortization of net loss (($12,900 − $8,100)/10)	480
Net pension expense	$19,980

Review 23-5

January 1—To record deferral of prior service cost

Assets	=	Liabilities	+	Equity
		+30,000		−30,000

PBO		OCI—PSC
	300,000 Bal.	30,000
	30,000	

OCI—Prior Service Cost	30,000	
Projected Benefit Obligation		30,000

December 31—To record pension expense

Assets	=	Liabilities	+	Equity
+15,000		+49,500		−38,000
				+500
				+3,000

Plan Assets		Pension Exp
Bal. 350,000		38,000
15,000		

PBO		OCI—PSC
	300,000 Bal.	30,000 | 3,000
	30,000	
	49,500	OCI—Pension G/L
		| 500

Pension Expense	38,000	
Plan Assets (expected gain)	15,000	
OCI—Pension Gain/Loss ($5,000/10)		500
Projected Benefit Obligation ($33,000 + (0.05 × $330,000)) . .		49,500
OCI—Prior Service Cost ($30,000/10)		3,000

December 31—To record deferral of unexpected gain on plan assets

Assets	=	Liabilities	+	Equity
+1,000				+1,000

Plan Assets		OCI—Pension G/L
Bal. 350,000		| 500
15,000		| 1,000
1,000		

Plan Assets ($16,000 − $15,000)	1,000	
OCI—Pension Gain/Loss.		1,000

December 31—To record funding of plan assets

Assets	=	Liabilities	+	Equity
+40,000				
−40,000				

Plan Assets		Cash
Bal. 350,000		| 40,000
15,000		
1,000		
40,000		

Plan Assets	40,000	
Cash		40,000

December 31—To record benefits paid to retirees

Assets	=	Liabilities	+	Equity
−22,000		−22,000		

Plan Assets		PBO
Bal. 350,000 | 22,000		22,000 | 300,000 Bal.
15,000		30,000
1,000		49,500
40,000		| 357,500
384,000		

Projected Benefit Obligation	22,000	
Plan Assets		22,000

Review 23-6

Income Statement	
Operating expenses	
Periodic pension cost, net.	$50,000
Nonoperating expenses	
Other components of periodic pension cost, net.	25,000

Statement of Comprehensive Income	
Other comprehensive income (loss)	
Unexpected gain on plan assets.	$ 8,500
Amortization of prior service cost	(2,500)

Balance Sheet at Year-End

Noncurrent assets	
Net pension asset ($350,000 − $310,000)	$ 40,000
Liabilities	
Stockholders' equity	
Accumulated other comprehensive income	
Net pension loss	(12,000)
Prior service cost.	(40,000)

Review 23-7

	Reported Net in Financial Statements		Reported on Balance Sheet				Reported in Comprehensive Income		
			Net Pension Asset/ Liability	Accumulated OCI		Cash Outflow	OCI		
	Plan Assets	PBO		Prior Service Cost	Pension Gain/Loss		Pension Expense	Prior Service Cost	Pension Gain/Loss
Balance, Jan. 1.	$200,000	$(223,000)	$(23,000)	$ 0	$30,000				
Prior service cost amendment		(15,000)	(15,000)	15,000				$15,000	
Service cost		(80,000)	(80,000)				$80,000		
Interest cost [0.08 × ($223,000 × $15,000)]		(19,040)	(19,040)				19,040		
Expected return on plan assets (0.07 × $200,000) . . .	14,000		14,000				(14,000)		
Unexpected loss on assets ($10,000 − $14,000)	(4,000)		(4,000)		4,000				$ 4,000
Actuarial loss on PBO.		(8,000)	(8,000)		8,000				8,000
Prior service cost amortization.				(1,500)			1,500	(1,500)	
Pension gain/loss amortization.					(620)		620		(620)
Contributions to fund	70,000		70,000			$(70,000)			
Retiree benefits paid.	(30,000)	30,000							
Balance, Dec. 31	$250,000	$(315,040)	$(65,040)	$13,500	$41,380		$87,160	$13,500	$11,380

1. Beginning balances for Plan Assets, PBO, Net Pension Asset/Liability and AOCI—Pension Gain/Loss.
2. Prior service cost amendment, $15,000 debit to Prior Service Cost in both the AOCI and OCI columns and credit to Projected Benefit Obligation.
3. Service cost, $80,000 (given) and interest cost, $19,040 (0.08 × $238,000 ($223,000 + $15,000)) credit to Projected Benefit Obligation and a debit to Pension Expense. *Interest cost is calculated based upon the adjusted PBO balance as of January 1.*
4. Expected return on plan assets, $14,000 (0.07 × $200,000) debit to Plan Assets and credit to Pension Expense.
5. Unexpected loss, $4,000 ($10,000 − $14,000) debit to Pension Gain/Loss in both the AOCI and OCI columns and credit to Plan Assets.
6. Actuarial loss on the PBO, $8,000 debit to Pension Gain/Loss in both the AOCI and OCI columns and credit to Projected Benefit Obligation.
7. Prior service cost amortization, $1,500 ($15,000/10 years) debit to Pension Expense and credit to Prior Service Cost in both the AOCI and OCI columns.
8. Amortization of pension loss, $620, debit to Pension Expense and credit to Pension Gain/Loss in both the AOCI and OCI columns. (Amortization equals beginning of year AOCI—Pension Gain/Loss of $30,000 less the corridor of $23,800, divided by service years of 10. Corridor is 10% of the greater of *the adjusted beginning of year PBO* or Plan Assets [$238,000 × 10%].)
9. Contributions, $70,000 debit to Plan Assets and credit to Cash.
10. Benefits, $30,000 debit to Projected Benefit Obligation and credit to Plan Assets.

January 1—To record prior service cost amendment

OCI—Prior Service Cost.	15,000	
Projected Benefit Obligation		15,000

Assets = Liabilities + Equity
+15,000 −15,000

PBO	OCI—PSC
223,000 Bal.	15,000 ǀ
15,000	

December 31—To record pension expense

Pension Expense	87,160	
Plan Assets.	14,000	
Projected Benefit Obligation		99,040
OCI—Pension Gain/Loss.		620
OCI—Prior Service Cost		1,500

Assets = Liabilities + Equity
+14,000 +99,040 −87,160
        +620
        +1,500

Plan Assets	Pension Exp
Bal. 200,000 ǀ	87,160 ǀ
14,000 ǀ	

	OCI—PSC
	15,000 ǀ 1,500

PBO	
223,000 Bal.	
15,000	
99,040	

	OCI—Pension G/L
	ǀ 620

December 31—To record deferral of unexpected loss on plan assets

OCI—Pension Gain/Loss.	4,000	
Plan Assets		4,000

December 31—To record deferral of actuarial loss on PBO

OCI—Pension Gain/Loss.	8,000	
Projected Benefit Obligation		8,000

December 31—To record funding of plan assets

Plan Assets.	70,000	
Cash		70,000

December 31—To record benefits paid

Projected Benefit Obligation	30,000	
Plan Assets.		30,000

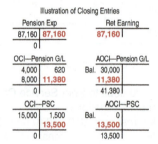

Review 23-8

a. 14 years

b.
Present value benefit stream	$55,201 (PV of annuity of $7,500, 10 years, 6%)
Present value on January 1, Year 5	$23,033 (PV of $55,201, 15 years, 6%)

c.
APBO ($23,033 × 4/14)	$ 6,581

Review 23-9

Measurement of Postretirement Benefit Expense	
Service cost	$320,000
Interest cost	15,000
Expected return on plan assets (0.06 × $125,000)	(7,500)
Amortization of prior service cost.	10,000
Total postretirement benefit expense	$337,500

Future Value of a Single Amount—Computation through Formula

Assume that we have a lump-sum amount of $10,000 to invest today for 3 years, earning 5% interest, compounded annually. What is the future value of this lump-sum amount at the end of 3 years? Today's (present value) amount increases to a future value amount from **compounding** of interest and is illustrated as follows.

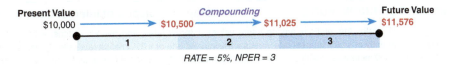

FYI: We use variable names similar to those used in Excel.

The future value of $10,000 after one year is $10,500, computed as $10,000 × 1.05. The future value of $10,000 after two years is $11,025, computed as $10,000 × 1.05 × 1.05. After the full three years, the future value is $11,576, computed as $10,000 × 1.05 × 1.05 × 1.05.

The formula for calculating this **accumulation** of interest is in **Exhibit 6-2**. This formula for the future value of a single amount calculates *FV* (future value) in terms of *PV* (present value), *RATE* (interest), and *NPER* (number of compounding periods).

$$FV = PV \times (1 + RATE)^{NPER}$$

We use this formula to solve for the future value of $10,000 on deposit for 3 periods at an interest rate of 5%; this yields a future value of $11,576.

$$FV = PV \times (1 + RATE)^{NPER} = \$10,000 \times (1 + 0.05)^3 = \$10,000 \times (1.15763^*) = \$11,576$$

EXHIBIT 6-2

Future Value of a Single Amount Formula

*To simplify this calculation, prepared tables (at the end of this chapter) can be used that include these factors. For example, the factor from the *Future Value of $1 Table* for 5% and 3 years is 1.15763. This factor of 1.15763 is multiplied by $10,000 to arrive at a future value of $11,576.30. Use of tables is explained further in Appendix 6B.

Future Value of a Single Amount—Computation through Excel

We obtain the same result using Excel because the formula to solve for future value is preset in the **future value function** in Excel. The inputs to the function are called **arguments** (commonly referred to as **variables**). After entering values in Excel for each argument, the function will return the future value. The arguments in Excel are defined as follows.

Excel Argument	Description
RATE	Market or effective rate of interest for each compounding period.
NPER	Number of compounding periods.
FV	Future value or the value at a future date that assumes an investment increased by interest accumulation.
PV	Present value or the value today of a future amount that is discounted to the present with interest discounting.

After selecting the future value (FV) function in Excel, enter the known arguments: interest rate (5%), number of periods (3), and present value (–$10,000). The **syntax** (or the layout of the function and its related arguments) of the future value function in Excel is =FV(RATE,NPER,PMT,PV). The FV function in Excel solves for the future value of $11,576 using the values of the arguments entered. When we enter a present value amount as a negative number (representing a *cash outflow*), Excel reports a future value amount as a positive number (representing a *cash inflow*). The opposite is also true—when entering a positive number for the present value (representing a *cash inflow*), Excel reports a negative number as the future value (representing a *cash outflow*). In **Demo 6-2**, we compute the future value of different amounts under different compounding scenarios.

	Excel Arguments				Excel Function
	RATE	NPER	PV	FV	=FV(RATE,NPER,PMT,PV)*
Given	5%	3	(10,000)	?	= FV(0.05,3,0,−10000)
Solution				$11,576.25	

*In the future value function, we enter zero for PMT because there are no periodic payments in this example—we discuss periodic payments in LO 6-4.

Future Value of a Single Amount—Change in Values of Arguments

The following table demonstrates how changing the values of the arguments affects the future value of $11,576.25 (from the previous example). In the first case, the interest rate is increased from 5% to 7%. Because interest is compounded at a higher rate of return, the future value increases to $12,250.43. In the second case, the number of periods that the investment earns interest increases from 3 periods to 5 periods. Additional compounding periods cause an increase in the future value to $12,762.82. In the last case, the initial investment increases to $15,000, resulting in an increase in the future value to $17,364.38.

	Excel Arguments				Excel Functions
	RATE	NPER	PV	FV	=FV(RATE,NPER,PMT,PV)
Original	5%	3	(10,000)	11,576.25	=FV(0.05,3,0,−10000)
Increase interest rate	7%	3	(10,000)	12,250.43	=FV(0.07,3,0,−10000)
Increase number of periods	5%	5	(10,000)	12,762.82	=FV(0.05,5,0,−10000)
Increase present value	5%	3	(15,000)	17,364.38	=FV(0.05,3,0,−15000)

EXPANDING YOUR KNOWLEDGE   Graphical Display of Interest Compounding

The following chart illustrates the relations among future values, interest rates, and periods of time. A $10,000 initial investment grows differently at a 10% interest rate versus a 5% interest rate or a 0% interest rate. After 10 years at a 10% interest rate, the $10,000 increases to $25,937, while at a 5% interest rate, the initial investment increases to $16,289. As you can see by looking at the trend lines, the future value grows at an increasing rate as the interest rate increases.

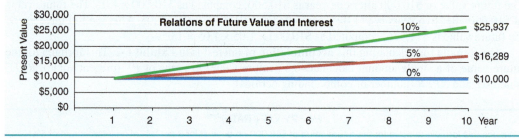

DEMO 6-2   **LO6-2**   **Future Value of a Single Amount**

Demo

MBC

For the separate investments *A* through *F*, complete the following table by indicating (1) the Excel function required to calculate the future value of the investment, and (2) the future value amount of the investment.

Investment	Compounding	Annual Interest Rate	Initial Cost	Investment Period	Excel Function	Future Value Amount
Investment A	Annually	6%	$ (5,000)	3 years	FV(0.06,3,0,−5000)	$ 5,955.08
Investment B	Annually	8%	(6,000)	5 years	FV(0.08,5,0,−6000)	8,815.97
Investment C	Semiannually	6%	(5,000)	4 years	FV(0.03,8,0,−5000)	6,333.85
Investment D	Semiannually	8%	(4,000)	6 years	FV(0.04,12,0,−4000)	6,404.13
Investment E	Quarterly	6%	(10,000)	5 years	FV(0.015,20,0,−10000)	13,468.55
Investment F	Quarterly	8%	(8,000)	4 years	FV(0.02,16,0,−8000)	10,982.29

REVIEW 6-2   **LO6-2**   **Future Value of a Single Amount**

Review

MBC

Laurel Inc. is considering a $5,000 investment with an expected annual return of 6%, compounded semiannually over 5 years. Compute the estimated future value of the investment with these terms. Next, compute the estimated future value of the investment assuming that the following arguments change while other arguments remain the same: (1) interest rate increases to 8%, (2) number of years increases to 10, (3) initial cost of the investment increases to $6,000, and (4) compounding is adjusted to quarterly. Consider each change separately.

continued

continued from previous page

Terms	Original Investment	Increase Interest Rate	Increase Periods	Increase Present Value	Increase Compounding
Annual interest rate ...	6%	8%	6%	6%	6%
Compounding........	Semiannual	Semiannual	Semiannual	Semiannual	Quarterly
Number of years......	5	5	10	5	5
Initial cost..........	$(5,000)	$(5,000)	$(5,000)	$(6,000)	$(5,000)
Future value........	$ a	$ b	$ c	$ d	$ e

More Practice:
BE6-2, E6-1, E6-2
Solution on p. 6-49.

Apply present value concepts to a single amount   LO 6-3

Present value refers to an amount earlier than the end-point of an investment. To determine the present value of a future amount, the future amount must be discounted to the present. **Discounting** is a mathematical process for reducing a future value to a present value. If the dollar amount at the end of an investment period (future value) is known, the amount of money needed at the start of the investment period (present value) can be determined, as long as the *interest rate* and *number of interest compounding periods* are known.

Present Value of Single Amounts
- Compute *current value* of a future single amount (discounting)
- Compute *current value* of a future estimated amount(s)
  - Discount Rate Adjustment Technique
  - Expected Cash Flow Technique

LO 6-3 Overview

Present Value of a Single Amount—Computation through Formula

Assume that we desire a future value of $11,576 in 3 years. If we assume an interest rate of 5% (compounded annually), what lump-sum amount must we invest today to have an accumulated future value of $11,576 in 3 years? The present value of this single amount is illustrated as follows.

We again illustrate this computation in two ways: through a formula and through Excel. The formula for the present value of a single amount is in **Exhibit 6-3**, where *PV* (present value) is defined in terms of *FV* (future value), *RATE* (interest), and *NPER* (number of compounding periods). This formula is derived by taking the future value of a single amount formula from **Exhibit 6-2** and dividing each side by $(1 + RATE)^{NPER}$. The present value of $11,576 discounted back one year is $11,025, computed as $11,576/1.05. The present value of $11,576 discounted back two years is $10,500, computed as $11,576/(1.05 × 1.05). Discounted the full three years, the present value of $11,576 is $10,000, computed as $11,576/(1.05 × 1.05 × 1.05).

$$PV = \frac{FV}{(1 + RATE)^{NPER}}$$

EXHIBIT 6-3

Present Value of a Single Amount Formula

We use this formula to solve for the present value of $11,576 for 3 periods at an interest rate of 5%; this yields a present value of $10,000.

$$PV = \frac{FV}{(1 + RATE)^{NPER}} = \frac{\$11,576}{(1 + 0.05)^3} = \$10,000$$

Present Value of a Single Amount—Computation through Excel

We obtain the same result using Excel. After choosing the present value (PV) function in Excel, we enter values for the arguments: interest rate (5%), number of periods (3), and future value ($11,576). The **syntax** of the present value function in Excel is =PV(RATE,NPER,PMT,FV). The function solves for the present value of $10,000 (rounded) using the values of the arguments entered.

	Excel Arguments				Excel Function
	RATE	NPER	PV	FV	=PV(RATE,NPER,PMT,FV)
Given	5%	3	?	11,576	=PV(0.05,3,0,11576)
Solution			$(9,999.78)		

Present Value of a Single Amount—Change in Values of Arguments

The following table demonstrates how changing the values of the arguments affects the present value of the investment from the previous example. In the first case, the interest rate is increased from 5% to 7%. Because interest is compounded at a higher rate of return, the present value required to return $11,576 decreases to $9,449.46. In the second case, the number of periods that the investment earns interest increases from 3 periods to 5 periods, which also results in a decrease in the investment required to return $11,576. In the third case, the desired future value increases to $12,000, which requires a higher upfront investment of $10,366.05.

| | Excel Arguments | | | | Excel Functions |
	RATE	NPER	FV	PV	=PV(RATE,NPER,PMT,FV)
Original	5%	3	11,576	(9,999.78)	=PV(0.05,3,0,11576)
Increase interest rate	7%	3	11,576	(9,449.46)	=PV(0.07,3,0,11576)
Increase number of periods	5%	5	11,576	(9,070.10)	=PV(0.05,5,0,11576)
Increase present value	5%	3	12,000	(10,366.05)	=PV(0.05,3,0,12000)

In **Demo 6-3A**, we compute the present value of different amounts under different compounding scenarios. In **Demo 6-3B**, we examine situations where a present value amount and a future value amount are known, and instead solve for the interest rate or the number of periods. In Excel, the syntax of the RATE function is =RATE(NPER,PMT,PV,FV) and the syntax of the NPER function is =NPER(RATE,PMT,PV,FV).

DEMO 6-3A ▶ **LO6-3**   **Present Value of a Single Amount**

For the following separate investments *A* through *F*, complete the table by indicating (1) the Excel function required to calculate the present value of the investment, and (2) the present value amount of the investment.

Investment	Compounding	Annual Interest Rate	Future Value	Investment Period	Excel Function	Present Value Amount
Investment A	Annually	6%	$ 8,000	3 years	PV(0.06,3,0,8000)	$ (6,716.95)
Investment B	Annually	8%	4,000	5 years	PV(0.08,5,0,4000)	(2,722.33)
Investment C	Semiannually	6%	15,000	4 years	PV(0.03,8,0,15000)	(11,841.14)
Investment D	Semiannually	8%	6,000	6 years	PV(0.04,12,0,6000)	(3,747.58)
Investment E	Quarterly	6%	5,000	5 years	PV(0.015,20,0,5000)	(3,712.35)
Investment F	Quarterly	8%	10,000	4 years	PV(0.02,16,0,10000)	(7,284.46)

DEMO 6-3B ▶ **LO6-3**   **Solving for Unknown Arguments**

Solve the following two separate questions.

a. Jacob invests $10,000 today and leaves it on deposit for three years to accumulate to a future amount of $11,576. What is the interest rate earned on this investment?

b. Josie invests $10,000 today earning 5% and wants to achieve a future amount of $11,576. How many periods must Josie invest $10,000 to accumulate to $11,576?

Solution

a. **Solving for Interest Rate**   The RATE function is illustrated as follows.

We choose the RATE function in Excel, and then enter the known variables of present value (–$10,000), future value ($11,576), and number of periods (3). The result of 5% is the interest rate that Jacob must earn on a $10,000 investment over 3 years to accumulate to $11,576. Because we are entering both an inflow and an outflow, we enter the cash outflow of $10,000 as a negative amount and the cash inflow of $11,576 as a positive amount. *Entering both values as either negative or positive will result in an error in Excel.*

| | Excel Arguments | | | | Excel Function |
	RATE	NPER	PV	FV	=RATE(NPER,PMT,PV,FV)
Given	?	3	(10,000)	11,576	= RATE(3,0,–10000,11576)
Solution	5%				

continued

continued from previous page

b. Solving for Number of Periods   The NPER function is illustrated as follows.

| Present Value | | | | Future Value |
| $10,000 | | | | $11,576 |

RATE = 5%, NPER = ?

We choose the NPER function in Excel, and then enter the known variables of present value (–$10,000), future value ($11,576), and interest rate (0.05). The result of 3 is the number of periods that Josie must invest $10,000 to return $11,576, assuming an interest rate of 5%. We again enter the cash outflow of $10,000 as a negative and the cash inflow of $11,576 as a positive amount.

| | Excel Arguments | | | | Excel Function |
	RATE	NPER	PV	FV	=NPER(RATE,PMT,PV,FV)
Given	5%	?	(10,000)	11,576	= NPER(0.05,0,–10000,11576)
Solution		3			

Fair Value Measurement—Discount Rate Adjustment Technique and Expected Cash Flow Technique

In Chapter 4, we introduced different approaches to determine fair value measurements. However, in applying these approaches, companies are able to choose a specific technique that fits the facts and circumstances of the situation. Two techniques outlined in the guidance are the (a) **discount rate adjustment technique** and (b) **expected cash flow technique** (also called *expected present value technique*).

820-10-55-4   Paragraphs 820-10-55-5 through 55-20 describe the use of present value techniques to measure fair value. Those paragraphs focus on a discount rate adjustment technique and an expected cash flow (expected present value) technique. Those paragraphs neither prescribe the use of a single specific present value technique nor limit the use of present value techniques to measure fair value to the techniques discussed. The present value technique used to measure fair value will depend on facts and circumstances specific to the asset or liability being measured (for example, whether prices for comparable assets or liabilities can be observed in the market) and the availability of sufficient data.

Discount Rate Adjustment Technique. The discount rate adjustment technique uses a single interest rate to discount future cash flows. The single interest rate reflects the risks associated with the cash flows.

820-10-55-12   When the discount rate adjustment technique is applied to fixed receipts or payments, the adjustment for risk inherent in the cash flows of the asset or liability being measured is included in the discount rate. In some applications of the discount rate adjustment technique to cash flows that are not fixed receipts or payments, an adjustment to the cash flows may be necessary to achieve comparability with the observed asset or liability from which the discount rate is derived.

Expected Cash Flow Technique. An alternative technique is the expected cash flow technique, illustrated in **Demo 6-3C**. This technique incorporates a range of potential cash flows and assigns probabilities to cash flow amounts within the range. In this way, the risk is applied directly to the cash flows, allowing accountants to recognize uncertainties in groups of cash flows. The expected cash flow technique may be appropriate for situations where payments are estimated and not contractual.

820-10-55-13 The expected present value technique uses as a starting point a set of cash flows that represents the probability-weighted average of all possible future cash flows (that is, the expected cash flows). The resulting estimate is identical to expected value, which, in statistical terms, is the weighted average of a discrete random variable's possible values with the respective probabilities as the weights. Because all possible cash flows are probability-weighted, the resulting expected cash flow is not conditional upon the occurrence of any specified event (unlike the cash flows used in the discount rate adjustment technique).

For example, a cash flow might be $100 (30% probability) or $400 (70%) probability. The expected cash flow is $310.

$100 × 30%	$ 30
$400 × 70%	280
Expected cash flow.	$310

These cash flows are discounted using the **risk-free rate of return**, which is the rate of return on an investment with zero risk, such as the return on a ten-year U.S. Treasury instrument.

820-10-55-9   b. Method 1 of the expected [cash flow] present value technique (see paragraph 820-10-55-15) uses risk-adjusted expected cash flows and a risk-free rate.

| DEMO 6-3C | LO6-3 | Fair Value Measurement—Expected Cash Flow Technique |

Demo
MBC

Briggs Inc. offers a two-year warranty on defects for all engines sold. Briggs uses the expected cash flow technique, discounting cash flows using a risk-free rate, to measure the fair value of its warranty obligation. In using this method, Briggs assigns the following probabilities to estimated cash flows over the two-year warranty period.

Year	Estimate of Cash Outflow	Probability	Expected Cash Flow
Year 1	$ 80,000	30%	$ 24,000
	95,000	40%	38,000
	105,000	30%	31,500
		100%	$ 93,500
Year 2	$ 95,000	20%	$ 19,000
	110,000	60%	66,000
	120,000	20%	24,000
		100%	$109,000

Assuming that cash flows occur at year-end, and the risk-free rate of return is 5%, calculate the fair value of the warranty obligation.

Solution

The present value of the warranty cash flows using the expected cash flow technique is $187,913.83 ($89,047.62 + $98,866.21).

Thus, the fair value of the warranty obligation is estimated to be $187,913.83.

	Excel Arguments				Excel Function
	RATE	NPER	PV	FV	=PV(RATE,NPER,PMT,FV)
Given	5%	1	?	(93,500)	=PV(0.05,1,0,−93500)
Solution			$89,047.62		

	Excel Arguments				Excel Function
	RATE	NPER	PV	FV	=PV(RATE,NPER,PMT,FV)
Given	5%	2	?	(109,000)	=PV(0.05,2,0,−109000)
Solution			$98,866.21		

| REVIEW 6-3 | LO6-3 | Present Value |

Review
MBC

Part One—Present Value of Single Amount   Laurel Inc. is considering an investment that will grow to $8,000 with an expected annual return of 6%, compounded semiannually over 5 years. Compute the amount that must be invested today (present value) under those assumptions. Next, compute the estimated present value assuming that the following variables change while other variables remain the same: (1) interest rate increases to 8%, (2) the number of years increases to 10, (3) the future value increases to $10,000, and (4) compounding is adjusted to quarterly. Consider each change separately.

Terms	Original Investment	Increase Interest Rate	Increase Periods	Increase Present Value	Increase Compounding
Annual interest rate ...	6%	8%	6%	6%	6%
Compounding........	Semiannual	Semiannual	Semiannual	Semiannual	Quarterly
Number of years......	5	5	10	5	5
Future value........	$8,000	$8,000	$8,000	$10,000	$8,000
Present value........	$(a)	$(b)	$(c)	$(d)	$(e)

Part Two—Solving for Unknown Argument   The following four investment cases are missing the value of one key argument. Solve for the unknown argument in each separate case. Assume interest is compounded annually.

continued

continued from previous page

	Investment 1	Investment 2	Investment 3	Investment 4
RATE ...	(a)%	6%	6%	5%
NPER ...	8	(b)	4	3
PV	$ (8,000)	$(7,734)	$ (c)	$(10,000)
FV	$12,000	$10,350	$3,900	$ (d)

Part Three—Expected Cash Flow Technique   Laurel Inc. is estimating legal costs related to an environmental remediation anticipated in 10 years. Due to uncertainties related to legal services required at that time, the company prepared the following estimates.

Legal Cash Outflow	Probability
$250,000	40%
200,000	30%
100,000	20%
50,000	10%

a. Compute the expected cash outflow for legal costs.

b. Assuming a 4% risk-free rate, determine the fair value measurement of the remediation liability using the expected cash flow technique.

More Practice:
E6-3, E6-5, E6-7

Solution on p. 6-49.

EXPANDING YOUR KNOWLEDGE   **Applications of Time Value of Money**

Where does time value of money apply to topics in this text? In Chapter 1, we introduced the *fair value hierarchy*, which requires fair value estimates to be classified as a Level 1, 2, or 3. A Level 3 estimate is based on unobservable inputs that reflect a company's assumptions. An example of a Level 3 estimate is where a company estimates the fair value of an asset or liability based on the *present value* of expected future cash flows. A preview of upcoming topics follows.

Topic	Chapter	Application
Notes receivable	Chapter 8	Noncurrent note receivables are recorded at the *present value* of cash flows discounted at the market rate.
Asset retirement obligations	Chapter 11	Obligations for asset retirements (such as dismantling, closure, and removal costs) are capitalized at the *present value* of those future costs.
Noncurrent fixed asset impairment	Chapter 12	When an asset's carrying amount is adjusted to fair value and when quoted market prices are unavailable, fair value is estimated by taking the *present value* of future net cash inflows using a rate reflecting the risk involved.
Intangible assets impairment	Chapter 13	Similar to noncurrent assets, in certain cases, fair value is estimated by taking the *present value* of future net cash inflows using a rate reflecting the risk involved.
Held-to-maturity debt securities	Chapter 14	Discounts (or premiums) on held-to-maturity debt securities are amortized over the debt term using the effective interest rate method and the *present value* function.
Noncurrent payables	Chapter 16	Noncurrent payables (notes, bonds) are recorded at the *present value* of cash flows discounted at the market rate.
Leases	Chapter 17	Measurement of lease liabilities and right-of-use (lease) assets requires the discounting of lease payments to *present value*.
Pensions	Chapter 23	Projected benefit obligation is the actuarial *present value* of benefits attributed to employee service rendered to date, as measured by the benefit formula using estimated future salary levels.

LO 6-4 Overview

LO 6-4 > Apply future value concepts to an ordinary annuity and an annuity due

Future Value of Annuities

Compute end-point value of a series of uniform payments

- Ordinary annuity: end of period payments
- Annuity due: beginning of period payments
- Deferred annuity: Delayed annuity payments

An **annuity** is a series of *uniform payments* (sometimes called rents) occurring at uniform intervals over a specified investment time frame. We determine the future value of an annuity using a *single interest rate*. The term *payments* is used because it includes annuity amounts that take the form of either cash payments into an annuity type of investment or cash withdrawals from an annuity type of investment. In cases where payments or withdrawals are uneven or unequal, each cash amount is considered a lump-sum amount and not an annuity.

There are two distinct types of annuities: an ordinary annuity and an annuity due. With an **ordinary annuity** (or an annuity in arrears), the payments (or receipts) occur at the **end** of each interest compounding period. With an **annuity due** (or an annuity in advance), payments (or receipts) occur at the **beginning** of each interest compounding period. Unless otherwise stated, all annuities are assumed to be ordinary annuities, meaning that each payment occurs at the end of each interest period.

The payment at the end of the first year earns interest for two years, accumulating to a future value of $5,618. The payment at the end of the second year accumulates interest for one year, so it has a future value of just $5,300. The third payment does not accumulate any interest because it is made at the end of the final period.

Future Value of an Ordinary Annuity—Computation through Formula

Assume that we make a payment of $5,000 on deposit at a financial institution at the **end** of each of the next 3 years, earning interest of 6%. What is the future value of this ordinary annuity of three $5,000 payments? The future value of this ordinary annuity is illustrated as follows.

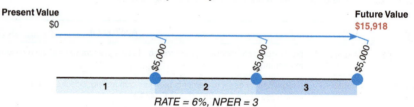

Present Value
$0

Future Value
$15,918

$5,000 $5,000 $5,000

1   2   3

RATE = 6%, NPER = 3

To compute the **future value of an ordinary annuity**, we use the formula to find the future value of each payment and sum them.

$$FV = PV \times (1 + RATE)^{(NPER - 1)} + PV \times (1 + RATE)^{(NPER - 2)} + PV \times (1 + RATE)^{(NPER - 3)}$$

Assuming an interest rate of 6% and that the $5,000 payments are made at the **end** of each period, the calculation follows.

$$FV = \$5,000 \times (1 + 0.06)^2 + \$5,000 \times (1 + 0.06)^1 + \$5,000 \times (1 + 0.06)^0 = \$15,918$$

$$= \qquad \$5,618 \qquad + \qquad \$5,300 \qquad + \qquad \$5,000 \qquad = \$15,918$$

The payment at the end of the first year earns interest for two years, accumulating to a future value of $5,618. The payment at the end of the second year accumulates interest for one year, so it has a future value of just $5,300. The third payment does not accumulate any interest because it is made at the end of the final period.

Future Value of an Ordinary Annuity—Computation through Excel

We obtain the same result with Excel using additional arguments.

Excel Argument	Description
PMT	Fixed payment per period.
TYPE	Enter *0* or leave blank: signifies that payments are made at the end of the period (ordinary annuity).
	Enter *1*: signifies that payments are made at the beginning of the period (annuity due).

After choosing the future value function (FV) in Excel, we enter the known arguments: interest rate (6%), number of periods (3), and annuity payment (–$5,000). The **syntax** of the future value function in Excel is =FV(RATE,NPER,PMT,PV,TYPE). We use the same future value function that we used for the lump sum calculation earlier, except now we include PMT (the annuity payment) and exclude PV (the lump sum), or enter as 0. The default in Excel is an ordinary annuity, so no entry is required for *TYPE*, although a zero may be entered. The result is $15,918, the future value of the ordinary annuity stream based on the values of the arguments entered. See also **Demo 6-4A**.

	Excel Arguments						Excel Function
	RATE	NPER	PMT	PV	FV	TYPE	=FV(RATE,NPER,PMT,PV,TYPE)
Given	6%	3	(5,000)	—	?	—	= FV(0.06,3,–5000,0,0)
Solution					$15,918.00		

Future Value of an Ordinary Annuity—Change in Values of Arguments

The following table demonstrates how a change in an argument affects the future value of the annuity stream from the previous example. In the first case, the interest rate is increased to 8% from 6%. Because interest is compounded at a higher rate of return, the future value of the $5,000 annuity payments increases to $16,232. In the second case, the number of periods that the investment earns interest increases from 3 periods to 5 periods, resulting in a future value of $28,185.46. In the third case, payments increase to $6,000, resulting in a higher future value of $19,101.60.

	RATE	NPER	PMT	FV	Excel Function
Original	6%	3	(5,000)	15,918.00	= FV(0.06,3,–5000)
Increase interest rate	8%	3	(5,000)	16,232.00	= FV(0.08,3,–5000)
Increase periods	6%	5	(5,000)	28,185.46	= FV(0.06,5,–5000)
Increase payment	6%	3	(6,000)	19,101.60	= FV(0.06,3,–6000)

Future Value of an Ordinary Annuity   LO6-4   DEMO 6-4A

Demo

MBC

For the following *end of period* annuities A through F, complete the table by indicating the (a) Excel function required to calculate the future value of the ordinary annuity, and (b) future value amount of the ordinary annuity.

Investment	Compounding	Annual Interest Rate	Payment	Investment Period	Excel Function	Future Value Amount
Annuity A	Annually	5%	$(15,000)	3 years	FV(0.05,3,–15000)	$47,287.50
Annuity B	Annually	7%	(10,000)	5 years	FV(0.07,5,–10000)	57,507.39
Annuity C	Semiannually	5%	(6,000)	4 years	FV(0.025,8,–6000)	52,416.70
Annuity D	Semiannually	7%	(2,500)	6 years	FV(0.035,12,–2500)	36,504.90
Annuity E	Quarterly	4%	(500)	5 years	FV(0.01,20,–500)	11,009.50
Annuity F	Quarterly	8%	(1,000)	4 years	FV(0.02,16,–1000)	18,639.29

Future Value of an Annuity Due—Computation through Formula

Assume now that we make a payment of $5,000 on deposit at the beginning of each of the next 3 years, earning interest of 6%. What is the future value of this annuity of three $5,000 payments, with the first payment due at the beginning of the first period (annuity due)? The future value of this annuity due is illustrated as follows.

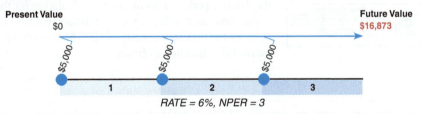

To compute the **future value of an annuity due**, we use the formula to find the future value of each payment and sum them.

$$FV = PV \times (1 + RATE)^{NPER} + PV \times (1 + RATE)^{(NPER-1)} + PV \times (1 + RATE)^{(NPER-2)}$$

Assuming an interest rate of 6% and that the payments are made at the **beginning** of each period, the calculation follows.

$$FV = \$5,000 \times (1 + 0.06)^3 + \$5,000 \times (1 + 0.06)^2 + \$5,000 \times (1 + 0.06)^1 = \$16,873$$
$$= \qquad \$5,955 \qquad + \qquad \$5,618 \qquad + \qquad \$5,300 \qquad = \$16,873$$

Because the payments are made at the beginning of each year, the future value of the annuity due of $16,873 is greater than the future value of an ordinary annuity of $15,918 in the example on the previous page.

Future Value of an Annuity Due—Computation through Excel

After choosing the future value function (FV) function in Excel, we enter the known arguments: interest rate (6%), number of periods (3), annuity payment (–$5,000), and type (1). By entering a value of *1* for type, the future value is calculated assuming beginning of period payments. The result is $16,873.08, the future value of the annuity due stream based on the arguments entered. See also **Demo 6-4B**.

	Excel Arguments						Excel Function
	RATE	NPER	PMT	PV	FV	TYPE	=FV(RATE,NPER,PMT,PV,TYPE)
Given	6%	3	(5,000)	—	?	1	= FV(0.06,3,–5000,0,1)
Solution					$16,873.08		

DEMO 6-4B	LO6-4	Future Value of an Annuity Due

Demo

MBC

For the following *beginning of period* annuities A through F, complete the table by indicating (1) the Excel function required to calculate the future value of the annuity, and (2) the future value amount of the annuity.

Investment	Compounding	Annual Interest Rate	Payment	Investment Period	Excel Function	Future Value Amount
Annuity A	Annually	5%	$(15,000)	3 years	FV(0.05,3,–15000,0,1)	$49,651.88
Annuity B	Annually	7%	(10,000)	5 years	FV(0.07,5,–10000,0,1)	61,532.91
Annuity C	Semiannually	5%	(6,000)	4 years	FV(0.025,8,–6000,0,1)	53,727.11
Annuity D	Semiannually	7%	(2,500)	6 years	FV(0.035,12,–2500,0,1)	37,782.58
Annuity E	Quarterly	4%	(500)	5 years	FV(0.01,20,–500,0,1)	11,119.60
Annuity F	Quarterly	8%	(1,000)	4 years	FV(0.02,16,–1000,0,1)	19,012.07

Future Value of a Deferred Annuity

A **deferred annuity** occurs when an annuity is delayed (see **Demo 6-4C**). This means that the payments do not begin until some future period.

For example, after two years, LA Bakery deposits $5,000 into an account at the end of each of the next 5 years at an interest rate of 7%. The future value of this ordinary annuity is illustrated as follows.

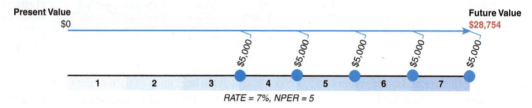

The initial period is ignored for this future value calculation because no investment took place during the deferral period. This means the calculation for the annuity is the same as it is for a 5-year ordinary annuity. The future value of the ordinary annuity is $28,754, calculated using the future value function in Excel.

	Excel Arguments						Excel Function
	RATE	NPER	PMT	PV	FV	TYPE	=FV(RATE,NPER,PMT,PV,TYPE)
Given	7%	5	(5,000)	—	?	—	= FV(0.07,5,–5000)
Solution					$28,753.70		

DEMO 6-4C	LO6-4	Future Value of a Deferred Annuity

Demo

MBC

After a 3-year deferral, Laurel Inc. deposits $8,000 at the *end* of each year for 10 years (which is years 4 through 13). The annuity is expected to earn interest of 6% annually.

a. What is the future value of the ordinary annuity?
b. What is the future value of the ordinary annuity if the first payment is deferred for three years?

Solution

a. The future value of the annuity at the end of the 13 years is calculated as follows.

   FV(0.06,10,–8000) = $105,446.36

b. If the first payment is deferred for three years, the future value of the annuity is still $105,446.36. Because no investment took place during the deferral period, the future value is equivalent to an investment that has no deferral.

Future Value of Annuities   LO6-4   REVIEW 6-4

For the following separate annuities A through F, complete the table by indicating the future value amount of the annuity stream.

Investment	Frequency of Payments	Annual Interest Rate	Payment	Payment Period in Years	Beg. or End of Period Payment	Deferral of Annuity Payment*	Future Value Amount
Annuity A	Annually	6%	$(1,250)	2 years	End	0 years	$_____
Annuity B	Semiannually	8%	(4,000)	3 years	End	0 years	_____
Annuity C	Semiannually	6%	(8,000)	4 years	End	0 years	_____
Annuity D	Annually	8%	(4,100)	6 years	Beginning	0 years	_____
Annuity E	Semiannually	6%	(800)	5 years	Beginning	2 years	_____
Annuity F	Semiannually	8%	(3,000)	4 years	Beginning	1 year	_____

Review   MBC

More Practice: E6-8, E6-9

Solution on p. 6-49.

*Deferral period falls before the payment period.

Apply present value concepts to an ordinary annuity and an annuity due   LO 6-5

A common business question is, "What's the current value (in today's dollars) of an annuity of future cash flows?" We measure this value using the present value of an annuity function, considering whether the uniform payments occur at the end of the period (ordinary annuity) or at the beginning of the period (annuity due).

Present Value of Annuities

Compute *current value* of a series of uniform payments
- Ordinary annuity: end of period payments
- Annuity due: beginning of period payments
- Deferred annuity: Delayed annuity payments

LO 6-5 Overview

Present Value of an Ordinary Annuity—Computation through Formula

Assume that we make a payment of $5,000 at the **end** of each of the next 3 years, earning interest of 6%. What is the present value of this ordinary annuity of three $5,000 payments, with the first payment due at the end of the first period (ordinary annuity)? The present value of this ordinary annuity is illustrated as follows.

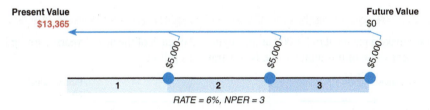

To compute the **present value of an ordinary annuity**, we use the formula to find the present value of each payment and then sum them.

$$PV = \frac{FV}{(1 + RATE)^{(NPER - 2)}} + \frac{FV}{(1 + RATE)^{(NPER - 1)}} + \frac{FV}{(1 + RATE)^{(NPER - 0)}}$$

Assuming an interest rate of 6% and that the $5,000 payments are made at the **end** of each period, the calculation follows.

$$PV = \frac{\$5,000}{(1 + 0.06)^1} + \frac{\$5,000}{(1 + 0.06)^2} + \frac{\$5,000}{(1 + 0.06)^3} = \$13,365$$

$$= \quad \$4,717 \quad + \quad \$4,450 \quad + \quad \$4,198 \quad = \$13,365$$

The first payment is discounted for one period, and so has a higher present value ($4,717) than the payment discount for two periods ($4,450) or the payment discounted for three periods ($4,198).

Present Value of an Ordinary Annuity—Computation through Excel

After choosing the present value (PV) function in Excel, we enter the arguments: interest rate (6%), number of periods (3), and annuity payment (–$5,000). The **syntax** of the present value function is =PV(RATE,NPER,PMT,FV,TYPE). No entry is required for TYPE because the default in Excel is for an *ordinary* annuity. The result is $13,365.06, the present value of the annuity based on the variables entered. This result means that if $13,365.06 was invested today at 6%, it would produce a pay-

	Excel Arguments						Excel Function
	RATE	NPER	PMT	PV	FV	TYPE	=PV(RATE,NPER,PMT,FV,TYPE)
Given	6%	3	(5,000)	?	—	—	=PV(0.06,3,–5000)
Solution				$13,365.06			

ment of $5,000 at the end of each of three annual periods. After the 3 payments, the investment would have a $0 value. See also **Demo 6-5A**.

Present Value of an Ordinary Annuity—Change in Values of Arguments

The following table demonstrates how a change in an argument affects the present value of the annuity from the previous example. In the first case, the interest rate is increased to 8% from 6%. Because interest is compounded at a higher rate of return, the present value of the annuity decreases to $12,885.48. In the

	Excel Arguments				Excel Functions
	RATE	NPER	PMT	PV	=PV(RATE,NPER,PMT,FV,TYPE)
Original	6%	3	(5,000)	13,365.06	=PV(0.06,3,–5000)
Increase interest rate	8%	3	(5,000)	12,885.48	=PV(0.08,3,–5000)
Increase periods	6%	5	(5,000)	21,061.82	=PV(0.06,5,–5000)
Increase payment	6%	3	(6,000)	16,038.07	=PV(0.06,3,–6000)

second case, the number of periods that the investment earns interest increases from 3 periods to 5 periods, resulting in an increase in the present value to $21,061.82. In the last case, the payment increases to $6,000, which increases the present value of this annuity to $16,038.07.

DEMO 6-5A   **LO6-5**   **Present Value of an Ordinary Annuity**

Demo

MBC

For the following *end of period* annuities A through D, complete the table by indicating (1) the Excel function required to calculate the present value of the ordinary annuity, and (2) the present value amount of the ordinary annuity.

Investment	Frequency of Payments	Annual Interest Rate	Payment	Number of Years	Excel Function	Present Value Amount
Annuity A	Annually	5%	$(15,000)	3 years	PV(0.05,3,–15000)	$40,848.72
Annuity B	Annually	7%	(10,000)	6 years	PV(0.07,6,–10000)	47,665.40
Annuity C	Semiannually	5%	(6,000)	4 years	PV(0.025,8,–6000)	43,020.82
Annuity D	Semiannually	7%	(2,500)	6 years	PV(0.035,12,–2500)	24,158.34

Present Value of an Annuity Due—Computation through Formula

Assume that we make a payment of $5,000 at the beginning of each of the next 3 years, earning interest of 6%. The present value of this annuity due is illustrated as follows.

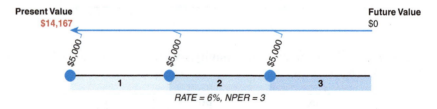

To compute the **present value of an annuity due**, use the formula to find the present value of each payment and sum them.

$$PV = \frac{FV}{(1 + RATE)^{(NPER - 3)}} + \frac{FV}{(1 + RATE)^{(NPER - 2)}} + \frac{FV}{(1 + RATE)^{(NPER - 1)}}$$

Assuming an interest rate of 6% and that the payments are made at the **beginning** of each period, the calculation follows.

$$PV = \frac{\$5,000}{(1 + 0.06)^0} + \frac{\$5,000}{(1 + 0.06)^1} + \frac{\$5,000}{(1 + 0.06)^2} = \$14,167$$

Present Value of an Annuity Due—Computation through Excel

After choosing the present value (PV) function in Excel, we enter the arguments: interest rate (6%), number of periods (3), annuity payment (–$5,000), and type (1). The result is $14,166.96, the present value of the annuity based on the arguments entered. See also **Demo 6-5B**.

	Excel Arguments						Excel Function
	RATE	NPER	PMT	PV	FV	TYPE	=PV(RATE,NPER,PMT,FV,TYPE)
Given	6%	3	(5,000)	?	—	1	=PV(0.06,3,–5000,0,1)
Solution				$14,166.96			

Present Value of an Annuity Due   **LO6-5**   **DEMO 6-5B**

Demo

MBC

For the following *beginning of period* annuities A through D, complete the table by indicating (1) the Excel function required to calculate the present value of the annuity due, and (2) the present value amount of the annuity due.

Investment	Frequency of Payments	Annual Interest Rate	Payment	Number of Years	Excel Function	Present Value Amount
Annuity A	Annually	5%	$(15,000)	3 years	PV(0.05,3,–15000,0,1)	$42,891.16
Annuity B	Annually	7%	(10,000)	6 years	PV(0.07,6,–10000,0,1)	51,001.97
Annuity C	Semiannually	5%	(6,000)	4 years	PV(0.025,8,–6000,0,1)	44,096.34
Annuity D	Semiannually	7%	(2,500)	6 years	PV(0.035,12,–2500,0,1)	25,003.88

Present Value of a Deferred Annuity

A deferred annuity occurs when an annuity is delayed—see **Demo 6-5C**. When computing the present value of a deferred annuity, interest is recognized during the deferral period.

For example, after two years of deferred rent, Leasing Inc. receives rental income of $20,000 a year for 8 years, beginning at the end of year 3. Given an interest rate of 6%, what is the present value of the annuity? The present value of this annuity is illustrated as follows.

The first step is to measure the present value of the ordinary annuity of $20,000 for 8 years. This present value is $124,196. The next step is to measure the present value of the lump-sum amount of $124,196 discounted at 6% for two years. This final present value is $110,534. This means that the present value of 8 rental payments of $20,000 beginning at the end of year 3 is $110,534.

	Excel Arguments						Excel Function
	RATE	NPER	PMT	PV	FV	TYPE	=PV(RATE,NPER,PMT,FV,TYPE)
Given	6%	8	(20,000)	?	—	—	=PV(0.06,8,–20000)
Solution				$124,196			

	Excel Arguments						Excel Function
	RATE	NPER	PMT	PV	FV	TYPE	=PV(RATE,NPER,PMT,FV,TYPE)
Given	6%	2	—	?	(124,196)	—	=PV(0.06,2,0,–124,196)
Solution				$110,534			

Present Value of a Deferred Annuity   **LO6-5**   **DEMO 6-5C**

Demo

MBC

Johnson received a defined retirement benefit, which will commence in 10 years. At that time, Johnson receives monthly cash payments of $2,000 for 15 years, with the first payment scheduled for the end of the initial month of benefit. Assuming an interest rate of 6%, what is the value of the annuity today? Assume annual compounding during the deferral period.

Solution

The present value of the ordinary annuity of $2,000 per month for 15 years (or 180 months), discounted at 6% (or 0.005 per month), is calculated as follows.

     PV(0.005,180,–2000) = $237,007.03

The final step is to calculate the present value of the lump sum of $237,007.03 in 10 years.

     PV(0.06,10,0,–237007.03) = $132,343.49

REVIEW 6-5   LO6-5   Present Value of Annuities

Review

MBC

For the following separate annuities *A* through *F*, complete the table by indicating the present value amount of the annuity.

Investment	Frequency of Payments	Annual Interest Rate	Payment	Payment Period in Years	Beg. or End of Period Payment	Deferral of Annuity Payment*	Present Value Amount
Annuity A	Annually	6%	$(1,250)	2 years	End	0 years	$_____
Annuity B	Semiannually	8%	(4,000)	3 years	End	0 years	_____
Annuity C	Semiannually	6%	(8,000)	4 years	End	2 years**	_____
Annuity D	Annually	8%	(4,100)	6 years	Beginning	0 years	_____
Annuity E	Semiannually	6%	(800)	5 years	Beginning	0 years	_____
Annuity F	Semiannually	8%	(3,000)	4 years	Beginning	1 year**	_____

More Practice:
E6-10, E6-11, E6-18

Solution on p. 6-49.

*Deferral period falls before the payment period.

**Assume semiannual compounding during the deferral period.

LO 6-6 Apply time value of money concept to common accounting scenarios

Applications of Time Value of Money
- Issuance of bonds
- Lease payments
- Pension obligations
- Capital investment decisions
- Debt retirement

LO 6-6 Overview

The time value of money concept has many applications in accounting for monetary assets and liabilities, both in recording entries and in disclosures accompanying financial statements. Monetary assets and liabilities are defined in the accounting guidance as follows:

ASC Glossary Monetary Assets: Money or a claim to receive a sum of money the amount of which is fixed or determinable without reference to future prices of specific goods or services.

ASC Glossary Monetary Liability: An obligation to pay a sum of money the amount of which is fixed or determinable without reference to future prices of specific goods and services.

In this section, we review monetary items related to bonds, notes, leases, and pensions. See also **Demo 6-6**.

Bond Issuance Price

A **bond** is a debt security issued by companies and governmental units to secure large amounts of capital on a long-term basis. In return for capital, the issuing company formally agrees to pay periodic cash interest based upon a stated interest rate during the bond term and to return the principal (face value or maturity value) at the end of the bond term.

While cash interest payments are based on the stated interest rate, the **market or effective rate** is used to discount the bond's cash interest payments and principal to the bond's issuance price. The market rate of a bond varies with the bond's risk, driven by economic, industry, and company conditions. The bond's issuance price is equal to the present value of the periodic cash interest payments (annuity) plus the present value of the return of principal (lump-sum amount).

Issuance of Bonds—Annual Interest

Assume that Wings Inc. issued $100,000 of 10-year 8% bonds on January 1 with cash interest payable annually on December 31. The market rate for bonds of similar risk is 9%. To determine the issuance price of the bonds, we calculate the present value of the cash interest payments of $8,000 per year (8% × $100,000) and the maturity value ($100,000) using a 9% discount rate, which results in an issuance price for the bonds of $93,582.34. We see how the present value of the principal lump sum amount and the present value of the cash interest payments are computed in one function in Excel.

	Excel Arguments						Excel Function
	RATE	NPER	PMT	PV	FV	TYPE	=PV(RATE,NPER,PMT,FV,TYPE)
Given	9%	10	(8,000)	?	(100,000)	—	=PV(0.09,10,–8000, –100000)
Solution				$93,582.34			

In this example, the bonds are issued at a **discount**—meaning the issuance price ($93,582.34) is less than the face value ($100,000). A discount exists when the market rate used to discount the cash outflows (9%) is greater than the stated interest rate (8%). If the market rate was less than the stated rate, the bonds would be issued at a **premium**—meaning an amount greater than the face value.

Issuance of Bonds—Semiannual Interest

Assume instead that $100,000 of 10-year, 8% bonds are issued on January 1 with cash interest payable semiannually on July 1 and January 1. The market rate for bonds of similar risk is 9%. Because the bonds pay cash interest semiannually, the interest rate and periods must be adjusted to reflect semiannual compounding as follows.

- Semiannual market rate: $9\% \div 2 = 4.5\%$
- Semiannual periods: 10 years $\times$ 2 = 20 periods
- Semiannual cash interest payment: $8\% \times \$100,000 \div 2 = \$4,000$

The issuance price of $93,496.03 for these bonds is computed by discounting the semiannual cash interest payments and principal to the present. Again, see how the present value of the principal lump sum amount

	Excel Arguments						Excel Function
	RATE	NPER	PMT	PV	FV	TYPE	=PV(RATE,NPER,PMT,FV,TYPE)
Given	4.5%	20	(4,000)	?	(100,000)	—	=PV(0.045,20,–4000, –100000)
Solution				$93,496.03			

and the present value of the cash interest payments are computed in one function in Excel. For further discussion on bonds, see Appendix 6A.

Lease Payment

Time value of money concepts are used in determining the lease payment that the **lessor** (owner of the asset) charges to the **lessee** (entity who is leasing the asset). Assume that Leasing Inc. leases equipment to Wings Inc. over a 5-year period, with payments due annually starting immediately on January 1. The equipment has a fair value of $50,000, a useful life of 5 years, and no salvage value. Leasing Inc. requires a rate of return on this lease of 12%. We calculate the lease payment of $12,384.36 using the PMT function in Excel. Because the payments are due at the beginning of each year, we enter a value of 1 for type.

	Excel Arguments						Excel Function
	RATE	NPER	PMT	PV	FV	TYPE	=PMT(RATE,NPER,PV,FV,TYPE)
Given	12%	5	?	(50,000)	—	1	=PMT(0.12,5,–50000,0,1)
Solution			$12,384.36				

Pension Obligations

In a **defined benefit plan**, employers pay an amount to eligible employees during their retirement period, as specified by the pension agreement. The benefit is earned over the years of an employee's service to the company. In measuring the pension obligation, employers must estimate the eventual retirement payments to employees and discount the payments to the present.

Assume that Wings Inc. pays retirement benefits to one employee (Justin) who is estimated to retire in 10 years. According to the pension agreement, Justin's annual benefit payment is equal to 50% of his annual salary at the date of retirement, estimated to be $70,000. The benefit is

	Excel Arguments						Excel Function
	RATE	NPER	PMT	PV	FV	TYPE	=PV(RATE,NPER,PMT,FV,TYPE)
Given	6%	15	(35,000)	?	—	—	=PV(0.06,15,–35000)
Solution				$339,928.71			

to be paid at the end of each annual period of retirement, which is estimated to be 15 years. Assuming an interest rate of 6% and annual compounding, the present value of the deferred annuity of $35,000 (50% $\times$ $70,000) *at the start of the retirement benefit period* is equal to $339,929, using the present value function in Excel. Next, discounting the deferred annuity of $339,929 10 years to the current period is equal to a present value of $189,814.42.

	Excel Arguments			Excel Function
	RATE	NPER	PV	FV	=PV(RATE,NPER,PMT,FV)
Given	6%	10	?	(339,928.71)	=PV(0.06,10,0,339928.71)
Solution			$189,814.42		

Lease or Buy

Companies often face situations where they must choose between the purchase or lease of a noncurrent asset. Assume that Northern Airlines is negotiating to acquire four new planes. Three alternatives are available.

1. Purchase the aircraft for $35 million each, payment due immediately.
2. Purchase the aircraft by paying $20 million each year for 12 years, with the first payment due immediately.
3. Lease the aircraft for $21.5 million payable at the end of each year for 12 years.

The relevant market rate (the discount rate) for ventures of this type is 10%. Assuming that Northern has sufficient resources, which alternative is least expensive? Ignore tax considerations. To compare the three options, the present value of each is determined.

			Excel Arguments				Excel Function
	RATE	NPER	PMT	PV	FV	TYPE	=PV(RATE,NPER,PMT,FV,TYPE)
Given	10%	12	(20,000,000)	?	—	1	=PV(0.1,12,−20000000,0,1)
Solution				$149,901,220			

Option One   The present value is $35 million × 4 planes = $140 million.

			Excel Arguments				Excel Function
	RATE	NPER	PMT	PV	FV	TYPE	=PV(RATE,NPER,PMT,FV,TYPE)
Given	10%	12	(21,500,000)	?	—	—	=PV(0.1,12,−21500000)
Solution				$146,494,374			

Option Two   The present value of an annuity of $20 million for 12 years with the first payment due immediately is $149.9 million.

Option Three   The present value of an annuity of $21.5 million for 12 years with the first payment due at the end of the year is $146.5 million.

Based on an interest rate of 10%, the least expensive option is option one.

Debt Retirement

Similar to lease payments, loan payments are calculated using the time value of money concept. Assume that on January 1, Wings Inc. signed a note payable for $75,000. The debt is to be paid off in 10

			Excel Arguments				Excel Function
	RATE	NPER	PMT	PV	FV	TYPE	=PMT(RATE,NPER,PV,FV,TYPE)
Given	10%	10	?	75,000	—	—	=PMT(0.1,10,75000)
Solution			$(12,205.90)				

years with annual payments due on December 31. The note accrues interest at a rate of 10%, compounded annually. The annual payment on this note is $12,205.90 calculated using the PMT function in Excel.

DEMO 6-6 ▶ **LO6-6**　　　　　　　　　　**Application of Time Value of Money**

Demo

MBC

Answer the questions for each of the following applications of the time value of money. Use Excel for calculations.

Topic	Application	Solution
Bonds	New Co. issued $50,000, 6%, 10-year bonds payable on January 1. Calculate the issuance price of the bonds if the bonds pay cash interest semiannually ($50,000 × 3% = $1,500) and the market rate on similar bonds is 7%.	**$46,446.90** **PV(0.035,20,−1500,−50000)**
Lease	Lessor Inc. leased equipment to Williams Inc. for a 10-year term, which is the estimated life of the equipment. The fair value of the equipment is $30,000 and the first annual payment is due at the inception of the lease. Calculate the annual lease payment Lessor Inc. will receive, assuming they want to earn a 10% return on its investment and the equipment has no salvage value.	**$4,438.51** **PMT(0.1,10,−30000,0,1)**
Debt	Debtor Co. borrowed $35,000 and agreed to pay off the loan over 5 years by making equal semiannual payments. What is the payment amount if the first payment owed by Debtor Inc. is due at the end of the first 6 months and the interest rate is 8%?	**$(4,315.18)** **PMT(0.04,10,35000)**
Capital Decision	Retail Inc. is considering two options for leasing equipment: pay $40,000 upfront or pay 5 annual installments of $10,000, with the first installment due immediately. If Retail Inc.'s borrowing rate is 8%, what option is better?	**PV of annual installments:** **$43,121.27** **PV(0.08,5,−10000,0,1)** **The $40,000 upfront payment is the better option as it is less than the present value of installment payments.**

Application of Time Value of Money	**LO6-6**	**REVIEW 6-6**

Answer the questions for each of the following applications of the time value of money. Use Excel for calculations.

Topic	Application	Solution
Lease	Lessee Co. leased a building beginning on December 31 for 15 years requiring annual lease payments of $80,000 with the first annual lease payment due immediately. Calculate the present value of the lease liability at the inception of the lease assuming an interest rate of 6%.	
Pension	A CEO will retire on December 31 of the current year. Retirement benefits are fixed payments of $10,000 at each month-end for 15 years. What is the present value of the pension liability on December 31 of the current year assuming an interest rate of 6%?	
Bonds	New Co. issues $50,000, 6%, 10-year bonds payable on January 1. Calculate the issuance price of the bonds if the bonds pay cash interest semiannually and the market rate on similar bonds is 5%.	
Debt	Debtor Inc. would like to establish a debt retirement fund to pay off a $250,000 debt due 5 years from today. If the fund is estimated to earn interest at 4% per year, what amount must be deposited semiannually (beginning in six months) to reach $250,000?	

More Practice:
BE6-16, BE6-17, BE6-18, E6-19, E6-21, E6-25

Solution on p. 6-49.

Management Judgment

Management judgment does *not* apply to the mechanical process of calculating a present value or a future value amount. However, management judgment is involved in determining the amounts that are entered into these calculations. For calculations in this chapter, these variables were provided. However, in practice, some variables are easily determinable, like a fixed payment, but many variables are estimated, such as an interest rate.

Estimated Rate Requires Judgment

Management judgment is required in estimating interest rates such as in the following cases.

- A bond issuance price is determined by taking the present value of contractual payments, discounted at the market rate. The market rate is determined based on bonds of similar risk.
- A lease payment is determined given the terms of the lease, the present value (and residual value) of the leased asset, and the rate. The rate is estimated based upon the lessor's desired rate of return.
- The future value of a bond sinking fund is calculated by using planned funding payments, number of periods, and the estimated rate of return on those funds.

Estimated Payment Requires Judgment

Management judgment is required in estimating future payments such as in the following cases.

- In the case of certain pension funds, the payment to employees expected to retire in the future must be estimated. The payment is determined by a pension formula, but may be based upon the employee's estimated salary at the time of retirement.
- The fair value of an asset in some cases is estimated by the present value of its net cash flows. For example, the gross profit obtained from selling goods produced on equipment over its useful life could be estimated as payments in calculating the fair value of the equipment.

Estimated Number of Periods Requires Judgment

Management judgment is required in estimating the number of periods such as in the following cases.

- In our above pension example, the number of periods must be estimated when determining the present value of the payments if the pension benefits will be paid until the retiree is deceased.
- In our above equipment example, the estimated useful life of the equipment (number of periods) must be estimated in determining the present value of the estimated payments.

Discount Rate Adjustment Technique vs. Expected Cash Flow Technique

Management must determine whether to use the discount rate adjustment technique or the expected cash flow technique in determining present value when there are risks in the cash flows. In other words, when the payments are not fixed or easily determinable, management must factor in risk by choosing an *appropriate interest rate* or factor in risk by using *expected cash flows* by assigning probabilities to cash flows. The latter was illustrated in Demo 6-3C where the fair value of warranty obligations was determined using the expected cash flow technique. While the probabilities related to potential cash flows were provided in this demo, these values must be estimated by management in practice.

APPENDIX 6A
LO 6-7

Apply time value of money concept to bond discount amortization

Bond Discount Amortization
- Amortize bond discount (premium) using effective interest method over bond term

A bond payable is a long-term debt instrument that typically requires cash interest payments over the bond term and payment of principal at the end of the bond term. A bond can be issued at an amount below the principal amount (discount) or at an amount above the principal amount (premium). The difference between the principal amount and the issuance price is amortized over the life of the bond. Present value concepts are applied in calculating both the issuance price and the amortization of the discount or premium over the bond term.

Effective Interest Method of Amortization

The price of a bond is determined based on the present value of both the principal paid at maturity (lump-sum amount) and the periodic cash interest payments made over the bond term (payments). The present value of the lump-sum payment and the interest payments are computed in one function in Excel.

Starr Inc. issued a $200,000, 5% bond due in 5 years, with cash interest payments due at the end of each year. The market rate of debt of similar risk is 6%. The cash flows with this bond are illustrated here.

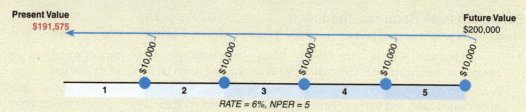

The $191,575 present value of the bond is computed using Excel. The bond discount of $8,425 is the difference between the bond's principal ($200,000) and the bond's issuance price ($191,575).

	Excel Arguments						Excel Function
	RATE	NPER	PMT	PV	FV	TYPE	=PV(RATE,NPER,PMT,FV,TYPE)
Given	6%	5	(10,000)	?	(200,000)	—	=PV(0.06,5,−10000,−200000)
Solution				$191,575			

The **effective interest method**, illustrated in **Demo 6-7**, is used to amortize the bond discount to interest expense over the life of the bond. With the effective interest method, interest expense is determined by multiplying the effective (market) rate of interest by the carrying value of the bond at the *beginning* of the interest period. For a discount bond, interest expense increases each period because interest expense is calculated based on the increasing bond carrying value. This means that the base for calculating interest expense each period is increasing as the bond moves toward the face value.

The cash interest paid each period is calculated by multiplying the face amount of the bond by the stated interest rate. The difference between the market interest amount and the cash interest amount is used to adjust the bond carrying amount each period until the bond reaches its face amount. The following amortization table illustrates how interest expense is recognized over the life of the bond. Amortization of interest on notes receivable is illustrated in Chapter 8 and amortization for bonds and notes payable is illustrated in Chapter 16.

Annual Period	Cash (Stated Interest)[a]	Effective Interest Method—Discount Interest Expense (Market Interest)[b]	Discount Amortization[c]	Unamortized Discount[d]	Bond Payable, Net (Carrying Amount)[e]
				$8,425	$191,575
1	$10,000	$11,495	$1,495	6,930	193,070
2	10,000	11,584	1,584	5,346	194,654
3	10,000	11,679	1,679	3,667	196,333
4	10,000	11,780	1,780	1,887	198,113
5	10,000	11,887	1,887	0	200,000
	$50,000	$58,425	$8,425		

[a] Stated rate × Bond face value
[b] Market rate × Bond payable, net, beginning of year
[c] Interest expense – Cash
[d] Bond discount beginning of year – Discount amortization
[e] Bond face value – Unamortized discount

Bond Discount Amortization   **LO6-7**   **DEMO 6-7**

Prepare an amortization schedule applying the effective interest method for $75,000 of 6%, 5-year bonds payable issued on January 1 of Year 1. The bonds pay interest annually on December 31. The market rate is 8%.

Demo

MBC

Solution

Date	Cash (Stated Interest)	Effective Interest Method—Discount Interest Expense (Market Interest)	Discount Amortization	Unamortized Discount	Bonds Payable, Net (Carrying Amount)
				$5,989	$69,011
Dec. 31, Year 1 . . .	$ 4,500	$ 5,521	$1,021	4,968	70,032
Dec. 31, Year 2 . . .	4,500	5,603	1,103	3,865	71,135
Dec. 31, Year 3 . . .	4,500	5,691	1,191	2,674	72,326
Dec. 31, Year 4 . . .	4,500	5,786	1,286	1,388	73,612
Dec. 31, Year 5 . . .	4,500	5,889	1,388	0	75,000
	$22,500	$28,490	$5,989		

Note Discount Amortization Schedule   **LO6-7**   **REVIEW 6-7**

Sicily Inc. purchases equipment on January 1 by issuing a 3-year, $20,000 note requiring no periodic cash interest payments. The market rate is 7%. Prepare an amortization schedule applying the effective interest method for this note issued for equipment. Do not show a separate column for the unamortized discount. *Hint:* The amounts in the cash column will be zero.

Review

MBC

More Practice: AppE6-1, AppP6-1

Solution on p. 6-49.

Apply time value of money concept using a financial calculator and compound interest tables

APPENDIX 6B
LO 6-8

Financial calculators and compound interest tables are additional tools available to help evaluate time value of money situations. Financial calculators operate similarly to Excel in that known variables are entered and the calculator computes the unknown variable, as shown in **Demo 6-8A**. Compound interest tables provide factors that can be used to simplify the process of determining present and future values through formulas, as shown in **Demo 6-8B**.

Alternative Ways to Solve Time Value of Money Problems
- Financial calculator
- Compound interest tables

LO 6-8 Overview

Time Value of Money—Financial Calculator

While different models of financial calculators can operate differently, most financial calculators have keys for present value (PV), future value (FV), payments (PMT), number of time periods (N), and interest (%*i*). Hewlett Packard and Texas Instruments manufacture popular types of financial calculators; however, the time value of money operations differ. When using a financial calculator such as the Hewlett-Packard 10Bii Financial Calculator, it is important to understand the functionality of the type and model of financial calculator used. After clearing data stored in memory, enter each variable followed by the appropriate calculator key.

DEMO 6-8A	LO6-8	Time Value of Money—Financial Calculator

Demo

MBC

Demonstrate time value of money functions through a financial calculator in the following two cases.

a. **Future value of a single amount**   Lowe Inc. has a lump-sum amount of $10,000 to invest today for 3 years, earning 5% interest compounded annually. What is the future value of this lump-sum amount at the end of 3 years?

b. **Present value of an ordinary annuity**   Lowe Inc. is to receive $1,000 per year, beginning one year from today, for a period of 5 years, earning 6% interest compounded annually. What is the present value of this ordinary annuity?

Solution

a. **Future value of a single amount**   Each of the following inputs is entered followed by the appropriate variable. Financial calculators are typically programed to enter percentages as whole numbers (such as 5 instead of 0.05). Also, the number of rounded digits can be adjusted, which is usually up to 12 digits.

Inputs		
−10000		PV
5		I/YR
3		N
Press	FV	
Output		
11576.25		

b. **Present Value of an Ordinary Annuity**   Each of the following inputs is entered followed by the appropriate variable calculator key.

Inputs		
1000		PMT
6		I/YR
5		N
Press	PV	
Output		
−4212.36		

Time Value of Money—Compound Interest Tables

Published **compound interest tables** can be used to solve time value of money situations, as shown in **Demo 6-8B**. These tables contain **factors** based on a $1 amount, with different combinations of interest rates and number of periods that are derived from present and future value formulas. These factors can then be multiplied by the actual amount for the situation to obtain the present or future value. Six tables are included at the end of this chapter.

Table 6B-1: Future value of $1
Table 6B-2: Present value of $1
Table 6B-3: Future value of ordinary
              annuity of $1

Table 6B-4: Present value of ordinary
              annuity of $1
Table 6B-5: Future value of annuity due of $1
Table 6B-6: Present value of annuity due of $1

One advantage of using tables is it eliminates many tedious calculations required in formula calculations. The disadvantages of using the tables are that it is more time consuming than using a financial calculator or Excel, and the situations are limited to the interest rates and number of periods published in tables.

Future Value of a Single Amount—Computation through Table

Assume that we have a lump-sum amount of $5,000 to invest today for 5 years, earning 8% interest, compounded annually. What is the future value of this lump-sum amount at the end of 3 years?

If using the tables to solve for this problem, first locate the appropriate table. In this case it is the *Future Value of $1 table* (**Table 6B-1**). Then find the interest rate column and read down the column to the intersecting line representing the number of interest periods involved, found at the left-hand side of the table. For our example, the intersection of 5 years and 8% rate results in a factor of 1.46933. We take this future value factor and multiply it by today's $5,000 amount.

$$\text{Future value} = \text{Present value} \times \text{Factor}$$
$$= \$5,000 \times 1.46933 = \$7,347$$

Present Value of a Single Amount—Computation through Table

Assume that we will receive $8,000, 10 years from today. Also assume an interest rate of 5% compounded annually. What is the present value of this $8,000 future lump sum?

If using the tables to solve for this problem, first locate the appropriate table, which is the *Present Value of $1 table* (**Table 6B-2**). Then find the interest rate column and read down the column to the intersecting line representing the number of interest periods involved, found at the left-hand side of the table. For our example, the intersection of 10 years and 5% interest results in a factor of 0.61391. Multiply this future value factor by the $8,000 future amount.

$$\text{Present value} = \text{Future value} \times \text{Factor}$$
$$= \$8,000 \times 0.61391 = \$4,911$$

Determination of Interest Rate—Computation through Table with Interpolation

Determination of an unknown interest rate or unknown number of periods sometimes requires interpolation because the table values are limited. Assume that $5,000 is deposited in a savings account at compound interest and that a $15,000 balance is expected at the end of year 10. What is the implicit interest rate, assuming annual compounding?

$$\text{Future value} = \text{Present value} \times \text{Factor}$$
$$\$15,000 = \$5,000 \times \text{Factor}$$
$$\text{Thus: Factor} = \$15,000/\$5,000 = 3.000000$$

From the *Future Value of $1 table*, the 3.00000 value for 10 periods falls somewhere between 2.83942 (which is compounded at 11%) and 3.10585 (which is compounded at 12%). The interest rate that corresponds to the 3.00000 value being sought is closer to 3.10585 (12%) than it is to 2.83942 (11%)— approximately 6/10 of the way from 11% to 12%. As an approximation, 11.6% might be used.

Future Value of an Ordinary Annuity—Computation through Table

Assume that an annuity payment stream of $5,000 is deposited annually at the end of each period at 8% interest for 6 years. What is the future value of this annuity stream?

To use tables to solve for this problem, first locate the appropriate table, which is the *Future Value of Ordinary Annuity of $1 table* (**Table 6B-3**). Then find the interest rate column and read down the column to the intersecting line representing the number of interest periods involved. For our example, the intersection of 6 years and 8% interest results in a factor of 7.33593. Multiply this future value factor by the $5,000 annuity amount.

$$\text{Future value} = \text{Present value} \times \text{Factor}$$
$$= \$5,000 \times 7.33593 = \$36,680$$

Future Value of Annuity Due—Computation through Table

Assume that an annuity payment stream of $5,000 is deposited annually at the *beginning of each period* at 8% interest for 6 years. What is the future value of this annuity stream?

To use tables to solve for this problem, first locate the appropriate table, which is the *Future Value of an Annuity Due of $1 table* (**Table 6B-5**). Then find the interest rate column and read down the column to the intersecting line representing the number of interest periods involved. For our example, the intersection of 6 years and 8% interest results in a factor of 7.92280. Multiply this future value factor by the $5,000 annuity amount.

$$\text{Future value} = \text{Present value} \times \text{Factor}$$
$$= \$5,000 \times 7.92280 = \$39,614$$

Present Value of an Ordinary Annuity—Computation through Table

If an annuity payment stream of $10,000 is deposited annually at the end of each period at 6% interest for 5 years, what is the present value of this annuity stream? To use tables to solve for this problem, first locate the appropriate table, which is the *Present Value of an Ordinary Annuity of $1 table* (**Table 6B-4**). Then find the interest rate column and read down the column to the intersecting line representing the number of interest periods involved. For our example, the intersection of 5 years and 6% interest results in a factor of 4.21236. Multiply this present value factor by the $5,000 annuity amount.

Future value = Present value × Factor
= $5,000 × 4.21236 = $21,062

Present Value of Annuity Due—Computation through Table

If an annuity payment stream of $10,000 is deposited annually at the beginning of each period at 6% interest for 5 years, what is the present value of this annuity stream? With an annuity due, each payment is made one period sooner than in the case of the ordinary annuity. This means that one way to find the annuity due factor is to multiply the equivalent ordinary annuity factor by $(1 + i)$.

To use tables to solve for this problem, first locate the appropriate table, which is the *Present Value of an Annuity Due of $1 table* (**Table 6B-6**). Then find the interest rate column and read down the column to the intersecting line representing the number of interest periods involved. For our example, the intersection of 5 years and 6% interest results in a factor of 4.46511. Multiply this present value factor by the $5,000 annuity amount.

Future value = Present value × Factor
= $5,000 × 4.46511 = $22,326

DEMO 6-8B ▶	**LO6-8**	**Time Value of Money—Compound Interest Tables**

Demo

MBC

Complete the following schedule by indicating (1) the relevant factor from the present value or future value table, and (2) the amount of the present or future value for each separate case *a* through *f*. Assume that the number of periods is 10 and the interest rate is 6% with annual compounding for each case. Round each answer to the nearest $1.

	Time Value of Money Case	Table (source)	Factor	Answer
a.	Current value of $5,000 to be received in 5 years.	Present value of $1	0.55839	$2,792
b.	Current value of a stream of $100 payments made at the end of each period.	Present value of ordinary annuity of $1	7.36009	$ 736
c.	Future value of a stream of $100 payments made at the end of each period.	Future value of ordinary annuity of $1	13.18079	$1,318
d.	Future value of a stream of $100 payments made at the beginning of each period.	Future value of annuity due of $1	13.97164	$1,397
e.	Current value of a stream of $100 payments made at the beginning of each period.	Present value of annuity due of $1	7.80169	$ 780
f.	Future value of $2,000, 10 years from now.	Future value of $1	1.79085	$3,582

Future Value and Present Value Interest Tables

Table 6B-1   Future Value of 1: FV1 = $(1 + i)^n$

This table shows the compound amount (future value) of $1 at various interest rates and for various time periods. It is used to compute the future value of single payments, where i = interest and n = number of periods.

n	2%	3%	4%	5%	6%	7%	8%	9%	10%	11%	12%	15%
1 ...	1.02000	1.03000	1.04000	1.05000	1.06000	1.07000	1.08000	1.09000	1.10000	1.11000	1.12000	1.15000
2 ...	1.04040	1.06090	1.08160	1.10250	1.12360	1.14490	1.16640	1.18810	1.21000	1.23210	1.25440	1.32250
3 ...	1.06121	1.09273	1.12486	1.15763	1.19102	1.22504	1.25971	1.29503	1.33100	1.36763	1.40493	1.52088
4 ...	1.08243	1.12551	1.16986	1.21551	1.26248	1.31080	1.36049	1.41158	1.46410	1.51807	1.57352	1.74901
5 ...	1.10408	1.15927	1.21665	1.27628	1.33823	1.40255	1.46933	1.53862	1.61051	1.68506	1.76234	2.01136
6 ...	1.12616	1.19405	1.26532	1.34010	1.41852	1.50073	1.58687	1.67710	1.77156	1.87041	1.97382	2.31306
7 ...	1.14869	1.22987	1.31593	1.40710	1.50363	1.60578	1.71382	1.82804	1.94872	2.07616	2.21068	2.66002
8 ...	1.17166	1.26677	1.36857	1.47746	1.59385	1.71819	1.85093	1.99256	2.14359	2.30454	2.47596	3.05902
9 ...	1.19509	1.30477	1.42331	1.55133	1.68948	1.83846	1.99900	2.17189	2.35795	2.55804	2.77308	3.51788
10 ...	1.21899	1.34392	1.48024	1.62889	1.79085	1.96715	2.15892	2.36736	2.59374	2.83942	3.10585	4.04556
11 ...	1.24337	1.38423	1.53945	1.71034	1.89830	2.10485	2.33164	2.58043	2.85312	3.15176	3.47855	4.65239
12 ...	1.26824	1.42576	1.60103	1.79586	2.01220	2.25219	2.51817	2.81266	3.13843	3.49845	3.89598	5.35025
13 ...	1.29361	1.46853	1.66507	1.88565	2.13293	2.40985	2.71962	3.06580	3.45227	3.88328	4.36349	6.15279
14 ...	1.31948	1.51259	1.73168	1.97993	2.26090	2.57853	2.93719	3.34173	3.79750	4.31044	4.88711	7.07571
15 ...	1.34587	1.55797	1.80094	2.07893	2.39656	2.75903	3.17217	3.64248	4.17725	4.78459	5.47357	8.13706
16 ...	1.37279	1.60471	1.87298	2.18287	2.54035	2.95216	3.42594	3.97031	4.59497	5.31089	6.13039	9.35762
17 ...	1.40024	1.65285	1.94790	2.29202	2.69277	3.15882	3.70002	4.32763	5.05447	5.89509	6.86604	10.76126
18 ...	1.42825	1.70243	2.02582	2.40662	2.85434	3.37993	3.99602	4.71712	5.55992	6.54355	7.68997	12.37545
19 ...	1.45681	1.75351	2.10685	2.52695	3.02560	3.61653	4.31570	5.14166	6.11591	7.26334	8.61276	14.23177
20 ...	1.48595	1.80611	2.19112	2.65330	3.20714	3.86968	4.66096	5.60441	6.72750	8.06231	9.64629	16.36654
21 ...	1.51567	1.86029	2.27877	2.78596	3.39956	4.14056	5.03383	6.10881	7.40025	8.94917	10.80385	18.82152
22 ...	1.54598	1.91610	2.36992	2.92526	3.60354	4.43040	5.43654	6.65860	8.14027	9.93357	12.10031	21.64475
23 ...	1.57690	1.97359	2.48472	3.07152	3.81975	4.74053	5.87146	7.25787	8.95430	11.02627	13.55235	24.89146
24 ...	1.60844	2.03279	2.56330	3.22510	4.04893	5.07237	6.34118	7.91108	9.84973	12.23916	15.17863	28.62518
25 ...	1.64061	2.09378	2.66584	3.38635	4.29187	5.42743	6.84848	8.62308	10.83471	13.58546	17.00006	32.91895

Table 6B-2   Present Value of 1: PV1 = $1/(1 + i)^n$

This table shows the present value of $1 discounted at various rates of interest and for various time periods. It is used to compute the present value of single payments.

n	2%	3%	4%	5%	6%	7%	8%	9%	10%	11%	12%	15%
1 ...	0.98039	0.97087	0.96154	0.95238	0.94340	0.93458	0.92593	0.91743	0.90909	0.90090	0.89286	0.86957
2 ...	0.96117	0.94260	0.92456	0.90703	0.89000	0.87344	0.85734	0.84168	0.82645	0.81162	0.79719	0.75614
3 ...	0.94232	0.91514	0.88900	0.86384	0.83962	0.81630	0.79383	0.77218	0.75131	0.73119	0.71178	0.65752
4 ...	0.92385	0.88849	0.85480	0.82270	0.79209	0.76290	0.73503	0.70843	0.68301	0.65873	0.63552	0.57175
5 ...	0.90573	0.86261	0.82193	0.78353	0.74726	0.71299	0.68058	0.64993	0.62092	0.59345	0.56743	0.49718
6 ...	0.88797	0.83748	0.79031	0.74622	0.70496	0.66634	0.63017	0.59627	0.56447	0.53464	0.50663	0.43233
7 ...	0.87056	0.81309	0.75992	0.71068	0.66506	0.62275	0.58349	0.54703	0.51316	0.48166	0.45235	0.37594
8 ...	0.85349	0.78941	0.73069	0.67684	0.62741	0.58201	0.54027	0.50187	0.46651	0.43393	0.40388	0.32690
9 ...	0.83676	0.76642	0.70259	0.64461	0.59190	0.54393	0.50025	0.46043	0.42410	0.39092	0.36061	0.28426
10 ...	0.82035	0.74409	0.67556	0.61391	0.55839	0.50835	0.46319	0.42241	0.38554	0.35218	0.32197	0.24718
11 ...	0.80426	0.72242	0.64958	0.58468	0.52679	0.47509	0.42888	0.38753	0.35049	0.31728	0.28748	0.21494
12 ...	0.78849	0.70138	0.62460	0.55684	0.49697	0.44401	0.39711	0.35553	0.31863	0.28584	0.25668	0.18691
13 ...	0.77303	0.68095	0.60057	0.53032	0.46884	0.41496	0.36770	0.32618	0.28966	0.25751	0.22917	0.16253
14 ...	0.75788	0.66112	0.57748	0.50507	0.44230	0.38782	0.34046	0.29925	0.26333	0.23199	0.20462	0.14133
15 ...	0.74301	0.64186	0.55526	0.48102	0.41727	0.36245	0.31524	0.27454	0.23939	0.20900	0.18270	0.12289
16 ...	0.72845	0.62317	0.53391	0.45811	0.39365	0.33873	0.29189	0.25187	0.21763	0.18829	0.16312	0.10686
17 ...	0.71416	0.60502	0.51337	0.43630	0.37136	0.31657	0.27027	0.23107	0.19784	0.16963	0.14564	0.09293
18 ...	0.70016	0.58739	0.49363	0.41552	0.35034	0.29586	0.25025	0.21199	0.17986	0.15282	0.13004	0.08081
19 ...	0.68643	0.57029	0.47464	0.39573	0.33051	0.27651	0.23171	0.19449	0.16351	0.13768	0.11611	0.07027
20 ...	0.67297	0.55368	0.45639	0.37689	0.31180	0.25842	0.21455	0.17843	0.14864	0.12403	0.10367	0.06110
21 ...	0.65978	0.53755	0.43883	0.35894	0.29416	0.24151	0.19866	0.16370	0.13513	0.11174	0.09256	0.05313
22 ...	0.64684	0.52189	0.42196	0.34185	0.27751	0.22571	0.18394	0.15018	0.12285	0.10067	0.08264	0.04620
23 ...	0.63416	0.50669	0.40573	0.32557	0.26180	0.21095	0.17032	0.13778	0.11168	0.09069	0.07379	0.04017
24 ...	0.62172	0.49193	0.39012	0.31007	0.24698	0.19715	0.15770	0.12640	0.10153	0.08170	0.06588	0.03493
25 ...	0.60953	0.47761	0.37512	0.29530	0.23300	0.18425	0.14602	0.11597	0.09230	0.07361	0.05882	0.03038

Table 6B-3   Future Value of an Ordinary Annuity of n Payments of 1 Each: $FVA = \left[\dfrac{(1+i)^n - 1}{i}\right]$

This table shows the future value of an ordinary annuity of $1 at various rates of interest and for various time periods. It is used to compute the future value of a series of payments made at the end of each interest compounding period.

n	2%	3%	4%	5%	6%	7%	8%	9%	10%	11%	12%	15%
1	1.00000	1.00000	1.00000	1.00000	1.00000	1.00000	1.00000	1.00000	1.00000	1.00000	1.00000	1.00000
2	2.02000	2.03000	2.04000	2.05000	2.06000	2.07000	2.08000	2.09000	2.10000	2.11000	2.12000	2.15000
3	3.06040	3.09090	3.12160	3.15250	3.18360	3.21490	3.24640	3.27810	3.31000	3.34210	3.37440	3.47250
4	4.12161	4.18363	4.24646	4.31013	4.37462	4.43994	4.50611	4.57313	4.64100	4.70973	4.77933	4.99338
5	5.20404	5.30914	5.41632	5.52563	5.63709	5.75074	5.86660	5.98471	6.10510	6.22780	6.35285	6.74238
6	6.30812	6.46841	6.63298	6.80191	6.97532	7.15329	7.33593	7.52333	7.71561	7.91286	8.11519	8.75374
7	7.43428	7.66246	7.89829	8.14201	8.39384	8.65402	8.92280	9.20043	9.48717	9.78327	10.08901	11.06680
8	8.58297	8.89234	9.21423	9.54911	9.89747	10.25980	10.63663	11.02847	11.43589	11.85943	12.29969	13.72682
9	9.75463	10.15911	10.58280	11.02656	11.49132	11.97799	12.48756	13.02104	13.57948	14.16397	14.77566	16.78584
10	10.94972	11.46388	12.00611	12.57789	13.18079	13.81645	14.48656	15.19293	15.93742	16.72201	17.54874	20.30372
11	12.16872	12.80780	13.48635	14.20679	14.97164	15.78360	16.64549	17.56029	18.53117	19.56143	20.65458	24.34928
12	13.41209	14.19203	15.02581	15.91713	16.86994	17.88845	18.97713	20.14072	21.38428	22.71319	24.13313	29.00167
13	14.68033	15.61779	16.62684	17.71298	18.88214	20.14064	21.49530	22.95338	24.52271	26.21164	28.02911	34.35192
14	15.97394	17.08632	18.29191	19.59863	21.01507	22.55049	24.21492	26.01919	27.97498	30.09492	32.39260	40.50471
15	17.29342	18.59891	20.02359	21.57856	23.27597	25.12902	27.15211	29.36092	31.77248	34.40536	37.27971	47.58041
16	18.63929	20.15688	21.82453	23.65749	25.67253	27.88805	30.32428	33.00340	35.94973	39.18995	42.75328	55.71747
17	20.01207	21.76159	23.69751	25.84037	28.21288	30.84022	33.75023	36.97370	40.54470	44.50084	48.88367	65.07509
18	21.41231	23.41444	25.64541	28.13238	30.90565	33.99903	37.45024	41.30134	45.59917	50.39594	55.74971	75.83636
19	22.84056	25.11687	27.67123	30.53900	33.75999	37.37896	41.44626	46.01846	51.15909	56.93949	63.43968	88.21181
20	24.29737	26.87037	29.77808	33.06595	36.78559	40.99549	45.76196	51.16012	57.27500	64.20283	72.05244	102.44358
21	25.78332	28.67649	31.96920	35.71925	39.99273	44.86518	50.42292	56.76453	64.00250	72.26514	81.69874	118.81012
22	27.29898	30.53678	34.24797	38.50521	43.39229	49.00574	55.45676	62.87334	71.40275	81.21431	92.50258	137.63164
23	28.84496	32.45288	36.61789	41.43048	46.99583	53.43614	60.89330	69.53194	79.54302	91.14788	104.60289	159.27638
24	30.42186	34.42647	39.08260	44.50200	50.81558	58.17667	66.76476	76.78981	88.49733	102.17415	118.15524	184.16784
25	32.03030	36.45926	41.64591	47.72710	54.86451	63.24904	73.10594	84.70090	98.34706	114.41331	133.33387	212.79302

Table 6B-4   Present Value of an Ordinary Annuity of n Payments of 1 Each: $PVA = \left\{\dfrac{1 - [1/(1+i)^n]}{i}\right\}$

n	2%	3%	4%	5%	6%	7%	8%	9%	10%	11%	12%	15%
1	0.98039	0.97087	0.96154	0.95238	0.94340	0.93458	0.92593	0.91743	0.90909	0.90090	0.89286	0.86957
2	1.94156	1.91347	1.88609	1.85941	1.83339	1.80802	1.78326	1.75911	1.73554	1.71252	1.69005	1.62571
3	2.88388	2.82861	2.77509	2.72325	2.67301	2.62432	2.57710	2.53129	2.48685	2.44371	2.40183	2.28323
4	3.80773	3.71710	3.62990	3.54595	3.46511	3.38721	3.31213	3.23972	3.16987	3.10245	3.03735	2.85498
5	4.71346	4.57971	4.45182	4.32948	4.21236	4.10020	3.99271	3.88965	3.79079	3.69590	3.60478	3.35216
6	5.60143	5.41719	5.24214	5.07569	4.91732	4.76654	4.62288	4.48592	4.35526	4.23054	4.11141	3.78448
7	6.47199	6.23028	6.00205	5.78637	5.58238	5.38929	5.20637	5.03295	4.86842	4.71220	4.56736	4.16042
8	7.32548	7.01969	6.73274	6.46321	6.20979	5.97130	5.74664	5.53482	5.33493	5.14612	4.96764	4.48732
9	8.16224	7.78611	7.43533	7.10782	6.80169	6.51523	6.24689	5.99525	5.75902	5.53705	5.32825	4.77158
10	8.98259	8.53020	8.11090	7.72173	7.36009	7.02358	6.71008	6.41766	6.14457	5.88923	5.65022	5.01877
11	9.78685	9.25262	8.76048	8.30641	7.88687	7.49867	7.13896	6.80519	6.49506	6.20652	5.93770	5.23371
12	10.57534	9.95400	9.38507	8.86325	8.38384	7.94269	7.53608	7.16073	6.81369	6.49236	6.19437	5.42062
13	11.34837	10.63496	9.98565	9.39357	8.85268	8.35765	7.90378	7.48690	7.10336	6.74987	6.42355	5.58315
14	12.10625	11.29607	10.56312	9.89864	9.29498	8.74547	8.24424	7.78615	7.36669	6.98187	6.62817	5.72448
15	12.84926	11.93794	11.11839	10.37966	9.71225	9.10791	8.55948	8.06069	7.60608	7.19087	6.81086	5.84737
16	13.57771	12.56110	11.65230	10.83777	10.10590	9.44665	8.85137	8.31256	7.82371	7.37916	6.97399	5.95423
17	14.29187	13.16612	12.16567	11.27407	10.47726	9.76322	9.12164	8.54363	8.02155	7.54879	7.11963	6.04716
18	14.99203	13.75351	12.65930	11.68959	10.82760	10.05909	9.37189	8.75563	8.20141	7.70162	7.24967	6.12797
19	15.67846	14.32380	13.13394	12.08532	11.15812	10.33560	9.60360	8.95011	8.36492	7.83929	7.36578	6.19823
20	16.35143	14.87747	13.59033	12.46221	11.46992	10.59401	9.81815	9.12855	8.51356	7.96333	7.46944	6.25933
21	17.01121	15.41502	14.02916	12.82115	11.76408	11.83553	10.01680	9.29224	8.64869	8.07507	7.56200	6.31246
22	17.65805	15.93692	14.45112	13.16300	12.04158	11.06124	10.20074	9.44243	8.77154	8.17574	7.64465	6.35866
23	18.29220	16.44361	14.85684	13.48857	12.30338	11.27219	10.37106	9.58021	8.88322	8.26643	7.71843	6.39884
24	18.91393	16.93554	15.24696	13.79864	12.55036	11.46933	10.52876	9.70661	8.98474	8.34814	7.78432	6.43377
25	19.52346	17.41315	15.62208	14.09394	12.78336	11.65358	10.67478	9.82258	9.07704	8.42174	7.84314	6.46415

Table 6B-5   Future Value of an Annuity Due of n Payments of 1 Each: $FVAD = \left[\frac{(1+i)^n - 1}{i}\right] \times (1+i)$

This table shows the future value of an annuity due of $1 at various rates of interest and for various time periods. It is used to compute the future value of a series of payments made at the beginning of each interest compounding period.

n	2%	3%	4%	5%	6%	7%	8%	9%	10%	11%	12%	15%
1	1.02000	1.03000	1.04000	1.05000	1.06000	1.07000	1.08000	1.09000	1.10000	1.11000	1.12000	1.15000
2	2.06040	2.09090	2.12160	2.15250	2.18360	2.21490	2.24640	2.27810	2.31000	2.34210	2.37440	2.47250
3	3.12161	3.18363	3.24646	3.31013	3.37462	3.43994	3.50611	3.57313	3.64100	3.70973	3.77933	3.99338
4	4.20404	4.30914	4.41632	4.52563	4.63709	4.75074	4.86660	4.98471	5.10510	5.22780	5.35285	5.74238
5	5.30812	5.46841	5.63298	5.80191	5.97532	6.15329	6.33593	6.52333	6.71561	6.91286	7.11519	7.75374
6	6.43428	6.66246	6.89829	7.14201	7.39384	7.65402	7.92280	8.20043	8.48717	8.78327	9.08901	10.06680
7	7.58297	7.89234	8.21423	8.54911	8.89747	9.25980	9.63663	10.02847	10.43589	10.85943	11.29969	12.72682
8	8.75463	9.15911	9.58280	10.02656	10.49132	10.97799	11.48756	12.02104	12.57948	13.16397	13.77566	15.78584
9	9.94972	10.46388	11.00611	11.57789	12.18079	12.81645	13.48656	14.19293	14.93742	15.72201	16.54874	19.30372
10	11.16872	11.80780	12.48635	13.20679	13.97164	14.78360	15.64549	16.56029	17.53117	18.56143	19.65458	23.34928
11	12.41209	13.19203	14.02581	14.91713	15.86994	16.88845	17.97713	19.14072	20.38428	21.71319	23.13313	28.00167
12	13.68033	14.61779	15.62684	16.71298	17.88214	19.14064	20.49530	21.95338	23.52271	25.21164	27.02911	33.35192
13	14.97394	16.08632	17.29191	18.59863	20.01507	21.55049	23.21492	25.01919	26.97498	29.09492	31.39260	39.50471
14	16.29342	17.59891	19.02359	20.57856	22.27597	24.12902	26.15211	28.36092	30.77248	33.40536	36.27971	46.58041
15	17.63929	19.15688	20.82453	22.65749	24.67253	26.88805	29.32428	32.00340	34.94973	38.18995	41.75328	54.71747
16	19.01207	20.76159	22.69751	24.84037	27.21288	29.84022	32.75023	35.97370	39.54470	43.50084	47.88367	64.07509
17	20.41231	22.41444	24.64541	27.13238	29.90565	32.99903	36.45024	40.30134	44.59917	49.39594	54.74971	74.83636
18	21.84056	24.11687	26.67123	29.53900	32.75999	36.37896	40.44626	45.01846	50.15909	55.93949	62.43968	87.21181
19	23.29737	25.87037	28.77808	32.06595	35.78559	39.99549	44.76196	50.16012	56.27500	63.20283	71.05244	101.44358
20	24.78332	27.67649	30.96920	34.71925	38.99273	43.86518	49.42292	55.76453	63.00250	71.26514	80.69874	117.81012
21	26.29898	29.53678	33.24797	37.50521	42.39229	48.00574	54.45676	61.87334	70.40275	80.21431	91.50258	136.63164
22	27.84496	31.45288	35.61789	40.43048	45.99583	52.43614	59.89330	68.53194	78.54302	90.14788	103.60289	158.27638
23	29.42186	33.42647	38.08260	43.50200	49.81558	57.17667	65.76476	75.78981	87.49733	101.17415	117.15524	183.16784
24	31.03030	35.45926	40.64591	46.72710	53.86451	62.24904	72.10594	83.70090	97.34706	113.41331	132.33387	211.79302
25	32.67091	37.55304	43.31174	50.11345	58.15638	67.67647	78.95442	92.32398	108.18177	126.99877	149.33393	244.71197

Table 6B-6   Present Value of an Annuity Due of n Payments of 1 Each: $PVAD = \left[\frac{1-(1+i)^{-n}}{i}\right] \times (1+i)$

This table shows the present value of an annuity due of $1 at various rates of interest and for various time periods. It is used to compute the present value of a series of payments made at the beginning of each interest compounding period.

n	2%	3%	4%	5%	6%	7%	8%	9%	10%	11%	12%	15%
1	1.00000	1.00000	1.00000	1.00000	1.00000	1.00000	1.00000	1.00000	1.00000	1.00000	1.00000	1.00000
2	1.98039	1.97087	1.96154	1.95238	1.94340	1.93458	1.92593	1.91743	1.90909	1.90090	1.89286	1.86957
3	2.94156	2.91347	2.88609	2.85941	2.83339	2.80802	2.78326	2.75911	2.73554	2.71252	2.69005	2.62571
4	3.88388	3.82861	3.77509	3.72325	3.67301	3.62432	3.57710	3.53130	3.48685	3.44371	3.40183	3.28323
5	4.80773	4.71710	4.62990	4.54595	4.46511	4.38721	4.31213	4.23972	4.16987	4.10245	4.03735	3.85498
6	5.71346	5.57971	5.45182	5.32948	5.21236	5.10020	4.99271	4.88965	4.79079	4.69590	4.60478	4.35216
7	6.60143	6.41719	6.24214	6.07569	5.91732	5.76654	5.62288	5.48592	5.35526	5.23054	5.11141	4.78448
8	7.47199	7.23028	7.00205	6.78637	6.58238	6.38929	6.20637	6.03295	5.86842	5.71220	5.56376	5.16042
9	8.32548	8.01969	7.73274	7.46321	7.20979	6.97130	6.74664	6.53482	6.33493	6.14612	5.96764	5.48732
10	9.16224	8.78611	8.43533	8.10782	7.80169	7.51523	7.24689	6.99525	6.75902	6.53705	6.32825	5.77158
11	9.98259	9.53020	9.11090	8.72173	8.36009	8.02358	7.71008	7.41766	7.14457	6.88923	6.65022	6.01877
12	10.78685	10.25262	9.76048	9.30641	8.88687	8.49867	8.13896	7.80519	7.49506	7.20652	6.93770	6.23371
13	11.57534	10.95400	10.38507	9.86325	9.38384	8.94269	8.53608	8.16073	7.81369	7.49236	7.19437	6.42062
14	12.34837	11.63496	10.98565	10.39357	9.85268	9.35765	8.90378	8.48690	8.10336	7.74987	7.42355	6.58315
15	13.10625	12.29607	11.56312	10.89864	10.29498	9.74547	9.24424	8.78615	8.36669	7.98187	7.62817	6.72448
16	13.84926	12.93794	12.11839	11.37966	10.71225	10.10791	9.55948	9.06069	8.60608	8.19087	7.81086	6.84737
17	14.57771	13.56110	12.65230	11.83777	11.10590	10.44665	9.85137	9.31256	8.82371	8.37916	7.97399	6.95423
18	15.29187	14.16612	13.16567	12.27407	11.47726	10.76322	10.12164	9.54363	9.02155	8.54879	8.11963	7.04716
19	15.99203	14.75351	13.65930	12.68959	11.82760	11.05909	10.37189	9.75563	9.20141	8.70162	8.24967	7.12797
20	16.67846	15.32380	14.13394	13.08532	12.15812	11.33560	10.60360	9.95012	9.36492	8.83929	8.36578	7.19823
21	17.35143	15.87747	14.59033	13.46221	12.46992	11.59401	10.81815	10.12855	9.51356	8.96333	8.46944	7.25933
22	18.01121	16.41502	15.02916	13.82115	12.76408	11.83553	11.01680	10.29224	9.64869	9.07507	8.56200	7.31246
23	18.65805	16.93692	15.45112	14.16300	13.04158	12.06124	11.20074	10.44243	9.77154	9.17574	8.64465	7.35866
24	19.29220	17.44361	15.85684	14.48857	13.30338	12.27219	11.37106	10.58021	9.88322	9.26643	8.71843	7.39884
25	19.91393	17.93554	16.24696	14.79864	13.55036	12.46933	11.52876	10.70661	9.98474	9.34814	8.78432	7.43377

More Practice:
AppE6-2
Solution on p. 6-49.

| REVIEW 6-8 | LO6-8 | | | | | | | Compound Interest Table | | |

Review

MBC

Complete the following schedule for investments *a* through *f* by indicating the relevant factor from the present value or future value table and the final present or future value amount.

Investment	Compounding	Annual Interest Rate	Amount	Investment Period	Payment at Beg. or End of Period	Future Value or Present Value	Factor	Answer
a. Annuity	Annually	5%	$1,000	2 years	End	Future	_____	$_____
b. Annuity	Semiannually	4%	500	3 years	Beginning	Present	_____	_____
c. Annuity	Semiannually	6%	7,000	4 years	Beginning	Future	_____	_____
d. Single Payment	Annually	5%	4,500	6 years	n/a	Present	_____	_____
e. Single Payment	Semiannually	6%	8,000	5 years	n/a	Future	_____	_____
f. Single Payment	Semiannually	4%	4,800	4 years	n/a	Present	_____	_____

Questions

Q6-1. Explain what is meant by the time value of money.

Q6-2. Assuming that the annual rate of interest is stated as 12%, what is the interest rate for the following compounding periods: (a) semiannual, (b) quarterly, (c) monthly?

Q6-3. What is the fundamental difference between simple interest and compound interest?

Q6-4. Briefly explain each of the following:
   a. Future value of $1.
   b. Present value of $1.
   c. Future value of annuity of *n* payments of $1 each.
   d. Present value of annuity of *n* payments of $1 each.

Q6-5. What is the future value of $10,000 earning 10% per year for two years?

Q6-6. Contrast a future value of $1 with the present value of $1.

Q6-7. If $15,000 were deposited in an account at 8% interest, compounded annually, what would be the balance in the account at the end of (a) 10 years? (b) 15 years? (c) 25 years?

Q6-8. Assume that we have a legal contract that specifies that we will receive $200,000 cash in the future. Assuming a 9% interest rate, what would be the present value of that contract if the amount will be received (a) 10 years, (b) 15 years, or (c) 25 years from today?

Q6-9. Assume that we deposit $20,000 in an account for a three-year period. How much cash would we receive at period end if 12% simple interest per annum is accumulated in the fund at the end of each quarter?

Q6-10. Assume that we will receive $100,000 cash from a trust fund six years from now. What is the present value of the $100,000, assuming 12% interest on a quarterly basis?

Q6-11. What are the three characteristics of an annuity? Explain what would happen if any of these characteristics were changed.

Q6-12. If $20,000 is deposited in an account at the end of each of *n* annual periods and will earn 9%, what will be the balance in the account at the date of the last deposit (an ordinary annuity), assuming that *n* equals (a) 10 years, (b) 15 years, and (c) 25 years?

Q6-13. Explain the difference between (a) future value of an ordinary annuity, and (b) future value of an annuity due.

Q6-14. Explain the difference between (a) present value of an ordinary annuity, and (b) present value of an annuity due.

Q6-15. Compute the present value of an annuity of five payments of $9,000 each using a 12% interest rate, assuming (a) an ordinary annuity, and (b) an annuity due. Explain why the two amounts are different.

Q6-16. Compute the future value of an annuity of six payments of $5,000 each using a 10% interest rate, assuming (a) an ordinary annuity, and (b) an annuity due. Explain why the two amounts are different.

Q6-17. A company creates a building fund by contributing $100,000 per year to it for 10 years. Explain how we identify whether this situation is an ordinary annuity or an annuity due.

Data Analytics

The Excel file associated with this exercise includes cash flows and probabilities associated with the environmental cash outflows under different scenarios. In this exercise, we use the Goal Seek function to determine how variables would change to arrive at different desired outcomes.

Data Analytics DA6-1
Analyzing How a Liability Computation in Excel Is Impacted by Changes in Estimates **LO3**

Data Visualization

Data Visualization Activities are available in **myBusinessCourse**. These assignments use Tableau Dashboards to expose students to visual depictions of data and introduce students to data analytics through data visualizations. These exercises are assignable and auto graded by MBC.

Data Visualization

Multiple Choice

MC6-1. **Identifying Interest Rate per Compounding Period and Number of Compounding Periods**   **LO1**
Ashford Inc. invested $20,000 in a three-year, 6% interest bearing investment with interest compounded semiannually. What are the values of the following?

	Interest Rate per Compounding Period	Total Number of Compounding Periods
a.	6%	3
b.	3%	6
c.	3%	3
d.	6%	6

MC6-2. **Identifying Future Value Excel Formula**   Which of the following arguments for the Excel FV   **LO2**
function will return the future value of an investment of $85,000 in an account with an annual 6% rate, held for 5 years compounded monthly?

   a.   =FV(0.06,5,0,-85000)   *c.*   =FV(0.012,20,0,-85000)
   b.   =FV(0.03,10,0,-85000)   *d.*   =FV(0.005,60,0,-85000)

MC6-3. **Calculating Present Value**   In evaluating an equipment purchase, Fortunate LLC. estimates the sal-   **LO3**
vage value of its equipment using the expected cash flow technique. Estimates of salvage value at the end of 20 years are $100,000, $120,0000 and $150,000 based on probabilities of 20%, 50%, and 30%, respectively. Assuming a risk-free rate of 5%, calculate the present value of the salvage value amount.

   a. $ 47,111   *c.* $15,704
   b. $125,000   *d.* $52,125

MC6-4. **Solving for Missing Excel Argument**   Assuming interest is compounded annually and assuming   **LO3**
no payments, solve for the missing argument.

       RATE: ?
       NPER: 6
       PV: $60,064
       FV: $76,000

   a.   4.0%   *c.*   3.5%
   b.   3.8%   *d.*   3.4%

MC6-5. **Determining Payment Amount**   If Center Inc. wants to make annual payments at the start of each   **LO4**
of the next 10 years into a fund paying 6% compounded annually, what should the payment be if the company wants to have $120,000 in the fund at the end of the 10th year?

   a. $ 9,852   *c.* $8,589
   b. $10,443   *d.* $9,104

MC6-6. **Calculating Present Value of Investment**   After 5 years, Jade will receive payments through an   **LO5**
annuity investment of $1,500 per year for 10 years. Assuming an interest rate of 5% and that Jade will receive the first payment at the end of Year 6, what is the present value of the investment today?

   a. $11,583   *c.* $15,569
   b. $ 9,075   *d.* $14,783

MC6-7.   Calculating Bond Issuance Price   On January 1, Aero Corp. issued $400,000, 10 year, 5%, bonds with cash interest payable on July 1 and January 1. The market price for bonds of similar risk is 6%. What is the issuance price of the bonds?

a. $370,560
b. $431,178

c. $430,887
d. $370,245

MC6-8.   Calculating Lease Payment   Assume that Leasing Inc. leases equipment to Rocket LLC. over a 10-year period, with payments due annually starting immediately on January 1. The equipment has a fair value of $80,000, a useful life of 10 years, and no salvage value. Leasing Inc. requires a rate of return on this lease of 10%. What is the annual lease payment calculated by Leasing Inc.?

a. $13,020
b. $12,580

c. $11,836
d. $ 8,000

Brief Exercises

Brief Exercise 6-1
Identifying Number of Compounding Periods and Rate per Period **LO1**
Hint: See Demo 6-1

Complete the following schedule.

Investment	Cost	Annual Interest Rate	Term	Compounding	Interest Rate per Compounding Period	Total Number of Compounding Periods
Investment A	$ 50,000	6%	5 years	Quarterly	_____	_____
Investment B	50,000	6%	5 years	Monthly	_____	_____
Investment C	100,000	8%	10 years	Quarterly	_____	_____
Investment D	100,000	9.6%	10 years	Monthly	_____	_____

Brief Exercise 6-2
Computing Future Value of a Single Amount **LO2**
Hint: See Demo 6-2

Evans invested $50,000 today in a mutual fund earning 5% interest, compounded annually.

a.   What is the value of the mutual fund in 5 years?
b.   What is the value of the mutual fund in 20 years?

Brief Exercise 6-3
Solving for Number of Compounding Periods **LO2**

Lawren plans to invest $10,000 today. Assuming that the investment earns 8%, compounded quarterly, how many quarters must Lawren invest the amount to achieve a goal of $15,000?

Brief Exercise 6-4
Computing Present Value of a Single Amount **LO3**

Depp is reviewing an investment that will provide a payout of $30,000 in five years. If Depp considers a 7% interest rate (compounded annually) acceptable, what amount is Depp willing to pay for the investment today?

Brief Exercise 6-5
Computing Present Value of a Single Amount **LO3**
Hint: See Demo 6-3A

Reynolds must accumulate $40,000 in eight years to purchase replacement equipment. Reynolds plans to invest funds today to have the $40,000 accessible at that time.

a.   Assuming a 6% return compounded annually on its investment, how much must Reynolds invest now to reach the goal?
b.   Assuming an 8% return compounded annually on its investment, how much must Reynolds invest now to reach the goal?

Brief Exercise 6-6
Solving for Interest Rate per Period **LO3**
Hint: See Demo 6-3B

Scarlett has $25,000 available today to invest for 20 years. Scarlett desires an investment fund balance of $100,000 at that time. What interest rate (compounded annually) must Scarlett earn to reach the desired balance in 20 years?

Brief Exercise 6-7
Solving for Compounding Periods **LO3**
Hint: See Demo 6-3B

Foxx has $25,000 available today to invest at a rate of return of 8%, compounded annually. How many years would it take for the initial balance to reach $75,000?

Stone will deposit $7,500 at the end of each year for 10 years in a fund that earns 7%, compounded annually. What is the total amount of the fund at the end of 10 years?

Brief Exercise 6-8
Computing Future Value of an Annuity **LO4**
Hint: See Demo 6-4A

Referring to information in BE6-8, what amount would be accumulated in the fund if the annual deposits were instead made at the *beginning* of each year?

Brief Exercise 6-9
Computing Future Value of an Annuity **LO4**
Hint: See Demo 6-4B

Nicholas receives loan proceeds today from a financial institution. Nicholas agrees to pay the financial institution $1,000 at the end of each month over a 3-year period, beginning one month from today. Assuming the interest rate on the loan is 8.5%, what is today's amount of the loan?

Brief Exercise 6-10
Computing Present Value of an Annuity **LO5**
Hint: See Demo 6-5A

Referring to information in BE6-10, what is the loan amount if the first payment is made immediately?

Brief Exercise 6-11
Computing Present Value of an Annuity **LO5**
Hint: See Demo 6-5B

What is the present value of 4 years of annual cash receipts of $8,000 at the end of each year that begins 2 years from today, assuming a 6% interest rate?

Brief Exercise 6-12
Computing Value of Deferred Annuity **LO5**
Hint: See Demo 6-5C

Samuel borrowed $25,000 to purchase a vehicle on January 1 by signing a 5-year note with a 6% interest rate. Assuming end-of-month payments and monthly compounding, what is the monthly payment on the loan?

Brief Exercise 6-13
Solving for Annuity per Period **LO5**

Leonardo Inc. invests $20,944 at the end of each year in an investment fund that earns 5% interest. How many years will it take for the company to reach $200,000?

Brief Exercise 6-14
Solving for Compounding Periods **LO5**

Wick borrowed $8,000 and agreed to make 10 annual payments of $1,036 at the end of each year. What is the interest rate of this loan?

Brief Exercise 6-15
Solving for Interest Rate per Period **LO5**

On January 1, Arrow Inc. issued $100,000, 5% bonds due in 10 years. The bonds pay annual interest at the end of each year equal to 5% of face value. The current market interest rate for bonds with similar risk is 6%. Determine the issuance price of the bonds.

Brief Exercise 6-16
Determining Bond Price **LO6**
Hint: See Demo 6-6

Applied Inc. signed a 10-year lease for its corporate office space on January 2. The first annual payment of $40,000 is due immediately. Assuming an interest rate of 7%, what is the present value of the lease liability?

Brief Exercise 6-17
Determining Lease Liability **LO6**
Hint: See Demo 6-6

Americ Inc. borrowed $80,000 on January 1 with repayment scheduled over a 10-year period, with payments due at the end of each year at an interest rate of 7%. What is Americ's annual payment on this loan?

Brief Exercise 6-18
Determining Annual Loan Payment **LO6**
Hint: See Demo 6-6

Aflack Inc. borrowed $10,000 and agreed to pay off the loan over 5 years by making equal year-end payments, compounded annually at 10%.
a. What is the annual payment amount?
b. What is the annual payment amount if the interest rate increased to 12%?

Brief Exercise 6-19
Solving for Annuity Amount per Period **LO5**

Exercises

Exercise 6-1
Computing Future Value
of Single Amount with
Changes in Compounding
Periods **LO1, 2**
Hint: See Demo 6-2

Vision Inc. is considering the following investment opportunities.

Investment	Compounding	Annual Interest Rate	Cost	Term
Investment A....	Annually	6%	$100,000	5 years
Investment B....	Semiannually	6%	100,000	5 years
Investment C....	Quarterly	6%	100,000	5 years
Investment D....	Monthly	6%	100,000	5 years

Required
a. Compute the future value under each of the investment options.
b. Which option is preferable if we desire the lowest cost?

Exercise 6-2
Computing Future
Value of Single Amount
under Different
Assumptions **LO1, 2**
Hint: See Demo 6-2

Abbot Inc. is considering the following investment opportunities.

Investment	Compounding	Annual Interest Rate	Cost	Investment Period
Investment A....	Semiannually	6%	$50,000	5 years
Investment B....	Quarterly	8%	60,000	10 years
Investment C....	Monthly	12%	40,000	8 years
Investment D....	Monthly	6%	80,000	10 years

Required
Compute the future value under each of the investment options. Round interest rate percentages to two decimal places.

Exercise 6-3
Computing Present
Value of Single Amount
under Different
Assumptions **LO3**
Hint: See Demo 6-3A

Consider the following four separate investment scenarios.

Future Amount	Compounding	Annual Interest Rate	Investment Period
$10,000	Annually	5%	5 years
50,000	Semiannually	6%	10 years
60,000	Quarterly	8%	5 years
80,000	Monthly	12%	10 years

Required
Compute the present value under each of the four separate investment options.

Exercise 6-4
Computing Present
Value of Several Single
Amounts **LO3**

The following cash inflows are predicted over the next five years: $10,000, $15,000, $20,000, $25,000, and $30,000 at the end of years one, two, three, four, and five, respectively.

Required
Compute the total present value of the five cash flows at the beginning of year one, assuming annual compounding at a 6% interest rate.

Exercise 6-5
Solving for Unknown
Variables for Different
Investments **LO2, 3**
Hint: See Review 6-3

Consider the following four *separate* investment scenarios.

	Investment 1	Investment 2	Investment 3	Investment 4
RATE	?%	6%	5%	8%
NPER	5	?	10	12
PV...........	$(5,000)	$(22,000)	$?	$(82,000)
FV...........	$ 8,000	$ 35,000	$18,000	$?

Required
Solve for the unknown variables in each of the four separate investment scenarios. Assume interest is compounded annually in each case.

Answer the requirements in the following two separate cases.

1. On January 1 of Year 1, Etna Inc. has $40,000 that is deposited in an investment account until needed. It is anticipated that $111,000 will be needed at the end of 10 years to expand manufacturing. What approximate rate of interest is required to accumulate $111,000 on December 31 of Year 10, assuming compounding on an annual basis?
2. Visi Inc. plans an addition to its building as soon as adequate funds are accumulated. The company has estimated that the addition will cost $200,000. At today's date, $90,600 cash is available for investment, and such a fund pays 6% interest (compounded annually). How many periods would be required to accumulate the $200,000?

Exercise 6-6
Solving for Unknown
Variables for
Different Investment
Needs **LO2, 3**

Minerals Inc. anticipates environmental costs at the end of a 10-year production cycle. Due to the uncertainties of the remedies available in 10 years, the company has developed the following estimates.

Exercise 6-7
Computing Fair Value
of Environmental
Liability **LO3**
Hint: See Review 6-3

Cash Outflow	Probability
$500,000	30%
550,000	25%
600,000	25%
700,000	20%

Required

a. Compute the expected cash outflow for the environmental costs.
b. Determine the fair value of the liability for environment costs assuming a risk-free interest rate of 5%. Apply the expected cash flow technique, discounting cash flows using a risk-free rate.

For the following separate annuities *A* through *F*, complete the table by indicating the future value amount of the annuity.

Exercise 6-8
Computing Future
Value of Annuities,
Deferrals **LO4**
Hint: See Review 6-4

Investment	Frequency of Payments	Annual Interest Rate	Payment	Payment Period in Years	Beginning or End of Period Payment	Deferral of Annuity Payment*	Future Value Amount
Annuity A	Annually	5%	$(5,500)	6	End	0 years	$_____
Annuity B	Annually	6%	(6,500)	4	Beginning	0 years	_____
Annuity C	Annually	7%	(20,000)	8	End	3 years	_____
Annuity D	Semiannually	4%	(3,400)	3	End	0 years	_____
Annuity E	Semiannually	6%	(2,500)	2	Beginning	0 years	_____
Annuity F	Semiannually	8%	(22,000)	4	End	2 years	_____

*Deferral period falls before the payment period.

On January 1 of Year 1, Fargo Inc. decides to accumulate a debt retirement fund by making 10 equal annual deposits of $15,000 at the end of the next 10 years, beginning on December 31 of Year 1. Assume the fund accumulates annual compound interest at 7% per year, which is added to the fund balance.

Exercise 6-9
Computing Future Value
of Annuity Deposits—with
and without Deferred
Payment **LO4**

Required

a. What is the balance in the fund immediately after the last deposit on December 31 of Year 10?
b. What is the balance in the fund after the last deposit assuming that the first payment is deferred until December 31 of Year 3?

On January 1 of Year 1, Cyber Inc. is considering the following four separate investment scenarios.

Exercise 6-10
Computing Present
Value of Annuity
Payments under Different
Assumptions **LO5**
Hint: See Demo 6-5A,
5B, 5C

	Investment 1	Investment 2	Investment 3	Investment 4
Annual interest rate	8%	6%	6%	8.4%
Investment period................	5 years	6 years	5 years	10 years
Compounding periods	Quarterly	Annually	Semiannually	Monthly
Payment per compounding period ...	$5,000	$18,000	$10,000	$1,000
First payment in Year 1	January 1	December 31	June 30	January 1

Required

Compute the present value of the annuity for each of the four investment scenarios.

is separately identifiable from providing a finished building. The customer can benefit separately from both the plan and from the finished building.

606-10-25-19   a. The customer can benefit from the good or service either on its own or together with other resources that are readily available to the customer (that is, the good or service is capable of being distinct).

Distinct within the Context of a Contract

A performance obligation is distinct within the context of a contract if that promise can be identified separately from other promises within the contract. This means that the promises in the contract are (1) not integrated or bundled into a combined product or service, (2) not the result of goods or services modifying other goods or services, or (3) not interrelated.

For example, the software on a phone (such as camera, clock, and navigation guide) is not distinct from the phone itself because the phone is necessary for the operation of the software. In another case, providing a sweetener in an iced tea at a coffee shop is not a separate obligation from providing the iced tea. Another example is that a nonrefundable registration (joining) fee for a fitness facility and a monthly facility usage fee are considered to be one performance obligation, even though the fitness facility can charge separately for these items. Overall, the objective is to determine whether the promise, in the context of the contract, is to transfer goods and services individually or to transfer them combined (or as an integrated bundle).

606-10-25-19   b. The entity's promise to transfer the good or service to the customer is separately identifiable from other promises in the contract (that is, the promise to transfer the good or service is distinct within the context of the contract).

606-10-25-21   . . . Factors that indicate that two or more promises to transfer goods or services to a customer are not separately identifiable include, but are not limited to, the following:

a. The entity provides a significant service of integrating goods or services with other goods or services promised in the contract into a bundle of goods or services that represent the combined output or outputs for which the customer has contracted. In other words, the entity is using the goods or services as inputs to produce or deliver the combined output or outputs specified by the customer. A combined output or outputs might include more than one phase, element, or unit.

b. One or more of the goods or services significantly modifies or customizes, or are significantly modified or customized by, one or more of the other goods or services promised in the contract.

c. The goods or services are highly interdependent or highly interrelated. In other words, each of the goods or services is significantly affected by one or more of the other goods or services in the contract. For example, in some cases, two or more goods or services are significantly affected by each other because the entity would not be able to fulfill its promise by transferring each of the goods or services independently.

Materiality Threshold

The revenue standard does not require companies to *separately* account for promised goods or services if they are immaterial in the context of the contract. For example, if as part of a service contract, a seller provides an email with a monthly account statement, the seller might consider the providing of a monthly email to be immaterial within the context of the contract. This means the service would not be considered a separate performance obligation. (However, immaterial items that are material in the aggregate within the context of the contract, require further analysis.)

606-10-25-16A   An entity is not required to assess whether promised goods or services are performance obligations if they are immaterial in the context of the contract with the customer. . . .

Licenses, Warranties, and Customer Options

Further explanations of licenses, warranties, and customer options are provided in the paragraphs below.

License   A contract can include a license combined with other promises. Each promise must be evaluated to determine whether it is distinct. A license establishes rights to intellectual property and the obligation of a seller to provide those rights. As an example, a franchise establishes rights for a franchisee. The franchisor grants rights to individuals or business entities to use a particular name and offer specified services or products for a period of time. In this chapter, we consider the recognition of revenue from the perspective of the franchisor. In a later chapter, we consider the accounting for franchise costs from the perspective of the franchisee.

Service-Type Warranties Companies can offer a warranty as part of a contract. Certain warranties (service-type warranties) that provide assurances in addition to agreed upon specifications of the related product are considered separate performance obligations. The accounting for warranties is addressed in Chapter 15.

Customer Options Sometimes sellers grant customers options or the right to acquire additional goods and services as part of a contract. The right to purchase additional goods and services is not an enforceable obligation of the customer but an option. A customer option may or may not represent an additional performance obligation of the seller. A customer option is considered a separate performance obligation when it is *material in the context of a contract*. In these cases, the customer would not have the option or right to free or discounted services or goods, unless they entered into the original contract. This means the customer is paying for two things in the context of the contract: a good or service now and the right to a good or service in the future.

> `606-10-55-42`   If, in a contract, an entity grants a customer the option to acquire additional goods or services, that option gives rise to a performance obligation in the contract only if the option provides a material right to the customer that it would not receive without entering into that contract . . . If the option provides a material right to the customer, the customer in effect pays the entity in advance for future goods or services, and the entity recognizes revenue when those future goods or services are transferred or when the option expires.

Volume discounts that are *prospective* (rights to discounts that apply only to optional purchases in the future) should be evaluated to determine whether the customer is provided a material right considered a separate performance obligation. Volume discounts that are *retroactive* (adjustments to prior purchases because a certain volume was reached) are evaluated as variable consideration and affect the transaction price (see **LO 7-4**).

Determining whether a customer option is material requires judgment. To make this determination, consider this question: Would the same class of customer receive the same option to acquire additional goods and services if they had not entered into the revenue contract? For example, a customer enters into a contract to purchase a good and receives a 50% discount coupon on a subsequent purchase. If 15% discount coupons are widely available to the public, the net benefit to the customer is a 35% discount coupon (50% – 15%). The contract would have two performance obligations—one for the purchase of the good and one for a 35% coupon on a future purchase. This means that the customer is actually paying the seller for two items: for the good received now and for a discount on future goods.

Evaluation of materiality should also consider *qualitative factors* such as what a new customer would pay for the same option, the pricing of similar items by competitors, availability of options during a renewal period, and whether benefits accumulate (such as points in a loyalty rewards program accumulating with each dollar of customer purchases). If the option or right granted to a customer is determined to be material within the context of the contract, it is considered to be a separate performance obligation. **Determining the number of separate performance obligations in a contract is important because the remaining steps of the revenue recognition process are applied separately to each performance obligation.**

DEMO 7-3 ▶	**LO7-3**	**Identification of Separate Performance Obligation(s)**

Demo
MBC

Determine how many separate performance obligations are included in the following *separate* contract examples.

a. A builder enters into an agreement with a customer to build an addition to the customer's home for $80,000, payable when completed. The builder (also acting as contractor) is responsible for all aspects of the project including construction services, plumbing, electrical, carpentry, painting, design, preparation, and cleanup.

Solution
Construction services can be sold separately to a customer and the customer could benefit from the individual services. However, the promise is for a finished addition to the house. These individual services cannot be separated from the overall promise in the contract to provide a finished addition because the services are highly interrelated and one or more services modifies another. Therefore, the building of the addition is considered **one performance obligation**.

continued

continued from previous page

b. Congo Inc. enters into a contract with a customer to sell an electronic tablet and two years of data services. The customer receives an electronic tablet at a discounted value of $75 (retail value is $200) and agrees to pay a monthly fee of $20 for data service. Congo also sells the tablet without data service and sells data services without the purchase of a tablet.

Solution

There are **two performance obligations** in the arrangement: the tablet and monthly data service. The tablet and monthly data service can be purchased separately; thus, the tablet and monthly data service each provides a benefit and represents a separate promise. Further, because the tablet can be used without the data service, and the data service can be used with a different device, the two elements are not highly interdependent. (Allocation of a transaction price to various performance obligations is discussed in a later step.)

c. Bitware Inc. enters into a contract with a customer to provide a software license. The customer accesses the software by entering a unique 10-digit code. The software is functional on the customer's own computer. Within this contract, the customer has access to Bitware's customer service by phone or online for 12 months after the software download. Customer service contracts for this software are available from other service providers.

Solution

The seller has **two performance obligations**: to provide the software license and to provide customer support. The first promise, the license, grants the customer the right to use the intellectual property. The second promise, the right to customer service, benefits the customer and is separately identifiable from the right to use the software.

d. Epik, a healthcare software provider, enters into an arrangement to provide software and 1,000 hours of consulting services for $750,000. The software and the consulting services are distinct. Epik also provides an option to its customer to purchase 100 additional hours of consulting services over the next month at a rate of $225 per hour, which represents a 10% discount off the price of consulting services. During the same period, Epik launches a general advertising campaign to offer a 10% discount for consulting services.

Solution

There are **two performance obligations**: the transfer of the software and the transfer of the 1,000 hours of consulting services. The option to purchase 100 additional hours of consulting services at a discount does not provide a material customer option because similar customers can receive the discount without entering into a contract.

e. Gapp Inc. sponsors a customer loyalty point program where customers earn one loyalty point for every $5 spent on clothing and accessories at any Gapp Inc. store. Loyalty program members often exchange accumulated loyalty points for free products at Gapp. An individual customer makes a purchase of denim jeans at Gapp on June 1 for $60 and earns 12 loyalty points.

Solution

There are **two performance obligations**: the purchase of denim jeans and the loyalty points distributed. The loyalty points are a material customer option for additional goods because they can accumulate and equate to free products.

RAYTHEON   **Real World—PERFORMANCE OBLIGATION(S)**

Raytheon Company is a technology and innovation leader specializing in defense and other government markets. The vast majority of revenue is from long-term contracts associated with the design, development, manufacture, or modification of complex aerospace or defense equipment or services. Raytheon reported the following revenue recognition policy in a recent Form 10-K, which indicates that contracts can contain single or multiple performance obligations.

A performance obligation is a promise in a contract with a customer to transfer a distinct good or service to the customer. Some of our contracts with customers contain a single performance obligation, while others contain multiple performance obligations most commonly when a contract contains multiple distinct units (such as engines or certain aerospace components) or spans multiple phases of the product life-cycle such as production, maintenance and support.

EXPANDING YOUR KNOWLEDGE   **Material Customer Option?**

The revenue recognition standard requires a customer option to be defined as a separate performance obligation only if the option is material in *the context of an individual contract*. FASB's intent is to allow companies to disregard immaterial items at the contract level. If a company establishes thousands of contracts in a year, a sophisticated system is required to review materiality at a contract level. Consider, for example, a cell phone provider.

Case One A customer has signed a one-year agreement for cellular service for a total price of $1,200. The customer also receives an option to renew service at a discounted price. The renewal option has a standalone selling price of $20. The cell phone provider considers the $20 option *to be immaterial* to the contract price of $1,200.

Case Two A customer has entered into a month-to-month cellular contract for $100 per month. The customer also receives an option to renew cell phone service at a discounted price. The standalone selling price of the renewal option is $10. In this case, the cell phone provider considers the $10 option to be *material* to the contract price of $100.

As outlined in these cases, a $10 option can be material, whereas a $20 option might not be material considering the context of the individual contracts. Because the standard does not require a review of options in total in determining materiality, the total value of options considered immaterial at a contract level, can be material at a company level. Still, these options will not be considered separate performance obligations.

REVIEW 7-3	**LO7-3**	**Identification of Separate Performance Obligation(s)**

Review

MBC

In each of the following *separate* contract scenarios, determine and describe the number of performance obligations.

a. An optometrist enters into a contract with a customer to sell a pair of contacts along with two free boxes of contact solution. The optometrist sells contacts and solution separately, but the contacts require solution to work properly. Alternative brands of solution are compatible with the contacts.

b. A manufacturer purchased specialized industrial equipment for $350,000 plus installation services with a cost of $35,000. Due to the nature of the equipment, the installation is highly specialized and involves additional modifications of the equipment at the site of the installation.

c. A retail customer enters into a contract for a three-year license for anti-virus software. The purchase includes an initial software download and subsequent software updates over the three-year license period. Because new viruses emerge quickly, the software is expected to change and adapt extensively over the three-year license period.

d. A service provider enters into a contract with a customer for one year of home security monitoring for $360. Under the sales contract, the service provider guarantees a rate of $295 per year for years two and three as long as there is no lapse in service. The rates for security monitoring are expected to increase by 10% per year without the renewal options.

e. A franchisee enters into a contract with a franchisor for the right to operate a fast food location, using the company's (1) logo, design, and advertising materials; (2) menu items, recipes, and supplier contacts; (3) store designs; and (4) daily operating instructions for a five-year period beginning on January 1. The upfront fee of $250,000 also includes the purchase of equipment for $50,000, to be delivered 3 weeks after the date of the contract.

f. A retailer sells barbecue sauce with a coupon attached for 50 cents off the next purchase of barbecue sauce. The barbecue sauce typically sells for $2.00 a bottle.

g. A customer purchased a refrigerator from a home improvement retail store. Because the customer had no means to transport the refrigerator to her home to benefit from its use, she also rented a truck through the store for two hours. At the same time, the customer purchased vehicle insurance from the store because she was not sure if she would be covered through her own insurance plan.

More Practice:
BE7-7, BE7-8, BE7-9, BE7-10, BE7-11, E7-6, E7-7

Solution on p. 7-84.

h. An owner of a rental property enters into a contract with a service provider to manage its property over a one-year period. Management services vary each day but include items such as managing occupancy, maintenance, and accounting services.

Determine the transaction price—Step 3

LO 7-4

The next step in the revenue recognition process is to determine the **transaction price**, which is the amount of consideration that the company expects to be entitled to in exchange for the transfer of promised goods or services to a customer. The transaction price *excludes* amounts collected on behalf of third parties such as certain sales taxes.

Step 3: Determine Transaction Price
- Fixed consideration (*determines transaction price*)
- Variable consideration (*estimates transaction price*)
  - Expected value method
  - Most likely amount method
- Consideration payable to the customer (*reduces transaction price*)
- Refund liability (*reduces transaction price*)

LO 7-4 Overview

In this section, we explore how the transaction price is determined. The transaction price is made up of fixed consideration, variable consideration, or elements of both. The transaction price can also be affected by items such as consideration payable to customers, refund liabilities, time value of money, and noncash consideration. In addition, as shown in LO7-8, when a company simply arranges for services to be provided, the transaction price includes only the fee or commission that the company is entitled to for the transfer of the goods or services.

Determine Transaction Price					
Fixed Consideration	Variable Consideration	Consideration Payable to Customer	Refund Liability	Time Value of Money	Noncash Consideration

Fixed Consideration

With **fixed consideration**, determination of the transaction price is simple. For example, a builder enters into a contract with a customer to construct an addition to a customer's home for $80,000. The transaction price is stated in the contract and is not contingent on other events. In another example, REII Inc. sold one ski sweater for fixed consideration of $100. The transaction price is *fixed* and easily determinable.

Variable Consideration

Variable consideration results when the price of goods or services a seller is entitled to depends on future events, or when a price varies due to discounts, incentives, credits, or other similar items. If the consideration promised in a contract includes a variable amount, the company must estimate the amount of consideration the company is entitled to upon the exchange. Examples of variable consideration include the following:

- Price concessions
- Retroactive volume discounts
- Rebates and refunds
- Bonuses, incentives, and royalties
- Revenue contingent on future event occurring
- Cash discounts (see Chapter 8)

The revenue recognition standard provides two choices to estimate variable consideration: the expected value method and the most likely amount method. See **Demo 7-4A**. Companies should choose the method that is the better predictor of revenue and that method should be applied consistently with the following constraint outlined in the accounting standards:

606-10-32-11   An entity shall include in the transaction price some or all of an amount of variable consideration in accordance with paragraph 606-10-32-8 only to the extent that it is probable that a significant reversal in the amount of cumulative revenue recognized will not occur when the uncertainty associated with the variable consideration is subsequently resolved.

Expected Value Method

606-10-32-8 An entity shall estimate an amount of variable consideration by using either of the following methods, depending on which method the entity expects to better predict the amount of consideration to which it will be entitled: a. The expected value is the sum of probability-weighted amounts in a range of possible consideration amounts. An expected value may be an appropriate estimate of the amount of variable consideration if an entity has a large number of contracts with similar characteristics. . . .

To use the expected value method, a company needs data necessary to consider and quantify the possibilities of all possible outcomes.

$100 × 35%	$ 35
$200 × 35%	70
$300 × 30%	90
Variable consideration	$195

For example, assume consideration is variable due to the potential for a retroactive volume discount if specified sales volumes are met. Consideration to be received might be $100 (35% probability), $200 (35% probability), or $300 (30% probability). Under the expected value method, variable consideration is estimated at $195.

Most Likely Amount Method

606-10-32-8 b. The most likely amount is the single most likely amount in a range of possible consideration amounts (that is, the single most likely outcome of the contract). The most likely amount may be an appropriate estimate of the amount of variable consideration if the contract has only two possible outcomes (for example, an entity either achieves a performance bonus or does not).

For example, if the consideration to be received might be $400 or $0 but the most likely amount is $400, variable consideration is estimated at $400.

The seller is required to use the method that best predicts the amount of revenue to be collected. The availability of alternative methods does not imply companies have a free choice to use either if one is significantly more predictive than the other.

DEMO 7-4A ▶ **LO7-4**   **Estimating Transaction Price When It Includes Variable Consideration**

Demo
MBC

Example One—Expected Value Method   Diaz Inc. develops website ads for customers. Contract terms and conditions are similar across its various contracts. Contracts typically include a fixed fee plus variable consideration for a performance bonus earned when website ads are delivered ahead of schedule. Based on Diaz's historical experience, the bonus amounts and associated probabilities for achieving each bonus on a new customer's contract follow.

Bonus Amount	Probability of Outcome
$ 0	15%
5,000	40%
10,000	45%

Diaz has a large number of contracts that have characteristics that are similar to the new contract. As a result, Diaz determines that using the expected value method would better predict the amount of consideration to which it will be entitled than using the most likely amount method. What is Diaz Inc.'s transaction price for the performance bonus based upon the *expected value method*?

Solution

Diaz estimates $6,500 of variable consideration to include in the transaction price using the expected value method, calculated as follows.

Bonus Amount		Probability of Outcome		Revenue Recognized
$ 0	×	15%	=	$ 0
5,000	×	40%	=	2,000
10,000	×	45%	=	4,500
Variable consideration				$6,500

Example Two—Most Likely Amount Method   Diaz Inc. develops website ads for customers. Contract terms and conditions are similar across its various contracts. Contracts typically include a

continued

continued from previous page

fixed fee plus variable consideration for a performance bonus related to the timing to complete the website ad. If the website ad is finished by the deadline stated in the contract, Diaz Inc. will receive a bonus of $5,000. If the website ad is not finished by the deadline, Diaz Inc. receives no bonus. Based upon its historical experience, Diaz believes that the most likely amount of the bonus consideration is $5,000. What is Diaz Inc.'s transaction price for the performance bonus based upon the *most likely amount method*?

Solution

Diaz estimates $5,000 of variable consideration to include in the transaction price using the most likely amount method, calculated as follows.

Bonus Amount	Revenue Recognized
$ 0	$ 0
$5,000	$5,000

EXPANDING YOUR KNOWLEDGE   Constraint on Variable Consideration

A seller recognizes variable consideration only to the extent a probable significant reversal of revenue will not occur in the future. The revenue recognition standard outlines factors that could increase the likelihood of a revenue reversal (not all inclusive).

606-10-32-12   In assessing whether it is probable that a significant reversal in the amount of cumulative revenue recognized will not occur once the uncertainty related to the variable consideration is subsequently resolved, an entity shall consider both the likelihood and the magnitude of the revenue reversal. Factors that could increase the likelihood or the magnitude of a revenue reversal include, but are not limited to, any of the following:

a. The amount of consideration is highly susceptible to factors outside the entity's [seller's] influence. Those factors may include volatility in a market, the judgment or actions of third parties, weather conditions, and a high risk of obsolescence of the promised good or service.
b. The uncertainty about the amount of consideration is not expected to be resolved for a long period of time.
c. The entity's [seller's] experience (or other evidence) with similar types of contracts is limited, or that experience (or other evidence) has limited predictive value.
d. The entity [seller] has a practice of either offering a broad range of price concessions or changing the payment terms and conditions of similar contracts in similar circumstances.
e. The contract has a large number and broad range of possible consideration amounts.

Consideration Payable to a Customer

As part of a contract, a seller can pay consideration to a customer. Examples of consideration paid or payable to a customer include credits (coupons), volume discounts, rebates, cooperative advertising arrangements, and slotting fees (shown in **Demo 7-4B**). The payment of consideration need not take place at the same time as the revenue contract. Expected **consideration payable** is generally treated as a reduction of the transaction price.

Selling price
Less: Consideration payable
Transaction price recorded as sales revenue

Unpaid consideration at a reporting period is recorded as a current liability. If however, the payment to the customer is in exchange for a distinct good or service received from the customer, the transaction is recorded separately as a typical purchase from a supplier. Further, if consideration payable is greater than the fair value of the distinct good or service received from the customer, the excess is treated as a reduction to the transaction price.

606-10-32-25   An entity shall account for consideration payable to a customer as a reduction of the transaction price and, therefore, of revenue unless the payment to the customer is in exchange for a distinct good or service . . . that the customer transfers to the entity.

606-10-32-26   If consideration payable to a customer is a payment for a distinct good or service from the customer, then an entity shall account for the purchase of the good or service in the same way that it accounts for other purchases from suppliers. If the amount of consideration payable to the customer exceeds the fair value of the distinct good or service that the entity receives from the customer, then the entity shall account for such an excess as a reduction of the transaction price. If the entity cannot reasonably estimate the fair value of the good or service received from the customer, it shall account for all of the consideration payable to the customer as a reduction of the transaction price.

DEMO 7-4B ▶ **LO7-4** **Reducing the Transaction Price for Consideration Payable**

Kallog Inc., a cereal manufacturer, sells its cereal line to a large grocery store chain. Kallog also pays the grocery chain a **slotting fee**, which is a payment for desired shelf position in the store. The slotting fee is negotiated as part of the sales contract. For the month of June cash sales to a grocery store were $10,000, cost of inventory was $4,000, and the slotting fee was $500. Kallog did not receive a distinct good or service in exchange for the $500. What is Kallog's transaction price?

Solution

The slotting fee is consideration payable because it is paid by the seller in connection with the contract and is not paid for a distinct good or service. The transaction price (recorded as sales revenue) is measured as follows.

Selling price	$10,000
Less: Consideration Payable	500
Transaction price recorded as sales revenue	$ 9,500

Instead of recording the consideration payable (slotting fees) as an advertising expense, it is reported as a reduction to the transaction price because it was negotiated as part of the contract.†

† Recognition of revenue is in a later section (LO 6). Looking ahead, the following summary entries for the month of June are required by Step 5 for revenue recognition assuming Kallog pays the slotting fee in a future month.

To record sales

Cash	10,000	
Sales Revenue		9,500
Consideration Payable		500

To record cost of goods sold

Cost of Goods Sold	4,000	
Inventory		4,000

Refund Liability—Sales with Right of Return

A company recognizes a refund liability (usually a *current liability*) if the company receives consideration from a customer and expects to refund some or all of the consideration in the future. The **refund liability** is the amount of consideration received (or receivable) that the company does not expect to be entitled to. The amount of refund liability should be adjusted at the end of each reporting period. The most common refund liability is a sale with right of return. Other refund liabilities include retroactive price adjustments and refunds due to poor customer satisfaction with a service provided.

The transaction price, and ultimately the amount of revenue recognized, is reduced by estimated full or partial returns. (The right of return is *not* considered to be a performance obligation.) The expected value of sales returns is estimated in the same way as other variable consideration: using either the expected value method or the most likely amount method. The transaction price recorded as sales revenue in the income statement is reduced by the refund liability. In other words, sales revenue is recorded only for goods not expected to be returned. The recording of returns is discussed further in Chapter 8.

Time Value of Money

The revenue recognition standard provides guidance on accounting for arrangements with significant financing components. The determination of whether a financing component is significant is assessed at the contract level and involves judgment, with an evaluation of both qualitative and quantitative factors. In determining the transaction price in contracts with significant financing components, companies adjust consideration amounts for the effect of the time value of money when the timing of payments provides the customer with financing benefits. A contract with a customer does not have a significant financing component if any of the following factors exist.

606-10-32-17 Notwithstanding the assessment in paragraph 606-10-32-16, a contract with a customer would not have a significant financing component if any of the following factors exist:

a. The customer paid for the goods or services in advance, and the timing of the transfer of those goods or services is at the discretion of the customer.

b. A substantial amount of the consideration promised by the customer is variable, and the amount or timing of that consideration varies on the basis of the occurrence or nonoccurrence of a future event that is not substantially within the control of the customer or the entity . . .

c. The difference between the promised consideration and the cash selling price of the good or service . . . arises for reasons other than the provision of finance to either the customer or the entity, and the difference between those amounts is proportional to the reason for the difference. For example, the payment terms might provide the entity or the customer with protection from the other party failing to adequately complete some or all of its obligations under the contract.

In addition, the following practical expedient is applicable to contracts with short-term payment receipts.

606-10-32-18   As a practical expedient, an entity need not adjust the promised amount of consideration for the effects of a significant financing component if the entity expects, at contract inception, that the period between when the entity transfers a promised good or service to a customer and when the customer pays for that good or service will be one year or less.

See Chapter 8 for recording significant financing components involving notes receivable.

Noncash Consideration

The fair value (at a contract's inception) of noncash consideration received from a customer must be included in determining the transaction price. If the fair value of the consideration is not reasonably estimable, the value of the consideration is estimated indirectly by reference to the standalone selling price of the goods or services promised to the customer. Noncash consideration can be in the form of property, plant, and equipment, or a financial instrument. A customer might contribute goods or services to facilitate a seller's fulfillment of a performance obligation. An entity should include the customer's contribution of goods or services in the transaction price as noncash consideration only if the entity obtains control of those goods or services.

As an example, assume that on January 1, Atlanta Inc. enters into a contract with Green Mfg. to build equipment. Atlanta Inc. pays Green Mfg. $2 million cash and agrees to provide necessary materials with a fair value of $250,000 to be used in the manufacturing of the equipment. Atlanta Inc. will deliver the materials to Green Mfg. approximately three months after Green Mfg. starts the manufacturing process. Green Mfg. obtains control of the materials upon delivery by Atlanta Inc. and could elect to use the materials for other projects. In this case, Green Mfg. determines the transaction price to be calculated as follows:

$2 million cash + $250,000 noncash consideration = $2,250,000 transaction price

Transaction Price	**LO7-4**	**REVIEW 7-4**

In each of the following separate revenue contract scenarios, determine the transaction price *and* determine whether the transaction price is fixed, variable, or some combination of both.

Review

MBC

a. Merc Inc. sells $100,000 of inventory during the year to customers for $130,000. Merc Inc. accepts returns up to 6 months after the date of purchase. Based on historical trends, 5% of inventory that Merc Inc. sells is returned.

b. Krowgar Co. sells a brand new cereal product to Mart Inc. for $3,000. Krowgar agrees to reimburse Mart Inc. $500 for anticipated shortfalls in the selling price collected by Mart Inc. for the launch of the product.

c. IT Inc. enters into a contract with Smit Co. to install a new technology system. IT Inc. will receive a bonus of $5,000 (in addition to a fixed fee of $50,000) if the installation is completed before year-end. The bonus decreases by $1,000 per week after year-end. IT Inc. estimates that there is a 70% probability that the contract will be completed by the agreed-upon completion date, a 20% probability that it will be completed one week after year-end, and a 10% probability that it will be completed two weeks after year-end.

d. Sisko Inc. enters into a contract with Davi Co. to install a new technology system. Sisko Inc. will receive a bonus of $5,000 (in addition to a fixed fee of $50,000) if the installation is completed before year-end. The bonus decreases by $1,000 per week after year-end. Based on Sisko's history of meeting deadlines, Sisko estimates that the most likely amount of the bonus to be received is $5,000.

More Practice:
E7-12, E7-13, E7-14, E7-15

Solution on p. 7-84.

LO 7-5 ▸ Allocate the transaction price to performance obligations in the contract—Step 4

Step 4: Allocate Transaction Price Based on Relative Standalone Selling Prices
- Observable standalone selling prices
- Estimated standalone selling prices
  - Adjusted market assessment approach
  - Expected cost plus a margin approach
  - Residual approach

LO 7-5 Overview

After the performance obligations are identified and the transaction price is established, the next step is to allocate the transaction price to the separate performance obligations.

| ① Identify contract(s) with customer | ② Identify performance obligation(s) in the contract | ③ Determine transaction price | ④ **Allocate transaction price to performance obligation(s)** | ⑤ Recognize revenue when (or as) each performance obligation is satisfied through a transfer of control |

The transaction price is generally allocated to each performance obligation based on the **standalone selling price** or the price at which a company would sell a promised good or service separately to a customer. The company must determine the standalone selling price for each material distinct performance obligation and then allocate the transaction price based on each item's relative standalone selling price compared to the total standalone selling price of all performance obligations in the contract.

606-10-05-4 d. Step 4: Allocate the transaction price to the performance obligations in the contract—An entity typically allocates the transaction price to each performance obligation on the basis of the relative standalone selling prices of each distinct good or service promised in the contract. If a standalone selling price is not observable, an entity estimates it. . . .

Determine standalone selling price of each performance obligation			
Observable	Estimated: Adjusted Market Assessment Approach	Estimated: Expected Cost Plus a Margin Approach	Estimated: Residual Approach

Allocate transaction price to performance obligations based on relative standalone selling prices

Observable Selling Price

The strongest evidence of a standalone selling price is when goods or services are sold separately. In such a case, standalone prices are **observable**.

606-10-32-32 The standalone selling price is the price at which an entity would sell a promised good or service separately to a customer. The best evidence of a standalone selling price is the observable price of a good or service when the entity sells that good or service separately in similar circumstances and to similar customers. A contractually stated price or a list price for a good or service may be (but shall not be presumed to be) the standalone selling price of that good or service.

Estimated Selling Price

The standalone selling price must be **estimated** when not observable. Three methods for estimating a standalone selling price are the (1) **adjusted market assessment approach**, (2) **expected cost plus a margin approach**, and (3) **residual approach**.

606-10-32-33 . . . When estimating a standalone selling price, an entity shall consider all information (including market conditions, entity-specific factors, and information about the customer or class of customer) that is reasonably available to the entity. In doing so, an entity shall maximize the use of observable inputs and apply estimation methods consistently in similar circumstances.

Adjusted Market Assessment Approach In the adjusted market assessment approach, a company estimates the price that a customer in a market (in which it is actively selling goods or services) would be willing to pay for these goods or services. Information can be obtained from competitors' prices. This method is easier to apply if a seller has been active in a market for a period of time or a competitor offers a similar product and it can be used as a basis for this analysis.

Expected Cost Plus a Margin Approach In the expected cost plus a margin approach, a company forecasts its expected costs of satisfying a performance obligation and then adds an appropriate margin for that good or service to compute the standalone selling price of that good or service.

Residual Approach In the residual approach, the standalone selling price of one (or more) of the goods or services is known. The remaining good or service is valued at the sales price left to be allocated. This method can *only* be used to estimate the standalone selling price of a good or service if one of the following criteria is met.

- The seller sells the same good or service to different customers for different amounts.
- The good or service does not have an established price because it has not been sold before.

Due to restrictions placed on usage of the residual method, practical usage of this method is limited.

In **Demo 7-5A** we show the allocation of transaction price when the standalone selling price for each separate performance obligation is observable or known at the start of the contract. In **Demo 7-5B** we show the allocation of the transaction price when not all of the standalone selling prices are observable, which means that some must be estimated.

In the examples and assignments in this chapter, we state the price that the goods or services are sold for including the price that is stated to the customer for each component. The objective, however, is to determine how to *allocate revenue to the performance obligations according to the revenue recognition standards for financial reporting purposes*. For example, a customer might be told that after buying ten products, the eleventh is free. However, for financial reporting purposes, the revenue recognition standard requires that revenue be allocated to all eleven products.

Transaction Price Allocation—Standalone Selling Prices Are Observable LO7-5 **DEMO 7-5A**

Example One—Total Standalone Selling Price Equals Total Transaction Price
A customer enters into a contract with B-Buys Inc. to purchase a computer and computer services for a combined price of $1,200 (stated to the customer as $1,000 for the computer and $200 for the computer services).The sale of the computer and the services are considered separate performance obligations. B-Buys Inc. sells the same computers to other customers for $1,000 each and provides computer services (technical assistance) to other customers for $200 per year. This means that the standalone selling price for the computer is $1,000 and the standalone selling price for computer services is $200. *In this case, the total transaction price of $1,200 equals the total standalone selling price of $1,200.* Allocate the total $1,200 transaction price to each separate performance obligation.

Solution

Performance Obligations	Transaction Price as Stated	Standalone Selling Price	Allocated Transaction Price
Computer	$1,000	$1,000	$1,000
Services	200	200	200
	$1,200	$1,200	$1,200

The transaction price of $1,200 is the amount recognized as revenue in Step 5, with $1,000 allocated to the computer and $200 to the computer services.

Example Two—Total Standalone Selling Price Does Not Equal Total Transaction Price
Assume the same circumstances as in Example One except that the customer pays a *combined discounted selling price of $900 (stated to the customer as $800 for the computer and $100 for the service)*. In this case, the total transaction price of $900 does not equal the total standalone selling price of $1,200. Allocate the total $900 transaction price to each separate performance obligation.

continued

continued from previous page

Solution

Performance Obligations	Transaction Price as Stated	Standalone Selling Price	Selling Price Ratio	Allocated Transaction Price	
Computer	$800	$1,000	1,000/1,200 or 5/6	$750	(5/6 × $900)
Services	100	200	200/1,200 or 1/6	150	(1/6 × $900)
	$900	$1,200	1,200/1,200 or 6/6	$900	

The transaction price of $900 is the amount recognized as revenue in Step 5, with $750 allocated to the computer and $150 to the computer services. The total allocated revenue recognized can never exceed the total transaction price.

ALPHABET   Real World—MULTIPLE PERFORMANCE OBLIGATIONS

Alphabet Inc. reported the following revenue recognition policy in a recent Form 10-K indicating the transaction price is allocated to performance obligations based upon the relative observable standalone selling prices of the performance obligations.

Arrangements with Multiple Performance Obligations Our contracts with customers may include multiple performance obligations. For such arrangements, we allocate revenue to each performance obligation based on its relative standalone selling price. We generally determine standalone selling prices based on the prices charged to customers.

> **DEMO 7-5B** **LO7-5** **Transaction Price Allocation—Standalone Selling Prices Are Estimated**

Demo
MBC

Example One—Adjusted Market Assessment <u>and</u> Expected Cost Plus a Margin Approaches
5M Inc. enters into a contract with a customer to sell three products in exchange for $200, the total transaction price (stated to the customer as $75 for Product A, $100 for Product B, and $25 for Product C). 5M regularly sells Product A, so the market price is directly observable at $75 per product. The standalone selling price of Products B and C are not observable. 5M Inc. gathers additional information regarding Products B and C. Two competitors sell an item similar to product B for an average selling price of $100. The estimated cost of Product C is $36 and the company expects a markup on cost of 40%. Allocate the total $200 transaction price to each separate performance obligation.

Solution

The standalone selling prices of Products A, B, and C are estimated as follows. The customer received a discount because the combined price of the bundled goods was $200, which was less than the estimated standalone selling prices of the individual products, which total $225.

Product A	$ 75	*Directly observable*—known standalone selling price
Product B	100	*Adjusted market assessment approach*—estimated based upon competitors' prices
Product C	50	*Expected cost plus a margin*—estimated based on cost plus margin ($36 × 1.40)
	$225	

Because there is no observable evidence of where to allocate the $25 ($225 − $200) discount, the discount is allocated proportionately as follows. The $200 transaction price is the amount recognized as revenue in Step 5, with $67 allocated to Product A, $89 to Product B, and $44 to Product C.

continued

continued from previous page

Performance Obligations	Transaction Price as Stated	Standalone Selling Price	Selling Price Ratio	Allocated Transaction Price*	
Product A	$ 75	$ 75	75/225 or 3/9	$ 67	(3/9 × $200)
Product B	100	100	100/225 or 4/9	89	(4/9 × $200)
Product C	25	50	50/225 or 2/9	44	(2/9 × $200)
	$200	$225	225/225 or 9/9	$200	

*Amounts rounded.

Example Two—Residual Approach

5M Inc. enters into a contract with a customer to sell three products in exchange for $200, the total transaction price. 5M regularly sells Product A for $75 and Product B for $95 on a standalone basis. The standalone selling price of Product C is not observable because it is a new product and is currently not sold by competitors. Because Product C has not been sold before and does not have an established price, the residual approach can be used to estimate the selling price of Product C. Allocate the total $200 transaction price to each separate performance obligation.

Solution

The standalone selling prices of Products A, B, and C are summarized as follows. The $200 transaction price is the amount recognized as revenue in Step 5, with $75 allocated to Product A, $95 to Product B, and $30 to Product C.

Performance Obligations	Standalone Selling Price	Allocated Transaction Price
Product A	$75 (*Observable*)	$ 75
Product B	95 (*Observable*)	95
Product C		30*
		$200

*$200 – $75 – $95 = $30

Estimating Standalone Selling Price for Customer Options

Recall that a customer option is the right to acquire additional goods and services as part of a revenue contract. As with other performance obligations, the standalone selling price must be determined. If the standalone selling price is not observable, it must be estimated. The discount offered through the customer option should be adjusted for any discount the customer could receive without the option and the likelihood that the customer will exercise the option.

606-10-55-44 Paragraph 606-10-32-29 requires an entity to allocate the transaction price to performance obligations on a relative standalone selling price basis. If the standalone selling price for a customer's option to acquire additional goods or services is not directly observable, an entity should estimate it. That estimate should reflect the discount that the customer would obtain when exercising the option, adjusted for both of the following:

a. Any discount that the customer could receive without exercising the option
b. The likelihood that the option will be exercised

Transaction Price Allocation—Customer Options　　　　　**LO7-5**　　**DEMO 7-5C**

A sporting goods store sells a tennis racquet for $40 and offers the customer an option to purchase tennis balls for 60% off the retail price of $10. Based on past promotions, the store estimates that the customer will exercise the option 40% of the time. The typical store coupon allows for 10% off a store purchase.

Demo

MBC

continued

continued from previous page

The store estimates the standalone selling price of the customer option as $2.00, calculated as follows.

$$\textbf{\$10 tennis ball price} \times (60\% - 10\%) \times 40\% \textbf{ likelihood of exercising the option} = \$2.00$$

Allocate the total transaction price of $40 to each performance obligation.

Solution

Now that we have the standalone selling price of the tennis racquet of $40 and the standalone selling price of the customer option of $2.00, we can allocate the transaction price of $40 to the two performance obligations. Based on relative standalone selling prices, the transaction price of $40 is allocated $38.10 to the tennis racquet and $1.90 to the customer option.

Performance Obligations	Transaction Price as Stated	Standalone Selling Price	Selling Price Ratio	Allocated Transaction Price
Tennis racquet	$40.00	$40.00	40/42	$38.10 (40/42 × $40, rounded)
Customer option . . .	0	2.00	2/42	1.90 (2/42 × $40, rounded)
	$40.00	$42.00	42/42	$40.00

EXPANDING YOUR KNOWLEDGE   Estimating Standalone Price

Estimating standalone price *requires judgment.* The revenue recognition standard indicates that we cannot presume that a list price or a contractually stated price is a standalone selling price. The revenue recognition standard provides examples of items to consider in estimating a standalone selling price.

Market Conditions to Consider
- Potential limits on the selling price of the product
- Competitor pricing for a similar product
- Current market trends that will likely affect the pricing
- The entity's market share and position
- Effects of the geographic area on pricing

Entity-Specific Factors to Consider
- Profit objectives and internal cost structure
- Pricing practices and pricing objectives
- Effects of customization on pricing
- Pricing practices used to establish pricing of bundled products

---

REVIEW 7-5   ▶ LO7-5   Allocation of Transaction Price

Review

MBC

Cellular Inc. is offering a promotion for new customers signing a contract: purchase a new handset, a one-year service agreement, and set of headphones for $710. The transaction price as stated to the customer is $150 for the handset, $480 for the one-year service agreement, and $80 for the set of headphones. Allocate the $710 transaction price under the following separate cases.

a. The three items (service, handset, and headphones) are sold separately by Cellular. The standalone selling prices of the handset, one-year service agreement, and headphones are $150, $480, and $80, respectively.

b. The three items (service, handset, and headphones) are sold separately by Cellular. The standalone selling prices of the handset, one-year service agreement, and headphones are $200, $480, and $80, respectively.

c. Two of the three items (service and handset) are sold separately by Cellular. The standalone selling prices of the handset and one-year service agreement are $200 and $480, respectively. Because Cellular has never sold headphones prior to this promotion, Cellular determined the average selling price of similar headphones in the market place to be $100.

d. Two of the three items (service and handset) are sold separately by Cellular. The standalone selling prices of the handset and one-year service agreement are $200 and $480, respectively. Cellular purchased the headphones for $64 a pair and expects a markup on cost of 40%.

e. Two of the three items (service and handset) are sold separately by Cellular. The standalone selling prices of the handset and one-year service agreement are $200 and $480, respectively. Cellular has never sold headphones prior to this promotion and is not able to obtain a reliable comparable market price because the headphones are unique and nothing comparable is available on the market.

More Practice:
BE7-18, BE7-19, BE7-20, E7-22

Solution on p. 7-84.

Recognize revenue when (or as) the seller satisfies a performance obligation—Step 5

The final step of revenue recognition is to recognize revenue as distinct performance obligations are satisfied. According to the accounting guidance:

Step 5: Recognize Revenue When Seller Satisfies a Performance Obligation
- Revenue recognized at a point in time
- Revenue recognized over time

606-10-25-23   An entity shall recognize revenue when (or as) the entity satisfies a performance obligation by transferring a promised good or service (that is, an asset) to a customer. An asset is transferred when (or as) the customer obtains control of that asset.

| ① Identify contract(s) with customer | ② Identify performance obligation(s) in the contract | ③ Determine transaction price | ④ Allocate transaction price to performance obligation(s) | ⑤ Recognize revenue when (or as) each performance obligation is satisfied through a transfer of control |

Control can transfer to a customer **at a point in time** or **over time**. Control implies the customer can direct the use and obtain the benefits of that good or service. In evaluating the transfer of control, management should consider guidance mainly from the perspective of the customer to determine if revenue is recognized at a point in time or over time. **When a company has multiple performance obligations, each performance obligation is analyzed to determine when control has transferred to the customer for each respective performance obligation.**

Recognition of Revenue	
At Point in Time	Over Time

Recognition of Revenue Over Time

Revenue is recognized *over time* if *any one* of the following three criteria in **Exhibit 7-3** is met.

Revenue Recognition Over Time Criteria	Contract Example
606-10-25-27a The customer simultaneously receives and consumes the benefits provided by the [seller's] performance as the [seller] performs . . .	24-month security monitoring at a retail store.
606-10-25-27b The [seller's] performance creates or enhances an asset (for example, work in process) that the customer controls as the asset is created or enhanced . . .	Contract to build customized equipment for a customer where the customer owns the work in process.
606-10-25-27c The [seller's] performance does not create an asset with an alternative use to the [seller] . . . and the [seller] has an enforceable right to payment for performance completed to date . . .	Contract to build customized equipment for a customer where the customer does not take physical possession of the equipment until fully built. The customer is obligated to pay costs incurred plus the agreed upon profit if a cancellation occurs.

EXHIBIT 7-3
Revenue Recognition Over Time Criteria

If one or more of the criteria are met, the seller must recognize revenue over time, proportionately with the rate of satisfaction of the performance obligation. How is revenue recognized over time? With some service revenue contracts, revenue is recognized evenly over the contract period on a **straight-line basis**. Other times, as in many long-term contracts, revenue is recognized based on the **extent of progress toward satisfaction of performance obligations**. Progress toward the satisfaction of performance obligations can be measured through input measures or output measures.

606-10-25-31   For each performance obligation satisfied over time . . . an entity shall recognize revenue over time by measuring the progress toward complete satisfaction of that performance obligation. The objective when measuring progress is to depict an entity's performance in transferring control of goods or services promised to a customer (that is, the satisfaction of an entity's performance obligation).

606-10-55-17   Output methods recognize revenue on the basis of direct measurements of the value to the customer of the goods or services transferred to date relative to the remaining goods or services promised under the contract. Output methods include methods such as surveys of performance completed to date, appraisals of results achieved, milestones reached, time elapsed, and units produced or units delivered. . . .

606-10-55-20   Input methods recognize revenue on the basis of the entity's efforts or inputs to the satisfaction of a performance obligation (for example, resources consumed, labor hours expended, costs incurred, time elapsed, or machine hours used) relative to the total expected inputs to the satisfaction of that performance obligation . . .

Judgment is needed to determine what is the measure that best captures progress that has been made. One common input method to estimate the amount of revenue to recognize over time is the **cost-to-cost method**, which measures the input of costs incurred relative to total expected costs to be incurred. In computing the percentage completion, costs due to inefficiencies (such as unexpected amounts of wasted materials, labor, or other resources) that were not reflected in the price of the contract are *excluded* from the calculation. The percentage completion is applied to total contract revenue (transaction price) to measure the amount of revenue to recognize to date. *Note:* If the company estimates a net contract loss, the net contract loss is recognized immediately. Appendix 7A and Appendix 7B show journal entries for long-term construction contracts.

$$\text{Percent complete} \quad = \quad \frac{\text{Total costs incurred to date (excluding inefficiencies)}}{\text{Most recent estimate of total project costs}}$$

$$\text{Recognized revenue} \quad = \quad \text{Percent complete} \times \text{Total contract revenue}$$

Recognition of Revenue at a Point in Time

If none of the criteria included in **Exhibit 7-3** are met, revenue is recognized **at a point in time**—when control of the asset passes to the customer. The five factors in **Exhibit 7-1** are key in determining whether control has passed to the customer. For example, examining whether the customer has physical possession of the asset or whether the seller has the right to payment are some of those key factors.

Contract Liabilities and Contract Assets

The definition of contract liability and contract asset are important and are defined as follows.

Balance Sheet Accounts	Point of Revenue Recognition
Contract liability	**ASC Glossary** An entity's [seller's] obligation to transfer goods or services to a customer for which the [seller] has received consideration (or the amount is due) from the customer.
Contract asset	**ASC Glossary** An entity's [seller's] right to consideration in exchange for goods or services that the [the seller] has transferred to a customer when that right is conditioned on something other than the passage of time (for example, [the seller's] future performance).

When a customer performs first (a prepayment), the seller recognizes a contract liability. This means a seller records a liability if a customer's payment occurs before transfer of control of the good or service to the customer. The seller recognizes revenue at the point when the performance obligation is satisfied. As shown in Exhibit 2-10, a variety of account names are used to refer to a contract liability such as deferred revenue, deferred service revenue, and deferred royalty revenue.

When a seller performs first and satisfies a performance obligation by transferring control of a promised good or service, the seller has earned a right to consideration from the customer. The seller then recognizes either a receivable or a contract asset. A **contract asset** represents a *conditional right* to consideration. The right would be conditional, for example, when a seller must satisfy another performance obligation in the contract before it is entitled to payment from the customer. If an entity has an *unconditional right* to receive consideration from the customer, a **receivable** is recognized and presented separately from other contract assets. A right is unconditional if nothing other than the passage of time is required before payment of that consideration is due.

606-10-45-1   When either party to a contract has performed, an entity [seller] shall present the contract in the statement of financial position as a contract asset or a contract liability, depending on the relationship between the entity's [seller's] performance and the customer's payment. An entity [seller] shall present any unconditional rights to consideration separately as a receivable.

For example, a seller enters into a contract to deliver two products to a customer which will be delivered at two different times. The delivery of each product is considered a separate performance obligation. The customer is not required to pay for both products until 30 days after *both* products are delivered. After the first product is delivered, the seller debits Contract Asset (not a receivable) and credits Sales Revenue. This is because the seller does not have an unconditional right to consideration until the second product is delivered. After the second product is delivered, the contract asset is reclassified to a receivable. If however, the customer is required to pay for each individual product 30 days after delivery of the product, the company debits Accounts Receivable and credits Sales Revenue after delivery of the first (and second) product.

606-10-45-2   If a customer pays consideration, or an entity has a right to an amount of consideration that is unconditional (that is, a receivable), before the entity transfers a good or service to the customer, the entity shall present the contract as a contract liability when the payment is made or the payment is due (whichever is earlier). A contract liability is an entity's obligation to transfer goods or services to a customer for which the entity has received consideration (or an amount of consideration is due) from the customer.

606-10-45-3   If an entity performs by transferring goods or services to a customer before the customer pays consideration or before payment is due, the entity shall present the contract as a contract asset, excluding any amounts presented as a receivable. A contract asset is an entity's right to consideration in exchange for goods or services that the entity has transferred to a customer. . . .

In **Demo 7-6A**, we review three examples where revenue is recognized at a point in time. In **Demo 7-6B**, we review three examples where the satisfaction of at least one performance obligation is recognized as revenue over time.

Recognition of Revenue at a Point in Time   **LO7-6** ◀ **DEMO 7-6A**

Demo

MBC

Example One—Revenue Recognized at a Point in Time

A seller, REII Inc., enters into a contract to deliver customized ski equipment to a customer for $500 (cost is $250). The customer pays a $100 deposit upfront on October 15, while the remaining $400 ($500 − $100) is due on delivery, expected in three weeks. Prepare the journal entries required on October 15 and on November 7 (the date that the customized ski equipment is picked up by the customer and balance is paid in full).

Solution

Revenue is recognized upon delivery of the ski equipment because that is the point at which control of the product is transferred to the customer. Only at this point is the fifth step of the revenue recognition process complete. Because the $100 was received in advance of the delivery of the product, REII Inc. will recognize deferred revenue (a contract liability). Deferred revenue will be derecognized and revenue will be recognized when delivery of the customized product takes place.

October 15—To record customer prepayment

Cash	100	
Deferred Revenue		100

Assets = Liabilities + Equity
+100   +100
C:o   DRev

Cash	Deferred Rev
100	100

November 7—To recognize revenue and reduce inventory

Deferred Revenue	100	
Cash	400	
Sales Revenue		500

Assets = Liabilities + Equity
+400   −100   +500
C:o   DRev   Rev

Cash	Deferred Rev
100	100	100
400	

	Sales Rev
	500

Cost of Goods Sold	250	
Inventory		250

Assets = Liabilities + Equity
−250   −250
Inv   Exp

Inventory	COGS
250	250

Example Two—Revenue Recognized at a Point in Time

Gapp Inc. sponsors a customer loyalty point program in which customers earn one loyalty point for every $5 spent on clothing and accessories at any Gapp Inc. store or through online purchases. Loyalty program members can exchange accumulated loyalty points for free products at Gapp Inc. (such as one loyalty point equals $1 of free products). It is common for loyalty program members to accumulate and redeem loyalty points for free products. During June, customers purchased products with a sales value of $20,000, earning $4,000 in loyalty points. Based on past history of promotional programs, Gapp Inc. estimates a standalone selling price of $0.75 per loyalty point or $3,000 in total. The standalone selling price of the products purchased is $20,000.

continued

continued from previous page

Required

a. Assuming that there are two performance obligations (product sales and loyalty points), allocate the transaction price to the products and loyalty points.

b. Record the entry for sales for the month of June. (Ignore the cost entries.)

c. Assuming that 1,600 loyalty points were redeemed in June, and Gapp Inc. still expects 3,000 points to be redeemed in total, record the entry to recognize revenue on the redeemed loyalty points. (Ignore the cost entries.)

Solution

a. The transaction price is allocated as follows (Step 4).

Performance Obligations	Transaction Price as Stated	Standalone Selling Price	Selling Price Ratio	Allocated Transaction Price*
Sale of product	$20,000	$20,000	20/23	$17,391 (20/23 × $20,000)
Loyalty points	—	3,000	3/23	2,609 (3/23 × $20,000)
	$20,000	$23,000	23/23	$20,000

*Amounts rounded.

b. Gapp Inc. records the following journal entry for the month of June for the transfer of control of product to the customer (point in time sale). Revenue allocated to the customer option (loyalty points) is deferred until the rewards are redeemed for additional product.

Assets	=	Liabilities	+	Equity
+20,000		+2,609		+17,391
C:o		DRev		Rev

Cash		Deferred Rev	
20,000			2,609

	Sales Rev	
		17,391

June 30—To record sales transaction

Cash	20,000	
Deferred Revenue		2,609
Sales Revenue		17,391

c. Gapp Inc. recognizes revenue related to the customer options for June for $1,391 or [(1,600 pts/3,000 pts) × $2,609]. Gapp Inc. records the following entry.

Assets	=	Liabilities	+	Equity
		−1,391		+1,391
		DRev		Rev

Deferred Rev		Sales Rev	
1,391	2,609		17,391
			1,391

June 30—To record customer redemption of loyalty points

Deferred Revenue	1,391	
Sales Revenue		1,391

Example Three—Revenue Recognized at a Point in Time

A contractor enters into a three-year construction contract with a customer to build an office building. The contract has the following conditions.

- The office building plan is based upon a standard model frequently built by the contractor.
- Non-refundable payments are required including 10% of the contract up front, 50% of the contract at the end of 18 months, and 40% at the end of the contract if the project meets the prescribed requirements.
- The customer can cancel the contract at any time (with a termination penalty); any work in process is the property of the contractor.
- Physical possession and title do not pass until completion of the contract.
- Total estimated contract revenue is $300 million and total estimated contract cost is $200 million.
- Year one cost is $120 million (including $20 million related to contractor-caused inefficiencies).

Determine the revenue that the contractor should recognize during the first year of the contract.

Solution

The contractor must evaluate whether revenue should be recognized at a point in time or over time. In reviewing the revenue recognition criteria in **Exhibit 7-3**, this situation does *not* warrant revenue recognition over time.

- The customer does not enjoy use of the building or have control of the building over its life, as it does not own the work in process.
- The building has alternative uses (is not customized).
- The contractor does not have an enforceable right of payment for work to date. Payments are not based upon performance but on a preset schedule, thus, at any point in time, the contractor may not have been compensated for the work completed.

Therefore, no revenue (or expense) is recorded during the current year.

Instead, revenue (and expense) is recognized in income at the completion of the project when control of the building is transferred to the customer.

| Recognition of Revenue Over Time | **LO7-6** | **DEMO 7-6B** |

Demo

MBC

Example One—Revenue Recognized Over Time

On June 1, Forde Auto Manufacturer sells for cash, 500 maintenance contracts, each covering 36 months, to its customers for $1,000,000. The customers will benefit from the maintenance contracts over the 36-month protection period. The standalone selling price of each maintenance contract is $2,000. Prepare Forde's journal entry (1) to record the sale of maintenance contracts, and (2) to record any adjusting entry on June 30. Ignore cost entries.

Solution

Revenue on the maintenance contract is recognized over time because the customer will benefit from the service over the 36-month period. The entries to record the deferral of revenue on June 1 and the entry to record the recognition of revenue on a straight-line basis follow.

June 1—To defer service revenue

| Cash | 1,000,000 | |
| Deferred Service Revenue | | 1,000,000 |

Assets = Liabilities + Equity
+1,000,000 +1,000,000
C:o   DRev

| Cash | | Def Serv Rev | |
| 1,000,000 | | | 1,000,000 |

June 30—To recognize revenue for one month

| Deferred Service Revenue | 27,778 | |
| Service Revenue ($1,000,000 / 36 months) | | 27,778 |

Assets = Liabilities + Equity
              −27,778   +27,778
              DRev   Rev

| Def Serv Rev | | Service Rev | |
| 27,778 | 1,000,000 | | 27,778 |

Example Two—Includes Revenue Recognized Over Time

On January 1, Top Buys Inc. enters into a contract with a customer for a combined discounted selling price of $940 (stated to the customer as $700 for a computer, payable at the date of sale, and $240 for one year of computer service, payable at $20 per month). Standalone selling price of the computer is $960 and the standalone selling price of the computer service is $240. The allocation of the transaction price of $940 is calculated as follows (Step 4).

Performance Obligations	Transaction Price as Stated	Standalone Selling Price	Selling Price Ratio	Allocated Transaction Price
Computer	$700	$ 960	960/1,200 or 4/5	$752 (4/5 × $940)
Services	240	240	240/1,200 or 1/5	188 (1/5 × $940)
	$940	$1,200	1,200/1,200 or 5/5	$940

Record journal entries for Top Buys Inc. on (a) January 1 at the point of sale, and (b) January 31, the date of the first monthly payment. Assume that service revenue is recognized on a straight-line basis.

Solution

The allocated transaction price for the computer ($752) is recognized as revenue when the customer takes control of the computer at the time of sale. The $188 service revenue is recognized over the one-year contract term at $16.00 per month ($188/12, rounded). A contract asset of $52 ($752 – $700) is established at the time revenue for the computer is recognized. The contract asset represents a right to consideration, conditional on Top Buys satisfying the computer service performance obligation. The contract asset represents the difference between the revenue recognized (allocated transaction price of $752) and the consideration received (amount billed to the customer for the computer of $700). This asset is reduced each month by the portion of the monthly computer service fee that was allocated to the computer of $4.00 per month ($52/12, rounded). On January 1, the following entry is reported upon the sale of the computer.

January 1—To record sale of computer

Cash	700	
Contract Asset	52	
Sales Revenue		752

Assets = Liabilities + Equity
+700   +752
C:o   Rev
+52
ContrA

| Cash | | Sales Rev | |
| 700 | | | 752 |

| Contract Asset | |
| 52 | |

On the first date of the monthly service payment (and for each of the 11 months remaining in the contract), Top Buys Inc. records the following entry.

continued

continued from previous page

Assets	=	Liabilities	+	Equity
+20				+16
C:o				Rev
–4				
ContrA				

Cash		Sales Rev	
700			752
20			16

Contract Asset	
52	4

January 31—To record service revenue

Cash ($240/12)...................................	20	
Contract Asset ($52/12)*		4
Service Revenue ($188/12)*		16

*Amounts rounded.

Example Three—Includes Revenue Recognized Over Time

A contractor enters into a three-year construction contract with a customer to build an office building. The contract has the following characteristics.

- The office building is highly customized to the customer's specifications.
- Non-refundable, interim progress payments are required.
- The customer can cancel the contract at any time (with a termination penalty); any work in process is the property of the customer.
- Total estimated contract revenue is $300,000 and total estimated contract cost is $200,000.
- Year one cost is $140,000 (including $20,000 related to contractor-caused inefficiencies).

Determine the amount of revenue that the contractor recognizes during the first year of the contract, assuming that the company uses the cost-to-cost method to estimate progress toward satisfaction of its performance obligation.

Solution

The contractor must evaluate whether revenue is recognized at a point in time or over time. In reviewing the revenue recognition criteria, this situation warrants revenue recognition over time because:

- Customer has control of the building over its life, as it owns land and the work in process.
- The building is highly customized, thus built for a specific use.
- The contractor does have an enforceable right of payment for work to date because progress billings are required.

Therefore, revenue is recognized over time.

Progress toward satisfaction of the performance obligation is estimated as follows. Contract inefficiencies are not included in the cost-to-cost measurement.

$$\text{Percent complete} = \frac{\$120{,}000 \text{ (Costs incurred to date excluding inefficiencies)}}{\$200{,}000 \text{ (Total estimated costs)}} = 60\%$$

Computation of recognized revenue

Revenue ($300,000 × 60%)	$180,000
Costs (excluding inefficiencies)	120,000
Gross profit...................................	60,000
Contract inefficiencies	20,000
Adjusted contract margin	$ 40,000

Under the cost-to-cost method, 60% of revenue is recognized (or $180,000) which results in a gross profit of $60,000 and an adjusted contract margin of $40,000.

TESLA

Real World—REGULATORY CREDITS—REVENUE RECOGNIZED AT POINT IN TIME

Automotive regulatory credits are issued by certain governments as an incentive for auto manufacturers to build low-carbon emitting or electric vehicles. For example, a state may require auto manufacturers to maintain a certain number of regulatory credits each year, which are earned by producing vehicles that meet certain environmental standards. Generally, if an auto manufacturer accrues more than the minimum credits required, it can sell the excess credits to other auto manufacturers who fall short of the standards. Tesla Inc. sells its excess credits and discloses this in its revenue recognition policies. Tesla accounts for the sale of regulatory credits at the time control is transferred to another party as explained in an excerpt from its 2023 Form 10-K.

continued

continued from previous page

> **Note 2. Summary of Significant Accounting Policies**
> **Automotive Regulatory Credits** We earn tradable credits in the operation of our automotive business under various regulations related to ZEVs, greenhouse gas, fuel economy and clean fuel. We sell these credits to other regulated entities who can use the credits to comply with emission standards and other regulatory requirements.
>
> Payments for automotive regulatory credits are typically received at the point control transfers to the customer, or in accordance with payment terms customary to the business. We recognize revenue on the sale of automotive regulatory credits, which have negligible incremental costs associated with them, at the time control of the regulatory credits is transferred to the purchasing party. Deferred revenue related to sales of automotive regulatory credits was immaterial as of December 31, 2023 and 2022. Revenue recognized from the deferred revenue balance as of December 31, 2022 and 2021 was immaterial for the years ended December 31, 2023 and 2022. During the year ended December 31, 2022, we had also recognized $288 million in revenue due to changes in regulation which entitled us to additional consideration for credits sold previously.

Licenses

A license establishes the rights of a customer to intellectual property of an entity (such as software, motion pictures, music, franchises, and patents). The revenue recognition standard provides guidance on whether to recognize revenue over time or at a point in time for a license depending on whether the customer has the right to *access* or *use* the intellectual property.

606-10-55-58A An entity should account for a promise to provide a customer with a right to access the entity's intellectual property as a performance obligation satisfied over time because the customer will simultaneously receive and consume the benefit from the entity's performance of providing access to its intellectual property as the performance occurs. . . .

606-10-55-58B An entity's promise to provide a customer with the right to use its intellectual property is satisfied at a point in time. . . .

To determine whether a customer has the right to access or the right to use the intellectual property, the seller considers the classification of intellectual property.

- **Functional intellectual property** Functional intellectual property has significant standalone functionality. For example, if a license transfers a right to use intellectual property, the intellectual property has significant standalone functionality. Thus, the customer's use of the intellectual property is not affected by the seller's continuing activity. A functional intellectual property has the ability to perform a task or be played, such as game software or film content. In this case, revenue would generally be recognized at a *single point in time*. (If, however, the functionality of the intellectual property is expected to substantively change during the license term and the customer is required to use the updated property, the license grants a right to access.)

- **Symbolic intellectual property** Symbolic intellectual property does not have significant standalone functionality: substantially all of the utility is derived from association with the seller or the seller's ongoing activities. If a license provides the right of access to the seller's intellectual property, the customer's use of the intellectual property is affected by the seller's continuing activity. In this case, revenue would generally be recognized *over time*. Symbolic intellectual property includes items such as brands, trade names, and logos.

In **Demo 7-6C**, we review the process of revenue recognition of a license.

Recognition of License Revenue	**LO7-6**	**DEMO 7-6C**

On January 1, a franchisor grants a license to a franchisee to use the franchisor's trade name of Tasty Taco and to sell the Tasty Taco menu for 10 years. The license (franchise) is a contract between the franchisee and the franchisor. The franchisor receives a fixed franchise fee of $500,000 on January 1 plus a royalty equal to 5% of customer's sales over the term of the license of 10 years. In addition to the license, the franchisor provides restaurant equipment for $150,000 (cost of $130,000), due upon delivery of the equipment on February 1. The price of the equipment and the franchise fee represent standalone selling prices. The franchisor expects to provide services related to the license evenly over the license term. These activities are customary business practices of the franchisor and include product improvements, pricing strategies, advertising campaigns, and operational suggestions to support the franchise name and menu. None of these activities directly transfers goods or services to the franchisee.

Demo

MBC

continued

continued from previous page

Record the journal entry on (a) January 1, the date of contract, (b) February 1, the date of the delivery of the equipment, and (c) December 31, assuming that the franchisee reported sales of $350,000 for the year ended December 31.

Solution

The contract has two distinct performance obligations, a promise to grant a license and a promise to transfer equipment. Each promise is distinct because the license and the equipment are not interdependent. The franchisee benefits from the license separately from the equipment (the equipment could be used for other purposes or even be sold for cash.)

The transaction price consists of fixed consideration ($500,000 plus $150,000) and variable consideration (fee based upon sales). Because the license and equipment were sold at standalone selling prices, the price allocated to the license will be $500,000 plus the fee based upon sales, and the price allocated to the equipment will be $150,000. The fee based upon sales is allocated entirely to the franchise license because it relates entirely to the franchisor's promise to grant the franchise license.

Because the franchisor's continuing activities affect the value of the franchise over the 10-year period, revenue will be recognized over time. Therefore, the franchisor defers the initial franchise fee on January 1, and recognizes revenue over the license term.

January 1—To record receipt and deferral of franchise fee

Assets = Liabilities + Equity		
+500,000 +500,000		
C:o DFRev		

Cash	Def Franch Rev
500,000	500,000

Cash	500,000	
Deferred Franchise Revenue		500,000

On February 1 the revenue (and cost) related to the equipment will be recognized when control of the equipment is transferred to the franchisee.

February 1—To record transfer of control of equipment

Assets = Liabilities + Equity		
+150,000 +150,000		
C:o Rev		

Cash	Sales Rev
500,000	150,000
150,000	

Cash	150,000	
Sales Revenue		150,000

Assets = Liabilities + Equity		
−130,000 −130,000		
Inv Exp		

Inventory	COGS
130,000	130,000

Cost of Goods Sold	130,000	
Inventory		130,000

Because the service related to the license is provided evenly over the lease term, fixed franchise revenue will be recognized on a straight-line basis. The franchisor records the following entry on December 31, which also includes an accrual for the royalty fee.

December 31—To record franchise revenue

Assets = Liabilities + Equity		
+17,500 −50,000 +67,500		
AR DFRev Rev		

Accounts Rec	Def Franch Rev
17,500	50,000 | 500,000
	Franchise Rev
	67,500

Deferred Franchise Revenue ($500,000/10)	50,000	
Accounts Receivable ($350,000 × 0.05)	17,500	
Franchise Revenue...................................		67,500

REVIEW 7-6 ▶ **LO7-6**	**Revenue Recognition**

Answer the requirements for each of the following separate cases.

a. Face North Co. required an advance payment of $200 on January 15 from a customer for a customized order of sweatshirts. The customer picked up the sweatshirts on January 31, and paid the remaining balance of $100. Determine the amount of revenue that Face North Co. would recognize on January 15 and January 31.

b. Roote Co. sold backpacks to customers in September at full price for $10,000. At the point of sale, Roote Co. provided customers 100 coupons for $40 off the purchase of a backpack in October. The coupon is considered a separate performance obligation. Roote Co. estimates the standalone selling price of the backpacks to be $10,000 and the standalone selling price of the coupons to be $2,000 ($40 × 50 coupons expected to be redeemed). Determine the revenue that Roote Co. records in September for the sale of full price backpacks, and the amount of revenue deferred for the coupons.

c. On January 15, Construction Inc. entered into a contract with a customer to build an addition to its corporate headquarters for $4,000,000. The customer owns the construction in process during the construction period and the customer is under obligation to pay for any work completed, even

continued

continued from previous page

if the contract is cancelled. The addition is expected to be completed in two years for a total cost of $2,400,000. Actual costs incurred through December 31 of the current year are $1,400,000. Determine the amount of revenue to recognize in the current year ended December 31.

d. On January 15 Quality Inc. entered into a contract with a retailer to build a parking ramp for $2,000,000. Quality Inc. owns the construction in process and the parking lot is located in a commercial district accessible to a number of businesses. The parking ramp is expected to be completed in two years for a total cost of $1,600,000. Actual costs incurred through December 31 of the current year are $900,000. Determine the amount of revenue to recognize for the year ended December 31.

e. On January 1, Franchisee Inc. enters into a contract with Franchisor Inc. for the right (beginning immediately) to operate a fast food location, using the company's (a) logo, design, and advertising materials, (b) menu items, recipes, and supplier contacts, (c) store designs, and (d) daily operating instructions for a five-year period. The upfront fee of $250,000 also includes accounting services for the franchise for one year only, beginning on January 1. The standalone selling prices of the franchise services and accounting services are $245,000 and $5,000, respectively. Determine the amount of revenue to recognize for Franchisor Inc. on January 1 and for the remainder of the year ended December 31.

More Practice:
BE7-22, BE7-25, E7-27, E7-28, E7-31
Solution on p. 7-85.

Recognize revenue after a contract modification   LO 7-7

It is not uncommon for modifications to contracts to take place at some point during the contract term. **Contract modifications** create or alter the rights and obligations of parties to the contract.

`606-10-25-10`   A contract modification is a change in the scope or price (or both) of a contract that is approved by the parties to the contract . . . A contract modification exists when the parties to a contract approve a modification that either creates new or changes existing enforceable rights and obligations of the parties to the contract. A contract modification could be approved in writing, by oral agreement, or implied by customary business practices. . . .

> **Contract Modification**
> - Adds distinct goods or services at standalone selling price(s)
>   - Account for as a new separate contract
> - Adds distinct goods or services not at standalone selling price(s)
>   - Terminate original contract and account for under new combined contract
> - Adds nondistinct goods or services
>   - Cumulative catch-up adjustment
>
> *LO 7-7 Overview*

Accounting standards guide the treatment of contract modifications depending on whether the modification provides for additional distinct goods or services at standalone selling prices. The three options outlined below are illustrated in **Demo 7-7.**

Contract Modification			
	(1) New Separate Contract; No Change to Original Contract	**(2) New Combined Contract after Terminating Original Contract**	**(3) Cumulative Catch-up with No New Contract**
Adds distinct goods/services	Yes	Yes	No—Additional goods or services are not distinct
Increase in contract price is reflective of standalone prices	Yes	No—Contract price increases are not reflective of standalone prices of additional goods and services	Not applicable

- **Modification (1).** For a modification to be accounted for as a new separate contract, both conditions must be met: meaning the modification provides distinct goods or services and the change in contract price reflects standalone prices. For example, a manufacturer modifies a contract to sell additional distinct goods at an observable standalone selling price. In this case, revenue is recognized under the new and old contract separately.

- **Modification (2).** A contract modification is treated prospectively if the additional goods and services are distinct, but the contract price is not adjusted for standalone prices. This means that the remaining consideration will be allocated to the remaining performance obligations, including those added in the modification. For example, a service contract is modified to extend service for an additional year at a reduced rate (below the standalone selling price.) In this case, the original contract is terminated and a new combined contract is created for all remaining goods and services. The revenue for all remaining goods or services to be provided is recorded at a **blended price** of the new and old contract.

- **Modification (3).** If the additional goods or services are not distinct, the modification is accounted for as a cumulative catch-up adjustment. For example, a contractor and customer modify a long-term construction contract to build an office building which causes an increase in costs and the transaction price. In this case, the contract modification is considered part of the original contract and is, therefore, part of a single performance obligation. The effect of the modification on the transaction price and on percentage of completion are recorded as an adjustment (increase or decrease) to revenue on the date of the contract modification.

DEMO 7-7 ▶ **LO7-7**   **Revenue Recognition with a Contract Modification**

Demo
MBC

Example One—Contract Modification Resulting in a New Separate Contract

Over a 9-month period, Diaz Co. promises to sell 220 units of product to one of its customers for $2,200 ($10 per unit). After Diaz Co. has transferred control of 100 units of product to the customer, the contract is modified to require the delivery of an additional 50 units (a total of 270 units) to the customer. When the contract is modified, the price of the contract increases by $400 ($8 × 50 units). The standalone selling price of the 50 additional units at the time of the contract modification is $8 per unit, and the additional units are distinct from the original units. Determine the amount of revenue that will be recognized for (1) the 120 units remaining in the original contract, and (2) the 50 additional units resulting from the contract modification.

Solution

Because the 50 new units are distinct and have a standalone price, the agreement to sell the 50 units is considered a *new separate contract* and is accounted for as follows.

Remaining Contract Revenue to Recognize	
Remaining sales in the original contract: 120 (or 220 − 100) units × $10 (original contract price) . . .	$1,200
Sales under the contract modification: 50 units × $8 (modified contract price)	400
Total remaining revenue to recognize.	$1,600

Example Two—Contract Modification Resulting in a New Combined Contract*

Assume the circumstances with Diaz Co. in Example One are the same except that the customer identifies a quality issue unique to the first 100 units purchased. As a result, Diaz Co. agrees to a price concession on the additional 50 units to compensate for the quality issue. The price of the additional 50 units is determined to be $5 per unit. (Standalone selling price of the new units is still considered to be $8 per unit.) Determine the amount of revenue that will be recognized for the (1) 120 units remaining in the original contract, and (2) 50 additional units resulting from the contract modification.

*Adapted from ASC 606-10-55-114.

Solution

While the additional 50 units are distinct, the units are not sold at their standalone selling price because the price concession is related to quality deficiencies of the previous units of product sold. Therefore, the modification results in the termination of the original contract and the creation of a new combined contract. Revenue per unit for the remaining units will be recorded at a blended price of the new and old contract.

Remaining Contract Revenue to Recognize		
Remaining sales in the original contract: 120 (or 220 − 100) units × $10.		$1,200
Sales under the contract modification: 50 units × $5.		250
		$1,450
Blended revenue per unit:	$1,450/170 (or 120 + 50) units	$ 8.53
Total remaining revenue to recognize	(1) $8.53 × 120 units	$1,024
	(2) $8.53 × 50 units*.	$ 426

*Answer adjusted due to rounding.

continued

continued from previous page

Example Three—Contract Modification Resulting in a Cumulative Catch-Up Adjustment

A builder enters into a two-year contract with a customer for $350,000 to manufacture customized equipment (a single performance obligation). After 6 months, the builder and customer agree to modify the floor plans which results in an increase in both the transaction price and total expected costs by $75,000 and $50,000, respectively. Is the contract modification treated as (1) a new contract or (2) as part of the original contract? What type of adjustment is required?

Solution

Contact modification is treated as part of the original contract and accounted for with cumulative catch-up adjustment. If the company uses the cost-to-cost method to measure its progress toward satisfying the performance obligation, the percentage of completion takes into account the adjusted transaction price and estimated total contract costs. The updated percentage of completion is applied to total contract revenue to measure revenue recognized to date.

Contract Modification	**LO7-7**	**REVIEW 7-7**

Answer the requirements for each of the following separate cases.

a. On January 1, Manufac Co. enters into a contract with a retailer to sell 250 distinct items of merchandise for $50,000 ($200 per item) over a 12-month period. On March 31, the parties to the contract agree to a contract modification to add an additional 80 items for $220 each within the original contract period. The $220 per unit price for the additional items represents the standalone selling price of these items on the date of the modification. If 200 items had already been sold under the original contract, how would revenue be allocated to the remaining 50 items under the original contract and the 80 items per the contract modification?

b. Assume the same information as in part *a* except that the $220 per unit price for the additional items does *not* represent the standalone selling price of these items on the date of the modification. If 200 items had already been sold under the original contract, how would revenue be allocated to the remaining 50 items under the original contract and the 80 items per the contract modification?

More Practice:
MC7-10, MC7-11, BE7-28, BE7-29, E7-32

Solution on p. 7-85.

Recognize revenue in more complex revenue arrangements

LO 7-8

In this section we explore four situations that add complexity to Step 5 of revenue recognition in determining whether control of the asset has transferred to the customer: (1) bill-and-hold arrangement (**Demo 7-8A**), (2) consignment arrangement (**Demo 7-8B**), (3) repurchase arrangement—**Demo 7-8C**, and (4) principal/agent arrangement—**Demo 7-8D**.

Complex Revenue Arrangements
- Bill-and-hold arrangement
- Consignment arrangement
- Repurchase arrangement
- Principal/agent arrangement

LO 7-8 Overview

```
①                  ②                  ③              ④                  ⑤ Recognize
Identify           Identify           Determine       Allocate           revenue when (or as)
contract(s)        performance        transaction     transaction price  each performance
with               obligation(s)      price           to performance     obligation is
customer           in the                             obligation(s)      satisfied through a
                   contract                                               transfer of control
```

Bill-and-Hold Arrangement

A **bill-and-hold arrangement** takes place when a customer is billed for goods that are completed and ready to deliver, but the seller does not actually ship the goods until a later time period. Even though the physical asset has not passed to the customer, the seller must still evaluate whether control of the physical asset has passed to the customer. The revenue recognition standard identifies the following additional criteria (beyond the criteria previously outlined for a transfer of control in **Exhibit 7-1**) that *all* must be met in order for control to be considered passed to the customer and revenue recognized. These criteria prevent companies from shifting sales into the current period (overstating revenue) when the risks and rewards of ownership have *not* passed to the customer in the current period.

606-10-55-83   In addition to applying the guidance in paragraph 606-10-25-30, for a customer to have obtained control of a product in a bill-and-hold arrangement, all of the following criteria must be met:

    a. The reason for the bill-and-hold arrangement must be substantive (for example, the customer has requested the arrangement).

    b. The product must be identified separately as belonging to the customer.

    c. The product currently must be ready for physical transfer to the customer.

    d. The entity [seller] cannot have the ability to use the product or to direct it to another customer.

For a bill-and-hold arrangement to be substantive, it would generally need to be requested by the customer, not initiated by the seller. A seller would need to determine whether the customer request for a bill-and-hold arrangement has a substantive business reason.

DEMO 7-8A ▸ **LO7-8**   **Transfer of Control under a Bill-and-Hold Arrangement**

Demo

MBC

Brow Inc. enters into a contract during August to supply 1,000 units of product to a retailer, at a date to be specified by the retailer. The retailer expects to have sufficient shelf space at the time of delivery but does not currently have the shelf space to hold the order. Even though the 1,000 units of product are interchangeable with other units, the 1,000 units are ready for immediate shipment at the request of the customer, segregated from inventory (beginning on September 1) and will not be used to fulfill other orders. Payment for the 1,000 units is due September 30. The units are sold at $50 per unit while the cost to Brow Inc. is $30 per unit. Record the entry for Brow Inc. on September 1.

Solution

Brow Inc. should recognize revenue on September 1 when the 1,000 units are segregated from the rest of the inventory because the inventory cannot be used to fulfill other orders and is ready for transfer to the customer. The reason for the bill-and-hold transaction is substantive (lack of shelf space).

Assets = Liabilities + Equity
+50,000   +50,000
AR   Rev

Accounts Rec		Sales Rev
50,000		50,000

Assets = Liabilities + Equity
−30,000   −30,000
Inv   Exp

Inventory		COGS
	30,000	30,000

September 1—To record sale of units in bill-and-hold arrangement

Accounts Receivable	50,000	
Sales Revenue (1,000 × $50)		50,000
Cost of Goods Sold	30,000	
Inventory (1,000 × $30)		30,000

Consignment Arrangement

A **consignment arrangement** occurs when a company (**consignor**) ships goods to a distributor (**consignee**), but retains control of the goods until a predetermined event occurs, such as the sale of the product to a customer. This means that even though the consignee has physical possession of the asset, the consignee might not have control of the asset. The following indicators from the revenue recognition standard can be used to evaluate whether an agreement is a consignment arrangement.

606-10-55-80   Indicators that an arrangement is a consignment arrangement include, but are not limited to, the following:

    a. The product is controlled by the entity [consignor] until a specified event occurs, such as the sale of the product to a customer of the dealer [consignee], or until a specified period expires.

    b. The entity [consignor] is able to require the return of the product or transfer the product to a third party (such as another dealer).

    c. The dealer [consignee] does not have an unconditional obligation to pay for the product (although it might be required to pay a deposit).

The consignee exercises due diligence in holding the product and selling the product for the consignor. The consignee forwards the selling price to the consignor after the product is sold while the consignor pays the consignee a commission related to the sale. The consignor carries the inventory on its balance sheet; the consignee does not carry the inventory on its balance sheet. The consigner records sales at the selling price of the product while the consignee records commission revenue.

LO7-8 **DEMO 7-8B**

Demo

MBC

On June 1, Consignor Inc. ships 50 items of inventory to Consignee Inc. who has agreed to sell the products to the end customers in exchange for a 10% commission on the sale. The products sell to the end customer for $250 while the cost to Consignor Inc. for each product is $140. On June 30, 25 items are sold by Consignee Inc. for cash, and Consignor Inc. is automatically notified at month-end. On July 2, Consignee Inc. remits cash less commission to Consignor Inc. electronically. Record the entries on June 1, June 30, and July 2, for Consignor Inc. and for Consignee Inc.

Solution

June 1—Consignor ships products to Consignee
No entries required. (Consignor may or may not record a journal entry to reclassify inventory from finished goods inventory to consigned inventory.)

Consignee
June 30—To record cash collection on sale of products

Cash (25 × $250)	6,250	
Commission Revenue (0.10 × $6,250)............		625
Payable to Consignor ($6,250 – $625)		5,625

Assets	=	Liabilities	+	Equity
+6,250		+5,625		+625
C:o		PayCons		Rev

Cash		Pay to Consignor	
6,250			5,625

		Commission Rev	
			625

CONSIGNOR
June 30—To record sale of inventory held by Consignee

Due from Consignee ($6,250 – $625)................	5,625	
Commission Expense (0.10 × $6,250)................	625	
Sales Revenue (25 × $250)		6,250

Assets	=	Liabilities	+	Equity
+5,625				–625
DueCons				Exp
				+6,250
				Rev

Due from Consignee		Sales Rev	
5,625			6,250

		Commission Exp	
		625	

Cost of Goods Sold	3,500	
Inventory (25 × $140)		3,500

Assets	=	Liabilities	+	Equity
–3,500				–3,500
Inv				Exp

Inventory		COGS	
	3,500	3,500	

Consignee
July 2—To record remittance of cash (net) to Consignor

Payable to Consignor.............................	5,625	
Cash		5,625

Assets	=	Liabilities	+	Equity
–5,625		–5,625		
C:o		PayCons		

Cash		Pay to Consignor	
6,250	5,625	5,625	5,625

CONSIGNOR
July 2—To record receipt of cash (net) from Consignee

Cash	5,625	
Due from Consignee		5,625

Assets	=	Liabilities	+	Equity
+5,625				
C:o				
–5,625				
DueCons				

Due from Consignee		Cash	
5,625	5,625	5,625	

Repurchase Arrangement

A repurchase arrangement allows for a repurchase of a good after it is sold to a customer. This right might be specified in a sales contract or in a separate arrangement with the customer. Repurchase rights can be a

- Seller's obligation to repurchase the good (**forward arrangement**).
- Seller's right to repurchase the good (**call option**).
- Customer's right to require the seller to repurchase the good (**put option**).

Forward Arrangement and Call Option

Revenue is not recognized in the forward arrangement or call option because the seller's obligation or repurchase rights *limit the customer's ability to control the good*. If the repurchase price is less than the original selling price of the asset, the transaction is accounted for as a lease by the seller (see chapter on lease accounting). If the repurchase price is equal to or greater than the original selling price of the asset, the transaction is accounted for as a financing agreement by the seller. In this case, a liability is recorded and any corresponding interest expense is recognized.

Forward Arrangement or Call Option (ASC 606-10-55-68)
Repurchase price < Original selling price → Lease
Repurchase price ≥ Original selling price → Financing Agreement

Put Option

In a put option, *the customer has control over the good* and has the choice of retaining the good, selling it to a third party, or selling it back to the seller. Thus, the accounting treatment depends on whether the repurchase price is less than or greater than the expected market value of the asset. If the repurchase price is less than or equal to the expected market value, the customer is expected to retain the good, so this is treated as a sale with the right of return. However, if the repurchase price is greater than the expected market value, the customer has a significant economic incentive to sell back to the seller

Put Option (ASC 606-10-55-72 to 76)		
Repurchase price ≤ Expected market value → Sale with Right of Return		
Repurchase price > Expected market value → Depends on the following:		
Repurchase price < Original selling price → Lease		
Repurchase price ≥ Original selling price → Financing Agreement		

(exercise the put option). In this case, and similar to the forward arrangement and call option described above, the seller accounts for the transaction as a lease if the repurchase price is less than the original selling price. If the repurchase price is equal to or greater than the original selling price, the transaction is accounted for as a financing agreement.

DEMO 7-8C ▸ **LO7-8**   **Transfer of Control under Repurchase Arrangement**

Demo

MBC

Example One—Forward Arrangement in which Repurchase Price Exceeds Original Sales Price

Manufacturing Inc. enters into a contract to sell equipment on January 1 of Year 1 to a customer, Bell Corp., for $51,440. As part of the contract, Manufacturing Inc. agrees to repurchase this equipment two years later for $60,000. The interest rate for a financing arrangement with commensurate risk is 8%. The equipment is repurchased from Bell Corp. on December 31 of Year 2 for the agreed upon repurchase price. Manufacturing Inc.'s accounting period ends on December 31. Record the entries for Manufacturing Inc. on January 1 of Year 1, December 31 of Year 1, and December 31 of Year 2, ignoring the cost entries.

Solution

Because the seller is obligated to repurchase the equipment, the transaction is a *forward arrangement*. The transaction is accounted for as a financing agreement (not a sale) because the repurchase price is greater than the original sales price. The equipment is not derecognized by Manufacturing Inc. because it is considered collateral for the loan rather than a sale of equipment to Bell.

Assets = Liabilities + Equity
+51,440   +51,440
C:f   Liab

Cash	Liab to Bell
51,440	51,440

January 1, Year 1—To record initiation of financing transaction

Cash..	51,440	
Liability to Bell Corp.		51,440

Assets = Liabilities + Equity
+4,115   −4,115
Liab   Exp

Liab to Bell	Interest Exp
51,440	4,115
4,115	

December 31, Year 1—To record interest on financing transaction

Interest Expense...	4,115	
Liability to Bell Corp. ($51,440 × 0.08)		4,115

Assets = Liabilities + Equity
+4,445   −4,445
Liab   Exp

Liab to Bell	Interest Exp
51,440	4,115
4,115	4,445
4,445	

December 31, Year 2—To record interest on financing transaction

Interest Expense...	4,445	
Liability to Bell Corp. [($51,440 + $4,115) × 0.08]		4,445

Assets = Liabilities + Equity
−60,000   −60,000
C:f   Liab

Cash	Liab to Bell
51,440 | 60,000	60,000 | 51,440
	4,115
	4,445
	0

December 31, Year 2—To record settlement of liability

Liability to Bell Corp. ($51,440 + $4,115 + $4,445)................	60,000	
Cash..		60,000

Example Two—Put Option in which Repurchase Price Exceeds Expected Market Value

Refer to Example One but assume instead that the contract gave the option to the customer to require the seller to repurchase the asset for $65,000 when the fair value of the asset at the end of two years is expected to be $61,000. The repurchase price of $65,000 is greater than the original selling price of the equipment of $51,440. How do the journal entries differ from the entries shown above?

continued

continued from previous page

Solution
Because the customer can require the seller to repurchase the asset, it is considered a *put option*. In this case, the customer would have an economic incentive to sell back the equipment because the expected fair value is less than the repurchase price. **Therefore, the transactions are recorded as a financing arrangement as shown above in Example One for the forward option.**

Example Three—Put Option in which Expected Market Value Exceeds Repurchase Price
Refer to Example Two but assume instead that the repurchase price is $61,000 and the fair value is expected to be $65,000. Again, the repurchase price (of $61,000) is greater than the original selling price of the equipment of $51,440. Record the entry on January 1 of Year 1.

Solution
In this case, the repurchase is unlikely so the transaction is treated as a sale with a right of return. The seller estimates the refund liability to be zero because it does not expect the customer to return the equipment.

January 1, Year 1—To record sale of equipment		
Cash	51,440	
Sales Revenue		51,440

Assets = Liabilities + Equity
+51,440   +51,440
C:o   Rev

Cash		Sales Rev	
51,440			51,440

Principal/Agent Arrangement

A **principal** promises to provide goods or services to its customers. An **agent** arranges for goods or services to be provided by the principal to an end customer, usually for a fee. A principal (not an agent) has substantive control of the goods or services before they are transferred to a customer. Indicators to consider in deciding who has control of the goods or services before transfer include:

- Who is primarily responsible for fulfilling the promise to provide a good or service?
- Who bears inventory risk before transfer to the customer?
- Who has discretion in establishing prices for the goods or services?

Accounting implications of being an agent or principal follow.

- **Principal** Recognize revenue at *the gross amount* paid by the customer and recognize the full cost of the product or service. Revenue is recognized when control of the good or service is transferred from the principal to the customer.

- **Agent** Recognize revenue in the *amount of the fee or commission it expects to be entitled to* for facilitating the transfer of goods or services. Revenue is recognized when the agent fulfills its performance obligation to facilitate a transaction between a principal and a customer.

`606-10-55-37B` When (or as) an entity that is a principal satisfies a performance obligation, the entity recognizes revenue in the gross amount of consideration to which it expects to be entitled in exchange for the specified good or service transferred.

`606-10-55-38` An entity is an agent if the entity's performance obligation is to arrange for the provision of the specified good or service by another party. An entity that is an agent does not control the specified good or service provided by another party before that good or service is transferred to the customer. When (or as) an entity that is an agent satisfies a performance obligation, the entity recognizes revenue in the amount of any fee or commission to which it expects to be entitled in exchange for arranging for the specified goods or services to be provided by the other party . . .

Estimating Revenue for Principal and Agent   **LO7-8**   **DEMO 7-8D**

Demo

MBC

Example One—Recognizing Revenue as a Principal
Find-a-Hotel Inc. contracts with major hotel chains to purchase overnight stays at reduced rates and sells the overnight stays to its customers. Find-a-Hotel Inc. must pay for purchased overnight stays regardless of whether it is able to resell them. Customers search for available overnight stays on Find-a-Hotel Inc.'s website where overnight stays are priced according to the discretion of Find-a-Hotel Inc. After purchase, Find-a-Hotel Inc. emails the confirmation number to the customer and resolves

continued

continued from previous page

any booking service complaints. The hotel chains fulfill the obligation of providing the hotel stay and remedies for any service complaints with the hotel stay.

On June 1, Find-a-Hotel Inc. purchases an overnight stay from a hotel chain in Miami for $75. A customer purchases the overnight stay through Find-a-Hotel Inc. on its website for $90 on June 7, to be used on June 10.

a. Determine whether Find-a-Hotel Inc. is a principal or an agent.
b. Record Find-a-Hotel Inc.'s entries on June 1, June 7, and June 10.

Solution

a. Find-a-Hotel Inc. is the **principal** and should recognize revenue at the gross amount charged to customers. Find-a-Hotel Inc. controls the overnight stays prior to transfer of the hotel stay to the customer. Find-a-Hotel has the ability to direct the use of the overnight stays, has the inventory risk in holding the overnight stays, and has discretion in pricing the overnight stays. The indicators support Find-a-Hotel Inc. as the principal.

b. Find-a-Hotel Inc. records the purchase of the overnight stay on June 1 when control of the overnight stay passes from the hotel chain to Find-a-Hotel Inc.

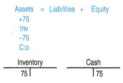

June 1—To record purchase of overnight stay

Inventory	75	
Cash		75

Find-a-Hotel Inc. would record revenue at the time that control of the overnight stay is transferred to the end customer from Find-a-Hotel Inc. on June 10. Therefore, revenue would be deferred as a contract liability by Find-a-Hotel Inc. when cash is collected on June 7.

June 7—To record sale of overnight stay to end customer

Cash	90	
Deferred Revenue		90

June 10—To record revenue for sale of overnight stay

Deferred Revenue	90	
Sales Revenue		90

Cost of Goods Sold	75	
Inventory		75

Example Two—Recognizing Revenue as an Agent

Assume instead that Find-a-Hotel Inc. enters into a contract with a major hotel chain to sell overnight stays online. For any overnights stays sold on its website, Find-a-Hotel Inc. facilitates payment between the end customer and the hotel chain. The price of the overnight stays are set by the hotel chain and Find-a-Hotel Inc. receives a 10% commission on each overnight stay sold through its website. Find-a-Hotel Inc. is not responsible for any hotel cancellations. The hotel chain fulfills the obligation of providing the overnight stay and remedies for service complaints.

A customer purchases an overnight stay through Find-a-Hotel Inc. on its website for $90 on June 7, to be used on June 10. Find-a-Hotel collects the full amount from the customer and electronically forwards this amount, less its commission, to the hotel chain on June 8.

a. Determine whether Find-a-Hotel Inc. is a principal or an agent.
b. Record Find-a-Hotel Inc.'s entries on June 7, June 8, and June 10.

Solution

a. Find-a-Hotel Inc. is the **agent**, facilitating a transaction between the principal (hotel chain) and the customer. Find-a-Hotel Inc. does not control the overnight stays before they are transferred to the customer. Find-a-Hotel Inc. does not control the price of the overnight stays, nor is it responsible for any cancellations by the customer.

b. Find-a-Hotel Inc. recognizes revenue when the overnight stay is purchased by the customer. At this point, Find-a-Hotel fulfilled its obligation of facilitating a sale for the hotel chain.

continued

continued from previous page

June 7—To record cash sale to customer

Cash...	90	
Accounts Payable (hotel chain) ($90 × 0.90).................		81
Commission Revenue ($90 × 0.10).......................		9

Assets = Liabilities + Equity
+90   +81   +9
C:o   AP   Rev

Cash		Accounts Payable	
90			81

Commission Rev	
	9

June 8—To record payment to hotel chain

Accounts Payable..	81	
Cash...		81

Assets = Liabilities + Equity
−81   −81
C:o   AP

Cash		Accounts Payable	
90	81	81	81

June 10—Customer stays the night

Find-a-Hotel records no entry on June 10, because revenue was recorded at the date that Find-a-Hotel facilitated the transaction between the hotel chain and the customer.

Complex Revenue Arrangements   LO7-8   REVIEW 7-8

Review
MBC

Answer the requirements for each of the following separate complex revenue cases.

a. On December 31, Batteries Inc. sold 5,000 batteries to a retail customer with payment terms net 30 and with shipment scheduled for February 15 of the following year. On December 31 of the current year, the units are clearly segregated in Batteries Inc.'s warehouse for shipment to the customer, but the units may be used to fulfill other customer orders as long as the units are replaced before the scheduled shipment date. Determine the type of complex revenue arrangement and the date that Batteries Inc. should record revenue for the sale of the 5,000 batteries to its customer.

b. Chocolate Inc. entered into a contract with Supplier Inc. in which it only is responsible for purchasing the product that it sells to the end customer. Any unused product can be returned to Supplier Inc. at no cost to Chocolate Inc. Also, Supplier Inc. can recall any unsold product held by Chocolate Inc. at any time for sale at other locations. On February 1, Supplier Inc. shipped product to Chocolate Inc. with a sales value of $5,000. For the month of February, Chocolate Inc. sold $4,000 of product and paid Supplier Inc. for the purchase electronically on February 28. Chocolate Inc. will hold the excess product into March, as it is likely that $500 of the amount will be sold. Determine the type of complex revenue arrangement and the amount of revenue that Supplier Inc. should record in February.

c. TicketMajor Inc. purchases tickets in large blocks for various live concerts. TicketMajor Inc. then sells the tickets online to the customers. TicketMajor Inc. is responsible for pricing the tickets and is responsible for any unsold tickets. Ticket purchases are nonrefundable after the customer purchases the tickets online. In February, TicketMajor Inc. purchased tickets worth $50,000 and sold tickets worth $35,000 for which concerts had taken place. Determine the type of complex revenue arrangement and how much revenue TicketMajor Inc. reports in February.

d. On January 1, Zappit Inc. sells equipment to Solo Inc. for $15,000. As stipulated in the revenue contract, Zappit Inc. will buy back the equipment on December 31 for $15,000. The relevant interest rate is 5%. Determine the type of complex revenue arrangement and the amount of revenue that Zappit Inc. should record on January 1.

More Practice:
BE7-30, BE7-31, BE7-32, BE7-33, E7-43
Solution on p. 7-85.

Describe accounting for contract costs and disclosure requirements for revenue recognition   LO 7-9

Revenue and the associated bad debt expense are presented on the income statement. Assets and liabilities associated with revenue contracts are presented on the balance sheet. These include contract assets, contract liabilities, and accounts receivable (net of the allowance for doubtful accounts). In addition, ASC 340 requires a number of disclosures in notes to financial statements and provides guidance on the reporting of contract costs.

Disclosure Requirements
- Disaggregated revenue
- Contracts with customers
- Performance obligations
- Significant judgments
- Practical expedients
- Contract cost assets
  - Costs to obtain a contract
  - Costs to fulfill a contract

LO 7-9 Overview

Contract Costs

Sellers may incur costs to obtain a contract or fulfill a contract, both of which are illustrated in Demo 7-9.

Cost to Obtain a Contract Included in costs to obtain a contract are items such as marketing costs, bid and proposal costs, sales commissions, and legal costs. These are amounts due to third parties (including company employees), not to customers. Costs incurred to obtain a contract are recognized as assets if they meet both of the following criteria.

1. Costs are incremental (costs that would not have been incurred if the contract had not been obtained). Costs incurred regardless of whether a contract is obtained (such as legal fees to draft a contract) are *not* considered incremental costs.

2. Costs are recoverable (directly charged to customer or expected to be recovered through the margin in the contract).

   340-40-25-1   An entity shall recognize as an asset the incremental costs of obtaining a contract with a customer if the entity expects to recover those costs.

Generally, all *other* costs incurred to obtain a contract are expensed as incurred. However, the accounting guidance offers the following **practical expedient**.

   340-40-25-4   As a practical expedient, an entity may recognize the incremental costs of obtaining a contract as an expense when incurred if the amortization period of the asset that the entity otherwise would have recognized is one year or less.

The asset recognized from capitalizing costs to obtain a contract is amortized on a systematic basis consistent with the pattern of the transfer of the goods or services to which the asset relates. For example, if a sales commission were paid on the origination of a contract (and not on contract renewals), the contract asset would likely be amortized over the expected length of the customer relationship. Assets recognized from the costs to obtain a contract are subject to impairment testing.

Cost to Fulfill a Contract Sellers can incur costs to fulfill a contract before transferring goods or services. Costs to fulfill a contract are recognized as an asset if the costs meet all of the following criteria (ASC 340-40-25-5).

1. Costs relate directly to a contract or an anticipated contract that the seller can specifically identify.

2. Costs generate or enhance resources used to satisfy performance obligations in the future.

3. Costs are recoverable.

The asset recognized from capitalizing the costs to fulfill a contract is amortized on a systematic basis consistent with the pattern of the transfer of the goods or services to which the asset relates. Assets recognized from the costs to fulfill a contract are subject to impairment testing.

Fulfillment costs include direct labor, direct materials, and allocation of costs that relate directly to the unsatisfied performance obligations in a contract. Fulfillment costs do not include general and administrative costs, costs of wasted resources, costs that relate to satisfied performance obligations, or where it is unclear whether the costs relate to unsatisfied performance obligations. Shipping and handling activities performed *before* the customer obtains control of the good are activities to fulfill the entity's promise to transfer the good.

The revenue recognition standard allows an **election for shipping and handling fees** incurred *after* the title has passed to the customer. Shipping costs that occur *after* title has passed to the customer can be recognized as fulfillment costs (in which case, the associated revenue is recognized when control of the asset passes to the customer) rather than as an additional performance obligation. This election simplifies the accounting for the seller—see the Amazon Real World box on shipping costs.

   606-10-25-18B   If shipping and handling activities are performed after a customer obtains control of the good, then the entity may elect to account for shipping and handling as activities to fulfill the promise to transfer the good. The entity shall apply this accounting policy election consistently to similar types of transactions. An entity that makes this election would not evaluate whether shipping and handling activities are promised services to its customers . . .

Example One—Costs to Obtain a Contract

On January 1, Arrens Co. enters into a contract with a customer where a sales staff member receives a 10% commission on the contract, totaling $5,000, to be paid during the year. The contract calls for Arrens to deliver product throughout the calendar year, and Arrens expects to recover the commission on the contract. The contract does not have a renewal option. How would Arrens account for the contract cost on January 1?

Solution

Because the cost to obtain the contract is incremental and recoverable, Arrens can recognize the commission cost as an asset and amortize it over the life of the contract as one alternative.

January 1—To record contract cost

Contract Cost	5,000	
Salaries Payable		5,000

Assets	=	Liabilities	+	Equity
+5,000		+5,000		
ContrC		SalP		

Contract Cost	Salaries Payable
5,000		5,000

Alternatively, because the contract is not longer than a year, Arrens could expense the commission cost as incurred under the practical expedient.

January 1—To record contract cost

Contract Cost Expense.	5,000	
Salaries Payable		5,000

Assets	=	Liabilities	+	Equity
		+5,000		−5,000
		SalP		Exp

Salaries Payable	Contract Cost Exp
	5,000	5,000	

Example Two—Costs to Fulfill a Contract

Hampshire Inc. enters into a service contract with a customer for a three-year period. Hampshire incurs costs of $5,000 at the outset of the contract that relate directly to the contract and are critical to Hampshire's obligation to fulfill the contract. There are no refund rights in the contract, and automatic billing takes place monthly. Costs are expected to be recovered. How would Hampshire Inc. account for the contract costs on January 1?

Solution

Hampshire should recognize the costs incurred at the outset of the contract as an asset since they (1) relate directly to the contract, (2) enhance the resources of the company to perform under the contract, and (3) are expected to be recovered. An asset is recognized and amortized on a systematic basis consistent with the pattern of transfer of the services to the customer.

Assets	=	Liabilities	+	Equity
+5,000				
ContrC				
−5,000				
C:o				

January 1—To record contract cost

Contract Cost	5,000	
Cash		5,000

Contract Cost	Cash
5,000		5,000

Financial Reporting

Revenue is presented in the income statement when the five steps of the revenue recognition process have been satisfied. The balance sheet displays contract assets and contract liabilities. As discussed earlier in the chapter, a contract asset is recorded when a company transfers goods or services to a customer before payment is due, excluding any amounts reported as receivables. Similar to accounts receivable, a contract asset is a company's right to consideration in exchange for goods or services that the entity has transferred to a customer. However, accounts receivable is recorded when the company has an unconditional right to consideration. This means only the passage of time is required for the company to receive the consideration. A contract asset is conditional in that the company may have to perform additional services or deliver additional goods to the customer prior to being entitled to the consideration. A contract liability is recognized when a customer pays in advance for a seller's performance obligation to transfer goods or services in the future.

Because they are interdependent, contract assets and liabilities (excluding accounts receivable) should be presented on a **net basis**, as either a contract asset or a contract liability. The netting of contract assets and contract liabilities is performed at the contract level.

31 October 2014 TRG Meeting; agenda paper no. 7   The boards decided that the remaining rights and performance obligations in a contract should be accounted for and presented on a net basis, as either a contract asset or a contract liability. The boards noted that the rights and obligations in a contract with a customer are interdependent—the right to receive consideration from a customer depends on the entity's performance and, similarly, the entity performs only as long as the customer continues to pay. The boards decided that those interdependencies are best reflected by accounting and presenting on a net basis the remaining rights and obligations in the statement of financial position.

The net contract asset or liability is presented separately from the refund liability. Management should evaluate any resulting contract asset or receivable for impairment in accordance with the accounting guidance in evaluating the impairment of receivables (ASC 310).

Financial Statement Disclosures

The **objective** of the disclosure requirements is to provide sufficient information to enable users of financial statements to understand the nature, amount, timing, and uncertainty of revenue and cash flows arising from contracts with customers. To achieve that objective, a seller shall disclose qualitative and quantitative information about all of the following:

- **Disaggregated revenue**   Sellers shall disclose revenue disaggregated into categories that illustrate how economic factors affect the nature, amount, timing, and uncertainty of revenue and cash flows.

- **Contracts with customers**   The opening and closing balances of contract assets and liabilities should be provided. Significant components of changes in balances should be provided, including the amount of revenue recognized in the current period that was deferred in prior years. The company should disclose information about significant payment terms, the nature of goods and services promised, obligations for returns, and warranties provided. The revenue recognition standard includes examples of required disclosures and addresses more complex topics such as cumulative catch-up adjustments and impairments.

- **Performance obligations**   The company should provide information about performance obligations, including when they are typically satisfied, the nature of goods and services provided, the allocation of transaction prices to distinct obligations, and the timing of revenue recognition.

- **Significant judgments and changes in judgments**   Sellers shall disclose information about the timing of satisfaction of performance obligations, determination of the transaction price and the amounts allocated to performance obligations, methods used to recognize revenue over time, and justification for those methods.

Real World—SHIPPING COSTS: A PERFORMANCE OBLIGATION?

In the revenue recognition standard, the FASB provides an election which allows an entity to account for shipping and handling activities performed *after* control of a good has been transferred to the customer as a fulfillment cost. This means that the shipping obligation would not need to be considered a separate performance obligation. Consider Amazon Inc., who serves retail customers through the web. Without this election, it is quite possible that Amazon would have three performance obligations: to provide the good, to ship the good, and to insure the good through the shipment process. If that were the case, Amazon would have had to allocate the transaction price to the three performance obligations, including shipping, whether the customer paid for shipping or not. Even further, the timing of the recognition of the three performance obligations would be different: revenue for shipping and insurance would be recognized over the shipping period, while revenue on the product purchase would be recognized when control of the good was transferred to the customer. The election simplifies the accounting for such transactions, allowing companies that ship free on board to elect to avoid treating shipping as a separate performance obligation.

Contract Costs and Revenue Disclosures   LO7-9   REVIEW 7-9

Match each term or phrase, 1 through 9, with its best description, *a* through *i*.

Term or Phrase	Description
____ 1. Net basis of presentation	*a.* Practical expedient to allow immediate expense treatment
____ 2. Capitalized costs to fulfill a contract	*b.* Direct and recoverable contract costs, incurred to satisfy future performance obligations
____ 3. Objective of financial disclosure for revenue	*c.* Incremental and recoverable costs incurred prior to contract
____ 4. Performance obligation or cost to fulfill a contract	*d.* Offsetting contract assets against contract liabilities on a contract basis
____ 5. Accounts receivable	*e.* Shipping costs incurred after title has passed to a customer
____ 6. Capitalized costs to obtain a contract	*f.* Unconditional right to consideration
____ 7. Short-term costs to obtain a contract	*g.* Results from a transfer of goods or services to customer before payment is due
____ 8. Contract asset	*h.* Increase the understanding of the nature, amount, timing, and uncertainty of revenue arising from contracts
____ 9. Contract liability	*i.* Prepayment for a good or service

Review

MBC

More Practice: MC7-13, BE7-35, BE7-36

Solution on p. 7-85.

Management Judgment

The aim of ASC 606 is to establish the principles for companies to use when recognizing revenue. A *principles-based approach* requires management judgment.

606-10-10-1   The objective of the guidance in this Topic is to establish the principles that an entity shall apply to report useful information to users of financial statements about the nature, amount, timing, and uncertainty of revenue and cash flows arising from a contract with a customer.

Management considers all relevant information in applying the standard and consistently applies the standard across all of its revenue contracts.

606-10-10-3   An entity shall consider the terms of the contract and all relevant facts and circumstances when applying this guidance. An entity shall apply this guidance, including the use of any practical expedients, consistently to contracts with similar characteristics and in similar circumstances.

Each step of the revenue recognition process requires judgment. We highlight some of the judgments described in this chapter.

Step 1: Identify contract(s) with customer

- Determining whether a contract meets the five conditions of validity (p. 7-6).
- Determining when and how to account for contract modifications (p. 7-32).

Step 2: Identify performance obligation(s) in the contract

- Determining whether a promise meets the criteria to be treated as a separate performance obligation (p. 7-9).
- Determining whether a separate performance obligation (such as a customer option) is material (p. 7-11).

Step 3: Determine the transaction price

- Estimating variable consideration through the expected value method or the most likely amount method (p. 7-14).
- Determining whether consideration payable is made for a distinct good or service (p. 7-16).
- Estimating a refund liability (p. 7-17).
- Determining whether a financing component is significant (p. 7-17).

Step 4: Allocate transaction price to performance obligation(s)

- Determining standalone selling prices when the amount is not observable using the adjusted market assessment approach, the expected cost plus a margin approach, or the residual approach (p. 7-19).
- Considering all relevant information when estimating standalone selling prices (p. 7-23).

Step 5: Recognize revenue when (or as) each performance obligation is satisfied through a transfer of control

- Identifying the point of transfer of a promised good or service using indicators (p. 7-4).
- Evaluating the criteria to determine whether revenue should be recognized over time (p. 7-24).
- Estimating the amount of revenue to recognize over time, as progress is made toward satisfying the promise(s) of the contract (p. 7-25).
- Determining whether a customer has the right to access or use intellectual property (p. 7-30).
- Determining when to recognize revenue under a bill-and-hold arrangement, consignment arrangement, repurchase arrangement, and a principal/agent arrangement (p. 7-34).
- Determining whether a contract cost meets the criteria for capitalization (p. 7-41).

In general, management must determine the proper disclosures, including the disclosure of significant judgments made and changes in judgments (p. 7-43).

APPENDIX 7A
LO 7-10

Apply the revenue recognition process to long-term contracts expected to be profitable

LO 7-10 Overview

> **Long-term Contracts—Profitable**
> Single performance obligation satisfied over time
> - Gross profit recognized over time
> - Single performance obligation satisfied at a point in time
> - Gross profit recognized at end of the project

This section reviews the accounting for profitable long-term contracts where the performance obligation is satisfied over time (formerly called *percentage-of-completion method*) and where the performance obligation is satisfied at a point in time (formerly called *completed contract method*). The criteria included in LO7-6 is used to classify a long-term contract into its proper category.

Revenue Recognized Over Time

In **Demo 7-10A**, we demonstrate the journal entries for a long-term contract where revenue is recognized over time. As construction costs are incurred, they are accumulated in **Construction in Process**, an inventory account. Progress billings are not directly recorded as revenues but are debited to **Accounts Receivable** and credited to **Billings on Contracts**, a contra inventory account used for billings on long-term contracts. Cash collections on the contract from customers reduce **Accounts Receivable**. Up to this point, the contract is accounted for on the balance sheet only.

Revenues and expenses on long-term contracts are recognized in the income statement on a periodic basis. For each reporting period, actual construction costs are debited to **Cost of Construction** (expense account) and *estimated* revenues are credited to **Revenue from Long-Term Contracts** (revenue account). The difference between the two is gross profit and is debited to Construction in Process. While recording actual expenses is generally straightforward, determining the revenue to recognize requires management judgment. The cost-to-cost method (see **LO 7-6**) is often used by management to estimate the revenue to recognize each period. The following graphic displays the balance sheet and income statement accounts used in accounting for long-term contracts.

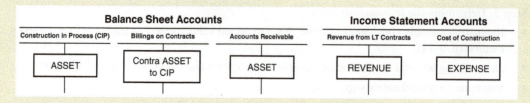

Balance Sheet Accounts			Income Statement Accounts	
Construction in Process (CIP)	Billings on Contracts	Accounts Receivable	Revenue from LT Contracts	Cost of Construction
ASSET	Contra ASSET to CIP	ASSET	REVENUE	EXPENSE

On a reporting date, companies will report the rights and obligations in a contract (Construction in Process and Billings on Contracts) on a net basis. If Construction in Process exceeds Billings on Contracts, the net difference is reported as a *current asset*. The net debit balance represents the contractor's net ownership interest in the construction project. If Construction in Process is less than Billings on Contracts, the net difference is reported as a *current liability*. The net credit balance represents the customer's net ownership interest in the project. Upon completion of the long-term project, a journal entry is recorded to close the Construction in Process account and Billings on Contracts account.

Revenue Recognized at a Point in Time

In **Demo 7-10B**, we demonstrate the journal entries for a long-term contract where revenue is recognized at a point in time. In this case, all revenue and expense recognition is deferred until the end of the contract. This means that over the contract period, we record entries to accumulate Construction in Process, progress billings, and cash collections.

At the completion of the contract, the entire gross profit on the construction project is recognized and all the accounts are closed. Income is recognized as the difference between the accumulated credit balance in Billings on Contracts and the debit balance in Construction in Process, assuming that the total price of the contract has been billed. The accumulated amount of billings on contracts is recognized as revenue from long-term contracts, and the accumulated amount of construction in process inventory on completion of the contract is recognized as cost of construction (an expense). In the financial statements, Construction in Process inventory is carried at cost on the balance sheet and the income statement reflects no impact from the contract until the time of completion of the contract.

Long-Term Contract: Revenue Recognized Over Time—Cost-to-Cost Basis LO7-10 ◄ DEMO 7-10A

Demo

MBC

Ace Construction Co. has contracted to erect a building for $1.5 million, starting construction on February 1 of Year 1, with a planned completion date of August 1 of Year 3. Total costs to complete the contract are estimated at $1.35 million, so the estimated gross profit is projected to be $150,000 ($1.5 million − $1.35 million). Progress billings payable within 10 days after billing will be made on a predetermined schedule. The company uses the cost-to-cost method to estimate revenue on long-term construction projects. Assume the following data pertain to the construction period spanning three calendar years.

Construction Project—Three-Year Summary (Contract Price: $1,500,000) As of December 31	Year 1	Year 2	Year 3
1. Costs incurred.....................	$ 350,000	$ 550,000	$ 465,000
2. Costs incurred to date...............	350,000	900,000	1,365,000
3. Estimated costs to complete...........	1,000,000	460,000	0
4. Estimated total costs................	1,350,000	1,360,000	1,365,000
5. Billings	$ 300,000	$ 575,000	$ 625,000
6. Billings to date	300,000	875,000	1,500,000
7. Collections	270,000	555,000	675,000
8. Collections to date	270,000	825,000	1,500,000

Estimated completion costs increased by $10,000 in Year 2, and by another $5,000 in Year 3. The total cost to complete the project is $1,365,000 at the end of Year 3. Estimated contract profit as of December 31 of Year 3, is therefore revised from the original estimate of $150,000 to $135,000 ($1.5 million − $1.365 million). Assume the contract meets the three criteria to recognize revenue over time. Thus, for each year of the construction project (a) record construction in process inventory, progress billings, and customer collections; (b) record expense, revenue, and gross profit; (c) close out balance sheet accounts (at job completion); and (d) prepare the financial statement presentation.

Solution

a. **Record Construction in Process, Progress Billings, and Collections of Progress Billings**
  (1) Cost incurred on the long-term project are initially classified as Construction in Process.
  (2) Billings to customers are recorded as a debit Accounts Receivable and a credit to Billings on Contracts. Recall that Billings on Contracts is a contra account to Construction in Process.
  (3) Cash collections from customers increase cash and reduce the accounts receivable balance.

continued

continued from previous page

CIP	
350,000	
550,000	
465,000	

Cash & Payables	
	270,000	350,000
	555,000	550,000
	675,000	465,000

Accounts Rec	
300,000	270,000
575,000	555,000
625,000	675,000

Billings	
	300,000
	575,000
	625,000

		Year 1		Year 2		Year 3	
(1)	Construction in Process	350,000		550,000		465,000	
	Cash and Payables*		350,000		550,000		465,000
(2)	Accounts Receivable	300,000		575,000		625,000	
	Billings on Contracts ...		300,000		575,000		625,000
(3)	Cash	270,000		555,000		675,000	
	Accounts Receivable ...		270,000		555,000		675,000

* If construction costs are initially recorded as expenses, then expenses are credited, which is a reclassification.

b. Record Revenues and Expenses

The cost-to-cost method is used to determine percent complete as follows.

Calculation of Percent Complete, as of Dec. 31	Year 1	Year 2	Year 3
Costs incurred	$ 350,000	$ 900,000	$1,365,000
Estimated total costs	1,350,000	1,360,000	1,365,000
Percent complete	25.926%	66.176%	100.000%

The percent completed is computed as costs incurred divided by the estimate of total costs to complete. For example, estimated total costs at the end of Year 1 ($1,350,000) equals costs incurred to date ($350,000) plus estimated costs to complete at the end of Year 1 ($1,000,000). For Year 1, the percent complete of 25.926% is equal to $350,000 (costs incurred to date) divided by $1,350,000 (estimate of total costs). Revenue recognized to date is equal to the percent complete multiplied by the total contract price of $1.5 million.

Calculation of Revenue to Date	Year 1	Year 2	Year 3
$1.5 million × 0.25926	$388,890		
$1.5 million × 0.66176		$992,640	
$1.5 million × 1.00000			$1,500,000

To determine revenue for each year, revenue recorded in prior years is subtracted from the total revenue recognizable.

Current period revenue = (Percent complete × Total contract revenue) – Revenue recognized in prior periods

In Year 2, for instance, the revenue to be recognized is the total revenue recognizable of $992,640 minus the revenue recognized in Year 1 of $388,890, or $603,750. The gross profit to be recognized is the difference between revenue and costs incurred in the period.

Calculation of Gross Profit	Year 1	Year 2	Year 3	Total
Revenue	$388,890	$603,750	$507,360	$1,500,000
Costs incurred	350,000	550,000	465,000	1,365,000
Gross profit	$ 38,890	$ 53,750	$ 42,360	$ 135,000

The entry to record the recognition of revenue and expense in each period follows.

CIP	
350,000	
38,890	
550,000	
53,750	
465,000	
42,360	1,500,000
0	

Billings	
1,500,000	300,000
	575,000
	625,000
	0

Cost of Construct	
350,000	
550,000	
465,000	

Rev from Contracts	
	388,890
	603,750
	507,360

	Year 1		Year 2		Year 3	
Construction in Process	38,890		53,750		42,360	
Cost of Construction	350,000		550,000		465,000	
Revenue from Long-Term Contracts ...		388,890		603,750		507,360

c. Close Balance Sheet Accounts

The following journal entry closes out Billings on Contracts and Construction in Process at the completion of the project.

continued

continued from previous page

Year 3—To close Construction in Process and Billings on Contracts

Billings on Contracts......................................	1,500,000	
Construction in Process..................................		1,500,000

d. **Financial Statement Presentation**
Construction in process exceeds billings on contracts in Year 1 and Year 2; thus, on the balance sheet, the net amount is presented as an asset in Year 1 and Year 2. On the income statement, revenue, costs, and gross profit are presented.

Revenue Recognized Over Time	Year 1	Year 2	Year 3
Balance Sheet:			
Current assets			
Accounts receivable	$ 30,000	$ 50,000	
Inventory			
Construction in process..................	$388,890	$992,640	
Less: Billings on contracts.................	300,000	875,000	
Construction in process in excess of billings...	$ 88,890	$117,640	
Income Statement:			
Revenue from long-term contracts	$388,890	$603,750	$507,360
Cost of construction	350,000	550,000	465,000
Gross profit.................................	$ 38,890	$ 53,750	$ 42,360

Long-Term Contract: Revenue Recognized at a Point in Time   **LO7-10**   **DEMO 7-10B**

Refer to **Demo 7-10A** but assume instead that the Ace Construction contract did not meet the criteria to recognize revenue over time. For the three years of the construction project (a) record construction in process inventory, progress billings, and collections; (b) record revenue and expenses at the project completion; (c) prepare the financial statement presentation; and (d) compare the gross profit recorded in **Demo 7-10A** and **Demo 7-10B**.

Solution

a. **Record Construction in Process, Progress Billings, and Collections of Progress Billings**
The journal entries to record the construction in process inventory, progress billings, and collections of progress billings each year follow. This step is the same as we illustrated above when revenue was recognized over time in **Demo 7-10A**.

	Year 1		Year 2		Year 3	
Construction in Process	350,000		550,000		465,000	
Cash and Payables		350,000		550,000		465,000
Accounts Receivable	300,000		575,000		625,000	
Billings on Contracts ...		300,000		575,000		625,000
Cash....................	270,000		555,000		675,000	
Accounts Receivable ...		270,000		555,000		675,000

CIP

350,000	
550,000	
465,000	

Cash & Payables

	270,000	350,000
	555,000	550,000
	675,000	465,000

Accounts Receiv

300,000	270,000
575,000	555,000
625,000	675,000
0	

Billings

	300,000
	575,000
	625,000

b. **Record Revenue and Expense Recognition at Project Completion**
The journal entries to recognize revenue and expense upon completion of Ace's contract in August of Year 3 follow.

Year 3—To recognize revenue and expense

Billings on Contracts	1,500,000	
Revenue from Long-Term Contracts		1,500,000
Cost of Construction	1,365,000	
Construction in Process..............................		1,365,000

Cost of Construct

| 1,365,000 | |

Rev from Contracts

| | 1,500,000 |

CIP

350,000	1,365,000
550,000	
465,000	
0	

Billings

	300,000
	575,000
1,500,000	625,000
	0

continued

continued from previous page

c. **Financial Statement Presentation**

The balance sheet and income statement presentations of the contract follow.

Recognized at a Point in Time	Year 1	Year 2	Year 3
Balance Sheet			
Current assets			
Accounts receivable	$30,000	$50,000	
Inventory			
Construction in process	$350,000	$900,000	
Less: Billings on contracts	300,000	875,000	
Construction in process in excess of billings ...	$50,000	$25,000	
Income Statement			
Revenue from long-term contracts.............	—	—	$1,500,000
Cost of construction........................	—	—	1,365,000
Gross profit	—	—	$ 135,000

d. **Compare Gross Profit Recognized**

The following table shows the differences in gross profit between the two methods on a year-to-year basis. We see that total gross profit totaled over the three years is the same for each method.

Gross Profit When:	Revenue Recognized at Point in Time	Revenue Recognized Over Time
Year 1.............	$ —	$ 38,890
Year 2.............	—	53,750
Year 3.............	135,000	42,360
Total	$135,000	$135,000

REVIEW 7-10 ▶ **LO7-10** **Long-Term Profitable Construction Project**

Review

MBC

BuildMore Construction Co. contracted to construct an addition for $400,000. Construction started in January of Year 1 and was completed in November of Year 2. Data relating to the contract follow.

As of December 31	Year 1	Year 2
Costs incurred	$150,000	$170,000
Estimated costs to complete.........................	190,000	
Billings	200,000	200,000
Collections	140,000	260,000

Required

More Practice:
AppE7-1, AppE7-6, AppE7-7

Solution on p. 7-85.

a. Record the journal entries for Year 1 and Year 2 under the assumption that revenue is recognized at a point in time.

b. Record the journal entries for Year 1 and Year 2 under the assumption that revenue is recognized over time.

Apply the revenue recognition process to long-term contracts expected to be unprofitable

When the costs necessary to complete a contract result in contract losses, two situations are possible.

1. Loss results in an unprofitable contract.
2. Contract remains profitable, but there is a current-year loss.

In **Demo 7-11A**, we demonstrate the accounting for a contract with an overall loss. Whether revenue is recognized at a point in time or over time, the projected loss is recognized in full in the period in which the loss is estimated. In **Demo 7-11B**, we demonstrate the accounting for a contract with a current-year loss, but overall, the contract remains profitable. When revenue is recognized at a point in time, no additional entry is necessary because all gross profit is deferred, and an overall loss is not expected. However, with a contract for which revenue is recognized over time, a period reporting a loss results from the usual computation of the percent complete applied to total revenue, which ends up being less than costs incurred.

> **Long-term Contracts**
> - Overall loss on unprofitable contract
>   - Recognize loss in full in period when loss is known
> - Current period loss, but overall profitable contract
>   - Revenue at a Point in Time: No periodic loss recognized
>   - Revenue Over Time: Partially reverse previously reported profits
>
> *LO 7-11 Overview*

Overall Loss on an Unprofitable Contract   **LO7-11**   **DEMO 7-11A**

Demo

MBC

Refer to information in **Demo 7-10A**. Suppose that Ace's costs incurred are $350,000 in Year 1 and $550,000 in Year 2. At the end of Year 2, Ace's estimate of costs to complete the contract increases from $460,000 to $625,000. This means costs incurred through Year 2 total $900,000, and the total estimated cost of the contract becomes $1,525,000. Thus, at the end of Year 2 there is now an expected loss on the contract of $25,000 ($1,500,000 – $1,525,000). Assume that actual costs incurred in Year 3 are $625,000.

Required
a. Record the loss in Year 2 assuming revenue is recognized at a point in time.
b. Assume the contract meets the three criteria to recognize revenue over time. For each year of the construction project, (1) record construction in process inventory, progress billings, and collections; (2) record revenue and expenses ; (3) close out balance sheet accounts (at job completion); and (4) prepare the financial statement presentation.

Solution
a. **Reporting Loss—Revenue Recognized at a Point in Time**
The entry to record the expected overall contract loss of $25,000 at the end of Year 2 follows.

December 31, Year 2—To record contract loss

Loss on Long-Term Contracts	25,000	
Construction in Process		25,000

Assets = Liabilities + Equity
−25,000   −25,000
CIP   Loss

CIP	Loss on Contracts
25,000	25,000

b. **Reporting Loss—Revenue Recognized over Time**
1. **Record Construction in Process Inventory, Progress Billings, and Collections of Progress Billings**
The three journal entries to record the construction in process inventory, progress billings, and collections of progress billings each year for Ace Construction follow.

	Year 1		Year 2		Year 3	
Construction in Process	350,000		550,000		625,000	
Cash and Payables		350,000		550,000		625,000
Accounts Receivable	300,000		575,000		625,000	
Billings on Contracts ...		300,000		575,000		625,000
Cash	270,000		555,000		675,000	
Accounts Receivable ...		270,000		555,000		675,000

CIP	Cash & Payables
350,000	270,000 | 350,000
550,000	555,000 | 550,000
625,000	675,000 | 625,000

Accounts Rec	Billings
300,000 | 270,000	300,000
575,000 | 555,000	575,000
625,000 | 675,000	625,000

continued

Exhibits included in the index with a corresponding "e" following the page numbers.

Exhibits included in the index with a corresponding "e" following the page numbers.

Exhibits included in the index with a corresponding "e" following the page numbers.

Exhibits included in the index with a corresponding "e" following the page numbers.